THE CAMBRIDGE ECONOMIC HISTORY

VOLUME II

SECOND EDITION

THE

CAMBRIDGE ECONOMIC HISTORY OF EUROPE

VOLUME II

TRADE AND INDUSTRY IN THE MIDDLE AGES

SECOND EDITION

EDITED BY

M. M. POSTAN

Late Professor of Economic History in the University of Cambridge

AND

EDWARD MILLER

Fellow of Fitzwilliam College in the University of Cambridge

ASSISTED BY

CYNTHIA POSTAN

The right of the University of Cambridge to print and sell all manner of books was granted by Henry VIII in 1534. The University has printed and published continuously since 1584.

CAMBRIDGE UNIVERSITY PRESS

CAMBRIDGE

LONDON NEW YORK NEW ROCHELLE

MELBOURNE SYDNEY

Published by the Press Syndicate of the University of Cambridge
The Pitt Building, Trumpington Street, Cambridge CB2 1RP
32 East 57th Street, New York, NY 10022, USA
10 Stamford Road, Oakleigh, Melbourne 3166, Australia

First edition published 1952
Second edition published 1987

Printed in Great Britain by the University Press, Cambridge

British Library cataloguing in publication data

The Cambridge economic history. – 2nd edn,
Vol. 2: Trade and industry in the Middle Ages
1. Europe – Economic conditions
I. Postan, M. M. II. Miller, Edward, 1915–
III. Cambridge economic history of Europe
330.94 HC240

Library of Congress cataloguing in publication data

The Cambridge economic history of Europe.
Vol. 2 – has title: The Cambridge economic history.
Includes bibliographies.
Contents – v. 1. The agrarian life of the Middle
Ages, edited by M. M. Postan. – v. 2. Trade and industry
in the Middle Ages, edited by M. M. Postan and Edward
Miller, assisted by Cynthia Postan.
1. Europe – Economic conditions. 2. Europe – History.
I. Postan, M. M. (Michael Moïssey) ed.
II. Habakkuk, H. J., ed. III. Miller, Edward,
1915– . IV. Title: Cambridge economic history.
HC240.C312 330.94 66-66029

ISBN 0 521 08709 0

UP

CONTENTS

CHAPTER IV

The Trade of Medieval Europe: the North

by MICHAEL POSTAN, Late Professor in the University of Cambridge

CHAPTER V

The Trade of Medieval Europe: the South

by ROBERT S. LOPEZ, Late Professor in Yale University

CHAPTER VI

Asia, Africa and the Trade of Medieval Europe

by DAVID ABULAFIA, Lecturer in History in the University of Cambridge

CHAPTER VII

Trade and Industry in Eastern Europe before 1200

by ALEKSANDER GIEYSZTOR, Professor in the University of Warsaw

CHAPTER VIII

The Trade of Eastern Europe in the Later Middle Ages

by MARIAN MAŁOWIST, Professor in the University of Warsaw

CHAPTER IX

The Woollen Industry

by ELEANORA CARUS-WILSON, Late Professor in the University of London

CHAPTER X

Mining and Metallurgy in Medieval Civilisation

by JOHN U. NEF, Professor Emeritus in the University of Chicago

CHAPTER XI

Building in Stone in Medieval Western Europe

by GWILYM PEREDUR JONES, Late Professor in the University of Sheffield

CHAPTER XII

Coinage and Currency

by PETER SPUFFORD, Lecturer in History in the University of Cambridge

MAPS

PREFACE

This new edition of the second volume of *The Cambridge Economic History of Europe* is substantially as it was planned, and as much of its contents had been approved before his death, by the late Sir Michael Postan. His principal object was to fill gaps in the first edition, published in 1952, that were attributable to the circumstances of the war and post-war years during which it was written. The most important gaps were the absence of studies of Eastern European trade, of the Asian and African dimensions of European trade and, among 'background' topics, of the money and currencies of medieval Europe. These vacant spaces have now been filled. In only one particular has Sir Michael Postan's plan for the volume not been realised. It had been his intention that it should also include a chapter dealing with medieval land transport and shipping, a chapter which he had hoped to write himself. In the event this task was still uncompleted at the time of his death and it did not prove possible to arrange for its completion by another hand within a period that would avoid still further delaying the appearance of a volume which had already been long in preparation. It seemed best, therefore, to abandon this part of the plan for it, the more particularly because much of the evidence for trade routes and transport is reviewed, often in considerable detail, in the chapters on the main trading regions.

In addition to chapters which fill gaps in the first edition it also appeared desirable, given the rapid accumulation of archaeological knowledge in recent decades, to commission a new study of trade and industry in barbarian Europe up to Roman times. The rest of the chapters have been brought forward from the first edition – all, with the exception of the chapter on building in stone, with revisions that in most cases are substantial. Inevitably, not all the contributors to a volume which, in its original version, appeared more than thirty years ago, have lived to see its revision completed. In addition to Sir Michael Postan himself, G. P. Jones, R. S. Lopez and E. M. Carus-Wilson of the contributors to the first edition, as well as David L. Clarke, all died in the course of the volume's preparation. The assistance of others in providing or revising bibliographies in particular is noted in the table of contents and gratefully acknowledged. In one respect, too, the extension of the volume's scope to include the East European lands has created its own problems. Partly as a result of boundary changes many places since 1945 have come to be known by new names in current usage, although they may be more familiar under their older names. For the sake of clarity both names have sometimes been given in the text and an attempt has been made to indicate alternatives in the index.

The arrangement of the volume, like that of the first edition, involves some repetition and a certain number of overlaps, but to remove them would have detracted from the individual contributions. Again, as in the first edition, there are some differences of opinion between contributors which there has been no editorial attempt to reconcile or conceal. In this respect the volume reflects a consistent editorial policy which was succinctly stated by Sir Michael Postan in the preface to the first edition. 'The whole principle of the Cambridge Histories, made up as they are of separate contributions of reputable historians, must take differences of interpretation for granted. In a series devoted to economic history these differences are not only inevitable but also essential... The facts and theories with which economic historians operate are even more provisional than the facts in the older and more stabilised branches of historical study. The authorised and established versions of economic history are therefore very few... In their absence the study of economic history has done very well, for the striking advances in recent years have been greatly stimulated by the clash of opposing views.'

It fell to the present editor to come upon the scene only at a very late stage in the preparation of the volume. There are, in consequence, probably a variety of obligations which have been incurred along the way in its preparation which lie outside his direct knowledge and for which he can express only general gratitude. On the other hand he has received generous help from the staff of the Cambridge University Press, and from Mr William Davies in particular; and he is indebted above all to Lady Cynthia Postan not only for much work on the text of the volume but for her help in preserving a degree of continuity in bringing it to completion.

1986 E. M.

CHAPTER I

Trade and Industry in Barbarian Europe till Roman Times

I. *Introduction*

The antecedents of trade and industry in the European continent extend continuously through time to the activities of the earliest hominids, a million years ago, in a Europe that we would now scarcely recognise; a Europe with an unfamiliar geography, a different climate and an exotic fauna and flora. In Man's own knowledge and continuing experience there have been not one Europe but a succession of Europes through time, each with its own distinctive character. Indeed, the minute penetration of the European environment which mapped the resources of later trade and industry was the cumulative consequence of this successive experience of every aspect of Europe, under every kind of condition, collectively stored in the cultural traditions of its inhabitants. It might almost be said that Man stayed still and let Europe fluctuate about him in its oscillation trajectory. But this, of course, is not true, for Man's ancestors continuously adapted both biologically and culturally in such a way as to intensify his branching penetration deep into the interstices of his environment. In this process Man's cultural adaptations have increasingly insulated his population from environmental fluctuations by means of the increasing regulatory variety of his material and social artefact assemblages.

It at once seems incongruous to take historical concepts of trade and industry back into a series of contexts in which ultimately Man is not even Homo sapiens and in which perhaps formalised speech itself may be doubted. Nevertheless, the most primitive tool-using hominids practised complex economies – elaborate time and role allocation strategies, combining various subsistence methods and extraction processes with which to feed and equip the community and ensure its continuity. Even in these earliest contexts commodities were gathered, shared and exchanged on a limited scale whilst a multiplicity of raw materials were regularly exploited by the repetitive employment of special technological skills. This much archaeology tells us with certainty.

The incongruity – the anachronism – is to imagine that in these ancient contexts the communities concerned viewed these economic activities in the highly peculiar, highly formalised way conditioned in us by our contemporary background. We may even legitimately talk about the economic strategy of the troop of baboons, but it would surely be unwise to attribute to them that selectively atomised perception of their activities which is indeed a peculiar product of our own minds. When we analyse the economics of ancient European societies and scrutinise their trade in commodities, or the organisation of their industries, we must constantly recollect the retrospective astigmatism of our own transient view, accustomed as it is to the peculiarly idiosyncratic and asymmetric emphasis of contemporary industrial economies. It is our own cultural astigmatism which seeks to polarise functional and non-functional transactions, to separate utilitarian from ceremonial activities and, above all, mistakenly seeks an 'economic purpose' behind the cultural manifestations which are the multipurpose spicules of group activities. Although it is true that our astigmatism grows less as the activities approach our own times, it remains no less a distorting factor in attempts to understand the economy of the Medieval village than it is for a similar study of a Neolithic village, perhaps four thousand years earlier. We must remember that in other sociocultural contexts the exploitation of resources, the processes of production, the distribution of commodities by exchange and the concepts of wealth are all pursued on a different scale, in terms of different philosophies and with the conscious emphasis on quite other facets of these activities. The cultural models that constrain the activities of other cultures differ from our own and consequently those activities are not entirely explicable in terms of our concepts of economics, trade and industry.

In order to understand the appropriate contextual dimensions of exchange and production in ancient Europe we must be careful to use reconstruction models closer to those of anthropology than to the more formal models of modern economics; indeed, it is probably necessary to use a mixture of models derived from animal behaviour, social anthropology, and economics.[1] In the first three-quarters of a million years of European hominid activity the primate behaviour factor will dominate the patterns fitted by the mixed model; in the last quarter of a million years social anthropology will more extensively map the variations, until in the remaining millennium formal economic

[1] For anthropological approaches to economic theory, see G. Dalton (ed.), *Tribal and Peasant Economies* (New York, 1967); R. Firth, *Economics of the New Zealand Maori*, 2nd edn (Wellington, 1959); D. Kaplan, 'The Formal-substantive controversy in economic anthropology: reflections on its wider implications', *Southwestern Journ. of Anthropology*, XXIV (1968), 228–51. For archaeological approaches, see D. L. Clarke, *Analytical Archaeology* (London, 1968) and D. L. Clarke (ed.), *Models in Archaeology* (London, 1972); E. S. Higgs (ed.), *Papers in Economic Prehistory* (Cambridge, 1972) and *Palaeoeconomy* (Cambridge, 1975).

factors will dominate the modelling activities in which, nevertheless, the three factors still coexist. To these factors we should correctly add those accidental and stochastic elements which are the necessary ingredients of any realistic interpretative model. This approach suggests that it need not be inappropriate to use modern terms for ancient activities as a predictive analogue – an indication of hidden potential – nor is it entirely inappropriate to use the mathematical methods of modern economic analysis upon primitive economies. These procedures simply serve to show what aspects of ancient activities can be immediately comprehended in the dimensions of our own modern minds, at the same time establishing those irreducible residual aspects for which explanations must be sought amongst the other factors in the context. The best that we can do is to stretch the data of prehistory over a conceptual framework incorporating behavioural, cultural, economic and stochastic models, using each factor in turn to control the others, thereby noting the most adequate model in the particular context and learning from the discrepancies between the models – a kind of mental regression analysis.

Since we are familiar with the contemporary conceptions of industry and trade it is mainly necessary to sketch some of the dimensions in which the elements of these activities differ in the contexts of other societies. It is not that our cultural network and its structure is substantially different from those of the ancient Europeans, merely that the selective emphasis of the bonds are rather different. In human societies both past and present the population is everywhere networked by the cross-cutting web of kinship relations and the superimposed mesh of social acquaintances. Groups of kinsmen may cooperate to produce, distribute and consume commodities, or join together in other activities, whilst at the same time the individual members will be variously interlinked with non-kin groups in age sets, status classes, recreational cliques, ceremonial fraternities, religious bodies, military regiments, political factions and exchange partnerships. All of these linked lattices have the effect of extending special obligation relationships throughout a finite population, with advantageous reciprocal consequences. Production and consumption may be regulated in the network, famine or natural disaster may be cooperatively overcome and fresh advantages may be more effectively exploited by sharing their development with others – with a reciprocal gain in prestige status. Internal conflict will tend to run contrary to some relationships shared by various parties and these interested bystanders may therefore move to minimise and heal the disruption. In such an intricately adjusted web of relationships, economic activities and exchange partnerships are an integral part of the social, religious, psychological and material culture nexus and these latter factors can never be separated from any hypothetically 'pure' economic considerations.

So much for the static network of social obligations, but cultures are dynamic systems with moving and circulating contents and changing internal and external relationships. A significant proportion of this dynamism is bound up with the circulation of commodities within the system and at any one time the relationship between individuals in the network is connected with the distribution state of the commodities within the network at that time. In many ways culture systems run on the circulation of commodities within a distribution flow operated by the social machinery. For example, in most communities, the nodal regularities of the daily, weekly, monthly, seasonal, annual and life cycle activities of the individuals in the social group are selectively but strikingly marked out by appropriate ceremonies, in which special commodities are consumed, manufactured, or dispersed in a continuous cycle conferring birth gifts, age-group and status insignia, maturity emblems, bride price, dowries, wedding feasts, gift exchanges, religious sacrifices and dues, communal levies and the requisites for burial ceremonies. In this context the consumption and display of commodities is a conspicuous and outwardly meaningful communication serving many purposes other than strictly utilitarian ones; especially serving to restate in an intricate symbolism the mutual rank, status and roles of the individuals in the network at that time – a kind of decorated pecking order. The commodities used in this symbolic decoration of values may be of any kind and represent an idiosyncratic and stochastic selection. Nevertheless, the continuous definition, maintenance and fulfilment of mutual roles within an elaborate machinery of status and prestige relationships is a factor in even the most modern economic activities.

The arbitrary units of exchange recognised by a society are a particularly important and selected subset of commodities within the larger set of commodities in circulation. Some commodities may be circulated freely in any direction and from amongst these favourite staples are usually selected as media of transaction – durable commodities with a certain scarcity value but not so scarce or capricious as to fail to keep a constant flow through the social machinery. These units of exchange may be utilitarian, consumable or non-consumable, manufactured or natural objects: favourite commodities are shells, teeth, tusks, furs, feathers, hides, beads, bracelets, torques, ingots, axes, mats and fabrics; or consumable staples such as pigs, cattle, sheep, tobacco, salt, yams, bananas and cereal grains. The use of foodstuffs as exchange media may at first seem surprising but they are quite sufficiently durable and are only consumed when absolutely necessary; in this way an active trade in foodstuffs may have no primary connection with nutritional requirements. The corn bins of the Neolithic chieftain, the horse herds of the Scythian prince, the cattle of the Celtic noble and the *pithoi* of olive oil in the Minoan potentate's magazines represented actual capital wealth as well as potential food.[2]

However, apart from the commodities in free circulation and the media of exchange there is usually a third set of commodities which on no account may be used as media of exchange – the symbolic insignia marking certain castes or elites, often intricately decorated and elaborately finished artefacts, conspicuously enshrining the consumption of much labour, food surplus, rare resources and rare materials. The existence of these exotic prestige insignia, which cannot be obtained by free exchange, constitutes an important set of barriers marking subcultural castes or cliques into which it is not possible to 'buy' oneself, however wealthy the individual may be. Nevertheless, prestige itself, whether symbolised by restricted regalia or by an impressive surplus of ordinary commodities, has the capacity to exert influence and is a source of power in the society at large. In all societies prestige is a cashable commodity, a form of capital on whose account loans may be borrowed, expeditions financed and obligations and treaties secured. The New Guinea 'big man' relies on his hoard of imported boars' tusks and shell *lunulae* not only to mark his rank and thus gain the proper deference appropriate to it, but as a means of gaining followers and the services of sorcerers and canoe masters. The Aunjetitz chieftain of Early Bronze Age Europe similarly relied on his hoard of imported amber nuggets, faience beads, bronze ingots and weaponry to endorse his rank and gain specialists for his retinue, and the Mycenaean princeling on his treasury to gain the obeisance of his villagers and as surety for the expensive tackle and gear for his mercantile speculations.

The anthropological model of commodity production and circulation outlines the way in which extensive 'kula' trade rings might be mainly circulating strange prestige kickshaws which primarily served to increase the local status of the exchange partners and to strengthen their partnership, whilst almost incidentally and on sporadic occasions facilitating the additional circulation of some 'useful' staples. All in all, we can appreciate that commodities were exchanged, and raw materials were regularly exploited with special technological skills, in

[2] J. G. D. Clark, 'Traffic in stone axe and adze blades', *Economic History Review*, 2nd ser. XVIII (1965), 1–28; Clarke, *Analytical Archaeology*, 94–5; T. G. Harding, *Voyagers of the Vitiaz Strait: a study of the New Guinea trade system*. Monographs of the American Ethnological Society, XLIV (Seattle, 1967).

the most ancient societies of Europe but that the context of those activities was very different from the contexts that we extrapolate to them when we think in terms of trade and industry. It is no longer surprising to find that commodities of many kinds circulated over vast areas of prehistoric Europe without long-range movements by individuals and involving not so much commodities of economic 'utility' as decorative gewgaws or display weaponry. Commodities more congruent with our own ideas of utilitarian trade were produced and circulated in this context and clear memories of these later media of exchange are preserved in our European vocabularies – salt (salary), a handful of iron spits (*drachma*), ingots (*aes*), cattle (pecuniary), land (fee), and grain. These 'useful' commodities were, however, only part of the system and would rarely be the cause of the exchange system coming into existence.

The history of trade and industry in barbarian Europe is therefore essentially the history of activities which have been transformed almost beyond recognition. In the anthropological model the production and circulation of commodities is secondary to the proper functioning of a culture and operating only to satisfy its essential needs. In the modern economic model, society is deliberately reorganised in an attempt to optimise its economic sector – a reorganisation frequently to the detriment of large sections of the society's population but to the marked benefit of other sections. This aspect alone should be sufficient to help us resist the temptation to see this transformation in terms of an older primitive arrangement and a more recent advanced configuration, with a steady, simple, onward-and-upward, evolutionary trend linking one to the other; the overwhelming temptation to write the economic history of Europe in a few paragraphs – the farming villagers replace the hunters, metals replace stone technology, surplus supports the city, the city state becomes the nation, and all the while the mines get deeper and deeper and society better and better. Alas, because archaeological information is such a peculiar sample and so difficult to interpret, some resemblance between this caricature and this chapter is almost inevitable.

Nevertheless, the economic development of Europe has been a good deal more complex and uneven than such an approach would suggest. Europe has always been an area with a great diversity of habitats, an intricate nested tessellation of different soils, routes, barriers, fauna, flora and climate, a varied mosaic of intersecting macro- and micro-environments. At the crudest level we will repeatedly contrast the developments in the Mediterranean zone with the differing patterns of temperate middle Europe and coniferous northern Europe – a contrast stretching back to the primeval habitat requirements of the earliest hominids and primates. European cultural development and diversification has followed a mosaic and multilinear pattern congruent with the diversity of the continent. The economic developments have been simultaneously interacting and cumulative, discrete and divergent, fluctuating and convergent. Former centres of development periodically became peripheral and frontiers became central; archaic survivals suddenly became advantageous bases for fresh development and elaborate economic formats periodically revealed an incapacity for further adaptive development. The pattern is one of repeatedly reticulating development, hunting-and-seeking in many directions in constantly changing environments; one can at best trace only the diverse trajectories of certain economic innovations and trade conditions, marking their successive contributions to particularly localised but critical thresholds.

It is a well-known property of complex systems that the successive introduction of unrelated factors may cumulatively approach a threshold beyond which the system cannot survive unchanged. At the same time the introduction of new elements or conditions into such a context may result in the emergence of unforeseen consequences or capacities – the development of fresh potential. Now, the cultural systems of prehistoric Europe may be approximately portrayed as dynamic information and activity systems locked in complicated processes of interchange with other changing societies and with their changing environments. The individual social, economic, religious and psychological configurations of these systems were certainly very diverse but they were all richly-networked complex systems coupled within their territorial environments. It is not entirely surprising, therefore, that certain broad thresholds can be discerned in the developing economic pattern of prehistoric Europe, thresholds which have important implications for the growth of trade and industry.[3]

The elements which mark these putative thresholds in the archaeological record do not appear suddenly, together, at single points in time, neither are they simultaneously found all over Europe. The individual elements inevitably have long antecedent trajectories; it is, however, the cumulative effects of the successive introduction and integration of these elements and conditions that combine to mark the emergence of a fresh economic capacity which particularly interest us here. Although often initially restricted to the Mediterranean zone of Europe, the contemporary subsequent repercussions of many of these successive system-repatternings were increasingly widely felt through the continent. The elements combining to define these broad economic

[3] Clarke, *Analytical Archaeology*, 77–81.

thresholds necessarily include a great diversity of factors – environmental, social, religious, historical, political, economic and technological. It is the very comprehensive diversity of such a complex of changing factors which makes their reinforcing ramifications the more powerful. Unfortunately, the archaeological record gives us only an irregular sample of information on these diverse changes and in some important aspects no information at all. The archaeologist is still particularly prone to ignore the catalytic importance of the contemporary social, political and historical factors – how things came to be the way they were, the restrictive effect this had on further outcomes, and the advantageous or disastrous exploitation of successive situations organised by social, political, religious and military leaders.

The thresholds that we are going to use to segment the continuity of European development are, of course, determined by our present interest in trade and industry within the economic context. We know far more about the later thresholds from their greater mass of archaeological material and the enormous quantity of contemporary written records. For these later periods we can make some clumsy attempt to assess the political and historical factors which are so conspicuously missing from the earlier phases. In contrast, the Palaeolithic epoch is so huge chronologically, so environmentally diverse, and so little understood, that its appearance as a featureless monolith in the economic record is mainly a monument to our ignorance, to be passed over with great rapidity in the shortest possible space. Yet to assume any degree of economic or social homogeneity, or lack of change, over such a vast and diverse era is clearly absurd. Nevertheless, the apparently quickening pace of development with passing times does not appear to be entirely an illusion – the expansion in hominid population, the exponential growth in artefact variety, in environmental control and in political unit size is an unequivocal sign of this. But once again we must remember that this overall trend is a composite of many oscillating, fluctuating and desultory individual cultural developments; no one community has continuously crested this curve of development, indeed the continuously shifting focus of climax development is one of the features of analytical interest.

The multiple factors and their cumulative effect in defining the particular thresholds will be briefly outlined at the beginning of the time segment which they crudely define. The dates attached to these transitional thresholds are merely rough indicators based on radiocarbon dates relevant to Europe; they must be carefully distinguished from the much earlier appearances of similar thresholds and elements in adjacent areas, especially to the south and east.

The most significant thresholds can thus be usefully employed to define six interlocking phases in which the economic patterns, and therefore the trade, the technology and the industrial potential, of Europe were cumulatively repatterned –

1. The gathering-hunting-fishing economies: *c.* 1,000,000–6000 B.C.
2. The agrarian economies: *c.* 6000–2000 B.C.
3. The Aegean network and the Early Bronze technologies: *c.* 2000–1400 B.C.
4. The Mycenaean network and the Developed Bronze technologies: *c.* 1400–1200 B.C.
5. The colonial networks and the Late Bronze technologies: c. 1200–600 B.C.
6. The colonial empires and the pre-industrial Iron technologies: *c.* 600–0 B.C.

II. *The Gathering-Hunting-Fishing Economies: c. 1,000,000–6,000 B.C.*[4]

The opening threshold for Man in Europe is made increasingly complex by the inappropriate nature of the term 'Man' and by the long-term mosaic development which physical anthropologists are now demanding for these creatures, even in Europe. It now seems increasingly probable that Mediterranean Europe was actually within the boundaries of the earliest incipient hominid developments – thus already emphasising the important ecological frontier separating the European interior from the north littoral of the Mediterranean sea. Several varieties of superior ground apes, the earliest known hominids, now date back into the late Miocene, *c.* 10,000,000 B.C., with an already extensive middle-latitude habitat ranging from the Mediterranean and Africa to India and China. Many of these hominids had developed a bipedal gait and these groups with free hands probably made regular use of unmodified sticks and stones as implements for knocking down fruit and nuts, for digging out roots and for killing insects and small animals; these capacities are even within the range of the abilities of most of the modern apes today.

The middle-latitude distribution of the earliest hominids was no accident – the middle latitudes of the globe are the richest in plant life, the polar regions for sunshine and photosynthesis. The wealth of plant and animal life provided a great diversity of ecological niches from

[4] For general surveys, see F. Bordes, *The Old Stone Age* (London, 1968); J. M. Coles and E. S. Higgs, *The Archaeology of Early Man* (London, 1969). For evidence of environment and subsistence, see K. Butzer, *Environment and Archaeology*, 2nd edn (Chicago, 1971). For hominid evolution, see D. Pilbeam, *The Ascent of Man* (New York, 1972).

the forest canopy to the undergrowth floor and from the savannah parkland to the montane grasslands; a diversity of habitat widely reflected in the great variety of early pongid and hominid populations exploiting these micro-environments. The dentition and skeletal structure of the early hominids similarly reflects the agile pursuit of these multiplex resources to provide an omnivorous diet with the emphasis on vegetable matter – basically leaves, shoots, roots, fruits, seeds, nuts, insects and small animals. A diet which could be held to the mouth by the grasping pentadactyl hands of the free forearms, secured in the mouth by unspecialised canines, bitten by chisel incisors and adequately ground by powerful molar teeth of relatively simple structure. Man's first toolkit included his hands and feet, his nailed fingers and toes, and his mouth with its varied array of equipment. Man's first artefacts were in many respects simple material imitations and extensions of these integral and inherited tools of survival.

The archaeological evidence from the contexts of the fossil hominids does not contradict this dietary pattern although there is some uncertainty about the quality and importance of meat in the hominid diet. Several lines of enquiry suggest that meat was much less important than has been assumed and although it was an important and regular part of hominid diet it may never have formed either the bulk or the staple of that diet. Modern dietary observations demonstrate that a multiplicity of vegetable elements have probably always formed the bulk of the diet of man and apes in the middle latitudes; it is only in the photosynthetic deserts of near Arctic or Antarctic conditions that man must rely predominantly on animal and marine foods and substitute the moss from reindeer stomachs and the plankton from fish gullets for the missing vegetal elements.

The archaeologically bemusing evidence of the 'big kill' sites, with the dismembered carcasses of big herbivores amidst a scattered variety of stone butchering tools, must be set against the missing vegetable, wood and basketry evidence, lost to decay. Vegetable and insect foods hardly require better artefacts than the hands and teeth with the addition of a few wooden sticks and points, whereas a constellation of specialised stone artefacts is necessary for the particular tasks of killing, skinning, gutting, butchering and otherwise processing animal carcasses – especially those of large beasts. Other evidence combines to suggest that stone artefacts may be quite asymmetrically correlated with the special requirements of hunting, butchering and secondary tool production, clustering densely around these activities in the hominid spectrum, whilst the more persistently intensive pursuit of leaves, stalks, roots, fruits, seeds, nuts, grubs, insects, rats, snakes and lizards may be sparsely represented, if at all, in the stone artefact record.

A balanced economic assessment has been made even more difficult by the marginal habitats now occupied by vestigial gatherers-hunters-fishers, wherein extraordinary conditions now prevail, as well as by the cultural emphasis on meat, hunting prowess, and domestic animal numbers which often perversely bears no proportional relationship to their dietary importance in the culture concerned. However, the evidence from fossilised human faeces and the rare survivals of wooden digging-sticks, harvesting-crooks, and clubs combine with the general purpose design of the earliest hand-picks to suggest that grubbing-out tools may have been a more frequent hominid occupation than hunting big game. In order to redress this longstanding mis-emphasis we shall adopt the term gatherers-hunters-fishers, rather than the traditionally misinformed categorisation of hunters-fishers-gatherers with its questionable emphasis on hunting.[5]

Implement-using, and consequently a detailed interest in raw materials, probably goes back to such widespread late Miocene hominids as Ramapithecus punjabicus. Artefact-making, however, which requires a greater degree of mental symbolling and forethought, probably developed more slowly but also on the widespread basis of modifying natural implements. By early Pleistocene times, *c.* 1,000,000 B.C., several varieties of Australopithecus africanus were habitually bipedal, displayed less specialised jaws and developed various refinements in hand structure in addition to an expansion of brain capacity and complexity; in all probability these changes were coupled with the widespread development of tool-making. Australopithecine populations may have partly evolved in the Mediterranean zone of Europe, although centred in the latitudes of the south. Traces of putatively Australopithecine pebble tools have been found at several sites within the Mediterranean zone of Europe, including finds from the Vallonet cave at Roquebrune-Cap-Martin on the Mediterranean coast, Monte-Peglia in Italy, and possibly at other sites in Romania and Spain. However, by middle Pleistocene times, *c.* 600,000 B.C., varieties of Homo erectus had evolved in populations barely distinguishable from those within the range of variation of contemporary Homo sapiens. It was probably bands of Homo erectus that first succeeded in penetrating the European interior and thus commenced the infiltration of this marginal environment by reaching peripheral

[5] For studies of modern hunters and gatherers, see M. G. Bicchieri (ed.), *Hunters and Gatherers Today* (New York, 1972); M. A. Jochim, *Hunter-Gatherer Subsistence and Settlement* (New York, 1976); R. B. Lee and I. Devore (eds), *Man the Hunter* (Chicago, 1968). For alternative views about the importance of plant foods, see D. L. Clarke, 'Mesolithic Europe: the economic basis', in G. de G. Sieveking *et al.*, *Problems in Economic and Social Archaeology* (London, 1976), 449–81; C. Vita-Finzi and E. S. Higgs, 'Prehistoric economy in the Mount Carmel area of Palestine: site catchment analysis', *Proc. of the Prehistoric Society*, XXXVI (1970), 1–37.

Britain, Germany, France and Hungary from the littoral of the Mediterranean and Black Sea.

This penetration of 'Outer Europe' was materially affected by the periodic climate oscillations of the Ice Age, *c.* 1,000,000–10,000 B.C., which in interglacial spasms lasting some hundreds of thousands of years supported a 'Mediterranean-like' environment deep within central Europe. Magnolias flowered amidst mixed woods of beech and hornbeam interlaced by lianas and vines, whilst elephants, hippos and rhinos grazed quietly beyond the reach of the puny, baboon-stalking, Australopithecine pygmies, although soon within the regular hunting capacity of robust Homo erectus with his more elaborate artefacts and projectiles.

In the intervening and equally long glacial phases, this European middle-latitude 'natural habitat' zone for hominids was gradually displaced southwards by the increasingly cold conditions which swept around the expanding northern Ice Cap and the converging Alpine glaciers. Now, mammoth, woolly rhinoceros and reindeer grazed, whilst musk-oxen stamped on the frosty, moss-covered tundra or tore up the dwarf willows, polar birch and dwarf pine trees; in warmer pockets bison and horse herds migrated swiftly across bands of sparsely wooded steppe. Initially, at least, the hominids seem to have retreated to the Mediterranean littoral in these severe phases, encapsulated within their traditional habitat ecology and abandoning the European interior to its new denizens. Latterly, at the end of the Riss glaciation, *c.* 200,000 B.C., and throughout the Wurm glaciation, *c.* 80–10,000 B.C., small hominid groups seem for the first time to have succeeded in exploiting the alien tundra environment immediately south of the ice sheets of northern Europe. Amongst these frontier groups hunting must certainly have played an unusually important role and skilful micro-environmental control, employing fur cloaks, fire, communal tented dugouts and screened caves, together enabled them to survive the somewhat less severe climatic rigours of such favourable areas as Atlantic France and periglacial Poland. Full cultural adaptation to steppe and tundra life, including the use of tailored fur clothing ultimately enabled the late Pleistocene hominids to conquer and survive the Wurm glaciation *in situ*, in middle Europe, virtually wherever the land was ice-free. The hominids had finally broken through the northern ecological threshold constraining their habitat zone, using the same means with which they were subsequently able to transcend every boundary – by cultural adaptation.

During the interstadials of the Wurm glaciation, *c.* 40,000 B.C., the variety of Man known as Homo sapiens first became apparent as a population variety of developed Homo erectus in the Near East and in eastern Europe. The archaeological record tells us of an accompanying and widespread technological change from making flint tools on flake blanks to making flint tools on blade blanks which could be hafted in composite tool forms. However, these developments took many millennia to materialise and most of the 'innovations' accompanying Homo sapiens have long antecedent histories. Bone, antler and, probably, wooden artefacts were more intensively produced, but these materials were already used by Homo erectus; ceremonial burial with red ochre, food and equipment became a regular feature, but had long been practised by Homo sapiens neanderthalensis; group hunting of the large herd herbivores was organised on a large scale but had been practised regularly since Acheulean times; painted and engraved art flourished conspicuously, but may have long existed on wooden objects and the walls of skin tents, as the Mousterian painted and engraved objects from Tata in Hungary might suggest.[6] Formalised speech communication can hardly be doubted for Homo sapiens, but even this development probably stretches back to the time of the appearance of Homo erectus. It is only the further intensification of Man's culture, accidents of preservation, our own ethnocentricity and the extremely localised but impressive evidence of elaborate social organisations in a very few advantageous areas, which have cumulatively combined to lay undue stress on the significance of the transition from Homo sapiens neanderthalensis to Homo sapiens. Nevertheless, this Upper Palaeolithic phase marks the arrival of the genetic diversity of the hominids within the set of variety still to be found within the racial range of modern man.

Hominid group organisation over the million years, or so, of the Pleistocene was probably as varied as the climatic and ecological environments which provided the oscillation context. This mosaic variety in band organisation probably diversified progressively with the development of the later hominids, especially with the successful adaptation of peripheral groups to specialised survival within fresh ecosystems such as the temperate forest, steppe and tundra conditions in Europe north of the Mediterranean. Except in very advantageous coastal areas, perhaps including parts of the Mediterranean littoral, the diverse populations must have moved cyclically around large territories in order to take advantage of the seasonal harvests of groups of resources in turn through the year. Such bands will have varied in social organisation, role allocations, economic strategies, territorial areas, rotational schedules and varied in size from tens to perhaps hundreds, both from group to group and from season to season. It is

[6] Bordes, *The Old Stone Age*, 110.

probable that in the richer resource areas and seasons family bands could temporarily come together to form substantial tribes with a developed and elaborate social structure. But these are unusual conditions which seem to have prevailed from time to time in the Dordogne, the Ukraine and in one or two other environmentally favoured areas of middle and Mediterranean Europe. It is not surprising, therefore, to find in these favoured areas and periods many of the material trappings of rank insignia, prestige and display equipment and commodities, and therefore a developing system of exchange in rare and attractive materials and resources.

Sea shells, animal teeth, boars' tusks, fossils and ivory plaques were perforated and sewn in hundreds on the caps and clothing of elite individuals, or strung in crescentic spacer-plate necklaces around the fur-caped shoulders of the powerful. The same restricted individuals also displayed their rank in intricately decorated and elaborately finished bone and probably wooden spearthrowers and batons of various kinds; super-elaborate versions of the focal artefacts of the community. Every kind of coloured stone was now collected and their sources noted – including amber, ophite, coloured jasper and quartz crystals, and red, yellow and black ochres. Equipped in the finery of fur and feathers, shells and teeth, his face fiercely painted in reds and yellows, the Gravettian and Magdalenian hunting-chiefs and shamans must have presented a deliberately impressive sight as they performed the ceremonial rituals which enshrined and conveyed their perception of Man's relationship with the world of nature.

Mediterranean and Black Sea shells were carried hundreds of miles inland to the Gravettian sites of the Ukraine, to the Mousterian sites of Hungary and to many French Aurignacian and Solutrean sites. The Magdalenian culture group of southern France was especially rich in perforated sea-shell finery – mainly dentalium, nerilium, columbella, petunculus and spondylus shells brought from the Mediterranean and the Atlantic littoral. Utilitarian commodities also circulated within the same limited territories. Distinctive and desirable siliceous raw materials for artefacts were often selectively obtained from particular outcrops and sources. Slovakian obsidian and radiolarite was used, for example, at Polish Aurignacian sites such as Zwierzyniec. White flecked flint from Świeciechów on the middle Vistula circulated over an area of some 120 miles radius in Aurignacian and Szeletian contexts. Baltic flint from Silesia was exploited by Gravettian bands from Moravia, occurring at their winter sites a hundred miles away through the Carpathian passes to the south. Bitumen from the Styrian tar wells may also have circulated widely in central Europe for tool-hafting and waterproofing. Obsidian from Hungarian Mousterian and Aurignacian sites such as Ballavolgyer and Keckesgalyer seems to have come from the deposits a hundred miles away in the Hegyalia range of the Carpathians. Grand Pressigny flint was widely distributed amongst the Aurignacian and Gravettian groups of France.[7] It is therefore quite apparent that the European stone and flint resources were already known in especially minute detail within particular territorial boundaries; as one might expect for the main technological raw material of the period. Doubtless other organic commodities may have circulated to the same limited extent – the furs and feathers of the tundra game; the hides, horns and antlers of the steppe beasts; and the wood, bark and resins of the timber stands.

One consistent pattern emerges from the surviving distributions of shells, pigments and special stones – with very rare exceptions the distributions are restricted to a limited area, usually no more than one hundred miles in radius, often much less. This strongly suggests that these movements of raw materials and commodities must be placed within the context of mobile gathering-hunting-fishing bands, which of necessity continuously moved around large territories in their annual subsistence cycle. In this context, one resource or quarry outcrop might often serve, simultaneously yet successively, as a focus within the peripheral intersection of several group territories, and the group itself might exploit that resource at different seasons of the year. Since a gathering-hunting-fishing territory of 120 miles radius is not unusual for recent groups of this kind, it is not at all surprising to find a resource-distribution unit of similar dimensions operating in Palaeolithic Europe. The rare cases of wider distribution can largely be accounted for in terms of peripheral gift exchanges or of the simultaneous yet successive exploitation of a common resource by several intersecting groups. On this simple model the latter would therefore be capable of a distribution unit of about 240 miles radius – perhaps in this respect fitting the distribution of Carpathian obsidian from the middle Danube to the Ukraine.

In terms of this territorial model we can perhaps discern the groups from the Garonne moving into the Pyrenees with the spring migration of bison and returning in the autumn with ophite and minerals from Isturitz. From the Dordogne valley other groups will have moved west to fish and seal on the Atlantic coast, returning with skins, shells and salmon vertebrae beads. Some will have followed the northern herds making the spring migration to the freshly exposed pastures of the Loire and Paris basin in the north and the Auvergne plateau in the

7 J. G. D. Clark, *Prehistoric Europe* (London, 1952), 182–3; K. Jazdzewski, *Poland* (London, 1965), 37–47; L. Vertes, 'Das Moustérien in Ungarn', *Eiszeitalter und Gegenwart*, X (1959), 21–40.

east – returning with Parisian fossil shells (Grotte du Renne), Grand Pressigny flints (Fontenioux) and coloured ochres from the rocks of the Auvergne. Presumably other groups centred on the Mediterranean littoral will have carried sea shells northwards into the Cevennes above the Dordogne, perhaps during spring and autumn movements from their Mediterranean winter bases.[8] Much the same pattern may have framed the spring movements of Moravians trekking northwards onto the Silesia plain, with their Czech flint, Styrian bitumen and Hungarian obsidian artefacts, returning through the Moravian Gates in the autumn with their Baltic flint, amber nodules and northern furs.

In this way the gathering-hunting-fishing bands will have moved around their territories exploiting a sequence of material and organic resources in a formalised rotation, changing their group configuration and size in a rhythmic family dispersion and congregation as the resources seasonally permitted. Almost incidentally raw materials and commodities would have been gathered from one spot and circulated with and amongst the family bands in their annual movements; perhaps occasionally, some commodities might be exchanged with peripheral bands of other groups in largely ceremonial gift exchanges of partly symbolic and partly useful foreign commodities. Naturally, it would be such rare, colourful and exotic acquisitions that elite individuals would above all treasure and display as part of their prestige and status insignia. To some extent, therefore, the long-distance movement of desirable commodities will have been directly stimulated by the more elaborate ceremonial and social roles which the economies of the more advantageous areas could support – the chiefs and sub-chiefs, lineage headmen and hunt leaders, shamans and spirit doctors, tribal functionaries and skilled semi-specialists who might operate advantageously in uniting the temporary tribal band gatherings of the Dordogne, Moravia and the Ukraine. In these situations territories rich in natural resources could support unusually elaborate social structures with an unusual variety of social ranks, each requiring distinctive display insignia and therefore together stimulating gift-exchange systems to satisfy these needs.[9]

[8] A. Leroi-Gourhan, 'Les Fouilles d'Aroy-sur-Cure (Yonne)', *Gallia Préhistoire*, IV (1961), 3–16; P. Mouton and R. Joffroy, 'Les Gisements Aurignaciens des Rois à Mouthiers (Charente)', *Gallia*, Supplement IX (1958); L. Pradel, 'La Grotte Périgordienne et Aurignacienne du Fontenioux, commune de Saint-Pierre-de-Maillé (Vienne)', *Bull. de la Soc. Préhistorique Française*, XLIX (1952), 413–32. See P. G. Bahn, 'Seasonal migration in South-west France during the Late Glacial Period', *Journ. of Archaeological Science*, IV (1977), 245–57 for more recent discussion.

[9] The author would like to acknowledge the debt he owes to Paul Wilkinson for help and advice in preparing this section on Palaeolithic commodities.

III. *The Agrarian Economies:* c. *6,000–2,000 B.C.*[10]

Post-glacial conditions, *c.* 10,000–6,000 B.C., reintroduced heavily forested landscapes to middle and northern Europe, largely replacing the grasslands, steppe and tundra and their big, herd herbivores with thick forest vegetation and the mainly small or scattered game associated with these environments. The gathering-hunting-fishing bands responded to these changes with more scattered and less specialised social structures and economies – the agile individual stalking of forest deer with the bow replaced the communal *battue* and the open-country spear and spearthrower techniques. In the Mediterranean zone of Europe these post-glacial changes were less dramatic and, indeed, hardly detectable outside a general trend towards drier conditions and fluctuations in marginal mountain and plateau zones. The Mediterranean gatherers-hunters-fishers, therefore, show a marked continuity of Palaeolithic techniques in interrelated Epipalaeolithic complexes which remained comparatively densely deployed in advantageous areas of the Mediterranean littoral.

The threshold marking the establishment of the first simple agrarian economies in Europe is therefore as complex a series of events and changes as any we have to discuss. Gathering, hunting and fishing continued as vigorously as ever, both beyond the territories of the peasant settlers and, indeed, as a significant subcultural activity within the agricultural communities. Stone technology remained the basis of artefact manufacture, and the Palaeolithic cognitive map of the primary resources of Europe still contributed the main framework for exploitation; everywhere the continuity of the aboriginal gathering-hunting-fishing communities is to some extent attested.

Nevertheless, from the seventh millennium onwards southern Europe was increasingly networked by new kinds of sociocultural unit which gradually repatterned the social, economic, religious and psychological configuration of most of the population of Europe. Within the space of two thousand years, *c.* 6,000–4,000 B.C., peasant villagers had cut and burnt their way from one end of forested Europe to the other, spreading a lattice of village communities with a population density per square mile hitherto unparalleled in any except the most advantageous aboriginal territories of the continent – and therein quite unmatched for economic stability and potential. The basis for this population deployment was cereal agriculture backed by

[10] For general surveys, see S. Piggott, *Ancient Europe* (Edinburgh, 1965), chap. 2; A. C. Renfrew, *Before Civilization* (London, 1973); H. T. Waterbolk, 'Food production in prehistoric Europe', *Science*, CLXII (1968), 1093–1102; D. Collins, *The Origins of Europe* (London, 1975).

stock-rearing and balanced by gathering, hunting and fishing as before; the forest-consuming stone adze and fire, the antler and crook-branch hoe, the ceramic pottage bowl and the storage jar were the artefacts of the age. The slow retreat of the Scandinavian ice cap and the collapse of its peripheral glacial weather system set the context of this threshold in European development. The ensuing post-glacial optimum introduced the Atlantic climatic phase in Europe north of the Mediterranean – a warm, wet phase with a mean annual temperature some 2–2½ °C above those now prevailing and lasting almost three thousand years, *c.* 5,000–2,000 B.C. The period of optimal warmth fell broadly *c.* 4,000–3,000 B.C. and brought to a climax the dense mixed forest of oak, elm, lime and alder which then stretched almost without interruption from the Carpathians to the North Sea, parted only occasionally by the sinuous highways of the major river systems and the Alpine heights.

The expansion of the agrarian frontier from the Mediterranean littoral to the fringes of the northern coniferous forests was a process of the greatest importance for the subsequent economic development of Europe. The initial foci in which the separate elements of this new and complex set of economic strategies had first appeared were further east – in that elliptical football which encloses the Anatolian and Iranian plateaux.[11] These two great middle altitude plateaux, with their rain-trapping mountain rims and their then moderate climate, were for the most part rolling grasslands filled with herbivore herds and scattered belts of oak, cedar and pistachio woodlands. Amongst these wild grasses were the ancestors of the agrarian cereals – emmer, einkorn, barley, millet and oats; amongst the herbivores grazing on these grasses and woodlands were the ancestors of the domestic animals – sheep, goats, pigs and wild cattle. The trees of the plateau parkland also included most of the orchard fruit and nut trees – almond, pistachio, wild grapes, figs, apples, pears and others. On the northwestern flanks of this area the Anatolian cereal, wild einkorn, spilled into adjacent Mediterranean Balkan Europe and Greece. To the south of the plateaux emmer and barley were also to be found in scattered stands along the temperate altitudes of the Lebanon range, probably extending as far south as Sinai. It was in these plateaux and peripheral territories that the gathered food supplies were at first trivially augmented by fencing and resowing small patches of wild grasses for their seeds, and by protecting and propagating the trees which

[11] K. V. Flannery, 'The ecology of early food production in Mesopotamia', *Science*, CXLVII (1965), 1247–56; P. J. Ucko and G. W. Dimbleby (eds), *The Domestication and Exploitation of Plants and Animals* (London, 1969). For an alternative view of the origins of agriculture, see Higgs, *Economic Prehistory*.

produced fruit or nuts; other techniques were also developed for capturing alive female animals and their young and penning them up against hard times; the simplest way to preserve food supplies was to keep the staples alive. The gatherers-hunters-fishers in these limited but diverse territories were thus increasingly able to stabilise their food supply in a run of good years and bad years by a little supplementary horticulture and stock-rearing.

The initial mosaic of regional experiments in food regulation took place between *c.* 19,000–6,000 B.C. around and within the primary plateau areas, assisted by the fluctuating desiccation of some of the more marginal terrain in conjunction with the breakdown of the ice-cap weather system in northern Europe. The gatherers-hunters-fishers of these southern areas had already for many millennia seasonally harvested and pulverised the seeds, fruits, nuts and legumes of the proto-domesticates, including the cereal seeds, alfalfa, ryegrass and flax seeds, wild caper, almonds, pistachio nuts, acorns, peas, beans, lentils, astragalus and trigonella, wild grapes, figs, apples and pears. Over the same vast inland area, with its negligible river and lake resources, the wide absence of fish, shellfish and other forms of aquatic protein helped to emphasise the prolonged and intimate hunting acquaintance of the gatherers-hunters with the ancestors of the domestic animals – sheep, goats, cattle and pigs. Retrospectively, it is possible to distinguish markedly regional and localised gatherer-hunter band economies, stabilised with idiosyncratic combinations of semi-domesticates – sheep, goats and barley here, goats, legumes and orchard there, cattle, pigs and einkorn elsewhere. Band contact and interaction coincided with convergent conditions to pool the economic strategies and staples of the local groups until, by the seventh millennium, these had stabilised into a limited set of widespread agrarian systems based on combinations of principal staples – sheep, goats, pigs, cattle with emmer, einkorn, barley cereals, plus peas, beans, lentils and apples, pears and nuts balanced against continued gathering, hunting and fishing. A large number of semi-independent regional subsistence props were thus increasingly and successively integrated within a smaller number of balanced economic systems, in which the props had become the main pillars of the new, more extensively mixed strategies. The three-sided equilibrium triangle of the gatherer-hunter-fisher economies was now a stabilised polygon with fresh agrarian resource dimensions and a capacity for the territorially dense occupation of long-term settlement sites producing an annual food surplus.

Around 6,000 B.C., perhaps earlier in places, the first definite traces of agrarian settlers are found in Europe. These settlements are restricted to the Balkan Mediterranean zone immediately adjacent to the Anatolian plateau and tightly confined to the ecological niches already occupied by the wild prototypes of the new domesticates; it is even possible that the territories of this area were fully within the zone of primary developments but this has yet to be demonstrated. On the fertile plains of Macedonia and Bulgarian Thrace settlers from north-western Anatolia extended a growing network of substantial villages of flat-roofed rectangular houses, using ceramic containers for their cereal gruels and stews. The grassy plain of Thessaly, directly linked with southern Anatolia by the island chain from the Gulf of Volos, now began to support numerous small villages in which pottery was still unknown, although emmer wheat, barley, peas, beans and lentils were grown, sheep and goats reared, and the same fruit and nut trees maintained as those found in the Anatolian and Iranian plateau areas.

However, the ecological personality of Europe is not so closely similar to that of the Mediterranean plateaux and littoral as to permit a wholesale intrusion without adaptive modification. Geological contortions have contrived to rim the Mediterranean basin on its northern periphery with a semi-continuous chain of formidable mountains which drop precipitately to the narrow littoral plains. The altitude of this chain, together with its consequent rainfall and winter snows, combine to extend fingers of temperate middle European and Alpine ecology to the very edge of the Mediterranean itself. The plains of Bulgarian Thrace, Macedonia and Thessaly are abruptly walled by plateaux and peaks which then carried belts of temperate European deciduous oak forest below an Alpine beech and fir band, the whole populated by elements of middle European fauna – deer, mountain goat, wild cattle, boar, bear and wolf. The indigenous European gatherer-hunter-fisher band territories must already have embraced most of the surface area of the continent but with these largely mobile populations the occupation density was insignificant, except along the Mediterranean, Atlantic and Baltic littoral zones, where marine and land resources were complementary; in these latter areas there is every evidence that the ancient populations continued and gradually re-equipped and repatterned under agrarian acculturation.

Northwards again, beyond the Mediterranean outliers of the mid-European ecology, there lay a far more formidable environmental cordon barring the north-eastern exit of the great Hungarian plain in a broad diagonal band, where the Austrian Alps threaten to join the Little Carpathians, only forty miles away across the Danube. The formidable character of this natural Maginot line was complicated for the Mediterranean agronomists by the ever wetter-than-present Atlantic climate which prevailed beyond it and by the reinforcing complexity of its separate ecological factors which provide a cumulative defence in depth. North-west of this band lay the European glacial soils and clays, the long, snowy European winters, the heavy annual rainfall, the short cloudy summers and the primeval deciduous oak forest, in a climax form several millennia old – an uncleared tangle of massive, fallen, dead and decaying trunks three to ten feet thick, interlaced by the formidable undergrowth which a damp, ungrazed forest supports. That this primary forest exists nowhere in Europe today, is a tribute to generations of peasant farmers and a relentless clearance against which the forest finally capitulated only in late Medieval times. The aboriginal gatherers-hunters-fishers had always lived in and through the forest, their own friendly englobing environment; to the land-using peasant farmer this forest was a hostile ogre which must be felled with the axe and burnt with fire. It is little wonder that European peasant folktales to this day are uniformly dominated by the contrast struck between the friendly open villages and the threatening forest, with its stock of menacing inhabitants – from wolves and bears to magical shamans and bands of little forest people; the socio-economic significance of the young woodman as a folk hero was perhaps similar to that now reserved for Russian tractor drivers.

The Mediterranean farming communities simply skirted and outflanked the southernmost European defences, utilising but not settling the higher zones of the Pinduc and Balkan mountain massifs. The seventh-millennium villages therefore extended their network along the rivers and coasts, where important supplementary food supplies were always available and communication was easy. They moved inland around the peripheries of the great ranges, following the fertile valley soils and the Mediterranean micro-environments which extended far up the ascending Danube, Maritsa, Kara Su, Struma and Vardar rivers. By exploiting this deep peripheral penetration of aspects of Mediterranean ecology into lowland Bulgaria and Macedonia, some peasant groups were able to infiltrate the great Hungarian plain without the necessity for drastic cultural adaptation. However, those communities on the north-western Hungarian frontier and those on the higher headwaters of the Balkan-Serbian plateau rivers were gradually forced into closer and closer mutual adjustment with middle European fauna and flora in its less dense development. In these transitional areas an important first acquaintance and elementary knowledge of European resources was gradually established; timber increasingly replaced pisé in house construction, ridge roofs were adopted against the wet Atlantic climate, the range of stone axe and adze proliferated in response to the forest environment. Suitable stone for adzes and artefacts rapidly became a resource of great importance and doubtless some knowledge of the properties of the strange stones, timbers, edible roots, berries, nuts, animals and plants will have been gained from the aboriginal groups into the midst of whom the peasant settlers were moving.

A peasant community of this period may be usefully illustrated by the riverside village at Lepenski Vir, on the Danube east of Belgrade, carbon dated at 4950±150 B.C. The village of thirty to thirty-five trapezoidal houses was set on a terraced spur above the whirlpool which has given the site its name. The whirlpool, it materialised, was an important resource in its own right – sucking surface water and food down to the depths where sturgeon, catfish, and carp permanently hovered and ate their fill, to be netted and harpooned by the villagers. The situation of the village within the steep Danube gorge tightly restricted the agricultural land to small garden-size pockets, but this could be set against the advantages of the immediately adjacent river resources and those of the limestone cliffs which soar from 300–700 metres above the site. In effect, the limestone canyon concentrated at one locus the separate resource and micro-climate zones of the Danube, its shallows, the warm environment of the beach terraces and the village site, the temperate forest and animals of the middle slopes and the cool montane peaks beyond. The strategy of this site location may reflect the relatively small part played by cereal 'garden horticulture' in the Lepenski Vir economy and certainly the plentiful fish bones, wild boar, wild cattle, deer and small carnivore remains eloquently reflect the natural resources of the vertical hierarchy of resource zones adjacent to the site.[12]

By the fifth millennium similar small village communities were strung along the Mediterranean littoral and islands, from the Aegean and Adriatic to the coasts of Spain, France and North Africa. These coastal communities also relied heavily on the rich harvest of sardine, tunny, shellfish and Mediterranean seals to augment their small patches of cereals and their herds of sheep and goats. Many of these coastal communities seem to represent convergent acculturation and spread of artefacts and techniques amongst the pre-existing and relatively populous, interrelated gatherer-fisher-hunter bands of the Epirote-Adriatic, Franco-Italian and Ibero-Mauritanian Epipalaeolithic complexes. The inland penetration of Europe was only slightly slower, the village network rapidly extending to the boundaries of the Hungarian plain by the end of the sixth millennium. Villages were strung along

[12] J. Nandris, 'Lepenski Vir', *Science Journ.* (Jan. 1958), 64–70; R. Tringham, *Hunters, Fishers and Farmers of Eastern Europe* (London, 1971).

the river networks of the Balkans and deployed in chains north from Thessaly and Macedonia, up the river Vardar, down the river Morava to the Danube and thence northwards along the well-drained terraces of the Körös. Along this filigree linkage, large shells from the Aegean Spondylus mussel were exchanged from hand to hand in the form of necklaces of cylindrical shell beads, or as bracelets cut from entire shells; the mute surviving traces of what was once probably an intensive two-way exchange of Mediterranean against European commodities.[13]

The infiltration of the Balkan uplands had already acquainted the peasant farmers with some aspects of European fauna and flora in the atypical Mesomediterranean bioclimatic zone. However, the north-western Hungarian threshold to the true mid-European ecology required the relentless peasant persistence of the whole fifth millennium before successful adaptations and mutations amongst the societies, material culture, crops and animals of the farmers enabled them to emerge with a stable, integrated, cultural format; one capable of penetrating the mid-European environment – the inner frontier of reinforcing glacial soils, thick deciduous forest, sharp winters and wet summers. This pioneer penetration was apparently accomplished by the Danubian peasants from the north-western fringes of the Körös network. Tightly organised in small lineage communities, these pioneers slowly forged a technique of slash-and-burn hoe agriculture in forest clearings on loess slopes, thus exploiting the virgin fertility of the finest, well-drained glacial soils in a rotational schedule around the settlements of neat, large, timber longhouses. Cattle and stock were few and even these were probably stalled for much of the inclement winter in the aisles of the great thatched longhouses. Adzes of carefully selected and widely exchanged tough igneous stones characterise the challenge presented by the forest to these peasants; a challenge successfully overcome only by a careful integration of selected soils, cereals and domestic animals, within a skilful strategy combining settlement stability with the repetitive short-term exploitation of fresh loess plots, meeting the forest with socially organised cooperative effort using fire and the adze.

The favoured loess soils were originally precipitated in long narrow bands by the prevailing winds blowing moraine rock dust southwards from the ice face of the long-withdrawn Eurasiatic ice cap. Almost by accident, therefore, these fertile and well-drained soils form a narrow discontinuous fillet of settlement areas, extending from the

[13] N. J. Shackleton and A. C. Renfrew, 'Neolithic trade routes re-aligned by oxygen isotope analyses', *Nature*, CCXXVIII (1970), 1062–5.

Ukraine to the Paris basin in one direction and from Iran to the Hwang-Ho in another. Within the space of little more than two or three hundred years the Danubian peasants had multiplied and proliferated their villages along the whole loess chain to the coasts of the North Sea. Over the same period other very similar communities, using closely similar economic strategies, dispersed eastwards from northern Iran into north-western China.

This peasant penetration of continental Europe has often been compared with the European frontier in forested America. The frontiersmen in both situations showed that cultural adaptation was the key to survival and the first European peasants found a very great deal to learn from the sparse but minutely adapted indigenous gatherer-hunter-fisher bands. This must especially have been the case with regard to information on forest craft, hunting-fishing-gathering schedules, local resources and the peculiar properties of the European fauna and flora. The outcrops of hard rocks, decorative coloured ochres and the sharp siliceous stones essential for tool production, were, as we have seen, already well known to the local aborigines and widely distributed within the mobile bands themselves. Now we have a context of a more static village network, supporting a relatively dense population actively engaged in forest clearance; a context which therefore required the intensive exploitation and regular dispersal of the commodities by deliberately adjusted exchange mechanisms operating over far wider fields than the unit band territory and its simple multiples, observed in the preceding phases of European prehistory.

The quarrying of stone, obsidian, flint and coloured ochres had already been extensively practised by some of the gatherer-hunter-fisher bands and even in these early contexts it now appears that a limited amount of shallow shaft mining was already practised before the sixth millennium. Szeletian gatherers seem to have quarried a considerable quantity of soft ochre pigment from 'paint' mine shafts near Lovas, in Hungary, as early as Wurm I–II, *c.* 35,000 B.C., and comparable workings for haematite pigment are known from the Kamienna river valley in Poland; significantly, both sites document an intensive Palaeolithic exploitation of coloured pigments in areas where no Palaeolithic painting now survives.[14] The shallow surface quarries for flint at Grand Pressigny and the Belcayre plateau, in France, were already being exploited by Palaeolithic bands, whilst later gatherers-hunters-fishers extracted quartzite from the quarries at Wommersom in Belgium and flint nodules from the pits at Cronsko

[14] Jazdzewski, *Poland*, 56–7.

in central Poland.[15] At the latter site, several hundred pits had been cut some ten feet deep into the clay to recover the chocolate coloured flint; the nodules were then worked into rough-outs on extensive surface working-floors, dating *c.* 5,600–5,000 B.C. It now seems probable that shallow pit and shaft mining had been a frequent practice amongst the large gatherer-hunter-fisher communities of the post-glacial north European forests and that the more intensive Neolithic mining over the same territory represents yet one more element in the cultural continuity of this area from late Gravettian, through Maglemose and Ertebølle times, to the early Funnel-Beaker farmers of the fourth millennium.

However, even the most elaborate quarrying sites of the gatherer-hunter-fisher bands only represent the cumulative consequences of thousands of annual visits, in the course of their enforced movements around the resources of their territories: activities largely, but not entirely, confined to satisfying only the immediate needs of the groups concerned. In contrast, Neolithic mining developed a more advanced semi-specialist status, supported by the increasingly populous agrarian communities and pressured by their voracious demand for axe and adze blades for use in forest clearance. Hundreds of shafts were now successively sunk from 30–60 feet through the chalk at focal mining centres, from the Malmo area of Sweden and adjacent Denmark, the Spiennes in Belgium, Grimes Graves and Easton Down in England, to Krzemionki in Poland. In the Mediterranean, too, flint was mined from deep tunnels in the limestone at Monte Tabuto, Sicily, and at mainland sites in Apulia; these supplies were also supplemented by limited exchange networks circulating the highly prized obsidian from Lipari, Italy, and the Aegean islands.[16] In most of these centres of intensive mining, there is evidence of an organisation and output superior to that found in the simple pits of the gatherers-hunters-fishers. Special raw materials were gathered from widely distant areas to facilitate the mining operations – hundreds of short-lived antler picks were required, special tough mining axes and mauls were employed, quantities of fat were needed for the dish lamps, not to mention wedges, mallets, shovels and baskets. No less than 244 discarded antler picks were recovered from two of the pits at Grimes Graves, Norfolk. Especially tough igneous stone tools were also imported for the mining activities – Cornish greenstone was employed at Grimes Graves, and picks, hammers, adzes and mauls of Silesian gabbro and basalt were used at Krzemionki.

[15] Clark, *Prehistoric Europe*, 182–3; D. de Sonneville Bordes, *Le Paléolithique Supérieur en Périgord* (Bordeaux, 1960); Jazdzewski, *Poland*, 56.

[16] Clark, *Prehistoric Europe*, 174.

The output of such mining centres is likely to have reached many thousands of finished rough-outs per person and at the Norwegian island quarry of Hespriholmen alone, it has been estimated that some 20,000 boat loads of greenstone had been extracted.[17] This degree of organisation and redistribution is obviously far greater than that necessary to satisfy the requirements of local communities. The periodic exploitation of these resources had clearly been transformed into at least a long annual season of preparation and mining by semi-specialists from nearby villages – probably twenty or thirty men and women successively opening-up four or five deep mines in the dry season necessary for safe shaft sinking. Although only a few people may have been involved, supplies had to be gathered on a large scale and the mined nodules worked into tool blanks by surface knappers, repetitively employing their special technological skills. Finally, the flint, obsidian or stone ingots had to be distributed over a wide area in exchange for other commodities.

The distribution patterns of these thousands of surplus blades, cores, axes and adzes fully confirm the implications of the more extensive deep mining activities. Whereas the gatherer-hunter-fisher distribution units spanned a hundred or so miles of sparse dispersion, now it is commonplace to find quantities of these 'factory' products extending in asymmetrical distribution fans, frequently stretching two or three hundred miles from the self-same resource centres. It is significant that these factory centres developed a mutually adjusting distribution pattern such that every area could gain supplies from several centres, although one source was usually predominant. This complex outfall could only have been sustained within the context of very active and well organised systems of interlinked ceremonial gift-exchange cycles. These exchange rings will also have circulated other commodities in both directions – pigs, dogs, axes, shells, teeth, boars' tusks, orchres, pitch, furs, feathers, amber, beads, bracelets, pots, obsidian, copper trinkets and display gear, selected artefacts and cereals. The stone-axe and copper-artefact distribution patterns are therefore of the greatest interest mainly as the only surviving skeletal trade of this continuous but swelling traffic in European commodities of all kinds.

The premise of 'Neolithic self-sufficiency' is therefore only relatively acceptable, if at all. The circulation of European commodities may not have been quantitatively very large, nor very essential in terms of subsistence, but nevertheless the elaborate network of exchange partners, village markets and resource centres successfully distributed local commodities far beyond the territories within which

[17] Clark, 'Stone axe and adze blades', 1–28.

they had formerly been restricted; the new mobility of commodities thus serving to compensate for the growing requirements of the more static agrarian communities. This traffic incidentally, but significantly, extended the transmission of many new artefacts and materials, customs and games, stories and religious tenets, and other novel items quite unrelated to the formal commodity content of the exchange networks. The drive in this traffic was the display and consumption of commodities required for the continuous 'rites-of-passage' of the tribesman's life-cycle. The circulating machinery for this traffic was the cross-cultural gift-exchange network, involving short-distance movements of porters or canoes. The outcome of this traffic was the expanding development of extensive trade networks, linking hundreds of otherwise unrelated communities in the rapid dissemination of innovations and commodities with mutually beneficial results; a traffic which supported an important rise in the territorial potential of formerly marginal environments now coupled in a multilinear direction with various areas of more stable output.

IV. *The Aegean Network*[18] *and the Early Bronze Technologies:* C. 2,000–1,400 B.C.

Throughout the fourth and third millennia the agrarian tribesmen of Europe continued to hoe and weed, hunt and fish, gather and store, whilst the exchange networks serving the settled communities increasingly replaced the old forest trails of the mobile gatherers-hunters-fishers. Even the inhabitants of the northern coniferous forests had adopted limited aspects of the new subsistence patterns and in the West almost every Atlantic island had become the home of settled communities. Thus the wide range of European ecology was increasingly reflected in the diversified mosaic of cultures, from the peasant fishermen of the Mediterranean littoral to the lineage communities collectively cultivating the clearings of the Scandinavian forests, and from the lakeside cabins of the Alpine farmers to the large, timber and pisé fortified villages on the Balkan mounds. However, significant innovations had already begun to appear; restricted to the Balkan and Mediterranean zone at first but spreading to the inland territories through the intercommunicating village network. Copper metallurgy, including the production of simple arsenical alloys, slowly became an important feature of the Balkan village centres after *c.* 3500 B.C., although the new mineral remained disadvantageously expensive and

[18] For general surveys, see M. Gimbutas, *The Balts* (London, 1963); Piggott, *Ancient Europe*, chap. 3; A. C. Renfrew (ed.), *The Explanation of Cultural Change* (London, 1972).

rare in middle and northern Europe until the Alpine Saxo-Thuringian and Bohemian lodes were opened up, after *c.* 2500 B.C.[19] An innovation with far more extensive repercussions also spread through the same areas about the same time – the ard, or simple plough. Between *c.* 2500–2000 B.C. the ard widely replaced the hoe as the primary agricultural tool of the peasant farmers of Europe, rapidly transforming the amount of land one man could bring under cultivation, increasing the demand for land and the surplus from it, and revolutionising attitudes towards land, property, inheritance and kinship obligations. The complex dissemination of the ard, yoke, ox-traction, wheeled vehicles, the sled, copper-alloy technology jointly combined cumulatively with the drier conditions of the developing sub-boreal period to transform middle Europe, crossing the threshold *c.* 2500–2000 B.C.

Meanwhile, major developments in Egypt and Mesopotamia had already advanced to a critical state, affecting the economic and social patterns of their own and immediately adjacent peoples. Sprawling townships began to manifest a higher degree of central organisation and an increasing degree of subcultural specialisation; urban chiefdoms were developing into regional city states, dependent on the surplus of a penumbra of scattered villages. The enlarging spheres of political interest of these urban centres began to tessellate the countryside and inevitable boundary conflicts about peripheral resources became a frequent source of conflict along the great river valleys. In the ceaseless mutual adjustment of conquest and submission, organisation and reorganisation, larger and larger political units emerged to redistribute the expanding food surplus from the villagers' irrigation and plough agriculture. By *c.* 3500 B.C. the competitive conflict between city and city, nome and nome, had already fully developed; by *c.* 3000 B.C. great states and territorial kingdoms had condensed from this aggregating and segregating process. Menes, the king of Upper Egypt, conquered the delta nomes and ruled the Nile from the first cataract to the Mediterranean; in Mesopotamia, the copper-sheathed phalanxes and battle-waggons of the kings of Ur, Lagash and Eridu, fought for temporary ascendancy until Sargon of Akkad established his short-lived empire in the twenty-fourth century B.C.

The emergence of new social and political units in the valleys of the Nile, the Tigris and the Euphrates had wide repercussions. The rambling tribal towns of Anatolia, Syria, and Palestine were already two and three millennia old, but they did not compare in size, degree of organisation or potential with the new cities and the new city states;

[19] For recent discussion, see A. Sherratt, 'Resources, technology and trade in early European metallurgy', in Sieveking *et al.*, *Problems in Economic and Social Archaeology*, 557–81.

the 'civis' and civilisation had arrived. The new urban centres were deliberately aimed at the objective of optimal economic output for the greater aggrandisement of the city managers and their state; in this world of competing powers, only the most powerful could remain independent. The focal urban centres drew surplus resources from the countryside on an increasing scale and the central authority organised scribes and officials, with their scripts and seals, to note, count and reallocate the stored surplus to other specialists and artificers, these in turn produced more consumer goods and more complex artefacts. The cities were vast amplifying units plugged into the old Neolithic network of villages: raw materials were sucked in and complex social and material products turned out, but since power and prestige centred in the possession of these complex new products, this output largely remained the restricted property of the temple staff and the king's servants. The temple and the palace were not merely the centres of political and religious power, they were impressive factory centres with whole wings set aside for the reserve of raw materials and magazines of finished products together with the workshops of the tied artificers; these buildings were simultaneously centres of state wealth and finance, commercial banks, arsenals, granaries and storehouses for state reserves of all kinds. The palace and temple were the commercial and industrial centres of the revenue state and they survived in these capacities until the collapse of the Byzantine Empire and the political elevation of the merchant classes and the self-made capitalists.

These events were seemingly remote from the European tribesmen of the third millennium but the consequence of these new political organisms, deep in Asia Minor and far across the Mediterranean, reached out to the very borders of Europe, whilst their indirect repercussions sped far beyond direct contacts. The new network of cities and city states expanded over and above the existing lattice of simple villages, which in many ways continued almost unchanged; the new phenomenon was largely a subcultural revolution in which certain restricted castes could benefit from the enlarged revenue extracted from groups of villages. The new political powers therefore depended upon an uninterrupted supply of resources and raw materials. Initially, the bulk of the food requirements could be supplied from local territories, but it was certain strategic raw materials which now necessitated the efficient organisation of commodities which had previously trickled in by gift-exchange – formal trade was the solution. In the alluvial valleys of the Nile, the Tigris and the Euphrates the strategic raw materials primarily included big timber for chariots, carts, ships and buildings as well as metals for the tools of production and the weapons of military power. Large and regular quantities of copper were necessary together with the more limited tin supplies later required to make hard bronze. In time, the consignments of tin came to assume the strategic importance and political significance that has been attached in modern times to tungsten for steel armour plate and machine tools, or latterly to oil supplies and uranium deposits.

The dynasts of Egypt and Mesopotamia organised increasingly more extensive land and sea networks to supply the raw materials necessary for the maintenance of the state against its rivals.[20] At first, this supply organisation was less in the form of continuous flow, two-directional trade as we now understand that term, and rather more in the form of annual military expeditions to the resource areas; if the resource area was peripheral to several major states it would thus become a politically and militarily contested area. Should the population of the resource area prove hostile it was regularly attacked and looted; if it was more pragmatic it supplied the expedition's requirements and in return the elite caste was given rich embassies and treasures and left in peace; thus royal gift-exchange became a political and economic precedure for the diplomatic ratification of certain mutual obligations, at the same time linking elite castes cross-culturally to an extent often endorsed by intermarriage. Under more peaceful conditions these expeditions could increasingly be left to professional merchants under armed escort, with regular caravans of pack donkeys and two-wheeled ox carts. These merchants were often required by local rulers to reside only in limited quarters of their towns and such merchants' quarters or 'karum' then provided all the local facilities of commercial banks and caravanserai. In this way the local potentates in distant towns were able to take advantage of the routes through their territories to tax and tithe the merchandise passing through, thus materially augmenting the riches and political power of their own dynasty and town.

The proliferating trade networks, therefore, had the general consequence of inducing the formation and agglomeration of many small buffer states and dynasties amongst the already populous tribal townships and chiefdoms of Anatolia and the Levant. Thus, the economic activities of the great states seem to have been instrumental in the rise of the barbarous Hittite kingdom under its earliest dynasts, Pitkhana and Anittas, around their town of Kussura, *c.* 2000 B.C. and in the similar rise of the enriched city states of Levantine Aleppo, Alalakh, Byblos, Tarsus, Carchemish and Ugarit. Beyond these the network stretched to the earliest palace kingdoms of Knossos, Mallia

[20] J. Botteró, E. Cassin and J. Vercoutter (eds.), *The Near East: the Early Civilizations* (London, 1967); J. Mellaart, *Earliest Civilizations of the Near East* (London, 1965); Recontre Assyriologique Internationale, 1976, in *Iraq*, XXXIX (1977).

and Phaistos on the Cretan plains, and Alasia in copper-rich Cyprus. Even at the most distant boundaries of Anatolia and Europe the nameless dynasts of Troy II and Dorak seem to have governed small frontier states which may have respectively encompassed Lemnos, Imbros, Tenedos, Gallipoli and the Troad at one end of the Straits, and the Bosporus at the other – barbarous kingdoms with their feet both in Anatolia and Europe. Even beyond these fringes of urban civilisation lay the diminutive but proud halls of the petty Helladic chiefdoms of Lerna on the Gulf of Argos, at Orchomenos on Lake Copais, at Dimini in the Thessalian plain, and at the lesser sites of the Ezero culture in the plains of Bulgarian Thrace. By 2000 B.C. the great imperial powers were focally set amidst an expanding mosaic of vassal kingdoms and free city states, distantly tessellated into a peripheral band of greater and lesser urban and non-urban tribal chiefdoms – a replicating pattern partly precipitated by the organisation of the great powers themselves.[21]

It is only when one grasps the scale and dimensions of the new trading enterprises in comparison with the preceding scale of these activities that their indirect importance for Europe becomes apparent. About 2350 B.C. Sargon of Akkad led an expedition northwards into central Anatolia to assist his merchants in the city of Puruskhanda, returning by way of the Silver Mountains (Taurus) and the Cedar Mountains (Amanus). Simultaneously, the same king could boast that his southern trade network was such that ships lay at harbour in front of his Mesopotamian palace from Tilmun (Bahrain), Makkan (Persian Gulf), and Meluhha (Gulf of Oman); thus Sargon's network directly drew upon commodities within a radius of 1000 miles and indirectly even beyond that. Caravans of 300 donkeys and a dozen carts travelling 500 miles became a regular occurrence, carrying on occasion $12\frac{1}{2}$ tons of tin in a single load – sufficient for 125 tons of hard bronze, or enough to equip the total armoury of a small state. The pharaohs of the earliest dynasties also regularly sent annual expeditions to Sinai for copper and to Lebanon for timber; in 2650 B.C. alone, the Pharaoh Sneferu brought back 40 shiploads of cedar logs in a single expedition to Byblos. The Levant was becoming a crucial area of resources simultaneously sought by Egypt, Mesopotamia and Anatolia; only thirty years before the maritime expedition of Sneferu, in 2680 B.C., King Gudea of Lagash had been collecting timber in the same area of his expedition from Mesopotamia. With these intersecting spheres of economic interest the great powers of Egypt and Mesopotamia

[21] See S. Hood, *The Minoans* (London, 1971); R. W. Hutchinson, *Prehistoric Crete* (Harmondsworth, 1962); S. Loyd, *Early Highland Peoples of Anatolia* (London, 1967).

were inevitably brought into a military and political involvement which culminated in the Egyptian conquest of the entire Syrian coastline from Sinai to Byblos, under the pharaohs of the XIIth dynasty *c.* 2050–1900 B.C., broadly contemporary with the Sumerian empire of the IIIrd dynasty at Ur, *c.* 2150–2000 B.C.

Even at the distant Troad, the kings of Dorak could receive a gold-sheathed throne from the Pharaoh Sahure, *c.* 2553 B.C., probably as a diplomatic present indirectly exchanged through Tarsus or Byblos for commodities shipped through those intermediate ports.[22] Beyond the frontier kingdoms of Troy and Dorak, donkey caravans may even have trekked annually to the barbaric chiefdoms on the defended mounds of Bulgaria to load woollen cloth, gold, timber and incidental curiosities. More distant still, there now arose tribal chiefdoms scattered along the Danube and in adjacent areas of middle Europe, marked by the rich burials of the chieftains themselves and by the scattered bronze and gold hoards of their personal treasuries. These chiefdoms were the original consequence of economic surplus, advantageous location and the indirect stimuli emanating from the Aegean, a political precipitate of efficient village agrarian economies using the plough, bronze tools, the cart, the sled and the canoe. The chiefdoms stimulated the exploitation of local copper, gold and tin resources, and organised the exchange networks bringing amber, furs and other products from the north and faience beads, metal vessels and prestige weaponry from the south.

The rise of the middle European Aunjetitz and Tumulus tribal chiefdoms and their shortlived, unstable confederacies were directly related to the rise of intensive European cereal and pastoral agriculture; the more dense population and its more complex economic organisation stimulated the redistribution of produce and commodities within more centralised tribal configurations. In this context, and with these early bronze technologies, the metalwork was almost entirely the expensive vehicle for status and rank manifestation, the caste marks of the chief, his kin, and his dependent artificers. The showy bronze weaponry and the gold and amber gewgaws commanded respect and even the few bronze tools only served to produce more equipment to further distinguish the owners of the means of production and to endorse their right to redistribute the communal surplus. The social consequence, although expressed with particular cultural variations, was a cumulative cycle tending to make the elite even more wealthy and powerful, stimulating more and more subcultural specialisation and differentiation, thus promoting an overall proliferation in cultural castes and social subdivisions.

[22] J. Mellaart, 'The Royal Treasure of Dorak', *Illustrated London News* (18 Nov. 1959). The Dorak finds were not subsequently verified and are not accepted as authentic by all authorities.

The intensive plough agriculture produced a surplus for redistribution by the elite; the elite exchanged the surplus for weaponry, display trinkets and tools for their smiths and artificers; the elite became more powerful and took more surplus from more villages and hired more specialists. One man with a plough could free many women from hoeing to specialise in household industries, especially weaving. The surplus cloth joined the surplus foodstuffs, the products of the specialist bronze smiths and carpenters, and the land ploughed by a man's own efforts, to add to the increased diversity of property. Property itself increased the importance of vertical genealogies and thus formalised inheritance patterns within kin groups rapidly became an important and complex machinery for the restriction of property within the bounds of increasingly well-defined complex castes.

Elaborate feuding and hospitality systems probably developed, which at one and the same time could ensure the safe conduct of trade commodities, metal supplies, artificers, merchants and caravans and yet, beyond an invisible line, would permit wholesale piracy, the taking of captives, looting, warfare and murder in pursuit of valuable staples. The increased importance of wealth hoards, and the economic desirability of male captives as miners and slaves, or female captives for weaving and handicrafts, would probably have played an important part in a general increase in raiding and therefore in the escalation of settlement defences and in weaponry. Indeed, all the traditional elements of the 'heroic societies' were now emerging: the increasingly integrated functional development of intensive economy, metal-using cultures – tribal chiefdoms, socially stratified castes, dependent specialists, elaborate property inheritance, genealogies, feuding and hospitality systems.[23] Although doubtless taking many different regional forms, amidst a variety of surviving archaic social patterns, the rise of the European chiefdoms nevertheless witnessed the rise of centrally coordinated redistributional societies, in which ceremonial gift exchange as an activity of largely sociological importance was increasingly supplemented by organised trade as an activity of major economic significance.[24]

The elaborate bronze technology and the social apparatus for its maintenance seems partly to have spread through Europe by acquisitive diffusion and internal social reorganisation, and partly by tribal movements along the Danube. South of the Carpathian-Sudeten ring the existing cultures widely adopted the Balkan-Anatolian ceramic and artefact styles of the Proto-Aunjetitz group *c.* 1800 B.C., including plain burnished and metallic ceramics, tin, bronze, bivalve moulds,

[23] J. R. Goody, 'Inheritance, property and marriage in Africa and Eurasia', *Sociology*, III, 1 (1969), 55–76.

[24] E. R. Service, *Primitive Social Organization* (New York, 1966).

riveted metalwork, rapiers, daggers, helmets, halberds, and dress pins. North of this basin these innovations seem largely to represent the cross-cultural aggrandisement of existing castes, so that 'Aunjetitz' metal styles are found widely outside the restricted boundaries of that particular culture. The local chieftains seem to have quickly developed the exploitation of their territorial metal ores, and intensive shaft mining, smelting and casting were linked to an efficient redistribution network marked by hoards of copper-ingot torques and ingot bars for alloying and reworking in the chief's smithy. In this context a single hoard from Altenburg, on the Austrian border is reputed to have contained 1,000 Aunjetitz copper-ingot torques.[25]

The unsettled conditions developed by the feuding chiefdoms themselves have left us a range of such metalwork caches, from heterogeneous wealth hoards of weapons, trinkets, scrap, gold, amber, tin and faience to the ingot depots abandoned on the routes radiating from the mining centres. Markedly regional schools of bronze technology inherited an occupational caste and were trained by an interlinked set of bronze masters. Not only did these regional bronze schools flourish around the mining areas of Iberia, north Italy, the Alps, Bohemia, Moravia, Saxo-Thuringia, Brittany and in the Hiberno-Scottish zone, but the redistributional capacity of the trade network was now such that major bronze schools could be supported in areas without metal ores – notably the remarkable Danish bronze tradition and the Wessex school in Britain.

The period *c.* 2000–1400 B.C. in Europe, therefore, frames the rise of sophisticated political chiefdoms, a restricted but capable grid of regional bronze technologies, the organisation of efficient trade systems carrying many commodities other than the bronzes, and the proliferation of social subdivisions and subcultures. On the Mediterranean, the expansion of the Great Powers proceeded amidst the peripheral development of palace economies and urban chiefdoms, linked by the caravans and carts of the land network and by the sailing ships of the intersecting Aegean, Levantine and Egyptian maritime networks. Along the Mediterranean coastline of Europe the sailing ship for the first time allowed and stimulated direct connection between the eastern and western basins of the Mediterranean through the interlinking triangle of the Tyrrhenian Sea. On the islands and rocky headlands of Italy, Sicily, Sardinia, Lipari and Malta exotic fortified settlements now sprang up with an evolved copper metallurgy and heterogeneous pottery traditions directly linked to regional wares of Greece, Cyprus, the Cyclades and Crete. These Tyrrhenian centres

[25] V. G. Childe, *The Danube in Prehistory* (Oxford, 1929), 233.

seem, in turn, to have developed secondary connections with Mediterranean France and Spain, by way of the Balearic Islands and the North African littoral. By this time the traditional Mediterranean mixed economy combining fishing, sheep and goats, barley plots and olive, vine and fig orchards, seems to have already made its finally integrated appearance and doubtless materially helped the more intensive population and exploration of the Mediterranean shores.

Meanwhile, in the rather different environment of middle Europe, the onset of the sub-boreal warm climatic phase must have speeded the indigenous mastery of the forested terrain and assisted the more rapid northward spread of Mediterranean innovations. The copper and bronze tools now built effective plank boats, carts and ploughs so that the harnessing of the wind for sail power was hardly less important than the harnessing of oxen for traction purposes. A single boat or cart could carry a cargo of at least one ton, at several miles an hour for long distances, a task which would formerly have required relays of more than fifty porters for each load; now a single ploughman could till, in less than two days, family fields that would have taken a team of women a week to hoe. In Bronze Age Europe the agrarian communities could, with less manpower, maintain larger fields and produce a greater surplus than their predecessors, freeing man and womanpower for other specialist pursuits, including the trade of more commodities, further and faster than was within the capacity of their ancestors.

V. *The Mycenaean Network*[26] *and the Developed Bronze Technologies:* C. *1,400–1,200 B.C.*

If our frame of reference had not been especially focussed on European economic development there would probably be little or no justification for separating the Mycenaean period from the general context of Mediterranean developments between *c.* 2000–1200 B.C. However, from a European point of view there are several reasons for distinguishing this short phase, if only as a threshold to the events that followed. In this phase mainland Greece joined the lattice of urban chiefdoms, palace economies and intersecting maritime networks, thus becoming a European centre of civilisation in its own right, literate, powerful and markedly Mediterranean. Politically, there is strong

26 For general surveys, see M. Gimbutas, *Bronze Age Cultures in Central and Eastern Europe* (The Hague, 1965); Piggott, *Ancient Europe*, chap. 4; Lord W. Taylour, *The Mycenaeans* (London, 1964).

evidence that Greek-speaking Mycenaeans were able to annexe the Cretan kingdom of Knossos *c.* 1450 B.C., introducing a dynasty of aggressive character, with strong mainland connections. At Knossos this transition is marked by the conversion of the old Linear A script to the Linear B idiom for writing Greek and the introduction of the idiosyncratic 'Palace Style' in ceramics (Late Minoan II), together with mainland features in fashions, weapons and chariotry. Hereafter, Mycenaean Greek interests not only embraced those of the former Aegean thalassocracy of the Keftiu islanders, formerly headed by the Cretans, but extended their merchant ventures over an area covering the entire basin of the eastern Mediterranean, from the Tyrrhenian to the Black Sea. An urban civilisation was thus established on the mainland of Europe with maritime interests stretching from Italy to the Danube delta, and with a strong commercial interest in securing supplies of raw materials from unexplored Europe as an alternative to the very expensive, highly competitive and politically involved markets of the Near East.

Outside Greece this threshold is marked by the full expansion and developing confrontation of the Egyptian empire, pushing its frontiers to the Euphrates under Tutmosis III (*c.* 1450 B.C.) and the rising power of the Hittite empire under Tudhaliyas II (*c.* 1460–1440 B.C.). Although probably never a politically unified empire in the integrated sense of these great powers, the Mycenaean states, nevertheless, seem occasionally to have acted together in varying loose federations, and they certainly jointly constituted a third major power on the 'world' scene at that time – the first European culture to achieve that scale of political significance. In more remote inner Europe, the barbarian chiefdoms and tribes were achieving a rough degree of parity with Mycenaean bronze technology and military equipment, as well as beginning to form unstable political confederations of some size. The fully developed bronze technologies of the Alps, Bohemia and the Carpathians were now based on regular, deep gallery mining which produced a sufficient quantity of copper to extend the previously limited array of display weaponry and restricted tools to a more comprehensive set of bronze equipment, probably available to all higher caste tribesmen. For the first time bronze displaced stone as the primary raw material for everyday tools and a technical regression in the standards of most flintwork was now accompanied by the contemporary cessation of work at most of the stone-axe factories, quarries and mines; important focal resource centres had become unimportant, and formerly unimportant Alpine, Bohemian and Carpathian mountain valleys now became centres of radiating bronze networks.

The scale of European bronze production and distribution was accelerating to industrial proportions, although the peak was reached in the ensuing phase, *c.* 1200–900 B.C., under the Urnfield culture group. Already, however, remote mountain lodes were being tunnelled by deep shafts and timbered galleries. The ore was cracked away by fire-setting, followed up by teams of miners using specialist bronze pick-heads, stone mauls and hammers. The debris was dragged to the surface on small sleds, and later by windlasses, where the ore was crushed, milled and separated by flotation in wooden troughs. The ore was then roasted to vaporise impurities and finally smelted in clay crucibles over charcoal furnaces boosted with skin bellows. It has been estimated that these pithead activities at some Tyrolean sites would have required 180 workers or slaves, employed in mining, surface refining processes and cutting timber for props, fuel wood, troughs, pipes, structures and artefact handles. The timber consumption alone would deforest perhaps 19 acres locally every year; an activity which over a period of centuries must have dramatically augmented the open pasture on the mountain treeline, with a consequent growing stimulus towards the transhumant exploitation of these expanding resources by the valley farmers.[27]

From the pithead the bronze was taken to the smithies in the form of bun-shaped copper ingots from the crucible bottoms, or recast in bars or rings which have been found in hoards of up to seven hundred and twelve hundred pieces.[28] The precious tin was brought by other trade routes to the same smithies from sources in the Carpathians, Bohemia, Brittany, Cornwall and Galicia. However, very little new tin was needed, except to keep pace with the expanding production and demand, for the scrupulously careful salvage of scrap bronze and worn tools by itinerant merchants served to recover all but a fraction of the original bronze output for recasting. The same merchants bartered the fresh cast tools and weapons on the trip out from the smithing centres, collecting scrap in part exchange to return to the smithy. The hoards, therefore, often present a seemingly heterogeneous collection of new and old artefacts, not to mention other oddments collected in exchange and perhaps other organic merchandise long since decayed without trace. Smiths themselves seem to have increasingly specialised in the production of particular lines: goldsmiths worked at their delicate anvils with tiny bronze hammers, swordsmiths produced aesthetically superb and functional blades widely traded in bundles, sheet-metalworkers skilfully raised and riveted bronze kettles,

[27] V. G. Childe, 'Trade and industry in Barbarian Europe till Roman times', in *Cambridge Econ. History of Europe*, II, 1st edn (Cambridge, 1952), chap. 1.

[28] M. Ebert, *Reallexikon der Vorgeschichte* (Berlin, 1924–32).

cans and cauldrons, whilst the village smith turned his hand to most things but especially to casting popular lines of axes, sickles, knives, pins, trinkets and to carrying out general repairs. Specialisation continued in all spheres of life and many new 'life styles' are marked by the repetitive occurrence of subcultural artefact kits. The capacity of the increasingly organised trade routes widely reflects the use of canoe, sled and cart in the sheer size of the surviving hoards; two to three hundred objects are quite common and some late examples are even larger – 14,800 bronze items and scrap coming from a single cache at Prato di Francesco, Bologna, for example.[29] The societies requiring this output, capable of maintaining these specialists, and sustaining and protecting the vital trade flow, must have included political organisations only slightly less complex than those of the Mycenaean states themselves.

With the emergence of a European society into the comparative light of literacy one can amplify the purely archaeological record with the evidence of the tablets.[30] The Mycenaean states seem to have covered territories averaging about 25–35 miles in diameter, so that a roughly central capital was never more than a day's march from its own territorial borders and the tributary towns were almost all within a day's march from one another. The state territory was held from these urban sites, which were often fortified, imposing their will upon a network of dispersed villages and themselves loosely controlled from the focally situated seat of the dynastic clan. The kingdom of Pylos encompassed most of Messenia which was administratively divided into two provinces: a near province of nine tributary towns around the capital of Pylos and a distant province of seven towns around the Messenian Gulf. Similarly, Knossos, at this time *c.* 1200 B.C., was apparently capital of the whole of central Crete and lord of more than a dozen towns.

The largest burgh would contain the palace-factory of the king (*wanax*) and the smaller establishments of his immediate kin, all enclosed within a precinct amidst the simple housing of their dependent retainers, grooms, men-at-arms, artificers and slaves, which constituted an outer or 'lower' town extending over several acres. Under the authority of the king were the feudal lords (*pasireu*) of the outlying towns, each of whom would command a retinue and a palace establishment on a lesser scale in their regional capitals. Some of these lords would be kinsmen of the king himself, but others would represent other dynastic families and thus presented a constant source

[29] Childe, 'Trade and industry', 21.

[30] L. R. Palmer, *The interpretation of Mycenaean Greek texts* (Oxford, 1963); M. G. F. Ventris and J. Chadwick, *Documents in Mycenaean Greek* (Cambridge, 1956).

of potential instability. The king exercised his authority through his commander-in-chief (*lawagetas*) and his assembled knights (*eqeta*); here, the legends strongly suggest that the 'commander-in-chief' was a senior kinsman of the king, often a brother of the king's father and thus an experienced veteran with the capacity to act as regent in the event of disaster, or on the succession of a young monarch. The 'knights' were apparently a war-host of the younger men from the estate-owning families (*tereta*) who could afford to support the expensive equipage required by their military rank.

However, the substratum of this state society remained the network of simple villages under village headmen and a caste of craftsmen and serfs, some of whom belonged bodily to the establishment of the king or of the shrines. Some, at least, of this labour force were slaves and captives from border raids, which would accord with their status as the 'property' of the captor. Young women were especially prized in this respect because of their wide variety of skills – handicrafts, weaving, menial duties and their ability to produce slave offspring. The Homeric picture of noble heroes contending for the fine equipment of a fallen enemy and squabbling over the allocation of particularly fine chariot horses and slave girls seems to enshrine the flavour of this social pattern in a realistic way.

The Mycenaean states represented an important social and economic innovation in Europe at this time, *c.* 1450–1200 B.C. These complex organisations marked the integration of uncoordinated urban and tribal chiefdoms within centrally organised revenue states which permitted an elaborate cultural development, surpassed only by the metropoli and political empires of the great powers. The Mycenaean dynasts appear to have superimposed a system of revenue obligations to a political caste upon earlier patterns of tribal obligations within kinship networks. These archaic tribal patterns continued in peripheral areas of Greece and in the substratum of villages and village headmen, surviving the collapse of the Mycenaean states to re-emerge in the countryside of classical Greece.

The staples of the Mycenaean economy seem to have been barley, wheat, figs, olives and sheep. From these and other staples the palace industries manufactured and stored oil, ewes' milk and cheese; wove and dyed cloth; manufactured unguents with herbs; accumulated reserves of dried foodstuffs; hoarded and reworked metal supplies; amassed stock-piles of imported commodities; and maintained an arsenal of weapons and chariot parts, keeping the whole neatly sealed and recorded on the clay tablets and dockets of the quartermaster's stores. Once again it is the scale of the units recorded in the palace transactions which reminds us of the potential of the state economy –

64,580 litres of wheat, 9,000 figs, 5,520 olives, 10,157 sheep, 380 woollen cloths.[31] These mainland products and other commodities were then traded for scarce and foreign goods, especially copper from Cyprus. Assyrian tin from Cilician retailers, Egyptian gold from Crete, ivory from Syria, wine and oil from the islands. Amber too was imported, especially to the Ionian shores; some apparently came from Sicily, some from Scandinavia via the head of the Adriatic, but other amber supplies probably trickled in from Black Sea sources – Buzau in Roumania, Kiev in Russia and the Caucasus deposits. The importance of the Mycenaean amber trade has been exaggerated, however, to a degree only paralleled by the inflated distortion of the extent of direct Mycenaean intervention in the European Middle Bronze Age as a whole.[32]

The commodities regularly imported by the Mycenaean states seem to have come from a relatively restricted marine network. Almost all the imported goods were shipped by seasonal, circular expeditions sailing east through the Cycladic archipelago to the Carian coast, Rhodes, Lycia, Cilicia, and north Syria, then returning via Cyprus, Crete and the Peloponnesus; a round voyage of *c.* 1,400 miles, probably requiring two or three weeks out from Greece and a similar period for the return. It is precisely along this route that we find Mycenaean commercial and political activity developing, at first in the Cyclades, then in central Crete, next in Rhodes and eventually in Cyprus. A chain of Mycenaean merchant 'karum' quarters were set up in restricted districts of the main foreign ports from Carian Miletus at the foot of the northern Anatolian littoral routes to Syrian Al Mina at the mouth of the Crontes on the tin and ivory trail. The great hoards of copper ox-hide ingots are strewn along the links of this maritime chain, from shipwrecks between Cape Gelidonya and Kyme harbour in Euboea, and from wayside palace treasuries like those ingots stacked against Syrian elephant tusks in the storerooms of the palace at Kato Zakro, at the easternmost tip of Crete.

Similar ingots and tusks appear on the shoulders of alternating Levantine porters on a copper tripod from Curium, Cyprus.[33] Indeed, there is considerable evidence that Levantine as well as Mycenaean shipping circulated along this network: the 'Phoenicians' of the Homeric epics might therefore equally be restored to this more ancient

[31] *Ibid*, 214, Knossus No. 87; 219, Knossus No. 94; 198, Pylos Totals; 322, Mycenae No. 228.

[32] For recent discussion of Mycenaean links with Europe, see K. Brannigan, 'Wessex and Mycenae: some evidence reviewed', *Wiltshire Archaeological Magazine*, LXV (1971), 89–107; A. C. Refrew, 'Wessex without Mycenae', *Annual of the British School at Athens*, LXIII (1968), 277–85; Refrew, *Before Civilization*; A. Snodgrass, 'Mycenae, northern Europe and radio-carbon dates', *Archaeologia Atlantica*, I (1975), 33–48.

[33] S. Casson, *Ancient Cyprus* (London, 1937), 128–9, Pl. VIII.

horizon together with the Achaeans with whom they are said to have dealt. A motley assemblage of Syro-Cilician seals and Levantine trinkets have appeared in Mycenaean contexts from more than fifty sites, ranging from the sealstones from the Palace at Thebes to the scores of cheap little votive Baal mascots in lead and bronze – good luck mascots for the voyage, perhaps? The Gelidonya wreck certainly makes patent the risks implied by the Storm-God votives and confirms that some of this trade was carried, with the mascots, in Syro-Cilician shipping as well as between the thwarts of the Mycenaean penteconters – a new type of ship traditionally introduced by the Asiatic Danaus of Argos and thus perhaps from the coastal Danaans of Syro-Cilician Adana.

No single find so richly illustrates the nature of the maritime networks at this time as the shipwreck already alluded to. The ship had apparently been driven onto Cape Gelidonya by a gale which had turned her broadside on, unable to turn into the wind – a navigational weakness of early galleys, graphically described by St Paul from his own experience off Malta. Cape Gelidonya is the most notorious hazard on the Lycian coast between Rhodes and Tarsus and the wreck was found at its foot by skindivers who carefully excavated the hulk underwater.[34] The vessel was a small wooden sailing ship, about 35 feet long by perhaps 12 feet at the beam, probably carrying a light cabin in the stern. The laden freight included about one ton of copper ingots, quantities of bronze scrapmetal and perhaps half a hundredweight of tin ingots. The cargo was very carefully stowed amidships, the 55 lbs copper ox-hide ingots and the small tin bars were stacked and wrapped in protective matting, with the scrap bronze and newly cast bronze tools kept separately in wicker baskets; the whole burthen was packed around with brushwood bundles to insulate the hull from internal battering in rough weather. The extremely interesting evidence strongly suggests the presence of a smith or smiths on board, and this might reasonably be deduced not only from the mixed cargo of pure copper and tin, bronze scrap and untrimmed, freshly cast, bronze tools, but also from a large cushion-stone anvil amidships, together with two stone forging hammers, a bronze swage block, sandstone polishers, whetstones for sharpening and finishing and a beam with weights, perhaps for estimating the weight of tin to copper for the various bronze alloys.

The Gelidonya ship's master probably occupied the small stern cabin, lit with its small oil lamp. The captain carried with him his personal bronze razor and his Syro-Cilician cylinder seal and five

[34] G. F. Bass, *Archaeology under Water* (London, 1966); G. F. Bass, 'Cape Gelidonya: a Bronze Age shipwreck', *Amer. Philosophical Society*, LVII, 8 (1967).

scarabs to seal up his cargo against theft, as well as a few chunks of Taurus crystal — perhaps a sample for customers or a private profit-making investment. The rest of the small crew probably slept on deck and one may perhaps attribute to them the knuckle-bone gaming dice and the food bowls with remains of a meal of fish, fowl and olives. The extensive complement of bronze woodworking tools might suggest that the ship's carpenter was already an essential and specialised craftsman, with his chest of axes, adzes, chisels, gouges, axe-adzes and knives. The bronze spearheads were perhaps part of the ship's armoury against marauders and may even suggest an escort of a marine or two with this rich cargo. Although by no means a treasure vessel by the standards of the time, the Gelidonya galley would certainly have made a handsome prize. A ton of copper and half a hundredweight of tin would produce something like 50 bronze helmets, 50 bronze corselets, 500 long bronze spearheads and 500 bronze rapiers; sufficient to armour fully the commander-in-chief of Pylos, his sixteen feudal lords and their immediate kin, together with nearly five hundred properly equipped knights, the whole war-host of the state of Pylos in fact. By an illuminating chance the accounts of the Pylos palace preserve a summary of bronze-ingot reserves at a time when the state was being put on a wartime alert; these reserves total just over one ton, or almost exactly the cargo of the Gelidonya wreck.[35]

The observation that one ship might carry the equivalent of the strategic bronze reserves of the palace and possibly of the state of Pylos, raises other interesting points in this context. We may recall that even by *c.* 1900 B.C. a single Assyrian caravan could re-export 12½ tons of Elamite tin on 200 beasts of burden travelling from Assur to Cappadocia. This caravan was part of a regular trade network carrying tin north-westwards to Anatolian Kanish, which in turn re-exported much of this tin westwards to the Syro-Cilician coastal cities, the ports from which the Mycenaean 'karum' shipped tin back to the Mycenaean states.[36] Now this state of affairs does not suggest that the Mycenaean states would ordinarily find tin in short supply – the absence of Mycenaean bronze hoards proclaims the efficiency of their re-utilisation system and, furthermore, the 12½ tons of tin from the single Assyrian caravan would probably suffice to stock the tin reserves held by all of the dozen or so Mycenaean states taken together. What this export and re-export trade does suggest is that tin would normally be plentiful but very expensive, and that supplies would be extremely

[35] Ventris and Chadwick, *Mycenaean Greek*, 356, Pylos No. 256.

[36] J. C. Gardin, 'Reconstructing an economic network in the ancient East with the aid of a computer', in D. Hymes (ed.), *The Use of Computers in Anthropology* (The Hague, 1965), 378–91.

sensitive to the political situation far beyond the Mycenaean sphere of intervention; diplomacy with the Syro-Cilician potentates, often against Hittite interests, must have much exercised Mycenaean political activities.

It would appear that the Mycenaean state economies could, in theory, have been self-supporting except in respect of copper and tin supplies and the many luxury items that a caste society demands to bedeck its ranks and statuses. The sea peoples of the Anatolian and Levantine coasts retailed most of these requisites, but at a price. Mycenaean maritime enterprises therefore seem to have increasingly probed the coastline of Europe, from the Tyrrhenian Sea to the Danube delta, for cheaper, more reliable supplies of staples and exotica. The effects of these Mycenaean expeditions were mainly peripheral and indirect in their impact upon middle European cultures but Mycenaean wine and oil jars regularly found their way to many southern sites on the coasts of metal-rich Italy whilst rapiers, spearheads and faience beads of Aegean-Anatolian type appear in a few coastal Bulgarian and Roumanian hoards.

From the Danube delta, the wealthy chieftains of the intervening chiefdoms of the Wietenberg and Monteoru cultures controlled the reciprocal flow of middle Danube commodities to the coast and Aegean-Anatolian trinkets and innovations to the cultures beyond the Carpathians. Chariots and chariot harness appear to have been one of the innovations which rapidly passed into the repertoire of the chieftain caste in such central European cultures as the Otomani group. One interesting feature of the chariot harness is the much favoured 'rick-rack' motif found on bone cheekpieces, chariot inlays and whip handles from central Europe to the Aegean; perhaps the undulating 'roiko' ornament described for similar Mycenaean harness in the tablets.[37] The antecedents of this motif are obscure, but they are linked through variations on Otomani and Wietenberg ceramics and bronzes with motifs on Gumelnitza and Salcutza artefacts of the southern Balkans, suggesting that the harness form, the motif and the horses may have reached the Mycenaeans from the famous horse pastures of Thrace, rather than vice versa. Nevertheless, in general one might compare the mercantile activities of the Mycenaean states off the coasts of south-eastern Europe with those of the Arab traders along the East African coastline from the ninth to the twelfth centuries A.D.

The development and significance of the late Mycenaean maritime network can best be assessed against its general economic and political context. Initially, the Mycenaean chiefdoms were no more than the

[37] Ventris and Chadwick, *Mycenaean Greek*, 408.

barbarous beneficiaries of the maritime network linking the Aegean peoples of the islands, the Keftiu, amongst whom Crete had latterly assumed the dominant status *c.* 1660–1450 B.C. The rise of the urban states of the Greek mainland seems to have culminated with a Mycenaean conquest of Knossos and the subjugation of Crete within an independent Mycenaean kingdom *c.* 1450 B.C. At about the same time Mycenaean merchant colonies began to spring up and infiltrate other centres of the former Cretan mercantile network – in Miletus, Rhodes, Tell Atchana, Ras Shamra, Byblos, Gezer, Lachish and in the Nile delta. After *c.* 1400 B.C. Cos and the Dodecanese islands came within the Mycenaean hegemony and more bases were planted on Rhodes and Cyprus, allowing a far more intensive commercial penetration of the Syro-Cilician coastline. The Greek mainland and the islands were thus able to form a reciprocal network well equipped to supply the resource deficiencies of individual members and well situated to exploit Levantine and Cypriot commodities to the south-east, Anatolian and Black Sea trade to the north-east and Italian and Sicilian resources to the west. It should not be imagined, however, that the expansion of the Mycenaean network was a coordinated imperial venture. Initially, at least, it was probably no more than a competitive race for Minoan footholds by the younger sons of various Mycenaean dynasts, only occasionally and temporarily acting in concert in the famous, quarrelsome expeditions of the great epics. Indeed, the Homeric epics, with their fairly exact factual knowledge of the Aegean and their more misty acquaintance with the coasts and islands beyond the Straits of Messina and the Bosporus, seem accurately to embody the navigational experiences of this period and to have drawn upon a corpus of mariners' tales to decorate old and famous stories, in the manner of the medieval minstrels.

VI. *The Colonial Networks and the Late Bronze Technologies: c. 1200–600 B.C.*

The Mycenaean period marked the extension of the Near Eastern network of interconnected urban, revenue-state economies to the Greek mainland and thus linked the fringe of Europe with the world of the two great powers, the Hittite and the Egyptian Empires, and the bustling trading cities of the Levant. The centralised authority and the literate bureaucracy of the Mycenaean palace economies represented an important expansion of the frontiers of urban civilisation – the world of city states, kingdoms and military empires – and correspondingly, a slight contraction of the barbarian world of the totemic bands, tribes and tribal chiefdoms of innermost Europe. Nevertheless, the dynasts of the Mycenaean elite remained a ruling caste and its subculture, superimposed upon a tribal society surviving in the substratum of villages dispersed in the countryside beyond the burghs; a tribal society which remained a functioning system well into the period of classical Greece.

The century around 1200–1100 B.C. forms the threshold for momentous events which transformed the then civilised world and stimulated repercussions directly involving the tribesmen of middle Europe. Historically it would be tempting to represent these changes purely in terms of a sequence of political events, but here, as in other instances, the real threshold integrated a multiplicity of mutually interacting factors, cumulatively made manifest in the political sequence noted by the scribes of the great powers. This century of events witnessed the collapse of the Hittite Empire, the disintegration of the Mycenaean states, and imperial Egypt thrown back and attacked on its own frontiers, together with extensive population resettlement from the Troad to Gaza. The east Mediterranean was in turmoil and the colonial penetration of the west Mediterranean commenced in earnest with the settlement of whole communities replacing former commercial enclaves.

In middle Europe the contrasting evidence suggests the development of tribal confederacies and possibly kingdoms of unparalleled wealth and size for the area. In eastern Europe there are signs that important new socio-economic configurations now emerged with a novel pattern and fresh potential – the rise of the horse-mounted pastoralist societies. Whilst in central, western, and northern Europe the Late Bronze technologies reached a climax of production, providing a full range of metal tools as well as weapons and incidentally disseminating the earliest elements of iron metallurgy, released and dispersed by the collapse of the Hittite empire. The exchange networks of these regional bronze technologies now reached to the fringes of the Arctic Circle and deep into the coniferous forest zone of the north and east. At their core, elaborate chiefdoms provided markets, ensured supplies of labour for the deep mines and maintained a flow of carts and porters, canoes and ships, bartering and circulating staples and trinkets. Even at the outermost peripheries, the lives of the hunter-fisher-gatherer bands in the Norwegian forests and the Siberian Taiga were increasingly modified in order to exchange furs and skins for bronze and cereals; the development of full chieftainships, the growth of individual property and territorial ownership, more display equipment and imported finery accompanied the changes in these archaic band organisations.

The principal factors which combined to transform the Mediterranean scene and to modify the cultures of middle Europe at this time seem to have included climatic trends, the rise of the mounted pastoralist economies and the coincidence of political circumstances amongst the great powers. These factors are themselves interrelated and were certainly modulated by a far more complex interaction of many other contributing elements. Amongst the Mediterranean states these developments threatened the restless equilibrium between the elite castes administering the sophisticated economies and the peasant substratum beneath. Sequences of unusually severe famine, aggravated by epidemics and by the continuous obligation to supply revenue, could easily stimulate unrest and minor population movements which would in turn contribute to the internal instability. Social unrest of this kind could be seriously exacerbated by external military commitments and inflamed by the conflicting policies of rival dynastic clans within the states, finally erupting into an internal revolt led by an opportunist commander-in-chief, by a brother or an uncle of the ruler, or by a rival faction. The foundation legends of the new colonial towns of the west Mediterranean repeatedly described such refugees, fleeing to fresh prospects and resources in the 'new world' beyond Scylla and Charybdis to metalliferous and fertile Italy at first, but soon to North Africa, southern France and eventually to the Spanish 'el dorado'.

In central Europe the evidence suggests that external pressures were less important than the internally expanding economic capacity of a growing population which was throwing up increasingly larger and more complex political organisations. The climatic factors which unsettled the east Mediterranean at this time were positively advantageous in central and northern Europe. The barbarian chiefdoms were themselves rapidly converging upon at least incipient state organisations centred on fortified timber townlets, focally placed amidst the scattered agrarian tribal communities. Small political and economic centres of this kind emerged early on in the lower and middle Danube basins and soon proliferated on the upper Danube, amidst the fertile and metalliferous Alpine valleys, in equally rich Bohemia and amongst the lakes and streams of the Baltic Vistula valley. These townlets of the Urnfield culture group covered some 2–15 acres with two to three hundred timber houses, holding populations of perhaps five hundred to two thousand persons under the authority of a chief and his retinue, either in a fortified hall in the settlement, or in a separate residence close by. The analogy with the medieval timber towns of the same areas and with the Mycenaean burghs to the south are equally appropriate. Except in degree of organisation, overall size and aspects of construction, these Urnfield townlets reflect the foundation of social organisations only slightly less potent than the Mycenaean and continuing in many respects into the medieval pattern. The similarity of these social patterns is made apparent as they emerge into the historical daylight of both the Mycenaean tablets and the medieval chronicles respectively. One may compare the state of Pylos, already discussed, with the Baltic province of Volhynia in 1219, ruled by five grand dukes from their fortified halls in timber burghs of *c.* 15 acres and administered by sixteen regional dukes from lesser establishments in townlets of 2–10 acres.[38]

The expanding middle European pattern of wealthy chiefdoms and incipient state organisations, or kingdoms, is mainly associated with the regional cultures of the Urnfield culture group, so named from the dense cremation cemeteries adjacent to the settlement sites. The 'expansion' of this culture group may probably be best understood as the vector of a number of components — as the spreading material trappings of an expanding social pattern increasingly adopted by similar peoples in similar circumstances, supplemented by tribal population movements and the convergent acculturation of adjacent ethnic groups. The social pattern spread by these processes, the economic systems that they represented and the ethnic groups spreading with them, were responsible for much of the cultural pattern of Europe as it emerged in later history; the historical European scene was set in many essentials *c.* 1200 B.C.

The factors involved in the east Mediterranean collapse are therefore mainly of interest for their repercussions amongst the middle European cultures and for their colonial consequences in the European littoral of the west Mediterranean and beyond. The climatic factor is the least understood and the most difficult to assess realistically. However, in essence we may say that the period *c.* 1200–600 B.C. falls at the juncture between the closing phases of the warmer and drier sub-boreal climate, *c.* 2000–800 B.C., and the opening sub-atlantic phase with its wetter and colder climate, *c.* 800–400 B.C. This transition seems to have been accompanied by shortlived but locally important oscillations, as is so often the case in climatic changes. The evidence is circumstantial, uneven and insecure, but its sheer bulk suggests a measure of probability for the general trends involved. The inference is that the inland areas of the Greek and Anatolian peninsulas were subjected to unusually severe and recurrent bouts of desiccation and drought over the period *c.* 1250–1000 B.C., broadly corresponding to a period of unusually mild climate in inland Europe – the setting for the great cultural florescence in that area and perhaps relevant to the rise of the

[38] Gimbutas, *The Balts*, 171.

steppe pastoralists. Whether we accept this climatic evidence or not, there is at least supporting evidence for drought in inland Greece and Anatolia in this period, accompanied in some areas by famine, epidemics and small population movements to the more reliable rainfall areas of the littoral.[39] Although it must be heavily stressed that this putative evidence is not interpreted as a cause for contemporary events, but merely as one factor amidst many, important in some areas but less important in others.

The second factor cited was the rise of the mounted pastoralist economies of the western steppe and their expansive infiltration into a selection of peculiar niches which this freshly integrated economic strategy now permitted. Here again the evidence is incomplete and difficult to interpret but some clarification is possible. The available evidence suggests that the fertile Pontic prairies were at first occupied by various agrarian village communities practising mixed farming. Domestic animals flourished in the steppe environment and local wild horse herds were certainly domesticated by *c.* 2500 B.C. as merely another variety of 'hornless' stock. Between *c.* 2500–1500 B.C., village pastoralist communities from the Caucasus flanks increasingly expanded onto the eastern steppe, apparently controlling large herds from tented ox-waggons and possibly from chariots. In any event, it seems likely that the various communities of the eastern and western steppe practised a stable village economy with subcultural symbiosis between those whose duties operated the stock around the village pastures and those who raised grain and fruit in the fertile soil. This strategy continued until recent times in the Cossack villages and, as Herodotus confirms, there was never a time in which the steppe was occupied only by nomad pastoralists.

The horse was used for chariot traction by *c.* 1500 B.C. but seldom ridden except by grooms or messengers. However, the development of an adequate saddle and bridle harness between *c.* 1500–1200 B.C. seems to have transformed the steppe situation much as the arrival of horse-riding transformed some of the Indian prairie farmers into plains buffalo hunters. Given comfortable and controlled horse-riding, the herdsmen on horseback could now manoeuvre vast herds with ease and exploit a far wider range of pastures in succession. By a kind of social binary fission, the division of labour between social subcultures now became an independent cultural symbiosis between separately specialised economies; the agrarian villages continued with the pastoralists circulating in their interstices. On the Carpathian fringe, it was apparently some elements of the local Cimmerian, Thracian and

[39] R. Carpenter, *Discontinuity in Greek Civilization* (Cambridge, 1966).

Phrygian tribes who increasingly took to the relatively unexploited pastures, which in this dry sub-boreal phase extended discontinuously from the Roumanian Dobrudjam through Bulgarian Thrace to parts of Macedonia and Thessaly. Thus, by *c.* 1200 B.C., a group of mounted pastoralist communities deployed amongst their agrarian kinsmen of the plains of Thrace; a militarily formidable but disorganised force poised opposite the closely congruent grasslands of northern Anatolia.

Before pursuing the Phrygian infiltration of northern Anatolia it is necessary to outline its context, the political circumstances amongst the great powers *c.* 1250–1100 B.C., the third factor in the events which followed. These circumstances follow from the traditional role of the Levantine city states as the direct or retail source of important strategic raw materials, staples and luxuries, tapped in common by successive Egyptian, Mesopotamian and Anatolian dynasts, and now by the Mycenaean princelings. With the efflorescence of the Hittite empire, between 1460–1220 B.C., the Levant increasingly became the middle ground for the power play between the Hittite kings and the Egyptian pharaohs. This confrontation reached a climax with the indecisive battle of Kadesh *c.* 1286 B.C., in which the Hittite King Muwatallis massed his allies and mercenaries from the Anatolian coastline against the military expedition of Rameses II and his vassals and auxiliaries.

As an effective basis for the pursuit of their southern imperial aims, the late Hittite kings reorganised their empire into two provinces; the home province in the rear included the old Hittite homeland and the capital at Hattusas under the command of a royal governor, whilst the forward province in southern Anatolia was the military base of the armies and the Hittite king, as commander-in-chief. This unbalanced stance assumed that the northern province could be lightly held, whilst the king and his armies pursued a policy of southward expansion. In quick succession, the imperial capital at Hattusas was sacked by northern Kaski tribesmen, the western vassal states of Arzawa and Assuwa came out in revolt with the aid of their Mycenaeanised coastal neighbours in Lydia, Caria and Lycia, and in 1275 B.C. the uncle of the absent king usurped the throne and after a brief civil war became Hattusilis III. The new Hittite kings now fought to stabilise the home province with successive expeditions against the rebel areas, including a campaign towards the Troad about the period of the Mycenaean expedition against Troy *c.* 1260 B.C.

Under Arnuwandas IV, the northern and western situation rapidly deteriorated under renewed, and this time partially coordinated, attacks from the west by the vassal states and their allies, the 'peoples of the coastlands', and from the north by the Kaski and also the Mushki – Phrygian horsemen from across the Bosporus, perhaps related to the Kaski themselves. The Arzawa was seized *c.* 1230 B.C. by a Lydian vassal, King Madduwattas, aided by Attarissiyas, a prince of coastal Ahhiyawa, possibly an Achaean state in Caria centred on Miletus. The more northerly Assuwa area was seized by the Kaski and the Phrygian horsemen, now present in force under a prince Midas. However, the unprecedented military advantage of the Phrygian horsemen and the internal dislocation of the Hittite allies soon turned the new force against Arzawa and the Lydian, Carian, Lycian and Cilician peoples of the coastlands; with the arms of imperial Hatti fighting for survival around Hattusas nothing could stem the flood of invaders and the turmoil of refugees. Within a hundred years of their first foothold, the Phrygian Mushki tribes had consolidated in western Anatolia and had even sallied into northern Syria and Mesopotamia to confront the Assyrian King Tiglath-Pileser I with an army of 20,000 cavalry under five chieftains.

The Hittite empire was smashed and the repercussions for the economically interconnected states of the Levant, Egypt and Mycenaean Greece were only slightly less severe. In 1227 B.C. 'northerners from many lands' attacked the Nile delta by boat, including in their number many of the Hittites' former coastal allies from the battle of Kadesh – the Lycians, Ahhiyawans and possibly Sardians. This first wave probably represented adventurers from the initially successful revolt by the coastal peoples of Anatolia, mercenary freebooters armed in the latest Anatolian–Aegean fashion with tribal variations, crested helmets, plate cuirasses, Aegean rapiers, and the round cavalry and infantry shield; it is significant that later Greek traditions attributed these military innovations to Caria and Lycia.

However, this first raid was of little consequence by comparison with the second in 1196 B.C., probably corresponding to the full Phrygian invasion of coastal Anatolia and their drive down the south-western littoral. On this occasion a large fleet of northerners moved down the Levantine coast, in conjunction with a land army with chariots and men, women and children in bullock carts – whole peoples were on the move. The Egyptian scribes noted:

> The coastal peoples joined together, they were displaced from their lands and their peoples scattered. No land stood before their weapons, from Hatti (the Hittites), Kode, Arzawa and Alashiya (Cyprus) onwards. They camped in Amurru (Syria), they desolated its peoples and its land was destroyed; they came with fire before them, onwards toward Egypt.

The imperial Egyptian forces retired to the delta and there Ramesses III successfully resisted the invasion, abandoning Palestine to the invaders. The motley refugees settled the Palestinian coast and parts of Cyprus where they became known as the Philistines, after the Peleseti, the subsequently dominant group amongst the confederation of Mycenaeanised 'sea peoples'.

Unfortunately, the Mycenaean collapse is not documented by their inventory tablets and we must rely on archaeological evidence, eked out by the oblique indications of the tablets and the later traditions. However, the archaeological evidence outlines two severe spasms, the second cumulatively more decisive than the first; one upheaval *c.* 1230–1200 B.C. and the second *c.* 1130–1100 B.C. In the first spasm the network of Mycenaean states was severely dislocated by burning and destruction at many of the main citadels, including Mycenae, Tiryns, Midea, Pylos, Gla, Zygouries, Prosymna, Berbati, Korakou and others, but with no evidence of any alien invaders. The ceramic distributions suggest some accompanying population movements outwards from the interior areas towards the west coasts of the Ionian islands and Epirus, as well as eastwards to Rhodes and Cyprus; movements which might link with the growing desiccation of the Greek interior. In this first convulsion the majority of the political centres show destruction and abandonment, although the citadel of Mycenae survived the destruction of its outer town. The second spasm, *c.* 1130–1100 B.C., was marked by the complete destruction of Mycenae, the abandonment of a hastily built bastioned wall across the Corinthian isthmus and decisive changes in the culture of the Peloponnesus – no more written records, no more palace bureaucracies, the adoption of Thessalian protogeometric modes and apparently a revival of the underlying substratum of tribal peasant organisation. Individual citadels such as Athens survived but the interdependent network of centrally organised Mycenaean states had been forever destroyed and its administering castes rendered impotent.[40]

The indications of the late Mycenaean tablets can only be used to infer the kinds of upheaval which might be generically likely in this kind of state system. The Mycenaean state was apparently a fiscal superstructure in the palaces and towns financing and organising trade with other states and empires in a mutually adjusted international network based on the exchange of revenue for commodities. The village communities of Mycenaean Greece were in many respects beyond the subcultural frontiers of the dynasties which ruled from the great palaces, except for the collection of revenue from the village surpluses. The village network provided the economic substructure of the society and displayed a far greater stability in the face of violent changes; foreign trade might fluctuate, dynasts and feudal lords

[40] Carpenter, *op. cit.*

plunder townships and palaces, but the village communities farmed on in stoic continuity. The state administration was very little concerned with the organisation of the rural communities beyond the extraction of revenue. Tribute was heavy and in times of bad harvests and famine the surplus could be ill-spared; should these times coincide with external unrest and disruption, then the dynasts would tend to levy larger and larger contributions in manpower and commodities to prop up their administration and organise its defence. This in turn would cause further peasant unrest; left with decreasing reserves, on the margins of famine and despair, such a cumulative system of interacting disasters could, if conditions correlated effectively, combine to bring down the state by a combination of civil rebellion and external assault, catalysed by the inevitable opportunist intervention of rival dynastic parties; the same model which seems to outline the general components of the Hittite collapse, already described.[41]

Finally, we can appeal for enlightenment to the epic tales that survived into the Homeric period, although we must remember that, like the Saxon Chronicle, their main purpose was to provide a respectable explanation of the ancestry and rise to power of the new upper class. Nevertheless, the tales needed to be entertaining distortions of the truth rather than outright lies and the picture they extrapolate into the Mycenaean period is wholly reasonable.

Significantly, the epics sketch a period genealogically covering roughly ten generations before the Doric period and, regardless of the particular tale, the frame is always the same – the quarrel between the Perseid clan of 'the sons of Heracles' and the upstart Pelopids, 'the sons of Thyestes and Atreus'; the return of the Heraclids to their rightful domains representing the cue for Doric intervention and the happy ending. In general the tales portray a ruling caste composed of a relatively few interrelated royal clans, so that the dynasties at various ruling centres were involved in a constantly changing pattern of family alliances and feuds.

The traditions claim that the intrusive Pelopid dynasty became paramount at Mycenae, having dispossessed the Perseids, who thereafter constantly schemed their return to power in the Peloponnesus – the kingdom of Pelops. True to form, the Pelopid houses of Thyestes and Atreus themselves disputed the succession at Mycenae until the Atreid rival Orestes was banished to the Asiatic coasts of his forefathers, whilst the descendants of Thyestes reigned at Mycenae. The epics then relate a period of great upheaval, separated from a second convulsion by a period of two or three generations dogged by notorious bad

[41] F. G. Bailey, *Caste and Economic Frontier* (Manchester, 1957).

luck – the 'struggle with the fates' (Erinnyes). The first upheaval is the return of Orestes and his extensive campaign of vengeance against the Perseid strongholds. The sons of Orestes then suffered a period of successive ill omens, disasters, famine and pestilence, only brought to a close by the triumphant return of the Heraclids with their Thessalian allies, the Dorians, and the eventual success of their long drawn out campaigns against the High King Tisamenes fortified in the Peloponnesus. The two spasms separated by two or three generations take us back to the two archaeological convulsions *c.* 1230–1200 B.C. and *c.* 1130–1100 B.C., separated from one another by about one hundred years and from the historic epics by another three hundred years.

We may not trust the ancient epics in any detail but the tradition seems broadly plausible and corresponds well with the inferences of the tablets, the archaeological record and the general parallel of the Hittite collapse. It seems that some Mycenaean states collaborated in opportunist expeditions in the Troad and perhaps against other parts of the Anatolian coastline, at a time of general disturbance amongst the outer Hittite vassal states and their coastal allies *c.* 1260 B.C. In the absence of these expeditions political rivals fomented unrest and brought about a coup for the Thyestid house, shortly after the return of the Atreids from their famous exploits overseas. Subsequently, the exiled Atreid contender, Orestes, returned, recaptured Mycenae and proceeded to campaign against the hostile Perseid citadels; this episode would then correspond with the first major dislocations *c.* 1230–1200 B.C. This civil war combined with coincidental economic factors and civil disorder to upset the precarious equilibrium of the Mycenaean hegemony, creating a rapidly declining political and economic situation helped by the contemporary collapse of the Hittite and Levantine commercial networks. Perhaps we are also at liberty to attribute the unrest of the Doric tribes around Olympus, and the traditional exploits of the Heraclids against the Centaurs of Thessaly, as the southernmost repercussions of marauding bands of Thraco-Phrygian 'horsemen'. In any event, dynastic intrigue, economic troubles, civil disorder and famine may thus have conspired to bring down the commercial network of Mycenaean states as quickly as they had disintegrated the the Hittite empire.

The collapse of the east Mediterranean states broadly corresponds with the period of expansion of the central European chiefdoms and confederacies; in terms of economic surplus, bronze technology, social organisation and weaponry, a broad degree of parity now existed between middle and Mediterranean Europe. The flourishing group of Urnfield cultures had already expanded to the Macedonian and Italic fringes of the Mycenaean world; some tribal mercenaries and armourers from these sources even seem to have been involved on a small scale in the closing dynastic squabbles of the Achaeans – apparently carrying their slashing swords, leaf-shaped spears and bossed shields in defence of the Mycenaean kingdoms with western maritime contacts. Beyond the centrally expanding Urnfield peoples were a mosaic of diverse Atlantic and Iberian tribes, a peripheral zone of motley peoples using archaic bronze technologies and weapon fashions long outdated in central Europe. However, it appears that the central developments of the expanding Urnfield network created a situation in which the major metal resources of inner Europe were increasingly devoted to the production and distribution of Urnfield equipment for Urnfield cultures, forming a kind of central 'common market' area. This situation seems gradually to have forced the heterogeneous maritime cultures of the Atlantic and Iberian littoral into closer and closer interdependence for metal supplies which increasingly circulated within this outer 'free trade' area; Britain, Ireland, Brittany, Galicia and Spain thus exchanged trade goods in a network peripherally including Denmark and Sardinia and which mainly exchanged tin, copper, bronze, silver and gold metalwork.

This 'Atlantic Bronze Age' first emerges as an economically significant linkage between the west Mediterranean and the Atlantic after *c.* 1000 B.C. and reached its peak with the penetration of its southernmost outlets by the highly organised Phoenician mercantile marine *c.* 900–300 B.C. These later, large-scale commercial dealings in metal supplies seem to have stimulated the development of 'middle-man' Iberian kingdoms based on redistribution economies, like that of King Arganthonios of Tartessos. The Phoenician trading off the European coastline thus played a significant role in catalysing the development of more complex social organisations in barbarian Europe – just as the Arab and Portuguese slave, ivory, and gold trade stimulated the African states of Ghana, Mali, Songhay, Ife, Benin, Zimbabwe, Bakongo and Dahomey.

The Atlantic maritime network probably only moved into effective existence with the introduction of the sail and the keeled galley from the Mediterranean, probably at the hands of the Phoenicians themselves *c.* 900 B.C. The arrival of the sailed ship in southern Atlantic waters now permitted regular, long-distance, two-way commerce on an economically significant scale. Even so, the distribution evidence suggests that the Atlantic maritime network was based on relatively modest, seasonal, short-distance voyages to and fro between adjacent centres – from Britain to Brittany to the Garonne, the Garonne to Galicia, Galicia to the Tagus, the Tagus to Gades and Tartessos. It was probably not until the long-distance exploratory voyages of Himilco the Carthaginian, *c.* 450 B.C., and the Massiliote Pytheas, *c.* 310 B.C., that any one captain attempted the full length of this trade route.

The nature of the cargoes carried on the Atlantic network is preserved in the distribution of idiosyncratic bronze artefacts and in the records noting the early voyages by Colaeus, Midacritus, Himilco, Pytheas and other earlier unnamed captains. Apparently, pottery, salt, bronze tableware, oil and wine were traded northwards against Irish copper, gold and bronzework, Cornish and Breton lead and tin, amber and furs reshipped from Heligoland and cereals, slaves, hides and dogs from various ports. Once again we are fortunate in having the inorganic remains of two ships' cargoes salvaged from different parts of this network. One such cargo is probably represented by the densely packed hoard of bronze tools, weapons and scrap metal dredged from the Odiel estuary at Huelva in southern Spain; a cargo which included bronze swords, axes, spearheads and tools of mainly Iberian origin in association with a few Irish, French and Sardinian types and several Phoenician fibulae of Cypriot type, *c.* 700 B.C. The other shipwreck comes from the eastern wing of this same commercial network and has been recovered by divers from Béziers, in the Gulf of Lions near the emporium of Narbo. The vessel contained 760 bronze tools, weapons and trinkets, together with more than half a ton of copper ingots, perhaps from the Iberian or Sardinian mines; the whole cargo dating from *c.* 800 B.C.[42] Irish artefacts, including bronze cauldrons and gold collars, are known from other Atlantic Iberian hoards and Atlantic bronzes from several Sardinian hoards complement the scatter of Sardinian types from Huelva to Hengistbury Head; embossed bronze shields and horned or crested helmets of the same general pattern also link Ireland, Spain, Sardinia and Denmark. The evidence of the wrecks suggests that the shipping was mainly handled by the skilled seamen of native kingdoms, like the Veneti and the Tartessians, but that they were moving freely through areas and into ports from which Phoenician middlemen were also operating. The Phoenician–Iberian trade was thus part of an extensive commercial network which coupled the coastline of Atlantic Europe to the markets of the Mediterranean states and which transported commodities by the ton load.

The expansion and deployment of the Phoenician colonial network was therefore of paramount importance is expanding the development of the Atlantic trade and its social and economic consequences amongst the tribesmen of outer Europe. The Phoenician seamen of the Levantine ports were amongst the most experienced of the ancient

[42] Bass, *Archaeology under Water*, 87.

world, the inheritors of a maritime tradition as old as the sail itself. The Mycenaeans had nick-named these bronzed traders 'red skins' (*Phoenikes*) and the Gelidonya wreck reminds us that probably the great bulk of east Mediterranean marine traffic was in Levantine hands. The Mycenaeans had their commercial 'karum' in Levantine and Cypriot ports but their marine network was largely complementary to that of the Levantines, centring on the Aegean coast of Anatolia and the Ionian coast of Italy and Sicily, only peripherally exploring European possibilities to the mouth of the Danube, into the Adriatic and into the Tyrrhenian Sea. However, the collapse of the Mycenaean states *c.* 1100 B.C. removed the market, the financial backing and the social environment which had stimulated Mycenaean investment in competitive commercial exploration by the young mercantile princelings, eager to finance the rise to power of their own dynastic clans; it is no accident that the argosies of the epics were crewed by noblemen, or that their ventures should have been a recurrent theme for the dependent court bards. Individual trading by sub-Mycenaean vessels must certainly have continued but the scale and daring of the enterprises must have diminished with the market which had supported them – the competitive Mycenaean elite.

The Phoenician merchants were therefore able to exploit the demise of their Mycenaean competitors to the north and west by rapidly deploying into the Aegean markets and through the Sicilian straits already mapped by the Mycenaean mariners. The earliest Phoenician explorations in the west Mediterranean probably date to this phase, *c.* 1100–1000 B.C., gradually plotting the anchorages of the North African littoral and thus providing the traditional 'foundation' dates for Leptis, Carthage and even Gades beyond the Pillars of Hercules. The rapidity of the Phoenician expansion westwards is understandable, given the existing knowledge of the Sicilian channel, the excellent supply facilities of the North African littoral and the pre-existing maritime connections between the peoples of that area and Iberia. By the tenth century the southern arc of the west Mediterranean was a Phoenician Sea, bounded by new urban and literate settlements on western Sicily, Sardinia, and the Balearics, continuing in a chain of ports to the Almerian harbours of Lucentum, Abdera, Malaca and ending at the Atlantic outposts of Gades and Onoba on the coast of Taressos.

The early Phoenician explorations were by no means confined to the southern arc of the west Mediterranean which later became the main focus of the Punic league. There is increasing evidence that the subsequent alliances between the Etruscans and the Carthaginians were simply continuing an intimate relationship going back to *c.* 1000–900 B.C. The Phoenicians seem to have retreated from the Tyrrhenian Sea after a very early expansion from the Mycenaean bases in the south to emporia actually on the Etruscan and Latin coastline and on the flanking shores of Sardinia and Sicily. Etruria now emerged from Villanovan tribalism into the federation of incipient state organisations focussed on new Italian urban centres, around the Phoenician station of Punicum and other trading ports. The so-called 'orientalising' art styles marking the rise of the Etruscan states from their Villanovan peninsularity are in fact the trademark of the ornate, eclectic pastiche of the Phoenician 'art nouveau', found from the Levant and Cyprus, to Greece and Crete, North Africa and Iberian Tartessos. Phoenician glass, ivories, jewellery, gold and silver bowls, bronze metalware and fibulae appeared in the richer Etruscan chiefdoms which could now pay for them with quantities of copper and iron from the enormously rich mines of Vetulonia and Populonia. The rustic Villanovan chiefdoms rapidly emerged as the twelve states of the famous Etruscan federation and Tyrrhenian thalassocracy *c.* 800–500 B.C. The kingdoms of Etruria and Tartessos were thus indirectly the offspring of the mercantile enterprise of colonial expansion into the west Mediterranean and doubtless, even beyond these coastal states, there were more distant political repercussions of a similar nature.

The Phoenician and later the Greek penetration of the west Mediterranean was a new phenomenon; it was not confined to the establishment of small commercial 'karum', it was the permanent settlement of complete communities in a network of advanced and literate colonial cities. The Phoenician colonists first extended this replicating pattern of urban states to the west Mediterranean shores, established a colonial thalassocracy and introduced full iron technology and all the concomitants of literate state organisation to within range of the European tribesmen of Mediterranean Italy, France and Iberia. The infiltration of the southern end of the Atlantic maritime network by the Phoenicians, *c.* 900 B.C., finally harnessed the economies of outer Europe to the urban markets of the Mediterranean, a process rapidly intensified by colonial Greek settlement and trade with Celtic France and Italic Italy, *c.* 750–600 B.C., and by the colonial Etruscan Alpine trade with central Europe, *c.* 600–300 B.C.

VII. *The Colonial Empires and the Pre-Industrial Iron Technologies: c. 600–0 B.C.*

This closing epoch marks the great acceleration in the progress of the 'Mediterraneanisation' of Europe, a process which continued until in recent centuries the rising economic supremacy of the northern industrial nations reversed this flow of variety. The threshold of this accelerated transformation of European culture was defined by the sub-Atlantic climatic oscillation, the European adoption of full iron technology, the development of European urban centres, the economic and political intervention of Mediterranean states in European affairs and the Mediterranean introduction of coinage and cash market economies. Uneven in their distribution and significance, more apparent in the south than the north, these changes nevertheless combined to foretell the end of European tribalism and the rise of the feudal nation states.

The sub-Atlantic climatic oscillation rapidly displaced the prevailing warm and dry conditions of the sub-boreal Bronze Age and introduced our current European climatic pattern. This oscillation opened *c.* 800–400 B.C. with a preliminary extreme phase, even colder and wetter than at present. Beech and hornbeam woods displaced the oak forest in the south, under the more rapidly circulating cool and wet air cover which then made for improved agricultural conditions in middle and Mediterranean Europe. In the far north, however, this oscillation tended to waterlog the rich, valley pastures and killed them with creeping peat bogs; the poorer glacial soils rapidly deteriorated to sandy heathland, and the Atlantic coastal woods were finally deforested. In the mountainous interior of Scandinavia, Britain and the Alps, the tree line retreated some 600 ft from the summits; thus, in favourable situations, further developing the high grazing meadows available for transhumance or hunting. In the lower lands of middle Europe the fat loam soils were increasingly liberated from the forest by the iron axe and ploughshare, whilst further north the acid German heaths developed their modern guise, stretching into the zone of inland Hiberno-Scandinavian bogs and meres. As the marginal conditions for Scandinavian farming retreated, the context for intensive hunting, trapping and reindeer grazing in Norway and in the Scandinavian mountains expanded: everywhere the farmers of the European high valleys increasingly developed the art of the seasonal exploitation of the exposed mountain pastures. In short, the folkways of historic Europe now began to emerge from amidst the more ancient patterns of existence.

Under the sub-Atlantic climate the mainly Celtic lands of middle and Mediterranean Europe flourished, whilst the Teutonic area astride the German Sea suffered the unfamiliar constraint of an expanding population and a contraction in the area and quality of available farming land. The agrarian frontier which had been pushed towards the Arctic Circle itself, now recoiled to a more southerly horizon and the Teutonic tribes were faced with increasingly severe problems in territorial adjustment. Whereas the Celtic tribes expanded westwards into the flourishing lands between the Rhine and the Ebro, and eastwards into the Balkans, the Teutonic tribes sought *lebensraum* to the south-east, pushing beyond the Elbe into the Slav territory of the south Baltic forests. The Slavs were thus pinched between the expanding Teutons, Celts and Scythians and were themselves obliged to erode the territory of their eastern Balt neighbours. The climatic, economic and political factors were beginning to emerge which ultimately combined to stimulate the expansive redeployment of northern populations in the Migration Period.

The rapid adoption of iron technology by the European tribesmen between *c.* 800–500 B.C. contributed to the increasing dislocation of political and economic patterns which had been relatively stable throughout the later Bronze Age; old centres now became peripheral and former peripheral areas became of central importance. The European interior was far richer in high quality iron resources than the lands of the Mediterranean littoral, with western and central Europe richer in their turn than the Balkans; the broad parity that had already been established with the Mediterranean was now firmly displaced in favour of the centre and west of Europe. The new strategic raw material gave the barbarian territories a far greater economic potential, eventually realised with the rise of coal fuel. Iron and steel now provided cheaper, more plentiful, more durable and sharper weapons and tools, whilst bronze production was released for ornaments and tableware. The expensive flow of bronze artefacts was displaced by a more egalitarian flood of iron and steel implements; even the plough, the mattock and the spade could now be shod with iron, and the cheap iron nail or clamp could be freely employed in more complex structures. Furthermore, the new iron shares and coulters could tackle the more fertile, heavy loam and clay soils of vast untapped areas of glacial Europe, whilst the old Bronze Age centres on the thin chalk and gravel topsoils became of more marginal importance.

The old patronage group of the bronze-equipped elite certainly continued as the iron-equipped elite of the new societies, but the military and economic capacity of the great mass of ordinary tribesmen was no longer so closely controlled by the chieftain's central role; iron was a more 'democratic' raw material than any since the days of the flint and stone technologies. This subcultural shift in the internal balance of tribal power was no less significant than the territorial displacements in the foci of European agricultural and economic importance. Widespread social unrest within the tribes of Europe was thus as significant a factor in these times as the unrest between tribes. Young nobles and warrior band 'impi' could now more easily usurp tribal power, or even detach themselves entirely and wander as marauders and mercenaries to the fringes of the civilised world, to the despair of the pedant palaeologists. Chiefdoms and kingdoms were tending to become oligarchies, detribalisation was beginning and the tribally 'free man' was now almost a social and economic possibility.

The crucial iron technology spread into Europe along a broad front and after a long period of infiltration as an expensive and peculiar metal, fit for decorative purposes only. Iron would not melt at the available furnace temperatures and therefore could not be cast by the mass production technique used for bronze tools – enigmatically, iron could be uselessly soft, or hard and brittle to the point of intractability, sharp and bright, or dull and corroded; the operating factors controlling these properties of iron thus required a new understanding. However, the early Anatolians had solved these problems and the Hittites quickly appreciated the stiffness of thin iron blades for daggers and rapiers, which were produced in restricted quantities from before 2000 B.C. down to the collapse of the empire *c.* 1200 B.C. The Hittite collapse and the dispersal of its border tribes has always been taken as the traditional starting point for the spread of iron technology through the Mediterranean and into Europe. However, modern evidence points to an earlier and more gradual spread of iron with a pronounced lag before its technology was properly appreciated by the rather differently orientated bronze smiths.

A knowledge of iron had certainly reached the eastern Danube by the close of the Middle Bronze Age, as can be seen from the iron-hilted bronze dagger from the Otomani site of Ganovce *c.* 1300 B.C.[43] The evidence now points to an early 'import phase' in which Anatolian iron objects were sent as gifts to distant potentates and were redistributed even beyond these recipients – iron probably appearing in this way in the Balkans, Mycenaean Greece and Crete, the Levant, and Egypt between *c.* 1500–1200 B.C. This initial period of iron imports and the reworking of imported iron introduced iron trinkets and iron wire-inlay to the middle Danube *c.* 1200–1100 B.C. at the same time, or slightly earlier, as the same features arrived in the Italian mainland by sea. However, between *c.* 1100–800 B.C., the native production of iron began and it increasingly displaced bronze for most weapons and tools which were at first slavishly copied in the new metal; the Balkans, the Danube valley, Greece and Italy now began

[43] R. Pleiner, 'The Iron Age: a notion in history,' in R. W. Ehrich (ed.), *The Flagstaff Symposium*, (1969), 13ff.

to mine and smelt their own iron ores. In the west the Phoenician trading-posts introduced iron artefacts to the southern Iberian peninsula *c.* 900–800 B.C., whence some slight knowledge of the metal spread into the Atlantic maritime network. Nevertheless, the abundance of local bronze supplies in both the Atlantic west and Scythian east prolonged the continuing production of some bronze weapons and tools down into the fourth century B.C. in those areas.

The second factor contributing to the political and economic transformation of the European tribal kingdoms was the development of urban centres in Europe itself. One may waste a great deal of energy in arguing the definition of urban units, but, broadly speaking, it is possible to distinguish four categories of early European urban settlements; the first two classes were Mediterranean in style and the latter two categories were partly indigenous native developments and partly the convergent consequence of indirect Mediterranean stimuli – the Timbuctoo and Benin of Europe. In the areas remote from the colonial zone, the earthen ramparts and palisades of the earlier timber townlets proliferated within the tribal areas of Europe, the nodal points of individual chiefdoms. These occupied hill forts rarely exceeded 25 acres of low density housing and probably seldom held populations of more than two thousand people, leaving ample room for cattle, refugees and garden plots within the earthworks, which usually enclosed an area roughly double that covered with housing. In the closing centuries of this era, however, far vaster timber towns or *oppida* had appeared, still with low density housing but sprawling over 50–200 acres within undulating sites defended by linear earthworks; extreme examples such as Kelheim and Heidegraben on the Upper Danube enclosed 1,500 and 3,500 acres respectively. These *oppida* were usually the focus of a confederacy of kingdoms and besides enclosing the royal hall and mint they might house from two to ten thousand inhabitants, including industrial specialists of all kinds and often embracing in the outer ward of the fortifications the fields necessary for their support. However, lest one should be dazzled by the scale of European urban centres at this time one should match them not only against the colonial towns but against the many Mediterranean cities which enclosed 200 acres at high density and the metropolitan capitals of 400 acres and more with some thirty thousand inhabitants.

The Near Eastern urban network now stretched in a continuous economic superstructure over the littoral of Mediterranean Europe and in a discontinuous lattice stretching far out across the European hinterland. At the centre of this network lay the Persian Empire and its metropoli, surrounded in the west by smaller urban confederations and leagues, such as those of the Greeks, Carthaginians and Etruscans, and beyond these again there now extended the native towns of the Iberian, Celtic, Thracian, and Scythian tribal kingdoms. As far as peripheral Europe was concerned, one of the most important agents in the coastal colonisation was the Greek maritime leagues. The Phoenician and Etruscan thalassocracies continued but first the Assyrian and then the Persian conquests of the Levant isolated Carthage at the head of the western Phoenician colonies and at the same time stimulated the resurgence in Greek colonial activities.

Early Greek colonial activity continued the Mycenaean pattern with the Ionian settlement of coastal Anatolia and coastal Sicily and southern Italy *c.* 750–700 B.C. Again, following the Mycenaean lead, exploratory voyages were made from these two major trading areas north-eastwards into the Black Sea and westwards into the west Mediterranean. In the Black Sea a chain of early colonies was established *c.* 700–600 B.C. in the coastal lands of the Thracians, Gatae and Scythians, strategically placed at river mouths conveying staples from deep in the interior, and regularly spaced at one or two days' sail along the coast. The most important centres, Panticapaeum, Olbia and Tomis, rapidly became wealthy cities with regular trading relationships stretching hundreds of miles into innermost Europe.

Panticapaeum lay in the Crimean wheatlands at the mouth of the Sea of Azov, with the river Don stretching away into distant Muscovy and a coastline adjacent to the metalliferous Caucasus. Olbia was founded at the joint mouth of the rivers Bug and Dnieper which Herodotus' informants knew intimately for some forty days' travel inland towards Kiev. As the northernmost port in the Black Sea, Olbia was at the point where the Baltic trade emerged and where the steppe, deciduous forest and coniferous forest resources were closest to the sea. The Olbian merchants knew all about the Scythian mare-milkers of the steppe, the gold-winning Agathyrsi of the Carpathians, the wolf-skin clad warriors of the Slav Neuri around the south Polish swamps and even something of the distant fur-trappers of the coniferous forests. Greek wine, oil, pottery, jewellery and metalware passed upstream in quantity as far as Kiev, whilst amber, furs, hides, pitch, gold, slaves, wheat and horses passed to the coast for redistribution by the maritime network. Similar products were brought to Tomis, the strategically sited outlet for the entire Danube trade. Avoiding the dangerous marshes of the Danube delta, the colony of Tomis was cunningly situated to the south, where the meandering channel of the Danube comes closest to the coast, thus an easy portage of 50 miles to Tomis on the coast cut out 250 miles of perilous delta swamp navigation. By *c.* 300 B.C. the inland trail of Rhodian wine and oil amphorae was matched by a scatter of silver coins of Thasos, reaching as far as the Theiss and Maros rivers, although concentrated in the hoards of the middlemen south of the Iron Gates. Together, these colonies on the Black Sea regularly supplied the Greek mainland with very large quantities of important staples including cereals, salt, iron ingots, hides, timber, slaves, ship's tar, salted meat, salted sturgeon and tunny fish, as well as such luxuries as honey, amber, fine furs, Carpathian and Caucasian gold and Thracian silver.

In the west Mediterranean, the Greeks fought their way into the highly competitive market by a mixture of intrigue and violence launched from the homeland and from the eighth-century footholds in southern Italy and Sicily. The Carthaginian league already embraced all the Phoenician cities of North Africa, western Sicily, Sardinia, the Balearics and the annexed kingdom of Tartessos, whilst from their Iberian bases the voyages of Hanno and Himilco respectively explored the African coast down to Sierra Leone and the European coast as far as Brittany by *c.* 450 B.C. In the north the Etruscan confederation was at the height of its power and both politically and economically controlled the area from the Campanian and Adriatic coasts to the foot of the Alpine passes. The colonial Greeks skilfully usurped the Punic trade with Etruria, whilst at the same time inciting and aiding the Latin tribes against their overlords. The wedge between the Punic and the Etruscan leagues was then driven home by the defeat of their combined fleets at Alalia off Corsica by the Phocaeans in 535 B.C. and by the successful land and sea operations of the successive tyrants of Syracuse over several centuries. By these devices the Greeks managed to infiltrate the gap between the southern Iberian colonies of the Carthaginians and the western Ligurian colonies of the Etruscans. The Phocaeans quickly founded a major colony at Massilia *c.* 600 B.C. to command the Rhone trade and by 500 B.C. a belt of Greek towns extended from Nice to Alicante under the general patronage of the flourishing Massiliotes. Even earlier, *c.* 640 B.C., Colaeus of Samos had successfully slipped through the Pillars of Hercules and returned with a cargo of Iberian silver. But although other Massiliote captains, like Pytheas in *c.* 300 B.C., repeated the voyage of Himilco to the British Isles, the subsequent Carthaginian seizure of southern Spain forced the Massiliotes to concentrate on outflanking this Atlantic blockade by trading overland to the Atlantic estuaries of the Gironde and Loire and to the headwaters of the Rhone itself.

In general, the Greek settlement of the Gulf of Lions resembled the colonial pattern adopted in the Black Sea – a string of coastal towns carefully placed at the natural outlets of rivers and routes running deep into the interior. The luxuries and manufactured goods of the Mediterranean now flowed inland in exchange for cereals, hides, wool, iron, tin and slaves, ferried in a continuous flow from the distant bounds of the Celtic territories. However, the competitive commercial enterprises of the Massiliote Greeks and the Etruscans seem to have clashed deep in Alpine Europe. The Etruscan expansion to the foot of the Alps intensified the ancient trade with the Celtic tribes of the upper Danube, importing salt, tin and amber whilst exporting jewellery, bronze wine services, wine and oil. About the same period the Massiliote merchants appear to have established a commercial connection with the same Alpine area from the headwaters of the Rhone valley and a trade war seems to have ensued, on a military footing in the Mediterranean and on a commercial basis in the interior.

The nodal triangle between the headwaters of the Saone, Seine, Rhone, Rhine and Danube, only one hundred miles broad, thus became the competitive focus attracting all the luxuries of the Greek and Etruscan world. Glass, coral, gold jewellery, fine Italian metalware, wine services, Greek pottery, oil and wine now flowed into the tribal strongholds of this crucial area, whose chieftains controlled the redistribution of British and Breton tin from the Seine, Belgic iron from the Rhine, amber, salt and copper from the Danube valley. One stronghold, at Heuneburg on the upper Danube,[44] suddenly sported a novel bastioned brick wall in provincial Greek style – surely planned by some Greek adviser; other sites in the same general region have revealed the princely wealth of the chieftains' burials with their Rhodian flagons and south Italian wine services. However, amidst the riches of Kappel, Vilsingen, Grachwil and Berne the grave of the Celtic queen at Vix, on the upper Seine, is the most remarkable.[45] This innominate Boudicca lay on a dismantled waggon with a Graeco-Italian gold torque at her throat, quantities of ornaments of bronze and amber around her and a complete bronze table set of south Italian origin, with accompanying Attic wine cups. In the corner of the grave there stood an import of regal proportions, a huge bronze volute-krater, five feet tall and magnificently decorated, probably the work of the best Tarentine workshops. The Vix krater, together with the accompanying wine service and the gold torque, may well have been part of a Massiliote diplomatic embassy of especial importance in the commercial rivalry with the Etruscans; a royal gift of prodigious value commissioned and brought from the finest south Italian ateliers to the wharves of Massilia, then laboriously shipped to the upper Seine and presumably presented by a deputation of merchant ambassadors,

[44] W. Kimmig, 'Early Celts on the Upper Danube: the excavations at the Heuneburg', in R. Bruce-Mitford (ed.), *Recent Archaeological Excavations in Europe* (London, 1975), 32–64.

[45] R. Joffroy, *Le Trésor de Vix* (Paris, 1962); J. V. S. Megaw, 'The Vix burial', *Antiquity*, XL (1966), 38–44.

anxious to secure the continued flow of trade upon which their livelihood and that of Massilia depended.

A fascinating picture of the Mediterranean penetration of Europe now emerges, with the first definite evidence of Mediterranean merchant-explorers sailing the Atlantic coastline, operating deep in Iberia, following the Rhone to the umbilical communications' centre of Europe, crossing the Alpine passes from Etruria to the Celtic homelands, following the Danube to the Iron Gates, exploring the Dnieper northwards to Kiev and probing the Sea of Azov to the mouth of the Don. These expeditions were not the work of the epicurean Greek literati who all too rarely allude to their taller stories, but the achievement of largely anonymous freebooters, speculative merchants, mercenary artificers and artisans, renegade riff-raff, outlaws of the frontiers of civilisation; the opportunists of the colonial world, destined to remain nameless unless they returned with the fortune which could transform their venality into nobility, as happened to Colaeus of Samos. These hybrid frontiersmen, sparingly literate, clad in the outlandish mixture of Greek and native dress so carefully depicted on colonial works of art, but the joke of the Attic comedies, these were the men who penetrated the southern flanks of Europe to a depth of some 300 miles and talked with Herodotus of their forty-day journeys inland.

This largely riverine penetration of southern Europe was not a uniform process; on the contrary the trade goods often show a markedly polarised distribution in which the largest quantities of finest products appear mysteriously concentrated at the most distant extremities of exploration. The richest presents and the finest wines were destined for those distant kings and chieftains who could most fundamentally control the flow of desirable European commodities and their redistribution. The very finest products of the civilised world appear in the distant treasuries of the Celtic elite at Vix, Mont Lassois, Camp du Chateau, and the Heuneburg, in the hoards of remote Geto-Thracian aristocrats at Craiova and Agighiol, or amidst the wealth of faraway Scythian princes at Chertomlyk and Kul Oba.

Everywhere in the wake of these deep commercial penetrations of middle Europe are found the coins of the Greek colonial cities. At first these coins were probably accepted as so much convenient gold or silver bullion, but gradually their convenience as a medium of exchange for certain restricted transactions became apparent. The earliest Mediterranean coins were struck by the Lydian kings, *c.* 700 B.C., possibly for the express purpose of paying mercenary soldiers unable to take payment in kind, a purpose for which much early coinage was specifically minted. These early coins were not, however, the first currency – they were merely another medium of exchange circulating in addition to the variegated iron spits, bars, and ingots, gold and silver rings and lumps, bronze rings, axes and even arrowheads. The superiority of coins lay in their standardisation in convenient units of exchange, visibly authenticated by the stamp of the issuing authority; a cash market economy was now possible. From the Lydian kingdom the production of coinage rapidly passed to the adjacent Ionian cities and by *c.* 600 B.C. most of the cities of the Greek maritime leagues were already minting their own coinages. Some especially reliable, plentiful and pure coinages rapidly gained confidence as international currencies – the Persian 'archers', the Corinthian 'foals', the Athenian 'owls' and the Macedonian 'Philippi', for example, but the majority of coinages circulated internally within a more restricted group of local markets.

The Iberians, Celts, Geto-Thracians and Scythians rapidly became acquainted with the coinage of the Greek merchants, and coin balances are a frequent find in the European tribal *oppida*. The employment of coinage for military pay, for provisioning armies in the field and for the widespread employment of tribal mercenaries also trailed coinage in the wake of every military expedition into Europe; from the Persian invasion of Dacia and Scythia in 515 B.C., the expeditions of the Macedonian kings into Bulgaria and Yugoslavia between *c.* 450–350 B.C., to the Celtic mercenaries hired by the Etruscans, Graeco-Italians and Syracusans from *c.* 450–300 B.C. and the Punic forays into central Iberia, *c.* 400–200 B.C. By *c.* 300 B.C. there was widespread familiarity with money transactions in middle Europe. Soon after this date the Celts of France and central Europe began to mint careful copies of the Philippus and the coins of Massilia, whilst the Geto-Dacians simultaneously copied the coins of Larissa and Thasos as well as the Macedonian series. Likewise the northern Iberians struck inscribed coins based on the *drachmae* of Greek Emporion and the southern Iberians copied the Punic silver of the Barquidae. These earliest coinages were initially very close copies of the original Mediterranean models and even carried intelligible inscriptions either taken from the original source or, more significantly, introducing the name of the issuing dynast or tribe and thus giving evidence of a growing acquaintance with Mediterranean letters and language. This same evidence also suggests that the earliest tribal coins, with their neat filleted borders and accurate inscriptions, were designed and produced for the local chieftains by Mediterranean craftsmen working in native service. Perhaps the same renegades who helped negotiate with grasping merchants and advised on matters varying from the best wines and tableware to problems in fortification, or even those early artificers who stimulated the rise of the great native art styles with their Mediterranean embellishments. However, after the art of coin-striking was learnt and the foliate basis of Mediterranean art appreciated, the tribal artificers took over with their own weird elaborations. Neither the coinage nor the art styles can be said to degenerate; they are simply transformed.

The native European coinages circulated primarily within the restricted markets of particular tribal kingdoms and their distributions clearly define the territories belonging to various tribal unions. These local coinages probably gave a great economic stimulus to the internal production and retail of goods of all kinds in a market economy, at the same time tending to accelerate detribalisation by their increasing substitution in transactions formerly fulfilled by mutual obligations. In many respects the subsequent emergence of the European, feudal-state economies represented the further development of these early changes. The feudal economies embrace a category of systems employing redistribution mechanisms intermediate between those of the tribal societies and those of cash-economy, revenue states. At first sight the feudal machinery is apparently based on the minutely detailed, formalised and institutionalised hierarchy of personal obligations and services in return for land held. In fact, the minute evaluation and codification of these obligations can be shown to have evolved largely in order to convert these theoretical statutory services quickly and conveniently into pecuniary or other equivalents. Ultimately, the European systems elaborated an almost ritual formalisation of the tribal clientship system in terms of a calculus of archaic obligations long since superseded, in order to harness an ancient social pattern to an economy based in reality on revenue, taxes, coinage and manufacturing towns; a calculus in which '*x* equals obligation' was substituted by '*x* equals cash equivalent'.

However, it is unlikely that the earliest European tribal coinages were used in quite the advanced manner already in vogue throughout the Mediterranean cash markets. Initially at least, these tribal coins, struck with mystic insignia at the royal *oppida*, may have served very restricted and carefully prescribed internal tribal purposes; hence their restricted distributions. What these various restricted transactions might have been can only now be guessed, but in northern Europe there long survived the custom of treating the small issues of tribal coinage as symbolic wealth medallions in the gift of the chief or king, bestowing status and approval on the holder, circulating in society at large as wealth held for services to the tribe and its royal family and exchanging for material commodities only when necessary. Perhaps we should take in this context the curious stories of the 'potlatch' ceremonies of Luerna, the king of the Arverni, who distributed gold and silver coins to his tribesmen by his own hand from his chariot. Certainly, the acceptable media of exchange for barter, clientship, blood-money, bride-price, dowries, tribute and taxes long continued to involve the traditional commodities – cattle, grain, salt, iron, tools, weapons or garments – and to what extent coin could be substituted in these transactions we do not know.

Within the span of this closing period, the entire lateral band of middle Europe was penetrated by the commercial and political agents of the Mediterranean powers. This infiltration operated at many social and cultural levels and proceeded on a series of broad fronts from western Punic Iberia to Greek Celtica, Etruscan Rhaetia to Greek Illyria, Thracia and Pontus. This intensive subcultural interpenetration nevertheless had repercussions far beyond those limited areas directly penetrated by Mediterranean merchant-adventurers; the whole area south of the Rhine and Danube was directly or indirectly exposed to massive new stimuli, as well as lesser influences in restricted areas even further to the north. Barbarian mercenaries, artisans and slaves now served in the armies, factories and cities of the Mediterranean powers. Conversely, Mediterranean adventurers, advisers and artificers also entered the service of the barbarian potentates and introduced them to literacy and the other delights and achievements of the civilised worlds. At a more direct level, there was outright interaction between the armies of civilised Persia, Macedon, Etruria, Massilia, Punica and those of the barbarian Scythians, Thraco-Getians, Celts, Ligurians and Iberians – battles in which the Scythians and Celts were able to defeat the fine field armies of the ancient world and permanently to seize southern France, northern Italy, Anatolian Galatia and the coastal Pontus, respectively. Even at more indirect levels the mutual interaction was a significant factor in stimulating novel social, material, economic, religious, political and artistic developments that were not entirely one-sided. This intensive subcultural ferment extended not only along the entire geographical frontier between Mediterranean civilisation and the tribal kingdoms but also proceeded in depth, down the whole social frontier from the luxury-loving elite to their dependent artificers, from the surplus-producing tribesmen and the mercenary warriors to the industrial slaves and captives.

It would be quite untrue, however, to portray the economic development of Europe purely in terms of an increasing degree of Mediterranean penetration. The economic development of Europe, like that of historical Africa, was indeed transformed by colonial intervention and its repercussions, but the pattern that was thus transformed was already a European pattern long before the changes began and long after their withdrawal. The general analogies between the Mediterranean impact on ancient Europe and the colonial impact on historical Africa are quite striking, especially in relation to the rise of the tribal chiefdoms, urban development, detribalisation and the rise of the native states, with their initial instability.

In ancient Europe we can note the transition from a phase in which European products were an economic curiosity for the Mediterranean states, *c.* 2000–1400 B.C., through a period of their increasing, but still peripheral, importance, *c.* 1400–600 B.C., to a phase in which European commodities were a small but crucial element in the expanding Mediterranean economies, *c.* 600 B.C. This latter phase commences with the full deployment of the urban colonial bases along the southern European coastline and the expansion of their role in the political and economic affairs of tribal kingdoms far beyond their immediate vicinities. This external colonial stimulus, aided by the development of coinage and redistributional cash-market economies, catalysed the formation of larger kingdoms and confederate chiefdoms, centred on increasingly more complex *oppida* and townlets. Everywhere, imported objects and artificers stimulated the European development of new but markedly hybrid native art styles, initially the distinctive livery of the subcultural equipment and insignia of their Mediterraneanised patrons, the tribal elite. The parallel inceptions of the Ibero-Punic Tartessian, Graeco-Celtic La Tène, Thraco-Getian and Graeco-Scythian art styles were the artistic offspring of this seminal episode.

It is during this transitional phase, *c.* 600–0 B.C., that Spanish, French, north Italian and Carpathian metal resources first became essential to the exponentially expanding requirements of the Mediterranean world. At the same time, the Iberian, Celtic and Scythian supplies of cereals, salted meat and fish, wool, hides and slaves had become only slightly less important reserves for the increasingly industrial and decreasingly agrarian Mediterranean cities. The situation was rapidly approaching the point at which leading Mediterranean powers could no longer afford to allow the flow of such vital European resources to fluctuate at the whim of distant despots and at the risk of interception by political rivals. The European Greeks, however, were more interested in the superior resources and tempting challenge of the Near East, commercially following the conquests of Alexander into India itself, but firmly holding their Celtic and Pontic granaries nevertheless. The Carthaginians and Etruscans began to appreciate and militarily to exploit the European trade routes on their immediate borders, in Iberia and north Italy. But these developments were rudely interrupted by the rise of Rome, the former Italic puppet of the

Hellenic league, which now began to exploit its central location and the divisions between its Etruscan, Punic and Greek rivals.

Rome quickly overthrew its Etruscan overlords, with the tacit acquiescence of the Greek colonists of Italy and aided by the devastating raids of the Celts through the Alpine passes, *c.* 410–390 B.C. Subsequently, the rapid expansion of the Latin league, headed by Rome, alarmed the Graeco-Italian cities into united actions under Pyrrhus, king of Epirus, but although actions were lost the new power was not crushed and opportunist Carthaginian activities in Sicily intervened, *c.* 278 B.C. The Romans then absorbed Syracusan Sicily and Massiliote Gaul in return for protection against the expanding Carthaginian domain, *c.* 210 B.C. The great duel of the Punic wars finally culminated in the triumph of the Roman legions, the surrender of Carthage and the Roman occupation of Iberia, *c.* 200 B.C. Greece fell next in *c.* 146 B.C. and Mediterranean Europe had finally become a Roman province. From this broad beachhead the Roman military machine expanded inexorably – Scythia followed in *c.* 70 B.C., northern Gaul *c.* 50 B.C. and by the reign of Augustus the Roman legions were deployed on the new Rhine and Danube frontier, *c.* A.D. 9. The colonial leagues of the old Mediterranean world were now engulfed in the military empire of a European super-power, the western successor to the eastern empires of Alexander and the Persian Achaemenids. Henceforth, the detribalised, but dependent, Europeans, south of the Roman frontier, were tax-paying members of one huge revenue state. North of the Rhine–Danube frontier there now developed a new trade zone, and new barbarian chiefdoms competed in unstable perturbation; to the north, the Germans and Slavs, to the east the Huns and Parthians. The threshold of the European German empire and the Slav kingdoms, the medieval feudal nation states, the Renaissance colonial powers and the empires of the industrial Iron Age were yet to come.[46]

[46] The author is deeply indebted to Dr Andrew Sherratt for help in reading and checking the MS of this chapter.

CHAPTER II

Trade and Industry under the Later Roman Empire in the West*

In the year of our Lord 301, 'aroused justly and rightfully by the abuse of immoderate prices and an uncurbed passion for gain, which is lessened neither by abundant supplies nor by fruitful years', the Emperor Diocletian issued an edict in which, after analysing the evils of the times (in curiously pompous and tortuous Latin), he laid down for their improvement a tariff of maximum prices, to be observed on pain of death throughout the whole Empire. This edict is significant not so much for its results (which were trivial), but as a symbol of the change that had come over the life of the Mediterranean world since the setting up of the principate by Augustus three hundred years earlier. A world of free, private economic activity had given place to one of state control. Machinery had been devised for the organisation of production and trade. Forms of free association had been transmuted into organs of rigid regimentation. The imperial authorities, once content merely to provide facilities for the trader, to act as 'night-watchman for the business-man', now sought to direct his whole life and his very movements from place to place.

The process of this transformation was involved. It had its ramifications in every branch of social and economic life; and it embraced the provinces no less than Italy, the original core of the Empire. Its beginnings can be traced in the earliest period of the principate; but unfortunately the critical time when the new outlines were solidifying is one of the most obscure in the whole history of Rome. In the absence of reliable literary sources, the economic history of the third century has largely to be reconstructed with the aid of archaeology, and by deductions made from such later evidence as the legal codes afford, and from a comparison of earlier conditions with the system set up by Diocletian and Constantine. Inevitably, therefore, a review of the trade and industry of the later Empire must begin with the principate.

* This revision of the chapter published in the first edition of this volume was carried out in 1966 and a few additional amendments were made ten years later.

ATLANTIC
OCEAN
XII
Maxima Caesariensis
Britannia I et II
Flavia Caesariensis
Germania II
Belgica II
Belgica I
Germania I
Lugdunensis II
Lugdunensis I
XI
Sequania
Aquitanica II I
X
Novempopulana
Viennensis
Narbonensis
1
2
3
Gallaecia
Tarraconensis
Lusitania
IX
Carthaginiensis
Baetica
Baleares
Raetia
Noricum ripense
Noricum Mediterraneum
VII
Venetia et Histria
VI
Savensis
Aemilia et Liguria
Flaminia et Picenum
Tuscia et Umbria
ROME
Corsica
Sardinia
Campania et Samnium
Lucania et Brutii
Sicilia
Mediterranean
Mauritania Tingitana
Mauretania Caesariensis
Mauretania Sitifensis
Proconsularis Zeugitana
Numidia Cirtensis
VIII
Valencia Byzacena
Tripolitana
Key to the numbers of the Dioceses:
I Oriens
II Pontus
III Asiana
IV Thrace
V Moesiae
VI Pannoniae
VII Italia
VIII Africa
IX Hispaniae
X Viennensis
XI Galliae
XII Britanniae
Note: The representation of the four provinces making up the Diocese of Britanniae is conventional, since the names, but not the position or limits of these provinces, are known.

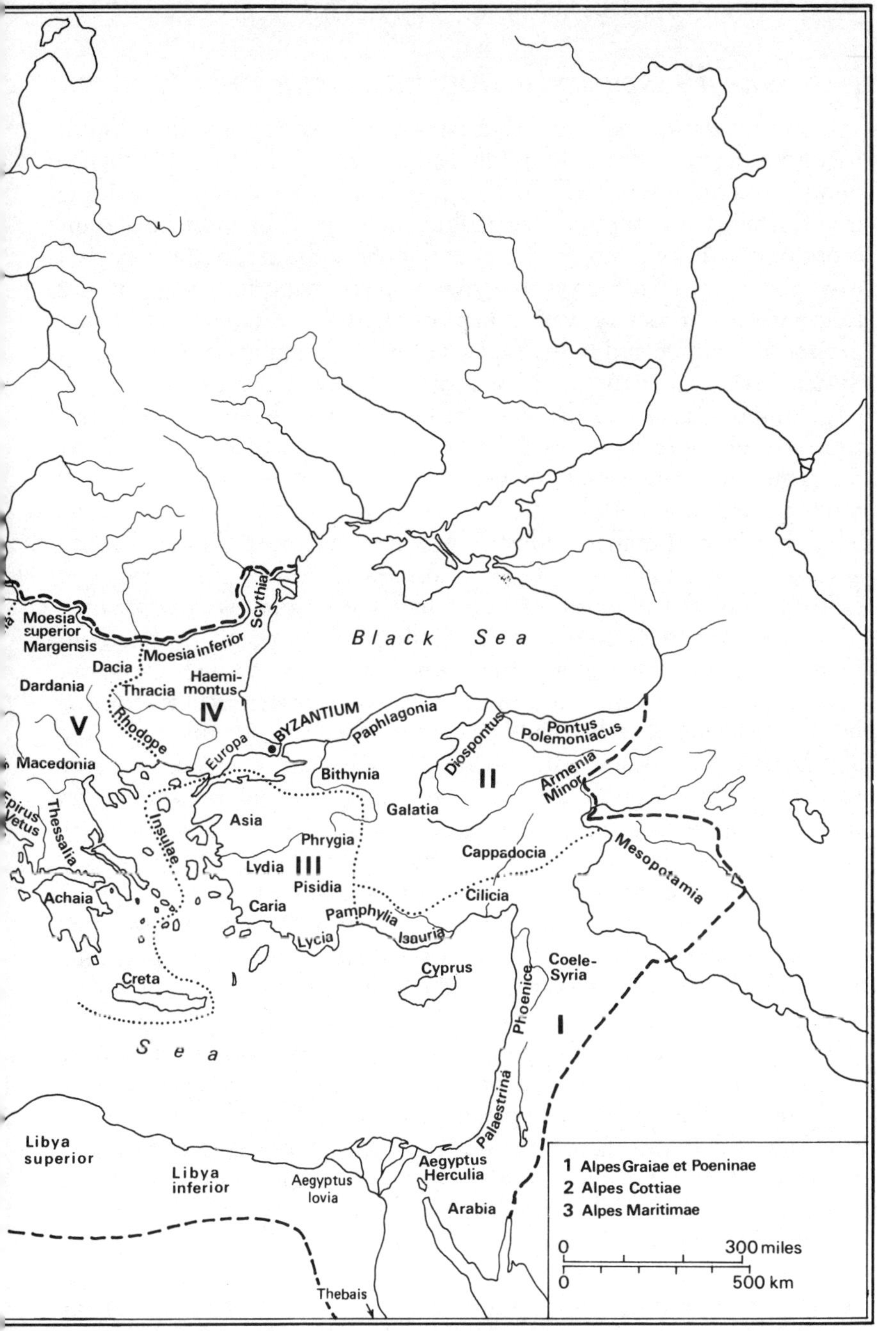

Map 1. The Empire under Diocletian

I. *The Prosperity of the Early Empire*

The annexation of the old-established provinces of the eastern Mediterranean under the Republic had exercised a profound influence upon the economic life of the West. Basically of course – and this is true throughout antiquity – agriculture remained the most important economic activity both in the countryside and among the city and town dwellers. It has been estimated that the contribution of agriculture to the wealth of society was perhaps of the order of twenty times that produced by trade and industry. Nevertheless, an influx of Greeks and Syrians, who came to the West mostly as slaves, but rapidly and in large numbers achieved the status of freedmen, was responsible at this time for an appreciable rise in the technical level of production. At the same time, new standards were set up, and the demand for more refined wares was stimulated by the actual import of eastern products. The character of Italian industry was not, however, fundamentally altered, but remained one of small businesses. Workers were engaged either in casual labour or in individual workshops, *tabernae*, which frequently served as booths for the selling of the goods produced in them. Naturally this was a pattern which allowed of much variation. Sometimes the customer might bring his own materials, his cloth or his gold and silver, to be made up into garments or ornaments by the appropriate workman. But there is plenty of evidence for the craftsman himself providing the raw materials and in some cases making it up for the market. The existence of bazaars and the presence of pedlars on the streets and in the public baths presupposes a considerable amount of production of this kind.

Moreover, in some instances industry is known to have developed on a larger scale, and with the aid of slave labour to have approached something like a factory system; and despite the old Roman prejudice against trade, inscriptions reveal the presence of upper-class rich business men, who were organised in companies, *societates*, and were prepared to contract for the provision of public and even private buildings, and occasionally to speculate in the buying up, repairing and reselling of damaged property. Usually the men engaged in this kind of lucrative activity were socially obscure. All the more remarkable therefore is the case of the Domitii, who between A.D. 50 and A.D. 150 established what was almost a monopoly in the brickyards of Italy, and so provided perhaps the only example in Roman history of political fame resting upon industrial wealth. The beginnings of the firm go back to the demand created by the great fire of Rome in A.D. 64; and judging by its stamped products, which reveal the existence of fifty-three slaves, twenty-two freedmen, and twenty-two others of uncertain status, the actual number employed must have been far in excess of this. By A.D. 155 the Domitian brickworks were employing no less than forty-six foremen; and the wealth of the Domitian family helped to lay the foundations of the Antonine dynasty, with which it had marriage connections. There are other examples of fairly large concerns, such as the pottery of Gaius Laekanius Bassus at Fasana near Pola, which produced *amphorae* for the marketing of Istrian oil and employed at least fifteen slaves; and the export business in oil and wine of Calvia Crispinilla, a lady of infamous reputation at the court of Nero, is attested by stamps on *amphorae* found in north-east Italy and Pannonia. The bronze industry of Capua, too, must have been highly organised; and we know the names of thirteen female slaves who worked in a weaving shed at Pompeii. In Rome itself there are records of two large factories during the early Empire, one for the reprocessing of papyrus and another for handling Spanish red-lead. In general, however, these larger enterprises were exceptional and were to remain so throughout antiquity. Thus the lead pipes provided under contract for the imperial authorities were mainly the product of small firms; and the predominant form of industrial organisation remained one of private individuals working for themselves, or small firms undertaking modest contracts.

The division of labour between free men, freedmen and slaves varied from one industry to another; nor is it always easy to assess the value of the inscriptional evidence on which our knowledge rests. It has, however, been calculated that among the owners and entrepreneurs in business in Rome during the first two centuries of the Empire, there was a preponderance of freedmen over men of free origin in the proportion of two to one, and that a similar but much smaller preponderance also existed in the rest of Italy. The labourers, however, were mainly slaves, with some freedmen whose manumission had been qualified by a clause exacting continued duties of this kind; free wage earners were exceptional anywhere in Italy, though their occasional use is implied in a story of Vespasian, who is said to have rejected the adoption of a labour-saving hoisting machine with the words: 'I must feed my poor' – a story not perhaps to be taken very seriously, since benefactions rather than schemes for public work were the more usual imperial answer to poverty. In the early Empire there was no kind of regulation of the conditions of labour in the various industries. Under a system of free contract, working hours normally stretched from sunrise to sunset, and child labour was used where it was profitable. Wages were paid sometimes by the day, sometimes by the piece.

What then were the main results of the setting up of the Augustan principate in the sphere of production and commerce? They are to be seen essentially in the quickening of economic activity, and the extension of commerce which came with a higher standard of living. When Pliny says that every servant girl has her silver mirror, he is probably guilty of rhetorical overstatement. But the first period of the Empire undoubtedly saw the fruits of security – peace, and a good system of roads and safe sea communications – in the rise of a class of Italian business men, sometimes free and sometimes of freedman origin, who took the initiative in developing the western provinces. In particular these men extended the wholesale trade, which Roman sentiment had always regarded as almost respectable. 'Business on a small scale', writes Cicero (*De officiis*, I, 150–1), 'is despicable; but if it is extensive and imports commodities in large quantities from all over the world, and distributes them honestly, it is not so very discreditable; nay, if the merchant satiated, or rather satisfied, with the fortune he has made, retires from the harbour and steps into an estate, as once he returned to harbour from the sea, he deserves, I think, the highest respect.' Earlier in the same passage Cicero expresses his contempt for manual work, which he describes as degrading. It is the typical attitude of the Republican nobility, of an aristocracy which was content to see its physical work done by slaves; and in so far as this attitude persisted under the Empire, its results were not happy. The capital accumulated by the *nouveaux riches* of the Augustan revolution tended to be invested in land rather than in manufacture or commerce; and these activities were left largely to freedmen and foreigners. Contempt for those who practised them was to persist throughout antiquity and in A.D. 436 we find Theodosius demanding that public service be 'purged of the infection' of certain silversmiths and jewellers who had managed to secure modest posts.

Thus Italy still preserved, if in a modified degree, the parasitical character which it had established under the Republic. Cicero's big business man, it will be observed, is one who imports and distributes; and this definition reflects the function of Italy in relation to the rest of the Mediterranean world. This aspect of the Italian economy should not, however, be exaggerated. Strabo describes the Egyptian corn boats returning empty from Puteoli, which had been a flourishing export harbour serving the rich districts of Campania; but recent research has shown that this is misleading and that Puteoli remained a prosperous commercial city down to the early decades of the third century, though with a slight shift towards land as the source of wealth for the local aristocracy. Pliny asserts that India, China and Arabia between them received annually the vast sum of a hundred million *sesterces* from the Empire, a statement supported by the discovery of numerous Roman gold coins in India, and even in Ceylon and China. It may fairly be assumed that these coins represent payment for the luxuries – dancing girls, parrots, ebony, ivory, pearls and precious stones, spices, perfumes, silks and drugs – which the Far East sent to Rome. But there is now evidence that as trade with India increased, imports from there – especially pepper, precious stones and muslin – began to be paid for in copper and tin, wine, glass and woollens, and no longer in precious metals. On the other hand, during the first century of the Empire Italy enjoyed a flourishing trade with the undeveloped provinces of the north and west. Africa, Spain, Gaul, Germany, the Danube areas and Britain were all markets for Italian bronze, glass and pottery, and this trade laid the foundations of the prosperity of Aquileia, through which much of it passed. From here the trading houses of the Barbii and the Statii despatched overseas goods, together with the products of Italy, northwards to the Danube and eastwards to Istria in exchange for slaves, cattle, hides, resin, pitch, wax, honey and cheese, and for the iron and wool of Noricum.

Other parts of Italy also flourished under the early principate. The bronzework and glassware of Campania, the pottery of Arretium, the textile industries of Apulia and Calabria in the south and of the Po valley in the north (where linen was also manufactured), all enjoyed a season of prosperity; and there was a considerable local trade and exchange of commodities throughout the peninsula. Gradually, however, this declined. Italy lacked the skill to compete with the East; and once the new western provinces were developed, they were able to exploit certain advantages of labour which quickly put them ahead of Italy. By the second century Italian overseas trade was reduced to a trickle.

For this regression in the economic life of Italy the provinces of the north and west were in part responsible. Here the setting up of the Empire had been more than a mere stimulus. It was rather a creative act, which carried the benefits of Graeco-Roman civilisation and town life to fresh areas, and extended the civilised way of life as far as the Roman legions went. The process had, of course, already begun earlier. Under the late Republic, Provence and Languedoc had been for some time a second Italy, with rich olive groves and extensive vineyards. But now the consolidation after Caesar's conquests carried Roman civilisation to the English Channel and the Rhine, and northern Gaul began to show the marks of a more developed economy. New towns, centres of Roman culture, and inhabited by craftsmen and merchants, began to spring up in all parts, not large indeed by modern standards, or even in comparison with an Alexandria or an Antioch – the populations of Nîmes, Toulouse, Autun and Trier were never more than 50,000, nor their areas above 500–850 acres – but nevertheless important centres for the dissemination of civilised ways of thought and behaviour. In Spain too the cities grew in number and size. According to Strabo, there were more commercial entrepreneurs in Gades than in any other city of the Empire except Patavium in the Po valley.

The first stage in the Romanisation of a new province or frontier area usually came with the presence of the Roman army, which would supervise the building of forts, harbours, bridges and roads, and for this purpose frequently set up its own brickworks and opened up its own quarries. Thus the potteries of Xanten and Neuss, and the lamp factory at Weisenau near Mainz, which dates from the time of Augustus, were directly worked by the army. The next stage was the arrival in the new area of the Italian trader with goods to serve the army and, incidentally, the native population. In the wake of the trader colonies and markets such as Cambodunum (Kempten in Allgäu) sprang up; and very soon, with the stimulus given to native industry, the third stage was reached, in which the colonial area developed its own economy. The net result was a decline in the demand for Italian products and a shift in the location of industry outward from Italy to the provinces.

This tendency can be most easily traced in the history of the production of the fine red-ware pottery – *terra sigillata* – which is so typical of most important Roman sites, and fills so many of the display cabinets of local museums. About the end of the Republic we find *sigillata* produced at various centres in Italy, including Rome itself, Puteoli, and above all Arretium in Etruria; gradually, by the time of Augustus, Arretium has forged ahead, and captured the main markets. Its products appear in every province of the Empire, and especially in Spain, North Africa, North Gaul and Germany. The workshops seem to have been large, and organised on a basis of slave labour; thus we known of fifty-eight slaves in that of Publius Cornelius. Sometimes, too, it is possible to trace the manumission of a slave and his subsequent appearance as an independent master. However, the centre of production soon began to shift. After a short period during which work from Modena, which lies nearer to the frontier, appears on Gallic sites, a brand of Gallic ware from la Graufesenque (Aveyron), and several minor centres such as Banassac (Lozère) and Montans (Tarn), makes its appearance and begins to supply Aquitania. By the beginning of Tiberius' principate pots from la Graufesenque were reaching the Rhine and the camp at Haltern on the Lippe. From its potteries, one square kilometre in extent, there poured forth thousands of vases, which by A.D. 40–70 had a complete control over the market. They are found all over Gaul and Roman Germany. The contemporary camp sites at Hofheim in Taunus and Aislingen in Württemberg contain virtually none but la Graufesenque ware. In the British Museum there are over a thousand sherds mainly from London; and under Domitian some even reached Scotland. From Narbonne they were exported to Spain, where they competed with the declining industry of Arretium, and even to Italy itself.

However, by Domitian's principate la Graufesenque too had passed its prime. The sites in southern Baden now begin to show sherds of a type which has been traced to Lezoux, the scene of a large collection of potteries with several hundred kilns seventeen miles east of Clermont Ferrand, and not far from the Allier, which served for purposes of transport. These potteries, which were pre-Roman in origin, reached the acme of their success from about A.D. 75 to A.D. 110. By this time Italy had completely lost its hold on the foreign market. Even under the Flavians the only Italian pots exported went to North Africa; and in the ruins of Pompeii there was discovered an unopened crate of pottery, largely from Gaul – so powerful had the competition of the new centres become. The main markets for Gallic ware were, however, in the military zones, along the Rhine and Danube and, to a lesser extent, in Britain. Very soon, therefore, the industry once more began to move eastward towards Germany.

Under ancient conditions land transport was always excessively slow and expensive. To bring an oil-crushing machine from Suessa twenty-five miles away to Cato's farm at Venafrum cost 72 *sesterces*, or 14.5 per cent of its cost; but to bring it the 75 miles from Pompeii cost 290 *sesterces*, which is 73 per cent of the cost. In Diocletian's time, to transport a waggonload of hemp worth 4,800 *denarii* 240 miles exactly doubled its price. So prohibitive was the cost of transporting cheap or heavy articles by land, and so little had the situation improved in nearly half a millennium. This fact explains not only the tremendous advantages enjoyed by a country with good river transport like Gaul, but also why the pottery industry migrated eastward into Germany. About A. D. 100, men from Lezoux had established a flourishing centre at Heiligenberg in Alsace, and a little later the pots from Faulquemont-Chémeny, twelve-and-a-half miles east of Metz, were reaching the Rhine, the Moselle, the Rhine–Danube *limes*, and other parts of Germany. In A.D. 83 civilian potters occupied the kilns at Rheinzabern between Mainz and Strasbourg, which had been abandoned by the army when it moved forward to Heddernheim at the junction of the Nied and Main near Frankfurt; in A.D. 125 they were joined by a group from Heiligenberg, and from this time onwards under Hadrian and the Antonines the pots of Rheinzabern dominated the markets of the whole Rhineland. Finally, in about A.D. 170, when Marcus Aurelius transferred the armies to the area of danger along the Danube, the Rheinzabern potters moved out to Werstendorf in Bavaria. The Rhenish factories survived until the invasions of the third century; and in Gaul, meanwhile, the process of decentralisation had taken on a secondary form in the appearance of a multiplicity of centres and zones producing local imitations of *sigillata* and vaguely associated with the old sites. This new production served a small market and cannot compare in style, efficiency or organisation with Lezoux and la Graufesenque. There were, however, other types of pottery which achieved both merit and popularity, such as the black ware of Tongres in Belgium and a similar pottery with grey slip and decorations reminiscent of Celtic motifs, produced in the Nene valley and near Colchester in Britain.

The movement towards frontiers could be paralleled in other industries; and it was the result of several related causes. Some of these – the cost of transport, and the attraction of a market closely related to the frontier armies – have already been mentioned. In addition, as we saw, Gaul had a system of good waterways, and easy communications with both the Ocean and the Mediterranean. Technically too the Gallic products have the advantage over those of Arretium: they are harder baked, and have a brighter glaze. Yet another factor lay in the development of the internal Italian market, which was essential as a basis for the industry. During the first century of our era the upper classes in Italy turned more and more to rich metals for their table ware, and the poor of course could afford only the cheapest crockery. The few who still desired *sigillata* preferred the superior products of la Graufesenque and other Gallic sites.

Together these factors are no doubt sufficient to explain the migration of the pottery industry to newer lands. But in addition the organisation of production in Gaul was superior to that in Italy. Some forty *graffiti* discovered among the potsherds of la Graufesenque record the numbers of various kinds of vases included in a single firing, listed under the names of separate potters. These lists suggest that a common kiln was shared by a number of independent craftsmen, whose free status is clear from their signatures on their wares; yet there is evidence for an exchange of moulds between them, for we have copies of identical vessels turned out by different firms. The problem is to discover who ran the kiln. Was it some local *seigneur*, such as Tiberius Flavius Vetus, whom we find acting as *patronus* to a group of free iron-workers and stonemasons at Dijon? Or did the potters themselves own a kiln communally? The second view is the more likely, and it has been suggested that this form of cooperation between free labourers was the continuation of an old Celtic tradition. Traces of a similar system have been found in the later Gallo-Roman potteries of the Argonne.

Free labour working in this way within the framework of a cooperative society provided a very marked contrast to the conditions in Italy, where vase-signatures indicate that the potter was usually a slave. Indeed, out of 132 workers at Arretium, whose names have survived from the period before A.D. 25, no less than 123 are slaves. This contrast in itself affords a good reason why the pottery industry should have shifted outwards to Gaul and Roman Germany.

The history of Gallo-Roman pottery in Gaul is, however, no isolated phenomenon. On the contrary, the first two centuries of the Empire saw a similar expansion in all branches of economic life in these provinces. The application of classical techniques to the resources of a fertile land with an industrious and skilful population of free men brought quick returns. Primarily Gaul produced agricultural goods. Grain from the rich plains of Gascony was shipped from Narbonne to Ostia; and the freshwater boatmen of Lyons brought the corn harvested along the Loire and the Seine down the Saône and Rhône to the shippers of Arles. Alternatively the northern harvest went via the Escaut and the Meuse to help in the provisioning of the Rhine armies. Gaul played only a small part in the feeding of Rome; but the presence of a *procurator annonae* at Arles is not without its significance.

In addition to grain the province produced large quantities of timber, olive oil and wine. Much of the country was still under forest, and the lumbermen built their logs into rafts and floated them down the broad rivers for eventual export to Rome, where between 800 and 900 public baths consumed a vast amount of wood fuel. The vineyards of Provence were already famous under the Republic. By Pliny's time they stretched along the Rhône valley, and the wines of Vienne were highly rated. *Apéritifs* made from smoked Narbonese wine with aloes, or from wine of Vienne with an infusion of resin, were both known at Rome, though it is unlikely that Gallic wines offered serious competition to those of Italy during the first two centuries of our era; indeed the *vinarii* of Lyons imported Italian wine for distribution in Gaul. Similarly, until about A.D. 150 merchants from the same town dealt in olive oil from Spain and Italy; after that date there is some evidence that Gaul itself began to export this important commodity.

The advent of the Romans also brought an impetus to industry. The manufacture of woollen cloth and linen is assigned by Pliny to the whole of Gaul. In the main it was a domestic industry, though Strabo mentions linen-workers among the Cadurci, who may have been employed in a factory. Textiles flourished especially in the north, with its abundance of wool, and in the east, where the export trade of Trier was stimulated by the presence of the Rhine armies. There was also an increased exploitation of the mines; and the building of towns was directly responsible for the opening up of quarries. Many of these appear to have belonged to the state, and were organised under imperial procurators and exploited by contractors. This is true, not only of the Pyrenean marble quarries, which helped to civilise the valleys of the south-west and created the prosperity of Lugdunum Convenarum (Saint Bertrand-de-Comminges), their port on the Garonne, but also of the silver mines near Villefranche (Aveyron), and perhaps of the argentiferous lead mines of Melle in Deux-Sèvres. Others belonged to municipalities or to individuals like the *femina clarissima*, Memmia Sosandris, referred to as the owner of a group of *ferrariae* on an inscription of A.D. 226 from Lyons. Whether these *ferrariae* are iron mines or foundries is not clear: probably the term covered both, for it was customary to smelt iron near the mine and to bring it to the forge in long, lozenge-shaped ingots. The work of the smith was generally carried on locally, and in small independent smithies, though occasionally groups of iron workers are found, such as the clients of Tiberius Flavius Vetus of Dijon. Nevertheless, the mineral wealth of Gaul proved disappointing, especially in the precious metals. In some fields great strides were made. The tin plating of bronze was a Gallic discovery, and silver-plating was practised in Alesia before the coming of the Romans; and though the bronze-ware of Capua maintained its pre-eminence in the markets of the West until about A.D. 100, after it had to face the competition of both Gallic and German wares, which are found on sites along the lower Rhine, in Britain, Hungary, free Germany, and the Siebenbürgen. In particular the discovery of calamine (silica-zinc) at Gressenich, near Stolberg, on the north slopes of the Ardennes, led to the manufacture of brass objects which were both cheaper and in some respects technically superior to bronze; Gressenich was probably the origin of the famous Hemmoor pails, which are found on sites in free Germany dating from about A.D. 150 to the fourth century. Free Germany also absorbed bronze goods from Gaul; many of the *paterae* and sieves from German sites were probably manufactured at Eisenberg in the Rhenish Palatinate, and another workshop, that of Lucius Cusseius Ocellio, has been localised at Nyon in Switzerland.

In the production of glassware too Gaul soon became a rival to Italy. About A.D. 50, Pliny tells us, glass workers migrated from Italy to Gaul, and we find workshops at Arles and Lyons. But the movement did not stop here. As in the case of *sigillata*, the industry spread northwards and eastwards to the Rhine. By A.D. 100 works had been opened at Namur in Belgium, and at Trier, Worms and Cologne. Very soon Cologne had become the main centre for glassware, supplying the whole of the western provinces except Italy. Finally, jewellers, goldsmiths and silversmiths lived in all the large towns, especially at Narbonne and Lyons. They were mainly freedmen of eastern origin, like the Lydian *aurifex* whose name appears on an inscription from Avenches.

In all this development a primary part was played by the presence of the German frontier, with its armies of the Rhine and Danube and the vast plains and forests of free Germany beyond. The presence of the legions was a great stimulus to trade and also – as in the case of *sigillata* and glassware – it exercised a magnetic attraction upon industry itself. The wages of the army and the imperial administration made it easy for the frontier districts to import luxuries, and such necessities as could not be produced locally – special wines, oil and olives, papyrus – without corresponding exports. Thanks to these advantages Roman Germany became rich, and rapidly outgrew its early character as a colonial area. Settlements based on trade sprang up along the lines of communication in western Germany and Switzerland, where the lakes and rivers were exploited to the full, so that even after the legion abandoned its camp at Augst near Basle in A.D. 100 the prosperity of the district was maintained. Further east the direction of trade was mainly south to Aquileia, which took iron from Noricum in exchange for Italian manufactures; and from the Danube at Carnuntum in lower Austria the ancient amber route ran north to Samland, through the Moravian Gates, Kalisz, and Osielsk on the bend of the Vistula. This route was already known to Pliny, and continued to be used until the middle of the third century. But west of it in Pomerania, the markets were gradually captured by Gaul and the Rhineland; while in Bohemia, where first-century cemeteries show large quantities of Roman goods, native German products gradually grow more common in the graves of the second century, and finally predominate in those of the third.

The economic influence of a fortified frontier is also to be felt in Britain. Britain, however, was a distant province which had been late to enter the Empire – Claudius' invasion was in A.D. 43 – and it long remained a colonial market for made-up goods and a source of raw materials. Strabo lists its exports as wheat, cattle, iron, hides, slaves and hunting-dogs; and there were also oysters and (for a short time in the early second century) brooches. In return Britain imported the necessities of army life (there were three legions and their auxiliaries stationed in Britain) and considerable amounts of *sigillata*, most of which was brought up the Thames to London, as is clear from both the large amount found in the London district and from the discovery of the wreckage of a ship carrying *sigillata*, which ran aground on the Pudding Pan Rock near Whitstable in the late second century. *Sigillata*, however, never superseded the local wares from the native potteries, and these (which account for almost 96 per cent of the sherds found in Britain) show a development from many different varieties to a smaller selection of successful types produced in a few large centres. A feature of British economic life, which can be paralleled in the early history of the occupation of the Rhine frontier, is the part played by the army in satisfying its own needs for manufactured products. There were for example several legionary potteries, that at Holt in Denbighshire turning out wares of a Roman type, and there were also legionary smithies. The one gold-mine, at Dolaucothy, and most of the lead-mines were state-owned, managed by imperial procurators, and probably worked by slave labour. Copper and tin were smelted to make bronze, and indeed bronze ornaments show local characteristics down to the early years of the second century. With the opening up of Cornwall in the third century, pewter begins to appear as a luxury for the owners of country villas who could not afford silver. But this takes us forward to the conditions of the later Empire, which in Britain coincided with the highest peak of prosperity.

In general, British economic life remained backward and retarded, though from the end of the first century the province became more or less self-sufficient in all but wine and oil. Inscriptions illustrate the commercial links between Britain and the continent – with Bordeaux, Mainz and Zeeland; and inside Britain itself the dedication of an altar at Bowness-on-Solway, for success in his enterprise, by a trader just about to venture beyond Hadrian's Wall, is a vivid reminder of the traffic up both coasts of Scotland, which continued until the fourth century, taking glass, brooches and Rhenish pottery to exchange for slaves, cattle, leather, furs and the other commodities of the North. Trade with Ireland was desultory and insignificant: goods were carried in Irish ships, and the finds suggest that the Irish were most concerned to obtain Roman coins.

Gaul, wrote Pliny, was the equal of Spain for cereals, oil, wine, horses and metals; but Spain was superior in esparto grass (for ropes), vitreous rocks, and delicate dyes, and in the keenness and industriousness of its slaves, and the toughness and ardour of its people. This is on the whole a fair summary, if perhaps a little unjust to the character and enterprise of the Gallic people, and certainly inadequately appreciative of the superiority of the Spanish mines. Gold, silver, lead, tin, iron, copper, cinnabar, mercury, mineral dyes, marble and salt are all to be found in various degrees of profusion in the soil of Spain; and elsewhere Pliny (who probably overestimated the promise of Gaul rather than underestimated the achievement of Spain) pays a generous tribute to this abundance. Modern authorities have estimated that the mines of New Carthage produced eight-and-a-third tons of silver per annum. Both Pliny and Strabo have left detailed accounts of the technique of extracting metals which the Romans employed in Spain. In some cases gold could be obtained by surface washing, elsewhere deep shafts were driven into the mountain; and finally there were long tunnels 'outdoing the work of the Giants', which were excavated in the bowels of the earth and underpinned; then, when all was ready, the arches were removed and the whole mountain side would collapse. The soil thus laid bare was washed for gold with the aid of water often brought for many miles and precipitated from a height upon the debris. Within the shafts Diodorus mentions the use of Archimedes' screw for draining the flood water from the lower levels, and at least nine examples of this device have been found, each one capable of raising the water over a yard and a half. Ctesibius' pump and various types of drainage wheel were also employed.

From the time of Tiberius onwards most mines were in the hands of the imperial authority, which sometimes handed over the exploitation to a company under contract. Thus the large cinnabar mine at Sisapo was worked by *socii Sisaponenses*. More often, however, the emperor kept a closer control of extraction through his procurators. Mines near Hispalis in the Sierra Morena, for example, were under the management of a *procurator Montis Mariani*, who was responsible for sending the ingots to Ostia, where they were received by his opposite number, the *procurator Massae Marianae*. Such procurators might manage their mines directly, with the aid of slaves and convicts; alternatively, they too might pass on the work to large or small groups of contractors. Under Hadrian especially the authorities favoured a system reminiscent of that adopted about the same time in regulating the conditions under which *coloni* occupied parts of the large imperial estates of North Africa. The mines were handed over to the direct exploitation of small individual contractors; and two documents from Vipasca (Aljustrel) in southern Portugal throw light on how this system worked out in practice. The first of these, usually known as the *Lex Metalli Vipascensis* and probably dating to the Flavian era, contains some of the very detailed regulations which the procurator laid down for the mine and its adjoining village, which was independent of any municipality. The surviving sections of this inscription enumerate the conditions under which the various economic activities of the village are farmed out as monopolies to separate lessees: thus the auctioning of property (and the collecting of the sales tax associated with it), shoemaking, barbering and fulling, are all concessions, leased out on monopoly terms and protected against any infringement of the monopoly by specified penalties. The local baths – important in a mining village – are also run on a lease, and the hours of opening (sunrise to noon for women, 1.0 p.m. to 8.0 p.m. for men), the prices of admission, and the other obligations of the lessee are all laid down. Among other items of interest the document records the exemption from the usual taxes of schoolmasters living in the village. A second document, dating from the time of Hadrian, contains part of the imperial regulations for the actual exploitation of the mines, and defines the obligations of the contractors (who as small men work their own sections). From this inscription it is clear that half the ore went to the *fiscus* and the other half to the contracting miners. This system seems to have persisted under the later Empire. We hear of some mines and quarries worked by convicts or forced labour, but in the main miners continued to be free workers living in closely-knit hereditary groups, though perhaps from preference rather than compulsion.

Besides its metal ore (which mainly went abroad unworked) Spain exported a variety of products, agricultural and industrial, particularly from Baetica in the south. Fruit, wax, honey, pitch, drugs and dyestuffs were regularly sent abroad from all parts of the peninsula, and there was an export of wool to Italy from the districts of the Turdetani, from near Cordoba and from Salaecia in Lusitania. Most of this was sold in the raw state, but there was also a trade in Spanish cloaks from Baetica, where inscriptional evidence for weavers and dyers in several towns confirms the references in Martial and Juvenal; at Hispalis for instance there were *centonarii*, makers of patchwork quilts and felt coverings.

Another important and peculiar Spanish product was its fish-sauce. There were two main types, *muria* and the more highly prized *garum*. *Muria* seem to have been a liquid obtained from pickling tunny-fish in brine: *garum* was a juice distilled from the blood and entrails of the scomber or mackerel, and subsequently allowed to ferment in the sun for several months. Dealers from Malaca distributed the most famous brand of this delicacy, *garum sociorum*, in Rome; but despite the implications of this trade name, there is no evidence for a monopoly of either manufacture or distribution.

In general, Baetica was the richest and most prosperous part of the country. The valley of the Guadalquivir was the only district with a surplus of wheat for export; and it was Baetica too which furnished the two most important trading commodities – olive oil and wine. Samples of sherds taken from the so-called Monte Testaccio, a vast mound of broken pottery 140 feet high and 3,000 feet in circumference, which lies beside the Tiber emporium at Rome, have shown it to consist mainly of fragments of second-century *amphorae* from Spain. Marks similar to those inscribed upon these sherds are also to be found on fragments of pottery all over the western provinces, for instance at Augsburg and Bregenz, along the whole Rhine valley from Switzerland to Holland, at York and London in Britain, in every part of Gaul and in North Africa. The *amphorae* of which these sherds formed part appear to have been in the main of two types, one with a long neck for wine, the other with a short broad neck for oil. Some may have held grain, but the majority were beyond doubt used for the transport of Spanish oil and wine. The chief centres of their manufacture are Astigi and Arva in Baetica, and it is estimated that Monte Testaccio contains the fragments of about forty million *amphorae*, each with a capacity of over eleven gallons. These figures indicate the success of the Spanish producers during the second century in capturing the Italian market (as well as the markets of the other western provinces of the Empire) through either the low price or the high quality of their wines and oils.

The sherds from Monte Testaccio also give information on the shippers; and these, somewhat strangely, seem not to have been Spaniards. Their three names show that they were free citizens, though many were clearly freedmen, and may have obtained full citizen rights by virtue of an edict of Claudius, which offered special concessions to such shippers, *navicularii*, as built a vessel of 10,000 *modii*,[1] and employed it in the grain trade on governmental call for six years. Shippers from all over the Mediterranean appear to have taken part in the Spanish trade, often working in partnerships; but there is evidence for a particular connection between the Baetican oil merchants and the shippers of Narbonese Gaul. A Roman knight, for example, who is described as an oil merchant from Baetica and a patron of oil merchants at Rome, appears on another inscription as a shipowner on the Saône and patron of the local shipowners' gild. On the whole, one has the impression of a greater degree of initiative in Gaul than in Spain; and Gallic merchants increasingly dominate trade in the west as the Syrians and Greeks dominate that of the eastern Mediterranean and beyond.

The remaining western provinces, Sicily and Africa, were both primarily granaries for Rome. The regular imports of foreign grain were a life-line without which the capital could not exist. Each year

[1] Such a vessel had a carrying capacity of 3,083 cubic feet, which is approximately the equivalent of 31 registered tons (net registered tonnage).

Egypt sent five million, Africa ten million, and Sicily perhaps two million bushels of grain[2] to Ostia, whence it was conveyed up the Tiber to Rome either in smaller ocean-going craft using sail and oars or in barges, probably towed by slaves (though from the fourth century onwards there is evidence for the use of oxen). This tremendous task of provisioning a city of perhaps a million inhabitants was the particular concern of the emperors from Augustus onward, and it was carried out by private shippers working on contract for the government. From time to time concessions were held out to those who would undertake this work. Claudius, for instance, was not content merely to regulate and subsidise the selling price like Augustus and Tiberius, but built a new harbour at Ostia linked by canal with the Tiber and issued his edict granting privileges to those who undertook to ship grain; thus corn merchants were indemnified for losses incurred in storms and received bounties according to their social status. The importance of the corn trade to Ostia is illustrated for a slightly later period by a set of mosaics representing scenes connected with it, which are preserved in the so-called Piazzale delle Corporazioni, a large portico situated behind the theatre and administered by the local authorities in Ostia. These mosaics, which date from after the reconstruction of the portico by Commodus in A.D. 196, are some indication of the occupation of many members of the audience which frequented it as a social centre during the intervals in the theatre. Surviving inscriptions from this building give us information concerning African, Sardinian, Gallic and Alexandrian shippers who did business here; but our records are incomplete, and there may have been others, including *navicularii* from Spain and Sicily.

In conjunction with its production of wheat Sicily was also famous for its stock raising; but notwithstanding some evidence for a flourishing internal trade in wines, mineral products and woollen goods (Syracuse produced *trimitoi*, probably a kind of drill), and also for the conveying of grain to Ostia by Sicilian shippers from Messina who took back pottery in return, Sicily never played a vital part in the commerce of the early Empire. Rather it remained a land of *latifundia*, large estates belonging to absent landlords of senatorial rank, which often attained the size of miniature principalities. Nevertheless, the towns remained prosperous down to the third century, and this implies an active local industry and retail trade. Catania, for example, which we know as a centre for fine woollens and a town containing quarrymen and ship builders, brought its water supply from Licodia,

[2] For discussion of these figures, which are controversial, see T. Frank, *Economic Survey of Ancient Rome* (Baltimore, 1933–40), V, 218–20; V. Scramuzza, *ibid.*, III, 338ff.

sixteen miles away, over a three-tier aqueduct, and possessed a theatre and a huge amphitheatre holding fifteen thousand spectators, five or six public baths, and other large and impressive public buildings. Despite the paucity of records, these achievements point to a flourishing if somewhat parochial economic life.

African industry too makes little showing. The primary importance of the province lay, of course, in its export of grain and, as a secondary commodity from Caesar's time at least, of olive oil. Oil presses have been found in several areas of North Africa; and we have a second-century dedication at Rome in honour of the prefect of the imperial corn supply(*annona*) by the 'African grain and oil merchants'. It is curious, therefore, that there is not more evidence concerning the pottery industry. The evidence for the manufacture of earthenware lamps is plentiful, and allows one to trace the gradual ousting of Italian by local wares. But of the samples taken from Monte Testaccio only fifteen sherds showed markings identifying them with certainty as of African manufacture. Trade within the province was on a small local scale, with the town market as the main focus of distribution. Some records of industry have survived; inscriptions refer, for example, to silver workers from Caesarea and to various kinds of textile operatives in Carthage and other towns. Cloth made from the wool of indigenous sheep was the only manufactured product from Africa which achieved anything like an international reputation; and the clothing workers alone appear to have been widely organised into gilds, the usual indication of a flourishing industry. Another trade of some importance – and a measure of the prosperity of the upper classes in the province – was the making of mosaics. Over two thousand have been discovered, many representing African scenes, and most of them of very mediocre workmanship. The absence of any references to gilds among the workers in the mosaic and pottery industries has been taken as evidence that the craftsmen concerned in them were mainly slaves. On the other hand Baetica too is singularly lacking in evidence for the existence of gilds. Both here and in Africa there may have been special local conditions or traditions working against the usual organisation of industry and trade.

Together, such details as these create a general picture of the western and more recently developed provinces of the Empire, which fit into a whole, impressive in respect of both its size and its achievements. Within an area extending from the Scottish lowlands to the Euphrates, from the Black Sea to the Atlas Mountains, a single economic system[3]

[3] M. I. Finley (*The Ancient Economy*, London, 1973, 33f) condemns this formulation as anachronistic: the different parts of the Empire differed so widely in social structure, land tenure and organisation of labour that such a phrase cannot be meaningfully used. Moreover, he

was organised under one central authority. From the setting up of the principate in 31 B.C. the Empire enjoyed almost unbroken peace for nearly a quarter of a millennium. Freed from the threats of war and the burdens of military service, and protected by well-devised frontiers and a standing army several hundred thousand strong, its population could devote itself to the activities of peace, to agriculture, commerce, and industry.

They were of course not insulated from outside contacts (though these were never very significant). Trade with free Germany and the north has already been mentioned; and from the end of the first century there was a growth in the amount of commerce passing along the caravan route through Parthian territory to the Far East. The Romans imposed a high customs duty on such trade – in the first century it was 25 per cent – but there is evidence for an interchange with China under the Han dynasty via Bactra (Balkh) and Antiochia Margiana (Merv). Chinese records show one Kan-Ying gathering information about an area which was probably Syria, and it was probably in the second century that the merchant Maes Titianus reached the Tarim Basin (where Graeco-Roman finds have been made). The main contacts with the Far East were, however, by sea. The discovery of the monsoon by a Greek sea-captain named Hippalus sometime before Augustus' death in A.D. 14 had immeasurably shortened the time needed for a voyage to India, so that it was now possible to reach the Malabar coast sixteen weeks after leaving Puteoli and to complete the round trip to India within a year. By the late century the southern Deccan was familiar to western traders, and during the second century Greeks sailed beyond Ceylon and Sumatra to reach the Mekong delta in Vietnam and Caltigara, which is perhaps Hanoi. Chinese records show Greek merchants who claimed to be envoys of An-Tun (Marcus Aurelius) visiting the court of Huan-ti at Loyang on the Hwang-Ho in A.D. 166. However, this trade beyond India always remained tenuous and was of no great economic importance either in quantity or in its effect on the economic situation within the frontiers of the Empire.

The prosperity of the early Empire was attained with a minimum of governmental interference. Normally the Emperor left trade to the private individual, intervening rarely and guardedly. The state revenues, it is true, had a direct interest in commercial prosperity, in so far as taxes were imposed on sales and on commerce. The *portoria*, which

argues, the top people in the hierarchical society of Rome were interested not in profits but in status, and agricultural self-sufficiency, not wealth acquired from trade, remained their ideal. For a critique of his thesis, in relation to trade and manufacture, see M. W. Frederiksen, *Journal of Roman Studies* (hereafter *JRS*), LXV (1975), 166–8.

embraced customs levied along the eastern frontier and at certain stations between provinces (for this purpose the Spanish, Gallic and Danubian provinces were each regarded as composite units), local octrois, and tolls exacted at fixed points along the main routes, were designed as a source of revenue, not as a bar to trade; the rate varied at different times and in different places, but it was never a serious burden – though early in Nero's reign an abortive attempt was made to give an additional impetus to trade by the abolition of both the *portoria* and the 5 per cent tax on sales. Both these taxes were farmed out to contractors, who were *equites* during the first century of our era, and subsequently, from Hadrian's principate onwards, freedmen acting under the control of imperial procurators.

Apart from these taxes, however, trade was left in private hands. In the course of romanisation, splendid roads had been built all over the West. Quick communications between the frontiers with their legionary camps, provincial centres like Lyons, and Rome itself, were essential to effective control; the goods of the traders followed the same roads, frequently in the same direction as the legions. Even the corn supply, on which the very existence of Rome depended, was left to private *navicularii*, who were merely encouraged by concessions to enrol on contract with the government. Thus the profits went to the individual entrepreneur, while the imperial authority patrolled the seas, protected the roads and trade routes, and guaranteed the peaceful conditions which would allow trade to develop. Moles, quays, lighthouses, and canals – such as those joining the Rhine and the North Sea, or the Red Sea and the Nile – were constructed at the public expense; inns were built by the government, water supplies charted. Indeed, in the whole economic field of the early Empire, the mines were almost the only exception to the general rule of free enterprise. Tiberius here initiated a policy of concentrating ownership in the hands of the emperor. Even so, the exploitation was frequently carried out by contracting companies or, as at Vipasca, by groups of small contractors who worked their own concessions.

The apparent success of this economic system (which was not the result of any conscious policy), and its impressive accomplishments, should not, however, be allowed to obscure the serious weaknesses which undermined it. Despite the phenomenal growth of cities in the West, it must be remembered that many of these were very small. The bulk of the population, even in the East, where cities were of ancient standing, and still more in Gaul, Spain, Germany and Britain, lived on the land in only the most superficial contact with Roman civilisation or trade. Moreover, the cities themselves, with their elaborate public buildings, fora, baths, amphitheatres, circuses, statues, triumphal columns and arches, lawcourts, and temples, together with the festivals, the banquets, and all the tremendous outward paraphernalia of Roman life, tended to exaggerate the contrast between the comfortable townsman and the toiling peasants of the countryside. Yet his luxuries could only be paid for by their efforts; for the alternative – the increase of wealth through a decisive advance in technique – would have required not only a different form of social organisation, but also the acceptance of a different set of concepts about social and economic aims by the dominant classes in ancient society. If we except a few devices such as the gear and the screw, the rotary mill and the water-mill which was developed from it, glass-blowing, the use of concrete in building, hollow bronze casting and the invention of the valved bellows in the fourth century of our era, which for the first time made complete smelting possible, the level of technique under the Empire never surpassed that already reached in Hellenistic Egypt. Transport by land remained cumbersome, slow and expensive; the Romans never learnt to use the horse-collar, which makes it possible for a draught-animal to drag a heavy wagon without choking, and oxen, which were usually employed for heavy loads, did not average more than two miles an hour. Sea-transport, though cheaper, was also slow. Many of the ships were of low tonnage, and the captain normally crept along the shore, putting in frequently to take on board water and provisions, or to spend the night at anchor, as his Greek and Phoenician predecessors had done six hundred or a thousand years before; normally there would be little or no navigation during the winter. The adventures of St Paul, including a shipwreck and considerable discomfort, on board the three vessels which he employed to make the journey from Palestine to Rome, must have repeated an experience common to many whose business took them overseas.

Finally, the picture must be qualified by the reminder that it was not static. This very system – or lack of system – with its freedom from control, its relatively benevolent – because in the main indifferent – state apparatus, which had led to such positive achievements in the new provinces of the West (as well as in the older Greek lands of the East) developed in a little over a hundred years into its direct opposite – the highly controlled caste state of the later Empire. How was this change effected? In particular, is it possible to detect the seeds of the new order germinating within the old?

II. *Crisis and Inflation in the Third Century*

The fifty years from Severus Alexander to Diocletian are shadowy and obscure. Assailed by Goths along the northern frontiers and by Persians in the East, the Empire passed from crisis to crisis. Under Gallienus, the son and successor of the ill-fated Valerian, who died a captive in Persian hands, Gaul temporarily broke away from the Empire, and Italy was ravaged by the Alemanni and Greece by the Heruli. Only the superhuman efforts of a series of soldier-emperors like Claudius the vanquisher of the Goths, Aurelian 'restitutor orbis' and victor over Zenobia, the queen of the break-away desert-state of Palmyra, and Probus who restored the Rhine and Danube frontier, enabled the Empire to survive. Even so the cost was tremendous.

In the West the towns suffered severely, particularly in Gaul, where the ravages of barbarian enemies were exasperated by the rising of the *Bagaudae*, a native *jacquerie*, described by Paulinus of Pella as 'a servile faction with an intermixture of freeborn youths, raving mad and armed for the especial murder of the nobility'. Here, for several centuries open towns had grown and prospered behind the defences of the Rhine frontier; once those defences were down, the enemy could run riot through the provinces, burning and plundering. The commercial elements and small artisans virtually disappeared. From the time of Postumus' rising against Gallienus the towns, now too big for the remnants of their former populations, shrank into fortresses, and from Aurelian's reign (A.D. 270–5) onwards, these are rarely more than seventy acres in area, often less. Thus Bordeaux is exceptionally large with its perimeter of 2,275 metres and an area of seventy-five acres, the new *castrum* at Strasbourg has forty-eight acres, Nantes, Rouen and Troyes have each forty, Beauvais, Tours and Rennes twenty-five, and Senlis a mere seventeen. A particularly noteworthy example is that of Autun (Augustodunum), which was 500 acres in area when it fell before the Gallic armies of Tetricus and the pillaging of the *Bagaudae;* Constantius rebuilt it with an area of twenty-five acres.

Such a reduction in size seems to imply at least some decline in the population. In some instances, such as Strasbourg, the civilians may still have lived outside the *castrum*, prepared to fall back on it in time of need. But Strasbourg was a military town, the headquarters of the *comes Argentoratensis* and the eighth legion down to the latest times, and therefore not typical of Gallic towns in general. It seems likely that by the middle of the third century most of the cities of Gaul had suffered some decline in the number of their inhabitants as a result of the invasions and depredations. But unfortunately we are without the means of assessing the extent of this decline in population,[4] especially in respect of those living on the land, nor can we safely assume that what was true in Gaul was true elsewhere. Clearly invasion, massacres and the toll of civil war must have made their mark on many provinces. Plague too may have contributed to a fall in numbers; but a population such as that of the Roman Empire, living near to subsistence and with a high death-rate, is usually resilient and quick to make up the losses due to plague and famine. What perhaps did more to create the symptoms of man-power shortage was the growth of governmental pressures. This may have been in part a reaction to a fall in the number of available tax-payers but, through the exactions of the *fiscus* and the demand for more troops along the frontiers, itself made the situation worse. Consequently, although there was indeed a shortage of man-power, it is not possible to say with assurance whether it was due to an increased demand for men and money, a drop in the number of available hands, or both. But however it is to be explained, such a shortage had been felt well before the third century. Already under Marcus Aurelius it had become expedient to fill up the empty lands of the Empire with barbarian prisoners; and Augustus' legislation, designed to encourage the birth-rate, would not have remained in force for three centuries, had it not been felt to be both necessary and at least partially effective.

The practice of settling barbarians within the Empire continued in the third century, when we hear of groups of Chamavi and Frisii being established behind the frontiers; Constantine similarly settled Franks. The restoration of Gaul was accomplished by the settlement, first of Gauls rescued from captivity, and then of barbarian prisoners. In the course of the fourth century this practice continued and increased. Barbarians were brought into the province in ever larger numbers and settled in veritable colonies under the control of prefects. Many a town or village in modern France, a Bourgogne, a Sermaize, an Alain, an Allemagne, betrays the original influx of some group of Burgundians, Sarmatians, Alans or Alemans. Thus one result of the third century crisis was a gradual barbarisation of the western provinces: and this has to be kept in mind in assessing the output and quality of its industry and commerce.

In particular, the conditions of uncertainty which prevailed during the greater part of the third century tended to discourage trade in

[4] How far the population declined, and the significance of any such decline as a factor in the decay of the Empire, have been much debated. Against A. E. R. Boak, *Man-power Shortage and the Fall of the Roman Empire in the West* (London, 1955), who assumes a large drop in the population and makes this a major cause of decline, see Finley, *JRS*, XLVIII (1958), 156–64; cf. Jones, *Later Roman Empire*, II, 1040–5.

distant commodities and to reinforce the strong urge towards local production and local self-sufficiency. A period of disorder imposed new strains on a financial system which had devised virtually no machinery for creating credit through negotiable bills but relied on hard coin for almost all transactions. There was never any ancient equivalent of the joint-stock company with limited liability; hence risks were personal, interest rates were proportionately high, and it was impossible to amass the capital for large-scale enterprises. There was thus a constant temptation to reduce risk and expense, which takes its place along with the many other motives already discussed, which drove craftsmen out towards the market and the new centres of raw material. Moreover, as we saw, this movement was naturally accelerated when, as in Gaul, there was a free labour force which may have proved more effective than the slave labour of Italy.

The fact that so much ancient industry was based on slave labour was important for another reason. As an institution slavery had been adversely affected by the Roman peace. From the first century onward, but increasingly in the third and fourth centuries, fewer slaves were available. The Emperors had made it their concern to end war within the frontiers and to wipe out piracy, and in both aims they had been comparatively successful. War and piracy had been the chief source of slaves; and though there continued to be a diminished flow across the frontier (where, as Symmachus remarks, 'slaves are easy to come by and the price is usually reasonable'), the great days of the Delian slave market, when, Strabo records (perhaps not without some exaggeration), 'the island could admit and send away tens of thousands of slaves in the same day', were long since over. Though we hear of various ways in which the law forbidding the enslavement of a Roman citizen on Roman territory could be circumvented, and though the increasing humanity of the early Empire made it possible for many slaves to contract marriages and bring up families, the additional numbers thus gained were not sufficient to fill up the gap – especially since as early as the principate of Augustus, and even during the last decades of the Republic, this increase in humanitarian sentiment, coupled with the attractions of the free corn which was available for all citizens of the capital from the time of the *Lex Clodia frumentaria* of 58 B.C., also led slave-owners to manumit on so grand a scale that the government was compelled to introduce limiting legislation. If there were fewer slaves, that did not of course mean that no labour was available; and indeed there are signs of a changing attitude on the part of those in authority towards free workers. 'There is nothing noble about a workshop', wrote Cicero contemptuously. But by the time of Constantine tradesmen are being granted exemption from public duties, in order that they may have the leisure to improve their skill. Unfortunately this change of heart – if such it was and not a practical recognition of necessity – came rather late. For by the time of Constantine there is evidence that a system of economic and political compulsion was already operating. In the meantime any centralisation and concentration of industry in Italy had ceased to correspond to economic realities. Concentration only brings an appreciable reduction in overhead expenses when considerable capital is involved and there is a high degree of specialisation of labour. But under the Empire – even assuming that there was an understanding of such factors or an interest in such goals – equipment was still simple, a few tools and the skill of the individual. To migrate was easy and it made good sense for a potter from Arretium to move off to the flourishing potteries of la Graufesenque.

The development of the western provinces in the first hundred and fifty years of the Empire has thus a double aspect. In so far as it led to the release of new productive forces in hitherto primitive lands it was progressive. But at the same time it was accompanied by a reduction in the scope of inter-provincial commerce. From the time of Claudius it is possible to identify several large trading areas, not indeed wholly isolated from each other, but including within their frontiers (which might embrace several administrative provinces) the bulk of their trade. Thus Spain, Germany and to some extent Britain (though Britain is a special case) were grouped around Gaul; another block was formed by the African provinces from Mauritania to Cyrenaica; Italy, together with Sicily, Corsica and Sardinia, made a third grouping, which was increasingly driven back upon itself; and finally (to limit ourselves to the West) Rhaetia and Noricum were linked with the other Danube provinces of Pannonia and Dacia (and later with South Russia) in a block which remained anchored to Italy through the trade of Aquileia until the end of the second century. By this date the West as a whole had made itself self-sufficient for all its main needs, such as grain, wine, oil, salt, glass, textiles, brass-ware, and pottery. The converse of this independence was the decay of Italy. More and more the peninsula became parasitical upon the rest of the Empire, which supported it by subsidies in the form of taxes to maintain the civil service, and the vast income from the Emperor's private estates; and with the removal of the imperial court from Rome in the third century, even this prop was withdrawn. Gradually the economic links were being broken. From the middle of the third century onwards these large inter-provincial blocks fell yet further apart. For example, the latest dated Spanish *amphorae* from Monte Testaccio date from 257. It is a fair inference that the German invasions of Spain in Gallienus' reign had crippled the flourishing export trade of wine and oil to Ostia.

The strain and tension, and the general economic regression of the third century are also reflected in the history of the coinage; and this was another factor affecting the nature and level of commerce. Its importance, it is true, must not be exaggerated, since in the Roman world the use of coinage as a means of exchange was by no means common or fundamental outside the direct influence of the cities, especially in the northern provinces, nor were coins issued by the state with an economic purpose. The emperors coined primarily to pay their soldiers and civil servants and to provide the wherewithal to pay taxes, and the use of coinage to facilitate trade was an accidental, if useful, side-effect of a fiscal operation. Augustus had attempted to regularise the coinage by stabilising the relationship between the gold *aureus* weighing one-fortieth of a pound and the silver *denarius* weighing one-eighty-fourth of a pound at 25:1. But before long pressure on the treasury led to interference with these weights. According to Pliny (*Nat. hist.* 33. 47) the *aureus* was reduced by Nero (A.D. 54–68) to one-forty-fifth and the *denarius* to one-ninety-sixth of a pound, and his statement is confirmed by the ascertained weight of surviving specimens, which average 7.29 g for the *aureus* and 3.41 g for the *denarius*. In addition, Nero reduced the silver content of the *denarius* to 90 per cent, a figure which Trajan (A.D. 98–117) brought down to 85 per cent and Marcus Aurelius (A.D. 161–80) to 75 per cent. It has been argued that these changes in the silver content of the *denarius* were designed to compensate for a fall in the value of gold and to maintain the ratio between the two metals; and indeed it appears from Lucian that the ratio between the two coins was still unchanged under Pius (A.D. 138–61). But the reduction in size of both silver and gold coins by Nero is difficult to explain except as a concession to strained finances, and it seems more likely that the debasement too was forced on the government by financial pressure and was intended to cover the heavy expenses of Trajan's wars in Dacia and Parthia and those of his successors in the east and the north.[5] In further reducing the silver content of the *denarius* by a third Septimius Severus (A.D. 193–211) – who in addition raised the pay of the troops – was clearly following the same policy. Caracalla (A.D. 211–17) raised legionary pay yet again and, to meet this expense and that of a new Parthian war, issued – for the last four years of his reign – a new silver coin, the *antoninianus*, of a weight equivalent to one and a half *denarii* but tariffed

[5] See, against Mickwitz, *Geld und Wirtschaft im römischen Reich des vierten Jahrhunderts nach Chr.* (Helsinki, 1932), 32f, A. H. M. Jones, *The Roman Economy* (Oxford, 1974), 191–2.

at two *denarii*. He also slightly reduced the size of the *aureus*, which had hitherto remained constant in size and quality since the Neronian reduction to one-forty-fifth of a pound.

Despite the growing disparity between the gold and silver content of the coins, there is evidence that the ratio of 1 *aureus*:25 *denarii* remained unchanged down to the time of Severus Alexander (A.D. 222–35),[6] and that there was no substantial rise in prices during this period. From the death of Maximinus in 238, however, a rapid inflation took place, and this was perhaps due to a realisation of the extent to which the silver content of the *denarius* had been reduced, rather than to any increase in the number of *denarii* in circulation.[7] From 238 onwards the quality of silver coins deteriorated at a catastrophic rate, until they were little more than silver-washed bronze. Under Philip the Arab (A.D. 244–9) inscriptions from Nubia show a ratio of 1 *aureus*: 40 *denarii*, and the *antoninianus*, which had been revived by Pupienus and Balbinus (A.D. 238) and soon superseded the *denarius* as the standard 'silver' coin, was in turn debased until by the reign of Aurelian (A.D. 270–5) it contained only one per cent silver. From about this time the price graph moves rapidly upwards, followed from about 280 onwards by the level of wages.[8] Aurelian minted a new issue of billon (silver-bronze) coins, which had some temporary success, though his successors perhaps reduced their face value.

The *aureus* too had not come through the third century unscathed. After a period of fluctuation its weight had dropped to one-seventieth of a pound under Carus (A.D. 282–3), and shortly afterwards, in 294, Diocletian (A.D. 284–305) stabilised it at one-sixtieth of a pound, as part of a general currency system containing gold, silver, silver-bronze (billon) and bronze coins and operating throughout the Empire (including Egypt, which had hitherto had a coinage of its own). Alongside the larger *aureus* he issued a new silver *argenteus* at 96 to the pound, and laid down a ratio between gold and silver coins and those of base metal, as Augustus had done. The latter, however, were evidently over-valued, for in A.D. 301, at about the same time as he issued the price-edict Diocletian published a decree on the currency,

[6] See on this subject, which is disputed, M. H. Crawford, *Aufstieg u. Niedergang der römischen Welt* (Berlin-New York 1972) (hereafter *ANRW*), II, 2, 566–7. Against the view of Heichelheim, *Klio*, XXVI (1933), 96ff, that there was an inflation under Commodus, see A. Passerini, 'Sulla pretesa revoluzione dei prezzi durante il regno di Commodo', *Studi G. Luzzatto*, I (Milan, 1950), 4ff. For an inflation under the Severi, see T. Pekáry, 'Studien zur Römischen Währungs- u. Finanzgeschichte von 161 bis 235 n. Chr.' *Historia*, VIII (1959), 460–3.

[7] For the contrary view see Pekáry, 'Studien', 456–7; R. P. Duncan-Jones, *Papers of the British School at Rome*, XXXIII (1965), 232.

[8] On this see J. P. Callu, *La Politique monétaire des empereurs romains* (Paris, 1969), 395ff.

declaring that silver coins (and no doubt gold) were to be valued at double in terms of debased *denarii* (which by this time were units of calculation only).[9] By this measure he gave official recognition to the existing ratio between the two currencies, as indicated by the accepted run of prices, and he did this in conjunction with his bold attempt to impose universal price controls. It was either then, or in 294, that the *aureus* began to be called the *solidus*, a name which it was to carry into Byzantine times.

In A.D. 309 Constantine (A.D. 306–37) reduced the *solidus* to one-seventy-second of a pound (4.55 g), but he continued to strike *argentei* on the Diocletianic standard of 96 to the pound. The size of the silver coins was, however, eventually also reduced, to give 144 to the pound in 348 and 240 to the pound in 396. Various readjustments took place in the course of the fourth century, but very little silver was in fact now minted and by about A.D. 400 it ceased altogether; silver coins do not re-appear until a century later in the barbarian kingdoms. The *solidus*, however, persisted virtually unchanged until the eleventh century. It has been argued that the *solidus* was not a true coin, since it was weighed in commercial transactions or upon being paid into the treasury and credited only at its actual weight and not at its nominal value, and since, when they exchanged bronze for coin, people spoke of buying and selling *solidi* for money (*pecunia*). This argument is not, however, to be pressed, for it has been pointed out[10] that much the same was true of English sovereigns paid into the Bank of England between 1819 and 1889, a period when the sovereign was unquestionably a coin in the full sense of the word.

Bronze or billon coins also continued to be minted as small change, and since this was not treated as token-money, its size (and real value) suffered a series of reductions to meet the financial pressures operating on the government; by now, as a result of the retariffing of existing coins, the *denarius* had become a mere unit of calculation, with no coin equivalent. The billon *nummus* of Diocletian's system was reduced in weight by Constantine in 307 and again about 310, and four years later

[9] On Diocletian's currency reform see K. T. Erim, Joyce Reynolds and M. H. Crawford, *JRS*, LXI (1971), 171–7; Crawford, *ANRW*, II, 2, 577ff. The relationship between this currency reform and the price-edict is disputed. A new fragment of the latter found at Aezani gives the price of a pound of gold as 72,000 *denarii* and of a silver pound as 6,000 *denarii*, which shows the gold:silver ratio under Diocletian to have been 1:12, almost exactly what it had been under Augustus. However, the currency decree, which is dated to 1 September 301, implies a far higher value of the gold pound calculated in *denarii*, and this creates a problem on the usual dating of the price-edict to November–December 301, inasmuch as a sudden fall in the value of gold to 72,000 *denarii* and its rise again shortly afterwards are hard to explain. Possibly, then, both decrees were issued simultaneously in September 301, and the lower figure for gold in the price-edict reflects a set of prices assembled over a period of time and already out of date by the time the edict was promulgated.

[10] See G. Mickwitz, *Die Systeme des römischen Silbergeldes im vierten Jahrhundert* (Helsinki, 1935), 3.

it had depreciated to a quarter of its Diocletianic value. As has been already suggested, the rate of 72,000 *denarii* to the gold pound (which is equivalent to 1,200 *denarii* to the *solidus*) was probably too low when it appeared in Diocletian's Edict of A.D. 301, but the subsequent rapid rise in this figure indicates an exceedingly high rate of inflation in terms of billon coins and notional *denarii* during the fourth century. Evidence from Egypt, where sums are reckoned either in *denarii* or in notional *drachmae*, worth each a quarter of a *denarius*, shows that by A.D. 324 a *solidus* was worth 4,350 *denarii*.[11]

Why the government acquiesced in an inflation in base metal coins of these proportions can only be conjectured. But the likelihood is that under Diocletian and Constantine it had succeeded by fiscal means in accumulating enough gold and silver to issue a sound currency in those metals and no longer needed the debased *denarii* – not even to any great extent in the payment of the army, since the soldiers' main emoluments were now paid in kind (see below, pp. 107ff). Consequently the government had no real interest in maintaining a base metal currency, and so made only occasional, half-hearted attempts to correct the inflation by issuing better coins. It was probably not realised that by minting more and more bronze and drawing none back in taxation the government was itself making further inflation inevitable.

What did such an inflation mean in the ordinary life of the population of the Empire? Not so much as similar inflations in modern times. Prices of course tended to rise in terms of the currency that was being debased, though not always immediately. On the other hand, the rural and peripheral parts of the Empire, especially in the western provinces, made only marginal use of coinage; for them barter and a largely self-sufficient economy gave adequate protection against the effects of the debased currency. Those dependent on wages were more vulnerable. In any inflation wages tend to lag behind prices, and the third century inflation certainly had a permanent effect in reducing the real wages and salaries of soldiers and state employed.[12] This in turn resulted in a move towards tax-collecting and paying those on the state list in kind rather than cash, and in a sudden drying-up of new charitable foundations of the kind which had been so noteworthy a

[11] *P. Oxy.* 1430. The history of the Roman currency and the inflationary changes of the third and fourth centuries cannot be written with confidence, partly because of the difficulty of equating the recorded names of coins with existing specimens and partly because of the fluctuations in relative value not only between gold and silver, but also between both these metals and bronze or billon; nor do we adequately understand currency policy, if indeed there was any clear policy. On this, see the works of A. H. M. Jones quoted in the bibliography and especially *Economic History Review*, 2nd ser., V (1953), 293–318 (reprinted with additions in *Roman Economy*, 187–227) and the account in *Later Roman Empire* (Oxford, 1964), I, 438–48.

[12] See Jones, *Roman Economy*, 208ff.

feature of municipal life in the early Empire. But in ancient times there were not the accumulations of savings to be wiped out overnight. Since the fall in the value of the *denarius* resulted from the fall in its silver content, older and better specimens maintained their previous exchange value or (what amounts to the same thing) were retariffed as multiples of the new debased coins; there is epigraphical evidence for a sharp distinction between 'old coins' and 'new'. Thus hoarded money – the commonest form of saving – maintained its value; and the only people to be hit, other than public employees, were those who had lent large sums with an agreement for fixed repayments, and those who accepted the debased coins before the new rate became established. Nevertheless, the inflation introduced an element of uncertainty into commercial life, which is reflected in an increase in the number of leases in which the rent was payable in kind rather than in money, and in a shortening of the periods stipulated for repayment of money loans. This uncertainty is well illustrated by a remark of Constantine (*Cod. J.* v. 37, 22) that loans were not a safe form of investment. Our evidence is mainly from Egypt; but the effects of the same process must have been similar in other parts of the Empire, where the element of hazard thus introduced into trade will have contributed to the tendency to restrict and localise it. Similarly, an analysis of the volume of coinage circulating in the Empire at various times during the first three centuries shows a significant change from the time of Severi onward, when a pattern of circulation hitherto substantially uniform throughout the whole Empire gives way to haphazard and apparently disorganised variations from province to province, which may signify a breakdown in the attempt to sustain a coherent imperial currency system.[13]

Inflation can be seen as the response of the government to the difficulties of financing the imperial machine. In the conditions of the third century in particular the cost of maintaining the structure of the civil service, and of buying the loyalty of an army increasingly recruited from barbarians, was a burden which the depleted resources of the provinces were not strong enough to shoulder. In raising the legionaries' wages Septimius Severus and Caracalla had added a crippling addition to the annual state expenditure. Yet the population was probably declining and technique remained more or less stagnant. Faced by this problem the emperors had a limited choice open to them: they could sell public property, confiscate private property (belonging to rich men conveniently charged with treason and

[13] I owe this information to Professor M. K. Hopkins, who kindly made unpublished work on this subject available to me.

convicted) or debase the currency; and at various times they adopted all these methods. The last provided a real, if temporary solution. For though sooner or later the debased coins were bound to be retariffed in terms of gold, and their value to sink in terms of goods, the vast sums which were constantly being paid out to the civil service and the army could meanwhile be met in the new currency. Any measure which would relieve the tremendous strain on the treasury presented great attractions to any emperor in times of crisis.

It is against this background that Diocletian's price-edict of A.D. 301 must be considered. The discovery of fragments of this remarkable document in Egypt, Crete, Cyrenaica, Greece and Asia Minor[14] confirms the statement made in its introduction that the maximum prices therein prescribed for all types of services and commodities and for freight charges were applicable throughout the Empire (though its setting up seems to have depended largely on the energy and conscientiousness of the various provincial governors). The introduction also gives a clear hint of the purpose behind the edict, a subject on which there has been much argument, when it complains that 'sometimes in a single purchase a soldier is deprived of his bonus and salary, and the contribution of the whole world to support the armies falls to the abominable profit of thieves'. Primarily the emperor was concerned to ensure that the soldiers' pay was adequate for their needs, and to prevent a repetition of the price increases of the last century, which could only be followed by further demands for increases in salaries. The decree is especially detailed in its enumeration of foods and types of clothing, male and female; for example, it lists eighty-four different articles of wool and over two thousand of linen; and five linen centres are named for the eastern half of the Empire, each of which produces nine different qualities. The significance of this fact will be considered below. Here it may be observed that the prices for food are almost all higher than those calculated in terms of gold for similar commodities in Egyptian papyri of the second century. In short, Diocletian's *maxima* were high, and therefore not likely to interfere seriously with normal trade. They would, however, act as a check on any raising of prices in the vicinity of the armies or imperial courts.

The edict was a failure. According to Lactantius (*De mort. pers.* 7, 6), goods were withdrawn from the market, thus forcing up prices more than before, and there was 'great bloodshed on account of small and paltry details' – either through riots or the invocation of the death

[14] In addition, a fragment of a Greek version dealing with marble and animals for the amphitheatre has been found at Pettorano in Italy, but it seems likely that it is not of Italian provenance; cf. J. Bingen, *Bulletin de Correspondance héllenique*, LXXVIII (1954), 349–60.

penalty. Whether the edict could have succeeded inside a virtually closed economy of substantial size such as the Roman Empire is a subject for speculation. Its interest for us here is rather in the light which it throws on the more important developments of later Roman economic organisation. In particular it raises three questions: the growth of compulsion by the government as an essential feature of economic and political life; the extent to which the state was operating a money economy; and the amount and character of inter-provincial trade still carried on under the later Empire.

III. *State Intervention and Economic Decline*

An edict such as Diocletian's would have been completely at variance with the economic practice of the early Empire. Whereas the Hellenistic age provides evidence of several Greek cities legislating to fix prices, the Roman government by contrast had hitherto taken for granted (and asserted in official decisions) the free operation of bargaining. But since the days of the principate a radical change had taken place in the organisation of labour. It was customary for free tradesmen, craftsmen and professional workers in the Hellenistic world to organise themselves in gilds, whose functions were partly religious and partly social. Through their contributions the gild members provided for their funeral expenses and subsidised their periodic banquets; and the gild sometimes controlled and protected the professional status of its members, though it never played the part of a modern trade union in fixing wages. Similar gilds, with the name of *collegia*, sprang up at Rome, probably under Greek influence. During the Republic they were treated with suspicion and repeatedly banned as sources of political disturbance; but the emperors realised their possibilities as machinery for the official control of the workers.

The growth of *collegia* is perhaps most easily to be traced in connection with the *navicularii*, the shippers responsible for the transportation of the grain with which the capital was provisioned. They were the object of special imperial solicitude. The concessions granted by Claudius were confirmed by later emperors: but from Hadrian's time it was insisted that a shipper must employ the bulk of his capital on state duties to qualify for them. For some time these privileges were granted to the shippers as individuals. But an inscription from the time of Antoninus Pius, in which *navicularii marini* of Arles honour their 'excellent and most upright patron', the procurator of the corn supply, signifies the importance which the gilds were now acquiring. Marcus Aurelius laid it down that no one should belong to two *collegia*; and an item from the *Digest*, dating to the reign of

Septimius Severus, which specifically asserts that concessions are to go to individuals for their services and not to gildsmen promiscuously, is an indication that the gilds were being drawn into the state apparatus. By the end of the second century there is evidence for the existence of various privileged gilds at Rome, including the shippers engaged in the corn trade, the smiths (who may have had public duties as a fire-brigade even under the late Republic), the oil merchants, the bakers, the 'corn-measurers' and the swine merchants; and in A.D. 200 the five *collegia* of Arles shippers went on strike to enforce higher rates.

The further development of these gilds during the third century is unfortunately obscured by the paucity of the sources. The *Life of Severus Alexander* (33) in the *Historia Augusta* states that this emperor (A.D. 222–35) established *collegia* 'of all the wine-merchants, dealers in lupins, makers of soldiers' shoes, and of all craftsmen', and that he granted these gilds legal advisers and assigned appropriate lawcourts to each. Unfortunately the *Historia Augusta* is unreliable, and this extract may reflect fourth-century conditions. All that can be said with certainty is that by the time of Diocletian (A.D. 284–305) the *collegia* are no longer voluntary, privileged bodies, but controlled organisations, the members of which are tied to their trade and pass on their obligations to their heirs. The *collegia* were frequently treated with honour: they possessed *fundi dotales*, which might include estates, and premises, as well as technical equipment. They had patrons and a religious cult; their members were exempt from many taxes, and often their retired presidents were rewarded with honorific titles. But this show of esteem disguised a form of harsh tutelage. The gilds were increasingly integrated into a unified state system; more and more their members were compelled to work in the service of the state. From A.D. 395 onwards a series of laws was promulgated in the West (but not in the East) forbidding the *collegiati* to leave their gilds and their work; and in some occupations – for instance in that of baker – marriages had to be endogamous within the families of fellow gildsmen.

The typical pattern can be illustrated from the *navicularii*. Claudius had given special concessions to anyone who would build a ship of 10,000 *modii* and employ it in the service of the *annona*. In the fourth century anyone owning a ship of this tonnage was obliged to put it at the disposal of the state, but was in return entitled to exemption from an appreciable amount of tax. In A.D. 326 Constantine gave such a shipowner complete immunity from all fiscal charges in a rescript which somewhat grandiloquently asserted the privilege to apply to 'all shippers, throughout the whole world, throughout every age'. These privileges were reaffirmed in A.D. 334 and 337, and in 380 Gratian gave shippers the status of knights (*equites*). This, however, was only one side of the picture. For meanwhile the *navicularius* had been effectively tied to his occupation through the linking of this with the individual's property; thus the heir to the property also inherited the obligations of the occupation.

The shipper's duty was to assemble a crew and organise the voyage of his ship in the state service. During the time that it was thus in commission, he was compensated by the state at a rate which was defined by Constantine in A.D. 334, for the *navicularii* provisioning Constantinople, as 4 per cent of the value of a cargo of corn in kind, together with a grant of one-thousandth of its value in gold, in order that they might carry out their duties with enthusiasm and 'scarcely any cost to themselves' (*Cod. Theod.* xiii. 5.7). Whether this marked a deterioration or an improvement in the position of the *navicularii* since the publication of Diocletian's edict in A.D. 301 cannot unfortunately be determined, for although newly discovered fragments prescribe a special tariff for fiscal goods, which appears to be lower than that for normal cargoes, the text does not allow us to determine by how much. But by the early fifth century, in A.D. 412 and 414, the percentage paid to the *navicularii* bringing corn to Rome from Africa was only one per cent. A series of regulations hedged the shipper about, to ensure that he – or strictly speaking his ship's captain, the *magister navis* – did not speculate with his cargo, delay in port or attempt illicit trading, all of which were offences carrying the death penalty. Any shipwreck was food for imperial suspicion. An enquiry must be held and the crew examined under torture. If on the other hand all went well, the captain must proceed by the shortest route to his destination, where he received a state *relatoria* or *securitas* (receipt), which he must present within two years (later reduced to one) from the beginning of his present period of service; in what was left of this time he had to make his way back to his own port, but could undertake further trading voyages on his own account without fear of requisitioning. In conjunction with the *navicularii* we hear of a large group of subsidiary *collegia* with special functions and all equally under state control – the small lightermen, dockyard workers, caulkers, ballast-loaders, divers, stevedores, and corn-measurers, the *caudicarii*, or bargees, who conveyed grain up the Tiber from Ostia to Rome, and the *lintriones*, who brought the fuel by water to the many baths of Rome. The duties of all were closely defined.

This special state concern with the *navicularii* sprang from their importance for the provisioning of Rome. A sum of 3,600,000 bushels of corn (14,400,000 *modii*) was required annually to meet the claims of the public service and those entitled to free distributions; and in addition it was the duty of the *fiscus* to organise a supply of cheap corn for the rest of the population of the capital, so that the total annual imports may have been of the order of 17,000,000 bushels (see above, pp. 87–8). Some time before the reign of Aurelian (A.D. 270–5) the distribution of bread was substituted for that of corn, and the gilds of bakers, which had been officially recognised under Trajan, now assumed special importance. By the fourth century they were completely organised in the state service; and because the work was hard and unpleasant, the regulations were harsh. As in the case of the shippers, their property was linked with the trade, which was inherited with it. If a man became heir to the estates of both a shipper and a baker, he was liable for both duties; moreover, anyone, of whatever status, who married a baker's daughter, must himself adopt the occupation. It was the baker's task to collect corn from the state granaries, grind it in his own cellar, bake it into bread, and distribute this at the appointed place in each quarter of Rome. After the widespread adoption of the water-mill during the fourth century, in place of that worked by human or animal power, we hear of the setting up of a separate gild of millers (*molendinarii*) at Rome, with headquarters at the foot of the Janiculum; this is but one example of the specialisation of function, and subdivision into subordinate gilds, which took place in this important industry.

However, the state did not confine its incursion into trade to corn. Free distribution of olive oil, which had been sporadic since the later Republic, became regular from Septimius Severus' time onwards. Two gilds of oil merchants dealt with Baetica and Africa respectively. Similarly the gild of pork merchants acquired official duties towards the end of the third century, when the regular distribution of pork was organised at Rome. These *suarii* had to receive the pigs from various Italian landowners who were liable to provide them as part of their tax, bring them to Rome, slaughter them there, and deliver the meat to those entitled to it. As we shall see below, there grew up a system by which the taxpayer was allowed to commute his liability by a payment in cash, which the *suarii* would use to buy the equivalent animals in the open market at or near Rome.

The same forms of gild organisation are to be found in most of the provinces of the West during the later Empire. Here the *collegiati* operated under the control of the municipality, represented by its *curia*, or town council. The *curiales*, who enjoyed a higher social status than the gildsmen, gave the latter their orders, and were responsible to Rome for their implementation. Although those gilds connected with the feeding of the people offer the earliest and most typical examples of state control, they are by no means the only ones. By the fourth century most trades and professions are organised in *collegia*, and there are records of gilds of innkeepers, fishmongers, potters and silversmiths, as well as the public employees in the state enterprises, which have still to be considered below.

The existence of these gilds is the background against which Diocletian could attempt the tremendous feat of regulating all prices throughout the Empire. Yet, even in the time of Diocletian, it is plain that the economic system is not one of complete nationalisation: it is rather a hybrid form of controlled private enterprise, a logical development from the uncontrolled private enterprise of the early Empire. Most industrial and commercial property is still privately owned. But in place of the earlier relationship, by which the individual bound himself to the state for a prescribed period, with his property as a pledge, but emerged a free man at the end of the six years or so of his contract, the state has now attached the property to the occupation, and the gildsman is obliged to work for the benefit of the state in virtue of his ownership. The state compensates him for his loss of income; but in the fourth century this *solacium*, or 'consolation', as it was officially termed, increasingly takes the form of payments in kind.

Why this form of semi-planned economy was evolved is a problem on which there is no unanimity. No doubt special factors applied to the various branches of production and distribution. But, in the main, it appears that the state assumed the responsibility because the people had to be fed, the goods had to be produced and distributed, and private enterprise, left to itself, was proving unequal to the task. The same phenomena are clearly apparent in political life, where the crises of the third century, with its widespread destruction of wealth, brought with them a dearth of citizens willing to shoulder the increasingly heavy burdens of municipal office. From the time of Diocletian and Constantine onwards municipal office becomes the duty of a hereditary caste of *curiales*, who have lost most of their initiative to imperial officers, but remain responsible not only for financing the greater part of the town's activities out of their own private fortunes, but also for collecting the taxes and provisioning the town through the agency of the local *collegia*.

Thus nationally and locally the feeding of much of the population of the Empire became a public responsibility; and this, as we have seen, was largely accomplished by side-stepping the use of money. The extent of this development must, however, be carefully defined. For the fourth century in particular it has been argued that over vast areas of the Empire a declining economy led both the imperial authorities and individual citizens to abandon the use of money, and to substitute a system of barter, by which all payments, including wages and taxes, were made in the form of foodstuffs, clothing, or any other articles of common use, rather than in a now worthless currency. It is suggested that under the stress of the upheavals of the third century the Roman world reverted to 'domain-economy', in which the large landowners maintained every class of workman on their estates, which they sought to make economically self-sufficient. This system, it is urged, is reflected in the taxation established by Diocletian, in which payments in kind play a primary role.

Now it is true that at all times many parts of the Roman world got on very adequately without coinage as a means of exchange. But the thesis of a universal lapse into barter is hard to reconcile with the evidence provided by Diocletian's price-edict. With its very full and precise list of prices covering a wide range of commodities and services – commodities moreover coming from every part of the Empire – this document gives no indication of a decline from a money economy to one based on barter. Moreover, it has already been shown that the crises and disturbances of the third century had not been sufficiently severe to drive out money. Even the inflations had merely brought a slight increase in the number of contracts stipulating payments in *natura* in areas where this type of contract had always existed. On the other hand, perhaps from the time of Septimius Severus (A.D. 193–211)[15] the provisioning of the armies had been made the regular responsibility of the provinces through which their route lay. A special order (*indictio*), which tended to be of more and more frequent occurrence, laid down the details of the supplies to be furnished, and this impost in kind was known as *annona*. When Diocletian introduced his new fiscal system, based on double taxation units – the area of cultivable land (*iugum*) and the single unit of human labour required to work it (*caput*), combined in a twofold tax of *capitatio* and *iugatio* (see Volume I, 2nd edn, pp. 113–14) – he made the annual payment of *annona* its central feature, thereby perpetuating and intensifying the far-reaching effects which had already been produced.

First, the payment of taxes in *natura* inevitably raised problems of transport. The large quantities of oil, grain, meat, wine, clothing, etc., which had to be paid annually into the *fiscus* required the setting up of vast numbers of public storehouses (*mansiones*) along the main routes of the Empire. Since, moreover, land transport was so difficult and expensive, this led to a progressive decentralisation of economic life. Outgoing payments in kind, for example allotments of food or the provision of uniforms for the army, were linked directly with the

[15] Cf. D. van Berchem, 'L'Annone militaire', *Mém. de la soc. nat. des antiquaires de France* (1937), 177ff.

income from certain adjacent provinces, in order to avoid burdening the treasury with the cost of transport over long distances. Thus, state employees received their wages in vouchers, which served as drafts on specified public storehouses in the vicinity. The recipient went to the *mansio* to draw his allowance of corn, wine or oil. His salary, varying according to his rank, was calculated in units (also known as *annonae*), which were equivalent each to sixty *modii* (fifteen bushels) of wheat per annum.

The payment of public employees, civil and military, in kind was very much in their favour during a period of inflation.[16] For clearly the debasing of the currency, carried out under the pressure of a succession of crises, would have defeated its own ends unless state employees, whose salaries were the main item in the bill of imperial expenses, could be paid in the new depreciated money. Naturally, this procedure aroused resentment; and it was an obvious advantage for soldiers and civil servants if they could enforce payment in goods rather than in debased silver. In order that wages might be paid in *natura*, however, the goods must first be in the hands of the government; and this could best be effected by levying taxes in *natura* upon the agricultural population. Such were the considerations which seem to have led Septimius Severus to institute[17] (and Diocletian to develop) a system which ensured the satisfactory provisioning, originally of the army and later of the bureaucracy, on whom depended the existence of the whole imperial machine.

The payment of taxes in kind affected both the peasants and the *collegiati*. The institution of serfdom by the binding of the *colonus* to the soil soon followed the establishing of an annual tax in *natura*, which made the landlord personally responsible for the returns throughout his whole estate. But the gildsman equally found the new fiscal system tending to diminish his freedom. The collection of taxes in kind raised vast problems of transport: and the task was entrusted to the gilds. It is an example of the strong hold of tradition on the emperors that they preferred to use the system of compulsorily requisitioning the services of the gilds rather than create new branches of the imperial administration. The hardships to which this policy gave rise can be illustrated from the system of land transport. Just as the *navicularii* had been pressed into government employment for the transport of the *annona* by sea, so the moving of fiscal products by land was carried

[16] See Mickwitz, *Geld und Wirtschaft im römischen Reich*, 176ff.

[17] For the view that Septimius Severus introduced the system abruptly, see van Berchem, 'L'Annone militaire', 117ff; this is queried by A. H. M. Jones, *The Greek City from Alexander to Justinian* (Oxford, 1940), 329–30, nn. 94–5 and *The Roman Economy*, 197–8, n. 27, tracing a more gradual growth of requisitioning. For the view that the system developed as a result of the currency debasement from A.D. 238 onwards, see Crawford, *ANRW*, II, 2, 571ff.

out, first by the requisitioning of humble muleteers (*catabolenses*), and later by the adaptation of the public post. This too, despite its fourth-century name (*cursus publicus*) – earlier it was known as *vehiculatio* – was in fact worked by a system of requisitioning.

There were two speeds. The horses or light mule carriages employed by individual travellers would cover almost fifty and twenty-five miles a day respectively; whereas produce was conveyed slowly in ox-drawn wagons at an average speed of six to seven miles a day. The routes followed lay along the main imperial roads, and every six miles or so there were stables, and changes of horse for couriers. At longer intervals, of up to fifteen miles, were built *mansiones*, where a traveller could stay, and associated with these, and often fortified against brigands, were the warehouses for the *annona*. In the fourth century the whole organisation was controlled by the *vir illustris magister officiorum*, who possessed the right to compel members of families associated with the municipal councils to undertake the supervision of the *mansiones*, including the responsibility for the prompt departure of postal services, the conserving of supplies and the protection of the nearby rural population against arbitrary acts of requisitioning; and if Libanius' evidence from Antioch is typical, the craftsmen and shopkeepers of nearby towns were likewise pressed into supplying the furniture and replacing the breakages as well as serving in person as cooks, cleaners and servants in these posts. Far the greater part of the service was carried out by this unpopular method. The stables were built by *corvées* of forced labour; and though the animals were public property, they were acquired, and a quarter of them renewed annually, by requisitioning. On the other hand, the skilled employees of the post, grooms, muleteers, veterinary surgeons and carpenters (to repair the waggons), were hereditary public slaves, who received clothes and rations, but no wages.

It is clear that a system such as this was capable of inflicting great hardship and injustice. Moreover, in time of war, when armies moved rapidly from one front to another, the transport system was likely to suffer dislocation. The ultimate destination of large stores of meat, oil, timber, clothing etc. might have to be changed at short notice; or the kind of commodity required might itself change, and where building stone had been wanted in peace-time, the urgent need might now be for bricks, or timber to construct artillery. When these dislocations resulted in intolerable burdens being laid upon certain *collegia*, their members frequently abandoned their duties and took refuge in flight. It was primarily to prevent this that the practice grew up of binding a man to his occupation with the sanction of law. Henceforward *collegiati* must keep to the same profession and carry out duties for the state in return for a nominal *solacium*.

This evolution of the Roman Empire during the third century from a system of *laissez-faire* to one of controlled private enterprise, working within limits sharply defined by the state, removed a considerable body of the population outside the range of money economy for the bulk of its needs. But though the importance of money was thus partly reduced, the effects of this trend should not be exaggerated.

In the first place, money did not cease to fulfil its primary purpose in imperial finances. The furnishing of *annona*, whether under the terms of the *iugatio–capitatio* tax, or of the modified form of it found in the western provinces, was obligatory only for those living on the land. For other sections of the population there were taxes in gold and silver. Senators, for example, in addition to the *annona* payable on their estates, were liable to a super-tax (which persisted until A.D. 450), known as the *follis* or *collatio glebalis*, and also to the payment of a sum of gold (*aurum oblaticium*) on the occasion of an emperor's accession and each quinquennial anniversary of it. Similarly, the magistrates and council members of the various cities were obliged to contribute *aurum coronarium*, originally as a theoretically voluntary gift to celebrate special occasions, and later, by a rescript of A.D. 364, as a compulsory donation. Finally, there was a special tax, instituted by Constantine, the *collatio lustralis*, which applied strictly to the trading classes, but was extended to include money-lenders, inn-keepers, brothel-keepers, and virtually everyone who followed an occupation for gain (though rural craftsmen, doctors, teachers, painters and the lower clergy were specifically exempt). This tax, which was levied every five years, was paid on the amount of capital involved in a business, with a minimum payment for those whose capital was negligible; and it had to be paid in gold and silver or, from A.D. 372 onwards, in gold alone. This *chrysargyrum*, as it was therefore commonly called, was abolished in the East in A.D. 498, but, as Cassiodorus shows, it continued to be exacted in the West down to the sixth century – thus outliving the Empire. It went largely to pay for shows given by the emperor and for the donations which the army demanded and received on all important occasions. It was felt as an overwhelming hardship by the taxpayers, and Zosimus and Libanius speak of fathers prostituting or even enslaving their children (despite the law) in order to raise the required sum.

All these taxes, except the *annona*, were paid in silver and gold, and are reflected in the gold coinage instituted by Constantine. During the fourth century, moreover, following a practice which is found as early as A.D. 213 in Egypt, the *annona* itself gradually evolved into a tax paid in gold rather than in kind; and the substitution of gold for goods, *adaeratio*, also appears in the payment of government employees. In A.D. 325 Constantine specifically forbade the use of *adaeratio* in paying out the *annona* of tribunes; but in A.D. 364 and 365 it is permitted to certain categories of state employee, including the soldiers along the Danube, the *riparienses milites*, who are to receive nine months' wages in kind and three months' in gold. In A.D. 389 *adaeratio* is accepted as a general practice in Illyricum; and this decision is followed by various rescripts defining the rate at which the calculation shall be made. In the course of the fifth century the practice grows. In A.D. 423 a rescript of Honorius and Theodosius makes it compulsory in the payment of officials, and implies that it is already recommended for the army. An interesting example of its application comes from an edict of the same year, dealing with the payment of troops, which lays down that five-sixths of the gold shall go to the first line troops in person, and one-sixth to the weavers in the imperial factory, who in return are to provide uniforms for the *iuniores* and *gregarii milites*. In this way misuse of the money by the younger and less responsible troops was prevented. Finally, by A.D. 439, *adaeratio* was compulsory for army and officials alike.

The issue around which the main controversy concerning *adaeratio* centred was the rate of conversion. A calculation of the equivalent of any tax in gold might be made according to a fixed rate, or according to the market price current either in the district where the tax was levied, or at Rome. Thus in A.D. 324 the landowner who had to supply the *suarii* from Rome with swine was allowed to pay in gold at the local rate, which was fixed for the year. Later in the century, however, the *suarii* successfully appealed against this ruling, which might involve them in a loss, should the price of swine near Rome prove dearer than that in the local market; consequently in A.D. 367 the price at Rome was substituted for the local price as a basis for *adaeratio*, and such taxpayers as still preferred to pay in kind were allowed to do so, provided that they added $\frac{1}{20}$ of the value of the swine to cover the cost of transport to Rome. A similar clash of interest existed between the recipients of *annona*, the army, the civil service and the employees in public concerns on the one hand, and the landowners who paid taxes on the other. The former were less likely to lose if their salaries were in kind; but if payment was made in money, they were concerned to ensure that its purchasing power should not fall through a rise in the price of goods. Consequently they preferred *adaeratio* to be carried out at the current market rate of the district where they lived or were stationed. The landowner, on the other hand, benefited from voluntary *adaeratio* at a fixed tariff. He could then decide on each occasion whether it paid him to meet his obligations in kind or in gold. The danger for the state was that of falling between the two parties and shouldering the loss; and eventually a flexible system was devised, whereby the praetorian prefects laid down tariffs with fixed rates each season and *adaeratio* became compulsory. This system, which was in full operation by the early decades of the fifth century, in effect brought with it the end of fiscal payments in *natura*, though *natura* remained the basis on which the obligation in gold was calculated.

Thus, for upwards of two centuries taxation in kind removed from the workings of the market (though to a decreasing extent) vast quantities of commodities in everyday use; and accordingly it reduced the area and scope of the money economy. There is also evidence that many of the large landowners, who had been strengthened by the institution of the colonate, began to make their estates partially independent of the market, accepting a proportion of their rents in kind – corn, wine and agricultural produce – and some even adding branches of industry to the normal activities of the domain. The *Theodosian Code* draws an important distinction between those merchants who buy in order to sell, who keep a shop, attend markets and fairs, and in general live from the fruits of their trade, and those who merely sell the produce of their estates. The former are of course subject to the payment of *chrysargyrum*, whereas the latter are taxed only on their land and the number of their employees (*capitatio–iugatio*). Thus the landowner who mined iron or copper on his estate, set up workshops and smithies, producing tools, ornaments and household utensils even beyond the needs of his own establishment, still remained exempt from any further tax, such as his competitors in the town would have to pay.

That some degree of industrial activity was associated with country houses and estates has been proved by excavation. There are for example remains of a fulling or dyeing establishment in a villa at Darenth in Kent, which contained large tanks and a vast series of hypocausts. Its size suggests that it was capable of handling cloth woven at several weaving establishments, and these were probably situated in nearby villas. Gaul provides what are at first sight still more impressive examples of the same tendency. The most notable is the luxurious villa excavated at Anthée in the Belgian province of Namur. Here, within a walled enclosure 650 metres in extent, stood the villa itself, dating to the middle or perhaps the second half of the first century, and beyond it in the east some twenty separate buildings, of which at least half appear to have been used for industrial purposes; there are furnaces belonging to a forge, iron foundries, and shops for the making of bronze and enamelled articles, for brewing, and for pottery, harness and leather work. Among the debris have been found large numbers of small objects, buttons, bells, hairpins, brooches, both plain and enamelled, rings, bracelets, keys and box-fittings, all on a scale far beyond what could be expected if this industry was merely to satisfy the needs of the villa. Even larger and more impressive, if less definitely industrial, is the establishment associated with a villa found at Chiragan in the plain of Martres-Tolosanes, a little to the south of Toulouse. The fortunes of this villa, which was frequently rebuilt between the time of Augustus and the fourth century, were at their greatest under the Antonines. Here, in close association with the villa itself, are some eighty smaller buildings, some of which at least show signs of having been used for domestic crafts: loom-weights and occasional tools have been found. Nevertheless the remains of Chiragan do not impose an assumption of industrial activity in a wider sense, as do those at Anthée. It is by no means impossible that the rich Gallic family of the Aconii, whose home this villa probably was, maintained an entourage of some four hundred persons simply to minister to their personal needs and those of the estate. Moreover, both Anthée and Chiragan appear to have been at the height of their activity from one to two hundred years before the date when the widespread reversion to domain economy is usually assumed to have taken place, and perhaps merely illustrate the growth of large estates which had already been noted under the late Republic and was a feature of the Empire from the first and second centuries onwards. Recent investigation has thrown new light on this development both in Greece, where many classical towns were absorbed by large estates, imperially or privately owned, and in southern Italy, where a period of economic prosperity under the early Empire was sometimes (though by no means always) associated with a growth of villas and the flourishing of a rural economy.

Literary evidence also throws some light on the problem of industrialised domains. Palladius, in a much quoted passage (1, 6, 2), advises landowners to have iron-workers, carpenters, and makers of casks and barrels available on the estate, lest it should be necessary to interrupt the agricultural tasks in order to send labourers into the town. This does not of course mean that the landowner should attempt to make himself independent of the town, but merely that there should be men on the estate able to do the simpler jobs and restrict the number of occasions on which the help of the town has to be called in. The presence of such craftsmen on an estate implies that they were regularly employed: they will hardly have been kept idle in the expectation of emergencies. But the text is not to be pressed too far, the more as Palladius himself gives many indications of the dependence of the manor on the town market. In general, the estate which has developed specialised industrial activities is to be regarded as exceptional. Normally the slaves on an estate of the late Empire would not be professionally trained workers. Carpenters and joiners, wicker-workers and rope-makers one would expect to find; and Palladius is evidence for ironsmiths. But it seems clear that for anything more complicated the landowner fell back on the town, or called in the aid of travelling tinkers and other itinerant craftsmen. If the estate produced raw materials, these would usually be worked up in the towns; and from here too would come the bulk of the slaves' tunics, cloaks and felted woollen overalls, even though the domain would normally carry out some weaving and spinning. From the town too came pottery, metal ware, finer baskets and ropes, and farm wagons.

A far greater inroad into the realm of private economy was made by the state factories, which are mentioned in various rescripts in the *Codes* of Theodosius and Justinian, and in particular in the *Notitia Dignitatum*, a list of the dignitaries and departments of the imperial bureaucracy, especially in the western half of the Empire, which probably dates in its present form to the early decades of the fifth century, though the original on which our version is based was most likely compiled about A.D. 395. Already under the early Empire some of the needs of the army had been met by military factories for the production, for instance, of tiles and bricks. Examples are plentiful along the Rhine frontier, with its army potteries at Xanten and Neuss, and at Weisenau near Mainz. Now, under the directed economy of the later Empire, factories were employed to supplement the use of controlled private enterprise, and state arsenals, weaving mills and dyeworks were set up in various places. The date of this new development cannot be exactly determined. The evidence of the *Historia Augusta*, which would take them back to the reign of Severus Alexander, is unreliable; indeed there is no certain proof of their existence before Diocletian, though they may have developed in the latter part of the third century.

The supreme official responsible for the imperial factories of the West was the *vir illustris comes sacrarum largitionum* stationed in Rome; under him were the procurators of the individual factories, and the activities of these officials were closely controlled. The sanctions constantly laid down by the legal codes suggest that it was the practice of these officials to try both to cheat the state and to extort money from the provincials. Their appointment was for a limited period only, and was covered by the giving of surety beforehand and the rendering of accounts at the end of the term of office. Four kinds of factory are mentioned from the western part of the Empire, weaving mills (*gynaecia*), linen mills (*linyfia*), dyeworks (*bafia*), and the *barbaricaria* or *argentaria*, which were works originally carrying on embroidery in gold and silver thread (though in the East, where a little after A.D. 374

they were transferred to the control of the *magister officiorum*, and perhaps also in the West, they also produced the bronze armour with gold and silver decorations worn by officers); these *barbaricaria* were in the charge of *propositi*, perhaps subordinate to the *procuratores* of adjoining weaving establishments. In addition there were two *gynaecia* controlled separately by another official, the *vir illustris rerum privatarum*, and therefore perhaps regarded as being in some special sense the personal property of the emperor. Finally, there were various ordnance factories under the control of the *vir illustris magister officiorum*.

The weaving mills were at Bassiana, between Sirmium (Mitrovica) and Belgrade, Sirmium itself, and at Iovia, in Illyricum; at Aquileia and Milan; at Rome; at Canusium and Venusia, both of which were long famous for their fine undyed cloaks, and also for an inferior material dyed with cheap purple and made up into tunics; at Carthage (where the 'slaves in our factory' are mentioned in a rescript of the *Theodosian Code* from the year A.D. 380); at Arles, Lyons, Rheims, Tournai, Trier and Autun; and at Venta *in Britannis*, which is perhaps Winchester, near the sheep runs of Salisbury Plain and the Hampshire Downs.[18] The two private factories are at Trier and another town, which may be Viviers. Only two linen mills are mentioned, at Vienne and at Ravenna. The dyeworks were at Tarentum, at Salona, on the island of Cissa (off Istria), at Syracuse, at Girba (in the Syrtes in North Africa), in the Balearic Islands, and at Toulon and Narbonne in southern France; in addition there were several dyeworks in North Africa under the control of a single procurator, perhaps stationed in Carthage. The *barbaricaria* were at Arles, Rheims and Trier and were probably run in conjunction with the *gynaecia* in those towns.

The location of these factories seems to have been determined by two factors, their proximity to raw materials and their convenience as bases for equipping the armies. Transport difficulties made it essential to place them at a safe but not excessive distance from the frontier: Bassiana, Sirmium, Trier and Tournai all fulfil these conditions. Moreover, where there are records of the moving of a factory, for instance from Salona to Bassiana or from Autun to Metz, the purpose seems to be to bring it nearer to the armies it supplied. It is significant that, despite the obvious facilities which south-west France and Spain afforded, there were no woollen factories in these provinces, and this is presumably due to their distance from the armies on the frontier. Similarly the imperial arms factories of the West were all situated in Illyricum, northern Italy or Gaul. In Illyricum shields were manufactured at Sirmium, Aquincum (Alt-Ofen), Lauriacum

[18] Other possibilities are Caerwent and Caistor-by-Norwich.

(Lorch) and Carnuntum, and arms of various kinds at Sirmium and Salona; in Italy shields came from Verona and Cremona, arrows from Concordia, bows from Ticinum (Pavia), and broad-swords from Luca; and in Gaul arms of every type were manufactured at Argenton (Argentomagum – unless Argentoratum, Strasbourg, should be read), arrows at Mâcon, broad-swords at Rheims and Amiens, shields at Trier and Amiens, artillery (*ballistae*) at Trier, and some unrecorded arms at Soissons.

In view, therefore, of both the precedents of army workshops of the early Empire, and the situation of these late imperial factories, there can be little doubt that they were designed to meet some of the needs of the army and bureaucracy – which were, however, far greater than they could satisfy; there is no evidence that they produced for the market as well. As we saw, Diocletian's edict is particularly comprehensive in its lists of articles of clothing, and in one place it lays down prices for a soldier's *chlamys* and a tunic, which are described as '*indictionalia*', which presumably means 'of the type specified in the imperial *indictio*'. It has been argued that these articles of clothing were products of the imperial factories, and that their procurators took an active part in the fixing of the prices in the edict. This is possible; on the other hand the price fixed may simply be that at which an independent craftsman was to sell certain articles of uniform to the taxpayer who was liable to provide them in his *annona*. Nor can one draw analogies from the dyeworks, which certainly sold to the public, for purple dyeing, unlike weaving, was an imperial monopoly.

Doubts have been expressed whether these factories were all factories in the modern sense, that is, concentrations of workers employed under a single roof, or whether the terms *gynaeceum*, *linyfium*, etc., merely refer to a collection of hand workers employed within their own homes on conditions laid down by the authorities.[19] Evidence exists that weavers and mint workers at Cyzicus in the fourth century worked on the cottage system. But it would be obviously unsound to generalise from this one instance; and in favour of the traditional view of these establishments as genuine factories is the fact that the work in them, which was arduous and unpopular, was increasingly carried out by forced labour, which would require careful supervision. The dyeworks in particular, where the raw materials included human urine and shell-fish which might have been six months dead, were largely manned by slaves and convicts. And frequently the law laid down labour in the woollen mills and dyeworks as a penalty for Christians and other malefactors. In A.D. 336 the son of one

[19] A. W. Persson, *Staat und Manufaktur im römischen Reiche* (Lund, 1923), 91.

Licinnianus, who had been apprehended after absconding, was put in chains and assigned to the woollen mill at Carthage. Moreover, by an edict of A.D. 365, published at Milan, any freeborn woman who married a textile slave was herself compelled to become a weaver, unless she had already published particulars of her own status before marriage. One is reminded of the similar stipulation which forced the husband of a baker's daughter to become a baker; and indeed one can trace a tendency to make the status of both *collegiati* and employees of imperial factories unchangeable and hereditary. Thus an edict of A.D. 380 forbade the children of workers in the imperial mints to marry outside their class. As a safeguard against attempts at escape, mint workers were branded on the arm; and the Codes are full of penalties for the concealment of runaway textile workers.

As imperial employees, the workers in the textile mills, mints, dyeworks and arms factories will have received their wages in kind, like the troops; and like them they were branded on the arm, for identification. The labourers in the arms factories (*fabricenses*), whose status was higher than that of most other workers, were described as performing *militia*, military service; and the *bastagarii*, or baggage carriers, responsible for bringing up the armies' supplies, were also treated as a militarised ordnance corps. The status of these various imperial workers was ambiguous. *De iure* it was servile and Eusebius could describe textile hands, without any sense of incongruity, as 'slaves of the treasury'; but *de facto* they were more like free persons tied to their occupation, and in comparison with such social groups as the *curiales*, theirs was often an enviable lot. They form, however, a further, considerable section of the population which is withdrawn from the money economy.

Nevertheless this economy was never completely effaced, despite the system of tax collection and payment of imperial employees in kind. The edict is evidence of this at the outset of the fourth century; and it is confirmed throughout the whole of the later Empire by the background of the writings of the Church Fathers, which consistently presuppose a world in which transactions are carried out with the aid of money. In this respect there is no appreciable difference between writings of the fourth century and those of the fifth. In both the rich man with money to spare lends it for interest, perhaps through the agency of a banker, to those who require it, sometimes to the poor, but also to business men. The landowner is more than once spoken of as profiting by scarcity and fearing a good harvest, a clear piece of evidence for the effect of the market on the price of his produce. His customers include both the city poor and also rich men without land, who buy their victuals and even their bread outside their own establishments. Further, there are craftsmen working either for themselves or as wage-earners for others; some work at home, others are itinerant. In the towns there is an active retail trade in foodstuffs and everyday articles and for all this money is used. Other evidence tends to confirm the same picture. There is, for example, the case of Melania, a rich member of the Valerian family, with a palace on the Caelian hill at Rome and properties widely distributed throughout the western half of the Empire, bringing in 120,000 *solidi*; between A.D. 404 and 417 she succeeded in selling these, mainly for gold, and thereafter distributed the sum raised among the poor. Such a financial undertaking would have been quite impossible in an economy which had reverted predominantly to barter.

Indeed, during the fourth and fifth centuries, despite the state control of all large-scale undertakings, most provinces possessed a flourishing small industry in the hands of private craftsmen, organised of course in *collegia*. Even at this time state monopolies only applied to a very few commodities. From the time of Diocletian the provincial currencies disappeared (except in Egypt) and minting was completely restricted to the state mints. Otherwise the only true monopolies were purple dyeing with the finer products, which was reserved for the state by an edict of A.D. 369, and the making of purple and gold embroidered cloth, *paragaudas*. Neither of these monopolies is fiscal in origin, but they form part of a policy which ended by restricting the wearing of purple to the imperial house. Otherwise private competition was allowed in the most unlikely fields. We even hear of Thalassius, a friend of Libanius, who owned an arms factory, perhaps at Antioch, towards the end of the fourth century. Small craftsmen, payers of *chrysargyrum*, existed widely in both halves of the Empire. The wages laid down in the price-edict, and calculated on time rates, piece rates with keep, or piece rates without keep, most probably represent the maximum that an independent craftsman could ask from a casual employer (or customer), rather than the wages paid to the hands in a large-scale enterprise; and from the price of precious metals there recorded it may be assumed that, as in the early Empire, craftsmen such as goldsmiths and jewellers bought their own materials and produced to some extent for the market. However, when this independent activity is considered in relation to the compulsory duties exacted by the state from all these craftsmen as members of the *collegia*, and the obligation to pay burdensome taxes in gold, their hardships become apparent. Technically they are free men; but their low repute is indicated by the fact that the craftsman now usually carries only one name in place of the three on which the Roman had always prided himself.

In so far as craftsmen worked for themselves and sold their goods on the market they used money. But it was the debased silver and bronze of the inflations, and even the amount of this available varied from province to province. As we have seen, the government minted with an eye on the army and its military needs rather than on trade. This explains why Spain possessed no mint under the late Empire but had to rely on southern Gaul for currency, and why, except for a short-lived mint at Carthage from A.D. 296 to 307, Africa had to get its coinage from Italy. The virtual absence of a mint from the frontier province of Britain (there was one at London between A.D. 296 and 324) is less easily explained. Perhaps its distance led to a lack of interest in an unprofitable province. Even in those provinces well supplied with coinage, however, Constantine's *solidus* was too large a unit to finance small transactions, and these had to depend on the bronze currency. Throughout the fourth century the government made constant efforts to increase the supply of gold. For instance by an edict of Valentinian and Valens, dating to A.D. 365, anyone willing to go prospecting for gold might leave his present occupation, on condition that he subsequently remitted eight (later seven) scruples of gold annually to the treasury. Conditions cannot, however, have been very attractive, for in A.D. 376 measures had to be taken against Thracian miners who were seeking a refuge from their hardships with the Goths; and two years later a further edict laid down severe penalties for such miners of Gaul and Italy as might attempt to reach Sardinia. There are, moreover, repeated references to gold-miners who concealed themselves, took up agricultural work and were to be apprehended and brought back to their place of origin.

However, the fourth century saw what Symmachus describes as *enormitas auri crescens*; and by the time of Theodosius, the state had apparently sufficient gold and silver at its disposal to mint large quantities of small coins in these metals (but mainly gold) which served as a sound currency for small-scale trading. The source of this gold is not certain. But, though some of it no doubt came from prospectors, and some from the treasures of pagan temples or from eastern campaigns, the bulk of it no doubt represented the fruits of a consistent policy of attracting all the silver and gold within the Empire to the imperial *fiscus*. With the exception of the corn for Rome and Constantinople, which continued to be requisitioned, the restoration of a full money economy (for the growth of *adaeratio* was gradually eliminating *natura* from fiscal transactions as well) was complete in the East by the fifth century. In the West, however, wars and political stresses were more acute. Moreover the failure of the government to produce any more silver coins after the fourth century resulted in a shortage of any convenient currency unit between the *tremissis* (a gold coin worth a third of a *solidus*) and the small debased bronze, and this hampered the restoration of a true money economy. British fourth-century hoards show a unique preponderance of silver coins, which points to a shortage of gold in that province. From about A.D. 400 onward small coins disappear from both Britain and the Danube area. Indeed, Britain received no new coins at all after A.D. 407, and existing coins tended to be hoarded, not spent. By A.D. 430 coinage as a medium of exchange in Britain was a thing of the past. In other western provinces too the restoration of a money economy was hampered by the relative shortage of precious metals. The economy as a whole was much enfeebled, and the growth in the power of large landowners had weakened the central government. The truth about natural economy, in the western half of the Empire at least, appears to be this. From the time of Diocletian onward virtually two economies coexist. The needs of the ordinary man were satisfied by the public distribution of the main necessities of life, supplemented by small purchases in the free market with the debased bronze currency (which, however, gained somewhat in value in the fifth century in the absence of new issues). Simultaneously, a sound gold coinage, helped out by a little silver up to the end of the fourth century, and again after the resumption of minting by the Goths and Vandals in the late fifth century, circulated among the rich, enabling a landowner like Ausonius, who wished to refurnish his household, to buy every kind of luxury from all parts of the known world.

This raises the third problem suggested by the price-edict. To what extent was inter-provincial trade still maintained during the last two centuries of the western Empire? This is a question not easily answered, largely because of the difficulty of deciding just how much weight is to be attached to the scattered evidence available. Where items of information are rare, the survival or disappearance of any one must be largely a matter of chance, and it is easy to exaggerate the importance of what evidence we happen to have. Some new light has, however, been thrown on this problem by the discovery of fragments of a Latin version of Diocletian's edict from Aphrodisias in Caria, which provide new and decisive evidence for widespread Mediterranean trade in everyday articles at the outset of the fourth century.

These Carian fragments for the first time give us the rates for the tariffing of sea transport. Hitherto the only transport charges known from the edict were the rates for conveying various loads by wagon, ass or camel; and this worked out at $1\frac{1}{3}$ to $1\frac{3}{4}$ *denarii* per hundred pounds for every mile (without the driver's wages) – a rate which was prohibitive against the conveying of goods long distances by land. For example, a wagon-load of wheat weighing 1,200 pounds cost 20 *denarii* per mile to transport. The cost of wheat was 100 *denarii* per *castrensis modius*, so that if we can assume (on the evidence of Pliny) that an Italian *modius* of wheat weighs 22 pounds, the wagon-load in question would be worth either 5,450 *denarii* or 2,725 *denarii*, depending on whether the *castrensis modius* was the same as, or double, the Italian *modius*.[20] Hence a journey of only 270 (or 135) miles would double the cost of the load. And the cheaper the commodity transported, the more quickly transport costs would become prohibitive. The new rates for sea transport give a very different picture. They lay down the maximum prices to be charged per *castrensis modius* for some fifty-seven trips between five export regions, mostly in the eastern half of the Empire – Alexandria, Oriens (which probably include such ports as Seleuceia-in-Pieria on the Orontes), Asia, Africa and Nicomedia (in Bithynia) – and every part of the Mediterranean; altogether thirty items preserve both the terminals and the rate, but there is no reason to think that other journeys were not listed.

These fragments justify new and important conclusions. The fact that eastern ports are mentioned by name, but for the West only provinces, may be due to the fact that the edict in many ways reflects conditions in the eastern rather than the western half of the Empire. It is not evidence for a predominantly one-way traffic, for return rates from Rome to Asia would be the same as those from Asia to Rome. The rates themselves are a remarkable contrast to those for land transport. Thus, the maximum price of wheat is 100 *denarii* per *castrensis modius;* but the cost of transport is only twenty-six *denarii* for the trip from 'Oriens' to Lusitania. To be able to ship a cargo the whole length of the Mediterranean for 26 per cent of its maximum value made distant trade a feasible proposition, even after full allowance has been made for the risks entailed;[21] and the edict presupposes a trade of more than local dimensions in objects of ordinary use. A few fragmentary items from the tariff for river transport serve to complete the picture of a fairly considerable inter-provincial trade, with products from Britain, Gaul and Africa going to all parts of the Mediterranean as late as the end of the third century. The same picture may appear at first sight to be confirmed by the *Expositio totius mundi*, the Latin translation

[20] On this controversial subject see S. Lauffer, *Diokletians Preisedikt* (Berlin, 1971), 213; R. MacMullen, 'Diocletian's edict and the *castrensis modius*', *Aegyptus*, XLI (1961), 3–5, who points out that the larger figure for the *castrensis modius* would produce more acceptable maximum food prices in the edict.

[21] R. Duncan-Jones, *The Economy of the Roman Empire* (Cambridge, 1974), 367–8, suggests that some of the prescribed figures for sea-transport may be out of line with the wheat costs and so uneconomic; but this does not change the general picture.

of a description of the Empire compiled by a Greek of Alexandria or Antioch about A.D. 350. But the *Expositio* is more reliably informed about the eastern provinces than the western; and, despite one probable reference to the imperial court at Trier, much of the account of Gaul and Spain seems to reflect earlier sources. An assessment of the intensity of trade in the western half of the Empire during its last centuries must be based on the evidence surviving from the various provinces; and this considered *en bloc* points to a very marked economic regression from the position of the earlier Empire, though indeed roads, harbours and inland waterways continued to be maintained, and piracy only became a real nuisance in the Mediterranean with the Vandal conquest of Africa.

Gaul, despite the tremendous material damage done by the barbarians and the *Bagaudae* (see above, p. 93), still continued to produce textiles. Apart from the imperial factories, there is evidence for Gallic clothing in the edict of Diocletian; cloaks came from the Treviri, the Ambiani and the Bituriges, and we hear too of wool from the Atrebates, and of a linen cloak from Aquitania as late as the fifth century. Moreover, in at least one industry, there was progress beyond anything achieved under the earlier emperors. The manufacture of glass, in imitation of that produced in Italy, was introduced into Gaul in the time of Pliny (see above, p. 82); but it began to make real headway only from the middle of the second century, when we hear of factories in Bourbonnais, Poitou, Vendée, Loire-Inférieure, Argonne, Eifel, and above all at Cologne. Technical improvements in the course of this century resulted in a fine transparent glass, which was frequently adorned with geometrical motifs, and even scenes of a mythological character, gladiatorial combats and the like. Various ordinances from the time of Constantine onwards gave special protection and concessions to the *vitriarii* (glass workers) and *diatretarii* (filigree workers), provided they taught their skill to their children. This policy, which was designed to repair the ravages of the third century among skilled workers, was tantamount to a subsidy of the glass trade, and throughout the fourth century it continued to flourish, especially in Gallia Belgica, where the proximity of the army and the court at Trier acted as a strong stimulus to production. The merits of the great output of glass in this period are hard to assess. The shapes, based on those of gold and silver vessels, remained good; and new refinements of technique were evolved, such as gilding or painting between two layers of glass. On the other hand, there is a general decline in quality, and a yellow or greenish tinge begins to appear in the later specimens.

In its earlier stages the glass industry appears to have used foreign personnel. We have, for example, an inscription referring to a Carthaginian citizen, an African, named Julius Alexander, who practised as a maker of glass in Gaul. Later, for about a hundred years, from A.D. 275 to 380, the large factories of Frontinus seem to have operated with slave labour, producing a single type of monotonous barrel-shaped glass bottle. Frontinus' headquarters were probably Cologne, but his firm may have had branches near Boulogne and Beauvais, judging by the diffusion of specimens found. However, impressive though this industry may be, with its suggestion too of specialisation of types, it never reaches the scale of the earlier potteries. Glassware was used by the aristocracy, not by peasants or small artisans and traders, and, though some of it was exported to Asia and Scandinavia, it remained a luxury. Nor is the revival of pottery in the Argonne, with a new type of decoration imparted by the potter's wheel rather than the mould, evidence for a widespread commercial renaissance. The decline of the corporations is in itself against such an assumption. The shortage of inscriptions makes generalisation dangerous; but the badness of the lettering of those we have is symptomatic of the general regression. The vigorous Gallic shipping trade of earlier years now seems to have disappeared. Fourth-century texts mention *navicularii* from Africa, Spain and Egypt, but none from Gaul; and the new fragments of the price-edict, which tariff the trade routes from the eastern ports, only confirm the impression that such emporia as Arles and Narbonne were frequented mainly by merchants from the East. Similarly there are no late references to the gilds responsible for Gallic river transport. How far the work formerly undertaken by these gilds had been transferred to the *bastagarii* (see above, p. 118) and the militarised flotillas of the lakes and rivers of France and Switzerland, remains a subject for speculation.

Further to the east, in Roman Germany, similar trends are apparent. The court at Trier and the frontier armies provided a stimulus to Gaul and Germany alike, and Cologne glass circulated in both areas. On the Danube too, for similar reasons, the late Empire saw the flowering of an economy that had developed slowly. The price-edict refers to clothing from Rhaetia and Noricum, and to 'cloaks from the Danube area'; and the state factories of Illyricum are likely to have been founded where the textile industry was already in existence. Trade over the frontier, however, was more and more restricted by imperial policy. References to *pelles* – especially beaver and marten furs – in Diocletian's edict may point to the beginnings of a fur trade with the North. But the export of iron and bronze to the barbarians was forbidden from the early fourth century onwards; and an edict of A.D. 374 not only forbade the export of gold, but somewhat naïvely urged that 'wherever gold should be discovered in the hands of the barbarians, subtle guile should be employed to remove it'. About the same time the number of points at which trade with the barbarians was permitted was strictly limited; the Goths, for example, were allowed only two trading posts along the Danube. Shortly afterwards we find arms, wine, corn, oil and fish sauce also included in the list of articles which must not cross the frontier. These restrictions undoubtedly hampered the remnants of trade from the North; and the removal of the court from Trier to Arles in A.D. 413 was a further blow. There is evidence that such rich men as could fled south about this time, leaving an impoverished area which rapidly deteriorated to something like the economic level of free Germany.

Britain, on the contrary, enjoyed an Indian summer in the fourth century, due in part to a growing economic self-sufficiency and also to the fact that the island had escaped the worst ravages of the previous hundred years. There is now evidence that earlier scholars exaggerated the decay of the towns in the fourth century, but it remains true that the prosperity of the villas is in striking contrast to the picture elsewhere in western Europe. Whereas in Gaul, where in the early third century there was a recrudescence of indigenous decorative forms, especially in the art of enamelling and in the appearance of a native style which foreshadows that of the fourth century and later barbarian work, British craftsmanship during the third and fourth centuries shows a break with Celtic types, and instead we have a flood of standardised articles such as brooches, of which some may be importations from the continent, but others are certainly native imitations. Celtic art was not, however, driven underground, but survived to create a Romano-Celtic synthesis in some of the best work that has survived, especially in sculpture and pottery.

The imports of *sigillata* from the continent virtually ceased shortly after A.D. 200 owing to the disruption of the Gallic potteries in the civil war between Albinus and Septimius Severus. They were superseded – though on a much smaller scale – by glass-ware and pottery from the Rhineland. From about A.D. 150, however, local potteries were producing fine wares. The excellent Castor ware from the Nene valley is found all over Britain and continued to be produced down to the fifth century. But there were many other local wares as well, some unsuccessful imitations of Samian, and others whose producers obtained army contracts and were thus able to secure a wide distribution of their products. One such centre was at Colchester, but the most widely used vessels, made in a coarse dark fabric known as black burnished ware, perhaps came from Staffordshire; the factory which produced them has never been located. Like the Danube provinces Britain also developed a textile industry. The imperial factory at Venta was no doubt set up to provide uniforms for the army in Britain; but a reference to British cloaks in Diocletian's edict points to some amount of export trade. There is also evidence for fourth-century exports of corn from Britain, but it is not clear whether this went in the ordinary way of trade or as a fiscal levy. Similarly the British workmen who helped to rebuild Autun may have gone voluntarily to Gaul, but were more probably a corvée. In general the economic trend in Britain, as elsewhere, during the fourth century, was towards local self-sufficiency. The province had now a more balanced economy and could retain more of the wealth it produced. There was indeed a slight increase in the amount of exports of both basic commodities like corn and textiles and luxuries such as jet and pearls. Excavations have revealed few foreign products in the villas of this period; and the absence of a mint and the exceptional hoarding of silver coins have already been noted (above, pp. 120–1). But largely for geographical reasons, it was an age of quiet prosperity, until the neglect of the imperial authorities and the withdrawal of the legions paved the way for the overrunning of the province, the destruction of the villas and the coming of the Saxons.

Spain too continued to enjoy a modified prosperity. The large number of late milestones which have survived points to energetic work in maintaining the roads and this activity, especially in the north-west, may connect with the importance of the gold mines of Galicia. But these roads also served the needs of internal commerce, much of it, no doubt, as in Britain, carried out by hawkers and pedlars. The presence of a synagogue at Elche, however, and the canons of the Council of Elvira, which regulated the commercial as well as the social relations between Jews and Christians, points to a considerable body of Jewish traders in Spain by the end of the third century. Some export trade undoubtedly continued. Even in the fourth century, Ausonius in Gaul receives gifts of olive oil and fish sauce (*muria*) from Barcelona, and bears witness to the survival of the old trade name, *garum sociorum*. The *Expositio totius mundi*, too, though awarding pride of place to the learned men of Spain, *viri docti*, deigns also to notice its olive oil, fish sauce, lard, garments and esparto grass – 'sufficient for the whole world'. Its baggage animals too – if this document is to be trusted – were still renowned; but there is no mention of race-horses, though Julian presented one to Constantius, and both Symmachus and Vegetius sing their praises. The edict of Diocletian lists the hams of the Cerretani and Spanish wool; and though for reasons already considered there were no state textile factories in Spain, the Balearic Islands contained dyeworks. Both before and after the foundation of Constantinople, in A.D. 324 and in 336, there is evidence from the *Theodosian Code* that fiscal corn was being sent from Spain to Rome. Spain also continued to import goods on a considerable scale, *sigillata* and other wares from Africa, luxury goods from the East and sarcophaguses from Rome. However, a steep decline in the amount of available evidence is clear proof of the decay which the province suffered under the impact of civil war and invasion. Spain had no mint, and the coins in the mining districts became rarer, though some bear names as late as those of Theodosius (A.D. 378–95) and Honorius (A.D. 395–423). Altogether we know little of the real state of the country at this time, not even whether Avienus is to be believed when he speaks of the once famous western port of Gades as lying in ruins, or Ausonius, when he describes Hispalis, Cordoba and Tarraco as still flourishing.

Sicily, records the *Expositio*, is a land of unlimited wool and baggage animals; it abounds in rich and learned men, who speak both Greek and Latin; it grows fine wines on the slopes of Etna; and both Syracuse and Catania are famous for their circuses. In fact the province seems to have remained a centre of primary production, and in the late fourth century it was still sending corn to Rome, and breeding world-famous horses for use in the gladiatorial games, the circus and the postal service. As before, Sicily still imported pottery; fourth-century earthenware lamps from Africa have been found both at Syracuse and at Camarina, and there was some trade with Narbonese Gaul and the eastern provinces. Tiles were manufactured locally and also imported from Africa. Through its equable climate, its landscape, and its antiquities, the island attracted tourists; but even though they were mainly drawn from the richest classes, the senators, who were forbidden to visit other provinces, they will hardly have constituted an important economic factor. In general, Sicily was still a land of large estates and ranches, and these with their *coloni* controlled the main pattern of life outside the towns.

After the foundation of Constantinople, Rome was provisioned mainly from Africa, and until its seizure by the Vandals a hundred years later the province – together with Mauretania – remained primarily a storehouse for the capital. Its people, says the *Expositio*, were crafty. Their main passion was for gladiatorial games; there were few good men among them, and they were unworthy of their rich country. Those of Mauretania were, however, still worse, for their habits and way of life were barbarous; Mauretania was significantly one of the few places which still furnished slaves. From the *Expositio* we also learn that Africa supplies olive oil 'sufficient for nearly the whole earth' (but the phrase, which has almost the character of a refrain in this work, should not be pressed too closely), and that it was rich in fruits and baggage animals. African woollens are not mentioned, though both Numidia and Mauretania are said to export clothing; however, the presence of a textile factory and several dyeworks under the control of a procurator stationed at Carthage is consistent with the independent references to African rugs, cloaks and linen tunics, in both the *Historia Augusta* and the price-edict.

The important quarries of North Africa had apparently fallen into disuse during the third century, for in A.D. 320 Constantine issued a rescript authorising anyone who so wished to quarry there for marble – a policy subsequently extended to several eastern provinces. This shortage of quarrymen is an example of the growing failure of free labour to provide the necessities of life under the later Empire. At the quarries of Fruschka-Gora in Pannonia the workers consisted of convicts, mainly Christians *damnati ad metalla*, and some 620 slaves under the charge of five technical overseers with the somewhat inappropriate name of *philosophi*, and a troop of soldiers to give them moral support. No doubt the same system was also tried in North Africa, and similar conditions may well have existed in such a quarry town as Simitthus. The fact that even so attempts had to be made to encourage individuals to embrace the career is some indication of the decline in the population. Carthage, it is true, remained one of the great cities of the West even under the Vandals. Both St Augustine and the author of the *Expositio* mention the famous Street of the Silversmiths, the *vicus argentariorum*. But the province as a whole appears never to have recovered from the pillaging which followed the suppression of the revolt of A.D. 238, which set the Gordians on the imperial throne. This rising of the propertied classes was crushed by Capellianus, the *legatus* of Numidia, and his campaign was probably attended by a tremendous destruction of wealth. Later, in the fourth century, some of the more extreme supporters of the Donatist heresy formed themselves into wandering bands, whom their opponents dubbed *Circumcelliones*, 'wandering monks'. They were evidently poor and, according to St Augustine, Punic-speaking; they protected tenants against landlords, debtors against their creditors, and slaves against their masters, and they used violence against their enemies, burning down their houses. This movement was unusual in being a religious heresy with a strong social undercurrent.[22] The *Circumcelliones* remind us in many ways of the *Bagaudae* who continued

[22] The question how far ancient heresies concealed social and nationalist aims is discussed sceptically by Jones, *The Roman Economy*, 308–29.

to be active in Gaul and revolted on three occasions between Diocletian and Valentinian III (A.D. 425–55); they also penetrated Spain. The *Bagaudae*, so far as we know, had no religious aspect; but both movements represent the ineffective retaliation of an oppressed class. In Africa, too, the fourth century saw a growing decay in the towns. Diocletian had attempted at the end of the third century to restore the municipalities to prosperity by direct governmental action and by orders to the *curiales*; but the shock and setback had been too great, and there is little evidence from Africa of even the modest degree of economic revival which the fourth century showed in many provinces of the West.

Of these, however, Italy was not one. The continued primacy of Rome is reflected in the new fragments of Diocletian's edict, which place Rome first among the western destinations of ships leaving ports in the eastern half of the Empire; but its role had been established in the early Empire, and it continued to be provisioned out of the taxes. Under Diocletian Italy was divided into two *dioceses*, of which the southern was exempt from the normal *annona*, but was specifically responsible for providing the capital with meat, wine, wood and lime. Northern Italy on the contrary was assessed for *annona* and its administrative centre was Milan. The general decline of the peninsula, already a feature of the early Empire, now shows itself in the fact that many previously prosperous towns such as Puteoli and Tarracina join the list of those provisioned from abroad. Much of the countryside had fallen out of cultivation, the roads had deteriorated, and by the middle of the fourth century brigandage was so serious that in A.D. 364 the use of horses was forbidden to shepherds and even landowners in seven provinces. By the end of the century half a million *iugera* in Campania, one of the richest regions, were lying fallow; and in A.D. 450 the legal codes speak of famine compelling men to sell their children into slavery. In these conditions trade could hardly flourish; and indeed Italy had long played a passive role in imperial commerce. In the early fourth century Italian wines has still some reputation. The price-edict of Diocletian tariffs the prices of Picene, Tiburtine, Setine, Surrentine and Falernian vintages; but this does not necessarily imply that they were widely exported. In the same document there is evidence for trade in Marsian and Messapian hams, and for Lucanian pork sausage. This modest list may be reinforced from the *Expositio*; but the glowing picture which is given here of the cornlands of Calabria, and of Campania as the home of rich men and the pantry (*cellarium*) of Rome, induces justifiable suspicions that this description has little relation to the real conditions in the middle of the fourth century. The only evidence of Italian manufactures is in connection with the woollen industry. The old centres, it appears, are still active; we hear of woollens from Canusium and from Mutina (which is famous for its light cloaks), and the market contains both wool and woollens from Tarentum. Of these towns Canusium was the site of the imperial weaving mills; others were situated at Milan, Aquileia, Venusia and Rome; and the purple works of Tarentum lay in the second great area of Italian wool production. The north of Italy must also have enjoyed some prosperity from the imperial arms factories established there (see above, pp. 116–7). But there was little independent economic life. As the fourth century advances it is possible to trace the increasing power which the state exercises over the gilds; and with the Gothic invasion of the fifth century, the interruption of the corn supply from Africa, and its final cessation after the Vandal conquest, references become fewer and their significance more obscure. Whether the Italian *collegia* survived the fall of the western half of the Empire is debated. There were gilds in existence in Ravenna in the tenth century; but since Ravenna was under strong influence from the East, they are more probably revivals than survivals from the fifth century.

IV. *Summary*

These scanty records of trade and industry give some indication of the economic decline of the West during the last century and a half of the Empire. The large enterprises, the provisioning of the big centres, the army and the civil service, have been taken over by the state and they remain state responsibilities even after the growth of *adaeratio* has largely put an end to the experiment of taxation in kind; for though the taxes are now paid in gold and silver, it is the imperial authority which buys the goods and supervises their transport and distribution through the tied corporations. The pressure of taxation is now so great that no large-scale independent enterprise can survive. Yet it would be wrong to imagine the late imperial economy as one from which the independent man has vanished. Retail trade continues to flourish, especially of the type in which the craftsman makes and sells his own goods. Moreover, the wholesale trader does not die out, although his scope is reduced and his risk has increased. The price-edict shows a prosperous inter-provincial commerce for the beginning of the fourth century, including articles of common consumption as well as the luxuries which are the more obvious objects of later trade.

In the main, however, it is the rich man's market which trade in products from a distance seeks to satisfy; and not least, the large landowners living on their estates, which are self-sufficient for many of the prime necessities of life, and rely on itinerant labour and the local market for the rest, expend their fortunes on rare goods brought from the ends of the Empire. The cleavage between these large landowners, who had gained increased power through the institution of the colonate (itself a secondary result of the introduction of annual taxes in *natura*) and the imperial administration on the other hand, was one of the factors which made for the break-up of the western part of the Empire. Less united and less vigorous than the East, more torn by peasant risings such as those of the *Bagaudae* and the *Circumcelliones*, poorer, and lacking the bulwark which Constantine's new capital had given to the East, the western half gradually weakened and dissolved into the successor states of the Franks, Goths, Vandals and Lombards.

With the collapse of the imperial state, that large section of the economy which depended on it simply disappeared. The residue – small artisans and traders in the towns, local markets, itinerant craftsmen, the villages around the manor or the monastery, and, for the rich, an irregular trade in luxuries from all parts of the Mediterranean – was left as the economic foundation of the new states of medieval Europe.

CHAPTER III

Byzantine Trade and Industry

I. *The Economic Policies and Organisation of the Byzantine Empire*

Byzantine economic history shows a marked contrast to the economic history of other medieval states. Its evolution does not correspond with that of the peoples of western Europe with their steady advance towards modern economy, nor does it resemble the story of the Arab Empire, the story of a vast loosely-knit dominion, rich in natural resources of every sort but never fully developing them. Byzantium was a carefully administered state, dominating a large but not naturally very wealthy territory, and aiming at the greatest possible amount of centralisation in its capital, Constantinople, a city whose size and organised activity made it unique in the medieval world.

Byzantine history falls into clearly differentiated periods. The first, from the foundation of Constantinople till the Arab conquests in the seventh century, is a continuation of the history of the Roman Empire. The emperor still possessed all the eastern provinces of the Empire, and his problems were similar to those of his predecessors. There follows a period when the Empire, reduced in size and at first in danger of collapse, gradually adjusts its life to reach a high state of prosperity in the tenth and early eleventh centuries. Then comes a period of new invasions from the East and military and economic aggression from the West, Byzantium apparently recovers, then rapidly declines, till the capture of Constantinople by the Crusaders in 1204. The Empire of Nicaea and the recovery of Constantinople in 1261 again suggest a revival; but the last two centuries of the Empire tell a story of impoverishment and decay.

Throughout these periods the basic aims of the Byzantine government remained the same. The first was to provide and maintain a strong centralised administration. The emperors, from Diocletian onwards, had diagnosed the main cause of the decline of Rome as being the lack of uniformity and control in the provincial government. Diocletian had thought the Empire too big to be ruled from one centre; he envisaged two or four. But Constantine's new capital which was both easily accessible and easily defensible, and the loss of western provinces to the Barbarians made further concentration feasible, though it was resented by the rich provinces of Syria and Egypt, each with a great metropolis of its own; and it was not completed till the Arab conquests further reduced the size of the Empire. The centralisation went deep. Not only were the market towns in closer connection with the capital than in the West, but the villages were in closer connection with the market towns, on which they depended for most of their supplies.[1] The connections were made possible by good communications. The Byzantines kept up and improved the Roman road system in their dominions and always had an adequate mercantile marine. At the same time the administration was elastic. Local governors enjoyed considerable autonomy and responsibility; but they were periodically inspected by officials from the central government, which controlled them further by paying their salaries.[2] The system worked well until the emergence, from the late tenth century onwards, of a provincial nobility, rich enough to defy the central government[3] and the destruction of communications in the course of the Turkish wars of the late eleventh century.

The second aim of the government arose from the first. It was to keep the population of Constantinople well fed and contented. Disorder in the capital of so centralised a state might seriously damage the whole administrative system. Consequently everything possible was done to ensure a steady flow of cheap food and essential articles to the city, to the welfare of which, except under the Iconoclastic emperors, the provinces were often sacrificed.

Thirdly, the government aimed at obtaining a steady revenue through taxation, to pay for the upkeep of the administration and an army largely composed of mercenaries, and at building up large stocks of gold. In Byzantine eyes a good emperor was an emperor who left behind him a well-stocked treasury. The gold was necessary as a reserve against national emergencies and to provide a backing for the imperial coinage. The government also understood the possibility of controlling prices by the regulation of the amount of gold in circulation.

In pursuit of these aims the Byzantine government issued laws and ordinances that affected every aspect of the economic life of its subjects. This state control was potential rather than actual. It did not

[1] See *Cambridge Economic History*, I, 2nd edn, 211.

[2] Governors of some unruly or frontier provinces obtained all or part of their salaries from the taxes that they collected. This gave them an incentive to collect the taxes efficiently. Such provinces were liable to particularly frequent visits by inspectors, to see that there was no extortion or corruption.

[3] See *Cambridge Economic History*, I, 2nd edn, 215ff.

represent a systematic policy but was for administrative purposes. If the administration did not seem to require the enforcement of these regulations, they remained dormant. Diocletian's law which ordered sons to follow their fathers' profession was retained throughout Byzantine history, but there is no evidence that it was ever enforced; and the official ban on unrestricted travel round the Empire and on a change of residence seems to have been generally ignored. The Lives of Byzantine saints, which provide our best evidence for the way of life of the average citizen, give the impression of very little governmental interference with the individual, except in times of crisis, such as famine, civil unrest or war. Even the *Book of the Prefect*,[4] the compilation made by Leo VI of the rules governing the gilds of Constantinople, probably shows an ideal rather than an actual state of affairs.

The Byzantine authorities were at no time concerned with the balance of trade. Exports from the Empire were of political rather than of economic interest to them. In fact, from Roman times onward, many more goods were imported than exported, and the balance was paid for in gold. This meant that the prosperity of the Empire largely depended upon the availability of gold. The Roman Empire had been able to support itself in the necessities of life but had imported luxuries, such as silk, precious stones and spices, from the East. In exchange gold, and to a lesser extent silver, had been exported to the East. This gold came mainly from Nubia, to which the Romans had access, and, if the diplomatic situation permitted, from the Caucasus and the Urals. But stocks of gold within the Empire were steadily diminishing. Moreover, the gold exported to Persia went out of circulation, as the Persians used silver for their currency and used gold either for ornaments or as stores of treasure. At the same time, owing to the unreliability of the Roman coinage, individuals and institutions within the Empire began to hoard precious metals. Constantine the Great's reform of the coinage, by restoring confidence, released some of these hoards; but this was countered by the desire of the newly established Christian ecclesiastical institutions to build up their own stores. Meanwhile barbarian migrations on the Russian steppes and in Africa, in the fourth and fifth centuries, and wars with Persia in the sixth, prevented easy access to the stores of gold. By the time of Justinian's reign (527–61), the position was beginning to alarm the authorities.

There was, however, a certain amount of gold coming from the western half of the Empire. The establishment of barbarian kingdoms there had not much affected trade across the Mediterranean, except for

[4] See below, pp. 154ff.

a period in the middle of the fifth century when the Vandals of Africa used their fleet for piratical purposes. The new rulers and their subjects were eager to obtain the luxuries of the East, for which they paid mainly in gold, as their own exports were few. But the trade was conducted by Syrian and Egyptian merchants in Syrian and Egyptian ships; and the gold went almost entirely to Syria and Egypt. Only a little of it reached Constantinople in the form of taxes. Some was used for the imperial mints of Alexandria and Antioch; more went further east to pay for Asiatic goods. Some, too, went into the treasuries of Syrian and Egyptian churches and monasteries and so was withdrawn from circulation. Till the seventh century Egypt and Syria were far richer than the provinces round Constantinople. The new capital provided a market for local goods and for imported luxuries; but as yet its factories could not compete with those of Alexandria. It was Egypt that manufactured the glass, the high-class pottery, the jewellery and the woven stuffs that were exported to the West; and Alexandria contained the chief ship-building yards of the time. The timber for the ships came from the Lebanon; and the Lebanese ports, especially Berytus, also built ships. Moreover, the Far-Eastern trade reached the Mediterranean through Egypt or Syria. Arabian spices, of which incense was the most important, came by caravan from southern Arabia to the Gulf of Akaba and were carried thence either to the Mediterranean through southern Palestine or northward through Transjordan, Damascus and the Orontes valley to Antioch. Spices from the Far East, such as pepper and cloves, and a certain amount of Chinese raw silk were brought by sea by Egyptian merchants sailing in Abyssinian ships from Malaya or Ceylon across the Indian Ocean, taking advantage of the monsoons, and up the Red Sea to Clysma on the Gulf of Suez, and thence to Alexandria. An imperial official stationed at Clysma superintended the trade and himself made yearly visits to the Indies. Gold, together with ivory and ostrich feathers, was obtained from East Africa, again by Abyssinian ships carrying Egyptian merchants.[5] The Persian trade, consisting mostly of raw and made-up silks from China, came chiefly through Iraq to Antioch, though silk for the Constantinople market might travel through northern Persia and Armenia to Trebizond on the Black Sea.

[5] The Egyptian–Abyssinian trade is described by Cosmos Indicopleustes in his Christian Topography, a work written, in about A.D. 530, with the aim of proving that the world is flat.

II. *The Economy of Byzantium up till the Arab Invasions of Syria and Egypt*

In spite of political problems caused by the religious and administrative grievances of Syria and Egypt against the government at Constantinople, the fifth century was a period of growing prosperity. The Emperor Justinian on his accession in 527 found the treasury well enough filled for him to embark on an extravagant internal policy of public works and an ambitious foreign policy of expansion. Unhappily, a war with Persia had already broken out, caused largely by imperial annoyance at the rising prices charged by the Persians for silk. It continued intermittently but with increasing ferocity for over a century. Northern Syria in particular suffered from the war. Her trade with Persia was interrupted; and she was the first target of the Persian armies. Antioch was captured in 540; and the ensuing sack, following soon after two great earthquakes, in 526 and 529, dealt it a blow from which it never fully recovered. Justinian tried to preserve the eastern trade by diplomatic negotiations with the Abyssinians, aimed at keeping the Red Sea open and ensuring supplies of African gold. But before his reign was over the collapse of the Abyssinian dominion in Arabia and the Blemmyes' invasion of Nubia made his efforts fruitless. The establishment of a Turkish empire in Central Asia opened up a new route for raw silk from China that by-passed Persia to the north; but it closed down when the Turkish empire disintegrated at the end of the century. It was, however, by this route that Nestorian monks travelled to Constantinople with eggs of the silk-worm hidden in their hollowed staffs, thus founding the silk-growing industry that was later to be the pride of Byzantium. Meanwhile the stocks of gold in the West were declining and were further diminished by Justinian's wars in Italy and Spain, wars which used up much of his own reserves of treasure.

The political and economic decline of the Empire continued under Justinian's successors. In the early seventh century, under the Emperor Phocas, the whole administration was on the verge of collapse; Phocas himself, when he found that he could not escape from his foes, deliberately sank the contents of the imperial treasury in a shipwreck. His successor Heraclius was left without financial resources to carry on the government at a moment when the Persian war had been renewed with heightened intensity. For fifteen years the Persians held Syria and Palestine, annexing all its stores of treasure; for ten years they held Egypt, though they seem to have interfered less with its economy. Heraclius could only finance his government by taking over the treasures of the Church in Constantinople and Anatolia. He was at last successful in the war; and a large part of the Persian royal treasure fell into his hands. But he used it to repay his loan from the Church, for which he raised in addition what money he could from the reconquered provinces of Syria and Egypt. Much wealth had been lost in the war; and now great stocks of gold went again to be idle in ecclesiastical treasuries. In A.D. 630 there was about 20 per cent less gold in circulation than there had been two centuries earlier.

The Arab conquest of Syria and Egypt followed swiftly on the Persian war. The ease of the conquest had its economic causes. The Syrian merchant had bought his goods from Persia and sold them direct to the West. He resented having to pay high taxes to a distant government in Constantinople which had done nothing for him except involve him in wars with Persia. The Egyptian merchant was mainly interested in the Red Sea route. When the Abyssinians were replaced by the Arabs as the chief power there, he needed to make friends with the Arabs. Egypt was also a great corn-growing country, from which Constantinople had obtained its corn. Shortage of gold had already forced prices down, to the detriment of the farmers; and during the Persian occupation of Egypt Constantinople had been forced to develop corn-fields nearer home. Egyptian corn had lost its main market; and, like the Syrians, the Egyptians resented the high taxation imposed by Constantinople. The Arabs from the outset demanded far lower taxes from their subjects; and when their empire expanded to stretch from India to the Atlantic they provided access to far vaster sources and markets than Byzantium could provide. But transport along the Mediterranean now tended to be by land, along the North African coast, as the Arabs did not control the sea. The Syrian merchant marine, the most vigorous in the Mediterranean since Phoenician days, declined, never to recover.

III. *Trade and Industry from the Eighth to the Twelfth Centuries: Re-adjustment and Prosperity*

With the loss of Syria and Egypt Byzantine economic history properly begins. The Empire was now a unit centralised in Constantinople. It is hard to imagine a better centre. The city was an almost impregnable fortress, surrounded on three sides by seas into which it was difficult for an enemy fleet to penetrate, though they were easy of access for peaceful voyagers and merchants. It also lay on the most convenient land-bridge from Europe into Asia and on the one outlet from the Black Sea. It thus commanded the junction of two of the great trade-routes of the world. So long as supplies were available the victualling necessary for a great city could be managed without trouble. The population of the city seems to have remained fairly constant from the sixth till the later twelfth century, and may be roughly estimated as about 800,000, if the suburbs on both sides of the Bosporus and along the Marmora coasts are included.[6] The population consisted of the court, the huge civil service, the central Church organisation and vast numbers of monks, lawyers, doctors and lay teachers, the small shop-keepers and retailers to be expected in so large a city, market-gardeners whose plots lay within the walls, artisans and factory-workers, many of them slaves of foreign origin, and the destitute, some cared for in hostels provided by both the state and the Church, others living in hovels or homeless. Before the tenth century there was no hereditary aristocracy or upper bourgeoisie. Till it was possible to invest in land, family fortunes seldom lasted for long. No one was too grand to engage in commerce: though the Emperor Theophilus in the ninth century was shocked when he discovered that his empress was part-owner of a merchant-ship. The imperial family ought not to indulge in trade.

It was some time before Byzantine trade adjusted itself to the new circumstances. The Arab conquests and migrations in Asia cut the Empire off from its supplies of gold; and it was only by a strict control of circulation that the Byzantine currency kept up its value. Early in the eighth century diplomatic moves reopened access to the Urals. The kingdom of the Khazars, a commercially-minded Turkish race, had been established to the north of the Caspian during the seventh century. Byzantine craftsmen were employed by the Khazar Khan, for whom they constructed his one stone-built city, at Sarkel on the Sea of Azov; and in return Ural gold began to come through to Byzantium. About the same time contact was made again with the Caucasian gold-mines, whose output, however, was diminishing. In the later eighth century the anti-ecclesiastical policy of the Iconoclastic Emperors brought a large amount of monastic treasure into circulation. But the chief source of gold for the Empire was now provided by the Arabs themselves, who imported raw materials from western Europe through Spain and from northern Europe by the Volga route and paid

[6] The population within the walls of the city was probably not more than 600,000. See the discussion of various estimates given by P. Charanis, 'Observations on the demography of the Byzantine Empire', in *Thirteenth International Congress of Byzantine Studies, Main Papers*, XIV (Oxford, 1966). There was probably a slight drop in population during the seventh and eighth centuries. At the end of the eleventh century the population was swelled by refugees from parts of Anatolia occupied by the Turks.

for them in gold, thus enabling western and northern nobles to buy for gold the expensive luxuries of the Byzantine factories. By the ninth century the Empire had rebuilt large stocks of gold and could once more take imports from the East.

Wars with the Arabs had obliged the Far Eastern trade to take more northerly routes. The route across Turkestan to the Black Sea was kept open by the Khazar kingdom whose prosperity lasted from the eighth to the tenth century.[7] During those years the Khazar capital of Itil, on the lower Volga, was a market where merchants of all races could be found. From Itil goods destined for Europe were taken to the Crimean port of Cherson, the northerly outpost to Byzantium, whence Greek ships carried them to Constantinople. This was the usual route for Chinese goods, which consisted, as far as Byzantium was concerned, almost entirely of raw silk. Indian and Malayan goods, ivory, precious stones and spices, usually came through Afghanistan and Persia; and in Persia carpets and made-up silks would be added to the caravans. Armenian merchants collected the goods in Persia and conveyed them to Trebizond, where Greek ships picked them up. Direct trade between the Arabs and Byzantium was rare at first, though cotton from Egypt seems to have reached Constantinople without much interruption; but before the end of the ninth century woven goods from Syria and Baghdad were imported from St Symeon, the port of Antioch, or overland through Asia Minor.

Till the late ninth century imports from the north, slaves and furs and wax from the steppes and amber and dried fish from the Baltic, were brought by local traders to Cherson, where they were collected by Greek merchant ships. By the beginning of the ninth century the Russians had taken over all this trade. Goods from the Balkan peninsula and from central Europe, such as Serbian minerals and Transylvanian salt, usually came by land to Thessalonica and thence to Constantinople. From western Europe there was imported a small quantity of slaves, timber, weapons, and, later, rough woollen cloth. Most of these goods came through the markets in Venice.

Goods coming to Constantinople from the Black Sea were stopped by customs officials at the entrance to the Bosporus, at Hieron, where a 10 per cent *ad valorem* duty was imposed. Goods from the Mediterranean and the Aegean paid a similar duty at Abydos or at Gallipolis on the Hellespont. For Asian goods there were customs houses at Trebizond, at Attalia and at Cilician Seleucia and, inland, at Ancyra.

[7] The history of the Khazars is still a matter of controversy, much of it being based on early documents of doubtful authenticity. See D. M. Dunlop, *The History of the Jewish Khazars* (Princeton, 1954), and Z. Ankori, *Karaites in Byzantium* (New York, 1959). For the role of Khazaris in international trade see W. Heyd, *Histoire du commerce du Levant* (Leipzig, 1936), II, 48–9.

Customs officials at Thessalonica controlled the Balkan trade.[8] Till the late sixth century the customs organisation was controlled by the Count of the Commerce at Constantinople. Afterwards it was decentralised and the local customs officers, the *commerciarii*, were allowed considerable autonomy. At the end of the eighth century the Empress Irene allowed free imports; but the advantages to the city's trade were felt not to make up for the loss to the imperial revenues; and her successor restored the duties, appointing new posts so that importers of goods from the south or west should not evade them by landing their wares at some port west of Abydos. This had been the practice with regard to slaves in particular. Henceforward wherever such slaves were sold a special tariff of 2 *nomismata* (about 30 gold francs) was imposed.

It is impossible to estimate the volume or value of all this trade. We do not know what proportion of the imperial revenues was acquired from import duties.[9] They must have formed a considerable item in the budget; but if Irene could carry on her government without their help, they cannot have made a vital difference. She may have thought that consequent lowering of prices and stimulus to trade would bring in larger sums in direct taxation; and there is reason to believe that the import trade was suffering from a slight slump in her time. In any case, her experiment was not repeated. Of the commodities imported the largest sums were probably spent on raw silk. Even when silk-worm farms were established round Constantinople and in Greece, the raw silk merchants and dressers bought most of their material from abroad. Made-up cloth of all sorts, especially damasks and brocades, were similarly imported in large quantities, despite a considerable local production. Such precious materials as ivory and jewels can only have come in small quantities, as there were few buyers that could afford them outside of the imperial court; and the demand for furs was restricted to the rich. On the other hand, vast amounts of spices were imported. The list that the perfumers' gild was entitled to sell includes many items, such as pepper, cinnamon and musk, all

[8] The evidence of seals shows that at various times there were customs officials also at Mesembria, Develtus, Heracleia and Kerasount on the Black Sea, and in the Aegean Corinth, Andros, Rhodes and Chersonese in Crete, and at Sylaeon and Korykos on the southern Anatolian coast, and, when it was recaptured, at Antioch. There are casual references to officials in a number of other towns, but most of them probably dealt with local octrois. See H. Antoniadis-Bibicou, *Les Douanes à Byzance* (Paris, 1963), for a full discussion.

[9] Estimates of the total imperial revenue vary from 8,000,000 *nomismata* per annum to 50,000,000. The evidence is so scanty that any calculation must involve guess-work. It was certainly large enough to enable a thrifty emperor to build up a big reserve. After a peaceful reign of 27 years Anastasius I, a financier by profession, left the sum of 320,000 lbs of gold in the treasury when he died in 518. The Regent Theodora, when she retired in 856, left 109,000 lbs of gold in the treasury. Basil II, in spite of all the wars of his reign, left about 200,000 lbs of gold, as well as piles of precious stones and metals. In each case these reserves were quickly dispersed by subsequent rulers.

coming from the East; and Byzantine medical treatises, such as that of Symeon Seth, assume that all manner of Indian spices, such as nutmeg, galingale and cloves, are easily obtainable in Constantinople. The slave trade was never large; the Church disapproved of it. Most of the slaves who worked in the mines or the palace factories were prisoners of war.

Exports from the Empire were less numerous. The East bought a few products of Byzantine factories, such as glass *tesserae* for mosaic work, and some dyes and spices, such as Peloponnesian cochineal and mastic from the Aegean islands. The West and North provided customers eager to buy any of the luxury products of Constantinople. Though this trade brought gold into the Empire, the imperial authorities did not encourage it too far. They preferred their products to have the value and mystery of comparative rarity. Export of the finest silks was forbidden. They might occasionally leave the country as an imperial gift to some foreign potentate, but that was all. Silks of lesser quality could be exported, but the supply for export never seems to have equalled the demand. Linens and cottons were exported in larger quantities, and from the tenth century onwards Peloponnesian carpets were popular in the West. Works of applied art, enamels, carved ivories and steatites and so on, though there was always a demand for them, were too costly to be exported in large numbers. Goods for export paid a duty similar to that on imported goods, at the same stations. The customs examination was very strict. Otto I's ambassador, Liudprand of Cremona, found that his diplomatic status, which permitted him to export ordinary goods duty-free, was of no avail when he tried to take out silks on the prohibited list.

A large quantity of the goods imported from the East seem to have been re-exported straight to the West or the North. It is uncertain what transit-dues were charged on them.

Most of the carrying trade between eastern countries and Byzantium, and all the coastal trade within the Empire, was done in Greek ships. They had a complete monopoly in the Black Sea, conveying all the goods from Cherson and Trebizond, until the end of the ninth century, when the Russians began to develop their trade and the Khazar trade began to decline. Thenceforward goods from the steppes were brought in yearly Russian expeditions which sailed down the river Dnieper and along the Bulgarian coast to the Bosporus. In a desire to cultivate Russian friendship as well as to encourage this trade, registered Russian traders were allowed by a treaty, signed in 907 and renewed a few years later, to import their goods duty-free.[10] In the

[10] This exemption seems to have lapsed when the Russian trade declined in the eleventh century, owing to the invasion of the southern steppes by the Polovtsians.

western trade the Greeks lost their monopoly about the same time. By the tenth century Bari, the capital of Byzantine Italy, had a merchant marine of its own, while the vassal city of Amalfi was steadily increasing its connections with a colony of its merchants in Constantinople. But the dangerous competition came from Venice, itself also nominally a vassal city and, as yet, tactfully respectful in its attitude to its imperial overlord. By the end of the tenth century Venice already had a large merchant fleet which not only carried all the trade between the Western Empire and central Europe and Byzantium but also provided the regular passenger and mail services. Nevertheless Greek ships still sailed to Italy. The merchantman that rescued the Western Emperor Otto II after his defeat by the Muslims at Stilo in 982 was not an isolated phenomenon.

Goods imported overland seem usually to have been brought by foreign merchants. There were annually companies of Syrians in Constantinople who had conveyed Syrian stuffs and Indian goods imported through Iraq by road across Asia Minor. A mosque was maintained in the city for the use of Muslim visitors. Men from the Balkan countries could be found in Constantinople and in Thessalonica selling their local products to the gild organisations. Foreigners were never discouraged. It was only right that they, and not the Byzantines, should pay the import and export duties. But their lives during their visits to the capital were carefully circumscribed and superintended. On their arrival they had to report themselves to the city authorities who kept in touch with them. Special khans, called *mitata*, were allotted them, and none of them were permitted to remain more than three months in the city. These rules applied to ordinary Muslim and west European traders. Later the chief Italian cities set up consulates in Constantinople, and the consular officials took over the surveillance of their fellow-citizens, with the approval of the imperial authorities. The Russians, being considered more barbarous, had their own arrangements. They were given free lodging and free baths, but they were housed in a suburb and not allowed within the city walls without an escort. Bulgarian traders had to register themselves and their goods. This took place at Constantinople; and when in the late ninth century a corrupt minister had the registration office moved to Thessalonica, Bulgarian trade was so badly dislocated that the Bulgarian king went to war to right it.

Despite occasional interruptions due to wars, Byzantine foreign trade increased in volume till the international convulsions of the later eleventh century. It received very little encouragement from the government, which only interfered when revenue was concerned or the acquisition of gold and of the raw materials needed by the imperial factories. The merchants' welfare would be sacrificed in the interests of diplomacy or of maintained order in Constantinople.

Internal trade consisted primarily in the supplying of Constantinople with the necessities of life and the comforts that its citizens increasingly demanded. The corn that fed the city grew for the most part in Asia Minor and was conveyed by sea from the port nearest to the corn-fields. If the Asian crop failed corn could also be brought in from other provinces. During the Asian famine of 1037 the government bought up 100,000 *modii* (650,000 kg) of corn in Hellas and the Peloponnese. Thrace, which provided corn after the Turkish occupation of most of Anatolia, used mainly to produce cattle and swine, driven in herds to the city abattoirs. Sheep came for the most part from the highlands of Bithynia. Fruit and vegetables were grown locally and along the sheltered shore of the Gulf of Nicomedia. Fish was plentiful in the Bosporus. Fishermen had to purchase licences, the proceeds from which went to pay for the oil for the lamps in Saint Sophia. Spices and flavourings came from all parts of the Empire, mastic from the islands, saffron from Cilicia, gum from Pisidia. Cloths of local manufacture were supplemented from Peloponnesian looms. Carpets were made both in the Peloponnese and in Anatolia. Stocks of raw silk were replenished from farms near Thebes or Corinth. Flax grown in the western Peloponnese and along the Asiatic coasts of the Aegean came to be made up into finished cloth in Constantinople, with the help of Peloponnesian dyes and alum from Kerasount to fix them. Other large cities such as Thessalonica and Trebizond needed to have their local produce supplemented in order to maintain their considerable populations.

With the exception of foodstuffs, goods carried from one province to another paid an octroi at their ultimate place of destination. This was not applied to goods destined for the court or for the army. Agricultural machinery seems also to have been exempt, and goods for personal use. Exemption might also be specially granted to monasteries, and it was usually granted to sea-captains for cargoes that they personally owned.

The mercantile marine was carefully controlled. The rules that governed it were published in a code known as the Rhodian Law, because, in the days of the early Roman Empire, Rhodes was, it seems, supposed to have the best maritime code. This was reissued without alteration at intervals from the eighth to the thirteenth century. It gives us some idea of the organisation of Byzantine shipping. Every ship had an owner or hirer who was distinct from the captain, though a captain could own or hire his ship. The captain had complete command of the ship once the voyage was begun. His pay was twice that of the ordinary sailors. The petty officers (the mate, the carpenter and the helmsman) received one-and-a-half times the sailors' pay, and the cook one-half of it. The captain was responsible in cases of theft and when the cargo was damaged by bilge water. He had also to see that suitable skins were provided to protect the cargo, according to its nature. Silk and linen goods required special care. In a crisis the captain was empowered to raise a loan to obtain anything necessary for the ship. Merchants always accompanied their goods. Consequently passengers had a right to join in any discussion about the jettisoning of cargo, though presumably the final decision was the captain's. They had to deposit their gold and valuables with the captain, who would not otherwise accept any liability for their loss. When the cargo was lost by shipwreck or any other cause the shipowner was liable to pay compensation according to its nature. He was charged one-fifth of the value if it were silver, one-tenth if it were gold, pearls or dry silk, less if the silk were wet. Cargoes of less value, such as corn or oil, carried no such liability. Passengers were entitled to a space not exceeding three cubits by one; women had less. Their daily ration of fresh water was regulated.

Ships were valued at 50 gold pieces (about 750 gold francs) per 1,000 *modii*, the *modius* being apparently a measure of capacity based on the *modius* of corn (6.5 kg), or 30 gold pieces if they were over a certain age. The loss of a ship in the days before marine insurance was therefore a serious matter for its owner. Sea travel was full of perils. Shipwreck was avoided as far as possible by closing the seas from October to March, but both the Black Sea and the Aegean are liable to suffer storms at all seasons. The former has few snug anchorages, and the latter has many dangerous reefs and currents. Wreckers existed in plenty. Pirates were a less constant danger. In the Black Sea they were rare, but the Aegean with its innumerable islands was well suited for them. From 824 to 961 Crete was the headquarters of Saracen pirates. Even the harbours contained thieves who would cut cables and steal anchors. Various precautions were taken against fire. The galley fire was the only fire permitted on board. Passengers were specifically forbidden to fry fish themselves. In view of these dangers investment in shipping was highly speculative, though the rewards of a successful voyage were great. The authorities therefore permitted maritime loans to command a higher rate of interest than was allowed to ordinary loans. Throughout the middle Byzantine period the rate was 16.66 per cent per annum. It is doubtful whether this was high enough to tempt many investors. A removal of the limit would probably have helped Byzantine shipping, especially when competition from the West became keen.

The chief centre for the exchange of goods was Constantinople where, to facilitate supervision, each trade had its own quarter and the conditions of sale were fixed in the regulations of the various gilds. The bazaars of Constantinople were busy at all seasons, though activity lessened during the winter months when the seas were closed and came almost to a standstill when snow blocked the roads in Thrace and Asia Minor. Other towns had their own annual fairs, of which one, the fair of St Demetrius at Thessalonica, was pre-eminent. This opened on 20 October and closed on the first Monday after St Demetrius's Day (26 October). By the eleventh century it was already an annual event and was still flourishing on the eve of the Turkish conquest. During those centuries it was the greatest fair in the Near East. An early twelfth-century satirist describes it as the height of its prosperity.[10a] It took place on the open plain outside the walls, in two long lines of tents with side streets at right angles to them. It was here that most of the silken stuffs of Corinth and Boeotia were exposed for sale, and it was here that the produce of the Balkan countryside found its market, together with skins and salt from the Carpathians. Muslim merchants brought Syrian damasks and Egyptian cotton. Italian merchants came chiefly to buy. All the trade of the Near East was reflected in St Demetrius's Fair. No other town within the Empire held a fair of such dimensions, though the bazaars of Trebizond were full of merchants of all nationalities during the summer months, and Antioch, after its reconquest by the Empire in 969, was the chief meeting-place of Greek and Muslim traders.

IV. *Trade and Industry in the Thirteenth and Fourteenth Centuries: Decline*

Towards the end of the eleventh century Byzantine trade began to undergo drastic changes from which it was never to recover. The Seljuk conquest of the bulk of Asia Minor altered the whole of Byzantine economy by robbing Constantinople of the main source of its corn supply and of much of the solid peasant population which was one of the foundations of its strength. Constant wars in Asia Minor upset its land and even its coastal trade. At the same time the Norman conquest of southern Italy led to piratical raids on the prosperous Greek peninsula and seriously threatened all the European provinces of the Empire. Meanwhile the Italian maritime cities were increasing their merchant fleets and encroaching more and more into eastern markets. Finally, the Seljuks disrupted the pilgrim routes to the East and appeared to threaten all Christendom and this led to an outburst

[10a] *Timarion*, an anonymous imitation of a dialogue by Lucian. See J. H. Tozer, 'Byzantine Satire', *Journal of Hellenic Studies*, II (1883), 235ff.

of religious enthusiasm in western Europe. This emotional upheaval combined with a colonising instinct and Norman ambitions to produce the movement that we call the Crusades, a movement that was to revolutionise the trade of the Levant to the lasting detriment of Byzantium.

In 1082 the Emperor Alexius I, worn out by wars against the Turks in Asia and barbarian invaders in the Balkans, had to meet a Norman attack on Epirus. He was reduced to asking for both naval and financial help from Venice, whose Adriatic policy was equally endangered by Norman aggression. In 1092 Alexius issued a Golden Bull which stated the arrangements for the repayment of this loan. The Venetians were to be free to trade without any interference from customs officials in a list of imperial cities which included every important port, except those in Crete and Cyprus and a few on the Black Sea coast. In other words, while every other merchant, Greek or foreign, had still to pay the 10 per cent duty, the Venetians could export and import goods duty free. They were also to take over the Amalfitan warehouses and establishments within the Empire, Amalfi having by now been engulfed in the Norman kingdom.

Alexius probably did not foresee the results of his action. To excuse the Venetians from paying duty seemed to him to be the easiest way to settle his debt out of revenue, while he thought the stimulus to trade would be useful to Byzantine manufacturers at a time when Byzantium had lost much of its merchant fleet owing to the Turkish and Norman wars. He could not have realised how damaging the concession would be to the rebuilding of his mercantile marine, and this was perhaps because there seemed to be sufficient scope for it in the Black Sea where Russian ships no longer sailed. Trouble soon followed. Alexius's son, John II, and his grandson, Manuel I, each in turn tried to withdraw the concession but had to restore it when Venice took hostile action. Other Italian cities inevitably and forcibly demanded like privileges. In 1111 Alexius reduced the tariff rate for Pisan merchants to 4 per cent and allowed them an establishment in Constantinople. In 1155, under Manuel, the Genoese were given similar terms, and a little later their liability to the 4 per cent duty was restricted to Constantinople alone. In all other ports, with the exception of two on the north coast of the Black Sea, they could trade freely. These two, Rossia and Matracha, were the ports which exported dried fish from the Don and the Caspian. The emperor did not wish to be dependent on foreigners for so important an article of his subjects' diet, to say nothing of his own caviare. The Pisan and Genoese concessions were periodically withdrawn and almost immediately restored.

As a result the carrying trade passed almost entirely into Italian hands. Even the Black Sea trade passed largely into Genoese hands. A large Italian population grew up in Constantinople. In 1180 it was estimated at more than 60,000 souls. At first the Italians lived amongst the local population and intermarried with them; but as they grew more numerous they brought out their own wives and families, and acquired a special position. They were known as *burgesii*, a graecised form of *bourgeois*, and were settled in quárters each with a quay and a church along the Golden Horn, each quarter administered by its own officials. The officials paid homage to the emperor after the western fashion, and the whole community was charged large sums in taxation, often levied quite arbitrarily. Indeed, the treasury was probably well compensated for its loss in tariff revenue by this direct taxation of resident foreign merchants.

The effect of the Crusades on the trade of Byzantium was vast but not immediate. Constantinople was at first on the Crusaders' main route, and their comings and goings, though trying for the Byzantine police, brought new buyers to the city's markets. But the success of the First Crusade resulted in the opening of Syrian ports that had been closed to European traders for five centuries, and so provided a route for oriental goods to reach western Europe without passing through imperial territory. This did not at first make much difference. Italians settled in the Crusaders' cities and encouraged visits from the interior; but the Crusader lords supported themselves in their castles by levying exorbitant tolls on the caravans. Ironically, it was only after the Arab world had been united under Nur ed-Din and Saladin and its trade had revived and expanded, and after the Crusading states had been reduced to the Syrian littoral and the lay lords replaced as the guardians of the frontiers by the Military Orders who liked to dabble in commerce, that the Crusader ports flourished. It is clear from both Venetian and Genoese records that during the twelfth century Alexandria and Constantinople were each far more important to the Italians than all the Crusader ports put together. Owing to movements in central Asia and the growth of the kingdom of Georgia, which reached its zenith under Queen Thamar at the end of the twelfth century, the Far Eastern trade was mainly taking the route through northern Persia to Trebizond. A more immediate effect of the Crusades was to embitter relations between eastern and western Christendom.

In the middle of the twelfth century Constantinople still seemed to be fantastically prosperous. The Jewish traveller, Benjamin of Tudela, who was there in 1166 or 1167, was deeply impressed by its commercial activity and the merchants of many nationalities that he saw in its bazaars, 'from Babylon and Mesopotamia, Media and Persia, Egypt and Palestine, Russia and Hungary, Patzinacia and Bulgaria (the Black Bulgaria of the upper Volga), Lombardy and Spain'. Only Baghdad, he thought, was in any way comparable. He added that the Emperor Manuel derived from Constantinople alone a revenue of 20,000 lbs of gold. A large proportion of this must have come from foreign settlers and merchants.

However, it was soon afterwards that the decay in Byzantine commercial life became obvious. The Emperor Manuel's splendid government had been costly, and the military disasters of his later years used up his resources. Rivalry between the various Italian communities caused endless rioting in the city, damaging store-houses and interrupting trade. The rivalry extended to the seas. Each Italian city maintained a pirate fleet to prey on its neighbours' ships, and all would prey on Greek shipping. Manuel had not been able to afford to keep up a fleet strong enough to curb them. After his death in 1180 the regency of his widow, a Crusader princess, adopted a pro-western policy which so added to the exasperation of the Greeks of Constantinople that in 1182 they overthrew her and began to massacre the Italians in the city. Large numbers perished and their quarters were burnt. The Italian cities demanded heavy compensation and backed their demands by devastating the coasts of the Empire. Before the end of the century their merchants were back again, enjoying all their old privileges. But too much hatred had been aroused and was intensified by the growing mutual mistrust of the Greek and Latin Churches to allow for any stability or confidence. The Venetians who had most to lose determined on sterner action. They could not afford the periodical unfriendliness of the imperial government. They were jealous of the Genoese, whose slightly better relations with Byzantium had enabled them to capture most of the Black Sea trade. They wished to control the whole government of Byzantium; their opportunity came with the Fourth Crusade, when the Crusaders, already in debt to them, agreed to join them in a successful attack on Constantinople. A Latin Empire was set up (1204–61), in which Venice had the lion's share.

The commercial history of the brief Latin Empire is part of the history of Venice. The Greek Succession States followed commercial policies suited to their respective positions. The Nicean emperor, who controlled western Asia Minor, sought to be self-sufficient. The Emperor John Vatatzes (1222–54) for most of his reign forbade all foreign imports and did not encourage exports. His lands did not lie on any of the great trade routes of the time, and they could supply their inhabitants with all the essentials of life. Luxury and extravagance were frowned upon. John only bought his empress a new crown when he could pay for it out of the profits from his poultry-keeping. The emperor of Trebizond, the Grand Comnenus, was better placed for international trade as his capital was still the terminus of the caravan route through northern Persia, a route that grew in importance as the Mongol Empire expanded. By charging low tariff dues on the caravans that entered his territory and on the ships, mostly Genoese, that met the caravans, he stimulated trade and kept himself in affluence and his people prosperous, despite the natural poverty of his land whose only asset was its silver mines. The Despotate of Epirus seems to have enjoyed a prosperous local trade, and the Empire of Thessalonica, set up when the Epirotes ejected the Frankish invaders from the city, though its history was turbulent until it fell into Nicaean hands, remained a busy trading centre: the Fair of St Demetrius was held every year without interruption.

Constantinople was recovered by the Byzantines in 1261, but the restored Empire can scarcely be said to have had any foreign trade. The city had been recaptured with Genoese help, and the Genoese were the main beneficiaries. They were given free access to all Byzantine ports. At Pera, across the Golden Horn, they maintained a station that attracted trade away from Constantinople itself. Owing largely to the Mongol Empire, the Black Sea trade was highly prosperous in the late thirteenth and fourteenth centuries, and the Genoese carried the greater part of it. They had their own colonies at Kaffa and Tana on its northern shore, and they enjoyed preferential treatment in Trebizond. The Venetians were soon allowed to trade free of duty in all imperial ports and had a small colony in Constantinople itself; but these concessions were only granted after the Genoese had had time to establish themselves, so that the Venetians were obliged to play a secondary part. They did so with a bad grace, and there were endless skirmishes between the two great Italian seaports, which were not conducive to peaceful trading. Pisa had fallen out of the running. Her merchants had to pay a 2 per cent duty on all imports and exports to and from the Empire, and the same duty was charged on merchants from other cities with which the Empire had a trade agreement: Florence, Ancona, Narbonne and the Sicilian towns. The Catalans paid 3 per cent. Rates were apparently raised by the Emperor Andronicus III. The Narbonnais were charged 4 per cent, which was now preferential treatment. Pera was the main entrepôt for the oriental goods bought by these merchants for re-export to the West; but the Venetians and Pisans preferred to buy in Constantinople rather than in a Genoese colony. As trade was free across the Golden Horn, prices were the same.

It seems, however, that there was still a considerable Byzantine merchant marine, mainly engaged in cabotage. Foreign ships trading between Byzantine ports had to pay a duty at the port of delivery as though they had been importing goods from abroad. The local trade was therefore not worth their while. Greek ships paid no duty. The corn merchants of Constantinople and Thessalonica by now usually bought their own ships in which to import corn, often from abroad, and sold them at the end of the season. The shipping corporation at Thessalonica in the fourteenth century was an important body, perhaps more important than the corresponding body in Constantinople. This marine lasted till the fall of the Empire. One of the last ships to fight its way into the Golden Horn through the Turkish blockade in 1453 was a Greek merchant ship bringing corn from Sicily. Minor Byzantine ports such as Mesembria or Monemvasia each had their ships for local purposes, but the products of Thrace and the Peloponnese, such as the wine called Malmsey after Monemvasia, were exported in Italian ships. The Empire of Trebizond seems to have had no marine, largely, no doubt, because it lacked a harbour of any size that gave protection from winter storms. Trebizond itself had only an anchorage that is exposed to the north. The semi-independent Despotate of Epirus maintained a small merchant fleet.

The numerous tariff regulations obliged the Empire to employ a large body of customs officials in every port, to discover the nationality of each ship that came in and to assess the value of her cargo. At Pera, and probably also at Constantinople, there was a further series of charges to be paid, taxes on tonnage and measurage. The Byzantine customs officials were strictly supervised and do not seem to have been particularly corrupt. But the elaborate regulations encouraged smuggling by the nationals who had to pay tariffs. The Narbonnais were especially notorious for it.

Before the fourteenth century was out the Ottoman Turks were established on both sides of the Hellespont. Early in the next century they reached the Asiatic shore of the Bosporus and the European shore shortly before they captured Constantinople. Inevitably they used their position to levy tolls on shipping passing through the straits and at times even to close them entirely. The added burden soon became too heavy for the Genoese. But so long as Constantinople remained a Christian city foreign traders still came to the Golden Horn. Its fall ended it all and for a time the Levant was closed to commerce. It was fortunate that European enterprise was soon to discover the ocean route to the Far East.

V. *The Organisation of Trade and Industry: the Book of the Prefect and the Gilds*

To medieval eyes Constantinople had the air of a great industrial city. Travellers were struck by its active industries, by the building work, by the furniture factories and potteries, and by all the other works necessary for a great city's life. The manufacture of luxuries was especially impressive. Of these the silk industry was the most remarkable. Since the earliest days of the Empire vast quantities of raw silk had been imported into the Empire to be made up in Constantinople. After Justinian's day these had been supplemented by an increasing amount of home-grown silk, from worms farmed in or near the capital and in certain of the provinces, especially the Greek peninsula. It seems, however, that the silk grown within the Empire was never sufficient for the demand. Importation continued throughout Byzantine history.[11] In Constantinople the silk was dressed, woven and dyed, and put on the market as finished cloth. Linen was also made up in Constantinople but it seems to have arrived from the flaxfields in Macedonia or Pontus or elsewhere already woven, and only received at the capital the superior dyeing and finish that distinguished it from provincial products. Cotton goods were also finished in Constantinople, but in much smaller quantities. The Byzantines of the capital never troubled much about fine woollen cloth, though coarse woollen cloth was imported in large amounts to clothe the numerous poor. Each family seems to have made up its own woollen garments.

After the silk industry the metal industry was the most renowned. It was even more luxurious. Gold and silver plate were made in considerable but controlled quantities. More elaborate work, cloisonné enamel, Damascene, the carving of semi-precious stones and all jewellers' work, including ivory carving, was in great demand; but the supply was limited owing to the cost of the materials and the highly technical workmanship required. But the cash turnover of the industry must have been enormous. There were also large glass factories, making mosaic tesserae as well as glass for domestic use. The third great industry of the city was the manufacture of armaments. This, for obvious reasons, was a state monopoly. In particular, the secrets of Byzantine chemical warfare were very carefully guarded,

[11] Bury and Andreades believed that by the end of the sixth century Byzantium grew all its own silk. But both the Rhodian Code and the Book of the Prefect (*c.* 900), as well as other casual references, indicate that silk was still imported in very large quantities.

though the manufacture of Greek Fire must have employed a fair number of workmen.

Some of the provinces had their own industries. In Cyprus gold was woven, and the product was much sought after in Constantinople. Samite had been woven in the Greek islands since early times. By the ninth century woollen and linen cloth was made up in the Peloponnese. The widow Danelis of Patras owned a large carpet factory. By the middle of the eleventh century Thebes and Corinth manufactured large quantities of silken cloth, made from locally grown silk. It was not considered as fine as silk made up in the capital. Before the Seljuk conquest various towns in Asia Minor were manufacturing for export the pottery later known as Kutahya ware. There were cloth factories in Thessalonica, and in the later days of the Empire its carpets were famous.

These industries were organised in two main groups, industries run by the state or by individual magnates, and industries run by the gilds. Throughout Byzantine history the emperor was the greatest industrialist in the Empire. The chief silk factory of the Empire was situated within the imperial palace. Silk-worms fed on the emperor's mulberry trees, and their silk, supplemented by imported raw silk, was taken through the various stages of dressing and weaving in different buildings within the precincts. Women workers dealt with the primary stages, and men provided the finishing touches. Certain dyes were set apart for the sole use of this factory. It was only here that the purple murex could be used in full strength; and it seems that only here was it permitted to mix gold and silver thread in with the silk. The finished goods were mainly patterned brocades, over the designs of which great trouble was taken. The best entered the emperor's or the empress's ceremonial wardrobes, or might be sent as gifts to foreign courts. The others included the official uniforms of the upper grades in the court hierarchy or the civil service. Uniforms for the lower grades were apparently bought by the government in the city cloth market. Whether officials had to pay the emperor for their uniforms or received them free is uncertain. Probably they were perquisites of office, as the imperial silk factory was not primarily a profit-making concern. On the contrary, the intention seems rather to have been to prevent the finest products of Byzantium from being launched on the market. By keeping them rare the Emperor raised their value to an enormous height and so enhanced the effect of his gifts. The palace factories had been founded in the early days of Constantinople, when the emperors wished to bring the whole silk industry under their immediate control. Despite popular opposition this control was completely established in Justinian's time, when the high price of raw materials drove private dealers out of business. It proved to be unworkable and seems to have been relaxed during the following century. Thenceforward only the finest silks remained an imperial monopoly. The workers in the palace factories were organised into three imperial or 'public' gilds, the clothiers', the dyers' and the gold embroiderers'. There was a Prefect at the head of each; and general supervision was maintained by an office dependent on the Prefect of the City.

Armaments, as we have seen, were another imperial monopoly, for obvious reasons of state. None were put on to the market and no profit was expected from their manufacture, which took place in the arsenal buildings, close to the imperial palace. The minting of money was similarly an imperial monopoly. Much of the bullion, especially gold, was imported, but much also came from mines within the Empire, which were all the emperor's property. Metal not needed for the arsenal or the mint was sold at a profit. The highest class of jewellery, especially the finest enamel-work, seems, like the best brocades, also to have been produced in the palace factories. But here the regulations were less strict. If the palace was responsible for the best jewelled work, it was because the emperor alone had sufficient capital for such a costly industry.

Labour in the imperial enterprises was servile or semi-servile. The mines were worked by prisoners of war and their descendants or by non-Christian slaves bought in wholesale quantities from northern Europe and the Steppes. The women who worked in the *gynaeceum* seem also to have been tied to their jobs till they were past work. More specialised labour was mostly in the hands of freedmen, though occasionally they might be joined by an able slave. Even the descendants of freedmen were usually required to follow in their fathers' occupation, unless there was a superfluity of labour; and it was sometimes possible to break away by determining to become a priest or a monk.

The emperor was probably the only large employer of labour in Constantinople itself. For political reasons it was thought unwise to allow any private person to manufacture there on more than a petty scale. In the provinces, about which little evidence survives, it seems that industry was almost entirely carried on by magnates using servile labour. In country districts, where markets might be distant and free labour hard to obtain, only someone with capital could get a business going. The parents of St Theophanes the Confessor employed hundreds of slaves on their properties in the Aegean islands in the eighth century; and the century later the widow Danelis had some three thousand slaves working in her carpet factory and her other enterprises. It was probably this dependence of Byzantine provincial industry on individual rich capitalists that made its history so spasmodic. Members of established families could receive permission to make up and sell silk. But the later silk industry of Corinth and Thebes seems to have been on a more co-operative basis and not to have employed slave-labour. The great monasteries had their own individual enterprises, producing wax and oil and, in the case of the monasteries of Mount Athos and Bithynian Olympus, timber. The monks, from Christian sentiment, did not possess slaves; but each monastery had a number of lay servants who worked for very exiguous wages. In the larger provincial cities, such as Thessalonica, there seem to have been both industrial magnates and co-operative gilds.

It was slave-labour that made the chief difference between the enterprises of the industrial magnates and those of the gilds. In Constantinople all the smaller manufacturers were organised into gilds, 'private' gilds, as opposed to the 'public' gilds of workers in the imperial factories. These gilds differed from those of the West, though many of their regulations were almost identical with western gild regulation. But they were not primarily associations created for the mutual self-interest of the members and the preservation of the industry. On the contrary, though they probably descended from similar Roman organisations, they were used in Byzantine times to enable the imperial authorites to exercise control, particularly for fiscal purposes, over every industry in the city. The official in whose department control of the gilds was placed was the prefect of the city. Fortunately the book of regulations issued by Leo VI in about the year 900 for the instruction of his prefect has survived. It does not contain new orders but is a summary of the orders then existing; and it gives the clearest picture that we possess of Constantinople industrial life, though it is unlikely that all the controls that it mentions were continuously put into effect.[12]

Of the industries mentioned in the *Book of the Prefect* the silk industry occupies most space. It was extraordinarily specialised. The raw silk, whether imported from abroad or collected from local farms, was bought by the raw-silk merchants who might not go outside of the city to buy it. Raw silk sold in the market was bought by the merchants co-operatively; each contributed to the fund and received silk in proportion to his contribution; but apparently it was possible

[12] The tendency of modern historians, such as Andreades, Mickwitz and Lopez, is to minimise the strictness of the governmental control and to show the gilds developing more on the lines of those in the West. Certainly the government did not insist on all tradesmen being members of an appropriate gild. But the government's potential control was on a scale unparalleled in the West; and gild regulations were a matter for imperial legislation.

to buy the silk privately from itinerant importers. The raw-silk merchant retailed his silk to authorised buyers, either private persons who made it up at home, or to the raw-silk dressers. He thus seems to have been an unnecessary middleman; but his value to the government was that he paid a small tax on all the silk that he handled, a tax collected through the masters of the gilds.[13] The silk dressers, whose business was to clean, twist, double and wind the silk and, probably, in most cases to weave it, either bought the raw silk collectively as a gild at an agreed price from the raw-silk merchants' gild, or bought individually from individual raw-silk merchants, who might not make a profit of more than 1 *miliaresion* per *nomisma*, that is, 8.33 per cent. The amount that they required had to be registered at the prefect's office; they could not buy where and what they pleased. Above all, no silk dresser could retail any raw silk that he had bought.

There is no mention of any gild of silk weavers or of tailors. The dressers must have been weavers too; and tailoring and the making up of the cloth was done either by the silk dyers or by the silk-stuff merchants, each of whom had their gilds. Much weaving and tailoring was also done by the customers in their homes. There were restrictions on the dyes that might be used and on the cut of the garments, though Leo VI withdrew most of them on the ground that it was unsuitable for an emperor to be an arbiter of fashion; but sufficient safeguards were left to prevent the gilds' products competing in any way with those of the imperial factory. The merchants of silk stuffs simply retailed the finished article. But it was part of their duty to see that foreigners or unauthorised persons did not buy for export silks that were on the list of goods forbidden to leave the country. There was also a gild of *prandiopratai*, merchants who bought foreign finished silk goods, chiefly from Saracen countries, dealing as a gild with the Syrian importers. Syrian residents of ten years' standing, though not members of the gild, could share in its purchases.

Despite all the regulations the relative functions of the gilds were never clearly defined. A silk dyer could buy raw silk from the raw-silk merchant and could apparently retail the finished article, though he was not allowed to be a member of the gild of merchants of silk stuffs. Entrance to a gild usually cost 10 *nomismata*, though the entrance-fee to the dyers was only 3 *nomismata*, and the applicant had to find five members of the gild who would testify to his suitability. The usual punishments for contravening the laws of the gild were flogging, shaving and the confiscation of property. Each craft had to expose its

[13] The text is too corrupt for it to be possible to decipher the rate of taxation.

wares in a fixed place and had to permit thorough inspection by the authorities. It was possible for a slave to become a member of a gild (though not, it seems, of the gild of silk dressers) if his master stood surety for him and provided him with any capital required. Or apparently a master could delegate his authority to a slave who was then responsible for seeing that the regulations were obeyed. These were probably household slaves, as it was assumed that the gildsman employed free labour in the industry. The workman had a monthly contract and could be paid a month in advance. It was strictly forbidden to try to induce a workman to break his contract. There were a few dealers in silk, the *metaxarii*, who were not enrolled in a gild. The state gave them special protection, paid for, no doubt, by special taxes.

The linen merchants' gild, the only other cloth gild mentioned, had similar regulations; but the linen merchants were retailers rather than manufacturers. Of the other gilds mentioned in the *Book of the Prefect*, the most important in the eyes of the authorities were those of the dealers in bullion and the bankers. The former included jewellers, goldsmiths and money-lenders. They were not only obliged to provide small change for *nomismata* on market days but also made valuations. It was their business to see that precious metals were not sold to foreigners for export; and they themselves could not buy for any purpose more than one pound of gold at a time. The rates for lending money were strictly fixed. The dealers in bullion were allowed to charge an interest fixed in Justinian's day at 8 per cent, while the private money-lender could only charge 6 per cent. But by the ninth century 6 per cent had been altered to 6 *nomismata* per lb of gold, that is to say 8.33 per cent and the gildsmen's 8 per cent rose correspondingly to 8 *nomismata* per lb, or 11.11 per cent. The function of the bankers' gild is unclear. In Justinian's time the name *trapezitai* was given to the official cashiers in the public service; and the *Book of the Prefect* assigns to the dealers in bullion the work that one would expect bankers to perform and allots no specific duties to the *trapezitai*.

The position of the notaries' gild is a matter for legal rather than economic history. But we may note in passing that a notary was required to pay to his clerk a salary fixed at one-twelfth of his earnings, whatever they might be. The other gilds were all concerned with the daily necessities of life. The perfumers sold scents and dyes but also the spices that were an essential part of medieval diet. It was laid down that they might only sell goods bought by scale as opposed to goods bought by steelyard, which were the grocers' business. There had been an apothecaries' gild, but before the tenth century it had been absorbed into the perfumers'. Most of the other goods were bought from importers and, to facilitate inspection, the transactions could only take place on certain fixed days. The wax chandlers and the soap chandlers formed two separate gilds. The former bought their raw materials mainly from abroad but also from the great monasteries, and made them up into candles. They also dealt in lamp oil. The soap chandlers who were concerned solely with the making of soap, seem to have had the highest entrance fee of any of the gilds, 6 *nomismata* payable to the imperial treasury and 6 more to the imperial *vestiarius*. The leather trade had three gilds, the pelters', who prepared the raw skins, the tanners' and the saddlers', who sold the finished leather. The leather gilds could be called upon to work for the emperor when required for whatever remuneration he might choose to bestow on them. This was owing to the importance of leather in making the armaments of the time.

Of the gilds dealing with foodstuffs the grocers' was the largest. The goods that they were empowered to sell included, beside regular groceries, greengrocery, poultry, salt fish, earthenware, bottles and nails, all of them goods sold by steelyard. Grocery was a profitable business; the grocers were allowed to make a profit of 2 *miliaresia* per *nomisma*, that is to say 16.66 per cent. The butchers and the pork butchers had separate gilds. The former dealt in beef and mutton. They were urged to go and meet the herds of sheep driven in from Asia Minor at some point beyond the river Sangarius, so as to buy them cheaper, rather than wait for them at towns nearer to the capital such as Nicomedia. Sheep-owners who brought sheep themselves to Constantinople had to sell them at fixed prices and in fixed places, sheep and lambs separately, and pay a tax on each,[14] or to sell to certain authorised butchers. Cattle, too, seem to have been bought outside of the capital. Government officials had to be present at the slaughter of cattle, one beast in each lot being cut up before their eyes. Pork butchers on the other hand had to buy their swine in Constantinople, in the market square of the Bull. The fishmongers, who were apparently more numerous, fish when in season being a major article of diet in Constantinople, sold their fish at several markets in the city. They could buy it from the fishermen only on the quays or from boats at anchor. They were forbidden to deal in salt fish. The bakers' gild had special rights. So important was it to the welfare of the city that no member could be called upon to perform any public service. The bakers bought corn and ground it themselves. They were allowed to make a profit of one *keration* and 2 *miliaresia* per *nomisma*, the 2 *miliaresia* being calculated to be the cost of labour

[14] The rate of the tax is not clearly stated

and the *keration* the net profit, just over 4 per cent. Bakeries had to be built of stone to minimise the risk of fire. The innkeepers also had a gild. They were the only accredited wine merchants, but the wine did not have to be consumed on the premises. Closing time was at 8 p.m. All the gilds dealing with comestibles were liable to severe penalties if convicted of hoarding against times of scarcity. But non-perishable foodstuffs, such as dried fish, might not be sold to persons leaving the city.

There was also a gild of *bothri*, agents who disposed of remainders of all sorts of livestock. Very often there would be more beasts for sale than the butchers required; the *bothri* could then sell them to private individuals.

The *Book of the Prefect* also provides regulations for building contractors and specialised members of the building industry, such as carpenters, masons, locksmiths and house-painters, though none of them seemed to have formed a gild. The contractor was usually, but not invariably, a master-builder himself. Builders were not allowed to take on another job if they were already engaged on one. Contracts could not be altered except after a valuation conducted by the prefect's officials. A stone house that fell within ten years had to be rebuilt at the contractor's expense, unless the cause was an act of God. If the house was built of mud bricks the contractor's liability lasted for six years.

Most of the gilds occupied specific quarters in the city, mainly along the great Middle Street that ran from the imperial palace to the church of the Holy Apostles. The butchers and the fishmongers had their own special markets. The grocers, however, for the convenience of the public, were scattered throughout the city, and the same was presumably true of the bakers. The perfumers' gild was stationed close to the bronze gate of the palace, so that the pleasant scent should be wafted up to the great icon of Our Lord that was carved over the gate. On the other hand, travellers reported that the stench which came from the pelters' and tanners' quarter was so foul that no respectable person could live nearby. The concentration of each trade in a particular district naturally facilitated the supervision exercised by the prefect's officials. This supervision was often minute. When prices and profits were not specified in the articles of the gild the prefect could fix them according to the circumstances of the moment. All weights and measures had to bear the prefect's seal and were periodically tested. All cases of broken contract or complaints of bad behaviour between employer and employee came not before any gild court but before the prefect's bureau, as did disputes between vendor and customer. The prefect had also to see that regulations of a religious nature affecting the gilds were obeyed. Sunday closing was ordained; but, to judge from the frequency with which the order was repeated, the rule must often have been broken. Even in the early fourteenth century we find the Emperor Andronicus II trying to reimpose it. Business was to stop also on major feast days. On Sundays and feast days taverns might not open before 8 a.m. The soap chandlers were forbidden to use animal fats during Lent or on other fast days. The dealers in bullion had to report on the sale of any sacred object, in an attempt to prevent the dispersal of holy relics out of the Empire. The smuggling of such objects was highly profitable, as western European potentates and churches would pay enormous prices for the relics of any early Christian saint.

Little is known about the officials of the gilds. The head of the notaries, the *primicerius*, was a personage high in the imperial hierarchy. It seems that there was an official at the head of all the silk gilds, but casual references to him confuse him with the superintendent of the imperial silk factory. The *prandiopratai* had an *exarch* at their head. The raw-silk merchants had more than one *exarch*, doubtless because of their greater numbers. The pelters, tanners and saddlers were each headed by a *prostates*. The fishmongers had a *prostates* in command of each fish-market. The pork butchers had a *protostates* and the innkeepers a *proestotes*, the terms being probably variants of *prostates*. No mention is made of heads of any other gild; but they presumably existed. The *exarchs* enjoyed a higher rank than the *prostatai*. Probably all the cloth gilds had an *exarch* and the provision gilds a *prostates*. These officials were certainly appointed by the prefect, probably on the recommendation of the gildsmen, but such salaries as they received were obtained from the gild. The prefect himself employed two ranks of superior inspectors, the *episkeptetai* and the *epoptai*, and lesser officials, the *bullotai*, whose duty was to stamp and inspect weights and measures. In official tables of precedence the first two ranked above the *exarchs* and the *bullotai* between the *exarchs* and the *prostatai*. At the head of the prefect's commercial bureau was the *symponus*, or assessor, sometimes called the *legatarius*. He kept the register of all imports and exports and was in charge of the customs. It was also for him to see that no foreign or provincial merchants stayed for more than three months in the capital. Each gild seems to have had its own *symponus*, who was probably the representative of the chief *symponus*.

It is uncertain whether there were definite regulations about apprenticeship. Apprentices certainly existed, as we know from casual references, but there is no mention of fixed rules or time limits for their services. Though Diocletian's law forcing a son to follow his father's trade had necessarily been relaxed, it was apparently usual for at least one son in the family to continue in the family business. This provided an automatic solution for much of the problem of apprentices. The question of labour in the various crafts is equally obscure. As we have seen, in the silk trade it is assumed that the manufacturer or dealer employs one or more free workmen on a monthly contract, and that the bakers also employ labour. Smaller concerns were probably family affairs. But the whole question is cut across by the question of slavery. Throughout the Byzantine period there was a growing sentiment, fostered by the Church, for the lessening and even the abolition of slavery. But slaves in private households existed to the last in Byzantium, though by the twelfth century they were rare and were almost entirely prisoners of war. Household slaves ranked higher than state-owned slaves, and if they misbehaved the usual punishment was to send them to join the latter. A manufacturer or merchant who owned slaves could presumably employ them in his business; and, as we have seen, a slave could, at least in the cloth trade, have an establishment of his own. In this case he was financed by his master, to whom he paid a regular proportion of his profits; in the end he might purchase his freedom out of his savings. The process represented one of the few ways in which a rich Byzantine could usefully employ surplus capital. A large number of the artisans in Constantinople were women, a fact that was particularly noted by foreign travellers. At first most of these women, in particular those employed in the imperial workshops, were tied to the job with no hope of escape from it; a man who married any of them was reduced to the same servile condition, as were the children of the marriage. This rule, which dates from Justinian's time, seems to have been gradually relaxed. By the twelfth century the imperial factories probably used mainly free labour. Indeed, by the ninth century we hear of work-people seeking admission into the imperial factories because of the security that it offered.

Of the other trades that flourished in Constantinople, such as that of ship-chandler (the Emperor Michael V was a ship-chandler's son) or undertaker or fisherman, too little is known for us to be able to describe their organisations. Fishermen, ship-owners and sailors could all be called upon to perform public duties in an emergency.

There was no unemployment. The demand for goods remained more or less constant, and most trades catered only for the local market and so were little subject to fluctuation. If any able-bodied men were found to be out of work they were put by the prefect under the *quaestor*, who gave them employment in the state bakeries or the market gardens that supplied the charitable institutions of the city. 'Idleness', wrote Emperor Leo III in the *Ecloga*, 'leads to crime, and any superfluity resulting from the labour of others should be given to the weak, not the strong.' Occasionally a bad harvest caused a shortage of corn and hence distress among the poor. At such times the prefect intervened to keep prices down and supplies were supplemented out of the stores kept by the government against emergencies. When Nicephorus II made use of a shortage to corner the whole wheat supply of the Empire and sell it at a profit to the bakers' gild, everyone was deeply shocked. The infirm poor were cared for in great charitable institutions, some of which were founded by emperors or great personages who provided them with ample endowments in property and issued strict rules for their governance, and were thenceforward controlled by the state; others were organised and run by the monasteries. The monasteries with their growing hoards of wealth have earned a bad name amongst the economic historians of Byzantium; but in fact they performed several useful functions. They provided education for children of all classes, they ran hospitals and they provided refuges for the elderly. The Byzantine official or business man might earn a good income, but there was nowhere for him easily to invest his savings. When he retired, he, or his widow when he died, might find themselves a drag on the community. The monasteries provided homes for such people where they could give themselves over to devotion or where they could have the leisure for intellectual studies or for useful open-air pursuits such as gardening. Thus monastic institutions played a valuable part in the Byzantine social economy. For a rich man there was an alternative form of insurance against old age. He could buy a title. The price varied according to the rank, but each title commanded a yearly salary averaging $2\frac{1}{2}$ per cent of the original cost.

Owing chiefly to governmental regulations about rates of interest, no one seems to have made a fortune out of any form of trade in the capital, though an enterprising trader could make a comfortable living so long as he stayed in business; but his death might leave his dependants destitute. In the provincial cities the supervision was less exact. In ports, such as Thessalonica, the local prefect saw to customs business and registered exports and imports, and there was probably an attempt to keep prices fixed. But there was no organised gild system as in the capital. When later, about the late thirteenth century, trade corporations appeared they were bodies founded by the tradesmen themselves in self-defence against the magnates. In consequence, society in Thessalonica became more complicated than in Constantinople. Beside the land-owing nobility there developed a rich bourgeoisie of merchant magnates and ship-owners who were at permanent enmity with the small shop-keepers and the artisans and eventually provoked them into the strange democratic movement known as the Revolt of the Zealots, which is more closely paralleled by movements in western Europe than by anything in Constantinople. There was a general trend in favour of municipal self-government noticeable in all the provincial cities of the later Byzantine Empire. The details are very obscure. In many cases the city fell under the power of the local nobility, who provided some constituted authority in control of prices and local taxation.

The great fortunes of Byzantium were made in the provinces, or in the government service, many posts in which were very highly paid.[15] The Melisseni, the first great Byzantine family to arise and the last to disappear, probably derived their fortune from property in Constantinople and for that reason remained eminent for some six centuries. But they were exceptional. Till the ninth century there was no part of the imperial countryside free from the periodical devastation of foreign armies or rebellious tribes. But once land became a safe investment, enterprising land-owners, like the Peloponnesian widow Danelis, founded industries on their estates, or, like the Cappadocian Philaretes, indulged personally in large-scale farming. In troubled times land might be bought cheap and far-sighted investors would be rewarded. Most of the wealthy families of tenth and eleventh century Byzantium were descended from some successful soldier or government official who had either been given a grant of government land by the grateful emperor, or who had invested part of his salary in land. Under careful management rents and local industries would soon enhance the value of the estate. Less scrupulous officials had further opportunities for making money; but they, too, in view of the restrictions on profit, invested their ill-gotten gains in land rather than entrusting them to a commercial enterprise. Land was not always obtainable, however; and the land hunger on the part of the magnates was one of the problems that most worried the imperial government. The failure to solve it was disastrous to the Empire. But a solution by means of providing alternative facilities for investment was unthinkable at the time. In consequence few fortunes, except for those invested in land, lasted for more than one generation. Even when a rich man owned servile shopkeepers, his piety usually made him free them on his death. The fluidity of private capital was reflected in the social organisation of the Empire. In direct contrast with western Europe the

[15] The largest private fortune recorded in Byzantium was that of Archbishop Theophanes of Thessalonica, a man famed for avarice, who in 1038 was found to have 3,300 lbs of gold in his treasury, mainly obtained by the dishonest use of church funds. Five years later the Patriarch Alexius of Constantinople, an equally unscrupulous cleric, left 2,500 lbs of gold. Both fortunes were confiscated by the state.

aristocracy remained open to any wealthy newcomer, and the connection between the nobility and commerce was never broken in Constantinople, though in the provinces in the later centuries, in towns such as Thessalonica and Trebizond, and particularly in districts that had been subject to Frankish influence, land-owning families with a tradition of culture behind them began to despise the *nouveau riche* bourgeoisie.

VI. *The Coinage, Prices and Taxation*

The merchant Cosmas Indicopleustes, writing in the sixth century, declared that the prosperity of the Empire was due to two causes, Christianity and the coinage. It is to be hoped that Christianity brings its reward on earth, but there is no doubt of the value of a good coinage. Constantine the Great had established the lb of gold as the basis of the coinage. The *nomisma*, or gold piece, which was originally called the *solidus* and after the thirteenth century the *hyperpyron*, was fixed at the rate of 72 to the lb. The silver and bronze coinage had at first been variable, but about the year 500 Anastasius divided the *nomisma* into 12 *miliaresia* or 24 *keratia*, and the *miliaresion* was divided into 12 *pholles*. Silver coins were related in a fixed ratio to the gold, a silver lb being valued at 5 *nomismata*, a ratio that did not need to be altered till the later Middle Ages. The *nomisma* contained a quantity of gold to the value roughly of 15 gold francs, with a fineness of theoretically 24 carats. Existing examples are all just slightly below these theoretical figures, and weights are between 4.30 and 4.32 grams. The government tried to maintain a good reserve of gold, largely in order to control prices by regulating the amount of currency that it issued. The Byzantines were well aware of the value of their coinage. Historians who wished to blacken an emperor's reputation were apt to accuse him of trying to debase it. Nicephorus II was attacked for having introduced a light-weight *nomisma*, the *tetarteron*; but it seems that the intention of the *tetarteron* was to provide the provinces newly conquered from the Saracens with a coin equivalent in value to the Saracen dinar to which they were used.[16]

Debasement began in the extravagant reign of Constantine IX. He issued five types of *nomismata* and two of *tetartera*, each with diminishing real value. His successors, Theodora, Michael VI, Isaac I and Constantine X, seem to have maintained the *nomisma* at Constantine

[16] This is Grierson's interpretation in his 'Nomisma, tétartèron et dinar', which seems preferable to Lopez's view in his 'La crise du besant au Xe siècle'. See bibliography for both articles; also article by H. Ahrweiler, 'Nouvelle hypothèse sur le tétartèron..', *Zbornik de l'institute byzantin de l'Académie Serbe*, VIII (1963).

IX's lowest level, about 18 carats, and 17 carats for the *tetarteron*. Under Romanus IV there was another slight fall, with the added disadvantage that coins of the same issue varied in content. The fall was accelerated under Michael VII and reached a low level of 8 carats for the *nomisma* under Nicephorus III, when the *tetarteron* disappeared.[17] His successor Alexius I Comnenus tried to restore the position, calling in the debased coinage; but he was driven by financial needs to issue *nomismata*, partly of brass, or two-thirds of the value of the gold *nomisma*. He insisted on taxes being paid in gold *nomismata*, while he paid governmental expenses in the debased coin. He succeeded in rebuilding a gold reserve, but insufficiently for him to restore the coinage. Fiscal calculations continued to be made on the assumption that the *nomisma* was still worth 72 to the lb of gold, but it never recovered its old value. The debased coins passed into general circulation; and foreign creditors usually insisted on being paid in *michaelata*, the coins of Michael IV, the last to contain the proper amount of gold.[18]

The *nomisma*, or *hyperpyron* as it usually came to be called,[19] fell slowly at first. At the time of the First Crusade it could be exchanged for 15 silver sous of the Franks. In 1156 the Genoese valued it at 10 of their silver sous, and at $9\frac{1}{2}$ in 1157. In 1204 it could be exchanged for 3 English sous, about 14.60 gold francs; but the English sou was not easily exchangeable in the Levant and was cheaper than its metallic value. In 1228 the Venetians gave the *hyperpyron* of the Nicaean emperors a value equivalent to 11.81 gold francs, but in 1250 it was rated considerably higher in relation to the currency of the French monarchy. This was because the Nicaeans had been selling agricultural produce to the Turks in return for gold. Actually at the time it had 16 carats and ought to have been valued a little lower. In 1261 the *hyperpyron* had 15 carats, and 14 in 1282. By 1310 it had 12 carats and 12 alloy, and the fall was continuing. By the mid-fourteenth century traders, even in Constantinople itself, preferred to use Venetian or Genoese ducats, as the *hyperpyron* had lost its international credit.

Of the purchasing power of money in Byzantine times and the general level of prices it is difficult to speak with confidence. The price of wheat in 960, before Nicephorus II speculated in the corn market, was 3 *keratia* per *modius*, which was roughly the same as that in Greece in July 1914. Other foodstuffs were probably five or six times less expensive than in 1914. In about 950 a pair of oxen cost 8 *nomismata* in Constantinople, about 6 times cheaper than in 1914; and horses

[17] See the tables given by Grierson in his 'The debasement of the bezant in the eleventh century'.

[18] *Michaelata* are usually assumed to be the coins of Michael VII; but as these were already debased, they must be the coins of Michael IV. None were issued in the brief reign of Michael V.

[19] The word *hyperpyron* is loosely used, but usually means the *nomisma*.

were about 4.5 times cheaper. Silk on the other hand was costly and considered to be literally worth its weight in gold. It seems that prices had been lower up till the end of the seventh century. In the eighth century, under the Isaurians, there was an increase in monetary stock, which raised the price level. Nicephorus I in the early ninth century checked a further rise by reducing the amount of money in circulation; and prices seem to have remained much the same till the end of the eleventh century, when political disasters, the devaluation of the coinage and the growing impact of Italian currencies, began to make their effect. By the fourteenth century corn cost about twice as much as in the tenth century. This was largely due to the fact that the corn fields of Asia Minor were now in the hands of the Turks.

The cost of living in Byzantium was enhanced by the heavy taxation, far heavier than in any other contemporary country. Country communities had to pay the *epibole*.[20] For town-dwellers there was the *kapnikon*, a hearth tax which was rated at 2 *miliaresia* per head in the early ninth century but was certainly increased later. There was a capitation tax, the *kephaletion*, but it seems to have been charged only on non-Christians and foreigners. There was a tax called the *aerikon*, introduced by Justinian and still existing in the ninth century, which was perhaps a tax on town property.[21] Augustus had introduced a system of death duties on property inherited from a collateral or a friend. Justinian repealed it; but at some time it was re-introduced to include direct inheritance also. Nicephorus I evolved a tax on unearned increment on the ground that it ranked as treasure trove and so the state should have a share in it. But it proved difficult to assess and to collect and was soon abandoned. Indirect taxation consisted of the various tolls, import and export duties, market dues and harbour dues, registration fees, and, for a time, a stamp duty on receipts. Tax collecting was efficient; evasion was almost impossible. The tax collectors were reputable government officials who were carefully supervised so as to prevent corruption. They were not unnaturally an unpopular class but, as far as we can tell, seldom corruptible, though they were sometimes accused of raising assessments in order to enlarge their commissions. There was, however, in the later Empire a growing tendency to introduce tax-farming and to reduce the employment of collectors directly dependent on the state. By the twelfth century, after

[20] The villages were taxed as communities, and the *allelengyon*, introduced by Basil II, obliged the wealthier members to make up any deficiencies due to the poverty of the peasants. The *allelengyon* was repealed by Romanus III. In some more primitive districts taxes were paid in kind. An attempt to make the Bulgarian peasants pay taxes in money sparked off the Bulgarian revolt of 1040.

[21] The *aerikon* has been interpreted differently by every historian of Byzantium. No interpretation is entirely satisfactory.

the disorganisation caused by the Turkish invasions, this became general in the provinces. This undoubtedly increased the chances of extortion. Already the customs dues on certain commodities had been farmed out from time to time to imperial officials or favourites. There seems to have been little objection to this, unless the farmers sacrificed the welfare of the trade to their own interests, as when Leo VI's friends who were farming the customs dues on the Bulgarian trade diverted it to suit their convenience from Constantinople to Thessalonica. In times of crisis an emperor could charge a supertax, such as the *dikeraton*, an extra twelfth on the *kapnikon* raised by Leo III to pay for the repair of the city walls; or he might add to his revenue by exacting forced loans from his subjects; and the usual punishment for disgraced officials included the confiscation of their property. On the other hand, emperors freely disbursed large sums of gold, as well as of land, to favoured officials; and gold was constantly sent out as subsidies to foreign or vassal potentates.

VII. *Conclusion*

There are many aspects of Byzantine economy that remain unknown to us owing to the inadequacy of the sources. Published laws and administrative manuals provide some details. Lives of the saints and a few biographical sketches embodied in funeral orations tell us something of the social life of the Empire. But Byzantine historians took very little interest in economic affairs in comparison with ecclesiastical affairs and personal politics. Moreover, especially from the late tenth century onwards, they were nearly all conscious stylists who disliked having to use technical terms for which they could not find an elegant classical equivalent. In consequence their descriptions of economic questions are vague and often misleading. This objection was purely intellectual. Every Byzantine had a proper respect for industry and commerce. Pride in his family origins never kept him from wishing to enrich himself however best he could. Even amongst the landed nobility of late Byzantine times there was seldom any of the arrogant contempt for trade that characterised the feudal houses of the West. Money-making was always a highly respectable preoccupation.

The general picture of Byzantine economic life shows a paternalist state with no idea of a fully planned economy but with the legal right, often but by no means regularly exercised, to interfere in every detail of its subjects' lives. Its main faults were an arbitrary readiness to sacrifice the long-term interests of the Empire for immediate gains or for purely political ends, a taxation so high as often to be crippling in its effects, and the failure to provide any useful provision for the investment of capital. Its main assets were an outlook which was for its time enlightened and unprejudiced, a genuine care for the welfare of the old and the unfortunate, a determination that lasted for seven centuries to maintain a sound currency, and the possession of a superbly placed administrative and commercial centre in Constantinople.

CHAPTER IV

The Trade of Medieval Europe: the North

I. *The Trade in General*

(1) COMMODITIES

The international and inter-regional trade of northern Europe and its principal industries bear little resemblance to the conventional image of medieval economy. The traffic across the continent of western Europe, or between the European mainland and the lands immediately to the north and to the north-east, evokes in a modern reader none of that romance which clings to the trade of southern Europe. The latter brought to western Europe exotic goods of every kind: pepper, ginger and other spices of the East Indies, silks, brocades and tapestries, sweet wines, oranges, raisins, figs and almonds. It enticed the merchant into the mysterious lands of the Near and Middle East, to Byzantium and Syria, often to Africa, and sometimes even to China. It was also the trade of the caravans, the galleys, the junks; and of the Venetian, Genoese and Florentine adventurers and merchant princes. This was the medieval trade as popular writers know it, and this is the trade which some serious writers have in mind when they insist on the luxury character of medieval commerce.

The trade of northern Europe was quite different. It was not greatly concerned with oriental and Mediterranean commodities. At various times between the sixth century and the tenth, traders and warriors brought goods from the extreme north of Europe to Byzantium and re-imported Byzantine goods into northern Europe. Much more frequently the Italian merchants of the later centuries sailed into the harbours of England and Flanders, bringing with them all the infinite variety of Levantine and oriental products. Still more regularly – in fact throughout the Middle Ages – Italian merchants and the men of the north, Germans, Flemings, English and French, mingled in the great international marts of central and northern Europe: in Champagne during the twelfth and thirteenth centuries, in Bruges in the fourteenth and the early fifteenth centuries, in Geneva, Antwerp and Bergen-op-Zoom in the fifteenth; and there exchanged the Italian and the Italian-borne products for other goods.

Yet generally speaking, in the economic life of northern Europe these contacts were of secondary importance. The main currents of trade across northern Europe and between northern Europe and other countries flowed with products of the northern hemisphere, cruder, bulkier and altogether more indispensable than the luxuries and the fineries of the text-book convention. This convention is not altogether true even of the south, for foodstuffs or raw materials also entered into the trade of the Mediterranean region. Nevertheless, what gave the southern trade its peculiar character was not the trade in the bulky essentials, but those luxury trades which we associate with it. By contrast, the trade of northern Europe was almost exclusively devoted to the necessities of life.

Of the luxuries originating in the North and circulating in northern Europe furs were probably the only one worth noting. Modest furs of local origin – the 'conies' of England, the Low Countries and France, the goatskins and the sheepskins of peasant wear, could perhaps be counted among the modest pre-requisites of humble existences. Not so the rare and rich furs of Scandinavian and Russian origins – fox, bear, beaver, sable, ermine. They were ceremonial wares, an insignia of wealth and standing; they rivalled the senatorial purple in the early Middle Ages, the Italian brocades and oriental silks in the later centuries, as marks of rank and worth. And so important did they become in European trade that by the end of the thirteenth century they formed one of the mainstays of Hanseatic commerce and wealth.

Furs, nevertheless, were something of an exception, for the main articles of northern trade were bulkier and cheaper necessities of life. Its main, and certainly the most permanent, branch was traffic in food. The very conditions of Germanic settlement in north-western Europe made it inevitable that some areas should early in their history have come to depend on food imports. Throughout the Middle Ages large portions of Scandinavia could not grow on the spot all the food they needed. Ever since the early days of the great migrations, a relatively large population settled in the water-logged and sandy lands of the estuary of the Rhine – the Frisian country of the seventh-century nomenclature – which could not raise crops large enough to feed their population in normal years. Later in the Middle Ages, i.e. from the middle of the twelfth century onwards, the regions of the north-western littoral, Flanders, Brabant and Holland, maintained an industrial population which they could not feed out of their own agricultural production. In the words of a late fifteenth-century description, the Dutch of that time still largely subsisted on dairy produce, birds and fishes. Further south and west, on the Atlantic coast of France, lay the rich lands of Gascony which specialised in wine and had to bring in some of their food from outside.[1]

What made it possible for these needs to be covered was that side by side with the regions deficient in foodstuffs there were to be found regions with exportable surpluses of food. It is doubtful whether the estuary of the Rhine before the ninth century and the flourishing areas of Flanders and the Netherlands in later centuries could ever have fed themselves had not rich grain-growing areas existed at their very backdoors. In the early Middle Ages grain came down the Rhine from the rich agricultural areas served by the upper reaches of the river. In the later centuries some grain came from the agricultural areas bordering on German Rhineland (Guelders, Jülich and Cleves), but the bulk came from northern France. The valleys of the Somme and the Seine were the granaries of northern Europe. The agricultural surpluses of the lower Seine went mainly to the south, to feed Paris. But the wheat of the rich loam lands of Santerre, Vermandois and Cambresis, went not only by the Oise to Paris, but along the Scheldt to Flanders and along the Somme to Rouen and overseas. Amiens, Abbeville and St Valéry became the *foci* of grain trade between France and the Low Countries, and the trade continued till the very end of the fifteenth century. Throughout the earlier Middle Ages, but more especially in the thirteenth century, England was an exporter of foodstuffs, including grain. Later still, another and much more important source of grain appeared. As a result of German colonisation of the Slavonic lands beyond the Elbe vast new agricultural resources were opened up, and from the end of the thirteenth century onwards east German and Polish rye flowed to the West. By the beginning of the fourteenth century Baltic grain began to contribute to the Flemish food supplies, and by that time also it ousted English grain from Scandinavian markets.[2]

Grain, however, was only one of the essential foodstuffs carried across the continent and the seas of northern Europe. The history of European dairy farming and milk trade is a somewhat neglected topic of economic history, but the importance of butter and cheese as articles of international commerce is now beyond doubt. There are apparently several regions of specialised butter production whence butter was exported to other countries: Holland, Scandinavia, southern Poland, and to a smaller extent England. In historical records of the late thirteenth and fourteenth centuries butter appeared so suddenly as to suggest to some historians that there was a sudden change of diet

[1] Quoted in J. E. Niermeyer, *De wording van onze volkshuishouding* (The Hague, 1946), 34.
[2] W. S. Unger, 'De Hollandsche graanhandel en graanhandelspolitiek in de middeleeuwen', *De Economist* (1916). Also Z. W. Sneller in *Bijdragen tot de Vaterlands. Gesch*, VI, 2 (1925).

among the inhabitants of northern Europe as a result of which oil was displaced by butter. In England, however, the high-water mark of the dairying industry is in the years around 1300 – a time when the earls of Lancaster pastured vast herds of cows on their *vaccaries* in Lancashire and Yorkshire, and when Ipswich, Boston and Lynn exported butter and cheese by the ton.

Even more important was fish, for the consumption of fish in the Middle Ages was high, and sea fisheries were many. Some fish was caught in and off all the estuaries of Europe and along its sea coasts. In the early Middle Ages the fishermen of Brittany and Normandy may even have brought in the flesh of whales and seals. But great international fishing grounds were relatively few. One such fishing ground was largely exploited by English fishermen: it was the herring fisheries off the coasts of Norfolk and south Lincolnshire. Its centres, and especially Yarmouth and its fishing suburb of Gorleston, became famous as the home of England's herring, though it is doubtful whether the red herring of Yarmouth, so important in the food supplies of England, ever figured prominently in international commerce. More international was the Scandinavian fishing industry, that of the white herring and the stockfish. From Norway the art of 'white' curing or salting spread to other countries, and it was very largely from Iceland that the bulk of medieval supplies of stockfish came. Further south, the estuary of the Rhine formed throughout the Middle Ages another centre of the fishing industry. In the sixth and seventh centuries much herring must have been fished by the Frisians in their estuary waters and exported from there all over north-western Europe. But throughout the greater part of the Middle Ages, and certainly from the thirteenth century onwards, by far the most important of the fishing grounds of Europe and also the busiest centre of the curing industry and of the herring trade were the Baltic fisheries of Skania off the south coast of what is now Sweden. It rose to prominence at the turn of the thirteenth and fourteenth centuries, and as late as 1537 more than 90,000 tons were still salted there. By that time, however, the herring fisheries off the coasts of the northern Netherlands, modern Holland, had risen to rival those of Skania as the main source of fish supplies.

It would not be difficult to catalogue a whole list of other staple foodstuffs which entered the international trade of north European countries. In the twelfth and thirteenth centuries England exported bacon from her eastern counties, largely from Ipswich. Throughout the later Middle Ages vegetables, especially very large quantities of cabbages, garlic, onions and onion seed, regularly came from France and the Low Countries, and apples – the pippins of Normandy – from

Norman ports. Towards the close of the Middle Ages hops and beer began to come in from Holland and west Germany. Indeed so important had become the beer traffic that historians have sometimes ranked it among the primary causes of Holland's rise in the fifteenth century.

Nevertheless, with the exception of grain and fish, no other comestible product was more indispensable to medieval diet, or was carried in larger quantities than wine. Large quantities of wine were apparently drunk in northern Europe as well as in the growing areas of France and Germany. In the eleventh-century *Colloquium of Alfric*, Alfric did not drink wine because he was not rich enough to buy it. Four centuries later, on the morrow of thc battle of Agincourt, Henry V would not allow his soldiers to celebrate on the heavy wines of Champagne, for they had been brought up on ale and beer and were not used to strong wines. But men of all stations above the lowest drank it in large and, as far as England goes, increasing quantities.

The significance of wine in international trade was not only in the quantities in which it was drunk, but also in the conditions under which it came to be produced. In the course of centuries the commercial production of wine, once widespread over the face of Europe, gradually concentrated in regions of highly specialised viticulture. There had once been vineyards in what would now be regarded as most unpropitious parts of England and the Low Countries. In France itself wine of some repute was grown everywhere. But by degrees the wines of three or four areas – Poitou, Gascony, Burgundy (Auxerrois) and the Moselle – all of them seats of flourishing viticulture since the days of Rome, rose to dominate the international demand. In a thirteenth-century *fabliau* narrating the combat of wines an English priest is made to pass in review some thirty or forty regional vintages. Having excommunicated a dozen or so of unworthy wines he leaves the field of battle to the northern vintages of Argenteuil, Meulent, Auxerre, Soissons, Épernay, the various wines of Guyenne and Limousin, and above all, the wines of Angoulême, Saintes, Bordeaux and Poitou. The prize goes to what were undeniably the most highly valued of medieval wines, the sweet wines of Cyprus, and the troubadour himself shows a true gift of prophecy in preferring the white wines of Chablis and Beaune. But the wine most generally drunk 'all over England, among Bretons, Flemings, Normans, Scots, Irish, Norwegians and Danes and bringing in return good sterling is the wine of La Rochelle.

Had the *fabliau* been written a century or so later, it would not only have excluded from the list a number of local vintages, but would also have placed La Rochelle as a source of sterling-earning wine in a second place after Gascony. By the beginning of the fourteenth century these two regions had come to supply the bulk of wine entering into international trade. But whereas the products of Poitou and La Rochelle went mostly to other parts of France and to the Low Countries, the clarets of Gascony went mostly to England, forming a close and continuous link between the two countries.

As a result of the wine trade the two countries developed economic systems which were mutually supplementary. Wine was Gascony's chief product, and she was not self-supporting in either food or textiles, while England was one of Europe's chief importers of wine (she imported over four million gallons in 1415), and was also from time to time able to supply Gascony with grain – with her own in years of good harvests and with re-exported Baltic grain in other years.

Yet although the 'French' wines flowed between countries in quantities far greater than any other, the wine of other nations also contributed their quota. There was a regular flow of sweet wines from Spain and the eastern Mediterranean to the countries of northern Europe: the 'Malmsey', the 'vin muscadet', and a few others. Above all, there were the wines of the Rhine valley. They were one of the staple commodities of Frisian trade in the sixth and seventh centuries; they were also one of the principal commodities imported into this country by the merchants of Cologne when they began to come here in large numbers at the end of the eleventh and twelfth centuries. And it was Rhenish wine that German merchants sold in Scandinavia before they had large surpluses of eastern grain to dispose of.

So much for trade in food. It was large and, being food, was indispensable, but both in value and in bulk it was rivalled by the trade in basic raw materials. Of these, one of the most important and certainly the bulkiest was timber. Timber resources were unevenly distributed over the face of Europe, and were all but lacking in the areas where the population was at its thickest: in Flanders, in the Netherlands, and eventually in southern England. As a rule, timber was becoming scarcer as the countries of western Europe were getting settled and as forest was giving place to fields and pastures. But even in those regions of northern Europe which were still well wooded, as in parts of this country, hardwoods predominated, and 'tall timber' suitable for shipbuilding and for standard domestic structures had to be brought in by water. In this trade water transport was even more important than the ecology of native forests. For timber growing away from navigable rivers and seaports, like much of the timber in the forests of west and north Midlands of England, was often more difficult to transport to other places within the country and much costlier than timber imported from abroad by sea.

Timber was therefore an important article of water-borne trade. In the earlier centuries, from the eleventh to the thirteenth, the chief exporters of timber were Scandinavia and the wooded regions of south Germany; but in the fourteenth century, with the opening of the Baltic, this trade, like the grain trade, changed in direction and volume. The vast coniferous forests of eastern Europe including Russia, Poland and Livonia now became available, and from the middle of the fourteenth century onwards eastern timber shipped from the Baltic and more especially from Danzig all but ousted from the western markets the other types of 'white' timber. Pine, yew and fir of Baltic origin and occasionally some birch, both in logs and in sawn boards – 'wainscot' and *klapholz* – became one of the main articles of Hanseatic imports into this country and also one of the chief magnets which drew English merchants to the Baltic regions. At one time in the fifteenth century hulls of boats and whole ships came to be imported from Prussia in lieu of shipbuilding material. Some wood shipped from Baltic ports may have come from countries even further afield. The bowstaves which won the battles of Crécy and Agincourt probably came from the Carpathian mountains and were shipped to England through Hungary and Prussia.[3]

The forest resources of eastern Europe and Scandinavia were not exploited for timber alone. Russia was by far the most important source of medieval pitch and tar, and pitch used in this country in the later Middle Ages was nearly all of Baltic origin, though a little came also from Bordeaux and Bayonne. From Russian and Polish woodlands also came potash, obtained by the burning of wood.

The industrial raw material *par excellence* was wool. The cloth industry was the first, and for a long time the only, medieval handicraft to grow into a *grande industrie*. It was also the first industrial occupation to transform whole parts of Europe into specialised manufacturing regions. In southern Europe specialised industrial centres of this kind sprang up in Florence, and centres of cloth industry were also to be found in Champagne and the south of France. But it was mainly in northern Europe, at its north-western corner, that an industrial society wholly based on the cloth industry came into existence.

Industrial societies, in the plural, would perhaps be a better term. Several contiguous regions of northern Europe became successively industrialised as the Middle Ages drew to their close, and all this industrial activity – ever shifting but never broken – grew up on imported wool. Some of the wool came from central France, and the

[3] Th. Hirsch, *Danzigs Handels- und Gewerbgeschichte unter der Herrschaft des deutschen Ordens* (Leipzig, 1858). For a comprehensive, though possibly exaggerated, survey of Norwegian timber exports, see A. Bugge, *Den Norske Traelasthandels Historie*, I (Skien, 1925).

original prosperity of the Artois cloth industry was largely based on the wool of Auvergne and the Cevennes. But by far the most important centre of wool, a source which at the turn of the thirteenth and fourteenth centuries overshadowed all others, was Britain. By the second half of the thirteenth century the average annual exports of wool from England averaged more than 30,000 sacks, or about eleven million pounds. Some of it went to Italy, but most was worked into cloth in the north – in the Low Countries and later, to an ever increasing extent, in England herself.

Cloth, thus made, was in itself a very valuable and by far the most important example of a 'wholly manufactured' export. In the seventh century we hear of English cloth exported to Carolingian Francia, and throughout that and subsequent centuries we find in the records stray references to traffic in Frisian cloth, which may have been cloth made in the Frisian lands and in their immediate vicinity or English cloth distributed on the continent by the Frisians. Various other regional varieties of cloth entered into the international trade of the ninth, tenth and eleventh centuries. But from the end of the eleventh century onwards, Flemish cloth began to overshadow all other cloths of Europe, and by the end of the thirteenth century we find it exported to the remotest corners of the then known world. In the later centuries it became the chief commercial *quid pro quo* for the grain, furs and timber products which the Baltic countries yielded up to the West, and therefore one of the pillars of German strength in Novgorod, Riga and Reval. When in the late fourteenth century English and Dutch cloth began to appear in large quantities on the continent it naturally flowed in the wake of the Flemish exports, gradually replacing them in all their ancient channels. Like the Flemish cloths they were soon to be found all over the civilised world – in Hungary, Russia and the Asiatic East as well as in countries nearer home.

Compared to cloth, the other textiles, though worn by men of all ranks, were not of very great importance in the inter-regional trade of northern Europe. Silks and other luxury fabrics of Byzantine, Italian and oriental origin came in from the South throughout the Middle Ages. More important were linen and flax of northern growth. The damp and cool flax-growing areas of Europe were as clearly defined as its sheep-farming regions. They were as a rule to be found on land ill-suited to the growing of good quality wool, just as the chalk uplands and the salt marshes of Europe, which carried the largest and the best flocks of sheep, were ill suited to the cultivation of flax. Hence the broad geographic demarcation between the flax areas of the Low Countries, north-west France, Poland and Russia and the wool-growing areas of England, central France and Spain. Yet in some areas the two textiles were mutually competitive, if not mutually exclusive, and in no other country were they more so than Flanders. Parts of the Low Countries were well suited to the growing of flax and in fact grew and worked it throughout the Middle Ages. From the end of the eleventh century, however, the making as well as the wearing of woollen cloth spread so rapidly that to an observer the change might well appear as a combat between flax and wool. In a rhymed pamphlet of the eleventh century an anonymous pamphleteer defined the problem as *conflictus ovis et linis*. In the end, linen became one of Flanders' secondary exports. Some linen goods were still imported from there into England in the fourteenth and fifteenth centuries, but by that time the bulk of linen imports came from other sources; mostly from northern France and from regions of central and eastern Europe controlled by the German Hanse. From Brittany and Baltic regions came also most of the canvas for sails and much of the hemp for ropes and cordage.

Wool and flax, however, were not the sole raw materials needed for the manufacture of northern textiles. Other subsidiary clothmakers' materials entered into northern commerce, and chief among them were woad and madder, the two commonest dyes of the Middle Ages. Both were to some extent grown in northern Europe. Some woad came from Italy and was in the late fourteenth and fifteenth centuries carried in Venetian galleys. A great deal of woad for English use came also from the region of Toulouse via Bordeaux. But before the fourteenth century Picardy was the chief northern home of the woad industry, and it was on woad that the economic prosperity of Amiens and Corbie and the fame of their merchants were based. More exotic dyes, especially the much valued and highly priced *granum*, came from Portugal, the still more precious ultramarine came from the East. Of the other materials used in the making of cloth, alum, black soap, mostly Spanish, and potash, mostly eastern European, were the most important.

Potash, though a product of the Baltic timber industry and a raw material of the clothmakers, should perhaps be classified with the next important group of commodities in northern trade – the minerals. The basic mineral of modern times, coal, was worked in Northumberland throughout the Middle Ages – certainly in the thirteenth century – and was carried from there by sea to London and to the Low Countries. From the thirteenth century onwards coal was also mined in Hainault and, perhaps, Westphalia and elsewhere.

By far the most important of the mineral products was salt – one of the essential ingredients of medieval food, the indispensable preserver of meat, and the mainstay of the great fish-curing trades. Salt was both mined and obtained by evaporation from salt pans, and local centres of both kinds of salt industry were to be found all over Europe. The economic rise of Venice in the ninth century may well have begun with the development of local salt supplies. Further north the salt deposits of the eastern Alps, already exploited in prehistoric times, revived in the closing stages of the Middle Ages. In this country the salt deposits of Worcestershire were also worked throughout the Middle Ages. But for the purposes of north European trade the most important salt-producing areas were the Lower Saxon region of Lüneburg and, still more, the Bay of Bourgneuf on the Atlantic coast of France. The Lüneburg salt deposits were conveniently situated for export to the Baltic as well as to the Netherlands. But in the course of the late fourteenth and the fifteenth centuries Lüneburg deposits, like most other important salt industries of Europe, shrank in importance by comparison with those of western France. The shallow waters and flooded areas between the mouth of the Gironde and the Isle of Oleron – mainly in the Bay of Bourgneuf – formed natural salt pans of great extent and remarkable productivity. They were worked from early times, but it was not until the later centuries of the Middle Ages that they began to attract buyers from all over the world. In the first half of the fifteenth century, when our documentary evidence about Bourgneuf becomes most abundant, we find it frequented by great salt fleets of all the northern nations. Hanseatic 'Bay fleets' sailed there several times a year, and Dutch and English ships and merchants also resorted there in large numbers. By that time Bay salt also entered northern politics as well as northern trade. The lawless and riotous life of this salt 'Klondyke' generated international conflicts and quarrels, and the safety of the 'Bay route' preoccupied the Hanseatics throughout the fifteenth century, and gave rise to at least one war – that between England and the Hanse in the middle of the fifteenth century.[4]

Relatively less prominent in the annals of northern trade and in the records of its shipping were the exports and imports of metal. The mining of precious metals, especially of silver, was a great industry, and its products played a part in economic development of Europe so crucial that they should not perhaps be treated as mere items in a list of commodities. But bullion was not the only metal worked. Some ironstone was mined in most places, and some iron was smelted in almost every great country in the Middle Ages. But of important centres there were only three or four; one was Westphalia, others were in Saxony, in the Basque country in the Pyrenees, and above all in

[4] A. Agats, *Der Hansische Baienhandel* (Heidelberg, 1904). About the importance of salt for Zeeland, see H. J. Smit in *Bijdragen etc.*, VI (1930).

Sweden. It is doubtful whether there ever was a period since the twelfth century when the high-quality iron of Swedish origin, the 'osmund' of medieval records, was not exported from that country to other parts of northern Europe. We find it in the documents referring to Swedish trade in the twelfth century, in the records of Westphalian trade to Sweden in the thirteenth and fourteenth, in the English customs accounts of the fourteenth and fifteenth centuries. It was the most highly priced and internationally the best known of medieval irons.

Of other metals and metal wares, copper, mostly of Swedish and Hungarian origin, and lead and tin, mostly of English and German origin, were distributed all over northern and western Europe by Hanseatic merchants. So were also other miscellaneous metal goods, most produced in the area of Liège, Dinant and Cologne, and pewter goods of English make – altogether a current of trade not very abundant in comparison with grain, wool or timber, yet sufficiently important to attract the attention of the makers of commercial treaties and of legislators.

This catalogue of goods entering the commerce of northern Europe could be continued almost indefinitely. Miscellaneous commodities of European origin crossed and recrossed the frontiers of northern countries and passed its tolls. Bricks from the Low Countries, swords and helmets from Cologne, tapestries and painted images from Flanders, books from France and the Low Countries, amber 'paternosters' from Prussia, wax and honey from Russia, thread and lace from Cologne and Brabant, hawks from Bruges and Calais, feathers for pillows from all over Germany. But it is not from these commodities, whether luxuries or playthings, that the commerce of northern Europe took its colour. Its essential feature was trade in bulk, its characteristic commodities were the necessities of life and industry, its economic function was to bind the peoples of northern Europe by real economic ties – ties without which life in many places would have been difficult if not altogether impossible.

(2) QUANTITIES

The catalogue of commodities cannot be complete, and as long as it is confined to the main branches of trade it cannot be even wholly representative. Above all, it cannot do full justice to the complexity of medieval commerce. The regions of Europe depended on each other's products or, to use the jargon of the economists, benefited from the geographical division of labour, to a far greater extent than a mere list of commodities would suggest. In spite of all the difficulties of long-distance trade the network of commercial exchanges had in the course of the Middle Ages come to be woven into a tight and complicated mesh. That whole industrial societies, like those of Flanders and Italy and later that of Holland, should have come into existence even though the essential raw materials, as well as food, had to be imported, is an instance familiar enough. Less familiar, but equally characteristic, is the example of the export of beer from north-western Germany and later from Holland where it was brewed from grain imported from abroad. But nothing illustrates better the complexity of multilateral exchanges than the various secondary currents of trade which crossed and recrossed the main lines of commercial traffic. In the same years in the fifteenth century we find England exporting grain through Chester and Bristol to Ireland; importing grain through the eastern ports from the Baltic; exporting red herring from Yarmouth (to Holland of all countries!) and importing white herring through every port; exporting malt and ale and importing beer; exporting faggots and stakes and importing every other kind of timber; exporting figures made of alabaster and importing saints carved in wood; importing wax and exporting tallow; exporting pewter and importing Dutch pottery. And although these subsidiary currents were all small, they went far to give the economic geography of Europe the shape it has borne ever since.

Eloquent as these facts are, they cannot provide a full substitute for the missing statistics. They might, however, be sufficient to demonstrate how wide was the range of needs which inhabitants of northern Europe covered by purchases from outside, and they might even support the surmise that the volume of the trade must have been high. For bulky goods would not be worth exporting or importing except in bulk, and a regular trade in essentials over long distances presupposed exporters relying on regular and substantial deficiencies in the importing countries as well as importers relying on a regular and substantial flow of suppliers from abroad.

Here and there this general argument can be illustrated by numbers drawn from an occasional *cache* of figures. Thus the English trade returns, which are more abundant than those of any other country – they will be discussed later – make it clear that in the first half of the fourteenth century the value of British exports was at times not less than £250,000, or the equivalent of about $1\frac{1}{2}$ million quarters of wheat or $2\frac{1}{2}$ million quarters of oats at prices prevailing in the last decade of the fourteenth century. The evidence of the Hanseatic *Pfundzoll* – a war tax on sea-borne imports – suggests that in the seventies of the fourteenth century the annual value of the taxable sea-borne trade of the principal Hanseatic ports for which evidence is available was in excess of three million Lübeck marks, or about 600,000 of contemporary pounds sterling.[5]

Even more concrete, though not necessarily more precise or relevant, may be the few surviving figures of individual commodities imported and exported. We are told that the total amount of herring salted on the fishing grounds of Skania in a good year could be as high as 120,000 tuns and that some 24,000 tuns of salt were imported in a curing season. In some years at the beginning of the fifteenth century Dutch grain imports by the Somme route may have been as high as 230,000 quarters. At the beginning of the fourteenth century wine exports from Bordeaux reached 100,000 tuns (some 25 million gallons)[6] per annum. In 1334 a few English merchants received royal licences to export to Bordeaux more than 50,000 quarters of grain. The English records show that in the late thirteenth and early fourteenth centuries this country at times exported as much as 35,000–40,000 sacks, the equivalent of about 15 million lb of wool. In the good years of the fourteenth and fifteenth centuries this country exported more than 50,000 pieces of cloth of 28 yards per piece, and it is possible that at the height of their prosperity the Flemish cloth towns turned out a number of cloths at least three times as great.[7]

Similar estimates could be cited for a number of other places and other commodities, but however varied, they cannot and perhaps need not be turned into true measurements. The show of precision which they may impart to the history of trade is largely deceptive. Some of the figures are, to say the least, ambiguous; but even those which are not, have survived more or less in isolation and cannot be fitted into reliable estimates of total trade and still less into measurements of social income. It may be significant that in a petition of the prelates and barons in 1297 it was confidently asserted that the wool of England represented half the total produce of the land; but what was the total produce of the land? It might also be important to know that the value of English exports in the thirteenth century was probably equivalent to the annual earnings of approximately 100,000 agricultural labourers. But even this figure, large as it is and close as it comes to a real measurement, does not mean very much unless related to the total size of English population or to the distribution of income between the various classes of the English people: a subject still shrouded in darkness.

[5] The value of sea-borne exports of the four Hanseatic ports listed by Stieda approached 1.5 million marks in 1370. W. Stieda, *Revaler Zollbücher*, lviiff. The other German figures in this and preceding paragraphs come from G. Lechner, *Die Hansische Pfundzollisten des Jahres* 1368, 57–8.

[6] Below Table IV; also M. Gouron, *L'Amirauté de Guienne*, 47. [7] Below Table III, p. 242.

The most that these figures can do is to build up in a cumulative and circumstantial fashion the general impression that the volume of medieval trade was considerable; the least they can do is to make it unnecessary to disparage the part trade played in medieval life. No doubt, in comparison with the nineteenth and twentieth centuries, medieval trade at its highest would appear very small. But why compare with the nineteenth century, and indeed why compare at all? For all we know, the record of international trade in the nineteenth century may well turn out to have been a mere aberration in the economic development of the world. It has been argued that in the course of that century factors of production – land, labour, capital – were distributed more unequally over the face of the globe than in any other period of world history. As a result, inter-regional trade may have been greater in relation to total income than it would have been had the movable resources and especially capital been more evenly spread. By the same argument the international flow of resources has been slowly reducing the relative importance of trade, even though it may have raised its total volume and value. But even if the argument with all its implications were not accepted, it would still remain true that in the nineteenth century foreign trade was so great that, by comparison, the trade of all other centuries, the seventeenth and eighteenth as well as the thirteenth, would appear insignificant. And if historians and economists insist on matching century against century, they would be less open to accusation of irrelevance if they compared the Middle Ages with the earlier centuries of the modern era, the sixteenth, the seventeenth, the eighteenth. Thus compared, medieval trade of European countries would appear (and the argument is one of appearances and not of measurements) both smaller and greater than that of, say, the seventeenth century: smaller in the fifteenth century, greater in the thirteenth.

All such comparisons, however, are highly questionable. Not only must the magnitudes of commercial exchanges always be matters of vague surmise, but they must remain mutually incomparable even if they were capable of exact estimate. From this point of view more relevant than any attempt at a measurement of foreign trade are the simple historical facts indicating the place of trade in medieval life – the existence of specialised economies, the number and relative wealth of towns, the attention paid by kings and parliaments to trade and navigation, the readiness to engage in political and military conflicts on behalf of trade. The geographical and political implications of medieval trade will be discussed separately, but they must also be borne in mind in considering the problem of quantity. Did not the wool trade supply a link between Flanders and this country stronger than political, dynastic or cultural ties with France? Did not the Gascon wine trade to England forge a link of political loyalty stronger than affinities of race, language and distance? In the twelfth century interruption in English imports could produce famine in western Norway. In the early fourteenth century disturbances in northern France could produce famine in the Low Countries. In the fourteenth century conflicts with England could result in unemployment all over the Low Countries. And in the fifteenth century the seizure of the salt fleet homeward bound from the Bay of Bourgneuf could produce a major crisis all over northern Europe.

The economic interdependence of distant regions and the essential character of certain branches of trade may appear out of scale with the small quantities of goods in fact exchanged. In the middle of the sixteenth century, Thomas Barnaby, an enthusiastic sponsor of the coal trade, could argue that 'the thing that France can live no more without than the fish without water; that is to say the Newcastle coals, without which they can neither make steel work nor metal work nor wire work nor goldsmith work nor guns nor no manner of things that passes the fire'. In the Middle Ages coal exports were probably smaller than in the sixteenth century. The French were as yet rare visitors to the coal wharves of Newcastle: their calls there did not become at all frequent until about 1500. And before the advent of the French, the Flemings and the Zealanders did not apparently take out of this country more than about 10,000 tons in a good year. Yet, even then, coal was, as in the nineteenth century, a bulky return cargo without which the voyages might not have paid and would not have been undertaken.

It is therefore not surprising that in time of war some countries appeared to be even more vulnerable to blockade than in more recent times. The readiness with which embargoes and economic boycotts were used as political weapons is in itself evidence of the store men laid by foreign trade: indeed, of foreign trade in its most specialised manifestations.

(3) IMPEDIMENTS AND FACILITIES

The scope of medieval trade is all the more remarkable for the various obstacles which beset the merchant. It is perhaps true that medieval commerce could not have functioned as it did, had the obstacles in its way been quite as formidable as their history might suggest. Yet formidable they doubtless were, and none more so than the innumerable payments on the frontiers, along the rivers and roads, on town markets and in sea ports: payments which must have burdened commerce nearly as much as similar payments were to burden the trade of France on the eve of Colbert's and Calonne's reforms or the trade of Germany on the eve of Napoleon's conquest.

England was perhaps the largest area of northern Europe in which trade was free from any but small tolls. If tolls were paid at all, they were usually in the nature of a *pontage* or a *viage*. Like the turnpike tolls of a later age they were levied to defray the cost of constructing or of maintaining a road or a bridge. As a rule the king's government seldom granted the right to impose a toll except in exchange for a true equivalent in road service; and grants were frequently preceded or followed by inquisitions into the revenue of tolls and their employments.

By comparison with these service tolls, or 'tolls-thorough' as they were known to a later age, the 'tolls-traverse' – payments based on ancient right and functioning as a customary source of revenue irrespective of the road service rendered – were not many. They were remarkably few in comparison with similar tolls in medieval and post-medieval France and Germany. There, at the best of times, no major trade route was entirely duty-free. Thus, even the much frequented international land routes from Flanders to France in the thirteenth century had to pass numerous toll stations, of which several, those of Bapaume on the French border and those of Péronne, Nesle, Compiègne and Crépy-en-Valois on the roads of northern France, were more or less inescapable. There were also provincial tolls all over the internal roads beyond Paris, and there were payments at the frontier stations on the south and the east leading to the upper Rhine and the main Alpine passes. Above all, there were innumerable tolls on the Loire, the Somme, the Oise, the Rhone and the Garonne. The allegation that towards the end of the fourteenth century there were 130 toll stations along the Loire is probably far-fetched. But it is known that the tolls on the Loire, such as there were, grew as much in the following 25 or 30 years as they had grown in the preceding fifty. The Garonne and the Rhone were no freer than the Loire, and even on the Seine the toll charges on grain shipped in the late fifteenth century over a distance of 200 miles equalled more than half of its selling price.

The German picture was less uniform, for the country contained the relatively free arteries, like the great Hanseatic routes to the East, as well as the much taxed and restricted roads which connected the route with the interior. The surviving lists of tolls along the main German rivers may exaggerate the actual weight of impositions, but however much discounted they make formidable reading. At the turn of the thirteenth and fourteenth centuries there were said to have been more than 30 toll stations along the Weser and at least 35 along the

Elbe. In the middle of the thirteenth century there were more than fourscore tolls along the Austrian stretch of the upper Danube and a score of tolls on the river Main. But the most advertised, the most bitterly resented and, from the point of view of trade, the most damaging, were the tolls on the Rhine. According to a recent account there were about 19 toll stations along the Rhine at the end of the twelfth century, about 35 or more at the end of the thirteenth century, nearly 50 at the end of the fourteenth, and more than 60 at the end of the fifteenth century; mostly belonging to the great ecclesiastical princes of western Germany. Writing in the middle of the thirteenth century, an English chronicler, Thomas Wykes, could find no other way of describing the system on the Rhine than 'the raving madness of the Teutons' (*furiosa Teutonicorum insania*).[8]

The total weight of the internal tolls was thus heavy and growing, and may in part account for the gradual clogging of internal trade in the closing centuries of the Middle Ages. At the same time it is important not to misunderstand their incidence and their effect on commerce. The system as a whole may have been sufficiently exorbitant and sufficiently anarchical to impose here and there a weight of charges greater than the traffic could bear. Yet the yield of the main toll stations on the Rhine, the Main and the Elbe remained to the end sufficiently valuable to justify their owners, and especially the great ecclesiastical princes, in fighting for their retention to the bitter end. The presumption, therefore, is that, generally speaking, they did not choke trade altogether. Extortionate as were the lords of the Rhine tolls, the trade of certain towns, and Cologne in the first instance, remained relatively free over long stretches of the river. And although in the later Middle Ages grain from upper Germany was eventually forced out of the river and took to the land route, timber could still be floated downstream to Holland. The same is broadly true of the Elbe, for the merchants of the Wendish towns never ceased to use the river for the bulkier goods originating beyond Magdeburg and for shipments of fish and salt up the river.

The general impression is that the main weight of the toll taxes fell upon local traffic, thereby reinforcing the particularism and self-sufficiency of local economies. Their chief effect on long-distance trade was to raise local prices for imports and to reduce local prices of exportable surpluses. This in turn may have reduced production for exports and narrowed down the markets for imports. But how great the reduction in fact was in different fields of trade will not be known until local prices have been studied in greater detail than has so far

[8] *Annales Monastici* (Rolls Series), IV, 222.

proved possible. The general impression is that among the factors, which at times held back the output of industry and agriculture, high tolls *en route* to distant markets were of relatively little importance. The ability of medieval agriculture to yield surpluses for export, or its failure to do so, depended much less on differences in costs of distribution (including tolls) than on variations of climate, of soil, of seasons and, above all, of social structure. The same argument may not apply to products of industry and mining. The supply of most industrial products was greatly affected by costs, and the demand for textiles, metal articles and luxuries was apparently quite elastic. Everything that helped to raise their final costs was therefore bound to restrict the volume of production and sales. But for reasons to be expounded later, long-distance trade was not as a rule greatly affected by local taxes, from some of which it was exempted and most of which it could avoid.

From the point of view of inter-regional and international trade, more effective because more unavoidable, were the national or princely taxes at the frontiers or the great international toll stations, like those of Bapaume. But in the nature of things these taxes were not as a rule so high as to be crippling. Among the highest was the English export duty on wool in the late fourteenth and fifteenth centuries. The taxes, i.e. customs and subsidy, at times rose to about £2 to £2 13*s.* 4*d.* per sack, to which about 1*s.* should perhaps be added for various local dues in English ports and 6*s.* 8*d.* for customs charged in Calais and sometimes levied as a special excise on wool shipped to Italy. The total customs payments thus computed were equal to about 20 per cent of the value of good quality wool in Calais. The tax in the end penalised British wool exports and greatly stimulated production of cloth at home, but it never stopped the wool exports altogether; and had it threatened to do so it would almost certainly have been moderated. Tax on cloth exports at a rate which varied from 1*s.* to 2*s.* 9*d.* or from about 1.5 to 4 per cent *ad valorem* was not much higher than stamp duties and registration fees were to be in the free-trade decades of the nineteenth century. Miscellaneous imports paid a tax of 3*d.* in the pound, to which frequently the poundage of 1*s.* in the pound was added. The additional duties levied on imports and exports were on the whole very small. Local dues such as 'anchorage' on boats or tolls on merchandise brought into ports varied from place to place and, on the whole, fell less heavily on distant trade than it might appear from the toll lists. In the Cinque Ports in the thirteenth century the tolls on wine, their main imports, varied from 2*d.* to 4*d.* per cask. The charges in Southampton averaged about 2*d.* per pound worth of merchandise; in Winchester they were at the rate of 1*d.* per cwt of wool. But in all these ports most merchants and merchandise coming from other English towns were exempt from local tolls by royal charter or else paid reduced tolls by inter-urban agreements. In a port like Yarmouth where remission was not so general, local dues might vary from about 2*d.* per cloth to 4*d.* per pipe of wine or a last of herring: by no means an exorbitant charge. No doubt in a number of foreign ports where local taxation was employed as a means of enforcing the monopoly of the residents the taxes could at times be much higher than they were in English ports. The various dues which were levied on strangers along the roads leading from the vineyards to the port of Bordeaux were sufficiently high to deter them from buying wine directly from the growers. But customs in Bordeaux itself were not such as to impede the flow of wine exports.

There was indeed every reason why most taxes and tolls actually borne by long-distance trade should not have been as heavy as those which weighed on local trade. Where princely authorities were so many and so ill-coordinated, as on the Rhine, the total weight of dues might in fact pass the limit of what the international traffic would bear. Yet even at times and in places where this limit was passed, trade was merely forced into alternative routes.

For alternative routes there always were. In considering the much misunderstood history of medieval trade routes, it is important to remember that what made a route was not the physical attributes of a road – a stretch of tarmac or an immovable railway track – but a combination of conveniences, mostly of political and social character: residential and trading facilities *en route*, guarantees of safety and security and, above all, comparative freedom from imposts and taxes. Geographical and physical conditions were of course essential; mountains could only be crossed by passes, rivers by fords and bridgeable places. In general the medieval carrier stuck as long as he could to navigable rivers and to the greater ancient highways, many of which were Roman in origin and construction, and most of which contained sections made and maintained by the work of men. But, within limits set by geography, the man-made conveniences – even such conveniences as bridges – could be duplicated and multiplied, and their sites could be shifted. In a famous capitulary Charlemagne had to lay down that if the twelve bridges over the Seine were to be reconstructed they should be placed *ubi antiquitus fuerant* and not moved to new sites. The same motif recurs more than once in the history of European bridges, as in the clause of the Magna Carta providing that no man should be distrained to work on bridges on sites where they had not been *ab antiquo*. When in the later judicial proceedings we find the parties pleading that the bridges in question still were in *locis quibus esse consueverant tempore Ioannis regis* the main object was to prove that the bridges still had to be maintained, but the presumption was that the permanence of a bridge site could not be taken for granted.

What is true of bridges is even truer of the social and institutional components of a trade route. These could be combined and re-combined into linked chains stretching across the face of Europe in double, treble, and multiple strands. Thus between England and Flanders on the one hand and the Mediterranean on the other there were during the Middle Ages at least a dozen of geographically feasible lines of communication from which merchants could take their choice. There was, in the first place, the major alternative of land routes and sea routes. The latter did not become important until the closing of the Champagne routes by the action of the French kings in the late thirteenth and the fourteenth centuries; but eventually they rose to great prominence. In the last hundred years of the Middle Ages the bulk of English wool exports to Italy went that way, and whereas in the early fourteenth century the Genoese wool importers paid toll on wool in Milan, in the fifteenth century the merchants of Milan paid toll on their wool in Genoa. Among land routes, the Italians and the other merchants trading to the south rang the changes over a wide scale of trade routes across Flanders and France. There were in the first place the main lines of the Flemish rivers, and there were routes which were wholly or largely land-bound. In the thirteenth century, in addition to a number of secondary routes, there were two main arteries – that of Arras and that of Douai – which crossed Flanders to the south; and there were also at least several routes from Brabant to France which grew in importance in the later Middle Ages: a network of routes across northern France, most of them converging on Compiègne and Troyes, and spreading out from there to Paris or to Saulieu, Dijon and the other places *en route* for the south-east. Marc Bloch has drawn attention to the several routes between Paris and Orléans, but a cursory study of French internal trade would reveal the several variants forming the routes between Paris and Brest, Paris and Lille, Paris and Rouen, Paris and La Rochelle, some following the main rivers of France, others mainly land routes.[9]

The same variety of routes traversed the continent from the west to the east. The time when the *Hellweg*, which bisected northern Germany from Dortmund in Westphalia to Magdeburg or Bardowiek on the Elbe, was the sole line of communication to the Slavonic east passed away (if such time ever was) with the twelfth century. In the

[9] H. Laurent, *La Draperie des Pays-Bas en France*, 48ff., 246–53; Armand Deroisy in *Revue du Nord* (1939), 40ff; F. Imbertin in *Les Annales* (1939); and M. Bloch's postscript, *ibid.* 416.

thirteenth and later centuries there were at least four transcontinental routes between Bruges and the Baltic: the sea route by the Sound, the two older land routes via Lübeck and via Münster and Stettin, and eventually the new southern route via Frankfurt-an-der-Oder. Historians have uncovered at least six main routes between the German ports on the Baltic and south-east Europe; two in a northerly direction: one by Gnesen and Posen and the other by Kalisz and Breslau; four in the south: by Sandomir, by Cracow, by Lwów, and by Oposzno; and a network of other routes to and beyond Bohemia, round and into Hungary.[10]

The feasible lines of transcontinental traffic, whether complementary or competitive, were so many as to defeat the attempts of many a hopeful beginner at an exhaustive list or a comprehensive map. In this maze, trade could be relied upon to pick its way and to shift when necessary. The history of the embargoes and staple laws imposed during the Middle Ages is one continuous record of old routes abandoned and new routes opened up. If some arteries of trade were closed by excessive imposts and restrictions (as the Champagne route across France was closed by the vexatious policy of the French crown), others could be opened up by free-trade treaties negotiated between the interested parties. The early development of Brabant in the thirteenth century is generally ascribed to the liberal commercial policy of the far-seeing Counts of Brabant; the use of the eastern artery from Brabant via Lorraine in the late Middle Ages was made possible by 'free-trade' treaties which extended in an unbroken series from the fifties of the fourteenth century to the sixties of the fifteenth, and above all to the agreements between the merchants of Milan and Rudolf of Hapsburg for the remission of tolls and duties along the route which led from Bâle to Brabant. The Venetian merchants for a time developed the Bavarian route to the Alps, through Nuremberg, as an alternative to the French route, and there too the way was 'made' by agreements with princes for remission of dues and for greater safety of traffic.

The freedom of long-distance traffic was thus in essence a freedom of choice between routes. It was therefore imperfect and unstable and, from every point of view, inferior to the great liberty which European trade was to enjoy in periods as truly free as the honeymoon decades of the Victorian *laissez-passer*. For not only were routes newly chosen sometimes more expensive than the routes which had to be abandoned, but the whole system of communications suffered from lack of

[10] Hirsch, *Danzig's Handels- und Gewerbgeschichte*, 178–80 and *passim*. G. Köster in *Forschungen zur Brandenburgischen u. Preussischen Gesch.*, XLVIII (1936), 120ff.

permanence and stability. In addition it was often insecure. Political conditions on which it depended changed frequently; princely whims and aims were often unaccountable; and above all wars were apt to break out at all times. And the crippling effect of war on trade must not be underestimated. Here and there war demands might inject a stimulating dose of inflationary expenditure into certain branches of trade; but on the whole war meant taxation, forced loans, monetary disturbance and physical hazards. Contrary to all the current notions, medieval conflicts could approach very closely the recent models of total war, for medieval princes did not as a rule hesitate to sacrifice their long-term economic prospects to the strategic or fiscal necessities of war. It was not so much the mere fact of annexation by France as the exposure to the demands of Philip le Bel's war strategy and war finance that ruined the cloth industry of Artois, the transit trade of France and the prosperity of the fairs of Champagne. It was Edward III's war finance that brought havoc into the English wool-growing and wool trade and into the Italian investment in this country. It was the Hanseatic war policy and its accidents that all but ruined in the fifteenth century the German position in eastern Flanders.

Above all, in time of war and within the range of its operations, pillage and piracy reigned. Piracy and robbery along roads and rivers could at times develop into a major disaster, and it is therefore no wonder that it has now become one of the major themes of medieval history. The records are full of complaints, petitions and counter-petitions arising from the seizure of ships and goods on the high seas, and it is doubtful whether there was any major act of piracy which remained unrecorded in the surviving medieval evidence. It is therefore not surprising that in modern accounts of medieval trade piracy figures very conspicuously.

It may even be that piracy has received more attention than it deserves. For if on some continental land routes ambushes and attacks on convoys were endemic, piracy on the high seas was not. Generally speaking it was much less a permanent feature of the medieval scene than an accident of war. In some parts of Europe, on the south-west coast of England, on the west coast of Brittany, and along the creeks of Normandy, and no doubt elsewhere, there was to be found a sea-faring population who at all times engaged in occasional piracy. But most of the piratical acts in medieval records were committed not by professional pirates practising their occupation in all seasons, but by merchants who turned pirate and sometimes acted as privateers under offical letters of mark. They either were pressed into service by their princes or turned to privateering while trade was at a standstill, or were trying to recoup themselves for acts of piracy they or their compatriots had suffered at the enemy's hands. Pirates and privateers preyed on the French and English shipping in the Channel every time war between France and England broke out; with the result that during the Hundred Years War, i.e. for nearly 150 years, the sea-borne trade between Brittany and Normandy on the one hand and the English south coast on the other was reduced to a small and fitful trickle. The North Sea was thrown into a chaos of universal and promiscuous privateering of this kind in the fifties and sixties of the fifteenth century, and there were occasional outbursts of wholesale piracy in the disturbed periods in Anglo-Flemish relations in the early fourteenth century. But in the times when wars were not raging and in areas outside the range of privateering bases, the main channels of sea-borne trade were maintained more or less open.

On land the only true remedy was the enforcement of the king's peace. When and where the princes were strong enough to keep the roads safe – as in Flanders and Champagne in the eleventh, twelfth and thirteenth centuries, in Burgundy in the fifteenth century, in Prussia and Livonia in the fourteenth and early fifteenth centuries – merchant traffic flowed unmolested both in peace and in war, and the wealth of their countries grew at the expense of lands and routes not so blessed. In Germany the safety of the routes was sometimes enforced by the action of the towns. In the later Middle Ages the great Hanseatic routes to the east were almost wholly free from the dangers of piracy and robbery. Somewhat more restricted and on the whole less successful were the activities of the inter-urban police unions (*Landfriedensverbände*) of the thirteenth and fourteenth centuries, which, with the occasional assistance of local princes, waged battle against the robber barons and their nests along the west German rivers.

On the high seas however the security of traffic was almost entirely the concern of the merchants and shippers themselves. Where shipments were valuable and regular and followed established sea lanes, they were as a rule made in convoy. The English wool was shipped in two great bi-annual convoys elaborately organised and controlled. The German and Dutch ships carrying salt from the Bay also as a rule sailed together, and so did often the English cloth boats sailing to the Baltic and the Prussian and Dutch boats plying between Danzig and the west. The system must have been effective, for very few of the great convoys were ever seized or disturbed. There was hardly an instance of the Venetian galleys being seized or plundered in northern waters on their annual visits to England and the Low Countries; not one of the great wool fleets which sailed from the main wool ports of England was ever seized; and of all the great Bay fleets, which regularly passed through the Narrow Seas on their way from the

Atlantic coast to the Baltic, the first ever to be attacked was the great Bay fleet which was seized by the English in 1449. In short, piracy even more than the other disturbances of trade was a characteristic feature of the Middle Ages only in so far as the Middle Ages were specially prone to war. When and where peace prevailed trade flowed unhindered.

(4) TRANSPORT

In times of war and on routes which happened to be no more than ordinarily insecure the dangers of the routes must have added to the cost of trade. But in most years and especially in the years of peace they were by no means the main constituent of costs and could not be blamed for the high expenses of distribution. Commercial distribution was bound to be a costly service, but – tolls apart – the main element of cost was undoubtedly transport. It is not that transport was as primitive as it is sometimes represented, but like all transport of the pre-railway age it was wasteful of time, equipment and manpower.

On land routes goods were carried by horse and ox, but not necessarily by pack. Carrying services on medieval estates in this country and abroad consisted of both summage, i.e. carriage by horseback (indeed sometimes on human backs), and cartage; but English manorial accounts make it quite clear that, for bulky goods or for carriage over distances, carts and, where suitable, boats were used. On some stretches, e.g. across mountain passes, pack animals might be the only feasible means of transport, and the *vectuarii* of Genoa and Asti who ran the traffic across the Alps to Champagne at the end of the thirteenth century apparently employed horses for the purpose. But carts of varying sizes as a rule made up the bulk of medieval trade caravans. A thirteenth-century tariff of Péronne suggests that the purposes of local traffic were served by the *colliers* – the medieval coolies – who drew barrows and other small vehicles *ad collum;* and that some local traffic also went by pack-horses. But the bulk of the traffic was apparently borne by the *bronnette*, a cart on two wheels, which according to a text of 1327 was capable of carrying a fardel of thirteen cloths; and more still by *car* or the *carrette* on four wheels capable of carrying a cargo two or three times that of the *bronnette*.

The Péronne cart was not substantially different from the vehicle commonly used by peasants in the daily routine of their agriculture, and peasant carts therefore provided the main reserve of medieval transport. Wherever the accounts of local bulky traffic have survived, more especially of stone, brick, wood, or charcoal, we find it carried by horse and cart or ox and cart hired or requisitioned from nearby villages. Peasant carting was, however, in the nature of things seasonal and could not supply the needs of trade all the year round. It is therefore not surprising that regular traffic along the main lines of communication was in the hands of men who specialised in the business of transport and acted as common carriers. English records have preserved evidence of common carriers traversing the country in the thirteenth, fourteenth and fifteenth centuries from Southampton to Winchester and Oxford, from the Cotswolds by road and river to London, from the midland counties to the Stourbridge Fair near Cambridge, from Westminster and Oxford to York and Newcastle-on-Tyne. In towns like London there was a recognised profession of 'brokers of carts' who acted as intermediaries between carters and owners of cargo. Sometimes whole rural areas specialised in carting services. In the middle of the fourteenth century the carriers who transported wool from Flanders to Bâle were mostly Alsatians and Saarois; the Brabant route to the south was used mainly by carters from Lorraine, and the overland routes from Toulouse to the Atlantic seaports mainly by the wagoners of Béarn.

Wheeled traffic could not have been so general had roads been as impassable as some of the roads which Arthur Young depicted in the eighteenth century. Judged by modern standards they were certainly bad beyond all comparison, and most local roads were no more than mud tracks barely useable in bad weather. To conclude, however, that every King's road 'made and maintained itself', or to argue, as so well-informed a historian as Marc Bloch did, that medieval roads in general were no more than *l'endroit où on passe*, barely differentiated from fields and field tracks, is perhaps too disparaging a generalisation.[11] It may be true of the very early local example Bloch quotes: the village road which, in Flodoard's story, St Theodulph prevented from being ploughed up. On the other hand it could not possibly have applied to at least one local road in thirteenth-century Cheshire. For when the Cistercian abbey of Vale Royal in Cheshire was erecting its buildings, peasant carts transported stone from the quarry at Eddisbury about eight miles away, and made thousands of journeys, most carters managing to make two complete journeys – a distance of about 30 miles – per day for months at a time: and winter months at that.

The generalisation applies even less to main roads. Main roads artificially levelled and drained were not universal; roads with artificial

[11] C. T. Flower, *Public Works in Medieval Law*, II, p. xvi (Selden Soc. Publications, Vol. XL for 1923).

metal or paved surfaces must have been very uncommon. Yet road approaches to a number of towns were frequently paved, and artificial road beds were also to be found in the open country. In origin they were mostly Roman, for in spite of all the shifts and changes in medieval routes, Roman roads were used whenever possible. In England ancient Roman ways dominated the medieval road system, and the main roads on a surviving fourteenth-century map were little different from what they had been ten centuries earlier. Nor were they in this respect much different from what they were to be four centuries later, and it is also doubtful whether their surfaces were much worse. Their foundations were that many centuries 'newer' than in the eighteenth century, and in addition the average medieval cart was probably lighter than the later wagon. It was seldom furnished with metal tyres, which the Elizabethan legislators found so destructive of road surfaces.[12]

It is also probable that in England, parts of France and the Low Countries, surfaces and drainage were kept up to a standard well above that of a mere track. In most European countries the law of the road and the surveyance of roads were lax and rudimentary. Yet to assume, as Marc Bloch did, that roads were not subject to special legislation and control is not altogether true, even of France. For the legal notion of *strata publica* was part of the legal doctrine of thirteenth-century France, even if it may not have been greatly respected in practice. In this country, where documents have survived in greater abundance, they contain numerous indictments of people guilty of obstructing public roads, encroaching on them, or neglecting their duties of maintenance. And the indictments are evidence not only of the disrepair and neglect of roads but also of the legal and administrative provisions for their upkeep. For in Common Law, as defined by Bracton and enforced by royal courts, the definition of the King's Highway included not only military roads but all roads leading to ports and markets, and their destruction or obstruction was an offence against the king. In addition, law and custom charged landlords and vills with the maintenance of the *via communis* in good passable order.

That the law was not always enforced may be taken for granted; and at certain periods the gap between law and practice was bound to be wide. In England the work of maintenance was as a rule confined to the upkeep of drains and ditches, and the road was not deemed impassable except when flooded or barricaded. Moreover, in the late

[12] K. Lamprecht in his well-documented appendix on roads in Rhineland (*Deutsches Wirtschaftsleben im Mittelalter*, (Leipzig, 1886), II, 236ff.) emphasised the continued use of Roman roads in the early Middle Ages; but his evidence does not support his argument that as time went on waterways replaced the Roman roads.

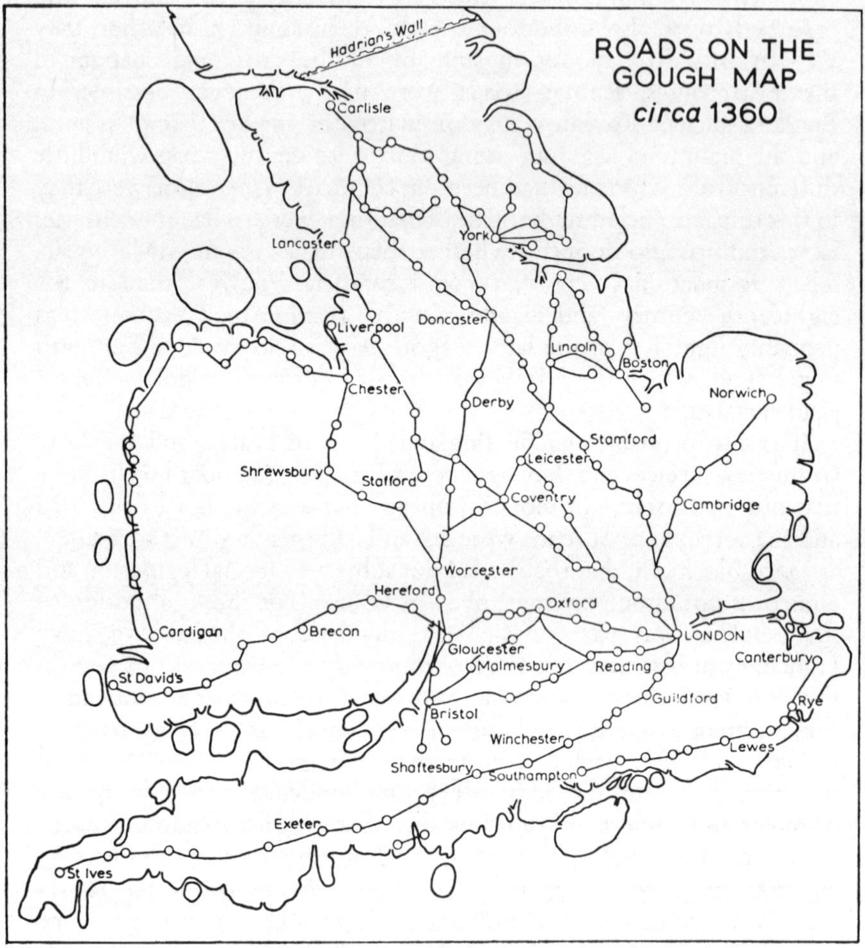

Map 2. The Gough Map. Reproduced from *Historical Geography of England*, ed. H. C. Darby, Cambridge, 1936.

fourteenth and fifteenth centuries the system, linked as it was with feudal obligations and manorial dues, may have suffered from the commutation of services and from the general tendency on the part of the landlords to cut their capital investments. The Royal Commissions of walls and dykes to some extent succeeded in checking the deterioration of bridges as well as of the main sea walls and dykes, but could not and were not expected to establish an effective national control over roads.

Yet, if in some respects daily practice fell short of legal ideal, in one or two respects the ideal was sometimes outstripped by practical achievements. Thus substantial towns paved their roads and levied a special pavage tax for the purpose. Roads across moors and fens often included causeways and reinforced beds which cost much to build and to maintain. The causeway by the Holland bridge near Boston was made up of thirty bridges; a road across Sedgemoor near Glastonbury was built of stone on a foundation of brushwood and alder sleepers held together by oak balks.

Some of the road works were carried out by princes. The French kings may have neglected to enforce the law of roads, but English thirteenth-century records have preserved evidence of work on roads and bridges undertaken by the crown on its own initiative. In England the crown in preparation for its military expeditions often undertook works on a very great scale, as in 1277 when Roger Mortimer was appointed to enlarge and widen roads and passes into Wales, or in 1283 when Royal Commissioners were appointed to widen the passes into Wales to a bowshot in width. But not all road works were fruits of state initiative. Religious houses, municipalities, landlords and private benefactors, all made their contributions. The Holland causeway was built by a religious house; the Glastonbury causeway was in fact maintained by another religious house. The Stecknitz canal which in 1398 cut across the base of Jutland peninsula was a part of Lübeck's endeavour to support the land road in competition against the sea route by the Sound. Similarly, when in 1332 the town of Ghent busied itself with the repair of a distant stretch of road near Senlis in the neighbourhood of Paris, this was taken for what it was – an act of enlightened self-interest of a community dependent upon traffic across France. History has not preserved the names of the anonymous masons (some writers thought they might have been smiths) or donors who by 1237 opened up the pass of St Gotthard by constructing a road and a bridge across the gorges at Schöllenen, thus opening up a great new line of communication between Italy and Europe. But records of all European countries have preserved scores and hundreds of references of charitable gifts, by will and otherwise, for the building and improvement of communications: gifts which contributed as much as acts of municipal and princely governments to the main system of European communications.

In the main, private enterprise and private benefactions were primarily concerned with bridges and causeways: so much so as to suggest to one historian of public works the generalisation that, whereas the Romans were road-conscious but were quite prepared to cross rivers by fords, the men of the Middle Ages were essentially bridge-conscious. The writer has cited the part bridges played in the ancient feudal obligation of *trinoda necessitas*, as well as the frequent references to pontage, a local tax levied for the upkeep of bridges.[13] But he could also have cited, if he wished, the English evidence of the building and repairs of bridges and the more stringent enforcement of legal obligations for the upkeep and maintenance of bridges. And if there is anything in this generalisation, it may well be connected with what is now known about Roman inefficiency in the use of draught animals. Where the Romans moved themselves and their goods on horseback, medieval men used carts.

A high proportion of bridges, both in France and England, are first mentioned in the twelfth and thirteenth centuries, pointing to the completion and perfection in that period of local road systems supplementing the older Roman grid where this survived and serving the specific needs of the medieval economy and society. The relationship of the development of this local system with the economic development of the countryside is clear: the numerous local roads of medieval Europe were linked with the general movement of economic development precisely because they served economic purposes.

The main alternative to wheeled traffic, however, was not the pack-horse but the barge and the boat. Here and there records have preserved curious instances of short sea routes for a time becoming unaccountably dear, but generally, in the Middle Ages as in modern times, carriage by water was much cheaper than by land; and this was one of the reasons why river traffic was able to bear the heavy tolls which weighed on it in so many countries. Traffic in heavy goods, such as timber and coal, over long distances was only possible where cheap waterways were available. Mineral coal was known as 'sea coal', not because it was necessarily mined by the sea but because in came to the south by river and by sea. Water transport explains also why in the south and east of England it was cheaper to import timber from the Baltic and Norway than from the north-west midlands and why it

[13] C. T. Flower, *Public Works*, p. XIX.

paid to import building stone from Normandy for the erection of cathedrals and castles in southern England.

Sea transport was cheap in spite of the small size of the medieval boat and in spite of the costly methods of navigation. Medieval shipping was as a rule coastal. Whether because navigation was mainly by sounding, or whether because the high seas were thought dangerous, masters preferred to hug the coasts. Whenever possible they left the sea and sailed by internal waterways, and Holland owes much of its importance as a centre of entrepôt trade to the medieval seaman's liking for the shallow and sheltered waters of Dutch rivers and canals stretched along the east to west route. Further east and west along the same route ships plied when possible in the narrow waters between the islands and within sight of dry land. As long as these methods prevailed, sea transport was bound to be relatively expensive, for it involved constant reloading at points where the coastwise route was interrupted by land masses. Lübeck and Hamburg were two such reloading places half-way from Bruges to Danzig. Amsterdam and Rotterdam, the two terminal points of the Dutch waterways, were two other ports serving the same function. There was also a great deal of reloading into lighters in seaports which, like Bruges, happened to be situated in silted-up river estuaries. Cranes – and they were to be found in a number of large ports – lightened the labour, but they could not do away with it altogether.

Both the size of the boats and the methods of navigation may have improved as the Middle Ages drew to their close. The history of the shipbuilding industry in the Middle Ages has not yet been written, and the technical history of medieval ships, though better known, is still incomplete. But in so far as it is possible to generalise from the present state of knowledge, it appears that in the later Middle Ages more merchant ships were carvel-built than in earlier centuries and that clinker-built boats were ousted from the main trade routes across the north seas. The Genoese and Spanish carrack, a swifter though not necessarily a larger vessel, did not as a rule go much further east and north than the ports of Flanders and southern England, but towards the end of the Middle Ages it dominated England's western approaches and the sea-borne trade in the Mediterranean. In addition, in the later Middle Ages once a year there came into Southampton and Bruges the great Venetian galleys. But the mainstay of the new merchant shipping in the northern seas were the slower and roomier boats of local origin. The typical ships of the English wool and wine fleets and of the Dutch and Hanseatic shipping in the North Sea and the Baltic were the cogs and hulks frequently displacing as much as 100 or 200 tons and sometimes approaching the 400 and 500 ton limit.

Whether as a result of these improvements or through the spreading use of the compass or through the growing knowledge of their element, the seamen of the later Middle Ages ventured more frequently than before into the open sea. Such voyages had, since times immemorial, been occasionally made by Irish, Scandinavian and English merchantmen trading to Iceland, but from the economic point of view the most important instance of navigation not wholly coastal was the *Umlandfahrt* – the route to the Baltic round the Sound which was probably opened by seamen of Zealand some time in the middle of the fourteenth century. The direct routes as well as the larger ships must have helped to reduce the freights, and it was on lower freights that the Dutch established their sea power in the course of the fifteenth century.

In addition there were the internal waterways. The classical country of river navigation was east of the Elbe and more especially east of the Oder – in Lithuania, Poland, Galicia. Among the western Slavs there were whole societies – villages and regions – which lived on and by their broad and sluggish rivers. In the course of centuries the Lithuanian and Slavonic peasants and fishermen had developed a system of river navigation ideally adapted to the transportation of timber and other bulky cargoes. The usual transport was by a local variant of a raft – the Slavonic *dubassy* – large timber platforms capable of carrying temporary huts and a great deal of miscellaneous cargo as well as large quantities of timber. Hence the importance of eastern river ports like Thorn, Kovno and Brest-Litovsk. Hence also the prominence which rivers and weirs occupied in the records of eastern European trade and in the trade treaties between the Germans and the Slavonic princes.

It is doubtful whether rivers were equally important in the west, but here and there they formed essential links in transcontinental routes. The Seine was a great trade artery of northern France and one of its main grain conduits, served and largely dominated by the rival companies of riparian traders of Paris and Rouen. The part which the Somme and the Oise played in the grain traffic has already been mentioned; the Scheldt and the Meuse never ceased to serve the needs of Flemish traffic. At times most of the great rivers of Europe, the Rhine, the Main, the Weser, the Elbe in Germany; the Loire, the Rhone, the Garonne in France, carried much of the heavy long-distance traffic. If they did not always do so and if, in spite of the greater economy of water carriage, traffic was at times apt to desert the great waterways, the fault lay with the owners of tolls who preyed upon them. It has already been shown how the general tendency was for the river tolls to multiply and how at times some rivers, mainly

German, came near to being deserted by the merchant and the barge-man. Yet even in the later Middle Ages they were not deserted altogether. Traffic was reduced but never stopped.

In England rivers were freer than in most other parts of Europe and formed an organic part of the English route system. The Thames, the Lea, the Stour, the Wye, the Severn, the Avon, the Humber, the Trent, the Yorkshire Ouse, the Witham and other rivers were busy trade arteries reaching far into the interior. The Thames was navigated well into Oxfordshire, although in the fifteenth century wool from the Cotswolds was as a rule loaded on barges no further west than Henley. Nottingham was connected with the sea through the Trent and the Humber. In conjunction with the Ouse and the Fossdyke the Trent formed a chain of waterways from York to Boston. The Humber was also a great waterway serving places as far inland as York and Beverley. Other and smaller rivers with their estuaries were linked to the main rivers and marked the points at which England's inland ports sprang up in the course of the Middle Ages.

In England, in Flanders, in the northernmost reaches of the North German rivers, the waterways were kept up more or less continually and more or less efficiently. We read of course of mills and fishing weirs obstructing the passage, of mudbanks allowed to form, but we also read of dredging operations, of repairs to banks and embankments, of prosecutions for neglecting and obstructing the care of the waterways. Indeed in this country the very frequency of complaints shows what medieval men expected from their waterways and bears indirect witness to the use men made of the transport facilities they found. Even in England, however, well served as that country was by its rivers, most traffic went by routes which combined overland and riverine ways or else went wholly by land. For this the facts that waterways might suffer neglect or be clogged by obstructions were not the sole reasons. River directions did not always correspond to the directions trade needed to follow and even for goods going by water overland feeder routes might be required. The meandering courses of rivers also meant that distances by water were often longer than by road and on some of their reaches navigability might be restricted by flooding or shallows or shifting sand banks. These difficulties coupled with the naturally sluggish pace of movement by river, especially upstream, made it expensive of time. Road transport might even be preferred to a roundabout sea voyage. Thus, in the later Middle Ages, much of the transit of goods between Southampton and London was by road, but this reliance on roads in no way prevented Southampton from becoming London's most important outport for trade to and from the Mediterranean.

Viewed in retrospect, medieval trade seems abundantly provided with means of communications – roads, sea lanes, rivers. Drawn on the map the network may indeed appear more imposing than it in fact was, for the final test of a transport system is not its density on the map but its effect on costs; and the costs were doubtless higher than the plethora of routes and quasi-routes might suggest to the uninstructed. What the average costs in fact were, no historian could now so much as guess, and it is doubtful whether the guess would be worth making even if it could be made. The most salient feature of trading costs in the Middle Ages was their infinite variety – a variety which would distort and falsify any attempt to strike an average for the system as a whole. Even a cursory survey of freights and charges would reveal striking contrasts in costs at one and the same time along routes of equal length and of similar physical character. In times unfavourable to commerce and on routes least favoured by governments, the charges could be very high and indeed prohibitive. But it would of course be a truism to insist that being prohibitive they must not be taken to represent the average costs of trade along the main lines of communication. For on routes which were so heavily taxed, or were so badly served by transport, or were so profoundly disturbed by war and piracy as to be unsuited to active trade, traders were not in fact active. They frequented instead those routes on which transport was relatively free and cheap. In theory this may have raised the costs of trade higher than they might have been had the merchants' choice of routes been unrestricted and had all the potential trade routes been in service; but in practice merchants engaged in the main branches of medieval trade could in most times find routes which were reasonably cheap or at least not so costly as to justify excessive 'traders' margins' or greatly to restrict the demand for commodities and their supply.

Thus the few surviving figures of costs of cartage in and around the Hanseatic towns suggest that in the second half of the fourteenth century it was sufficiently low to make it possible to divert the grain trade to land routes at a time when the river traffic was being choked up by tolls and taxes. The same conclusion also emerges from the English evidence which is sufficiently abundant to justify an impression more nearly statistical. The manorial rolls and other surviving accounts suggest that the existence of the peasant reserve of carts kept the level of cartage costs low. In 1278 a long and expensive transport operation on the king's behalf from Rhuddlan via Chester to Macclesfield, a distance of about 70 miles, was carried out at an average cost of 6*d.* per day per cart with two horses. The average charge elsewhere appeared to be from 3*d.* to 4*d.* per carthorse per day. Thorold Rogers computed that where the service was carried out over long distances by common carriers, who bore the legal responsibility of bailees of the goods and had to undertake loading and unloading, the charge worked out as about 3½*d.* per ton per mile for the double journey. But the services of peasant carts were much cheaper. According to Thorold Rogers a peasant cart could be hired at any time of the Middle Ages at an average charge of 1*d.* per ton per mile when the journey there and back was made in a day, and the charge did not appreciably rise even after the price revolution of the sixteenth century. For Norfolk a local historian has assembled the local carting charges in the fifteenth century, and these often worked out if anything lower than Thorold Rogers' penny. At these rates the cost of transporting goods over 50 miles would in the middle of the fourteenth century be rather less than 1.5 per cent of the value of the cargo if it were wool, and about 15 per cent if it were grain.

Sea transport was even cheaper, so long as it followed the well-established and regular sea lanes. The cost of shipping a tun of Gascon wine to Hull or Ireland at the end of the fifteenth century worked out at about 8*s.* per tun or rather less than 10 per cent of its f.o.b. price in Bordeaux. It appears that in the late fourteenth and fifteenth centuries the transport charges in relation to the f.o.b. prices were if anything lower than a century earlier. In the fifteenth century the transport costs of wool from London to Calais, including the costs of convoy, worked out at about 4*s.* per sack or rather less than 2 per cent of its f.o.b. price in London or Dover. A weigh (400 lb.) of coal cost about 2*s.* to transport from Newcastle to the south, presumably to the Low Countries, whereas transport charges of a certain shipload of about 200 tons of miscellaneous, mostly valuable, cargo from Bergen-op-Zoom to London in the middle of the fifteenth century worked out at £20, or 2*s.* per dead-weight ton.

These charges were not very high, and they may largely explain why it was that in such active and well-established branches of trade as English wool exports to the Low Countries or the Gascon wine exports to this country the distributors' margins were not exceptionally high even if judged by modern standards. The surviving evidence of the wool contracts and the figures given in a fifteenth-century treatise, the *Noumbre of Weyghtes*, make it possible to estimate the average cost of handling wool on its way from the grower to the foreign buyer. The total cost of packing, transport from a Midland county to London, custom and subsidy (the latter at the lower English rate), amounted to about £2 13*s.* 4*d* per sack. To this there has to be added the freight from London or another wool port to Calais, including the expenses of the convoy, which in the second half of the fifteenth century worked out at about 4*s.* per sack (6*s.* 8*d.* per sarpler of rather less than two sacks). The average price which an English exporter was expected to pay for a sack of high quality wool in the Cotswolds in the second half of the century averaged about £8, so that the total expenses would amount to about 40 per cent of the inland price and would bring the total cost of a sack to a stapler in Calais to rather more than £11. The selling price of the fine Cotswold wool in Calais and Bruges fluctuated between £12 and £13, thus leaving a nominal profit of £1 to £2 per sack of fine wool. A certain amount of disguised profit was also made on various allowances and premiums for differences of weight, wastage, etc.[14]

It is also possible to estimate with some accuracy the cost of distribution of Gascon wine. We are told that the f.o.b. prices at Bordeaux in the second half of the fourteenth century established themselves somewhere in the neighbourhood of nine Bordeaux livres and were made up of 5 li. paid for grapes, for the making of wine and for brokerage, 1 li. 10 sous paid for transport to Bordeaux, and 2 li. 10 sous for Great Custom from which the merchants of Bordeaux and the privileged merchants were exempt. Sea transport to English ports of the south and east coast varied between 2 li. 10 sous and 5 li. per tun and about 1*s.* 6*d.* had to be paid for various dues in English ports. The costs in England therefore worked out somewhere in the neighbourhood of 14 livres or about £5, and the wholesale price for Gascon wine in London appeared to be not greatly in excess of that figure. Considering the length of the route and the many hands through which the wine had to pass on the way from the Gascon grower to the English vintner, the added charges were by no means out of proportion to the costs of transport and handling which were to prevail in the wine trade of later ages.[15]

A somewhat similar conclusion would probably emerge from the study of other 'regular' branches of northern commerce – Baltic timber, Skanian herring, Bay salt. In the first half of the fifteenth century the price of salt in Danzig immediately on arrival of the Bay fleet was barely twice that which, following the English attack on the Bay fleet in 1449, the merchants claimed to be the cost of the salt at Bourgneuf. What is more, it competed in price with salt originating from Saxon and other nearby sources. Transport and expenses of handling were obviously not the main constituent of costs.

On the other hand, the trades which did not happen to enjoy the

14 '*The Noumbre of Weyghtes*', Brit. Mus. Cotton, Vespasian E. ix; E. Power and M. Postan, *Studies in English Trade in the Fifteenth Century* (London, 1933), 70–2.

15 R. Boutruche, *La Crise d'une société* (Paris, 1947), 151, n. 1; Francisque Michel, *Histoire du commerce et de navigation de Bordeaux* (Bordeaux, 1867–70) I, 123, 127.

advantages of relatively free and cheap lines of communication could at times be weighed down with vast expenses *en route*. What is more, even in favoured trades, like the English wool exports or the Gascon wine trade, war and commercial conflict sometimes obstructed the normal channels and added greatly to costs. Whereas in normal years, e.g. in the first two decades of the fifteenth century, the wholesale prices of Baltic timber in English ports were barely twice those in its Polish places of origin, in the years of 1437 and 1438, when trade between England and Danzig was opened after an interval of embargoes, prices were exceptionally low in Poland, very high in England, and the distributive costs and profits were inordinately high. Wainscoting then cost little more than 2 marks per hundred in Poland and 5 marks in Danzig and fetched 24 marks in Yarmouth; bowstaves which cost 14 marks per great hundred in Danzig were 51 marks in England; planks (*klapholz*) about 10 marks in Danzig and 35 marks in England.[16] Similarly, in the middle and second half of the fifteenth century, when direct relations between England and Gascony were broken by war and French occupation, and Gascon wine had to find its way through neutral countries and neutral hands, the cost of transport and of handling was so high as greatly to reduce both the price in Bordeaux and the price in England and indeed to reduce the English wine trade to a mere shadow. Even in the English wool trade the costs were not elsewhere as low as they appeared to be along the route which led from the wool grower to the stapler in Calais. Thus, the Italian merchants and the Englishmen who sent wool to Italy in the fifteenth century must have found transport and other charges very high. To begin with, the Italian merchants in England had to pay what amounted to disguised bribes for licences to avoid the staple of Calais and they also had to pay higher export duty. The transport was also costlier. According to the record of expenses incurred in the shipment of the King's wool to Italy in the late seventies and early eighties of the fifteenth century, the freight of a sack carried by a galley to Venice amounted to £3.3*s*. 4*d*. – which was much less than the costs by the land routes – and the total cost of a sack of wool to the exporter came to well over £14. The wool then sold in Venice at about £20 per sack, and the profit of £5 to £6 per sack was much higher than that earned by staplers on their shorter and safer route.

In short, medieval communications, like other trading activities, suffered much more from instability and uncertainty, political in origin, than from high costs of an inefficient transport service. Inefficient the service certainly was, wasteful of manpower and other resources; but

[16] Hirsch, *Danzig's Handels- und Gewerbsgeschichte*, VIII.

so was also medieval industry and agriculture. Judged by modern standards the making and growing of goods for sale may well have been costlier than the carrying of the goods to the consumer. To put it more abstractly, the proportion of trading costs to total costs was probably less in the Middle Ages than it is now, which is merely another way of saying that far greater economies have resulted from industrial revolutions of the eighteenth and nineteenth centuries than from the corresponding improvements in transport and distribution. If so, this may be one of the reasons why men in the Middle Ages found it not only necessary but also possible to trade and why commerce played the part it did in the economic life of the Middle Ages. And if it can be shown – as it appears probable – that local taxation, war and piracy became more disturbing and more difficult to circumvent as the Middle Ages drew to their close, this may also help to account for some of the 'long-term' trends of medieval trade. These trends will form the subject of the remaining sections of this chapter.

II. *The Age of Expansion*

(1) THE ORIGINS

The goods entering northern trade were as a rule products of local agriculture and industry and were often sold and bought in small quantities out of current production. From this point of view the great inter-regional currents differed in little but magnitude from the operations on the local markets. The staple commodities of international trade were handled in bulk and travelled over longer distances, but there was no hard and fast line between local and international trade. Both depended upon the surpluses of local production, rural and urban, and both grew with the general expansion of population and production.

It should therefore be possible to account for the 'origin' of northern trade without invoking any special cause not inherent in the general economic development of north-western countries themselves. Inter-regional trade, like the local trade from which it developed, was more or less endemic in the history of European society. Its use was familiar to prehistoric man, and there is therefore no reason why at the beginning of the Middle Ages men should have had to learn anew the lesson of its necessity and convenience. It has already been suggested that in the very choice of their *habitat* the tribal groups of northern Europe appeared to assume the existence of inter-regional exchanges. For otherwise it would be very difficult to account for their deliberate migration into the waterlogged plains of the Rhine littoral, the fiords and uplands of Norway and the fenlands of Britain; or for the emergence at the very dawn of the Middle Ages in most European countries of specialised communities of sheepfarmers, fishermen, charcoal burners, saltmakers and miners. It could of course be argued that in the early stages of medieval settlement men were able to wring a balanced supply of necessities from lands which eventually supported specialised economies. But some regions – fishing areas like the estuary of the Rhine, or wool-growing areas of northern England – were fully specialised very early in the Middle Ages; and regional specialisation implies inter-regional exchange.

This does not, however, mean that specialised societies were the only ones to engage in trade. Some trade must have been essential even to agricultural areas capable of highly variegated cultivation and of a highly self-sufficient economy. For, however self-sufficient the large estates or the villages in the continental interior of north-western Europe in the Dark Ages, they were never entirely independent of commercial supplies from outside or unaffected by division of labour within. Few agricultural villages themselves produced their salt, their iron or all their textiles. And however closed the economy of a village, not all households in it were equally self-sufficient. From the earliest centuries of the Middle Ages there were to be found in the medieval villages and estates craftsmen – smiths, potters, and sometimes even carpenters and weavers. Among the peasant cultivators themselves there always existed smallholders, who had to work for wages, and substantial peasants, who had surpluses to dispose of. Rents, reckoned and often paid in money, were older than the oldest manorial documents; while wages were seldom paid wholly or entirely in kind. In order to pay rents the peasants had to sell their produce; and whenever wages were paid in money the wage-earners presumably spent them at the market. Indeed an unbiased student of medieval agriculture cannot avoid the conclusion that social existence in medieval villages would have been impossible without some market and some trade.

This conclusion is in the nature of things hypothetical, but it is sufficiently obvious to shift the onus of proof from those who assume some trade at all historical times to those who wish to deny its existence at any period of the historical, as distinct from the pre-historical, past.

In this sense medieval trade never 'arose'; but it undoubtedly expanded and contracted. During the six or seven centuries of its documented history the quantities of goods entering European markets grew and declined; and so did the area in which they circulated. But whereas the territorial scope of medieval trade is on the whole easy to trace on the medieval map, the changes in the volume of northern trade are very largely a matter of guesswork. So scanty is the quantitative evidence of medieval trade that it is not surprising to find historians still differing about the scale as well as the chronology of economic growth. As late as the eve of the first Great War they were still able to assume a trend which closely corresponded to the distribution of the evidence. The paucity of records of trade in the early Middle Ages was taken to signify the scarcity of the trade itself, while the wealth of evidence in the fourteenth and fifteenth centuries was taken to mean that trade had grown in the intervening centuries. In dealing with individual regions historians may sometimes have been unable to fit them into the general curve, but when it came to the trade of western Europe as a whole they invariably represented the course of commercial development as a line steadily rising from the Dark Ages, when trade virtually disappeared, to the sixteenth century when it flourished abundantly.

Most obvious of all appeared to be the starting point of the story. Historians could take it more or less for granted that the irruption of the barbarians meant a complete break with the economic civilisation of the Roman Empire. The trade of Rome died a violent death, and with its demise European economy sank into a 'natural' condition, innocent of all industry and exchanges. Under the late Merovingian kings the Germanic societies were supposed to have moved forward far enough to acquire some trade and the rudiments of a settled urban life, but the advance did not become really rapid until the so-called Carolingian Renaissance. Soon after, the trade may for a time have been held back by the Norman and Saracen invasions and by the feudal anarchy of the ninth and tenth centuries. By the eleventh century, however, the pressure at the frontiers eased, and economic development and commercial expansion could be resumed and continued without break till the age of the 'great discoveries'.

The line, thus drawn, is straight and continuous – too straight and continuous for the present generation of historians. It is no longer possible to believe in the continued expansion of trade throughout Europe in the closing centuries of the Middle Ages, and more will be said about this later. There are also reasons for being doubtful about the beginning of the story. The starting point of the old version has been assailed and, probably, destroyed by converging attacks from two co-belligerent, though not necessarily allied, historical schools: Dopsch's and Pirenne's. Alfons Dopsch and his followers, basing themselves on their own interpretation of the literary evidence (principally Tacitus) as well as on recent archaeological evidence (principally the excavations in the Roman *Limes*), have attacked both the notion of the primitive barbarism of the German invaders and that of the complete break with the material civilisation of Rome. Dopsch found no difficulty in showing that in the 150 years between Caesar and Tacitus the Germanic societies had acquired most of the attributes of a fully articulated economic civilisation, including the use of coinage and the dependence on trade. He also discounted the accounts of the total destruction wrought by the Barbarians upon the material fabric of the Roman countries in which they settled. Urban life in the older Roman towns had declined but had not wholly disappeared. The Merovingian age, having thus inherited some of the commercial life of Rome, carried it on until it merged into the ascending movement of the Carolingian age.

But for this assumed continuity between the Carolingian and the Merovingian ages, Pirenne's view of Merovingian trade is not much different from Dopsch's. He also found it easy to show that the economic life of the Roman provinces in western Europe continued uninterrupted, even if impoverished, throughout the Merovingian age. Commercial relations with the east persisted; Syrian merchants and their goods circulated throughout Europe; and Marseilles still remained Europe's doorway into the Mediterranean and the Levantine world. A break did occur in the end, but according to Pirenne it took place not at the outset of the Dark Ages, but in the Carolingian epoch. In the eighth and ninth centuries Saracen invasions and Muslim domination in the Mediterranean broke Europe's commercial links with the South, while in the North, economic life – including urban life in general – dwindled and declined under the stress of Viking raids and conquests.

The difference between the two points of view is thus largely focussed on the exact role of the Carolingian age, and to that extent has not yet been fully resolved. The weight of the argument, however, appears to be against the theory of a violent break in the eighth and ninth centuries. The commercial links with the East and the traffic of costly luxuries may have suffered from the Muslim conquests and from the general insecurity of the times. But economic activity – settlement, colonisation, agricultural production – continued to expand; and in the history of European trade, economic activity within Europe mattered more than ease of communication with the outside world. For it has already been shown that northern trade was more dependent on the production of northern Europe itself than it was on the conditions in the eastern Mediterranean. The recurrent periods of disorder and anarchy during the Norman raids may have interfered with economic activities of every kind, but recent evidence from the north of France suggests that the ruin and devastation which the Norman invasions brought with them did not break the continuity of urban life in places like Arras. On the British side, the accumulating evidence points not only to the early development of trade across the Channel but to its continued functioning throughout the Dark Ages.

Yet, whatever is the final verdict on the Carolingian 'break', there can be little doubt about the continuity of development between the fourth and the seventh centuries. In Europe no violent break had intervened between the centuries officially Roman and those officially Barbaric, and there is equally little doubt that from the end of the tenth century onwards trade, like economic life in general, entered upon a period of rapid and general expansion.

(2) THE GROWTH

The course of medieval trade from the tenth century onwards can be traced both in its changing volume and in its expanding geography. From both points of view the trade grew until some time in the fourteenth century. The volumes of medieval production and of trade were on the increase, but expansion quantitatively considered was not its only significant feature. During this period northern economy was, so to speak, formed, for it was then that its separate regions, its trade routes and its commercial connections, composed themselves into a single trading area. In addition, throughout this period the trading area gradually spread eastwards and ended by absorbing the whole of central and eastern Europe.

The expanding volume of trade was a part of an economic process so general and so all-embracing that its story is easier to tell as an episode in the history of population and agriculture than as part of a narrower history of trade. For it was in agriculture and settlement that the signs of expansion were most obvious. In countries like England, where from the beginning of the thirteenth century onwards manorial documents can be made to yield something in the nature of statistical evidence, the growth of output can be traced for at least a century. But here and there, as on the estates of the bishopric of Winchester in 1209, production at the beginning of the thirteenth century already stood so high that the historian cannot fail to discern behind the later figures the dim outlines of an earlier increase stretching far back into the eleventh century and beyond.

The impression is greatly reinforced by what can be learned about settlement and population all over north-western Europe in the eleventh, twelfth and the thirteenth centuries. England and the continent west of the Elbe were rapidly filling up. In England the comparison of the population data in the Domesday Book with that of the manorial surveys of the twelfth century and the early thirteenth century, and of the latter with the Hundred Rolls of 1279 and the later manorial documents (rough and ready as such comparisons are bound to be), will show agricultural holdings multiplying manifold, and areas under cultivation growing apace. French evidence, mostly monastic, from Burgundy, Normandy and elsewhere in the tenth and eleventh centuries; German evidence from the Rhineland, Westphalia, Lower Saxony and Holstein; and, above all, the evidence from Flanders, tell the same story of growing population and expanding cultivation.

By the turn of the twelfth and thirteenth centuries the process had gone far enough for the surplus population to break out of the confines of what was now an old and relatively over-populated land and to spill over into new 'colonial' lands east of the Elbe. Here and there – as in Artois in the late eleventh and twelfth centuries, Flanders in the late twelfth and thirteenth, and possibly in parts of Champagne at the turn of the twelfth and thirteenth, and parts of westernmost Germany in the thirteenth – population was so abundant as to seek a solution to its economic problem in general industrialisation. It will be shown later that this period saw the rise of most of the great regional industries – that of cloth in Artois and Flanders, and probably Champagne; that of metal goods in Cologne, Liège and Dinant; that of iron and coal, lead and tin, in England, Hainault, eastern France and south Germany. But even in those parts of Europe which did not industrialise during this period the towns were receiving great and ever-growing reinforcements from the surplus population of the countryside.

This was indeed the time when the whole of western Europe became urbanised. Towns large and small sprang up all over the continent; most of them, whether old or new, grew fast throughout the period. In Flanders and in north Germany surviving topographical evidence, chiefly early maps, has enabled students to lay bare the main stages of urban expansion in the Middle Ages and to show how growing settlement added suburb to borough and repeatedly burst through successive girdles of urban fortifications. Elsewhere, and more especially in England and central France, the evidence of urban growth is less direct, but is none the less convincing. In the rural records of the time, as well as in its literary sources, the town figures as the place of opportunity to which the villein might flee in search of freedom and wealth. That in most of the greater towns of the eleventh, twelfth and thirteenth centuries opportunities were more or less unlimited is indirectly borne out by the prevailing freedom of immigration – a freedom which was not to be regulated and restricted until much later in the Middle Ages.

Growing production, both agricultural and industrial, and increasing population were bound to lead to greater trade and are sufficient to account for its expanding volume. Other favourable developments, more purely commercial and more directly involved with the processes of trade, may also have made their contribution; and one of them – the influx of bullion – may have played an important and certainly a conspicuous part. Increasing supplies of precious metals, and their expanding circulation, may at times have influenced the prices of commodities (and more about it will be said presently). Now and again they may also have influenced agricultural and industrial investment, and may thereby have given a further stimulus to both prices and production.

Recently, historians have laid special emphasis on the part which gold played as a means for the settlement of international accounts. It was Marc Bloch who first drew attention to the part which gold played in commercial exchanges between East and West, and it was he who first connected the main phases in the early history of international trade with the redistribution of gold in the world. Other students have supplemented Bloch's thesis and showed how dependent was the foreign trade of the Roman Empire on Rome's ability to pay for eastern supplies in gold. In the last two centuries of the Empire supplies of gold dwindled away and Rome's purchasing power in the East declined; yet in the early centuries of the Merovingian era enough Roman gold was still available in the west to make it possible for the Frankish society to make some use of the as yet open channels of travel and commerce with Byzantium and the Levant. With the Muslim conquests, however, the world supplies of gold were radically redistributed. The Muslim conquerors acquired both the accumulated stocks of precious metals and the monopoly of supplies of newly mined gold. Starved of gold, European commerce with the East languished, and its *malaise* continued until the tenth century. It was not until the turn of the millennium that Muslim countries began to import slaves, metal goods, timber and other commodities of European origin in quantities large enough to change the direction of gold movements. Eastern gold entered again into circulation, trade between West and East was resumed, and through it the whole economic life of Europe revived.[17]

This thesis, however questionable in detail, is in the main supported by a certain amount of evidence and can be accepted as a working

[17] M. Bloch, in 'Le Problème de l'or au Moyen Age', *Annales d'Hist. Econ. et Sociale* (1933), 4ff. M. Lombard, 'L'Or musalman du VIIe au XIe Siècle', *ibid.* (1947), 143ff. In England the issue of 1343 is generally regarded as the first effective gold coinage in the Middle Ages, even though gold coins had been minted some hundred years earlier by Henry III.

hypothesis. Yet, even if it were fully borne out by further researches, it would still be insufficient to account for the evolution of northern trade. The commercial currents directly dependent upon supplies of gold were those which flowed to and from the eastern Mediterranean. They doubtless touched economic life in the north at many points. Northern and western Europe as a whole may now have enjoyed (if 'enjoyed' is the right term) an active balance of trade, with the result that gold was now coming into many a country producing raw materials. Italian florins and ducats and perhaps Byzantine and Arabian gold coins now augmented the local resources of currency – mostly silver – and gold coinage began to be minted. But more important than the Italian supplies to Levantine and Byzantine gold was the real wealth which growing commerce generated. Much of it found its way into the hands of merchants all over Europe and could now be invested in industry and trade. Its chief beneficiary was doubtless Italy and, more especially, its great commercial cities, but from there radiating circles of investment and prosperity reached the outlying countries of medieval Europe, and it is doubtful whether any part of the continent escaped their effects altogether.

Yet, the effects on the trade of northern Europe could only be indirect. The opening of the Levant added relatively little to the demand for raw materials and manufactured commodities of European origin (metal goods being the chief exception). Slaves were the commodity which was most in demand in Islamic lands in the early Middle Ages and which, if we are to trust some recent studies, was mostly responsible for starting and maintaining the flow of gold from the East. But the traffic in slaves touched the economy of northern Europe at very few points, if at all. In the Dark Ages, i.e. between the seventh and eleventh centuries, the trade was largely in the hands of Jews and Syrians who took their 'cargoes' across Russia, Poland and western Germany to Spain and countries further east. Here and there they may have formed commercial *nuclei* within Europe: we are told that Verdun was an entrepôt centre of the slave trade, and it is possible that merchants resident there took part in the traffic. But from the point of view of western Europe generally, this was merely a transit trade skirting the outer fringes of its territory and leaving behind very little oriental gold. Later, from the eleventh century onwards, other commodities of European origin, such as cloth (and furs!), found their way east, and raw materials imported from the north went into the making of the Italian goods exported to the Levant. Yet the total quantities of continental goods thus exported were as yet barely sufficient to redress the entire balance of Europe's trade with the Muslim world and to support the commercial prosperity of the North.

Did the crusades make much difference? The idea that the crusades were a turning point in the history of European economy is one of the most cherished notions of economic history; and so also is the belief that having conquered the Holy Land the northern world proceeded to help itself to the wealth of the Levant. How true it is and whether true at all is a problem which more properly belongs to the history of Mediterranean trade. The repercussions of the crusades must however be mentioned here, even if the mention can only be of the briefest and vaguest.

An economic history of the crusades has not yet been written, but until it has been written, and the economic balance of the crusades has been struck, it will be difficult to say whether their consequence was to augment the flow of gold from Italy and the Levant to the continent of Europe, or on the contrary to drain the continent of its precious metals. Most probably the trickle of gold frequently changed direction, and at times contrary movements cancelled each other out. The occupation of the Holy Land may, to begin with, have brought in booty and ransom, and so must also have done the sack of Constantinople in 1204. On the other hand, ransom sometimes had to be paid and booty yielded to the Muslims. We are told that Richard I's ransom alone was the equivalent in value to 50,000 woolsacks, or much more than a whole year's exports. Similarly, crusading expeditions more often than not set up a drain on the western means of payment. The countries which sent them out financed them with levies and taxes; crusading nobles raised funds at home in many and various ways, but mostly by loans on which they could draw abroad. These methods of financing must have helped to mobilise the hoarded reserves of gold and silver, and thus indirectly to quicken the circulation and to influence prices and economic activity in general. Yet they must also have depleted the total supplies of gold in northern Europe, since they sent precious metals moving away from continental Europe towards Italy and the Levant. Ecclesiastical taxation in support of the Latin kingdoms, the voyages to the Holy Lands, the military and religious activities of the Templars and the Hospitallers, must all have acted in the same fashion and added to the continental debit balance with Italy and the east.

This does not of course mean that the crusades did not stimulate the economic development of Europe, but the stimulus, such as there was, must have come from factors more general than mere importation of bullion. If northern Europe felt it at all, it must have received it in the course of ordinary trading activities of the Italian merchants and through their expanding commercial and financial operations. In this revival bullion played its part, but it did so not by virtue of its function in international accounts, but as a result of its internal circulation and investment. And here again the Levantine current was a mere tributary, and probably a small one, of a far more abundant flow. Although Italians brought into Champagne, Flanders and England a certain amount of gold, mainly of their own coining, the bullion most in circulation was not Levantine or Byzantine and not even predominantly Italian. What is more, it was not gold.

Throughout the Middle Ages, and more especially in their earlier centuries, the precious metal most commonly used in coinage and in everyday payments was silver. The coins of northern Europe until the second half of the thirteenth century were all silver, and continued to be predominantly silver until the end of the Middle Ages. The evidence of mints, such as the accounts of the royal mints of England and the surviving registers or urban mints and exchanges, makes it quite clear that silver formed the bulk both of existing stocks of money and of the new accretion of metal. Gold and gold coins were relatively more common in international dealings presumably because gold was more convenient to transport and also somewhat more stable in value. In addition gold coins had the advantage of being as yet few – mostly Italian – and therefore free from the curse of variety and heterogeneity which afflicted the silver currencies of Europe. For these and other reasons, in clearing accounts of Italian merchants at the Champagne fairs of the thirteenth century as well as in commercial dealings with Italian merchants in other parts of northern Europe, payments were apt to be reckoned in gold coins. Similarly, royal debts to Italian bankers in England and France were frequently reckoned in ducats and florins. Yet there is no evidence that the Italian bankers in fact delivered equivalent sums in gold cash, and there is unmistakable evidence that loans reckoned in gold coins, such as the Frescobaldi loans to Edward I and the Bardi loans to Edward III, were often made and repaid in silver and in goods. And in international payments between merchants of other nationalities active in northern Europe silver pounds and marks, English and Flemish, were most commonly used both as units of account and of payment. So even if it remains true that gold figured prominently in international payments it did not wholly displace silver even there.

The bullion in circulation was thus predominantly silver, and it is very probable that the amount of silver circulating in the twelfth and thirteenth centuries increased. How large the increases were cannot be said with certainty, but it is obvious that the increases came from several sources. Some new silver doubtless originated from mines recently opened up. Although silver must have been mined in Europe throughout the Dark Ages, the main sources of European silver, in Hungary, in Saxony, in the Harz mountains and elsewhere, were not fully developed until the tenth, eleventh and twelfth centuries. Mines, however, were not the only and may not even have been the chief source of additional silver, for even in the earlier centuries of the Middle Ages the volume of currency depended not only on the additions of newly mined metal but also on the uses of accumulated stocks of bullion. For it appears highly probable that the economic changes of the twelfth century set into motion a great deal of wealth previously immobilised in hoards, plate or ornaments. And that the bulk of the bullion thus 'de-hoarded' must have consisted of silver is clearly brought out by the evidence of wills and mint accounts.

So whether any came in through the early medieval contacts with the Levant, or during the crusades, imported bullion could not be held responsible for the revival and growth of medieval trade. Some of the other monetary factors were more important, but even they were not and could not be decisive. Their influence on trade would normally be transmitted through changes in price levels; yet even changing prices had a limited effect.

The problem of prices is, in Italy at least, closely involved with that of monetary circulation. We know now that during the earlier centuries of the Middle Ages, i.e. before the thirteenth, some prices changed a great deal. From the very moment at which documentary references to them become at all frequent, i.e. from the middle of the twelfth century in England, and from the middle of the thirteenth century abroad, until the first quarter of the fourteenth century, food prices appeared to move steadily upwards. The English prices alone have so far been assembled for the earlier period. The work of collection and tabulation is as yet far from complete, but Thorold Rogers and, later, Lord Beveridge's team of archivists and historians have been able to analyse their data in a manner which enables a statistical trend to be traced.

Expressed in percentages the prices of 1150 were about 30 per cent of those in the first quarter of the fourteenth century; in other words the price rise in the intervening period was about three-fold. The price rise did not, moreover, begin in 1150, and, as far as the scanty evidence suggests, it went beyond that date. In so far as the figures of south-western Germany collected by Lamprecht can be relied upon, they suggest a progressive rise in prices from the eighth and ninth centuries to the tenth and eleventh, continued, though not so violently as in England, to the early thirteenth. Yet even Lamprecht's figures show a rise of at least 50 per cent between the second half of the twelfth century and the first half of the thirteenth.[18]

This was a veritable price revolution. Yet, in considering its economic effects, it is important not to argue by analogy with price revolutions of later centuries. For reasons which will have to be mentioned again more than once, the effect of price changes could not have been very general or widespread.

Table I. *English Wheat Prices, 1160–1339*[19]

(Twenty years' means)

Period	Wheat price in shillings (per qr)	Wheat price in grains of silver (per qr)
1160–79	1.89	534
1180–99	2.60	744
1200–19	4.33	1082
1220–39	4.19	1047
1240–59	4.58	1144
1260–79	5.62	1404
1280–99	5.97	1491
1300–19	7.01	1734
1320–39	6.27	1547

Agricultural output was bound to react to a secular rise in grain prices so steep and continuous, but its reactions may have differed from region to region. In the wine- and wool-growing areas of Europe, where the rural economy was one of cash crops, and even in certain areas predominantly arable, such as parts of western and northern France and above all southern England, estates continued to be run as large units producing mainly for the market, and even peasants marketed a considerable proportion of their output. And where the proportions to be sold were high, rising prices must have favoured and stimulated both output and sales. Indeed, the social historian of English agriculture cannot escape the conclusion that the high prices of the late twelfth and thirteenth centuries and the commercial boom in agricultural produce were to some extent responsible for the continued survival of the large-scale units of agriculture.

To this extent the agricultural boom left its impression on European trade. As cultivation of cash crops expanded, larger quantities of agricultural products came on the markets; as rural wealth grew,

[18] Lamprecht, *Deutsches Wirtschaftsleben*, II, 512ff; esp. tables, etc., on pp. 612–13.
[19] Cited by the courtesy of the late Lord Beveridge.

opportunities for miscellaneous trade widened. Thus far the effect of prices is clear enough. What is not so clear is whether regions where the bulk of agricultural production was in the hands of peasants were equally affected. And it is not known how far industrial commodities, industrial raw materials and industrial regions were directly involved in the price changes. Historians do not even know how the prices of non-agricultural commodities moved, if they moved at all. Evidence is very scanty and difficult to interpret. Such as there is suggests that prices for commodities like cloth and iron goods rose less steeply and less continuously than food prices. Prices for some commodities like coal and timber may even have fallen.

It is thus probable that price movements of the twelfth and thirteenth centuries were not 'general' in the sense in which the term is sometimes employed to indicate more or less simultaneous and synchronous shifts in the price levels in all the main groups of commodities. If so, the probability is that such changes as there were were not due to monetary causes. Not only the influx of foreign gold but even the far more important supplies of silver and the still more important changes in its employment and circulation, could not have been the prime movers in the great economic transformation of the period – a transformation of which the expansion of trade was merely a part.

There is no need, however, to end the discussion of prices on this agnostic note. For even if the price movements fail to establish bullion's responsibility for the commercial efflorescence of the age, they can still reveal the action of other and perhaps more effective causes. More especially, steep and continuous changes in food prices unaccompanied by similar changes in other prices make it more or less certain that the relative costs of agricultural production were rising, and this again indicates a growing pressure of population against land.

This is not the place to discuss general problems of medieval land and population; in so far as they are relevant to the history of trade they will be discussed again in a later section. Here it will suffice to note that all available evidence, especially for France and England, shows land rents, land prices and entry fines rising on a scale fully consistent with the hypothesis of 'pressure of population'. In this way the discussion of prices merely brings the argument of this chapter to the point at which it digressed to gold and monetary causes. Trade grew because Europe expanded. The lands of continental Europe carried an ever-growing population; growing population, in its turn, meant that agricultural production increased, that industries developed and that whole regions became industrialised. And growing wealth of rural Europe and economic specialisation of its regions meant bigger and better trade.

(3) THE PROFESSIONAL MERCHANT

Growth quantitatively considered was by no means the only important change in the history of medieval trade in its age of expansion. It was accompanied by other phenomena, less material, and more obviously related to the condition and behaviour of men.

One of them was the extension of professional trade. In general, the part which full-time merchants played in economic life, very insignificant to begin with, was becoming more important as time went on. Doubtless, some professional trade there must always have been. We are told of the Syrian and Jewish merchants visiting Gaul at the dawn of the Merovingian age, and probably forming in the predominantly rural societies of western Europe alien *nuclei* of resident merchants, not unlike the Jewish towns and townlets in the eastern states of nineteenth-century Europe. A travelling Jewish merchant of the eighth, ninth and tenth centuries arriving in western Europe from the east counted on finding there his coreligionists with whom he could trade, live and pray. When we are told by Gregory of Tours that, on his entering into Orléans, King Guntram was welcomed in Syrian, Latin and Hebrew, the presumption is that in the sixth century these were the native tongues of the merchants of Orléans.

Yet be it noted that merchants whose tongue was Latin were not altogether absent from the rudimentary communities of merchants. Evidence of indigenous merchants is scanty but is not altogether absent. We may know little about Philo, the merchant, whom Ausonius knew, or about Euphron of Bordeaux or about Eusebius of Paris, both mentioned by Gregory of Tours – their names like their age still appear to belong to Rome. But from the seventh century onwards evidence of merchants wholly indigenous becomes more frequent and more certain. In the seventh century King Dagobert founded the fair of St Denis which Franks, Frisians and Saxons (Anglo-Saxons?) frequented; in the same century we hear of Frankish merchants travelling into the lands of the Slavs and Avars.

Some of the indigenous merchants were doubtless men of substance, like Christophe of Tours, who, we are told, speculated in the wine of Orléans, but in the main they must have been small fry, travelling hucksters of foreign wares. Their stock in trade must have consisted almost entirely of the small luxuries required on the medieval estates and villages: spices, silks and other exotic fineries. For when it came to the buying and selling of agricultural commodities or of industrial articles locally produced, the services of the merchant were not always necessary. In medieval Europe, as in agricultural areas of our own day, the average producer was able to dispose of the petty surpluses of his household (eggs, cheese, hens, vegetables, milk, cattle and even grain) without the assistance of a professional trader. Similarly, wherever an industry happened to be organised in small handicraft units and goods were made in small quantities or to order, producers and consumers could deal with each other without the intervention of a trader. Not only the village smith and potter, but the urban butcher, baker and candlestick-maker themselves disposed of their produce. Even in the later centuries of the Middle Ages the distinction between craftsman and trader remained a very nebulous one, and men commonly traded with goods they themselves produced.

Merchantless trade, moreover, was not confined to transactions which were purely local. Manorial produce often travelled over long distances, and manorial trade in the early Middle Ages was sometimes in the hands of manorial officers themselves. Some of the larger estates were sufficiently large, and the quantities of marketable commodities which they produced were sufficiently great, to enable them to do their own selling, though perhaps it would be rash to assume that they always did so. Historians have made great play of the monastic *negotiatores* of the early Middle Ages, who were trade representatives of monastic houses selling their output in distant markets and sometimes making there the necessary purchases for their communities. The term *negotiatores* must not however be taken too literally. Some of the *negotiatores* were monks and manorial officials, but some may well have been professional merchants acting in the name of monastic houses and under their protection, just as the 'king's merchants' of the English kings of the thirteenth century traded under the protection of king's letters, but in a manner and on a scale wholly professional.

Much more important were certain other forms of non-professional or not wholly professional commerce, and most important of all was the commercial activity of certain semi-rural communities. There was nothing to prevent the members of the fishing and seafaring communities of Zealand and the Rhine estuary from venturing far away from their homeland in pursuit of markets and goods. The sea could not by itself provide for all their needs, but it enabled them to go anywhere they pleased in search of customers and supplies. Similarly, the fiords of Norway could neither feed nor occupy all the population throughout the year, and there was nothing to prevent the free Norse peasants from roaming the seas and visiting foreign lands.

In this way a great deal of trade could be conducted all over Europe by men who were, so to speak, part-time merchants.

There was thus a great deal of non-professional commerce: rather more in the early Middle Ages than later. Indeed, what historians sometimes describe as the period where medieval trade 'arose' may merely refer to the time when conditions favouring part-time trade disappeared and a professional merchant class spread.

Some such unprofessional commerce could of course be found even in the later Middle Ages. Monastic communities acted as traders whenever and wherever they happened to derive their income from large and regular production of marketable commodities. The English wool-growing monasteries of the twelfth, thirteenth and fourteenth centuries not only sold their wool clip regularly to foreign exporters but often undertook to supply them with *collecta*, i.e. wool they themselves bought up from the surrounding countryside. We can also find English landlords dabbling in wool trade in every century of the Middle Ages; squire and squireen of Gascony taking a hand in wine trade, landlords on both sides of the English Channel – in Devon as well as in Brittany – maintaining ships for piracy and trade. Similarly, seafaring communities of Zealand, Holland, Normandy and Brittany continued to combine a little trade and occasional piracy with their main occupations of fishing and shipping.

Broadly speaking, however, conditions in the later centuries were less favourable to part-time commerce than they had been at the dawn of the Middle Ages. In a number of medieval towns production of some commodities soon outstripped the potentialities of the local market. Cloth of the principal cloth-making towns of northern France and Flanders, metal goods of the towns of western Germany – to name only two most obvious instances – came to be made in large quantities for the distant and unknown demand; and whenever this happened the petty producer could not market his output, and the services of a merchant intermediary became unavoidable.

Still more significant and less obvious were the similar developments in the countryside. Feudal society and feudal law soon made it impossible for the average members of a rural community to combine agriculture with trade, while the passing of the large-scale demesne economy removed the *raison d'être* for the manorial *negotiatores*. In England it is possible to lay bare in the records of the wool trade the process whereby the social changes in wool-growing areas called forth a new merchant class. As the numbers of small sheepfarmers grew, so professional wool merchants interposed themselves between wool growers and wool exporters. The history of the grain merchant and fishmonger has not been investigated as fully as that of the wool merchant; but it seems more than probable that a similar connection was also to be found there.

The development of trade as a whole-time occupation played its part in the rise of towns. The story of the towns, their appearance and growth, does not belong to this chapter. Growth of towns has so far been mentioned as evidence of the general expansion of medieval economy, and need not be mentioned again except in so far as it was linked with the social transformation of trading activities. For so linked it doubtless was. Most historians are now agreed that the towns multiplied and grew in the two centuries following the tenth, for the simple reason that trade grew. Yet the logical and historical connection between growing trade and emerging towns is by no means an inevitable one. The Norsemen proved capable of engaging in active trade without towns; it is not at all certain that Dorstad and some of the other places mentioned as centres of Frisian trade in the seventh and eighth centuries were towns in the medieval and modern sense of the term and not merely clusters of fishing and seafaring settlements. At the very close of the Middle Ages most of the English wool trade was in the hands of merchants living in the country, and the bulk of cloth industry was in the hands of men who combined spinning and weaving with some agricultural pursuits and lived in what still were essentially rural habitations.

Indeed as long as industry and trade could remain part-time occupations and be in the hands of men who were also peasants, fishermen, landlords or monks, there was no need and little opportunity for commercial and industrial towns. The reason why at the height of the Middle Ages towns became necessary and indeed inevitable was not merely that trade expanded, but also that conditions of feudal society made it difficult for the expanding trade to remain in the hands of the rural classes and to be combined with other rural pursuits. At a time when life and all its vocations had become wholly professional, when war and government had become the exclusive occupation of the landlord and the freeholder, and when agriculture had become the whole-time occupation of the semi-servile peasant, trade had to become equally professionalised. Gone were the times when farmers from Norwegian fiords, fishermen of Frisia, and monk procurators of monastic estates or privileged officials of the Carolingian estates were able to run all the trade there was. Trade was becoming to an ever increasing degree the affair of whole-time merchants and artisans trading in a professional way.

The effect on towns was obvious. In order to be professional and to conduct trade all the year round merchants and artisans had to be exempt from the ties and liabilities which restricted the liberty of movement and freedom of contract of the lower orders of feudal society. Their houses and tenements with their shops had to be free from the obligations which burdened the rural tenures; their transactions had to be judged by a law better suited to dealings between merchant and merchant than were the feudal custumals and common law. Hence the essential function of the medieval towns, as non-feudal islands in feudal seas; and hence their appearance in large numbers in the eleventh century – the time when trade grew and feudal order matured. Hence also the crucial part which the charters of privilege (which were nothing else than guaranteed exemptions from feudal order) played in the origin and development of towns. Charters of this kind created boroughs out of villages, and cities out of castle suburbs; and charters of this kind punctuated the subsequent progress of urban communities on their way to full urban status. The rising town was thus essentially a political and legal phenomenon, even though it served an obvious economic function.[20]

The argument is obvious enough, yet it may at first sight appear to clash with what historians have recently discovered about the social history of the early medieval towns. The growing volume of historical studies of the so-called patrician families suggests that the upper layers of urban society in the Middle Ages sprang from the families which happened to own land in the towns in the early stages of their history, and got rich as the rents and land values of town property rose. In detail the process may have differed from region to region, but in general, towns as different as Arras in the eleventh century, Barcelona in the twelfth century, and Lübeck in the early thirteenth seem to conform to the common pattern. In all of them political and economic power in the early phases of their history belonged wholly or in part to the urban landowners or their descendants. Indeed, so general and so obvious was the landed interest in medieval towns that a generalising sociologist like Sombart was able to base on it his entire theory of medieval capitalism and to find in rising land rents the chief source of the 'initial' capital of medieval industry and trade.

Stated in terms so general and so simple the theory may indeed be difficult to reconcile with the impression of the town as the seat of a professional merchant class. But was the history of the 'patriciate'

[20] This argument is not affected by the well-known fact that agriculture continued to play a part, often an important part, in the economic activities of smaller towns. However agricultural the small town was, what differentiated it from the regions purely rural was its nucleus of traders and artisans.

in fact so uniform and so simple? In the first place not everywhere in northern Europe was the citizen landowner a linear descendant of the original owner of town sites. Some towns in the early Middle Ages had grown up on land belonging to their feudal overlords, whether kings or great feudatories. In some towns feudal landlords proceeded to alienate the income from urban property by sub-infeudation, by sub-letting and by outright sale of full property rights (burgage tenures in England, allodial tenements in France). But in some places, especially in the *villes neuves* of western Europe – artificial foundations of a somewhat later age – the feudal founders sometimes retained the superior title to property as well as its income. In the English boroughs and in some towns abroad, e.g. Bordeaux, the freehold and burgess tenures of urban sites were as a rule shared among a whole number of manorial landlords of the surrounding countryside: a fact which stimulated several German and English lawyers, and Maitland among them, to propound the famous garrison theory of borough origins.

Wherever the land was in feudal hands, and as long as it stayed there, the rising profits of urban landownerships largely by-passed the burgess inhabitants. Yet even in towns, where in the twelfth century the burgesses owned or otherwise held most of the land, they did so not so much by succession from the original landowners as through later investment. The famous history of the market of Lübeck, as expounded by Rörig, may indeed prove that the great Lübeck families had all sprung from a narrow circle of men who had taken part in the founding of Lübeck and owned the sites of the market place. But the same history also makes it clear that the urban landowners of Lübeck had come from merchant families of Westphalia and that their venture into landownership was merely an investment and part and parcel of their great commercial speculations beyond the Elbe.

Altogether the distinction between investment in trade and investment in land in the early medieval town can be drawn too rigidly. Not only did investments in land and urban rents come naturally to medieval merchants, but the reverse process – the investment into trade of wealth mainly derived from urban rents – was equally common and equally easy. Commercial partnership serving the purposes of investment had been known to European law since times pre-medieval. The sleeping partnerships of the *commenda* type were the general practice in Italian towns in the eleventh century; and the life of St Godric, which will be mentioned again presently, shows that the commercial partnerships were an established practice in eleventh-century England. And commercial partnerships, especially of the 'sleeping' kind, made it possible for urban wealth to be employed on a large scale in foreign trade, even if it happened to be derived from land.

Indeed this employment of wealth in speculative ventures to distant lands was more characteristic of the leading figures in medieval towns than their connection with land. If we are to trust Pirenne, the typical representatives of North European trade in the eleventh and twelfth centuries were the men he calls 'early capitalists', but who should be described more exactly as merchants trading abroad on a large scale. The trace they left in records is very faint, but here and there Pirenne was able to discern behind the fog and silence of early sources the fleeting shadows of the early capitalists. In one instance he was even able to draw a full-scale portrait of a merchant engaged in far-flung speculative trade. Godric, a trader of East Anglia at the turn of the eleventh and twelfth centuries, began as a beachcomber, became in the fullness of life a substantial merchant and a member of a partnership, and ended his life by becoming a saint and by inspiring a *Vita*.

In this the merchants of this age differed both from the class of small pedlars from which some of them must have originated and from the more sedate and less adventurous burgesses who were to dominate the trade in a later age. They were not primarily interested in the daily trade of the local market, and their indifference imprinted itself on the very economic character of the town. As long as they formed the governing group, the economic and social policy of the town itself was one of expansion, free immigration and relatively free trade. Our direct evidence of free immigration and free trade is of course very scanty: perhaps because it is in the nature of free trade to leave behind scanty traces in documents. But had settlement and local trade been as restricted as they were to become later, towns and town population could not possibly have grown as we know that they did. For growth and expansion was the hallmark of the age.

(4) THE MOVING FRONTIERS

The expanding and professionalised trade also had obvious geographical and political implications. Indeed, the economic geography of medieval trade and its involvement with international politics have been studied more fully and are understood better than almost any other aspect of the subject. For, unlike the other aspects of the history of trade, the story of moving frontiers and of emerging trade routes is compounded of war, politics and exploration, and has therefore been well illuminated by fully documented events. No wonder historians of trade have given them so much attention.

The attention, however, has been by no means unwarranted, for the political and geographical features of medieval commerce were not only conspicuous but also important. As trade increased and declined and as new regions were opened and old ones decayed, the whole balance of power in northern Europe altered. Nothing indeed proves more the essential function of inter-regional commerce in medieval life than the part it played in the rise and fall of European principalities or in their political, military and naval power.

The purely political implications of economic geography are perhaps most obvious in the opening phase of medieval trade. The one geographical feature of North European trade in the Merovingian and early Carolingian period which historians take more or less for granted is its withdrawal from the world economy of the Roman Empire. The fall of Rome meant that in the sixth century Gaul, Brittany and Rhineland no longer stood in the same relation to each other and to the rest of the world as three centuries previously. The economic links with Italy and the Mediterranean were not altogether severed, but the trade was undoubtedly becoming more localised. At the height of imperial prosperity, i.e. in the second century, the Empire formed an economic system dominated by the needs and the policy of metropolitan Italy. Needless to say, there were exchanges between the provinces and within each province taken separately, and it is a mistake to think that even at the height of the imperial era all roads led to Rome. Yet, broadly speaking, the main currents of Roman trade formed a co-ordinated system, to which each province made a distinct and sometimes a highly specialised contribution. This system began to disintegrate in the closing centuries of the Roman era and was all but gone in 473.[21] In the course of the fifth and sixth centuries, movements of inter-regional trade, such as there were, conformed ever more to the shifting needs and opportunities of the different northern regions and ceased to form part of an imperial network or to be dominated by imperial merchants.

Here are a few examples. In the third and fourth centuries Britain exported foodstuffs to feed the Roman legions on the Rhine. In the Merovingian age the exports to the lower Rhine did not cease – for all we know they may have grown – but they were dominated not by the needs of the Roman legions but by those of the population of the Rhineland and they now probably consisted of metals and cloth, both of which in the imperial times used to be taken elsewhere. Another example is the North Sea fisheries. At the height of the imperial era Roman merchants conducted from Utrecht an active fish trade between the delta of the Rhine and the more southerly provinces

[21] See above, pp. 121–31.

of the Empire. In the Merovingian times fish continued to be exported, but it now went in many other directions, including that of France and south Germany, and was carried by local merchants. Similarly, Flemish, Frisian and possibly English cloth, which may previously have been used to clothe the Roman legions, was now carried, among other places, to Scandinavia.[22]

This picture of northern trade, grown more local and directed away from the centres of the Empire, is wholly compatible with what we know of the activities of the Syrian merchants and the continued imports of oriental goods into Marseilles. What Syrian merchants and the port of Marseilles handled were probably the exotic goods of the Orient. The trade which was now becoming local and separate was the trade in the bulky and essential goods which was the northern trade *par excellence*; and such network of inter-regional exchanges as was now emerging was woven, not by Syrian merchants, but by other and more local groups of intermediaries.

Of the intermediaries, the earliest and the most prominent were the Frisians. They owed their importance to the geographical opportunities as well as to the geographical limitations of their land. Frisia stretched along the coast of the North Sea from the estuary of the Sincfal (now Zwin) to the estuary of the Weser. It was relatively infertile, but its network of navigable rivers opening into the sea, and its well-sheltered channels between islands, fitted it well for fishing, navigation and water-borne trade. Within it, the point which gathered to itself most of the commerce was Dorstad on the old estuary of the Rhine: a place of great renown, the 'city of forty churches'. Whether it in fact was a great city or merely a conglomeration of fishing and trading villages is a problem which archaeologists will have to decide, but it was already important enough to stamp itself upon most of the earlier references to Frisian trade. Later, especially in the ninth century, it rapidly lost its importance, partly through its destruction by the Normans, but chiefly through the change in the bed of the river from its old arm to the Waal. When this happened, the town of Tiel on the Waal took Dorstad's place, though in the process some of Dorstad's trade and much of its political importance may have passed to Utrecht.

From these centres, and from the delta of the Rhine as a whole, an entire network of routes radiated in every direction: to England, to Gaul and western Francia, to Scandinavia and the Baltic. When we read in an eighth-century history, such as Bede's, that London was an

[22] In Pirenne's view this orientation would not presumably take place until the eighth century. Cf. F. Vercauteren, *Civitates de la Belgique Seconde* (Brussels, 1934), 451–2.

emporium of trade housing many foreign merchants, we have to think in the first instance of the Frisians, for Bede expressly mentions Frisian merchants in another place. In most references to foreign trade and foreign merchants in the eighth and ninth centuries the Frisians invariably figure. Liudger, a visiting Frankish ecclesiastic of the eighth century, mentions Frisian merchants in London, and so does Alcuin.

We know much more about their trade to the south. Their main point of entry into western Francia was Quentovic (near modern Etaples), from which they visited Rouen, Amiens and the interior of western France. Certain records of the first half of the eighth century show them active at the fair of St Denis, which was at that time the most important internal market in France. But most of their commerce to the south probably flowed along the Rhine. Down the Rhine they shipped corn and wine from Alsace; up the Rhine they took their cloth, fish and other goods to pay for the corn. They established settlements in the chief Rhenish towns, in Cologne, Duisberg, Xanten near Düsseldorf, Worms; but Mainz was probably their most important destination. The town was well placed at the junction of the Rhine route with the routes which came from the south and the south-east, and there the trade of the Danubian plain and the Black Sea region entered the commercial currents of western Europe.

Even more ancient, if not more abundant, were their trade connections with Scandinavia. Archaeological and literary evidence points to the immemorial antiquity of Scandinavian trade. This trade was largely in the hands of Scandinavians themselves, but in one period some of it was in the hands of the Frisians. A ninth-century *Vita* of St Anscarius, a priest engaged in missionary work in Denmark and Sweden, reveals by a number of accidental details the commercial activities of the Frisians. Anscarius apparently travelled with Frisian merchants to Schleswig and from there to Birka, the Swedish trading centre in the Baltic.

Such was the territorial scope of Frisian trade. Yet the part the Frisians played in it must not be misunderstood. They were its chief intermediaries, but they did not dominate it. The commodities they exported did not all stay in Frisia and did not even necessarily pass through it. Nor were they alone to serve the trade routes on which we find them. Though very active in the Anglo-Saxon trade, they did not dominate it to the exclusion of English merchants. Similarly, Frisians seem to have traded very actively to western Francia, but we know that there was also direct trade between the Franks and their neighbours, and that some of this trade was in the hands of native merchants.

Even more independent and more important was the part played in the northern trade by the Scandinavians. In the economic history of the ninth and tenth centuries the Norsemen left, if anything, deeper trace than the Frisians had done in the preceding period. In doing so they, like the Frisians, were largely impelled by the necessities of their geography. Like the Frisians, they had to seek their livelihood on the high seas and in foreign lands for the simple reason that their own land was unable to feed them. Here and there, in eastern Denmark, in southern Sweden, in parts of southern Norway, men were able all through the Middle Ages to lead lives little different from those of agricultural communities in other parts of western Europe. But elsewhere in Scandinavia society was of necessity made up of part-time peasants – men who lived on their farms part of the year and roamed the seas or navigated distant rivers the rest of the year.

Some of them went to sea as fishermen, others as robbers, adventurers, colonists and conquerors, still others went as traders; in fact, most of them were fishermen, traders and conquerors in turn. It is very largely as Vikings, i.e. as sea robbers and conquerors, that they appear in history textbooks, but economic historians meet them as traders long before their Viking expeditions began and long after they had ceased.

The Viking expeditions began in the first quarter of the eighth century, but archaeological evidence shows that there had been some trade between Scandinavian countries and the rest of western Europe since pre-historic times. Even in the worst period of the Viking wars there was a great deal of purely commercial intercourse not only between the Viking settlements, but between Scandinavia and non-Scandinavian lands. The journey of St Anscarius, already mentioned, took place shortly after the reputed burning of Dorstad by the Vikings. Yet he travelled in a Frisian boat, and in Schleswig he met Danes who were apparently in the habit of going to Dorstad with purely pacific aims.

We must not therefore allow the tumult of the Viking era to obscure the story of common trade done in the ordinary way. The fact that it was both common and commonplace explains why so many of the contemporary sources pass it in silence. Our chief evidence of the raids are the sagas, and sagas were heroic stories about heroic men. Yet even in the sagas we find references to trade in its peaceful and prosaic forms. They sometimes refer to people who were merchants pure and simple, and also mention expeditions undertaken without any predatory aims. We also know that the Scandinavians built and navigated not only the swift assault boats in which they carried out their raids, but also the slower and roomier cargo boats for commercial traffic. It is indeed probable that some parts of Scandinavia specialised in trade to the exclusion of raiding expeditions. Thus the Gotlanders who traded with all the countries of northern Europe did not, as far as we know, send out a single identifiable Viking expedition, even though we find them occasionally engaged in Nordic wars.

Thus considered, Scandinavian trade formed part of that network of commercial connections which we saw taking shape in north-western Europe under the leadership of the Frisians. In some respects, however, its part in north-western commerce was different from that of the Frisians, the Anglo-Saxons or the Franks. In the first place, the Scandinavian trade reached its highest point after the Frisians had begun to decline. In the second place, it far transcended in its range the older limits of northern commerce. In their voyages the Norsemen penetrated to Greenland and the coast of North America in the west, to the Bosporus in the east; and while their western expansion was not of very great importance to European commerce, their eastern voyages were to have the greatest political and economic consequences. They forged a link between north-western Europe and the Baltic, and in addition they established important land routes across the continent of eastern Europe.

The Baltic and the lands round it were until the eleventh and twelfth centuries well outside the scope of western commerce, just as they were outside the range of Germano-Latin Christian civilisation. But they were well within the range of Scandinavian contacts. The Scandinavians crossed and recrossed the sea on their way to the Baltic islands and from there to the Baltic coasts of modern Mecklenburg, Pomerania, Prussia and Livonia, and apparently maintained an active commercial intercourse with the inhabitants of these shores, Slavonic and Ugro-Turkish.

We know very little about the trade and navigation of the Baltic before the tenth century. There is little doubt that the Slav tribes inhabiting the Baltic coast had navigated the sea routes and traded by them. Jumne, on the Isle of Wollin at the estuary of the Oder, was the site of a Slavonic centre, and legend has preserved the fame of an ancient Baltic seaport on the same or a nearby site, the Vineta of the Slavs, the 'nobilissima civitas' of the chronicles, the reputed residence of great merchants and the repository of fabulous riches. Like the other legendary seaports, Vineta is said to have been engulfed by the sea, and, like the other *villes englouties*, it was reputed to toll its submerged bells in times of ill omen. Whether Vineta was in fact a town in the western sense of the word we do not know. Other towns of the western Slavs depicted in the chronicles – Oppeln or Haithabu –

were, we are told, little more than haphazard huddles of cabins made of wattle and mud. Nor can it be said with any certainty that Vineta was ever regularly visited by Scandinavians. It is however certain that, on the very border of the Slavonic east, near Lübeck, the Scandinavians possessed a trading settlement known to the chronicles as Reric, and that another settlement, Truso, sprang up not far from modern Elbing in west Prussia. But of all the towns and settlements they established on the fringes of the Slavonic east, none were more famous or endured longer than Novgorod. Novgorod the Great, the ancient city on Lake Ilmen, guarding the western terminus of a trade route from the Baltic to the interior of Russia, had drawn Scandinavian traders to itself since very early times, possibly since the eighth century, and we know of a Scandinavian settlement there in the tenth century.[23]

Scandinavian penetration into Russia did not, however, end with Novgorod. Before the eighth century was out the Scandinavians under Rurik established themselves as rulers of the 'Russian' tribes. Both before and after their conquest of Russia they regularly crossed and recrossed the great Eurasian plain en route to the East. Starting from the Baltic they went up the Neva and the Great Lakes, recrossed the central Russian watershed by dragging their boats after them, and then sailed south and south-east by the rivers flowing into the Black and Azov Seas. Byzantium was their goal, and there they served as mercenaries, traded as merchants, and at least once pillaged the great city itself. But Byzantium was probably not the only eastern land they touched. We do not know whether they themselves penetrated into the trans-Oxian region of Baktria or into the trans-Caspian provinces of Persia. But they must at least have touched upon the fringes of the Asiatic steppes and traded with the Khazars and the Bulgars of the middle and lower Volga.

In this way the Scandinavians provided an economic link between northern Europe and the lands further east – a link which became more important after the direct maritime connections with the Orient had been severed in the eighth century. And this part they continued to play for several centuries. They were still active in the Russian, Polish, and Livonian centres in the twelfth century, still visited Utrecht in the second half of the same century and the east coast ports of England in the thirteenth century. But by that time their trade had already been overshadowed by the commercial activity in other parts of Europe, and before long it disappeared altogether under the pressure of the rising German tide.

[23] W. Vogel, 'Ein seefahrender Kaufmann um 1100', *Hansische Geschichtsblätter* (1935), 181; *idem* in *Festskrift* in honour of Professor Koht; cf. F. Rörig in *Hansische Geschichtsblätter* (1933), 22ff.

The time when the Scandinavian fortunes began to sink and the German flood rose to engulf them coincides with the beginning of the most rapid phase in the expansion of European economy and trade. The story of the expansion between the eleventh century and the thirteenth has already been told. So has also been the role of the Italians in starting it and in maintaining its momentum. Yet in spite of the Italian stimulus and the part they were beginning to play in the internal trade and finance of most continental countries, the two trading areas – the northern and the southern – remained more or less distinct. The great and growing exchanges between them were sometimes in the hands of the Italian houses with branches in England and France and the Low Countries. But most were carried on, so to speak, on the frontiers of the two areas – the places where the Italians met the merchants of the north-west and where the goods of northern origin and the Italian imports changed hands.

One of these frontier regions, at which the two commercial spheres touched, were the regions of east-central France, and in the first place Champagne. The story of the great Champagne fairs will be told elsewhere. Here it will suffice to note that the reasons why Champagne emerged in the twelfth century as the point of junction were to a large extent political. Under the rule of the counts of Champagne and Blois, their country was one of the earliest in Europe to benefit from the feudal peace which in the eleventh century replaced the feudal anarchy of the preceding epoch. Its population and production grew. As now appears probable, it acquired very early in the period a flourishing cloth industry. But what favoured most its development as an intermediary was its convenient position at the intersection of ancient land routes leading from the Mediterranean to the north German frontier, and from Flanders to central and eastern France. Its ancient towns, Troyes, Langres, Rheims and Laon, were well placed at the focal points of the transcontinental traffic and therefore provided convenient meeting places for the merchants of Italy and Provence on the one hand and those of Germany and the Low Countries on the other. It was at these meeting points that the great Champagne fairs sprang up in the twelfth century and developed into veritable nerve centres of medieval trade in the course of the thirteenth century.

What made the confluence of trade in Champagne so important is that the commercial currents which flowed into it had in the meantime swollen into broad rivers. It will be impossible in this chapter to describe them all, and still less to follow in detail their manifold courses. Thus the southern stream – that which flowed from the Mediterranean countries – was the most important of all, but its story is outside the territorial scope of this chapter. The western current, which issued from the central and western regions of France, may be part of this chapter's subject, but it has been little studied and may at first sight appear to be hardly worth studying. For it may be argued that so well-provided were each of the main regions of northern and western France that they were able to cover their needs from their own production and were not dependent on foreign supplies or markets. This notion of international trade as an occupation in which only poor countries need engage must not, however, be taken too literally or indeed too seriously. The richer provinces of France, perhaps because they were rich, had important surpluses to dispose of. There was grain to spare in Picardy and Normandy, wine to sell in almost every province of central and western France, wool in the uplands of Auvergne and the Cevennes, flax in the north-west, and other specialised products of agriculture elsewhere. As medieval countries go, France was a thickly populated country, and early in her history cities of Roman pedigree as well as towns of more recent origin began to attract large numbers of migrants from the country. By the thirteenth century, Paris, with its 30,000 inhabitants, was one of Europe's most important cities, and between the tenth century and the thirteenth urban centres of more than local importance sprang up everywhere – some of them, like Amiens and Orléans, were commercial capitals of large provinces; others, like Rouen and Bordeaux, great river ports or sea ports; others still, like Lille, Chartres, and Bourges, were seats of textile and metallurgical industry; others, like Paris herself, were all these things together.

A country so furnished could not remain a mere *congerie* of self-sufficient arcadias. That it in fact did not, is shown by such evidence of French trade as we have. The documents show foreigners visiting the fairs of northern France – St Denis, Boulogne, Chartres, Compiègne – long before the fairs of Champagne rose to their fame. The ports of northern France, Etaples (Quentovic) in the seventh and eighth centuries, Le Havre, Rouen, Barfleur and others in the eleventh and twelfth centuries, and countless other ports of call in the later centuries, figure prominently in the surviving records. In the English records the merchants of Amiens and Corbie importing woad are to be found among the earliest foreign visitors to London.

If, nevertheless, in the records of the Champagne fairs, the French current appears to be relatively unimportant, the reason for that is that by the end of the thirteenth century, when documents became abundant, commodities of other more highly commercialised regions (English wool, Flemish cloth) dominated the scene while France's economic connections with the outside world were beginning to suffer from the territorial conquests of Capetian kings, and from the consequent industrial conflicts, war taxation and military operations.

By comparison, more abundant and better illustrated was the stream which issued from the north and the north-east. It was fed from a multitude of tributaries and, of the latter, one issued from a region which was itself destined to succeed Champagne as a meeting point of north and south.

This region was Flanders. Flanders, like Champagne, was unusually fortunate in its political beginnings. In the course of the Dark Ages different political fortunes befell the two halves of the Roman Belgica Secunda. The southern part, that of the lower Seine and the Marne, plunged into feudal anarchy early in the Carolingian era and was just emerging from it as it fell under the domination of the rising power of the French Capetians. The economic prosperity it enjoyed at the turn of the eleventh century under the French kings proved ephemeral, for as a border country on the very front line of the Capetian expansion, it was not too well suited for active industry or trade. Not so the northern part of Belgica Secunda. By a fortunate accident the feudal fiefs and baronies of the south-western Low Countries were early in the tenth century assembled into a strong principality of the Counts of Flanders. Under their rule a large portion of the Low Countries, from Arras to Ghent, came to enjoy peace and order in advance of most other parts of Europe. And in the shelter of the count's peace, arts could flourish, trade could prosper, and towns could grow.

The geographical situation of the country was equally favourable. The country lay on the coast of the North Sea, open to sea-borne trade from almost every quarter; it was also cut across by navigable rivers, more especially the Scheldt, and was well provided with sheltered estuaries for harbours. Yet Flanders owes its industry as much to its geographical limitations as to its geographical facilities. While, under the shelter of Flemish peace, population grew, the yield of the land remained relatively small. The Flemings carried out a great work of internal colonisation, added polder to polder, erected dykes all along the coast and along the main water-courses. By the middle of the twelfth century they had acquired all over Europe a reputation as experts in land drainage, and their qualities – the Flemish system of reclamation, the Flemish freedom and the Flemish experience in organising new settlements – they carried with them at the invitation of German princes into the new lands beyond the Elbe. Yet neither internal colonisation nor emigration could solve their population problem, and the solution was found where such solutions normally lie, i.e. in industrialisation.

By the middle of the twelfth century Flanders became the foremost – and possibly the only – predominantly industrial country in northern Europe. The chief centres of its cloth industry, Ypres, Ghent, Douai, came to rank among the most important towns of northern Europe. Together with the commercial port of Bruges which served them they formed by the end of the century the four members – the Four *Leden* – of Flanders, which began to rival the political power of the Counts in the thirteenth century and were to challenge it in the fourteenth.

Flanders also possessed certain other industries and trades. But until the end of the fourteenth century none of the other occupations compared in importance with cloth, and cloth was also the mainstay of Flemish commerce. Cloth was also the magnet which drew to Flanders the merchants of the world and gradually helped to develop in Bruges another international mart, rival and eventual successor to the fairs of Champagne. Bruges' greatness was probably rooted in the function it fulfilled at the turn of the twelfth and the thirteenth centuries as the point of entry of English wool and of English merchants. Before long the Italians came there in search of English wool and English custom, but by the end of the thirteenth century the Germans had established themselves in Bruges as the chief exporters of Flemish cloth, and the principal buyers of Italian imports and the chief providers of eastern European foodstuffs and raw materials.

By that time the Germans had come to dominate the international economy of northern Europe. The thirteenth was indeed their century, but their pre-eminence in the economy of continental Europe was beginning to reveal itself at least a whole century earlier.

Eventually the range of predominantly German trade, like the area of predominantly German speech and culture, stretched from the eastern borders of north Holland and Lorraine to the heart of Central – and later also Eastern – Europe. But its focus, especially at its beginning, was in the Rhineland and its capital. For in the course of the twelfth and the thirteenth centuries all the trade routes and all the cultural influences which radiated from the Rhineland – its architecture, its crafts and its mystic art – came to centre upon one town, and that town was Cologne.

The early history of Cologne is shrouded in a certain amount of controversy. There is no doubt that its urban nucleus had survived from the Roman era and that as an administrative centre and as an episcopal residence Cologne preserved some semblance of urban life throughout the Dark Ages. It may also have preserved its economic function, for it could boast of an annual fair in the tenth century and housed merchants and artisans much earlier. By the end of the eleventh century Cologne had already become an emporium of trade and industry. Its two fairs – one at Easter and the other in August – were already well established, and so also was its fame for wealth and power. Writing early in the twelfth century Otto of Freising could assert that there was not a town in contemporary Germany or Gaul as rich as Cologne; and Cesarius of Heisterbach, a Cistercian compiler of miraculous stories, spoke of Cologne in somewhat the same way in which New York used to be spoken of in European books. There was something in the very air of Cologne that made men rich.

Some of Cologne's wealth was derived from industrial products: textiles, mainly linen, cloth and thread, and especially metal goods. Its bells were famous in thirteenth-century Europe, and so were other products of its copper-beating crafts. One of Cologne's masters, Frederick of St Pantaleon, ranks among the greatest metal workers of all ages. Still, it is in commerce and not in industries that the mainsprings of Cologne's wealth will be found. Its main field was the Rhine valley itself. Owing mainly to the growth of the hinterland, the estuary, once the focus of European trade, now ceased to occupy this position. Most of the delta's trade now passed through Cologne and, in the end, came to be handled by Cologne merchants. At the beginning of the period the merchants of Utrecht appear to have traded along the Rhine on their own account, but eventually Cologne ousted its competitors and succeeded in appropriating to itself the bulk of the valley's trade. In the twelfth century we find its merchants active as far south as Austria and Carinthia and also in Augsburg and Regensburg – a town which at that time gathered into itself the economic threads of the Danubian region.

Needless to say, the lands along the Rhine valley itself were not the only region to which Cologne's commercial connections extended; just as the Rhineland with Cologne was not the only area to play its part in the commercial development of the continent. Another such area was Flanders itself. Much of Flemish trade was with England, France and southern Europe, and in the early phase of their commercial expansion, and especially in the twelfth century, the Flemings appear to have frequented the markets of Cologne and also the upper Rhine and Saxony as far east as the Elbe. But in the course of the thirteenth century as the active trade of the Flemings died out, the Cologners gradually became the chief intermediaries between Flanders on the one hand and central and southern Germany on the other. For a time in the thirteenth century they even succeeded in penetrating into the

Anglo-Flemish wool trade and interposing themselves between the English wood growers and the Flemish cloth makers.

Another similar area lay to the west of the Rhine, between the Rhine and the Maas. The trade of this region, which the Germans usually describe as Maasland, was founded on the industries of its towns: Huy, Namur, Liège and Dinant. Huy and Liège produced some cloth for export, but their chief industry was metals, and Dinant was especially famous for its metal goods.

Almost equally important was the activity and greater still the future potentialities of the regions to the east of the Rhine. The territory between the Rhine and the Weser, usually described as Westphalia, was a valuable source of agricultural exports and of metal ores mined in the south-east of the region. Yet it was not in the export of domestic produce and not in western Germany that the historical destiny of Westphalia lay. Ever since Frankish times the region had served as a corridor to the lands further east. Several important east-to-west routes crossed it, and none were more important than the famous *Hellweg* which began at Duisburg, went between the Ruhr and Lippe and passed the towns of Dortmund and Soest before crossing the Weser into Saxony. On this route were to be found the Westphalian towns which were to lead in the commercial development of eastern Europe: and it was thanks to the men of these towns that eastern European trade before long fell into German hands.

The eastern specialisation of Westphalia was largely Cologne's own fault. Faced in the west with the barrier of Cologne's power, the rising towns of Westphalia naturally turned to the as yet virgin fields further east. And although the merchants of Cologne were as active in the east as the men of any other German town, they could not claim there that position of overwhelming economic privilege which they enjoyed elsewhere. It is therefore no wonder to find the Westphalian towns taking a leading part in the exploratory period of eastern trade and forming the earliest trading stations in the east. We find them also acquiring a lion's share in the work as well as in the profits of urban colonisation and town-building all over north-eastern Europe from Lübeck to Riga.

Some of what has been said about Westphalia applies also to the region immediately to the east, i.e. Saxony. Saxony, as the documents reveal it in the twelfth century, had for more than four centuries been part of the Holy Roman Empire and was now an integral part of the German homeland. Like Westphalia, it owed its first entry into the commercial system of Europe to its mineral resources, for by the late twelfth and thirteenth centuries the Harz mountains were rapidly becoming the principal mining area of continental Europe, the main source of copper and lead, as well as of precious metals. The industry was centred round Goslar, and the fame of Goslar as the capital of the mining industry outlasted, even if it did not outshine, its fame as the residence of the Saxon and Hohenstaufen emperors. Yet Goslar was not the principal commercial town of the country, for the simple reason that in Saxony, as in Westphalia, the most flourishing commercial activities were those which led its merchants to the east. To this activity Saxony and its towns were especially suited. In the early Middle Ages, i.e. before it was wholly assimilated to the Empire, it lay across the German route to the east like a barrier. Now the barrier had become a corridor. Whereas in the opening centuries of our period – eleventh and early twelfth – the regular overland traffic stopped at the Elbe crossings – chiefly at Bardowiek, but also at Magdeburg and at a few smaller places – at the end of the twelfth and all through the thirteenth century the frontiers of German trade moved eastwards, and men from the border towns of Saxony took part in the movement and greatly benefited from it.

The eastward spread was indeed the most characteristic trend of the epoch. Its beginning can be traced as far back as the Frankish era. From about the sixth century onwards the civilisation of the Latino-German West began to expand into the commercial interior of Central Europe; and, in consequence, the entire economic balance of the continent gradually shifted to the east. In the early Merovingian times the focus of the Frankish state and society was in Gaul, but in the sixth and seventh centuries it moved from the left bank of the Rhine to the right. In the centuries between the fifth and the eleventh the lands between the Rhine and the Weser were being fast reclaimed and settled by the overflow of their own population, and by the time Charlemagne become emperor, the eastern and more purely Germanic parts of his kingdom were able to supply him with the bulk of his power and of his armies. But no sooner was this transference completed than a still further move to the east began, and the Saxon lands beyond the Weser were laid open to Frankish conquest and assimilation. It has been argued that to the Franks the acquisition of Saxony was a military and a political necessity, for they had to subjugate the Saxons if they were themselves to be saved from being submerged by the next wave of Germanic invasions. Whether in fact Charlemagne's Saxon expeditions were nothing more than preventive wars we do not know, but we know that the Saxon lands had been an object of attraction long before they could possibly have become a source of danger. Their military conquest was well prepared by missionary activity and was itself preceded and followed by commercial ventures and trading settlements. Before long Saxony was wholly absorbed in the trading area of western Europe, and by the beginning of the eleventh century it had itself become the starting point for a further leap in the same direction. This time it was the turn of the Baltic and of the Wendish lands east of the Elbe.

This final phase of the process was also its most important one. It began with the conquest of Slavonic lands which was led largely by princes, and it continued as a great enterprise in settlement and colonisation. And long before the work of colonisation ended it brought fundamental change into European, and, more especially, German commerce. Urban colonisation by merchants and for commercial motives accompanied, and in some places even preceded, rural colonisation by knights and peasants. Not all the Westphalian merchants in search of Slavonic markets and sources of supply stopped at the line of the Elbe. As often as not they themselves ventured into the interior of the Wendish lands, and now and again penetrated into the Baltic region. With the permission of the Slavonic princes they began establishing trading stations all along the main routes leading to Novgorod and Smolensk, which were the two main points of entry into medieval Russia. In Schleswig, the starting point of the Scandinavian sea-route to the eastern Baltic, Westphalian merchants possessed something in the nature of a factory in the early twelfth century. At the next stage of the same sea-route, at Wisby on the island of Gotland, they established themselves at about the same time. But from the point of view of subsequent history, the most significant of their trading factories was the one they apparently built up very early in the twelfth century, or even at the end of the eleventh century, at the Slavonic town of Lübeck. Profiting by the liberality of the Wendish prince, they formed there a permanent settlement at least as early as the twenties of the twelfth century. But in the late thirties Adolph of Holstein conquered the land and burned the city, and in 1143 the new Lübeck, this time a purely German town, was founded.

Lübeck was to be followed by other new towns. In the extreme north-east the German merchants founded at the very beginning of the thirteenth century the town of Riga, henceforth the centre of their trade in Livonia. By the end of the twelfth century the trading settlement in Wisby grew to turn the entire town into a German port and strong-point, and at the opening of the thirteenth century the town of Hamburg rose to match Lübeck at the eastern foot of the Jutland peninsula.

Of this first generation of new German towns none could rival Lübeck. It soon drew to itself the trade which had previously gone

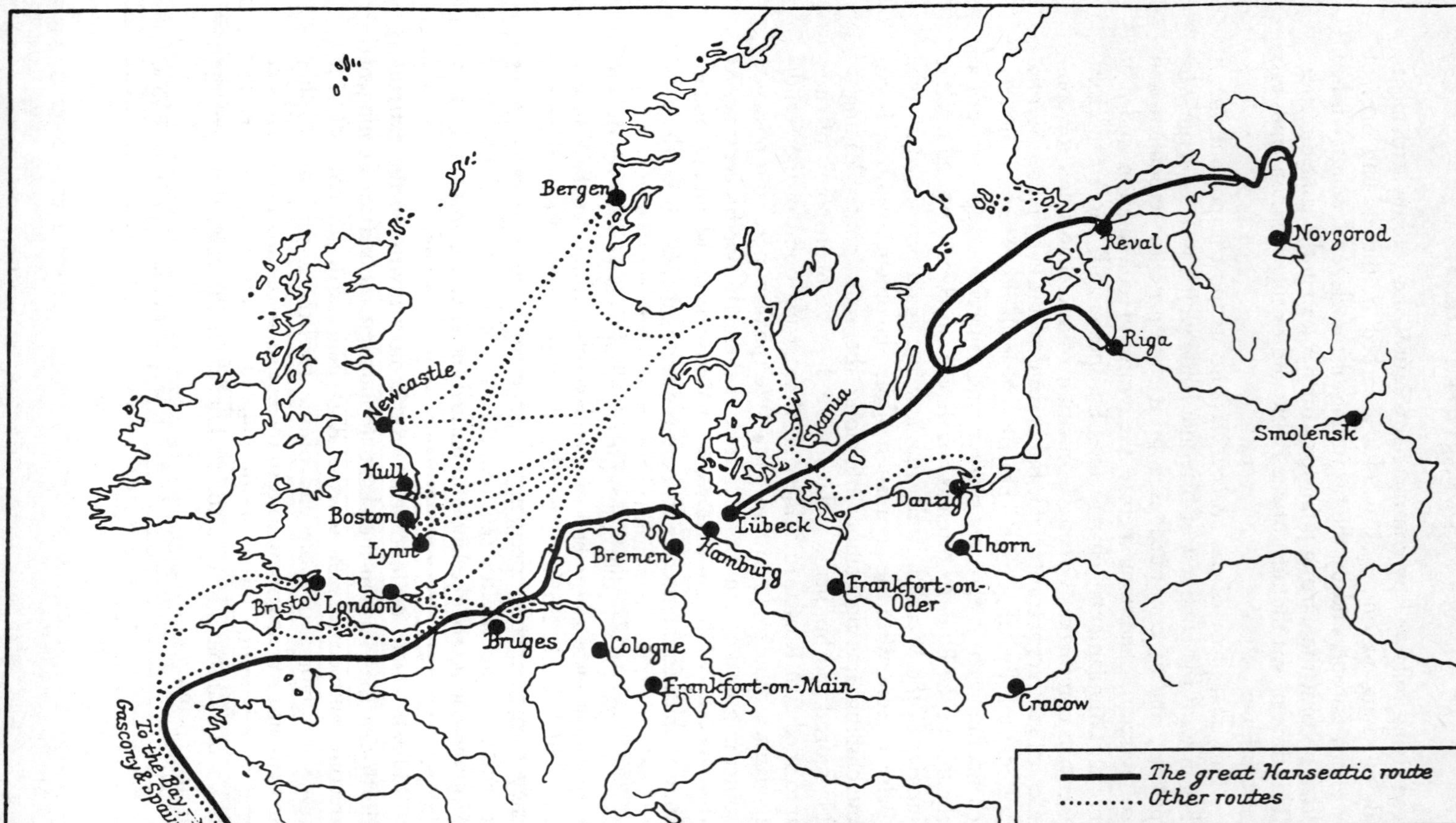

Map. 3. The Great Hanseatic Route. Reproduced from *Studies in English Trade in the Fifteenth Century* ed. Power and Postan

overland to Bardowiek, replaced Schleswig as the chief starting point for sea journeying across the eastern Baltic, established itself in the fisheries of southern Scandinavia and of the island of Rügen, and in the rising trade with Bergen and the interior of Sweden. By degrees the old overland routes as well as the old Scandinavian sea routes fell into desuetude, and the bulk of the trade with the east was forced into the channel which ran along the south coast of the Baltic and across the foot of the Jutland peninsula – the channel which Lübeck served and dominated.

This first generation of new German towns was soon followed by another and a larger crop of secondary formations. Lübeck, the first daughter town of the Westphalian cities, in itself became a generation or two later the 'mother' of other eastern towns. Immediately to the east, as to the south-east, it helped to found the towns of Schwerin, Wismar and Rostock, and a number of smaller towns. At the furthest east there sprang up Riga's sister towns of Dorpat and Reval, and the chief towns of Prussia (but not yet Danzig). The whole chain of German towns sponsored by the Westphalian towns and Lübeck was practically completed by the end of the thirteenth century.

These new towns had a double function to perform. In the first instance they connected the lands of the west with the sources of Slavonic goods: furs, honey, pitch, tar, timber and rye. This was essentially a Baltic trade, and Russia was its chief source and market. The second function was to serve as an outlet for the goods of the newly colonised lands. Bremen and, above all, Hamburg collected corn from the regions of the Weser and the Elbe and exported it to the west. Lübeck and Hamburg became the centres of the fishing industry of the western Baltic, the salt trade of the Elbe, and the forest goods of Brandenburg. Somewhat later the Prussian towns of Marienburg, Elbing, Thorn and Königsberg, and later still Danzig, became the outlets for the corn and timber trade of Prussia, Lithuania and western Poland.

To northern Europe as a whole, and to the German lands in particular, the rise of the eastern towns and of the great route on which they stood was of profound, almost of revolutionary importance. It transformed the whole composition and direction of northern trade. The industrial nations of the north-west and especially Flanders were now offered markets and new and very abundant sources of essential supplies. England, hitherto dependent on Scandinavian timber, began to import large and ever-growing quantities of Baltic wood. She also began to buy, sometimes for her own use, sometimes for re-export, quantities of Baltic grain. Other sylvan products – pitch, tar, potash, as well as furs and wax – now came from eastern Germany, or from the Slavonic lands tapped by the Germans. Flanders, hitherto fed by the corn supplies from northern France and southern Germany, was now beginning to be supplied by Baltic grain. The Germans were also able to take food to Scandinavian countries previously dependent on imports from Britain.

All this brought wealth and power to the east German towns and marked the final stage in Germany's commercial rise. Their hold over east European markets, foodstuffs and raw materials, also made them welcome and even indispensable all over northern Europe. They won predominant power in Scandinavia, great economic influence in the Low Countries, important privileges in England. Before long, economic power was buttressed by a political organisation, and the German towns combined into the great naval, military and political union of the Hanse.

With the formal establishment of the Hanse the eastern expansion of north European trade can be said to have been completed, and a new and different chapter in its history began. For, paradoxically enough, the official founding of the Hanse in the sixties of the fourteenth century was not so much a further step in German expansion as a manifestation of an entirely new phase in the history of European trade and of German power. It marks the end of eastward expansion – indeed of all expansion – and a new period in the economic history of Europe.

III. *The Age of Contraction*

(1) THE DEPRESSION

The great commercial expansion did not continue into the late Middle Ages and was not destined to merge without a break into the ascending economic movements of the sixteenth century. In some parts of Europe it slowed down; in others it ceased altogether. Historians will therefore be justified in regarding the two closing centuries of the Middle Ages, the fourteenth and the fifteenth, and more especially the second half of the former and the first half of the latter, as a period of arrested development, and even in speaking of a 'secular' depression succeeding the 'secular' expansion of the earlier centuries.

The contraction, like the expansion which preceded it, is easier to diagnose that to measure. Reliable figures capable of forming comprehensive statistical series are almost as rare in the records of the later Middle Ages as they are in the records of the twelfth and the thirteenth centuries. In England alone were national customs accounts kept in the later Middle Ages, and enough of them have survived to provide a broad statistical background to the history of English foreign trade. But even the English customs accounts are more complete and more reliable for some periods than for others. The figures for the fourteenth century are less comprehensive than those of the fifteenth and are not available in consecutive or comparable series except for wine, wool and cloth. The latter have been tabulated by Professor Gray in annual averages for two-yearly periods at intervals of about a decade. The fifteenth-century figures have been fully analysed elsewhere. The two series are in Tables II and III:

Table II. *Exports of Wool and Cloth from England in the second half of the fourteenth century (annual averages)*[24]

Years	Wool (sacks)	Broadcloths‡
1353–55	—	3,040
1355–57	—	7,485
1357–60	35,840*	9,346
1366–68	26,634†	14,593
1377–80	21,627	15,449
1392–95	19,359	43,072

* 1357–59 – 2 years.

† 1367–69.

‡ The figures in this column slightly underestimate the total and slightly exaggerate the rate of increase, for they do not include worsteds and other cheap cloths of the same kind which were relatively more important in the early period.

The figures tell their own tale. The only exceptions to the record of decline were the short-lived boom in the value of miscellaneous exports and imports in the mid-thirties of the fifteenth century which probably reflected the high cost of imports during an acute economic conflict with the Hanseatic League; and above all the high level of cloth exports throughout the period. The latter were rising throughout the second half of the fourteenth century and mounted with exceptional rapidity between 1380 and 1395; but from the high point they then reached they soon descended to an average of about 30,000 broadcloths, round which they fluctuated for some 25 years. In the two decades of active trade with Central and Eastern Europe following the, so-called, Vorrath treaty with the Hanse in 1437, the exports of cloth rose well above the average and exceeded 50,000 cloths, but in 1448

[24] These figures have been corrected and supplemented in E. Carus-Wilson, 'Trends in the Export of English Woollens in the Fourteenth Century', *Economic Hist. Rev*, III, no. 2, 1950, but the general trend they exhibit is the same.

Table III. *Exports and Imports of Dutiable Commodities in England, 1399–1482*

(Annual averages in 3-year periods)*

Years	Exports of wool (sacks)	Exports of broadcloth	Imports of wine (tuns)	Exports and imports of miscellaneous merchandise paying poundage (values in £)†
1399–1402	15,023	27,760	—	—
1402–05	10,864	24,502	6,237	60,887
1405–08	14,221	29,315	6,220	187,439
1408–11	14,393	30,718	13,696	150,368
1411–14	14,447	25,108	12,113	124,313
1414–17	14,131	29,488	17,063	136,683
1417–20	14,778	28,366	10,975	145,192
1420–23	13,893	36,359	5,168	135,994
1423–26	13,959	42,665	3,591	109,049
1426–29	15,437	38,417	6,821	129,420
1429–32	9,749	40,641	8,940	119,691
1432–35	8,294	39,693	9,950	146,754
1435–38	2,353	40,814	6,097	113,275
1438–41	9,101	56,097	10,509	127,221
1441–44	9,776	55,976	11,748	130,452
1444–46	9,279	52,482	12,275	106,168
1446–48	7,654	53,699	11,000	121,795
1448–50	8,412	35,078	9,432	91,456
1450–53	7,660	38,928	7,424	91,001
1453–56	9,290	37,738	6,826	82,533
1456–59	7,664	35,059	4,072	59,089
1459–62	4,976	31,933	4,190	65,503
1462–65	7,044	25,855	7,074	57,449
1465–69	9,316	39,664	5,942	93,942
1469–71	7,811	27,610	3,411	53,421
1471–76	9,091	43,129	4,729	115,475
1476–79	7,502	51,889	6,887	120,333
1479–82	9,784	62,586	6,927	179,340

* 1444–46, 1446–48, 1448–50, and 1469–71 are computed in 2-year periods; 1465–69 is a 4-year period, and 1471–76 a 5-year period.

† The figures do not include miscellaneous exports by Hansards.

they fell again to their pre-1437 level and remained there until the last quarter of the century.

For other parts of Europe there is little statistical evidence beyond a few figures of local imports and exports or occasional series of measurements reflecting the movements of the more important trades. The best known of the former are probably the returns of the Hanseatic *Pfundzoll*, a tax on sea-borne trade levied by the principal Hanseatic towns in the second half of the fourteenth and in the fifteenth centuries. Unfortunately, the returns have not survived in a series sufficiently consecutive to reveal a convincing trend; and with the exception of the Lübeck figures for 1368–69, they have not yet been presented to historians in a wholly usable form. The longest of the series so far available, that of Hamburg, suggests that the sea-borne exports and imports rose from 250,000 Lübeck marks in 1362 to 374,000 in 1371, and then dropped to 336,000 in 1400.[25] But the figures may well exaggerate the rise and underestimate the fall in Hamburg's trade, for the *Pfundzoll* was frequently imposed in times of strained international relations and sea war when a great deal of traffic, which would otherwise have gone through the Sound, sought the greater security of the overland route through Hamburg.

On the other hand, the evidence of individual trades covers a range of commodities and places so wide as to make up for the paucity of more general measurements. And though little of it is statistical in the narrow sense of the term it is sufficiently full and varied to reveal the main economic trend.

The trend and the facts from which it emerges may appear to be primarily concerned with agriculture and industrial production rather than with trade. But the distinction must not be pressed too hard. In an earlier section heavy emphasis was laid on the predominance in north European trade of products of European industry and agriculture. Where facts make it appear very probable that Europe's production declined, or at least ceased to grow, there is every justification for concluding that commercial exchanges must also have slowed down or stagnated.

Naturally enough, the evidence of agricultural production is most copious, though also most difficult to interpret. Superficial signs of agricultural crises abound in the records of the fourteenth and fifteenth centuries. Wars were more frequent and more continuous than at any other time since the tenth century; great pestilences visited Europe in 1348–49 and at least twice again in the second half of the century.

[25] W. Stieda, *Revaler Zollbücher*, lviiff.

Crops, buildings, equipment, as well as the agricultural calendar, were bound to suffer, and production was bound to decline. In addition, rural economy was undergoing a process of readjustment which helped to reduce the level of both agricultural production and of trade.

Arable cultivation contracted everywhere, but on large units, and especially on 'demesne' farms of great estates, the contraction was most rapid. Such demesnes as still functioned in the fourteenth century in various parts of France were wound up in the course of the late fourteenth and fifteenth centuries. In England, where the demesne farming has survived to a far greater extent than anywhere else in Europe, the transformation was most radical.

The contracting acreages of the demesnes must not of course be used as an accurate index of agricultural decline. Yet even if corrected and heavily discounted, they still bear witness to a general recession. By no means all the lands lost to the demesnes were acquired by tenants; and there is every sign of poorer lands, whether on the demesnes or on lands anciently in the possession of tenants, gradually going out of cultivation. Theoretically, the yield per acre or per man should have risen; but even if this happened in the fifteenth century (and there is no evidence to show that it did) the total output was bound to decline.

What is more, a smaller proportion of the output was now drawn into the main stream of inter-regional trade. The dwindling of demesne farming signified also the decline of commercial production. No doubt, in this country, some large-scale units continued to be run by substantial tenant farmers, but in general peasant tenancies increased and multiplied at the expense of large units of commercialised agriculture; and peasant landholders must have consumed a far greater proportion of their produce than the quasi-capitalist owners of the demesne farms.

Thus on the thirty-two manors of the bishopric of Winchester at the beginning of the thirteenth century some 1750 quarters of wheat were sold, nearly all outside the manors. This amounted to 48 per cent of the gross output and 82 per cent of the 'net' output (after deduction of seed). When a century later the yields, i.e. the 'net' output in relation to seed sown, had become considerably higher, the proportion of sales to gross output also rose to 70 per cent. On the six Wiltshire manors of the Duchy of Lancaster at the very beginning of the fourteenth century, the 'net' output of grain of all kinds (including some 75 quarters bought but excluding some 525 quarters of seed) was about 1,330 quarters, while the sales amounted to 1,208 quarters: indeed the output was so large that it must have included a carry-over of old grain. On the Wiltshire estates of Lord Hungerford, on which demesnes functioned until the middle of the fifteenth century, sales of grain reached similar proportions. On the Hungerford estate of Winterbourne-Stoke in 1448, 97 quarters out of the 'net' output of 112 were sold.

No such sales could be expected from peasant units, however commercialised some of them were. A little calculation, indeed mere commonsense, will show that at a time when on the holdings of the peasants of the top rank – the virgaters – the area under corn in any year averaged about 15 acres per household (in Cambridgeshire at the time of the Hundred Rolls of 1279 the area sown annually by an average peasant above the rank of cottar was 7 acres) and when the yield of wheat, allowing for seed, was no more than six bushels per acre, the marketable surpluses of an average peasant household were small. So even if the extent of cultivated land had remained the same, the change-over to peasant agriculture would inevitably have reduced the amount of grain available for sale, and with it the total volume of grain trade.

Hence also the reduced scale of inter-regional traffic in grain. The evidence of urban food supplies leaves the impression of a trade shrinking in volume and sometimes restricted in its range. We are told that in the late Middle Ages London was drawing its supplies from a much smaller area than earlier and had become more or less dependent upon the agricultural surpluses in the Home Counties. There is also some evidence to suggest that the grain supplies of other important English towns were becoming not only smaller (this could also result from decline in the town population), but sometimes also more local. Hence the growing pre-occupation of towns with their food supplies and with the grain stocks: a pre-occupation which overshadows the urban policies of most of the greater towns on the continent.

At first sight, no such shrinkage could be observed in the grain trade of the Low Countries, where the sea-borne supplies from the distant Baltic appeared to assume an even greater importance. Yet a shrinkage there must have been. It is quite possible that Baltic imports into the Low Countries grew in importance merely because the French sources of corn supplies had been running dry. The exports from the valleys of the Somme and the lower Seine, though by no means exhausted, were not, and could not be, as abundant as they had been in the middle of the fourteenth century. Anglo-French war, the English occupation of Normandy and Picardy, the choking up of river traffic by tolls, were bound to interrupt the flow; and there were also other signs of a more general agricultural depression. It was not therefore an accident that in some years in the fifteenth century we find the Norman towns importing grain from the Baltic, and the records have preserved an accidental report of a whole Hanseatic grain fleet arriving in the estuary of the Seine in 1450.

In some of these examples eastern Germany and the other Baltic regions figure as the only examples of unfailing bounty. Did then the grain production and the grain trade of eastern Europe escape the depression that prevailed elsewhere? To some extent they probably did, since they still continued to yield marketable surpluses large enough to feed Holland and Norway and to keep the great east-to-west trade flowing. But even if the flow never ceased it was no longer as full as it had been in the middle of the fourteenth century. Comprehensive statistics of the Hanseatic grain trade do not exist; such figures as we have are largely confined to the evidence of the grain deals of the Prussian Order, which are both incomplete and misleading. But all indirect evidence points to a slump in the fortunes of German agriculture throughout the greater part of the fifteenth century. An interval of at least a century separated the high-water mark of agricultural expansion in eastern Germany in the fourteenth century from the outburst of large-scale commercial agriculture on the *Rittergüter* in the sixteenth century. During that interval, the map of Brandenburg, Pomerania, Mecklenburg and Prussia became covered with abandoned holdings, deserted households and depopulated villages, all pointing to the economic tribulations of peasant agriculture. But large-scale units of production were also going through a period of economic difficulty, for labour was getting scarce and dear, and grain was falling in price. Before the century was out landlords sought and found a remedy in *Bauernlegen* – a policy whereby peasants were deprived of land and forced to work on the estates. But the movement did not get under way until the very turn of the fifteenth and sixteenth centuries. From 1400 to 1475 – these are approximate dates – the landlords found their old prosperity going and the new prosperity not yet arrived. Would it therefore be too fanciful to conclude that if in that century Baltic supplies in the west still appeared as abundant as ever it was not because supplies had grown but merely because the demand had shrunk?

For there is little doubt that the demand for grain in the main consuming areas was shrinking. On some of the main inter-regional markets, those of the greater towns and of the principal industrial areas of northern Europe, the numbers of inhabitants declined. The process was of course more complex in detail than it may appear on a broader view. Yet for all its complexity, it leaves little room for doubt about its effect on the grain market. The demand for grain apparently receded in the main consuming areas, and it must also have receded on the innumerable local markets throughout the length and breadth of Europe.

The importance of the local demand must not be under-estimated. In chapters dealing with the earlier centuries attention was drawn to the large proportion of marketable foodstuffs which went to feed the villagers, manorial servants and artisans who did not possess enough land to cover their needs out of their own production. This class included agricultural labourers, rural artisans and smallholders of every type and size, and was always to be found in the countryside. It was, however, more numerous at some times than at others, and in most countries – certainly in Germany and England – this class contracted in the later Middle Ages. What with the steep decline of rural population and with the new opportunities for larger holdings on the lords' land and elsewhere, the numbers of landless or all but landless labourers in English villages fell out of proportion to the general decline of population. And as the numbers of wage-earners and smallholders sank, sales for local consumption must have dwindled.

It is because demand declined that the reduced production and smaller sales did not result in a chronic, still less a mounting, scarcity of food. Over the later Middle Ages as a whole, bread grains appeared more abundant than ever before. They were especially plentiful in the second quarter of the fourteenth century when prices fell more than 20 per cent below their level in the first quarter. Soon afterwards came the succession of bad harvests and low yields following on the great mortality of 1348–49; but this again was followed in England and abroad by the 'good seventies'. According to several continental chronicles, the harvest of 1375 was the best for fourteen years, and was followed by four years so good that according to an Alsatian chronicle, people were 'fatigued by the abundance'. In 1377 the prices of bread in England touched their lowest point for thirty years, and in 1395 in Strasbourg grain became so plentiful and so cheap that bakers replaced the 'standard' penny loaf with a halfpenny one. Bread was never to be quite so plentiful again, but periods of relative abundance occurred in various parts of Europe throughout the fifteenth century at intervals frequent enough to justify historians in regarding the whole period as an age of low agricultural prices. Above all, the first and third quarters of the fifteenth century in western Germany, in the Low Countries, and in some parts of France and England, were times when supplies, relative to demand, were near their peak.

The recurrent phases of plenty raise problems closely linked with those of prices and will therefore be discussed again later; but they should be mentioned here if only in order to record a warning against a possible *non sequitur*. The decline of the grain trade and of arable agriculture could be accompanied by signs of abundance and must not be judged by them. On the other hand, in other branches of agricultural production the declining or stagnating output was not always matched by the decline in demand, and signs of abundance may be absent. Thus, for reasons which have not been fully accounted for, the supplies of foodstuffs of animal origin, and especially butter, were smaller in relation to demand than were the supplies of grain; and their values fell more slowly or even rose. Therein, however, lies a tale which properly belongs to another section of this chapter.

The category of animal products here discussed does not of course include Europe's most important industrial material – wool. English customs figures make it clear beyond all doubt that trade in wool was on the wane. Tables II and III above will show that English exports, by far the most important in western Europe and solely responsible for high-quality wool imported into Flanders, Holland and Italy, declined from about 35,000 sacks per annum in the first half of the fourteenth century to about 8,000 sacks in the second half of the fifteenth century. It would of course be wrong to ascribe the entire deficiency to falling production, for it is now well understood that in the meantime England had greatly increased her cloth industry and consumed a far greater proportion of her clip. Indeed, so marked was the shift from foreign users to the English cloth-makers that until recently historians have used the figures of declining wool exports as evidence of England's rising cloth production. This argument, however, no longer holds good. H. L. Gray and others have shown that, at its highest, England's cloth production could not possibly have accounted for all the difference between the high level of wool exports in the middle of the fourteenth century and their low level in the late fifteenth.

Declining supply, as well as other difficulties of trade, also accounts for the confused and broken pattern of the wine trade. We know little about the fortunes of the wine exports of the upper Rhineland or of the Moselle, and hardly more about those of La Rochelle, but much more is known about the conditions in the southern and by far the most important wine area, that of Gascony. The region experienced not only the general economic difficulties of the age, but also the direct effects of military operations of the Anglo-French wars. At times only Bordeaux and its immediate surroundings escaped wholesale devastation. The toll of the ruined vineyards has found faithful reflection in the statistics of fourteenth-century exports. The decline, interrupted for a while in the last decade of the fourteenth century, was resumed in the fifteenth. During the middle decades of the century, French occupation of Gascony led to a complete interruption of trade to England and all but deprived Gascony of its most important customer; and exports to England, which had averaged 8000–10,000 tuns in the thirties and forties and had sometimes been more than that at the beginning of the century, sank to little more than 5000 in the fifties and sixties. It was not before the eighties of the fifteenth century that English merchants appeared again in force on the wine-market of Bordeaux and only in the nineties did British imports of Gascon wine recover the volumes of sixty years earlier.

Table IV. *Exports of Wine from Bordeaux in the Fourteenth Century*[26]

(Annual averages)

Years	Tuns	
1305–07	95,650	
1308–09	102,724	
1310–11	51,351	
1328–30	81,366	
1335–37	45,315	
1348–50	9,675	
1352–58	19,681	(five years only)
1363–70	22,111	(six years only)
1372–73	14,373	
1374–79	13,297	
1379–81	7,842	

It is of course possible that the irregular and probably dwindling supplies of wine were in some parts of Europe compensated by increasing supplies of beer; for beer made with hops was the product of the Middle Ages in decline. From the middle of the fourteenth century onwards it was brewed in ever-increasing quantities in most of the North German towns, above all in Hamburg, and also in towns of the northern Netherlands. Historians do not, however, know enough about medieval consumption in different places and at different social levels to be able to judge to what extent wine and beer were true substitutes, and how far beer was merely ousting ales and other drinks of a humbler kind.

The light which the surviving records throw on the other branches of the victualling trade is equally uncertain and on the whole equally subdued. Enough is known about the salt trade of the Bay of

[26] The figures of fourteenth-century wine imports have been derived from M. K. James, *Studies in the Medieval Wine Trade* (Oxford, 1971).

Bourgneuf to suggest that here at least output and trade were growing in the fifteenth century. The documents, however are not sufficiently continuous to report the effect of piracy and war in the forties and fifties, nor do we know enough about salt exports from other areas, e.g. Lüneburg, Zealand or South Germany, to be able to set the buoyancy of the Bay trade against the possible decline elsewhere. The evidence from the English salt areas suggests that there production was, to say the least, stagnating. The feudal farm of the main salt-making centres in Northwich and Middlewich, which was largely, though not wholly, made up of revenues of the salt-pans, fell from £168 in 1301 to £130 in 1347 and £90 in 1368. Indirect evidence – figures are lacking – suggests that production remained low for at least another century.[27]

A more general, even if an indirect, indication of a probable decline in international salt industry will be found in the vicissitudes of its chief customer – the herring trade. The great fishing industry of Skania was still active in the fifteenth century and was not to enter upon its final decline for another century or century and a half; but it was no longer expanding and was frequently depressed by war and by bad catches. In the good years at the turn of the fifteenth and sixteenth centuries as much was caught and salted as ever before. In Falsterbö, where most of the Skania fishing was then concentrated, at least 100,000 tuns (about 10,000 long tons) were salted in 1537, which was only about 20,000 tuns less than may have been salted in the same place in 1368. But in some years during the intervening period the catches and the trade fell to a mere fraction of the volumes of 1368 and 1537. The recurrent wars between the Hanseatic League and the Scandinavian kings, and political friction with Flanders and England, repeatedly interfered with both fishing and export. Possibly the fishing grounds themselves were beginning to show signs of wear, and there were complaints of bad catches in 1411, 1412, 1416 and 1425. In the late twenties, war, in interrupting both fishing and trade, proved to be a blessing in disguise, for with the return of peace yields recovered to reach their highest levels between 1432 and the mid-forties. In the middle of the century, however, complaints of poor catches became frequent again and continued at intervals throughout the period.[28]

This record of the fishing trade, if true, bears a striking resemblance to what was apparently happening in the great extracting industries of the time. More especially, the mining areas were now going through a phase which the old-fashioned economist would have described as one of rapidly diminishing returns. The symptoms were

[27] H. J. Hewitt, *Medieval Cheshire* (Manchester, 1929), 118–19.
[28] D. Schäfer, *Das Buch des lübeckschen Vogts auf Schonen* (Halle, 1887), xxxixff.

all local, and the complaint did not turn out to be permanent; but for the time being most branches of European mining were, so to speak, 'due' for a recession irrespective of what was happening at the same time in industry and trade in general. Sooner or later they were bound to pay the penalty for the rapid and cumulative expansion of the previous century and a half; and for most of them the fourteenth and fifteenth centuries were their time of reckoning. By then seams became exhausted, or else had to be worked under conditions which were raising technical problems beyond the powers of medieval technology to solve.

From this point of view the most characteristic is the history of European silver mining. Exhaustion appears to have come over all silver-mining regions, secondary as well as primary. Derbyshire and Devonshire in England, Poitou and the Massif Central in France, and probably Sardinia in Italy, petered out in the later Middle Ages; but far more striking and much more important was the decline of silver mining in its main centres, in central and south-eastern Europe. The silver mines of Hungary had been exploited since the eighth century and reached full development in the twelfth and thirteenth centuries. The mining industry of Saxony and especially that of Rammelsberg by Goslar, which since the tenth century had been the principal source of European silver and copper, passed the peak of its output and prosperity by the thirteenth century. The highly important mining industry of Freiberg had risen in the twelfth century and reached the farthest limit of its development by the beginning of the fourteenth century; the development of the silver mines at Meissen, in Tyrol, in Carinthia, and especially of the rich Transylvanian deposits and of the Bohemian mines of Iglau and Altenberg was roughly contemporary; that of Silesia and perhaps Moravia somewhat later. But by the middle of the fourteenth century in nearly all these regions the mining industry was plunged into a depression from which it did not climb out until the second half of the fifteenth century. Water was the great enemy. The underground workings now reached the strata exposed to the danger of flooding, and in spite of all the experiments and abortive attempts to deal with the underground water it was not until the late fifties that the experiments of Martin Claus of Gotha solved the problem, and Saxon mining could be resumed on scale approaching that of the pre-crisis years.[29]

[29] See below, Chap. X, 721; Berhard Neumann, *Die Metalle, Geschichte, Vorkommen*, etc. *passim;* E. Reyer, *Zinn*, 6ff.; L. Lewis, *Stannaries*, 33ff.; C. Neuburg, *Goslars Berghau bis 1552*, 55ff., 78, 106; A. Weyhmann in *Jahrb. d. Gesellschaft für Lothringische Gesch. u. Altertumskunde* (1905), 3, 56ff.; Ludwig Beck's *Geschichte des Eisens* (Brunswick, 1891–2), is utterly unconcerned with quantities, but the medieval section of vol. 1 (pp. 643ff.) strongly supports the impression of a general advance in the use of iron and steel in the later Middle Ages.

The vicissitudes of silver mining have been well recorded and well studied. On supplies of silver the entire currency of medieval Europe depended, and with them the price level was inextricably involved. Historians therefore know more about silver than about any other branch of medieval mining. It appears, however, probable that with the exception of iron most other medieval mining and metal trades went through the same experiences as silver. Copper was mined in Saxony and Hungary as a by-product of silver and suffered a similar fate. The copper production of Sweden, which was of more recent origin and had developed relatively slowly, may have had a more even career. On the other hand, the tin industry of England – probably the most ancient of all the mining industries of Europe – contracted in the late fourteenth and fifteenth centuries. At least once before the industry had been faced with a similar prospect. In the early thirteenth century its ancient deposits in Devonshire had been showing signs of exhaustion and the industry had to move further west to Cornwall. In the fourteenth century it was the turn of the Cornish tin centres to suffer. The output fell from about 1,328 thousand weights per annum in the thirties of the fourteenth century to under 500 thousand weights in the mid-fifties. It recovered for a while at the end of the century when it reached a very high peak of 1,600 thousand weights per annum, but it soon slumped again and stayed low – mostly below 900 thousand weights – throughout the fifteenth century. The output was not to reach and pass the figures of the pre-Black Death decades until well into the sixteenth century. The decline was not so clearly marked and did not appear to continue for a period equally long in the other important tin area, that of Zinnwald and Altenberg in the Bohemian mountains, but there too the rising trend was interrupted in the first half of the fifteenth century (the Hussite wars were mainly responsible), and production could not wholly recover until the seventies.[30]

The iron industry alone appeared to have escaped the depression. For one thing, it was more dispersed and more dependent on local conditions than other branches of mining. And it is also possible that the very disorders and wars of the time, which did so much to disturb industrial development elsewhere, stimulated the making of guns, cannon and miscellaneous weapons, and created what appears to be a mild war boom in the main iron-making regions. For in at least two main European sources of high-quality iron – that of Sweden and that of Bayonne-Bilbao – output continued at a level which did not sufficiently differ from that of the previous centuries to attract the

[30] See below, Chap. X, 720–3.

attention of contemporary commentators. In most of the other important centres of the iron industry on the continent – even on the Lorraine deposits of the low-grade ore – the industry underwent in the second half of the fifteenth century a technical development – higher and better smelting ovens, greater use of water to work bellows and hammers – which suggests that the industry was expanding. How recent and how general this expansion was and how much it owed to war demand – all these are questions still awaiting an answer.

This catalogue of industries, sinking or just afloat, cannot be concluded without some reference to the most important of the medieval industries, that of cloth. This is not of course the right place in which to unravel its involved pattern in the later Middle Ages. If Europe is viewed as a whole, the later Middle Ages will appear as the time when cloth production both rose and fell. While it declined in Flanders and probably in France, it prospered in other places. In the fourteenth century the cloth industry of Brabant drew to itself some of the prosperity which seemed to be departing from Flanders. In the middle of the fourteenth century the English cloth industry made a sudden leap forward which brought it to its peak at the turn of the fourteenth and fifteenth centuries; in the fifteenth century the cloth industry of Holland, especially that of Leiden, got under way. We are told that a number of smaller centres of cloth production came to the fore at that time. However, nothing less than a statistical enquiry could show whether the industrial activity in the new areas was sufficient to match the declining production of Flanders; and comprehensive figures are lacking. But judging from the falling supplies of raw materials, the cloth industry, and more especially the output of the high-quality cloth for export, must also have declined. In Flanders, Brabant and Holland, by far the most important source of high quality wool was England, and English wool exports were declining.

The story of the cloth industry epitomises the entire history of commerce and industry in the later Middle Ages. The contemporary record of most other trades was equally broken and confused by local and contradictory movements. Regarded as a whole, European economy had its irregular rises and falls – what the economists call short-term fluctuations – which broke the continuity of the falling trends. Above all, the last quarter of the fourteenth century and the second quarter of the fifteenth were marked both in this country and abroad by signs of economic revival, however sudden and short-lived. Yet, on a broad view, European trade passed in the later Middle Ages through a trough long enough – sometimes longer than a century – to justify the diagnosis of a 'secular' slump.

There is now a broad agreement about the facts of the slump, but there is still much uncertainty about its explanation. Was the depression sufficiently 'general', i.e. common to a range of occupations sufficiently wide, to justify the assumption of a common factor? Some of the causes were undoubtedly accidental and contingent: misfortunes, local and temporary, which will be found in the record of every major industry and trade. The Hussite wars had their effect on Bohemian mines; Gascon campaigns disturbed the wine trade; Scandinavian wars interrupted the fishing and the curing of Skania herring; the Wars of the Roses may have interfered with English exports; and urban revolutions had their obvious effect on the Flemish cloth trade. All these were, so to speak, 'events': fortuitous happenings which sometimes coincided but were not deeply related. Some historians might therefore be forgiven for their reluctance to treat them as anything more than a series of accidents and coincidences.

Accidents and coincidences they doubtless were. Yet some of them, even if regarded in isolation, might on second thoughts appear to be not wholly fortuitous. It will not be too far-fetched to believe that the military and political conflict between the Hanse and the Danish kings was in fact due to the remarkable expansion of the Hanseatic interests in Skania fisheries and in Scandinavia in general during the previous century, or that the social war in Flanders was prepared by the previous century of industrial growth. Even less accidental and more obviously rooted in the expansion of the previous age were the seemingly unrelated experiences of miners struggling in different parts of Europe against the difficulties of deep workings and against the mounting dangers of water. And in a field less purely economic, it is possible to interpret the gradual clogging up of important trade routes, described elsewhere, as a more or less inevitable consequence of the political regime which had gradually evolved in the later Middle Ages in the territories of France and the Holy Roman Empire: the solidifying of local custom in the former, the withering of central authority in the latter.

It is not, however, on these considerations alone that the hypothesis of a common cause rests. Much more important is the manifestation of certain deep-seated factors similar to those which were responsible for the ascending movement of the earlier centuries. In the first place, there were prices. Just as the expansion of the twelfth and thirteenth centuries was accompanied by steep price rises all over Europe, so was the decline of the fourteenth and fifteenth centuries accompanied by price changes no less continuous, though possibly less spectacular. Some of these movements have already been mentioned; here they must be considered somewhat more closely. The series most easily available to the historian and most generally studied, that of grain, shows prices expressed in terms of stable exchange medium either falling or stagnating all over Europe. The 20-year means of English wheat prices collected by the late Lord Beveridge and his team of price historians moved in the following manner:

Table V. *Price of Wheat in 20-year periods*

Years	Wheat prices in shillings (per qr.)	Wheat prices in grains of silver
1300–19	7.01	1,734
1320–39	6.27	1,547
1340–59	6.31	1,372
1360–79	7.55	1,508
1380–99	5.57	1,113
1400–19	6.37	1,188
1420–39	6.65	1,107
1440–59	5.56	926
1460–79	6.02	812
1480–99	6.40	852
1500–19	6.91	920

Thus, apart from the high prices of 1360–79, which were influenced by a succession of bad harvests, the current prices sagged with a tendency to fall, while silver prices fell with hardly a break. Comparable foreign prices are not available for periods as early and in samples equally representative. The two collections most commonly used – Hanauer's for Alsace and d'Avenel's for France – do not lend themselves to close analysis and will not by themselves support any reliable historical conclusion. All that the two series can be made to yield is a vague and general impression.

Yet general impressions are not to be spurned, especially if they happen to agree with other and more reliable evidence; and the impression is that the continental prices, in terms of silver, exhibit the English trend to a greatly exaggerated degree. The exaggeration was obviously due to the currency troubles of the times, for whereas the English coinage remained comparatively stable (the silver content of the shilling stood at about 246 grains troy until 1344, and was thereafter reduced by slow steps till it fell to 133.20 grains troy in 1461) that of France and of most other continental countries was greatly debased throughout the fourteenth and fifteenth centuries. So fast and so continuous was the debasement that, however much the current prices rose, they never kept pace with it. According to recent authorities of the counts of Flanders at one time purposely manipulated their currency in the hope that the cost of living and wages would lag behind international prices.

Yet, however exaggerated the trend of the French and Alsatian prices, they moved in the same direction as the trends of other and more reliable series. Among the latter should perhaps be included the price series for Flanders since 1375, which has also been assembled by the International Price Committee. It shows the 'current' wheat prices fairly stable between 1375 and 1425 and then, after a brief and sharp rise in price in the second quarter of the fifteenth century, falling rather steeply for another twenty-five years. By the end of the third quarter of the fifteenth century they stood barely 9 per cent above the price in 1375 and barely 5 per cent above the price in 1400. In the same period prices measured in silver apparently declined.

Table VI. *Annual Wheat Prices in the Low Countries*[31]

(Index Number: 1375–99 = 100)

Years	Current prices
1375–99	100
1400–24	104
1425–49	138
1450–74	109

The importance of the figures in Flanders lies in their relation to the world prices. The Low Countries were heavy importers of grain which they drew from more than one distant source and commonly from the Baltic. They were thus more sensitive to the general trends in European production and commerce than were the prices for such comparatively self-sufficient countries as England. From this point of view, also worth quoting is the little evidence we possess of the movement of prices in the principal source of grain exports in the same period, i.e. in the eastern Baltic. In an anonymous mid-nineteenth century compilation based on the Koenigsberg records of the Prussian Order, the price of rye expressed in units of silver is shown to behave in a manner strikingly similar to that of grain prices in the west. The prices for rye in Koenigsberg in the fifteenth century moved as shown in Table VII. Owing to the heavy debasement of local currency in the fifteenth century 'current' prices may actually have risen, but

[31] I owe the Flemish prices to the late Lord Beveridge's courtesy. They are derived from printed sources, mostly from H. Van Houtte's *Documents pour servir à l'Histoire des Prix*. The Königsberg prices (Table VII) come from an anonymous mid-nineteenth-century summary of grain prices in the records of the Prussian Order, quoted in W. Abel, *Agrarkrisen und Agrarkonjunktur* (Berlin, 1935), 32–3.

the rise was probably gentle compared to the heavy depreciation of the mark.

A movement of prices so continuous must have had an obvious effect on economic life. The falling or sagging prices for agricultural products happened to be accompanied by steeply-rising costs of labour and must therefore have depressed the profits of demesne farming and discouraged commercial production for the market everywhere. In the absence of clear statistical evidence about trade in luxuries and semi-luxuries, it is difficult to say to what extent it was affected. Did the purchasing power of the upper classes and their demand for goods decline with the falling profits of industry and agriculture?

Table VII. *Prices of Rye in Koenigsberg*

(Index Number: 1399 = 100)

Years	Price (silver)
1399	100
1405	89.29
1432	85.32
1448	79.81
1494	49.84
1508	36.48

On general grounds some such correlation could be expected, but whether the effect of prices went further than that, whether it was also responsible for the slump in the major industries, depends on a number of other considerations. It depends, in the first place, on the extent to which price changes were general, i.e. common to the entire range of medieval commodities. It depends also on the susceptibility of medieval producers to price stimuli; above all on the susceptibility of those agricultural producers, who did not depend on 'cash' crops for their income.

On the whole the evidence on both points will not support the hypothesis of prices as the main, and still less as the sole, cause of the slump. Our knowledge of medieval prices is largely confined to grain, but in so far as other series are available they suggest that the fall in prices was highly departmentalised. Thus it does not appear that prices for cloth or those for iron, or indeed those for other commodities, fell at all or fell in the same proportion as prices for agricultural products. Heterogeneous and difficult to collate as are the figures in Thorold Rogers' great collection, they nevertheless leave a strong impression that industrial prices did not in any way synchronise with those of grain. Prices for building materials were rising till the middle of the fourteenth century, were more or less stable from 1370 to 1425, and thereafter fell at a somewhat slower pace than those of grain. The prices of textiles (the least reliable in the collection) appear to fall from 1375 to 1440 and to rise thereafter. Prices for iron were rising fast in the second half of the fourteenth century and falling gently in the fifteenth, finishing in 1475 about 4 per cent above their level in 1350. Expressed in bushels of wheat the index of iron prices in the second half of the century rose without a break from 100 in the first half of the century to 159 in the decade of 1351 to 1360, and to 352 in 1389 to 1400.

Thus the prices for separate commodities did not move together. Even the different agricultural products depreciated and appreciated at times and at rates somewhat different from those of wheat. As far as it is possible to judge from the variegated collection of prices for animals and animal products assembled by Thorold Rogers, the relation between their prices and those for wheat was not at all close.

The prices are here expressed in silver, and therefore somewhat exaggerate the fall in prices, but they reveal very clearly the difference between the two series. The prices for animal products in current coinage actually rose and were considerably higher in the period of 1401 to 1425 than in that of 1351 to 1375 and were not much lower in 1451 to 1475 than they had been a century earlier. Indeed, expressed in current prices, the series after 1351 continues the rising trend of the previous two centuries for at least another 125 years. Hanauer's figures for Alsace, however exiguous, and d'Avenel's collection for France, however heterogeneous, are nevertheless sufficient to suggest that in other parts of western Europe the two series were at least as divergent as in England. Taking Hanauer's silver prices for 1351 to 1375 as 100, we find that in 1400–25 the grain prices fell to 64 while the prices for animal products stood at 87. Hanauer's silver prices, but not his current ones, broke thereafter, but while the index of his silver prices for grain fell between 1351 and 1450 from 100 to 71, that of his prices for animal products stayed at 100. In the subsequent collapse of silver prices, largely reflecting the debasement of French coinage, the index of grain prices sank by the end of the century to as low a level as 40, but prices for animal products still stood at some 40 per cent higher at 54 to 56.

Similar – no more reliable but equally significant – evidence about most animal products could be quoted from almost every continental country, but none of these prices are more significant or have been better studied than those of butter. Trade in butter may appear to the uninitiated too slight a foundation for any argument, especially for an argument about medieval economy as a whole. Yet in spite of being cast on a small scale, it has turned out to be an important index of wider movements. For butter was a merchandise circulating over great distances and commanding an international price; and what is even more important is that it happened to be a semi-luxury entering into popular consumption. When we are told that in this period a Prussian labourer earned the equivalent of 30 kilograms of rye per day, it is not necessary to know what Alfred Marshall said about the elasticity of the demand for bread in order to conclude that agricultural labourers were now better able to indulge in a little butter, however expensive. The price of butter was therefore highly responsive to changes in demand and supply, and was more sensitive as a barometer

Table VIII. *English Prices of Animal Products and Wheat*

(Index Number: 1351–75 = 100)

Years	Wheat	Animal products and cattle
1351–75	100	100
1376–1400	71	88
1401–25	70	99
1426–50	70	89
1451–75	55	76
1476–1500	53	68

of markets than prices of more indispensable foods. It is therefore very significant that the price of butter and the price of grain diverged more widely than the prices of any other commodities. In the fourteenth and fifteenth centuries the butter prices rose very steeply, in both current coinage and in silver, in all the main sources of supplies, with the possible exception of Holland – in Sweden, in Norway, in western Poland. Steepest of all was the rise in Norway. There, after about seventy or eighty years of relatively stable prices, butter suddenly rose by about 10 per cent in the sixties of the fourteenth century and by about 33 per cent by 1400. In the course of the fifteenth century the prices continued to soar; and by 1457 reached a level 200 per cent above that of 1400, dropping to about 100 per cent above that of 1400 in the next decade. On the other hand, the prices for rye imported from the Baltic moved relatively little, and if anything sagged. A similar discrepancy between the prices of rye and butter developed in Sweden and in Prussia, and above all in the Polish hinterland from where Prussian seaports drew most of their butter. In Cracow the index of prices for rye between 1398 and 1450 sank from 33 to 10, but at the same time the prices of butter rose from 10 to 33 or more than threefold.[32]

[32] Julian Pelc, *Ceny w Krakowie w latach 1369–1600* (Lwów, 1935), 127ff.; for other butter prices, see J. Schreiner, *Pest og Prisfall in Senmiddelalderen* (Oslo, 1948), 82.

From the present point of view, the precise cause underlying the behaviour of butter prices is less important than the fact that they behaved differently from grain prices, and that they bear out more fully than any other price series the danger of generalising from a price trend which was apparently confined to grain. Indeed, even in the grain trade the influence of prices is not very obviously related to changes in production and trade. While in most European countries prices expressed in silver were falling, current prices in local coinage were rising, and in regions as self-supporting as most provinces of France and central Germany it was the current prices that mattered most, for it was in relation to current prices that the cost of living, the rate of wages and the profits of agriculture fluctuated. In England the break in the prices in the second quarter of the fourteenth century was unmistakable, but the downward trend was neither continuous nor very marked – certainly less continuous and less marked than the earlier rise. The line representing the long-term trend of English prices and based, say, in moving 25-year averages, is all but horizontal; the prices of 1500 being actually 10 per cent higher than those of the first quarter of the fourteenth century. The lowest prices of the period – those from 1450 to 1475 – were only 20 per cent below those of 1300 to 1325. Expressed in silver, the English prices fell rather more steeply; yet even they did not fall more than about 25 per cent: from 1372 to 1107 grains of silver per quarter of wheat in the century between 1340 and 1440. And it was in that century that English agriculture contracted most and its organisation changed most profoundly.

The economic and more especially the commercial trends of the time were thus out of scale with the movements of grain prices. Is that surprising? The only way in which changes in grain prices could influence production and trade was by calling forth greater or smaller supplies of marketable products. But earlier in this chapter it has already been emphasised that in agriculture prices were by no means the sole, or the main, conductor of economic stimuli. Peasant producers were far too self-sufficient to order their production and to regulate their marketable surpluses in direct response to commercial considerations; and in the later Middle Ages this element of self-sufficiency increased rather than diminished, or, what is the same thing, the proportion of agricultural producers sensitive to prices was smaller than before. There is thus even less reason for seeking in grain prices the main cause of the falling trends of the later Middle Ages than there is for seeking in them an explanation of the rising trends in the earlier centuries.

The doubts are reinforced by the uncertainty of the monetary factor. One of the reasons why prices offer such an obvious and tempting explanation is that at first sight they can easily be fitted into what is known of the contemporary changes in the supply of precious metals. The supplies of silver from the European silver mines gradually gave out, as silver mines entered upon their decline. The supplies from the Goslar region dwindled in the thirteenth century, those from the other mining areas of central and eastern Europe declined or ceased altogether in the fourteenth or early fifteenth centuries. There is also evidence of local scarcities of silver. Indeed, such re-minting as the English crown undertook in the fourteenth and fifteenth centuries, in 1344, 1346, 1351, 1412 and 1461, had for its object to bring the silver content of the English coins into line with the shorter supply and the higher price of silver.

This now appears to be the generally accepted view. Its relevance to the problem of falling prices, however, is not as clear as it might at first sight appear. In the first place, there is a purely historical difficulty of dates and places. The movements of prices cannot easily be synchronised with the dates at which the mining of silver is known to have declined, nor can they be put into geographical relation with areas in which silver was mined. Whereas the Goslar mining was already depressed in the thirteenth century, and silver mining elsewhere reached its lowest depths by the middle of the fourteenth century, the fall in prices did not begin till some time in the first half of the fourteenth century and did not become general till much later. Silver began to flow again from the Saxon mines in the fifties of the fifteenth century, yet, expressed in terms of silver, prices stayed low and, in England at least, continued to fall till 1480. Moreover, the price changes occurred no earlier and were no more spectacular in the regions nearest to the sources of new silver than they were elsewhere; and it is difficult to read into the regional differences between the price series in Cracow, Alsace, Holland and Norway the familiar sequence of concentric ripples by which falling investment and employment in the mining areas could normally be expected to transmit the effects of a mining slump over the entire face of Europe.

There are also the more general arguments some of which have already been mentioned in the discussion of the thirteenth-century rises. To begin with, the annual increments of new silver at their highest were not as great as other changes in silver supplies could be and, in fact, were. By 1300 or 1320, the dates at which supplies of silver from continental mines began markedly to fall off, the total stock of silver in Europe, in relation to annual output, must have been truly enormous, for it had been amassed in at least two centuries, and probably three, of large and steadily mounting output. And when the total stock was thus two hundred to five hundred times that of its annual accretions, the international price of silver was influenced more by the manner in which it was employed than by the current flow from the mines. The falling investment in industry and agriculture as a result of the low level of profits, the changing financial techniques, the diversion of currency into the hands of the crown and its soldiers, the greater demand for silver for buckles and buttons: each of these phenomena could and should have had at least as great an effect on the value of silver as the changes in the supply of new bullion.

What makes the hypothesis of silver supplies all the more difficult to accept is that, even if the flow of new metal from the mines affected international supplies of silver, it did not in the same degree, or indeed in any degree, determine the supplies to individual countries. Individual countries received the bullion by means of international trade, and such was the structure of foreign trade in the later Middle Ages that while some countries earned vast balances, others did not; and that the changes in trade balances did not synchronise with the ups and downs of silver mining. On the roughest calculation, England's favourable balance on the visible trading account oscillated in the course of the fifteenth century between £50,000 and £150,000, and was on the average equal to about half the total value of English foreign trade and more than twice the value of coinage drawn in and out of the mint in the years of recoinage. And if, in the fourteenth and fifteenth centuries, wool exports and grain exports declined, the deficiency was more than made up by the high taxes on wool, the development of English cloth exports, and the virtual cessation of Flemish cloth imports. There is thus every reason why silver should have continued to be imported, and there was nothing surprising or anachronistic in the verse of the fifteenth century, *Libel of English Policy*, in which its well-informed author describes the Prussians as importing

> plate of silver of weighes good and sure
> in great plenty which they bring and buy
> out of the lands of Bohemia and Hungary.

In times of reviving trade, such as the last quarter of the fourteenth century and the thirties and forties of the fifteenth, when the *Libel* was composed, the balance of trade and the imports of bullion may well have risen not only in relation to the total value of trade of those years but also in comparison with the trade balance of earlier centuries. True, that visible balance was apt to be eaten into by papal taxation and often frittered away in payments for war and garrisons abroad, but all this means is that the flow of silver in and out of this country was due to war and payments abroad, and not changes in silver output alone.[33]

Thus price movements there were, and from most of them important consequences followed; but they could not be entirely ascribed to monetary causes, and moreover they were not general. And price changes which are not 'general' but are mainly confined to grain, point to a factor which has already been shown to have operated in the opposite direction in the early centuries of the Middle Ages, i.e. population. On broad, and largely theoretical, grounds a fall in population would be compatible with all the phenomena which our evidence exhibits, and should raise none of the objections to which other general explanations are open. When population fell, some marginal lands would in all probability be abandoned and food would be produced on better land. Relative to the amount of land and labour engaged in food production and relative to the demand for food, supplies would then be more plentiful and therefore cheaper. There would thus be every reason to expect both smaller production and lower prices accompanied by the show of abundance which is so conspicuous in the late fourteenth and fifteenth centuries. A fall in population would also have, so to speak, a selective effect on prices, in that it would tend to lower the prices of agricultural products, which were previously being produced at high and ever-rising costs – or, to use the economist's terminology, under steeply diminishing returns – but would have little effect on commodities not greatly subject to diminishing returns, i.e. most industrial products. By increasing the proportions of silver per head it would counteract the effects of falling supplies from the mines, and might even counterbalance what economists would describe as 'deflationary changes in liquidity', but what historians would classify as greater tendency to hoarding. It would help to increase the 'effective demand' of large masses of population, i.e. stimulate their outlay on food and other goods, and thus lead to higher prices and greater supplies of semi-luxuries especially sensitive to fluctuations of demand.

All this is theory, and like all theories it may at first sight appear too

[33] The problem is further complicated by the use of gold. Most countries in Europe introduced gold coinage by the middle of the fourteenth century, and even before that happened, gold and gold coin of Italian and Byzantine origin was often used in settlement of international payments. The value of silver, or rather its local scarcities and superfluities, were therefore bound to be affected by the terms on which silver and gold coins were exchanged. And as commercial values of the two metals were often at variance with the 'official' or mint terms of exchange, flights to and from silver coinage were very frequent. When they happened they did at least as much to cause local scarcities and abundances of silver as any other changes in the supply of bullion.

simple to fit the infinite variety of medieval experience. But it so happens that this particular argument has emerged from evidence purely descriptive and from arguments largely empirical, and has in fact been first announced as a matter of historical fact by medievalists as innocent of population theory as only medievalists can be. To make this clear it may be worth marshalling some of the evidence even if this will mean transgressing the strict limits of this chapter's subject.

The most familiar evidence is that derived from the topographical record of depopulation, and, above all, from the evidence of vacant holdings and uncultivated fields in the later Middle Ages. In England neither the story of colonisation in the earlier centuries nor that of the depopulation in the later ones has been studied sufficiently closely to yield statistical estimates, but the historians who handled evidence abroad happened to be more quantitatively minded; and, if their results are to be trusted, the abandoned fields and holdings represented throughout the late Middle Ages a very considerable proportion of land erstwhile occupied. In south-western Germany the *Wüstungen* at the turn of the fourteenth and fifteenth centuries were so high as to account in some places for more than half of the holdings. Recent computation puts the proportion of vacant holdings in Scandinavian countries almost equally high.[34]

Needless to say, the evidence of abandoned holdings is apt to magnify the depopulation process it reflects. But allowing for fields abandoned for reasons other than shortage of population, allowing also for subsequent re-lets and re-occupation, there still remains a large balance of lands unoccupied and depopulated through shortage of manpower. Moreover the shortage was obviously general, i.e. not confined to agriculture alone. Contrary to what is sometimes assumed, the fall of population in the countryside was not the result of flight to towns, for population in towns was also dwindling. In this country the old corporate towns – Northampton, Lincoln – filled the air with protestations of poverty and with claims for reduction of royal taxes on grounds of depopulation. A German historian has computed that the population of North German cities declined in the course of the fourteenth and fifteenth centuries by at least 20 per cent. No such computation has been made for the towns of England or France, but those towns where the urban evidence has been studied at all closely – Bordeaux, Rouen, Arras – bear signs of contraction at least as great. The Flemish decline has already been noted.

[34] Wilhelm Abel, *Die Wüstungen des Ausgehenden Mittelalters* (Stuttgart, 1955), 5–31; Schreiner, *Pest og Prisfall i Senmiddelalderen*, 58–63 and *passim*. For a detailed quantitative analysis of German *Wüstungen*, see Heinz Pohlendt, *Die Verbreitung der Mittelalterlichen Wüstungen in Deutschland*, (Göttingen, 1950), ch. II and III.

Depopulation, both urban and rural, was of course a complex process, mostly discontinuous and sometimes compensated by new growth; and indeed some of the new growth was so boisterous that in the absence of quantitative data it might well give the impression of a balance successfully redressed. Thus, while the population of most English towns fell after 1350, it may have remained more or less stationary in London, Bristol and Southampton and two or three other seaports, and may for a time have grown in the cloth-making towns and villages of East Anglia, Yorkshire and the West Country. Similarly while the population in the towns of France, Flanders, northern and central Germany declined, that in north Netherlands (Holland) and in southern and south-eastern Germany may have grown in the course of the fifteenth century.

This was a redress in some measure, but the measure must not be exaggerated. Judging from the amount of cloth produced – say 50,000 cloths per annum – the numbers engaged in English cloth industry at its height could not have been greater than 25,000 persons, if as great.[35] Abroad the cloth industry of Holland was not yet on a scale sufficient to make up for the decline of the industry elsewhere, just as her towns could not as yet have grown sufficiently to balance the fall of urban population in Flanders and France. Similarly, the development of Augsburg and Nuremberg was also too much in its infancy to counter-balance the ebbing fortunes of Hanseatic economy.

Further evidence of falling population will be found in the falling land values. In various parts of France payments for land continually fell, in spite of the rising wheat prices in current coinage. On the estates of St Germain-des-Prés near Paris rents fell without a break from 84*d.* per *arpent* in the second half of the fourteenth century to 55*d.* in the middle decades of the fifteenth century and to about 30*d.* in the seventies and eighties. In Sweden, Denmark and Norway land prices – both rents and capital values – were falling throughout the period, at a pace which appeared to outrun the fall in prices of grain.

Finally, there is the evidence of wages. For whereas prices of agricultural products fell, wages rose. Evidence of rising wages will be found all over Europe, but the most complete as well as the most reliable series of wages so far available is that of the wage rates on the manors of the bishopric of Winchester published by Lord Beveridge. That series reveals a twofold rise in real wages between 1300 and 1350: a rise strangely suggesting a scarcity of labour through falling production.

35 There are several ways of computing the figures. The simplest is to compute from the price of cloth and the costs of production. See M. Postan, 'Some agrarian evidence of declining population...', *Economic History Review*, 2nd ser., II (1950), 232.

So, unless and until new evidence to the contrary is produced, the commercial and industrial depression of the later Middle Ages must be accounted for by decline in numbers. There were fewer hands at work, and there were fewer mouths to feed. This need not have left individuals any worse off; indeed there is every reason for believing that the working population of northern Europe was now more prosperous than ever before. Yet collectively Europe became smaller and poorer, and the decline in her trade and industry was merely one manifestation of a contracting continent.

(2) THE REGULATED TRADE

A long period of contracting trade left its mark on the men engaged in it. The economic status of the merchants, indeed their very behaviour, changed; and no change was more typical, more in tune with the times, than the passing of the great men. If the characteristic figure in commercial and industrial development of the early centuries was the adventurer-merchant depicted by Pirenne, the typical representative of the later Middle Ages was the sedate *bourgeois* of middle rank. Rich men were of course to be found in many large towns. Above all, the Anglo-French wars brought forth small groups of war financiers and speculators. But careers and fortunes like those of Jacques Cœur in fifteenth-century France remain isolated and shortlived; for this was no longer the time of the great speculators moving about the western world, founding cities, forcing open new trade routes, founding new commercial empires. Their race had all but died out and was not to be reborn until the very threshold of the Renaissance, the time when the Welsers and the Fuggers rose in the south of Germany, and the new generation of speculators appeared on the bourses of Antwerp and Amsterdam.

The fifteenth-century merchant new-style was a composite type made up of several elements of different antiquity. One of its components was that of a merchant turned financier; and both the type itself and the process by which he appeared on the scene were of course much older than the later Middle Ages. Medieval merchants of all centuries were prone to retire from active trade as soon as they had made their fortunes. Having retired, the more substantial business men in England often abandoned their towns and their urban associations altogether and established themselves in the country as gentlemen. On the continent, they would more frequently choose to stay in the town as *rentiers*. They might participate as sleeping partners in the active trade of others; they might buy urban tenements and rents, take up municipal and other public bonds and sometimes advance private loans.

The propensity to retire into a life of *rentier* is not difficult to account for. The physical hazards of active trade abroad were not always matched by opportunities for enrichment, and the opportunity grew poorer as the foreign markets grew smaller. At the same time it is probable that capital was still sufficiently scarce to command a high rate of interest. As far as it is possible to judge (and the problem has not been investigated as fully as it deserves), the return expected on the investment of sleeping partners in fifteenth-century England was on the average well in excess of 10 per cent per annum. The later Middle Ages also offered new and ever-growing opportunities for financing needy municipalities and kings at rates nearly as high.

There is therefore nothing incomprehensible or in any way mystical about that process of financial degeneration which seems to have come over a number of wealthy cities in the Middle Ages. When we find in the middle of the thirteenth century the ruling class of Arras made up largely of financiers advancing money to towns and princes all over northern Europe, we cannot explain this otherwise than by concluding that many of the families, which in the late eleventh and twelfth centuries had pioneered in the European cloth industry and in long-distance trade, had now 'made their pile' and sought in money-lending a quieter mode of life and a less adventurous occupation. Other cities might also, like Arras, pass out of the plane of active trade into mere money-lending. It so happens that the rise of Arras to the position of a banker city to the rest of northern Europe occurred very early (for Arras's industrial career had also begun very early) and has been well studied; but a historian with a practised eye will find no difficulty in detecting in the later Middle Ages the same process in most of the towns of northern Europe which had gone through a period of expansion and enrichment in the previous century or century and a half. Much of the mystery of the otherwise inexplicable withering away of the active trade of Flemish merchants might be found in the growth of the *rentier* class. The men, who would in an earlier age have acted as traders to foreign lands or even as employer-clothiers, were now tending to withdraw into quieter occupations: into brokerage and hostel-keeping in Bruges, into passive investment elsewhere.

In the later Middle Ages this process became more general, more, so to speak, disseminated, but it did not account for the entire change in mercantile society. It accounted only for one component of the new *bourgeoisie*, and there were other components as well. Above all, there were the men who looked for and found security not outside but within occupations still largely commercial. They did so by trading in a smaller way, within well organised and protected markets.

The typical figures of northern European commerce in the late Middle Ages were on the whole a humbler lot of men than the merchants of some other times and places. Historians have always noticed the social differences which distinguished the commerce of the great Italian cities from that of the Hanseatic towns. Whereas the bulk of Italy's foreign commerce and finance in the later Middle Ages was in the hands of great commercial and banking houses, the Frescobaldi, the Bardi, the Peruzzi, the Medici, the Datini, the trade of the Hanseatic towns was in the hands of a greater number of smaller people. The difference, however, was not so much geographical as chronological. The records of the earlier centuries, the time when the great Hanseatic cities were being founded, are filled with the acts of great families attempting great things. In a few cities like Cologne it is still possible to find in the later Middle Ages great traders and speculators, like Tidman of Limbourg who financed Edward III, or Gerard von Wesel who tried in the middle of the fifteenth century to lead Cologne's break-away from the Hanse. Elsewhere in the German north, men of this stamp were no longer to be found. It is not that the great families wholly died out, for there were still Castorps and Warendorps all over Hanseatic regions. What happened was that they no longer occupied the position in the Hanseatic trade which had been theirs when they were blazing its trails in the newly opened lands beyond the Elbe.

The bulk of the trade was now in the hands of men of middling substance. And being middling they looked for safety and found it in co-operation, in combination, and more generally in numbers. It was for their benefit that the Hanseatic League maintained in most foreign centres within its influence their great factories or *Kontors* with large bodies of resident agents or factors. It was their cargoes that were marshalled in convoys to the Bay of Bourgneuf, to the east coast of England, to Bruges. And it was their trade that was looked after by corporate organisations within the German towns – the *Bergenfahrers* and *Schönenfahrers* of Lübeck, the *Englandfahrers* of Cologne.

The English development was even more remarkable in that the dividing line was drawn more sharply. The early years of Edward III, coinciding as they did with the opening phases of the Hundred Years War and Edward's great fiscal operations, forced into bloom all the capitalist or quasi-capitalist elements in English life. Men like the brothers de la Pole, representing the upper rank of the English merchant classes, now rose to great wealth gained in supplying the armies, in arranging and transmitting payments abroad, in managing the king's taxes and levies on wool. Their economic power as well as their hold over the English wool trade reached their highest point in the thirties and forties when, having formed several syndicates, they were able to finance the crown and to monopolise the entire British export trade in wool. But Edward's insolvency in the fifties brought about their collapse; and their collapse meant also the demise of a whole social order. When in the last quarter of the century the Staple of Calais finally took shape it was made up of a larger number of smaller men – men who in the fifteenth century were to be represented by the three generations of Cely's: respectable, prosperous traders who, though in the highest rank of the wool trade, could not claim more than one fiftieth or even a hundredth share of England's wool exports. Needless to say, individuals of outstanding wealth did not wholly disappear from English trade and finance. The wars of Richard II call forth Brembre and Lyons; the trade of Bristol could boast of Robert Cheddar and William Canning. And in fifteenth-century London, there was Dick Whittington. Yet in a curious way none of these men were as typical of the fifteenth century as the great London dynasties were of the thirteenth. They were probably not quite so rich; they were certainly less numerous. Above all, they no longer dominated the trade of the country. The economic and financial power of the wool trade in its relations with the crown and with the outside world now rested not on the wealth or influence of individuals but on the power of the corporate organisation – the Company of the Merchants of the Staple of Calais.

The Company of the Staple was not alone. The 'general' traders of England, who specialised in importing and exporting miscellaneous merchandise other than wool, now for the first time appeared in records as the Company of Merchant Adventurers. By then the name was out of date. The time when English general merchants adventured furthest into distant lands and seas was the turn of the fourteenth and fifteenth centuries and preceded by at least two or three generations the establishment of a company claiming the title of Merchant Adventurers. It was in the fifteenth century, when the expansion of English trade both in area and in quantity was long over, and when most opportunities for commercial adventure had fallen away, that the merchants arrogated to themselves the name to which they were no longer entitled. Their company was coming into an ever greater prominence as the century drew to its close, and made up in collective power and influence for the more modest substance of its members.

Corporate trade was indeed the typical feature of the later Middle

Ages. Mediocre men combined to do what greater ones might have done in isolation. In later centuries, the late sixteenth and the seventeenth, corporate trade could be made to serve the ends of great speculative business. Similar corporations may also have existed in the earlier centuries of the Middle Ages. Did not the great Flemish capitalists of the thirteenth century operate in London through the Hanse of the Flemish towns, and did not the magnates of Cologne establish themselves in England at the same time through a similar Hanse? In the later Middle Ages, however, corporate action and corporate support became the mainstay of mediocre firms. With their support large numbers could share in the trade of northern Europe, and without it no merchant from northern Europe could successfully operate. For corporations both protected and circumscribed the trade they controlled; and they did not confer collective power on their members without acquiring collective authority over them. By virtue of this authority, they were now able to regulate the scale and the methods of individual enterprise and to lay down rigid rules for prices and credit, for terms of sales, for relations with agents, and for the latters' residence and conduct.

As the scope of individual enterprises contracted and their reliance upon corporate organisation grew, so their methods and organisation changed. This is not the place to deal with all the facts of medieval business technique. One fact, however, is strictly relevant here. The modest scope of individual enterprises, as well as their large numbers, forced upon them a method of trade which in at least one respect differed from the methods of the great houses of Italy and South Germany. They were less, so to speak, self-contained. An individual English firm trading abroad, or a Hanseatic firm trading in England, or a Dutch firm trading in Antwerp and Bruges, did not as a rule trade through channels entirely and exclusively its own. Whereas a great Italian firm might be served by bodies of servants and partners, a typical Hanseatic or English firm, being too small to maintain a large body of permanent servants, would try and avail itself of the services of more or less independent agents and brokers. The difference must not of course be driven too far. Most English firms trading in Flanders sent out for shorter or longer periods representatives of their own, and there were Italian merchants in Bergen, London and elsewhere ready to act for any client in Italy. But on the whole the north European machinery of factories and corporate companies as well as the smaller scale of individual enterprise favoured a far greater development of resident agencies and of a specialised profession of foreign factors.

The corporate tendency manifested itself, however, not only abroad and in dealings with foreign countries but also at home and in matters of local trade. The municipal governments at home began to take an ever greater interest in the commercial activities of their burgesses, and the age was one of mounting urban regulations and of accumulating urban legislation. The right to participate in the trade of the local markets and in the staple branches of foreign trade was being defined and circumscribed, the entry into them was being limited. Monopoly was indeed the prime object and the pre-requisite condition of urban regulations and became the guiding object of town policy. It was only the power of the king, as in England and France, or the political links with other towns, as in North Germany, that prevented the whole of Europe breaking up into a loose assembly of small but economically independent territories, each dominated by a monopolistic town. And even in England and France and the Hanseatic north, the monopolistic and corporate interests came to the fore in most towns.

Urban economy was indeed beginning to approximate to the textbook fiction of a medieval town: a diminutive region forming with its rural belt a self-sufficient unit, within which trade and industry were partitioned into equal shares and regulated by law. The reason why historians have so often been led to accept this fiction as a representative sample of medieval economy is that they know much more about regulated economy of the corporate town than they do about trade in its freer and less regulated aspects. For it is in the nature of regulation and control to breed documentary evidence and thus to perpetuate itself in history out of all proportion to its real importance in historical development.

The corporate and monopolistic features of fourteenth and fifteenth century towns have thus shielded from view the meagrely documented activities of freer trades and freer towns. There were 'open' towns, and 'open' trades within them, even in the Middle Ages. For we know that the great fair towns of northern Europe – Bruges, Antwerp, Bergen-op-Zoom – were free ports where strangers were allowed to enter and where trade with strangers was more or less unrestricted by any law, except perhaps the law of residence and brokerage. Greater or smaller elements of freer trade might also be found in great metropolitan centres like London, in seafaring communities like Middelburg. Yet, on the whole, it was not these towns that typified the new order, but Danzig, which ended by excluding even the other Hanseatics from its local trade; Bergen, where the German merchants who dominated it established a close and highly-regulated monopoly over its trade; Rouen and Paris, where local companies watched and fought jealously over their fields of operations; and countless other smaller towns in France and Germany, which now sank into that well-regulated stupor from which they were not to awake until the French revolution and Napoleon's conquests.

The monopolistic and regulated economy of medieval municipalities was of course related to the political as well as to the social changes within the towns. In the political struggles, which mark the history of the north European towns in the fourteenth century, the rising parties were the craft gilds, which voiced the interests of the smaller men rooted primarily in the local markets. In many German towns, in Wismar, in Rostock, in Bremen, indeed in Lübeck itself, craft gilds rose in the second half of the fourteenth century or the beginning of the fifteenth to sweep out of office the descendants of the patrician families entrenched in town government. Similar revolts took place elsewhere – the Flemish risings of the fourteenth century indeed belong to the mainstream of the politics and diplomacy of the age. Except in Flanders, most of the movements of revolt failed; in towns, in which the democratic governments established themselves, they were as a rule ousted from office after a few years and replaced again by representatives of the patrician families. Yet, even at times and in places at which the counter-revolutions succeeded what they re-established was the political ascendancy of illustrious families and not the conditions which had once upon a time helped them to acquire their lustre. As has already been said, the great families themselves were no longer the same. They were mainly landowners, *rentiers*, public servants, or else traders differing only in name and personal descent from the middling men around them. The time for capitalists was over or not yet.

(3) THE HANSE

The commercial depression, which for all its local variations, affected the whole of northern Europe, and which, for all its discontinuity, lasted for a century and more, was bound to influence the political history of European trade. More especially it was bound to influence the economic policies in regions which happened to be most exposed to the action of commercial change.

North Germany was thus exposed to an extent greater than other parts of Europe. It would be natural to expect that, at the time when both population and commerce ceased to grow, the territorial scope of German trade should have ceased to expand and its outer frontiers should have ceased to move. Danzig was the last great foundation of the German town builders. After the beginning of the fourteenth century no other towns of importance and no new commercial positions were founded in the Slavonic east. The newest and easternmost Germanic settlements – beyond the Oder and the upper Danube – were destined to remain isolated oases amidst a culture which they failed to assimilate and within an economy which they never wholly subdued or integrated with their own.

It is therefore not as paradoxical as it may seem that the age which saw the end of German expansion should also have given birth to the most important political formation in German history of the late Middle Ages – the Hanseatic League. At first sight the League was a step so novel and so forward that it may be difficult to see in it signs of decline. Yet viewed from the point of view of economic and geographical facts, it represented in the field of transcontinental trade the all-prevailing trend towards collective protection. For in the second half of the fourteenth century German commerce had all but reached the limits of its territorial expansion. From now onwards the German towns were more anxious to keep the positions they possessed than able to acquire new positions further afield. This indeed became the purpose of the Hanseatic League, and from this point of view the League was little more than a federation which the German towns established among themselves to maintain by political action that place in European trade which they had won for themselves in the course of the economic changes of the preceding epoch.

The rise of the League was thus essentially a political event; and its early development was largely a constitutional process. Its starting points were the unions of German merchants abroad. The organisations of German merchants in Wisby and London were the earliest unions of this kind. Indeed it was in England that the very term 'Hansa' was used for the first time to designate the right of merchants to form trading associations, and by the beginning of the thirteenth century the word ceased to be applied to the burgesses of English towns and was confined to the organisations of foreign merchants in London.[36] Thus a number of Flemish towns headed by Bruges formed in the thirteenth century a London 'Hansa', which represented them before English authorities and acted on their behalf in defence of their interests and privileges. Another such organisation was the Cologne 'Hansa', which was eventually to grow into the Hanse of the Steelyard comprising all, or nearly all, the German merchants trading in London.[37] The *Carta Mercatoria* of 1303, which greatly extended the privileges of foreign merchants in England and which in later centuries came to be claimed by the Germans as the constitutional foundation of their privileged status in this country, dealt with the North German merchants as a single body. Since then the English merchants knew only of the *mercatores alemanniae*, and in this way the London Hanse

[36] For a closely argued discussion of the evolution of the term, see R. Doehaerd, 'À propos du mot "hanse"', *Revue du Nord*, XXXIII, no. 129 (1951).

[37] It has been suggested, but not definitely proved, that there were originally two German *Hansae*, that of Cologne and that of the Easterlings, which later fused into one: see M. Weinbaum, 'Stalhof und Deutsche Gildhalle zu London' in *Hansische Geschichtsblätter*, Jahrgang 1928 (Lübeck, 1929).

of the Cologners became the London Hanse of the Germans. Under Edward II, moreover, the Hanseatic merchants acquired valuable exemptions from customs, which put them in a more favourable position than other aliens, or indeed the native merchants of England. Their corporate organisation of the Steelyard received extensive powers of self-government and jurisdiction and a share in municipal authority in London. All in all, the Hanseatic rights in England established the Germans in a position of privilege and autonomy comparable to the 'capitulations' of a later age.

England, however, was not the only place where the merchants from North Germany came to have a corporate organisation and a privileged status. There was hardly an important commercial centre in northern Europe, in which some German towns did not at one time or another receive grants of commercial liberties and did not organise into communal bodies of very much the same type as the German Hanse in London. Of these communal organisations the most important were the German 'factories' at the two termini of the great route: in Bruges and Novgorod.

The German factory, or *Kontor*, in Bruges was not as old as their London Hanse, but in the course of time it became their chief trading station abroad. At the time when the *Kontor* was established, Bruges was about to enter upon the most illustrious stage of its history. With the rise of the *Kontor* the active commerce of the Flemings themselves gradually declined, but, strange as it may seem, the importance of Bruges grew as the active trade of its burgesses dwindled. At the height of Flemish industrial and commercial development in the thirteenth and the early fourteenth centuries Bruges had been one of the economic centres of Flanders, one of its four *Leden*, but unlike the other three it was from the very beginning more important commercially than industrially. Its cloth industry was far behind that of Ghent, Ypres and Douai; nor did it possess any other important industries. And even in commerce Bruges had at first fulfilled a highly specialised function. Its geographical situation was inconvenient for internal trade: off the main artery of the Scheldt and on the periphery of the main internal land routes. But it proved very convenient as a port for commercial traffic between the Low Countries and England, and its trade expanded as the cloth industry of Flanders became more and more dependent on English supplies of wool.

Apparently it was this connection with England that attracted the Germans to Bruges in the first instance. There has been a certain amount of argument among German historians on this point, but on the whole it appears that the Germans had been in the habit of going to England long before they established themselves in Flanders. It was because Bruges had been the centre of Anglo-Flemish trade that it also became the centre of German-Flemish trade. But with the Germans there it soon developed into something more than an Anglo-Flemish trade junction and before long acquired many features of an international emporium. Bruges, the seaport and the seat of a great fair where the Germans and the English had been in the habit of going, now became also the port and the fair where the Bretons, the Normans, the Spaniards and later the Italians came to do their buying and selling. And as Bruges rose in importance, the Hanseatic *Kontor* drew to itself an ever greater proportion of German trade. In the course of time its privileges, its federal organisation and its hold over the Hanseatic trade became the standing, not to say the burning, issue of the inter-urban politics of the German Hanse.

The third important centre of the German foreign trade where the merchants from northern and eastern towns enjoyed important privileges and a communal organisation was the 'Petershof' of Novgorod. Novgorod was the eastern terminus of the great route and the chief centre of German trade in Russia. In the early Middle Ages the Scandinavians, and especially the Gotlanders, who were probably the first to establish a commercial factory in Novgorod, possessed there a 'Hof', i.e. a 'yard', with hostels and warehouses. But eventually the 'Hof' passed into the hands of the Germans and became the seat of a communal organisation of German merchants trading to Novgorod protected by treaties with Russian princes and enjoying liberties roughly of the same kind as those possessed by their factories elsewhere.

In addition to the three main corporations of Bruges, London and Novgorod, the merchants of the Hanseatic towns also possessed outposts in smaller places like the English 'treaty ports' of Lynn, Boston, Hull and Bristol, or the distant factory – 'Fondacho dei Tedeschi' – in Venice, and a more permanent stake in the municipal institutions of most Norwegian and Swedish towns, and more especially of Bergen. In addition, improvised corporate organisations were sometimes set up in the towns of the Low Countries to which German traders happened to transfer their activities in times of trouble. Thus a network of commercial stations enjoying exceptional treaty rights and valuable commercial privileges and often connected by routes completely dominated by German merchants, formed a commercial system as close and, by all appearances, as tightly knit as any Europe had ever seen.

This system in its main outlines was already in existence at the beginning of the fourteenth century, but at that time the system, like the 'informal' empires of a later age, owed its cohesion and unity to economic facts rather than to political ties. For, in theory, the corporate organisations in foreign places still led separate and independent existences and, so to speak, 'belonged' to the merchants trading in them. Viewed politically and juridically, the rise of the Hanseatic League in the closing decades of the thirteenth and the first half of the fourteenth centuries was nothing else than a gradual transformation of the informal system into a formal one, and of the separate corporations, *Hansae* of German merchants, into a single union of the towns themselves. How this transformation occurred is more or less clear and does not need much explaining. Equally clear is the process by which the union of the towns acquired a permanent organisation. Sporadic meetings of the 'home' towns to discuss matters raised by their merchants abroad could be, and were, held several times in the middle of the fourteenth century. All that was necessary to bring them together more or less permanently was a suitable occasion and a determined leadership. Both came in the second half of the century, at the time when trouble was brewing in Flanders and a growing tension in relations with Denmark led up to the first great Hanseatic war.

At the very outset of the conflict, in 1367, the towns met in Cologne to form a confederation which was this time to be provided with the rudiments of a permanent constitution and a common purse. The League survived the war, and the peace of Stralsund of 1370 which concluded the conflict is therefore regarded as the birthday of the Hanse. Furthermore, in both these conflicts, and particularly in the conflict with Denmark, Lübeck came forward as the leader of the towns and the spearhead of their attack. And from that time onwards it came to be regarded, both within the Hanse and outside it, as the guardian of Hanseatic unity and as the sponsor of its policies.

This concludes the political and constitutional story of the rise of the Hanseatic League. But the most significant part of the story was neither political nor constitutional. It was economic, and the economic processes behind the constitutional evolution of the League were not those of rising unity and strength. On the contrary, the necessity which drove the towns to unite sprang from the recent, and on the whole dangerous, deterioration in their commercial position.

The changes in the internal relations of the Hanse might conveniently be considered first. No sooner had the Hanse emerged fully fledged from the war with Denmark than fundamental disunity began to reveal itself in the affairs of the newly born League. In the past the economic basis of Hanseatic unity had been their common interests in the monopoly of the great route and in the common privileges which they had won for themselves in foreign markets. They exercised their monopoly and enjoyed their privileges as economic confederates rather than competitors, and in this non-competitive combination Lübeck was the cementing agent – a role for which it was well fitted both by its history and its geography. German urban colonisation owed much to Lübeck's enterprise, and many of the towns to the east of the Elbe had arisen more or less as Lübeck's colonies. Throughout that early period they continued to be bound to it by social and personal ties. Lübeck also exercised a strong economic influence by virtue of its peculiar position on the route from the Baltic to the North Sea. As long as navigation went along the sea coast and internal waterways, goods from and to Prussia had to be discharged for carriage by land across the Jutland Peninsula and thus had to pass through Lübeck. However rapidly the trade of the Prussian and Livonian towns grew, Lübeck stood to benefit by it; and as long as Lübeck continued to be indispensable, none of the other towns was likely to object to its exalted part in eastern trade.

This position could not last for ever. By the second half of the fourteenth century Lübeck was losing, even if it had not yet wholly lost, most of its special advantages. In the first place its social ties with the other towns grew weaker. The colonisation movement had spent itself before the end of the fourteenth century, and, after that, Lübeck all but ceased to send out settlers to the newer towns. In Prussia alone the towns continued to grow, but they appear to have drawn their population from Prussia itself. So, while Lübeck still remembered that it was the mother of the Baltic towns, the other towns were beginning to forget that they were Lübeck's daughters. In the second place, Lübeck was ceasing to be an unavoidable *entrepôt* on the east-to-west route. In the second half of the fourteenth century, the men of Zuiderzee – of Campen, Deventer and Zwolle – popularised the direct sea route to the east round Jutland, the so-called *Umlandsfahrt*; and their example was soon followed by the Prussians going west, and by the English and Dutch going east. Among the Prussian towns Danzig grew in the forties and fifties to become the chief city of Prussia; and the Danzigers from the very beginning preferred to trade to Flanders and to England by the direct sea route. Finally, Lübeck was losing its predominant share in the trade of Prussia and Livonia. By the second half of the fourteenth century the towns of Prussia and Livonia were not only learning to trade to the west without the assistance of Lübeck, but were also acquiring an ever-growing share in the exploitation of their own hinterlands. The time was not distant when they would begin to look upon their respective regions as fields exclusively their own. The towns of Prussia would then begin to claim a monopoly of the trade of the Vistula as against the other members of the Hanse; Riga and Reval would lay the same claims to the trade of the Dvina.

The economic exclusiveness of the Livonian and Prussian groups of towns was a symptom of a *malaise* the effects of which were to be felt by all the Hanseatic towns and not by Lübeck alone. The local policies of separate territorial groups asserted themselves with ever-growing vigour. Most vigorous of all were they in Prussia where they derived not only from the local economic interests of the towns but also from the peculiar position of the Teutonic Order. The Teutonic Knights were both the makers and the rulers of Prussia, for they had organised its conquest and ruled it as its sovereign princes. But unlike most other territorial rulers of Germany the Order was very efficient: its administration was highly centralised and well organised, and its towns never assumed the same degree of independence as they did in other parts of Germany. So when the Hanse emerged it had to accept as a participant not only the towns of Prussia, but the whole of the Prussian state, that is to say, the Teutonic Order and its High Master.

The affiliation of the Order was undoubtedly a source of political strength to the League, for the High Master possessed a standing in international politics which was not to be trifled with, and his membership gave the Hanse a formal position in the world of territorial states. It the constitutional parlance of the time, the High Master was the *Beschermer*, the protector, of the League; something like a prince of the Hanseatic empire. At the same time the insistent particularism of the Order was a source of weakness. And nowhere did the particularism manifest itself more clearly than in the Order's commercial enterprises. It traded on a very large scale in corn, amber and other commodities. It possessed an elaborate commercial organisation with central offices (*Schäffereien*) in Marienburg and Königsberg, with a whole fleet of commercial boats and agents in Prussia and other large centres of Europe. In all this trade the Order acted very much as a competitor of the Hanseatic towns and even of its own towns. What is more, it made use of its political power to regulate internal trade in a way most suitable for its own commercial interests.

So much for the separate attitude of Prussia. The other group with very strong separate interests was the western wing of the Hanse, especially the Rhenish towns with Cologne. The latter continued to find their chief fields of activity in the Netherlands and in England. Whenever the Hanse had to undertake any measure against England and Holland, the merchants of Cologne disobeyed and circumvented it and were ready to give up the membership of the Hanse rather than suffer a loss in any of their trade in the west.

The only towns whose interest and policy seemed to be directed all through the fifteenth century towards the maintenance of Hanseatic unity were those of the central groups of the Hanse, and especially the so-called Wendish towns with Lübeck at their head. But even here Lübeck's particular interests asserted themselves. It was determined to maintain its position as a barrier and an indispensable intermediary on the east-to-west route, and it strove for Hanseatic unity largely because that unity was the only means to maintain the *status quo*. Hence its constant attempts to prevent the direct connections between the eastern Baltic and the North Sea. Hence also its bellicosity in all the conflicts with Holland and later also with England, the two countries which made the widest use of the direct sea route through the Sound. In other words, what Lübeck strove to maintain was not the Hanse *per se*, but the particular version of the Hanse which pivoted upon its port: an attitude which the other towns understood very well and frequently resisted.

In this way the close of the fourteenth and the fifteenth centuries witnessed the ever-widening divergencies of policy among the main constituent groups of towns within the Hanse. The divergencies were largely due to the differences of regional interests which have already been described. But, behind the regional particularism of urban groups like the Prussian, the Livonian or the Rhenish, it is also possible to discover signs of an economic contraction and reaction – the latter in the literal sense of a recoil from a new and unfavourable situation.

Some of the symptoms of the recoil will be found in the growing urban exclusiveness. Its general spread in the fourteenth and fifteenth centuries has already been described, but nowhere was the change-over towards local protectionism more clearly marked than in northern Germany. In the centuries of German growth and expansion there was relatively speaking very little of what might be called a protective or exclusive tendency in municipal policy. Germans were expanding their trade with great confidence and seemed to fear no competitors. In their early treaties with Russia and England the foreigners were given liberties of trade in German regions, and the Baltic was treated as an open sea. The internal government of the towns matched the liberal spirit of their trade. It was largely in the hands of patrician 'founder' families: an expansionist and adventurous race of men who cared comparatively little for the internal trade of their towns, and, as a rule, allowed foreigners to trade and to settle among them.

By the time of the Stralsund Peace of 1370 this liberal period was over. The gilds of artisans and traders were becoming very powerful. The democratic revolts in a number of towns have already been mentioned. When the epidemic of petty-bourgeois movements subsided, the municipal governments, even where they were in the hands of the old families, found it easy to meet the wishes of the local gilds and to exclude the foreigner from the town markets and the surrounding rural regions. And some towns began applying anti-alien laws even against the Hanseatics.

The social changes in Hanseatic towns were of course a local reflection of an ageing process through which the whole of Europe was then passing. But at the same time they also reflected a change which was more economic than social, and as such peculiar to the Hanse. The reason why the towns now turned to their own regional trade and tried to protect their local markets was that their opportunities elsewhere had either dwindled or were seriously threatened. For since the middle of the fourteenth century the international position in northern Europe had been continually changing to the detriment of German trade.

It has already been said that the immediate occasion for the formation of a permanent Hanseatic League was a threat to the Hanseatic interests in Scandinavia. The threat was not economic in origin. It sprang from a political movement in the Scandinavian kingdoms and did not threaten to raise up a rival economic power. Yet it was sufficiently characteristic of the difficulties which the Hanseatics were henceforth to encounter all over northern Europe, and above all in Scandinavia, to be worth looking at more closely.

In the late twelfth and the thirteenth centuries the Scandinavian countries were, so to speak, an economic vacuum. The native merchant class had either disappeared or had not yet risen, while the rulers were too anxious to attract whatever trade they could and, besides, were too weak to resist the outright exploitation of their countries by the Germans. The Hanseatics first appeared in Scandinavia quite early in the Middle Ages, and the merchants of Cologne traded there in the thirteenth and probably in the twelfth century. But it was only when the Germans began to import their corn surpluses that they were able to appropriate to themselves the entire commerce of the region and to acquire there a position of overwhelming power. Towards the middle of the fourteenth century the German merchants dominated the economic life of the three countries, supplanted the native commerce and shipping, and, with the single exception of the English, had no rivals or competitors to fear.

In Sweden they controlled the chief source of her riches – the mines. So great was their power in that country that by the beginning of the fifteenth century they appointed from among themselves one half of all the municipal governments. Equally deep was their penetration of Norway. The Norwegians were still actively engaged in commerce and navigation in the thirteenth century, but towards the end of the century the Germans made rapid inroads into their trade. We find them extending their hold over the towns of Oslo, Tunsberg, Trondjem, and especially Bergen. Bergen was the Norwegian staple town for the trade in the products of Iceland and other Norwegian islands and of the northern provinces, and it was from these regions that the most valuable products of Norwegian export came – stockfish and fish oil. And in Bergen, more than in any other Scandinavian town, the Germans were a kingdom within a kingdom, with their own laws and jurisdiction.

Their power in Denmark was somewhat more localised. Germans were settled in every Danish town, and German law replaced the Danish in national courts. But the chief point of their activity was the north shore of the Sound, the coastlands of Skania with its famous fishing grounds. For a time – a century and a half – Skania was a focal point of north European fish trade, and the periodic confluence of merchants at Skania made it also an important centre of exchange in other commodities. No wonder that the East Germans regarded Skania as an economic possession of great, not to say crucial, importance.

In the second half of the fourteenth century this position, so valuable, above all so powerful, suddenly deteriorated. Waldemar Atterdag, who rose to the throne of Denmark in 1340, not only set out to unify the Scandinavian kingdoms and thus to fill that political void in which the German towns had built their power, but, by his taxation, he also directly encroached on the Hanseatic privileges. The Germans were compelled to fight the immediate threat of taxation as well as the further danger of a united Scandinavia. The result of the struggle was a victory enshrined in the Peace of Stralsund of 1370, which was followed by the formal establishment of the Hanse.

The debut of the League was thus very successful. As a political weapon it proved itself equally successful in the struggles which it was to wage in the subsequent hundred or hundred and fifty years. The Treaty of Utrecht of 1474, which concluded a somewhat similar conflict with England a century later, still found the League in full possession of its foreign privileges and as triumphant over its enemies as it had been in 1370. Yet, successful as the League was in direct political action, it failed, as it was bound to fail, in its attempt to arrest the march of economic and political forces which continued to shape the evolution of trade in northern Europe. It was unable to defend its position in Novgorod in the face of the rising power of the Tsars; unable to maintain its old position in Flanders in opposition to the new centres of northern trade which were rising under different auspices in Brabant and Holland; unable to maintain its monopoly of eastern routes; in fact unable to maintain the route itself, which came in the end to be rivalled and replaced by other routes crossing the continent further south. Above all it was incapable of preventing the rise of the two great rivals who were destined in the sixteenth and seventeenth centuries to supplant the Hanse in the economic leadership of northern Europe – England and Holland.

(4) THE ENGLISH CHALLENGE

The expansion of the western powers into regions hitherto monopolised by the Germans began to make headway in the second half of the fourteenth century, and at first it was with the English threat that the Hanseatics appeared to be concerned most. English commercial activity in the north had been gathering strength all through the fourteenth century, and came to a head in its closing years. Yet what requires an explanation is not that the challenge should have come so early but that it should not have come earlier still. For throughout the Middle Ages England formed an essential part of the north-western trading area, and throughout the Middle Ages English merchants were themselves active on the trade routes to and from their country.

England's economic geography fitted her well to play an important part in the trade of north-western Europe. The shores of England were easily accessible across the narrow seas, and it will be recalled that in the Middle Ages as in the modern era sea routes were on the whole more efficient and cheaper than land routes. What is more, the English coast was not only easy to reach but was also worth reaching. Throughout the greater part of the Middle Ages England supplied the more highly specialised regions of Europe with the food and raw materials which some of them lacked. In this sense England's economy in the Middle Ages could be represented, as it often has been, as 'colonial'.

Like the colonial countries of more recent times England may in some respects have lagged behind the neighbouring continental countries, but what justifies the appellation most is that the goods she exported were of the kind that would now be described as 'primary produce'. Some manufactured commodities were of course made in England and sold to foreigners throughout English history, and in the later Middle Ages wholly or partly manufactured cloth was to become the mainstay of English trade. But until the second half of the fourteenth century it was minerals, wool and foodstuffs that sustained England's trade and made the English connection so indispensable in the economic life of Europe. At the very dawn of European history England supplied the rest of Europe with rare minerals, mostly tin. There is also every reason for believing that until the very end of the thirteenth century England was an important source of foodstuffs, grain and animal products which made her valuable to the Low Countries and indispensable to Scandinavia. Above all, it was the wool of her grasslands that made it possible for the highly specialised cloth-producing economies of the Low Countries and Italy to develop. Not until the late fourteenth century did England's part in European trade cease to be mainly that of a supplier of raw materials. But as long as she played that part she was bound to attract foreign trade and foreign investment in a larger measure than many other regions of Europe and to figure prominently in the commercial fortunes of the western world.

It is thus not surprising that the history of commercial voyages to and from England should have reached to the very dawn of history. Phoenicians may or may not have paid regular visits to the West Country in search of tin, but it seems highly probable that in the Bronze Age bronze articles, manufactured from indigenous metals in Ireland and England, were exported or perhaps re-exported to the continent.[38] Even before they occupied the country the Romans may have imported minerals mined in Britain: Strabo mentions gold, silver and iron. There is also a strong presumption that southern England became a source of grain supplies to neighbouring provinces of Gaul. Strabo mentions wheat exported from Britain in pre-Roman times, and centuries later Roman writers speak of wheat shipped from Britain to Rhineland. And although one writer, Ammianus Marcellinus, describes the shipments as a wheat tax (*annona*), the probability is that England had a large exportable wheat surplus.[39]

What happened during the long interruption of the Anglo-Saxon invasions, indeed how long it lasted and how complete it was, we do not know. But no sooner does the darkness lift and the documentary evidence become available than references to England's commercial relations with the continent reappear. Miscellaneous Anglo-Saxon sources bear testimony to the wide range of Anglo-Saxon imports and exports and so do other surviving facts of Anglo-Saxon archaeology. King Æthelred's enactment about the tolls of London reveals that at the time of the tenth and eleventh centuries London was frequented by merchants of Flanders, Normandy and North Europe in general;

[38] S. Pigott, 'The Early Bronze Age in Wessex', *Proc. Prehist. Soc.* (1938).

[39] In the view of R. G. Collingwood and J. N. L. Myres, *Roman Britain and the English Settlement* (Oxford, 1937), 243, the exports were *annona* on a large scale; but was large *annona* exported from provinces not normally producing exportable surpluses?

men from Francia and the German Empire are explicitly mentioned.[40] England was then obviously within the trading area of central and northern Europe. From Britain came foodstuffs, raw materials and, for a time, slaves, and the famous letter of Charlemagne to King Offa complaining of the deterioration in the quality of English cloths bears witness to the existence of a well-established cloth trade. Some historians have gone so far as to suggest that the so-called Frisian cloth, to which there are numerous references in continental sources, was nothing else than Anglo-Saxon cloth distributed by Frisian merchants.[41]

Whether this particular hypothesis is right or wrong there is no doubt that the Frisians played an important part in Anglo-Saxon trade of the time. Bede mentions Frisian merchants settled in York and London, and there are other, less indirect, indications of Frisian participation. But the Frisians were not alone. In the first place there were also the Scandinavians. In English political history contacts with the Norsemen were mostly those of war, migration and conquest. There is, however, little doubt that both before and during the age of the Danish invasion Scandinavians were in the habit of trading to the British Isles, and the Norsemen continued to trade even after they had established their reputation as marauders and invaders. We find Danes settled in London, in York and Exeter, and there is widely scattered evidence of Scandinavians trading with Anglo-Saxon England not only from Scandinavia proper but also from Scandinavian settlements in Ireland and Iceland.[42]

The Norman Conquest did not break the commercial ties with Europe, but, if anything, added to them. The trade to Norway apparently continued uninterrupted and was very active in the twelfth century. In the Sverrir's Saga, King Sverrir is shown commending in a speech the trade of the English who brought wheat and honey, fine flour and cloth. The date of the speech in the Saga is 1186, but its sentiments might with equal justice have applied to the English trade a hundred years earlier or a hundred years later. There are continuous references throughout the thirteenth and the early fourteenth centuries to commercial shipments from Norway to the harbours of East Anglia, mostly to Lynn and the ports on the Humber,[43] laden with typical products of the north: timber, fish and fish-oil. But in addition

[40] Brit. Mus., Cotton, Titus A, fol. 140, cited here from text in *Hans. Urkundenbuch*, I, no. 2.

[41] C. J. Klumker, 'Der friesische Tuchhandel zur Zeit Karls des Grossen u. sein Verhältnis zur Weberei jener Zeit', *Jahrbuch d. Gesellschaft f. bildene Kunst etc. zu Emden*, XIII (1899).

[42] A. Bugge, *Die Wikinger* (Halle, 1906), 130–1. Cf. also *idem*, *Den Norske Traelasthandels Historie* (Skien, 1925), 47–8.

[43] *The Great Red Book of Lynn*, *passim*; *Diplomatarium Norwegicum*, IX, nos. 102, 159, 201, etc.; cf. Bugge, *Den Norske Traelasthandels Historie*, 138–86.

connections with Flanders were now developing very fast and the economic partnership between this country and the Low Countries, so characteristic of the European economy in the Middle Ages, was taking shape.[44]

That partnership was founded upon wool. English pastures with their persistent moisture and permanent grass, with their chalk subsoil or their salt-laden air, were ideally suited to the pastoral economy and more especially to the grazing of sheep. Pastoral pursuits therefore dominated the life on this island throughout the Celtic and the early Saxon ages. Livestock was then the mainstay of agricultural wealth, the standard unit of value and form of capital. Throughout the Middle Ages pasture continued to play an indispensable part in the process of internal colonisation as well as in the routine of settled agriculture. England's marginal lands were mainly used for grazing, and even in the boulder clay valleys, mostly heavily wooded, herds of swine were pastured. As population grew in the twelfth and thirteenth centuries and more land was put under plough, some of England's natural pastures, such as the uplands in the Cotswolds, the high grounds of the South Downs, the Lincolnshire wolds, or the marshes of Somerset, might be put under plough and made to yield grain, mostly oats. But no sooner did population recede than the marginal 'outlands' were again turned into pasture whenever suitable. And there were also areas, such as the downlands of Hampshire and Wiltshire, the uplands of Yorkshire and Lancashire, the wet grasslands of Cheshire, the Welsh borders in Shropshire and Herefordshire, where pastures remained inviolate through the Middle Ages and where flocks and herds grew with expanding population and settlement. Cattle and more especially sheep were also to be found in the purely champion parts of England, where they played an essential part in the prevailing economy of mixed farming. They manured the soil and they supplemented the income from arable farming; indeed, the entire routine of the common field system was adjusted to suit the needs of village herds and flocks.

It is therefore natural that in spite of the inroads which the plough occasionally made into grassland, English wool production should have been growing throughout the earlier centuries of the Middle Ages. How much this growth owed to large-scale commercial investment and how much its quality improved by selective breeding, we do not know for certain. There is clear evidence that in the twelfth and thirteenth centuries Flemish and Italian financiers (and they were

[44] For a view that commercial connections between England and Flanders in Merovingian and Carolingian periods were negligible, see P. Grierson, 'The Relations between England and Flanders before the Norman Conquest', *Trans. Royal Hist. Soc.* 4th ser., XXIII (1941).

the only ones who happen to have left behind them written records) made long-term loans to wool-growers. But by then English wool production was already at a very high level and its pre-eminence in Europe was already well established. As for breeding, there is every evidence to show that sheep-farmers in the Middle Ages understood the hereditary factor. They took care to mate the better animals *pro stauro meliorando*; they imported rams of good breeds, such as the Lindsey.[45] Whether as a result of breeding the quality of English wool as a whole was improving throughout the early Middle Ages is more difficult to tell. By the beginning of the fourteenth century wools of certain areas established their reputation for quality. The highest prices were paid for the fine and short wool of the scanty pastures on the Welsh marches, the home of the Ryeland sheep; and for the fine long wools of the Cotswolds, and of the wold and marshland of Lindsey and of Kesteven in Lincolnshire, the home of the 'old Lincolns'.

Wool exports grew with the wool production. Wool merchants from abroad figure in almost every early document in which commercial dealings are mentioned. At the turn of the twelfth and thirteenth centuries we find Flemings buying wool in large quantities, and involved on that account in complicated transactions with kings and landlords. One of them, William Cade, a Fleming active in the middle of the twelfth century, left a brief but very illuminating record of his commercial and financial transactions; but he was obviously not alone. It has already been mentioned that by the beginning of the thirteenth century the merchants of the Flemish towns formed in London something in the nature of a corporate organisation, the Flemish Hanse, which represented the Flemish merchants and presumably provided them with a common residence and essential commercial services. Some of the greater Flemish merchants of that age, Boinebroke, or Pied d'Argent, left almost as clear a mark in the English records as they did on the history of their native towns. They were capitalists of the purest water, speculators on a large scale, employers of large numbers of their countrymen, lenders of large sums to English monasteries and magnates, traders in cloth.[46]

Important as the Flemings were, they were not alone, and in the end they were not even the most important, among the foreign merchants drawn to England by her wool. In the second half of the thirteenth century the German merchants – the Cologners at first and later the Hanseatics – became active among the foreigners trading in

[45] H. Hall (ed.), *The Pipe Roll of the Bishopric of Winchester* (1903), 8, 40, 76.

[46] H. Pirenne, 'La Hanse Flamande de Londres', *Bulletins de l'Académie royale...de Belgique* (1899); Georges Espinas, *Sire Jehan Boinebroke* (Lille, 1933); G. Dept, 'Les Marchands flamands et le roi d'Angleterre, 1147–1216', *Revue du Nord*, XII (1926).

England and exporting English wool, but the lion's share of the trade was eventually acquired by the Italians. How and why the Italian merchants first came to England is a somewhat controversial question. As the twelfth century was advancing to its close Italians appeared all over western Europe, in France as well as in England, and there is no telling why individual adventurers from Lombardy and central Italy should have decided to try their luck in England. But there is little doubt that some of them were drawn to England and above all to English wool by the financial business with which they happened to be charged. Many of the Italian merchants from central Italy, who came to this country in the late twelfth and thirteenth centuries, were active in the first instance primarily as collectors of papal taxation, not as traders or as money-lenders. In the financial dealings between individuals and in the loans to the crown, it was still the Jews and not the Italians who were most active (indeed finance was the only occupation of the English Jews at that time). Such were, however, the economics of papal taxation that the Italian tax-collectors were bound to be drawn into wool trade and into private and royal finance. The proceeds of taxes had to be remitted and wool was the most obvious form which the remittance could take. Some of the ecclesiastical taxpayers would indeed pay their tax in kind even though the transaction might be clothed in monetary form. And in the process of their wool business the Italian merchant bankers were bound to come very close – as it proved, too close – to the royal exchequer. Export licences, exemptions from duties and miscellaneous royal favours had to be negotiated and paid for. Above all, the sums of money and of goods which passed through the hands of the Italian bankers and tax-collectors were so large as to attract the greedy eye of the needy kings. Some of the papal taxes in Henry III's reign were in fact levied for the benefit of the English crown and found their way into the royal coffer not as loans but as outright gifts.[47]

In this way wool trade and royal finance became inextricably mixed, and the mixture proved sufficiently potent to raise the Italians at the end of the thirteenth century to a dominant position in the English wool trade. By the turn of the thirteenth and fourteenth centuries, the great Italian houses of the Ricardi, the Frescobaldi, the Bardi and the Peruzzi, were dominating the English wool exports and in some years exercised a total monopoly of exports and entire control of the royal Customs.

[47] W. E. Rhodes, 'The Italian Bankers in England and their loans to Edward I and Edward II', *Historical Essays of Owens College Manchester*, ed. T. F. Tout and J. Tait (Manchester, 1907). C. Johnson, 'An Italian Financial House in the XIV Century', *Trans. St Albans and Hertfordshire Archt. and Archaeolog. Soc.* n.s. I (St Albans, 1903). A. Sapori, 'La Compagnia dei Frescobaldi en Inghilterra', *Studi di Storia Economica Medievale* (Florence, 1947; new edn, 2 vols. 1955).

From this position the Italians were eventually ousted by syndicates of native merchants and finally by the English Company of the Staple. In the last century of English trade in the Middle Ages English merchants controlled the bulk of the wool trade as well as a large share of other exports and imports. To a historian anxious to record the evolution of national power this *dénouement* might indeed appear as an act of fulfilment, and it was represented as such by Archdeacon Cunningham and other writers of the same generation. They saw the English merchants slowly and continually graduating to a position of pre-eminence in English trade. The early initiative and leadership belonged to foreign merchants, to Flemings, Hanseatics and Italians, but the English were good, if slow, learners, and by the middle of the fourteenth century they had acquired all the arts of commerce. Now at last, the Moor who had done his duty could be dismissed – it was Edward III who did the dismissing – and the English merchants were at last able to establish and enjoy the leadership for which they were now fully qualified.

This story, however, no longer appears as credible as it did once upon a time. The very notion of trade as a social art acquired by men at the end of their progressive ascent through history may have come naturally to a generation which not only believed in continuous progress, but valued the commerce of their own day as the highest manifestation and fulfilment of their culture. Present-day historians, rubbing shoulders as they do with anthropologists and sociologists, find it more difficult to treat trade as a characteristic attribute of a sophisticated civilisation. The processes of trade itself were sufficiently simple to be practised by medieval man at all stages of medieval development. What determined the exact place which trade was to occupy in their daily lives and in their development was the historical setting taken as a whole – their laws and customs, their distribution of wealth, their access to circulating capital, as well as the political circumstances of the time. And it so happened that neither the institutions nor the provision of capital in medieval England were so deficient as to prevent English merchants from taking an active part in English trade.

The first references to English or Anglo-Saxon merchants are probably as old as references to any merchants in England. We hear about Saxon, which is commonly taken to mean Anglo-Saxon, merchants visiting the Merovingian fair of Saint-Denis, the fairs of Rouen and Troyes in Charlemagne's time, and resident in Marseilles early in the eighth century. In his letter to King Offa Charlemagne promises protection to English merchants 'in accordance with ancient customs of trade'.[48] It is possible that the Saxons among the foreign merchants resident in Rome in the ninth century were also Anglo-Saxon, but, in general, references to English trade and English merchants in the ninth century are few, for this was a disturbed period both in England and on the continent. References to Englishmen abroad become more frequent in the tenth and the eleventh centuries, and one of them suggests that in 1050 Englishmen sailed to the Baltic. The evidence of Anglo-Saxon towns reveals the existence of native merchants throughout the last two or three centuries of the Anglo-Saxon era.

That the native merchants were not all hucksters serving the local market is perhaps indicated by the accidental survival of the life story of a merchant whose career bestrides the end of the Anglo-Saxon and the beginning of the Norman period, St Godric of Finchale, whose *vita* has been so tellingly exploited by Pirenne. The English merchants who visited Utrecht at the end of the twelfth century were probably wool traders. The Anglo-Norman documents repeatedly mention English wool merchants, and their numbers increase as the records of English trade accumulate. In 1273 the hostilities with Flanders led to a royal embargo on wool exports, and that in its turn led to the institution of licences for export; the surviving collection of licences reveals the existence of a very large body of native merchants engaged in wool trade.[49]

In general, the surviving evidence of English trade and finance of the thirteenth and fourteenth centuries abounds with names of great merchants who were either English born or permanently settled in England and who played a great part in every branch of English trade: acted as king's merchants, or on occasions helped to finance the king and to serve him in various financial and commercial capacities, administered his war chests, organised the remittance of funds abroad, purveyed goods for his household and armed forces, or merely supplied him with large quantities of imported commodities. In the twelfth century and the thirteenth there were de Waleys, de Haverhills, Finks, Fitz Alans, de Cornhills, Basings, Blands, Buckerels, de Rokesleys, Aswyks, de Ludlows: a small but powerful class which was fast acquiring the character of a hereditary caste, dominating the civic councils of London, active in every important branch of English trade,

48 Haddon and Stubbs, *Councils*, III, 496. Cf. also G. Jacob, *Der nordisch-baltische Handel der Araber* (1887), 112; A. Dopsch, *Die Wirtschaftsentwicklung der Karolingerzeit* (Weimar, 1922), Part II, 194–5.

49 A. Schaube, 'Die Wollausfuhr Englands vom Jahre 1273', *Viertelj. f. Sozial u. Wirtschaftsg.*, VI (1908).

and holding large investments in landed property and mortgages (Gregory de Rokesley at one time held a mortgage over the lands of no less a person than the Bishop of Ely). The class merges imperceptibly into the financial oligarchy of the mid-fourteenth century – the de la Poles and their associates.

True enough, it was not until the middle of the fourteenth century that the English merchants succeeded in establishing themselves in full control of the wool trade and in a condition of predominance in English trade as a whole. This development however did not come about by a gradual process of apprenticeship and graduation, but through a series of political and economic events of a kind that would have given English merchants an equivalent position at any time in English history. The effective cause was the financial crisis in the affairs of the crown in the early phases of the Hundred Years War.

That wool trade and wool traders should have become enmeshed in the tangled skein of fourteenth-century finance is not at all surprising. The annual wool crops may not have represented half of the nation's wealth as a petition of the barons would have it; but they undoubtedly represented a very large proportion of the nation's marketable produce or of what now would be described as the country's main 'cash crop'. The wool trade therefore had an obvious attraction for kings on the look out for money or for goods capable of yielding quick cash, and wool was bound to become an obvious object of royal finance. Taxes on wool grew throughout the fourteenth and fifteenth centuries. In addition to the 'old custom' of 6*s*. 8*d*. per sack fixed in 1275, a 'new custom' of 3*s*. 4*d*. was levied on foreigners since 1303. In the course of the fourteenth century the king repeatedly tried to force out of the reluctant Parliaments grants of high subsidies on wool. By the end of the century grants of wool subsidies became regular, and, with this addition total taxation on wool rose to 40*s*. per sack exported by Englishmen and 53*s*. 4*d*. per sack exported by foreigners. This new tax was not, however, established without a previous deal with the Commons over the control and the management of the wool trade.[50]

The wool trade was also involved with the royal debt. The wealth represented by the annual wool crop was frequently raided by the crown for short-term loans. Richard I's ransom had been paid out of a loan raised by the proceeds of English wool sales abroad, and loans raised in such fashion became common at the end of the thirteenth and the early fourteenth centuries. In 1297 Edward I tried to finance his Flemish expedition by pre-empting in England and selling abroad

[50] E. Power, *The Wool Trade in English Medieval History* (Oxford, 1941), 63–103.

8,000 sacks of wool. This device was later employed by Edward III on a much larger scale and with less regard for the interests of the wool traders and the wool growers.

In this way the wool trade was inevitably drawn into the machinations which mark the history of Edward III's war finance. With each successive crisis the conduct of the wool trade had to be reorganised, and each reorganisation brought it a step nearer to the monopoly of the Staple. The first and most important crisis led to the destruction of the Italian interests. The Italian commitments in the wool trade and in royal finance reached the highest point under Edward III. For the first thirteen or fifteen years of his reign, and more especially in the years of hectic war finance between 1337 and 1340, the Florentine house of the Bardi and from 1336 onwards also the great Florentine house of Peruzzi lent the king vast sums generally on the security of taxes, mostly the wool customs. In the end, however, financial operations in England and elsewhere overstrained their resources. As long as they were still able to add loan to loan they remained in possession of their privileges in English wool trade. But as soon as their liquid resources began to give out, as they did in 1343, the king inevitably defaulted. By 1346, the whole of the English business of the two houses was reduced to a vanishing point, and for a time the Florentine bankers had to withdraw not only from the English wool trade but from the English scene altogether.

The place of the Italians was at first taken by a consortium of the wealthier English wool traders and financiers. The consortia, made up of more or less the same group of commercial magnates and as a rule led by William de la Pole and his associates, were formed or re-formed on three of four occasions after 1345. They helped to finance the siege of Calais and the Crécy campaign by a series of large loans (up to £100,000) on the security of the wool customs. In return they received the virtual monopoly of the English wool exports. In several years all exports of wool were prohibited except under licence, and only the members of the consortia were allowed to export.

By 1349 the syndicates suffered the same fate as the Bardi and the Peruzzi, and the royal default led not only to the temporary eclipse of de la Pole's circle but also to a change of system. The king had now to turn to a larger body of wool merchants, and to do this at a time when he badly needed parliamentary consent for higher subsidies on wool. In the end he was able to obtain both the subsidies and the loans in exchange for important concessions. The parliament of 1351 granted the wool subsidies for three years in exchange for abolition of all monopolies, but in the end monopolies were not so much abolished as widened by being vested in the English Company of the

Staple. That Company became the main source of regular loans on the security of wool and wool customs.

The device of the Staple was by no means new. A staple of sorts was already in existence in the last quarter of the thirteenth century when, in order to operate his forced loan on wool of 1294–97, Edward I directed his own wool and that of the wool merchants at first to Dordrecht and then to Antwerp: both towns situated near the places where he needed funds for his war. But his was not yet a full-fledged staple. It was permissive and not compulsory and it did not create a monopolistic Company of the Staple. An attempt to make it compulsory was made in 1313 when it was fixed at St Omer, but even then the system was as yet very fluid and experimental. Between 1316 and 1326 the Staple was moved from one foreign town to another; between 1326 and 1337 it twice crossed the Channel to selected English ports, and for a brief interval the trade was altogether free. But after 1337 and more especially after 1350 the organisation of the trade rapidly moved towards the monopoly of the English Company of the Staple.

The process began with a full swing away from monopolies of any kind. It has already been shown that in 1351 parliament stipulated, as a *quid pro quo* for the grant of wool subsidies, that all monopolies should be abolished. In accordance with this stipulation the Ordinances of the Staple enacted in 1353 left the aliens free to buy and export wool as much as they liked, and no Englishman was allowed to engage in exports. This arrangement could not last. It was profitable to wool growers, entrenched in Parliament, but too unfavourable to the English merchants and consequently also to their ability to lend money. The system began to break down in 1357. By 1361 the English Company of the Staple was in possession of a virtual monopoly of wool exports to northern Europe; by 1399 it was safely and permanently launched in Calais. Even then Italians were able to export some wool under royal licence on condition that they took it to Italy and did not sell it in competition with the staplers on the wool markets of the Low Countries. But on the latter the English monopoly was now unchallenged.

The monopoly suited the bulk of the English wool merchants who now formed the Company of the Staple; it suited the rising interest of the clothmakers for it created wide discrepancies between wool prices at home and abroad. Above all, it suited the king. The custom and subsidy on the export of wool was the best possible security which he could offer, and a chartered company enjoying the monopoly of the trade was a much safer source of loans than the series of firms and syndicates which had, one by one, gone bankrupt in the early years of the Hundred Years War. The link with the crown was further reinforced by the Act of Retainer of 1446, by which the Company farmed the whole of the custom and the subsidy on wool, and undertook in return to pay the wages of the garrison at Calais and certain other fixed charges, repay itself for its past loans and deliver any surplus over and above a fixed sum into the exchequer. The only interest which suffered was that of the wool growers; and this may have been one of the reasons why the production of wool declined.

The English predominance in the wool trade was thus a product of political and fiscal causes. It was not a manifestation of English trade 'come of age', still less a stage in the economic growth of English trade and economy. It was brought about by successive acts of royal policy and as a result of a bargain between the king and merchants. Moreover it did not result in any increase in the volume of the wool trade handled by English merchants. If we are to trust the figures of the royal export licences of 1273 which have already been mentioned,[51] the English share in the wool exports of the time, though not more than one-third of the total, represented some 11,500 sacks, shared by some 280 exporters. By the middle of the fifteenth century about the same number of staplers exported eight to ten thousand sacks. The English predominance had grown, while the wool trade shrank.

More relevant to the story of English economic growth was the development of the cloth trade and the wine trade. English wine trade was in some respects one of the oldest branches of English commerce, and also one in which English merchants were predominant from the outset. Evidence of English imports of foreign wine – mostly French – go back to the early years of the Norman rule and beyond. Under the Angevins England found itself politically linked to Gascony, the main wine-producing area of Europe, and the connection thus established stimulated Gascon viticulture and also opened before English merchants a great and ever-expanding field of enterprise. Large, and for a time growing, quantities of wine were imported from Gascony, and most of the imports came to be handled by English merchants, mainly those of Bristol. In return Gascony had to be supplied with foodstuffs, cloth and other miscellaneous goods, which came from England or via England, and were mostly brought by English merchants and English ships. The trade reached its highest point at the beginning of the fourteenth century, when in some years more than 20,000 tuns of wine were imported into England.

The most spectacular event in the history of English trade in the

[51] See above, p. 289.

late Middle Ages – an event which did more than anything else to conjure up the spectre of the English challenge in the Baltic – came as a result of English cloth exports. Manufacture of marketable cloth was indigenous in this country, and some cloth was always exported. Exports of cloth to France in the seventh and eighth centuries have already been mentioned. A Norwegian saga mentions English cloth among imports to Iceland at the end of the tenth century.[52] English cloths of various kinds, sometimes described by the parts of England from which they came, continue to be mentioned in the records of the twelfth and thirteenth centuries. But although active, the trade was rather small: very much smaller than the Flemish cloth trade and the wool and wine trades of England. In the second half of the fourteenth century, however, the industry suddenly grew to rival and finally to overshadow all other branches of English industry and trade.

The factors behind the growth have been described elsewhere. Cloth manufacture was establishing itself outside the bounds of corporate towns and was thus better able to keep its labour costs low and to employ mechanical devices, mostly water power. The disorder in Flanders and emigration of artisans from there brought an addition of skilled labour to the English industry. Some protection to more expensive brands of cloth resulted from the prohibition of Flemish imports. But from the point of view of this essay most significant of all is the connection which undoubtedly existed between the growth of the cloth industry and the financial vicissitudes of the wool trade. Continuous interruptions and disorganisation of wool exports hit the rival cloth industries. Above all an export tax of some £2 10*s*. per sack greatly lowered the costs of production at home by comparison with foreign cloth, and it is also possible that English wool monopoly also helped to raise the price of wool to the foreign clothmakers. Thus assisted, the English cloth manufacture forged ahead until by the 1490s the English exports at times exceeded the high figure of 50,000 cloths or an equivalent of some 10,000 to 12,000 sacks of wool and about twice that in value.

With England cloth exports so great, the whole character of English foreign trade and the behaviour of English foreign traders were bound to be transformed. As long as English exports consisted mainly of wool, there was no need for English merchants to go far afield in search for markets and customers. Wool was a raw material of industry; its customers were foreign cloth manufacturers; and the only important cloth manufacturing centres were not only highly localised but also situated near at hand, mainly in the Low Countries. On the

[52] Bugge, *Die Wikinger*, 132.

other hand, finished cloth had to be sold to potential consumers, and in the main centres of potential consumption, or in other words, to men and women all over continental Europe and beyond. It is therefore no wonder that whereas the wool staplers were able to transact their business in Calais and had no need to venture beyond Bruges, English cloth exporters had to push out in every direction, and, in the first place, into east European markets where Flemish cloth had previously been sold. We find fleeting references to Englishmen in Stralsund and Danzig in the eighties of the fourteenth century. In Danzig they were well established by the nineties and possessed a settlement and a factory by the end of the first quarter of the fifteenth century. By that time there was also an English company in the Norwegian trading port of Bergen, where, in exchange for English cloth and other miscellaneous goods, goods of Norwegian and Icelandic origin, mostly fish, could be bought. It is quite possible that there was also an English component in the international mart at the fishing centres of Skania.[53]

The English appearance in the Baltic brought home to the Hanseatics the dangers of the English challenge. Unfortunately for Anglo-Hanseatic relations and for peace in the Baltic, the English penetration into the northern markets began in earnest at a time when conditions for it were least propitious. The English merchants began to frequent the east-to-west route at the very moment when foreign competition appeared to threaten the foundations of Hanseatic prosperity and unity. They tried to establish themselves in Danzig at the very time when the protection of the local market and regional monopoly was becoming the fundamental purpose of municipal policy. Their appearance in the Hanseatic system would have produced a considerable conflict in any case but, in the conditions of the late fourteenth and early fifteenth centuries, it was bound to result in a bitter and desperate struggle.

To begin with, the struggle was developing in English favour: mainly because for the time being the English drive was well backed at home, whereas the German opposition was not. In the English towns the relatively small and specialised groups of men trading to the Baltic found support from the main body of urban opinion which was strongly anti-Hanseatic. Left to themselves the towns could always be relied upon to act against all foreigners, the Venetians, the Genoese, the Flemings as well as the Hanseatics; but the Hanseatics offered the

[53] For these and most of the subsequent facts of Anglo-Hanseatic relations, see M. Postan, 'The economic and political relations of England and the Hanse', in E. Power and M. Postan (eds.), *Studies in English Trade in the Fifteenth Century* (London, 1933).

best and the easiest targets. Their exceptional fiscal privileges and their proud position in the City of London – a city within a city – were bound to draw on them the greater share of urban xenophobia. The anti-Hanseatic movement combined the demands of merchants threatened with exclusion from the trade of Prussian towns with the appetites of merchants anxious to exclude the Hanseatics from the trade of English towns. The common enemy produced a sense of common interest and ranged the mass of English urban classes behind the agitation.

At first this movement also enjoyed the full support of the government. In the conditions of the early fifteenth century the government, and more especially the House of Commons, found it easy to respond to the pressure of anti-Hanseatic interests and to understand their motives and their language. The temper of the age, fed by accidents of the Hundred Years War, was charged with nationalist pride; the social changes of the times were helping to draw together the official class in English government and the upper ranks of the merchant class. In addition the City of London had evolved in the fifteenth century an efficient 'lobby' in Parliament, and even the provincial towns sometimes elected special deputations 'to make suit in Parliament against Hanseatic privileges'. No wonder the Hanseatics came to regard Parliament as their chief adversary and never expected from it any favour or concession.

The policy of the Lords and of the King's Council was somewhat less definite, for individual lords and prelates sometimes shielded the merchants of the Hanse from enmity and vindictiveness of the Commons and were often referred to in Hanseatic correspondence as their only friends in England. Yet as long as the Council was capable of comprehending and obeying the *raison d'État*, the underlying assumptions of its policy towards the Hanse was little different from those of the merchant classes. On those occasions when personal and party interests of magnates were not much involved, and when conciliatory attitudes to the Hanse were not dictated by the military and political events in Flanders and France, the Council did its best to back the merchants over their demands in the Baltic.

Thus backed (and as long as it was thus backed) the English mercantile offensive appeared to be very formidable and was indeed scoring success after success. A conflict in the eighties of the fourteenth century ended somewhat to the advantage of the English merchants, and the treaty of 1388 which wound it up recognised for the English their 'old rights' and their freedom to come to the lands of the Hanse and Prussia and to settle there and to traffic freely and undisturbed. A similar conflict in the first decade of the fifteenth century ended by another treaty, in which the English were confirmed in their right to come to Prussia and there *mercari, ibidemque morari et ex inde ad lares et domicilia propria redire*. Under the cover of this treaty the English merchants established a flourishing factory in Danzig with a communal organisation, a communal house and a governor with disciplinary powers over its members. When difficulties again arose in the thirties, mostly over the position and privileges of the English company in Danzig, the treaty of 1437 conceded to the English merchants not only their old rights of entry, trade and residence, but also fiscal exemptions as exceptional as those the Hanseatics possessed in England. The English traders were to be free of all taxes imposed in the course of the previous hundred years or more.

On each of these occasions the English merchants benefited from fundamental disunity in the ranks of the Hanseatic towns. Even though the Danzigers were bitterly opposed to the English merchants in their midst, the Prussian Order and even some interests within Danzig itself set great store by their trade to England and were among the first to seek an end to the successive conflicts. Similarly, the western wing of the Hanse, especially Cologne, had no part in the quarrel over the English position in the Baltic and was always willing to compromise. Even the position of Lübeck was not as yet consistent and she could be found on occasions counselling moderation and concession to the English claims.

Thus aided, the English prospects appeared very bright indeed. To some Hanseatics the English danger appeared in a light curiously prophetic. Viewed in this light the English threat appeared greater than it actually was, more urgent and more threatening than that of the Dutch. This alone would be sufficient to explain why the strength of Hanseatic opposition stiffened in the middle of the century and why Lübeck swung in support of the anti-English policy. It was badly hit by English piracy, it had grown to fear the effect of great maritime links between Prussia and the west, and in general it was now adopting a belligerent attitude in defence of the Hanseatic hold of the Great Route. At the same time the English pressure was weakening. This was not altogether due to factors purely or mainly economic. The export of English cloth declined in the middle decades, but the decline was in itself due to failure of the English commercial offensive. The reason why the latter failed is more likely to be found in the political disorders of the middle decades of the century.

With the War of the Roses approaching, the Council became a mere instrument of the rival baronial parties and was no longer able to give support to the English claims against the Hanseatics. It is not that the economic policy of the late Lancastrian and the early Yorkist governments was inspired by any new and different principles. Its worst failing was that it ceased to be inspired by any principles whatsoever. The private interest of ruling magnates in and out of King's Council was allowed free licence, and matters of state policy were made to serve the predatory aims of powerful men. Not only were the merchants unable to rely on the latent power of English arms, but that power itself became a mere instrument of predatory sea-war and piracy. There were easy and substantial gains to be derived from attacks on Hanseatic shipping, and the Council not only did nothing to stop piracy on the high seas but itself directly and indirectly contributed to its extension. It was largely under the auspices of influential members of the Council that the first great attack on Hanseatic shipping in the Bay took place in 1449, and the second great attack in 1458 was led by no other person than Warwick. The outburst of piracy helped to consolidate Lübeck's anti-English policy and to cement the unity of the Hanseatic League and led to a naval war which threw the entire trade and navigation on the North Sea into chaos. At the same time, in spite of the raging naval war, the parties in the Council were not averse from making use of the Hanseatic assistance in their domestic struggles.

In the end a private deal between Edward IV and the Hanseatic League put an end to all English chances in the conflict with the Hanse. Under that deal the Hanseatics helped Edward to equip the expedition which brought him back to England, and in exchange they received back, in 1474, unaltered and unimpinged their old privileges without having to concede any rights to the Englishmen in the Baltic towns. They immediately stepped into the place they had occupied in English economic life in the first half of the century, and this place they were to preserve until well into the Tudor era. Their share in English foreign trade soon passed the highest point it had reached before. While they exported on the average about 6,000 cloths annually between 1406 and 1427, and about 10,000 annually between 1438 and 1459, their exports rose to well above 13,500 between 1479 and 1482.

The English merchants derived whatever profit and comfort there was to be derived from the restoration of peace and the resumption of Hanseatic trade. But their attempts at direct relations with the markets of central and eastern Europe received a set-back from which they were not to recover until the age of Elizabeth. Their chances of establishing themselves there were further reduced by political changes in Prussia. Danzig, now under the sovereignty of Polish kings, enjoyed almost a complete *Landeshoheit*, involving full autonomy in matters of government and economic policy. In confirming the treaty with England it postulated that the English were to be treated as all other foreigners. The English merchants themselves ceased to press for parity in the old and full sense of the term, since by now the Baltic trade was no longer vitally important to them. Whether as a result of the continued friction with Denmark and consequent closing of the Sund, or as a result of the war-time rearrangements in the organisation of English trade, the direct trade of English merchants to Danzig was dwindling very fast. Whereas on several occasions in the first half of the century there were over thirty English boats anchored in the port of Danzig, only twelve boats arrived from England during the three years following the cessation of hostilities, and in 1497, when the registers of the Sund tolls begin, not a single English boat passed the Sund. As late as 1503 there were only twenty-one English boats passing the Sund and it was not until 1547 that the English shipping to the Baltic could again stand comparison with that of the Dutch.

The effects of the English defeat reached further than the mere failure to establish a factory in Danzig. Its net result was to interrupt for nearly two generations the expansion of English trade into the outlying European markets and to canalise all English commerce into the single current which led to the Low Countries. The traffic in Baltic goods was taken out of English hands; some of it proceeded indirectly by way of Brabantine fairs, some of it was carried on by the Dutch and the Hanseatics. And with the end of the Baltic trade there also came the end of the Baltic trader. Not until the rebirth of direct Baltic connections in the middle of the sixteenth century and the rise of the Eastland Company did the Baltic 'interest' establish itself again among English merchants.

The loss of the Prussian connection happened to coincide with the lopping off of most other outlying branches of the English trade. In Norway the Hanseatics had since the beginning of the fifteenth century tightened their hold over the trade of Bergen and defeated all the attempts of the English merchants to restore that position. The cessation of the Bergen trade at first sent the English merchants directly to Iceland, but this new enterprise, however important in itself, only completed the ruin of the English trade in Scandinavia. It plunged England into a state of chronic conflict with Denmark, and in the second half of the century it finally shut the Dano-Norwegian waters to English trade and navigation. Even more damaging, though less enduring, was the interruption of English trade to Gascony. This connection, so old and so important in the economic life of the country, was to be disturbed and finally broken during the concluding phases of the Hundred Years War. The French reoccupation of Gascony put an end to the flourishing English exports of cloth and all but interrupted English imports of wine. For a time even the clarets of Gascony were not obtainable except through neutral markets in the Low Countries.

Thus, having lost the more distant markets on the periphery of their trading area, the English merchants were compelled to restrict their maritime and commercial ventures in northern Europe to the Low Countries; and the 'Merchant Adventurers', a corporation of merchants trading to Flanders and Holland, absorbed the bulk of English trade and the mass of English traders.

The effects of this concentration reached even further than commerce. The historians of the English cloth industry may also find a connection between concentration of English trade to the Netherlands and concentration of English production on undyed and unfinished cloth. There is no doubt that the bulk of English cloth exports in the late fourteenth century and beginning of the fifteenth century consisted of fully dyed and fully finished cloth. But when, with the falling off of the outlying markets, the English exporters lost direct contact with the main body of consumers, they had to adjust themselves to a trade on a market still largely dominated by local cloth industries. A *modus vivendi* was found in increasing the exports of undyed and unfinished cloth and selling it to the dyers and finishers from Flanders and Holland. These were essentially the terms on which the great expansion of English cloth exports under the Tudors was made possible, and the old symbiosis of England and the Low Countries was re-established.

(5) THE RISE OF HOLLAND

Compared with the English challenge that of the Dutch matured relatively late, but its late inconspicuous beginnings turned out, from the Dutch point of view, to be a blessing in disguise. It was very largely because the English attack opened rapidly and successfully that the Hanseatics, and especially the Prussians, read into it the dangers which it did not in fact spell. It had received strong backing from the English government in the first half of the fifteenth century, and thus added further weight to the German alarm. For, after all, at the beginning of the fifteenth century England was a first-class military power with a long record of successful aggression, and in the estimation of the Prussians it had already revealed some of its congenital propensities for empire-building. Did not the Danzigers argue in 1410 that if the English were allowed to settle and to trade in Prussia they would soon annex the country as they had annexed Bordeaux and Gascony? It was because the English danger loomed so large that the

Prussians at first and the whole of the Hanse in the end opposed it with remarkable vigour.

The strength of the Dutch position was that their rise owed little to political action, and that it was purely economic throughout its early history. They had insinuated themselves into the Baltic trade before the Hanse as a whole woke up to their menace; and so firmly was their power grounded in economic and geographical facts – and eventually in naval prowess – that it could not easily be countered by the political and naval measures at the disposal of the Hanse. Hence the paradox of their challenge: it turned out to be so strong in the end because it appeared so weak at the beginning.

One of the reasons why the so-called commercial rise of Holland in the later Middle Ages was so inconspicuous is that it was a product of local rather than of national development. The country which we know as the Netherlands consisted of at least four geographical regions, each with an economic history of its own: Zealand, Friesland, south Holland and north Holland. In the so-called Dark Ages the delta of the Rhine was the centre of northern commerce. Later, during the Middle Ages, the region of the delta, with Utrecht at its head, was still important as a centre of trade in corn, fish and wine. At the end of the same period, south Holland with Dordrecht was also showing signs of considerable commercial activity, and so did also the northernmost end of the Netherlands: Campen, Deventer, Zwolle, Groningen. These towns stood in a loose connection with the Hanse which seems to have paid them very well. But in the fourteenth century important centres of commerce began to appear in parts of the Netherlands hitherto relatively backward, i.e. in Zealand and in north Holland. It is this development of north Holland that is usually meant when the rise of the Dutch is discussed, and it was this development that hit the Hanseatic trade most.

The exact circumstances of the development are somewhat obscure. Dutch historians sometimes connect the rise of Amsterdam, and with it of the rest of north Holland, with the German transit trade through the waterways of Holland *en route* to Flanders and England. According to this view the new dykes obstructed the northern entrance into the Dutch system of rivers and made it necessary to transfer the goods into smaller boats. Amsterdam sprang up at the northern entrance to the dyke system, and Rotterdam at the southern, but other Dutch towns also began to take a hand in this traffic, and by the end of the fourteenth century Holland could already stand on her own feet and was able to enter into competition with the Hanse. On a somewhat broader view the trade of north Holland grew partly out of the internal trade of the country, and partly out of the sea-borne trade between some of its towns and other countries. Like the rest of the Netherlands, north Holland and south Zealand possessed ships and engaged in trade from time immemorial – they were forced to it both by the abundance of their waterways and by the one-sided economic development of the surrounding regions which necessitated a constant movement of foodstuffs. But, whereas in the earlier centuries the distant journeys of Hollanders were probably confined to England and Flanders, in the late fourteenth century they turned to the Baltic. One of the reasons why Hollanders went eastwards was probably the introduction of the *Umlandfahrt* round Jutland. But the chief cause was that the Dutch economy was expanding at the time when opportunities for sea-borne trade in other directions were limited.

Their economic expansion, though two or three centuries old, was gathering speed in the fifteenth century. The thirteenth century saw the Dutch completing the dyking system which protected them from the invasion of the sea. The following century saw a great development of agriculture and cattle breeding and industry, and the fifteenth was marked by a sudden efflorescence of the old cloth industry. When at the close of the fourteenth century events disorganised the Flemish manufacturers, Holland, together with England, rose to the leadership of the continental cloth production, and by the middle of the fifteenth century Leiden became one of the foremost cloth centres in the world. Simultaneously with the cloth manufacture there developed also other industries, and especially beer brewing and fishing. In the course of the fifteenth century Holland was also becoming an important source of herring for western Europe, and its salted fish was carried as far south as Bâle. In addition, both the industry and the trade benefited by the unification of the Netherlands in the fifteenth century by Philip of Burgundy and by the long spell of peace under his rule.

It was largely because their economy grew so gradually that their appearance in the Baltic passed almost unnoticed by their contemporaries. Apparently they entered the Hanseatics' preserves chiefly as carriers, and until the very end of the Middle Ages they were active in the Baltic as sailors at least as much as traders. On some routes they carried Hanseatic goods and were therefore very useful to those towns which had large quantities of bulky goods to carry, such as Riga, Reval or Danzig. By the same token they were most unwelcome to Lübeck. Lübeck was consequently the first to rise in opposition to the Dutch, and throughout the fifteenth century Lübeck was at the back of all the anti-Dutch activities of the Hanse. And for exactly the same reasons Prussia was unwilling to quarrel with the Dutch and on several occasions did its best to thwart Lübeck's plans against Holland.

The story of the Dutch penetration and of their successful combat with the Hanse cannot be told here with all the detail it deserves. By the end of the second decade of the fifteenth century, Dutch progress in the east had grown far enough to have drawn to itself the alarmed attention of the Hanseatic politicians and to have produced the first serious conflict. The issue was raised in 1417 by Lübeck and the other Wendish towns which managed to get through a Hanseatic Diet some limitations of the Dutch trade, but were unable to carry with them the Prussian towns in further attempts to close the Baltic to the Dutch altogether. This, however, was only the first of the many Dutch-Wendish clashes to come. By degrees friction became chronic and, for many years, peace was with difficulty maintained by temporary truces. In 1437 the truce was not renewed and a formal state of war lasted from 1438 to 1441. It was during that war that the Dutch revealed to the outside world how much their economic power had grown in the preceding fifty years. In the end the Hanse had to give way in spite of a whole succession of what seemed to have been political triumphs and to conclude the peace treaty of 1441 recognising the freedom of the Dutch trade in the Baltic.

The strength of the Dutch resistance during the war was something of a revelation to the German towns. But the defeat of the Hanse was clinched not so much by the power of Holland as by that conflict of interests within the Hanse, which appeared every time the Wendish towns tried to do anything against the Dutch. Prussia would not support Lübeck against Holland, and in addition the western wing of the Hanse, and especially the towns of the Zuidersee, Campen, Zwolle and Deventer, vacillated between their loyalty to the Hanse and their commercial interests in Holland. In the end, some of them concluded separate agreements with the Dutch and thus broke the ring of the Hanseatic blockade. With slight variations the same story repeated itself each time the Wendish towns proposed action against Holland, and all the active measures of the Hanse against the Dutch remained ineffective.

What made the Dutch especially difficult to combat was that very often the Hanse could not help handicapping itself by the aggressive policy it adopted towards other foreign powers. In their endeavours to arrest the course of economic change the Hanseatics repeatedly took measures which, whatever their avowed object, in the end merely contributed to the increase of Dutch trade. There were several such measures in the fifteenth century. In the fifties the Dutch trade received a great stimulus from a Hanseatic blockade of Flanders, when a great deal of Hanseatic trade passed to the south Germans and the Dutch. In the sixties and the seventies the blundering Hanseatic politicians offered the Dutch the greatest of all their opportunities by their short-sighted and aggressive defence of their Bruges 'staple'. The circumstances of this staple policy are indeed sufficiently interesting in themselves to be worth describing in greater detail.

As a result of the process already explained, Bruges had become by the first half of the fifteenth century the most valuable of Hanseatic markets abroad. It was the centre of German cloth trade and the terminus of the great Hanseatic east-to-west route – the point where this route tapped the channels that led to the French, the Italian and the Iberian south. But in the course of the fifteenth century Bruges began to lose its advantageous position. There were political complications in Flanders itself and there were also economic causes. In the first instance the Zwin, the waterway connecting Bruges with the sea, was silting up and no amount of dredging and dyking could stop the process. Secondly, in the course of the fifteenth century the Flemish industries migrated in directions unfavourable to Bruges. Partly as a result of Brabantine policy, but partly as a result of decline in south-west Flanders, economic leadership passed to the regions in the north-east, especially to Brabant. And, according as the trade and industry of Brabant grew, the old ports of Brabant, Antwerp, with its satellite market of Bergen-op-Zoom, began to rival Bruges as centres of cloth and wool trade. Before long they also began to rival it in other fields. In the same way as Bruges had grown to become the all-important western terminus of the great Hanseatic route to the Baltic, Antwerp now grew to become the terminus of more recent and rival routes: one to the south via Lorraine and one to eastern Europe via the Rhine valley, Frankfurt-am-Main, and Frankfurt-an der-Oder. The alternative routes appeared in response to a number of incentives, but it is probable that they owed much of their prosperity to the initiative of the Dutch and of the merchants of the south German towns seeking a way round the Hanseatic monopoly. And the tighter the Hanseatic hold over the northern trade, the more determined became the endeavours of the outsiders to develop the alternative routes.

To Lübeck the old route was of greater significance than to anybody else. Lübeck was the town of the Hanse most interested in maintaining the old Hanseatic lines of communication, but in addition it was also the town most closely linked with the Bruges *Kontor* by a network of interests woven together in the course of a hundred years. But the measures it adopted in defence of Bruges were doomed to failure. They were not supported by other parts of the Hanse and, what is more, they still further undermined the economic position of Bruges. This is especially true of the so-called 'staple' rules. In order to restore Bruges to its position in the Hanseatic trade, the Hanse laid down in the middle of the fifteenth century a series of rules by which costly goods and goods which constituted the monopoly of the Hanse, i.e. wax, furs, metals, Skania herring, had to be imported to Bruges before they could be sold elsewhere in Flanders or the Low Countries. In addition, all cloth, whether it was produced in Flanders or in Holland, had to be brought to Bruges before it could be exported to the east. At one time an attempt was even made to exclude Dutch cloth altogether, and to force every German boat carrying staple goods to call at Bruges even if the goods were directed to England or to the towns of the western Hanse. Needless to say this staple policy defeated its own ends. Hanseatic trade could not at one and the same time maintain its volume and be tied down to a decaying place. What happened was that the rules of the staple were evaded in spite of their energetic enforcement; and that in so far as they were obeyed they depressed the Hanseatic trade and stimulated the trade of the south German and the Dutch towns. The Hanseatics themselves began to call in ever-increasing numbers at Antwerp and the towns of Holland – Amsterdam, Middleburg, Haarlem, Delft and Vere – and to stay away from Bruges. Even the Flemings began to send their cloth to Bergen-op-Zoom and Antwerp, from whence the Dutch carried it to Amsterdam, which was now a very important centre of cloth trade.

In 1477 the Hanseatic Diet revoked the staple rules, but it was already too late, for they had done all the harm they could. By the end of the century Bruges was beginning to take on the aspect of 'Bruges le mort', Antwerp with Bergen became the chief mart of northern Europe, and the Dutch were in an impregnable position. They now traded as far east as Breslau and Cracow, and the towns of Prussia themselves began to look with dismay at the Dutch entering Poland. For 1495 we possess the earliest returns of the toll stations at the Sound, the famous *Sundtolls*, and in that year the Dutch vessels formed the bulk of all the shipping bound for the Baltic.

CHAPTER V

The Trade of Medieval Europe: the South

I. *The First Five Hundred Years*

(1) THE BASIC TRENDS

In the dim light of its scanty documentation, the first half of the Middle Ages in the European South looks like a multisecular trough of depression between the crest of the Roman prime and the higher crest of the late medieval Commercial Revolution. It started dismally: by 476, when a handful of Barbarians seized the last remnant of the Roman Empire in the West, the native population had been cut down by epidemics, thinned out by genetic infertility and soil exhaustion, oppressed by fiscal and political depotism, demoralised by military defeats and unnerved by prophecies of imminent doom. Commerce had taken crippling losses. Communications were breaking down, coinage was scarce and debased, fewer and fewer agricultural and industrial products were available for sale, the purchasing power of all but the wealthiest individuals had been eroded. The formerly tight network of laborious cities and well-cultivated fields was changing to a sparse pattern of virtually self-sufficient large estates surrounded by no man's land.

The crisis was not restricted to the European South alone – possibly its remotest roots went back to an unfavourable pulsation of climate affecting the whole temperate area of Eurasia ever since the second century of our era – but it was not everywhere irreversible. The eastern provinces of the Roman Empire, whose cities and merchants had long outshone their western counterparts, had a remarkable come-back after 476, as the settling down of a large proportion of the Barbarians in the West relieved pressure on the East. In turn, the victory of the invaders reduced the impact of war and taxation on the West; but the Barbarians were not numerous, efficient or concerned enough to refloat its sinking economy, and their inertia was more damaging than their impact. The high fever of Rome's agony was merely replaced by bloodless deflation and a general lowering of standards. There was no total disaster and commerce did not come to an end, but it could not soar again so long as a chronically undermanned labour force, with dwindling skills and inadequate tools, was hard put to produce the bare necessities for themselves while supplying to their coarse masters what was needed to keep them well fed and to enable them to purchase some goods in the market. As late as the tenth century, when unmistakable signs of an upturn emerge at long last from documentary haze, it is obvious that the level of trade and the quality of life were still far below those of the Roman prime.

Yet, retroactively, the first half of the Middle Ages may also be regarded as an over-extended fallowing, which through decay and readjustment paved the way for a more dynamic and better balanced economic set-up. Even in its heyday the Roman economy was geared for comfortable stability rather than restless growth, and commerce was its stepchild. It was stunted by overwhelming agricultural investment and prestige, by governmental monopolies and requisitions and by high transport costs. It was starved for working capital and credit, weakened by the inability of slaves and proletarians to buy what they wanted and restricted by the ability of every section of the Empire to produce nearly all it desired. During the early Middle Ages both the liabilities and the assets of the Roman legacy were eroded, but not everywhere at the same time and to the same extent. In the Byzantine Empire change was prompter but less sweeping than in the barbarian West: without renouncing its biases or its grip, the government gave some leeway to private initiative and international exchanges; without discarding old implements and techniques that were still usable, the merchants tried smaller and quicker ships, lighter and less breakable containers (wooden barrels instead of clay amphors), more flexible business contracts and other helpful innovations. In their wider geographical framework, and half-helped, half-hindered by their peculiar blend of anarchic tribalism and despotic militarism, the Islamic merchants brought to the Mediterranean more novelties. The West was much slower in moving from disintegration to reconstruction, but when it did, there was less interference from the past. Centuries of hardship had reduced the demands of government, shown the value of Byzantine and Islamic new practices, made slavery an obsolete institution, and bred a new kind of aggressive, self-confident merchant. In the tenth century the West was still underdeveloped as compared with the East, but was rapidly catching up with it.

A wretched beginning, a long depressed profile, a promising denouement: these simple generalisations are undisputed and seemingly indisputable, but it is difficult to elaborate on them. One has to shuffle and reshuffle disconnected scraps of information, laws that may have been unenforced, incidents that may have affected only a small corner of the European world, descriptions that may be mere rhetorical exercises, statements that may be sheer misunderstandings. Always difficult to retrieve, the progress of innovation from first conception to broader and broader diffusion becomes almost inscrutable when evidence is discontinuous. Quantitative data, ever so questionable even after the birth of statistics, become sheer guesses when one has to stretch them beyond the spot to which they refer. This explains the inconclusive outcome of the brilliant debate on the volume of early medieval trade and its variations that has until recently filled the scholarly world with excitement. Some credit was given to the Ostrogoths, the Visigoths, the Merovingians, the Lombards for checking at some point the decadence of the Barbarian period. The Carolingians were singled out for greater praise: Alfons Dopsch, arguing mainly from regulations of local trade, stressed the correlation between Charlemagne's political and economic reconstruction plans. Then Henri Pirenne, shifting emphasis to international trade, charged the Arabs with wrecking the commercial unity of the Mediterranean and forcing Charlemagne to fall back on an introverted continental economy. Lastly, Maurice Lombard contended that a massive infusion of Arab gold, swapped against European raw materials, promoted a revival at that very time. When the insights of the participants in the discussion were separated from their overstatements, many new facts had been added to the dossiers, but the debate had to subside as moot.

Absolute quantity, however, is only one dimension of economic history and not in every sense the most enlightening. The fact that Charlemagne's armies were smaller than Napoleon's, or that the readers of Paul the Deacon were fewer than those of Pirenne, does not make Charlemagne and Paul the Deacon unimportant: their resonance was amplified rather than muffled by the still and rarefied atmosphere in which they operated. Throughout the early Middle Ages one comes across incidental mentions of 'rich' merchants: thus they appeared to their contemporaries, whose yardstick may not be ignored. On the other hand, any attempt to chart economic change within a determinate period involves some kind of quantitative comparison. One wonders whether the cumulative number and average quality of surviving testimonies in all fields of activity could not be a more reliable indicator of the waning and waxing of commercial enterprise than the sole direct evidence on trade. Ever scantier written records and ever cruder artefacts over the first two hundred early medieval years bear witness to the faltering energy of generations that apparently make do with dwindling remnants of the Roman past or, at most, take a few hints from Byzantium. The bottom is touched in the second half of the seventh century and the first years of the eighth: there are decades – not precisely the same in every part of southern Europe – to which no record of any kind can be ascribed, as if people had been too exhausted to do more than hibernate. Then, gradually, documents and monuments reappear; they are generally unimpressive, but their language or style, even when it tries to reproduce older models, has a new ring. In the course of the tenth century the choir becomes louder, if not necessarily more pleasant, and novelty fills the air.

Granted that extrapolating from culture to commerce is normally an ill-advised procedure, in this particular case there is some confirmation from closer quarters. Most significantly, the recurrent epidemics that had sapped the population from the late second century on continued throughout the seventh; then, after a last major outbreak in 742–3, they faded out of the demographic forefront until the Black Death of 1346–8. Localised indications of population growth in fertile rural areas begin to appear in the Carolingian period, possibly in connection with a favourable pulsation of climate; but they may have been largely offset by the famines and wars that accompanied the collapse of the Carolingians, and at any rate it would take time before the increase could snowball to noticeable size. Besides, the impact on trade of this faint stirring cannot have been strong while the grain harvest of privileged Carolingian estates was barely twice the input of seed, and their managers were admonished that 'there should be no need to request or buy anything from the outside'. Special opportunities for commercial revival, however, were arising in the Italian fringe, where a few tiny seaports, backed by a less underdeveloped hinterland and open to Byzantine and Muslim air, were reaching for political and economic autonomy. In the tenth century, accelerated demographic growth turned the tide at long last.

This tentative reconstruction of basic trends neither embraces one of the conflicting theories aired in the now moot debate on the volume of trade, nor rejects totally any of them. The efforts of certain pre-Carolingian rulers to give ancient economy a new lease of life are not to be denied; but that economy could not be frozen, it needed rejuvenation, and the barbarian West was not up to it. The Arabs caused temporary disorder and destruction on first onslaught (especially in the seventh century), but could not and did not want to force foreign merchantmen off the sea. In the ninth century, Charlemagne strove to make his Empire militarily and economically self-sufficient, but had no intention to erect an iron curtain around it. No doubt the formation of three self-contained economic systems, whose centres of gravity were inland (Aachen, Baghdad and, to some extent, Constantinople, eccentric to the Mediterranean while pivotal between Balkans and Anatolia), tended to de-emphasise their links across the sea; so did their frequent hostilities. However, the increased diversity of products from three empires no longer encompassing the Mediterranean made those very links more valuable; war or no war, loopholes had to be created through which badly wanted commodities could be exchanged between one empire and another, while customs officers pretended not to notice that they were on the list of forbidden exports. This kind of trade could not be voluminous, but it offered substantial profits at a high risk. It had seminal effects on a new kind of merchant, who was to make commerce a more independent and prestigious activity than that of the old-style merchant living in the shade of government officials and landed proprietors.

Quality and style in early medieval trade – types and specialisations of merchants, business methods, commodities and means of exchange, sea and land routes – can be described better than quantities can be measured. A brief survey of these topics, some of which should be dealt with more specifically in other chapters and volumes, must precede the detailed chronological survey that will be offered in the next section. Coinage, 'barter' and credit supply the best transition between quantity and quality. As a matter of fact, coins are the only tangible evidence of which a fairly continuous series survives; their weight and alloy can be checked; their purchasing power can occasionally be inferred from documents of sale. But they cannot provide the precise quantitative answers many prominent historians have asked of them. Minting is influenced by political and psychological motivations irrelevant to the needs of trade; moreover, the coins that have been found, mostly in hoards, are neither an exact cross-section nor a fixed percentage of the actual circulation. Above all, they are only one of three possible means of exchange, along with what is too indiscriminately called 'barter' and with credit. Both of them, in the early Middle Ages, are exceedingly hard to measure.

Still, it is important to observe that Rome in its prime had issued a most diversified coinage in many denominations of gold, silver and copper, each apt to serve transactions of a specific size. Its abundance was partly a sign of prosperity and of a good balance of payments, and partly an indication that coinage had no alternatives: barter was hardly ever resorted to in trade, credit was scant except for usurious consumption loans. The barbarian kings, falling heirs to depleted treasuries and to a coinage thrown off balance by the long crisis of the Empire, sooner or later gave up the minting of all denominations except one, the *tremissis* (a fraction of the gold *solidus*). Gold was the fittest symbol of authority for a sovereign advertising himself through his coins, and it cost less to strike one *tremissis* than several pieces of silver embodying the same value. That the kings did not choose the full *solidus* (of 4.55 grams) may mean that they realised that it was too valuable for practical use in an impoverished economy; that they provided no small change shows that serving the people was not their main preoccupation. The purchasing power of precious metal had climbed so steeply that a single *tremissis* might buy the provisions of an entire family for several months; one wonders what means of payment could be used for small daily transactions in retail shops, and indeed whether such shops survived at all. On the other hand, one should not jump to the conclusion that coinage was undertaken only for non-commercial uses (to store wealth, pay tributes or taxes or fines, adorn necklaces or bracelets, and measure the value of other goods): there would have been no incentive to minting coins if they had lost their primary purpose of buying and selling.

The Lombards, whose commercial economy and organisation were closest to Byzantium (still a country of full *solidi* and lively trade), gradually debased the *tremissis*, but kept striking it until the Frankish conquest; so did the Visigoths, until the Arab conquest of Spain. But the Merovingian kings by the late seventh century had become too weak and indifferent to keep the mints in their hands. The local officials, prelates and self-employed moneyers who took over the minting discontinued the *tremissis* and replaced it with lighter coins of debased silver. Silver was traditionally preferred to gold by most Germanic and Slav peoples, and because its purchasing power was ten times lower than that of gold (still less when alloyed with copper) the new coins were more functional for medium-sized transactions though not for the smallest. Nevertheless, the Carolingians intended to reaffirm their authority on coinage and to restore the purchasing power of coins. Since Charlemagne got hold of the Lombard mints, where the gold *tremissis* of Roman ancestry was still produced, one might have expected that he would make it (or possibly the full *solidus*) the cornerstone of his monetary restoration. But this would have increased friction with the Byzantine Empire, which claimed the exclusive right to strike gold; moreover, silver by his time had won the day not only in France but in England and Spain as well; hence he opted for silver coins, but of a higher weight and better alloy than previously. The early collapse of his plans, however, handed back the silver coin (*denarius*) to decentralised minting and accelerated debasement. By the tenth century the denier had lost so much of its silver content that it became useful for fairly small transactions, while imported Byzantine and Islamic gold coins replaced to some extent the discontinued domestic *tremissis* as the means of exchange for large transactions. At the same time, prices left their moorings and began to rise.

Without grappling with another quantitative debate that seems bound for a moot point – the absolute volume of coinage and its possible connection with the international balance of trade – one is tempted to interpret the long deflation of monetary prices as a sign that the mass of coins in circulation tended to be inadequate even for the depressed commerce of the early Middle Ages. This is probably true, but the problem is not so simple. Because commerce was sluggish and daily shopping virtually non-existent, coins circulated but slowly and intermittently. Only a few professional merchants needed an ever-ready supply of coined metal; most other people would find it safer to hoard away what they did not expect to spend soon, and more pleasurable to convert it into the lavish jewellery and glittering sacred objects of which the early Middle Ages was so fond. As a consequence, coins were not necessarily as 'liquid', nor as promptly available and easily exchangeable for other goods as were grain, cattle, horses and commodities that could be used or consumed right away. One comes across documents requesting payment either in kind or in coin, whichever would be readier at hand. In the Christian territories of Asturias and León, the alternative was spelled out more precisely in the tenth century by the standardised equivalence of a *solidus* in silver coins to a sheep or a *modium* of grain. In northern Italy, bread loaves of a determined size (*panis de cambio*, exchangeable bread) were ascribed a specific monetary value as fractions of the gold coin, thus making up for the lack of coins usable for small transactions. Payment in kind, however, was not only suggested by scarcity of cash, but by the preference of the seller. In 768, an Italian moneyer (that is, a *manufacturer* of coins) bought a piece of land for 28 *solidi*. Presumably a man in this trade would have been in a position to pay cash, but he gave only 15 *solidi* in coin. For the balance he delivered a horse which he probably had to buy in the market. In the ninth century the lowering standard of coinage had persuaded a northern French monastery to give wandering beggars deniers rather than food; in the tenth, faster inflation drove many Italian sellers back to demanding payments in kind as preferable to cash.

If payments in kind and hoarding of cash were not incompatible with the survival of what older scholars called 'money economy' or 'economy of exchange' (as opposed to 'natural economy' or 'subsistence economy'), they certainly slackened the tempo of commercial activity. Credit would have had the opposite effect, if it could be diverted from usurious consumption loans to investment in trade; but the Roman record was far from brilliant, and the first medieval centuries did not even match it. In the Roman Empire money-lending and deposit-banking were mainly the business of *trapezitai* ('bankers') and *argentarii* ('silversmiths'), but Gregory the Great was forced to intervene to save from bankruptcy the last *argentarius* doing business as a banker in Rome, and from that time on the term seems to mean just silversmith. French, Spanish and less frequently Italian councils kept hurling harmless thunderbolts at *usurarii* – were they really plain loansharks? – but Lombard law mentioned interest-bearing loans as perfectly lawful, and a southern French text that has been traced to eleventh-century Italian works on Roman law listed various forms of loans, both in kind and in cash, including loans by merchants to merchants. By this time, too, the term *trapezita*, sometimes used as a synonym of *monetarius* or *cambiator*, reappeared in Italian and French sources. There are good reasons to believe that the political and financial prominence of moneyers, attested as early as the time of St Eloi of Limoges, goldsmith–minter, minister to King Dagobert, bishop and saint, hinged not only on the fact that they struck coins at a profit, but also on the opportunities they found to lend some of their products. Their number and wealth kept growing between the ninth century and the twelfth. Often literate in an age of widespread illiteracy, rubbing shoulders with the highest lay and ecclesiastical officials, commoners by blood and profession but intermarrying with the nobility, some of them were to play a minor role in the Investiture struggle and the emergence of the Communes. But they were not in the forefront of the Commercial Revolution, and this leads one to think that if they lent money it was not primarily for investment in trade.

Probably the normal way for a merchant to obtain credit and assistance was to join forces with other merchants. The basic contractual arrangements of Roman law for borrowing or pooling capitals survived with some adjustments: the loan tried to conceal its interest charges and look like an act of charity; the sea loan justified the charges as a premium (the lender waived his claims if the cargo was lost by an act of God); the partnership, involving the fullest solidarity and the fullest sharing of risks and profits, tended to slip back into the family cocoon from which it had emerged, so that there were special partnerships of brothers or cousins. Then, new forms of association and collaboration, perhaps pre-existing as informal customs from time immemorial, made their appearance in Byzantine and Islamic law of the seventh and eighth centuries, and were mentioned in Venetian and southern Italian records of the ninth and tenth; this transfer shows the persistence of a Mediterranean *koiné* of merchants in spite of political and religious rifts. Mutual trust was the binding force: the simplest new contract was a pledge by a merchant to transport (and trade with?) goods of another, ostensibly without compensation but presumably with the expectation that the courtesy would be returned (*rogadia*); the most archaic 'new' contract, reflecting the pattern of the

Hellenistic law of jettison, was an agreement between travellers in the same ship to share in predetermined proportions the risks and profits of a common venture (*colonna*); the most flexible joined in a maritime venture a lender who bore all risks of capital for a major share of profits with a managing borrower who bore all risks of labour for a smaller share (*commenda*). *Rogadia*, *colonna* and partnership of brothers (with an unlimited duration) were bound for early obsolescence as commerce picked up, but the *commenda* and the partnership of cousins with limited duration (*compagnia*) would become as central in late medieval business (the former, in sea trade; the latter, in land trade) as the corporation in modern economy.

Approximately at the same time as the new contracts, new types of ships, suited to fight as well as to trade, responded to the challenge of a Mediterranean no longer torpidly tranquil, but torn apart by Byzantine–Islamic duels and harassed by piratical raids. Their names, mostly derived from the Greek or the Arabic, indicate their origin; but the westerners selected and reshaped only such foreign models as would meet their modest needs. The galley, a Byzantine auxiliary warship of the tenth century, was later to become the queen of Mediterranean trade and warfare through a series of improvements conceived in the West. The story of shipping reflects that of a conflict that in the long run benefited only the neutral. While the Byzantine and Muslim governments imposed on their seamen the ties of blockades and counterblockades as well as the burdens of war taxes and war losses, the mariners of Venice and Amalfi, practically undisturbed by their own governments, developed their commerce with both sides and with the western hinterland. So did the Jews; but they had no flag and no ships of their own, hence they depended on the dubious goodwill of strangers. By the tenth century, Syrians and Greeks had entirely withdrawn from commerce in the western Mediterranean, and faced Italian competition in the international trade of their own countries.

It has been claimed that the Arabs dealt a terrible blow to long-distance sea trade (Pirenne), or, conversely, that they caused it to soar (Lombard). Truth probably lies in the middle: war and piracy are no boon for trade, but no war can destroy commerce, and pirates depend on ships to prey upon. In the lack of absolute quantitative data, all that can be ascertained is some change in the objects of trade. Egyptian papyrus, long displaced as a material for books by cheaper and more durable parchment, continued to be imported for official documents wherever and so long as Roman bureaucratic tradition prevailed. The Merovingian chancery let it go in the late seventh century, but the papal chancery held on to it until its fabrication in

Egypt was discontinued owing to the competition of paper. Italian and Spanish olive oil, whose transportation had become cheaper thanks to the replacement of amphors with barrels, lost some customers through changes of taste: the Barbarians preferred butter for cooking and did not mind the smell of burning tallow for candles. On the other hand, the attraction and prestige of Byzantine (and, later, Islamic) silk and purple textiles, enhanced by their functioning as symbols of religious and political authority, resisted all vagaries of fashion. So did the demand for spices, with their many uses as food seasonings and preservers, medicinals and colour dyes. No doubt the supply of those goods was often irregular, but temporary scarcity merely raised their value without affecting their central position in luxury trade.

A steeper price escalation seems to have occurred, over the last centuries of the early Middle Ages, in two interrelated branches of trade: slaves and war materials. In both cases the growing objections of governments against the export of essential resources were bolstered by moral scruples; but they failed to stop merchants whose prospects of gain increased faster than their earthly and other-worldly fears. By converting its economy and its ethics gradually from slavery to serfdom, the West had long kept the cost of slaves within reasonable bounds: as late as 725 a French boy was sold in Milan for 12 gold *solidi*, while a good horse could fetch from one to three *solidi* more. At that time, however, an untrained slave brought as much as 100 *dinār* in the Umayyad Caliphate, and one well versed in poetry 600 *dinār* (more than 500 *solidi*). Normally too expensive to be used as farm labourers, but irreplaceable in the harems and the armed forces, white slaves continued to be in great demand throughout the Muslim states; indeed, the recrudescence of raids along the Christian shores towards the end of the early Middle Ages has been linked to an urge to refill a stock that was inadequately provided for by trade. In the same period, western merchants turned from the exhausted domestic market to the heathen frontier, where it was possible to capture prisoners and sell them without qualms – even to infidels – since their souls were irretrievably lost 'pro peccatis'. This, in fact, was the time when the word 'sclavus', Slav, replaced 'servus' in the meaning of totally unfree. The Muslims also appreciated the quality of various western weapons, especially 'Frankish' and Scandinavian swords, and had increasingly to resort to imports of European timber, iron, tin, copper and pitch as their own reserves dwindled or were too far away from the Mediterranean region. No matter how objectionable, this trade with the enemy offered westerners their best chance to pay for their own imports of luxury goods and gather seed capital for the sea merchants who would later wrest from that very enemy the military and commercial control of the Mediterranean. Still, one must not imagine too much: Islamic and Byzantine sources indicate that as late as the tenth century, trade with southern Europe was far from crucial in their economic perspective.

What makes the difference between developed and underdeveloped commerce, however, is not long-distance trade in luxuries and war materials but everyday traffic in ordinary goods. Here, in the heart of the matter, was the most serious deficiency of the early medieval West, denounced by such symptoms as the unchecked decay of the Roman roads, the virtual disappearance of inns along them and of shops in the towns, the propensity of authorities to regard as a thief any unknown stranger offering a horse or an ox for sale, the prominence of salt as almost the only staple that still was the object of sustained trade. (Venice itself owed its start in business to the salt of its lagoon.) Extrapolating from these and other phenomena, some scholars have taken the dimmest view of the early medieval scene. In the sparsely populated landscape of that age, they claimed, every large estate, monastic body and village community took care of itself by raising its own food and producing the simple tools indispensable in rural life. In turn, most towns, deprived of a steady market and contracted into a small portion of their walled area, relied heavily on the produce of cultivated plots inside the walls and in the immediate surroundings, using the uncertain returns of their limited trade and craftsmanship to stock provisions for the unpredictable future. Professional merchants catered for emergencies and extravagances, pedlars offered curiosities on feast days, all other exchanges were carried out directly between one producer and another.

Such a gloomy picture is not wholly unwarranted, especially for backward areas and periods of distress, but fails to take into account the brisker activity of certain regions, the persistence of urban traditions in a large part of the South, the resilience and adjustment of people under trying circumstances. An examination of urban survival and revival would take more space than they may be allowed here, but a few instances will be of help. Milan and Pavia did not escape the general demographic decline, but in the reduced proportions of the time maintained their economic leadership in the Po valley and their thin commercial links ranging from the Levant to England. Arles, formerly the capital of Gaul, squatted for a while within the walls of the Roman arena, then expanded again as the main centre of trade and navigation in the Rhone valley. Oviedo and León, stepping stones of the Christian *reconquista*, recaptured some fragments of the trade lost to the Muslims in Toledo and Cordoba. The emergence of two brand new centres, Venice and Amalfi, offset the decadence of

Aquileia and Pozzuoli. Self-sufficiency may have been a widespread aspiration, but it was hardly attainable even in the largest estates, much less in the cities. Hence, as shops vanished for lack of daily customers, periodical markets and fairs took their place. Too uneventful to be mentioned in the rare sources of the early centuries, new fairs come up for notice in the Carolingian period, when they need to be 'granted' by official authorisation. Their progress is shown by such examples as that of Piacenza, which in 819 had only one fair lasting one day: three fairs of eight days each were added in 872 and 873, and a fifth fair of 17 days was established in 896. Weekly markets like that of nearby Pavia, where in 901 a *negotiator* (merchant) rented a stall for 6 pence a year, needed no special charter and were probably held throughout the early Middle Ages. Lastly, the richer documentation of the tenth century alludes to shops in a number of cities; some may have been just movable barracks (then and now, the Spanish term for shop is *tienda*, 'tent'), but others are included in houses and may have been rooted there for a very long time.

Travel and transportation could be very difficult but never impossible. Formal inns were normally replaced by private houses accepting paying guests, in Italy at least; one need not take too seriously the outbursts of a German bishop who complained that the Italian *hospites* often poisoned their guests and *always* presented a bill. On the other hand, free or inexpensive hospitality was offered to pilgrims and other wayfarers in hospices and *xenodochia* (guest-houses) supported by the Church or by lay foundations; merchants could put up there, and many pilgrims were notorious smugglers. Pious foundations and fraternities also developed an interest in roads and bridges after the Roman ones became impassable. Costly metalled highways were no longer necessary for a transportation entrusted chiefly to pack animals, especially towards the end of the early Middle Ages, when horseshoes came into use – to say nothing of the fact that men also served as pack animals in a depressed society; any trail could do. Above all, the breakdown of highways led to an unprecedented intensification of internal and coastal navigation, mainly with barges and very small boats. Salt, grain, wine, oil and other staples were thus transported over fairly long distances, often by small producers in person or by agents of larger producers, who sold them in the market, thus becoming part-time merchants, even as specialised craftsmen sold their products in their own house or in the town market. The Po, the Arno, the Rhone, the Aude, with their tributaries, became main routes of trade, joined by road or canal to the Rhine, the Meuse, the Loire, the Garonne, and other rivers flowing into the Atlantic. Boats laden with iron descended the streams of the central and eastern Alps with dangerous speed. Even the small lake of Wallen in the Swiss mountains, the swampy waters of the Sile river in eastern Venetia and the stony bed of the Scultenna in the Apennines became routes of boatmen.

One should not minimise the importance of these unimpressive ramifications of trade, nor take the cue from hagiographic tales of pious merchants who had started as thieves or pirates. Certainly many merchants made generous donations to religious institutions, but this was no extraordinary confession of guilt. Neither should one regard as mere serfs the local merchants and carriers who attached themselves to an ecclesiastic or lay patron, whom they served as suppliers and business managers. When certain abbeys entrusted what they called 'our merchants' to sell or buy what they defined as 'our necessities', they merely obeyed the prescriptions of canon law and Carolingian capitularies which authorised their dealings and exempted from tolls their boats, pack animals and carts on explicit condition that they transported only goods for the personal consumption of the monks and their dependants. The largest and best organised monasteries, however, organised their production with an eye to the production of surpluses exchangeable for other goods. By the tenth century, Santa Giulia (near Brescia) brought raw silk to the royal market of Pavia, where it sold for five *solidi* a pound. The monastery of Sant'Ambrogio in Milan employed moneyers and merchants in a variety of business deals, some of them smacking of usury; in turn those moneyers and merchants used their connections with the monastery to promote their own affairs. Had the archives of lay proprietors been preserved as carefully as those of some French and Italian religious institutions, one would probably recognise a closer symbiosis between landed noblemen and *negotiatores*: scattered Italian evidence from the early eighth century onwards show some of the latter marrying noblemen's daughters, buying land, and taking active part in the political life of cities. Once again, one is led to believe that the size of extant documentation may have a more than accidental relation to the state of things; for all other tokens indicate that urbanisation and commercialisation were brisker and earlier in Italy than elsewhere, although they developed mostly in the same forms as in other parts of the European South.

Merchants were few and trade was thin, of course; but rarity may add value to what little can be got. The Roman emperors had employed professional traders and carriers to purvey and transport, at state-controlled prices, foodstuffs and other materials needed for the administration and the army; but they saw no reason to pamper or protect their supply agents while the goods were easily available, and in the final crisis of the Empire found no better cure for dwindling supplies than trying to force the agents to deliver as usual. Plain, unarmed merchants would not easily gain the confidence of barbarian kings; yet Priscus and Solomon, Jewish merchants hired by two Merovingian kings, and their co-religionist Abraham of Saragossa, 'palace merchant' of Louis the Pious, supplied goods to the court and, in exchange, were backed by the sovereign in their trade. Louis' benevolence towards the Jewish traders of Lyons shocked Agobard, the bishop of that city. But there could be no objection when Charles the Bald, in 877, bestowed upon all 'negotiatores, vel qui in civitatibus commanent', the costly honour of paying a special quota of the tribute to the Normans. The Ottonian emperors went further: a rash of charters extended their protection collectively to all merchants from a number of cities (both in Italy and in Germany), so that nobody could place obstacles in their ways. Probably these promises were neither very effective nor entirely gratuitous, although no counterpart is mentioned in the charters; but they showed a respect for the entire class of traders that imperial Rome had never felt.

Two Italian documents deserve special attention as early tokens of the future. In 750, Aistulf, the Lombard king, listed side by side three classes of *possessores* (landed proprietors) and three classes of *negotiatores* who owed military service on horse or foot, with weapons proportioned to their wealth. In each class, landowners and merchants were expected to perform exactly the same duties, the only difference being that the latter had the option of redeeming their obligations in cash. Even though Aistulf's army went down to defeat before Pepin the Short's, the mere fact that merchants could be regarded as the equals of landowners is extraordinary for the early Middle Ages. In 829, Giustiniano Partecipazio, the Doge of Venice, mentioned in his will not only real estate and valuable objects, but also a substantial sum – 1,200 silver pounds – which he had invested in commercial ventures overseas. Venice at that time was not a part of the barbarian and pre-feudal West but an autonomous offshoot of the Byzantine Empire; but investing in trade was a dishonourable and illegal thing to do for a nobleman and a ruler according to Byzantine law. That the Doge in person gave the example of trying his luck as a merchant was still more extraordinary than a Lombard merchant on a war horse. Before exploring the consequences of Italy's early start, however, it seems necessary to shift the focus from basic trends to the chronological sequences of events in the various parts of the early medieval European South.

(2) A CHRONOLOGICAL SKETCH

There was no sudden change after the formal collapse of the Western Empire. The Barbarians, far from continuing their destructive work after the conquest, endeavoured to preserve the old institutions, both good and bad. They had neither the desire nor the ability to cure with radical means the economic and social disease which had spelled death for Rome. They did not substantially change the oppressive taxation of trade, though they enforced it less efficiently, and they made no serious effort to break up the large estates. There was no parallel in the West to the abolition of the sales tax in the Byzantine Empire, or to the renaissance of free peasantry as indicated by the slightly later Byzantine Agrarian Law. Merchants from the Eastern Empire continued to tighten their grip on the commercial life of western Europe and north-west Africa. Greek words – *cataplus*, *catabolus* – designated the dock areas and the incoming ships in all barbarian kingdoms. Since the Byzantine emperors were usually on good terms with the kings, oriental merchants found open doors everywhere.

Soon after the Vandal conquest, Africa apparently resumed the usual shipments of oil to Constantinople and Rome. Carthaginian merchants continued to go to Spain and Byzantine merchants remained in Carthage. After the Byzantine restoration in Africa and Italy, in the time of Gregory the Great, several ships went every year from Carthage to Rome. Southern Spain also became a Byzantine protectorate in the late sixth century, and this made the resumption of direct communications between the eastern Mediterranean and the Atlantic possible. There was a Greek colony in Cordoba; other Greek merchants, 'arrived by ship from the Orient', were found in Merida. Both cities, well inside Spain, were situated on rivers flowing into the Atlantic. In the seventh century there are indications that Byzantine ships may have reached England. The account of a Greek hagiographer, who speaks of a ship of the Alexandrian Church which carried grain to England and loaded tin there, was regarded until recently as historically worthless. But the unearthing of an Anglo-Saxon burial ship, containing Byzantine silver plate, in East Anglia has brought unexpected confirmation to the legendary account. Soon after, however, the Visigothic reconquest of southern Spain must have brought the direct relations between the Atlantic and the eastern Mediterranean to an end.

Law-books are almost the only source giving information on trade in Visigothic Spain. We catch glimpses of kings endeavouring to control the coiners and to maintain what was left of the Roman *cursus publicus*. We see *mercenarii* carrying on the roads and rivers of the kingdom the 'gold, silver, clothing and various ornaments' which the *transmarini negociatores* import into the sea towns. If we may judge from the story of a *mercenarius* of the late fifth century as related by Sidonius, men of this class were both carriers working for the overseas merchants and small merchants on their own account. It may be surmised that the *transmarini negociatores* were mostly orientals and belonged to a higher class than the local merchants. The Visigothic kings heavily taxed these 'oversea merchants', but tried to remove obstacles from their path. The royal protection, however, did not cover the Jews, who were very numerous in all the larger cities. A series of laws restricting their activity reached a climax under King Egiza (687–702) when he forbade them to approach the docks or to trade with Christians. No wonder that a few years later the Jews welcomed the Arab invasion. Before leaving the Iberian Peninsula, however, we must recall that Christian merchants from Urgel and Barcelona, in the Spanish March, maintained relations with Cordoba and other cities in the Spanish Caliphate. Slaves are the only item of trade specifically mentioned in the sources.

In Mediterranean France trade was much livelier, especially after the Frankish kings had wrested Provence from the hands of the Goths, making it the main outlet of the greatest barbarian state to the southern sea. Even Narbonne, which remained in Visigothic hands, benefited from its proximity to the Frankish border. In Provence not only Marseilles and Arles but also smaller centres such as Nice and Lérins maintained relations by sea with Italy, Spain, Africa and the Levant from the fifth to the early seventh century. They exported slaves, cloth and timber. They imported spices, wine of Gaza and Falerno, olive oil, rice, dates, figs, papyrus, leather goods and silk. Considerable quantities of these goods were forwarded from the coast to the most distant regions of Merovingian France by river and road. We still hear of 'constituta evectio tam carralis quam navalis' (state transportation by both carts and boats) in 716. Many Roman bridges had collapsed, but they were replaced by pontoon bridges like that of Arles. Local fairs were organised in the smaller centres such as Rodez and the neighbouring towns. In the larger cities the merchants had permanent residences and shops, but they were quick to go wherever the trade opportunities were favourable. Orientals seem to have outnumbered native merchants in wholesale trade. The entrance of a Frankish king into Orleans, which is today the linguistic capital of France, was cheered in Latin, Syrian and Hebrew!

Mediterranean France, which increased its boundaries when Charles Martel annexed Languedoc and Charlemagne the Spanish March, did not lose all commercial importance after the beginning of the eighth century. Reliable sources mention more than once the Italian ships which called at Marseilles in the ninth century. Less reliable accounts, referring to the later years of the reign of Charlemagne, mention a variety of 'Arab' wares in Arles and speak of African, Jewish and even Breton (or British?) ships along the Narbonnese coast as if they were a far from uncommon sight. A lost charter of Boso, the king of Provence (879–87), granted the church of Arles the tolls collected from the Greeks and other strangers in the *portus* of that city; the grant was confirmed by Boso's son in 921. In the ninth and tenth centuries the Rhone and perhaps a Provençal harbour may have been used by merchants of Verdun on their way to sell slaves in Spain. We only know with certitude that the route from northern France to Spain branched off from the *Via Francigena* – France to Rome – somewhere near Lyons; slavers and pilgrims went in the same caravan before having to part. Lyons itself was the home of many Jews, who owned synagogues and slaves, and who were well supplied with wine and other luxuries.

Nevertheless, it seems undeniable that Carolingian and early Capetian France gradually turned its back on its own Mediterranean coast. Among probable causes of this slow change one must give due importance to the political anarchy, local warfare and foreign invasions which grew steadily worse from the seventh to the late tenth century. Similar disasters, however, also affected the trade of the Italo-Byzantine cities with the Lombard hinterland without disrupting it. Probably a more specific factor of decline was the lack of normal and continuous diplomatic relations between France and the oriental powers. While no war has ever eliminated contraband, reciprocal trade agreements and favourable tariffs are essential for a full development of commerce. Even in the 'Dark Ages' a passport (*sigillum*) was required to cross the frontiers and to be admitted to the main markets of the Muslim states, the Byzantine Empire, Lombard Italy and the Carolingian Empire. It is significant that Muslim wares are mentioned in Arles when Charlemagne's relations with Cordoba and Baghdad were at their best, and that Greeks appear in the same city when the kings of Provence were negotiating for an alliance with Constantinople. As a rule, only the Jews could freely go back and forth between France and non-Catholic lands because they had no definite nationality and were politically harmless. Their ascendancy was no less helped than hindered by discrimination against them. In Carolingian France they became so predominant in trade that the texts often divide traders into two classes, 'the Jews and the other merchants'.

This does not mean that the commercial currents from the East ceased to reach France, but only that they had to follow devious channels. In the ninth and tenth centuries a new economic unit, Catholic Europe, was slowly emerging in place of the older Mediterranean unit. Contacts with the Byzantine and Muslim worlds were maintained mostly through peoples who lived near the frontier and who were admitted to the oriental markets: Slavs, Scandinavians and Italo-Byzantines. (Already in the seventh century caravans of Frankish *negociantes*, mostly slave traders, went to Slavonic and Avar territory for trade. Charlemagne established a series of frontier outposts across Europe, from the Danube to the northern shore, where his subjects could trade with the Slavs.) The frontier outposts shifted eastwards as Catholic Europe expanded. In the tenth century, Polish, Russian, Turkish, Muslim and Jewish merchants went to Prague to purchase slaves, furs, tin and other European wares, and no doubt to sell oriental commodities. This overland travel, however, was slow, expensive and frequently interrupted by war. The Scandinavian river and sea route via the Volga or the Dnieper and the Baltic was longer but cheaper. The Italo-Byzantine route via the Mediterranean, the Po valley and the steep Alpine passes was the shortest and probably the cheapest.

It would not be surprising if French trade with the East suffered from this change of routes. Germany, however, owed to the new routes unprecedented commercial opportunities and her cities along the great rivers of western and southern Germany benefited the most. Mainz is a good illustration. Local merchants carried grain down the Main to the city while traders from Magdeburg linked Mainz with Bardowiek near the mouth of the Elbe. Frisian merchants resided in the best houses of Mainz before 886. They brought with them not only the textiles of their country but also oriental wares purchased in Scandinavia or in Rome. Other wares were imported into the city by Slavonic merchants. Jewish traders obtained salt from central Germany, and boasted of bringing to Mainz some commodities imported directly from Palestine. A lone Muslim traveller from Spain who visited Mainz in 973 was surprised at the quantity of 'Indian' spices he found there. The spices might well have been bought by local traders in the Italo-Byzantine cities: one 'opulent merchant' from Mainz, Liutfred, appointed by Otto I as ambassador to Constantinople, went there via Venice. Certainly that was not his first journey by that route. His city, in the heart of Europe, could use equally well the Baltic, the overland and the Mediterranean supply routes from the Orient. German and Swiss centres farther south, however, definitely gravitated towards the Italo-Byzantine cities. So did southern France. We know that a good number of transalpine references point to the Italians as the principal if not the only suppliers of eastern wares to the larger part of Europe.

Italy at last had begun to exploit the advantage of her central position in regard to both continental Europe and the Mediterranean basin. A fruitful transformation took place in Italy during the first five centuries of the Middle Ages, in spite of recurring political and military disasters. A nation of moderately successful peasants and farmers, who in Roman times were dependent upon easterners for their trade and who did not produce enough food for their overgrown capital, now was on its way to becoming the first commercial and industrial nation in the West. An unimpressive but significant step in this direction had occurred before the end of the 'period of transition'. Italo-Byzantine merchants almost entirely replaced the Greeks and the Syrians as middlemen between the eastern and the western Mediterranean.

The transformation was slow at first. Jews, Greeks and Syrians still dominated commerce in Italy under the Ostrogoths. The administration imported grain and other foodstuffs from the non-Italian provinces of the kingdom and from Africa in larger quantities than it exported its own commodities. One wonders whether the survival of Roman municipal administration, craft gilds and taxation system was really a boon, since this burdensome structure had speeded the collapse of the Western Empire. A more substantial advantage was the continued upkeep of the Roman highways, even though this delayed the utilisation of internal waterways. Sea trade was promoted by the fact that the western Mediterranean for a few years became an Ostrogothic lake save for Africa, which was controlled by the friendly Vandals. However, we must not accept at face value the hyperboles of Cassiodorus, whose imagination placed in the harbour of Rome the traffic of bygone times and transformed the fishermen of the Venetian coast into shippers 'wont to cross infinite stretches of the sea'. Nor must we give much credence to a chronicler who spoke of *negotiantes* flocking in to enjoy Theodoric's perfect order; other sources of that allegedly fortunate period mention brigands in the country and armed bands in the cities.

At any rate, any recovery that may have occurred in the time of Theodoric was nullified by the frightful ravages of the Graeco-Gothic war (535–53) and of the Lombard invasion (568). The years of the lawless Lombard 'interregnum' (574–84) probably were still worse, but they were followed by a long period of comparative peace and steady if slow economic recovery. The Lombards, however, were unable to wrest from the Byzantines most of the coastal areas and the control of the sea. All along the hollow shell of the 'Roman' possessions, the inhabitants were gradually driven to rely upon sea trade for the means of subsistence they could no longer obtain from the lost hinterland. The letters of Gregory the Great point out the commercial importance of Ravenna and mention numerous ships leaving Naples and Rome practically every month from March to early October for the islands, Africa, Provence and the Levant.

Three centuries later (around 875), when Muslim and Norman raids were at their worst and the peninsula was in a state of anarchy, the sailing season in the Tyrrhenian had been contracted but slightly. Ships, usually grouped for security in large convoys, navigated in the period from April to September. Some of them succumbed to enemy attacks, but others attacked the enemy and reached friendly shores with their prizes. Naples and Rome were now less important than Amalfi and Gaeta. The tiny harbours of these seaports which were hemmed in by the mountains found this handicap a stimulus to commercial expansion by sea. Soon after, Salerno, a 'Lombard' city, forsook national ties and sought new fortunes by recognising Byzantine overlordship. Farther east, on the lower Adriatic, 'Roman' Bari hesitated to choose between agriculture and trade because it still had a wide hinterland. Eventually the proximity of the Balkan coast, where the *Via Egnatia* from Constantinople reached Durazzo, tipped the balance on the side of trade. Ravenna, the old political and maritime capital, continued to thrive. Farther north, along the fringe of Venetian islets from Comacchio to Grado, a people of fishermen was growing into a nation of traders. By the late tenth or early eleventh century a Lombard writer pointed out with lingering amazement that the Venetians 'do not plough, do not seed, do not gather vintage', but purchase all the grain and wine they want in exchange for their wares – salt, spices and silk.

The prosperity of these communities, as we have seen, was largely based on triangular trade with their Byzantine overlords and their Muslim and Lombard neighbours. The Byzantine Empire clung to the later Roman practice of channelling foreign trade through a number of market towns along the border, beyond which no alien could go without a permit. If he was allowed to reach Constantinople, he was expected to transact his business, within time limits established by treaties, in state-controlled lodging houses (*mitata*). A long list of forbidden exports – slaves, gold, war materials, essential foodstuffs, precious textiles reserved for the emperor and his court – set further limits for foreign and native citizens alike, and the very word *kommerkion* significantly designated a variety of taxes on both foreign and internal trade. Still, Byzantium offered an attractive variety of industrial art goods, perfumes and spices in return for simpler wares it needed, and smuggling was not too hard through its extended sea and land frontiers. The Italo-Byzantine cities were qualified to serve as border markets for legitimate trade, handy for contraband, and exempted from most restrictions imposed on aliens. The Venetians, who often lent ships for war, transportation and state mail, were rewarded with lower tariffs at the Dardanelles; the Amalfitans, whose loyalty was shakier, were not so privileged, but still passed as provincial citizens of the Byzantine commonwealth. One wishes more records from Byzantium had survived, but what little we have clearly indicates sustained and growing trade relations, apparently with a balance of payments favourable to the Empire.

The Italo-Byzantine merchants ought to have been treated as unfriendly aliens in the Muslim world, where restrictions on trade and residence of foreigners were milder but not substantially different from those of Byzantium. They were not, with a few exceptions such as a mob attack on Amalfitans in Old Cairo (996), belatedly repressed by a Nestorian vizier. They exported mainly spices, perfumes, ivory, textiles and oil; they imported slaves, timber, iron, wooden and iron objects, all of which could be used at war against the Byzantine Empire. But only the Venetian Doges made serious attempts at enforcing Byzantium's decrees forbidding that trade, with temporary success at best. The Italo-Byzantine seaports of the south Tyrrhenian more often than not allied themselves with Muslim powers. In the ninth century, Pope John VIII tried in vain to win over the bishop-duke of Naples and the local rulers of Amalfi and Gaeta either by a threat of excommunication or by an offer of customs exemption in Rome plus a gift of 10,000 silver *mancusi*; ironically, both the *mancusi* and the papyrus on which the Pope wrote his anti-Muslim appeal were of Islamic origin. In turn, ambassadors of the Tunisian Muslims aboard a Venetian convoy aided the crew in attacking a convoy of Spanish Muslims; then they carried out their mission of inducing the Byzantine governor of Sicily to renew the agreement which insured to the citizens of either country the right to trade in the other. In this tangle of conflicting political and economic interests, the Italo-Byzantine cities pursued the latter with the smallest encumbrance from official political postures. Whatever loss the Amalfitans may have suffered in Constantinople through their pro-Muslim leanings was compensated for by their gaining first place in African trade with the West and with Byzantium itself.

Italo-Byzantine commercial relations with the Lombard kingdom and, later, its Frankish conquerors were at the beginning an inescapable consequence of the fact that coastal towns without a hinterland and a hinterland without coastal towns were economically interdependent. The gradual conquest of wide stretches of the coast by the Lombards and the Franks did not alter these relations substantially; their rulers seldom were on good terms with Byzantium and the Muslims, nor were they in a position to catch up with the faster development of the Italo-Byzantine trading centres. In addition to foodstuffs, the latter found in the comparatively underdeveloped interior iron and timber that could pay for imports from the Muslim world and leave surplus money usable in trade with Byzantium. By the early eighth century, in the absence of formal trade agreements between the Byzantine Empire and the Lombard kings, local authorities under King Liutprand took the initiative of granting reductions from the usual 10 per cent tax on foreign trade to the boatmen of Italo-Byzantine Comacchio who carried salt, oil and pepper up the Po to Cremona. These homely comestibles actually bear witness to diversified trade: salt was extracted in bulk from the Italo-Byzantine lagoons, oil was obtained in substantial quantity from Africa, and pepper was imported in small amounts from Constantinople or Alexandria. To the same period (possibly to King Liutprand himself) is also ascribed an invitation to the Venetians to frequent the fairs of Pavia, the Lombard capital. In turn some Lombard merchants entered the Byzantine territory in Italy where the boundary line was not sharply defined, but as late as the tenth century they do not appear to have been admitted to the lodging houses of the Byzantine capital.

The commercial primacy of the Italo-Byzantine seaports was threatened for a time by the direct negotiations of the Carolingians with the courts of Constantinople, Cordoba and Baghdad. Perhaps the treaty of Charlemagne with Hārūn al-Rashīd, about which we have little positive information, was concerned only with the travel of pilgrims. These pilgrims, however, probably availed themselves of the market near the Christian *xenodochium* of Jerusalem, where anyone could exhibit his wares by paying two pieces of gold a year. Charlemagne's lost treaty of 813 with the Byzantine emperors apparently granted subjects of each empire access to all highways and waterways of the other as well as admission to the state-controlled markets of the respective capitals. This πάκτον, however, was abrogated almost immediately after ratification. Therefore the Carolingians, despairing of being able to patch up their differences with Constantinople, transferred to Venice the reciprocal facilities which the treaty of 813 would have insured to the entire Byzantine Empire. This seems to be the origin of the Franco-Venetian *pactum* of 840 which, through promulgation by Emperor Lothar and successive confirmations and improvements, laid the foundations for the absolute primacy of Venice over the other Italo-Byzantine seaports in western trade. In the following period the open collaboration of Amalfi, Naples and Gaeta with the Muslims eventually caused these cities to forfeit their privileged position in the Byzantine Empire. Other Italo-Byzantine cities – Comacchio, Ravenna and some Istrian seaports – were conquered by the Lombards or the Franks. The complaints of the Istrians to their Frankish governors show what this conquest meant: 'We are laughed at by our Venetian and Dalmatian neighbours and by the Greeks our former masters...(we cannot) give hospitality to foreigners.' At last, in order to retain some of their old trade, the Istrians begged the Venetians for a protectorate, while Comacchio was ruined and forced to submit to Venice. Even Ravenna began to decline, though her greater vitality is proved by the presence in the tenth century of a *schola* of merchants – probably a survival of Roman times and perhaps the earliest merchants' 'gild' mentioned in western sources of the Middle Ages.

By the first years of the eleventh century Venice by force of arms and diplomatic cunning had won a position of decided predominance among the intermediaries in commerce between East and West. The city was virtually independent of Constantinople and yet still enjoyed the privileges of Byzantine citizenship. Venice maintained diplomatic relations with all Muslim powers and dealt as an equal with the kings of Italy and the western emperors. A series of agreements with local authorities in Upper Italy ensured low tariffs for Venetian trade moving up the main rivers flowing from the Alps. Besides the Istrian cities, several Dalmatian towns and islands, formerly included in the Byzantine Empire, had accepted Venetian suzerainty in order to escape Slavonic occupation. With the Dalmatian raw silk coming in as tribute and with state-controlled *xenodochia* where foreigners were admitted on the same terms as they were in the lodging-houses of the Byzantine capital, Venice was a little Constantinople in the West.

The future rival of Venice, Genoa, in the early eleventh century was just beginning to recover from the long depression that followed the Lombard conquest about 642. The conquerors had torn down her walls and allowed the Roman highways along the coast and across the Apennines to break down. In three hundred years we hear only once of a convoy stopping in Genoa on its way from Rome to Provence (878), and it was not a commercial convoy. A Muslim fleet that sacked it in 934 or 935 must have been disappointed in finding it mainly a community of fishermen and peasants with very few merchants and ecclesiastic or lay landowners. The raid, however, set in motion a vigorous reaction; the community rallied, obtained privileges from the government, and readied its ships for commerce and for war.

Pisa fared better under the Lombards and the Franks. It was the main Tyrrhenian port of the kingdom, close to the main surviving highway of the kingdom (*Via Francigena*), to Lucca, Tuscany's provincial capital, and to Corsica, the only island loosely controlled by the kings. The Lombards apparently granted Pisa a measure of autonomy and protected a group of aliens (*waregangi*, no doubt Italo-Byzantines). Under the Franks, it continued to receive Greek slavers, to send convoys to Byzantine Sardinia and, possibly, to be in direct communications with Constantinople; like Genoa, it became a target for Muslim raids but fought back.

The cities of the Italian interior, too, seem to have preserved more of their vitality than those of the other barbarian states. By the end of the early Middle Ages their social texture and political behaviour had much in common with those of the Italo-Byzantine cities: a fair number of noblemen, free merchants (*negotiatores*) and craftsmen resided within their walls and took care of many tasks of local administration. On the other hand, the central government under Byzantine influence gradually became involved in economic control. Our information on this comes chiefly from an account describing tenth-century conditions, but it is clear that some elements went as far back as the middle or late Lombard period. In Pavia, and apparently in some other cities, the basic crafts and professions, including merchants and moneyers, were headed by *magistri* under the supervision of royal officers. The state claimed all gold found in the kingdom's rivers, presided over the mints, and punished counterfeiters under a Byzantine-inspired Lombard law. Foreign ships going up the Po had their terminus in Pavia, the capital; instead of *mitata*, however, the visitors found only an empty market square where they could pitch their tents, unless they were admitted to the houses kept in the city by ecclesiastical institutions from other cities. A Lombard official, akin to the Prefect of Constantinople, supervised the transactions and collected tributes from the Italo-Byzantine importers of textiles, spices, mirrors, oil and salt. To check merchants arriving overland, there were *clusae* or customs houses wherever a route crossed the Alps into Italy. In these border outposts, foreign merchants had to stop, pass inspection, and pay a 10 per cent tax on imported horses, slaves, tin, swords and textiles of wool, linen and hemp. Exceptionally the Anglo-Saxons, favoured by a special agreement, paid only every third year a lump sum and a tribute in kind.

While indicating an interest in the economic good order of the country, state control is not necessarily a boon for trade. In Italy it was less efficient, hence both less helpful and less oppressive than in Byzantium. The early Carolingians were impressed enough by what they saw in Italy to try to extend some of its aspects to the other parts of their empire, but lost power before they could make it work. The post-Carolingian kings of Italy endeavoured to keep it going for a while, but had eventually to yield to the growing initiative of their autonomous cities. These were better judges of the needs of commerce than the feudal lords who got hold of the Carolingian heritage beyond the Alps.

II. *The Age of the Commercial Revolution*

(1) THE MERCHANT IN THE ECONOMIC FOREFRONT

The startling surge of economic life in southern Europe between the mid-tenth and the mid-fourteenth centuries marks a great and irreversible turn in the history of western civilisation. The first phase in the long process that was eventually to uplift Europe from underdevelopment to full development (as one might say today), it raised the average standard of living well above that of the Roman peak, with a less inequitable distribution of wealth than had ever been known before. At the lower end of society, it completed the emancipation of native Christian slaves and enfranchised a large proportion of the serfs. Contradictorily, but not illogically, it lent strength here to urban self-government, there to monarchic consolidation. It influenced law and religion, literature and art, promoted education and communication at all levels, and at its peak made it possible for a few business men to encompass in their dealings the whole of Eurasia from England to China.

At the remote origin of the surge there must have been the first stirrings of the second half of the early Middle Ages, after epidemics subsided and the population began ever so slowly to grow afresh, on land rejuvenated by centuries of underexploitation, and possibly stimulated by a favourable pulsation of climate. By the late tenth century, sufficient manpower was available to break the lingering vicious circle of low production and low consumption, thus starting four centuries of agricultural growth. Agriculture remained fundamental, the occupation or the source of income for the overwhelming majority of the population. Its progress alone, however, would hardly have broken through the economic ceiling established in antiquity unless the leadership in economic development had passed from the hands of people who would rather spend than invest to those of men willing to postpone consumption for the sake of profit. Not necessarily greedier than the wealthy landowner, but usually more single-minded and professional in the pursuit of gain, the merchant became the catalyser in what may properly be called the age of the Commercial Revolution.

This change was prepared and accompanied by substantial shifts in the political status and social posture of the merchant class, in its top brackets if not in the lower ranks. No matter how thriving in the Graeco-Roman prime, traders had failed to attain the power and prestige vested in the landed classes. Entrenched in mediocrity, they were at best second-class citizens, at worst resident aliens in their native towns, forever tempted to retire from business and buy land for respectability. The early Middle Ages had reduced their numbers and their chances of gain to a minimum, but by the same token had sharpened the wits, the organisation and the aggressiveness of the remaining few. The merchant entrepreneurs who emerged from that tough apprenticeship and multiplied in the course of the Commercial Revolution were cast in a new mould: they cared less for recognition than for autonomy, less for security than for opportunity. They were perfectly adjusted to the warlike, disconnected society of their time. Some of them were members of the lower feudal nobility or passed as such. Whatever their origin, they knew that commerce was a dangerous venture, where capital and labour had to take the same calculated risks (from war as well as from trade), and where partners must be chosen above all on grounds of mutual trust. In exchange for privileges, they would pledge allegiance to higher authorities, but their normal aspiration was not to infiltrate the feudal and ecclesiastical hierarchy, which needed their services yet would not discard its biases against them. Their ultimate goal, fully achieved by the early thirteenth century throughout Italy between Alps and Tiber, and partly attained elsewhere along the French and Catalan coasts, was to become the masters of their own cities and make them the hubs of territorial states where agriculture itself would be subservient to trade. At no other time or place have there been as many governments by and for the merchants – a further reason to speak of an 'age of the Commercial Revolution'.

Commercialisation had to precede industrialisation: so long as artisans had inadequate machines, they could not, like merchants, make sufficient profit to accumulate capital or attract credit at a low cost. Leaving for treatment elsewhere an analysis of the commercial methods and tools that carried forward the Commercial Revolution, we must now describe in some detail its progress from take-off to full speed in the European South. Italy has the oldest records, the most numerous and enlightening ones; it was the home of nearly all the forerunners of the take-off, and played in further development a role as prominent as that of England in the early decades of the Industrial Revolution. What is more, Italy maintained its lead throughout the Commercial Revolution, even increasing it in some sectors toward the end of the period. Hence it seems helpful to cast the limelight on that

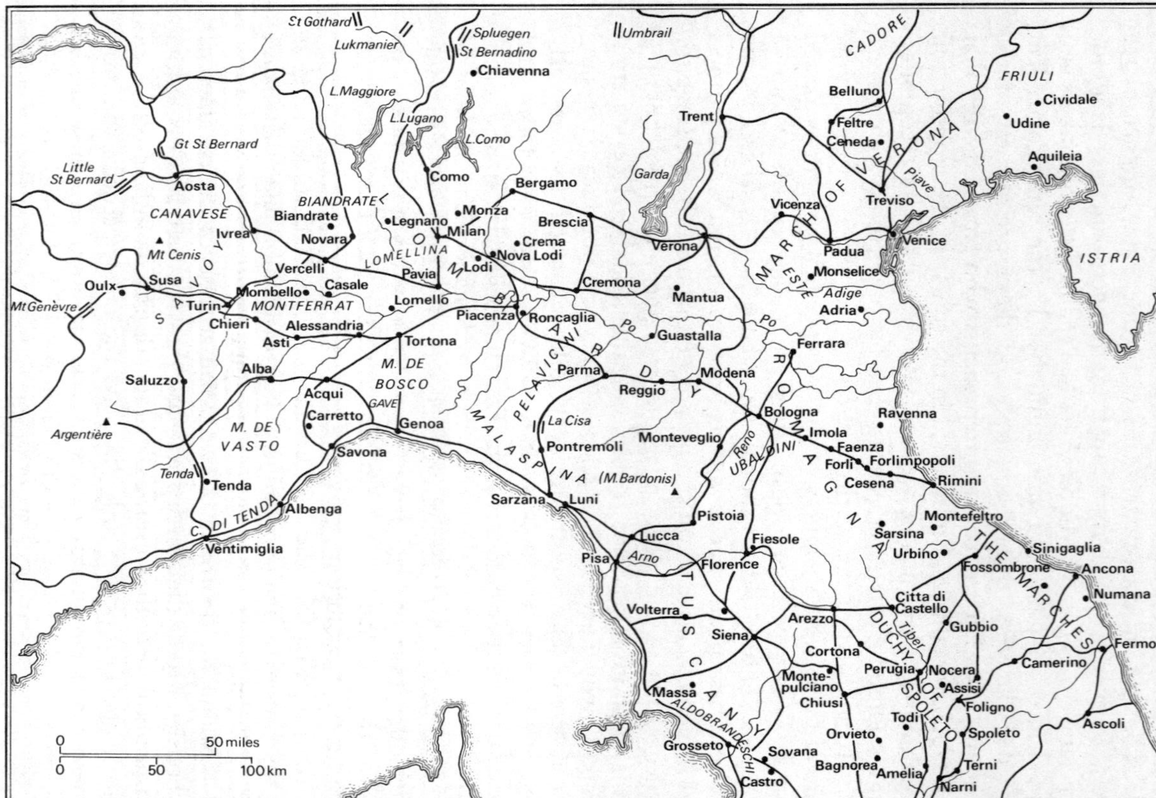

Map 4. North Italy in the Twelfth Century.

country, while pointing out as we go that other parts of the European South lagged behind, and that even in Italy there were backwaters as well as mainstreams. The dynamics of commercialisation will thus be explored by following chronologically but separately the growth of local trade, overseas trade, and overland trade. A concluding section will attempt to qualify these broad generalisations by focussing on local and regional aspects of the Commercial Revolution in its prime.

(2) THE PROGRESS OF COMMERCIALISATION

(A) *Expansion of the Home Market*

Local trade does not meet the eye as promptly as long-distance trade, but it has a stronger potential of expansion and contraction. It had been the greatest sufferer in the early medieval depression; its revival, connected with the increasing productivity and demand of a growing population, had paramount importance, even if it did not contribute as much as long-distance trade to the rapid formation of large fortunes.

Demographic history has made great progress in the last two or three decades, but is still severely handicapped by the dearth of reliable figures. Still, it is well established that the increase of population in all classes alike was steady and considerable throughout the age of commercialisation. At first only a small minority was directly involved in the Commercial Revolution, and even when the shift to trade reached its full tide most people remained engaged in agriculture. Yet the growth of the merchant class, no matter how small in absolute numbers, was sufficient to change the character of the entire society. Let us now trace those groups who engaged in commerce and see how they became involved in it.

Fathers of large noble families were forced either to disinherit all except their eldest sons or to split the ancestral holdings until the estate became 'pulverised'. From the great reservoir of landless, land-hungry knights which was thus formed came many of the fighters for the military enterprise which enlarged the commercial frontier of Catholic Europe. Most of them came from non-Mediterranean areas, although some were Italians, southern French or Catalonians. These fighters, however, merely opened new ground for trade without taking a direct part in commercial enterprises. Our interest in them ceases when the campaign in which they were engaged ends.

Much more important were those prolific families of the lesser nobility who lived in a town or in its suburbs, and whose landed property became insufficient to support them in a manner befitting a feudal lord. In many 'Lombard' towns of northern and central Italy descendants of city viscounts and of episcopal *advocati*, and other small

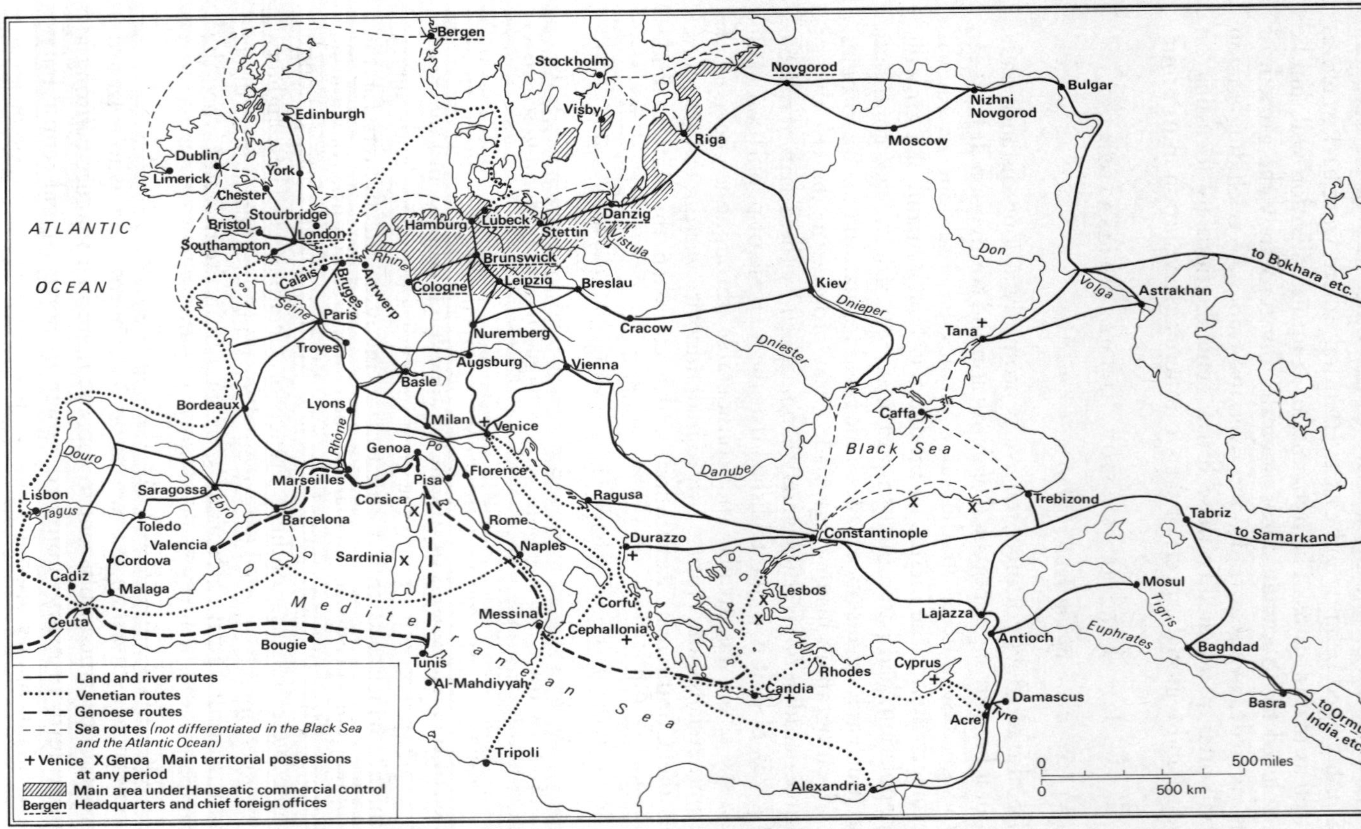

Map 5. Principal Trade Routes in the Thirteenth Century

fry of the nobility joined the upper bourgeoisie in a struggle against German overlords, Muslim invaders and other common enemies. United they won political liberty and economic opportunities for the city in the eleventh and twelfth centuries. Engaging in commerce was a natural step for noblemen whose feudal resources were insufficient, and who found themselves at the helm of free commercial communities. At the same period the members of the nobility played a prominent role in the commerce of the 'Italo-Byzantine' cities, which had gained or were gaining independence under their leadership. But this was not a new fact, for commerce there had always been the occupation of the larger part of the population including the nobility. On the other hand, the farther one goes from Italy, the smaller is the participation of noblemen in the rise of trade. The viscounts of Marseilles, Montpellier and Barcelona remained feudal lords, interested in commerce only in so far as they could levy tolls upon it. It is true that many landed proprietors, who probably belonged to the lowest strata of the nobility, seem to have been included among the early 'merchants' of southern France and Catalonia. But it is impossible to tell whether they had become traders because they owned land rents or whether they had become noblemen because they had accumulated money in trade. The second process can be followed easily in the documents of cities which developed in a later period. In fourteenth-century Lyons some ten non-noble families year after year supplied all of the consuls of the young commune. Eventually they made their entrance into the lower nobility, only one step below the feudal aristocrats whom they had fought for centuries.

It was, however, ordinary merchants, commoners rather than noblemen, who filled the ranks of the business class in Italy as elsewhere. As early as 1068 the Milanese non-noble *ordo negotiatorum* played an important role by the side of the *ordo capitaneorum vassorum* (the class of noblemen living in the city). Non-noble merchants formed the rank and file of the private associations which set up the communes – in some places before the end of the eleventh century, in others in the twelfth or the thirteenth. Soon they ruled the cities almost as if the cities had been their own property, making communal policy an expression of their own mercantile interests. In Milan their hegemony was not challenged by the humbler classes until 1198; elsewhere they remained sole masters for a longer period, and in some cities they never had to share their power with other groups. Their individualistic tendencies were somewhat restrained by the powerful bonds of relationship. Families formed units whose numerous members usually were closely bound by common political and business interests. There were confederations of families – often rallying around some party label, Guelf or Ghibelline, 'White' or 'Black' – but merchant gilds, where they were created, only made their appearance long after the consolidation of the communes. In Siena, Bologna and elsewhere they were formed simultaneously with the gilds of money dealers. In most of the maritime cities and in some important centres of the interior (Asti for instance) there never was a merchant gild of any sort, probably because commerce directly or indirectly was the occupation of the overwhelming majority. For the same reason the 'consuls of the sea' in Pisa, Marseilles, Montpellier and other seaports were not heads of a special group, but municipal officers entrusted with harbour and navigation police. In one way or another nearly everybody drew his means of subsistence from the sea.

As commerce absorbed larger and larger strata of the population in the cities, wealth rather than birth became the main basis of class distinction. In many Italian cities some merchants at least were descended from a very long line of early medieval *negotiatores*, but others were upstarts and newcomers to trade. In neither case can we discover their actual ancestors, because family names were not in use for ordinary people until very late. At the beginning of the twelfth century a Genoese notary copying a number of obscure family names – they were often derived from ridiculous or obscene nicknames – gave up the task and simply added: 'and many others whose names are difficult to write'. Some nicknames were destined to be transmitted to generations of great Genoese business men. Venice itself, when it closed almost hermetically the rolls of the merchant 'nobility' (1297), listed as noble both old and new 'patrician' families (*case vecchie* and *case nuove*). The Malipieros, who claimed aristocratic origin of great age, actually descended from a maestro Piero, a master merchant or craftsman. In most of the other cities 'nobility' became merely a social distinction which could entail indirect economic advantages, but no legal privileges whatsoever. The Florentine Commune liberally knighted rich merchants and shop-keepers, and these often imitated the ways of the old aristocracy by buying country estates and building palaces in the city. At the same period (1293) enrolment in one of the commercial, industrial or professional gilds was made a pre-requisite for holding public offices. A time was to come when men of noble origin in some towns, in an endeavour to win the support of the lower class, would insist upon being regarded as commoners. Outside northern and central Italy the dividing line between noblemen and merchants was not erased, but became thinner and thinner in the more 'commercialised' areas. In Majorca, for instance, noblemen and bourgeois were lumped together in one class, the *homens de honor* who lived in the capital and subjected the peasants to thorough exploitation.

Commerce also eventually opened new horizons to some branches of industry, which became major forces in the economic and political life of the city. To be sure, in many minor business centres the presence of craftsmen in the group which ruled the town merely meant that most of the merchants themselves were hardly richer than ordinary gild masters. This may have been the case even in Montpellier, where some representatives of the humblest crafts were commonly elected to the Consulate. But in cities such as Florence, Lucca, Bologna and Milan the only crafts which gained a place in the government usually were those capable of capitalistic development, that is, textile and metallurgical industries producing for export or trades working for mass consumption such as the butcher shops, whose number remained restricted by law while cities continued to grow. The master craftsmen who thus attained equality with the merchants and bankers were not plain artisans, but entrepreneurs who applied to industry some of the capital derived from commerce and finance. Their prosperity ultimately rested upon the increase in number of humbler gildsmen and industrial labourers who consumed or manufactured their goods, and this increase was a result of the general demographic growth. As one watches these masses struggling for better living conditions and for a share in what was called, with dubious accuracy, a 'government of the people', one may well wonder how far 'commercialisation' meant prosperity for all. It is true that salaries rose – between 1194 and 1228 those of the masons in northern Italy apparently more than doubled – but the debasement of coins sometimes reduced real wages to a bare minimum. Yet there are definite indications in the sources of the thirteenth century that the standard of living kept going up. The Commercial Revolution, not unlike the Industrial Revolution, increased the distance between the very rich and the very poor, but on the whole tended to improve the lot even of those who were unable to rise above their class – to say nothing of the fact that by rushing agricultural surpluses to disaster areas it converted famines from recurrent into exceptional events.

Still, the greatest gift of the Commercial Revolution was the continuous creation of new opportunities for everyone to climb from one class to another. To be sure, there were sharp fluctuations and crises, which we would probably call business cycles if we could gather complete commercial statistics. But the increase of the population continued, and with it continued the expansion of the home market which created the opportunities. Apprentices became masters, successful craftsmen became entrepreneurs, new men made fortunes in commerce and money-lending, merchants and bankers enlarged their business. The middle class waxed more and more prosperous in a seemingly inexhaustible boom.

Expansion was also stimulated by a constant immigration from the country, where the population was also increasing and becoming more and more open to the influence of the city. A scholar has stated, perhaps with some exaggeration, that family names of the inhabitants of Italian cities in the twelfth and thirteenth centuries indicate a peasant origin for two-thirds of the number. Entire villages gradually lost to nearby towns all of their inhabitants, peasants and landowners. After a few generations the newcomers might gain a place among the leading families. The Cerchi who headed the White Guelfs in Dante's Florence came from the Sieve valley; the Manduel who ranked with the greatest merchants in Marseilles in the early thirteenth century came from a village near Nîmes. The larger part of the immigrants, however, settled among the lower class, supplying cheap manpower to the leading industries and manual work to harbours and agencies of transportation, or, at best, becoming shop-keepers and masters in the humbler crafts.

Capacity to absorb further members in the already existing urban business class rather than political advantages offered by towns determined the size of immigration. Although the Aragonese serf could gain personal freedom and citizenship by residing one year in a town of the kingdom, the growth of towns there was slow. In the fourteenth century serfdom was still widespread at the very doors of Gerona and even in the surroundings of Barcelona. In contrast to this, 'foul smelling villeins' swarmed to the Italian towns. Unlike the bourgeois of northern Europe, who invited immigration to build up the strength of the city, the Italian burgher usually felt strong enough to conquer the feudal class unassisted, and regulated immigration according to the needs of specific branches of trade. He destroyed the imperial palace within the city walls and the country castle of the lord. Then he transformed the serfs into free men – with no political rights – and told most of them to stay where they were and produce cheap and plentiful food for the city. His demands and often his personal interest in agriculture stimulated economic activities in the country, both by introducing improved methods to secure larger yields of staple foods and by intensifying the production of raw materials for industry, such as flax in Romagna, silk in the Lucchese territory, saffron in eastern Tuscany, wool in Abruzzi, metals in Sardinia, Elba and the Alpine region. The increased returns of the land in turn enabled the peasants to buy more products from the cities. Literary sources represent the northern and central Italian rustic as possessing few fineries, but sufficiently well provided with necessities. Money economy, which already in the early Middle Ages was not unknown in the Italian rural communities, by the fourteenth century was almost as prevalent in the country as in the cities. This minor 'agricultural revolution' also spread to southern Italy, Provence and Catalonia, but only to a less degree.

The Commercial Revolution itself penetrated the smaller centres. Notwithstanding the inadequate documentation of country life, we catch glimpses of merchants, shop-keepers and artisans of the main crafts even in the smallest towns. In fact, the availability of water or the proximity of mines caused some industries to move away from the main towns. Smiths and armourers of the mining valleys north of Bergamo and Brescia wrought masterpieces which were sold by city wholesalers, the limpid streams around Fabriano enabled that tiny city to become the world's greatest centre for the production of paper, and artistic industries began to flourish in several townlets, some of which are still famous today. The fulling mills and almost all ship-yards were not located in the main cities. A third-rate Ligurian seaport, Noli, in the thirteenth century had local 'patricians', merchants, bankers, ship-owners, drapers, carders, weavers, fullers, dyers, furriers, farriers – all this notwithstanding the wretched conditions of the communications with the hinterland, which caused Dante to seek in the trail to Noli a term of comparison for the superhuman difficulties he met in climbing the mountain of Purgatory. Similar pictures can be drawn for many minor centres in northern and central Italy, Dalmatia and Provence, and for several in the other Mediterranean countries.

Inland in Languedoc and Gascony where old cities were few, some of the new agricultural settlements (*bastides*) assumed the functions of towns. In the early fourteenth century the Bonis brothers, merchants and bankers in the *bastide* of Montauban, carried on a trade worthy of many a large city business man and kept one of the best books of accounting that have come down to us from non-Italian areas before 1500. A number of new trading centres also sprouted up from the open fields and the rugged coastlines of Sardinia and Corsica, sometimes from an outgrowth of Genoese or Pisan *castelli*. But in the larger part of Italy, Provence and Catalonia, the old cities were too many and too strong to tolerate the growth of new rivals. In the Po valley Alessandria, founded by the Lombard League as a bulwark against Frederic Barbarossa, was the only notable addition to the galaxy of large towns of Roman origin.

The inevitable direction of the Commercial Revolution was through urban to metropolitan economy. The process, however, was far from complete even in Italy. As soon as they had completed the conquest of their own agricultural district, the Italian Communes engaged in competition with one another, for primacy or simply for breathing space, since chances for expansion were great but not unlimited.

Weapons of the struggle included embargoes, piracy, destruction of harbours, discriminatory tariffs, and the construction of new routes to displace old highways and canals. Eventually some cities emerged on top and increased their lead by leaps and bounds, whereas others – including glorious towns such as Pavia, Ferrara, Ravenna, Siena and Pisa – had to resign themselves to second rank. Other towns hopelessly trailed. But even the smallest cities usually retained some degree of autonomy and served as markets for the surrounding countryside, as stations along ways of communication and as homes of some highly specialised industrial skill. Therefore they continued to grow absolutely, while steadily losing men and capital to the larger cities. We must not imagine the smaller centres as cut off from the main commercial currents. In medieval Italy international trade always remained comparatively more important than local trade. The very smallness of the territory of most communes made it impossible for them to live as self-sufficient units, even though they tried to maintain a well-rounded economy by a series of measures which we may call 'pre-mercantilistic'.

When drawing a distinction between urban and metropolitan economy, we must consider the intensity rather than the extension of commerce. Not only the 'metropolitan towns' but also many minor cities drew their food from distant areas, exported their wares to all directions of the compass, played host to colonies of business men from other towns and sent colonies radiating through Europe and the Mediterranean. What especially singled out a 'metropolis' was the all-embracing influence of trade, so powerful that it dwarfed all other activities within the city. It was not the number of the inhabitants but their spirit that made the difference. While Paris, the largest city in Catholic Europe and the capital of a great kingdom, was not a business metropolis, one needs only to thumb through the cartularies (books of minutes) of the Genoese notaries of the thirteenth century to see how high ran the fever of commercial profit in that 'metropolis'. Men and women, widows and spinsters, adolescents and octogenarians, noblemen and servants, landed proprietors and artisans, laymen and priests, all alike engaged directly or indirectly in business. Practically every citizen had a stake in the galleys, the trains of pack animals, the fairs or the colonies and had investments with the bankers, the craftsmen or in the market of government bonds – be it a matter of many thousand pounds or only a few pence. Those who had nothing to invest contributed their labour and expected their reward from commercial operations.

Outside northern and central Italy, the picture was different. Cities grew more slowly and could not attain or maintain full independence.

While all political energies of free communes were directed to the support of economic expansion, feudal lords and monarchs often neglected the best interests of the cities under their rule in order to pursue political ambitions or to increase their income. But there were some rulers who adopted vaguely 'pre-mercantilistic' policies and employed feudal forces and income drawn from the agricultural hinterland on behalf of trade. Robert Guiscard and Roger II were pioneers in this practice. Under their rule the Italo-Byzantine seaports of southern Italy and the cities of Muslim Sicily underwent the difficult conversion from outposts of oriental trade to outlets of the new territorial kingdom. They managed fairly well. Agriculture flourished, industry was encouraged and there was a brilliant, if fleeting, beginning of oversea expansion. Before the end of the twelfth century, however, a series of invasions and internal disorders ushered in a decline, which also depended on the comparative poverty of the soil of southern Italy. To establish their power and to wage megalomaniac wars the kings imposed heavier taxes and became increasingly dependent upon Genoese, Pisan and Florentine seamen, merchants and financiers. Little by little the native merchants were confined to local trade, while northern and central Italians gained the control of international commerce and took from Sicily, Apulia and Campania more grain than these regions could safely export. Desultory measures of Hohenstaufen and Angevin sovereigns aimed at restoring the economy of the realm were either too little or too late. Even Frederick II, whose economic policy was intelligently planned, dealt a serious blow to agriculture by encouraging the spread of transhumance. Notwithstanding the splendour of the capital cities, Palermo and Naples, and the prosperity of such seaports as Messina and Trani, there were unmistakable marks of decline apparent by the mid-thirteenth century. The war of the Vespers (1282–1302) split the kingdom into two and made the decadence of the South incurable. The population nevertheless continued to grow, but this growth was not accompanied by a proportional increase of production and it could only lead to pauperism.

At the same period, the larger part of Provence and Languedoc, having fallen under Capetian or Angevin rule, had come to the end of a period of commercial growth which nearly matched that of Italy. The meagre sources of the tenth and eleventh centuries point to Arles as Provence's leading city. Prominent in late Roman times, but engulfed in the general depression of the early Middle Ages, it got a second wind as the capital and namesake of a post-Carolingian splinter kingdom embracing most of south-eastern France. The absorption of that kingdom into Conrad II's empire and the subsequent feudal disintegration did not arrest the economic progress of the city, whose commanding position on the lower Rhone remained an asset as long as the sea-coast was exposed to Muslim raids and internal trade flowed mostly through waterways. In the early twelfth century Arles was, with Pisa and Genoa, one of the three cities to which the bishop of Compostela turned for naval help against the Muslims; by the thirteenth, it had become a self-governing Commune but had lost its primacy. Marseilles, with the best harbour on the sea shore, had taken the lead and beamed with municipal pride. At its zenith around 1250 its overseas commerce, which reached as far as the Levant but was centred in the western Mediterranean, may have equalled that of Pisa though not those of Genoa and Venice. Then Charles of Anjou subdued Marseilles as well as Arles, Grasse, Nice and other thriving Provençal cities, and harmed their international relations by involving them in his ill-fated naval wars. Local trade, however, continued briskly. Narbonne and other Languedocian centres were less fortunate: their early growth was checked at the very peak of the Commercial Revolution, first by the disasters of the Albigensian crusade, then by the Capetians' efforts to divert all trade to Aigues-Mortes, a port built by St Louis on the malaria-ridden delta of the Rhone, and the fairs of Nîmes, established by Philip III. Narbonne rapidly decayed; by 1320 its harbour was completely silted up. Aigues-Mortes survived, but its trade was mostly carried out by Genoese and Florentine merchants.

The decline of the old Provençal and Languedocian seaports made the fortune of a new one, Montpellier, whose beginnings in the early twelfth century had been handicapped by an agreement between its lord and Genoa to limit its trade beyond local waters, but which breathed more freely under the protection of the kings of Aragon and Majorca in the fourteenth. Local trade and relations with Spain also helped the more modest development of Toulouse; but the rise of the Catalan star in the thirteenth and fourteenth centuries left little room for competitors in the long-distance trade of that region. Barcelona's trade, fairly significant in the late tenth century, grew concurrently with the power of the monarchs, who used the city as a counterpoise to the feudal nobility. At first they merely showed some interest in textile workshops and very little in commerce. But under King Jayme I of Aragon (1243–76) and his successors, the entire resources of the kingdom were mobilised for expansion overland and oversea. Catalan merchants were granted privileges throughout the new conquests, and royal ambassadors secured franchises for them far beyond the frontiers of the realm. Thus it was that Barcelona, latest of the Mediterranean harbours to come to prominence, 'every day must be enlarged because of the many ships coming to it', as King Jayme stated with pride. At the beginning of the fourteenth century the Catalans were the most formidable competitors of the Genoese and the Venetians and wrested from Pisa most of what Genoa had left to that unfortunate city after crushing its fleet at Meloria (1284).

Yet even Catalonia was far from approaching the commercial importance of northern and central Italy. Perhaps the best indication of the incomplete development of a native business class in Spain, France and southern Italy is the position which Jewish money-dealers and merchants continued to occupy in spite of severe legal restrictions and sometimes of pogroms. In Marseilles, for instance, no more than four Jewish merchants were allowed to embark in any one ship, and none at all were admitted to vessels bound for Alexandria. Yet notarial contracts of Marseilles prove that the Jews were successful in overseas trade and farmed out or purchased large shares of the taxes levied upon navigation and industry. In the Aragonese kingdom, where mob attacks were not infrequent, the Jews were still more numerous and influential. In contrast to this, in northern and central Italy they were almost unmolested, but their economic power was slight.

The difference of development between Italy and other countries can also be measured by comparing the sizes of their towns. The earliest reliable data upon which a comparison can be based are censuses of homesteads taken in the first half of the fourteenth century just before the Black Death suddenly interrupted the rising trend which had continued for some four hundred years. Different historians have variously interpreted the census figures by checking them against other contemporary documents, but even though there may be some doubt about the absolute figures the proportion between different towns can be accurately calculated. According to what seem to be the best estimates the population of Catalonia before the Black Death was roughly 600,000, or 42–3 inhabitants per square mile (Beloch; perhaps the figure is a little too low). The fertile kingdom of France had 16 to 17 million inhabitants in 1328, more than 100 per square mile (Lot, Marc Bloch). At the same period the mountainous kingdom of Naples had roughly the same density with a total of 3,300,000 inhabitants (Egidi, Beloch). The territory of Florence in 1328 had at least 330,000 inhabitants, or more than 200 per square mile (Barbagallo, Beloch). The density was still higher in central Lombardy. The dominant fact, however, was the size of the cities – even though the proportion of citizens engaged in trade was not the same everywhere. Both Milan and Venice had close to 200,000 inhabitants (Barbagallo, Luzzatto); Florence, Genoa, and perhaps Palermo and Naples, had some 100,000 inhabitants (Luzzatto, Doren, Carli) and a number of minor Italian cities had several tens of thousands. These figures, while low in themselves, are impressive if we consider that outside Italy only Paris surpassed 100,000, Narbonne had about 30,000 (Port) and Arras, one of the major centres of northern trade, barely surpassed 20,000 (Lestocquoy).

(B) *Expansion Overseas*

The Italian ascendancy in the Commercial Revolution was foreshadowed by the many facts we have already noticed in the early Middle Ages – the rise of Italo-Byzantine merchants as middlemen between Catholic Europe and the Muslim and Byzantine world, the wealth of the Italo-Lombard landowning *negotiatores*, and the diffusion of *commenda* and commission contracts among the former, of interest-bearing loans among the latter. When the hour came, the men were ready. The numerical increase of both the producers and the consumers kept adding momentum to trade.

But this explanation is only part of the truth. Venice in the later Middle Ages reaped larger profits in the fields which she had harvested for centuries before, but the Italo-Byzantine cities of the South saw their prosperity wither away in the midst of the general boom. Pavia, the Lombard capital, became a centre of third rate, while Milan, her smaller rival, grew into a metropolis. Cities like Genoa and Florence, which had been almost insignificant in the early Middle Ages, later jumped to the forefront. We must regard the incessant increase of the Italian population as a strain as well as a stimulus. The French at home found ample territory in which to settle the overflow of their people; the Spaniards spread over land seized in the *Reconquista*; the Germans colonised the East. But in Italy, so far as one can tell from inadequate evidence, most of the marginal lands were taken up at an early period. Very few *castelli* were built after the twelfth century, and new tracts of land were reclaimed only through costly irrigation or reckless deforestation. Agricultural methods improved, but climatic conditions limited the development of the three-field system. If some provinces of southern Italy exported grain, it was because the peasants lived on chestnuts and fruit – as many of them still do today. With the possible exception of Milan all the larger cities in northern and central Italy had to import foodstuffs from distant countries. Apart from Corsica and Sardinia, there was no near frontier open to emigration. Yet, on the whole, northern and central Italy were not only the most densely populated but also the wealthiest regions in Europe. Commerce was the frontier of the Italians.

Italian participation in the Catholic counter-offensive extending from the late tenth to the early fourteenth century was a commercial frontier movement as well as a religious and military enterprise. Italy's maritime towns won absolute mastery of the sea and permanent trading posts across the Mediterranean by fighting for 'God, glory and gold', alone or in conjunction with feudal armies. They accumulated capital by looting the enemy, while extending loans and supplying ships to the crusading powers. They added to their customers the former crusader who had learned to enjoy the luxuries of the Orient and the crusader's friend who had heard his tales of wealth and wonder. War, however, was only one instrument of commercial expansion. The 'Iliad of the barons' was preceded, accompanied and overstepped by the Odyssey of the merchants. Often the individual initiative of daring unarmed pioneers accomplished more than much bloody fighting; so did diplomatic pressure and sometimes missionary work. Even where conquest opened the way, peace and collaboration with the former enemy were necessary to exploit the gains. A Muslim writer philosophically stated that 'the military men are busy in the wars, the peoples trade in peace, and the world belongs to whoever takes it'. A Catholic archbishop candidly declared that commerce with the Egyptians 'always yielded us advantages and honour'. Yet a vague feeling of uneasiness remained in the innermost conscience of the merchant who had dealings with the man of another faith, much as it persisted in the conscience of the business man who took 'usury', that is, commercial interest. In spite of the steady progress of toleration the religious and racial antagonism between Catholics and non-Catholics, kindled especially by zealots who had never been overseas, continued to the end a disturbing element in the conduct of international trade.

It was a series of military enterprises, harbingers of the general Catholic counter-offensive, that brought to commercial greatness two hitherto inconsiderable towns, Genoa and Pisa. Ever since the Lombard conquest, Genoa had little if any international commerce, and even Pisa in the tenth century was more an agricultural than a commercial centre. Their earliest raids can hardly have been aimed at 'opening the high sea' to Christian merchant ships, as some scholars have suggested, since Venetian, Amalfitan or Byzantine convoys had never ceased to sail the waters of the Mediterranean. At first the Pisans and the Genoese only intended to destroy nests of Muslim marauders who were laying waste their fields and occasionally attacking their cities. They had practically completed this task with the liquidation of the last Muslim forces in Corsica and Sardinia (1015–16), when they decided to continue their raids and rapidly extended them to the entire western Mediterranean. They also expanded their trade, and by 1065 we hear of Genoese commercial convoys in the Levant. In 1088,

Pisans, Genoese and a few southern Italians joined forces under papal sponsorship in what may truly be called the dress rehearsal of the Crusades. They stormed al-Mahdiyyah, the strongest Muslim base in North Africa, and after offering the city to the Norman king (who refused it) they returned it to its ruler on condition that he pay an indemnity and exempt Christian merchants from every toll. Genoa and Pisa had come of age. Before the middle of the twelfth century they outpaced all Italo-Byzantine seaports except Venice. By the end of that century Genoa had surpassed Pisa and overtaken Venice itself.

This extraordinary transformation must have been the result of successful commercial exploitation of seed capital, mostly derived from local agricultural and natural resources, and of credit liberally 'put to work', to use a medieval formula for profitable investment. How rapidly investments could grow we know from a few examples of the twelfth century. The accounts of three contracts of *societas* and *commenda*, drawn up in 1156–8, show that within three years a descendant of the Genoese viscounts trebled his original investment of £250.4 Gen. even without leaving his city. His travelling partner, a 'new man' who had started without capital, earned almost £150 Gen. as his share of the profits. At the same period a Venetian merchant and shipowner could amass a fortune even when paying from 43 to 50 per cent interest on his loans for overseas trade. There were thousands of similar ventures. The earliest surviving Genoese notarial book, including entries for part of the period 1154–64, records investments of more than £10,000 Gen. for Syria alone, and almost as much for Alexandria.

The Venetians had used as 'initial capital' the salt of their lagoon; the Genoese and the Pisans must have added war booty to their smaller assets, mainly agricultural surpluses. We know, for instance, that in 1101 the Genoese helped the Crusaders to capture and sack Caesarea, a Palestinian seaport. They reserved rich prizes for their officers and remunerated the shipowners with 15 per cent of the loot. They distributed the remainder among 8,000 sailors and soldiers, each receiving 48 *solidi* and two pounds of pepper. Thus each of them was transformed into a petty capitalist. An incentive to exploit this capital came three years later, when the king of Jerusalem further rewarded his allies with the grant of one-third of Caesarea and full exemption from tolls. Probably similar if smaller raids in the early eleventh century had given the Genoese and the Pisans a strong gusto for adventure, a clear realisation of the wealth of the Muslim world and the initial capital necessary to build up their fleets and to engage in trade. Then, as commerce multiplied the original investments, they shifted their attention from mere plundering to the acquisition of tariff reductions. Finally, they followed the example of the Italo-Byzantines in founding autonomous and permanent overseas settlements. This last step was a great turning point, because it meant that there was a continuous flow of trade in the Mediterranean at a time when in so large a part of Europe commerce was still carried out intermittently at the fairs.

The first Italian colonies were established in Constantinople, Antioch, Jerusalem and perhaps in some African ports in the eleventh century, many years *before* the First Crusade. They probably became permanent settlements merely as the result of the gradual obsolescence of Byzantine and Muslim restrictions on residence of alien merchants, but autonomy and tariff exemptions must have been derived from formal grants. Some of them certainly were not obtained by war or threats of war, but by peaceful agreement. During the twelfth and thirteenth centuries Venice, Genoa and Pisa built up extensive networks of trading posts all along the Mediterranean shores. 'So many are the Genoese, so scattered world wide – that they build other Genoas wherever they reside', said a vernacular poet of the thirteenth century. Other maritime centres of Italy, southern France, Catalonia and Dalmatia and even some inland cities of Lombardy and Tuscany also sent forth settlers overseas, but their commercial colonies were fewer and either too scattered or too localised to constitute a complete system. The process of colonisation reached its peak in the late thirteenth and early fourteenth centuries. By this time the Italian merchants had penetrated deeply into three continents, opened new routes and turned to colonial imperialism.

At first most settlements were small. They sometimes were crowded into one large building, the *fondaco* (from Arabic, *funduk*) or into a group of buildings where the merchants deposited their wares, paid their duties, transacted their business, prayed to their God, and lived according to their national law as administered by their own officers. They felt safer and freer, and the state which had granted the *fondaco* found it easier to supervise them. The same principles led Venice to establish a *fondaco* for the Germans; in turn, many southern German towns kept lodging-houses for foreign merchants to prevent these visitors from taking part in local trade. In the Mediterranean, the *fondaco* system continued to prevail for a long time only in north-west Africa, Muslim Spain and Egypt. As late as the fifteenth century all Catholic merchants in Alexandria had to spend the night in their *fondaci*, which were locked from the outside. In the Crusaders' states, however, trading posts from the beginning constituted entire sections of cities including small orchards and cultivated plots. In the Byzantine Empire the Italian colonies also rapidly spread over large areas. By the late twelfth century there were some 10,000 Venetian residents in Constantinople, and their number greatly increased after the Fourth Crusade. In the thirteenth and fourteenth centuries Italian communes, individual Italian 'colony builders' (we cannot say 'empire builders' because the size of the colonies was never very large) or Catalan military adventurers conquered or were granted wide domains including fields and sometimes mines operated by local serf or hired labour.

Nevertheless, the importance of a colony was not necessarily proportional to its size. More often it depended upon the resources of the commercial hinterland and the privileges enjoyed by the settlers. In fact, true settlers were the exception in the early colonial 'settlements'. The trading post served as an advanced operational base rather than as a self-contained unit. Most of the inhabitants were young men who went to a colony to gain experience and capital and then returned home. Others were travelling merchants who lingered in the colony a few months or a few years, so long as their business required. Even later, when a large number of merchants took root in the colonies and developed interests, aspirations and special characteristics of their own, they were as little sedentary as the merchants of their motherland. They collaborated with the latter not as commission agents but more frequently as independent business men who accepted short-term *commenda* partnerships, sea-loan contracts and letters of exchange.

It did not take long before the Italians and other Catholic Mediterranean merchants had reversed completely the relations between their country and the highly civilised, but weary Muslim and Byzantine worlds. The Italians controlled the sea and the largest fleets, and found in the Alps and the Apennines timber for countless new ships. In many of their colonies they had won total exemption from duties or at least considerable reductions, whereas local merchants still had to pay full tariffs. Their capital and commercial organisation, though still unimpressive at the beginning of the twelfth century, grew quickly in the hands of men who had intelligence, initiative and courage, the invisible and indispensable tools of every success. At the side of these business men were the free artisans and the seafaring freemen of the home territory. Back of them was a continent in full growth. No wonder that the Italians practically monopolised the freight and passenger traffic throughout the Mediterranean, and took from the Muslims and the Byzantines not only all the trans-Mediterranean trade but also an ever-increasing share of local business in North Africa and the Levant. Their expanding commercial, financial and shipping activity powerfully stimulated both the young European industries and the old industries of the Near East. The latter, however, often tended to decline after a first period of boom. Let us take a typical instance. In the twelfth and thirteenth centuries the Italians exported woollen cloth and some linen of Syrian manufacture. At first this exchange seems to have favoured the orientals, whose products were perhaps less abundant but more expensive. Gradually the Italians with their growing demands induced the Syrians to shift to mass production, not without some sacrifice of quality and variety. At the same time they constantly increased their exports of French, Flemish and Lombard cloth to the Levant. Meanwhile Italian silk manufacturers so successfully imitated and improved oriental patterns, that they eventually became the main suppliers of Europe. Moreover, by the fourteenth or fifteenth century silk fabrics made in Italy even competed with oriental silks in the Levant itself.

Yet if one could reconstruct the trade balance of Europe with the rest of the world in the twelfth and early thirteenth centuries one might still find that Europe was not in a creditor position. To be sure, the excess of exports over imports in trade with the immediate hinterland of the colonies continued to grow. So did the shipping and commercial profits which the Italians reaped when taking part in local business of the Muslim and Byzantine world. But these credits may not have entirely balanced the debts contracted by importing increasing quantities of spices, raw silk, furs and other products of farther Asia, Africa and north-eastern Europe. The land and sea routes leading from the colonies to these countries were open only to Muslim and Byzantine merchants. The Byzantine emperors barred foreign traders from the Black Sea, the sultans of Egypt claimed the monopoly of trade beyond the coastal zone and the rulers of North-West Africa, by a conspiracy of silence, kept the Italians from learning the whereabouts of gold mines in Darkest Africa. The latter was not a serious handicap, since North-West Africa's very unfavourable balance of payments forced the Muslim traders of the coast to deliver to the Italians substantial quantities of the Senegalese gold dust. This gold and that mined in southern Germany helped the Venetians, the Genoese and the Pisans to strike a balance in their dealings with the Egyptian and Byzantine intermediaries who monopolised the long-distance trade extending beyond Constantinople and beyond Alexandria, Cairo and the Red Sea.[1]

In the twelfth century the Venetians, the Genoese and the Pisans

[1] It would be interesting to carry the investigation one step further to discover in what way the Muslims settled their apparently unfavourable balance of trade with China, India and Africa. The fact seems to be that the balance was not really unfavourable. The Senegalese gold miners exchanged their precious dust for salt and copper, both of which were abundant in Muslim North Africa. India imported horses from Arabia and ivory from Muslim East Africa. China imported so many wares that it developed an increasingly unfavourable balance of trade which was settled by payment in cash. In the mid-eleventh century the annual import of ivory, pearls, aromatics, etc. was paid by the Chinese with more than 53,000 'units of count', and it rose to more than 500,000 'units of count' – almost ten times as much! – in 1175.

did not resent too much being exploited by the oriental monopolists, because they themselves had the monopoly of the European end of this trade. The very high prices paid by the ultimate consumers inside Catholic Europe allowed large profits for both groups of monopolists. But when the number of Italian buyers increased and when other Catholic merchants entered the competition, the first group of monopolists – the Muslims or the Byzantines – were able to raise their prices. Since the ultimate purchasers inside Europe could not absorb this rise, it was the Italians and, no doubt, their Provençal and Catalan competitors who had to absorb it by reducing their profits. In Genoa the price of pepper, which had been £4–5 Gen. in the mid-twelfth century, was raised only to slightly more than £6 Gen. a century later. Even this apparent increase was offset by the decline of the Genoese pound in metallic content and in purchasing power. The decline of the profits is indicated by a number of Genoese *commenda* contracts of the mid-thirteenth century. These contracts show net gains ranging from an exceptional 50 per cent, which was high, but not excessive considering the risks, to less than 9 per cent; some contracts even show a loss. Venetian documents indicate much the same trend. Expressions of resentment against the oriental monopolists grow more and more frequent in literary sources of that period.

Meanwhile the Muslim counter-offensive had rekindled the flickering fire of the crusades. Saladin had united inner Syria and Egypt and had all but hurled the crusaders into the sea. Even in its best days the kingdom of Jerusalem had been a mere toe-hold in the Levant. Its trade depended on friendly relations with inner Syria, and Syria itself was not as good a commercial basis as was Egypt. The new 'kingdom of Jerusalem' which was rebuilt by the Third Crusade was only a narrow coastal strip. It depended wholly upon the Italian navy for defence and subsistence. To preserve that strip, which did not even include the Holy City, the Italians had frequently to engage in war against Egypt–Syria. Reluctantly they had to enforce the papal decrees forbidding export of war materials to Egypt, even in peacetime – and hence had to export more gold to purchase spices. While the situation deteriorated in the Muslim Levant, in Constantinople the old friction between Byzantines and Westerners also increased. In the numerous conflicts that ensued the Italians probably were wrong as often as the Byzantines. But the Byzantine emperors went to the extreme of encouraging or tolerating mobs to plunder the quarters of the wealthy Italians in Constantinople and to kill some of the merchants. Maritime circles in Italy increasingly felt that only the conquest of both Egypt and the Byzantine Empire would solve at once the military and the commercial problem. Such conquests would furnish large supporting bases for the crusaders' states and would break the bottle-necks through which trickled the goods from the Black Sea and from the 'Indies'.

These hopes may have spurred the Venetians and a number of feudal lords, with the knowledge if not the explicit consent of the popes, to begin the Fourth Crusade as an expedition against the Byzantine emperor.[2] The Crusade was not fully successful because Asia Minor remained to the Greeks and hence no overland communication with Palestine was obtained. Victory in Europe, however, enriched the feudal armies with more land and more booty than had the First Crusade; it secured for Venice the most valuable islands in the Aegean and quarters in every important seaport, and it opened the Black Sea to the Latin merchants. The Greek upper class and whatever was left of the bourgeoisie were ruined; the lot of the humbler labourers and peasants probably underwent little change. Fifty-five years of Venetian commercial hegemony (1204–61) ended when the Genoese aided the Byzantine emperor in recovering Constantinople, and thus followed the Venetians in being the privileged exploiters of the Empire. As a Byzantine historian sadly noted, 'the Latins incessantly increased their profits and their power on sea, while the Greeks were growing weaker and weaker.' In the early fourteenth century the Genoese suburb of Pera had a trade worth approximately fifteen times more than that of the Byzantine capital. Constantinople itself was thronged by merchants of the minor Catholic centres. Marseilles, Montpellier, Narbonne, Barcelona, Ancona, Florence and Ragusa (Dubrovnik) established colonies in the capital and some merchants even came from Spain, England and Germany. The shores of the Black Sea were studded with Genoese and Venetian colonies. The Genoese easily granted colonial citizenship to Latins, Greeks, Armenians, Turks and Jews, but the Venetians' jealousy excluded all outsiders.

In 1218, fourteen years after the conquest of Constantinople, the conquest of Egypt was the aim of another crusade led by a papal legate and manned largely by citizens of the three major Italian seaports. Damietta, the second-best Egyptian harbour, fell. Western merchants at once deserted the seaports of the Holy Land to rush to Damietta. But the expedition proved a failure, and Damietta was lost. Later Frederick II tried to rebuild the kingdom of Jerusalem by making agreements with the Egyptians, but this attempt was sabotaged by the

[2] In my opinion, the interpretation of the Fourth Crusade as a last-minute diversion imposed by the Venetians is untenable. But even if it were accepted, one would have to consider that the original purpose of the crusaders – replacing, in an essential position for the war against the Muslims, a usurper with the imprisoned legitimate rulers – was not totally reprehensible. Only when the restored emperors were murdered by another usurper did the crusaders partition the Empire among themselves.

Pope. A second expedition against Egypt, led by St Louis, temporarily recaptured Daminetta, but it finally ended in disaster. Since Egypt could neither be conquered nor befriended, commercial and military common-sense advised evacuation of the Holy Land. Whatever defence was attempted in the following years was prompted chiefly by religious sentiments. As the final catastrophe approached, the traders gradually transferred their business to the island of Cyprus and the little Christian kingdom of Cilician Armenia. Therefore the fall of the last beach-heads in Syria in 1291 caused no sudden crisis. The only disaster suffered was caused by the Pope, who prohibited all trade with Egypt. These 'economic sanctions' bore more heavily upon Venice and Genoa since the Catalans utterly disregarded the embargo and gained a predominant position in Alexandria. Other Catalans captured Athens in 1311. Sicily had become Aragonese in 1282. All this constituted a threat for the Italians, but not yet a vital challenge, because the Catalan merchant class was still small.

The importance of Egypt, however, was greatly reduced by the most momentous event of the thirteenth century – the Mongolian conquest and unification of the larger part of Asia and southern Russia. The Muslim world never recovered completely from this terrible blow. Splendid cities were wiped out; their population was decimated. Yet to the western merchants, who had been spared the horrors of the Mongolian war, the subsequent Mongolian peace disclosed immense horizons. The heart of the eastern Muslim world; the depth of Russia and Turkestan; the lands of the Farther East where the largest cities, the widest rivers, the greatest plains and plateaus were found and where gun-powder, coal, paper money and printing were everyday objects – the fatherland of silk and the fountainhead of spices – all this lay open for everyone to reach.

As the immense empire of Chinghis Khan was transformed into a loose confederation of four wide khanates, the friendly attitude of the western khans of Persia and of Kipchak (South Russia) attracted to these countries large groups of Italian merchants. Laias, Trebizond, Caffa, Tana and other seaports of the Syrian and Cilician coast, of the Black Sea and of the Sea of Azov became the golden gates through which a hitherto barred continent was entered. Tabriz and Astrakhan became almost as familiar to the Genoese and the Venetians as was Constantinople in the twelfth century. Genoese pioneers sailed the Caspian Sea and the Persian Gulf on ships built in their colonies. Some merchants went much farther into the eastern khanates of Turkestan and China. Between 1260 and 1269 the father and the uncle of Marco Polo reached Peking by land. In 1275 young Marco was received by Kublai Khan. Before he returned by sea to describe in an immortal book the wonders of the 'Indies', many others had left for the Farther East. In 1291 the Vivaldi brothers of Genoa endeavoured to reach the Indies by sea, sailing 'west' from the Straits of Gibraltar. One wonders what turn the history of the world would have taken if they had succeeded, two centuries before Columbus and Vasco da Gama. They never came back. Their fate seemed to spur other Italians to take the land routes to Central Asia, India and China. By the early fourteenth century Pegolotti, the Florentine merchant and writer, stated that the route from the Crimea to Peking was 'quite safe'. Chinese silk now reached the English market through Genoese or Tuscan intermediaries; in Italy it sold for about three times its cost at first purchase in China, which was easily enough to yield a substantial profit, but not an exorbitant one in view of the investment of capital and time required for the long journey, especially as silk from the Caspian region was closer at hand and fetched a slightly higher price in Italy. This made it essential to build up the exports of European commodities that would bring profit on the eastbound leg of the trip; gems, live horses, mechanical clocks and fountains, fine linen and woollen cloth. By the 1340s, a balance had almost been reached. Scores of Genoese merchants and a smaller number of Venetian ones regularly invested large sums in trade to and from Central Asia, India and China; some of them established residences there, thus making the Far East a new and promising Italian frontier.

The wealth of eastern and far eastern trade seemed to dwarf the commercial opportunities in the western Mediterranean and beyond the Straits of Gibraltar. The precipitous decline of North African economy under the attacks of the nomads and of the desert transferred nearly all coastal trade to European merchants and shippers. These men brought industrial products from their continent and even oriental wares to Tunis, Bougie and Ceuta, and purchased wool, hides, wax, indigo, alum, coral and sometimes grain, but usually not oil, since Africa no longer had surpluses to sell. Both the investments and the returns were comparatively small. This tended to make Africa the refuge of declining merchant communities such as Pisa, Marseilles and Messina. To be sure, some Genoese and Venetians continued to come, but they would have been more interested in reaching the mysterious Palola, the medieval Eldorado, which, as we now know, was a Senegalese island between two rivers where negro gold washers exchanged their precious dust for a little salt, copper and other necessities. Palola could not be found, but the search for it led to considerable expansion. In the early fourteenth century we hear of a Genoese merchant living in Sijilmāsa, deep inside the Sahara, and of another Genoese discovering one of the Canaries and building a castle there. Italian ships now more frequently sailed along the Atlantic coast of Morocco. In the twelfth century their terminus usually was Saleh, but after 1250 it was displaced farther south to Safi.

The fact that the same merchants who sailed fearlessly through Gibraltar to Morocco still hesitated to turn northwards along the European coast of the Atlantic can only be explained by considering that commercial opportunities in the western Iberian states seemed too modest to warrant the effort, while the Atlantic coasts of France and northern Europe could be reached faster by an overland shortcut. No doubt the complex, if meagre, long-distance trade of Castile and Navarre, entrusted to local merchants and ships, fed many small seaports on the northern shore from Bayonne to Corunna; iron mines and other local resources helped the Biscayan and Cantabrian towns to gain some prosperity. But the slow and destructive pace of the *reconquista* up to 1233 tended to stifle rather than to promote the economic development. The rapid conquest of Andalusia and Murcia, however, marked a turning point. Castile, through her new southern outlets, breathed more freely the air of the Mediterranean and of the Atlantic. Merchants from Genoa, Piacenza, Pisa, Lucca, Como and Marseilles flocked to Seville which had become Castilian in 1248, and met there Portuguese, English, French and German merchants. Special streets and a new *barrio* (suburb) were set apart for the privileged foreign traders. The export of Castilian wool, leather, alum and mercury mounted to new heights. The import of cloth and luxury goods also stepped up.

By 1277, if not earlier, a new advance was made. Genoese galleys began to sail via Cadiz and Seville to France, Flanders and England. Their lofty hulls dwarfed the northern ships in the ports of La Rochelle, Calais, Southampton and London, and were joined by Majorcan galleys. Lastly, the Mediterranean merchants successfully experimented with large and strong sailships, the carracks, which could reduce the detour involved by calling at intermediate ports all along the coast and steer straight to the northernmost destination of France and England. Spices, alum, grain, wine and other wares from the Mediterranean area and the Far East were exchanged for Flemish cloth, English wool and other wares. Some merchants made important remittances in cash to stimulate their promising business. Before the mid-fourteenth century England and Flanders had become regular destinations of one of the yearly convoys which both Genoa and Venice sent out with fixed schedules. No attempt was made by the Mediterranean merchants to extend their voyages to the Baltic, where they would have had to compete with the Hanseatic merchants. This competition might not have been a forbidding obstacle for the Italians, but neither the fish of the northern seas nor the grain of the Baltic attracted sailors who had access to the fish and the grain of South Russia. Newcastle and Sluys, the seaport of Bruges, were the farthest harbours where their galleys could profitably sail.

The returns of taxes derived from Genoese sea trade reflect the effect of oversea expansion in its latest and most sweeping phase. They indicate a more than fourfold increase from 1274 to 1293. In the latter year the incoming and outgoing wares subject to tax in the Genoese harbour were valued at £3,822,000 Gen. This figure, which does not include tax-free trade by sea or the important trade by land routes, is not very large in itself, even if we consider that at this period a bushel of grain cost in Genoa 3 to 5 *solidi*, a good ox £4 Gen., a piece of Flemish cloth from £6 to £14 Gen., and a Genoese sword with a curved handle 9 pence. But the sum indicated seems to be roughly seven times as high as the income of the French monarchy under Philip Augustus, and almost ten times as high as the exports by sea from Lübeck in Lübeck's peak year, 1368.[3] It must be noted that soon after 1293 Genoa's commercial progress was particularly hindered by civil wars. The tax returns of 1334 indicate a trade of only £1,806,000 Gen. In the same year, however, tax returns of Pera registered a movement of wares by sea valued at £1,648,000 Gen. Thirty years later similar documents place the sea trade of the Genoese colony in Alexandria at about one million pounds. The 'other Genoas' praised by the vernacular poet had grown to a size approaching that of the motherland itself.

(C) *Expansion Overland*

A contour map of the expansion of overseas trade is easily drawn by concentrating on the dominant seaports: smaller harbours tend to use the same basic routes and to carry the same fundamental commodities, although not as many and not as far. The expansion of overland trade lacks unity: it scatters out in every direction, involves the greatest variety of goods, and offers sufficient though not equal opportunities to centres of any size. The areas of salt trade around Hyères, Ibiza, Setubal and La Rochelle, those of wine trade around Gascony, the

[3] The comparison is based upon metallic contents according to the estimates of Desimoni (Genoese gold pound), Schaube (Parisian silver penny) and Grautoff (mark of Lübeck), and upon the assumption that a 10:1 ratio between gold and silver was prevalent during the thirteenth and fourteenth centuries. It does not take into account fluctuations in this ratio, differences caused by the simultaneous use in each place of various coins of different metals and alloys, variations in the purchasing power of the metals, and the other elements of error which make an accurate comparison impossible. It seemed useful to express roughly by figures the magnitude of Mediterranean trade as compared with other economic data. The writer, however, is fully aware of the basic inexactitude of comparisons between different times, places and moneys.

Rhone valley and Calabria, those of lumber, metals, dyestuffs, textiles of varying quality expanded each in its own way. So did credit: the most powerful and enterprising 'companies' of merchant bankers were built by Italians and, to a smaller extent, Languedocians from Cahors and Figeac, but they did not penetrate the underdeveloped and remote parts of Europe as fully and deeply as did the Jewish moneylenders, obliged by their insecure status to look for backward markets where Gentile competition would be smallest. Virtually all trading centres of the European South sent some people to the huge Champagne fairs, but other fairs of regional rather than international importance attracted a significant number of merchants from distant towns, colonies of Spanish and Portuguese traders eventually were formed in Flanders and Holland, and their fellow-citizens visited English centres. To track down these and other commercial connections, however, would take much space and drown the outline in details; besides, documents are inadequate in most cases. Though the Italians, whose movements are better known, did not dominate overland trade as much as they did overseas trade, they spread more widely and emerged more often on top. It seems proper, hence, to concentrate once more on them.

While the appearance of Italians in China and in the Sahara was in a way the outgrowth of a process begun in the early Middle Ages, their penetration inside Europe was substantially a new trend. In the tenth century as a rule it was northern merchants who went to Italy or southern France to exchange their wares with those of the Mediterranean world. In the later Middle Ages, however, Italians crossing the Alps gradually surpassed in numbers and importance the Northerners who visited the Mediterranean countries or who settled there. As early as 1034 we hear of merchants from Asti going to France through the Cenis. Forty years later, Pope Gregory VII assailed the king of France because the latter had seized 'infinite sums' from Italians visiting his fairs (St Denis?). In the twelfth century the fairs of Champagne, situated roughly two-thirds of the distance from the Mediterranean to the North Sea by the shortest land route, became the main meeting place between northern and southern merchants. The importance of these fairs continued to grow in the thirteenth century, and was not seriously threatened by the beginning of Italian voyages in the Atlantic, but it sharply declined after the first ten or twenty years of the fourteenth century. Long before that period, however, Italian business men had also established relations with other fairs and had settled in nearly every important city of France, Flanders and England. Smaller groups went to Germany, Hungary and Poland. Up to the late twelfth century northern Italians, especially from Asti,

Piacenza, Milan and Cremona, probably outnumbered the Tuscans and the Romans. In the thirteenth century the Tuscans took the lead. First Siena, then Florence, held the most prominent place, while Lucca maintained herself in the third place and Pistoia followed closely. Of maritime cities only Genoa contributed substantially to this emigration, but all of the major inland centres and even small towns such as San Gimignano witnessed the sorrow of the wives 'deserted in their couch because of France', as Dante bitterly complained. It is true that until the late thirteenth century this exodus, like that of the overseas colonies, had most frequently a purely temporary character.

The Italian diaspora of *Oltremonte* (beyond the Alps) was numerically smaller than that of *Oltremare* (across the sea), but its activities were so various that they defy summary description. Emigrants exercised one or several of the following professions: mercenary bowmen, sailors, shipwrights, captains of merchant ships and fleet admirals; textile manufacturers, mining entrepreneurs, lessees of mints; importers of Italian and oriental wares and exporters of cloth, linen and wool; staple traders in grain, wine and salt; pawnbrokers serving the lower class, moneylenders and supply agents serving the upper bourgeoisie, the great ecclesiastics and lay vassals and the monarchs; farmers of customs, tax collectors and bankers in the service of the Pope and the kings of France and England. Their status could be as high as that of the Florentine Franzesi brothers ('Mouche' and 'Biche') who became the revenue agents and financial wizards of Philip the Fair until the king sacrificed them to the wrath of the people who had been hit by an inflation. It could be as exalted as that of the Genoese Antonio Pessagno, who under Edward II was 'king's merchant', purveyor of the wardrobe, farmer of the Cornwall mines, seneschal of Gascony and founder of a *bastide* which he called Genoa, while his brother Leonard was Portugal's admiral-in-chief and obtained fiefs in that country. But it could also be as low as that of the moneylenders from Chieri, a little town near Turin, who competed with the Jews for the monopoly of petty usury in various towns of the North, where the legal rate of interest was higher than that allowed in their country. Again, an Italian in *Oltremonte* could be a member of a great *tavola* or *compagnia* of merchant-bankers, a great business man alternating trips to the Champagne fairs with voyages to the Levant, a transport agent (*vecturalis*) carrying goods for both Italian and northern international traders, a lone adventurer with little baggage of his own, or a prominent political emigré trying to make a living until his party regained control of his home city. Merchants from Gascony and Toulouse kept in their hands most of the export trade in French wines to Flanders and England, but in all other branches of international trade the Italians far surpassed the other southern groups in wealth, number and versatility.

Various as were the interests and the background of these Italians, their fortunes very frequently were allied directly or indirectly to the international influence of their most powerful fellow-citizen, the Pope. It was probably not an accident that the second earliest evidence concerning Italians at the French fairs comes from letters of the great Gregory VII on their behalf. Pontifical credentials opened many doors to the Italians, and other valuable connections resulted from each of the Crusades, often as a by-product of financial and shipping services rendered to crusading clergymen, knights and princes. Finally the Popes entrusted the great Tuscan companies with the transmission to Italy of ecclesiastical tithes collected throughout Europe. It was as papal agents that the employees of the Lucchese Scorcialupi company went as far as Greenland, where the tribute was paid in 'sealskins, whalebone and sinews of whales'. The money that was collected could seldom be reinvested in trade, because the Curia needed the cash promptly. But the Italians took a commission and benefited from the ready cash available throughout Europe. They also carried out commercial operations in behalf of the Pope. On 10 April 1336 the Avignon branch of the Florentine Acciaioli company received an urgent order to ship grain to the poor Armenians. It transmitted the order to the branches in Naples and Bari. By the end of the month more than 7,000 tons of grain had been purchased and the ships were ready to forward the relief to the Christian outpost in the Orient. Thus, paradoxically enough, one of the greatest vehicles of the papal charitable activities and of the moral and political supremacy of the Pope over the national monarchies was the experience of the Italian international business men and *campsores* who had flouted the canons against usury ever since the early Middle Ages. This 'sinful' activity placed at the disposal of the Pope, in the Pope's own country, the best organised group of financiers in the world. Similarly the old trade of Venice, Genoa and Pisa with the infidel and the schismatic had supplied the information, the ships and the money without which the Popes could never have planned the Crusades.

This association with the Roman Church was not an unmixed blessing for the Italians. It induced them to venture deep into the Catholic kingdoms where their navy could not protect them and where they enjoyed no self-government and often paid heavier duties than the local merchants. It also encouraged their natural tendency to couple extremely dangerous and hated lending activities with the healthier practice of international trade. The favours of temporal rulers had the same result. To be sure, many Italian companies did not succumb to the temptation of the high interest promised by loans and clung to strictly commercial activities. Even those companies most deeply committed to banking never abandoned the practice of trade, and indeed they constantly used loans to public authorities as a trump card to obtain commercial favours. Such favours met with no local opposition in regions economically strong. The great manufacturing communities of Flanders and Brabant and the wealthy merchants of the North who frequented the great fairs did not fear the Italian merchants, who bought from them much cloth and linen in exchange for spices, silk and useful dyestuffs. But in the larger part of France and England not only the sellers of oriental commodities, but also the Florentine and Milanese buyers of wool aroused the antagonism of the petty local craftsmen and wool merchants by outbidding them. King's officers and local authorities adopted all sorts of protectionistic measures to hinder the encroachment of the foreigner upon the citizen's preserve.

The benevolence of French and English kings often shielded the Italians, much as it had protected the Jews. But it was a precarious protection, which could at any moment be displaced by hostility and by decrees of confiscation or expulsion. Arbitrary seizures of wares already paid for, failures to pay ecclesiastical dues for which advances had been made to the Pope, and sometimes unilateral repudiations of debts rendered the risks of the Tuscan merchant-bankers in Catholic countries still greater than those of Mediterranean traders voyaging on stormy seas and doing business with Muslims and Greeks. All the ponderous companies which sprang up in the thirteenth and early fourteenth centuries from fortunes made partly through interest-bearing loans ultimately went bankrupt. Their collapse involved in ruin partners and depositors alike. Yet the crash of a bank did not destroy all the wealth that had been created. Some partners had succeeded in hiding part of their profits. Moreover, the raw materials a *compagnia* had imported had given employment to hundreds of craftsmen at home. Finally, much credit had been created – and credit was precious at a time when gold was scarce and trade was booming.

Southern Germany was the only important producer of gold in Europe. Was it partly because of this that it was far less affected than France or England by the Italian penetration? Was it rather because of the smallness of commerce and exclusiveness of commercial legislation in the southern German cities? Provisions to put foreign merchants at a disadvantage and to enforce equality among local merchants seem to have been stricter than anywhere else in southern Europe. The results of this policy can be observed in the exceptionally small size of the towns up to the fourteenth century, and in the gradual shrinking of the commercial horizon. The old supply line from the Levant through the Danube or Bohemia lost its importance. Though in the twelfth century we still hear of Ratisbonians in Kiev and of Germans in the Levant, in the thirteenth even the merchants of Prague depended on the Venetians for the supply of spices. Furthermore, the northern German city of Cologne expanded its trade into southern Germany and took from Ratisbon part of the Danubian commerce.

Some progress, however, was made in local trade and in the textile and iron industries. Danubian trade, though no longer prominent in world economy, continued to grow absolutely: it has been estimated that about 15,000 tons of merchandise went through the customs office of Linz in 1295. Vienna, Passau, Ratisbon, Nuremberg, Ulm, Constance, Schaffhausen and other cities attained a modest prosperity. Their merchants kept in their hands most of the trade of southern Germany with Italy; they went to Venice, Verona, Trento, Milan or Genoa to export their metals, timber and linen and to fetch eastern goods and many other wares. Their activity, humble as it was, held a promise which was later to be fulfilled by the tremendous growth of Nuremberg and Augsburg. Up to the mid-fourteenth century, however, southern Germany was rather a neglected corner than a serious competitor within the immense Italian commercial empire.

(3) THE HEYDAY OF MEDIEVAL TRADE

The hundred years that preceded the outbreak of the Black Death epidemic offer the best chance for a survey of the Commercial Revolution's achievements and limitations. At long last, one finds documents in relative abundance, even for the less-developed parts of southern Catholic Europe. Some of them include fairly reliable quantitative data, too spotty for extrapolation and generalisation but valuable as random indicators of size. On the whole, the period (1245–1345) encompasses the high tide of four centuries of accelerated commercial growth. It also shows some tokens of attrition, especially towards its end – a series of bank failures between 1298 and 1345, intensified warfare and mounting taxation, creeping deforestation and soil exhaustion in some areas – but no apparent threat to continuing progress.[4] The very dynamic of growth generates at every step its shortages and imbalances, but mends itself by turning obstacles, finding new channels and improving its material and mental equipment.

[4] It is worth noting, however, that the great famine which scourged northwestern Europe in the early fourteenth century had no parallel in the South. Overpopulation and food deficiencies were old problems there, but merchants were prepared to import foodstuffs from surplus areas in times of need.

That is precisely what merchants keep doing down to 1345, enlarging their own scope and involving craftsmen and agriculturists in their operations; one can hardly expect them to worry more about future consequences of immediately bearable strains than did the makers of the Industrial Revolution of modern times. On the surface at least, the ups and downs of the period in question resemble the cycles of boom and bust that spiralled around the multi-secular trend of expansion in the industrial age. Indeed, in Genoa, whose rich documentation enables one to look further back than elsewhere, one such cycle has been postulated as early as the mid-twelfth century. Another cycle is well documented a century later. The favourable conjuncture of the years 1248–54 led to overexpansion of naval construction, textile production, commercial investment, credit and coinage; this was followed by bank failures and political unrest in 1255–62, after which a new and faster acceleration began. Still another cycle took place around 1300 (expansion, roughly from 1280 to 1298; contraction, approximately 1299–1320); the evidence has not been sufficiently studied, but it may support the hypothesis that whatever slow-down may have occurred before 1345, in Genoa and elsewhere, was no more than a periodical adjustment in the course of rapid development.

Without picking up the old debate of whether true capitalism existed in the Middle Ages (not so much an economic as a semantic problem), one can easily see many facets of the Commercial Revolution that anticipate to some extent the revolutions of the modern world: a steady accumulation of capital in money and in goods; a growing use of credit and a trend toward gradual separation of management from both ownership of the capital and manual labour; a constant endeavour to improve the methods of business and to compete with other business men in the same field; a planning of large-scale operations with a view to expanding the market; an elevation of trade interests to the importance of state affairs; and, above all, a desire for profits as a leading motive for commercial activity. On the other hand, these phenomena occurred on a far smaller scale, affected fewer persons, and were much less pronounced than they are in the modern world. Furthermore, the anti-capitalistic religious theories of the Middle Ages had probably more widespread acceptance than anti-capitalistic Marxist theories have today. It is also true that important features of modern capitalism such as the joint-stock corporation cannot be found in the Middle Ages.

Late medieval trade of Mediterranean Europe seems gigantic only in comparison to early medieval or ancient commerce. True, the circulation of capital and goods increased in geometrical progression as money, credit and the economy of exchange decisively triumphed over economic isolation. Yet the absolute volume of trade in the early fourteenth century was still small, not only because the entire population of Europe was nearer to 50 than to 100 million, but also because large areas probably remained almost impermeable to the new commercial currents and because the purchasing power of the lower class developed too slowly to permit the demand of the common man to weigh very heavily. Outside Italy trade depended chiefly upon the demand of the upper class. Two-thirds of the 445 clients of the Holzschuher company of Nuremberg in 1304–7 belonged to the nobility or the clergy, and the amount of their purchases far outweighed the transactions of the bourgeoisie. In Italy the purchases of the growing middle class probably surpassed in quantity and value those of the upper class. But even the bourgeoisie was a small minority of the population, and it usually was more interested in quality and durability than in quantity and cheapness. Around 1338 the historian of Florence, Giovanni Villani, who was an employee of the great Peruzzi company, rejoiced when he noted that the cloth production of his city had doubled in value owing to the adoption of better wool. He saw no harm in the fact that the increased price had caused the output to fall from 100,000 to 70–80,000 pieces yearly.

There seems to be no sound reason to doubt Villani's figures, although they have been challenged. They definitely indicate mass production. Yet if we consider that the woollen industry was the greatest exporting trade of Catholic Europe, that Florence in the fourteenth century was one of its main centres and that according to Villani no less than 30,000 Florentines drew their livelihood from it, the figures appear low to a modern reader. Certainly the larger part of the population in Europe used homespun cloth except perhaps on Sundays. If we turn from industrial products to staple foods, we shall come to similar conclusions. A few large cities and densely populated areas imported grain from distant countries, but the larger part of the inhabitants of southern Europe depended on local production except in years of famine.

The comparative smallness of trade was probably both the cause and the consequence of the inadequacy of the revolution in transport. To be sure, technical improvements continued to be made after the three epoch-making innovations – the horseshoe, the horse collar and the galley, all gifts of the eastern world to Catholic Europe – that had opened the way for the Commercial Revolution. In the later period the compass, astrolabe, *martelojo* and other nautical inventions facilitated long-distance navigation, while the French *pavé du Roi* with its rectangular slabs and the Lombard circular stones improved the surface of roads in muddy regions. But these and other improvements did little to add speed and power to the desperately slow and weak means of conveyance used ever since the eleventh or tenth century. There was nothing in the Commercial Revolution to parallel the successive injections of the railroad, the screw propeller, the internal combustion engine and the aeroplane into the arteries of the Industrial Revolution. Hence effort had to be concentrated on making the best use of the already existing means of conveyance, on multiplying and improving the ways of communication, and on organising a more efficient and intensive circulation. Great as was the progress in these directions, it could scarcely have had a revolutionary effect. Cheap bulky goods, in particular, could seldom stand the costs of transportation over a long distance, unless that distance was covered by water – preferably on the *naves*, slow sailing ships that cost one-third as much as the galleys while they carried four times as much freight, or on the canal barges towed by men or horses. With such means of conveyance little improvement could be made. As late as the sixteenth century the Milanese Chamber of Merchants decided that 18 days was still a reasonable time to cover the distance downstream from Milan to Venice, perhaps 200 miles, by its regular line of internal navigation. Let us recall that in 943, according to Liutprand of Cremona, a fast boat went in three days from Pavia to Venice, about the same distance.

The lack of good communications was not unconnected with the smallness of many states and the decentralisation of others, which in turn led to monetary chaos, to physical insecurity and to arbitrariness of the customs system. In these respects there was hardly any progress since the early Middle Ages. Some coins had wider circulation than others and were less debased, but no coin up to the mid-thirteenth century had a stable value or was accepted everywhere, except the Byzantine gold *hyperperon*. The resumption of independent gold coinage in the Italian Communes in the second half of the thirteenth century caused the *hyperperon* to be displaced by the *genoin*, the florin and the ducat in the international market, but it did not eliminate disorder in local coinage. Furthermore, municipal and national wars in the later Middle Ages may have been perhaps slightly less frequent than the feudal wars of the earlier period, but they affected larger areas and were directed very frequently at the methodical destruction of the economic resources of the enemy. On sea, war between the major Italian seaports was almost continuous. If a merchant desired a minimum of safety, he usually had to join a convoy or a caravan as he did in the early Middle Ages. No matter where he went, he had to face vexatious restrictions. Most states, for instance, did not permit export of gold or basic foodstuffs except in special cases. Tolls were high except where a special agreement reduced or lifted them on behalf of the merchants of a given town. Their collection placed the merchant at the mercy of customs officers, who might sometimes be bribed into undervaluing his wares, but who might also extort much more than was due. A ship while at sea obviously had no tolls to pay, but it was subject to the menace of storms. Upon his arrival a merchant might be arrested because a war had broken out after his departure, or because the local authorities had issued a 'reprisal' order against all citizens of a state of which one citizen had defrauded one of their subjects. Reprisals were so harmful to trade that they were imposed only as a last resort, but they could not be eliminated so long as the fatherland of the offender neglected to force him to refund the damage. Only Genoa in 1296 set up a special tribunal to hear claims against its own citizens. Moreover, the inhuman custom of seizing the goods of shipwrecked vessels survived even after it had been outlawed in all civilised countries. Charles I of Anjou in 1270 enforced this custom against his own fellow-crusaders. Finally in the Mongolian states and in the Muslim principality of Ormuz the goods of a merchant who died when travelling were seized.

These and other risks prevented the original commercial partnerships from developing into more flexible and powerful instruments to pool capitals. Traders who sailed overseas continued for centuries to use chiefly the *commenda* contract, which brought together *for a short term* a resident party who supplied capital but no management and a travelling party who supplied management but no capital. In practice, if not in theory, liability towards third parties was limited to the amount of the investment. The short duration of the *commenda* contract made it possible for each party to take a very circumscribed chance with the other even if mutual trust was less than perfect. Nothing prevented the same parties joining again and again, if the first experience had been satisfactory, in *commenda* contracts of the same kind. Still, the travelling (managing) party could never count on renewals; he had to conclude his transactions as soon as possible and to return to his home city or send back the funds to the lender. On the other hand, traders who went overland used chiefly the *compagnia* partnership, which associated for many years a large number of partners, who supplied both capital and management and were alternatively travelling or resident. Each of the partners was *unlimitedly liable* toward third parties for the debts of the entire company. This collective responsibility may have been originally a legacy of the time when the *compagnia* really was, as the name indicates, a non-commercial association of members of the same family eating the same bread and working for the increase of the common patrimony. But liability remained unlimited when the 'table-companions' became merchants often unrelated by blood, no doubt because third parties were averse to dealing with a member of a company unless all partners shared full responsibility with the latter. Consequently any partner could ruin completely the others by a poor speculation, and the risks increased with the number of new partners admitted to the company.[5]

The advantages which neither of the main commercial contracts combined – indeterminate duration and limited liability – existed in other forms of investment, especially in the public loans. A prudent investor would buy shares in one of the numerous loans floated by the greatest Communes. Shares could be kept as long as desired, or sold in the market, if possible when the quotation was high. Another conservative form of investment was real estate. Commerce could compete with the state and the estate only if it offered very large profits. But large profits could be obtained only by maintaining prices at a high level. High prices made it hard to sell to the common man and kept down the volume of trade. We have now apparently closed the vicious circle and we are back to the point from which we started.

The circle, however, was not really closed. All brakes to commercial development were loosened by the continuous thrust of the ever-expanding market which we have previously described. This expansion made progress possible – a slow progress if measured in terms of nineteenth-century dynamics, but a fast progress if considered from the point of its modest departure and geometric rate of increase. By stimulating consumption at one end and production at the other, the merchant–middleman–entrepreneur kept converting the luxury of yesterday into the treat of today and the common requirement of tomorrow. Our picture has been gloomy enough so far. Now let us review briefly the positive aspects of medieval trade at the time when the Commercial Revolution reached its zenith between the mid-thirteenth and the mid-fourteenth centuries. Small trade in the small towns probably is a better starting point for our survey than would-be big business in the metropolitan cities. We will recall that in the early Middle Ages local exchanges between village and village or trade between the town and its agricultural hinterland had been comparatively rarer than long-distance trade in luxury goods. Hence the progress of 'commercialisation' in rural or semi-rural areas was in a way a more revolutionary change than the growth of international commerce.

The fact that in the later centuries of the Middle Ages most peasants

[5] We cannot discuss here special clauses which improved some *commenda* and *compagnia* agreements, and other commercial contracts which had smaller importance or shorter popularity. Some of the latter had advantages which the more popular contracts lacked.

in Italy and many peasants elsewhere in southern Europe were able to pay their rents in cash is by itself a significant indication of 'commercialisation'. Unfortunately, however, we lack a clear picture of commercial activities in the countryside, not only because the attention of most scholars has been almost monopolised by the glamorous long-distance trade, but also because the purchases and sales by the peasants usually were carried out orally and have left no trace in the records. Only occasional entries in the books of town notaries show that the country dweller in many parts of Italy was thoroughly familiarised not only with money economy, but also with the simpler commercial contracts. In the region of Nice at the border between Italy and France, however, traces of barter were still noticeable in the late thirteenth century; a Piacenzan merchant when dealing with the farmers had to insist that they should pay 'in hard cash and not in kind, without giving or offering goods in payment'. Significantly enough, the general store and the sedentary shopkeeper or trader had appeared in a number of central and northern Italian villages, whereas the itinerant merchant was still paramount in France. But he was no longer a humble pedlar. His business had grown large enough for him to become worried at the intrusion of outside competitors. In the fourteenth century we first hear of a general gild of mercers in Provence, headed by a man bearing no less a title than *roi des merciers*. Before the mid-fifteenth century similar gilds had been organised in nearly all regions of France, from Champagne and Ile-de-France to Blois and the Dauphiné. That the members as a rule were itinerant we may infer from their care to be sure of lodgings wherever they went.

A visit to Maître Ugo Teralh, notary and draper at Forcalquier, will take us one step higher in the commercial hierarchy. His town consisted of a cluster of houses built on the slopes of a mountain dominating a dead-end valley of northern Provence. Neither the main trail from Avignon to Mont Genève nor the Durance, which was used by boats as far as Manosque, went through Forcalquier. The counts 'of Forcalquier' themselves, in fact, lived in Manosque. Today Forcalquier has about 2,500 inhabitants; how many did it have in the Middle Ages? Perhaps only a few hundred – no more than a manor's population. To these few and to the inhabitants of the nearby villages Maître Teralh sold cloth by the auln. He required those who bought on credit to enter their names in a primitive book of accounts he kept. In May 1331 there were 36 entries; some of them were in Hebrew, since many Jews traded and lent money in the smallest Provençal villages. The cloth came mostly from nearby Languedoc, but some had been manufactured in St Denis, Rouen and Provins. What could

Forcalquier offer in exchange? Probably the cattle of its lean prairies, the wild rabbits whose preservation was so important that the hunt was open only every second year, and possibly some timber. Its trade, small as it was, is significant for a region where even the toll of Aix – a much larger city – often made no collection in one entire day.

Now let us move to a slightly larger town, Bonifacio – another new beneficiary of trade, since it was founded only in 1195 by Genoese subjects on a rock overlooking the strait between Corsica and Sardinia. Among the early settlers of Corsican Bonifacio was a Ligurian Bonaparte. But we are not interested in him. We shall stop at the store of the late Armanno the currier, deceased in 1238. When an inventory of his goods was made, there were in stock 947 skins of goat, lamb, deer, stag, fox and marten, 14 whole pieces and two bundles of woollen cloth of unidentified provenance, 12 smaller cuts of woollen, 2½ pieces of silk, 60 pieces of burlap, one of fustian from Pontremoli (a tiny city in the northern Apennines), some wine, some pepper and other wares. Armanno had bought houses and had received in partnership £1507 Gen. from 26 small investors. He had died too early to see his town develop into a lively commercial centre, which long before its first centenary maintained relations with every important harbour of the western Mediterranean and with its own rugged hinterland on both sides of the strait. Since Bonifacio had practically no manufacturing of its own, its resources were chiefly salt, skins and cheese from the hinterland. Petty piracy offered a pleasant alternative to the routine of peaceful trade. In a regular commercial contract of 1287 we have an extreme example of the length to which the business spirit in Bonifacio sometimes went, when a 'lady' hired herself out as 'servant and mistress'.

Even without extending our inquiry to other secondary towns a little larger than Bonifacio and Forcalquier, we have been warned by these examples of the importance of small centres. Hundreds of Ugo Teralhs and Armannos perhaps purchased only a few thousand pieces of cloth, but they were the men that partly filled the gap left in medieval trade by the weakness of marketing organisation in the metropolis. The most enterprising provincial merchants some day would emigrate to the larger cities to become big business men. The others remained obscure but precious cogs in the exchange of cheap industrial products of the larger cities with the surplus agricultural production of the forgotten areas.

Other regions which were better provided with communications brought their surplus to the markets of middle-sized industrial cities. Of these markets we know very little – again, not only because sources are insufficient but also because few historians have regarded them worthy of attention. Many markets remained as unimportant as most of them were in the early Middle Ages, but others rapidly grew, and there were so many of them. One of the fairs of Parma, for instance, specialised in transactions in cloth and in cattle, two main articles of exchange between city and country, ever since 1126. Parma was comparatively unimportant in long-distance trade, but we know that it was a thriving city. Its rural market explains the origin of many of the resources that enabled the Parmans to buy expensive products in the commercial cities and to build their splendid cathedral. Nor was trade of this kind restricted to intermittent markets. It was carried on almost continuously in eight successive fairs of the secondary cities in the valley of the lower Po, where cheap bulky goods were shipped by river or canal. Throughout Italy, towns and their districts were commercially interdependent.

In Italy, Provence and Catalonia local trade underlay greater commercial currents, but in the larger part of central and western France – the core of the kingdom – it was paramount. There were many middle-sized towns and a densely settled free peasantry, but no business metropolitan cities and no great native merchants. Even in Paris two Italians, who in 1292 had a yearly taxable income of £5,625 and £4700 Par. respectively, far outdistanced the wealthiest Parisian bourgeois, Pierre Marcel, who had a taxable income of £2,900; then there were four Italians whose income was more than £2,500 each. Yet France was a thriving country. In Castile, in Portugal and in Aragon proper the same phenomenon took place. Towns had not lost their rural characteristics; many of them, in fact, still look rural today. When they were not exclusively administrative and military communities, they were usually centres of local exchange of low-grade industrial products for slightly below average agricultural staples. Yet throughout the Iberian peninsula we witness the progress of fairs and markets, including the daily market (*azogue*), where foodstuffs and coarse cloth were the main articles of exchange. In southern Germany the towns usually carried out some long-distance trade, but they lived mainly on production of fustian, cutlery and other products consumed chiefly in their agricultural districts. This may explain the large number of 'cities' under 1,000 inhabitants and the comparative affluence of petty merchants (*kramer*) in the larger towns, very few of which surpassed 10,000 inhabitants.

Then we must consider that specialised merchant staplers lived in many seaports and road hubs from Barletta or Manfredonia in Apulia to Casablanca or Arisla in Morocco and to Libourne or Bordeaux in Gascony, to mention only a few such places. They offered the travelling merchant of the commercial cities and the sedentary agent (*fattore*) of the great companies considerable amounts of their staple commons in return for heavy consignments of cheap Lombard or Languedocian fustian or for a handful of spices. Their business was so organised that they could patiently wait until the products of the countryside reached their stores after a slow trip in barges, on mules, or on the backs of peasants. More often than not they had purchased in advance the harvest of the next year, in spite of the ecclesiastical prohibition of dealing in futures. They knew as well as did big business men how to handle the local officers whose duty it was to forbid the export of certain staples and to levy heavy tolls upon other commodities. 'Do remember', says Pegolotti, 'that if you treat the customs officers with respect and give them something...they will always reckon your wares for less than they are worth.' He spoke of Constantinople, a great market of grain as well as of precious goods, but he could have said the same for Messina, La Rochelle or Sandwich.

It was by these procedures that the metropolitan towns obtained the larger part of the raw materials of industry and basic foodstuffs which their immediate hinterland could not supply. Some grain, wool and wine and nearly all silk, cotton and best colour dyes came from the Levant and Africa, but the most important supply areas of food and raw materials were in Europe itself. The needs of the larger cities were far from negligible. Villani's figures, which seem to be substantially accurate, reckon Florence's daily consumption of grain at more than 1,300 bushels. Almost two-thirds of it came from territories not subject to the city. The Florentines ate 4,000 oxen and calves, 80,000 lambs and 30,000 pigs a year. They drank 25 million quarts of wine, or about a gallon a week per man, woman and child. Both Milan and Venice consumed much more. While Milan's territory was exceptionally fertile, that of Venice was far less productive than that of Florence. Marseilles exported wine produced in its district but had to import grain. So did Barcelona. The kitchens of pontifical Avignon swept almost clean of meat on the hoof the entire area between the Rhone and the Alps. Loftier appetites of the urban population were satisfied by increasing purchases of objects of industrial art, such as ivories of Paris, enamels of Limoges, glass ware and mosaics of Venice.

The consumption of the raw materials of industry was particularly important, not only in the metropolitan cities but also in secondary towns. All sources of iron and timber in Italy were exploited, but this was not enough. The smiths of Lombardy and the shipbuilders of the Italian maritime cities imported their basic raw materials partly from Germany and France. Cotton came mostly from the Levant. Lucca imported yearly some 165,000 pounds of silk (chiefly of Turkestanian and Chinese origin) in the period 1337–40. This may seem a very low figure for the greatest centre of silk industry in Europe, but we must consider that in 1317 a revolution had forced many craftsmen into exile. In the fourteenth century the Lucchese used water power to speed up the output of their throwing mills. This was the greatest technical invention in the textile industry since the introduction of the pedal loom, which was already in use in the twelfth century, both in the Byzantine Empire and in Western Europe. To feed these looms the manufacturing cities usually had to import wool from distant regions, except perhaps the minor centres of Languedoc and central Spain which may have been supplied entirely by the production of wool of their immediate hinterland. In Italy nearly every region produced wool, but the Lombard towns, whose output of cloth was the largest though not the finest in southern Europe, imported additional quantities from France, North Africa and Syria. Choice Spanish wool supplied the greater part of the needs of the Florentine manufacturers up to the last years of the thirteenth century, when it was displaced by English wool. Even in 1273, when the vogue of this wool had hardly begun, 44 Italian merchants in England exported 8,000 sacks (about 1325 tons); but this amount was sufficient for the manufacture of only 24,000 pieces of cloth – a very small percentage of the total Italian production. In the following years the demand for English wool increased many fold, and imports from other countries also stepped up.

The expansion of the city market led to the development of groups of wealthy cloth sellers, spice sellers, mercers, grocers, butchers, bakers and other specialised merchants who bought wholesale and sold retail. Their permanent stores largely displaced the weekly market and the craftsman's workshops as channels for distribution to the public, at least in the larger Italian cities. In a smaller city, Pavia, benches in the four main squares continued to be more numerous than stores, but they also became a permanent feature of what we may call the shopping centre. In a commercial metropolis such as Genoa the store (*apotheca*, *bottega*) had eliminated the bench at least by the mid-twelfth century. No article was either too precious or too humble to be offered for sale in large lots. We come across a seller of glass who purchased a hundred chamber pots, and a jeweller who in one sale disposed of 111 precious rings, 169 sapphires and topazes, 348 hardstones, 59 pearls and 132 cameos, one of which contained a piece of the Holy Cross. Individual trademarks and mail orders were introduced in different fields. Credit sales and sales by instalment were commonplace. Banking accounts were used not only for commercial operations but in everyday life. In extant documents of a single month in 1253 we meet with lodgers who paid their rent into their landlord's account, with a city employee who entrusted a bank to cash his salary and with a farmer who deposited in a bank money to discharge a debt due in nine months. Add to all of this the innumerable transactions of overseas and overland trade, the speculations on the money exchange and in the shares of public loans, the purchases, sales and mortgages in real estate, the operations of the loan-sharks, the contracts of shipbuilding, building and other industries, and you will then have some idea of the swirling activity in a business metropolis of the thirteenth or early fourteenth century.

At the head of all traders, of course, were the big business men – import and export merchants, international bankers, industrial entrepreneurs and 'colony builders'. Perhaps as much as nine-tenths of them were northern and central Italians. The balance was mostly made up of Provençal, Languedocian and Catalonian sea merchants, of wine exporters from Gascony, Toulouse and La Rochelle, of grain exporters from Sicily and Apulia, of salt exporters of the Aunis and of the upper Danubian region, and of linen exporters from Switzerland and southern Germany. The wealth of the Italian big business men can be estimated by such examples as that of Federico Corner, a Venetian merchant who *declared* a taxable estate of £60,000 Ven. (1379), or that of Salimbene Salimbeni, a Sienese merchant-banker who offered his city a loan of £236,000 Sien. to win a war (1260).[6] The splendid palaces of the Salimbeni and Corner families, still extant, testify to the humanism of these merchants, many of whom were close friends of literati and scholars. The medieval big business man most frequently was a very active politician and a dogged fighter in civil and external wars. But his love of fatherland, home and family did not prevent him from being always on the move, always ready, until old age prevented, to leave his comfortable home to wander *per diversas mundi partes*, wherever business opportunities might call him.

Unlike most big business men of our time, the great merchant of the later Middle Ages usually spread his activities into many different lines of trade and coupled large-scale operations with small retail purchases and sales. Of course a modern tycoon might smile at the methods and at the comparative smallness of the capital and credit of his medieval predecessor. He would probably feel less inclined to implore the assistance of heaven in his work, since his rate of travel

[6] Obviously much larger capital than the entire fortune of any individual could be concentrated through *compagnia* or *commenda* contracts. One of the many notaries who drafted contracts for the Genoese merchant Filippo Magnavacca recorded *commenda* contracts to a combined amount of £25,352 Gen. in three consecutive days of September 1227. The Florentine Bardi and Peruzzi companies lent King Edward III of England a total amount of 1,365,000 florins according to Villani's figures, the substantial accuracy of which has been proved by Armando Sapori. We lack data to evaluate the fortunes of non-Italian partnerships during the thirteenth and early fourteenth centuries, but it can be assumed that the figures were much lower.

does not depend on wind filling the sails or sun baking mud-caked roads. But who can tell whether in another five hundred years future business magnates will not smile at the methods, the capital and the transport used by business men of our time? Quantity is only one element in the evaluation of economic development, and it has little meaning if it is not seen against the general background of the times. Restrictions of capital and speed existed not only for the big business man, but for his contemporaries as well. No doubt the courier of a Venetian trading house who covered in four days the distance to Florence – usually a 22 to 25-day trip for pack animals – astonished his contemporaries even more than does the modern business man who travels by aeroplane while most of the laymen travel by railroad or car. Furthermore, in the Middle Ages absolute specialisation would have been unwise in view of the great hazards attending each kind of trade, and retail operations could not be spurned since the opportunities for wholesale operations fast exhausted themselves.

But let us leave to others the discussion of business methods and techniques and turn instead to survey briefly the main objects of import and export trade. The main axis of commerce continued to run from the north-west to the south-east, from eastern and southern Europe to Muslim and Byzantine countries, as it did in the early Middle Ages. Western textiles and eastern 'spices' (chiefly seasonings, dyestuffs and medicinals) occupied the first place, at least by value, among the various articles which were exchanged in ever-increasing quantity. Pegolotti in the early fourteenth century listed no less than 386 items under the heading 'spices'. He included also many commodities of western origin, and such wares as copper, glue and cotton, which we would hardly reckon as spices. Eastern 'spices', however, were usually more valuable and there was a greater variety of them. Pegolotti quoted 11 kinds of sugar (of which nine at least came from the Levant), 7 sorts of kermes dyes (from different parts of the Balkans, Provence and Spain) and 23 different types of raw silk (mostly from the Middle and the Far East). As for western textiles, every important centre of northern France, Belgium and England, as well as Florence, gave its name to one or more expensive woollens. Cheaper woollen cloth and fabrics containing cotton came mostly from the Lombard cities, from Languedoc, from Pisa and Siena and from South Germany. Linen was obtained especially from Champagne, Switzerland and South Germany. The finest linen was the only western article that could bear the cost of transportation as far as Peking. Bulky goods, however, were commonly shipped to any destination in the Mediterranean, the Black Sea and the Atlantic from Safi to Newcastle and Bruges. Venice, for instance, exported leather goods, furs, salt, grain, oil, iron, copper, tin, mercury, timber, fruit, soap, animals and slaughtering meat and slaves as well as expensive textiles and 'spices'. A secondary but not negligible source of income for the Mediterranean shipowners was passenger traffic. Pilgrims paid little but they were content with the poorest 'accommodation', and there were so many of them. Muslim pilgrims were almost as good customers as were the Christians. When it came to mass transportation of Crusaders, the larger seaports engaged in a cut-throat competition. Marseilles in 1268 tried to capture the market by reducing the fare to Palestine to 60, 40 and 35 *solidi* in first, second and third class respectively. If one was stoic enough to sleep in the stables aboard ship one paid only 25 *solidi*.

By the early fourteenth century the increased movement of goods and passengers had led to important changes in transport facilities both by sea and land. Different types of ships, ranging from the speedy but narrow war galley to the slow but roomy *navis*, were used for different wares. While in wartime even the strongest and fastest galley loaded with light expensive wares might be unable to go through the blockade, in 'normal' times (that is, when only minor wars and piracy threatened navigation) the regular convoys of heavy galleys, escorted by war galleys, were quite safe. In these larger galleys enough light precious wares were laden to cut the cost of transportation of the heavier goods. The value of the cargo of one of these ships could well surpass 200,000 ducats, and sometimes a single merchant supplied the cargo for as many as three of them. Convoys of *taride*, still heavier galleys which were almost as rounded as a *navis*, transported grain and fish from the Black Sea. At the same time, for the traffic directed to England and Flanders, larger, sturdier and faster sailing ships – the carracks – gained favour with independent entrepreneurs because they could replace a substantial number of fighting sailors with professional arbalesters (later, artillery men), and sail singly, straight through the Bay of Biscay to their northern destination relying on their own strength. Their use spread to the Mediterranean, but here their shortcomings weighed more: they missed the opportunities of local trade on their way, needed full cargoes to make any profit, and depended on mercenary soldiers whose zeal and expertise did not match those of sailors working partly for a share in the commercial operations. Convoys and more adaptable sailing ships such as the cogs continued to play a significant role. Toward the end of the fourteenth century Venice sent convoys almost entirely composed of comparatively few *naves* to take on cotton in bulk in the ports of Syria and Cyprus. The regular convoys were subventioned and supervised by the governments of Genoa and Venice, and were sent out every year on a fixed schedule to various destinations in the Mediterranean, the Black Sea and the North Atlantic. Usually they were open only from February or March to September or October, but the Genoese became the pioneers of winter navigation in the early thirteenth century, and the Venetians soon followed their example. The increased number of ships and voyages partly made up for the tonnage, which even in the heaviest *naves* was very small.

Overland traffic never completely overcame the handicaps which made it more expensive then overseas traffic, but it did become safer on the most frequented roads. Whereas merchants still had to travel in caravans (*caterve*) along certain trails infested by brigands, such as the route from Trebizond to Tabriz, elsewhere they went without escort or entrusted their goods to thriving organisations of transport agents. Competition between markets and toll stations led to substantial reductions of customs and to improvements of roads. As an instance we can recall the main episodes in the duel between Swiss mountaineers and French carters to capture the great commercial currents running across the continent. In the eleventh century most of the traffic between the valleys of the Po and of the Upper Rhine went through the passes of the Central Alps – especially the Septimer – even though wares had to be transported on porters' backs or on wheelbarrows over the steepest stretch. In the twelfth century that traffic was gradually diverted to the route through Champagne, the Rhone valley (or the Rhone river itself), the Provençal seaports, the sea as far as Savona or Genoa and the Apennines. This itinerary was almost three times as long, but it avoided the Alps and exploited to the utmost the possibilities of cheap transportation by water. In the thirteenth century the construction of a bridge across the Schöllenen gorge opened the St Gotthard to pack mules and restored part of the traffic to the Alps. Then the carters and boatmen of France began to lower their prices. In 1318 the Florentine Del Bene company, which imported French cloth, paid less per mile on the overland stretch from Paris to Marseilles than on the maritime stretch from Marseilles to Pisa. Exceptional as this case may have been, it indicates a sweeping change from the mid-thirteenth century, when (as it has been calculated) it would have cost about 3 *solidi* to ship 100 pounds of merchandise by sea from Civitavecchia to Genoa, but 80 *solidi* to send the same amount by land from Marseilles to Provins, a distance only a little longer. Nevertheless the Swiss did not give up the struggle. After 1338, work was begun in the old Septimer Pass to construct a road passable for small carts – the first of its kind in the Alps.

All available data on transport, tolls, business practices and volume of trade in the early fourteenth century convey the impression that there was a sharp distinction between what we may call the 'inner' and the 'outer' area of long-distance commerce – omitting the 'forgotten' areas such as Navarre and the core of the Balkan peninsula where there was very little commerce. The 'outer' area was a field of large risks and large profits, a frontier where good luck was almost as important as good management. Travel in the depths of Asia, for instance, still required more than ordinary resistance and courage in spite of Pegolotti's reassuring words about the Tana–Peking route. In 1338, when the Venetian merchant Giovanni Loredano prepared to go to Delhi with his brother and four other partners, his family and his parish priest besought him to desist. He died en route, as did two of his companions. The venture at first suffered losses, but thanks to the fabulous lavishness of the sultan of Delhi, it ended with a 100 per cent profit. This, however, was hardly a consolation to Loredano's wife, who later retired to a convent.

In the 'inner' area of long-distance trade, however, commerce had now ceased to be an adventure. It was a highly competitive market, where success depended mainly on efficiency, quickness and almost meticulous weighing of transport charges, tolls and marketing conditions. Investments were comparatively safe and profits were usually moderate, even if judged according to modern standards. Distance was not always the dominant factor in drawing the border between 'outer' and 'inner' areas, since war could at any moment render trade extremely dangerous even at the gates of a commercial metropolis. Similarly, the financial and political vicissitudes of France under Philip the Fair sometimes made Paris a less safe place for international merchants than Peking. Normally, however, the 'inner' area included the entire coastal zone of the Mediterranean, of the Black Sea and of the Atlantic from Ceuta to Safi and from Bayonne to London and Bruges, and the thickly populated internal regions of northern and central Italy, Champagne, Ile-de-France, Flanders and Brabant.

In some types of business, merchants endeavoured to reduce or to eliminate competition in the 'inner' area by forming monopolistic compacts and cartels. In 1255, a Genoese and a Venetian jointly controlled the production of alum in Seljuk Anatolia and were able to provoke an artificial rise of price. In 1283, the government of Venice ordered all Venetian merchants to form a cartel for the purpose of buying cotton and pepper in Alexandria. In 1331, the wine merchants of St Jean d'Angély, Bordeaux, Libourne and La Rochelle united to dictate their terms to the count of Flanders. Craft gilds, of course, worked in many ways like cartels. Notwithstanding all this, the margin between cost of production and selling price continued to shrink. In the early fourteenth century the Del Bene company purchased cloth in Flanders, finished it in Florence and sold it there, in the Champagne fairs or in southern Italy only 11.70 to 20.34 per cent dearer than they had bought it. Only efficient management – and low salaries to the finishers – enabled this company to make a 7 to 15 per cent profit. It would certainly be dangerous to generalise from the data furnished by this particular company alone. That this example is not exceptional, however, we may infer by noting that the interest rate for deposits in banks, government loans and real estate investments also had fallen to around 8 to 12 per cent from the 20 or even 25 per cent which had been the customary commercial interest rate *in Italy* in the early thirteenth century. Obviously profits from overseas commerce were subject to much greater fluctuations, but the average profit does not seem to have been very far from these figures.

The reduction of the margin of profit and the tremendous increase of the volume of traffic quickened the development of business techniques and slowly undermined the superiority of the travelling merchant over the sedentary business man. What we may call a process of rationalisation enabled traders not only to weather the serious crisis that came with growth, but also to reach new peaks of prosperity. Some scholars have considered these changes so important that they have spoken of a 'commercial revolution' in the late thirteenth and early fourteenth centuries. The revolution, however, had been on the march for at least three centuries and had caused a great number of transformations, not only in business techniques but also in many other fields. Improvements in management in the thirteenth and fourteenth centuries might be compared to the inventions of the railway, of the dynamo and of the diesel motor in the Industrial Revolution. They added speed and power to an already feverish and mighty economic expansion. They saved the Commercial Revolution from being choked by its own magnitude.

Let us not assume, however, that the sedentary merchant of the fourteenth century had a better grasp of economic opportunities than had, for instance, the travelling merchant of the old *commenda*. Both were adapted to the specific conditions of their times. In a regime of little competition and huge profits the travelling merchant had all the advantages except that of personal comfort. It was he who managed the enterprise, and those who entrusted capital to him had to accept his decisions and his accounting almost blindly. He shared with no one the profits of his own investment, and was entitled to no less than 25 per cent of the profits of the numerous investments he received in *commenda*. We know very well that more often than not he retained more than his legal share. Nevertheless people kept offering their money to him, much as men nowadays in times of boom rush to subscribe to new stock offerings, because they felt that even the most reckless and unscrupulous travelling merchant would earn enough to enrich them as well as himself. When, however, competition grew and many small profits were required to form a respectable capital, the cost of travelling became too heavy to bear. Then the sedentary merchant took over as well as he could the management of long-distance trade and carried out his business through branches manned by his employees and through overseas commission agents. He endeavoured to obtain more adequate accounting and to keep close track of his affairs by correspondence. Thus he saved the share which would have been paid to the travelling merchant, but he had to carry a heavy managerial structure which could be supported only on condition that business was continuous and intensive. The robust, but more inflexible, body of maturity had replaced the lean, but more pliable frame of youth.

Our survey must come to a close. We have begun it with a sketch of two very humble business men, Ugo Teralh and Armanno the currier. Let us conclude it with the quick portrait of two very great business men, Benedetto Zaccaria and Francesco Datini. The former was a travelling merchant, a great nobleman and a man of the sea. The latter was a sedentary business man, a self-made man, and a native of an inland town. Between the two, they summed up the best characteristics of the medieval merchant prince. They were utterly different, but two sentiments made them similar: a very medieval religiousness, and a very 'modern' eagerness for profit.

Benedetto Zaccaria, born some time before 1240, was one of ten Genoese brothers and sisters who claimed descent from the viscounts of the city. Most of his family was actively engaged in business and politics as he was. His triumphs as an admiral and a diplomat alone would make him one of the outstanding men of his time. He was one of the commanders at Meloria where Genoa destroyed the Pisan navy, and he commanded the Castilian fleet at Marzamosa where the Moroccans were crushed; he wrote, in witty French, a plan for a 'continental blockade' of England and helped Philip the Fair to execute it; he conquered Tripoli in Syria, witnessed its fall to overwhelming Egyptian forces, and later toyed with the idea of a crusade of women to recapture it; he engaged in both grand and petty piracy and carried out vital secret missions in various courts. Let us concentrate on his activities as a business man. With the typical eclecticism of his time he traded in spices, cutlery, cloth, linen, furs, salt, grain and other wares, and speculated in foreign exchange, in shares of the public loans and in real estate. What made him exceptional, however, was the way he exploited two fiefs he had obtained from the Byzantine emperor. One of them, the island of Chios, yielded a crop of mastic worth about £16,000 Gen. a year. Chios was the only place in the world where this aromatic herb, much appreciated in the Levant, was produced. Later records indicate that excess production of mastic in any year was destroyed since a larger crop would have lowered the price without increasing substantially the quantity sold.

More important were the alum mines of Phocaea, in the other fief jointly held by Benedetto Zaccaria and one of his brothers. Alum was an indispensable material for the dyeing industry. Phocaea's alum was the second best in the world, while the best quality came from Koloneia in northern Asia Minor. Zaccaria managed by political intrigue to keep all exports from Koloneia off the market while he was developing Phocaea's mines, and then exported Koloneia's alum as well as his own. In a few years a new city of 3,000 inhabitants, New Phocaea, sprang up near the mines, which yielded about 700 tons yearly. The ore was processed in the old town on the sea shore. In one recorded instance Zaccaria sold 33 tons of processed alum for £3,000 Gen., carriage free in Bruges. He used his own ships to distribute the alum in different countries, and employed all his diplomatic and military skill to enlarge his markets. In Genoa, his home town, he owned a dyeing house and financed a Florentine clothmaker. Some of the by-products of his business, which shows definite vertical and horizontal integration, were the building of a *fondaco* in the Crimea, a short-lived control of Puerto Santa Maria (the seaport of Seville) and the first recorded voyage through the Straits of Gibraltar to England. Zaccaria died in his palace in 1307, when he was about to sail on another business venture in spite of his old age. Four years later Empress Margaret, the wife of Henry VII, spent the last days of her life in the palace of Zaccaria's heirs. Her presence could not make more 'imperial' the house that had sheltered a true empire builder.

Francesco Datini requires fewer words than the less wellknown Zaccaria. Datini was born in 1335, the son of a taverner of Prato, a small but lively town near Florence. At thirteen he was an orphan and a shop-boy of a Florentine merchant. Shortly thereafter he left what appeared to be a hopeless future and settled in Avignon, working as a business employee (*fattore*). At twenty-eight he founded a company with a capital of 800 florins, one-half of which he contributed. At forty-seven he was back in Florence, a rich man, but still eager to increase his wealth. He died at seventy-five and bequeathed nearly all of his 70,000-florin estate to charity in spite of the fact that he had a numerous family: after all, his children were illegitimate, and he had created a trust fund for his legal wife. His public generosity shows his religious sentiments, but a sceptical man might think that his conscience disturbed him. Datini's first business had been the armament industry, which was undoubtedly the most profitable in Avignon during the Hundred Years War. But he was as eclectic as Zaccaria. We see him engaged in banking, international commerce, cloth manufacturing and dyeing, in the silk industry and still other activities – all this through a large number of small companies totally or chiefly financed by him. He had permanent *fondachi* (branches) in Avignon, Genoa, Barcelona, Valencia and Majorca and correspondents scattered throughout western Europe and the Levant. His account books show the entire evolution from the single to the double entry method of book-keeping. The pious foundation to which he left his estate still exists, and conserves all the papers of his firms. The books number 500, and there are more than 300,000 letters exchanged between Datini and his correspondents and employees. Some of the letters show Datini's close friendship with many outstanding literati and scholars of his time. Datini, however, carefully kept out of politics, which had caused so much trouble to so many merchants, including at times Zaccaria.

Zaccaria lived in the most glorious time of medieval trade, but Datini made his fortune after the best days had gone. We have told his story only because his methods were similar to those of many merchants of the early fourteenth century. But the calamity which had made him an orphan – the Black Death – ushered in far more serious crises than the difficulties which had given rise to sedentary merchants like him.

III. *The Waning of the Middle Ages*

(1) THE SIZE OF THE CRISIS

Incessant wars and invasions, scourging taxation and inflation, recurrent major epidemics, serious ecological damage, probably an unfavourable pulsation of climate, certainly a reversal from demographic growth to demographic decline: under these circumstances the Roman Empire in the West and its trade had declined and fallen. A thousand years later, a similar if not identical combination of calamities hit the West and the countries beyond it, almost relentlessly for a whole century (1346–1453) and then again, after a forty-year lull in the wars, during most of the sixteenth century. Stronger and more resilient than the Roman Empire, late medieval Europe did not collapse; but its economy was far more deeply and durably scarred than most historians admitted as late as fifty years ago. They could not and did not overlook the disasters, of course; yet they were so impressed by the artistic and literary splendour of the incipient Renaissance, by the conquests of some monarchs and world explorers and by the conspicuous consumption of the rich, that they tended to dismiss the worst quakes as if they had been isolated shocks, promptly absorbed by a forever rebounding and soaring society.

The truth of the matter is that while reacting vigorously against continuing adversity the Commercial Revolution wore its impetus out. No doubt its basic structures and techniques were preserved, and a good proportion of its material gains were salvaged or recovered (especially during the lull of the late fifteenth century); but the buoyancy of the age of open opportunities fell flat, social mobility waned, and conservation became a more desirable and attainable goal than growth. Still hazy and unorthodox when the first edition of the present volume espoused it, the interpretation of the waning Middle Ages and waxing Renaissance as essentially an economic depression has now become a majority opinion. It has not, however, entirely disarmed the opposition of a learned minority holding more optimistic views. The argument, which involves the whole transition from medieval to early modern economy, overlaps the chronological span of the present chapter, but its wider implications must be kept in mind. Actually the gap in opinions has been narrowing down: the fundamental trends – a crest before 1346, a trough approximately until 1453 (with a tendency to stabilisation towards the end), a second crest during the 1454–94 lull, a second trough thereafter – are no longer controversial. On the other hand, it goes without question that there were sharp deviations from the norm, islands of prosperity in the midst of depression, pools of stagnation in the fringe of recovery. The debate practically hinges on the effectiveness of recovery, that is, on whether the second crest was lower than, equal to, or higher than the first: a question that can be quantitatively tackled only to the extent that precise information is available not only on the second crest, but also on the first, for which documentation is scarcer.

This requirement cannot be met with a fair degree of approximation except in the field of demography. Inflated by four centuries of growth and sheltered by at least one century without major famines, the population of southern Europe suffered the heaviest losses in the first outbreak of the plague: about one-third of its total must be regarded as a conservative estimate. For those who contracted it in the bubonic form, a mortality rate well above 50 per cent was normal; it rose to more than 90 per cent in the rarer pulmonary form. The following outbreaks, occurring at intervals of fifteen to twenty years, were somewhat less catastrophic, probably because the survivors of earlier plagues were immunised, possibly because the virus was weakened in time, certainly because the patients were more effectively isolated. Gradually the population tended to be stabilised at approximately two-thirds to three-quarters of its pre-1346 maximum, and may have regained more ground between 1454 and 1494, when wars subsided and syphilis was not yet another major killer. It has been claimed that stabilisation at a lower level was a needed relief from an earlier overpopulation; but the Commercial Revolution had succeeded for centuries in increasing productivity faster than population, and there is no proof that it could not have continued to do so without the Malthusian brakes of disease, war, and hunger. In an age of still feeble consumption and slight mechanisation, the supply of manpower remained a crucial resource; it was not without some reason that the writers of the pre-industrial age often measured the wealth of a country by the density of its population.

Strictly economic quantitative data for comparison between the first and second crest are more fragmentary than the demographic ones, but some of them indicate even sharper contractions. In Florence, for instance, both the amount of capital and the number of employees of the Medici company of merchant bankers, Europe's largest business enterprise for most of the fifteenth century, were much smaller than those of the Peruzzi company, the city's *second* largest in the early fourteenth. The significance of this contraction is increased by evidence of a much greater contraction in the woollen industry, Florence's largest employer at the time, and scarcely affected by the better performance of the silk industry, which involved a smaller amount of capital and labour. At any rate, Florence's second crest seems to have waxed and waned earlier than elsewhere: in the second half of the fifteenth century the Medici company declined and fell, and Giovanni Rucellai, next to the Medici the richest banker, retired from business to avoid further losses and devote himself full time to collecting art. Again, tax farming records suggest for Genoa's maritime trade in the late fifteenth century an expected value of between one-third and one-half the amount expected in 1344; the credibility of this estimate, which would almost negate the existence of a second crest, is enhanced by data of the same kind suggesting for Marseilles approximately the same decline over the same period. The second crest is more perceptible in the states of Venice and Milan, both of which badly needed the partial respite of 1454–94 after investing in war an appalling proportion of their resources (in 1377–81 and 1431–41 the Venetian government had whisked away from its taxpayers respectively one-fourth and two-thirds of their assets through compulsory loans); but the main beneficiary of peace is agriculture, not trade. In Milan, the only certain tokens of growth are in the industry of arms and in luxury objects for the court. In Venice, the period of recovery is marred at the beginning by the failure of the Soranzo bank (1453), at the end by that of the Garzoni and Lippomani banks (1499), in the central years by a costly, losing war against the Turks (1463–79). Florence, Genoa, Milan and Venice were the 'Big Four' of the Commercial Revolution, whose ups and downs largely determined and reflected the basic trends of European and Mediterranean trade.

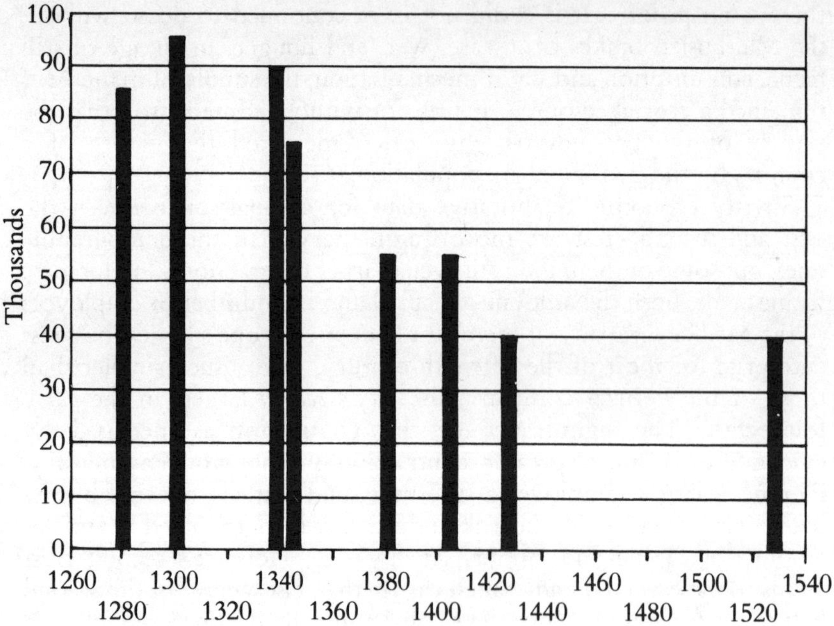

Fig. 1. Recorded Population of Florence, 1280–1530 (Clergymen and paupers are not included)

Reproduced from R. Lopez, *The Three Ages of the Italian Renaissance* (University of Virginia Press).

It has been argued that in the late fifteenth century a number of younger and smaller trading centres, mostly outside Italy, progressed enough to compensate for the decline of the old business establishment; but no figures have been produced to demonstrate that their second crest was actually higher than their first, and even if it was, one would hesitate to assume that their gains could balance the losses of the older and stronger commercial powers. Granted that the emergence of fresh forces was highly important as a promise for the future, every age must be judged by the realities of its present.

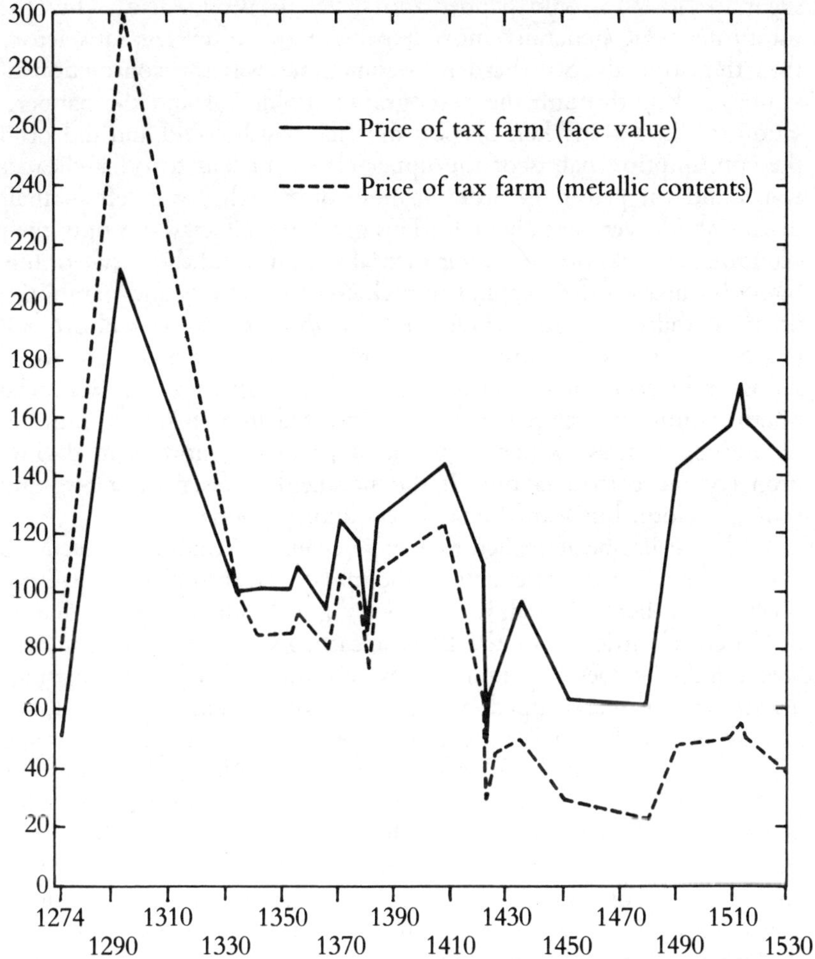

Fig. 2. Anticipated Maritime Trade of Genoa, 1274–1530 (1334–100) Reproduced from R. Lopez, *The Three Ages of the Italian Renaissance* (University of Virginia Press).

Changes in the quality, style and scope of trade convey a clearer message than incomplete and unreliable statistics. As the following section will show in greater detail, the eastern frontier of south European trade gradually receded from the sea of China to the edge of the Mediterranean, losing even there the secure shelters of the Italian commercial colonies; compensations were sought and found by developing in the West the production of merchandise no longer easily available in the East – silk in Granada and Calabria, alum in Latium, sugar in Madeira, wild pepper and slaves in West Africa – but the substitutes were generally more expensive and often less satisfactory than the originals. Still harder to counteract was the contraction of home markets through the demographic doldrums and the pauperisation of disaster-stricken masses; merchants still could and did prod the consumption habits of the upper class, but had to offer cheaper wares and cut profits in order to hold on to what was left of their middle and lower class clientele. This gradually affected not only their economic calculations, but their mental attitudes and their style of life. Some burned up their capital in reckless speculations and gambling; others withdrew it from trade and ploughed it into agriculture and real estate; still others invested it in the pursuit of power and social status or in books and works of art. Almost all over the European South, commerce tended to be concentrated in a shrinking number of business houses, which appreciated prudence more than daring, property more than labour. It did not neglect essential staples and ordinary cloth, but leaned heavily on luxury goods.

Of late it has been argued that these changes would have occurred even if the catastrophic events of the mid-fourteenth century had not precipitated them. Indeed, there was a slight decline in the population of Florence a little before the Black Death, a shortage of shipbuilding wood in the Genoese Apennines as early as the mid-thirteenth century, a scattering of overcropped, overgrazed, overpopulated or abandoned land all over southern Europe, a widespread recrudescence of war and high taxation, of bank failures, monetary disorder and diminishing profits in short-distance commerce before 1346 (though no food shortages like those that caused the great famine of north-western Europe in 1315–17). A recent study of Benjamin Kedar, based on thousands of commercial contracts and a variety of literary sources, brings out what one might call the subconscious expressions of declining self-confidence among Genoese and Venetian merchants; they grow much louder after 1346, but are not absent in the earlier decades. Their ships gradually abandon their lay augural names (such as *Wealth*, *Fortress*, *Merriment*) to be placed under the protection of a saint's name; their investments insist on the risk more than on the profit of a commercial venture; their successes are no longer credited to their own skill and courage but primarily to the assistance of God. Still, one must not place the first symptoms of hypertension of a mature economy, which needs some adjustment after growing incessantly for several centuries, on the same plane with the manifestations of total distress. To cite only one example, one hears many complaints from Siena, which in the eighty years before 1346 endures serious military defeats, a more than tenfold increase of public expenditure and the failure of its greatest bank, yet keeps trading and fighting, and in the last ten years finances two monuments to its own glory, Ambrogio Lorenzetti's fresco of the Good Government and Lando di Pietro's project of a Duomo Nuovo intended to eclipse the Duomo of its Florentine rivals. It took the Black Death to kill Lorenzetti and interrupt for ever the construction of the Duomo Nuovo.

Actually, it would be an exaggeration to say that the mid-fourteenth-century crisis drove all merchants to despair. In northern Europe, the cost of wars and conspicuous consumption will create serious shortages of cash in spite of the fact that the per capita amount ought to have grown with the decrease of the population; there are occasional shortages in Italy, too, but more refined manipulations of credit minimise their impact. For sailing through the economic storms, a Florentine manual of trade offered in 1442 the following prescription: 'Never be eager to remit money where there is dearth, nor to withdraw it where there is abundance...but make remittances in advance in order to have ready cash at good price wherever it is dear...for you must consider that abundance comes right after dearth.' To those who lacked cash, Benedict Kotrulic of Dubrovnik (Ragusa), whose little book *On Commerce and the Perfect Merchant* is an impassioned tribute to the merchant class, suggested in 1458 the following heroic remedies: 'When a Genoese is impoverished by some accident of adverse fortune, he becomes a pirate, and so do many Catalans; the Florentines help themselves by becoming brokers or artisans in some craft.' Coming five years after the fall of Constantinople to the Turks, this statement is only one of many that bear witness to a stubborn, widespread determination to stay in business against all odds. Forty years of recovery after 1453 strengthened that determination by bringing back a measure of 'abundance after dearth'.

Nevertheless, it seems appropriate to choose 1453 as the closing date for a chapter that begins with the fall of Rome. No doubt the long anticipated fall of Constantinople did not cause an economic upheaval – it was always possible to trade with the Turks – but it marked the first step in a succession of events that demoted the Mediterranean from its central position in trade and ultimately delivered to northern Europe the dominant role in world economy.

(2) THE LAST CENTURY OF MEDITERRANEAN-CENTRED TRADE

One of the greatest tragedies in history, the Black Death of 1348, burst open the doors to the depression which had already been foretold by other ominous tokens. No less than 35 per cent and perhaps as much as 65 per cent of the crowded urban population succumbed to the plague. The rate of mortality was less high in the country, but it was the fate of cities that mattered most, since cities were the leaders of economic expansion. The toll was heaviest where urbanisation was the most intensive and where the agrarian population had grown the thickest – which means that the cream of the economic world was skimmed. Nor was the Black Death the only calamity of that kind. The plague came back again and again, nullifying the growth of one generation after another.

Wars also were more protracted and more destructive than they had been since the time of the last wave of barbarian invasions in the ninth and early tenth centuries. The Hundred Years War in France, civil wars in Castile and in southern Italy, the ravages of the *condottieri* and innumerable local campaigns in northern Italy and southern Germany completed the work of disease and prepared that of famine. Other imponderable reasons, among which we must probably include birth control, prevented any prompt recovery. In the larger part of Europe the prosperous level of 1300 was not reached again before the sixteenth or the seventeenth century. The population of Florence, for instance, fell from about 110,000 inhabitants in 1338 to 45–50,000 in 1351; it increased only to 70–75,000 in 1380 and was still about 70,000 in 1526. Modena, a minor city in northern Italy, fell from about 22,000 inhabitants in 1306 to 8–9,000 in 1482 (Doren). Zürich, of which we have no data prior to the Black Death, had 12,375 inhabitants in 1350 and 4,713 in 1468 (Keller-Escher). Montpellier had 22,500 inhabitants in 1367 and 5,000 in 1379 (Germain). In France war was perhaps an even worse calamity than the Black Death and the later epidemics. Furthermore, the definitive expulsion from the kingdom of the Jews, who were accused of spreading the plague, entirely wiped out a useful if small commercial group. As for Germany, it will be enough to recall that fourteen major epidemics after that of 1348–50 are recorded for the second half of the fourteenth century. Catalonia alone owed a temporary recovery to the fact that its commercial development reached its peak after the middle of the fourteenth century. Homesteads rose from 86,895 to 95,258 between 1359 and 1369. But the figure fell to 77,973 in 1378 and it went below the 60,000 mark in 1497 (Vandellós).

A contemporary writer ascribed the spread of the Black Death to the 'microbic' war unleashed by the Mongolian Khan of Kipchak against the Genoese colony of Caffa in the Crimea. The Khan, he says, endeavoured to break the resistance of the besieged inhabitants by catapulting over the walls bodies of men who had died with the plague. The city held out, but returning colonists carried the disease to western

Europe. Be that as it may, the siege of Caffa, which was preceded by a pogrom of Italian merchants in Tana (Azov), was very bad news in itself. It was an instance of the sudden deterioration of the situation throughout the Mongolian states. The Khan of Kipchak made peace with Caffa, but a few years later his death was followed by prolonged anarchy. The Italians suffered still heavier blows in the Khanate of Persia, where their interests had grown in a few decades almost as large as those they had acquired in the Byzantine Empire in the course of several centuries. The death of Khan Abū Sa'īd in 1338 marked the collapse of a state which had been most friendly to the foreigners. Tabriz, the most important city, was seized by a tyrant who slaughtered or robbed those merchants who had trusted in his promises. Similar disasters occurred in the Khanate of Turkestan, beginning with a massacre of Europeans in its capital, Almaligh (1339), and ending with the total collapse of the state. So long as a friendly Mongolian Khanate remained in China, some Italian merchants continued their attempts to reach that country by devious routes. But even the Khanate of China was undermined by internal disorders which ended in its overthrow by the national dynasty of the Ming in 1368. The new rulers had neither the power nor the wish to maintain relations with Europe through the immense distances of the Asiatic continent or the Indian Ocean. It is true that in the fifteenth century Chinese warships and merchant junks sailed as far west as the Arabian coast, but these vessels did not reach shores frequented by European merchants.

The limitless possibilities opened to the Westerners by the Mongolian unification of Asia were lost. It was again necessary to use the Egyptian bottle-neck and to depend upon Muslim intermediaries to obtain the goods of the Farther East. Venice, which had sent no convoys to Egypt from 1323 to 1345, now entreated the Pope to cancel the embargo and the sultan to conclude a new commercial treaty. The Pope granted only individual licences upon payment of exorbitant fees. The sultan gladly resumed the exploitation of the Christian merchant in a manner much more drastic than hitherto. The bitter struggle for the last bastions of the Holy Land and the subsequent European desertion of Egypt for the Mongolian markets had withered the sprouting seeds of toleration. Furthermore, Egypt itself had been impoverished by maladministration and by the strain of a double battle for survival against both Mongolians and Christians. Its ships no longer sailed further than Aden. To this harbour the goods of the Farther East came, no doubt at an increased cost to the Egyptians, in Indian ships and, during the fifteenth century, even in Chinese junks. It was imperative for the Egyptians to seek a compensation for their financial and commercial decadence in the thorough exploitation of the monopoly of trade with Europe.

As the financial crisis of Egypt grew worse, European merchants in Alexandria traded on even harder terms. Already in the late fourteenth century they had to pay duties amounting in all to around 100 per cent of the value of goods. In 1428 the sultan took over the monopoly of the export of pepper, which had been sold hitherto by private Egyptian merchants, and raised its price in Alexandria from 80 to 130 *dīnār*. Still worse was to come. In 1480, when the Venetians refused to pay 110 ducats for a *sporta* (about 480 pounds) of pepper which sold in the market for 50 ducats, the sultan confined them for two days and three nights in their *fondachi*, then dragged them to the custom-house and did not permit them to go until they had paid 70 ducats for the pepper. If this could happen to the Venetians, who were backed by the strongest navy in the world and enjoyed the exceptional distinction of owning two extra-territorial *fondachi* in Alexandria, the other merchant communities must have fared even worse. Only mutual dependence and fear prevented a very tense situation from reaching a breaking point. The sultan needed Christians to buy his commodities and knew from experience that he could not outrage Venice without facing severe military reprisals. Venice and the other merchant communities needed Muslims to supply eastern wares and knew from experience that Egypt could be beaten but not conquered. Hence, in spite of constant friction, Venetian commerce in Alexandria mounted to new heights, although probably not as much as it has been claimed – as usual on the basis of incomplete statistics and without reference to pre-1346 figures.

Much more ominous clouds were gathering further north. From the early fourteenth century the Ottoman Turks had been gnawing at the Byzantine possessions in Asia. In 1352 they gained a foothold in Europe with the help of the Genoese, who needed allies against the Venetians. Before the end of the century they had conquered nearly all of the Balkan peninsula without having to break their alliance with Genoa or to cross swords with the Venetians. Although they were not necessarily hostile to foreign commerce and merchants, they certainly did not care to maintain the extraordinary privileges that the westerners had extorted from the weakness of the Byzantines. Here, as in Egypt, merchants tried appeasement as a remedy less costly than war. Some colonies even bought immunity from attack by paying tribute. Europe, however, had to fight back when the Turks began to blockade Constantinople. At this point Tamerlane emerged from the depth of Asia, defeated the Turks and was courted by the Westerners, including even the king of distant Castile, who sent him ambassadors. In spite of cruelty inflicted upon Italian colonies reached by his troops, Tamerlane seemed to many a new Chinghis Khan who would restore peace through destruction and commerce through peace in the immense territories he had subdued. But the conqueror died in 1405, and the Turks resumed their advance. The repercussions of these events upon the commerce of Constantinople can be judged from the returns of taxes levied on maritime trade in the Genoese suburb of Pera. These fell from £1,648,630 Gen. in 1334 to £1,199,046 in 1391 and to £234,000 in 1423. The decline will appear still greater if we consider the constant diminution of the weight and purchasing power of the Genoese pound.

Thus, contraction of eastern markets and shrinking of home markets reversed the trend which had made the Commercial Revolution possible. Nor were conditions more favourable to the expansion of southern European merchants into northern Europe, since northern Europe had also been scourged by epidemics and frequent wars. Furthermore, the Commercial Revolution of the previous period had brought distant regions more closely together and thus made them interdependent. The fluctuations of the international money market, of which the fall of the Genoese pound is an instance, had wide repercussions because most credit and commercial operations involved transactions in foreign exchange. To be sure, bankers and merchants tried to forecast the trends: in 1265, for instance, a Sienese merchant warned from Troyes one of his fellow-citizens in Lombardy to be on the alert for a probable fall in the quotations of the French currency in Italy as a result of an expedition then being prepared by Charles of Anjou. At a later period, however, as the margin of commercial profit and interest kept shrinking, unpredictable variations in the exchange rates could doom to failure an otherwise successful business operation.

It was not 'one world' as yet, but there was a sensitive world market, and it reacted quickly to crises in distant countries. Local difficulties, for instance, cannot entirely explain why the Florentine cloth industry declined so precipitously that in 1378 the revolting weavers demanded that industrialists should pledge a minimum yearly output of 24,000 pieces – which still was less than one-third of the production of 1338. Among the causes, we must mention the loss of the Persian market to which Venetians and Genoese had exported Florentine cloth before the collapse of the Mongolian Khanate; the impoverishment of the French nobility who were great consumers of luxury cloth before the Hundred Years War; the curtailment of exports of English wool which was the basic raw material before the war; and the bankruptcy of the Bardi and Peruzzi, Florence's greatest companies of merchant-bankers, which was connected with the war. Probably other distant events, of which we fail to see the connection with Florentine industry, also contributed to its decline. World-wide difficulties also must have formed the background of the social revolts which agitated all of Europe from London to Salonika and from Majorca to Flanders in the second half of the fourteenth century, although if we observe any one of these revolts too closely we discern only local causes and local peculiarities.

We are in the presence of an all-European depression. We must explain it chiefly by all-European causes. Though the last century of the Middle Ages has not yet been fully studied, it is not impossible to perceive a leading thread through the maze of its evidence.

Perhaps the most misleading factor, more misleading to the men of the fourteenth century than to us, is that the first disasters were followed by a wave of apparent prosperity. Terrible as the catastrophes were, they had struck a strong body which reacted vigorously. After the Black Death, the opening stages of the Hundred Years War, the Genoese–Venetian–Catalan clash of 1350–5 and other smaller conflicts there was a sharp increase in the demand for goods. Mortality had automatically increased the amount of money per capita and provoked a shortage of manpower. Wage-earners were able to demand higher salaries — in money terms if not in purchasing power – and debtors and tenants found it easier to pay their dues. While a stream of new immigrants from the country answered the demand for labourers in the cities, peasants who had not as yet been able to gain liberty now bought it. Their payments enabled the landlords to increase their purchases from the merchants and industrialists. The latter were able to pay larger salaries because they sold more – not only to the landlords, but also to the labourers and to the rest of the population which had abundant money to spend owing to the inflation. The increase of mass consumption lightened competition, which had heavily restricted commercial profits in the last few years before the Black Death.

Unfortunately this prosperity, born of inflation and of the diminished productive power of the population, did not last long. Even if its bases had been sounder than they were, the recurrence of the epidemics and the continuation or the recurrence of the wars would have brought it to an early end. As soon as the ranks of labour were filled sufficiently to ensure adequate production for the slowly but steadily shrinking market, both landlords and industrialists 'cracked down' on wages. The desperate revolts of workmen, petty artisans and peasants failed to turn the tide. The peasants at least did not lose their personal liberty, but the lower classes in the cities saw their condition become much worse than it had been before the Black Death. It was they who bore the main burden of the measures by which the industrialists endeavoured to compensate their diminished sales through reducing costs and increasing efficiency of production, especially in the textile industry. By supervising workers very closely and by imposing fines for technical errors, by hiring more women and fostering immigration of unskilled labourers from the country, by adopting the putting-out system for the initial stages of manufacturing, and by inviting artisans driven from Flanders on account of economic crisis and political disorders, the Italian clothiers were able to ride through the hard times. But over-production became a danger for the first time since the beginning of the Commercial Revolution. Gilds all over Europe gradually restricted the number of new masters who now shared only limited opportunities.

In commerce, also, the process of 'rationalisation' begun before the Black Death made gigantic strides. With so many markets in the Levant closing to European merchants and with the growing dullness of European markets, the *leitmotif* became to offer for sale 'only as much as one can sell in the place of destination', to quote the words of a fifteenth-century manual of business. Nor was it always possible to buy as much as was desired. The age of rapid fortunes won in daring overseas and overland ventures was over. Only the sedentary merchant who could make long-range plans to be executed with the help of numerous employees and commission agents and who could patiently wait for his investments to bring hard-won profits still had a fighting chance. In Italy, 5 to 8 per cent was now regarded as a fair interest rate in commercial loans. No wonder that commerce lost both capital and men to other forms of activity. Although banks increased their size and improved their methods, they used a larger part of their capital for loans to the idle upper class and more frequently to belligerent states. Genoa's funded debt, for instance, increased more than tenfold in thirty years. Moreover, a growing number of merchants retired from business, invested in real estate, lavished huge sums in magnificence, and became members of the new 'bourgeois nobility', whose high standards are described in Castiglione's *Courtier*. To be sure, this was not a new trend, but it was more stressed than ever before. It left durable gaps in the merchant class because, outside of war profiteering, there were few chances for new men to make fortunes and to take the place of old merchants becoming gentlemen. Meanwhile the Communes, the highest expression of the power of the Italian merchant class, were being overthrown by tyrants, ruled by selfish oligarchies or torn by civil wars.

These conditions dangerously increased the distance between the very rich and the very poor, and strengthened the tendency of merchants and manufacturers to cater mainly for a small group of wealthy customers. The surge of silk industry in those very centres where cloth production declined is a significant manifestation of the trend toward the growth of luxury industries. Other entrancing but alarming symptoms are the progress of industrial arts and the building of palaces of unprecedented splendour. In Florence, notwithstanding the decline of the textile industry and the shrinking of the population, the Medici family in the fifteenth century had a fortune of half a million ducats. Besides the small number of extremely wealthy families were more than two-thirds of the taxpayers who in 1399 paid taxes of less than one florin, or the 3,000 *miserabili* whose income in 1428 was too small to tax. Adverse economic trends and the hostility of the ruling oligarchy made the lot of these proletarians much harder than it was during the opening stages of the Commercial Revolution. Nor was the outlook any brighter for the lower classes in towns where capitalism had made slower progress. In Bâle 25.5 per cent of the citizens in 1424 did not have the minimum taxable capital of 10 florins; the proportion rose to 32 per cent in 1453. In contrast to this, 3 to 5 per cent of the population owned more than half the wealth of the city. Inequality grew deeper even within the upper class. In Venice, which was the wealthiest city in Europe towards the end of the Middle Ages, seven opulent merchant noblemen in 1379 made a tax declaration disclosing a fortune of 140,000 to 240,000 ducats each and almost 400 noblemen disclosed fortunes of more than 12,000. But 800 members of the nobility lived on the margin of decent poverty with 1,200 to 12,000 ducats, and many hundred who had still less were definitely poor. Good connections and assistance from the government enabled a few poor nobles to recoup their fortunes, but the majority sank, lower and lower. In France the Hundred Years War brought greater inequality along with the general misery. If the court often displayed extravagant pomp and if a Jacques Coeur amassed about one million gold *ècus*, there were 'great noblemen' who could spend no more than 20 crowns a year. The condition of most peasants and artisans was appalling.

If, however, these facts warn us against regarding the late fourteenth and the early fifteenth centuries simply as a prolongation of the economic expansion begun in the late tenth century, we must be careful not to overstress the dark side of the picture. A combination of adverse conditions had braked the wheels of commerce, but the progress accomplished during the Commercial Revolution in business methods was not lost. Indeed, depressions of necessity were times of greater improvements and rationalisation. Even if the merchants lost an entire continent in Asia, they opened new territories southwards in Africa and northwards and north-eastwards in Europe. Furthermore, some southern European countries which had formerly been backward now felt the full impact of the Commercial Revolution. Finally, even the greatest disasters were sources of profit for some men.

War, for instance, stimulated the arms trade. We have seen how the foundation of Datini's fortune was laid in the commerce of weapons in Avignon. Milan found in the metallurgic industries a compensation for the decline of its woollen production, even before it developed silk production. We hear that in 1427 two Milanese armourers alone were able to supply, in an emergency, arms for 4,000 horsemen and 200 infantrymen in a few days. Plain suits of armour made by the famous Missaglia arms-makers cost £200 Mil. apiece wholesale.

In France the turmoil which swept away the modest welfare of the common man piled up unprecedented fortunes in the coffers of the few. Jacques Coeur – a merchant from Bourges, but one who made Montpellier his second home and Mediterranean trade one of his main activities – climbed higher and fell faster than all of the others. Many less famous men found war profiteering an easier way to accumulate capital than peacetime trade. Jean Amici of Toulouse associated with an army officer to trade in booty taken from the English; Jean Marcel of Rouen amassed a fortune through all sorts of illegal speculations and through open collaboration with the English; Guillaume de Saint-Yon made fabulous profits selling meat at inflation prices to the Parisian rich. Other business men got rich by supplying the court or by assisting the French king in fleecing the king's flock. Some of them knew how to withdraw from trade as soon as they felt rich enough to identify themselves with the feudal aristocracy. A typical case is that of the Ysalguier family of Toulouse, who, though possibly of peasant origin, had made their fortune by administering the confiscated possessions of Jews and by serving the king in other ways. After a while they felt it below their dignity to continue their profession of money-changers and traders in hay and other humble staples. They purchased land, became courtiers and entirely associated themselves with the local nobility. This attitude was very common in the French business class as late as the eighteenth century, and it is not exceptional even today. But it must also be noted that throughout the Hundred Years War the state of the kingdom held little promise for anyone endeavouring to practise commerce on a large scale, while local trade, the mainstay of France's commercial economy, was too often impeded by obstructed communications and lack of surpluses for sale.

Wealth, even during intermissions between different phases of the Anglo-French struggle, was lost more rapidly than acquired, spent in lavish consumption more often than in productive investment. Demographic decline forced some industrial centres to override gild restrictions and to encourage immigration of both skilled and unskilled craftsmen, but the overall shortage could not be cured. The fairs of Champagne, which had lost their prominence when southern merchants had established direct relations with Belgium and England, were by-passed as international traffic sought safer routes through Germany; the older fairs of St Denis were discontinued for very long periods; those of Lyons, instituted shortly before the end of the war in competition with those of Geneva, grew but slowly. Woad trade and well-organised companies for the exploitation of water mills gave fresh impulsion to the economy of Toulouse and the surrounding region, but the Mediterranean seaports did not bounce back. Apparently Narbonne in 1378 had no more than a thousand inhabitants. Thanks to their connections with England, some of the Atlantic seaports which had been soaring in the early fourteenth century – Bordeaux, La Rochelle, Rouen – had periods of comparative affluence in the thick of the war, but their fortunes are hardly relevant to the history of southern trade.

Only the Byzantine territory suffered from war as thoroughly as France. From the traumatic interruption of what had been a promising commercial growth of Byzantium's Slav successor states in the Balkans, one seaport emerged as the principal neutral intermediary between the Turks and the Christian West: Dubrovnik (Ragusa). Its role reminds one of that of early medieval Venice; but Dubrovnik's merchants never could or would reach for military control of the sea, nor did they find in their ravaged hinterland anything approaching the economic backing Venice got in the developing Italy of the central Middle Ages. It was a sufficient achievement for the small Dalmatian city to keep its flag unfurled amidst its two larger neighbours, Turkey and Venice.

With a much earlier start and far greater demographic and military assets, Catalonia profited from the internecine war that weakened both Venice and Genoa to prolong and possibly increase its commercial prosperity well beyond 1346. For a few years the Catalans were able to exclude practically all other Europeans from North-West African commerce, and they became serious competitors of the Italians in the Levant. At first their methods and their spirit were markedly behind the times. Their greatest historian, Muntaner, who was also a 'colony builder', spoke with contempt of the bourgeoisie of the communes 'who do not know what honour means'. Sailors and settlers overseas had much of the rude, savage lawlessness of the early crusaders without their deep religious faith. The laws of Catalonia still punished by death the money-changer who was unable to pay his creditors; an unfortunate changer was beheaded in front of his *taula* (bank) as late as 1360. Narrow protectionistic legislation hindered the progress of Barcelona up to the end of the Middle Ages and in the long run enabled Valencia to acquire a larger international clientele. But the technique of the merchants made rapid progress and in some directions more than caught up with Italian business methods. A scholar has found in a Barcelonese contract of 1332 closer resemblance to the modern *société en accomandite* than can be noticed in the *commenda* and *compagnia* contracts most commonly used in Italy at the same period. The Catalan banking system was backed by comparatively small capital, but it was well developed: the public bank of Barcelona probably antedated all other public banks of the world. Jewish–Majorcan cartographers in the mid-fourteenth century drew maps as accurate as the slightly earlier *carte da navegar* of the great Genoese and Venetian cartographers. Textile and ceramic production were fairly well developed.

Nevertheless, none of the Catalan seaports ever built up commercial networks as wide as those of Venice and Genoa, and their decline was already pronounced in the first half of the fifteenth century. In 1387 they had lost to the Florentine Acciaioli family their main base in the Levant, the duchy of Athens. Soon thereafter they lost their quasi-monopoly of North-West African trade to the Italian cities. Their weakness may be ascribed partly to lingering indiscipline, but it was above all a consequence of the smallness of their population. Barcelona in the fourteenth century does not seem to have surpassed 30–35,000 inhabitants, the larger part of whom were petty craftsmen and other non-merchants. Valencia and Palma (Majorca) were still smaller, and Jews, Tuscans and Genoese maintained a prominent position in their trade. Behind these cities was not a region bustling with the activity of commercial and industrial towns, as was the hinterland of Venice, Genoa and Pisa, but a poorly developed kingdom of noblemen and peasants. In the fourteenth century – and to some extent even today – the Catalan coast was like the gilt façade of a building of mud and straw.

The golden age of Catalonia was already on the wane when both Portugal and Castile, initially with some assistance from Genoese admirals and traders, were opening those southern and western Atlantic routes that were to win for them a great place in the history of civilisation. Up to the late fourteenth century most of the scant long-distance trade of Portugal had been directed northwards, especially to Flanders, England and Normandy – therefore beyond the scope of the present chapter. But in the fifteenth century Prince Henry the Navigator promoted those famous voyages along the West African coast which enabled a group of Portuguese seamen and merchants to amass modest capital by purchasing the gold dust of Palola from Arab merchants and by buying or capturing negro slaves. The little island of Arguin near the Mauretanian coast became the main fortified outpost of these officially sponsored expeditions, which faced the competition of more advanced but more isolated Genoese and Venetian merchants. The Portuguese also landed in the Azores and Madeira, where they introduced the sugar cane. Norman adventurers established themselves in some of the Canaries, which had already been visited in the fourteenth century by the Genoese and the Portuguese, and ruled the islands in the name of the Castilian king.

These and other successes were great landmarks in world history, but their immediate impact on the development of Portuguese and Castilian trade was surprisingly small. Though recent studies have brought new light on the progress of both countries in the late Middle Ages, they do not quite dispel the impression that Castile and Portugal remained altogether underpopulated and underdeveloped, and that local gains barely made up for the all-European crisis which affected them and was aggravated (especially in Castile) by a worsening treatment of the Jewish and Muslim minorities. Agriculture was everywhere predominant, and it lacked manpower. Portugal exported salt, oil, cork and wine, mostly towards northern Europe. Fishing supported a fairly large number of seamen, and business methods were more up to date than in Castile. Larger than Portugal, but less open to the influence of international sea trade, Castile had a greater variety of vegetable and mineral products, but only two significant exportable surpluses. In the fifteenth century, it developed almost abnormally its production of fine wool, obtained by cross-breeding of the local flocks with African merinos. The largest, privileged company of sheep men, the *Mesta*, in 1477 owned 2,694,032 sheep, roughly one for every second inhabitant of the kingdom. While England, formerly the greatest exporter, was cutting its sales of wool in order to promote its textile industry, Castile chose the opposite course; thus it conquered the Italian wool market but missed all chances to become a great producer and exporter of cloth. Iron, the other (and older) trump card of Castile, was the special asset of the Basques, who in 1293 had exported about 4,500 tons of it, chiefly to northern Europe, and maintained a lively economic pace in the harder times that followed. By the fifteenth century a number of Basque merchant ships frequented the Mediterranean. But it would have been impossible for that peripheral region to convert to its tempo the rest of the kingdom, where the business class was exceedingly small, with the harrassed Jews precariously holding some of the key positions. One cannot improvise an enterprising commercial society: when the explorations paid off, Portugal and Castile had to turn to German, Italian and other foreign merchants for capital and advice, and they never quite made up for a delayed start.

In the fifteenth century the most rapidly advancing region lay in the heart of Europe. Commerce and industry were booming in the towns of southern Germany and Switzerland – Nuremberg above all, but also Augsburg, Ulm, Bâle, Zürich, St Gall, Geneva and many others. The 'great merchant company' of tiny Ravensburg, founded around 1380, had *fattori* in 21 foreign centres including Bilbao, Pest, Venice and Bruges. Ratisbon alone seems to have been on the decline after reaching its zenith around 1380; Vienna, rapidly growing up under the protection of the powerful Habsburgs, captured part of its trade, and fustian of Augsburg and Ulm eclipsed the 'Milanese' fustians made in Ratisbon. The golden age of Upper Germany came after the middle of the fifteenth century, but already in 1447 there were such men as the uncle and nephew Mundprat of Constance who amassed a taxable income of £132,424 in trade with Milan, Genoa and Spain.

Let us stop a moment to consider the rapid development of Nuremberg. If we may judge from the account books of one of its most prominent merchant companies, the Holzschuher firm, in the early fourteenth century the town did not yet have any particular importance. The firm's customers were residents of Nuremberg or lived within a thirty-mile circle. They were mostly noblemen and bourgeois who bought Flemish cloth, or Jews who borrowed money at the frightful average rate of 94 per cent. One wonders what interest the Jews in turn had to charge on those who borrowed from them. Certainly they took more than Nuremberg's legal rate of 43 per cent, which was the same as that generally allowed in Flanders, but was two to four times as high as the legal rate allowed in most Lombard towns. Nuremberg at that time (1304–7) produced linen and iron ware, but was not a great exporting centre. In 1332, however, we hear that its citizens enjoyed customs reductions in 69 cities, and a little later arms made in Nuremberg are mentioned in Spain, Italy and Flanders. Textile production also stepped up. In Venice the merchants from Nuremberg gradually overtook those of all the other German cities. In the early fifteenth century Nuremberg business men established connections with commission agents in Lübeck and in many cases went themselves to live in that great Hanseatic seaport. They imported

Baltic herrings to Salzburg and Polish oxen to Frankfurt-on-Main. Before the middle of the century they extended their business to East Prussia and, a little later, to Livonia. Thus they were competing with the Hanseatic merchants in the Hansa's own preserve. They distributed eastern spices and western textiles in many centres of the interior where few Italian big business men went. Nuremberg had become the central hub of a network of overland communications between eastern Central Europe and the Rhineland and between the Mediterranean and the northern seas.

It has been claimed that the surge of German trade was based on superior techniques, but the truth of the matter is that up to the end of the fifteenth century the business methods of the Germans remained more primitive than those of the Italians and the Catalans. Even later, though the great Augsburg bankers employed larger capitals than did the Florentine companies at an earlier period, they hardly used more advanced methods; moreover, they were much more narrowly attached to the tradition of excluding from key positions in their business any one who did not belong to their families. The general international situation was probably the largest factor in the rise of South German capitalism. Wars and the continued unfavourable balance of trade with the Levant increased the need for both non-precious and precious metals, of which South Germany and Austria were the main sources. Furthermore, the spread of the Commercial Revolution to eastern Central Europe, from Poland to Hungary, placed South Germany at the gates of an expanding frontier. Finally, the chaos of France and the troubles in Italy and Flanders hampered traffic across the continent via the Rhine valley or the western Alps, leaving the routes across the eastern Alps as the best available alternative. The progress of cities on the Italian side of the Brenner Pass – Verona, Trento, Bolzano, Merano – is a further indication of the same trend. The fact that before the fourteenth century few Italian big business men thought it worth while to penetrate the German market had permitted the growth of a comparatively modest group of long-distance merchants in every city from the upper Rhine to the upper Danube and the upper Adige. When the new opportunities matured, these men were ready.

It would be a great mistake to assume that Italy in the last century of the Middle Ages had lost its primacy in trade. In spite of the increased difficulties we have described, the Italian cities dazzled all foreign visitors with their magnificence, and merchants and bankers from Italy still towered above the business men of the rest of the world. Continued progress of commercial techniques and increasing concentration of capital had caused the influence of Italian big business men to increase rather than to diminish. The economic condition of Italy during the Renaissance has been rightly compared with that of England after 1870. The progress of other peoples took away from Italy its almost absolute monopoly of long-distance trade, but it also created new fields where the accumulated capital and experience of that people of commercial pioneers could be profitably employed. If all this implied decadence, neither the Italians nor their new competitors fully realised it.

Banking, maritime trade, industry and agriculture all alike were thriving in the country that had been the cradle of the Commercial Revolution. The Medici bank was by far the greatest financial organisation in Europe, roughly between 1430 and 1480. Its activities reached every region of Europe, the Levant and North Africa; they included not only banking operations but also trade in luxury articles and staple products, control of a few units of textile industry and monopolistic exploitation of alum mines. Many other banks in Florence and in other Central and North Italian cities had huge capital and world-wide business relations. On the other hand, Venice, having definitely outdistanced Genoa as a commercial centre, was undoubtedly the first seaport in the western world. Substantially accurate statistics, quoted in an official report of 1423 by Doge Tommaso Mocenigo, valued the Venetian sea trade outside the Adriatic at 10 million ducats yearly for exports and as much for imports. More than one-fourth of the exports represented trade with the duchy of Milan. The capital and the other cities of the duchy – among which Como held the first place in this respect – exported through Venice 48,000 pieces of cloth. Cheaper fustians, once the great speciality of most Lombard towns, were now an important industry only in Cremona; but that little town alone exported 40,000 pieces. Even granting that the figures may have been slightly exaggerated, it still was a large production considering that much cloth also was exported via Genoa or the Alpine passes and that German merchants often purchased it directly in the Lombard cities. Silk, however, was becoming a more important industry than woollen production. The diminished inflow of raw material from Turkestan and China did not discourage the Italians, who developed sericulture at home. Upper Italy, which today is the largest raw-silk producer in Europe, had not yet won its dominant position, though its agriculture was at that period far in advance of that of the other European countries. Most silk came to the manufacturers of northern and Central Italy from Sicily and Calabria through the seaport of Messina. The same regions also produced some cotton and a little sugar, thus turning to their own profit what originally had been a disadvantage, that is, the increasing difficulties in supply from the Levant. Saffron, once a staple of the Levant but in the thirteenth century cultivated also in Aragon and in eastern Tuscany, now was obtained almost exclusively in Italy, the mountainous province of Abruzzi being the greatest producer. Thanks to that trade, the little town of Aquila suddenly became a great commercial centre frequented by North Italians, Germans, and Dalmatians.

The Italians, not content with developing home resources, continued to expand abroad. Many had established residences in every important city of western Europe, from Lisbon and Cadiz to London and Bruges (or, later, Antwerp) as agents of home firms or as promoters of 'commercialisation' in less advanced countries. They also extended their influence to countries they had seldom visited in the earlier period. In Germany and Austria they used their capital, organisation and business methods to compete with local business men in banking and in export–import trade. In the kingdoms of Poland, Bohemia, Hungary, Serbia and Bulgaria, now for the first time entering fully into the circle of commercial economy, they introduced the luxuries of refined clothing and foodstuffs long familiar to the western gentlemen and bourgeois. They leased salt mines, mints and custom duties. Even when they became citizens of a foreign country, they usually kept very close relations with their fatherland, to which many of them retired to spend their last days. In the Levant and Africa, the oldest fields of their expansion, they adapted their methods to the changed situation. Since the colonies no longer were springboards for direct trade with the Farther East, the Italians intensified the exploitation of local resources and partly shifted their commercial activity from trade in luxuries to trade in cheap staple goods. In Africa and in the Caucasus, they had to learn how to trade with underdeveloped peoples, who had no use for the finer products of European manufacture. It was a profitable experience, although it entailed some disappointments. In 1447 a Genoese brought a lot of quality cloth to the oasis of Tuat, very deep into the Sahara. He hoped to sell the cloth for some gold dust of Palola. But Palola lay still far away, and the blacks of Tuat were all but naked! The unfortunate pioneer had to prepare his creditors for very bad news by writing a letter where he described his mischance. But a few years later a Florentine merchant, who was not looking for Palola, found Timbuktu on the Niger an excellent market for selling inexpensive Lombard cloth.

Still one must consider that by the fifteenth century Italian private initiative, unsupported around and inside Africa by naval power and state intervention, had to reckon with the new colonising ambitions of Portugal and Castile. Portugal, especially, still offered employment and fiefs to some Italian navigators, but in its pursuit of a route to the Indies relied mostly on its own subjects and plans. Even in the Levant, many Italian colonies had drifted away from their motherlands; but the power of Venice and Genoa still hovered on the eastern Mediterranean and the Black Sea as a reassuring if not unchallenged presence. In spite of its archaic underpinnings commerce with certain Caucasian regions was very profitable: Italian traders brought salt and coarse shirts, which served as money, and carried away caviare and slaves, more precious than gold in the exchanges with Egypt. The larger part of the Black Sea trade, however, was neither with primitive people nor with the decadent Byzantine towns, but with young and coming countries of eastern Europe. Caffa, the thriving capital of the Genoese semi-independent dominions in the Crimea, had lost its function as the terminus of Pegolotti's 'quite safe' route to Peking, but it had become the most lively commercial centre of south-eastern Europe, frequented by Tatars of the Golden Horde, Russians, Poles, Romanians, Bulgarians, Armenians, Greeks and Turks. Its cosmopolitan population probably approached 100,000. Further south-west in the Black Sea was the coast of the Balkan peninsula, where Genoese colonists of the lower Danube competed with the Venetian settlers in Greece and with the merchants from Dubrovnik and Zara for the growing trade of Walachia, Moldavia, Bulgaria and Serbia. Greece proper and the islands of the Aegean had acquired a new value for the Venetians, who gave fresh impulsion to the export of Malmsey, Cretan and Cyprus wines.

In 1453, however, the Turks conquered Constantinople. The capital and last stronghold of the Byzantine Empire had long before lost its commercial importance, but not its prestige, and it commanded both the entrance to the Black Sea and the shortest crossing from Europe to Asia. Its fall brought home the fact that the Mediterranean no longer was a lake dominated by Italian traders, and that no Italian state would make an all-out effort to recover its control. There are no sudden changes in economic history: Italy remained a great economic power, and the two states that emerged on top during the following hundred years, Turkey and Spain, also were essentially Mediterranean and South European; but the twilight of Mediterranean-centred trade began in 1453.

CHAPTER VI

Asia, Africa and the Trade of Medieval Europe

I. *Introduction*

(1) DISTINCTIVE FEATURES OF TRADE IN THE ISLAMIC WORLD

The medieval Islamic world, by comparison with western Europe, constituted a highly urbanised civilisation; and it combined distinctive regional specialities in industrial activity, agricultural production and cultural life. It was a civilisation whose great economic centres were tied together by successful and esteemed merchants, exploiters of the regional variety of the Muslim world; it was a civilisation which drew from the lands beyond its periphery – from Christian Europe, the spice islands and black Africa – many of the essential commodities upon which its wealth was constructed. Indeed, the economic dependence of the Islamic lands on non-Muslim regions helped to generate into life a new species of competitor: the mercantile republics of Italy and southern France, whose naval victories assured Christendom of command over the Mediterranean as early as 1200. The appearance of thriving communities of Christian merchants in western Europe only increased the commercial importance of the Islamic world, as the principal channel for the transmission of African gold and Indonesian spices to new centres of demand in the Latin West. In other words, the history of trade *through* the lands of Islam, towards Europe, becomes a dominant theme in the development of Muslim trade. In the late Middle Ages Egypt, Anatolia, Iraq all remained important consumers of the luxury articles which western merchants also required; but fluctuations in business, even the organisation of trade, were increasingly responsive to impulses from the West. Thus, a wealthy group of Egyptian spice traders, the 'Karimi' merchants, flourished partly in response to western demand for eastern spices on sale in Alexandria and other great ports.

This chapter seeks to investigate the major trade routes, carrying gold and spices towards Europe, textiles and slaves out of Europe. This is not to deny the continued vitality of trade within the Islamic world throughout the Middle Ages. Cairo and Baghdad were not under the remote control of western merchants; but even they, by the thirteenth

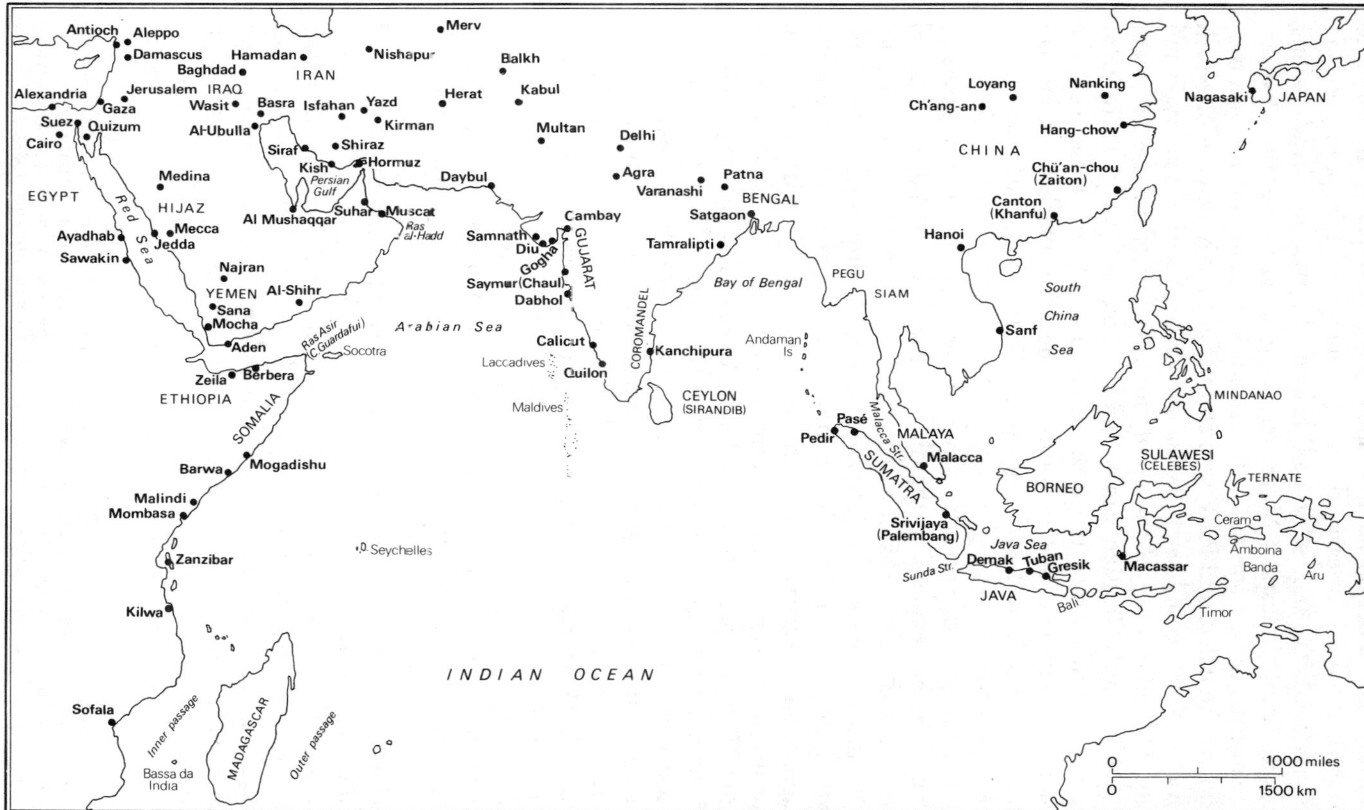

Map 6. Trading Ports and Cities in the Indian Ocean

century, fell under an Italian spell, and were partly in thrall to Westerners who had learnt the art of 'dumping' European goods in eastern markets, and who had helped throttle an already ailing Muslim textile industry.[1] Moreover, the gradual shift in the Mediterranean balance of trade towards western Europe meant the accumulation in the Italian and Provençal cities of gold siphoned out of North Africa before it could reach the Islamic heartlands of Egypt, Syria and Iraq. The suffocation of the textile industries of Islam, the diversion of gold towards Christendom and, finally, the discovery of a route to the spice islands which by-passed Muslim territory – these were the stages, to some extent consciously planned, by which the Christian merchants sought to snatch control of the movement of goods from the infidel foe.

The presence of powerful forces at work beyond the frontiers of Islam does not explain all the difficult paradoxes found in medieval Muslim trade. The urban civilisation of Islam, inheritor of centuries of Hellenistic, Syrian and Jewish expertise, encompassing a great part of the known world, from the Atlantic to Malaya, proved commercially stagnant in comparison with the once peripheral lands of western Europe: business methods, maritime skills, industrial technology in the Latin West outpaced those of Islam between 1100 and 1350. This is all the more remarkable since nautical language in the West and – to a lesser extent – terms of business show strong Arabic and Persian influence. It is too easy simply to explain this loss of primacy as the result of the naval successes of Byzantine and Italian fleets in the medieval Mediterranean. The issue reaches far deeper: the loss of naval primacy itself reflects a lack of sustained interest among Muslims in nautical technology – the romantic image offered by the modern dhow must not be confused with the more demanding conditions of heavy Mediterranean shipping. Equally, the decline of Muslim textile industries seems to suggest a more cautious attitude to investment in technological improvement than is visible in the Latin West.[2] Associated with this, there can be observed in the Islamic countries few well-established, well-heeled, politically influential merchant dynasties such as are to be found in the great Italian cities of the same period. An occasional family of Karimi merchants retained wealth and influence in late medieval Egypt for two or three generations; such families diversified their interests and operated small factories or purchased urban property. But there is no one in the Islamic world to

[1] For this phenomenon, see now the important final testament of Eliyahu Ashtor, *Levant Trade in the Later Middle Ages* (Princeton, 1983), which, however, appeared after this text was written.

[2] But it is now argued that the scale of agricultural innovation has been underestimated: A. Watson, *Agricultural innovation in the early Islamic World* (Cambridge, 1983), 5.

compare with the European urban patrician, with his say in the government of the city-state, with his blood-links to the local landed aristocracy, with his staying-power in trade, industry and often in politics too. The Islamic world, though rich in towns, had few city-states, and those merchants who acquired a major say in government did so mostly as civil servants – the *khawajas* of late Mamluk Egypt, the Muslims at the Cola court in India. The vast clans of the Italian cities which provided economic protection to their trading members, which provided a broad portfolio stretching far beyond the world of commerce, had no parallel in the fluid society of the Islamic town.[3]

It was a fluid society because the Islamic towns were the product of 'mushroom growth' – extraordinarily rapid growth. Basra grew from nothing to 200,000 inhabitants in less than thirty years, during the seventh century. The merchant class of the great Islamic cities, of Cairo, Baghdad or Cordoba, was not indigenous, as was the upper level of the merchant class in the western cities, which grew more slowly, often from Roman roots. Immigration from Persia to Spain fuelled the growth of the Spanish silk industry; the spread of new articles of production, and of artisan producers, across the breadth of the Islamic world was an expression of the breakdown of localism, of incorporation into a vast *oikoumene* unrivalled since the urban expansion of Hellenistic times. And, just as the localism of the Italian city-state – the local patriotism of all, the local origins of those in command – provided a powerful driving-force in the battle against competitors, the lack of localism in the Islamic lands deprived the cities of commercial aggressiveness. There is little to compare with the crusading zeal of the eleventh-century Pisans. Another expression of this lack of localism was government interference. The Mamluks were interested in trade because trade produced a major part of their revenues; but they did not think constructively about the expansion of commercial opportunities for their subjects, and, in the long run, their policies did more to destroy the commercial strength of the Egyptian spice-merchants than did external competition. A similar phenomenon is visible in contemporary Byzantium and Sicily. Thus, in the Islamic world the apparent lack of autonomous, well-armed trading cities is reflected in a more passive attitude to trade than western Europe displays.

Claude Cahen has pointed to the lack of interest in surplus

[3] These thoughts are generated by A. Udovitch's article 'Bankers without Banks: Commerce, Banking and Society in the Islamic World of the Middle Ages', in *The Dawn of Modern Banking*, ed. by Center for Medieval and Renaissance Studies, University of California-Los Angeles (New Haven, 1979), 255–73.

production as an important feature of the mercantile outlook of the medieval Islamic world. He characterises the merchant outlook as one of 'spéculation' and of 'acquisition'.[4] By the former term he means that merchants sought to purchase goods at acceptably low prices and to resell them at a handsome profit. By the latter term he means that the state and the wealthier classes aimed to draw from trade items that would enhance their style of living or their authority (under this heading purchases of weapons can be cited); there was no interest in the encouragement of trade and industry as sources of employment, nor even as sources of goods which could suitably be traded against imported luxuries or necessities. Such an economy could function largely because of the ease of access of the central Islamic lands to supplies of gold, which could be had quite cheaply on the Sahara trade-routes; this *grande aisance monétaire* sapped interest in the development of domestic centres of production. Cahen's analysis gains added point when the changes visible in the West are compared to the more static position of Islam. Although the Italian towns also experienced a degree of *aisance monétaire*, in ease of access to silver stocks, substitution of industrial products for bullion exports is clearly visible in the Genoese and Venetian records, even before 1200.[5] Moreover, the business class of northern Italy, Provence and Flanders placed little emphasis on easy living and aimed to supply princely courts and urban consumers rather than to enhance their own domestic luxury. Formed in a commercially more barren environment, the outlook of the western merchant was more adventurous, more experimental, than that of the Muslim merchant.[6]

At this point, it would be as well to dismiss any notion that the capacity for commercial expansion of the Islamic lands was deliberately limited as a result of sheer piety – that is, of obedience to the Islamic laws against usury. Similar restrictions were in fact applied to merchants in the West by the Roman Church and to Jewish traders

[4] C. Cahen, 'Quelques mots sur le declin commercial du monde musulman à la fin du Moyen Age', in *Studies in the Economic History of the Middle East from the Rise of Islam to the Present Day*, ed. M. A. Cook (London, 1970).

[5] See, for instance, M. F. Mazzaoui, *The Italian Cotton Industry in the later Middle Ages, 1100–1600* (Cambridge, 1981).

[6] So why did Venetians, Genoese and other Westerners aspire to wealth? Actually this remains an unsolved, and almost uninvestigated, mystery. Among the aristocratic clans who dominated the early Italian communes, the acquisition of wealth from trade was seen as a means to consolidate their standing at the head of society; wealth also offered status, in many towns, to *nouveaux riches* who sought respectability or even a political voice; and for poorer elements in the town the chance to make a profit by investing in trade made obvious sense, since such profits ensured survival during periods of famine or crisis. But for those who led the commercial expansion of the communes, it was status rather than high living that was required. The wealthy Muslim merchant had, under Mamluk rule, no hope of participation in the central organs of government, which remained in the hands of an ethnically distinct group of slave-soldiers; status was expressed through spending, rather than through the exercise of political control.

of East and West by eminent rabbis; equally, merchants of all three confessions knew there existed loopholes which made a variety of credit transactions possible.[7] In Tunisia at the end of the eleventh century there was active exchange of gold coins against silver, for profit; this was actually forbidden by the Malikite school of Muslim law, but, as Rodinson says, 'there was an everyday practice of violation of the canonical rules'. Non-Muslims in Islamic lands often found it preferable to follow Muslim commercial practice, which apportioned responsibility in the event of loss more conveniently than Jewish law. And the Jewish philosopher Maimonides expresses the position clearly when he says, in response to a query from Egyptian Jewish merchants, that deferment of payment in order to charge interest was not in breach of the Torah: far from being objectionable, it was necessary in order to sustain a great range of livelihoods.[8] Attempts to argue that the Muslim merchant of the Middle Ages was less 'capitalistic' in his use of money than his Christian or Jewish counterpart are the product of wishful thinking by Muslim apologists.[9]

Adept in commercial techniques, the Muslim merchant was nonetheless unadventurous in his travels beyond the Islamic world. There was major settlement by Muslim traders in China, and many Muslim merchants sailed the Indian Ocean, as far as Malaya. But it should not be assumed that the great geographers, such as ibn Battuta, were typical examples of Muslim enterprise. Geographical and zoological curiosity drew the Far East to the attention of Muslim and Jewish scholars, but practical enquiry based on commercial priorities was generally lacking. Marco Polo brought westwards an account of the nature and place of origin of luxury articles which, for all its overlay of wondrous romance, was more detailed and more accurate than the information available to Muslim merchants on the spice routes. Latin Christians explored the western shores of Africa and the Atlantic islands more thoroughly and successfully than anyone since the Phoenicians of Carthage, although western Africa was for a time part of a vast Islamic empire stretching north to Spain. Thus, the Vivaldi brothers had no known Arab precursors in their search for a maritime route to the Indies in 1291. And it is not surprising that the inhabitants of the Muslim world should have remained content with the trade routes they possessed. There were no ambitious groups seeking to bypass the

[7] For a comparison of Jewish, Christian and Muslim approaches, see M. Grice-Huchinson, *Early Economic Thought in Spain, 1177–1740* (London, 1978).

[8] S. D. Goitein, *A Mediterranean Society: the Jewish communities of the Arab World as portrayed in the documents of the Cairo Genizah*, I, *Economic Foundations* (Berkeley/Los Angeles, 1967), 197.

[9] M. Rodinson, *Islam and Capitalism* (London, 1974); but contrast the regrettable diatribes of e.g., N. Pacha, *Le Commerce du Magreb du XIe au XIVe siècles* (Tunis, 1976), or the views reported by B. Lewis, *History Remembered, Recovered, Invented* (Princeton, 1975), 84–5.

major routes to south and east through Islamic territory – across the Sahara, down the Red Sea or through Mesopotamia – except, predictably enough, in the Christian West, where such discoveries were seen as a potential blow to Islam. So the Muslim merchants tended to rest on their laurels.

Associated with this series of phenomena is the way Muslim communities at the edges of the world tended to develop. In China, a settled community of Muslim merchants existed from the eighth century onwards, but increasingly the Chinese Muslims concerned themselves with local trade and provisioning. Although links along the ancient silk roads were maintained, westwards to Sogdian and Iranian lands, the Chinese Muslims did not emerge as a new class of large-scale international traders. Islam furnishes few merchants to compare with the mysterious Radhanite Jews, whose caravans spanned Eurasia from the Seine basin and central Spain to the Chinese empire, and whose successors, albeit in more modest fashion, can be found among the Jews of Old Cairo in the eleventh century.[10] In particular, attempts by Muslim merchants and colonists to settle in Europe were never successful, outside southern Spain, Sicily and the Balearics. The fortified settlements of ninth- and tenth-century Provence proved ephemeral, though their commercial importance may have been under-estimated; the Muslims of south Italy settled the land and are soon lost to sight; the Muslims of Sicily vanished from the map by the early thirteenth century. The records of Genoa, Venice and Pisa rarely reveal Muslim merchant visitors to the Italian ports, though Pisa displays evidence for marriage ties between Tuscan patricians and Tunisian emirs. The real Muslim 'presence' in Europe had a very different character: a firm legacy was provided as a result of western importation of, or copying of, eastern industries – the silk industries of Spain, Sicily and, ultimately, of Lucca have some Islamic parentage, as do the European cotton and linen industries.[11]

It is evident that the term 'Muslim trade' is an unfortunate one, since it mixes two categories of activity, religious and economic, which were in fact separate. The trade of the Muslim world was carried on by Jews, Parsees, Copts, Greek orthodox, Hindus as well as Muslims; moreover, certain of these groups played an exceptionally important role. The Coptic monasteries in Egypt functioned for a time as staging-posts, where slaves were castrated and given a chance to recover from their disfigurement, before being trans-shipped to the great slave markets. The activities of Jewish merchants as intermediaries

[10] See now E. Ashtor, *The Jews in the Mediterranean Economy, 10th to 15th centuries* (London, 1983), a collection of articles of capital importance.

[11] See Mazzaoui, *Italian Cotton Industry*; Watson, *Agricultural Innovation*.

between Christian Europe and the Muslim lands have already been mentioned. And Hindu merchants penetrated quite far into the Islamic world – to the Persian Gulf and to the Red Sea entrance. In the late Middle Ages only one trade route under Muslim rule can really be described as the preserve of Muslim merchants, to the exclusion of 'protected peoples' and other unbelievers: the Red Sea route from the port of Aydhab, in eastern Egypt, to the straits of Aden, with the accompanying land route along the Arabian coast, through Mecca and Medina (which were, in any case, entirely closed to non-Muslims). Indeed, the reason for maintaining Muslim commercial control was largely religious: the fear that Raynaud de Châtillon would be emulated in his attempt to interfere with the pilgrim routes to Mecca in the 1170s, and that the centres of Islam would be placed under direct threat. It was only in the fifteenth century that Muslim merchants exported their beliefs to trading partners on the edge of the known world: the conversion of the Maharajah of Malacca will be discussed later. Aggressive islamisation was not a trade mark of Muslim merchants in the Middle Ages; in black Africa Muslim merchants peaceably serviced the needs of pagan courts and showed respect for the clearly drawn lines which divided the Muslim merchant communities from the traditionalist, animist ruling class.

In this chapter, then, the terms 'Islamic' or 'Muslim' trade will be used, as far as possible, to indicate trade by adherents of Islam. Equally, the term 'trade in the Islamic (or Muslim) world' will be used to describe trade by all those living in or entering lands subject to Muslim governments. The term 'Arab trade' will be avoided in general, since it is patently clear that many Muslim merchants were not Arab but Berber, Turkish, Iranian, Indian, Malay or Soninke.

(2) POSSIBLE APPROACHES TO THE HISTORY OF ISLAMIC TRADE

Attempts to provide a connected account of trade in, and through, the Islamic lands have been frustrated by the character of the source material upon which scholars have been forced to rely.[12] Struve's study of the trade routes of the Islamic world, published in the early nineteenth century, brought together information from travellers' tales, geographies and chronicles and made it possible to produce a rough map of the main routes; but little attention could be paid to processes of change. Heyd's history of the Levant trade, later that century, introduced valuable western evidence, though in consequence

[12] For further references, see the Bibliography on p. 905.

a largely Venetian and Genoese perspective was supplied; the trading life of the Muslim lands received less attention. Important new sources have come into view only since the 1930s: the Cairo Genizah letters, under Goitein's piercing eye; the Vienna papyri, whose value is not yet fully revealed; the *fatwas* or judicial decision of Muslim judges, which have much to say about economic conditions in the Maghrib. The study of tracts on taxation and agriculture, particularly by Claude Cahen, has greatly enlarged understanding of the links between commercial activity and the agrarian regime. And the horizons of the geographers have been extended by increased attention to Chinese sources which describe the topography and trade of the spice islands. Historical works by Malay and black African chroniclers have received serious attention, too. Archaeological work at the major Muslim trading centres – at Fustat or at Siraf – has brought to light material evidence of Sino-Egyptian commerce in the eleventh century and later; and close physical examination of Muslim coins and textiles has indicated the strengths and weaknesses of regional economies. So too, the attempts by Professor Eliyahu Ashtor to examine in tandem western archival sources such as the Datini letters in Prato, and oriental sources, effected a major advance in understanding the Levant trade of the Middle Ages. The intention here is to make maximum use of these 'new' sources, and to make relatively limited use of the more traditional geographical texts. The Genizah letters and the *fatwas* often say more clearly and more accurately what geographers and pilgrims report at second hand or through a fading memory. Thus, Idrisi's world geography, prepared at the court of Roger II of Sicily in 1154, incorporates contradictory reports of the economic condition of North Africa – the product of old and new sources, mingled together not always very successfully by a nonetheless remarkable Arab geographer. Another difference in emphasis in this account of the trade of Islam is the lack of attention paid in this chapter to the history of the Muslim fleets in the Mediterranean and other seas. The history of Islamic trade has been presented – by Archibald Lewis, for instance – as a by-product of Muslim naval history: a view which depends on untestable assumptions about the impact of local wars upon the freedom of movement of merchants.

Another departure from the norm is to lay particular stress on the centuries after about 1000. This is the period most clearly illuminated by many of the new sources; it is also the period when the Islamic world functioned increasingly as a channel through which luxury goods passed to western Europe, and the economic fortunes of western Europe and Islam became closely intertwined. Moreover, the sources for trade in black Africa and the spice islands become fuller after about

1300, so that the function of the extremities of the Muslim trade routes can be perceived more clearly in the late Middle Ages.

II. *Early Islamic Trade, 650–1000*

(1) INTERNAL VARIETY AND VITALITY

Islam inherited a rich mercantile legacy. The cities of Syria, Egypt and Mesopotamia had a long history of commercial prosperity; Damascus and Alexandria had for centuries benefited from their position at the cross-roads of several Levantine trade routes. But, generated by the Arab conquests, new cities also sprang into life in the seventh century: the fortified camps of Kufa and Fustat (whose very name, 'the Ditch', reveals the town's origins) grew into focal points for the immigration of artisans from far afield and for the transformation of Bedouin nomads into a settled Arab governing class. Mass movements of population, set in train by the breakdown of the old political order in Iran, Syria and North Africa, radically altered the ethnic composition of the former Hellenistic and Sassanian lands, and decisively shifted the emphasis in production from country to town. Eighth-century Baghdad or Fustat were inhabited by Arab conquerors, Persian and Syrian migrants, Jewish business men and artisans, mountain or desert peoples from nearby – united, if not in faith, at least in speech as Arabic became the *koine* of much of the Islamic world. The expansion of production within the towns, the lack of impenetrable frontiers, the use of a common speech, all encouraged the exchange of goods across considerable distances.

Another perspective can be adopted. The Byzantine Empire of the sixth century was experiencing a decline in industrial production and in population, especially within the towns. The Byzantine countryside, at least in Syria and Egypt, remained quite prosperous, as the large farms excavated in the Israeli Negev suggest. The trade of the Mediterranean was contracting, and a slow return to the soil seems visible in the Levant. One cause of this change was the series of plagues in the sixth and early seventh centuries, which afflicted the skilled manpower of the east Mediterranean cities. The rise of Islam suddenly turned these scales. The passages of Arab armies through Syria and the Holy Land led to the abandonment of the delicately maintained irrigation works of the Byzantine engineers; the settlement of former Bedouins in Byzantine lands meant a real decline in agricultural expertise; the emigration of the existing rural population to the new towns exacerbated decline. And the nomadic inheritance of the Arabs – their continuing care for flocks of sheep and goats – destroyed the fragile cover offered by desert foliage and induced severe desiccation. The urbanisation of the Islamic world thus reflects the rapid destruction of the economic base in the former Byzantine provinces.[13]

The movement of population had important consequences for urban, if not for rural, technology. In the eighth century southern Spain was settled by Syrian silk-workers, who laid the foundations of a long-lasting industry. So too Persian textile-workers brought their techniques westwards to Egypt and the Maghrib. Individual cities developed a special reputation for their industries: Mosul, Fustat for their cloth, Damascus and Toledo for their weapons. Yet many of the skills for which they were famous had been imported from further east; in the case of the Damascus and Toledo sword-makers, even the raw materials came from distant regions. In other words, regional specialities could flourish at some remove from the centres of production of raw materials. By the eleventh century, it was common for regions to enter into partnership with one another, one providing, the other processing, the raw material: the symbiosis of Sicily and Tunisia in the textile industry is a good example. The Islamic world of the eighth to the eleventh century is characterised by the ease of movement of raw materials towards specialised centres of craftsmanship, and of processed goods out of these centres and through the Muslim lands. By the tenth century this picture is becoming distorted: towns in Egypt and Spain were able to imitate each other's products and to undercut the market for specialised items manufactured in the classic centres. Isfahani textiles of Persian origin came to be made in Antioch; and the term 'Sicilian textile' lost some of its meaning when Spanish or Egyptian manufacturers hawked similar goods, locally produced, under that attractive label.

Two factors then – local specialisation and ease of communication across the vast Islamic world – greatly stimulated long-distance trade in the prize products of the Muslim towns, such as textiles, metalwork, pottery and leather. Long-distance trade in foodstuffs also developed, to service the large populations of the great cities: wheat was the staple diet of Baghdad and Cairo and – though shortages were frequent – it

[13] Watson, *Agricultural Innovation*, 5, seeks to remove blame from the Arab nomads for the worst destruction, and points rather to the positive achievements of Arab agriculture. It is important to distinguish between the first phase of nomadic upheaval in the Middle East (carried through into Tunisia as late as the eleventh century by the Banu Hillal) and later phases of major innovation, for instance in Moorish Spain and Sicily. Cf. M. Brett, 'Ifriqiya as a Market for Saharan trade from the 10th to the 12th century A.D.' *Journal of African History*, XIII (1972), 489–506 and D. S. H. Abulafia, 'L'attività commerciale genovese nell'Africa normanna: la città di Tripoli', *Atti del Congresso internazionale di studi sulla Sicilia normanna* (Palermo, 1973). Brett's view (but not my own) has points of contact with Watson's. Unfortunately, the argument about the devastation of the Holy Land has developed into one about modern politics.

is striking how successfully these cities provisioned themselves. Particularly successful was the expansion of market gardens on the edge of the Muslim towns, providing additional sources of non-staple food: onions at Palermo (the breath of whose onion-chewing inhabitants distressed ibn Hawqal in the tenth century); new vegetables, in Egypt and Spain, such as the artichoke and spinach. The bitter oranges of Persia and Mesopotamia reached Syria, Sicily and Spain by the end of the tenth century, and their peel and juice were blended with local cane sugar to make delectable sweets.[14] Nor were these fruits and delicacies aimed solely at a small aristocracy of consumers: they were packed and sent in trade across the sea. And, despite the rural decay which the Arab invasions had induced, the cities of the Islamic world were surrounded by intensively cultivated, highly productive gardens, whose owners imported the most efficient irrigation techniques and methods of terracing. Islam in the Middle Ages was so distinctively an urban civilisation that even the most successful agricultural innovations were conducted within or on the edge of towns. Of course, certain luxury foodstuffs could only be acquired in small quantities at very high expense from very far afield. In the early Middle Ages the major courts were not yet substantial purchasers of eastern spices (though Indonesian perfumes were much favoured); but by the tenth century the caliph was delighting in the taste of *sanbusaj* prepared in Baghdad with dough, meat and spices:

> And season well with cinnamon and rue;
> Of corriander add a handful, too,
> And after that of cloves the very least,
> Of finest ginger, and of pepper best,
> A hand of cummin, murri just to taste.[15]

And it was at this period that the maritime trade route carrying spices westwards, to Amalfi and Venice, was also re-established.

An important feature of the economy of the Islamic world was the reliance of the central lands – Egypt, Iraq – upon a bimetallic currency of gold and silver. The circulation of gold in the Muslim lands was encouraged by the reforms of Caliph Abd al-Malik at the end of the seventh century: he introduced a gold dinar of Muslim design to replace earlier coins which imitated Byzantine designs and precious metal content. The new dinar was slightly less pure than its Greek

[14] Watson, *Agricultural Innovation*, 42–50, and *passim*, charts these movements. He notes that bitter oranges had some appeal when sweet oranges were still unknown. In the Roman period the citron was the only citrus fruit cultivated in the Mediterranean, and it performed a role in Jewish liturgy during the Feast of Tabernacles.

[15] A. J. Arberry, 'A Baghdad Cookery-book', *Islamic culture*, XIII (1939); cf. C. Roden, *A Book of Middle Eastern Food* (London, 1968; Harmondsworth, 1970), 101–2.

counterpart, with the result that the dinar chased out the Byzantine *nomisma:* merchants preferred to hold back the *nomisma* for hoarding and to handle the inferior Arab currency in trade. But the successful creation of an Islamic currency, acceptable throughout the trading world, depended on the availability of good supplies of precious metals; the dinar, and its silver fraction, the *dirhem*, were minted from metals found mostly at, or beyond, the edge of the Islamic world, in Africa and the Caucasus, but over whose extraction Muslim merchants retained a very strong influence. Within Islam, there were still gold supplies to be had until the tenth or eleventh century: the Tulunid rulers of Egypt exploited the treasure trove of the ancient Pharaohs; the monasteries of Egypt and Syria were forced to release treasure – not just coin, but precious objects, deposited for safe-keeping by local Christians. Maurice Lombard saw these church treasures as the precious metal reserves of the Muslim rulers, available in time of crisis during the eighth and ninth centuries; and he pointed to similar usage in the Latin West, for example by the Frank Charles Martel.[16] Generally, gold supplies were easier to assure than silver, for the silver mines of Spain were soon exhausted and those of northern Iran and the Caucasus lay in a turbulent region. This meant that the price of gold was low, relative to silver: in the tenth century, a gold: silver ratio of about 1:8 is found in the central Islamic lands. To some extent, the problem of silver supply was alleviated by the growth of trade with Italy and western Europe: Sardinian and German silver was imported in increasing quantities from the eleventh century onwards. But European silver began to flow east when the Islamic world had already experienced a severe seepage of silver into the treasuries of Indian rulers and of Scandinavian pirate princes. In around 1000 Islam was probably losing silver faster than it acquired it.

The hoarding of Muslim silver outside the Islamic lands only decreased the availability of that metal as a medium for smallish or modest exchanges of goods. The regular use of silver and even gold coins in small villages was apparent to ibn Khurdadbah, writing in the ninth century. Payments of taxes in money were common, though in Egypt taxes in kind remained prominent throughout the Middle Ages. Under al-Hakam II (961–76) the treasury of the caliphs of Cordoba received a total of forty million dinars; at his accession it already held five million (250 cwt gold). Although the Moors in Spain must have received a handsome income from the poll-tax on Jews and Christians and from taxes on agricultural land, a high proportion of such figures

[16] M. Lombard, *The Golden Age of Islam*, translated from *L'Islam dans sa première grandeur, VIIIe–XIe siècle* (Paris, 1971) (Amsterdam, 1975).

represents trade taxes: taxes at the city gates, in the markets, on ships coming up river. In other words, the vast income of the early Islamic rulers testifies to the enormous volume of precious metals circulating as coin and the scale and success of inter-regional trade.

(2) EXTERNAL RELATIONS

(A) *The Age of the Radhanites*

Any study of early Islamic trade must consider the arguments of Henri Pirenne, suggesting a closure of the Mediterranean after the Muslim conquests in Syria, Egypt and North Africa, and after the Frankish conquests in Italy.[17] Pirenne maintained that commerce between western Europe and the Islamic world shrank to a very slight trickle during the eighth century; and he pointed to the disappearance of an active trade in spices, papyrus, wine and textiles, which the western Roman Empire had drawn from the East. Ashtor has continued to support the Pirenne thesis, observing that unremitting warfare between Muslim and Byzantine fleets made the free movement of merchant shipping all but impossible. He points to descriptions of Saracen pirate squadrons, lying in wait for Byzantine ships (or vice-versa), sacking coastal towns, seizing booty.[18] In criticism of this view, it might be wondered whether the references to Greek and Arab ships attacking merchant vessels do not reveal a continuation of Mediterranean maritime trade – not, to be sure, the massive movements visible in the later Middle Ages, but occasional, even unpredictable, sailings by Christian-owned ships of Marseilles and several Italian towns to the ports of the Maghrib, Egypt and Syria. Ashtor also notes that the ninth century saw Muslim navies land in Apulia, Sicily and Crete; he stresses too that war between Muslim pirates and Muslim governments was frequent – witness the occupation of Alexandria by Spanish Moors in 814. However, the same century sees the emergence of Amalfi, Naples and other south Italian ports which were active in trade between the central Mediterranean and Constantinople, Egypt and the Maghrib; Amalfi, as Wickham says, established its position 'by more or less consistently siding with the Arabs in their raids on the Italian coast in the ninth and tenth centuries'.[19] This makes plain both the difficulties Arab fleets presented and the opportunities that could be seized to

[17] H. Pirenne, *Mohammed and Charlemagne* (London, 1939); see now also R. Hodges and D. Whitehouse, *Mohammed, Charlemagne and the origins of Europe* (London, 1983).

[18] E. Ashtor, *A Social and Economic History of the Near East in the Middle Ages* (London, 1976), 102–4.

[19] C. Wickham, *Early Medieval Italy: Central Power and Local Society, 400–1000* (London, 1981), 150.

re-establish trans-Mediterranean trade. Trade between the edge of the Latin world and the edges of the Islamic world did not cease, but most commercial centres experienced serious decline by the ninth century; and even Amalfi, for all its success, could not create a strong economic bond between the European land-mass and the Levant. Moreover, the effects of the trade recession on the Islamic lands should not be underestimated. The coastal towns of the Nile delta and Syria were depopulated – their Greek orthodox inhabitants heading for Constantinople, their Muslim inhabitants choosing safer settlements away from the coasts.

Certain groups of merchants did, however, foster the limited luxury trade between western Europe and the East. The Saracen pirates of Fréjus and the Provençal coast founded settlements whose inhabitants remained active in trade and manufacture. The city of Marseilles contained a large and respected Jewish community, which may have kept links to Egypt and Syria open. But the best-known evidence for such links concerns another group of Jewish merchants, the Radhanites.[20] Ibn Khurdadbah describes how these intrepid travellers linked Spain and the French hinterland to the Near East, central and southern Asia, and China. The Radhanites must be assumed identical to the Jewish merchants who frequented the court of Charlemagne and Louis the Pious in the eighth and ninth centuries. They apparently worked alongside Syrian Christian merchants, who since Merovingian times had furnished northern European courts with rare eastern goods. Maurice Lombard saw a distinction between the *Judaei* and the *Syri*: the *Syri*, he believed, flourished earlier and specialised in the importation westwards of eastern luxury articles; the *Judaei* succeeded them and specialised in the export of furs, weapons and, no doubt, slaves to eastern outlets.[21] This distinction seems forced: the Radhanites too imported eastern spices, perfumes and drugs – the drugs formed part of the cabinet of the esteemed Jewish and Syrian physicians of the early Middle Ages. Moreover, it is not clear that references in western sources to 'Jewish' merchants should be understood to mean that those merchants were all Jewish by religion or descent. The terms *Judaeus* and *Syrus* became terms of convenience, more or less synonymous, to describe a certain type of merchant activity, rather than to provide an exact description of an individual merchant's origins. The Jewish merchants, for their part, probably benefited from the presence along the great trade routes of Hebrew communities some of which – in Prague, in Cochin India, in southern China – may have been founded by the Radhanites or earlier Jewish traders. Among the routes of the

[20] E. Ashtor, 'Aperçus sur les Radhanites', *Revue suisse d'histoire*, XXVII (1977), 245–75.
[21] Lombard, *Golden Age*, 212.

Radhanites was a route down the Rhone (whence perhaps their name, via the Latin *Rhodanus*), to the Provençal ports and across to Egypt; then down the Red Sea to India. Another route took the merchants to northern Syria; from Antioch they headed towards Iraq and thence by sea down the Persian Gulf to north-western India, Ceylon and the Far East. However, it was normal to cover the last stage, from India to China, by land, cutting out the Malayan peninsula. Yet another route eastwards ran through Prague to the kingdom of the White Bulgars and thence to central Asia, northern Iran and the remnant of the old silk road to China; along this route the Radhanites may have had the assistance of the Khazars, Turks whose rulers had adopted Judaism in the eighth century. Finally, there seems to have been a south Mediterranean route, from Spain along the African coast to Palestine and thence via Damascus to Iraq, Iran and the passes into India.

The Radhanites, as has been seen, exported some western products, such as furs and weapons. The demand for 'Frankish' swords in Islamic lands was high, because there were only limited supplies of iron for Muslim technology, and because the iron and steel technology of northern Europe was quite advanced. Even more important objects of commerce were the slaves of eastern Europe, the Turkish-speaking regions of central Asia, the horn of Africa and those Mediterranean coasts which suffered incessant pirate raids. The scale of the Zanj slave-revolt in southern Iraq, at the end of the ninth century, suggests too the scale of imports of slaves – in this case, from East Africa. The Saqaliba or Slav dynasties of southern Spain, in the eleventh century, were created by descendants of east European slaves who had been bought for service in the bodyguards of Moorish rulers. By 961 there were 13,750 male Saqaliba in Cordoba. And, in fact, the trade in west European slaves grew by the tenth century, while black slaves became less popular – partly as a result of the Zanj troubles. Even Egypt and Syria received large shipments of Slavs. Now, it is clear that the Radhanite Jews played a central role in the organisation of the slave trade. Certain of their major bases were also bases for the slave trade. At Verdun in northern Europe there was an important castration centre, though eunuchs were also 'manufactured' in Spain. Prague flourished as a great slave market, as did the northern Iranian towns – Samarkand, Bukhara. The slaves met very varied fortunes, depending on physical attributes – colour, beauty, strength. Sturdy Turks and Slavs faced a military career; Circassians were prized for their beauty, and the girls often entered the harem. Handsome boys fell into the possession of pederast princes. No more fortunate were the Zanj, who were put to work as sweepers and dredgers in the marshy lands of southern Iraq. When in 869 the Zanj were urged to revolt, they were promised not merely liberation, but many slaves of their own.

In the ninth century the Radhanites seem to decline. Partly this may reflect a change in attitude at west European courts: greater hostility to the slave trade[22] and hostility, too, to the presence at court of favoured groups of non-Christians – witness the fulminations of Agobard of Lyons against the Jews. More importantly, the ninth and tenth centuries saw the gradual re-awakening of Italian trade across the Mediterranean. A native business class began to emerge in southern Italy first of all, then in northern Italy, Flanders and the Rhineland; the last indications that the Rhineland Jews were in any way especially prosperous date from the First Crusade, when they suffered fearful pogroms. The revival of European trade was (Marseilles and Barcelona apart) a revival of Christian trade, and Jews were actually prevented from settling in large numbers in some centres of business, notably Genoa. In consequence, the Jewish merchant of the late eleventh or twelfth century possessed more restricted horizons than his Radhanite predecessor. If he lived, say, in Egypt or Spain he rarely interested himself in trade into the European land-mass. Most of the lands he knew were under Muslim rule, and even Constantinople was not a favoured trading centre for Jews.

The Radhanite traders were not the only Jewish business men to reach a peak before 1000. The Jewish bankers of Iraq and Egypt received high favour from the caliphs in the ninth century; though Jewish court bankers appear afterwards, in Mongol Iran, for instance, there seems nothing to rival the great merchant dynasties of the ninth and tenth centuries. Fischel picturesquely described one family firm in Baghdad as 'Joseph, Aaron and Co., Head Office, Baghdad'.[23] The court bankers were masters of the transmission of funds, using cheques and letters of credit; they were trusted servants who impressed rulers with their ability to provide and increase revenue; they made handsome loans when the ruler was short of money. Some capricious rulers did, it is true, force these loans against veiled threats of persecution of the local Jews. In Egypt Yaqub b. Killis even secured the office of vizier, though at the price of conversion to Islam; in 983/4 his private treasure contained at least 200,000 dinars. Quite apart from the fact that these bankers were also very active in long-distance trade, it is clear that the presence at court of such wealthy financiers, ready

[22] E. Ashtor, 'Gli Ebrei nel commercio mediterraneo nell'alto medioevo (sec. X–XI)', *Settimane di studio del Centro italiano di studi sull'alto medioevo*, XXVI: *Gli Ebrei nell'Alto Medioevo* (Spoleto, 1980), 454–6, repr. in E. Ashtor, *The Jews and the Mediterranean Economy, 10th–15th centuries* (London, 1983).

[23] W. J. Fischel, *Jews in the Economic and Political Life of Medieval Islam* (Royal Asiatic Society monographs, XXII, London, 1937).

to provide extensive credit, stimulated princely demand for luxury items and for high-quality armaments.

(B) *The Varangian Roads*

In the ninth century there emerged a group of merchants whose success in bringing furs and ironwork from north-eastern Europe bears comparison with the active trade of the Radhanites in the same commodities. The Scandinavian and east Slav traders linked the Baltic to Russia, Greater Bulgaria and the Black, Caspian and Aral Seas; they founded new markets along the Dnieper, Don and Volga. The ease with which these merchants transferred from the upper stretches of one river to the upper stretches of another led later geographers, notably Idrisi, to assume that the Aral Sea fed the Caspian and the Caspian the Black Sea. But the truth is remarkable enough: Varangian and Russian merchants regularly visited Azerbaijan, Khwarizm and, of course, Constantinople – Mickelgard, 'the Great City' par excellence. They also knew well the Turkic metropolis of Bulgar, which minted good silver coins copied from Abbasid models. Ibn Khurdadbah indicates what commodities these merchants carried:

> The Rus, who belong to the Saqaliba [Slav] tribes, travel from Saqlaba's most distant parts to the Roman Sea and there they sell beaver skins and black fox skins, and swords too. The prince of the Romans [the Byzantine emperor] claims one-tenth of their merchandise...On their way back they go by sea to Samakhars, the city of the Jews [Phanagoria, Black Sea], and from there they return to Slav country. Or else they sail down the Don, down the Slav's river [the Volga] and pass through Itil, the Khazar capital, where the ruler takes one-tenth from them. There they embark on the Caspian Sea and make for whatever point on the coast they have in mind. From Jurjan or Rayy [modern Teheran] they transport their merchandise by camel to Baghdad. There Slav eunuchs act as interpreters for them. They claim to be Christian and pay the poll-tax as such.[24]

Other Arabic writers, such as ibn Fadlan, shed further light on the activities of the Russians and their trading colleagues. Pagan practices survived among them – as ibn Khurdadbah says, they 'claim' to be Christian – and their lands were not often penetrated by Muslim merchants. Rather was it the Varangians and the Russians who sought out Muslim purchases anywhere from Bulgar to Baghdad.

The effects of these activities are visible in the great hoards of Iranian silver coins found in Sweden and on sites along the Varangian trade

[24] *Le Livre des routes et des provinces, par ibn Khordadbeh*, ed. C. Barbier de Meynard (Paris, 1865), 264.

routes. The northerners purchased from Iraq and Iran only limited quantities of Muslim produce, but they imported into the Muslim world great amounts of the wax, metals and furs of the remote forests. In Iran there was heavy demand for furs, to offset the often chilly climate. The Scandinavians and Russians thus carried away much silver, received as payment for these goods. This took the form of artisan work – silver ornaments such as buckles, small bowls and vases, or jewellery – as well as coined bullion. In Sweden oriental *objets d'art* formed an important part of the assets of a well-to-do trader or of a successful warrior. They could be converted back into precious metal, or melted down to manufacture local luxury articles – this was surely the fate of many Iranian *dirhems*. By contrast, very little gold coinage has been found in the Varangian hoards. Partly this reflects the direction in which much Varangian trade passed – through the silver-rich regions of Iran and the Caspian – but occasionally Muslim dinars were melted down to manufacture northern ornaments.[25]

The drainage of silver northwards could be tolerated in the tenth century; but during the eleventh century a silver famine developed in Iran. And these strains led to the decline of the northern trade routes: Iraq and Iran simply proved incapable of paying for massive imports of furs, swords and slaves, so long as the Varangians expressed little interest in Muslim textiles, ceramics and other non-metal goods. In addition, the trade routes fell victim to political changes in the steppes. The very expansion of the Scandinavian-Slav state of Rus' engendered serious difficulties: the Russians began to compete for control of territory with Khazar and Great Bulgar rivals. No doubt the ancient freedom of access to Iran, and freedom of choice of route, was increasingly denied to Varangian and Slav merchants. The irruption of the Cumans and Pechenegs into the Black Sea region, and of the Seljuq Turks into the Byzantine-Iranian borderlands, further reduced the security of the river routes during the eleventh century. And, most importantly, there emerged other European suppliers of certain items the Varangians had formerly conveyed: arms, slaves. The Italian merchant was less adventurous in attempts to penetrate Iraq or Iran, but his pockets were also full of silver when he came East, and empty of it when he returned West. Associated with this shift of the trade routes towards the Mediterranean is another major change: the economic eclipse of Iraq and the rise to greater prominence of the Nile valley as the commercial centre of the Islamic world.

[25] See below Chapter VII, p. 483.

III. *The Primacy of Egypt, 950–1500*

(1) THE LOSS OF PRIMACY BY IRAQ

The rise to economic primacy of Egypt coincides with the political separation of Egypt, under its Shiite Fatimid rulers, from the Sunni caliphs of Baghdad (969). Much of North Africa and Syria also acknowledged Fatimid overlordship. The presence of a large, powerful, luxurious court on Egyptian soil acted as a stimulus to local and foreign merchants: demand rose for silk, perfumes and other luxury goods; while the war needs of the Fatimids brought fortunes to suppliers of timber, iron, pitch and other military equipment. The trade in armaments points towards Venice, Pisa, Genoa and their western rivals – it is striking that the first mention of a Genoese merchant in an Egyptian document coincides with the rise to power of the Fatimids.[26] Despite papal condemnation of merchants who supplied the infidel's war needs, the traffic in contraband armaments only grew in the eleventh and twelfth centuries. By 1171 the Pisans were content to promise Saladin supplies for his navy. Even more important a factor in the economic rise of Egypt was the supply of silver from west European mines; this eased the silver shortage in Egypt, but relatively little western silver percolated into Iraq and other Islamic lands where the shortage was also felt. The westerners also stimulated the spice trade through the Red Sea; it is likely that the vigorous expansion of the Red Sea trade from the twelfth century onwards testifies to western demand for the drugs, dyes and flavourings of the East. But a side-effect was the slow decline of the alternative maritime route from India, which ran up the Persian Gulf to Iraq. Siraf and Kish slowly lost their importance; Aden became the principal transit centre for eastern spices. It would, of course, be wrong to underestimate the demand in the Muslim countries for eastern spices, but it does not seem that, before the Fatimid period, the India trade concerned itself heavily, perhaps primarily, with eastern perfumes, and that the new emphasis on spices reflects western taste at least as much as Muslim. In other words, a trade from East to West through Egypt was born, whose *raison d'être* was not so much the provision of Islamic centres of consumption, but the vigorous new courts and towns of western

[26] S. M. Stern, 'An Original Document from the Fatimid Chancery concerning Italian Merchants', *Studi orientalistici in onore di G. Levi dell Vida*, II (Rome, 1956), 529–38. Evidence – of a sort – for Pisan trade with Egypt is provided by the *bacini*, or ceramics, often of Islamic origin, inserted in the façades and towers of medieval Pisan churches; in the eleventh century a high proportion of *bacini*, originated from Egypt, though the route by which they reached Pisa is uncertain: David Abulafia, 'The Pisan Bacini and the Medieval Economy: a historian's viewpoint', *Papers in Italian Archaeology*, IV, *The Cambridge Conference*, Part IV (Oxford, 1985).

Europe. Paradoxically, Egypt owed some of its economic success in the eleventh and twelfth centuries to the defeats which Islam was suffering in the western Mediterranean at the hands of Pisan, Genoese and Venetian navies and of Norman, Castilian and crusader armies.

The strength of the Fatimid economy is perhaps most clearly revealed by the gold coinage of Egypt, which reached high levels of purity by the twelfth century (see Table I). Ehrenkreutz has analysed the fineness of the dinars of Iraq and Egypt, and his figures testify to the decline of the former and the rise of the Fatimid state:[27]

Table I. *Standard of fineness of Muslim gold dinars*

Number of coins from:	Per cent fineness below 90	90	91	92	93	94	95	96	97	98	99	100
Iraq *after* 946	7	1	—	—	—	—	—	—	—	—	—	—
Syria 891–969	2	1	1	2	4	1	2	2	1	—	—	—
Fatimid Egypt in reigns of:												
al-Amir 1101–30	10	1	2	—	1	3	—	8	3	9	8	40
al-Hafiz 1130–49	—	—	—	—	—	—	—	—	—	1	2	22
az-Zafir 1149–54	—	—	—	—	—	—	—	—	—	—	—	8

These figures also suggest how successfully Fatimid Egypt maintained access to supplies of gold from black Africa. Although some of this gold was siphoned off by the North African towns and by mints in Sicily and Spain, much of it was carried eastwards to Egypt, which formed a monetary rampart restricting the movement of gold into Iraq and the other Muslim lands – a function already observed in the case of western silver.

The Egyptian revival was generated by native producers, too. Taxation was fairly heavy, but direct intervention in the production of crops and industrial goods was limited – there was nothing to compare with the Mamluk war machine of the late Middle Ages, which often exploited the economic activities of the Egyptians in order to finance major military projects. In other words, there was no attempt to direct industrial production to specific ends, such as the manufacture of armaments. The caliphal *tiraz*, or textile workshop, was not intended to compete with the thousands of small factories aimed at the Egyptian public and at foreign consumers.[28]

While Egypt was flourishing, Iraq experienced serious internal strife.

[27] A. Ehrenkreutz, 'Studies in the Monetary History of the Near East', *Journal of the Economic and Social History of the Orient*, II (1959), 144, 256; *idem*, 'The Standard of Fineness of Gold Coins circulating in Egypt at the Time of the Crusades', *Journal of the American Oriental Society*, LXXIV (1954), 164, 166; Ashtor, *Social and economic history*, 176, 194.

[28] H. Rabie, *The Financial System of Egypt, AH 564–741/AD 1169–1341* (London, 1972), 72–132.

Peasant rebellions in the tenth century, Turkish irruptions in the eleventh, local separatism, all placed a severe strain on the Abbasid treasury. Collection of taxes must have become more difficult, and expenditure on the army became more burdensome. The Abbasids had recourse to debasement of their dinar. Under al-Muktadir, in 917, the dinar descended to a purity of only 85 per cent gold, though it rose to 90 per cent later in his reign. By the eleventh century dinars of only 90 per cent gold were commonplace; silver reserves were depleted. Moreover, pestilence in the towns and neglect of the countryside led to a decrease in industrial and agricultural production in Iraq and Syria. In fact, even when much of Syria fell under Fatimid control, this region did not participate in the economic success of the Nile region. Its agricultural regime was too severely battered by abandonment of the soil; its towns were tumultuously striving for autonomy and amongst themselves. It is probable that their fortunes only revived under crusader rule, when Syria came to play a similar role to Egypt as an intermediary in the west-bound spice trade. The process by which economic primacy was transferred from Iraq to Egypt is, then, intimately linked to that whereby western merchants came to dominate the Mediterranean and the markets of the Levant.

(2) THE CAIRO GENIZAH

(A) *The Evidence*

The period of Egyptian ascendancy is brightly illuminated by the hundreds of merchant letters discovered in the storeroom of a synagogue in Fustat (Old Cairo): the Cairo Genizah letters. These texts describe in detail trade routes and business methods; they list commodities and prices; other types of Genizah material, such as dowry lists and rabbinic *responsa*, furnish additional data on economic life. Nor was it simply the letters, judgements and prayer-books of the Cairo Jews which were preserved in the Genizah. Precisely because Fustat was regularly visited by Jews from other lands, and because its own merchants travelled to India, Yemen, Sicily, Tunisia and elsewhere, the Cairo Genizah provides exact information about commercial activity beyond Egypt. Equally, the very character of the Genizah generates serious problems. As Goitein has remarked, a Genizah is the very reverse of an archive: a collection of discarded texts ripe for oblivion rather than prepared in an orderly fashion for preservation.[29] Thus, the documents were discovered in a chaotic jumble, mostly torn or damaged; thus, too, few documents carry a precise indication of date, though most of the commercial letters that survive date from

[29] Goitein, *A Mediterranean Society*, I, 7.

the eleventh and twelfth centuries. The near impossibility of creating a chronological series from the Genizah letters handicaps the economic historian: problems of economic change can rarely be resolved on the basis of the Genizah texts alone. Moreover, the Genizah reflects the life of only one commercially enterprising community within the Islamic world. The Jews of the Ben Ezra synagogue in Fustat, the Genizah Jews, were Rabbanite, or orthodox, Jews of the Palestinian rite; but there were also Karaite Jews in Old and New Cairo (as there still are), as well as Rabbanites of the 'Babylonian' liturgy; and there are clear signs that the Ben Ezra Rabbanites steered away from a wide range of business enterprises which other Egyptians – Karaites, 'Babylonian' Jews, Copts, Muslims – must have handled. The Genizah merchants seem little involved, for instance, in the grain trade, or in trade in Morocco, the Spanish Levant, southern France and Byzantium. Here the 'Babylonian' Jews, whose liturgy was generally used in Spain, may have been much more active.[30] The Fustat Jews were indeed specialists, but it is impossible to do more than suggest ways in which their portfolio was different from that of other Egyptian merchants – what is clear is that their priority concerns, such as the spice and flax trades, brought great wealth to the Nile region between the tenth and the thirteenth centuries. In that sense, at least, they stood at the centre of the economic organisation of Egypt and the Islamic world. Moreover, the Fustat Jews seem to have possessed considerable commercial resilience, surviving as a major force in international business until 1150 or later. An explanation of this resilience may be hazarded. There exists an appreciable contrast between the cohesive community life of the Fustat Jews and what Goitein calls 'the shapeless mass of Muslims, who had little opportunity for self-government'; indeed, in certain respects the separate Jewish jurisdictions and community officials helped to create among the Jews an integrated self-governing 'republic' within the Fatimid state, albeit under strict controls; the Muslims were denied such autonomy. There were, too, important differences between the Jewish and the Muslim attitude to family life and the role of women in domestic, and hence in business, affairs.[31] The broader outlook of the Fustat Jews provided them with greater staying-power as merchants than their non-Jewish rivals possessed, for the Jews possessed powerful backing from their families; moreover, the dispersed Jewish communities of the Mediterranean maintained marriage relations over great

[30] For the possibility that the group of Jews following the Palestinian liturgy (ancestor to the modern Ashkenazi and Italian liturgies) maintained economic contacts with certain areas, such as the land of Israel itself, that were more intensive than those of the Jews of the Babylonian liturgy – (presumed ancestor to the Sephardi and to many Oriental liturgies), who had close links to Spain, see Goitein, *A Mediterranean Society*, I, 18–21. But this is mere supposition.

[31] S. D. Goitein, *A Mediterranean Society*, III. *The Family* (Berkeley/Los Angeles, 1978), 312–32.

distances, forming in fact a single great community which held in common certain of its business interests.

The Genizah documents provide essential clues to the question how the Islamic world acted as intermediary in the transfer of eastern spices and luxury items to the Christian West. The Genizah merchants are the middlemen of whom a detailed record survives – for all the lacunae; and the evidence from Fustat becomes richest just when the Mediterranean falls under Christian domination, and just as western demand for eastern luxuries begins to intensify. But because of the lacunae, the most sensible approach to the Genizah material is to offer a brief description of the trade routes, commodities and merchant class which it reveals, without forcing the evidence into a chronological framework.

(B) *Trade Routes and Business Methods of the Fustat Jews, 950–1150*

The Genizah merchants knew particularly well the shipping routes linking Egypt to Tunisia, Sicily and the coast of Syria. These major lines of communication were themselves serviced by shorter sea routes which tied the major Mediterranean ports to subordinate outlets; in addition, a lengthy network of land routes ran all along the coast of North Africa and far into the Saharan interior. The principal point of interchange between routes was al-Mahdiyyah in Tunisia – indeed, it is a clear reflection of the concentration of Genizah material in the eleventh and twelfth centuries that al-Mahdiyyah holds so prominent a place in the documents. Built as a political and commercial centre in the mid-eleventh century, this town seized local primacy from Qayrawan, before succumbing in turn to Tunisia.[32] Other towns in Tunisia, such as Sfax, channelled their major sea-bound trade through al-Mahdiyyah, although there were occasional visits by Egyptian merchants in search of textiles and olive oil. Whether the tendency to funnel trade through one or two major ports indicates that the volume of long-distance exports from the middle-range towns was not sufficient to warrant visits by large ships it is impossible to say. The Fustat merchants may have found it convenient to compare goods from a variety of sources by trading mainly through the larger ports, where they could expect to find the whole range of North African products: oil, textiles, coral, raw fibres. In these ports they made contact with a second stratum of local merchants, Jewish and Muslim, who handled the produce of the smaller towns and of the countryside, and who saw the shores of the Mediterranean as their farthest horizon.

[32] Brett, 'Ifriqiya as a Market', 347–64; cf. A. Lézine, *Mahdiya: recherches d'archéologie islamique* (Paris, 1966), and his shorter *Mahdiya* (Tunis, Société tunisienne de diffusion, 1968).

Another feature of 'Genizah trade' seems to cast the Fustat Jews as aristocrats of commerce. They favoured express travel, sailing on ships which avoided even quite important harbours – Tripoli, for example – and which headed straight for the cities of greatest renown. Thus, there was a direct link between Alexandria and Bougie, in North-west Africa, and there were fast boats bound for southern Spain – for Denia and Seville. This traffic could be quite intensive, in season. A letter written in Alexandria in the eleventh century reports in the late summer that 'until today, there arrived from the island of Sicily ten ships, each carrying about five hundred persons'.[33] It is true that the Genizah contains many letters describing the delays and frustrations of travel – shipwrecks, piracy, government interference – but these record relatively unusual events, and the trade routes westwards from Egypt seem to have operated fairly smoothly through much of the eleventh century. It was the routes northwards, to Syria and Anatolia, which were more seriously affected by war. Ships arriving from northern Syria seem often to have skirted the ports of Palestine, though about fourteen Syrian ports appear in the Genizah letters, including Laodicea, Tyre, Acre and Ascalon. The Egyptian Jews, partnered by Muslims, brought nuts, gums and raisins to the Nile along the Syrian coast.

The northern routes possessed additional importance: they were a stage on the long haul to Constantinople. Goitein mentions a letter describing a journey from Egypt to Constantinople via Jaffa, Rhodes and Chios, but he suspects that 'the trip, rather than following a regular route, might have been occasioned by military operations'.[34] In fact, it was normal for even the 'express' ships to hug the coast, and in consequence neither Cyprus nor Crete received the close attention of Egyptian shippers and traders.

The Genizah letters look eastwards, too, to the Red Sea and India. As Tunisia was the great way-station for merchants trading in the Far West, so Yemen was the point of concentration for those looking towards India. But Yemen was less visited than Tunisia: the Red Sea was regarded as less accessible, and India merchants were thought more foolhardy, or more venturesome. A merchant from Bône (Algeria) was anxious to collect debts due to him in Fustat before the arranged date; he therefore let it be known that he was passing through Egypt on his way to Yemen. But once he had recovered the debts he turned round and headed for the Maghrib. A debtor complained: 'Had I known he was only going to the west, I would not have paid him a thing.'[35] And there was a tendency for

[33] Goitein, *A Mediterranean Society*, I, 315.

[34] *Ibid.*, 214.

[35] *Ibid.*, 42. For the following see S. Shaked, *A Tentative Bibliography of Geniza Documents* (Paris/The Hague, 1964), 200.

merchants facing bankruptcy to flee to the Red Sea port of Aydhab, where they were less likely to be found than in the Mediterranean. This eastward route was closely tied to the westward one: goods were transmitted by the same groups of merchants from the Maghrib to Aden and back. In about 1100 the rabbinical court at Fustat adjudicated a case concerning Sicilian robes sent to Yemen. At the same period a Persian Jew living in Alexandria was handling herbs and dyes produced as far apart as Syria, Tunisia, Socotra and the East Indies, as well as coral from the Christian West and ambergris from the Atlantic. A leading eleventh-century merchant, Nahray b. Nissim (fl. 1045–96), exported flax from Egypt to Sicily and Tunisia, imported silk from Sicily and Spain, brought lacquer, indigo and brazilwood from the Far East for export westwards, and handled precious stones (turquoises, pearls, tortoise-shell), many of which had an eastern origin. Thus, it is clear that the Fustat Jews did not normally specialise in, say, the India trade as opposed to the Sicily trade; they operated on several fronts, spreading their portfolio widely; they tied together the Indian Ocean trade routes and the Mediterranean ones.

Specialisation in the India trade did, however, occur; and it seems that specialisation gradually became more frequent. Goitein has conjured a tempting explanation of this change out of the Genizah texts. In the eleventh century, he suggests, it was merchants from the Islamic world, not least the Fustat Jews, who dominated the trade routes of both the Mediterranean and the Indian Ocean. Then, as Italians gathered Mediterranean commerce into their own hands, the Jews of Egypt turned their attention increasingly towards the Red Sea and India; by the thirteenth century, a new force, the Muslim Karimi merchants, emerged to dominate the eastern trade and to service the needs of Italian visitors to Egypt; the Red Sea became a Muslim sea. The Karimis were granted extensive political favours, and, compared to them, the Fustat Jews possessed little leverage at the courts of Cairo and Aden. Thus, in the thirteenth century the Fustat Jews were obliged to concentrate more heavily on local Egyptian trade. The great age of the Fustat community was at an end. Indeed, non-Egyptian matters disappear largely from the Genizah, after about 1200, compared to the vast mass of mercantile correspondence which can be dated between the tenth and late twelfth centuries, and which concerned a much larger world, stretching from Andalusia to the Indies.

The Genizah letters illustrate this shift to more localised trading interests through descriptions of the overland routes which linked the city of Fustat to other African centres. Particularly important was the trade route through the desert to Aydhab on the Red Sea. There is a reference to a caravan which carried 500 camel-loads of eastern spices and luxury goods from the Red Sea to Cairo, as well as countless

Muslim pilgrims returning from Arabia.[36] Another land route tied Egypt to Tripolitania, Tunisia and – ultimately – Morocco. A certain Musa b. al-Majani travelled along this route, conducting business at many small towns. He would leave one caravan, do business, then wait for a new convoy; or he would make up a small party with other merchants, rather than search out a caravan – this method of travel was essential if a merchant was to reach lesser centres, off the main trade routes. But generally the Cairo Jews disliked land travel, and it is easy to see that the Italian supremacy in the Mediterranean afflicted them all the more, given their preference for the sea. Land travel was slow, and dates of arrival were even harder to predict than in sea travel; the danger from bandits was thought greater than that from pirates; and, for Jews, there were problems in travelling on the Sabbath which did not really apply on board ship. There was, therefore, a strong tendency to entrust goods bound overland to Muslim colleagues who would be able to exercise greater freedom of movement – such as the possibility of accompanying caravans of Muslim pilgrims free from the abuse Jews sometimes suffered. More successful were the attempts by the Fustat Jews to make use of inland waterways. Shipping penetrated the Nile as far south as Cairo, and there was particularly heavy local traffic in barges. In good conditions the Fustat to Alexandria run took less than a week. However, river traffic was more obviously subject to government interference than land or sea traffic. The rulers of Egypt saw in the Nile an ideal source of customs revenue, with tax stations all along the banks. One Genizah letter mentions the disappointment felt by a merchant coming by boat up-river to Fustat; the boat made an unscheduled stop at New Cairo, and the tax-farmer came on board to levy his dues.[37] It must be assumed that the river link between Cairo and Alexandria, Damietta and Rosetta was of prime importance, acting as a channel for the transfer of eastern goods to the markets of the Mediterranean. It is thus hardly surprising that the Genizah Jews achieved their high level of prosperity: their home city, Old Cairo, was, with New Cairo, the hub of the long-distance spice route.

The Genizah letters contain valuable information about business practice in the Islamic world. Although it would be unsafe to generalise from Jewish business practice and to apply the Genizah evidence to Muslims or Christians, it is clear that all Egyptians, not to mention Tunisians and Sicilians, had certain practices in common; a Jew wrote to Maimonides:

> Some fifteen years ago, I happened to travel to Sicily. So-and-so confided to me one and a third qintars of indigo, which had cost him $37\frac{1}{3}$ dinars. This

[36] Goitein, *A Mediterranean Society*, I, 276.
[37] See Goitein, *A Mediterranean Society*, I, 295–301.

was done without any specification. I did not know whether the merchandise was given to me as a *qirad* [a contract similar to the western *commenda*] or a shipment, and if it was *qirad*, whether it was according to Muslim or Jewish law.[38]

Thus, there were differences between Jewish and Muslim practice, but it was sometimes thought possible to ignore the issue when forming a trade agreement. What is at least clear is that the lone trader was a rarity. Even a merchant who relied on his own capital would try to travel in company: there were professional companions to be found. In particular, there existed a preference for short-term legal agreements, which guaranteed each participant's rights, over informal relations of trust where risks and profits were not formally apportioned. In the *qirad* contract, one partner provided capital, the other labour, and profits were divided; there also existed contracts in which a number of partners placed different shares, distributing eventual profits on the basis of labour provided and capital invested – an arrangement similar to the contemporary Genoese *societas*. A court record of 1162 reveals a merchant who provided 55 dinars out of a total of 150, and stood to gain one-third of all profits; his intention was to travel the Egyptian countryside with a cargo of silk.[39] It is worth adding that the late eleventh century exposes to view primitive insurance methods, so that, for instance, money could be invested in trade on behalf of young children, without excessive risk of loss of capital. But a warning should be sounded against the view that these commercial methods were exported to the West; Udovitch has presented the western *commenda* as a borrowing from the Islamic *qirad*.[40] These business methods were simple, uncluttered by legal complications, and they were capable of springing into life spontaneously at different ends of the Mediterranean. Indeed, the real analogy is not between the western *commenda* and the eastern *qirad*, but between the *commenda* and the commercial lease, equally familiar to Italian sharecroppers and Egyptian peasants.

It is clear that there is no single 'commercial law of the Genizah'. Maimonides himself counselled against this with a variant on the adage 'when in Rome, do as the Romans'. He stated that partnerships are binding subject to the customs of the country where they are made, unless the agreement stipulates otherwise. It is rare for Genizah contracts to follow Jewish law and to make the travelling partner responsible for losses – which can be explained in practical terms: the agent was usually younger and less affluent than his backer, and simply

[38] *Ibid.*, 183.

[39] *Ibid.*, 173.

[40] A. L. Udovitch, 'At the Origins of the Western *commenda:* Islam, Israel, Byzantium?', *Speculum*, XXXVII (1962), 198–207.

had less resources with which to cover losses. Rather was Muslim *qirad* practice followed, so that the investor carried the losses. As in the Christian West, detailed provisions were written into the contracts – often with little effect:

I have heard that my partner has gone to Damascus, although I have instructed him not to leave Ramle and that all his selling and buying should be done through Siba, the representative of the merchants.[41]

It has been seen that investors chose their partners from the Fustat community, from foreign Jews and from Muslims; yet an order of preference existed. At the head of this order was business contracted between members of the same family – which, in the case of Egyptian and Tunisian Jews, could mean business between merchants resident in Cairo or Tunis and their relatives in Aden or Palermo. Nahray b. Nissim of Fustat was closely related to the Taherti family of Qayrawan – itself of Algerian ancestry. Nahray also had relatives in Spain: the business and residence of one family encompassed the breadth of the Islamic world, from Andalusia to Aden, but, by comparison with medieval Venice where family assets were often pooled, the Genizah Jews did not tend to merge their business into a single family company. However, as in Italy, partnerships with non-relations took place, and partnerships with non-Jews, though frequent, often served specific ends, such as the use of the Muslim caravan routes.

(C) *Commodities and Prices in the Genizah*

It has been said that the Fustat Jews were active both in the transit trade through Egypt and in the supply to Egypt of items required by domestic consumers. In addition, they handled Egyptian industrial produce, especially cotton cloth and both processed and unprocessed flax. But there is little indication in the Genizah as to how business in individual commodities fluctuated. Other sources suggest that Egyptian textile exports declined in quantity by 1200; but the Genizah has little to say on the success of Italian rivals in intruding their own competing goods into the Near East. However, the Genizah merchants did maintain a strong interest in textiles from other parts of the Islamic world – from Muslim Sicily, from Tunisia and from lands to the east. They were particularly involved in the silk trade, and the Genizah provides valuable information on silk prices in the eleventh century. It is worth following Goitein through an examination of the price of several 'typical' commodities of the Fustat trade: pepper, silk and flax. The movement of prices in each case reveals specific peculiarities.

[41] Goitein, *A Mediterranean Society*, I, 178.

Fluctuations in pepper prices rarely seem dramatic, though there are predictable differences between prices in, say, Sicily and in Egypt, given the higher cost of transport to Sicily and the additional number of middlemen; the following prices (per 100 lb), unless stated otherwise, refer to Egypt:

1020s(?)	...	15 dinars per 100 lb
1050s/60s	...	22½ dinars 'official price'
1050s/60s	...	23¾ dinars
c. 1063	...	25 dinars
1050s/60s	...	33 dinars 'because in request by Europeans'
c. 1064	...	35¼ dinars
1050s/60s	...	36, 38 dinars – the latter 'sold to Europeans'
1050s/60s	...	37½ dinars, in Sicily
c. 1100	...	62 dinars[42]

Although there were different grades of pepper, they were rarely differentiated, and it is to silk that it is necessary to turn for major price variations determined by quality. From the 1030s to the 1150s there did exist a 'standard' silk fabric which sold at, or close to, 20 dinars for 10 lb of woven silk. But top-grade silk from Spain could reach 33 dinars per 10 lb at Tinnis on the Nile, as an example from 1075 indicates. Silk goods of a single origin varied considerably in style and price. In 1047 Sicilian silk cloth fetched about 2½ dinars per pound in Tunisia; but it could fetch 3 dinars, and inferior qualities sank below the Mediterranean norm of 2 dinars. Goitein sees in silk an article of investment and not merely of commerce; middle-class Egyptians of the Genizah period and later would try to exploit the fluctuations in silk prices to make a little extra capital.

By contrast with silk, flax and linen were traded in bulk. Prices for silk are for pounds, 10 lb units, occasionally for ounces; but for flax they are in far larger units – 100 lb or more. Unfortunately, Goitein does not distinguish carefully enough between processed textiles and unprocessed fibres, but he is probably right to stress what vast quantities of flax were exported westwards, raw, for processing. His statement that 'Tunisia and Sicily were the Liverpool and Manchester of the eleventh century, with Egypt providing the main raw material, flax', greatly exaggerates the role of Sicily and presents too grandiose a picture of the scale and organisation of textile production at this period.[43] But the involvement of the Fustat Jews in flax production

[42] Goitein, *A Mediterranean Society*, I, 221.

[43] S. D. Goitein, 'Sicily and Southern Italy in the Cairo Geniza Documents', *Archivio storico per la Sicilia orientale*, LXVII (1971), 10–13; cf. D. S. H. Abulafia, *The Two Italies: economic relations between the Norman Kingdom of Sicily and the northern communes* (Cambridge, 1977), 47; and Ashtor, 'Gli Ebrei', 447–9.

can be perceived at all stages: from the examination of the crop and its handling in the Egyptian countryside, via the sale of flax in Tunisia and Sicily (there are many mentions in the 1040s), to the retailing of finished linen goods. Prices in the raw flax market fluctuated more generously than those in the raw silk market, but the margin of profit tended to be greater. In part, the importance of flax to the Genizah merchants is simply a reflection of the importance of flax to the Egyptian economy of the eleventh and twelfth centuries. Twenty-two varieties of flax were recognised in Egypt. Muqaddasi, as early as the late tenth century, indicates that the industrial centre of Tinnis yielded 1,000 dinars each day in tax (*qabala*); and H. Rabie notes that – even if the figure is exaggerated – it implies that the rulers of Egypt sought to extract income from the textile industry.[44] The eleventh and twelfth centuries may have seen significant short-term expansion in the linen industry as a result of the importation of a quite different fibre, cotton, from India. Cotton plantations appeared in the Nile region and, on a large scale, in Sicily. A mixed weave of linen and cotton became known throughout the Mediterranean as 'cloth of Fustat' – that is, 'fustian'. It is less clear that pure cotton textiles were manufactured on a large scale; but cotton-rag was used for the production of paper, which in the mid-twelfth century was exported from Alexandria to Genoa and other ports.[45] Thousands of sheets were sent at a time from Egypt to Tunisia by Genizah paper-dealers. There was thus no sector of the textile industry – silk, linen, paper – in which the Genizah merchants did not have a very substantial stake.

Specialists in spices and textiles above all, the Genizah Jews contributed to the strength of state finances by smoothing the path through Egypt of the luxury items on which the Fatimid rulers levied their taxes. But the eleventh and twelfth centuries saw the gradual displacement, both from government favour and from the great trade routes, of the middle-rank Egyptian merchants. Imports from the western and central Mediterranean became the preserve of the Italians, whose importance to the Egyptian economy can be measured by the welcome they continued to receive while they gave active support to the Christian rulers of the Holy Land, new and serious enemies of the Fatimids and Ayyubids. Imports from the Indies via the Red Sea became the preserve of a group of Egyptian Muslims, the Karimis, who benefited from Saladin's favours, and were encouraged to oust Jewish

[44] Rabie, *Financial system*, 80.

[45] M. Amari, 'Nuovi ricordi arabici su la storia di Genova', *Atti della societa ligure di storia patria*, v (1873). The famous cartulary of Giovanni Scriba of Genoa, from the mid-twelfth century, is written on Egyptian paper,

or Coptic competitors. The Jews of Fustat became less interested in overseas trade, and many, as has been seen, concentrated on the home market; many, too, transferred from Old to New Cairo, and thereupon disappeared from the Genizah record. Moreover, the ancient ties between the Egyptian Jews and their co-religionists – even blood relations – in each corner of the Mediterranean were shattered by catastrophic events in the West. Bedouin raids in Tunisia, the Norman conquest of Sicily, the seizure of the Syrian coast by the crusaders and the Italians, all disrupted the trade routes on which the Fustat Jews had relied; more serious still were the fearful persecutions in western Europe, at the time of the First and Second Crusades, and the fundamentalist fervour of the Almohad conquerors of Andalusia. As early as 1107 countless European Jews, not to mention Spanish and Sicilian Jews, were seeking refuge in Old Cairo from the tribulations, commercial and religious, which they suffered at home.

It was not simply the Jewish merchants who felt the cold wind. The advance of Italian navies in the Mediterranean, to Sicily and the Holy Land, brought into prominence new, more northerly, trade routes which often bypassed Alexandria in favour of Tyre and Acre. At the same time, the European textile industry began to supplant the Egyptian, benefiting from superior technology and more aggressive sales techniques. Though the raw materials the Genizah Jews knew so well continued to pass out of Egypt and Sicily, they were increasingly processed on Lombard looms. So effective, indeed, was the European victory that Italian cloths made from Egyptian flax and Sicilian cotton unashamedly took their very name from the home-city of the Genizah; and these Italian fustians were sold back to the inhabitants of the region from which their name derived.

(3) COMMERCE AND THE STATE IN EGYPT, 1150–1350

The clearest evidence concerning the conduct of trade in the 'post-Genizah' era is provided by government records from Egypt – by handbooks, official or semi-offical, on taxation and financial policy under the later Fatimids and the Ayyubids. The value of this source material is enhanced by the fact that the rulers of Egypt involved themselves increasingly heavily in commercial matters from the late twelfth century onwards; they saw in the spice trade, in particular, a source of funds to cover their war expenses. This attitude itself altered the character of Egyptian trade in ways which will be discussed shortly. Of the handbooks on commerce and taxation the most illuminating is the *Kitab al-Minhaj*, written by a senior financial official, Makhzumi, in the late twelfth century.[46] This is a key work in two senses: it reports, on the basis of personal knowledge, the taxes on cultivation and trade levied in Makhzumi's own day; and it provided information to later writers, such as Maqrisi in the fifteenth century, and thus influenced future discussion of government involvement in trade.

Makhzumi mentions the leading commodities which passed through the ports of Egypt into the hands, very often, of Italian merchants. Unfortunately, his comments on Alexandria have not survived in full; but even for Damietta and Tinnis his lists are much richer than the occasional inventories of the Genizah merchants. In other words, Makhzumi's work makes it clear that the Fustat Jews did indeed neglect important sectors of Egypt's commerce. Among exports from Damietta and Tinnis he mentions, of course, linen, cotton and spices; but he also refers to fish, chickens (from Damietta), salt, dates and condiments (from Tinnis), grain (from Damietta) and – of particular importance – alum (from Alexandria and Damietta). His references to imports also compare interestingly with those known through the Genizah letters. Silk and brocades arrive in Damietta and Tinnis, while the latter also receives supplies of wool; both accept gold and silver, of course; and Alexandria receives coral, oil and saffron. Most notably, all three ports take in wood, and Makhzumi mentions arrivals of iron at Alexandria and Tinnis. The great importance attached in Egypt to supplies of war materials has been mentioned already. Cahen notes that Makhzumi mentions two types of product: those aimed at large-scale international trade and those intended for consumption by merchants and sailors aboard ship. Unfortunately, Makhzumi does not usually indicate the origin of the commodities he mentions, and it hardly needs to be said that the 'exports' include many items themselves imported into Egypt via the Red Sea or even the very ports from which re-export occurred.

Makhzumi's merchant community is a mixture of Muslims, *dhimmis* (non-Muslims resident in Islamic lands) and *rum*, or Greek and Latin visitors. There are references to Muslim merchants who cross the Mediterranean in both Muslim-owned and *rumi*-owned ships. There are tax reductions for Sicilian merchants which may reflect the fact that many Sicilians were still Muslim, as well as past trading pacts between Roger II and the Caliph al-Hafiz. A mysterious mention of Sardinian traders, also enjoying tax benefits, may refer to the former Saracen

[46] C. Cahen, 'Douanes et commerce dans les ports méditérranéens de l'Egypte médiévale d'après le *Minhadj* d'al-Makhzumi', *Journal of the Economic and Social History of the Orient*, VII (1964), 217–314; C. Cahen, 'Un Traité financier inédit de l'époque Fatimide-Ayyubide', *ibid.*, V (1962), 139–59; C. Cahen, 'Contribution à l'étude des impôts dans l'Egypte médiévale', *ibid.*, V (1962), 244–78.

settlements on the coast of Sardinia though they are unlikely to have survived the Pisan conquest in the eleventh century. By contrast, merchants – perhaps Christian – from the former Byzantine territories of Antioch and Laodicea were subject to slightly heavier taxes on trade than normal.[47] The main ports through which these merchant groups operated were Damietta, Tinnis and Alexandria, but the twin complex of Rosetta and Nastaru was also used – most often when weather or other pressing reasons demanded a landfall. Cahen observes that Makhzumi's picture of Tinnis and Damietta cannot really be projected into the thirteenth century, when Egyptian Mediterranean trade was heavily concentrated in Alexandria. Tinnis had already suffered from crusader attacks in the twelfth century – even, perhaps, from a Norman Sicilian raid – and the town rapidly lost its importance as a textile centre. Damietta continued to arouse interest among foreigners, though as much as a base for crusades against Egypt as a commercial centre. It remained important as a focus for regional trade in the Nile delta and towards the towns of Syria.

The *Minhaj* and its sister-sources suggest the level of government intervention in trade: a point of interest, since a very rough estimate of the volume of trade can be provided from the tax figures. Al-Fadil, Saladin's vizier, stated that total revenue from the *khums* tax was 28,613 dinars in Alexandria alone during A.H. 587 (1191–2); the *khums* was a tax on Christian merchants, levied on imports through the three great Nile ports. Its name means 'a fifth', but it was set at higher or lower rates for specific goods or groups of merchants. Rabie notes that al-Fadil's figure, if correct, 'represents a considerable part of the Egyptian revenue under Saladin'; and it also represents imports valued at over 100,000 dinars through the Mediterranean ports alone.[48] There is no need to examine in detail the complex tax structure of the ports; but it is of interest that particularly high taxes were levied on certain spices, produced locally or imported – coriander, caraway, aniseed, cumin – since these taxes must have produced extremely handsome revenue. By the late twelfth century the government began to levy commercial taxes more intensively, infringing the agreed rules in order to maximise income. The *zakat*, for instance, was technically levied for the benefit of the deserving: paupers, converts, bankrupts, volunteers for the holy war and, not least, the administrators of the *zakat*

[47] There are references to Greek, or at least eastern Christian, merchants from the former principality of Antioch in the acts of the Genoese notary Lamberto di Sambuceto, drawn up in Cyprus at the end of the thirteenth century; maybe these merchants had successful predecessors over a hundred years earlier: V. Polonio (ed.), *Notai genovesi in oltremare: atti rogati a Cipro da Lamberto di Sambuceto* (3 luglio 1300–3 agosto 1301) (Genoa, 1982), and the succeeding volume, R. Pavoni (ed.) (6 luglio–27 ottobre 1301) (Genoa, 1982).

[48] Rabie, *Financial system*, 91–2.

itself. But by 1200 the state was frequently demanding more than the legal amount ($2\frac{1}{2}$ per cent), was collecting the tax before it was 'ripe' (technically it could not be charged on merchandise acquired less than a year earlier), and was extracting it from exempt groups such as pilgrims. In 1181 a group of Karimi merchants coming from Yemen to Egypt found themselves paying *zakat* against the rules for four successive years. Under Saladin the *diwan al-zakat*, the financial department in charge of this tax, produced over 50,000 dinars per annum. Eventually the *zakat* came to be levied on shopkeepers' stocks, until the Mamluk sultan, Qalawun, late in the thirteenth century, decided that this practice severely afflicted trade and abolished this type of *zakat*.[49]

State interest in production extended deeper. The tax on cultivated land, the *kharaj*, was collected at different rates depending on the crop: about 3 dinars on flax, but less on cotton, and on local spices; sugar-cane and indigo were above average. All the way from the fields to the workshops flax was taxed, until Saladin alleviated the duty paid by spinning workshops. There is a constant sequence of abolition of taxes, where economic effects seemed serious, and of reimposition, when financial needs at court demanded funds. Saladin abolished a tax on sugar manufacture and on candy – notable exports to Asia and Europe – but the Mamluks operated the tax again in the early fourteenth century. Especial significance attaches to governmental interest in alum production. Egypt was a major source of alum in the the twelfth century, before the Italians gained regular access to the Anatolian interior; and the Egyptian ruler operated a monopoly. Burchard of Strasbourg told Frederick Barbarossa that alum 'is collected for the king's use' in Egypt.[50] European demand for alum grew as the European textile industry grew, so that the discovery of sources of alum in Asia Minor did not reduce the appeal of Egyptian alum before the end of the thirteenth century. Ibn Mamati explains that the government used alum in the settlement of debts for imported timber and other raw materials, in the Ayyubid period. If the government bought merchandise from a trader, and the value of that merchandise was greater than the *khums*, or 'one fifth', tax on the trader's goods as a whole, the *khums* was not charged directly; instead the trader was paid the difference between the *khums* and the value of the merchandise the government required from him; and this payment was made two-thirds in alum, and one-third in gold. Other commodities subject to state control and known from commercial

[49] Rabie, *Financial system*, 99.

[50] C. Cahen, 'L'Alun avant Phocée: un chapitre d'histoire économique islamo-chrétienne au temps des Croisades', *Revue d'Histoire Economique et Sociale*, XLI (1963), 433–47.

records included salt, natron and the gold discovered in the tombs of the Pharaohs. State emerald mines had considerable commercial significance, too: originally, in the tenth century, the government took a proportion of the emeralds discovered, but by the fourteenth century it appropriated everything. Thus, exported emeralds bought the ruler great profit, though untrustworthy mine-managers proved adept smugglers.

From Fatimid times onwards there existed a government office, the *matjar*, which managed the state monopolies and purchased produce or commodities required by the state: wheat from early times, then also alum, wood, iron, lead and soap.[51] The *matjar* had the power to enforce the sale of silk, lead, wax and olive oil to the state; but it had its benign side too, for it purchased merchandise at guaranteed prices even when the prices on the free market were very depressed. The emphasis on war equipment – wood and iron – is obvious. However, corruption became rife, and the officials of the *matjar* began to sell the stocks of timber to private merchants, so that when the state needed war supplies it had to buy back what had been its own property. In the Mamluk period, around 1310, the sultans accordingly enforced closer control over the *matjar*, which became their personal property.

The manner of state intervention in commercial life which was practised in Egypt was similar to that practised in other Mediterranean states which possessed an active, able bureaucracy and an effective war-machine: the kingdom of Sicily or Byzantium in its prime.[52] The protection of trade through Egypt took second place after the protection of supplies of war materials. Heavy taxation of flax shows that the state seized its opportunity to make money and did not concern itself with the possibly deleterious effect of high imposts on prime articles of production – the same phenomenon is visible at Tinnis, where textile enterprises were taxed quite heavily. Meanwhile, the movement of goods through Egypt generated funds for the state which could be directed back towards war finance.

(4) THE KARIMI MERCHANTS, 1150–1500

Towards the end of the twelfth century a new force in Egyptian trade seems to emerge, with commercial interests in Yemen, India and also nearer home in Damascus. The 'Karimi' merchants have attracted

51 Rabie, *Financial system*, 92.

52 For comparisons, see H. Antoniadis-Bibicou, *Recherches sur les douanes à Byzance* (Paris, 1963); D. S. H. Abulafia, 'The Crown and the Economy under Roger II and his successors', *Dumbarton Oaks Papers*, XXXVII (1983); J. Riley-Smith, 'Government in Latin Syria and the Privileges of the Foreign Merchants', in D. Baker (ed.), *Relations between East and West in the Middle Ages* (Edinburgh, 1973).

much attention from historians; Fischel's list of fourteen merchants distinguished by the label 'Karimi' has been extended by Wiet and Ashtor, so that about fifty Red Sea merchants are now known by name.[53] In certain cases their wealth, ancestry and – almost invariably – their religious affiliation can be identified. Moreover, there is increasing agreement about the origins and meaning of the term 'Karimi'. The most likely explanation of the word is that it is in origin a Tamil word, *karyam*, meaning 'business' or 'affairs'; in any case, it is almost certainly a foreign loan-word, since it appears in twelfth-century texts as 'karim', without any definite article. The word was, then, applied by Indian merchants with whom the future Karimis had extensive contact in a form such as, 'the Arabs are here for *karyam*'; its transformation into a title of honour for certain Muslim merchants was complete by 1200. At the same time, the Karimis displaced their Jewish and Coptic competitors, acquiring wealth and influence far beyond those of the earlier generation of India traders.

Goitein has found references in the Genizah letters not to 'Karimis' but to the 'Karim', meaning (so it appears) convoy, passing regularly between Egypt and India in the twelfth century. This convoy adopted several routes into the Indian Ocean – sometimes through Aden, but occasionally through the East African ports instead, bypassing the Arabian peninsula. He surmises that the route taken may have changed, in rotation, from year to year; though the experience of the Karimis later on suggests that, if the route changed, it was because Yemenite sultans, or even the Ethiopian Negus, were causing political difficulties in the Red Sea approaches. Goitein indicates that the twelfth-century Karim was renowned for the excellence of its wares: a letter mentions goods 'the like of which are not [even] to be found in the Karim'; moreover, large quantities were shipped in the Karim convoys:

> As far as the Karim is concerned – I received a letter from it, from my brother-in-law Mahruz from Sawakin, telling me that it contained 3000 bales and that it travelled homewards in the Karim of our Jewish business friends.

This letter probably dates from the 1120s or a little later. However, the India correspondence analysed by Goitein makes clear the fact that

[53] W. J. Fischel, 'Über die Gruppe der Karimi-Kaufleute (Ein Beitrag zur Geschichte des Orienthandels Ägyptens unter den Mameluken', in Fr. Rosenthal, G. von Grünebaum, W. J. Fischel, *Studia Arabica*, I (Analecta Orientalia, XIV, Rome, 1937), 67–82; W. J. Fischel, 'The Spice Trade in Mamluk Egypt', *Journal of the Economic and Social History of the Orient*, I (1958); G. Wiet, 'Les Marchands d'épices sous les soultans mamlouks', *Cahiers d'Histoire Égyptienne*, VII (Cairo, 1955), 81–147; E. Ashtor, 'The Karimi merchants', *Journal of the Royal Asiatic Society* (1956), 45–56.

many other merchants traversed the routes of the 'Karim', without forming part of the convoys.[54]

This picture of convoys of merchants, including many Jews, fades by 1181 when 'Karimis' (as opposed to a 'Karim') appear in the Arabic documents. A reference that year to Karimis who have to pay *zakat* for four years has already been mentioned. Around this time Saladin gave his protection to the Karimi merchants, and the *ancien régime* of Genizah traders began to crumble away. The Karimis – in the sense of India merchants enjoying protection by the sultans – thereafter remained the dominant group trading through the Red Sea, and their status was only substantially eroded in the fifteenth century, first under Sultan Barsbay (1422–38) and then in the face of Portuguese opposition. Throughout the Karimi period the prime interest of these merchants lay in the spice trade to Egypt from the East; but they also handled many of the *matjar* commodities, such as wood, wheat, flour, sugar, rice, weapons and textiles. The Karimis were a major source of armaments from India and the East, parallel to the Italians who were the major source from the West. Moreover, the range of their commodity dealings was in certain respects greater than that of the Fustat Jews, who were rarely involved in the movement of bulky foodstuffs. By contrast, however, the Karimis became rather conservative in their choice of trade routes. They limited their eastwards movements, establishing a terminus at Aden. In 1289 the sultan of Yemen arranged a banquet on his ships at Aden, and invited the Karimi and Indian captains who were in port to attend: an event which seems to indicate that, by and large, the Indian shippers controlled navigation between Aden and their homeland, while the Karimis controlled it up the Red Sea to Egypt. In addition, the 1289 banquet illustrates the existence of shipping entrepreneurs among the Karimis: they were not simply commercial passengers.

The problem whether the Karimi merchants possessed a corporate identity – a gild organisation, say – is particularly difficult. There were Karimi *funduqs*, or warehouses, at Cairo, Fustat, Aden, Alexandria, Jiddah, Qus, Zabid and Ta'azz: that is, along the Red Sea and Nile routes. These *funduqs* may bespeak a central directing body of the Karimis. There are references to individual merchants which suggest a corporate identity: 'he was chief of the Karimis'; 'he belonged to the Karimi merchants'; but too much emphasis should not be placed on figurative indications of status, such as these, supplied by the literary sources. If there were limits around the Karimis, these were limits prescribed by wealth, repute and confessional status. For, in the first

[54] S. D. Goitein, 'New Light on the Beginnings of the Karimi Merchants', *Journal of the Economic and Social History of the Orient*, 1 (1958).

place, all Karimis seem to have been Muslims. Ibn Qaysur, active in the late thirteenth century, was, it is true, the son of a Jew; another Karimi had a Coptic father. But they themselves were, or had become, Muslim. Ashtor has sought to show that there existed Jewish Karimis, but his explicit evidence is from an earlier epoch, that of the 'Karim' convoys known from the Genizah. On the other hand, Ashtor's characterisation of the Karimis as a whole carries great weight: 'The Karimis may have been a loose confederation of merchants bound together by mere professional interests. We may be sure that the richest and most esteemed Karimi always decided on questions which gave rise to discussion, that he, with some other prominent members of the group, represented them before the government, and that his authority was recognised by all the Karimis.'[55] Ashtor rightly warns against the assumption that the social organisation visible in the West at this period – with its gild statutes, and so on – must have been mirrored in the practices of the East.

One reason the trade of the Karimis prospered was that the Egyptian and, *pari passu*, the Yemenite rulers benefited enormously from taxation on Karimi traffic. There was a special controller appointed to look after the revenue from the trade of the Karimis, the *mustawfi al-buhar wal-Karim*. The Egyptian government provided armed protection for the Karimi fleets on the Red Sea, after a series of pirate attacks – in other words, the Karimis were worth protecting. The shock of Reynaud de Châtillon's Red Sea expedition in the 1170s, reverberates throughout the history of the Red Sea trade. Moreover, the Egyptian government cultivated good relations with the Rasuliyyid court in Yemen. Best of all, in the fourteenth century, the Mamluks extracted from Yemen an acknowledgement of Mamluk suzerainty; at other times, Karimis functioned as ambassadors – a feature which symbolises both the financial dependence of the Mamluks on Karimi trade and the high esteem in which individual Karimi merchants were held at the Mamluk court.

One reason for this high esteem was the availability of loans from the Karimis to the central government in Egypt. The Karimis put their surplus capital to use in moneylending, and certain of their clients were of outstanding importance: the Yemenite rulers, the Senegalese king Mansa Musa, who passed through Egypt in 1323 (though he proved a surprisingly bad debtor). The Mamluks were not, however, consistently gentle to the Karimi bankers. There were forced loans when the Mongols threatened the Mamluk empire in 1300; when Syria rebelled in 1352; when Tamerlane stood poised to march

[55] Ashtor, 'The Karimi Merchants', 52.

west in 1394. It is interesting to note how the same sultan who issued a generous *aman*, or charter of protection, to the Karimis, also pressed the Karimis to provide loans: in 1288 Qalawun brought some eminent Damascus merchants to Cairo and fined them; he then made the Karimis provide the Damascenes with a loan, since the latter did not have the money to hand. Generally, however, it was to war expenses that they were expected to contribute, with loans or even gifts. Burhan al-Din al-Mahalli, sometime ambassador to Yemen, helped pay for the defence of Alexandria in 1403. Excellent as the evidence is for the loans of the Karimis to the sultans, it is clear that the Karimis also lent to more modest clients. Maqrisi mentions a deal between a Karimi and a Christian, in which the former invested 20,000 dinars as capital.

Although something can be said about the business interests of the Karimis, the process by which a merchant was transformed, or transformed himself, into a Karimi is enigmatic. Many Karimis had very modest origins. Izz al-Din Abd al-Aziz b. Mansur started life as a humble tailor, and al-Mahalli rose to enormous wealth from poverty. In one case – that of Zaki'l-Din Abu-Bakr al-Kharrubi – we see a poor merchant acquiring wealth as a result of a lucky inheritance from an uncle. Apparent, too, is the diversity of origins of the Karimis: there were Muslims from Ethiopia and from the edges of the Turkish world. More typical, perhaps, is the career of Badr al-Din Hasan b. Suwaid al-Maliki; he had a legal training and inherited some money in 1387–8; he began to travel regularly between Egypt and Yemen. By his death in 1425 he had accumulated very big profits. Since the prime speciality of the Karimis was the spice trade, profits were especially handsome: up to 100 per cent on the Aden to Egypt run; and on arrival in Egypt virtually assured sales to Italian merchants. On the other hand, risks were high, above all in the Indian Ocean with its pirate-infested and rocky coasts, so that profits were eaten into. A twelfth-century 'pre-Karimi' merchant, Abu'l Abbas al-Hijazi, lost ten ships on the Indian Ocean at one time; fortunately he did not lose an eleventh ship which was carrying porcelain from China and aloe-wood. With these alone he was able to recover his former wealth.

The modest origin of some Karimis did not prevent the creation of short-lived merchant dynasties. The great Karimis married their sons into other Karimi families. Ashtor notes that the Karimis did not try to breach the ranks of the aristocracy as *parvenus*. And he attributes this concentration on marriage within their own social group to the lack of a Mamluk aristocracy, or at least of a fixed constellation of eminent families. Nonetheless, the Karimis gained a special *entrée* into the Mamluk sultan's inner circle. Al-Mahalli perhaps indicates this process most clearly. He traded on his father-in-law's behalf, and his son-in-law was a distinguished judge; he served as ambassador in Yemen and Egypt and was close to the sultans; but his son squandered much of his wealth. Interestingly, he was not merely a trader: he owned houses worth 50,000 dinars, and he used some of this wealth for the endowment of religious schools. The career of ibn Musallam was similar, though his origins are murkier. He made a good marriage and left each of his sons 20,000 dinars; one of his daughters married another India trader; and he owned houses and land. The fact that Karimis possessed urban property, sugar factories, warehouses and so on indicates that they did diversify their interests to a limited extent; but unlike contemporary Italian merchants of equal status they did not maintain a very strong interest in the acquisition of estates, and they were thus all the more at the mercy of a contrary trade wind.

Such a wind blew in the fifteenth century, in Egypt. The very government which had fostered Karimi trade so decisively turned against the India traders; and the reason for this desertion was not dissimilar to that for favouring them earlier – the Mamluks wanted money. There is no sign that the Mamluks interested themselves in the economic prosperity of their subjects, except insofar as they saw that an impoverished empire would be unable to sustain the heavy demands they made upon it for war funds. The reign of Barsbay marked the transition to a new Mamluk policy in which government involvement in the spice trade was more direct, and Karimi influence was correspondingly reduced. In 1438 the sultan forbade the Karimis to sell spices directly to the Italian merchants in Alexandria. State spice and sugar monopolies were created, and the government henceforth fixed the prices at which these items could be put on sale to the Europeans. Forced buying (*tarah*) from the Karimis helped prevent illicit stockpiling, or other resistance to the new policies. At the same time, Barsbay greatly increased the security of the Red Sea and made of Jiddah an important base for the disembarkation of goods brought from the East. This emphasis on Jiddah – that is, on a Mamluk-held town, with an efficient customs regime – detracted from the status of Aden as the principal intermediate trading station between Egypt and the Indies. As Darrag says, 'la fortune de Djedda s'était edifiée au detriment d'Aden'.[56] The Mamluks were able to exploit the weakness of the Rasuliyyid dynasty in Yemen, and to insist that Egyptian trade past Yemen should continue without interference even if it did not make use of Aden.

In the fifteenth century the financial difficulties of the Mamluk sultans only became worse. The decision to intervene directly in the

[56] A. Darrag, *L'Egypte sous le règne de Barsbay 825–841/1422–1438* (Damascus–Beirut, 1961).

spice trade was matched by the creation of a new merchant cadre whose tasks were dominated by the needs of the sultans themselves. The sultans commissioned merchants to buy spices on their behalf. Ali al-Kilani, who died in 1444, was entrusted with 5,000 dinars for the purchase of spices, and produced 12,000 dinars profit for the sultan alone. The spice trade was supervised henceforth by the 'king of the merchants' (*malik al-tujjar*), a government official who looked after the Red Sea and Indian Ocean traffic. The state merchants of the *khawajas* became in the fifteenth century a trusted body of financial bureaucrats; the private Karimi merchant lost ground to his better patronised successor, who combined a commercial career with public service. Another development may have contributed to the decline of the Karimis. There was increasing contact between the Mamluk government and rulers far to the east of Yemen. Even in the mid-fourteenth century diplomatic exchanges between Cairo and Ceylon had been valued. Barsbay cultivated contacts with the rulers of Delhi, themselves new to Islam and therefore full of interest in the Islamic heartlands further west. In Barsbay's time gifts, tribute and loose acknowledgement of Mamluk suzerianty were sent to Cairo and the Hejaz. The presence at the start of the fifteenth century of Chinese fleets in the East African approaches may also have stimulated the Mamluks into more careful consideration of their Indian Ocean policies, given the danger that the Chinese might compete for control of the trade routes and of the loyalty of the Indian princes.

The Mamluks, then, tried to rebuild the eastern spice trade without close reference to existing, Karimi, interests. The Mamluks were not concerned with the maintenance of the prosperity of a few hundred India traders; their first priority was to ensure that the India trade continued to exist, in order to produce funds for the government.

IV. *Muslim Trade in the Far East*

(1) SRI VIJAYA AND MALACCA, 600–1511

The two means of access to the Far East from the Mediterranean – overland through Central Asia and by sea round India – flourished at different times and only rarely competed directly with one another. This fact reflects important political changes within Asia – the division of China under the Sung, the rise of the Mongols under Chinghiz Kan, the seaward orientation of certain Ming rulers. Equally, internecine warfare among the Mongols of western Asia and the Steppes created breaks in, and diversions from, the classic trade routes overland to the

Far East. Broadly, it would be true to say that the overland routes flourished when the political control of the Chinese emperors (or their Mongol substitutes) extended very far to the west – over Turkestan, even – and when there existed comparative quiet in Persia, the Near East and the eastern Mediterranean. These conditions were fulfilled in the late Roman period, when the silk road brought luxury goods eastwards via Sassanid Persia and linked the three great territorial empires of the third and fourth centuries: China, Persia, Rome. The development in Byzantine lands of a silk industry, based on secrets revealed by eastern craftsmen, and the rise of Islam in former Roman and Sassanid lands led to the decay of the overland route; it is no surprise that silk ceased to hold its position as the most prized product of the Far East in the markets of the Mediterranean.

The fifth and sixth centuries saw independent developments in the Far East which gave slow birth to the overseas route. The division of China between northern and southern dynasties made access by foreign merchants to southern China less easy, at least by land. Moreover, the southern Chinese rulers began to take a greater interest in the barbarian peoples off the coast of Asia, attempting to win from them recognition of South Chinese lordship. This recognition itself entailed a sort of commercial relationship: the tributary states in Java and other islands sent vast quantities of their produce, perfumes above all, to the emperor in humble acknowledgement of his suzerainty, while the emperor sent in return munificent gifts graciously bestowed, which traditionally were of approximately the same value as the tribute received. Of particular importance in the movement of these goods were the Malay communities of Sumatra and the peninsula of Malaya.

Between the seventh and the fourteenth century the Malay state of Sri Vijaya (Çrivijaya) flourished on the Malayan straits, as the most important trading entrepot between the Indian Ocean and the Chinese seas. It possessed what can only be called natural commercial strength. Ships passing from India to China found their way blocked by the long tongue of the Malay peninsula; and a port which sat astride the route such shipping must take, as did Palembang, the Sri Vijayan capital, might become master of the communications system of South-east Asia. Moreover, the seasonal changes in the winds of South-east Asia forced shipping bound for China to sit out for several weeks in the Malayan region. But Palembang's success was not merely passive. The Malays themselves seem to have developed the art of sailing to a high level, and they were heavily involved in local Indonesian trade in aromatics even before the emergence of Sri Vijaya. But perhaps the most significant achievement of the Malay merchants was to introduce the Chinese to a range of commodities which had not greatly attracted attention before the fifth century: pine resin from the Indonesian islands to the east of Sri Vijaya, benzoin and other perfumes. These, Wolters has argued, served as substitutes for the resins transported into the Indian Ocean from Arabia – for the famous frankincense and myrrh whose high price and distant origin disadvantaged them in competition with humbler but respectable Indonesian produce.[57] Indeed, as early as A.D. 500 western Indonesian benzoin seems to have been appreciated even more highly in the Far East than western myrrh. Wolters also sees in Sri Vijaya a centre for the adulteration of genuine Arabian frankincense with Sumatran pine resin. The effect of Sri Vijayan substitution, honest and dishonest, of Indonesian for western resins is obvious. Palembang was catapulted into great importance as a paramount centre of exchange: a point of arrival for Arab merchants seeking to sell western produce to traders bound for China, an international warehouse for frankincense, pine resin and other perfumes of the East Indies. A Sung writer describes the frankincense trade; and, typically of Chinese writers, he sees this trade as a one-way link bringing what China desired to China's shores:

> The Arabs bring their goods by ship to San-fo-ch'i [Sri Vijaya] and exchange them for goods. Thus this perfume is usually found in great quantities at San-fo-ch'i. Each year great ships leave San-fo-ch'i for Canton or Ch'üan chou. At these two ports the shipping [officials] examine the amounts of perfume and establish its value. [Ch'ên Ching, *Hsin tsuan hsiang p'u*, quoting the lost *Hsiang lu* of Yeh The'ing-kuei.]

Further evidence for the strength of Sri Vijaya is provided by Chinese texts which refer to its embassies to the Sung court, for example in 988 and 1178; while Sri Vijaya also sought to confirm its standing locally, fighting vigorous wars against the Javanese, around 1000, and facing a threat from a South Indian ruler, the Cola Rajendra I (*c.* 1025). Rajendra's raids, recorded on a temple inscription at Tanjore, show that Sri Vijayan authority extended widely along the Sumatran and Malayan coasts – perhaps even as far as the Nicobar islands (*Nakkavaram* in the inscription, *Necuveran* in Marco Polo), which probably sent tribute to Sri Vijaya. The Arabic sources are interested in Sri Vijaya for additional reasons.[58] Masudi, writing at the end of the tenth century, insists that even the fastest ship could not circumnavigate Sri Vijaya in less than two years. Its products include

[57] O. W. Wolters, *Early Indonesian Commerce: a study of the origins of Srivijaya* (Ithaca, N.Y., 1967).

[58] P. Wheatley, *The Golden Khersonese: studies in the historical geography of the Malay Peninsula before A.D. 1500* (Kuala Lumpur, 1961) for all these sources.

camphor, aloes, cloves, sandalwood, cardamom and other spices; here, perhaps, the writer has confused Sri Vijaya itself with the other Indonesian islands, only a few of which acknowledged the authority of the Maharaja. But an essential point emerges: it was from Palembang and Sumatra that the Arabs obtained these precious spices, even though the Malays were themselves only middlemen between Sri Vijaya and the more primitive lands further east, where the spices and perfumes were actually cultivated.

Despite the commanding position of Palembang astride the Malayan straits, foreign ships did occasionally try to evade Sri Vijayan taxation and to sail straight past. Chao Ju-kua, writing in 1225, stated that San-fo-ch'i

> is master of the straits through which foreign traffic must pass, by sea or by land, in either direction...If a merchant ship passes by without putting in, ships come out to attack it, in a pre-arranged fashion. People there are ready to die [to achieve this]. Thus this land has become an important maritime centre.[59]

It is not surprising, therefore, that Arab merchants who came by sea rarely penetrated beyond, nor even saw reason to penetrate beyond, Sumatra. Equally, their knowledge of other parts of Malaya and Indonesia remained sketchy – neither northern Malaya nor even the lesser centres of trade, such as Temasek (Singapore), was frequented. The geographical works of the tenth to twelfth centuries written in the Islamic world repeat accepted truths about Sri Vijaya; Idrisi's report, for instance, composed in the 1150s, is a jumble of certainties and uncertainties, anachronisms and plain errors. There was a strong temptation to add monsters and mermaids to any description of the wondrous isles in the Far East, an attitude reflected in the tales of Sinbad the Sailor;

> And on the morrow we set out and journeyed over the mighty range of mountains, seeing many serpents in the valley, till we came to a fair great island, wherein was a garden of huge camphor trees under each of which a hundred men might take shelter. When the folk have a mind to get camphor, they bore into the upper part of the bole with a long iron; whereupon the liquid camphor, which is the sap of the tree, floweth out, and they catch it in vessels, where it concreteth like gum; but after this the tree dieth and becometh firewood. Moreover, there is in this island a kind of wild beast, called 'Rhinoceros', that postureth as do steers and buffaloes with us...It is a remarkable animal with a great and thick horn, ten cubits long, amiddleward its head; wherein, when cleft in twain, is the likeness of a man.
>
> [Second Voyage of Sinbad, transl. R. Burton].

[59] *Ibid.*, 298.

But there was some knowledge of the Malayan tin mines and of the Sumatran pearl fisheries, which were described by Idrisi.

Most historians accept that Sri Vijaya reached the peak of its prosperity before 1200. Palembang in its prime was cosmopolitan: even the parrots spoke several languages. But in 1178 Chou Kü-fei observed that Java (Sho-po) was richer than San-fo-ch'i; a modern authority, G. Coedès, has rightly remarked that it would be wrong to be misled by the physical remains of Borobudur and other Javan temples into the assumption that Java was more prosperous than Palembang, whose medieval remains are very meagre. Wolters, however, goes further: he argues that Sri Vijaya did not experience quite so dramatic a decline as is generally believed. He points out that the new commercial powers of late medieval Malaya – Temasek briefly, then Malacca in the fifteenth century – were ruled by dynasties which claimed Sri Vijayan royal descent, and that there was a gradual transfer of the seat of authority from Palembang via Jambi and Temasek to the glorious new capital at Malacca. In other words, Palembang was past its best by the late thirteenth century, but it was not without heirs: Jambi vied with it as a political centre as early as 1079–82; the continuity of royal blood and of commercial life from Sri Vijaya to Malacca means that, in a sense, Sri Vijaya never 'fell'.[60]

But it did decline. The changes inside Sri Vijaya had their origins further afield. Strong kingdoms in Java and autonomous states in northern Sumatra began to contest the authority of Sri Vijaya over the trade routes, as, perhaps, did the merchants themselves. The Javan kingdom of Singharasi came to rule over northern Sumatra and received tribute from parts of Borneo, the Moluccas and the peninsula. Even greater influence was acquired by the fourteenth-century Javan kingdom of Majapahit. These observations, however, do little to explain the decline of Sri Vijaya. Arab merchants still possessed customers in the West who sought the produce of the spice islands. The Karimi merchants were, at this very time, exceptionally active and successful in the Indian Ocean trade. The decline of Sri Vijaya has its roots, surely, in the process which also brought Sri Vijaya into life: the Chinese outlook on the barbarian world changed once again. The late thirteenth century is precisely the period when, under Yüan (Mongol) rule, China looked away from the southern seas towards the Asiatic expanses; when access to the West could be gained along a new, northerly, overland route, stretching from the Great Wall to the Caspian or the Black Sea; when daring western merchants penetrated to Zaytun and other Chinese ports, even establishing Italian settlements.

[60] O. W. Wolters, *The Fall of Śrīvijaya in Malay History* (London, 1970).

All this entailed the decline of the elongated Indian Ocean route through the Malay straits westwards. It did not entail the decline of Indies trade with the Chinese mainland, which, on the contrary, flourished: trade was now directed northwards from Java, the Celebes and the other spice islands, rather than focussed on a single centre of exchange in the capital of Sri Vijaya; and it was from the Chinese mainland, not from Indonesia, that the west-bound trade routes often now began. The effects of this shift were felt throughout the Islamic trading world, and beyond – in Alexandria, which suffered decline, no less than in Palembang. On the other hand, more opportunity was offered in the South China Seas to independent Chinese mariners who sailed their junks directly to the sources of supply of spices and perfumes. In consequence, China itself became a market for spices, attracting merchants from Christian and Muslim lands, whereas in the twelfth and early thirteenth centuries China had tended to acquire spices for domestic consumption and foreign merchants had operated out of Malaya. Under the grey rule of the boorish Yüan domestic demand for spices and perfumes may well have fallen. It would be interesting to know what effect these developments had on the Karimi and Tamil merchants who relied so heavily on the Indian Ocean trade routes.

Dramatic though these changes were, in their effect upon Sri Vijaya in particular they were not permanent. The divisions within the Mongol empire meant that the overland route was no longer safe by the mid-fourteenth century; in any case, western merchants seem to have become less adventurous by then. The Ming restoration in 1368 stimulated new thought in China about the southern seas, and the Chinese emperors returned to the Sung policy of southward orientation. At the start of the fifteenth century the eunuch Cheng Ho sailed the Indian Ocean, securing recognition of Chinese suzerainty as far west as the horn of Africa.[61] This renewed vigour stimulated the trade of Malaya in several ways. In the first place, the emperor whom Cheng Ho served – the so-called Yung-lo emperor – was a usurper and wished to demonstrate that his authority was at least as great as that of his more illustrious predecessors: a long series of tribute payments would bring him great renown. Secondly, the emperor sought to bring more securely under state control the private trade which had developed in the South China Sea. Wang Gung-wu sees this as an attempt to suppress the piracy which had developed alongside this trade, but the emperor presumably hoped for revenue from that trade, and financial

[61] Wang Gungwu, 'Early Ming Relations with S.E. Asia', in J. K. Fairbank (ed.), *The Chinese World Order* (Cambridge, Mass., 1968), 34–62; T. Filesi, *Le relazioni della Cina con l'Africa nel Medio Evo* (Milan, 1962).

motives cannot be ignored.[62] Thirdly, Yung-lo was to a degree continuing the policy of Emperor Hung-wu, his own father, who, before his death in 1398, had begun to look southward in the hope of securing allegiance from the Malay and Indonesian states.

This policy coincided with important, or rather pregnant, developments in those states. What seems to have occurred is that a Hindu adventurer, Paramesvara, created a small but very powerful base on the Malay Straits, a little before 1403, when the Chinese eunuch Yin-k'ing found him in control at Malacca. Paramesvara's origins are revealing. He was the husband of a princess from Majapahit, the Javanese political and commercial centre which had flourished in the fourteenth century. His place of origin is said to have been Palembang; but after rebelling against the Javanese ruler, he fled northwards, first of all to Temasek (Singapore), and then to a new foundation of his own, Malacca. And it was Malacca which was to wear the mantle which Sri Vijaya had worn in the early Middle Ages. Wolters has indicated that the Yung-lo emperor's policy did not directly benefit Malacca, which acknowledged Ming overlordship as did several other Indonesian states. But the principle applied by China was equal favour to all vassals. Thus, only when the Chinese fleet was in harbour was trade brisk – but, Wolters says, 'the trade was an abnormal one and depended on the survival of the *Yung-lo* policy'.[63] Malacca's success as a trading station should not, therefore, be attributed to its founder, but to later rulers who – without renouncing Chinese lordship – accepted another tie, that of the Muslim faith. The Ming expeditions were past history when, in 1436, the Malaccan ruler converted to Islam. This act may have been an attempt to attract Muslim merchants from the West towards Malacca, though local niceties were also observed, and some stress was laid on the continuity, real or imagined, between the dynasty of Sri Vijaya and that of Malacca.

Wolters' arguments provide an important warning against the assumption that Malacca was *ab initio* and by its very nature a major entrepot between East and West. But in identifying an earlier, less flourishing, phase of Malacca's history, Wolters only brings into greater relief the substantial commercial success of fifteenth-century Malacca. It was the obvious target for Dom Affonso d'Albuquerque if he were to seize control of the Indies trade on Portugal's behalf, as he did in 1511. Malacca grew to eminence not on the basis of its local

[62] Wang Gungwu, '"Public" and "Private" Overseas Trade in Chinese History', in M. Mollat (ed.), *Sociétés et compagnies de commerce en Orient et dans l'Océan indien. Actes du huitième colloque international d'histoire maritime, Beyrouth, 1966* (Paris, 1970), 215–26; *idem*, 'The opening of relations between China and Malacca, 1403–5', in J. Bastin and R. Roolvink (eds.), *Malayan and Indonesian Studies: essays presented to Sir Richard Winstedt on his eighty-fifth birthday* (Oxford, 1964), 87–104.

[63] Wolters, *The Fall of Śrīvijaya*, 157.

resources: the tin-mines of Kedah were only gradually brought under the city's rule; local food supplies were scanty; nearby rulers were reluctant to supply what seemed a parasite settlement. The strength of Malacca lay, rather, in its position on the straits at a time of reviving east–west maritime trade. It was a town which needed to trade, or to service trade, in order to survive; and it succeeded in gaining access to food supplies because it possessed the funds to pay for imports. These funds were themselves the produce of trade – of harbour taxes, market tolls and so on. In order to assure this income, the Malaccans extended their control over the nearby coast and fitted out patrol boats to force merchant ships to visit Malacca. Wheatley remarks: 'as in the days of *Sri Vijaya*, the Strait became again a private sea'.[64] Thus, Malacca sought to establish a monopoly of control of the trade routes. The Portuguese writer Tomé Pires, describing his country's new conquests, gave close attention to Malacca and its history. He says that 84 languages were spoken in the town's streets, but he also remarks that about a quarter of the merchants in Malacca in 1509 were Gujarati Indians.[65]

Malacca, like Sri Vijaya, benefited from the seasonal changes in the winds of South-east Asia. Shipping was forced to wait in Malacca for favourable winds to China, if coming from the West, and for the West, if coming from China. A through passage was rarely possible. Tomé Pires explains:

> Malacca is a city that was made for merchandise, fitter than any other in the world; the end of monsoons and the beginning of others. Malacca is surrounded and lies in the middle, and the trade and commerce between the different nations for a thousand leagues on every hand must come to Malacca.[66]

This trade consisted both of long-distance commerce with India and the Red Sea and of local commerce with the spice islands in search of the precious goods esteemed by the Gujaratis and Karimis. Moreover, Malacca fed itself from nearby stocks of rice, handled local cloths, such as Indonesian batiks, and received regular consignments of Chinese silk, raw and processed, metalwork, rhubarb and perfumes. Much of the Chinese trade came on a regular convoy of junks, which was sent back laden with pepper and spices. Wang Gung-wu has argued that Chinese relations with Malacca had their origin in information brought to the Chinese court in 1403 by Muslim merchants of South

64 Wheatley, *Golden Khersonese*, 306–20.

65 Tomé Pires, in A. Cortesão, *The Suma Orientalis of Tomé Pires, an account of the East, from the Red Sea to Japan, written in Malacca and India in 1512–5, and the Book of Francisco Rodrigues* (Hakluyt Society, ser. 2, XXXIX–XL, London, 1941), 285–6, 212–14.

66 Tomé Pires, 286.

India.[67] This supposition is of particular interest, since it suggests that the Gujarati role in the creation of Malacca must not be underestimated. Wolters has perhaps laid excessive stress on the purely Malay elements at Malacca; the Gujaratis were, for their part, experienced shippers who knew the China trade long before the rise of Malacca. In that sense, Malacca was already an Islamised town before the conversion of its ruler in 1436. Probably there was a distinction of function between Gujarati Muslims and other Indian merchants: Wheatley thinks the Gujaratis 'monopolised the cream of the Malaccan trade',[68] while the Coromandel merchants handled a greater bulk of Malaccan trade. Through the Indian merchants the spices of the East were then forwarded to Karimis, *khawajas* and, ultimately, Venetians, Florentines and other westerners. Albuquerque's conquests brought the nerve centre of this trade route under Portuguese control.

(2) THE ROUTE EAST

The extreme end of the spice route to the West has received more attention than the intermediate stages, partly as a result of van Leur's speculations on the character and significance of South-East Asian trade.[69] Although Arab merchants knew the route to the Indies from very early times, it is not clear that they continued to sail beyond Ceylon in large numbers during the late Middle Ages. Indian shipping, in rope-bound vessels, light but watertight, carried those western Muslims who did penetrate the eastern Indian Ocean; nevertheless these boats seemed flimsy by comparison with the great junks that came to Malacca from China. A distinction can be made between the period up to about 1200, when links between Iraq and the Far East were quite close, and a later period when contact was maintained not directly but by stages on a set route. As early as the eighth century Arab visitors to China, coming from Oman and Bassorah, are recorded, while Obolla in the Persian Gulf flourished until the ninth century as a centre of Indian Ocean trade. Subsequently, a new centre of Persian Gulf commerce emerged, at Siraf; around 916 there are references to shipping from Siraf to India, though the Sirafis also sailed to Aden and Zanzibar. The head of the Muslim community at Saimur, near Bombay, was a Sirafi. A Sirafi merchant of particular repute was Ramisht, active in the 1130s; he knew the ports of India and traded with China – one of his agents brought goods from Canton valued at

[67] Wang Gungwu, 'Early Ming Relations', 34–62.
[68] Wheatley, *Golden Khersonese*, 315; cf. Wolters, *Fall of Śrīvijaya*, 154–70.
[69] J. C. van Leur, *Indonesian Trade and Society: essays in Asian social and economic history* (The Hague–Bandung, 2nd ed, 1967).

half a million dinars in one year. In 1138 Ramisht provided the silk cover of the shrine at Mecca – using, of course, Chinese silk.[70]

By the middle of the twelfth century Siraf was eclipsed by competitors elsewhere in the Persian Gulf. The Yemenites promoted the interests of Kish (Kaïs), an island in the Gulf; in the thirteenth century Kish was, in its turn, displaced by Hormuz, and some of the leaders of the Kish community headed east for India, where they established worthy careers in government. From Hormuz an intensively used trade route ran to Cambay, in the north-west corner of the Indian sub-continent, and to Cochin India, much further south. It was often necessary to sit out the south-west monsoon in Cambay; indeed, it was best to allow a year and a half to reach Malacca via Cambay from the Red Sea. Tomé Pires observed that 'Malacca cannot live without Cambay, nor Cambay without Malacca'; and it was to Cambay that East African, Persian Gulf and Red Sea traders tended to come.[71] Trading associations were formed there for the next leg of the trade route eastward; typically, they would involve the carriage of Indian textiles to Malaya, though coral and worked copper were also prized commodities. Another route east linked Bengal to Malaya; the Bengali merchants tended to work towards Pegu, in southern Burma, before cutting across to the Malay straits.

There is no need here to examine in detail the interruptions in this trade occasioned by Yemenite activity against the Mamluks, or by Mongol attempts to suffocate the Red Sea trade. A letter of 1288 indicates that the Mamluks wished to welcome the merchants of Yemen, India and China into Syria and Egypt, but such attempts had no very marked success. For the secret of the Indian Ocean trade route was its segmentation: each group – Karimi, Gujarati, Malay, Chinese – had its own area of operation, in which it tended to control shipping, and where many or most of the merchants who travelled the route were members of the locally dominant commercial group. Only the Portuguese irruption induced dramatic changes in this manner of conducting business.

(3) MUSLIM TRADE IN CHINA

A brief mention of the attractions of China to Muslim merchants is necessary. Important settlements of Muslim merchants developed on Chinese soil as early as the T'ang period – the Ta-shih, or Arabs (from the term Tadjik, rather inaccurately) were one group; also there were

[70] S. M. Stern, 'Ramisht of Siraf, a Merchant Millionaire of the Twelfth Century', *Journal of the Royal Asiatic Society* (1967), 10–14; see also now, Hodges and Whitehouse, *Mohammed, Charlemagne and the Origins of Europe*; also S. Digby, 'The Maritime Trade of India', *Cambridge Economic History of India*, I, *c. 1200–c. 1750* (Cambridge, 1982), 125–59.

[71] Tomé Pires, 42–7.

the Po-ssu, or Persians, a term which was stretched to include even, perhaps, Indonesians. There are references to *Sa-po* visiting China as early as the fifth century; these may be Sabaeans, bringing frankincense and myrrh from Arabia. The Arabs left a strong legacy of Islam in China; the large Muslim population still existing in China bears witness to this. By the twelfth century Arab merchants in China were supplying the court; they owned sizeable ships. In 1136 P'u Lo-hsin, or Abu'l-Hasan, commissioned the construction of a junk. In the next century P'u Shou-keng served as Commissioner for Maritime Trade at the important trading centre of Zaytun (Ch'uan-chou). His son-in-law Bahran (Fo-lien) owned a fleet of 80 sea-going vessels. Professor Jung-Pang Lo has described how the rich Arab merchants provided ships to the warring Sung and Mongols in the late thirteenth century; some Arab-owned ships saw action in the Mongol assaults on Japan, Java and Indo-China, and presumably form part of the fleet discovered in 1981 off the coast of Japan – apparently one of Qubilai Kan's invasion fleets. But the Arab-owned ships were Chinese in design and construction; there was no through traffic of Arab merchant ships from China to the western Indian Ocean. On the other hand, the Arab merchants contributed to the port installations of the China coast: they built jetties at Wenchow and Kan-p'u; and, in the Sung period, the Muslim minaret of Canton was used as a lighthouse by captains entering port.[72]

Jung-Pang Lo believes that the private initiative of the Muslim merchants settled in China made a major contribution to the success of China's maritime trade in the Sung and Yüan periods. Moreover, these Muslims were not any longer newcomers, but native 'Chinese Muslims', descendants of merchant settlers of the T'ang and Sung period, rather than new blood. These merchants no longer looked to the West for their business contacts and were not simply specialists in the Indian Ocean or silk road trade; they were masters of local, China Sea, commerce above all else.

Nonetheless, Chinese artefacts reached the West along the maritime trade routes. Archaeological finds indicate where these objects were most prized; celadon wares have been discovered in Frederick II's palace at Lucera in Apulia; large quantities of Chinese pottery have been identified as Fustat and Siraf.[73] But it is unclear whether Chinese

[72] Lo Jung-Pang, 'Chinese Shipping and East-West Trade from the Tenth to the Fourteenth Century', in Mollat (ed.), *Sociétés et compagnies de commerce en Orient et dans l'Océan indien*, 167–76; cf. Wang Gungwu's contribution to the same volume, 215–26; also G. F. Hudson 'The Medieval Trade of Asia' in D. S. Richards (ed.), *Islam and the Trade of Asia* (Oxford, 1970), 159–67.

[73] G. T. Scanlon, 'Egypt and China: trade and imitation', in Richards (ed.), *Islam and the trade of Asia*, 81–95; D. Whitehouse, 'Ceramici e vetri medioevali provenienti dal Castello di Lucera', *Bolletino d'Arte* (1966), 171–8.

porcelain was valued as a curio or antique, or whether the latest products of the Chinese kilns and metal workshops were eagerly bought by wealthy consumers in the Muslim world as examples of the latest fashion. The copying of Chinese pottery by Egyptian craftsmen in the eleventh century and after suggests the admiration western Muslims felt for Chinese products. But it would be wrong to conclude that this imitation bespeaks a large volume of trade in Chinese goods. Michael Rogers suggests that, in the twelfth and thirteenth centuries, Chinese *objets de luxe* came west as gifts or as booty. There is sometimes a lengthy time-lag between the date of the original model – say, a T'ang figurine – and its Persian or Egyptian copy. In the thirteenth century Persian potters added Chinese motifs to their wares, but derived them from a wide range of Chinese artefacts, such as metalwork, rather than from known Chinese ceramics. 'Porcelains and Chinese bronzes', Rogers maintains, 'were much valued for their rarity, and thus were more or less well imitated, but they can never have been any more than goods of the utmost luxury.'[74] Excavations at Fustat have revealed significant quantities of T'ang, Sung, Yüan and Ming wares, celadons above all, but also, by the late fourteenth century, the distinctive blue and white wares which were to acquire special renown.

Revealing as the Fustat archaeological finds are, the China–Egypt trade was no more than a trickle. It was perhaps a sideline of Karimis and Gujaratis engaged in more important business, aimed at the spice islands. The Chinese silks which, in the late thirteenth and fourteenth centuries, reached western Europe often took a very different route, overland to Tabriz and thence through Anatolia to the Black Sea and Constantinople. Even the Italian communities of Zaytun were perhaps as interested in the chance to tap the spice trade as in the chance to acquire Chinese goods. It is noticeable that the explorers of the late fifteenth and early sixteenth centuries were keen above all to reach the spice islands and only secondarily to revisit the towns Marco Polo had seen on the Asian land-mass. Nor is this a matter for surprise. Marco Polo and the Muslim writers had all learned about the spice islands, but they had only, at best, visited their western edges. Given the lack of any precise description of the spice islands, Columbus's confusion of Hispaniola and Cuba with the East Indies was legitimate.

[74] M. Rogers, 'China and Islam – the archaeological evidence in the Mashriq', in Richards (ed.), *Islam and the trade of Asia*, 67–80.

V. *The Trade of Turkey, Iraq and Iran, 1050–1500*

(I) SELJUQ AND MONGOL TURKEY

It remains to consider Anatolia's role in the trade of the Islamic world. The conquest of Byzantine frontier territory in Anatolia is often assumed to have constituted a very severe blow to the Byzantine Empire, because it entailed the loss of well-populated, reasonably prosperous, provinces. Certainly, the Seljuq Turks inherited in eastern Anatolia an area of at least budding prosperity. The late eleventh and twelfth centuries saw the expansion of towns in Seljuq territory and the extension of important trade routes through eastern Anatolia. Moreover, the very existence of a major new power in Asia Minor led foreign merchants, especially Italians, to investigate ways of gaining an *entrée* into Seljuq lands: western merchants were reluctant to allow a region bordering on, and also supplying, other lands with which they traded to pursue acts of hostility against their ships and caravans. And from cautious approaches in the twelfth century came trading agreements by the early thirteenth; and from trading agreements came willingness to explore the opportunities Anatolia offered.[75] The Italians discovered that Turkey was a promising source of items they had previously bought in different areas of the Mediterranean. Particular interest attached to alum: Anatolian alum was known from the markets of Aleppo, where Tuscan purchasers congregated; but hopes grew of penetrating further inland to the sources of production.[76]

The Turks gave direct encouragement to visiting merchants in other ways than the provision of trade treaties. They worked hard to resettle the land and initiated vigorous building programmes in the towns. By the early thirteenth century Konya and Sivas were flourishing meeting-places for Italian merchants, for Iranian merchants and, occasionally, for the Greeks of Trebizond and the Muslims of Syria and Egypt. Khans, or caravanserais, were built at the main stopping-points along the classical Anatolian trade-routes. Industrial life was vigorous: at Akseray and in the Turcoman villages heavy fabrics, including knotted carpets, were woven – it is likely that the Turks brought to Anatolia advanced methods of carpet manufacture. Silver, alum and iron were mined, each attracting foreign merchants

75 M. Martin, 'The Seljuq-Venetian Treaty of 1220', *English Historical Review*, xcv (1980), 321–30.

76 For evidence that stocks of goods were maintained at Aleppo by thirteenth-century Italian merchants, see, for instance, D. S. H. Abulafia, 'Crocuses and Crusaders: San Gimignano, Pisa and the Kingdom of Jerusalem', in B. Z. Kedar, H. E. Mayer, R. C. Smail (eds.), *Outremer: studies on the Crusader Kingdom of Jerusalem presented to Joshua Prawer* (Jerusalem, 1982), 230–2.

from East and West. Anatolian wool was held in high repute, and the Turkish pastoralists probably increased production beyond Byzantine levels. Thus, whereas in the tenth and early eleventh centuries the Anatolian plateau had possessed rather little commercial importance, in the thirteenth century the same area became a major centre of production. Cahen remarks that the trade of Byzantine Asia Minor had a very different character to that of Seljuq Asia Minor: of trade in the Byzantine period he writes, 'in so far as it passed through its territory, it crossed the country without being of real concern to it'.[77]

The old caravan routes had as their destinations Constantinople at one end, the Muslim lands in Syria, Mesopotamia and Iran at the other, with subsidiary routes into the Caucasus. By the end of the twelfth century, however, these routes were utilised more intensively and new feeder-routes were generated. Michael the Syrian mentions how 400 merchants from Persia perished in the Anatolian snows – a large caravan. Further stimulus was provided by the creation of the Greek Empire of Trebizond, after 1204: Trebizond attracted Venetian and other merchants and brought foreign ships to the Black Sea coast of Anatolia. The Seljuq lands, despite uneasy political relations with Trebizond, benefited from the presence of these ship-borne merchants, who penetrated inland to Sivas in search of silver, nuts and eastern luxury goods. Sivas in particular flourished, since it stood at the cross-roads of several trade routes, running down to the Euphrates, up to the Pontos (at Samsun), and westwards through Ankara and the monotonous Anatolian plateau to the Bosporus and Constantinople. Russian merchants reached this part of the Seljuq empire even before 1204. A second major centre of trade was Konya, further south than Sivas. It had two bazaars, an 'old' and 'new', by 1201–2; it was visited by merchants from Tabriz and native Turkish traders. Thirdly, there was the port of Antalya, which became the principal Turkish outlet into the Mediterranean; its prosperity attracted the ambitious Tuscan adventurer Aldobrandini, who seized it and held it briefly in 1205. In 1220 the Venetians became well-entrenched at Antalya, as a result of their trade agreements with the Seljuqs. But Antalya possessed its own community of native merchants, too; they were known in the Black Sea and Cilicia, where the Christian kingdom of Leon the Armenian stood poised as middleman between the east Anatolian towns and Cyprus, Syria and Egypt. Konya and Antalya were linked to Cilicia by adequate roads, whose khans – erected even in remote countryside – greatly facilitated movement from the Black Sea through to the Mediterranean.

[77] C. Cahen, *Pre-Ottoman Turkey* (London, 1968), 163.

Further evidence that the Turkish economy was entering a period of prosperity around 1200 is provided by the coinage of the Seljuq rulers. As a matter of fact, the early Seljuq rulers only issued a very limited coinage, of copper, and the late twelfth century sees the first silver coins, under Kilij Arslan II; gold coins appear in the next century. Thus, from copper money, intended for small-scale business, there is a move to the precious metals of international trade, while the coins themselves become more assertive of their Seljuq identity – abandoning Byzantine models, but elbowing their way into the markets as an acceptable currency. The appearance of native silver coins in a region so well supplied with silver mines is no real surprise; but the presence of gold coins in the thirteenth century speaks for an accumulation of gold in the Seljuq heartlands; and this may signify big profits from trade, since Anatolia was as poor in gold mines as it was rich in silver mines. Turkey was in a similar trading position to western Europe at the same period: it was exporting silver, but acquiring gold.

In 1243 Seljuq Anatolia fell under the Mongol sway. Its prosperity was not, however, shattered. Italian visitors continued to buy silk and woollen cloths in Sivas and Erzinjan; the carpets of Akseray remained very popular. However, the Mongol conquest facilitated communication through Anatolia to more remote regions – to the Caucasus and the north Persian towns; foreign merchants began sometimes to miss the classic centres of Turkish trade, such as Sivas, and to cut across country instead, from Trebizond or Cilicia into Azerbaijan. Thus the region began to revert to its status in the Byzantine period, as a land to be crossed rather than visited for its own sake. Moreover, the opening of new, accessible trade routes running eastwards from the northern Black Sea, across the steppes to China, diverted some business from Asia Minor; by the late thirteenth century, however, the quarrels between the Golden Horde in Russia and the Il-khans in Persia meant that the safest route into Iran was through the Turkish vassal states in Anatolia, which acknowledged Il-khanid suzerainty. Merchants from the Il-khanid east visited Anatolia and even took ship on Italian vessels – bound, no doubt, more often for Cyprus and Egypt than for Genoa or Venice. Thus the Mongol period did not see a dramatic decline in Anatolia's commercial prosperity, so much as a redirection of trade partly to the detriment of the existing Turkish towns.

So, too, Mongol rule brought certain benefits, at a price. There were additional taxes; but in return the trade routes were policed. The coinage was reformed, and a new dinar was introduced; the mints of Anatolia became a major source of the new currency, which was intended to become accepted throughout the Mongol, or at least

Il-khanid, dominions. However, the small Turcoman states on the edges of Anatolia increasingly went their own way, issuing a great variety of their own money. Attempts by the Mongols to impose a paper currency (1294) were stoutly resisted.

During the thirteenth century Anatolia acquired additional attractiveness to foreign merchants. It became the major international focus of the alum trade: towards the end of the century the Zaccaria of Genoa tried to establish mastery over alum-bearing districts on the west coast of Asia Minor; and in 1346 the conquest of Chios by the Genoese assured the western cities of ready access to the alum of Phocaea, even though the sources of production were not in Italian hands. Much further inland, eastern Anatolian alum continued to find buyers in Aleppo and Cilicia. A merchant of San Gimignano disappeared into 'Turchia' in the mid-thirteenth century, while his more cautious colleagues ranged no further than Muslim Syria; it was probably alum he sought. More difficult to estimate is the importance of Anatolian links with Iran at the same period. A cursory glance at the culture of Seljuq Anatolia – at its art and architecture – reveals how potent Persian influence was; the close identity of some styles of Turkish and of Persian pottery suggests a lively trade in ceramics. These contacts may have acquired additional value in the fourteenth century, when western visitors to Anatolia showed increasing reluctance to tread the road to Tabriz and Persia; they thus relied all the more on Turkish middlemen for supplies of Persian goods such as textiles and ceramics.

The active alum trade and the close ties to Iran provide *prima facie* evidence for the continuing existence of a large group of native merchants in Seljuq lands, servicing a ganglion of trade routes linking Karahidar and the Anatolian interior to Phocaea, Cilicia and the Black Sea. After the loss of Acre in 1219 these trade routes acquired further importance. Italian merchants, unwelcome in the Holy Land, concentrated much of their Levant business in Cyprus and learned to rely on the sea-routes to southern Turkey, northern Syria and Egypt for supplies of Anatolian produce, eastern cloths and the spices of the Indies. It is to be presumed that, in the early fourteenth century, the native Turkish merchants serviced at least some of these vital links.[78]

[78] Further evidence of the vitality of the economy of Anatolia is provided by the silver coinage of Aydın and Menteshe imitated from Neapolitan models: P. Grierson, 'Le Gillat ou carlin de Naples-Provence: le rayonnement de son type monétaire', in *Catalogue de l'Exposition centenaire de la société française de numismatique (1865–1965)* (Paris, 1965), 43–56; see now also, E. Zachariadou, *Trade and Crusade: Venetian Crete and the emirates of Aydın and Menteshe (1300–1415)* (Library of the Institute of Byzantine and post-Byzantine studies, XI) (Venice, 1983), 142.

(2) ECONOMIC DIFFICULTIES IN IRAQ, 1250–1500.

The relative prosperity of Anatolia under Mongol overlordship, even compared to its Seljuq apogee, must be contrasted with the effects of Mongol rule elsewhere in the Islamic world: in Iraq. It has been seen that the economic primacy of Egypt over Iraq was established even before 1100. Nevertheless, the decline of Mesopotamian trade was not dramatic, at least in the twelfth and thirteenth centuries; rather was it a slow, continuous process, involving the increasing isolation of the Mesopotamian lowlands from the great trade routes of the spice merchants. The crusader conquests in Syria and the Holy Land may actually have stimulated the industries of some Mesopotamian cities: from Mosul and Baghdad fine cloths – local specialities such as the original 'muslin' – were carried to Damascus and Aleppo, where Latins from Acre could often be found. On the other hand, the late thirteenth century saw the eclipse of this trade link: Acre declined dramatically under the Mamluks, after 1291; but difficulties were engendered even earlier, in 1258, when the Mongol general Hulegu conquered Baghdad and incorporated Iraq as a peripheral province of the Il-khanid state. Heavy taxation, mass slaughter and large-scale emigration sapped the economic strength of the Iraqi towns and induced a severe fall in agricultural productivity. Much of Baghdad was abandoned by the mid-fourteenth century; moreover, the former capital of the caliphs was no longer the seat of a great court, attracting luxury goods from far afield and exercising a beneficial effect on the local market. However, it would be wrong to exaggerate the evils induced by the Mongol conquest. Ashtor indicates that some commercial enterprises flourished rather than contracted in the wake of the Mongol victory: weights and measures were standardised; there were coinage reform; rich merchants such as Imad-ad-din Ali b. al-Hasan al-Udhri acted as bankers to the new rulers.[79] But the direction of Iraq's trade changed, and the merchants of Baghdad looked eastwards to the Il-khanid courts in Iran and to the land routes through Khwarizm towards China. To that extent, the Iraqi merchants were beneficiaries of the *pax mongolica* of the late thirteenth century.

Sundered, however, were the links between Mesopotamia and Egypt or Syria. Mutual suspicion between the Il-khans and the Mamluks prevented the free movement of merchants between their territories. It was necessary for Iraqi traders to visit Cilician Armenia, or other entrepots linked to the Nile routes, if they wished to obtain Egyptian and Red Sea products in large quantities. At the same time,

[79] Ashtor, *Social and Economic History*, 249–67.

the Il-khanid capital at Tabriz began to flourish as an emporium where eastern spices, Persian silks and slaves were readily available. Tabriz drained the Persian Gulf of Indonesian spices; they were now carried directly to Tabriz rather than to Baghdad, Basra and the classic centres of trade. In consequence, Tabriz attracted the interest of western merchants, whose presence was strongly encouraged by the Il-khans.[80] It was closely linked to Cilician Armenia by trade routes across the mountains and around Lake Van; and, since the Italians were well-ensconced in Cilicia, it is not surprising that they responded to Il-khanid offers of commercial treaties – Venice still had an eye on Persia in 1320, when it arranged a trade agreement. Moreover, the Italians welcomed the opportunity to trade not merely in Iran but along the trade routes which fanned out northwards and eastwards to China and India. The early fourteenth century saw Italian visitors to Delhi; the Genoese sought to defend their interests by launching a fleet on the Caspian Sea, and by advising the Il-khan Arghun (1284–91) to attack Aden and to cut off the trade route linking Egypt to the Indies.[81] Although these Genoese schemes did not succeed, the Il-khanid state was able to interfere by different means in the Red Sea trade. An autonomous princedom, established at Hormuz on the Persian Gulf in the early fourteenth century, acted as a forwarding point for Indian goods bound for Tabriz. Thus, some of the spices of the East were diverted away from Aden and the Nile – away, also, from the traditional Persian Gulf route which ran from the island of Kish to Basra, Wasit and Baghdad.

The peak of the prosperity of the new trade routes via Tabriz was passed by the mid-fourteenth century. In part this may be due to the lack of responsiveness of the Venetians, Genoese and Tuscans to offers of trade rights at Tabriz – itself a reflection of that economic depression which had begun to grip the towns of Christian Europe.[82] Moreover, Persia lost its attractiveness when, in the 1340s, Turcoman generals seized power and the last embers of the *pax mongolica* flickered out. So, too, in China, after 1368, a non-Mongol dynasty looked away from central Asia and the Mongol trade routes and towards maritime dominion in South-East Asia. Obviously, the decline of the long-distance trade routes did not entail a collapse of interest in the local produce of Iran and Iraq: Venetian merchants did still visit the Turcoman dominions and were present at Basra and Baghdad in the

[80] Cf., however, B. Z. Kedar, *Merchants in Crisis: Genoese and Venetian men of affairs and the fourteenth-century depression* (New Haven, 1976).

[81] J. Richard, 'Les Navigations des occidentaux sur l'océan indien et la mer caspienne (XIIe-XVe siècles), in *Sociétés et compagnies de commerce en Orient et dans l'Océan indien*, 353–63.

[82] Kedar, *Merchants in Crisis*, 118–30; Ashtor, *Social and Economic History*, 275–6.

fifteenth century. The pearls of the Persian Gulf remained a special attraction. Hormuz, too, stood to gain from the persistence of maritime traffic between the Indonesian islands and the central Islamic lands. There were heavily employed trade routes linking Azerbaijan with Iraq and Aleppo or Damascus, while the revival of diplomatic links between the Turcomans and the Mamluks stimulated trade between Iraq and Egypt; particularly prized were Persian raw silk and processed textiles. But what is noticeable is that, although Iraq continued to channel its own goods into these east–west trade routes, it no longer stood astride the main routes; Iraq lay to the south of the overland route from Persia to Cilicia and the Black Sea, and to the north of the maritime routes which only touched its periphery. Ashtor remarks that 'the progressive decrease of Irak's share in the transit trade of the Near East resulted necessarily in the shrinking of its towns'.[83] And besides, competition from vigorous textile producers in Iran eroded the once prominent position of Iraqi industrial goods in the international markets.

The towns shrank not merely because of shifts in the trade routes. The arrival of bubonic plague in 1347 devastated Baghdad. As elsewhere, demographic recovery was rendered impossible by the recurrence of plague again and again in the late fourteenth and fifteenth centuries. In the 1470s a Venetian visitor, Giosafat Barbaro, described Baghdad as 'once a famous town, now to a great extent destroyed'; but it is only possible to speculate whether the plague had a more severe effect on the old population centres of the Mesopotamian lowlands than on their newer upland rivals in Persia and Azerbaijan. Certainly, the decline of Iraq was accentuated by warfare – most notably, by Tamerlane's massacres in Baghdad in 1401. It is likely, then, that the difficulties of Iraq were more profound than those of Iran or of lands to the west, since in Iraq the experience of plague was compounded by exceptionally severe warfare and by incompetent, ineffectual government. The Iraqi towns did not flower once more in response to rising demand from newly enriched survivors of the plague, as occurred in parts of western Europe. Iraqi industry was already severely ailing before the Black Death, and it was probably the textile centres of Iran which benefited instead from increasing demand for high- and middle-grade goods. Demand for Iraqi goods outside Mesopotamia was not sustained. Even the famous Baghdadi paper – a by-product of the textile industry – lost its markets, as competitors elsewhere in the Near East, and at Fabriano in Italy, produced paper of equal or higher quality.

[83] Ashtor, *Social and Economic History*, 277.

The economic decline of Iraq suggests an explanation of the wider economic crisis visible throughout the Muslim world in the fourteenth and fifteenth centuries. The Near East had lost its technological primacy to the textile factories of Italy, Catalonia and Flanders well before 1300; even agricultural expertise declined in the Near East, whereas it gained ground in Lombardy, Holland and other western lands. The heavy hand of military government, by Mamluks, Mongols and Turcomans, restrained innovation and limited opportunities for investment. The fortunes of the richer merchants were regularly confiscated, to bolster the shaky finances of the courts of Cairo or Tabriz. The result was that merchants concentrated on straightforward trading enterprises which produced predictable returns, and they tended to commit their capital predominantly to commercial investment. The growth of state monopolies in the Muslim world made investment in privately owned factories unattractive, since several sectors of production were government-managed, and since supplies of raw materials, such as precious dyes, needed to be negotiated through government offices. In consequence, there was a strong preference among merchants for high spending – for maintaining a high standard of living rather than for stockpiling capital in the hope of launching major new projects. The wealthy merchant ate, drank and was merry, for tomorrow was another day, when the sultan might well requisition his goods and question the right of his head to remain on his shoulders. An alternative – evinced by the Mamluk *khawajas* – was to join the ranks of the public servants, but this again meant that (corrupt practices apart) funds could not easily be accumulated for private investment.

Impatient Christian writers, from Marino Sanudo Torsello onwards, argued that the Islamic world could be strangled if trade relations were suspended – the arms trade, of course, but also the spice trade, which so enriched the princes through whose territory it passed. The Portuguese actually succeeded in diverting the gold trade directly towards Christian Europe without the use of Muslim intermediaries. What these writers and practitioners did not see was that they could leave the Islamic sultans and warlords to suffocate the trade of the Muslim world, without external help.

VI. *Muslim Trade in Africa*

(1) THE CRISIS OF THE MAGHRIB, 1050–1200

Just as Egypt was a major channel through which eastern commodities were passed to the Christian West, so, too, was North-West and

North-Central Africa a way-station for goods coming from the deep south – from the gold mines of Mali, across the Sahara. In two senses the towns of the Maghrib owed their prosperity to Saharan gold: it was partly to acquire gold that Christian merchants visited al-Mahdiyyah, Bougie, Ceuta and other ports; while markets further inland were also stimulated into greater activity by the availability of cheap gold and by the circulation of good quality gold currency. The peak of this prosperity was probably reached by the late eleventh century, when ambitious navies from Genoa and Pisa fought to establish trade counters at al-Mahdiyyah; agricultural prosperity existed, too, and the towns were able to supply their food needs at low cost from the surrounding countryside.[84] By contrast, the late twelfth and thirteenth centuries saw these successes badly compromised; indeed, the economic problems of North Africa were partly the result of the region's easy access to gold. The success of the Italian merchants in gaining privileged access to African gold and in dumping European goods, such as textiles, in the Maghrib generated a penury of gold in al-Mahdiyyah and its neighbours: paradoxically, gold passed so smoothly through the Maghrib to Italy and Spain that the North Africans themselves lost sight of, and ready access to, their most prized commodity. The Sicilian kings seem also to have 'sucked' gold out of the African towns, for use in their prestige currency; they returned wheat, which had earlier been a prime product of the African countryside, but was so no longer. Moreover, further difficulties were induced in the late eleventh century by bitter political struggles within North Africa – the rejection of Fatimid overlordship, the Almoravid threat from further west and, by the early twelfth century, raids and invasions by the Sicilian Normans.

Scholars have generally listed the Arab incursions into the Maghrib in the eleventh century among the catastrophes which crippled the prosperity of North Africa. The Banu Hillal and the Banu Sulaym, Bedouin nomads, were sent westwards by the Fatimids, partly to coerce the Zirid emirs of the Maghrib who had disowned Egyptian overlordship, and partly to disembarass Egypt of unwelcome visitors. There is, indeed, some evidence that the Fatimids expected the nomads to wreak enormous havoc in the Maghrib; and there is no denying that the Banu Hillal and their confederates changed the face of Tunisia and Tripolitania. Idrisi, writing for Roger II of Sicily in around 1154, describes how new cultivators, Arabs, displaced the Berbers. The abandonment of land by the Berber farmers meant the desertion of

[84] H. E. J. Cowdrey, 'The Mahdia Campaign of 1087', *English Historical Review*, XCII (1977), 1–29; Brett, 'Ifriqiya as a market', 489–506.

irrigation works; the delicately held supremacy of the farmer over the hostile environment of North Africa was rapidly eroded. In fact, the soil was deteriorating for additional reasons, too: the Sahara was advancing on all fronts; wadis were drying out; and it is likely that the irrigation works of the farmers were more difficult to maintain in the eleventh century in any case. The agricultural productivity of Tunisia declined dramatically; by the mid-twelfth century famines were frequent and, in the longer term, North Africa became heavily dependent on foreign supplies of wheat. And this change from earlier agricultural prosperity had an important effect on the character of commerce in the region. Because the nearest and most prolific source of wheat was Norman Sicily, the North African towns paid handsomely in gold for the wheat of the Regno and thus accentuated the outflow of gold from North Africa. The real beneficiary of the Banu Hillal invasions was not the Fatimid caliph, who recovered none of his authority over the Maghrib, but the Sicilian king, a Christian ruler, with whom, indeed, the Muslim jurists felt it improper to trade on such a scale.[85]

Major towns were also affected by the Hillalian invasion. From Qayrawan the focus of trade shifted westwards to the Mediterranean coast – to al-Mahdiyyah in the late eleventh century, and later still to Tunis. Partly this was to accommodate a new group of visiting merchants, the Italians, who sought gold, hides and wool; but it is noticeable that merchants whose home was within the Islamic world, such as the Fustat Jews, also congregated at al-Mahdiyyah. The decline of Qayrawan entailed a redirection of the gold caravans which had terminated there; now they headed directly for the coast and unloaded their goods for export, often outside the Islamic sphere. The caravans fanned out, to reach a number of ports spread between Ceuta and Tripoli; Michael Brett has linked this new distribution of caravan routes to the Hillalian invasions in a novel way. He refutes the view, often expressed, that the Banu Hillal sundered the trade routes carrying gold to North Africa, inducing economic misery in consequence. For Brett, the change that occurred was far more complex: gold continued to arrive, but not in Qayrawan; and the former masters of the Qayrawan gold trade, the Ibadi Arabs of the African hinterland, were toppled from primacy. The Hillalians did not themselves become gold merchants, but no single group survived to dominate the gold trade. This interpretation is particularly attractive since the Italian records show a growth in interest among Genoese and other merchants

[85] It will be obvious that this view differs from that of Michael Brett, expounded in 'Ifriqiya as a market'; cf. my 'L'attività commerciale genovese nell'Africa normanna'. For desiccation, C. Vita-Finzi, *The Mediterranean Valleys* (Cambridge, 1969) is suggestive.

in Ceuta, Bougie and other North-West African ports in which their trade seems to have been relatively slight before the late twelfth century.[86]

The late eleventh and twelfth centuries in North Africa are illuminated by an important, neglected series of documents: the *fatwas*, or legal decisions of Islamic judges, which provide information about the trading arrangements, commodities and centres of commerce along the Tunisian coast. It is clear that as early as 1091–3 there was a growing dependence of Tunisia on trade with the Sicilian granaries. A *fatwa* of that period raises the question whether it was legitimate to trade with Christian-conquered Sicily, even when that trade was in the very necessities of life. The judges argued that Allah would provide for his servants if they refrained from contact with the infidel – the problem was that Muslim merchants broke rank and continued to trade with the enemy in a way that could only incur divine displeasure. Similarly, any trade with the heathen only increased the power of the heathen: 'If we go to their country, the price of goods will rise in their land and they will gather considerable amounts of money out of our hands, and they will use this money to fight the Muslims and to fight Muslim lands.' But within half a century there was apparently no alternative: Sicilian grain was imported, not against exports of olive oil or textiles, but against gold payments. *Fatwas* of the 1140s explain how these payments were effected. Merchants would form an association to buy Sicilian grain, sending Almoravid and Tripolitanian dinars of pure gold. The head of the Sicilian mint would melt this gold down, adding one quarter of its weight in silver, and reminting the alloyed metal as the Sicilian *tari* (meaning 'fresh' coin), or quarter-dinar. The master of the mint would then hold back for the mint – and hence, presumably, for the royal treasury – as many *tari* as weighed the equivalent of the silver he had employed as alloy. Thus, the imported gold of the African merchants was handed back to them at considerably reduced purity: surviving Sicilian *tari* are invariably 661‰ pure gold, while the gold of Africa approached 1,000‰. It was also the practice for North African merchants to send bullion to Sicily in the form of rings, bracelets and other jewellery; it was then sold in the markets, and perhaps by this means merchants avoided the regular, distressing experience of the mint master's dealings.[87]

86 Brett, 'Ifriqiya as a market', seems to me here to make much sense.

87 For this source, see H. R. Idris, *La Berbérie orientale sous les Zirides, Xe-XIIe siècles*, 2 vols (Publications de l'Institut d'Études orientales, Faculté des lettres et sciences humaines d'Alger, no. XXII, Paris, 1962), II, 661–3. I have discussed this material further in my article 'Maometto e Carlomagno: le due aree monetarie dell'Italia medievale, dell'oro dell'argento', *Einaudi Storia d'Italia, Annali*, VI, ed. R. Romano and V. Tucci (Turin, 1983), 242–3, 253.

The *fatwas* are also eloquent about ties between the African towns and other parts of the Islamic Mediterranean. Around the year 1000, ships were being sent from Tunisia to Alexandria for sale. Qayrawan and al-Mahdiyyah sent their merchants as far as Mecca for trade. A long *fatwa* of al-Mazari, who died in 1141, includes a merchant's accounts. He went from North Africa to Alexandria, taking coral and silk; these he sold in order to buy indigo, bales of flax, cloves, musk, satin and women's veils. These articles were transported to Tunis by way of Bizerta, and the indigo was supplied to dyers. There were links, too, with Muslim Spain: Andalusian merchants bought coral from the central Mediterranean, as well as wool and honey – the former a distant ancestor of the merino wool later generations of Spaniards would produce on home soil. Algiers was an important entrepot in the early twelfth century, though after al-Mazari's day it ceded primacy to Bougie; its excellent port only became again of first significance in the sixteenth century. There is every sign that Moorish Spain, like Norman Sicily, developed a favourable trading relationship with North Africa, sucking gold out of the Sahara into its mints, via Algiers, Bougie and, of course, Ceuta.[88]

(2) THE GOLD OF SUDAN

So far allusion only has been made to the Saharan gold supplies. It is evident from even a cursory examination of the finances of the Muslim Mediterranean rulers how successfully they drew on Saharan gold: Andalusian separatism under Abd ar-Rahman III, Fatimid wars of conquest in Egypt and the Maghrib were made easier by access to the wealth of inner Africa. Gold coinages of high purity were minted on the Nile and at Cordoba, expressing in the clearest language the independence of the new caliphates from Baghdad and giving a sound monetary base to the economic activities of what, until the tenth and eleventh centuries, were not the real heartlands of Islamic prosperity. The gold dinars made this literally the 'Golden Age' of Islam. Later empires, too, were aided in their war efforts by the presence of trade routes bringing gold northwards: the Almoravids and the Almohads, in Morocco and in Spain, minted dinars of exceptional purity which, as has been seen, were eminently acceptable to the master of the Sicilian mint.

Until the eleventh century the Ibadi Arabs of the Djarid (southern Tunisia and south-east Algeria) had managed the movement of gold from their base at Wargla, on the edge of the Sahara. As the trade

[88] Idris, *Berbérie orientale*, II, 666–72.

routes diversified and moved west, important new centres emerged which serviced the supply of gold to Spain and the ports of North-West Africa. Sijilmasa was hailed by ibn Hawqal, as early as the tenth century, as an important focus for trade between the western Maghrib and the 'Sudan', that is, the kingdoms south of the desert; the same writer describes an order of payment he saw at Sijilmasa, worth 42,000 dinars.[89] For a time the income they received from Sijilmasa was a main prop of the authority of the Fatimids in the Maghrib. By the mid-twelfth century, however, Sijilmasa had passed its prime: although, as Idrisi indicates, southern Morocco remained the destination of many Saharan caravans, the Almohad invasions of the twelfth century caused jolts in the regularity of supplies. This may be because the authority of the Almohads did not extend so far to the south as had the authority of the empire of their Almoravid predecessors. Whereas in the late eleventh and early twelfth centuries a *pax morabitina* had reigned, the Almohad fanatics sundered relations with lands whose regime – Muslim or Christian – met their disapproval.

There were three main sets of routes across the Sahara towards the gold-producing areas: southwards from Sijilmasa and the western Maghrib; southwards from al-Mahdiyyah, Tunis and neighbouring centres; and an elongated route westwards from Egypt through the villages of what is now Chad. The last of these routes seems to have faded from prominence by the twelfth century, but to have undergone a revival in the fourteenth. Idrisi pictures the villages along the Egypt–'Sudan' route as deserted places which had lost their former importance. On the other hand, when the king of Mali, Mansa Musa, set out for Egypt and Mecca in 1324 the route to Egypt seems to have been in operation again; and it was known to Leo Africanus in the sixteenth century. Perhaps the Hillalian invasions did have cataclysmic effects on the easterly route, as well as stimulating into greater activity the westerly ones. But all these routes were only passable with the help of expert 'navigators': Levtzion has characterised the Sahara as a hostile 'ocean', with many small 'islands', that is, oases; there were few landmarks – indeed, the landscape shifted from day to day; and the best 'navigators' identified their location not merely by sight but by smell, by sniffing the sand. Archaeologists have discovered what cannot have been a rarity: a lost caravan of the twelfth century, buried in the sands.[90]

[89] N. Levtzion, 'Ibn Hawqal, the cheque and Awdaghust', *Journal of African History*, IX (1968), 223–33.

[90] T. Monod, 'Le Macden Ijafen: une épave caravanière ancienne dans la Majabat al-Koabra,' *Actes du premier Colloque international d'archéologie africaine* (Fort Lamy, Chad, 1969), 286–320. I am grateful to Dr David Phillipson of the University Museum of Archaeology and Anthropology for provision of this reference.

Beyond the desert were the towns where the caravans acquired their gold. The gold merchants of the Maghrib did not penetrate to the actual areas of production which lay further inland – there is an interesting analogy to the spice trade here, with the south Saharan towns playing a similar role to Palembang or Malacca. Even the local rulers were careful to avoid direct interference in the regions where gold was mined: an attempt by the king of Mali to extend his political control over the gold-bearing regions encountered the stubborn refusal of the gold-diggers to continue work for their new master. The Ghanaian and Mali rulers sought, rather, to extract benefit from the gold trade through taxes and the exercise of certain regalian rights: all large nuggets were reserved to the ruler, and the merchants were only permitted to handle gold dust. The black African rulers showed great willingness to protect Muslim merchants, even when they themselves were pagan. Excavations in the former royal capital of Ghana confirm al-Bakri's eleventh-century description of the town: the merchant settlement stood apart from the royal city; indeed the Muslim trading town was probably much grander than its royal pagan counterpart. The former possessed spacious stone houses, in which glass weights used for weighing gold and pottery from the Mediterranean shores have been found. Levtzion observes: 'the Muslim town was not only an appendage to the local town, but perhaps even more important than the latter'.[91] By 1400, however, the gold trade had become more centralised at the south Saharan end: Timbuktu emerged as a centre of Islamic trade in black Africa. Timbuktu in the fifteenth century also provided visible evidence of its prosperity: Leo Africanus mentions a mosque of Andalusian design there, while throughout the southern Saharan towns the practice of building with burnt tiles was borrowed from the Maghrib.

Further visible evidence of the region's prosperity was provided to the inhabitants of Cairo and the Hejaz in an altogether different manner. Mansa Musa's pilgrimage of 1324, from Mali to Mecca, gave rise to further legends about the limitless quantities of gold to be found in black Africa. On his arrival in Cairo the king of Mali scattered gold through the streets; the result was serious short-term inflation, since thousands of pounds of pure gold were suddenly injected into the Egyptian economy. So lavish, or wanton, was Mansa Musa that, on his return from Mecca, he found his money had run out, and he arranged loans with the Karimi merchants – who, as has been seen, were kept waiting for repayment much longer than they had been led to expect. Another effect of Mansa Musa's visit to Egypt was probably

[91] N. Levtzion, *Ancient Ghana and Mali* (*Studies in African History*, VII) (London, 1973), 25.

the revival of direct trade between Egypt and Mali. The Genoese merchant, Antonio Malfante, reached Tuat in 1447 and described the Egyptian merchants who had come there to trade copper and other goods against the black man's gold. Ashtor lays particular emphasis on the direct trade route between Egypt and black Africa in the late Middle Ages, because goods which moved along this route escaped the interference of Mediterranean merchants and rulers, such as the Catalans and the Aragonese.[92] Certainly their imagination, and that of the Portuguese, was greatly excited by tales of the Sudanese gold mines.

The most important commodity to come out of black Africa, after gold, was probably slaves. Spain, Sicily and Naples drew large numbers of Berber and black captives out of Africa throughout the Middle Ages: even in the fifteenth century Naples was a major 'consumer'. In the Muslim lands, especially Morocco, black slaves acquired trusted status in noble households, and in Christian lands they tended to perform domestic functions or, in Valencia, agricultural work.[93] They were also something of a prestige symbol, to judge from the possession of eighty black slaves by the Jewish treasurer of Castile, Don Samuel Abulafia (1320–60).[94] The slaves were often traded for horses, sent from North Africa. A Tunisian *fatwa* of the late tenth century indicates that the same merchants handled both horses and slaves, and there was still a link between the two commodities when Leo Africanus visited black Africa in about 1500: in Bornu it was customary to pay for horses with slaves, at a rate of fifteen or twenty slaves per horse, even though Bornu was also well supplied with gold. North African merchants found themselves servicing an efficient war-machine: horses helped in war; Bornu wars were consequently very successful; and so slaves were captured in war far in excess of Bornu needs.[95]

The southern Saharan towns were not simply sources of gold and slaves. In the mid-thirteenth century the Maqqari family traded via Tlemcen in Sudanese hides, ivory and kola nuts, as well as gold. They sent northern cloths south to Walata, where two of the brothers sold these goods to Saharan traders. Another brother, based at Sijilmasa, concentrated on forward planning and provision of information, sending lists of prices to his brothers at Tlemcen and Walata. The Maqqari brothers were active in other spheres, too: they dug wells on the Sijilmasa–Walata route, thereby assuring easier passage for

[92] Ashtor, *Social and Economic History*, 324–31.
[93] C. Verlinden, *L'Esclavage dans l'Europe médiévale* (2 vols., Bruges, 1955, and Ghent, 1977); J. Heers, *Esclaves et domestiques dans la Méditerranée médiévale* (Paris, 1981).
[94] H. Graetz, *History of the Jews* (English translation, Philadelphia, 1894), IV, 121.
[95] Levtzion, *Ancient Ghana and Mali*, 174–8.

merchants. This was an exceptionally wealthy partnership, handling the prestige products of black Africa. But there were more modest Sudanese goods on sale north of the Sahara: cloths, rougher than those the princes of Mali imported from the Mediterranean. In return, Maghribi merchants sent two commodities of special importance: copper and salt. Demand for salt is illustrated by al-Bakri's statement that the tax on imports of salt in Ghana was only half that on exports of salt, in 1067. The lost caravan discovered in the Sahara was carrying about a ton of copper, divided into rods. Glass, coral, tin and lead also went southwards; and in certain parts of Africa cowrie shells were in demand. They were brought from the East Indies and employed in Africa, as in the Far East, as a means of exchange. The lost caravan was also well supplied with these shells. Mostly they came via the Red Sea and Egypt.

The gold of Africa, for sheer quantity, had no real rival in the medieval world. The few gold currencies that existed in the Latin West before 1252 were minted from African gold, and the excellence of Egyptian coinage in the twelfth century has already been noted.[96] Access to African gold helped assure the economic primacy of the Muslim shores of the Mediterranean over Iraq, Iran or Byzantium, and, after 1200, it helped build the economic success of the Christian shores of the Mediterranean and the decisive dominance of the Italians and the Catalans. It is no surprise that Henry the Navigator and his successors should have sought to tap African gold from new outlets and to cheat Egypt of its traditional sources of the metal.

(3) EAST AFRICAN TRADE

Whereas West Africa enjoyed close ties with the Maghrib, Egypt and Spain, East Africa looked away from the Mediterranean and, to a considerable extent, away from the Islamic world. In the early Middle Ages slaves were supplied in vast numbers to the southern Mesopotamian marshlands, but they proved their unreliability with the Zanj rebellion in the ninth century. Timber and iron were listed by Idrisi and other geographers among the exports of East Africa, not merely to Islamic lands but also, significantly, to India – the home of fine-quality weapons. Rice was forwarded to Aden from Kilwa. And, of course, rhinoceros horn was highly prized – but, once again, in the Far East even more than in the Islamic world. Idrisi describes how men of Zabaj, apparently Sri Vijaya, visited the coast of East Africa; some

[96] To be more exact, the only evidence for acquisition of gold by the mint of the Norman kings of Sicily concerns African gold: Abulafia, 'Maometto e Carlomagno', 242–3. Cf. also R. S. Lopez, 'Back to Gold, 1252', *Economic History Review*, ser. 2, IX (1956), 219–40.

modern authorities, such as Chittick, consider such an elongated link unlikely, but it is not impossible that Malay merchants ventured so far west.[97] Somalia was a producer of frankincense, and there do seem to have been close commercial ties with Aden in the thirteenth and fourteenth centuries. But by the fifteenth century the conclusion is inescapable that East Africa aroused only very limited interest among Muslim merchants. Archaeologists have found little on the Kenyan sites of the fifteenth century that hailed from Egypt or Syria. Maybe the Arabs sent from the Red Sea principally perishable goods which have left no archaeological traces: textiles and foodstuffs. Certainly the horn of Africa had been receiving rice, wheat, ghee, molasses, textiles and sesame oil from as far away as India in very early times. Even the Muslim geographers tend to be fuller on the lands to the east – India and beyond – than they are on East Africa.

The other dimension to this picture is the evidence for continuous, intensive trade between East Africa and southern Asia, via Gujarati intermediaries. Chao Ju-Kua's description of Zanzibar, from 1225, is revealing:

> The Tsöng-po [Zanj-ba, Zanzibar] country is on an island in the sea south of the Hu-cha-la [Gujarat, India]. To the west it reaches to a great mountain. The inhabitants are of Ta-shi [Arab] stock and follow the Ta-shi religion. They wrap themselves in blue foreign cotton stuffs and wear red leather shoes. Their daily food consists of meal, baked cakes, and mutton.... The products of the country consist of elephants' tusks, native gold, ambergris and yellow sandal-wood. Every year Hu-cha-la and the Ta-shi localities along the sea-coast send ships to this country with white cotton cloth, porcelain, copper and red cotton to trade.

Links with the Far East grew stronger: there have been significant finds of fourteenth- and fifteenth-century Chinese porcelain on the Kenya coast; while the voyage of Cheng Ho to East Africa reveals an ephemeral desire to consolidate political and commercial ties with China still further. Kirkman remarks that the voyage of Cheng Ho was, after all, exceptional; but Indian contacts clearly are not.[98] Cambay in North-West India was especially active in trade with Africa. Kirkman even suggests that the arched doorways of fifteenth-century houses and mosques on the East African coast may be derived from Indian models – in other words, the relationship was not simply a casual commercial one. More eloquent still is the evidence of coin finds at Zanzibar and other trading towns shown in Table II. The large

[97] N. Chittick, 'East African Trade with the Orient', in *Islam and the Trade of Asia*, 101–3. But Idrisi may have confused men of Sri Vijaya with merchants trading there.

[98] J. S. Kirkman, 'The Coast of Kenya as a Factor in the Trade and Culture of the Indian Ocean', in *Sociétés et compagnies de commerce en Orient*, 247–53.

number of copper coins of Kilwa and Zanzibar also discovered suggests that local trade among the East African centres was also quite intensive. A letter from Diogo de Alcançova to the king of Portugal, dated 20 November 1506, indicates that merchants coming into Kilwa in the fifteenth century were heavily taxed in gold and cloth. It is hardly surprising, then, that another Portuguese writer should stress how the rulers of Pemba, Mafia and Zanzibar 'live in great luxury' and wear the cloth of Cambay.

Table II. *Origins of medieval coins found in East Africa to April 1959*

	Locations of finds and number of coins				
Sources of coins	Mafia	Zanzibar	Pemba	Kilwa	Somalia
Mamluk	—	—	—	2	6
Mongol	4	—	—	—	—
Unidentified Muslim	20	3	15	—	—
China: T'ang	—	4	—	—	1
Sung	9	185	—	—	16
Ming	—	—	—	—	6
Ceylon	—	—	—	—	4
S. India (13th cent.)	—	—	—	—	1
India (Bahmanid)	—	—	—	—	1

Source: G. S. P. Freeman-Grenville, *Journal of African History*, 1 (1960).

With the arrival of Vasco da Gama the trade route from Malindi to Calicut took on a new importance, and the relative isolation of East Africa from the great international trade routes came to a sudden end.

VII. *Conclusion*

It has not been possible to discuss here the trade of every corner of the medieval Muslim world. In any case, the boundaries of that world were fluid: Spain passed out of it, and the Balkans moved into it. But it is clear that the prosperity of the towns of, say, Umayyad Spain in the tenth century, or Fatimid Egypt in the twelfth, brightly outshone that of the late medieval Muslim cities. And the responsibility for this decline rests not merely with efficient, powerful competitors in Italy, Catalonia and the textile centres of northern Europe. There seems to be a contrast between the undemanding attitude of the early Muslim rulers, who milked the trade routes with relative moderation, and the stiff financial demands made by Mamluks in Egypt or Mongols and Turcomans in Iraq and Iran. The frequency of western visits to

Muslim ports, and the volume of trade with the West, increased steadily in the thirteenth century and, after jolts in the fourteenth, showed renewed vigour in the fifteenth century. Yet the continued, growing role of the Muslim world as an intermediary between the spice islands of Indonesia or the gold mines of inner Africa and the Latin West should not be interpreted as a sign of continuing commercial vitality within the Muslim world. Industrial production fell. Towns withered. The countryside remained desolate. Merchants from the West visited the Muslim lands not so much because of what they had to offer, but because of what they forwarded from lands on the fringes of Islam: Mali, Malacca.

At the root of the problems of Muslim trade is the attitude to investment of surplus capital adopted by merchants in the Islamic countries. The capriciousness of rulers – like the capriciousness of fate – were too well known to make long-term investment in industry very frequent, and merchant companies rarely survived more than three generations. Most telling of all is the lack of a securely based mercantile aristocracy, determining the interests of their home city and passing their wealth and power to later generations. In this sense the medieval Muslim merchant left no long-lasting legacy.

CHAPTER VII

Trade and Industry in Eastern Europe Before 1200

I. *Introduction*

It is hardly necessary to point out that what passed for trade and industry in the early Middle Ages bore little resemblance to the complex economic activity of the later Middle Ages and more modern times. The sources available to us and the conceptual apparatus of the historian cannot fully interpret the vaguely perceived forms of economic life during the early centuries of the Middle Ages in Eastern Europe. Such written sources as exist mainly tell us about long-distance trade. Within the last forty years, however, these documents have been reinforced by archaeological excavations which reveal fragmentary glimpses of the daily life of the Slavonic peoples. Typical finds in these excavations have thrown light on the various objects which were produced and consumed and this has helped us to reach certain conclusions of a qualitative, if not a quantitative, nature.

The exchange of goods and handicrafts in that early period is frequently referred to in the literature on the subject, but the dichotomy of a subsistence and an exchange economy in all its social and economic aspects is not a straightforward one, and the terms historians are forced to use when studying those far-off days are not altogether relevant.

Until at least the end of the eleventh century the peoples of the eastern and western Slavonic countries lived in a largely subsistence economy. It was a way of life in which the time and energies of small, widely dispersed groups of people, living in clearings in the huge forests, were devoted to producing goods to be consumed within the group. How sparsely populated that region was compared to other European countries can be gauged from estimates made for the year 1000: for every one Russian there were four central Europeans and more than eleven western Europeans. Neither then nor in earlier periods, however, was this small population an obstacle to the exchange of goods. The homogeneous economic unit (the tribe, the territorial community, the village or other settlement) could have produced some surpluses which, because of a better harvest, more favourable returns from fishing or hunting, or some other factor, were neither planned for nor needed. This was why a large number of individual or family households could exist. After the upper layers of society had taken what they wanted, other, similarly situated, members of the group could exchange goods with each other. As social differentiation proceeded, a group of landlords was formed and a state organisation emerged, the scope and dimensions of exchanges grew. Thus, primitive international trade assumed the trappings of a class phenomenon. There were sometimes other factors which helped to create new economic units in areas rich in natural resources, as happened at Kołobrzeg on the Baltic where there were salt deposits, or in north-eastern Europe with its wealth of animal furs.

The exchange of goods was usually bilateral, i.e. by barter, but this was not the only way of circulating goods. There were other methods such as plunder, tribute, gifts between rulers, dowries or ransoms. The reappearance of metal coins after the decline of the Roman Empire introduced into foreign trade yet another means of payment. But we may assume that between the seventh and the tenth centuries the produce of agriculture and stock-rearing and the artefacts of craftsmanship were still being bartered inside the home economy and that only those objects consumed by the upper classes (tribal and family chiefs and princes), other than their everyday necessities, needed metal coins. By this means luxury goods, gold and silver jewellery, bullion and other objects for the conspicuous display of their owners' social position could from time to time be obtained. Soon money came to indicate political power as well: according to the Oldest Russian Chronicle, Prince Izyaslav Iaroslavich 'went to Poland with great wealth saying that with its help he would find warriors' (a. 1073/6581). We know about the first stages of a commodity and money economy, at least on the local level, from the mid-ninth century in Moravia and from the tenth century in Bohemia: here various objects no longer having any intrinsic use occasionally took the place of money (e.g. small iron axes, pieces of linen, squirrel skins and lumps of salt). At the same time coins were being used for payments in the external trade.

The two systems – the closed economy of agriculture and the commodity-money economy – co-existed in several variants and in different proportions to an extent we cannot fully appreciate today. Nor are they much mentioned in written sources. The commodity-money economy is somewhat easier to study because of the considerable numismatic evidence which has survived. For this reason historians have tended to over-value the importance of monetary payments compared to the other forms of exchange and the general circulation of goods by barter. And there is a further tendency actually to make too much of the part played by external in comparison to internal trade which, as it was mainly an exchange of local products, was after all the decisive factor in the standard of living of ordinary people. One element in local exchange, artefacts made by craftsmen in the immediate neighbourhood (autochthonous production), appears increasingly in all the Slavonic countries from the mid-tenth century onwards, as we know from our studies of the early urban centres. But it is not clear whether these goods were made by craftsmen specially for the open market or whether they were made as forced tribute to the lords who then put them into circulation.

To these co-existing and contrasting systems of exchange we must add another aspect of economic life. Above the small-scale, homogeneous rural environment, there was the homeland of a tribe or the province of an early Slavonic state, and above them again there were larger spheres of operation, as big as the continent itself, dominated by such remote poles of economic magnetism as Muslim Central Asia and Byzantium.

Within these complicated, overlapping systems, about which our information is far from complete, were some stable areas, although even there we can discern changes taking place in the course of time. Some economic manifestations lasted for no more than a few scores of years (e.g. the commercial and military expansion of the Scandinavians), while others, such as the local market towns with their influence on the rural environment, endured for centuries. Bearing in mind how one system was superimposed upon another, we may distinguish three main stages in the development of trade and industry.

Chronologically our curtain rises on the stage when the features of long-distance trade were already discernible, that is, at the end of the eighth century, when Arab merchants had started to penetrate the lands of the eastern Slavs. We have a little earlier archaeological evidence of other distant contacts going back to the migration of Slavs in the fifth to seventh centuries. We have also a reference to Samo of Sens or Soignies (*pagus Senonagus*), who in the year 623 'joined with other merchants in order to go and do business with Slavs who are known as Wends' (Fredegar, IV, 48). Samo became ruler of Moravia and Bohemia and fought against the Avars who had political and economic control of the Danubian roads to Byzantium. But it was not until the ninth and tenth centuries that the consolidated Slavonic states of Moravia, Bohemia, Poland and Russia developed an active system of external trade. They were able to offer a regular supply of articles much in demand: not only slaves who were either prisoners of war or members of the native population, but also furs, honey and wax, all much sought after. These commodities were mostly payments in kind made to the prince's tax collectors, but they could also have been requisitioned without any economic quid pro quo. At the beginning of the eleventh century this trade suffered a severe setback, especially in the areas that were until then served by direct supplies of Muslim silver. The lands of the western Slavs were also much affected. Somewhat earlier, in the second half of the tenth century, a second, almost transitional, period had begun. At the same time as Arab commerce was declining and trade with western Europe was intensifying, and the state and the aristocracy were hoarding large amounts of precious metals, local centres of trade and industry had begun to develop in Slavonic countries mainly for the benefit of the upper ranks of society.

Our third and last period, beginning in mid-eleventh century, saw the rebuilding of trade after the break in the flow of eastern silver and the fall in the supply of western silver coins. To relieve the crisis, hoarded silver had to be put into circulation and non-monetary methods of payment had to be devised. New commercial contacts were established with a greater assortment of goods, and, what is more important, local craftsmanship started to develop in Slavonic countries. These movements gradually penetrated the countryside, and by the twelfth century the agriculture of the western Slavs was closely associated with the commodity-money economy. Our survey of these developments must end just before the great thirteenth-century urban explosion took place in the western Slavonic countries and the disastrous Mongol invasion overwhelmed the eastern Slavs.

The geographical limits of the scene to be described are somewhat ill-defined. They correspond roughly to the area occupied by the western and eastern Slavonic peoples in the early Middle Ages: this territory was from the middle reaches of the Danube northwards to the Baltic, and from the river Elbe in the west as far eastwards as the Volga and the Black Sea. This leaves out of account the southern Slavs who were part of the Mediterranean economy, but includes the Baltic lands and Hungary.

II. *Long-distance Trade in Central and Eastern Europe from the Eighth to the Twelfth Centuries*

Historians of the European economy, concerned with its medieval beginnings, have for long drawn attention to the importance of long-distance trade. In particular they have been interested in the links between the countries of western and eastern Europe in their dealings with central Asia and Byzantium. In the last fifty years the ever-popular subject of the Mediterranean and the continuing debate over Henri Pirenne's thesis concerning Muhammad and Charlemagne, have been joined as topics for research and discussion by the early medieval Baltic. A case has been made out for extending consideration to Muhammad, Charlemagne and Rurik. According to this thesis, Rurik and his Varangians were the symbols of compensation for the loss Europe had to suffer in its Mediterranean commerce after the Arab conquests. Their trade and military expansion, we are told, opened a Viking Age in international exchange. The Baltic is said to have become the axis along which economic life flowed on an even higher tide than in the Mediterranean countries.

It is not out of place in this chapter to reopen the question of Baltic trade in the early Middle Ages and in particular to challenge the slightly too rosy view of its stimulus to urban life and trade in post-Carolingian western Europe. Many scholars have put their ideas on this subject into print and all those beguiled by the idea of the Viking Age would do well to refer to these writings. Quite apart, however, from the Scandinavian contribution, which was certainly very important, the Slavonic countries and peoples can also claim our attention by reason of their economic and social vigour. The early Slavonic towns of the tenth and eleventh centuries bear eloquent witness to their productive and cultural activity.

The general lineaments of the economic geography of this long-distance trade are known to us through the writings of Muslim geographers of the time, while some detail is filled in by the diffusion of Islamic coins in Europe. The centre of gravity lay in the East, in the countries of the Islamic empire which from the early ninth to the early eleventh centuries were the chief customers for Slavonic goods, and in the South, in Byzantium. This made Russia the principal trading broker and clearing house for other Slavonic and Baltic countries. In comparison with this busy traffic, the influence of the western Muslim empire was limited. In the ninth and tenth centuries this trade reached some western Slavonic countries via western Europe or Venice, and even linked up with eastern trade through a fine network of land routes. The different features of the Baltic trade and the development of exchanges between Slavonic countries and western Europe will be discussed separately.

(1) EASTERN EUROPE BETWEEN SCANDINAVIA AND CENTRAL ASIA

The trade between the Slavonic countries and their nearer and further neighbours had its roots in the different economic and social features of the partners. In the early period of the Slavonic world, with its characteristically extensive rural economy, trade with Arab markets was initiated by the demand for articles of a semi-colonial type. The Arabs needed unlimited supplies of forest products and the Muslim world needed above all else slaves. The eastern Slavonic countries and their northern Finno-Ugric borderlands were able to fulfil demands of this kind and to organise exchanges from the time when that part of Europe established strong political systems of its own.

The needs of the Muslim world met with a ready response from the ruling aristocracy. Aiming to improve their military position and to assuage their demands for consumption and display, they looked for weapons and luxury articles of foreign craftsmanship. The special feature of Scandinavian and Slavonic exchanges with the East was that barter – product-for-product – formed only part of the trade; much more important was that it became the main channel by which oriental silver was introduced into north-eastern Europe. This particular aspect of the trade is all the more remarkable when we remember that Muslim merchants from the East were able to conduct the article-for-article barter with the nomads who lived on the shores of the Aral and Caspian Seas and Finnish tribes (Yugra and Ves) from the far north. We shall not be mistaken if we conclude that the exchange of article-for-silver was a result of a particular demand by the non-Arab organisers of that trade.

Distances of several thousand kilometres separating the economic wealth of eastern Europe from the Muslim centres of trade and crafts were overcome by the skill and energy of many merchants and middle men. For contacts with Muslim Asia the most important seem to have been the merchants from Khorezm (lying between the Caspian and Aral Seas, the Amu Daria River and Persia). From the eighth century they were pioneers in the Arab trade with eastern Europe, where they were known as the Khvalisi. In the Oldest Russian Chronicle the Caspian Sea was called Khvalisskoye Morye. The Khorezmians succeeded in monopolising the trade between eastern Europe and the different countries of the Baghdad caliphate in the ninth and tenth centuries. They began by taking over the trade in furs and slaves (including eunuchs). They penetrated up the Volga especially influencing the Khazars and Bulgars on the Kama. They were friendly with the Hungarians and one group of Khorezmians settled in Pannonia at the beginning of the tenth century preserving, as Izmailits or Kaliz, their mercantile function and the Islamic religion.

The outlet for the main westward stream of Islamic trade was originally the south-eastern shore of the Caspian Sea, connected overland on one side with central Asia and on the other with Baghdad. By sea, or by sea and land, people and goods reached the Volga mouth.

Ibn Fadlān wrote (*c.* A.D. 922) that travelling across the steppes of the middle Volga, it was easy to reach Bulgaria on the Kama. Another writer, Ibn al-Faquīh, states that the long journey from Russia to the caliphate was sometimes covered direct: Slav-speaking traders stepping out of ships on the Caspian shore and travelling from there to Baghdad on camels where slaves of Slav origin were their interpreters. However, such long hauls would be exceptional. Khorezmians as professional merchants came into contact with two Turkish tribes from the Volga, whose interest in trade was in exploiting politically and economically the territories they had conquered.

The first of those tribes, the Khazars, turned to Judaism at the beginning of the ninth century and they built a multitribal, but comparatively weak, empire on the lands between the Caucasus, the lower Danube, the Dnieper and the Volga. In the ninth and early tenth centuries it also included some Slavonic tribes (Polans of Kiev, Severyans, Radymichs, Vyatychs). The capital of Khazaria was Itil (Atil, or Hamlīh) on the lower Volga which from the ninth century served as a staging post in the transit to Russia and beyond. There were also colonies of Varangian, Slavonic, Muslim, Jewish and pagan merchants there with their own judges. The khagan of Khazaria took an obligatory tithe from the goods passing through his territory.

The Bulgarians on the Kama and middle Volga were also intermediaries. They adopted the Islamic religion at the beginning of the tenth century and liberated themselves from the Khazars. Their capital Bulgar played a part similar to Itil's. An Islamic writer of the tenth century called them 'silver Bulgarians' because of the abundance of this metal passing through their hands. They controlled the busiest route running from north-eastern Europe to Itil and the caliphate.

There were two variants of the Volga route: by land, which took about a month to travel, and by water, which took about two months upstream and twenty days downstream. There was also one land route from Itil to Kiev, with some 20 staging posts, and another via Sarkel on the Don and Chersonesus in the Crimea which brought goods like raw silk to Byzantium, and was used by Russian war expeditions toward the Caspian Sea.

The two states of the Khazars and the Bulgarians were destroyed by the Russian prince Svyatoslav, son of Igor, and Russia got closer control of the Volga trade and direct access to its products. But both Bulgar and Saqsin, the successor to Itil, remained respectively in Bulgarian and Khazar hands until the Mongol invasion. The shift of the centralised Russian state eastwards represented the summit of at least a hundred years of Varangian effort which started about the year 800 with the founding of the first forts and merchant hamlets not only on the eastern shores of the Baltic but also on Lakes Peipus, Ilmen and Ladoga. Their mercantile activities went hand in hand with robbery and conquest; the first mention of Scandinavian pirates on the Caspian and Black Seas dates from about A.D. 840.

The Scandinavian expansion, in this case Swedish, did not take the form of a rapid conquest of eastern territories or the mass colonisation of foreign countries. In eastern Slavonic lands the Varangians built up an exploitative warrior-merchant system maintained by well-trained troops settled in forts in commanding positions. They were interested in keeping to themselves the Volga route to the Arab world, and the Dnieper route to Byzantium. They kept contact with the local Slavonic aristocracy by maintaining alien dynasties in a few existing tribal states and keeping a well-organised military and fiscal apparatus. In the middle of the ninth century we hear about the Princes Askold and Dir in Kiev, about Rurik in Novgorod, or rather Old Ladoga; Rurik's putative son Igor (died 945) was the founder of the Russian dynasty with its capital and grand-prince in Kiev. A powerful state was created which took over foreign trade and put an end to the arbitrary expeditions of different Varangian chiefs as well as conducting a policy of expansion. The newcomers became more and more Slavonic during the tenth century in spite of their continuing contact with Sweden.

But even earlier, in the ninth century, the Varangian trading system providing links with the Baghdad caliphate and central Asia took over the main route from the Baltic to the Volga, as well as the Byzantium route 'from Varangians to Greeks'. The first of these routes consisted of a network of roads in northern Russia leading from Estonia and Latvia and the Gulf of Finland by many branches on land and water before it crossed the low watershed between the Baltic and the Caspian Sea to the upper reaches of the Volga. All over this huge region both Scandinavian and Arab imports have been revealed by excavations. There are also, occasionally, local names of hamlets deriving from Swedish terms for mercantile and transport functions. There are words deriving from technical terms which are also known in the old Russian terminology: *vaeringi/varyag* originally meaning 'member of a merchant gild' or in general 'a Scandinavian'; *kylfingr/kolbyag*, 'younger member of a gild'; *byringe/buryag*, 'transport assistant'. It is evidence of a well-organised trade between Sweden and the upper Volga, which included some articles of Scandinavian and Baltic origin but mainly goods produced by the people who exploited the forests of the entire north-eastern geographical region. The Varangians – who were called in Arab texts ar-Rus to distinguish them from Slavs (Sakāliba) – were from the very beginning helped by the latter, and in the mid-ninth century the Slavonic language began to be used internationally in all the trade of the caliphate.

What were the goods traded? The eastern Slavs provided forest products of relatively high quality and small bulk, such as furs, especially marten and fox, honey and wax. The calf leather imported into Khorezm took its Arabic name from the Russian *telatin*; horse leather was sought after, and Russia also exported linen. We know also that amber and weapons were sold. Next in importance, and equally easy to transport, were the slaves, about whom there are such copious records in the eastern countries of the caliphate from the ninth century onwards; among other occupations they became royal guards.

The enormous demands of the Islamic market could obviously not be satisfied by these imports, although there are some indications that amber was re-exported from Islam to China and in return a little Chinese silk reached the Slavs. From the Muslim world came spices, jewellery and ironware, semi-precious stones, beads and costly fabrics, traces of which have been found by archaeologists in Russia, Scandinavia and the Baltic coasts.

However, students of this trade have long been aware of the spate of precious metals, particularly silver, flowing into this sector of Islamic commerce, with the main stream of silver money passing through Bulgar on the Kama. It has even been supposed that trade with the Slavs and the Scandinavians could have been a unilateral commodity exchange: the products of eastern Europe being exchanged for oriental silver in the shape of Arab money – *dirhems*, bars and silver scrap, and ornaments broken up for transactions in which silver was measured by weight. Al-Gardīzī, a Persian historian from the mid-eleventh century, has left us information that is older than his own times about the Bulgarians on the Kama who 'give *dirhems* to the Slavs and ar-Rus, because the tribes do not sell their goods except for minted *dirhems*'. We know the supposed prices of some of the articles: one marten fur was valued at two-and-a-half *dirhems* in the tenth century on the Bulgar market (1 *dirhem* equals about 2.75 g of silver). A slave in Russia cost about 100 *dirhems*, but probably three times as much after he arrived in the caliphate.

The amount of silver of Islamic origin scattered around the vast area of northern Russia and the Baltic littoral (about 16–1700 finds with *c.* 2–300,000 coins forming no more than a tiny fraction of the total flow) places beyond question its extensive use by Islam to finance the trade with the Slavonic and Baltic worlds. Some explanation is required, however, for the fact that this circulation was limited to the silver *dirhem* whereas in the Mediterranean and, above all, in the Arab lands themselves bimetallism and even trimetallism (including a copper currency) was prevalent with the gold *dinar* featuring. The answer seems to be that the ratio of gold to silver, which in the West was 1 : 12, in Byzantium 1 : 18, and in Islam fluctuated between 1 : 12 and 1 : 17, never exceeded 1 : 10 in north-eastern Europe. Thus exports of gold were not a paying proposition, especially from the eastern part of the Arab world where silver always prevailed – quite apart from the fact that as a unit the gold *dinar* was too valuable since even the silver *dirhem* had to be broken up for some transactions in these countries.

The Muslim silver coins found in treasure-hoards buried in Russia and beyond during the ninth century originated mainly from the caliphates of the first six Abbasids, with a high proportion from the reign of Harun-al-Rāshid. Thus, they reached the Slavonic and Baltic lands long after their date of emission. Numismatists see in this delay yet another source of profit for the Islamic merchants trading with the Slavs: they sent to the West old coins withdrawn from circulation and bought for far less than the face value of the *dirhems* in actual currency. It was not till the tenth century that coins minted by the Samanids from their own local silver deposits were used to finance the European trade without any time-lag.

Silver – the main article in Scandinavian demand – came into the hands of the Varangians in exchange for furs and slaves, through custom duties taken from Khorezmian and Bulgarian merchants, or as booty taken during the plundering raids on Khazars, Bulgarians and the borders of the caliphate. The main current of silver, as is shown by the location of hoards with Arab coins, was absorbed by Sweden and Gotland where the silver was sent by Varangian merchant-warriors for safekeeping: according to provisional data, there are about 520 known hoards in Sweden and Gotland. But the current was syphoned off on the way: there are 18 hoards in Khazar lands and 20 in Bulgarian; northern tribes had 28 at Perm and 45 at Kiev. They were especially numerous in northern Russia (280), and the Baltic nations, Estonia and Latvia, had 65, all situated on the main route from Sweden to the Caspian. If the comparative size of these numbers reflects the real proportions of trade in the ninth and tenth centuries, then it is easy to see that the originally exploitative activities of the Varangians had the side effect of providing all the countries on the way, and especially northern Russia, with silver. Scandinavian silver also supplied other Baltic countries, as is shown by the 520 finds of Arab coins on the lower Elbe, the Oder, the Vistula and the Niemen. Some of the hoards were really big: 11,000 coins weighing 42 kg were found in Murom and 100 kg in Velikye Luki; other hoards with over a hundred coins in each of them were travellers' reserves.

Archaeological discoveries have made this trade comparatively easy to date. Its beginnings stem from the early ninth century; by the mid-century it had reached its peak and it began to tail off by the mid-eleventh century. Oriental scholars attribute the decline to a number of factors: the political crisis of the Muslim states in central Asia; the exhaustion or closing of the silver mines there; the destruction of Khazaria; the conquest of Bulgaria by Russia; and, finally, harassment of the caravan routes by the nomads of the steppes. Although communication was later re-established, as is shown by the twelfth-century account of Abū Hāmid, traffic was never again as big and it was once more in the form of article-for-article exchange.

The main reason for the cessation of the previous way of trading is to be found in the silver famine which, from the end of the tenth century, began to spread over the entire Muslim world. We cannot discuss here what caused the disappearance of silver from the East, and – nearly simultaneously – a return to gold in the West, but the two phenomena are thought to be inextricably bound up. The most interesting hypothesis implies that the already-mentioned disparity between the ratio of gold to silver in the East (including Byzantium) and in the West (including Slavonic and Scandinavian countries) caused the same forces which drained gold from the West to draw silver from the East. According to this interpretation the European gold famine is thus the reverse side of the same phenomenon. The significance for our subject is that vast quantities of silver were drained off towards neighbouring regions, partly perhaps towards India and China, but certainly towards eastern Europe. The amount proved to be so enormous that the output of the Arab silver mines, allowing for those either lost in wars or not being exploited for technical or political reasons, could not compensate for the mass outflow, even though this was spread over two centuries. Putting more and more hard currency into a commerce the balance of which was unfavourable was a recipe for disaster.

It appears that the contraction was felt more severely by the Muslim countries, especially because fewer slaves were shipped. The latter were able to regain their breath after the Scandinavian–Arab drainage of their resources; and there was less and less place for this commerce in the centralised Russian state which began in Vladimir Svyatoslavich's times. There are no archaeological traces of any intensive trade in the Russian countryside. The principal figures lived in forts and belonged to the ruling class. There they amassed treasures like the hoard of the Kievan prince Svyatoslav Iaroslavich, who had shown his wealth to the German envoys in 1075. 'They, seeing the vast amount of gold, silver and fabrics, said: it is nothing because it lies dead' (The Oldest Russian Chronicle, a. 1075/6583).

Attention must be drawn to the growing productive potentialities of the Slav countries themselves, which in the mid-tenth century set out to satisfy some of their luxury needs through their own crafts. At the same time the discovery of Saxon silver led to western money being diffused over eastern Europe, thus ousting Islamic coins.

The eastern trade, though on smaller scale, was still concentrated in Kiev in the eleventh century, until it again went northwards in the twelfth century to Vladimir-Suzdal Russia by the Volga route, which joined it to Asia and the Caucasus. Bulgar remained the transit point, where in 1226 Russia signed a treaty for six years, the last before the Mongol catastrophe. It ordered the Bulgarian merchants, provided they could show the appropriate sealed documents, to trade only in towns, and not either with manorial officials or with the peasants in the villages; reciprocally the Russian merchants could live and trade in Bulgar. From that part of Russia were imported buck- and sheepskins, articles of luxury metallurgy like vases of bronze and silver with niello decoration and chain armour made by town craftsmen, as well as linen from peasant tributes. Polovtsian nomads sought Russian bronze mirrors. In the other direction went spices, precious stones, whose Persian names are still preserved in the modern Russian language, and small quantities of artistic goods of eastern craftsmanship.

(2) SLAVONIC SLAVES IN THE MEDITERRANEAN

What of the Slavs' dealings with the western part of Islam? In the mid-ninth century only a trickle of luxury articles made its way across the heart of Europe through Spain, France and Germany, or alternatively through Venice, and thence to the Slavonic lands as far as the estuary of the Volga.

Ibn Hurdādbeh of Baghdad discusses the structure of this trade and the role of the merchants called Rhadanites (ar-Radaniya) in his 'Book of roads and kingdoms' dating from the mid-ninth century. They were Jews, and the most plausible derivation of their name is from the Persian word 'rahdan', meaning a guide: 'They speak Arabic, Persian, Roman, Frankish, Spanish and Slavonic. They travel from east to west, from west to east, by land and by sea. From the west they bring eunuchs, girl-slaves, young boys, brocade, beaver and sable furs and swords'. The two main routes they used, which Ibn Hurdādbeh mentions, one by sea and the other overland, point to their activities in the Mediterranean and the Black Sea, and their contacts with India. 'Sometimes they take a road via Rome (Italy) through Slav lands, and next to Hamlih (Itil), the town of the Khazars', whence they reach China via the Caspian Sea, Bactriana and Transoxania. The

Rhadanites brought nutmeg, camphor, cinnamon and aloes from the East. Although there have been attempts to play down their part in the slave trade, written records point the other way. There is no reason to doubt that it was the Jews who maintained the economic contacts – via a still lethargic Europe – with the other end of the Arab world. From the writings of Rabbi Iehuda ben Meir ha-Kohen of Mainz in the mid-eleventh century, we learn about a Jewish colony active at the beginning of that century in Przemyśl, situated on the route from Russia to Poland and Hungary.

The Rhadanites were surely also the intermediaries, although not the only ones, in the Slav trade with western Europe. A large part of the goods travelled no further than Germany or Italy and were consumed there. The case of the slaves was different since, under the agrarian structure of those countries, there was fairly little demand for them. On the other hand the export of Slav slaves to Spain and Africa is widely attested. They were used in the armies of those countries, in domestic service, and as assistants in the workshops of craftsmen; and moreover they were needed in great numbers. Their numbers in Cordoba during the reign of Abd ar-Rahmān III (912–61) rose to about 14,000. The Slavonic guards and the eunuchs who formed the administration achieved considerable political importance in the second half of the tenth and beginning of the eleventh centuries. Apart from numerous Muslim sources, Agobard of Lyons in the ninth century, and Liutprand of Cremona and the Life of St Adalbert in the tenth century, all mention the export of slaves to Spain through Mainz, Verdun and Lyons, where they were castrated. Among early Slavonic towns, Prague was famous for its slave market which even included *mancipia christiana* in the tenth century. This demolishes the view that these slaves were all captives taken by Frankish or Saxon lords on their forays, like Margrave Guncelin, who *familias multorum saepe id sibi querentium* (other lords), *Iudeis vendidit* (Thietmar, VI, c. 54). The powerful rulers of the new Slav states also sold their own subjects.

We must exclude from our discussion the seventh-century state of Samo, about which we know so little, as its development was soon arrested by the Avars. In the ninth century the first place belonged to the Moravians. At that time they controlled the junctions of the Danubian route and the routes from northern Italy to the Carpathians and beyond. Excavations in Staré Město, Mikulčice and some other residential castle-towns of lords have revealed an astonishing quantity of gold in the form of jewellery. Part of that gold may have originated in commercial or extra-commercial exchanges with Byzantium (gifts for princes and their lords). But there is still a question as to whether some of it did not come from Venice, which owed its earliest rise to the export of slaves to Muslim Africa in exchange for gold. We know for certain that in the early social structure of Czech, Polish and Hungarian states there was room for a large number of slaves, and traces of a trade in slaves are to be found in our sources up to the twelfth century; it is most likely that the Moravians also disposed of their slaves on the foreign market.

The quantity of Slav slaves on the Mediterranean markets of the period is indicated by two semantic phenomena. In the ninth century in the Arab world, the word *Saqlab* (plural *Saqāliba*) became widespread for slave. In the Latin West the word *sclavus*, and its derivatives in the various national languages, become common about the same time, originating probably in northern Italy, from *Sclavi*, the ethnic name of the Slavs.

The slave trade with the West was financed in a different way from the trade with Central Asia. Islamic money played virtually no part in it, coins from Spain and Africa remaining very rare in western Slav countries. The Rhadanites and other traders employed methods of exchange which were unlike those of the organisers of the Russian and Baltic trade.

On the other hand, the chronology in both cases is similar. The heyday of the Rhadanites also ends with the close of the tenth century. There is no reason to look for the cause in monetary upheavals. The decisive factor seems to have been the economic awakening of Europe as a whole, including the Slavonic countries where the early urban centres began to supply a large part of imports entering hitherto into lords' consumption. The period of ostentation and the slave trade was the period when the larger states emerged; and it came to a close simultaneously in the lands of both western and eastern Slavs. However it must be pointed out that the concurrent development of external trade and the founding of Slavonic states has meant that historians have sometimes assigned too much influence to this factor in the awakening of political life. The real heart of the problem is more complicated. There were social and political, not to speak of agrarian, changes at work among the Slav tribes. One such change was the appearance of an ambitious tribal aristocracy, which saw a way to establish its social position by external expansion. All these things began to happen in the seventh and eighth centuries and made the creation of large territorial units possible. The opening of trade routes was another stimulus to change which helped to consolidate the Slavonic ruling class, by absorbing ethnically alien elements and opening the lines of political expansion through foreign trade. But the fortunes of these states were not bound to the fortunes of the trade.

(3) THE CALL OF BYZANTIUM

Let us now examine the third path which long-distance trade took, in the direction of Byzantium. So far as the eastern and some part of the western Slavs were concerned, this trade had been cornered by Kievan Russia. Only Moravia appears to have had independent dealings with Byzantium; these were inherited in the tenth century by Hungary.

From Russian and Byzantine texts we can reconstruct the qualitative side of this trade and its organisation down to the very details of transport. There are many similarities between this trade and the exchanges in the estuary of the Volga, but, in its later development, the differences are profound. The sources call the route that 'from Varangians to Greeks' and it led from the Baltic either via the Gulf of Finland, up the Neva, to Lake Ladoga, the Volhov, and Lake Ilmen and the Lovat – or via the Gulf of Riga and the Dvina on boats, and so to the Dnieper, and thence down to the Black Sea; the rocky cataracts in the Dnieper had both Slavonic and Swedish names; boats were carried overland to bypass them, even at the risk of attacks from the steppes nomads, the Petchenegs. After travelling along the Black Sea coast, the merchants passed through the Bosporus to Constantinople. The journey took about ten days. Russia acquired ports for shelter on the mouths of the Dnieper, Dniester and Danube, like Oleshie on the Dnieper, or Kewe in the Danube estuary. Byzantine customs were paid at the mouth of the Dnieper during the tenth century; Chersonesus, in Russian Korsun, situated on the south-western coast of the Crimea, was a well-fortified northern emporium for the whole empire; after its conquest in 988–9, the Grand-prince Vladimir brought bronze horses and other masterpieces of art from there to Kiev. Russia and Byzantium struggled to possess Tmutarakan on the Don, as it was an important port on the route to the Caucasus and Trebizond.

Here also a group of adventurous Varangians took the initiative. From the beginning of the ninth century they founded small military–mercantile colonies which enabled them to penetrate the Slav regions up to Kiev. They found some degrees of political organisation there and their contacts with the local tribal aristocracy helped to draw the area into trade and political expansion toward Byzantium.

In the mid-ninth century a dynasty of Scandinavian origin followed the Slavonic tribal princes in Kiev and helped to organise a trade from there in much the same sort of goods as went to Arab countries. A passage in Constantine Porphyrogenitus (*De administrando imperio*, c. 9) describes the collection (*poludye*) in winter of levies in kind from the eastern Slavs which yielded commodities to be exported by the

Russian rulers to Byzantium. Kievan subjects – the tribes of Drevlans, Dregovichs, Kryvichs and Severyans – provided not only tribute but also transport: boats each of which was hollowed out of a single tree trunk complete with a crew of sailors, mostly Slav or Finno-Ugric slaves.

We may without exaggeration call this export a state-owned enterprise. The treaties between Russia and Byzantium (*dogovory*) of 911 and 944, which are known from reliable sources, throw some light on this strange trade. Armed forces played a large part in it by visiting the Bosporus in Russian ships and levying tribute on the strictly controlled external trade of the empire.

The first of these treaties, signed by Prince Oleg (we shall not discuss the text of 907 as it is now regarded as a compilation of later texts) abrogated the *ius naufragii* and, by suggesting help for shipwrecked men and goods, it settled the responsibility for unlawful acts; it guaranteed the exchange of war captives, made possible the enlistment of Russians in the Byzantine army and encouraged the search for runaway slaves. In 944 Prince Igor signed another treaty with the Byzantine regency which contained detailed trade decrees. He undertook to announce by letter to the Byzantine government the number of ships sent. The Russian merchants were to live in the neighbourhood of St Mamma monastery and were to get a monthly supply of food. The guests were welcomed only between spring and autumn: never in winter. They had to register themselves separately according to their town of origin: Kiev, Tchernigov, Pereyaslavl. A special town gate was designated by which they were to enter in groups of not more than fifty persons with an imperial official as guide. Everything they bought was free of duty (probably *kommerkion*). After the official conversion of Russia at the end of the tenth century a Russian quarter was established in Constantinople with its own monastery.

One of the motives behind the military policy of the early Slav states was the aim of extending and securing fiscal control over the trade routes. The Oldest Russian Chronicle, though written later, i.e. at the beginning of the twelfth century, well conveys the climate of the early Middle Ages and reveals the predatory basis of Prince Svyatoslav Igorevich's plan to leave Kiev and move his capital to the Danube. 'In the year 6477 (A.D. 969) Svyatoslav declared to his mother and his boyars: it does not please me to remain in Kiev. I desire to live in Pereyaslavets on the Danube for there lies the centre of my land. There is the store of all wealth: the gold of the Greeks, fine cloths, wine and divers fruits. From Bohemia and Hungary come silver and horses. From Russia skins and wax, honey and slaves.'

In return Russia bought in Constantinople local products, especially the costly coloured silk, usually called *pavoloki* in Russian. In the interests of the Byzantine merchants the 944 treaty limited the amount a Russian merchant could spend to 50 *solidi* (*zolotnik*). Two lengths of silk were the equivalent of one slave in Constantinople at that time, and the price of a young slave was 10 *solidi*. The Russian slave merchants had a special market-place in the eleventh century. A Russian merchant could not take more than ten lengths of silk out of the empire at any one time.

Russia received gold and silver from Constantinople partly in return for its products, partly as political gifts, and partly as the wages of the Varangian warriors in the imperial army. In 907 Byzantium paid the Russian troops 12 marks per man, which amounted to about 6,400 kg of silver in total. In 1043 the Russian fleet near Constantinople asked for a ransom of about 1,740 kg of gold, which was 6–7 per cent of the annual imperial income.

In the ninth, and even in the tenth, century most of this gold was going via Russia to the family hoards of Swedish warriors and merchants. The magnificent Gotland treasure room in the Archaeological Museum in Stockholm bears eloquent testimony to this traffic. But, starting from the mid-tenth century, part of the gold, on its way up the Dnieper, remained in the hands of the princes and the Russian aristocracy who amassed both secular and ecclesiastical plate and jewellery. And from the eleventh century we know of Byzantine gold *solidi* in the southern part of Russia. Certainly, some gold was going back to the Black Sea in exchange for luxury articles.

However, it seems that the Russian–Byzantine trade was usually a bilateral exchange of products with the economic potential of the partners being fairly equal. But even if Kiev, as the capital of a large state with a general demand, was the main customer for the Byzantine goods, it did not itself produce the majority of exports, but took commodities from other parts of Russia and especially from the North. This may well be why the Byzantine golden coins went no further than Kiev while silver coins went farther north.

In general, the Byzantine coins – occasional issues of the ninth century, but probably not reaching the Slavonic countries until the tenth – did not play an important part in that trade. Some other coins (silver *millaresia* from the reigns of Constantine Prophyrogenitus (913–59) and John I Tzimiskes (969–76)) are encountered only in northern Russia and, reaching these places via Scandinavia, in Pomerania, Great Poland and Mazovia. The exports of these *millaresia* was hampered by their differential nominal value: in tenth-century Byzantium this was twice the intrinsic value of the metal they contained.

Trade by mutual exchange and the equal balance of payments probably provide the reasons why these contacts lasted for so long. They were not interrupted even by the silver crisis which Byzantium also experienced from the beginning of the eleventh century. There was no break in the trade, even though the Dnieper route was always threatened by Polovtsian nomads, successors of the Petchenegs. Eventually, it declined because of the new route to the Black Sea via the Italian towns, though its final end was postponed until the fall of the Greek empire in 1204 and the Mongol catastrophe in the second quarter of the thirteenth century.

After the first period of quasi-state owned export trade, in the eleventh century a progressive emancipation of the merchants trading with Byzantium can be observed. They founded a corporation in Kiev, which attempted political pressure on the prince in 1069. In the twelfth century there was a sizeable Russian colony in Constantinople, situated inside the town close to the church of Forty Martyrs near the Golden Horn. In the tenth century Russia exported honey and beeswax beside slaves; eleventh- and twelfth-century sources add to that list – sables, Don caviar, smoked fish and walrus tusk carvings. A special organisation for transport was developed under the guards of the Russian princes on the 'Solny' (i.e. salt road) route leading to Halich, the 'Zalozny' route (a name derived probably from the sallows on the river banks) leading to the Don, and the 'Greek' route that went by the Dnieper, and later via Varna and Messembria. In the twelfth century the principality of Halich had its own route down the Pruth river to the Danube estuary, maintained lively trade contacts with Byzantium and, in the early part of the century, even owed it vassalage.

In the same period (eleventh–twelfth centuries) Salonica, with its yearly October fairs, began to serve as the second market for the Russian trade, which provided wine, salt fish, caviar and wax from the Don and the Danube. The trade in slaves extended as far as Alexandria as we know from Benjamin of Tudela (late twelfth century). Quite a special part was played by the holy Mount Athos on which the Russian monastery, Ksilurgu, was built at the beginning of the eleventh century with its own port and warehouses. In the twelfth century it was called the monastery of St Panteleimon vel Russian, and was partly supplied by Russia with goods and chattels like textiles and carpets. The Russian pilgrims did not limit their travels to Athos or Constantinople; we have a description of a voyage to Jerusalem in the years 1106–8 made by Hegumenos Daniel and his companions.

We also have details about Greek merchants dwelling near the church of St Elias in Kiev. Some of them came from Chersonesus, bringing materials for mosaics, sulphur, gold objects, glass, silk, velvet, samite, wine, olive, spices, fruits, well-cured leather (e.g. morocco), liturgical vases and vestments, and icons. They were also to be seen in Novgorod in 1106. Greek craftsmen worked in Kiev, and were especially famed for their enamel, pottery and glassmaking.

(4) THE BALTIC TRADE AND THE SLAVS

The part played by the Scandinavians in organising trade from the Baltic to Central Asia and the Greek world includes their activities within the Baltic itself. Did they provide the bridge over which some of the products from Asia and Byzantium travelled to the West? Or was the Baltic no more than a single economic zone forming the final link in the chain of eastern and western routes, which was not so much a staging post for the Scandinavian and Slavonic countries as the means by which their own needs were satisfied? The second hypothesis is probably preferable, although the Oldest Russian Chronicle implies that by 'sailing by Dvina to the Varangians and from the Varangians to Rome' the continent could be encircled and Spain and Constantinople reached.

Early medieval trade in the Baltic does not date from the appearance of the Scandinavians in eastern Europe. It was antedated by the contacts maintained in the seventh to ninth centuries between the Rhine estuary and Sweden via the Jutland peninsula. The *Vita Anskarii*, written in the second half of the ninth century, mentions three trade centres on the route: the Frisian Dorstad, the Danish Haithabu (Hedeby) and the Swedish Birka, and, when speaking about a town in *finibus Slavorum* (c. 19), it probably means Wolin. In 808 there was a Slavonic emporium called Reric (possibly Stargard (Oldenburg) in Wagria) destroyed by the Danes in the interests of Haithabu. King Alfred of Wessex sent his emissary, Wulfstan, in the years 887–90 via Haithabu to the mouth of the Vistula, where he found a market-place called Truso (nowadays Drużno near Elbląg) in Prussian territory. Excavations have enriched the picture with important information about those entrepôt centres which were the early form of urban life. Archaeologists have pinpointed some other centres, like Domburg on the Frisian coast, Skiringssal in Oslo fiord, or Lillö-Helgön between Birka and Stockholm.

The opening by the Swedes of the route up the rivers of eastern Europe and over the Volga watershed turned attention, both politically and economically, in that direction. In the same period the western Vikings interrupted the route between the North Sea and the Baltic, although they did not quite block it. The picture of the commerce of Birka on Lake Mälar (*c.* 800–975), however, reveals that ties with the West were weaker than those with Muslim East. Even when the harbour of Haithabu was in Swedish hands for a few decades at the turn of the tenth century, the Muslim silver accumulated in Sweden was not diverted towards the West.

In the tenth century, therefore, the entire Baltic area was the recipient of money skimmed from the eastern trade rather than a real promoter of economic contacts with the West, and it remains a fact that from the late ninth century Sweden and Gotland turned in upon themselves and became a dead end in which some part of the silver lay idle as their stock of money ceased to circulate.

It may be asked whether it was only the Scandinavian capacity to export that attracted these substantial quantities of gold and silver. These stocks, in fact, were at least partly generated by activities which were non-economic. Some of the wealth accumulated in northern Russia from the exploitation of its forests and other riches may have come to rest in the homeland of the organisers of this trade either as gifts to their kinsmen or as their own deposits. In any case the Muslim silver pumped into the Baltic basin fed trade within it. Few *dirhems* have been found in countries adjacent to Sweden. There have been only about 60 coin finds in Norway and Denmark, but the Slavonic and Baltic tribes absorbed the Swedish silver reserves much more freely: so far 65 hoards have been found in Estonia, Latvia and Lithuania, and 20 in Prussia; the whole of Poland 255 (Pomerania 143, continental Poland 112); Slavs on the Elbe 41. The wealth of Arab coins in the region of the lower Oder and the Vistula (i.e. the territory where in the tenth century the Polish state was formed) is very remarkable. The chronology of the inflow of Muslim coins is also interesting. They started to enter in quantity in the mid-ninth century. In Gotland the peak period for these hoards was between 920 and 930, after which time they began to dwindle rapidly. In Pomerania the decline did not start until after 960. The period in which exotic silver was introduced by Varangian activity lasted about a hundred years in all.

Why did the Swedes provide the southern, mainly Slavonic, Baltic coast with silver? One reason may have been that this area could supply products needed by Sweden for its own consumption or for re-export. It has lately been suggested that it was food – cereals, cattle, honey – which early Scandinavia may have been short of, and which Slavonic agriculture and cattle-breeding were capable of providing; for there are archaeological traces of Slavonic pottery – in particular receptacles for, e.g., honey – to be found in Swedish excavations. The Slav middlemen in the countries of origin may have purchased this food and handed it over to Swedish seafarers.

Without denying this, let us consider some other, wider possibilities, which are indicated by the role of the Slav states in amassing Arab silver via Sweden. Besides amber, which was not at the top of the list, their export of craft products (pottery), Pomeranian salt from springs, furs and slaves also appears probable. The political conditions in Pomeranian and Polish territory – the existence of tribal states – facilitated both the delivery of goods and the repeated re-organisations of trade from the ninth century. From the beginning of the tenth century conditions improved very much.

At the mouth of the Oder river, that is on its eastern branch, the Dziwna, flowing out of Szczecin Bay to the sea, at a safe distance from the open sea, a Slavonic castle-town and port called Wolin was founded in the first half of the ninth century. Adam of Bremen writes about it: *ad civitatem Sclavorum quae Jumme dicitur* (II, *c.* 27–28). It was known as Jóm (Jómsborg) in Scandinavian sources. From the mid-tenth century it was just as important as Haithabu and Birka. Excavations conducted there over many years have disclosed an early town settlement with a characteristic Slavonic material culture. Similar settlements have been found in Kołobrzeg (ninth century), whose inhabitants also exploited the saltpans and exported salt; and also at Kamień; and (from the beginning of the tenth century) at Szczecin.

They are paralleled by the first town settlements of the Elbe Slavs connected with long-distance trade – a manifestation of the wider social and economic changes taking place throughout the whole Baltic zone. Such centres may be identified with some of the main tribal fortified places, like Stargard (Oldenburg) in the Wagrian territory, two days' journey from Haithabu and considered as *civitas maritima* by Adam of Bremen, and overshadowed by Old Lübeck in the eleventh century; Mechlin (Mecklenburg) in the Obodrite region with its port Wismar, situated 5 km to the north on the sea-shore; Radgošč, a centre of a pagan cult, in the Ratarian area; Uznam (Usedom) at the mouth of the Peene, another branch of the Oder estuary; and Brenna (Brandenburg) in the Havelan area. In the ninth century there was, on the Sambia peninsula, a Prussian emporium, Wiskiauten, often visited by the Swedes. In the swampy mouth of the Vistula, on the eastern shore situated in the bay, near the modern Elbląg, a Prussian port Truso (Drużno) was established in the ninth and tenth centuries; the coast-line later changed, and this, together with the importance of contacts with the Polish state upstream on the Vistula, gave rise in the second half of the tenth century to Gdańsk (Danzig), the Slavonic port and town on the western shore of the estuary.

These centres of trade had much less interest in eastern silver than did the settlements near the Oder estuary, in Pomerania or in Middle

Poland. A heavy concentration of silver hoards appeared around Wolin, Kamień and Szczecin (29), 13 of which contained only Arab coins probably coming via Sweden. From 963 the lands on the lower Oder entered the sphere of the duchy of Poland's political activities which included attempts to seize the profits of long-distance trade in the Baltic by armed force. A study of the location of hoards in Poland has shown that, from the beginning of the tenth century, a powerful centre arose near Gniezno, which attracted the silver amassed by the local aristocracy and the prince's warriors; the fact that these deposits were concentrated in the northern part of the first Polish state points to its economic links with the Baltic. Even if the initiative for these contacts came from the Scandinavian side, there is no trace of a Swedish political presence on the southern coast of the Baltic or in Wolin. The growing commercial traffic was accompanied by an increase in piracy in the Baltic by crews of Scandinavian, Slav and certainly also Prussian origin. The Swedes and Danes still predominated in the ninth and tenth centuries.

On the other hand, on land, we can see local potentates taking a share in the Baltic trade. The Polish state, also created in the tenth century, by the end of the century controlled the Oder and Vistula basins. Its apparatus was autochthonic although it sometimes used foreign models, such as in the fiscal system.

Important changes took place in Baltic trade at the end of the tenth century. The cessation of the flow of Arab silver soon made itself apparent on the southern coast of the Baltic; the last Arab coin-hoards date from the end of the tenth century. Silver from the West took its place. Danish coins came from Haithabu, together with English and Irish coins. The appearance of English coins in the tenth century amongst the western Slavs is most easily accounted for by Danegeld imported into Denmark and re-exported to the Baltic. Any trade relations between England and Pomerania or Poland seem most unlikely. However, a British coin, the penny of Æthelred II, was taken as a model for the design of some of the Polish coins minted about 1010 by Boleslas the Brave.

The leading money was German. As soon as the danger of Magyar invasion had passed and the Saxon lords began to expand vigorously into the lands of Elbe Slavs, the discovery of silver in the Harz mountains had from about 965 made it possible to mint money, and a flood of German coins was released among the western Slavs. A growing demand for money inside Germany was accompanied by a clear incentive for the Saxon and Frisian mints to produce coins for export. The output not only financed German trade with the Elbe Slavs and Poland but also provided a powerful impetus for it. There is evidence that the mass influx of western money into the Baltic brought down the value of silver, thus further aggravating the crisis of Muslim silver and squeezing out its 'dear' money wherever such factors as the proximity of mints and silver deposits favoured the western money in the East. The area invaded by western money includes Gotland, northern Russia and the whole of Poland as well as the countries of the Elbe.

It is hard to resist the impression, however, that the role this money came to play was different from that of the Islamic money. Of course, it helped to attract Slavonic commodities into Germany, but it also combined with native Czech and Polish money in developing local trade and a money economy. From the middle of the tenth century, the Czech and Polish economies were also, though earlier than in Russia, faced with the problem of the next stage in their development. Long-distance trade benefiting only a small group of lords did not now suffice; there was need for a more broadly based foreign and local trade.

If the historical picture of the early and somewhat primitive trade of central and eastern Europe is relatively easy to distinguish in macro-economic terms, the transformation of the external trade of the Baltic coast and the continent has, it seems, a different character, and still needs many more detailed analytical studies. There are a few studies we can draw upon, however, like for instance those of the Swedish economy before the coming of the Hanseatics, or the origins of the western trade of Novgorod, or the mercantile and productive functions in Pomeranian, Polish and Elbian towns. These studies allow us to sketch out a picture of Baltic trade in the eleventh and twelfth centuries.

The origins of the early urban settlements in Wolin and elsewhere must be sought in the development of long-distance trade. But everywhere it was closely connected with the rise of local handicraft production. During the eleventh century the Baltic coastal towns became not only centres of trade but also of craftsmanship (amber-working, glassmaking, non-ferrous metal and iron work, horn work, carpentry, pottery, shoe-making) with a resident population also getting a living from agriculture, cattle-breeding and fishing.

The Pomeranian potentates (*primores*) living in those towns, as the *Lives of St Otto* colourfully describe them in the second quarter of the twelfth century, were engaged in both trade (among other things in slaves) and piracy. The Slav element gained military preponderance in the Baltic in the eleventh and twelfth centuries, but in the second half of the twelfth century the Danes succeeded in putting down western Slav piracy. This was one of the factors which led to the decline in the economic importance of Wolin, about which Adam of Bremen wrote about 1072–6 that 'celeberrimam prestat stacionem Barbaris et Grecis qui sunt in circuitu', and that 'urbs illa mercibus omnium septentrionalium nationum locuples nihil non habet iocundi aut rari' (II, 22). We know from that text that the journey overland from Hamburg to Wolin took seven days, and from Wolin to Great Novgorod by sea and land took fourteen days. During the eleventh century the old type of luxury trade continued, in which furs from Novgorod played a part, and a stream of silver, mainly Saxon, financed the operations of the merchants tapping the export opportunities of Elbian, Pomeranian and Polish lands. The same amassing of silver, this time from the West, shows how similar were the economic processes. The number of hoards increases and they are usually to be found near early urban settlements.

The next evident break does not come until the end of the eleventh century, when the quantity of hoarded metal falls, and in the first half of the twelfth century when the phenomenon of hoarding disappears. This could be explained by the inflow of silver from abroad coming to an end and local transactions increasing, with the result that all the available silver was put into circulation and the territorial rulers began themselves to mint on a larger scale.

The Baltic towns, both the Scandinavian ones like Lund and Roskilde in Denmark, or Sigtuna in Sweden, as well as the Slavonic towns mentioned above, began in the late eleventh century to put the products of their own craftsmen onto the local market and probably also into long-distance trade. They themselves organised the exploitation of their agrarian hinterland, stockbreeding and forests. On the lands of the Elbe a system of markets was created around the towns of the territorial administration, as, for example, in Demmin in 1128, 'cives Timinenses ante portam conventus forenses agebant' (Ebo, III, c. 5), a network of fairs and inns, paying taxes to a prince. On Rügen – until the decline of the pagan temple in Arkona in 1165 – the taxes were paid into the priests' treasury. Fairs existed there in the twelfth century also under the name of *vicus*. In western Pomerania the Christian mission conducted by Bishop Otto of Bamberg came across a market in Szczecin (second quarter of the twelfth century), which took place twice a week, with peasants from the neighbourhood visiting it *de rure* (Herbord, III, c. 26–29). Simultaneously the Szczecin merchants traded in Kamień and on Rügen, probably taking part twice a year in the exploitation of the herring fishery. Szczecin, which had, when local trade was increasing, a wider hinterland than insular Wolin, gained thereby a lead over its competitor and thus in the twelfth century succeeded in undermining the latter's long-distance trade as well. There were productive possibilities to assure the trade development of Kołobrzeg. When Bishop Otto arrived there, most of the inhabitants *institorum more* were on a journey *negociandi causa* (Herbord, II, *c.* 39); during the twelfth century the saltworks in that town were extended and fiscally reorganised and they provided even Silesia and Great Poland with salt. Most merchants in that area were Slavs closely connected with landownership, but in the eleventh century we know of Saxon and Danish merchants in Mechlin, Saxon merchants in Old Lübeck and, at the end of the twelfth century, German merchants, probably from Lübeck, in Gdańsk. Documents from the turn of the twelfth and thirteenth centuries show that the towns were under the laws of the local princes with a separate category for foreign merchants under the special protection of the princes.

Archaeological excavations as well as texts reveal a new assortment of goods in long-distance trade. For instance in the twelfth century English cloth ('frizal') and Flemish cloth ('burmit'), Baltic herrings, Rhenish glassware and ceramics, and Swedish ironware appeared in Gdańsk. Where exports are concerned, the Szczecin customs tariff in the third quarter of the thirteenth century enumerates the same classical goods from Pomerania, upon which it grew into importance: calf and horse leather; sheep and lambskins; beaver, otter, marten and fox furs; deer, honey and wax.

From the archaeological remains we know something about the sea transport of the western Slavs; the ships were never as big as the Scandinavian war-vessels. Besides small fishing boats, we know of multi-oared men-of-war, narrow but speedy, about 11–13 m in length, about 2.40 m in width, with a loading capacity of 3–5 tons, from Leba and Gdańsk, and cargo boats up to 11 m long, 5 m wide and loading about 10 tons; in both types sails could be used. It was probably at the end of the twelfth century (first mentioned in 1210) that the cog (*koga*, *navis maior*), of Frisian origin, appeared in the Baltic via Saxon merchants. This was a sailing vessel twice the size of the biggest Slavonic cargo boat. The speed of sailing ships on the Baltic can be deduced for the earlier period from the notes of King Alfred (ninth century); his sailor Wulfstan travelled from Haithabu to Truso (about 365 sea miles) in seven days and nights, which gave a speed of 2.2 sea miles per hour. A similar speed – 2.4 sea miles per hour – can be deduced from computing the fourteen-day journey from Wolin to Novgorod in the eleventh century. The *koga* doubled speeds hitherto achieved, thus opening up an era of Hanseatic supremacy.

After the decline in Varangian trade the eastern Slavs established Great Novgorod as the main centre for their Baltic contacts. The town was founded in the mid-tenth century (the earliest dendrochronological data comes from 953), and it was the junction of the trade routes into Russia. Its competitors were Polotsk, Vitebsk, Smolensk and Pskov, the latter being subordinate to Novgorod. Numismatic evidence indicates that beginning at the turn of the eleventh and twelfth centuries German silver coins penetrated northern Russia (122 finds as against 7 in the south), replacing Arab silver as it had done on the Baltic coast. The main intermediary for these contacts was Gotland, with its town Visby, known as 'the Baltic eye', and the eastern coast of the Baltic, where Riga was founded as a port in Semgal land before the German conquest. Trade between Novgorod and the West in the twelfth century is described fully in the chronicles; it seems that this coincided with qualitative changes in trade throughout the Baltic.

Contact with northern Germany in the thirties of the twelfth century is illustrated by evidence about Russian pilgrims to Hildesheim: a relic cross with a twelfth-century inscription in Russian belonging to one Ilya Lyudogochchin of Novgorod has been found. But we also hear about Bremen merchants on what seems to have been their first voyage to Novgorod in 1158, and in 1188 in Frederick I's charter for Lübeck there is a reference to Russian merchants. This was in fact a period of re-organisation of the Hanseatic merchants' trade with the Baltic and Novgorod Russia which in their hands quickly became a monopoly.

Foreign merchants from Sweden, Gotland, Bremen, and Lübeck lived on different streets in Novgorod and they had their own Catholic churches which also served as warehouses (*ecclesia mercatorum*), as for example the German church of St Peter. There was also a separate corporation of Novgorod merchants trading with the West with the Parasceve church. We know of their journeys from Novgorod to Roskilde, Sigtuna, Schleswig and Lübeck; we hear about wars and trade conflicts, as for example in 1188 when Novgorod proclaimed the closure of trade with the West. During the years 1189–99 a treaty was signed by Novgorod with the German and Gotlandic merchants confirming the traditional guarantees of peaceful mutual trade. A similar treaty dated 1229 and signed in Smolensk contains detailed agreements on law and credit.

What was the basis of the Novgorod trade? The wide assortment of goods of those taking part in it (from the West amongst other things: lead for church roofs; wine; spices for magnates' tables; enamels from the Rhineland and Limoges) should not obscure the fact that beeswax and especially furs soon played a large part in the exports of northern Russia, as did the import of silver from the West. The peculiar economics of Novgorod as a trading centre came into being in the twelfth century. The huge, sparsely inhabited territory was exploited mainly through political domination of the northern tribes. Various furs were sought, but white squirrel was preferred, fastened together in bundles of forties (*sorok*) and thousands, after their kind and quality had been carefully checked. Some territories offered wax, later sold in stones (circles) and barrels. About 1137 Novgorod fought for control of the hinterland of the northern Dvina and Petchora as far as the White Sea, and in the twelfth century for the Urals; it conquered the basin of the Kama up to Viatka and Tcheptsa. The territories of the Yugra and Samoyeds brought it into contact with people who did not know iron, and with whom trade had to be conducted by signs, for, as the Russian chronicle said, they did not 'understand our language'.

(5) OVERLAND TRADE BETWEEN SLAVS AND WESTERN EUROPE

Goods coming from western Europe to the Slav countries went by several routes as well as through the Baltic. En route they passed Elbe Slavs, Czechs, Moravians, Hungarians and some Balkan Slavs, making their way to Kievan Russia via Poland or Hungary. We have already discussed the passage to the Ummayad caliphate followed by Jewish and other merchants from central Europe (see pp. 485–6).

The archaeology of western Slavonic countries reveals that in the eighth century goods from the Frankish state reached the border territories in small quantities. A capitulary of Thionville dated 805 regulated the exchange by appointing the places where Frankish and Slavonic merchants were to meet: Bardowiek, Schessel, Magdeburg, Erfurt, Hallstadt, Forchheim, Bamberg, Ratisbon (Regensburg) and Lorch, and forbade the export of weapons to Avars and Slavs; there is also some information about the export of salt from the Frankish state to the East. The Russian legation visiting Louis the Pious at Ingelheim in 839 can be taken to confirm the possibility of contacts between Varangians and the Carolingian Empire. At the end of the ninth century, the Raffelstetten customs tariff refers to the presence in eastern Bavaria of 'Sclavi vero qui de Rugis – mercandi causa', who must, in spite of some doubt, be considered as merchants from Russia and Bohemia. Through this customs post male and female slaves were conducted (the latter, according to the tariff, twice as expensive as the former); also horses, wax transported on pack animals and food. From other sources we know that horses were exported to the West by Obodrites and Czechs; also that furs and leather were exported. The West provided swords from the Rhineland and the Danube with their makers' names on them (Ulfberth, Ingelred and others), some coming overland and some via the Baltic Sea. In Poland and Hungary there is some rare place-name evidence of the presence of Varangians and Kylfingers, but probably as mercenaries rather than as merchants.

Trade contacts flourished during the tenth century when both sides were organising their foreign trade on a nation-wide scale. At that time the Danubian route was closed because of the settlement of the Magyars and the Mediterranean trade was still taking its first steps. On the German side Bardowiek, Magdeburg, Halle and Ratisbon became prominent trading towns; and Prague was their counterpart establishing an enormous market for slaves and other goods from Russia, Hungary, the Balkans and Poland. There was also Cracow on the north side of the Carpathians, whence the road led to Kiev. Slavonic exports, and Bavarian and Saxon imports, were of the same character as formerly, but there were certainly more of them.

A fundamental change in the trade took place in the second half of the century on the part of the Germans, who, as we have already seen in the Baltic zone, wanted to make the exchange unilateral, paying for goods in silver. So far 1,210 finds have yielded 200,000 German *denarii* including about 84,000 in 88 sites in Poland; other major concentrations occur in Gotland (200 finds), Sweden (78) and northern Russia (122), all connected with the Baltic route. When compared with the number of finds in Bohemia and Moravia (23), Hungary (3), southern Russia (8), southern lands of the Elbe Slavs (88), the vitality of Poland's contacts with the Empire via the overland route is evident. But Poland, like Sweden, tended to amass silver without putting it into circulation. The point in time when the flow of coins was at its height was the mid-eleventh century and it came mainly from Saxon mints. It halted abruptly at the end of the century because of the general crisis of silver and the local monetary exchange in Poland. In the seventies of the eleventh century the latter state began to mint coins copiously from the reserves it had hoarded earlier.

At this time there is evidence of a certain restriction in western trade with Bohemia and Poland. The chronicler Gallus Anonymous had been able to write in 1116 that 'regio Polonorum ab itineribus peregrinorum est remota, et nisi transeuntibus in Russiam pro mercimonio paucis nota'. The transit trade was also profitable for Poland and its potentates who took advantage of the flow of luxury products for themselves, as is confirmed by the same chronicle, and also by excavations in Opole, Gniezno and Cracow, where silk, articles made of ivory, lacquer and silver, cowrie shells and seeds of figs have been found. The recovery of this trade route dates from the mid-twelfth century and was connected with the big economic offensive and partial German colonisation east of the Elbe. The transit route to Russia was still kept going, as we can deduce from rabbinical literature, which confirms the passage of traffic along the route from Cologne and Mainz via Ratisbon and Prague to Cracow and Kiev, and further on to the Crimea and the Caucasus as far as Baghdad, and the existence of small colonies on the way, and sometimes even Jewish quarters, as for example in Kiev during the twelfth century. The importance of Ratisbon as the centre of a very intensive eastern trade in the tenth to twelfth centuries is also confirmed by German sources. Its merchants travelled constantly to Kiev and lived there for some time, conducting money transactions with the mother-town, like the merchant Hartwig in 1178–80 with his debtor St Emmeram Abbey. Probably basing himself on Jewish information, al-Idrisi, a Sicilian geographer, knew the names of several Polish towns that were important in international trade; among others, Szczecin, Santok, Wrocław, Cracow, Sieradz, Gniezno, Sandomierz.

To the traditional exports of forest wealth, Russian craftsmen added some products, like cheap spindles made of Volhynian slate or encolpions made of bronze, probably of Hungarian origin. The Hungarian branch of the Kievan trade was centred in Esztergom and other towns which flourished in the twelfth century, thanks to gold and copper mines, and their position on the roads which led to Byzantium via the Balkans, to Venice via Croatia and up the Danube to the Germanic countries. Some of the exports and re-exports of Kievan Russia, especially from the principality of Halich, penetrated Poland by water down the rivers Bug, Narev and Vistula; in the border castle-town of Drohiczyn on the Bug about 3,000 lead seals of Russian princes have been found – evidence that there was a customs house there where goods were trans-shipped from Russian into Polish boats. The Polish customs tariff at Pomnichowo on the Narev in the twelfth century lists carts and boats loaded with salt, cattle, cloth and slaves. The principality of Halich in the twelfth century continued trading salt southwards, using the Dniester and Pruth rivers, and importing horses and copper from Hungary.

III. *The Local Market and Craft Production in Central and East Europe from the Tenth to the Twelfth Century*

By the second half of the tenth century at latest, two distinct economic systems existed side by side in the Slavonic countries of the Elbe, Poland and Bohemia. One was the system of local markets which, at the close of the tenth century, emerged from the needs of villagers and which, with minor variations in chronology, was consolidated in the course of the eleventh century. The other system was, of course, long-distance trade which supplied a small ruling group with the articles of luxury consumption which it demanded. We have seen how the metallic foundation of this trade crumbled away when the supply of Islamic silver gave out and how the new conditions of the eleventh century – the appearance and later disappearance of Saxon silver – transformed its operations.

Changes in the way these two systems interacted are difficult to describe for two important reasons. The first is the problems of interpreting numismatics which is the chief source of our knowledge. The second is that our economic terminology, a product of enquiring into later phenomena qualitatively very different from those of the Middle Ages, is irrelevant, inadequate and imprecise: whether we can legitimately apply it to this epoch is a recurring dilemma. But if the historian continues to use the terminology of modern economic history it is only because he feels obliged to keep asking his sources new questions which unfortunately they cannot always answer satisfactorily.

(I) MONEY CIRCULATION IN THE TENTH TO THE TWELFTH CENTURY

Let us begin with the specific features of metallic money circulation in Slavonic territories during the tenth, eleventh and twelfth centuries. The most striking phenomenon is the number of treasure-hoards, of which some 465 examples containing about 220,000 silver objects have so far been found in Poland. Chronological analysis has dated most of these hoards, Russian as well as Polish, to the tenth and eleventh centuries. Morphological analysis of their contents by Polish, Czech and Russian numismatists has yielded some highly interesting results.

The hoards have to be compared with the finds of single coins either lost by their owners, buried in graves, or found in other cult sites. It is quite probable that the hoards and the isolated coins could have come from the different, though connected, spheres of economic activity.

Let us recall the two economic aspects of the silver objects in the hoards. Dynamically their function was to be a medium of exchange. Statically their function was to be a store of wealth. The objects themselves consist mainly of a large quantity of Arab *dirhems* and west European coins; there are also silver ornaments of various kinds; and finally there are silver rods, bars and rings. All the objects – coins, ornaments and bars – are frequently broken, the coins into halves, quarters and even smaller fragments. During the eleventh century the silver ornaments and bars begin to disappear and the hoards gradually become stores of coins, mainly of western European or local issue, kept whole and no longer clipped. The monetary function of ornaments in the tenth century is beyond doubt; their clipping is evidence of how readily the artistic effort spent on fashioning silver into ornaments was squandered so that they could be used as units in a polymorphic metallic mass which were once again suitable for making payments. Obviously weight was the most important element in determining the circulation of silver in the course of commercial transactions in luxury products. It is worth noticing that Islamic coins do not occur amongst the individual finds inside *castra* and *suburbia*, but are concentrated in the hoards hidden nearby. The craftsmen and servants who inhabited these places did not use these coins: only lords and merchant-warriors did so.

The very fact that treasure was concealed, however, indicates the importance of the static aspect of the objects contained in the hoards. The basic function of the hoard was, after all, its capacity for transmitting the stored value over time and space. As a reserve of silver in the hands of the owner the accumulation of a hoard was linked to the conditions under which silver circulated at a given time, and its purpose was primarily related to the prospect of its being put back into circulation. It is impossible to accept the theory that the hoards were accumulated for non-economic reasons – for instance, because religious belief required provision for the after-life, or because of the need for psychological reassurance. The aim is certainly to be found in some aspect of the economic or political life of the individuals who laid up and concealed the treasure.

We may tentatively distinguish three stages in the formation of hoards among the Baltic Slavs: the first is up to the mid-tenth century: the second from the mid-tenth to the late eleventh century; and the third, from the end of the eleventh century until they disappeared. Hoarding before the middle of the tenth century appears to have been a side-effect of a still barbaric long-distance trade. It was encouraged by the relatively small number of commodities and their mainly luxury character, and by the irregularity and continually changing values of the transactions. Exchange was concentrated amongst a small group of people – local chieftains and warrior-merchants. The ultimate purpose of hoarding was to tap the circulation of Muslim silver for convertible reserves which could then be used, when opportunity arose, to purchase luxury articles which were, on the whole, expensive and in irregular supply. Since they were not always forthcoming, these stores of silver often lay fallow or were turned into ornaments for wear. From the end of the ninth century, throughout the tenth and into the eleventh, Baltic goldsmiths were engaged in converting imported silver into articles which were symbols of the social standing of the lords.

From the middle of the tenth century interesting changes appear in the contents of hoards, such as those in Pomerania. We find more and more ornaments and coins broken into smaller and smaller units of weight for use in minor transactions which were nevertheless large enough to require the use of silver. The average-sized *dirhem* contained from 2.7 to 3.5 grams of silver and in the ninth and early tenth centuries had been in demand undivided. By the second half of the tenth century the coin was found to be too heavy and too valuable and this explains why it was broken up into such tiny pieces. On the other hand, the European *denarius* of the kind put out by Saxon mints was a more serviceable unit of payment and, if clipped at all, it was divided into halves and quarters. It looks as if the owners of hoards were concerned with the liquidity of their assets, and that outlets for their use were increasing through the growth of external trade.

There are hints, however, that this development was stimulated not only by long-distance trade but also by the internal market. The latter, too, was beginning to supply commodities in greater quantity and variety and to assume permanent features as the number of transactions grew. Isolated western coins start to appear in castle-towns before the mid-eleventh century (about 10 per cent of all finds in Poland), and in graves in the middle of that century. This can be considered to be a sign of the wider diffusion of coins in internal exchange. Finally, we may assume that participation in this exchange was wider. It now embraced some of the primary agricultural and handicraft producers. Nevertheless, the overlords of the Polish and Russian states still dominated the trade and continued to drain off metallic reserves from the incoming western silver.

Finally, comes the third stage in the history of the hoards: their marked decline at the end of the eleventh century. Here we cannot agree with the verdict of some numismatists that many hoards mean a time of plenty and few hoards a time of scarcity. It seems more reasonable to suppose that as intensive hoarding was connected with a limited circulation of money, so decreased hoarding was now a result of a wider internal circulation. Everything goes to show that the expansion of local markets called forth a great demand for metallic money and other forms of currency, to which we shall return. An efficient circulation of silver money required an increase in the number of coins – among the western Slavs through the issue of their own money. About the mid-tenth century minting was organised in Bohemia and a hundred years later it was reformed by Bretislav I on the basis of periodical new issues which gave the prince a regular profit. The first coins in Poland appeared with the name Mieszko on them (Mieszko I, died 992), but most probably not until Boleslav the Brave's reign and then only on a small scale; the re-coinage of about 1070 was on a very much larger scale. The first coins in the Slavonic lands of the Elbe were struck by Pribislav Henry (1127–50), prince of Stodorans. The silver came partly from the mines in Bohemia and in the borderlands between Silesia and the territory of Cracow; partly also from imports, though these proved difficult after Muslim sources dried up and the export capacity of the German mints was exhausted at the end of the eleventh century, following a century of expansion; and finally from the release of hoarded silver. The money supply needed to meet the requirements of trade grew and the velocity of circulation speeded up. All these tendencies discouraged the hoarding of treasure, even by the lords, who began to release the silver they did not display as jewellery. New hoards dating from the end of the eleventh and the twelfth centuries tended to consist of coins withdrawn briefly from circulation. The situation in Russia was apparently different because it had no mints of its own, although even here the stores of precious metals were in fact reserves of money for large transactions based on silver.

The monetarisation of the local markets was a very complex process. The chronology set out above applies to metallic (i.e. silver) money. The development of urban centres, however, preceded the general use of metallic money as a medium of market exchanges, and in the Slavonic countries this metallic money was not the only money, even though its position was certainly paramount.

In 965 Ibrahim-ibn-Yaqub noted that in Prague scraps of open-weave cloth were used as a means of payment. He also gives us the prices of certain foodstuffs. While ten chickens could be bought for a silver *dinar* (1.2 to 1.5 grams), one chicken could be bought for one such strip of linen cloth. What are we to make of this medium of circulation? It is obviously substitute money. In discussing its economic significance it has been pointed out that even towards the close of the Middle Ages cloth was still comparatively expensive: in Cracow market it is probable that the equivalent of four chickens was one cubit of cloth. This is very close to Ibrahim's price of a chicken for one strip of cloth about the size of a handkerchief, or something like a quarter of a cubit. But the main point is that Ibrahim makes some play with the fact that the cloth is open-weave, which would suggest that ordinary cloth had already at an earlier time been treated as a standard of value.

Philologists say the derivation of the Slav verb 'to pay' = *platit*, *placic* was *plat*, meaning a scrap of cloth. These strips could therefore have been a kind of debased utilitarian form of cloth which had to come into existence when the number of transactions based on the 'cloth standard' became sufficiently large. However, we are still some way from token money, properly so called, of a purely nominal value independent of its real value. This view is supported by the conclusions of Czech numismatists who have drawn our attention to the disproportion between the commercial activity of Prague in the tenth and eleventh centuries and the small number of monetary finds from that period. The high price of metallic money would explain this fact. Exchange through its medium was possible only for the wealthy foreign merchants trading in expensive commodities. In the suburban market, on the other hand, exchanges were either wholly natural (commodity against commodity) or through the medium of these strips of cloth (commodity against commodity-money). Such dealings would embrace small, day-to-day purchases.

A similar use of non-silver commodity-money seems to have been current a hundred years earlier in Moravia and southern Poland. Excavations have revealed about 500 iron objects shaped like axes but unfinished and made of low quality metal which would make them useless as tools. Again, it is a plausible conjecture that this was a peculiar kind of money substitute. What is worth noting is that it comes from a period – the ninth century – when only the germ of urban life existed, for the imposing fortified settlements of the Moravian lords at Staré Město and Mikulčice can hardly qualify as developed towns. If the hypothesis of cloth and iron as commodity-money in the sense of a standard of value and medium of circulation were to be accepted, it would mean having to push back the beginnings of an organised local exchange to a period before the general distribution of silver money; and also to a period when the Slavonic agricultural communities and their lords conducted, alongside the exchange of luxury articles for silver, another kind of trade on a local scale involving transactions of low value. This line of thought would lead to a revision of current views about a natural economy and to a wider application to the early Middle Ages of knowledge derived from observation of peasant economies in today's under-developed countries.

In later centuries Russia, above all Novgorod, presents us with another kind of non-metallic money: this was furs which retained their full intrinsic and utilitarian value. Recently we have gained access to the account of the twelfth-century traveller, Abū Hāmid al Gharnāti (died 1169/70). In it he describes the habit in Russia of using for payment shorn skins which, as he writes, 'are of no use to anyone', but were tied in bundles of eighteen and marked with the sign of the prince. What is meant by forced money? The question remains open, since using skins which were of full intrinsic and utilitarian value as a medium for the circulation of goods raises many doubts. Opinions on this point are conflicting. Though Russia was, relatively speaking, saturated with foreign money, for reasons of prestige it issued its own coins during the reigns of Vladimir the Great (the gold zolotnik of about 4 grams) and Yaroslav the Wise (gold and silver – 3 grams), after which, apart from some occasional issues by Oleg-Michael, duke of Tmutorakan at the end of the eleventh century, there was no minting for several centuries. How are we to reconcile the absence of its own money with Russia's well-known internal and external trade between the eleventh and fourteenth centuries? How are we to reconcile the reports of silver flowing into Novgorod from the Hanseatic League with the paucity of coins found in excavations of the city? Finally, how are we to reconcile the developed system of Russian monetary units with this absence of a money of its own?

It seems necessary first to separate the period up to the end of the eleventh century since the plentiful supply of foreign silver on the Russian market gave it a real function as a standard of value, a medium of circulation and a means for the storage of value. There can be no doubt that silver was first preceded and then accompanied in these functions by furs, though to a limited degree and mainly as a standard of value in exchanges of the commodity for commodity-money type. Evidence for this is provided by Russian words for money: apart from the common Slavonic term *platit* which, as we saw, was derived from *plat* (a piece of cloth), such measures as *kuna* (a marten), and *vyeveritsa* or *vyeksha* (a squirrel) clearly point to the spread of animal pelts as a commodity-money.

However, the second phase, beginning with the twelfth century, appears to have brought a division of the spheres of circulation of silver. That which came in from the outside was, as in Great Novgorod, either frozen in ecclesiastical and secular treasuries or used by the lords of this city-state for private payments requiring silver. Both metals, and particularly the more common silver, were calculated as units of account and also of weight. In the twelfth century the system was arranged as follows: the highest unit was the *grivna* (*marca*) with 68 grams of silver in southern Russia and about 51 grams in the north, which was divided into 20 *nogatas*, 25 *kunas*, 50 *rezanas* and 100 *vyekshas*. The next highest unit, therefore, was the *nogata* with 2.46 grams of silver, equivalent to 1.25 *kunas*, 2.5 *rezanas* and 5 *vyekshas*. The third unit was the *kuna* with 1.97 grams worth 2 *rezanas*, and 4 *vyekshas*. The lowest unit was the *vyeksha* with 0.49 grams of silver. The silver weights were the approximate counterparts of coins.

In the twelfth century there appeared in circulation silver discs, hexagonal nuggets and other metal pieces of fixed weight, usually the equivalent of a Cologne mark (154 grams) which would suggest they were used as payments to, or more likely from, western traders. Presumably they also circulated in large transactions inside Russia. But many puzzles still remain. We cannot, for instance, state with any degree of certainty to what extent the system of monetary units was a system of silver weights only and to what extent it could be used to establish the values of goods other than silver.

The point is a crucial one. Various forms of token money became current in the internal market of Russia during the twelfth and thirteenth centuries. The most picturesque was the bundle of squirrel skins sealed by princely officials which we have already mentioned, though it is not attested for Novgorod but only for southern and eastern Russia. But the needs of circulation stimulated other forms of token money such as furs of full value counted in bundles (e.g. 40 skins equalled a *sorotchka*) or in single skins. We may also surmise that certain products wholly or partly without utilitarian value, but valuable in themselves, might have assumed the character of a local money (a weight of marine salt measured in *puzy*, Greek nuts, amber or cowrie shells). Scholars are now examining the evidence of archaeological excavations from this angle.

Even among the western Slavs who were never without their own mints or a supply of foreign money, similar phenomena can be found in the twelfth and thirteenth centuries. Here, too, the need to offset the chronic shortage of silver, as markets became increasingly busy, led to the revival or emergence of token money. Helmold writes of the island of Rügen in the twelfth century: 'Porro apud Ranos non habetur moneta', nec in comparandis rebus nummorum consuetudo, sed quicquid in foro mercari volueris, panno lineo comparabis' (c. 38). In medieval Poland fines imposed by the princes' officers were settled in furs with the following order of value: ermine, calabre, weasel, marten, fox. In the thirteenth century the rural population paid tithes of squirrel skins which in Poland too had roughly the value of commodity-money. There existed also a unit called *marca cunarum*; four of those units made one *marca argenti*, just as in Russia; but at the same time *cuna* (Polish *kuna*) probably did not only mean marten (*Mustela Martes Lin.*), but like the Latin equivalent *asperiolus* it meant small wild animals, including calabre (*Glis glis*) and squirrel (*Sciurus vulgaris*). We know that in Russia a *grivna* consisted of 25 and later 50 *cunas*; and the same was probably true of the Polish *marca cunarum*, each *cuna* being worth about 2 grams of silver. What is more, in Cracow, during the whole of the thirteenth century 'cum nigro argento et pelliculis de capitibus asperiolinis communiter forisabantur' (*Annales Cuiaviae*, a. 1305), which points to a peculiar kind of circulation of non-metallic money, similar to that of Russia.

This seems to provide evidence that in Poland as well as in Russia, apart from skins used for clothing, i.e. with all the attributes of a commodity, there were other skins in circulation which were not so used, but which still possessed an intrinsic value restricting their unchecked supply on the market. Contrary to the commonly-held view about the primitive character of such a currency, it is probable that it could originate and function only in big towns where it was easy to maintain a system whose existence required government intervention and a certain degree of social credit. In the rest of the country where non-metallic currency was in circulation, token money had to have all the attributes of a commodity.

In twelfth-century Russia one loaf of bread could be bought for the lowest unit, *vyeksha* (about 0.49 grams of silver), enough to feed one man for one day. It would thus seem to correspond to the lowest market transaction. Its measure also indicates its sphere of currency: the local market and its rural and handicraft base. The same area of circulation is signposted by another medieval Polish unit: this is the *krusza*, or lump of salt, which represented a real micro-unit since it was used to pay the *poena trecentorum* '*trzysta*' (300 grains of salt), the lowest penalty imposed for minor breaches of the old Polish law.

This survey of the forms of token money gives us an idea of the extent of money circulation on the local market. As we can see, it was considerable and had spread to the small trader and producer of market goods.

(2) CRAFTS, TOWNS AND MARKETS IN THE WESTERN SLAVONIC COUNTRIES

Can the moment when the pulse of the local market quickened be given an approximate date? We have to pose the question separately for each Slavonic country and for some the state of research makes any answer premature.

Let us describe this break-through as it occurred in the Moravian, Czech and Polish territories, and relate it to the emergence of the town as a centre for both local and long-distance trade. In recent years the light shed by written sources on the origins of towns has been supplemented by evidence from excavations which has revealed that a rudimentary urban life existed as early as the ninth century. Earlier there had been a series of castles in which one or even several chieftains resided. In Moravian territory big castle-towns were founded in the ninth century and excavations on their sites have revealed groups of lords' houses, each with its chapel (12 of them in Mikulčice) and graveyard. The graves can be graded according to the goods they contain: in Staré Město about 1.6 per cent of graves have an astonishing amount of gold in them; about 29 per cent are much poorer; another 10 per cent contain only knives and the remainder (about 53 per cent of the total) have no grave goods at all. It seems that these proportions approximate, *grosso modo*, to the social and cultural structure of the town's inhabitants: lords (*comites*, *principes*, *primates*) surrounded by warriors and servants, as well as by craftsmen and peasants of various levels of dependence, including slavery. The economic structure of such a town or fortified residence was based on the consumption of local goods with the addition of foreign goods brought in by extra-economic means and a trade in luxuries. In the ninth and tenth centuries the Baltic ports mentioned above, together with their inhabitants, seem to have lived off this foreign trade. Some kind of local exchange – whether compulsory or not – must have existed, but it appears that the two sectors, long-distance and local, were quite distinct and only loosely connected. The real need for markets arose from an external exchange of luxury, or complementary, products with an alien population.

It was not, however, until a settlement or *suburbium* of craftsmen and traders grew up around a castle that we can really talk of an embryo medieval town. Bohemia and Poland became states and were to some degree centralised during the reigns of Boleslav I (929–72) in Bohemia, Mieszko (*c.* 960–92) and Boleslav the Brave (992–1025) in Poland, and the old pattern of regional castles was arranged in a new way. The organisation of Hungary was somewhat similar. The castles were occupied by lords and military garrisons with growing consumer needs which had to be met by an extensive traffic in market goods, and this breathed life into local resources. An interesting attempt to awaken and utilise the productive and service potentialities of surrounding villages was the system of services established around the princely castles. This was a plan conceived by the monarch which functioned between the mid-tenth and the late twelfth centuries. Craftsmen and dependants (*ministeriales*) exercised a wide range of up to forty different trades, including those of cobblers (*sutores*), cooks (*coci*), honey gatherers (*mellifices*), and beaver wardens (*castorarii*) while still remaining agriculturists. Division of labour between these secondary occupations was imposed by the state and it was in the exercise of these occupations that bond services were performed and dues paid.

However, this division harnessed a part only of available productive capacities and skills and directed them only into channels essential to the business of the state apparatus. Its inefficiency soon became apparent. Though traces of this organisation have survived in the form of place-names signifying the various trades, by the mid-twelfth century it was on the wane. The craft sector was the first to disappear, followed much later by herding and hunting services. During the eleventh century crop and animal surpluses on peasant holdings were increasing, artisan workshops were springing up and both peasants and craftsmen were gradually taking part in local exchanges.

The arena in which this economic expansion took place was originally the castle and the *suburbium* which together deserve to be regarded as the first form of urban life in Bohemia, Poland and the neighbouring countries. The state furnished the castles with more powerful fortifications and an infrastructure of churches and chapels, *suburbia* and market-places. At the foot of the castles proper (*castrum* or *castellum* in the Latin of the contemporary records) was the *suburbium* with one of its boundaries usually touching the walls. During the tenth and eleventh centuries the castle and *suburbium* continued to attract rural craftsmen and helped to make crafts into permanent and skilled trades and to assure full employment and an outlet for their products through an expanding demand. Archaeological sites provide evidence that by the middle of the tenth century specialisation and the improved workmanship that went with it were apparent in pottery, shoemaking and tanning, boneworking, goldsmithing and blacksmithing. The conditions in which artisans lived and worked are still somewhat obscure, but probably the latter were rather closely dependent on the prince. There were dues in kind to be paid either as craft products or as services, while fishermen and peasants, for example, were obliged to supply the castle with part of what they produced, even though urban dwellers were still to a large extent also agriculturists.

Through their growing consumption the castles and *suburbia* were encouraging an expansion and differentiation of crafts, and despite their liabilities to the state the artisans were able to widen their margin of economic freedom and thus to engage in barter for food and other necessaries. We have already mentioned the sites in Bohemia and Poland where transit and exchange of luxuries on a continental scale took place. Market-places and their facilities (*pons mercati*) which had, according to written sources, first appeared during the reign of Boleslav the Brave were in Poland places of public exchange and were protected by ducal law.

When did the local need for exchange of foodstuffs and craft products come to be sufficiently pressing to make such market activities more important than the lords' foreign and luxury trade? We have two ways by which we can identify the eleventh-century watershed in the life of these early Bohemian and Polish towns. The first body of evidence comes, as previously pointed out, from the study of numismatics which, in Bohemia, indicates the reign of Bretislav I (*c.* 1050) with his reforms involving minting smaller dinars and active fiscal measures. In Poland economic activity can be dated to the reign of Boleslav the Bold (*c.* 1070) and the first large-scale issues of metallic money. Coins struck at home were now in circulation, and these coins, stamped by the prince, were an indispensable medium of exchange and standard of value. Metal was now needed for market commodities, especially in the local market, in the form of coins with a nominal value. The circulation of money quickened, coins became too valuable and too useful to be hoarded and currency shortages led to the spread of those substitute forms of money already described. Metallic money was paramount, however, as is shown by the payment of tolls and duties, either partly or wholly in coin, in twelfth-century Poland. Another indication was the introduction in Poland in 1138–46 of a system of frequent compulsory renewals of the coinage (*renovatio monetae*) involving withdrawal of the old money under the supervision of the princes' minters and issue of a new currency. This lucrative operation was only practicable when the output of the mints was sufficiently large, and it only profited the rulers when metallic money was in general and rapid circulation.

The second source of our knowledge comes from the charters. It is no coincidence that records of markets (*fora*) become more plentiful in the second half of the eleventh and during the twelfth centuries. These *fora* had grown up by the *castra* and *suburbia*, or in other localities. But, not every fort-compound had a market: we know of many princely fortresses which never became the nucleus of a town. Markets arose and multiplied in places which satisfied the needs of an agricultural hinterland. In the course of the twelfth century the number reached 250 in Poland and this included western Pomerania which at that time was connected with Poland. In Bohemia and Moravia the number was probably half as many again. If we compare the number of points where craft goods and services were exchanged at this time with the number at the end of the tenth century, the increase cannot simply be ascribed to population growth. This had less effect on the development of urban and market centres than did changes in the structure of economy and society.

The impetus came not only from the expansion of crafts but also from the greater productivity of agriculture, which in itself stemmed mainly from the increase in the area of land under cultivation and the number of livestock. The variety of urban crafts whose products have been excavated was clearly on the upgrade in the second half of the eleventh and during the twelfth centuries. We can also detect many features in the timber construction of Polish towns which point to a new stage of development at the close of the eleventh century: in the archaeological stratification of Gdańsk the last brushwood hut appears in the stratum estimated to date from 1090–1115. After that there are only houses to be found. Finally, town architecture from the twelfth century onwards is more monumental in character.

Only a few crafts – excluding metallurgy and mining – were still carried on as auxiliary occupations in the countryside, but in the towns archaeologists have counted well over twenty crafts that were pursued as full-time trades. The working of iron and non-ferrous metals, potting, tanning, shoemaking, bone- and horn-carving, wheelwrighting, boat-building, glass-making, quarrying and stone-cutting and so on, are revealed from the remains of workshops, tools and waste products found in Gniezno, Gdańsk, Opole and elsewhere as having been carried on by manufacturing methods of considerable variety and requiring a high degree of skill. Some of these craft occupations were combined with other trades.

Specialisation also led to a vertical organisation, i.e., some crafts exercised their skills in one of the various stages of production needed to transform raw materials into the finished products in, for example, cloth-making, woodturning or cooperage. At the same time the rudiments of a horizontal system existed, with, for instance, tanneries supplying shoemakers with leather. We can also see the modest beginnings of a territorial division of work: metal trades in towns used iron and non-ferrous metals furnished by mining and smelting undertaken as an ancillary occupation on farms (*rustici argenti fossores* are mentioned in Poland *c.* 1136).

More is known about the social conditions of craftsmen, though many points are still controversial: in particular the part played by manorial handicraft production in the market organisation of the twelfth and thirteenth centuries. Presumably some handicraft products were made to order, and there is proof of levies taken by lords which the latter then sold for cash, but it is also safe to assume that craftsmen sold the goods they made in the market directly. Convincing evidence of this is to be found in the moulds for the mass production of metal objects and the considerable quantity of semi-finished goods, waste and raw materials archaeologists have discovered, and by reference in our sources to *opifices res suas vendentes* (1177) in the market-place. There is less information about how far afield these articles were sold: probably the extent to which they were distributed depended on the kind of product and the needs of the socially differentiated local market. On this point historians of the Slavonic Middle Ages can learn a good deal from anthropologists who study African countries. A self-sufficient village economy may co-exist and interact with a commodity- and money-economy for a long time; some members of the rural population, mainly the lords and knights, probably used the market frequently and extensively; others, the peasants, had only casual and limited access to the market when buying knives or salt. From the second half of the eleventh century the lords took to extending their landed estates and erecting their mansions outside the princes' *castra*.

As the requirements of commerce grew, the number of markets held in the *suburbia* proved insufficient, and from the turn of the eleventh century more of them were needed. In addition to their numerical increase (in Cracow there seem to have been several markets in the twelfth century) they were held more often: in Szczecin beginning in the twelfth century market day was twice a week. During the twelfth century many small trading centres came into being, and concurrently with the markets set up on ducal initiative, others created by the great feudal lords also made their appearance. In principle, however, the state's monopoly remained undisturbed, and all changes, e.g. moving the market-place elsewhere, required the monarch's agreement. The ruler also retained many fiscal and judicial rights, although these were gradually encroached upon by various, mainly church, immunities. The distance between the bigger towns, originating either as princely fortresses or *suburbia*, was from 50 to 60 km in densely populated areas; but new centres of medium or small size cut the intervening distance by half or even a quarter, and some urban centres are also found on the fringes of settlement. They were often half-way between a town and a rural agglomeration providing – with the exception of trade – few non-agricultural goods and services. In the following period the competition between them resulted in the typical mid-European pattern of towns of various sizes, ranging from the smallest market town to the capital city.

Some of these new markets were given names signifying the day of the week on which they were held, e.g. Wtorek (Tuesday), Sroda/Sródka (Wednesday), Czwartek (Thursday), Piątek (Friday), Sobota/Sobótka (Saturday). Other names like Tarczek, Targowisko, Targowa Góra (Market Hill) etc., came from the term *targ* which means 'market'. Other places still, trying to indicate their new social and economic rank as against the older forms of settlement, assumed such names as Miejsce or Meszcze (*locus* in Latin sources), meaning 'town' in old Polish (*miasto* in modern Polish). This name was also applied to some settlements adjacent to *castra* (locus St Gothardi in Poznań) and was to be very popular in Poland (as it was in Bohemia); it later supplanted, or restricted, the use of the word *grod* (fortress) until then generally accepted as indicating a town.

Goods exchanged at local markets of every size were mostly products made in the larger, and sometimes also the smaller, communities. Although we do not hear of the 'forum quod fiebat ante atrium ecclesie eiusdem annuale' until the beginning of the thirteenth century, we may assume that fairs already existed in the twelfth century, and that they served long-range trade. Great significance may be attributed to imported goods for mass consumption, like cloth from western Europe which – according to excavations at Gdańsk – appears at the end of the eleventh century; but also Baltic herring, mostly salted, apparently at Kołobrzeg; Pomeranian, Kujavian, Ruthenian and Cracovian salt; bar- and wrought-iron; Russian and other pottery; glass; or golden ornaments. Towns and markets received a few luxury articles in return for their own wares, but principally they got agricultural products (corn, cattle, pigs) and forest produce, honey, wax and furs. An attempt has been made to estimate the quantities of food Opole in Silesia needed at the close of the twelfth century: it appears that, to sustain itself, the town needed cereals from 60 villages each with ten farms, sending 10 per cent of their produce to market. It should be added that, in that period, inhabitants of even larger towns were also engaged in agriculture, stock-breeding and fishing.

Markets and small towns possessing only rudimentary crafts acted mainly as intermediaries between customers and the big centres of handicraft production. But it was not only trade which had called them into being and kept them alive; they also developed another important town function, i.e. the provision of services. One of the chief service institutions was the tavern. Taverns made their appearance at the beginning of the eleventh century and multiplied alike in the bigger towns and the smallest settlements. A market always had its tavern (*forum cum taberna*) – a place where beer, entertainment and lodging could be had, which was also open, even on days when there was no market. It was also used for the collection of duties and carriage fees, for minting, and also for selling salt and handicraft articles. An interesting attempt to calculate the total volume of trade of about twenty taverns in Płock at the turn of the eleventh century suggests a weekly sum of 30 silver *marcae* (about 7,200 *denarii*), and this may represent the usual money turnover and volume of trade in taverns in early Polish towns. Even taverns in minor market-places recorded their income in money, though certainly some purchases were paid for in foodstuffs, as is shown by tavern incomes in western Pomerania which were reckoned in lumps of beeswax, dairy produce and poultry. Taverns, however, not only provided a service for ordinary people; since some part of their income, or even their entire business, might belong to a ducal household or a church institution, they were used to supervise the taxation of trade and also as a retail outlet for dues in kind collected from the peasants.

Fortresses and market settlements also satisfied some of the cultural needs of the rural population. Parochial churches were usually established beside the markets, and urban churches often extended their dominion over parts of surrounding countryside. Finally there was also an administrative role. Ducal power exercised from the castellan's fortress was felt by the peasant whatever liberties he had acquired, and, from the reign of Boleslav the Brave onwards, market gatherings provided an opportunity for the duke to demonstrate his authority. We should also mention some urban amenities like the butchers' or bakers' stalls which mushroomed at the end of our period and helped to increase rural consumption.

There must have been considerable variety in the social and legal position of the inhabitants of these places, particularly of the bigger towns like Szczecin, Wrocław, Gniezno or Cracow, and so far as the mass of the people is concerned it escapes the historian's eye. The population was still largely dependent on representatives of ducal authority in both the socio-political and economic sense, but the development of crafts and participation in the local market undoubtedly offered the people considerable economic opportunity.

Everyone, regardless of social status, were he craftsman, trader or customer coming to buy at the market, enjoyed the market peace (Polish *mir-pax*, or sovereign's hand = *ręka pańska*) – the safety of person and estate guaranteed by the prince's castellan and his deputies. During the twelfth century the trading place obtained a separate market judge (*iudex fori*) who – apart from his jurisdiction – was probably charged with the general and some part of the fiscal administration, sharing the fees involved with the duke's minter who attended the periodic exchanges of money.

Because there are so few written sources we cannot say exactly when in the twelfth century the market rallied around the traders' group. That group continued to remain under the control of the lord of the town, who in the Poland of that period was almost always the duke. We may presume that the decisive moment came in the second half or even as early as the middle of the century, and from then on our study of the rise of Polish towns joins the subject common to a vast part of Central Europe, i.e. the emergence of *ius fori*.

At the turn of the twelfth century we may observe in the Polish towns a small group of well-to-do people, presumably merchants, occupying a leading position among the population thanks to a various privileges acquired from the lord of the town, i.e. the duke or bishop. This group was able to invest and to exert an economic influence over the rest of the townsmen. In Poland it was headed, with the duke's authority, by the *soltys* or bailiff (*scultetus*), less frequently by the *włodarz* (*villicus*, *procurator*) or *zupan* (*supanus*), who was probably an official exercising – as we can see at the beginning of the thirteenth century – market jurisdiction and administering the growing urban community. But the community did not include all their permanent and temporary inhabitants, only citizens (*mercatores*, *cives*, *burgenses*) and 'guests' (*hospites*) enjoying rights of inheritance. In such few instances as can be traced the latter were local men, some of knightly origin. Small wonder then, as happened in Płock in 1237, that, in seeking a suitable legal privilege for these *hospites*, they were given those of Mazovian knights. Foreign traders, however, who were mainly German merchants, are occasionally encountered even earlier in the twelfth century, and more often from the first years of the thirteenth century. They reinforced the economic and social standing of the citizens of the larger towns, such as Cracow, Wrocław, Poznań or Gdańsk, and secured separate immunities for their own linguistic groups in those places.

Towards the end of the twelfth century markets and towns began to receive, in return for a fixed rent, the right to hold a free market (*forum liberum*) allowing all buyers and sellers access to it without payment of fees to the duke, or submission to the jurisdiction of the *advocatus* or castellan; they were also exempted from services in kind, charges or payments to the treasury and ducal officers. From the first decades of the thirteenth century there are indications that the words *burgum* and *burgenses* were coming to be accepted as describing the communities developing around the markets. The extent of the privileges received varied according to the role of the particular town. Some towns continued slowly to shape their own local town law evolving from the *ius fori*. Some towns, especially the smaller ones, continued to live within an economic and social framework that hardly changed until the fourteenth and even fifteenth centuries. They mostly abandoned it at a late date for another type of legal organisation, tested and in use in Silesian towns from the second decade of the thirteenth century. This was the German law (*ius teutonicum*).

(3) CRAFTS AND INTERNAL EXCHANGE IN RUSSIA

We may learn something about Russia's internal trade and the goods produced in that country during the years between the tenth and the thirteenth centuries from the few surviving texts; archaeological excavations provide us with further information on the state of material culture. However, the interpretation of the evidence, in the light of our knowledge of the urban and agrarian economy of that period, is still subject to debate. One fundamental problem relates to the number and function of the castle-towns (*gorod*, also old Russian *grad, grod*) at the beginning of the thirteenth century: how many were there and what was their function? A figure as high as 271, which has been quoted, seems somewhat improbable when compared to the number known to exist in the sixteenth century, when Russia excluding Siberia had 220 towns. It seems that the 271 medieval centres must include fortresses, defensive castles and fortified rural settlements not exceeding one hectare in area. Not more than a hundred of these could have had a fortified or, more often, an open *suburbium* (old Russian *posad, podol, predgradiye*) in which the inhabitants were concentrated around a castle (old Russian *grad, detinets*). The existence of a *suburbium* was the essential pre-requisite of an urban settlement, and although the literature on the subject is not in total agreement on this point, the origins of this kind of town can hardly have been earlier than the tenth century. Their predecessors of the eighth and ninth centuries were the fortified settlements of lords and princes which were both residences and seats of authority where payments in kind were received and where, from the tenth century onwards, craftsmen congregated. Even after craftsmen had made their appearance in the towns of the eleventh century scattered county handicrafts on a considerable scale were also active. It seems that about the year 1000 the main feature of agrarian settlements, both inside and outside the land occupied by the eastern Slavs, was that they consisted of small groups of people spread over a large territory with a density of approximately 1.6 inhabitants per square kilometre. This kind of settlement had a subsistence economy based on peasant households in which rural crafts were developed and goods produced for a restricted sale amongst neighbours as well as for the requirements of the manor.

According to our archaeological evidence the output of a village potter in the tenth to thirteenth centuries would have been distributed among nearby settlements with a common cemetery; the potter would have been a farmer working in the slack period of the agricultural year. In Russia, as elsewhere, the blacksmith's profession was a full-time occupation. His products can be found within a circle between 5 and 15 km in diameter and his output was intended for exchange, most probably by barter, against cereals, meat or fish. Bronze and silver ornaments of female dress have, after careful examination, been ascribed to country workshops serving an area 10 to 15 km in diameter. The proportions of this area suggest that its nucleus was a local market even though we have no information about any permanent rural fairs. As well as local products, ornaments showing the techniques of town manufacture are to be found in graveyards, though rarely in country graveyards.

On the other hand, from the beginning of the eleventh century up to the Mongol invasion, spindle whorls made of pink slate and produced in many of the hamlets of the Volhyn land near Ovrutch had an extensive sale. They are to be found distributed over the whole of Slavonic Russia in the mid-eleventh century, replacing the local spindles made of clay; they also reached Poland, the banks of the Volga and the Crimea. Other fancy goods, such as beads, small enamelled bronze crosses and glass bracelets, were similarly dispersed; the last two items seem to have been manufactured in Kiev. The explanation can only be that they were distributed by small-scale merchants, i.e. pedlars, who carried these small fancy articles around the countryside; goods of foreign manufacture are never found there. Some information about the social condition of country craftsmen leads us to think that in the eleventh and twelfth centuries they were dependants of the great estates owned by princes or boyars and that they paid their taxes in the form of the goods they themselves made; how much economic initiative they had we simply cannot tell.

The hundred towns referred to above, lying as they did in an area of 5.3 million square kilometres, were obviously few in number and anything but equally dispersed. According to our evidence, some already had quite a large population by the eleventh century; Kiev in particular may have had some scores of thousands of inhabitants; Novgorod, too, had 10,000 at the beginning of the eleventh century and 20,000 by the thirteenth. Their food supply was a perennial problem. In the eleventh and twelfth centuries the Novgorod chronicle is particularly sensitive to the years of famine and dear victuals. In the eleventh century meat, honey, salt, corn, hops, vegetables, fish, milk, bread, cheese and butter could be bought in the market at Kiev. Where did these foodstuffs come from? Did they come from peasants' deliveries to the market from an undefined area surrounding the town, or were they sales of the tribute in kind that the prince received from his estates and manors? Written sources suggest that a town's basic food supply came from the arable and stock-breeding farms and from the gardens belonging to the inhabitants, but the sources tell us nothing about the techniques of food production. A characteristic of the town settlement was the large area it covered because of its fruit and vegetable gardens. Letters written on birch bark and found in Novgorod give us details about supplies in kind from a village to its lord's house in town. We also know that the corn produced by Novgorod's hinterland was often insufficient, and that cutting off its deliveries of cereals was a potent political weapon in the hands of the duchy of Vladimir-Suzdal. The tributes princes received in corn were destined for consignees far away in other parts of Russia, or even abroad. It was possible to buy garments, cloth, shoes and weapons in a town market; archaeologists have distinguished more than forty different handicrafts represented by articles made to a high technical level and sometimes even to a degree of uniformity.

Apparent improvements in metallurgy can be seen in the weapons, craftsmen's tools and utensils of everyday town life. The fashioning of copper, silver and gold provided a wide assortment of articles from bells and cauldrons to jewellery made to order or for general sale, as is proved by moulds and casts for mass production: the ornamentation and shapes of urban pottery are richer than those to be found in the countryside. Carpentry, turnery, wood-carving and leather crafts have a distinctive urban character, but weaving apparently continued to be a rural craft carried on in peasant farms and country manors. Linen and cloth were sent from the latter to towns where they competed with imported products for the higher class of customer. Traces of glass production and luxury articles made of bone, horn and stone have been found. Some town craftsmen were still dependent on princes and lords; their tools marked with the princes' seals in Kiev and other southern Russian towns are testimony of this; workshops for handicrafts have also been found in princes' residences.

Whether these manorial craftsmen were in a position to produce anything over and above their manorial duties we cannot say, but monasteries were also centres of manorial crafts in which groups of men – under regular rule like the western *conversi* – worked for the benefit of the abbey or themselves and also for the market. This we know from the eleventh-century evidence that monks from Lavra Petcherskaya bought corn in the market at Kiev in exchange for articles – stockings and hats – they themselves had produced. The icon painters at the monasteries worked to order and they had others to help them.

All other craftsmen were subject to the prince's authority and while they had more freedom as to what they made, they were subject to greater economic risk; one of the causes of the popular uprisings in Kiev in 1113 and Novgorod in 1209 was the indebtedness of craftsmen, although we know nothing about the exact circumstances. Our sources suggest that the major part of their output was to order with materials provided by the customer. Whether Russian craftsmen reached the stage of organising themselves into any form of corporation seems still to be an open question. All we know is that the different craftsmen had separate quarters in Kiev (potters, tanners, blacksmiths) and in Novgorod (potters, shield-makers and groups of carpenters organised for specific jobs).

How far did the goods bought and sold at markets travel? Here archaeological analysis has helped us to distinguish between articles of high luxury, distributed from Kiev to towns throughout Russia, and other less expensive articles found only in a much more restricted number of towns. Goods bought in Smolensk are limited to an area of about 200–250 km radius, and in the principality of Kiev 400 km is the greatest distance separating places in which the same type of ornament has been found. One thing only is certain: the goods made by urban master-craftsmen were transported to other towns, but hardly ever to the surrounding villages. The customers of all categories of craftsmen came from an elevated social class of consumers. In these circumstances, therefore, the notion of the local market as it existed in Central Europe cannot be shown to apply to Russia. The markets in Russian towns during the eleventh and twelfth centuries were still dominated by the demands of the ruling class; their clientèle was wide but from one level of society only; the network they constituted was a tenuous one, but nevertheless it effectively connected territories remote from each other and integrated them into international trade routes. It would have been difficult to have linked the urban network more closely because population and settlement were so thinly distributed over the countryside; moreover the villages were insulated from the exchange of goods by the workings of the manorial system.

Thanks to the chronicles we know how the exchange of goods worked in an urban market. There were at least two such markets in Kiev, one in a suburb on the river bank, and the other on a higher terrace in the town itself. Some sessions took place weekly and some daily. About the middle of the eleventh century the age of merchant-warriors came to an end; until then their burials reveal to us the imposing arsenal of weapons they needed to guard their goods (*tovar*) when they travelled even in groups (here we find the etymology of the word *tovarishch*). Professional merchants began to operate with the help of short- and long-term credits bearing monthly interest. The Russian Law (*Russkaya Pravda*) in its three eleventh- and twelfth-century versions was much concerned with usury and trading credits; and there is evidence from other sources of a fall in interest rates from

50 per cent (considered usurious) to 20 per cent or even 6 per cent, as recommended by Vladimir Monomachos after the uprising in Kiev in 1113. When a debt was liquidated, the first creditors to be repaid were the foreign merchants, next the prince, then 'the others can divide whatever is left'. There are also short notes on how goods were to be consigned to alien merchants for trading. In Novgorod there were merchants' gilds from the mid-twelfth century; one of them was based near the church of St John the Baptist on Opoky (Ivan Predtetcha na Opokakh) and was governed according to a written charter of the twelfth century by which its autonomy was guaranteed. Its members were merchants specialising in the wax trade and they also had a monopoly of weights and customs payments. The gild had its own church and port; its elected leaders (*starosty*) held important political positions in the town. Another gild, near the Parasceve church (*Pyatnitsa*), was concerned with overseas trade.

In both Russia and the territories of the western Slavs towns made their first appearance at a time when a subsistence economy predominated and the movement of goods was still restricted. But the very different geo-historical conditions obtaining in Russia meant that the rhythm of urbanisation there was also different and until the thirteenth century the process impinged hardly at all on the life of the countryside, although it certainly helped to activate the levels of external exchange in the hands of lords. The Mongol catastrophe halted tentative beginnings of the penetration of urban economic activity into the countryside. The latter, even around Novgorod which preserved its big town status, remained impervious to the expanding foreign trade of Novgorod and its satellites which was based on the handicrafts needed to meet the demands of the ruling classes living in the fortified towns.

IV. *Conclusion*

An analysis of the ways in which the larger economic regions took shape suggests that the process was the result either of a specialisation of economic functions; or of the division of those specialisations in space and between different social groups; or else of the unification of small, differentiated regions with their own exchanges of local surpluses into larger economic regions, the whole reinforced by a political and institutional superstructure.

At the beginning of the Middle Ages the Slavonic peoples were quickly brought together by means of a long-range luxury trade into vast economic regions which by their very nature remained weak and whose very limited commerce was guaranteed by the first large states. The next stage was the slow and patient development of quite another structure, one based upon a money economy and exchanges between urban communities of merchants and craftsmen on the one hand and the arable farmers and cattle-breeders of the countryside on the other, but one which also relied on economic relations between the towns themselves as the latter developed into a hierarchy of urban centres. Thus, both locally and on a countrywide scale, economic regions took shape which also acquired the characteristic political superstructure of the epoch: that was, of course, the feudal principality.

CHAPTER VIII

The Trade of Eastern Europe in the Later Middle Ages

I. *Introduction*

The region under discussion stretches from the Oder and the Bohemian Forest eastwards as far as the Caspian Sea; it is bordered on the north by the Baltic and on the south it extends beyond the Carpathian mountains and Transylvania down to the Black Sea. In the late Middle Ages the various regions making up this territory were not all at the same stage of economic development and there are thus important differences in the timing and pace of the changes which occurred. In common with the rest of Europe at that time the larger economic units had still to make their appearance. Thus, when we wish to find out about the trade of the area, we have to consider disparate regions whose economic contacts were haphazard, for no state in eastern Europe had as yet created a uniform economic organisation even though some such tendencies could already be observed in, e.g. Bohemia and Poland.

The territory can usefully be divided into two main regions – the western, including Bohemia, Poland and the Slovak provinces of Hungary, and the eastern, comprising present-day Russia. The western region had by the thirteenth century already experienced a period of rapid development. In Bohemia this had probably come to an end by the latter part of the fourteenth century, whereas elsewhere it lasted, with some important exceptions, into the following century. On the other hand the Mongol invasion had caused a serious economic setback in a large part of the eastern region during the first half of the thirteenth century. Conclusive evidence of economic recovery can only be found in the second half of the fourteenth century when a period of relatively rapid growth began which continued into the succeeding centuries. The separation of these two main regions by the vast territories of the great Lithuanian duchy is a further complication, for the duchy was itself economically very varied and it exhibited features characteristic of both the western and eastern regions.

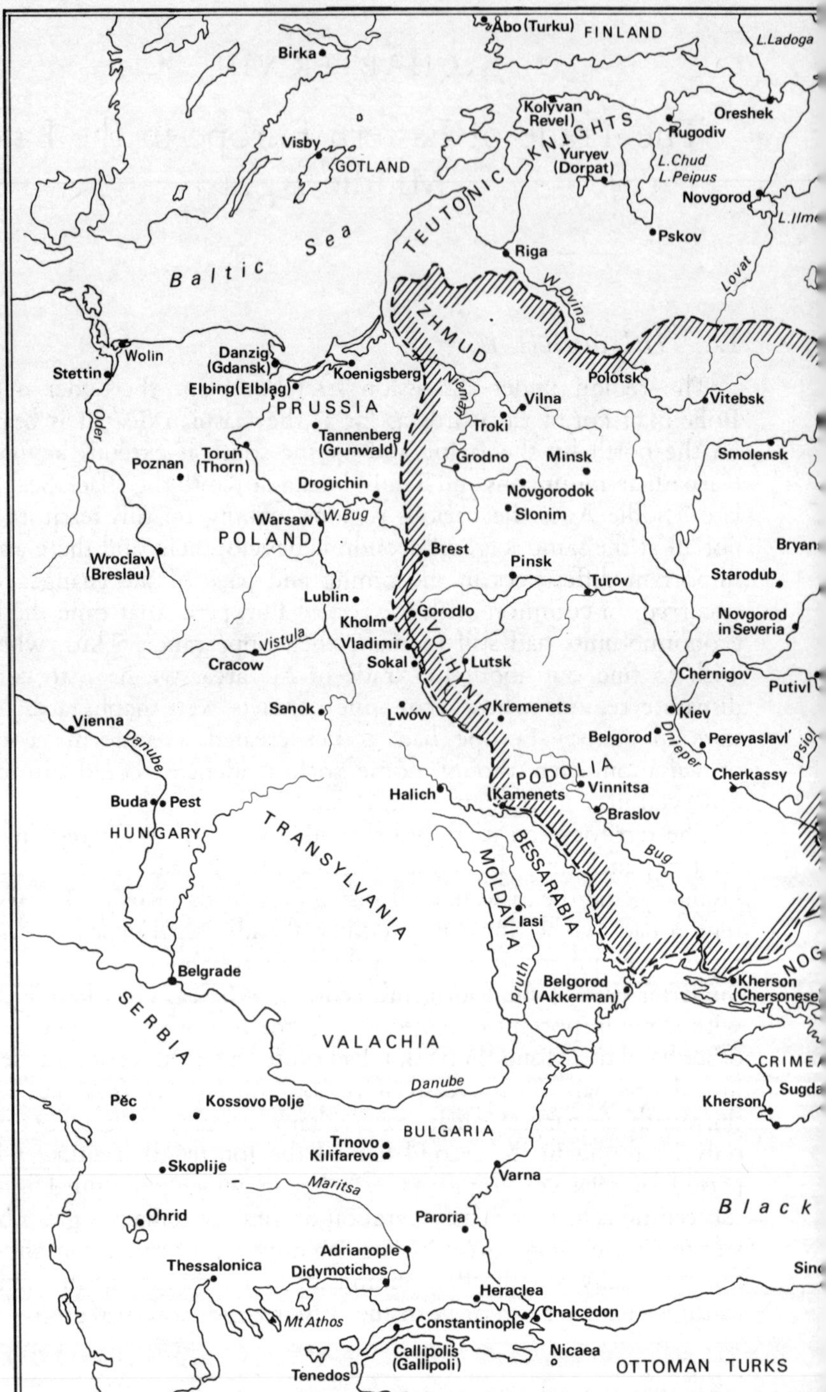
Åbo (Turku)
FINLAND
L. Ladoga
Birka
Kolyvan
Revel)
Oreshek
Rugodiv
TEUTONIC KNIGHTS
Visby
GOTLAND
Yuryev
(Dorpat)
L. Chud
L. Peipus
Novgorod
L. Ilme
Pskov
Sea
Baltic
Riga
W. Dvina
Lovat
ZHMUD
Wolin
Stettin
Danzig
(Gdansk)
Koenigsberg
Elbing (Elbląg)
Niemen
Polotsk
Vitebsk
Oder
PRUSSIA
Vilna
Troki
Tannenberg
(Grunwald)
Smolensk
Torun
(Thorn)
Poznan
Grodno
Minsk
Drogichin
Novgorodok
Slonim
Warsaw
W. Bug
POLAND
Brest
Wrocław
(Breslau)
Pinsk
Turov
Bryan
Starodub
Lublin
Gorodlo
Novgorod
in Severia
Kholm
Vistula
Vladimir
VOLHYNIA
Cracow
Sokal
Lutsk
Chernigov
Putivl
Sanok
Kremenets
Lwów
Kiev
Vienna
Danube
Belgorod
Dnieper
Pereyaslavl'
Psiol
PODOLIA
Halich
Vinnitsa
Cherkassy
Buda
Pest
Kamenets
Braslov
HUNGARY
TRANSYLVANIA
BESSARABIA
MOLDAVIA
Bug
Iasi
Belgrade
Pruth
Belgorod
(Akkerman)
NOG
Kherson
(Chersonese)
SERBIA
VALACHIA
CRIMEA
Danube
Pěc
Kossovo Polje
Kherson
Sugda
BULGARIA
Trnovo
Kilifarevo
Skoplije
Varna
Maritsa
Black
Ohrid
Paroria
Adrianople
Thessalonica
Didymotichos
Sin
Heraclea
Chalcedon
Mt Athos
Constantinople
Callipolis
(Gallipoli)
Nicaea
OTTOMAN TURKS
Tenedos

Map 7. Eastern Europe in the Later Middle Ages

II. *Trade in the Southern Half of Eastern Europe*

Let us start by considering the westernmost part of central-eastern Europe. Attention needs first to be drawn to the far-reaching regional differences in this area that historians and scholars working in this field have either summarily passed over or completely ignored. Thus, by the thirteenth century, in the area including Bohemia, Śląsk (Silesia), Małopolska (Little Poland), Upper Hungary and south-west Russia there was much greater economic activity than in the lands further north, and this activity was not only economic but also political and cultural. Central Poland developed at a slower pace, the greatest economic activity in the thirteenth and fourteenth centuries occurring in the Baltic region which at that time formed the springboard for a powerful German expansion into the heart of the continent. However, by the end of the fourteenth and the beginning of the fifteenth centuries the trends were reversed. Expanding economically and politically, the Polish, Lithuanian and Russian peoples took advantage of the favourable state of the market for their goods and tried to open up for themselves a route through the Baltic to western markets. In the course of the fifteenth century there were various signs of the emergence of large economic units, although it was a long time before these were fully formed. All these tendencies were particularly obvious where trade was concerned, and research in this field throws much light on the entire economic life of eastern Europe. It is also worth mentioning that, by contrast with the many countries in western Europe which experienced a period of grave economic and social crisis in the fourteenth and part of the fifteenth centuries, Poland, Lithuania, and later Russia, developed relatively very rapidly at that time, and in doing so overcame many aspects of their historical backwardness. But this was not the case in Bohemia where at the end of the fourteenth century a severe economic and social crisis helped to precipitate revolution and far-reaching change.

The Sudeten and Carpathian mountain chains constituted the axis of the most southerly territories of central-eastern Europe. The adjacent regions were, in the twelfth century, the scene of a rapid growth in settlement and rural economy and because the process was considerably accelerated in the thirteenth century it led to some fundamental structural changes. These found expression not only in a considerable extension of the land under cultivation, but also, in the Carpathians, in the growth of stock-rearing and an advance in agricultural techniques, as well as a change in the system of peasant dues. First in Bohemia and Silesia and later, though at a slower rate, in Little Poland (Małopolska) there was a change-over from labour dues and payments in kind to a system of dues paid in money at a strictly regulated level. This process, connected with the diffusion of so-called German law, was cause and result of an intensification of the agricultural economy which already had at its disposal large surpluses for sale in rural and urban markets. In the same period the expansion of already existing towns was accelerated and many new craft and trade centres came into being. In Polish studies it is now generally accepted that settlement according to German law was accompanied by a notable improvement in the economic condition of a large number of peasants. These improvements were the result of stabilising the level of dues and also of securing the peasants' hereditary right to their holdings. Some Czech historians, on the other hand, hold that by imposing many additional duties on the peasants, the landowners nullified the advantages the peasants had gained from the imposition of the new law and the gradual depreciation of money dues.[1] This assumption seems scarcely justified in face of the fact that a network of trading settlements rapidly developed in Bohemia in the thirteenth and fourteenth centuries in which peasants sold their produce and bought industrial products. Had economic conditions really deteriorated, it would be hard to explain this phenomenon. An expansion of crafts points also to the greater prosperity of many peasants in the territory under consideration. It must be emphasised that the concentration of crafts in towns did not take place merely to satisfy the needs of the local market, but also the needs of the surrounding peasant population. It can safely be claimed that, from the thirteenth century onwards, there was a noticeable increase in the economic ties between town and country in this area, and thus, as in the West, merchants and craftsmen gained ascendancy over the peasants. Bohemian merchants took advantage of the peasants' straitened circumstances before the harvest or in the period when dues had to be paid, either to buy grain, wine or other products cheaply or to give the peasants advances on future supplies of agricultural produce at relatively low prices. Craftsmen applied similar methods when they tried to limit the freedom of action of the rural population in towns by fixing prices at a level favourable to themselves.[2] Polish sources of the thirteenth and fourteenth centuries are less informative on this aspect; it may be supposed, however, that conditions in southern Poland were similar, although the towns, much less developed than in Bohemia, were not in a position to exert as much pressure on the rural population as they

[1] F. Graus, *Dejiny venkovskeho lidu* (Prague, 1957), II, 171–88.
[2] *Ibid*, II, 106–13.

did in Bohemia. There can be no doubt, however, that trade between town and countryside developed throughout the whole region, as the relatively widespread increase in prosperity shows.

The rapid, though uneven, development of towns in this area in the thirteenth and fourteenth centuries constituted a powerful stimulus to the growth of the rural economy, but both of these phenomena were also influenced by other factors, namely an expansion of mining, characteristic of the whole region at that time, and a new and very advantageous system of major trade routes. Bohemia was in a very fortunate position because of its natural resources, of which silver and tin were the most important. From the thirteenth century Bohemia led Europe in the field of the exploitation of metals. It is obvious that economic and political development stimulated the exploitation of these natural resources, but the abundance of silver and the presence of a certain amount of gold, tin and iron had a powerful influence on economic activity by simultaneously accelerating the growth of a money economy. From the beginning of the thirteenth century, first Jihlava, then Kutná Horá and the smaller centres, supplied the Bohemian economy with silver and this partly explains the introduction into circulation of the Bohemian *grossus* and *florinus* which provided a model for the monetary systems of many neighbouring countries. The development of silver and gold mining in Bohemia slowed down at the end of the fourteenth century. Technical difficulties arising from the exhaustion of the shallower seams of ore and from the pressure of subterranean waters provoked a grave crisis in Bohemian mining particularly in the fifteenth century.

Similar conditions may be observed in the Slovak and Transylvanian provinces of Hungary where, from the middle of the thirteenth and on into the fourteenth centuries, the exploitation of copper, silver and also gold (the latter particularly in Transylvania) developed on a large scale. Because the level of economic development was less advanced here than in Bohemia, however, these metals were more important for foreign trade. In these regions, also, technical difficulties caused a considerable fall in output during the fifteenth century. These difficulties could only be overcome by very large investment which was not undertaken in Bohemia and Upper Hungary until the end of the fifteenth century.

Silesia from the beginning of the thirteenth century, and Little Poland and south-western Russia somewhat later, were also the scene of mining development, though the last two areas had less valuable deposits at their disposal than those mentioned earlier. In Silesia lead ores with an admixture of silver were extracted in the region of Bytom from the twelfth to the second half of the fourteenth centuries; iron and lead ores, and a little gold, were mined at the foot of the Sudeten mountains. This was extracted in large quantities for the last time in the thirteenth century but occasionally even in the fourteenth century in the region of Złotorya, Lwówek and Mikołajowice; in addition the gold deposits in Złoty Stok and the duchy of Opawa were tapped. The extraction of iron ore by mining techniques began at the latest in the fourteenth century. From the twelfth century the natural resources of Silesia, particularly gold, attracted settlers from the West, especially from Germany, and this had a powerful influence on the whole economic development of the area.[3]

The turning point in the exploitation of salt in Little Poland also occurred in the thirteenth century. It had previously only been extracted from salt springs, but in this period salt mines were opened up in Bochnia and Wieliczka, and later in Galician Russia. It is impossible to separate these happenings from the growth and general development of the needs of southern Poland's population. Furthermore Little Poland's salt became an important factor in the development of long-distance trade, particularly with Hungary and Silesia. A similar phenomenon, generally under-rated by Polish historians, may be observed in the mining of lead and silver ores in Olkusz and, later, in Trzebinia and Chęciny, where the admixture of silver was smaller than in those countries mentioned above. However, the abundance of lead was an important element in the trade of Little Poland. Here the mining of iron to serve the internal needs of the country also developed.[4]

The general economic expansion in the region under discussion and the characteristic exploitation of natural resources had a powerful influence on long-distance trade in central-eastern Europe, and on the establishment of a serviceable system of trade routes in that period. Certain external features of great significance also came into play. In the second half of the thirteenth century important trading centres sprang up on the Black Sea, the Lower Don and the Volga; such centres as Soldaia (Sudak) and Caffa in the Crimea, Tana and Sarai. These were at the end of the great caravan routes coming to the West from China and Persia. Genoese colonies in the Crimea maintained their ties with Constantinople and had, in addition, constant contact with Trebizond and other ports on the Black Sea which had connections with the Persian Gulf and India. Thus they acted as a magnet to all the countries of eastern Europe and even to regions considerably further away. All these circumstances led to to the formation of a new

[3] H. Aubin, *Geschichte Schlesiens* (Breslau, 1938), I, 365; *Historia Śląska* (Wrocław/Breslau, 1961), II, 100–6; *Zarys dziejow hutrictwa na ziemiach polskich* (Katowice, 1960), I, 120–30.

[4] D. Molenda, *Górnictwo kruszctwe na terenie złóż ślasko-krakowskich do połowy XVI wieku* (Wrocław, 1963), 49ff; B. Zientara, *Dzieje małopolskiegio hutnictwa żelaznego XIV–XVI wieku* (Warsaw, 1954).

system of routes, particularly favourable for southern Poland, south-west Russia, Hungary, Moldavia and Wallachia. An attempt will be made later in this chapter to show that this formation, allied with the whole system of great transport routes, had a favourable influence not only on the growth of the long-distance trade of central-eastern Europe, but that it also acted as a stimulus to other economic activities, especially mining, which played such an important role in the region.

(1) THE TRADE ROUTES

The convergence of trade routes on the Bohemian Plain was closely connected with its resources of metals. The junction was Prague, capital of the Bohemian state, already by the thirteenth century both wealthy and powerful. Through Regensburg, and a little later through Nuremberg, Prague was linked with the routes to Venice coming from Bruges and Cologne through Frankfurt-on-Main and Bavaria. There was another road via Brno (Brünn) in Moravia, Vienna and Carinthia, although it was less important for Bohemia because of the staple laws in force in Vienna. The same road to Brno led on south-eastwards to Buda, from whence a land route continued as far as Transylvania and the Balkans and on to Chilia at the mouth of the Danube. It was possible to reach northern Hungary from Prague by the road via Olomouc (Olmütz) in Moravia. The routes leading from western Europe to the Black Sea via Bohemia were not, however, so important as the great parallel roads running further north. These roads could be reached from Prague by travelling north or north-east to Zgorzelec (Görlitz) in Upper Lusatia (Lausitz) or to Wrocław (Breslau) in Silesia. They led from the southern Netherlands, or from Frankfurt-on-Main, or Nuremberg, through Erfurt towards Wrocław. From there several roads went further east to Cracow. From the Polish capital they ran first through Vladimir in Volhynia, and afterwards through Lwów (Lvov) and the south Russian steppes to Caffa and Tana. At the end of the fourteenth century, as a result of the decline of Tana, this route turned further south-east and led via Suçeava in Moldavia to Bielgorod (Akkerman, Maurocastro) at the mouth of the Dniester. This port maintained close contacts primarily with Caffa and other towns in the Crimea and with Constantinople. The group of parallel routes for long constituted the chief link between the Netherlands, German and Italy on the one hand and the states on the Black Sea on the other, and played a very important role in the economic life of medieval eastern Europe, forming as it were the chief axis of its foreign trade. Its links with Bohemia have already been mentioned. At various points, particularly at Wrocław and at Cracow, routes coming from Austria and Moravia and from the direction of

Hungary and Transylvania reached the east–west routes from the South. Northward these routes led to the shores of the Baltic, making possible close contact between the southern and northern regions of central-eastern Europe.

When considering the significance of this system of communications, it must be emphasised that it did not by itself decide the character of the trade in the area under review. The structure of economic life in the different parts of the region exercised a far greater influence on the exchange of goods: and it is precisely the economic life of the individual regions that showed such important variations.

Bohemia, with its well-developed agriculture and mining, was undoubtedly the most economically advanced in the thirteenth century. Urban development in Bohemia was also considerably ahead of other eastern European countries. There was a relatively large number of towns and in the thirteenth and fourteenth centuries these showed marked signs of growth. By the beginning of the fourteenth century the population of Prague had certainly reached about 30,000 people, and this placed the capital of Bohemia amongst the large towns of Europe north of the Alps. Other Bohemian towns were considerably smaller, the number of inhabitants as a rule amounting to less than a third of the population of the capital.[5] There is no evidence that the great epidemics of the fourteenth century caused a permanent fall in urban population; probably the gaps caused by plague were quickly filled by an influx of peasants. In the thirteenth and fourteenth centuries the majority of wealthy inhabitants of Prague, Kutná Horá and many other towns were German. It was this rich merchant group, strongly supported by the last rulers of the Přemislid dynasty, and by John of Luxemburg and Charles IV, which governed the towns. Craftsmen and the large numbers of poor people were mostly Bohemians.

In the thirteenth and fourteenth centuries, crafts in the Bohemian towns were almost exclusively geared to the needs of the local and regional markets; foreign trade offered no incentive. This was because the wealthy merchants of Bohemia were almost exclusively interested in the import trade whose costs were defrayed by the export of silver in the form of money.[6] This Bohemian metal was a commodity of the highest value, attracting to the country foreign goods destined for the wealthy groups of nobles, clergy and townsfolk. Its role in the trade was, however, an obstacle to the expansion and improvement of native Bohemian craft production.

[5] F. Graus, *Chudiná mestska v době předhusitske* (Prague, 1949), 116.

[6] F. Graus, 'Die Handelsbeziehungen Böhmens zu Deutschland und Österreich im 14. und zu Beginn des 15. Jahrhunderts', *Historica*, II (1960), 107–8.

(2) THE TRADE OF BOHEMIA

It is possible to distinguish three consecutive phases in the history of Bohemian long-distance trade during the late Middle Ages. In the first period, lasting from the thirteenth to the last decades of the following century, trade developed rapidly. Then at the end of the fourteenth century there was a collapse as a result, perhaps, of the general socio-economic crisis and fall in metal production. During the Hussite revolution (1415–37) economic contacts with western and south-western Europe were seriously weakened. The emigration of the wealthy German merchants had an unfavourable effect, at least initially, upon mining. The Germans were replaced by Bohemian merchants who had less capital at their disposal. In this period some economic contacts began to develop between Bohemia and the countries of eastern and south-eastern Europe. Finally with the end of the revolution there was a renewal of trade ties with the Germans, although these were markedly less close than in the fourteenth century. However, it appears the Bohemian trade with its eastern neighbours increased somewhat.

The absence of sources of a statistical nature prevents a proper explanation of these three phases. Czech historians believe strongly that there was much more foreign trade between Bohemia and the Netherlands, the Germanic countries (including Austria) and Italy, than with north-eastern and southern Europe, especially in the thirteenth and fourteenth centuries. Their thesis seems to be fully justified. The Netherlands, Germany and Italy were in a position to supply those goods demanded by the wealthy classes of Bohemian society and at the same time they themselves needed silver and other metals. Contacts with these countries enabled Bohemia to obtain a supply of many goods for general consumption like salt, herring, etc. The exchange of goods between the borderlands of Bohemia and their German and Austrian neighbours was also very important: this exchange was especially active when long-distance trade was seriously disrupted by the Hussite revolution. However, Bohemian contacts with Poland, and even with Hungary, appear to play a smaller role in the thirteenth and fourteenth centuries.

Cloth was undoubtedly the most important item in Bohemian long-distance trade. It is possible that fabrics from Flanders made their way to Bohemia as early as the twelfth century, though Bohemian sources provide evidence of the existence of such imports only from the end of the thirteenth century, which seems too late a date for the beginning of the trade. According to information gathered by early scholars and more recently by Graus, scarlet cloth was imported from

Ghent in the fourteenth and fifteenth centuries, but textiles from Ypres, Poperinghe and Courtrai were more important. As in many other European countries in the fourteenth century, cloth from Brabant, but especially from Brussels, began partially to supersede products from Flanders. According to a well-known list of foreign goods imported at the end of the thirteenth century, wax, tin and silver were supplied to Bruges by Bohemia.[7] The fact that these goods were constant items on lists of goods appearing in the town markets shows that some economic contacts between Flanders and Bohemia had existed for a long period. Other sources seem to show that the chief *quid pro quo* for the exports from Flanders to Bohemia was Bohemian silver coin. Similarly, close economic ties grew up between Bohemia and the Rhineland and western Germany: from the thirteenth century Bohemia imported much cloth from Cologne and also from Aachen, Mainz, Frankfurt-on-Main and other towns. English textiles also appear in Bohemia from the second half of the fourteenth century, but the development of these imports, as of a supply from the northern Netherlands, occurred in a later period.

Western cloth was transported by routes leading from Flanders through Cologne and other Rhineland towns, and thence through Nuremberg, Amberg, Plzen (Pilsen) or Cheb (Eger) to Prague, or by a less direct route through Regensburg. From an early period Regensburg had lively contacts with Bohemia and eastern Europe as far as Kiev. This trade was seriously weakened in the second half of the thirteenth century owing to the fall of Kiev and changes in the network of trade routes; none the less, the contacts between Regensburg, the Bavarian towns and Bohemia remained very close.

During the fourteenth century, Nuremberg became more important. With the help of their own metal and, later, textile production and their contacts with Venice and the Netherlands, Nuremberg merchants expanded their trade to include the whole of eastern Europe and, particularly, Bohemia, Poland and Hungary. Prague was the chief centre for the distribution of western cloth in Bohemia. From there it found its way to Brno in Moravia and still further to Bratislava (Pressburg), at that time part of Hungary. To a certain extent, Brno was supplied with cloth and other goods from western Europe by the route through Wrocław, whence goods came via the Baltic or the north-west.

We have no data that would support any statistics about the supply of western cloth to Bohemia. However, there seems to be no doubt that imports increased markedly in the thirteenth century, i.e. during

[7] F. Graus, *Česky obchod se suknem ve 14, a počatkem 15. stoleti* (Prague, 1950), 13ff.

Bohemia's period of economic development, and lasted into the following century. Obviously western textiles were only accessible to the relatively wealthy sections of the population, and thus the volume of imports must have been limited.

Bohemia's economic contacts with Italy were undoubtedly looser than those with Germany, though trade with Venice played a considerable role. Bohemia received silk textiles and spices which it certainly paid for mainly with its silver coinage, although occasionally there appear references to a supply of Bohemian knives to Venice. A similar outflow of silver accompanied the monetary transactions of John of Luxemburg and Charles IV in Florence; however, it appears that Bohemia imported practically no Florentine goods in the fourteenth century.

Sources from Bohemia, the Netherlands and Germany provide evidence of the active participation of merchants from Bohemian towns, particularly Prague, in long-distance trade. In the fourteenth century, and perhaps even earlier, they set out for Bruges and frequented the fairs in Frankfurt-on-Main, where more than once they cleared their liabilities. In the fourteenth century they appeared also in Venice. In spite of this, foreigners were more active in long-distance trade. Merchants from the Rhineland occupied an important position in this field while the Flemings, who formerly travelled to Bohemia, vanished from the region. Regensburg and Nuremberg merchants, who supplied Bohemia not only with goods from Germany and the Netherlands but also from Italy and the Levant, were particularly active. Ties with Austria, otherwise very important for Bohemia, did not play a large part in the long-distance trade because of the strictly enforced staple regulations in Vienna from the middle of the thirteenth century. For their expeditions to Venice, Bohemian merchants probably used the road via Regensburg and Straubing to the Adriatic and vice versa. Vienna certainly participated in the transit trade to Bohemia and Moravia. Some Italian and French wine, and undoubtedly goods from Venice and the Levant, came there via Vienna. However, the exchange of grain from Bohemia for cattle from Austria was significant in Austro-Bohemian relations and of the greatest importance to both countries. Already in the first half of the fourteenth century, cloth of rather low quality from Brno appeared in Vienna, which was also the centre for exporting a large quantity of Austrian wine to Bohemia: this return trade in wine, however, was not very frequent. Access to Moravia, a part of the kingdom of Bohemia, was important for Viennese trade because the routes leading to north-eastern Europe, and particularly to the Baltic via Poland, ran through it. However, neither Polish nor Austrian trade along this route gained greater impetus, although in the fourteenth century Poland made attempts to increase it, and in any case, Polish cloth reached Vienna by the Moravian route via Brno or Olomouc.

It must be assumed that there was a rough balance between Bohemian grain exports to Austria and imports from Austria, and that less Bohemian money flowed abroad along this route than to the west and north-west.

The significance of Bavaria and Salzburg in Bohemian long-distance trade has already been indicated. From early times, salt from the Salzkammergut was brought to Bohemia via Passau. In return Bohemia supplied cattle. The Bohemian town of Prachatice played a large part in this border trade.

Local and foreign wines were exported from Bavaria to Prague. From the Carolingian period onwards the most important Bavarian town trading with Bohemia was Regensburg, but Augsburg, Munich, Landshut Rothenburg and especially Nuremberg were also actively concerned. The accounts of the Runtinger company from 1383 to 1407, edited by Bastian, include valuable material on the foreign trade of Bohemia at the end of the pre-Hussite period. The Runtinger company was engaged, first and foremost, in transporting Levantine goods from Venice, Italian silks and cotton materials (Milanese fustian) and spices such as ginger, Aragon saffron etc. to Bohemia, while goods from Bavaria and Upper Germany played only a very limited role in its trade.[8] The Runtinger accounts throw light on the export of Bohemian silver coins to Bavaria, although this was by no means the only Bohemian commodity the Runtingers were interested in. In Prague they were able to acquire Hungarian florins, much sought after by western European merchants. They also made contact through Prague with merchants from Cracow. It is possible to agree with the view of Czech scholars that there was a considerable outflow of metals from Bohemia to Upper Germany. However, the problem requires further research since it is probably unwise to generalise from the accounts of one company which was so closely connected with Venetian trade.[9] It may be assumed that the Bavarian merchants of more modest rank, and particularly those from Nuremberg, were much more interested in the Upper German trade in fustian

[8] A. Dietz, *Frankfurter Handelsgeschichte*, I (Frankfurt, 1910), 30, 31; Graus, *Česky obchod*, 30, 31; H. Simonsfeld, *Der Fondacho dei Tedeschi in Venedig und die deutsch-venetianischen Handelsbeziehungen* (2 vols., Stuttgart, 1887), I, 96, 101; Z. Winter, *Dejiny remesla a obchodu ve 14.–15. stoleti* (Prague, 1906), 357, 358; F. Bastian, *Das Runtingerbüch und verwandtes Material zum Regensburger–Südostdeutschen Handel und Münzwesen* (3 vols., Regensburg, 1935–40), I, 151, 152.

[9] Bastian, *op. cit.*, I, 26–8, 632–9; II, 52, 53, 57, 61, 62ff.

and metal products than were the wealthy Runtingers, for this trade required a smaller cash investment and satisfied a wider demand than did luxury articles. There is no doubt that cheaper goods for everyday use played a significant role in the earlier, expansionist, phase of the Nuremberg merchants' activity in Bohemia in the fourteenth century, as they certainly did in Poland, which the merchants reached through the St Wenceslaus crown territories. Undoubtedly they, too, took away some silver coins from Bohemia but they were also interested in copper, Bohemian tin and certain other goods. We are forced to conclude, nevertheless, that these imports from Germany, the Netherlands and elsewhere, though the goods may not necessarily have been expensive, must have had a depressing influence on the conditions of Bohemian craftsmen who were protected neither by the state nor by the wealthy merchants governing the cities. Thus it seems likely that the disadvantageous aspects of Bohemian trade with the West should not be confined to the outflow of metals. We must take into consideration competition from the more highly developed Upper German crafts, which certainly drew some of their raw materials from Bohemia.

Economic ties with its northern neighbours were important for Bohemia, even though the bulk of Bohemian external trade went to the West. At the end of the thirteenth century Bohemia was maintaining contacts with such distant centres as Hamburg, Szczecin (Stettin) and Lübeck, though in a later period the Hanseatic towns, with the exception of Torún (Thorn), did not show much interest in Bohemian affairs. According to Graus, the staple regulations in force in Dresden and Magdeburg, by preventing the use of the Elbe as a waterway to the north, closed the door to the Hanseatic region against Bohemian merchants. This did not hinder the development of trade between the towns of northern Bohemia and Saxony, Meissen and Lusatia (Lausitz). Thus, merchants from the town of Litoměřice reached Magdeburg: Žatec, Chomutov and other Bohemian centres were also engaged in this trade. Salt was taken from Halle by way of Leipzig and for this the upper reaches of the Elbe were used. Dried and salt fish, including Baltic herring, were bought in Pirna, Dresden and Meissen: mead and other goods were also obtained from Meissen. Some cloth from the Netherlands and Germany and woollen materials from Lusatia, particularly from Zgorzelec (Görlitz) and Zittau where production of medium quality cloth had developed on a large scale in the fourteenth century, were taken by northern routes. Perhaps already in the fourteenth century some cattle were driven to Bohemia from the northern borderlands. In return Bohemia sent its grain and metals, as well as a little cloth and beer. Attention has recently been drawn to the fact that, in the north and north-west border towns of Bohemia, coins from Meissen were in use, just as in the German territories bordering on the Bohemian plain Bohemian coins often appeared in transactions. It is possible to argue that the trade of Bohemia was roughly in balance, but the possibility still remains that the situation was unfavourable to Bohemia: in that good quality money flowed out of the country while inferior coinage forced its way in.[10]

Bohemia's contacts with Silesia are not very clear. This territory, originally a part of the Polish state, came in the first half of the fourteenth century under the rule of the Bohemian crown; at the same time, as will be shown later, it was closely tied economically to Poland. Wrocław (Breslau), the chief Silesian trade centre, developed first and foremost because of the trade between Poland and Germany. Nevertheless, throughout this whole period, important trade routes passed through Wrocław, connecting the mouths of the Oder and Vistula with Prague. Wrocław supplied Bohemia with some cloth from the Netherlands. Baltic herring, and perhaps also Russian furs and other goods from the Hanseatic trade area, reached Prague by the same road. Wrocław, trading with the south Russian territories in the fourteenth and fifteenth centuries and obtaining by the same route some goods of Levantine origin from Tana and Caffa, sent some of these on to Moravia and Bohemia. The whole problem would benefit by further research. Wrocław, the chief Silesian trading town, closely tied to Zgorzelec, was most certainly the export centre both for its own cloth and that of Zgorzelec; cloth and beer from Świdnica (Schweidnitz), quite popular in the area in the fourteenth and fifteenth centuries, and from Opava, were brought into Bohemia from Silesia. Imports of cattle from Poland via Silesia, which later became very important for Bohemia, are not confirmed by fourteenth-century sources. So far no work on Silesian imports from Bohemia has been published. In the thirteenth and fourteenth centuries it was undoubtedly confined to a little grain, cloth, ore and metal goods, though in the field of mining and crafts, Silesia was not only self-sufficient but, in the course of time, even began to export its own products. In the fourteenth century, up to the outbreak of the Hussite revolution, the chief route for the expansion of the business done by Nuremberg merchants in eastern Europe led through Prague and Wrocław. Italians

[10] Graus, 'Die Handelsbeziehungen', 104, 105.

also came to Silesia and to Poland by this route in the fourteenth century, and even at the beginning of the fifteenth. There are no grounds for asserting that economic ties between Bohemia and Silesia were strengthened as a result of Bohemian rule over that region. The well-known separatist policy of Wrocław was apparent during the Hussite period in the fifteenth century. Obviously during the revolution the social and national aspects of its policy were decidedly unfavourable to the German and Catholic patriciate governing Wrocław. None the less, during the reign of George of Podiebrad, Wrocław and the Silesian merchants treated the moderate Hussite king with hostility and inclined towards Poland or Hungary. It was unthinkable that Silesia could have been closely tied to the Bohemian economy in this period. When, after the loss of the German throne in 1404, the Bohemian King Vaclav IV (Wenzel) came into conflict with many of the German principalities, there was a plan to carry on the bulk of the trade with the Prussian Order of the Teutonic Knights through Silesia and Wielkopolska (Great Poland). The accounts of the Order from the end of the fourteenth and beginning of the fifteenth centuries point to some contacts between Prussia and Prague; however, these were probably not very important.[11] The revolution in Bohemia and the uncertain conditions in Silesia later made it difficult to use routes which passed through these regions.

Economic relations between Bohemia and Poland in the thirteenth and fourteenth centuries were very flexible. Polish sources often pass over this question in complete silence. Poland exported very cheap, plain and dyed cloth, which, as is well known, carried the lowest duty of all textile products.[12] The import of Polish cloth, lead and, perhaps, salt which was probably exported from Little Poland to Bohemia via Silesia, balanced the supply of Bohemian goods to Poland. We may suppose that already in the fourteenth century, some knives and other Bohemian metal goods known from fifteenth- and sixteenth-century Polish sources, reached Little and Great Poland. Bohemian wine could not rely on finding a market in Poland which imported its wine from Hungary and other countries. Amongst the towns belonging to the Bohemian crown, only Wrocław was actively engaged in trade with south-west Russia and, indirectly, with Tana and Caffa. From the middle of the fourteeth century the rulers of Poland and their towns endeavoured to hinder this trade, though they were usually unsuccessful. It is possible that, as a result of trade along the Bohemia–Silesia–

[11] C. Scattler, *Handelsrechnungen des Deutschen Ordens* (Leipzig, 1887), 36, 210, 266.
[12] Graus, *Česky obchod*, 46, 47.

Little Poland–south west Russia route, limited quantities of Bohemian silver coins reached the Black Sea regions, and already by the thirteenth century or even earlier, a few industrial products, such as limestone distaffs produced in the district around Owrucz, came in the opposite direction from south-west Russia. It is doubtful whether Levantine goods reached Bohemia, at that time so closely tied to Upper Germany and hence to Venice, via Cracow and Wrocław in any quantity. But it is clear from other sources that Upper German merchants carried Venetian and oriental goods to Poland via Bohemia and Silesia.

We may assume that the rather limited trade between Bohemia itself and Poland produced a favourable balance for Poland. This partially explains the flow of Bohemian silver coins to Poland in the fourteenth and fifteenth centuries. The probability is, however, that there must have been other reasons for this quite considerable flow, but, because of the absence of recent research into the monetary history of Poland from the thirteenth to the fifteenth centuries, it is difficult to say anything more definite on this score.

Economic contacts between Bohemia and Hungary were different in character. In the late medieval period Hungary, like Bohemia, was an important producer of gold, silver, copper and iron; deposits of these were present in Slovakia and Transylvania. However, cattle were reared in large numbers on the Hungarian plain. In addition there was a wave of German migration into Hungary in the thirteenth century which led to the development of mining there too. Thus mining products and cattle were Hungary's chief exports from a very early period and they went mainly to Vienna, Upper Germany and Italy. The staple regulations in Vienna, the growing activity of merchants from Nuremberg and other south German towns from the fourteenth century, combined with the relative weakness of the Hungarian middle classes, meant that its export trade to the West was in the hands of foreigners. Bohemian merchants also tried to build up connections with Hungary in the fourteenth century in which the most valuable goods for Bohemia were again Hungary's gold and cattle. Bohemia's exports to Hungary were different from those to other countries. The question has been very little investigated; none the less one may say that Bohemia supplied Hungary with its own and foreign industrial goods, the latter coming from Bohemia's transit trade. Thus, some cloth from the Netherlands and Germany and certainly textiles from Italy reached Hungary via Bohemia. This trade was not carried on by Bohemians alone: merchants from the Rhineland and Upper Germany, and (in the fourteenth century) newcomers from Cologne and Nuremberg in particular, using the roads via Prague, Brno in Moravia and Bratislava in northern Hungary, endeavoured to bypass Vienna. In the fourteenth century Bohemian merchants reached Buda, but they did not penetrate further. Hungary was a market for the sale of cheap Bohemian cloth. By the middle of the fourteenth century at the latest this cloth was taken from the Hungarian plain as far south as Dubrovnik. It was also sent east to Transylvania and Moldavia. However, these may have been Silesian textiles, which were much in demand in Transylvania, Moravia and Wallachia, passing as Bohemian cloth. There is no proof that these exports, which are confirmed by sources from the end of the fourteenth and beginning of the fifteenth centuries, assumed greater proportions at that time; none the less they must have been important for the under-developed Bohemian cloth industry which, even at home, could scarcely cope with foreign competition. It is safe to assume that some goods from the Levant reached Hungary via Bohemia, even though Hungary received supplies from many other directions. The chief Hungarian exports to Bohemia were cattle and gold money, and a considerable part of the latter passed through Bohemia into Germany. The trade between Bohemia and Hungary cannot, of course, be compared with that passing between Hungary and Vienna: however, during the fourteenth century both sides set great store by it. Its importance finds particular expression in the policies of the kings of Bohemia, John of Luxemburg and Charles IV, who sought privileges for Bohemian merchants in Hungary, and in the active attention the Hungarian rulers gave to this question.

Thus, during the thirteenth and fourteenth centuries, Bohemia was deeply engaged in long-distance trade and this fact influenced the growth of towns, particularly the capital, Prague. But the appraisal of the situation by German scholars and earlier Czech historians has been very onesided, since they attribute the growth to the unusually active part Charles IV played as ruler of Bohemia. They point to the countless immunities from customs duty which he granted to Bohemian merchants in Germany, as well as to the privileges secured for them in Hungary and to his initiative in re-directing the main trade route from Bruges to Venice via Prague. Recent Czech research, however, correctly draws attention to the fact that the policy of the kings of the Luxemburg dynasty mainly favoured Bohemian economic ties with Germany, and thus indirectly increased the outflow of silver, so characteristic of this trade. Czech historians also point out that the huge sums of money collected in Bohemia by King John and his successor to finance their dynastic policies had important and unfavourable effects which led to the depreciation of Bohemian currency and, at the end of the fourteenth century, to more widespread economic and social difficulties. The crown's energetic support for wealthy merchants, who were mostly Germans primarily engaged in trade with the West, had the same effect. Bohemian crafts were victims of these political and economic policies. They could not develop because of foreign competition, lack of protection and fiscal pressure from the patriciate and state government. All these factors contributed to the great social crisis which finally exploded in the Hussite revolution.[13] The revolution itself provoked the flight of the German clergy, nobility and town patricians: in all the large towns, particularly Prague and Kutná Horá, the German patriciate was gradually replaced by a Bohemian one. At first, however, these men had less financial resources at their disposal than the German merchants had possessed. As the patricate's control over the craft gilds was considerably weakened the gilds began themselves to influence the fate of the towns. This should have favoured an expansion of crafts, but their growth was hindered by foreign and civil wars. In contrast with the views held by earlier scholars, Janaček has recently shown that the breach in economic relations with the Germanic countries was not complete. It is true that Upper German merchants from Nuremberg withdrew from Prague and promoted a blockade of Bohemia; but some of them, more enterprising than others, penetrated Hussite territories, particularly the borderlands, for the did not wish to lose the opportunity to obtain silver. Catholic Plzen became the avenue into Bohemia for the merchants of Nuremberg. At the same time there can be no doubt that the previously much-frequented trade route, running from Bavaria to Hungary or north-eastern Europe, was abandoned. By-passing the Hussite territories, the Nuremberg merchants used the roads joining Saxony and Lusatia to Catholic Silesia or Great Poland. In turn the Wrocław merchants went to Upper Hungary via Catholic Moravia. This new network of roads was consolidated during the fifteenth century.

Recently Czech scholars have drawn attention to the fact that the border trade suffered little during the revolution and sometimes even expanded. Some Bohemian towns in the South and West like Cheb (Eger), Plzen (Pilsen), Domažlice (Taus), Tachov (Tachau) and Jindřichuv Hradec (Neuhaus) profited by this: and in many of these centres there was an increase in the production of cloth intended for export to Linz, Vienna, Bratislava, Nuremberg, etc. The border trade

[13] Graus, *Česky Obchod*, 46ff.

with Austria, which imported Bohemian grain, was maintained. It seems that border contacts with the Meissen region were also strengthened. Rather later, in the fifteenth century, the export of fish to Upper Germany gradually developed as a result of the increase of fisheries on the estates of the great nobles in southern Bohemia. Janaček is of the opinion that the Bohemians did not greatly suffer from a lack of imported goods during the revolutionary period, though at certain times there was a dearth of salt and spices. One may add that when the Hussites attacked Silesia and other neighbouring territories they seized many cattle and this fact points to a scarcity caused by interruptions of foreign trade.

The general limitation of imports from Nuremberg and Upper Germany during the revolutionary period opened up opportunities for the crafts meeting basic needs, particularly metal and textile manufactures. It is interesting to note that the import of cheap Polish cloth into Bohemia ceased in the fifteenth century and was certainly replaced by domestic output.

In the post-revolutionary period (after 1437), economic contacts with south-eastern Europe and particularly with Poland and Russia were strengthened, and this process may have begun somewhat earlier. At the same time trade with Bohemia's southern and south-western neighbours increased: the expansion of agriculture and fisheries in southern Bohemia favoured this by stimulating trade with Austria and Bavaria. The export of knives and Bohemian cloth to Hungary, Transylvania, Moldavia and Wallachia (Oltenia) undoubtedly developed though it did not assume large proportions. Later, in the second half of the fifteenth century, some Bohemian textiles and metal goods appeared in the territories of Poland and south-west Russia: this trade, however, did not acquire importance until the following century.[14] Incessant wars with Hungary, which temporarily controlled Catholic Silesia, made trade with the north-east difficult, but did not interrupt it completely. In fact, it was through Poland that cloth from England, Holland and, to some extent, the southern Netherlands reached Bohemia from the mouth of the Vistula. Doubtless it was also imported from Lübeck and Hamburg via Saxony, Meissen and Lusatia. In the fifteenth century the cloth industry developed rapidly in Zgorzelec in the region of Meissen and Lusatia, and its products were very popular in Bohemia. Salt was again brought from Saxony (as well as from Austria) and, at the end of the fifteenth century, cattle began to be a constant import from Poland.

[14] J. Janaček, 'Der böhmische Aussenhandel in der zweite Hälfte des 15. Jahrhunderts', *Historica*, IV (1962), 39ff.

The merchants from Nuremberg and from Upper Germany only gradually re-established their old contacts with Bohemia, the reason being the mutual distrust carried over from the revolutionary period, as well as the political disturbances and the war which lasted until 1475. The low productivity of silver mining in Bohemia, continuing until the rich new resources in the north of the country began to be exploited at the turn of the sixteenth century, was also partly responsible. It should be noted that the growth of copper and silver mining in Saxony in the second half of the fifteenth century drew the attention of the former German contractors in search of these metals away from Bohemia. King George of Podiebrad, hoping to rebuild Bohemian foreign trade, launched a plan to strengthen contacts with Venice and intended to use the roads running through Little Poland, south-west Russia and Moldavia to the centres of Levantine trade on the Black Sea: these, however, had lost much of their earlier importance by the second half of the fifteenth century.

With research at its present stage, it is difficult to say definitely whether Bohemian merchants were more actively engaged in foreign trade during the Hussite period or in the previous epoch, but there is no doubt the revolution influenced the structure of Bohemian trade considerably. It strengthened the position of home industries on foreign markets up to a point but its main effect was of course on the home market. The improvement in the economic position of the lower and middle ranks of the Bohemian nobility, of a great many townsfolk and of the wealthier peasants, probably provided a powerful incentive to home industrial production which was growing because of a diminished foreign competition. The gilds, whose number and political influence had increased considerably, were able fully to preserve and even to add to the privileges protecting them from rural producers. The royal towns gained in strength, though some private ones, such as Jindřichuv, Hradec and Sobeslav, also developed remarkably. The new merchants relied to some extent on Bohemian products in their activities at home and abroad and made it possible for these goods to reach foreign markets in the south and north-east. Compared with the pre-Hussite period, contacts with these regions were stronger, but did not result in an outflow of metals – a particularly valuable consideration in a period when less silver was being mined. The export of Bohemian grain and wine to neighbouring countries continued and even increased to the South. In addition to the grain, wax and other commodities which had been exported from an early period, new products from the countryside, mainly fish from the southern part of the country, appeared. Home as well as foreign demand gave a considerably greater incentive to Bohemian urban and rural production than had been the case in the fourteenth century. Obviously this process, which cannot be presented statistically because there are no relevant figures, did not run smoothly. The revolutionary war, Hungarian pressure and the numerous political misfortunes of George of Podiebrad, had an unfavourable effect on the country's general situation. King George's successor, the weak Władislaw Jagellon, wholly surrendering himself to the influence of the powerful magnates, could not protect his towns against the competition of the nobility where trade was concerned, and particularly against those private towns which were dependent on the nobles. At the end of the fifteenth century the great lords of southern Bohemia began to consolidate their estates and somewhat later this process was to threaten both peasants and towns. However, in the period under discussion, these disturbing phenomena were scarcely apparent and certainly were not felt on a large scale.

(3) THE TRADE OF SILESIA

Silesia, which began to enter the Bohemian orbit in the second half of the thirteenth century, and became a part of the territories of the crown of St Vaclav in the first half of the following century, was in many respects similar to Bohemia. The development of Silesian mining from the twelfth century onwards has already been mentioned, though its growth was not to be compared to that in Bohemia, or to the great advances in agriculture. Already in an earlier period, there was considerable urbanisation and the process accelerated in the thirteenth century. Some scholars estimate the population of Silesian towns in the middle of the fourteenth century, on the basis of the payment of Peter's Pence, as about 23.1 per cent of total population. This was about 490,000 people (according to other estimates only 376,000) and its growth in the succeeding hundred years was minimal. In the mid-fourteenth century Wrocław (Breslaû) already had between 11,000 and 15,000 inhabitants; by 1403 it had close on 20,000: Glogow (Glogau) had some 11,000 and Nysa (Neisse) about 6,000. The population of most of the remaining towns did not exceed 1–2,000.[15] The growth of Silesian towns is proved by the fact that they were early granted self-government on the basis of Magdeburg law. Złotoryja (Goldberg) obtained its charter as early as 1211, Lwówek (Löwenberg) in 1247, and Wrocław for the first time in 1242. This coincided with

[15] J. Mitkowski, *Uwagi o zaludnieniu Polski na poczatku panowania Kazimierza Wielkiego* (Poznan, 1910), x, 121–35; W. Kula, 'Stan i potrzeby badan nad demografia historyczna dawnej Polski', in *Roczniki Dziejòw Spoleczanychi Gospodarczych*, XIII (1951), 23–109; *Historia Slaska*, II, 17, 19.

the influx of foreigners, particularly wealthy German merchants, miners and craftsmen; even earlier newcomers from the southern Netherlands had settled in Silesia. They were attracted by the mining, especially of gold, a rapidly developing agriculture and, in consequence of these, the favourable perspectives opening up for immigrants. Thanks to the convenient availability of raw materials, the production of cloth, linen and metal goods increased rapidly in Silesia. However, in contrast to Bohemia, production in Silesian towns did not rely upon raw materials of home origin alone. Long-distance trade was an important factor for growth and supplied raw materials as well as providing a large market for the sale of industrial goods.

The network of trade routes already described was immensely favourable to Silesia since it gave access to the great lines of communication running from Germany via Poland and Russia to the Black Sea, and from Bohemia and south-west Europe to the east and to the Baltic.

The long-distance trade of Wrocław and other large Silesian towns can be summarised as consisting of industrial goods from Flanders, England and Germany and of articles of Levantine trade purchased in Bruges or Venice, the latter also reaching Silesia from the Black Sea. A part only of imports from the West were consumed in Silesia. The rest, together with numerous Silesian products, was re-exported to Poland, south-west Russia or Hungary. This, in return, made possible the import of salt, agricultural products, livestock, forestry products and some articles from the Levant, and consequently Silesia's foodstuffs and raw material supplies were considerably augmented in the thirteenth and fourteenth centuries. Since Wrocław belonged to the Hanseatic League, it was also to some extent engaged in maritime trade: nevertheless its activities on the Bruges–Novgorod route were not especially developed. However, the contacts with the Hanseatic League, and particularly with Prussia, enabled Silesian merchants to participate in the supply of cloth, herring and furs to Bohemia, Austria and Venice. Apart perhaps from wine and Italian and Levantine goods, some silver was exported from Bohemia to Silesia, but trade in this direction was of a rather secondary importance to the Silesian towns. Contacts between Wrocław, Nysa, Legnica (Liegnitz) and Świdnica (Schwednitz) on the one hand and Flanders on the other are attested by some thirteenth-century sources, although they were probably in existence much earlier as is suggested, amongst other things, by the presence of a colony from Flanders in old Wrocław even before German law was imposed on the town in 1242. Wrocław sources from the end of the thirteenth and the first half of the fourteenth century point to the import of cloth from Ghent, Ypres and many other Flemish and Brabantine textile centres, and the *schonlaken* which are frequently mentioned probably originated in Flanders or Brabant. Some of this cloth was finished in Wrocław. It reached Silesia through Germany and later also through the mouth of the Vistula as well, for the staple regulations in Frankfurt-on-Oder made it difficult for Silesian merchants to use the Oder as a route leading to the Baltic. The register of goods imported into Bruges at the end of the thirteenth century, already quoted, included copper, silver and gold from 'Polane' (Poland). This gold, as indicated above, most probably originated in Silesia which at this period, and during the following two centuries, was often identified with Poland even after the latter province had passed to the Bohemian crown.[16] It is possible that the same is true of the silver. Wrocław's trade relations with Bruges and later with Antwerp were very lively throughout the whole of the later Middle Ages. Its merchants made their way to England from whence, perhaps in the second half of the fourteenth and certainly in the fifteenth century, they imported cloth.

Throughout the whole period Silesian economic contacts with the Rhineland and Saxony were very active. Cloth from Cologne, Aachen, later Frankfurt-on-Main, Zgorzelec and many other centres flowed into Silesian towns, particularly Wrocław. In the fourteenth and even more in the fifteenth centuries, Zgorzelec, a large textile centre in Upper Lusatia, exported many of its products to Wrocław, sometimes for re-export. In return it bought from Silesia local and Polish wool, raw materials, and grain and cattle imported from the East. In addition Rhenish, French and Italian wines, dyes from Thuringia, metal goods, silks from Italy, spices etc. reached Silesia from Germany.

Wrocław's trade with the West was both passive and active. German merchants often visited the town and its own merchants often journeyed to the West. From the second half of the fourteenth century, they attended fairs in Frankfurt-on-Main. In the same period merchants from Wrocław, Świdnica and a few other Silesian towns began to visit the Fondaco dei Tedeschi in Venice.[17] But in spite of the undoubted activity of Silesians all over Europe, it is certain that foreign merchants played a very large, even a dominating role in its trade.

In the fourteenth century, despite the decrease in mining, Nuremberg merchants expanded their activities in Silesia. Venetians, and perhaps Genoese, merchants frequently appeared, the former occasionally settling in Wrocław. For all these foreigners, Wrocław constituted an

[16] M. Małowist, 'Le Développement des rapports économiques entre le Flandre, la Pologne et les pays limitrophes du XIIIe au XIV siècle', *Revue Belge de Philologie et d'Histoire'*, x (1931), 1020ff.

[17] Simonsfeld, *Der Fondacho*..., II, 152, 197, 227, 239; II, 72.

important link with eastern Europe, a staging post on the route to the East. The second half of the fourteenth century was a period of outstanding development for Silesian trade and particularly for that of Wrocław. Its merchants had for a long time maintained close contacts with Cracow and other trade centres in Little Poland and south-western Russia, and with Toruń (Thorn) and Gdańsk (Danzig), as is proved by the numerous settlements of Silesians in these territories, and particularly in Cracow, where relations were close though not always friendly. The Polish state and south-western Russia supplied Silesia with salt, lead, Hungarian copper, wool, wax, hops for brewing beer, leather and furs. Probably some of these goods were carried further west and south-west. It is not clear when the import of grain and cattle, so important from the fifteenth century, began on a large scale. In spite of the lack of statistical material, sources clearly point to the fact that the states bordering on eastern Silesia imported relatively large quantities of Silesian and western goods: these imports were fostered by the dynamic growth of these areas in the fourteenth and fifteenth centuries.

Silesia's economic position became more complicated in the fifteenth century. Symptoms of a serious agricultural crisis began to appear. Though the Hussite revolution did not extend to this territory, it gave rise to a constant state of war, and the Hussite army, which was often supported by the poorer elements in the population, inflicted cruel damage on agriculture and stock-rearing. (The Hussites carried off many cattle because of their scarcity in Bohemia.) It is possible that the fluctuations in Silesian rural production during the fifteenth century caused grain and cattle imports from Poland to rise and this was a factor of increasing significance. In spite of political uncertainty and the wars of the nobles in the fifteenth century, Silesian and specially Wrocław merchants maintained their close links with Cracow and Great Poland; by entering into relations with the growing towns of Warsaw and Vilno, they reached Novgorod and Moscow via Lithuania. Regular and close contacts with Poznań, Warsaw and Vilno (perhaps more at that time than with Cracow), provided Wrocław merchants, and indirectly merchants and producers from other Silesian towns, with access to markets, foodstuffs, raw materials and indeed the whole of north-eastern Europe. Herds of cattle were driven from Little Poland and Moldavia to Brzeg (Brieg) and Wrocław, and the latter town became an important international trading centre for furs and cattle. Some of these goods were intended for re-export to Germany, Bohemia and even to Italy, especially Venice. It appears that by the fifteenth century Silesia was evidently tied economically to the kingdom of Poland.

Like many other countries, Silesia experienced a revival of mining and a growth of metallurgy in the second half of the fifteenth century. The merchants of Wrocław and Cracow invested heavily in this field. The rise of gold production in Złoty Stok encouraged new attempts to exploit metals in other places. Iron mining increased. In the fifteenth century, the manufacture of metal goods, particularly agricultural tools intended for export to Poland, developed. While the Hungarian King Mathias Corvinus reigned over Silesia (1445–90), its merchants had a route to Cieszyn (Teschen) thus gaining access to the natural resources of Upper Hungary, and sharing in the export of local copper and silver. Agents of the large German companies from Augsburg, Ulm, Nuremberg and elsewhere also took advantage of this to establish houses in Wrocław. Representatives of the Fuggers were active there at the end of the century. They were interested in the Silesian mines and also organised the smelting of copper together with lead largely imported from Little Poland, as well as its further export.

Throughout the fourteenth century, but even more during the fifteenth, bitter conflicts arose between Wrocław and the towns of the Polish kingdom which, supported by the king, managed successfully to bar the way to the East against the Silesian merchants. Because of this struggle, Wrocław found itself at the end of the fifteenth century in a very difficult position, which underlines how far-reaching was its economic dependence on the territories of Poland.

It was not clear how profitable Silesia's trade was during the whole of this period. Transit trade was in the hands of the rich merchants, who made large investments in mining, bought up estates and also governed the towns. In the fourteenth and fifteenth centuries many town 'patricians' even moved up into the ranks of the greater nobles. The lower rungs of the social ladder were filled by the *institores parvi*, who confined themselves to local and regional trade.

Wrocław was undoubtedly one of the largest trade centres in central-eastern Europe. As in the other towns of this region, there is no proof that a banking system existed or that goods were insured, even in the fifteenth century, despite the economic troubles which favoured all kinds of speculation. It is possible that, not only in Silesia but also in the neighbouring states, investments in mining and the purchase of real estate in town and country swallowed up a very large part of the capital accumulated in trade, and that this produced more reliable, and in some periods, greater profits than banking operations or insurance transactions of a highly speculative nature would have done.

(4) THE TRADE OF LITTLE POLAND

Like Silesia and Bohemia, Little Poland entered into a phase of accelerated growth in the thirteenth century which was interrupted neither by the Mongol invasions (from 1241) nor by the great epidemics of the fourteenth century. Modern estimates of Little Poland's population in the first half of the fourteenth century, based on the collections of Peter's Pence, vary between 250,000 and 300,000. At that time Cracow is supposed to have had about 14,000 inhabitants, while the other towns of Little Poland seldom had more than 1,000.[18] In trying to evaluate fifteenth-century conditions we are faced by a difficult problem. The continuous growth of agriculture, stock-rearing and mining, their expansion into new areas, and the undoubted further development of the towns, though perhaps not so rapid as in the two previous centuries, to some extent contradict the conclusions reached by Pelc, not altogether accurately, from material concerning the history of prices in Cracow. He found that, although the level of prices of manufactured goods was high in the second half of the fourteenth century, in the course of the following century it fell by about 19 per cent.[19] Apart from this, however, there are no other signs of a weakening of the rate of demographic and economic growth in Little Poland in the fifteenth century in comparison with the preceding period.

With research in its present state it is not possible to resolve these contradictions. One may suppose that the money incomes of the nobility fell with the heavy depreciation of Polish money. This did not in any way harm the position of the peasants and hence of the vast majority of the inhabitants of Little Poland. Proof of this is the presence of peasants even amongst the students of the Cracow Academy: judging from the protests of the nobles, peasant youths were also sent quite frequently to learn crafts in the town, though this too was expensive. The poor from the countryside streamed into the towns looking for work and even found seasonal work in neighbouring states. This led at the end of the fifteenth century to a rise in the price of labour in the countryside and later on this was a powerful incentive for the introduction of serfdom. Mining and metallurgy developed throughout the whole period and, in spite of increasingly strong foreign competition, handicrafts also expanded. From the thirteenth century, but particularly in the fourteenth and fifteenth centuries, capital from Italy and Germany flowed into Little Poland and wealthy

[18] Mitkowski, *Uwagi*..., 127; Kula, 'Stan i potrzeby', 39; *Historia Polski* (Warsaw, 1957), I, I, 509.

[19] J. Pelc, *Ceny w Krakowie w latach 1369–1600* (Lwów, 1935), 51.

newcomers from these countries settled in the towns, especially Cracow. All this points to Little Poland's continued economic growth and not to its stagnation or regression. It is possible that Pelc's conclusions apply to a more limited sphere than is generally supposed. Could they perhaps be true of only a part of Little Poland, in particular of the Cracow region? The large imports of foreign goods, including craft products, could have been responsible for some fall in prices in this sector. The countryside of the region was also very densely populated and, even in the fifteenth century, may have experienced difficulty in finding markets for its products and that, in turn, may have had a depressing effect upon the price of foodstuffs. This is, however, no more than a hypothesis. It is worth adding that, in the fifteenth century, rural settlements developed in the eastern border of Little Poland, e.g. in the fertile Lublin region. Thus, from the rise in the number and size of these towns, we may assume that there were probably no serious difficulties in the economy of the countryside. The changeover to paying peasant dues in money, begun in the thirteenth and consolidated in the following century, confirms the existence of economic links between town and country. Crafts were concentrated in the towns, though the process was not complete in the Middle Ages. Also the burghers of Little Poland were partly successful in their struggle to restrict the freedom of peasants to engage in trade and handicrafts, though it seems that, in the light of the weakness of the majority of the towns, this victory was not very effective. There are some grounds for assuming that, in the first half of the fifteenth century, the ratio between the prices of urban and rural products was not favourable to the country dwellers, but there is no clear proof of this. Perhaps the market was glutted with agricultural products and even with livestock. This would, to some extent, explain the growth in exports of these products, the results of which, in the case of wool, affected the cloth industry throughout Poland at the end of the fifteenth century. As in Bohemia, Silesia and Upper Hungary, though not so strongly since Little Poland was less favoured in this respect, Little Poland's mining industry influenced the expansion of long-distance trade. The convenient proximity of the great trade routes, described earlier, also as we shall see, provided an important incentive for mining and other branches of the economy.

By way of introduction it should be emphasised that Little Poland's economic contacts with the other territories of the Polish state were very weak, particularly in the fourteenth and fifteenth centuries: significant change in this sphere occurred only gradually in the following century. To begin with, Cracow and the other towns of Little Poland were most closely connected with Silesia and the Slovak areas of Hungary, while trade with Wrocław was an important factor enabling Cracow merchants to take part in the exchange of goods with the West and the Black Sea area. In turn, the trade of Cracow, and of many smaller towns in Little Poland, was based primarily on close contacts with Hungary. In spite of this, however, it would be an exaggeration to describe, as is traditional in Polish studies, the long-distance trade of the towns of Little Poland as an exclusively transit trade.

Thus, from the thirteenth century Little Poland exported salt from Wieliczka and Bochnia to Silesia, gaining control over a permanent market there. As the output of iron in the Częstochowa area rose, some of it was sent to Silesia. Lead, leather, wool, furs, wax, timber, and, at the latest by the fifteenth century, increasing quantities of cattle and grain, were constant exports, some of these products coming from south-western Russia. Already in the thirteenth century, some eastern products reached Silesia from Cracow. They were purchased at first at Vladimir in Volhynia, but from the fourteenth century mainly in Lwów and to a smaller extent in the towns of the Black Sea regions. In turn, Little Poland was a market for cloth from Flanders and Brabant and woollen materials, in general of medium or even low quality, from Silesia or Lusatia, and for metal goods and beer; beer from Świdnica was particularly highly valued. Levantine and Italian products, the latter chiefly of Venetian origin, came to Cracow from Wrocław. Economic ties with Silesia led to its merchants frequently settling in Cracow. These contacts were so strong that, at the end of the thirteenth century and at the beginning of the fourteenth, the wealthy Cracow merchants inclined more towards political unity with Silesia and Bohemia than with the other Polish territories. This situation led to formidable political complications for Poland. Trade relations with Silesia remained close throughout the whole period, and the Polish state, gathering momentum from the fourteenth century, strengthened the position of its merchants.

Sources relating to Little Poland's trade with Upper Hungary date only from the beginning of the fourteenth century, but trade along this route had certainly developed during the preceding century. The trade was so essential for both parties that we can say that the two countries engaged in it were partners. The Carpathian passes provided a comparatively easy line of communication between Little Poland and Upper Hungary. Lead from Olkusz and the smaller mining regions was, perhaps from the thirteenth century and certainly in the two following centuries, an important export from Little Poland to Hungary. It was indispensable to Hungarian copper mining. There is no data on which to base any statistics, but it is clear that some individual deliveries of lead sent to Košice, the chief Cracow contractor, amounted to 4,000 cwt. Salt from Little Poland was also exported to Hungary: the Hungarian crown however, having its own salt deposits, strove to confine this import exclusively to the small border regions. Little Poland also sent to Hungary cheap cloth, perhaps mainly manufactured in Cracow and Biecz; but it is also possible that Great Poland's textiles penetrated deep into Hungary and even as far as the towns of Transylvania. This certainly was true of Silesian cloth re-exported south from Cracow. All these materials, however, constituted only a small percentage of the cloth exported to Hungary, mainly from Cracow. In the fourteenth century, cloth from Flanders predominated, but later, at the beginning of the fifteenth, it was Brabantine cloth from Brussels, Malines, Louvain, etc. The quantity of English kerseys, and perhaps later Dutch textiles, also increased at that time. Cloth from the Netherlands was often sent to Hungary from Cracow in large lots of one to four hundred lengths. Apart from lead, cloth was the chief commodity exported from Little Poland to Hungary.[20]

Copper, the output of which developed in Slovakia on a large scale in the second half of the thirteenth and in the fourteenth centuries, was the most important item exported from Hungary to Little Poland, and particularly to Cracow. The growth of metal crafts in Little Poland was thereby greatly encouraged, but above all Hungarian copper became the basic commodity in Cracow's trade (and that of some smaller towns like Sandomierz, Bochnia and Sącz) with Prussia, Bruges and later with Antwerp. The export of copper declined in the fifteenth century, mainly because output of this metal dropped due to the exhaustion of shallow deposits, flood problems in underground workings and increasingly fierce competition from the Nuremberg merchants who were exporting copper to the West and Venice. Wealthy Cracow merchants were, in the second half of the fifteenth century, actively interested in rebuilding the north Hungarian mining industry and were prepared to invest capital there. Jan Thurzo, a German from Upper Hungary but a citizen of Cracow, was heavily engaged in this. Around 1475 he founded a large metal works in Mogiła near Cracow where, with the aid of Polish lead, he extracted silver from the Hungarian copper. Copper mining in Slovakia flourished after the mines were taken over by the partnership between the Fugger company and the Thurzo family (1494); this led to a renewed growth of copper imports into Poland, and via Poland to the Baltic and Antwerp, though the merchants from Little Poland profited considerably less from this than they had done earlier.

[20] S. Kutrzeba, 'Handel Krakowa w wiekach srednich', *Rozprawy Polskiej Adademii Umiejetności*, 14 (1910), 58–72; J. Dabrowski, 'Kraków a Wegry w wiekach średnich' ('Cracow and Hungary. Their commercial relations'), in *Rosznik Krakowski* (Cracow, 1911), 218–22.

The import of silver from Upper Hungary was of fundamental importance for Little Poland because the Polish mints depended on this source of supply. Hungarian and Polish scholars have remarked on the absence of gold exports from Slovakia to the North, although it did supply Little Poland with some high quality iron, upon which, in the sixteenth century, there grew up in Sącz, on the route from Hungary, the manufacture of knives and sickles. In the fourteenth and fifteenth centuries, supplies of horses, wax, lead, furs and wine from Hungary were less significant for Little Poland than were metals. Wine did not become important until the sixteenth century.

In their economic contacts with Upper Hungary, the men of Cracow were ahead of their competitors – chiefly merchants from Košice and, to a smaller extent, from Bardiov. Most frequently merchants from these towns concluded their transactions at home or in Cracow without being tempted to go much further afield. In the fourteenth century Cracovians and Prussians were dominant in this field, while later on the former were more important. Also in the fourteenth century Cracow managed to crush attempts by the smaller towns of Little Poland to become agents in the trade between Hungary and the Baltic regions; later they used their victory to make it difficult for Prussian merchants to cross the Carpathians.

Any discussion of Little Poland's trade with the East in the late Middle Ages, should take account of the trade of south-western Russia, as this region was conquered by the Polish king, Casimir the Great, in the mid-fourteenth century. The notion of controlling the lines of communication to the Black Sea and the Lower Don, played an important, though not the only, part in this expansion. It is not clear how far Cracow and the other towns of Little Poland were, in the thirteenth century, linked economically with Vladimir in Volhynia, an important centre at that time for the trade in eastern goods. The effects of the Tatar invasion, and the later wars over these territories between the Russians, Poles and Lithuanians, were clearly felt in this region. After Casimir the Great gained control over south-western Russia, he energetically sponsored rural and urban settlements there. He placed special emphasis on the development of Lwów: this town had enormous potentialities because of the convenient network of trade routes leading from the west and north-west to the Black Sea. Cracow merchants who, in the second half of the fourteenth and in the fifteenth centuries, had endeavoured to gain access to Tana, and especially Bielgorod (Akkerman) and Caffa, were, in the course of time, forced to restrict their expeditions to Lwów which was transformed into the largest centre for trade between East and West in that area. Isolated periods when merchants from Cracow were active on the Black Sea, and even in Chios and Alexandria, do not change the picture as a whole. Armenians, Jews and Greeks coming from the East were very active in Lwów and, to a certain extent, in the smaller towns of south-western Russia. They settled in relatively large numbers, particularly in Lwów, and were in contact with their many fellow-countrymen living in Caffa, Bielgorod and other towns on the Black Sea. They imported into Poland pepper, ginger, nutmeg, saffron and other spices; pearls; silk and cotton materials; and Greek wine. Lwów merchants also established close contacts with Moldavia where, in Suceava, they had their own warehouses by the end of the fourteenth century. Large herds of cattle, an important item of export to Poland from the fifteenth century at the latest, came from this region, and the trade stimulated a considerable growth in the manufacture of leather goods in Poland. Herds of cattle from Moldavia and Podolia (western Ukraine) occupied an increasingly important place in Polish exports to Silesia, Germany, Bohemia and even to northern Italy. At the turn of the fifteenth and sixteenth centuries herds driven by individual merchants often exceeded a thousand head. The fairs in Jaroslav and Lublin became centres for the cattle trade in eastern Poland: and in the fifteenth century Lublin increasingly took part in trade with the south and north-east, thanks to which it grew rapidly.

Articles supplied by the Levantine trade which reached Poland from the East were intended both for home consumption and for re-export. In the fourteenth century, Polish merchants sent them to the West by the land routes, but they were chiefly exported by Prussian merchants to Prussia and thus some of them went to the Baltic lands and Bruges by sea. In the fifteenth century there were important changes in this trade and the flow of goods was to some extent reversed. This was perhaps because Prussian merchants were barred from Russia. It is possible that with Timur's invasion of the Near East and the wars accompanying the dissolution of the Byzantine Empire, the flow of eastern goods to Caffa was curtailed for some time, and this could have indirectly diminished their import into Poland. Perhaps as a result more eastern goods reached Poland in the fifteenth century from Venice and from Bruges. Nevertheless, the prices of articles provided by Levantine trade in Cracow in that century did not deviate from the general price levels in the Polish capital.

There is very little information about exports from Little Poland and south-western Russia to the East in the later Middle Ages and it is not therefore possible to estimate exactly its volume or to indicate how it developed. It should be noted though that goods originating in the West and taken to Poland by road via Silesia and Prussia are the most important here. One private inventory of customs houses on the route from Toruń to Vladimir in Volhynia and to Lwów, from the middle of the fourteenth century, points to a supply of cloth from Ghent, Bruges and Poperinghe and to considerably cheaper textiles from Toruń itself. At the end of this century, the Teutonic Order exported cloth from Ypres, Hernthals, Thuin, Valenciennes and Malines to Lwów and Lublin.[21] Perhaps English and Dutch textiles also appeared on the Lwów market in this or in a somewhat later period. They were widespread throughout Poland although the sources pass over them in silence. The grant of a charter to Lwów in 1472 to hold fairs mentioned Polish and Bohemian cloth as the chief object of trade. Probably the export of these products to the East increased in the fifteenth century, but we cannot imagine that they ever replaced western fabrics. Merchants travelling from Prussia and from the Black Sea towns also brought to Lwów and to other south-western Russian towns Baltic amber and Bohemian and Nuremberg metal products. Russian wax, furs and cochineal were exported subsequently from Caffa to the Italian textile producing centres. At the end of the period, beside Lwów and Lublin, wealthy merchants from Brześć (Brest) on the Bug and Kamieniec Podolski were engaged in trade with the East; Kiev, its early glory past, took only a small part in this trade.

It may be assumed that Little Poland and south-western Russia had an unfavourable balance of payments with the East, as they were to have in the following century. From 1466 onwards the number of slaves on the Crimean market increased: these were carried off from south-western Russia by the Tatars, subsequently sold to the Genoese and Turks and then taken to Egypt and Syria, while a certain number also probably went to Italy and other Christian countries on the Mediterranean. In this and a later period the Genoese from time to time drove slaves purchased in Caffa and in the Caucasus through south-western Russia and Little Poland, from 1461 onwards paying a per capita transit duty to the Polish king.[22]

It is not possible to say that the conquest of Caffa by the Turks in 1475 and their occupation of Bielgorod and Chilia in 1481 caused Polish trade with the East to sag for long. Lwów moved closer to Constantinople and later to the trade centres of Asia Minor. There is also no evidence that the Portuguese discovery of the road to the East led to radical transformations in the economic relations of Poland and the Near East, though recent research has shown that some changes did occur in this field.

Foreign merchant capital began to penetrate Poland actively in the

[21] *Hansisches Urkundenbuch* (10 vols., Halle-Munich-Leipzig, 1876–1918), III, n.559; Sattler, *Handelsrechnungen*, XXXIII, 136, 157.

[22] Ł. Charewiczowa, *Handel średniowiecznego Lwowa* (Lwów, 1925), 53, 89; M. Małowist, *Kaffa – kolonia genueńska na Krymie i problem wschodni w latach 1453–1475* (Warsaw, 1947), 52–6, 69ff, 76.

thirteenth century, but the process was at its height in the two following centuries. This may be one of the reasons why Little Poland and south-western Russia, where this phenomenon appeared most clearly, experienced a period of rapid development in the late Middle Ages, to which the flow of capital obviously contributed. It is possible that the check in the rate of economic expansion in many western European countries stimulated merchants from Nuremberg, Upper Germany and Italy to greater activity in the rapidly developing trade of Poland. That country offered them many advantages as a market for industrial goods and as a source of supply of many important indigenous and eastern products; its expanding mining industry offered many possibilities for the profitable investment of capital, and, finally, contact with Poland opened the door to the Black Sea. In 1365, the Nuremberg merchants obtained a charter granting them freedom to trade on payment of ordinary duties.[23] It is worth noting that the inhabitants of Nuremberg who, in this period, enjoyed numerous immunities from these duties in the West and in Bohemia, not only accepted the conditions offered, but increased their activities in Poland on a large scale. In the fourteenth century and at the beginning of the fifteenth, Nuremberg hucksters were active in Little Poland and south-western Russia supplying cheap metal goods like needles, scissors, knives, etc.; but in addition they also sold cloth from Germany and the Netherlands, Upper German fustians etc. It is clear from a collection of letters of Nuremberg merchants of 1444–5, and from other sources, that this aroused bitter protest from the craftsmen in Polish and Prussian towns.[24] These hucksters were the vanguard of the wealthy Upper German merchants who poured into Poland and sent their agents there in the second half of the fifteenth century. In this period they supplied, mainly to Silesia, Little Poland and south-western Russia, not only German goods but also many oriental wares acquired in Venice. In Poland they bought leather, furs, wax, cochineal, and in the course of time cattle from Russia and Moldavia, with increasing frequency.[25] According to H. Ammann, in the fourteenth and fifteenth centuries, the merchants of Nuremberg also journeyed through Little Poland and south-western Russia to the Black Sea and Constantinople;[26] however, Polish sources show that the chief items interesting them in Poland were Polish, Russian and Lithuanian

[23] J. Ptaśnik, 'Akta norymberskie do dziejów handlu z Polska w XV wieku' in *Archiwum Komiski Historycznej Polskiej Akadmii Umiejetności* (Cracow, 1909–13), X, 296.

[24] M. Scholz-Babisch, 'Oberdeutscher Handel mit dem deutschen und polnischen Osten nach Geschäftsbriefen von 1444', *Zeitschrift des Vereins f. Geschichte u. Alterthums Schlesiens*, LXIV (1908), 66, 67. [25] *Ibid.*, 61, 62.

[26] H. Ammann, 'Wirtschaftsbeziehungen zwischen Oberdeutschland und Polen im Mittelalter', *Vierteljahhschrift f. Sozial- u. Wirtschaftsgeschichte*, XLVIII (1961), 433–43.

products. During the fourteenth and particularly the fifteenth centuries, many wealthy merchants from Nuremberg, Upper Germany and Alsatia settled permanently in Cracow. They invested their capital not only in trade, but also extensively in lead, silver and salt mining, urban real estate and in the land. The majority of these men, like the Boners, Morsztyns, Bers, Kiesingers and many others, were quickly polonised; some held high positions in the treasury administration and entered the ranks of the nobility.

The Italian penetration into southern Poland was of a similar character. The Italians, appearing in Silesia and Little Poland in the thirteenth century, were mainly papal tax-collectors connected with the banking houses of Florence (the Bardi company amongst others), Asti, Lucca and Pisa. The sums collected were, in the fourteenth century, remitted to Italian trade agents in Bruges through Cracow merchants travelling there through Wrocław. With the expansion of the trade routes leading through southern Poland to the Black Sea, the Florentines and then Venetians and Genoese visited Poland, and even settled there with increasing frequency. Trade was not their sole interest. For a long time they held the leases of the royal salt mines in Bochnia and Wieliczka and invested in lead-mining in the region of Olkusz and Trzebinia. Some, like Goffredo Fattinanti from Genoa, settled in Cracow; he leased the royal mint and bought much urban, and some rural, real estate. In the first half of the fifteenth century, the Genoese appeared in Poland somewhat less frequently; but after the fall of Constantinople they were again very active, particularly in Lwów and south-western Russia. Cristoforo di S. Romolo, members of the De Veletariis family, Lorenzo Lomellino and others invested heavily in salt-mining in south-western Russia and in Little Poland, bought up country estates and acquired the right to levy taxes in Lwów.

The inflow of merchants from Florence, Genoa and Venice became in the fifteenth century quite an important factor in the economic life of Little Poland and south-western Russia. Florentines, often operating in partnership with merchants from Nuremberg, Wrocław and Cracow, supplied Wrocław and Cracow with Italian and Levantine goods by south-western routes; in return they bought considerable quantities of cochineal, furs from Lithuania and northern Russia, leather and wax. They also invested their capital in salt and lead mining. They purchased in addition much real estate, particularly in Cracow, where, in the fifteenth century, the amount of land owned by Italians considerably increased.[27]

[27] J. Ptaśnik, *Kultura włoska wieków średnich w Polsce* (2nd edn., Warsaw, 1959), 23–117.

Mention has frequently been made of the importance of cloth from the Netherlands and England in the trade of Little Poland and south-western Russia. Many products from Flanders, together with German textiles, must have penetrated by road from Silesia to the Upper Vistula in the thirteenth century. The beginnings of a more regular contact between southern Poland and Flanders occurred later in the second half of the thirteenth century. The list of goods imported into Bruges at the end of the century, quoted earlier, mentions that 'du royaume de Polane vient or et argent en plate, cire, vairs et gris et poivre'.[28] The gold and silver perhaps originated in Silesia, or from Hungarian exports to Cracow. The wax and furs could have been either of Polish, or – as seems more probable – of Hungarian or Russian origin. Undoubtedly the pepper was purchased in south-western Russia. Thus everything points to the fact that at the end of the thirteenth century, some metals and luxury goods were exported to Bruges from Poland; and this was probably not a sporadic trade; had it been so, the goods would not have been mentioned amongst the commodities constantly appearing in Bruges.

In the fourteenth and fifteenth centuries, the variety of goods supplied by Little Poland and south-western Russia to Flanders was considerably enriched. Hungarian copper, a little iron, fur and leather of similar origin, and some Polish lead became constant and permanent items. Finally, small quantities of silver may have reached Flanders via Little Poland and Prussia. In the fourteenth century, however, supplies of eastern goods from Lwów and Cracow to Flanders via Prussia certainly increased. At the end of the century, Cracow merchants exported cotton, silks, alum, pepper, ginger and saffron to Flanders. At the same time, all these goods were also bought, chiefly in Lwów but also in Lublin, by merchants from Prussia and the commercial agents of the Order of Teutonic Knights. It seems, however, that in the course of the fifteenth century, exports of eastern goods from Poland to the Netherlands fell somewhat as the result of the reduced supply from the Black Sea towns. In the fourteenth century and perhaps earlier, a little timber was already being exported to Flanders from the Carpathians, though the famous yews from this region were intended rather for England where they were made into cross- and long-bows. The rapidly developing export of forest products, and later of grain, to the northern Netherlands and to England relied, however, not on the resources of southern Poland, but of the central and northern parts of the country.

[28] *Hansisches Urkundenbuch*, II, n. 264, note 1.

Obviously cloth made up the great bulk of imports into Little Poland and south-western Russia from Flanders: at first, the costly fabrics of Ghent, Ypres and Bruges. Then, at the end of the fourteenth century, perhaps more Brabantine cloth from Malines, Brussels and Louvain, etc. was to be found amongst the expensive textiles on the Cracow market. During the fourteenth century medium quality cloth imported from the smaller towns of Flanders and other parts of the southern Netherlands became increasingly significant in all the Polish territories. Towards the end of the century and during the fifteenth, Flemish and Brabantine textiles gradually lost their customers first to English and then to Dutch cloth. However, the rivalry between these goods had still not finally been settled by the second half of the fifteenth century.[29] Apart from cloth, certain other goods, such as French and Spanish fruit and wine, were also brought from Flanders to Little Poland and Russia.

During the fourteenth century, the participation of Cracow merchants in the active trade with Flanders greatly increased and from information which has been preserved about the relatively numerous expeditions of rich Cracow burghers to Bruges, we know that the collectors of papal levies often entrusted them with the transport of money to that great Flemish city. Cracow merchants formed special companies to conduct this active trade with Flanders, though these were relatively short-term agreements.[30] At that time Cracow was recognised as a member of the Hanseatic League, but, although it profited from its authority, it was not completely identified with the League's political policies. The bitter war will be described later which, from the second half of the fourteenth century, the Cracow merchants waged with the merchants from Toruń in this connection. It seems, however, that at least until the beginning of the fifteenth century, the Toruń merchants predominated in Poland's transit trade with north-western Europe. In this period they penetrated not only to Cracow, Sandomierz and Lwów, but also to Hungary. During the fifteenth century fundamental changes occurred in this field. Toruń gradually declined, unable to withstand competition from the more powerful and conveniently situated Gdańsk. In the first half of the century Cracow merchants themselves sent their goods by ship from Gdańsk to Flanders with increasing frequency. At that time they led the other towns of the kingdom in the fight for freedom of access to maritime trade.[31] Later, however, they withdrew from this commerce. This

[29] Kutrzeba, 'Handel Krakowa w wiekach średnich', 26, 27; Ch. Verlinden, 'Brabantsche en vlaamsche laken te Krakau op het einde der XIV eeuw', in *Mededelingen van der konniklike Vlaamsche Akademie* (1949), *passim*.

[30] Małowist, 'Le Développement', 1039, 1040, 1047, 1049.

[31] Kutrzeba, 'Handel Krakowa', 39, 44, 45, 47.

was, perhaps, because of the drop in the supply of Hungarian copper to Poland, and it was this metal that constituted the chief *quid pro quo* for imports from the Netherlands to Little Poland. Poland's economic relations with north-western Europe took on a completely new character at that time.

(5) CONCLUSION

This outline of the trade of the countries composing the southern part of central-eastern Europe demonstrates that, during the thirteenth and fourteenth centuries, the exchange of goods throughout the whole region showed a marked increase, with Bohemia and Silesia holding the leading position. In the fourteenth century, the rate of growth of trade in Little Poland and south-western Russia also accelerated and continued to grow into the following century when the territories of the Bohemian crown were suffering a severe setback. Some of the symptoms of a deterioration in trade in the southern territories of the Polish provinces did not appear until the second half of the fifteenth century.

It must be emphasised that in the fourteenth century, which was when western Europe was experiencing economic difficulties, the region whose axis was the Sudeten and Carpathian mountain chains entered a phase of rapid development which is particularly clearly illustrated in the field of trade. The economic structure of the countries that have been discussed here exhibited many common features. Thus the whole period was characterised by a relatively rapid and unified growth of the rural economy and a progressive urbanisation. It has been shown that the exploitation of metals and other natural resources contributed largely to the general growth and exercised a positive influence on the exchange of goods. How important the structure of the great trade routes was to the economic life of the whole region, and particularly to Silesia, Little Poland, Upper Hungary and later-developing Moldavia and Wallachia has also been stressed.

The general economic growth and increase of wealth in the Sudeten–Carpathian region attracted foreign capital and the wealthy merchants who owned it, and they undoubtedly stimulated the rise in imports of foreign goods. One can already see this happening in the thirteenth and fourteenth centuries, but in Little Poland and south-western Russia it continued into the following century as well. If the expansion of trade and mining was thereby accelerated, in another sense the growth of indigenous crafts was seriously hindered by foreign competition. But for a time this was not too damaging since the markets were increasingly able to absorb supplies.

The economic development of the whole of this part of Europe resulted in the formation, in the thirteenth century, of strong unitary states. Bohemia became an important power; Poland, united again at the beginning of the fourteenth century, swiftly grew in power based mainly on its southern regions. During the fourteenth and fifteenth centuries Bohemia and Little Poland also experienced a rapid cultural development with particularly close trade contacts with Italy, while the Netherlands and southern Germany also had considerable influence on the culture of Bohemia and Poland during the later Middle Ages and the early Renaissance.

III. *Trade in the Northern Half of Central-Eastern Europe: Great Poland, Pomerania, Prussia and Mazowia*

Turning now to the problems of trade in the northern part of central-eastern Europe it should be emphasised that in many respects the situation was less favourable than it was further south. This is specially true of natural resources which were confined to some deposits of salt around Kołobrzeg in western Pomerania and in Kujawy, and to low quality iron ore found in many places. Where trade routes are concerned, changes occurring in the late Middle Ages in some measure reflect the fundamental economic and political transformations taking place throughout the region. Already by the thirteenth century the Baltic was important as a sea route not only for trade, but even for the migration of people into the northern part of our region. The same is true to some extent of the coastal land routes connecting trade centres between the Netherlands and Livonia and Russia. Somewhat further south another parallel route ran from Flanders and Cologne via Westphalia, Lower Saxony, Brandenburg and Great Poland as far as the mouth of the Vistula. However, the economic importance of these land routes could not, in the thirteenth and fourteenth centuries, be compared with the trade routes of the southern region.

P. Johansen has rightly drawn attention to the fact that the influence of trade along the so-called Bruges-Novgorod axis on the economic life of the Hanseatic towns on the Baltic and the North Seas has been overestimated in earlier historiography.[32] These towns could never have prospered without links with their respective and often vast

32 P. Johansen, *Der hansische Russlandhandel, insbesondere nach Novgorod, in kritischer Betrachtung* (Cologne – Opladen, 1962), 45, 46.

hinterlands. This holds good not only for Hamburg and Lübeck, a fact recently emphasised, but also for the towns of western and eastern Pomerania. Already in the thirteenth century there were land routes connecting the mouths of the Oder and Vistula with their deep hinterlands which made possible contacts with Silesia, Bohemia, Little Poland, Hungary and the Black Sea regions. Control over these routes became, from the middle of the fourteenth century, a cause for bitter conflict between the towns of the Baltic region and their southern competitors and rivals. The waterways, particularly the Oder and the Vistula with their tributaries, had only a limited economic significance in the thirteenth and fourteenth centuries. As a result, the exchange of goods between the coastal areas and the countries of the southern region was mostly made up, in that period, of light weight and expensive commodities suitable for transport by land. The land routes joining the mouth of the Vistula with Silesia, Bohemia and Austria via Wrocław, and with Hungary and south-western Russia via Cracow and Sandomierz, were much more important than was the Vistula and its tributaries. The position of the Oder region was to some extent different.

A gradual change in the situation did not begin until the end of the fourteenth and beginning of the fifteenth centuries, when first of all forest resources and then the growing grain supplies of central Poland and Lithuania came to play an important part in the internal and external trade of that region. In this connection, the necessity then arose of developing water transport. Under these changed conditions, the network of waterways (principally the Vistula and its tributaries, but also the Niemen and the western Dvina) greatly helped to unify the economy of the Baltic coast with that of the entire southern hinterland, even though serious economic and political obstacles arose in the process.

As were the territories further to the south, the northern region of central-eastern Europe was, in the thirteenth century, the scene of an intensive development of the rural economy, and particularly of agriculture. The pace of development, however, was not everywhere the same. An intensification of rural settlement in which German newcomers played an important part occurred in the twelfth century in western Pomerania and eastern Brandenburg, and in the following century it spread also to eastern Pomerania and Great Poland. But in sparsely populated and backward Mazovia (Mazowsze) there were not many new settlements. It must be pointed out that in the westernmost part of the region a catastrophic collapse of settlements and of the rural economy followed during the fourteenth century, which some modern scholars have attributed to the use of unsuitably heavy agricultural tools on the light soils of western Pomerania and Brandenburg.[33] However, in Great Poland and around the mouth of the Vistula rural settlement continued to develop despite the fact that immigration from Germany ceased completely. Certain signs of crisis in the rural economy appearing in the territories of the Teutonic Order at the beginning of the fifteenth century cannot be explained on purely economic grounds. This was the period in which Mazovia began to develop rapidly, soon to be followed by Lithuania, recently freed from the threat of constant raids by the Teutonic Knights who had harassed it throughout the fourteenth century and on into the first years of the fifteenth.

The developing rural economy stimulated the growth of towns in the thirteenth century although, with the exception of backward Mazovia, this was, of course, no new phenomenon. It is sufficient to mention here the expansion of the old towns of western Pomerania in the eleventh and twelfth centuries and the significant number of urban settlements in the remaining territories. The prospect of urban development attracted German immigration particularly to Pomerania and Brandenburg, and to a lesser extent to Great Poland. Mazovia's urbanisation came rather from its native population.

As mentioned earlier, from the point of view of trade, Great Poland and the adjacent territories of Brandenburg were, in the thirteenth century, worse off than the lands situated near the Sudeten Highlands and Carpathian Mountains. The lack of natural resources and important trade routes resulted during this period in a slower rate of growth in these countries than in Bohemia, Silesia and Little Poland. The transformation in rural society brought about by German law was less rapid there than in southern Poland. The introduction of money payments into the system of dues owed by peasants to their lords was also slower. This in its turn shows that the links between the rural and urban economies were weaker than in the South. At the same time, the towns throughout these northerly regions were relatively small. Poznań, the chief city of Great Poland at the beginning of the fifteenth century, could scarcely claim 4,000 inhabitants and was thus far behind Cracow and Wrocław.[34] With research in its present unsatisfactory state, it is not possible to do more than advance the hypothesis that, in the thirteenth and fourteenth centuries, the growth of the towns of Great Poland and neighbouring Kujawy, like those in the eastern

[33] B. Zientara, *Kryzys agrarny w Marchii Wkrzańskiej w XIV wieku* (Warsaw, 1960), 181.
[34] *Historia Polski*, I, I, 509.

territories of Brandenburg, was based solely on the agricultural, pastoral and forestry activities of the countryside. Frankfurt-on-Oder, lying at the intersection of roads leading south from the mouth of the Oder to Silesia and Bohemia, and from west to east, was something of an exception. Already by the thirteenth century the so-called *schonlaken* (perhaps cloth from Flanders), had appeared there. In the following century merchants from Frankfurt sometimes came to Bruges. Around 1351 the Hokemann brothers' company even had their representative there.[35] Poznań, which had already in 1253 obtained the 'Magdeburg law' and later was exempted from duties in the whole principality, was the most active town of Great Poland. But in spite of this, its growth was so slow that it was not capable of extracting any real profit from the right, obtained in 1390, of the staple on the 'Flanders road' projected in Poland at that time: this route was intended to connect Little Poland, via Great Poland, with the ports of western Pomerania, as a possible jumping-off point for Polish trade with the Netherlands.

We know very little about the long-distance trade of Great Poland in the thirteenth and fourteenth centuries. Its princely charters from 1238 anticipated that what were described as *panni nobiles et non nobiles* would pass along the route leading from the West to Włocławek and Pomerania.[36] This may mean Flemish cloth and the inferior German material. In this document there is also mention of the possible sale of wine by foreign merchants in Poznań and Gniezno. It is doubtful, however, whether Great Poland was in a position in this period to import any very great quantities of expensive foreign goods, since it probably lacked the means to pay for them. At the end of the thirteenth century, or somewhat later, the trade routes joining the Prussian towns of the Teutonic Knights with Silesia, Bohemia and Austria probably had some influence on the economic boom in western Great Poland. This road passed through a region on the borders of Great Poland and Silesia of moderately well-developed, though doubtless primitive, cloth manufacture.

This is a matter on which there is very little information in Polish sources. It is now possible, as a result of the researches of Warschauer, Graus, H. Ammann and Mączak, to assume that a cloth industry existed on both sides of the Great Poland-Silesian border in the fourteenth century, but it was certainly established even earlier in Kościan, Miedzyrzec and Wschowa. If we take into consideration the probable volume of output of these textiles, we may assume that they

[35] Małowist, 'Le Développement,' 1015. [36] *Ibid.* 1056, 1059.

were already also being manufactured in the fourteenth century in eastern Great Poland, around Sieradz, Brzeziny and Łęczyca, where, in later periods, this industry was well-established, and much cheap, so-called peasant, cloth was produced. Graus supposed that the term 'Polish cloth' included also cheap Silesian products. It must be mentioned, however, that in Poland itself local textiles were distinguished from those of Silesia. It is clear that in the first half of the fourteenth century Polish cloth was an item of trade in Prague, Kutná Horá, Brno in Moravia and other Bohemian towns. Already about 1335 it was probably imported from Vienna into Styria, Carinthia and Venice. In the mid-fourteenth century it appeared in Buda in Hungary and from thence it went to Transylvania. There, in Sibiu and Brašov, the customs tariffs mentioned it in 1412. It was exported from Transylvania to the Wallachian territories. In the fifteenth century deliveries to Caffa must be taken into account. In the West it is mentioned in the customs tariffs of Zurich between 1379 and 1400. This cloth was certainly taken to Prussia from the second half of the fourteenth century and at the end of the century Prussian merchants intending to export it to Novgorod met resistance from the Lübeck merchants. The supply of grey Polish cloth to Prussia reached significant proportions in the fifteenth century and continued to do so. In the same century we can also find it in Saxony, Vienna, Bratislava and Salzburg, while it was also exported from Austria to Venice.[37]

We may conclude from all these documents that Polish cloth was graded as one of the cheapest woollen materials. It is frequently described as 'thick', 'grey', 'white' or undyed, but sometimes it seems to have been blue, red, etc. The question arises as to why, when transport costs were so high, it was worth transporting such poor and cheap goods to distant parts. It is possible that demand for these inferior goods increased in the late Middle Ages when relatively large numbers of very poor people were concentrated in many towns. Prussian sources clearly point to this group being customers for Polish cloth.[38] It is also possible that the exporters profited from the particularly sharp depreciation of Polish money in the fourteenth century: the resulting difference between buying and selling prices ensured them a respectable return. Because the merchants of Great Poland in the thirteenth and fourteenth centuries were not able to

[37] A. Warschauer, *Geschichte der Provinz Posen in polnischer Zeit* (Poznan, 1916), 150; Graus, *Česky obchod*, 105, 106; Ammann, 'Wirtschaftsbeziehungen', *passim*; A. Mączak, *Sukiennictwo wielkopolskie XIV–XVII wieku* (Warsaw, 1955), 200, 201, 222ff.

[38] M. Małowist, 'Podstawy gospodarcze przywrócenia jedności panstwowej Pomorza Gdańskiego z Polska w XV wieku', *Przeglad Historyczny*, XLV (1954), 161, 162.

compete, the cloth trade was probably chiefly in the hands of foreigners, particularly Prussians and Silesians. In a later period the wealthy Jewish merchants of Poznań played a large part in this trade. In any case, it is clear that long-distance trade was an important incentive to the expansion of the cloth industry in Great Poland and this, in turn, facilitated the area's participation in this trade.

These exports, chiefly to Silesia, Bohemia and Hungary, could even, to some extent, have caused a flow of silver coins to Great Poland. The latter occupying, in the fourteenth century, a rather secondary position within the Polish state, gradually acquired in the course of the next hundred years relatively important political, and perhaps even economic power. It should be noted that, at least from the beginning of the fifteenth century, Nuremberg merchants began to appear with their goods in Great Poland, for this region was of increasing interest to them as a developing market and also as a place where they could buy not only local but also Lithuanian and Russian goods, a matter for discussion later (p. 580).[39] There were more signs of economic growth along the Baltic coast in the thirteenth and fourteenth centuries than in the hinterland immediately to the south. The immigrant German population played an important role here and it was supported in western Pomerania by the local authorities and further to the north-east by both groups of the Teutonic Order. Youthful scions of the German nobility who had joined the Order were able, thanks to their membership, to make a profitable career in the Baltic region. German economic and political expansion was not the same in all the Baltic territories, but everywhere it took place at the expense of the local population who were relegated to a lower social position. Rörig undoubtedly exaggerated the role of Lübeck as organiser of the settlement of German burghers on the Baltic and it is preferable to emphasise the colonising function of the Teutonic Knights. In the thirteenth and fourteenth centuries, they had an important military force at their disposal, with which they were not only able to assure security and relatively convenient living conditions to those who settled in the conquered territories, but also to acquire extensive economic privileges in the hinterland. The economic rivalry and competition between the Order and its subjects did not lead to violence until the fifteenth century, though there were signs of conflict considerably earlier. The fact that most of the Baltic towns belonged to the Hanseatic League was undoubtedly very important for their development. A. von Brandt, however, rightly points out that the

[39] Scholz-Babisch, 'Oberdeutscher Handel', 59–62; L. Koczy, *Handel Poznania do Połowy XVI wieku*, 226ff.

Hanseatic League was a very loosely knit organisation and that the differences in the interests of its members and even of individual towns were very sharp indeed.[40] Von Brandt's views ought perhaps to be qualified to the extent that the differences, as revealed by him, did not in fact appear until the end of the fourteenth century: but clearly we cannot regard the League as a homogeneous union of towns.

In western Pomerania the old towns headed by Szczecin (Stettin) suffered from the effects of the Danish and German invasions in the twelfth century. In the following century a new epoch in their economic expansion began in which the Germans played a decisive role. It was based on the rapid growth of the rural economy, and particularly of agriculture in western Pomerania, and the powerful position gained by the merchants from Szczecin in the Danish fishing grounds off the coasts of Skania. Szczecin also established contacts with Flanders and England. Zientara was probably correct in arguing that much of the grain supplies, by means of which the merchants of Lübeck and the other Hanseatic towns gained control of the Norwegian economy, originated in western Pomerania and that grain was also sent from there to Flanders and perhaps even to England. In any case, Szczecin was deeply involved in the struggle for the monopoly of grain exports in the thirteenth and fourteenth centuries. It successfully took advantage of its position near the mouth of the Oder to the detriment of Stargard and other towns. At that time Szczecin was also an important intermediary in the transport of Baltic herring and Low Countries cloth to the south. Kołobrzeg, at one time a fairly important centre for trade and the distribution of salt, was in a weaker position. Its salt works produced too little during the period of economic and demographic growth in the Baltic regions and could not compete with the salt imported by the Lübeck merchants from the district around Lüneburg and later with Bay salt from Brittany.

The collapse of the agricultural economy in western Pomerania in the fourteenth century dealt a serious blow to its towns. The position of Szczecin and the smaller trade centres deteriorated and the situation was also made worse by the powerful nobles in Mecklenburg and western Pomerania who behaved in an increasingly lawless way. The struggles of the Pomeranian princes against the advancing Brandenburgers had also an adverse effect. Frankfurt-on-Oder, supported by its Brandenburg rulers, blockaded the road to Silesia and Bohemia by the exercise of its staple powers. Long-standing anarchy in the so-called 'New March' made communications with Great Poland difficult. The

[40] A. von Brandt, *Die Hanse und die nordischen Mächte im Mittelalter* (Cologne, 1962), *passim*.

control gained by the Teutonic Knights over the New March at the beginning of the fifteenth century upset the plan conceived in 1390 to direct Polish trade with Flanders along the road leading to the western Pomeranian ports. We must assume that the deterioration of the herring catches along the coasts of Skania in the first half of the fifteenth century also affected the position of the western Pomeranian towns unfavourably. Its smaller ports became, in the fifteenth century, havens for pirates. The Dutch, however, were at that time already coming to buy grain and this no doubt stimulated the recovery of agriculture to a certain extent. It was still a long time, however, before there was any great improvement in the situation. Unfortunately research into the history of western Pomerania is still in its early stages and there may perhaps be surprises in the future although it is doubtful whether the picture we now see will be radically altered.

A different state of affairs prevailed in eastern Pomerania. In the thirteenth century it was, economically speaking, far behind its western neighbours and in a somewhat similar situation to Great Poland. In the course of the century Lübeck merchants began to appear in Gdańsk and in 1298 they obtained from the prince of Pomerania the right to maintain a trade agency there: even earlier he had granted them passage through his state to south-western Russia and Hungary. At that time some grain from the heart of Poland was already reaching Gdańsk by way of the Vistula, probably intended in the main for home consumption, but it seems that a little salt from Kołobrzeg, cloth from the Netherlands, herring, wine, etc. were being transported in the opposite direction.

In 1230 the Teutonic Knights, having subdued the Chełmno (Kulm) district, began a systematic conquest of Prussia, while at the same time energetically promoting the German rural and urban colonisation of their state. Both old and newly-founded towns of the region, like Toruń (Thorn), Elbląg (Elbing), Chełmno (Kulm) and others, begun to develop during the thirteenth century. Königsberg came into being on the mouth of the river Pregel. At an earlier period in its development, the state of the Teutonic Knights had been to a large extent dependent for supplies on Kujawy, the neighbouring and highly productive Polish border province. Later, in spite of enormous advances in agriculture, Toruń and, perhaps, the other towns of the southern borderlands continued to obtain their supplies of cattle, leather and, to some extent, grain from the adjacent Polish territories – as is quite conclusively proved by evidence dating from the first quarter of the fifteenth century.[41]

[41] Małowist, 'Le Développement,' 1060; *Idem.*, 'Podstawy...,' 159.

In the second half of the thirteenth century, Toruń and Elbląg already had an active maritime trade, and Toruń merchants certainly penetrated Poland and into south-western Russia and perhaps Hungary. In 1308–9 the Teutonic Knights were in control of the area around the mouth of the Vistula.

In spite of a wide literature on the subject, very little is known about the economic history of Prussia under the Teutonic Knights in the thirteenth and in the first half of the fourteenth centuries; nor are the available sources very helpful. Attention must be drawn here to what was, for that geographical region, an exceptionally wide and early resort to the use of money in the Teutonic Knights' state. It is worth noting that peasants living under German law paid their dues in money and that peasants living under Polish law quickly followed suit. Payments in labour and kind were important only for peasants using Prussian law. The economic links between town and country in Prussia are well-authenticated and provide an explanation of how peasants could make money payments. But there is no answer to the question as to where Prussia, quite without deposits of metal in its own territory, obtained the silver necessary to produce such good quality money. Foreign trade could have been the only source of a supply of metals, and this points to its importance in the life of the country. Indeed, the fundamental role and widespread use of money in the economy of Prussia under the Teutonic Knights means that we must assume that the balance of payments for long-distance trade could not, in the long term, have been unfavourable and, in the thirteenth and fourteenth centuries, was mostly rather favourable. The first serious money crisis in which an outflow of Prussian money was linked with its depreciation came after the Teutonic Knights' military defeat in 1410 and this coincided with profound disturbances in its trade with Poland and Lithuania.

In the thirteenth, and particularly in the fourteenth, century, Toruń, Elbląg and Gdańsk maintained both direct and indirect contacts with Bruges and London. They imported cloth from Ghent and Bruges, but, in the course of time, medium-quality products from Ypres, Poperinghe, Courtrai and many smaller centres in Flanders and Brabant seem to have predominated. From the second half of the fourteenth century, shipments of kerseys and other English cloth developed, and later also quantities of Dutch textiles appeared.

In the thirteenth and fourteenth centuries French and Spanish wine was carried to Prussia from Flanders, and at the end of the period the Prussians imported increasingly large quantities of salt from Brittany, wine from Poitou, Gascony and Spain and wine and southern fruits from Spain and Portugal. At the end of the fourteenth century a little salt began to be imported from Lisbon. Cloth, however, was definitely the dominating import. In spite of actively participating in the maritime trade to the Netherlands and to England via the Danish Straits, the Prussians bought and sold many goods at this period in Lübeck and the other 'Wendish' towns. Lübeck was an important trading partner for Prussia. The Prussians bought fish, particularly herring, fats, Swedish iron ore and a little copper from Sweden and Denmark; in both these countries, however, they played a very modest role compared with the merchants of Lübeck. In Novgorod too Prussian trade could not be measured in the fourteenth century against that of Lübeck or even of Livonian merchants. Like other members of the Hanseatic League, the Prussians acted as agents in the exports of furs and beeswax from Russia to the West, and in the import of cloth and other goods to Livonia and Novgorod. By the end of the fourteenth century the importance of the Prussians, and particularly of the agents of the Order, in Russian markets was already great; indeed, as Lesnikov and Khoroshkevitch assert, the Teutonic Order was at that time one of the chief suppliers of silver to Novgorod.[42] During the fifteenth century the merchants of Gdańsk developed quite an active trade by land routes with Polotsk, Pskov and particularly Novgorod, thus evoking bitter protests from the merchants of Livonia and Lübeck. In all probability, however, it was local articles and, particularly in the thirteenth and fourteenth centuries, goods brought from Hungary and south-western Russia by roads leading through Poland, which constituted the real basis of Prussia's long-distance trade. It is also a reasonable assumption that considerable imports from Bruges into Prussia of Flemish and Brabantine cloth would have been unthinkable at that period without the supplies of Hungarian copper and eastern goods acquired in Cracow and Lwów for the Bruges market. Toruń merchants were probably already visiting south-western Russia, Silesia and perhaps Hungary by the thirteenth century and by the beginning of the fourteenth century the traffic was well established. A list of roads to Vladimir in Volhynia and to Lwów, drawn up in Toruń in the first half of the fourteenth century, clearly points to it by distinguishing between the *viae antiquae* and the *viae novae*. It also mentions cloth from Ghent, Ypres and Bruges and woollen materials (at half the price) from Toruń as the only objects of Prussian export to south-western Russia.[43] It is known from many other sources that pepper, ginger and

42 M. P. Lesnikov, 'Torgovye snoshenya V. Novgoroda s Tevtonskim Ordenom', *Istoritscheskye Zapiski*, XXXIX (1952). 262; A. L. Khoroshkevich, *Torgovla V. Novgoroda s Pribaltikoy i Zapadnoy Evropoy* (Moscow, 1963), 281ff.

43 *Hansisches Urkundenbuch*, III, n.559.

other spices, as well as silk and cotton materials were brought from Vladimir and later from Lwów to Toruń; some of these were intended for re-export, chiefly to Flanders.

Even at the beginning of the fourteenth century we know very little of Prussian trade with Hungary. But copper and silver from Upper Hungary were already reaching Bruges in the thirteenth century, and doubtless the Prussians played an important part in this trade. Cracow, however, must already have been afraid of Prussian competition since in 1306 the town procured the right of the staple in Hungarian copper, though it was soon deprived of it. In the later years of the fourteenth century the import of copper and of some silver from Hungary was a very important item of Prussian trade, particularly for the Toruń merchants. Some wax and furs were also brought from Hungary, and from Little Poland lead, silver, cochineal and, from the Carpathians, some very valuable yew wood. In the middle of the fourteenth century the Polish king, Casimir the Great, having conquered south-western Russia, and probably acting in close agreement with the Cracow merchants, tried to obstruct the route to the West used by the Prussian and Wrocław merchants. Most probably he intended to transform his capital Cracow into a large entrepôt centre for the trade between the East and the Baltic region, but this plan was never realised because the Teutonic Knights acquired an alternative, though less convenient, door for the eastern trade of their subjects.

After a long period of free trade, the situation began to change at the end of the century. Supported by the crown, from 1372 Cracow established its staple rights. Poland, which in this period already had important economic and political power at its disposal, not only helped its merchants in their struggle to dominate the trade with Hungary and the East, but also endeavoured to clear a passage for them to north-western Europe. One such attempt was the unsuccessful opening in 1390–1 of the 'Flanders road' from Cracow to the ports of western Pomerania already referred to. Toruń, supported by the Teutonic Knights, made use of the right of the staple secured by them in 1403 which was clearly directed against trading expeditions from Cracow to Flanders via Gdańsk. The conflict over trade became interwoven with Poland's war with the Teutonic Knights. The victory of Poland and Lithuania over the Knights at Grunwald in 1410 was a crucial event not only for the political structure in north-eastern Europe: the trade of the Order and its subjects was also driven onto the defensive, and Toruń, deprived of the assistance of the Teutonic

Knights, began to decline. From then onwards Gdańsk became Poland's chief trading partner in Prussia, and the economic relations of the two countries acquired new foundations.

During the thirteenth and particularly the fourteenth centuries, the significance of local goods, including forest and agricultural products, markedly increased in Prussia's foreign trade with the West. This was the result of Prussia's rapid economic and demographic growth in this period and is particularly evident at the end of the fourteenth and the beginning of the fifteenth centuries, thanks to the Order's accounts which have been preserved, and to the sources relating to town trade which are more abundant for this period than for earlier times. The trade in the most valuable Prussian product, amber, was monopolised by the Order. Their agents, the so-called Schäffers, concluded long-term agreements with the gilds of rosary makers in Bruges and Lübeck to supply them with amber. Apart from this they exported amber to other towns, particularly Lwów and Lublin and thus to the centres of trade with the East where it was sold to local merchants and visitors from the Black Sea ports.

It is difficult to say exactly when Prussia began its export of agricultural products. At the end of the fourteenth century it was probably already an important item in its foreign trade. The buyers were the English and, later, mainly the Dutch merchants in Prussia. There are also some figures from the beginning of the fifteenth century concerning the supplies of rye and wheat to Norway, England and elsewhere.[44] Flanders was not active in this trade since it had sufficient western grain at its disposal. Though the direct sources relating to the problem of grain exports from Prussia are few, evidence exists throwing indirect light on the question. Thus, already at the end of the fourteenth and the beginning of the fifteenth centuries, the Prussian merchants frequently protested bitterly against the Teutonic Knights' plan to secure a dominant position, and even a monopoly, in the export of grain. This was chiefly rye which came in all probability from the dues collected by the Knights from their subjects. However, purchases of grain in Włocławek in Kujawy, a very fertile border province of Poland, are also mentioned in the Order's accounts. This same source refers to the export by the Knights of Kujawian wheat to England. Prussia's economic ties with Kujawy were of very long standing. In the mid-thirteenth century supplies of foodstuffs from Kujawy were indispensable for the Teutonic Knights' state, and supplies of leather, cattle, meat, fats and, perhaps, grain from Kujawy

[44] Sattler, *Handelsrechnungen*, 21, 23, 77, 78, 96, 97, 120, 165, 201.

and the neighbouring Mazovia continued to be necessary for Toruń. The craftsmen of this town clearly emphasised this fact in 1425.[45]

Throughout the whole period the export of timber and its products – pitch, tar, ashes, etc. – was of enormous importance for Prussia. The conclusion based on the Teutonic Knights' accounts and the Toruń town records from the later fourteenth and early fifteenth centuries is that only part of this timber came from Prussia itself. It seems that already at this time Prussia imported as much as, or even more than, it produced itself from Mazovia and from other parts of Poland, e.g. the densely forested regions of Radom. In the period under discussion, timber supplies from the Carpathians were already of secondary importance. Some export items were wainscot (*wagenschott*), pine and beech wood, staves, masts etc. in addition to considerable quantities of pitch, tar and ashes. The Order's agents were able to secure a regular supply of these goods, frequently paying their contractors certain sums in advance of future supplies to be delivered by a specified date, usually in the spring when the Vistula and its tributaries were best able to carry the goods. The Order's trading partners were mostly middle-ranking and lesser nobles and burghers of the Mazovian towns situated on the middle reaches of the Vistula and its tributaries, the Narev and the Bug. They organised the purchase of goods on the spot and subsequently transported them to Gdańsk where they were supposed to receive the rest of the agreed amount. Very often agreements included several deliveries and were of a long-term character.[46] Here we are dealing with the same system which the Hanseatic merchants used in Bergen and Livonia and which we come across in many European countries at that time. Thus many Polish suppliers were economically dependent on their creditors, but we cannot say whether they felt themselves to be exploited; we certainly hear of no complaints. We should add that a constant supply was essential for the buyer because of the considerable and growing needs of the Prussian ship-building industry and because of the considerable and growing exports of timber and its by-products to England, Holland, Flanders and, a little later, also to Portugal and Spain, and, to some extent, Normandy. On the other hand the still primitive economy of Mazovia was expanding rapidly in the fourteenth and fifteenth centuries, but beyond doubt its lack of merchant capital was acutely felt. Prussian credit, therefore, was one way of obtaining it.

The general impression is that the Teutonic Knights were pioneers

[45] *Ibid.* 201; M. Toeppen, *Acten der Ständetage Preussens unter der Herrschaft des Deutschen Ordens* (5 vols. Leipzig, 1874–86), I, n. 36, 79, 81, 82ff, 345.

[46] Małowist, 'Podstawy,' 150, 151.

of this system of trade with Poland, although it was also practised at the beginning of the fifteenth century by merchants from Toruń and Gdańsk, though to begin with, it seems, on a smaller scale.[47]

The increasingly frequent appearance of Polish forest and agricultural products on the Prussian markets at the beginning of the fifteenth century, resulted from changes in the economic life of Poland and Prussia and in the structure of international trade during this period. Mazovia, until then a backward region, and Great Poland and Kujawy, economically far behind the southern provinces of the state, entered during the fourteenth and fifteenth centuries a period of relatively rapid economic and demographic growth. The process of rural settlement and urbanisation speeded up, and throughout the whole region we can observe towns expanding as never before. Doubtless the favourable state of the international market for the forest and agricultural products of this region was not the only decisive factor; but it had, nevertheless, considerable influence, particularly on the development of Mazovia. Demand for its forest resources caused excessive deforestation, reaching into the heart of the neighbouring province of Podlachia, but the land thus cleared could be used for agriculture. The swift rise in the population of eastern Mazovia, still sparsely populated (around 58,000) in the first quarter of the fourteenth century, meant that this was particularly important.[48] In the following century, however, the expanding population was already seeking areas for settlement not only at home, but even in eastern Podlachia and the neighbouring virgin forestlands of Prussia. The level of agricultural production already attained made it possible for the inhabitants of central Poland to profit from external markets. In the fifteenth century this process gradually included the whole of the Vistula basin and its tributaries.[49] The Vistula network acquired in this period widespread communications and economic significance.

The growth of trade in forest products and later in grain, which can be proved by sources dating from the end of the fourteenth century, is explained by the rising demand for timber in England, the northern Netherlands, and somewhat later, when its colonial expansion got under way, in Portugal. This was the origin of the interest of these countries in the Baltic lands, and particularly in Prussia. The English and the Dutch who, at the beginning of the fifteenth century, already maintained close contacts with Prussia, probably did so to begin with mainly because of its timber resources. In spite of the prohibitions

[47] *Ibid*, 157, 167.
[48] See above, note 15.
[49] M. Biskup, *Zjednoczenie Pomorza Wschodniego z Polska w połowie XV wieku* (Warsaw, 1959), 95–106.

imposed by the Hanseatic League, at certain times in the fifteenth century they also bought ready-made ships in Prussia and thus profited from the growing ship-building industry at Gdańsk. Besides timber, grain is mentioned with increasing frequency and, in this connection, the nobility of the interior waged a fierce campaign in the first half of the fifteenth century for the right to sell grain in Gdańsk directly to the English, and especially to the Dutch.[50] The Prussian merchants, mainly those from Gdańsk, were the victors, but rural delegates to the Prussian parliaments several times claimed that the monopolistic policies of the towns in this matter would ruin country dwellers; this, however, was probably only propaganda. At the same time rivalry between the merchants and the Teutonic Knights over the grain trade became fiercer, its export being the issue at stake. Unfortunately it is not possible to estimate the volume of grain exported from Prussia in the first half of the fifteenth century.

Attention has already been drawn to the fact that the supply of wood and corn from the Baltic region, but chiefly from Prussia, had become an important element in the economic life of the northern Netherlands. By the end of the fourteenth century, the Prussian towns, particularly Toruń and Gdańsk, were importing forest products and a little grain from Poland. They, too, made use of the system of advance payments described above. Like the agents of the Teutonic Knights, the merchants made advance payments, mainly in cash but sometimes also in cloth from the Netherlands or England. During the years 1410–36 the numerous Polish wars with the Teutonic Knights waged over Prussian territory were damaging to agriculture in the most fertile areas of the country. In some years the Prussians did not have enough food to satisfy their own needs, and certainly not enough to export. The import of grain from Poland came to be indispensable. We may add in parentheses that this caused a flow of money from the Order to Mazovia and other Polish territories and was one element in the severe monetary crisis in Prussia after 1411. In the depreciation of money brought about by this crisis, there was also a motive for the attempts made at that time to increase the bondage of the peasants and to subject them to forced labour on the estates of the nobles and the Order.

At this time Gdańsk's trade with Poland and Lithuania was markedly intensified. At the end of the fourteenth century Poland and Lithuania permitted the Prussian merchants to set up a 'factory' of the Hanseatic type in Kovno (Kaunas). The Gdańsk merchants were

[50] M. Małowist, *Studia z dziejów rzemiosla w okresie kryzysu feudalizmu w Zachodniej Europie w XIV i XV wieku* (Warsaw, 1954), 421ff.

concerned with the export of timber and its products, but imported into Lithuania chiefly Breton salt, some cloth and other goods. At the same time the trade in sylvan and agricultural produce with the Polish territories expanded rapidly and in this the Gdańsk merchants made extensive use of the system of credit transactions described above. In 1448 the nobility of Prussia asserted that the flow of grain from Poland to Gdańsk was already having very unfavourable effects on the Prussian producers through changes in the price level.[51] Here it should be mentioned that many sources in the first half of the fifteenth century point to the fact that several Polish towns were developing trade with Gdańsk solely on their own account. Of first importance were such rapidly developing centres as Warsaw, Bydgoszcz, Nieszawa, Poznań and many others, but in the struggle over access to the sea they were led initially by Cracow. Cracow was not, however, engaged in any new branch of trade, even though the gradual drop in the inflow of copper from Hungary in the course of time had an adverse effect upon its trade with Prussia. The Polish and Lithuanian towns profited at this time from the energetic support of their successive rulers, who were mainly interested in the export of their own grain and timber. Supplies of grey Polish cloth and beer to Prussia also increased in the period, and the import of cattle from Mazovia acquired increasingly greater significance in the course of the fifteenth century.

As already pointed out, during the first half of the fifteenth century, the Prussian economy gradually became linked with the territories of the Polish state, and in mid-century this led to a political union.[52] The departure of the Teutonic Knights from the lands around the mouth of the Vistula and the union of Prussia and Poland facilitated the further development of economic processes already under way. During the second half of the fifteenth century the whole Vistula basin became involved in the trade in Polish grain, timber and other goods with Gdańsk, but the inhabitants of the old Polish territories were not able to take full advantage of the new situation. Already by 1442 Gdańsk had prevented them from making direct contact with foreign merchants in their own territory by reserving for itself the role of intermediary, and this situation remained unchanged after the war of 1453–66 since the Polish kings, hoping to tap Gdańsk's important financial resources, then withdrew support from their old subjects in the trade with Prussia. Because of this, the Gdańsk merchants were able to consolidate their hold over their Polish and Lithuanian

[51] *Ibid.*, 421, 422.
[52] Małowist, 'Podstawy', 164; Biskup, *Zjednoczenie*, 106.

contractors (in spite of the collapse of the Hanseatic house in Kovno) and they retained this position for several centuries. Only in the economic war with Wrocław did the support of the crown secure any important successes for Polish merchants at the end of the fifteenth century.

It is difficult to estimate the size of Polish grain and timber exports which, at the end of our period, formed the basis of the country's overseas trade. According to Biskup's calculations, in the year 1463, at the end of the war with the Teutonic Order, no more than 690 tons of grain were supplied to the port of Gdańsk along the Vistula: from 1461 to 1465 inclusive the amount was 5,000 tons and by 1465 around 5,750 tons. However, the author emphasises that these are minimum estimates. According to Samsonowicz's data, the years 1470 and 1475 show rather similar figures for the export of grain (mainly rye) from Gdańsk. The years 1490–2 saw a clear rise: in 1492 exports exceeded 20,000 tons,[53] though, according to later information, there were enormous fluctuations due to harvest yields in Prussia and the rest of Poland, as well as the level of prices in Amsterdam, and elsewhere. It should be added that exports of forest products from Poland seem to have reached their peak in the fifteenth century. The growth of the country's own demand for timber and its products, in conjunction with the undoubted destruction of the forests, resulted in Lithuania and Byelorussia becoming the chief exporters of forest products in the Baltic, with Gdańsk sharing the trade with Riga and Koenigsberg.

In the course of the fifteenth century Gdańsk's importance for the entire Polish economy increased enormously. The expansion of exports encouraged a growth in imports, which, apart from traditional goods like cloth from the Netherlands and England, salt, herring etc., included some spices supplied directly from Antwerp or purchased in Amsterdam. In spite of this, research reveals that Gdańsk's balance of payments became increasingly favourable.[54] Despite doubts which have been expressed on this question, the indications, in the light of everything that has been said above, are that Prussia's favourable trade balance at the end of the fifteenth and beginning of the sixteenth centuries was no new phenomenon. Gdańsk's close ties with its hinterland and the growth of forest, agricultural and cattle production

[53] M. Biskup, 'Handel wiślany w latach 1454–1466', *Roczniki Dziejow Spolecznych i Gospodarczych*, XIV (1953), 177–9; H. Samsonowicz, 'Handel zagraniczny Gdańska w drugiej połowie XV wieku', 346.

[54] H. Samsonowicz, *Badania nad kapitalem mieszczańskim w Gdańsku w drugiej połowie XV wieku* (Warsaw, 1960), *passim*.

in Poland in the fifteenth century would suggest that some money was already flowing into the country via the mouth of the Vistula, and the trend increased considerably in the years that followed.

During the fifteenth century important new factors appeared in Poland's long-distance overland trade which were in part the result of the monopolistic position of Gdańsk and some other towns of Prussia and Livonia as middlemen in the maritime trade between eastern and western Europe. Attention was drawn earlier to the increase in the rate of growth of rural and urban economy throughout the whole of central Poland, and particularly in Great Poland, Kujawy and Mazovia. Again, as in the earlier epoch, foreign merchants, perceiving openings for trade, began to penetrate Little Poland, to Poznań, Gniezno and Warsaw. In this instance they were the agents of the merchant companies of Nuremberg and other Upper German towns, and they appeared particularly often in Poznań which they reached by road through Leipzig, at that time closely tied economically to Nuremberg. Agents from Gdańsk and immigrants from Wrocław and Upper Germany were also active in Warsaw and often settled there. This, however, was not the decisive factor for towns in central Poland. It seems that merchant capital coming from the West, and frequently from Italy, played a smaller role there than it did in Little Poland. Merchant capital was limited to long-distance trade, but in this field native merchants were even more active. It was the inhabitants of the towns in the Vistula basin who were, in this period, more and more often to be found engaged in exporting forest and agricultural products and importing in return. They maintained, at least until the mid-sixteenth century, a clear ascendancy over the nobility, who only gradually started trading in the produce of their estates.

In the fifteenth century, however, new and encouraging trade prospects opened when Poland was united with the grand duchy of Lithuania, and when the economies of Lithuania, Byelorussia and north-west and central Russia started to grow at a more rapid pace than heretofore. The towns of the grand duchy, but primarily Vilno, Polotsk, Vitebsk and Smolensk, tried to establish direct contracts with western buyers of furs, leather and wax. During the fifteenth century the Vilno merchants succeeded in closing the Hanseatic house in Kovno and developed an active trade with Gdańsk and Königsberg, while still preserving their old contacts with Riga; but in all these ports, native merchants hindered the growth of direct contacts with the western newcomers. The situation was the same in Polotsk, where Hanseatic merchants maintained their privileges until the end of the fifteenth century. The Polish–Lithuanian union gave rise to frequent economic contacts between the two countries and this trade also extended eastwards towards Novgorod and Moscow. By the end of the fourteenth century at latest, there were already trade links between Lithuania and the grand duchy of Moscow, and the exchange of goods in this area became markedly more active in the course of the following centuries. It opened up several trade routes leading from Moscow and the towns of Byelorussia to Vilno, and then via the rapidly-developing towns of Warsaw and Poznań to Wrocław, or later by-passing it to Leipzig. Other less important eastern routes ran from Vilno or Brest to Lublin and so westwards to Silesia and Saxony.

In this way Polish, Lithuanian, Byelorussian and Moscow merchants obtained direct access to western markets where demand for furs, leather and wax was intense. From the West in return, cloth from the Netherlands and north-western Europe, metal goods and also silver coins reached Poland, Lithuania and Russia. This whole area of trade which, in the second half of the fifteenth century, had already assumed significant proportions, has been very little investigated. The town records of fifteenth-century Poznań and other documents show that important transactions were involved. The role played in all this by the wealthy Jewish merchants of Poznań, Lithuanian Brest and some other towns, as well as by citizens of Polish, Russian and German origin, was by no means unimportant. Merchants from Saxony and Upper Germany were certainly engaged in this trade. Leipzig was virtually its terminal point, and consequently its markets acquired great significance in international trade. Wrocław, however, also profited from it, as did Poznań, Warsaw and Vilno.[55] The import of Lithuanian and Russian furs and leather resulted, at that time, in the growth of tanning and fur-dealing in Poland. At the moment it is not possible to do more than advance the hypothesis that trade along the route mentioned here must have caused money to flow from the West and from Poland into Lithuania and Russia. By the sixteenth century this phenomenon was already clear.

Enormous transformations in the trade of the northern part of central-eastern Europe had taken place in the period we have been discussing and they were accompanied by a considerable growth in production and wealth. The characteristic feature was a much closer economic relationship between the respective territories. The political consequences of the economic changes were that Poland regained a large part of Prussia and the changes probably also helped to preserve the union between Poland and Lithuania. The importance of locally

[55] Koczy, *Handel Poznania do Polowy XVI wieku* (Poznań, 1930), 49–106, 204–22, 262–77; Małowist, *Studia...*, 440ff; A. Wawrzynczyk, *Studia z dziejów handlu Polski z W. Ksiestwem Litewskim i Rosja w XVI wieku* (Warsaw, 1956), 5–15.

produced goods in Poland's internal and external trade increased and this was obviously a continuing process. In the fifteenth century the most important items of export were timber and other forest products, grain and livestock, though handicraft and mining products also played their part. Certain factors which would later threaten the growth of the Polish economy in all its aspects were as yet hardly visible. One of these factors was the growing export of vital raw materials such as wool, which was already beginning to be in short supply by the end of the fifteenth century. In addition Polish exports stimulated the import of foreign industrial products that were widely in demand and this made things difficult for local producers. In the fifteenth century, however, when economic growth was in full swing, Polish crafts were not seriously damaged. Here it should be mentioned that the increase in demand for Polish agricultural and forest products checked a threatened crisis in the rural economy in the fifteenth century and helped to maintain the ability of the home market to absorb supplies. The wave of so-called 'second bondage' which led Polish peasants and the majority of town-dwellers to their ruin did not occur until a later period. A characteristic feature of the Polish economy in the thirteenth, and particularly the fourteenth century, was a continuous influx of foreign capital. This was perhaps connected with weaknesses in the main stream of economic life in the West during the crisis of feudalism. Obviously foreign investors saw opportunities in Poland for the advantageous investment of their capital in mining, trade and real estate. Some estimate of the flow of Upper German and Prussian capital into Poland should be attempted. It continued into the fifteenth century, long after it had ceased in Bohemia. These investments accelerated Poland's economic growth while at the same time releasing a dynamic force within the country itself. From this point of view it is also possible to see that the increasing import of foreign goods into Poland was connected with a rising demand for articles of which not enough were manufactured locally. The gap between Poland and the countries which had developed earlier rapidly diminished between the thirteenth and the end of the fifteenth centuries. Nor were the advances merely economic: they were political and cultural as well.

IV. *Trade in Russia*

In the twelfth century, and even more in the thirteenth, economic conditions in the greater part of Russia were far more backward than they were in Bohemia and Poland. The lands bordering the Dnieper suffered severely from the disintegration of the state of Kievan Russia and the attendant struggles between the Russian princes. In 1164, and again in 1182, Kiev, the chief political, commercial and craft centre, was plundered by the warring princes. As historians have always emphasised, nomads controlled the Black Sea steppes, thus obstructing trade between the Russian towns and Constantinople, the Caucasus and Persia. In addition the rapidly growing trade between Italy on the one hand, and Alexandria and the Syrian towns on the other, caused the trade routes connecting Byzantium with Russia and the Baltic region to decline in importance. However, in the twelfth and early thirteenth centuries, there was an expansion of settlement in north-eastern Russia and Novgorod grew rapidly in importance as a state centre and as a nucleus for trade and crafts.

The Mongol invasions (1237–40) and the consolidation of the Tatars' supremacy over Russia dealt the country, and particularly the basins of the Dnieper, Don and Upper Volga and their towns, a catastrophic blow. However, the Tatars never reached Novgorod and north-western Russia and this area was therefore relatively better off, even though it suffered some ill effects from the Tatar victory. It was the weakness of many of the Russian principalities, however, which enabled Novgorod, Pskov and even Polotsk, Smolensk and Vitebsk to develop, and it is precisely in these territories that we can see, relatively speaking, a marked growth in population in the late Middle Ages. It was this growth and economic development by the mid-thirteenth century which enabled Novgorod and Pskov to resist pressure from the Livonian Order and the Swedes. Lithuania's eastward expansion which led, in the thirteenth and fourteenth centuries, to the conquest of Byelorussia, was, from an economic point of view, less damaging, since the victors did not wish to change the status quo. The fate of south-western Russia which fell under the rule of Poland and Lithuania in the fourteenth century has already been described.

The results of the reconstruction and economic development of north-eastern Russia began to appear by the fourteenth century, particularly in the region of the Oka and Upper Volga where politico-economic centres, of which the most important was the duchy of Moscow, developed. This region was separated from the area conquered by the Tatars by huge forests (whence came the name 'Rus Zalesska' – Russia behind the forests), and for this reason the area suffered less from their incursions, with obvious benefits for human settlement. It was also helped by relatively more favourable natural conditions than those in the state of Novgorod. The positive influence on the economy of Europe, and particularly of eastern

Europe, exerted by the trade routes formed after the Mongol states came into being has tended to be overestimated by western scholars. Russia, devastated and exploited by the Tatars, had to undergo an initial period of reconstruction before it could draw any real advantage from the trade arising out of its geographical position. To participate in the trade with the Orient doubtless required quite considerable material resources, and it seems that, by the mid-fourteenth century at the latest, these had become available. The territories in the basin of the Upper Volga and Oka were then specially favourably sited to develop trade as well as their economy as a whole.

For Novgorod, and also even for the state of Moscow, the economic penetration of the northern territories had already become significant during the thirteenth century and this increased in the fourteenth century. Furs, wax and other commodities drawn from that region were the most important items in their long-distance trade and this fact in the course of time greatly reinforced Moscow's economic potential, as it did, to a lesser extent, Novgorod's.

By the end of the fourteenth century Moscow had become the most powerful Russian state. It gradually gained control over the lands in the basin of the Upper Volga and Oka, and hence over Novgorod's south-eastern hinterland, upon whose resources the maintenance of the state and its trade was increasingly dependent. Novgorod's key position in the sphere of economic relations with the West, which enabled the town to exploit its Russian neighbours, was an obstacle to Moscow's expansion, and Novgorod's eventual subjection to the Muscovite state should be seen as the inevitable sequel to this inconvenient circumstance. The entire situation was very like what happened when Poland was united with Prussia, though in the event Moscow gained more from unification than Poland did. But the long-drawn-out conflict which ensued over the national and economic barriers preventing Russia from having free access to the Baltic coastlands is outside the scope of this chapter. At the end of the period in which we are interested signs of Russia's economic and political expansion into the middle reaches of the Volga also appeared.

(I) THE TRADE ROUTES

The rise of the great Mongol empire in the first half of the thirteenth century and the final fall of Kievan Russia in 1238–42 could hardly fail to influence the structure of the trade routes in that part of eastern Europe. The great eastern caravan route leading from China and central Asia via Urgeng, Hadži-Tarkhan (Astrakhan) to the capital of the Golden Horde – Sarai-Berke (near present-day Volgograd on the middle Volga) – and to Tana (near present-day Azov) on the Don, grew in importance. We know that, in the thirteenth and fourteenth centuries, it continued westwards through south-west Russia and Poland to western Europe. It was also possible to get from Sarai via the Don, the Sea of Azov and the Black Sea to the towns of the Crimea, Asia Minor and Constantinople. Astrakhan, moreover, had links by sea and land with the system of routes leading to the Persian Gulf and to India. This whole expanding communications system operated quite satisfactorily in the second half of the thirteenth century and on into the fourteenth, in spite of the conflicts between the Golden Horde and the Persian state of the Il-Khans. But at the end of this period, during Timur's destructive invasion and the prolonged war that accompanied the later swift dissolution of his state, trade could not function normally. No doubt the concentration of eastern trade in the Syrian ports, and particularly in Alexandria, contributed to the decline in economic significance of this great trade route, even though the difficulties along the northern caravan routes must have been the main reason. We must assume that these difficulties made the Caspian Sea and the eastern Caucasus even more important as links between eastern Europe on the one hand and Persia and India on the other. The old river routes – along the Dnieper, Don and Volga – which connected the Black Sea and sub-Caspian region, and thus the Near and Middle East, with the Baltic territories, fulfilled a more limited function at the beginning of our period than they had done in earlier times.[56] During the three following centuries these rivers mainly served the traffic moving goods between the territories adjoining the Black, Azov and Caspian Seas, and the Upper Volga region. In the course of time, however, the development of the river and land communications leading from the Upper Volga to the basins of the northern Dvina and the Pechora gave these routes greater significance.

In addition there already existed in the thirteenth century another great system of communications linking the Baltic countries with north-western Russia. It too dated from a much earlier epoch, but experienced considerable development in the late Middle Ages. This was mainly the old waterway from the Baltic up the Neva into Lake Ladoga and the river Volkhov to Novgorod, but as the town of Reval developed, another starting point for routes leading via the river Narva or Dorpat to Pskov and Novgorod was available. Both these towns could also be reached by land routes coming from Riga and, in the fourteenth and fifteenth centuries, from Gdańsk. Novgorod

[56] See Chapter VII; F. Bruns and H. Weczerka, *Hansische Handelsstrassen* (Weimar, 1968–9).

was, in its turn, the point of departure for waterways and land roads running further north-eastwards into the regions of the northern Dvina and the Pechora towards the borders of Siberia, and south-eastwards into the heart of Russia. There was another starting point on the Baltic coast for a road from the mouth of the western Dvina into Byelorussia and the towns of Polotsk, Vitebsk and Smolensk, though from the thirteenth to the fifteenth centuries its importance cannot be compared with the great routes leading to Pskov and Novgorod.[57]

This elaborate system of communications reached into the very heart of the upper Volga region, but in the thirteenth and fourteenth centuries it was utilised to only a very limited extent. It was not until north-east Russia, and especially the state of Moscow, developed economically and politically that any changes occurred.

This description of the structure of the main Russian trade routes reveals the existence of several different regions whose trade was very loosely linked and of which the following may be distinguished:

(a) the Black Sea and Caspian regions, together with the steppes of central Russia;
(b) Livonia and north-western Russia with Great Novgorod as its chief trading centre; and
(c) the basin of the Upper Volga.

The vast territories in the north-east constituted the hinterland of both Novgorod and Moscow and will be discussed with them. A natural economy prevailed everywhere in medieval Russia, and the economic links between the individual areas in the thirteenth and fourteenth centuries were consequently very loose.

(2) THE BLACK SEA, THE CASPIAN AND THE STEPPES

Trade was most active in the second half of the thirteenth and in the fourteenth centuries around the Black Sea and the lands bordering on the Azov and Caspian Seas. This is confirmed by the system of routes discussed in the last few pages. Nevertheless, the intensification of trade here was primarily dependent on other factors. The Mongols had amassed considerable wealth largely through plunder, while the eventual stabilisation of Tatar authority in Russia promoted a regular outflow of goods (including slaves) from the subject states, even though it was perhaps at a lower rate than formerly. Other important factors in the economic development of the Golden Horde were the

[57] W. Goetz, *Deutsch-russische Handelsgeschichte des Mittelalters* (Lübeck, 1922), 195–245; F. Bruns and H. Weczerka, *Hansische Handelsstrassen, Atlas*, 36–40.

stock-rearing activities of the nomads on the steppes and the exploitation of the salt works in the Astrakhan area and on the Perekop isthmus, etc. These circumstances, together with a favoured position on the great intercontinental routes, helped to create and develop powerful centres of local and long-distance trade in the state of the Golden Horde during the thirteenth and fourteenth centuries. One fundamental pre-condition for this development was an efficient state apparatus which could provide security for merchants. These favourable conditions no longer prevailed in the second half of the fourteenth century. The effects of the great epidemics were aggravated by those of the bitter internal struggles within the Golden Horde itself. Timur's military invasion at the end of the century brought a wave of destruction, and later on the dissolution of his empire plunged the whole region into permanent political chaos which precipitated economic collapse.

Little is known of the fate of Sarai-Batu on the middle Volga, the first capital of the Golden Horde. Khan Usbek (1312–40) moved the capital to Sarai-Berke near present-day Volgograd. Thanks to the treasures assembled there and its geographical location, it quickly became the centre for a lively trade with central Asia and the Far and Near East.

Mention has already been made of Sarai and the Italian colony at Tana on the Don, and of the significance of their trade with central and western Europe in the fourteenth century and even earlier. Sarai, and to some extent Astrakhan and Tana, were not only important centres of the exchange of silk and cotton cloth from China, Turkestan and Persia but also, though perhaps to a lesser degree, of spices from south-west Asia. Other important items in the trade were furs, leather and grain – coming mainly from the land of the Bulgars on the Kama and Volga – whilst furs, walrus tusks and falcons were brought to southern towns via these lands from the regions of the far north. Goods sent into the heart of Russia in return were of eastern origin, also probably salt, and perhaps some western products, including cloth supplied by the Italians via Constantinople, the towns of the Crimea and Tana; sometimes cloth was transported by road from the West.[58]

It was suggested earlier that the trade between the towns of the Golden Horde and Russia could only develop when the latter had recovered from the damage done by the Tatar invasion, and that this probably did not happen before the fourteenth century. It is not possible to say when the Black Sea and Caspian territories began importing the handicraft products from the Upper Volga and Oka region that were so characteristic of Russian trade with the East in the

[58] B. Grekov and Ya. Jakubovski, *Le Horde d'or* (Paris, 1939), 133–47.

sixteenth and seventeenth centuries, but doubtless they had already made their appearance by the fifteenth century, a period when craft output in the Moscow state grew rapidly.[59]

Since the Tatars controlled the steppes and extended their supremacy over Russia, the latter was not only forced to pay a large tribute, but in addition suffered severe losses from slave-hunting raids. Sarai and Tana, and later especially Caffa, became important markets in the fourteenth century for slaves brought by the Tatars from Russia, the Caucasus and the steppes. The growth of trade in the towns of the Golden Horde attracted Italian merchants. The Genoese colony in Caffa (Feodosia) was established in the second half of the thirteenth century, but in the course of the following century it became the centre for a system of trading posts situated in the Crimea, on the coasts of the Black Sea, the Sea of Azov and south-western Caucasus. There was also a Genoese outpost in Tana, though it was weaker than the Venetian one. The Genoese maintained contact with Sarai too and, in the course of time, infiltrated into the grand duchy of Moscow, while some of them even penetrated as far as the Pechora region and helped to exploit it.

The disintegration of the state of the Golden Horde in the second half of the fourteenth century and the military invasion of Timur dealt a fatal blow to the inland towns of the area. Tana also fell, although Italian colonies lingered on there until the Turkish invasion in 1475. In the mid-fifteenth century the Venetian senate referred regretfully to the earlier heyday of its once-celebrated trading post.[60]

From the middle of the fifteenth century the most important town in the region was Caffa, inhabited mainly by Armenians with smaller numbers of Greeks, Jews and Tatars and a very small (2–3,000) but influential group of Genoese. As a centre it relegated the previously very wealthy town of Sudak (known to the Russians as Surozh and to the Italians as Soldaia) to a secondary position. Caffa, as the figures taken from a list probably compiled by the Turks after they conquered the town in 1475 show, had about 8,000 houses and 70–75,000 inhabitants; in earlier, and more favourable, periods its population had allegedly reached 100,000.[61] Caffa owed its powerful hold on the trade in oriental products less to the caravan routes linking it directly with the Middle and Far East than to its contacts with Constantinople and the towns of Asia Minor, the Caucasus and western Persia which all took part in the trade with the ports of the Persian Gulf. It appears that, together with the import of goods from these regions, the

[59] M. V. Fehner, *Torgovla Russkogo Gosudarstva so stranami Vostoka v XVI veke* (Moscow, 1956), 51–60.
[60] Małowist, *Kaffa*, 53, 91.
[61] *Ibid.*, 18, 21ff.

production of silk fabrics developed in Caffa. In the fourteenth century, Caffa was famous for the distribution of many kinds of oriental products in eastern Europe and for their export to the West. Reference has already been made to the great activity of the Italians, Armenians, Jews and Greeks of Caffa, in Bielgorod, Chilia, the towns of Moldavia, Lwów and Little Poland. Caffa's relations with Moscow and the other towns of the Upper Volga basin were also important for its trade; we shall have to return later to this matter.

It seems that the inflow of oriental goods into the Crimea slackened somewhat in the fifteenth century, because of the endless wars and disturbances in the Middle East. Caffa, however, continued to trade with Poland, Moldavia and Russia, although the supply of oriental goods from these countries to western Europe declined. In the fifteenth century, particularly after the fall of Constantinople, Genoese interest in its Crimean colonies diminished.

Caffa's economic role was not confined to participating in the oriental trade. The development of the Crimean towns stimulated agriculture. The production of wine in the Crimea was initiated at that time, and the output of sea salt increased on the Perekop isthmus. All this helped to supply the inhabitants of the towns with foodstuffs, and was also the basis of grain exports to Constantinople, the northern ports of Asia Minor and even Genoa. It was anticipated in 1465 that 5–10,000 *modii* of grain could be conveyed from Caffa to Genoa if the sultan would grant permission for deliveries to pass through the straits. It is likely that grain exports were made possible by the fact that supplies came not only from the Crimea itself but also from Bielgorod (Akkerman) in Moldavia and from the district by the mouth of the Dnieper; the import of grain from these territories is well documented. In addition, when the harvest in the Black Sea regions was poor, grain was often brought from as far away as Italy. Other items in Caffa's trade were: Crimean timber sent to Constantinople and Egypt; fish purchased at the mouth of the river Kuban in exchange for sea salt extracted on the Perekop isthmus; western and Polish cloths; local textiles; cochineal from Kiev and Lwów for the Italian textiles centres; and leather and furs from Tatar and Russian lands for despatch to various destinations. Thus, the Crimean trade centres stimulated economic life over a very wide area. On the other hand their slave trade did untold harm to neighbouring territories.

Caffa was the main slave market in the fifteenth century, though many other nearby towns had similar, but smaller, markets. In the second half of the fifteenth century, the successive khans of the Crimea also endeavoured to promote a slave trade in their towns to the great annoyance of the Genoese who were, it seems, at that time more actively engaged in this trade than any of the other inhabitants of their colonies. It is clear that each year the Genoese in Caffa bought slaves in the Caucasus at La Copa on the mouth of the Kuban and at Sebastopol (Sukhum). They even purchased slaves from the Tatars in Caffa itself and in Tana, Kerch, Inkerman and other places, which naturally encouraged the nomads to raid the settled peoples in Russia and Poland. The children of impoverished Tatar parents were also sold as slaves. In the fifteenth century everyone took part in this trade, even the Catholic bishops of Caffa. Slaves were mainly recruited from amongst the inhabitants of Russia, the Caucasus (the sources often mention Georgians), less frequently Poland and very often from amongst the Tatars themselves. A large number, perhaps the majority, were sent to Egypt, Syria and Turkey. There is no lack of information about slaves being conveyed by ship or even being driven along the land routes (via Moldavia and Poland) to Italy and other Christian countries in the Mediterranean. Verlinden has drawn our attention to their presence as far afield as Spain and southern France. My own earlier researches revealed a large number of transactions concerning slaves in Genoa in the second half of the fifteenth century, and that for the most part these slaves were women employed as domestic servants. It is possible that the majority of those exported to Turkey, and more particularly Egypt and Syria, were men destined for craft work and for the army.[62]

The occupation of Caffa and the other Black Sea towns by the Turks in 1475 and 1481 was not economically disastrous, though the inhabitants suffered from the extortions and atrocities of the invaders.

In the following period, Caffa and Akkerman increasingly became markets for slaves supplied by the Tatars, sometimes clearly at the request of the local merchants who financed the raiding expeditions.[63] However, Caffa's trade in Levantine goods fell away. This reveals a continuation of the process begun considerably earlier. At the end of the fifteenth century Constantinople's direct trade links with Oltenia and the Polish state were strengthened, whereas Caffa was now playing a very limited role in this direction, while maintaining its trade with the rapidly developing towns of north-eastern Russia.

(3) LIVONIA AND NORTH-WEST RUSSIA

As already pointed out, in the mid-thirteenth century the peoples of north-western Russia suffered considerably less from the Tatars than those living in other parts of the country. They also successfully

[62] *Ibid.*, 48–94, 157; see above p. 588, note 59.

[63] A. Dziubinski, 'Handel niewolinikami polskimi i ruskimi w XVI wieku i jego organizacja', in *Przeglad Historyczny*, LVII (1966), 36–49.

resisted pressure from the Germans who, at the beginning of the thirteenth century, had begun the conquest of Livonia and who gradually gained control over it; in the following century what remained of Danish authority was expelled from Estonia.

There is no doubt that the possibility of sharing in the trade with neighbouring Russia was the main motive for German merchants settling in Livonia. Nonetheless, the rural economy of Livonia itself constituted not only an indispensable pre-condition for the existence of the towns in which they settled, but also began in due course to influence their long-distance trade even more strongly.

The Livonian Order, which became a part of the Teutonic Order although preserving much of its autonomy, was less powerful than the Prussian Teutonic Knights. Up to the end of the fifteenth century it even managed to spread its authority over the whole of Livonia, but had to share it with the other German feudal lords. In fact both these groups, together with the inhabitants of the towns, were powerful enough to master and hold in servitude the conquered population of the country, although from the thirteenth century onwards, they quarrelled bitterly among themselves. This was particularly true of the relations between the Order, and the archbishop and town of Riga. One of the causes of friction was of course trade. So far as economic links between town and country were concerned the divergent interests of nobility, Order and townsmen did not appear clearly until the fifteenth and sixteenth centuries. The Order could not lend the Livonian towns such effective aid in their contacts with the Russians as the Teutonic Knights gave to their Prussian subjects. In the thirteenth and fourteenth centuries the political, military and economic relationship between the Order in Livonia and the towns of Novgorod and Pskov was considerably less advantageous for the Germans than in Prussia. In addition, as also happened in Prussia, the Livonian merchants suffered from the trade competition of the Order. Finally, the Order's frequent wars with the Russian city republics and Lithuania hindered the activities of the merchants in spite of the fact that both Hanseatic and Russian merchants did their best to eliminate these obstacles by special agreements. Many of the Livonian towns, and especially the three largest (Reval, Riga and Dorpat), belonged to the Hanseatic League, constituting the so-called Livonian section which yielded in turn in the thirteenth and fourteenth centuries to the powerful impact of Visby and Lübeck. In the fourteenth century, but particularly in the fifteenth, the diverging interests of local and Lübeck merchants became increasingly sharp and led to the rights of the foreign Hanseatic merchants in Livonia and of the Hanse posts in Russia being restricted.

At the end of the thirteenth and beginning of the fourteenth centuries Riga, Reval and Dorpat were already large local centres of internal trade for the whole of Livonia. The peasants either supplied their products direct to the markets of the bigger towns, or else they had them conveyed there by the inhabitants of the smaller towns and numerous market settlements (*Flecken*). An important element in internal trade was the advances against future supplies of rural products made by the merchants of Riga and Reval to their lesser contractors living in town and country. This system, established in Prussia and northern Poland by the fifteenth century, was developed in Livonia considerably earlier. To judge from the sources, the peasants suffered bitterly from the usurious activities of the nobility and clergy. It is quite clear too that some of the richer peasants took advantage of the loans granted them by the townsmen to interpose themselves between their urban creditors and the bulk of poor peasants, and extracted thereby considerable profit. Doubtless the system of the permanent contracts between town merchants and the richer suppliers of rural products analysed by Mickwitz on the basis of data from the second half of the sixteenth century developed in the same way. By the early fourteenth century small-town pedlars supplying peasants with cheap home-produced and imported craft products, and particularly with salt, were also very active in the countryside. The Livonian towns were never able to eliminate entirely the independent trade carried on by the peasants. Amongst others engaged in this trade were the so-called carriers transporting goods within the country. In many of the so-called illegal ports the peasants made contact with travellers from abroad and this particularly irritated the townsmen. At the end of the fifteenth century, the foreign trade of the towns was also threatened by the active part undertaken by the nobility and clergy. Their trade was based on peasant dues paid mainly in grain, but, beginning in the sixteenth century, the trade came to rely on serfdom on the developing estates of the nobility and church.

The country supplied the towns with grain, flax, hemp, cheap native furs, leather, wax and livestock and timber products. Some of these goods were intended for export. The foreign markets for the sale of Livonian goods were Lübeck, Bruges, England and, from the second half of the fourteenth century, Holland and later Portugal. In special demand was the Livonian and Russian flax which passed through Lübeck, and perhaps the Frankfurt fairs, even into the textile centres of Swabia (which, of course, chiefly used local flax). During the fifteenth century exports of timber, pitch and ashes to the Netherlands, England and Portugal increased. The first references to the export of grain, particularly of Livonian rye, date from the end of the thirteenth century. In the following century some Estonian rye was also exported to the West from Reval. However, grain did not play an important role in the exports from Livonia to the West during the fifteenth century; it was, however, always supplied in small quantities to neighbouring Finland and occasionally to Prussia, Sweden and Novgorod.[64]

During the period from the thirteenth to the end of the fifteenth centuries, the long-distance trade of Livonia was largely based on brokerage between Russia and the countries of central and north-west Europe. The Livonian towns of Reval and Dorpat were mainly partnered by Novgorod and Pskov, while the external trade of the towns in the Dvina basin – Polotsk, Vitebsk and Smolensk – came in the course of time to be linked with the merchants of Riga. The network of routes described above was the decisive factor in determining the areas of influence. What chiefly attracted the Hanseatic merchants to the Russian trade was its vast resources of furs and beeswax. Novgorod was the leading supplier of furs, while much of the wax produced in these regions was purchased in Pskov and Polotsk where furs were less important.

As mentioned earlier, north-western Russia did not suffer very much from the Mongol invasion. Novgorod and Pskov also managed to resist German pressure. Polotsk, Smolensk and Vitebsk, however, came in the thirteenth and fourteenth centuries under the domination of Lithuania. Recent research into the history of Novgorod has revealed many new facts bearing upon the history of its trade. It is now clear, for instance, that in spite of unfavourable natural conditions, the rural population of the republic of Novgorod was dependent upon agriculture and stock-rearing, even though fishing and hunting were also important.[65] It seems, however, that in relation to its growing population the agricultural basis of the Novgorod republic was most insecure. In our period, the land passed almost completely into the hands of a ruling group of boyars and clergy, with only a small area belonging to merchants. The peasant population paid dues to their lords in the products of agriculture, stock-rearing, fishing and forestry and, in the fifteenth century, also in money; furs and leather derived from this source were mainly intended for resale.[66] The social rank of Novgorod merchants was much below that of the boyars with whom they were economically linked. Nevertheless a certain group of merchants, particularly a rich body called 'the St Ivan hundred',

[64] W. Niitemaa, 'Der Binnenhandel in der Politik der livländischen Städte im Mittelalter', *Annales Academiae Scientiarum Fennicae*, LXXVI (1952), 52ff, 270ff; J. Ahvenainen, *Der Getreidehandel Livlands im Mittelalter* (Helsinki, 1963), *passim*.

[65] L. V. Danilova, *Otcherki po istorii zemlevladeniya i hoziaystva v novgordoskoy zemle v XIV–XV vv* (Moscow, 1955), 20ff, 45ff.

[66] *Ibid.*, 97ff; Khoroshkevitch, *Torgovla*, 53–68.

wielded great economic power. Archaeological research has revealed that Novgorod was also an important centre of craft production.[67]

It is difficult to agree with Johansen's view that, in the Middle Ages, external trade was not essential for north-western Russia.[68] Recent Soviet researches have shown that north-western Russia had inadequate resources of salt, even of low quality; that it was almost completely without either base or precious metals; and that its supply of essential food (i.e. grain) was unreliable.[69] This situation improved somewhat in the fifteenth century, by which time the distant regions of the north-east were more widely exploited. However the profits that accrued were primarily enjoyed by Moscow rather than by Novgorod. This state of affairs forced Novgorod and the other Russian towns in the area to maintain economic contacts with the Hanseatic merchants who were partners capable of supplying the goods they lacked.

Lesnikov and other Soviet scholars have recently noticed another important factor. Despite earlier views, it transpires that Novgorod was primarily a centre for the trade in cheap furs, particularly squirrel skins, and that these furs came mainly from the central regions of the republic. In fact, in the twelfth and thirteenth centuries, Novgorod had already extended its sphere of economic influence as far as the Urals and had in this period established colonies. But the tribute in furs demanded from the conquered population was very irregular, and the expeditions that were undertaken to collect them were not so successful as had until recently been assumed; indeed they often ended unsuccessfully. By the thirteenth century the grand duchy of Moscow had begun to spread its influence into the basins of the northern Dvina and Pechora, and this also occurred at the expense of Novgorod.[70] In addition the main region of medieval Russia supplying the more valuable furs was the land of the Bulgars on the Kama (the present-day Kazan), which had to be reached by semi-raiding expeditions from Novgorod, but in which the economic influence of the republic was unfortunately weak. Thus valuable furs, like sable and ermine, did not play a large role in the trade of Novgorod. We have to assume that the vast export of furs from Novgorod, which, in the fourteenth century, probably amounted to as much as half a million skins a year, was only possible because they were relatively so cheap. For it is difficult to imagine that the markets of medieval Europe could, over

[67] B. A. Ribakov, *Remeslo drevney Rusi* (Moscow, 1948), 594, 611, 623ff; A. V. Artsikhovski, *Novgorodskie remesla*, 6.

[68] Johannsen *Der hansische Russlandhandel*, 40ff.

[69] Khoroshkevitch, *Torgovla*, 213–30, 307–18, 320–2.

[70] M. P. Lesnikov, *Ganzeyskaya torgovla pushninoy v natchale XV veka* (Publications of Potemkin Institute, XIII, 1954), 61–93; *Idem*, 'Torgovye snoshenia', *Istoritcheskye Zapiski*, XXXIX (1952), 259ff; Danilova, *Otcherki*, 204–10.

a long period of time, have absorbed quantities of this order of goods that were very expensive, not to mention the fact that the Hanseatic customers did not dispose of a purchasing power comparable with that of the richer Italians. It is worth adding that in Novgorod the Hanseatic merchants wanted to buy only unprepared furs,[71] the reason being that not only were they afraid that prepared goods would inevitably be adulterated, but also that they themselves wished to reap the benefits of the higher prices charged to the final consumers. The bulk of furs sold in Novgorod came from peasant dues. The boyars probably sold them to local merchants who re-sold them to foreign buyers. The latter were, perhaps, also supplied directly by the boyars and, to the extent that this was possible, by dealers from the heart of the country, though the merchants of Novgorod opposed this practice. Russian peasants did not come to Novgorod to sell furs until the fifteenth century.[72] Wax, the second main item in Novgorod's exports, does not appear amongst the peasant dues paid to the lords; perhaps therefore the town merchants bought this commodity direct from the peasants who probably also supplied certain quantities to the urban markets.[73] By controlling the main source of supply of such valuable goods as furs and wax, not to speak of leather and other less important articles, and furthermore by virtue of their important political and military presence, Novgorod and, to a lesser extent, Pskov were in a strong position *vis-à-vis* travellers arriving from the West. Yet to take full advantage of their position they needed to have regular access to their distant customers, but, in the course of the thirteenth century, the Hanseatic merchants managed to oust the Russians from maritime trade with the northern coasts of the Baltic. Thus, both exports out of Russia and imports into Novgorod and the other Russian towns were in the hands of German merchants. Even so, however, the division of economic and political power between the German merchants and the Russians in the thirteenth and fourteenth centuries was considerably more to the advantage of the latter than was, for example, the position of the townsmen of Great Poland and Mazovia *vis-à-vis* the Prussian merchants. The Hanseatics had considerable successes in Novgorod and Pskov during the thirteenth and fourteenth centuries and their 'factory' or counting house, in Novgorod, which was at that time dominated by merchants from Visby and Lübeck, acquired extensive legal and economic powers. Although Hanseatic merchants managed to limit Russian commercial activity in Livonia, Novgorod and, to a large extent, Pskov, the Russians were in practice able to prevent the Germans from

[71] Khoroshkevitch, *Torgovla*, 97ff. [72] *Ibid.* [73] *Ibid.*, 47–72.

penetrating into the heart of Russia where its most valuable resources lay. They kept the trade between the German merchants and their vast hinterland in their own hands. We might even go so far as to speak of a balance of power between the two partners, albeit a somewhat shaky one. In the light of such a conclusion it is not difficult to accept Lesnikov's view that, at the end of the fourteenth and the beginning of the fifteenth centuries, the difference between the prices of goods from the Hanseatic–Russian trade in the markets of Bruges and Novgorod respectively (after subtracting freight charges) was relatively small and that the net profit of the Hanseatic merchants from their trade with Novgorod varied between very little and 12 per cent.[74] Lesnikov's conclusion has not so far been satisfactorily documented, but if it were to be confirmed then we should have to conclude that the relatively greater power of the Russian merchants in relation to their partners had an influence upon the price structure.

The quantities of furs, chiefly squirrel and other fairly cheap kinds, with which Novgorod supplied the Hanseatic merchants were considerable. In the 1350s the Lübeck company of Wittenborg exported from Novgorod and Livonia furs to the enormous value of between 200,000 and 500,000 Lübeck marks. At that time the Wittenborgs sold in the course of about three years an average of 20,000 skins a year. On one ship sailing from Reval to Lübeck in 1368 there were 75–100,000 skins in seventeen barrels. In 1403 English pirates captured 142,268 skins from Novgorod and Pskov in two ships sailing from Riga to Flanders. In 1398 the Order of Teutonic Knights exported up to 136,430 skins from Novgorod, but in the course of the following few years exports dropped to less than one-third of this quantity. In 1441 Novgorod confiscated 200–280,000 skins from Hanseatic merchants.

The export was thus a bulky one. Khoroshkevitch assumes that it increased in the course of the fourteenth century, was at its height at the beginning of the fifteenth century and was maintained at that level for a time. According to this authority, however, by the second half of the fifteenth century Novgorod was already suffering from the effects of the exhaustion of its resources; the hunting grounds shifted considerably further north and the main profit from this shift accrued to the Muscovite and not the Novgorod merchants.[75] Novgorod probably obtained its beeswax from the forests on the middle Volga, from the Oka, from the land of the Bulgars on the Kama, from the Riazan region and from Carelia; however in the export of beeswax Novgorod had also to yield to the towns in the basin of the western

[74] See above p. 594, note 70.

[75] Khoroshkevitch, *Torgovla*, 108–17.

Dvina. It is not possible to estimate the total yearly export of this commodity to the Hanseatic towns. In the middle of the fourteenth century, individual German merchants sometimes exported more than 7–800 kilos of beeswax from Novgorod, while the wealthy Wittenborgs sold about 6.6 tons per annum. Their case, however, was an exceptional one. According to the Reval customs books of 1368–9, around 18.5 tons of wax, probably chiefly originating in Novgorod and Pskov, went through the port in 1368. In 1393 one ship alone plying from Reval to Flanders carried about 6 tons of wax, and between 1399 and 1404 the Teutonic Knights exported around 43 tons from Novgorod and Pskov.[76] It is possible to agree with Khoroshkevitch's view that Russia was the chief supplier of beeswax to the European markets in the fourteenth century, with the western Dvina region playing a considerably larger role in this export than Novgorod and Pskov. Later the situation changed, for Novgorod became the chief entrepôt for the transit trade in beeswax from central Russia to central and western Europe. At the end of the fifteenth century probably over 300 tons were exported every year from Novgorod.[77] The output of leather in Novgorod was also highly developed, although it chiefly satisfied the domestic needs of Russia itself.

Novgorod's imports were considerably more varied. Doubtless the supply of cloth was most important, followed by salt and precious metals. It is probable that Novgorod and other Russian towns did not have an urban cloth industry of their own until the sixteenth century. This was probably due to the climate and the small number of sheep that were raised. The import of western cloth into Novgorod most probably dated from the twelfth century, and later increased. By the middle of the fourteenth century some Novgorod merchants were purchasing large consignments of western cloth; more was being imported at that time through Riga than through Reval or Dorpat. The volume of imports into Novgorod cannot be gauged. According to Khoroshkevitch, in 1410 the Hanseatic merchants had around 80,000 metres in store; this was, however, only the smaller part of their annual import. Flanders cloth, coming from Ghent, Bruges, Ypres, Arras and other towns, dominated the Novgorod market, but in the fourteenth and fifteenth centuries cloth known as the *nouvelle draperie* from centres on the river Lys was coming in, and cloth from Poperinghe was likewise increasingly available. The expensive cloths from Ypres enjoyed a relative success in Russia. They were intended for wealthy people not only in Novgorod but also in central Russia. From the middle of the fifteenth century imports of Dutch materials,

[76] *Ibid.*, 134. [77] *Ibid.*, 145ff.

mainly the cheaper cloths from Naarden and to a lesser degree from Leyden, the Hague and Amsterdam, increased considerably. In addition German, English and, to a much lesser extent, Polish cloth played a secondary role in Novgorod which, it seems, was rather conservative in its choice of textiles. Only at the end of the fifteenth century did English cloth gain for itself the same position in Livonia as textiles from Flanders and Holland; and maybe there was a similar change in Novgorod and Pskov.[78]

Recent Soviet researches have shown that the production of salt in the Novgorod area was very low. In the fifteenth century the situation improved owing to the growth of salt exploitation in Staraia Russa within the territory of the republic. However the great advance in salt production evident in the fifteenth and sixteenth centuries in north-east Russia did not mean that Novgorod received a much better supply. Novgorod was perhaps dependent to a large extent from the thirteenth century on salt imported from the Hanseatic towns, and the rise in population further increased the demand. In the thirteenth century Pomeranian salt from the district around Kołobrzeg was imported into Novgorod and Pskov, but in the following century the highly valued salt from the Lüneburg region was already predominant. In 1368 around 1,500 tons of salt, of which, perhaps, one-third was intended for Russia, were imported into the three chief Livonian ports. In later years salt imports into Livonia fluctuated greatly, sometimes increasing considerably; it was in this period that the cheaper Breton salt gained a distinct ascendancy over both the eastern Baltic and the Russian markets. In the 1430s about 3,000 lasts of salt (or about 6,500–7,000 tons) were imported annually into Reval alone. In the fifteenth century supplies of Portuguese salt also began to arrive, although still in limited quantities. During the whole of the period under discussion, salt was exported from the Livonian towns to Russia and Byelorussia, in amounts often constituting the greater part of what was imported. In all probability some of the salt supplied to Novgorod was re-exported to central Russia.[79]

Novgorod was self-supporting in respect of its iron requirements, but nevertheless imports of copper, lead and tin, often forbidden by the Livonian Order for military reasons, were indispensable. In spite of the ban the Hanseatic merchants, particularly those from Lübeck, supplied the Russians with these metals, as did the Nuremberg merchants who penetrated into Livonia perhaps as far as Novgorod in the fifteenth century.[80]

Amongst many other goods imported into Novgorod we should

[78] *Ibid.*, 164, 168ff. [79] *Ibid.*, 216–62. [80] *Ibid.*, 308ff.

mention the quite considerable quantities of wine and beer; herrings and small shellfish; amber from Prussia; and, finally, grain, the latter mostly when the Russian harvests were bad. Too little importance seems to have been accorded in recent Soviet studies to the last item, especially as far as the thirteenth and fourteenth centuries are concerned. In a later period Novgorod imported grain in times of scarcity, mainly from central Russia.

The constant and very important import of silver into Novgorod, and perhaps Pskov, suggests that the Hanseatic imports, although they were very diverse, often did not cover the price of the exports of Russian furs and beeswax. This is made clear by the accounts of the Lübeck Wittenborgs from the middle of the fourteenth century which have already been mentioned. The grave shortage of silver throughout Europe in the fourteenth and a large part of the fifteenth century caused the Hanseatic merchants to try to ban the export of this metal to Russia and to maintain a bilateral exchange of goods in Novgorod. Their attempts were not successful, in particular because of competition from the Order of Teutonic Knights. At the end of the fourteenth century and at the beginning of the fifteenth the Order's agents were very active in Novgorod – in this period, according to Lesnikov's calculations, they delivered there each year about 200 kilos of silver, probably mainly coming from Upper Hungary, but also from Little Poland and Silesia. It is possible that the revival of the mining of metals in central Europe during the second half of the fifteenth century influenced the supplies of silver to Novgorod. In the whole of the period under discussion silver came mostly in the form of ingots, but also as coins, though in lesser quantities. Gold coins, chiefly English nobles, also appeared as tender used by German merchants in Novgorod, but obviously much less frequently than silver coins. Recently Soviet scholars have correctly emphasised the significance of the import of metals, and particularly of silver, to Russia in the late Middle Ages, for precious metals were still not being extracted within its borders. From Novgorod the metals penetrated into central Russia and were undoubtedly an important factor favouring its economic growth and especially the reconstruction and diffusion of the monetary system in the fourteenth and fifteenth centuries, although Russia was forced to give the Tatars quite a large proportion of these metals as tribute.[81] The brisk flow of silver from central and western Europe into Russia throws additional light on the severe monetary crisis which was so widespread in the fourteenth and the first half of the fifteenth centuries.

[81] *Ibid.*, 268, 271–305; Lesnikov, 'Torgovye snoshenya', 262.

In practice all the large towns of the Hanse were engaged in active trade with Novgorod. For a long time Riga, Reval and Dorpat were too weak to take advantage of their convenient geographical position to reduce the influence of Lübeck and the other members of the powerful Wendish group in the Novgorod factory. But gradually, starting from the end of the fourteenth and the beginning of the fifteenth centuries, they began to achieve results, with Reval and Dorpat (Novgorod's closest partners) having the greatest success; Riga, which had already begun to do so in an earlier period, concentrated its efforts mainly on trade with the towns of the western Dvina basin. Nevertheless, the task of the merchants in the chief Livonian towns was not an easy one. They found themselves in increasing competition with men from the Finnish towns of Viborg and Åbo (Turku), who were energetically supported by the great resident Swedish feudal lords having a personal interest in the growth of these towns and in the trade with Russia. The German merchants, who were able in this way to break Novgorod's boycott and carry on a lively trade with the Russians, flocked to both these Finnish towns, particularly during the frequent conflicts between the Hanse and Novgorod in the fifteenth century. Prussian merchants, mainly from Gdańsk, also travelled by land routes to Pskov and Novgorod despite the efforts of the Hanse, and in this way undermined the position not only of Reval, but also of Lübeck, *vis-à-vis* their Russian contractors.[82] The impression that remains is that, in the fifteenth century, the number of merchants interested in trade with Russia markedly increased. The English and Dutch were also trying to penetrate the Russian centres of trade, but owing to determined resistance on the part of Reval and Riga they were forced to be satisfied, in general, with the supply of salt, cloth and other less important goods to the Livonian ports, where in return they purchased native and Russian products from the local merchants. In Livonia itself, however, the three large towns were not in a position fully to control the situation. Narva and, to a lesser extent, Pernü, neither of which belonged to the Hanseatic League but which were supported by the Livonian Order, became centres where Russian merchants were able to meet travellers from across the sea, particularly during the disputes and struggles between the Hanse and the Russians. The importance of Narva clearly increased in the fifteenth century.

All this relieved Hanseatic pressure on Novgorod and Pskov. Unfortunately we do not know a great deal about the merchants of these Russian towns. In any case much of our information concerning

[82] Goetz, *Deutsch-russische Handelsgeschichte*, 95ff, 109ff, 135.

the large-scale transactions concluded between the Novgorod and Hanseatic merchants points irrefutably to the fact that the accumulation of merchant capital in Novgorod was relatively far advanced in the fifteenth century, and that the Novgorod merchants did not lag behind their Livonian contractors in this respect. At that time they felt themselves to be increasingly restricted by the limitations imposed by the Hanse; they were not satisfied with active trade in Livonia and constantly claimed that the Hanse should guarantee them freedom and security in maritime trade.[83] Thus, in the Russian sphere we come across the same general phenomenon characterising the contemporary situation in England, Prussia and the Scandinavian countries. The Livonians reacted in a similar way when they tried, at whatever cost, to hinder direct trade contacts in their own territory between Russians and travellers from the West while spasmodically maintaining their privileges in Novgorod and Pskov. Neither of these republics was strong enough to break through the German barrier on the eastern coasts of the Baltic and in the fifteenth century they became increasingly dependent economically on their developing southern hinterland whence they derived a large quantity of grain and increasing amounts of furs and beeswax. In 1478 Novgorod was finally conquered by the grand duchy of Moscow which was already very powerful and was pressing for reasons of trade towards the Baltic. One ought to treat the closure in 1494 of the Hanse's factory in Novgorod as not only a victory for Moscow over the boyars and merchants of Novgorod, but also as a consequence of the struggle against the already anachronistic privileges of the German merchants in all foreign territories, not only in Russia.

The Hanse's trade with the towns of the western Dvina basin has not been studied in the same detail as has the history of its economic relations with Novgorod and Pskov. In the thirteenth century German merchants, mainly from Riga, came into direct contact with Polotsk, Vitebsk and even with the more distant Smolensk. In a somewhat later period, when the whole region came under the control of Lithuania, Riga merchants penetrated as far as Vilno, where they were active certainly by the end of the fourteenth century and at the beginning of the fifteenth, and perhaps even earlier. As in the Novgorod trade, they were chiefly interested in furs and beeswax. Lithuanian and Byelorussian wax became an item of prime importance in the trade of Riga, from whence it was exported to England, Flanders and elsewhere. Byelorussian and Lithuanian furs, however, were of lower

[83] *Ibid.*, 114ff.

value than those purchased in Novgorod and Pskov. Soviet scholars have recently questioned the view that flax and hemp were exported from Byelorussia and eastern Lithuania in the later Middle Ages, arguing that their cultivation did not develop to a degree sufficient to supply a surplus for local and foreign markets until the sixteenth century. The export of Byelorussian forest products to Riga, so important in the sixteenth and seventeenth centuries, only began in the fifteenth century. Thanks to this, Riga already exported in mid-century large quantities of ashes and a little timber. Exports from Riga to Byelorussia were similar in content to Hanseatic imports into Novgorod, i.e. they consisted chiefly of cloth and salt, the latter perhaps in relatively large quantities. Considered as a whole, however, the Hanse's trade with the Byelorussian towns, which were much weaker than Pskov and Novgorod, was smaller than German trade with either of the latter towns. In the fourteenth and fifteenth centuries, Polotsk became Riga's chief contractor, while Smolensk's contacts with Moscow to the East and with Vilno and Gdańsk to the west became much closer. In the fifteenth century the merchants of Polotsk, with the support of the grand duke of Lithuania, also limited the Hanseatic merchants' freedom of activity and themselves called in at Riga with increasing frequency, trying in this way to gain access to maritime trade. They were not satisfied with partial successes and managed to establish direct contact with Gdańsk as well as taking advantage of the increasingly frequent appearance in Polotsk of merchants from western Lithuania and Poland. We should see in all this one of the reasons why the great land route already referred to, running from Russia via Lithuania and Poland to Wrocław and Leipzig, came into existence. The ability of the Hanseatic merchants to trade with Russia and Lithuania was thereby weakened and that of the Byelorussian merchants strengthened. In 1498, no doubt under the influence of the latter, Grand Duke Alexander of Lithuania granted Polotsk the 'Law of Magdeburg', together with the staple rights and in so doing he cancelled all the privileges of the Hanseatic merchants.[84] We must assume that he was guided by the example of Ivan III and was able, with a single stroke, to strengthen the border towns and to obtain the support of the Byelorussian population. This did not mean, as it did in Novgorod in 1494, a permanent breach with the old economic contacts with Livonia. It did no more than bring these contacts into line with the new structure of economic and political power.

[84] *Ibid.*, 512ff; G. Hollihn, 'Die Stapel-und Gästepolitik Rigas in der Ordenszeit 1201–1562', in *Hansische Geschichtsblätter*, LX (1935).

(4) THE BASIN OF THE UPPER VOLGA

The reconstruction of the territories situated in the basin of the Upper Volga began in places immediately after the departure of the Tatars in 1240.[85] Nevertheless, the massacre or abduction of a large part of the population during the invasions and the long exploitation of the conquered Russian territories meant that the actual results of the reconstruction of the urban and rural economies could only be realised in the second half of the following century. It is not impossible that the epidemics which swept across central Russia in the second half of the fourteenth century added to the delay.

In the fourteenth and fifteenth centuries the agricultural regions of north-eastern Russia expanded quite considerably. The consequent increase in grain production facilitated the formation of groups of peasants employed in mainly non-agricultural occupations, such as the collection of wild honey (which amongst other things added to the supply of beeswax for external trade), fishing, hunting, etc., and in small-scale trading. Grekov, Vesolovski and Tcherepnin have all drawn attention to the fact that many villages acquired the character of market centres for the exchange of goods in their district and that craftsmen tended to congregate in these settlements.[86] Documents dating from the end of the fourteenth and fifteenth centuries show the peasants actively participating in trade. Some of them in the districts around the towns of Vladimir, Dmitriev and Byeloozero bought fish and other things from their nearer or more distant neighbours for sale to town merchants, who went out into the countryside both to buy and to sell goods.[87] There can be no doubt that there were peasants in the markets of even the largest towns in the fifteenth century. In spite of this, however, Soviet scholars seem convinced that the peasant economy of the period was completely natural and to support their belief they point to the fact that peasant dues were rarely paid in money; it must be remembered, however, that, in the later Middle Ages, peasants participating in trade, and sometimes even in long-distance trade, may be observed throughout Scandinavia, Livonia and to some extent Prussia, even though money was not always their medium of exchange. The extent of this phenomenon is enough to prove that a certain section of the peasantry, made up perhaps of the wealthier members, had already advanced beyond the confines of a natural or

[85] A. M. Sakharov, *Goroda Severo-Vostotchnoy Rusi XIV–XV vv* (Moscow, 1959), 45, 47, 60ff.

[86] B. D. Grekov, *Krestyanye na Rusi s drevneishikh vremen do XVII veka* (Moscow–Leningrad, 1945), 556ff; L. V. Tcherepnin, *Obrazovanye Russkogo Centralizovannogo Gosudarstva v XIV–XV vv* (Moscow, 1960), 297ff.

[87] Tcherepnin, *Obrazovanye*, 312–20; Sakharov, *Goroda*, 160.

barter economy. The dues paid in kind by the peasants of all the countries mentioned, including Russia, did not serve merely to satisfy the direct needs of their lords. In many cases they stimulated the lay and ecclesiastical lords to engage in trade. This can be seen clearly in the sources relating to Sweden, Finland, Livonia and the Teutonic Knights in Prussia. It may be explained by the relative weakness of the merchants of these countries, especially in Sweden, Finland, Denmark and Norway, in comparison with the great feudal lords; by the depreciation of money which hampered the process of commuting peasant dues; and finally by the still tenuous links between peasant and urban economies.

In north-eastern Russia the great landlords, especially the ecclesiastical ones, were, in the fourteenth and particularly in the fifteenth century, very actively engaged in trade. This was just as true of the metropolitan archbishop of Moscow as it was of such great monasteries as Troitse-Sergiev, Simonov, Kirillo-Byelozerski, Blagoveshchenski, etc. The great increase in the output of salt in northern and eastern Russia in the fifteenth century helped to foster the growth of these monasteries' commercial activities. The monasteries often took part in large-scale trade in salt, fish, sometimes grain, furs, etc. and obtained from the princes various exemptions for duty and market charges. Fairs of some importance sprang up around the monasteries. Many sites in Russian towns upon which were buildings (*dvori*) belonging to church institutions, or to boyars and princes, and inhabited by their subjects and servants, were used for trade and handicrafts and brought considerable profit to their owners.[88] Judging from the studies by Russian scholars, church institutions and the great monasteries particularly, had a much greater share in trade than the princes and boyars did, and they may even have dominated the internal trade of north-eastern Russia in the fourteenth and fifteenth centuries. They fostered the formation of a geographical division of labour between the different regions of the country. While their economic power was in some sense the result of the weakness of the towns, it was also no doubt a factor hindering their growth, and the fact that the feudal lords themselves owned urban property hampered the emergence of the citizen class as a social and legally unified group. We are dealing here with phenomena which are familiar in other central European countries, but which appeared in north-eastern Russia in a much more visible form.

In the fourteenth and fifteenth centuries the region in which we are

[88] Grekov, *Krestyanye*, 556ff; Sakharov, *Goroda*, 146–51; M. N. Tikhomirov, *Srednevekovaya Moskva v XIV–XV vv*. (2nd edn, Moscow, 1957), 107ff; Tcherepnin, *Obrazovanye*, 320ff, 346–63.

interested witnessed a marked growth in the number and size of towns. The debate generated by A. M. Sakharov's interesting study shows that the earlier view that there were about seventy-eight towns in central-eastern Russia which were centres of trade and handicrafts in the fifteenth century was too optimistic. However, Sakharov in turn goes too far when he reduces their number to twenty-five.[89] In north-eastern Russia the towns developed principally in the region of the Upper Volga as far as Nizhni Novgorod, particularly in the territory bordered by the Upper Volga itself and the Oka and Kl'azma, where natural and strategic conditions were favourable. The area was reached by the trade routes coming from the Black Sea and Caspian regions as well as from the North and the Baltic. Moscow was particularly conveniently located and so also were Tver and Nizhni Novgorod. The colonisation of the northern territories led to the foundation of important urban centres like Ustiug, Byeloozero and many other smaller towns of this type.[90] The towns and market settlements springing up in the region of the northern Dvina and Pechora were from the very beginning dependent upon the supply of foodstuffs, especially grain, coming principally from the agricultural region of the Upper Volga. The cost of these imports was covered by the exports of valuable furs, fish and salt. This dependence was probably one of the reasons why the northern territories gravitated towards the grand duchy of Moscow rather than the republic of Novgorod, which could not have assured them of an adequate food supply. When considering Moscow's growing political and military superiority over Novgorod during the fourteenth and fifteenth centuries, the increasingly close ties between Moscow and the north-eastern regions of Russia appear to be attributable to these economic facts. Because of them, Moscow became, in the course of time, the leading centre for the trade in luxury furs – sable, ermine, arctic fox, etc. – whereas the markets of Novgorod dealt, as we have already seen, in the cheaper kinds of furs. The grand dukes of Moscow, anxious to gain control over the lands of the northern Dvina and the Pechora, not only supported settlement in these areas and endeavoured to root out the influence of Novgorod by force, but, in certain cases, even exempted the merchants coming from the North from the payment of duty.[91] Though their plans were not fully realised till the fifteenth century, Moscow had already achieved important successes in the north-east even in the first half of the preceding century. This greatly strengthened its position in the trade with the East and West.

89 Sakharov, *Goroda*, 17ff; Tcherepnin, *Obrazovanye*, 329ff.
90 Sakharov, *Goroda*, 65ff; Tikhomirov, *Srednevekovaya Moskva*, *passim*.
91 Sakharov, *Goroda*, 198.

All Soviet scholars are agreed that in the fourteenth and fifteenth centuries trade with the East played a much greater part in the economic life of the Upper Volga basin than trade with the West did. M. V. Fehner notes that, even in the sixteenth century, oriental goods were much more widely used in Russia than were the products of central and western Europe.[92] It was mentioned earlier that the great trade centres on the middle and lower Volga had developed and the important Italian trading colonies in the Crimea had appeared during the time of the Mongol Empire. It is doubtful whether Russia, devastated by the Mongols, could have immediately established much in the way of contacts with the commerce of the Black Sea and Caspian region. However, the ravages perpetrated by the invaders were gradually repaired. One unequivocal sign of the revival of economic life in north-western and north-eastern Russia was the introduction of silver money into circulation and the increasing number of mints from the second half of the fourteenth century onwards. By the beginning of the fifteenth century there were already twenty-one mints.[93] Even if they probably did not all function at the same time nor issue large quantities of coins, their appearance should be taken as proof of the marked growth in the economy's need for money.

Researches into the history of Russian trade in the fourteenth and fifteenth centuries have not yet advanced very far, but it is clear that Sarai-Berke and Astrakhan during their fourteenth-century heyday maintained lively contacts with the territories of the Bulgars and of the river Kama. Kazan grew up at the point where this river flowed into the Volga and, in the course of time, became the rich capital of a separate Tatar khanate. It imported from the south and south-east silk and cotton materials, morocco, pearls, precious stones, spices and other goods from Persia, Turkestan, Asia Minor and India. In exchange it exported leather, Russian furs, falcons from the far north wax, honey, etc. Kazan was visited by many Russian merchants, especially during its great fairs.[94] The fall of Sarai and Astrakhan after the invasions of Timur accelerated the further growth of Kazan in the fifteenth century. Perhaps certain changes connected with the growth of handicraft production in Russia during this century affected Kazan's trade structure. Siroetchkovski and Fehner argue that, at the end of the century, considerable quantities of Russian leather and other leather goods, many artefacts made of iron, weapons and also, in a later period, firearms were imported from the Russian towns. The Tatar

92 Fehner, *Torgovla*, 5.

93 Ribakov, *Remeslo*, 680; G. B. Federov, *Dengi Moskovskogo Knyazhestva vremeny Dimitrya Donskogo (1359–1425)* (Moscow–Leningrad, 1949), 162; Sakharov, *Goroda*, 172; P. J. Lyashtchenko, *Istorya naradnogo hozyaystva SSSR* (Moscow, 1947), I, 212.

94 Tikhomirov, *Srednevekovaya Moskva*, 132; Fehner, *Torgovla*, 44.

territories, the Caucasus, Persia and later Turkestan, made up the vast region to which Russia sent the products of its crafts.[95] Nizhni Novgorod, the nearest trading centre to Kazan, was the first to have trade relations with it, though the share of Moscow and Tver as well as the smaller towns increased rapidly. In the fifteenth century Moscow, with its large population (according to Tikhomirov it had about 30–40,000 inhabitants)[96] and the seats of the grand duke, the metropolitan bishop, wealthy princes, boyars and clergy, in addition to its especially favourable position on the main lines of communication, was able to become a great trading centre with the East. Merchants from Moscow, Tver, Kolomna and other towns of the Upper Volga region, did not merely deal with Kazan, but went on, via the Volga and its steppes, to Astrakhan and from thence by sea to the Caucasus and Persia. Afanasi Nikitin, a merchant from Tver, reached India between 1462 and 1472, but recognised that the country did not offer any possibility for serious trade with Russia.[97] Ambrogio Contarini and Giosaphatto Barbaro, journeying to Moscow via the Volga region in the fifteenth century, drew attention to the relatively large-scale traffic along its roads. The traffic existed in spite of the risks the merchants ran of being attacked by bands of nomads and other brigands. In the second half of the fourteenth century and the beginning of the fifteenth, the famous Novgorod *uzhkuyniki* reached Kazan in their boats and plundered the town and the merchants staying there. Russian and eastern merchants journeying in these countries in large caravans frequently attached themselves to the Russian and Tatar envoys also travelling in this region.

In the fourteenth and fifteenth centuries the trade route up the Volga and its steppes was perhaps somewhat more important for Russia than were the roads running further to the west. However, the roads leading from the north to the Don and subsequently to the Sea of Azov and the Black Sea, and to the Crimea and Constantinople, were probably almost as important.[98] In the fourteenth and fifteenth centuries Moscow and the other large centres on the Upper Volga maintained lively contacts with Constantinople for both religious and economic reasons. The Byzantine capital was familiar to many Russian merchants and ecclesiastics. Contacts were also close with the Crimean towns: initially with Sudak (Soldaia) and later on with Caffa. Russia

95 Fehner, *Torgovla*, 51ff.

96 Tikhomirov, *Srednevekovaya Moskva*, 67.

97 *Khozhenye za tri morya Afanasiya Nikitina 1466–1472*. Izdatelstvo Akademii Nauk SSSR (Moscow–Leningrad, 1948), *passim*.

98 V. E. Siroetchkovski, 'Puti i uslovya snoshenyi Moskvy s Krimon na rubezhe XVI veka', *Izvestya Akademii Nauk SSSR*, III (1932), 194, 195; *Idem.*, *Gosti–Surozhanye* (Moscow, 1935), *passim*.

imported oriental goods from these places and perhaps some small quantities of cloth from Italy and north-western Europe. Luxury furs and wax were the chief exports and perhaps also leather and falcons and, later on, handicraft products. Trade relations with Caffa were particularly active in the second half of the fifteenth century and successfully survived the town's conquest by the Turks.[99] Quite independently of this trade, Caffa was the chief market for slaves captured in Russia by the Tatars. Moscow and the other towns of the region had perhaps by the fifteenth century established contacts not only with Sinope and Trebizond but with other trading centres in Asia Minor as well, and this connection later became very important for both sides.[100] We cannot reach any definite conclusion about Russia's trade balance with the East but, bearing in mind that both sides had many luxury goods to dispose of, we may assume that it was more or less in equilibrium.

A very powerful merchant group connected with the trade with the East, the so-called *Gosti Surozhanie*, emerged in the larger towns of north-eastern Russia and particularly in Moscow.[101] Their name shows that originally they traded mainly with Sudak (Russian, Surozh: Italian, Soldaia) in the Crimea. Thanks to the researches of Siroetchkovski, Tikhomirov and other scholars we know that they were the wealthiest group of merchants engaged in long-distance trade. Russian merchants themselves often took part in expeditions to distant parts, hence the name *gosti* (*hospites*). We also know that they must have had considerable cash resources at their disposal for they frequently made loans to the princes and boyars. Some, like the Moscow family of Hovrin (later the princes Hovrin-Golovin), also acquired extensive lands and gradually entered the highest ranks of the aristocracy.[102] As well as those advanced through office, wealthy merchants ranked highly in the social hierarchy of Russia.[103] Remembering what kind of goods they imported, we can guess they often provided exclusively for the needs of the richest members of society. We are concerned here with a group of wealthy merchants, typical of the Middle Ages, who formed an integral part of the social structure of their times. It is possible that the *Surozhanie* were engaged in distributing oriental goods throughout the Upper Volga area and in supplying certain quantities of them to Novgorod. However the main bulk of oriental goods imported into north-western Russia came through the Hanseatic merchants. This state of affairs does not seem to have changed until the sixteenth century. Amongst the group calling themselves

[99] Siroetchkovski, *Gosti–Surozhanye*, *passim*.

[100] Fehner, *Torgovla*, 68, 69.

[101] See above, p. 607, note 98.

[102] Tikhomirov, *Srednevekovaya Moskva*, 155.

[103] *Ibid.*, 160.

Surozhanie there were not only Russians but also Greeks from Byzantium and perhaps from Caffa, and Italians who had settled in Moscow over the years and had gradually become russified. Grand Duke Dmitri Donskoy (1359–89) conferred on a certain Andriei Friazin the right to an estate on the river Pechora, previously granted to his paternal or maternal uncle, Matviei Friazin.[104] The name 'Friazin' (plural 'Friagi') means in Russian 'Italian'. Assuming that the nickname 'Friazin' was not also applied to people trading with the Italian colonies, then both the 'Friagi' mentioned here came successively from the Italian Black Sea colonies. Could this mean that they were Genoese whom we know to have been both courageous and enterprising? Tikhomirov correctly saw in these two 'Friagi' merchants anxious to organise the export of furs and falcons from the far North.[105] In the second half of the fifteenth century a large group of Venetians arrived in Moscow: they were not all merchants; some may have been building specialists, etc. Armenian and Tatar merchants connected with the eastern trade also settled in Moscow and other towns.[106]

Sometime after the *Surozhanie* another group of Moscow merchants known as *Sukonniki* (cloth merchants) emerged. They should be associated with western trade and therefore regarded as being involved with imported cloth. Trade with the West had only a limited significance for north-eastern Russia during the fourteenth and early fifteenth centuries; but more was heard of it as time went on.

Here it is necessary to underline the fact that, in the fourteenth and fifteenth centuries, Novgorod was becoming increasingly dependent on the supply of grain from the south-east. Furs imported from north-east Russia, particularly from the lands of the Kama and the Volga, were all-important for Novgorod. The route along which they were brought led through the principality of Tver where in the second half of the fourteenth century Torzhok (little market) grew up as a centre for trade with Novgorod. Tver probably played a considerably greater part in the trade with Novgorod in the early days than did Moscow. Cloth from north-west Europe, copper goods and perhaps some iron reached the basin of the Upper Volga through Novgorod and Pskov.[107] We must also assume that most of the silver and money flowing into the heart of Russia during the fourteenth and fifteenth centuries came via Novgorod. It came not only in payment for goods but also as part of the tribute the inhabitants of Novgorod had to pay to the rulers of Tver and later to the grand dukes of Moscow.[108]

104 *Ibid.*, 130. 105 *Ibid.* 106 *Ibid.*, 205–20.

107 *Ibid.*, 136ff; Sakharov, *Goroda*, 114, 125, 126; Goetz, *Deutsch–russische Handelsgeschichte*, II, 65, 219. 108 Khoroshkevitch, *Torgovla*, 271.

Novgorod's far-reaching dependence in the fourteenth century on the territories unified under the rule of the grand dukes of Moscow was in stark contrast to the hostile behaviour of its boyars towards Moscow and also to its privileged position as the go-between in Russia's trade with the West. But that important trade centre was finally subordinated to the wider interests of the Russian economy by its conquest in 1478. The closure of the Hanseatic 'factory' in Novgorod in 1494 was no more than the direct consequence of the town's absorption into the Muscovite state and was intended to give Russian trade a greater freedom of movement. The energy with which Ivan III and his successor competed with the Livonians served the same purpose: Ivan built Ivangorod on the river Narva not only as a fortress but also as a focus for Russia's Baltic trade. Since the Russians never succeeded in breaking through the German barrier into the Baltic, from the fifteenth century onwards the significance of Moscow's trade with the Lithuanian towns of Byelorussia, and hence with Vilno, Warsaw, Poznań, Wrocław and Leipzig, was all the greater. Toruń, in the second half of the fifteenth century, and Gdańsk later, suffered from the increasing activity of the Russian, Polish and Lithuanian merchants on these new roads along which the Russians in particular probably made their way as far as Venice. In return Polish and Lithuanian merchants visited Moscow. Their trade was dominated by cloth imports into Russia from the Netherlands, England and Germany and the export to the West of high quality furs, beeswax, Russian leather, etc.[109] It must be concluded that a fair amount of money flowed along these routes into Russia. However, all these developments did not impair Great Novgorod's importance as a trade centre. On the contrary, it retained its position well on into the sixteenth century.

V. *Conclusion*

This outline of how trade developed in eastern Europe during the later Middle Ages fully confirms the original assertion regarding the differences between the economic conditions prevailing in the individual regions. In the thirteenth and fourteenth centuries a distinct group of territories can be discerned, comprising Bohemia, Silesia and the Polish and Slovak lands at the foot of the Carpathian mountains. Here, in addition to an expanding agricultural economy, the existence of a mining industry and a favourable conjunction of important long-distance trade routes exerted a powerful influence on events. At that

[109] L. V. Tcherepnin, *Russkiye Fyeodalnye Arkhivy* (Moscow, 1948), I, 231; *Idem, Obrazovanye*, 402ff; Khoroshkevitch, *Torgovla*, 295; Tikhomirov, *Srednevekovaya Moskva*, 138ff; Wawrzyńczyk, *Studia*, 14–29.

time Bohemia was undoubtedly the most advanced country, and it is no accident that at the end of the fourteenth century it was also the scene of a grave economic and social crisis very like the one that had already made itself felt in western Europe earlier in the century. In Bohemia the crisis precipitated an upheaval in the production and exchange of goods, even though these changes were not so far-reaching as in England or the Netherlands. In addition a regression in the mining industry hindered the growth of foreign trade in that country, which had previously been such an important exporter of precious metals.

Conditions in Poland, Lithuania and Russia were different again. The initial and most intense phase of Poland's economic growth took place in the thirteenth century, although the economy continued to grow without serious interruption during the following two or even three centuries. Lithuania and the Russian territories followed suit in the fourteenth century. While the economies of all these countries were displaying such dynamic features, the countries of western Europe were showing in the later Middle Ages symptoms of economic stagnation, if not regression, together with some significant socio-economic and political transformations. The pace of economic growth in the East and West was clearly different in the fourteenth and fifteenth centuries: later on the differences were less obvious, though they nevertheless existed. All these developments were reflected in the political events of the times.

The economic expansion of the countries of eastern Europe encouraged a significant inflow of trading capital and the emergence of a group of merchants, many of whom were immigrants. The process was interrupted in Bohemia and Silesia during the fourteenth century, but in the territories of the Polish state its pace quickened during the two following centuries, thereby encouraging the expansion of trade and mining. In Russia economic activity was less visible, although there was a steady immigration of foreign merchants from the south and south-east. But it should be pointed out that the import of capital and the immigration of merchants was the result of, rather than the reason for, the continuing economic growth. Both money and men were seeking opportunities for profitable investment. It may be that the various forms taken by German colonisation in the East from the thirteenth to the fifteenth centuries should also be considered in the light of this motive.

While Bohemia and, to some extent, Silesia exported their own precious metals mostly in the form of money, there are grounds for thinking that considerable sums of money were also flowing into central and northern Poland, Lithuania and Russia from the West and that this flow played an important part in the economic development and social transformation of these regions. It is difficult to imagine how such fundamental changes as the introduction of money and the gradual commutation of peasant dues could have occurred in these three countries without the import of silver from the West.

Already by the fourteenth century foreign trade was also attracting a powerful flow of western handicraft goods into eastern Europe, and by the fourteenth century these were by no means confined to luxuries. This would suggest that popular demand had increased beyond the level at which it could be met by the output of locally based crafts. The dangers inherent in that state of affairs did not appear in Poland and Lithuania until a later period, when economic expansion gave way to a long period of stagnation and eventual decline.

CHAPTER IX

The Woollen Industry

Europe was as renowned for its textiles in the Middle Ages as today. Many and various fabrics were produced, whether from indigenous fibres such as wool, flax and hemp, from fibres primarily imported such as silk and cotton, or from mixtures of both such as that of cotton with wool or flax. But of all its textiles woollens may well take pride of place. Not only were they manufactured in all parts of the continent and worn by all classes of the community, from the humblest rustic in his coarse burel to the man of rank and fashion dressed in cloth so fine that it was almost like silk. But they were one of the chief articles of exchange within Europe itself, and they were Europe's principal export to the continents of Asia, Africa and, for a short space, America. The Vikings, venturing westwards across the Atlantic in the eleventh century, carried cloth to barter with the North Americans for furs; so too the Italians, traversing Asia to the court of the Great Khan in the thirteenth century, took with them presents of cloth, and to the end of the Middle Ages Europe's woollens were marketed in bulk at the Mediterranean gateways of Asia and Africa. Widely dispersed as the industry was, three regions became pre-eminent above all others for the large-scale manufacture of woollens – Italy, England, and what may best be described by the Latin term Belgica, that is to say the land between the Somme and the Moselle. In these three regions the development of a great export industry may be studied through a thousand years of medieval history, dimly at first, then more distinctly as the centuries pass, until there can be discerned shifts in its location and changes in its technique not unlike those of more recent centuries, and an industrial organisation as complex and a social structure as unstable as any known today. The problems of an industrial society, with its many thousands of workers dependent upon distant markets and distant sources of raw materials, were all too familiar to Flanders in the thirteenth century, to Italy in the fourteenth, and to England in the fifteenth century.

I. *The Roman World*

Already in Roman days clothmaking was firmly established in these regions as an export industry producing for distant markets. Though comparatively few specimens of its work have survived to incite the speculations of the archaeologist, yet there can be no doubt that it developed as rapidly under the Empire as did the pottery and metal industries, showing not less marked, if less easily detected, changes in volume, location and organisation. Demand was expanding with the increase of wealth and the growing needs of city-dwellers and the army, and the *pax Romana*, bringing with it free trade, improved communications, a stable currency, and a reduction of risk in river, road and sea transport, created new possibilities for the long-distance exchange of raw materials and finished products; a high degree of local specialisation was thus facilitated. Moreover, the woollen industry was an ideal one for a newly developing province. For woollen cloth was in almost universal demand throughout the Empire; being neither fragile nor perishable it was admirably suited to long-distance traffic; and its production could be developed from an already existing domestic industry with comparatively little expenditure of capital. Thus while in every sheep-rearing land clothmaking flourished, in some it acquired an international reputation, and its importance in the trade of the Empire is amply attested by the sections devoted to it in Diocletian's famous edict fixing maximum wages and prices throughout his realms.

Doubtless the primitive household industry, making cloth to be worn by the family which produced it, survived to a considerable extent throughout the Empire, as it still does in some places even today. But it was increasingly giving way to commercial production. Augustus, mindful of the old Roman virtues and shocked at the extravagant garments worn by the Romans of his day, attempted to stem the tide of fashion, setting a royal example of simple living by wearing only clothes spun and woven at home by his sister, his wife and his daughter. And many great Roman ladies of the early Empire, who themselves spurned such manual labour, supervised the making of cloth by their own household slaves, like those spinners, weavers and fullers commemorated in the family vault of the consul Statilius Taurus at Rome. But in the city itself 'homespun' was fast disappearing as rich and poor took their choice from the ever-increasing range of commercially produced fabrics with which the shops were filled. In country districts it lingered longer, both among the peasants and in great households which grew their own wool. Slave women skilled in spinning and weaving were legally regarded as part of the equipment of an estate, and on cold and rainy days when farm work in the open was impossible they were set to their tasks, with wool combed and prepared for them beforehand. Even so the allurements of speciality fabrics were great. Wives, lamented Columella, disdained stuffs made at home, and with perverse desire took a fancy to clothing that cost large sums, perhaps as much as a whole year's income. Giving way to luxury and idleness they 'deigned not to carry the burden of manufacturing wool', so that stewardesses had to be appointed to supervise the work in their place. And just as luxury clothing was being purchased on the market by the rich, so cheap mass-produced clothing was coming into vogue for the poor. Homespun was too good for the ordinary slaves on a great estate. It might be used with advantage to the owner's purse, says Columella, for stewards, overseers and the better class of slaves; for the rest it was cheaper to buy.

Very largely, then, the Romans of the early Empire, rich and poor, supplied their need for cloth from a specialised industry. In part this was what may be described as a handicraft industry, if we may use this term for an industry of independent, isolated artisans, living by the produce of their craft and working usually on commission direct for their customers, often making up the customer's own material. But to a considerable extent it was a large-scale industry, often located in regions far from Rome, operating under the direction of capitalist entrepreneurs, and organised for export to distant markets. It is with this *grande industrie* that we are here concerned.

In lands of the Middle East, with civilisations much older than that of Rome, such a 'great industry' had long existed. New impetus was no doubt given to it by the growth of imperial trade, and fine woollens from Greece and Phrygia found their way to the Roman market. But there was no marked development or intensification, no startling change in organisation or technique, and it was for other textiles that the region became especially famous. Egypt, most highly industrialised of all, grew rich not by woollens but by linens, mass-produced for the natives of Somaliland and shipped also to India, and by cloths woven from Indian cottons and Chinese silks, sent westwards to Rome to compete with the old-fashioned woollens of which the toga had always been made.

The really striking advance was in the West. First to develop a large-scale woollen industry here was southern Italy. Her rapid industrialisation in the first century of the Empire was doubtless due as much to close contacts with Alexandria and the more highly developed regions of the Middle East as to the growing demands of the Roman market. From time immemorial the Romans had clothed themselves in the wool of their own sheep, and in southern Italy sheep were to be found on every farm; they flourished particularly on the slopes of the Apennines, especially in Apulia and Calabria. There, in the little market towns at the foot of the mountains, the wool was sold to discriminating buyers, quick to appreciate differences of quality and texture; the wool of Canusium, for instance, was known to be softer than that of Tarentum, but not so glossy. There, as at Telesia, *lanariae* were built by the town officials for the sale or perhaps the preparation of the wool, while Beneventum had its 'clerk of the wool accounts'. There too, as at Cannae, Corfinium and Amiternum, congregated the *lanipendiae* who most probably organised the putting out of the wool for spinning. For spinning then, as indeed until power was applied to it in the eighteenth century, was a process commonly entrusted to women working in their own homes. It was a stage in the making of cloth in which use could profitably be made of part-time as well as whole-time labour, in the countryside as well as in the towns, provided there were adequate arrangements for the distribution of the wool and for the collection and scrutiny of the finished yarn, to ensure that this was of full weight and of even quality. These little market towns throve on the traffic in wool and yarn. Sometimes, too, they became manufacturing towns, making up the yarn into cloth, particularly of the cheaper sorts. Such was Canusium, whose serviceable russets, 'like in colour to turbid mead', were sold in vast quantities at Rome in the first century for slaves like those Syrians of Martial's epigram who, 'dressed in Canusian wool, sweated beneath their litter poles'.

But much of the wool went down to the coast, in the form of raw wool, of yarn, or of unfinished webs, there to be fulled, dyed, finished and marketed as high-priced cloth. At Pompeii, for instance, it was taken in hand by the fullers, who were also concerned with the cleaning of soiled garments; their work is vividly depicted in the frescoes of the House of the Vettii and on the walls of a *fullonica* there. First the raw webs were pounded under foot in a trough, with water, soap and fullers' earth. This served to cleanse them and free them from grease and also to shrink and to felt them, thus producing a firm, compact, unshrinkable cloth some two-thirds the length, perhaps, of the original web. Then they were stretched on a frame so that they would dry to precisely the right size. Finally, while still damp, the nap was raised with a hedgehog skin or an instrument set with the *spina fullonia* (predecessor of the medieval teasel), and, when dry, cut with shears to a level surface, giving the cloth a smooth and even silky face after it had been pressed. Fulling was a process which demanded not only skill and a certain amount of equipment but also a considerable space of open ground for drying and a plentiful supply of clear, fresh water. From this it followed that fulleries were often set up along a watercourse in close proximity to each other and that there was need for regulating the use of the water. This may well have been one of the reasons for the frequent formation of gilds among the fullers, in Roman as in medieval times. At any rate it is clear that at Pompeii the owners of the fulleries were associated together and also that they were men of substance, concerned not merely with fulling the cloth but with selling it, and possibly acting as entrepreneurs organising its production. The great hall built at Pompeii for the fullers by the lady Eumachia is scarcely suited to a fullery, but, with its large court and colonnaded corridor, it is admirably designed for an exchange. Chance has preserved for us these tangible evidences of the fuller's trade in what was probably one of Italy's smaller industrial centres. Elsewhere in southern Italy the fullers may have been equally, if not more, important, but little record of them has survived beyond the fact that at Arpinium there were fulleries built by the town, while there and at Spoletium, Falerium and Rome there were fullers' gilds.

Further south, Tarentum was noted for its fine wool and for its russets in the first century, and it became yet more famous for its dyeworks as the purple fisheries of the Mediterranean were developed to meet the rising demand for luxury cloths; only the wealthiest could go clothed in such purple, for the cost of dyeing a garment in this exotic medium was nearly one hundred times the cost of the wool required for weaving it. And when in the later days of the Empire private enterprise gave way more and more to state enterprise and the state itself engaged in industry on a large scale, then imperial dyeworks (*bafia*) were established at Tarentum, as imperial weaving shops also (*gynaecia*) were set up in South Italy at Venusia and Canusium.

Northern Italy, too, produced fine wool on the slopes of the Alps and the Apennines, and in the first century of the Christian era there was a woollen industry in the Po basin, whence Patavium sent quantities of clothing of all sorts to Rome. In the second and third centuries this industry continued to flourish and, stimulated no doubt by the development of the Danube provinces and the proximity of the Danube armies, it developed yet further until it quite outstripped the industry of the South, whose decline became apparent. In the great industrial towns of the North, such as Parma, Mutina or Altinum, standardised fabrics were mass-produced on a scale which implied considerable specialisation of labour and a high degree of organisation. There was a woolcombers' gild at Brixia and a woolcarders' gild at Brixellum. Verona was known for its blankets; Patavium for its stout frieze called *gausapa*; Pollentia, like Canusium, sold coarse cloth for slaves. Here too the state set up its factories when state enterprise became the fashion under the later Empire. Mediolanum and Aquileia had imperial *gynaecia*, weaving perhaps for the frontier armies, and the needs of these legions may also have been met by the *gynaecium* close to the Danube at Sirmium and by that on the Adriatic at Salona. There was also a *gynaecium* in Rome.

So actively did the cloth industry of Italy develop that her own wool, on which it at first depended, was soon insufficient to feed her looms, and from the first century of the Empire she was importing supplies from other regions, particularly from Asia Minor, Sicily, Spain and Gaul. Most important as a source of raw materials was Spain. Once Spanish cloth had been much in request in Rome. Spanish cloaks had been taken as tribute from the conquered Celtiberi, and much cloth had come from Baetica. But now it was wool rather than cloth which was in demand. Cheaper varieties came from the North and a very fine quality from the South. Finest of all was the surpassingly beautiful black wool from the pastures of Baetica, where sheep were scientifically reared by Roman farmers such as Columella's uncle, who sent to Africa for breeding rams. From this was made a much admired dark cloth which could compete on the market even with that made of Tarentine wool dyed in Tyrian purple, boasting of itself:

Non est lana mihi mendax nec mutor aheno;
Sic placeant Tyriae: me mea tinxit ovis.

In southern Spain the Romans also developed the production of dyes, procuring thence red dyes such as cinnabar, Sinopean earth and, more especially, large quantities of kermes. Kermes was made from the dried body of an insect (*coccus ilicis*) which feeds on a species of oak found in Mediterranean lands. It was imported from Asia Minor as well as from Spain and yielded a scarlet dye of exceptional brilliance and permanence, vying in excellence with Tyrian purple, which in time it came wholly to supersede in the West. Though costly as compared with vegetable dyes it was cheap as compared with those from the purple fisheries. To dye 1 lb of wool with Nicene kermes, according to Diocletian's edict, might cost as much as 1,500 *denarii*, as compared with 600 *denarii* for orchil purple and 16,000 *denarii* for Tyrian purple.

Thus Spain, though continuing to make some cloth of her own, became primarily a supplier of raw materials to the Italian industry. So too it was with Mediterranean Gaul. Sheep were reared on the slopes of the Cevennes and the Pyrenees, where still they may be seen depicted on the funereal monuments of the Roman period, and wool was shipped thence to Italy through the port of Narbo. At Narbo also, and at Telo, imperial dye-works were established, completing a chain of such state factories round the western Mediterranean, for in addition to those in the gulf of Tarentum there were a number in the province of Africa and in the Balearic Isles. But apart from an imperial *gynaecium* at Arelate and another higher up the Rhone at Lugdunum, there is no trace of any large-scale woollen manufacture in southern Gaul. In western Gaul there seems to have been some development of the industry on the lower Garonne, for cloaks of the Bituriges were listed at a high price in the edict of Diocletian.

The most remarkable development of the industry was in northern Gaul, which witnessed an advance even more striking than that of north Italy, and one typical of the decentralisation of industry in imperial times as the centre declined in importance and economic activity on the periphery increased. In part no doubt this indicated a transference of production to the region of consumption. But it was more than this. For northern Gaul, like northern Italy, became an exporter on a considerable scale. The extent of her industrialisation is shown by the profusion of sepulchral monuments to workers in the woollen industry; only in Italy is there any comparable number. The manufacturing region stretched right across the country of the Belgae, from the Somme to the Moselle, through the modern Picardy, Artois, western Belgium, Champagne and Lorraine, then occupied by the tribes of the Ambiani, Atrebates, Nervii, Remi, Treveri and Mediomatrici, with their Romanised cities of Ambiani (Amiens), Atrebates (Arras), Turnacum (Tournai), Remi (Rheims), Augusta Treverorum (Trier), and Augustoduno (Metz).

Gallic cloaks and Gallic wool were finding a market in Rome in the first century of the Empire, but the wool was then rough and flocky and the fabrics woven from it coarse. Hence Gallic garments were at first the dress of the common folk, bearing the same relation, remarked Martial, to purple-dyed garments made in Rome as did Arretine pottery to the finest crystal. Nevertheless they became increasingly popular, if only for the warmth and protection afforded by the stout cloaks to which capacious hoods were attached. The development of the industry was therefore a profitable field for investment, and before long Roman sheep-farmers had succeeded in producing a much improved fleece, with the result that in due course Belgica was exporting to Italy both high-grade wool and high-grade cloth, fetching as good a price as any. The quantity of wool produced was as notable as its quality, particularly in the region of the Atrebates. It is related by Orosius that one year real wool, mixed with rain, here fell from the clouds, and whatever the origin of his tale there can be no doubt that in the fourth century the wool of this district was peculiarly abundant and excellent. In the price edict of Diocletian it was rated more highly than any other wool, even that of Tarentum.

Garments made from it were no longer scoffed at by fashionable Romans, but competed with the finest Italian clothing. Not only were they worn by Romans living in Gaul, but in Italy too they became the rage; an Atrebatic *sagum* was as indispensable in the fourth century for a well-to-do Roman as linen from Egypt. Equally famous for cloaks of high value, according to Diocletian's edict, were the immediate neighbours of the Atrebates – the Ambiani, the Treveri and the Nervii; indeed Nervian *birri* (long hooded cloaks) were so popular that they were being imitated in Asia Minor. It is scarcely surprising that in a region so amply provided with fine wool and skilled craftsmanship, four imperial *gynaecia* were set up – at Turnacum, Remi, Augusta Treverorum and Augustoduno.

Apart from the existence of these state workshops little can be said with certainty as to the organisation of the industry in Belgica. We do not even know to what extent it was concentrated in the towns. Some of the clothing was probably exported in a semi-finished state, for there is mention in Diocletian's edict of the price for fulling new Nervian *birri*. But that some fulling and finishing was carried out in Gaul would seem to be indicated by the tomb at Sens which shows the fuller trampling cloth in a trough and, above, his three-foot-long shears. Much dyeing was certainly done, though here the Gauls could not hope to compete with Mediterranean lands since, much as they loved gaudy colours, they had neither the Tyrian purple nor the scarlet kermes. Vegetable dyes, however, they cultivated extensively, and with these, relates Pliny, they imitated all the colours, even producing a substitute, if not a fast, Tyrian purple, 'without running the risk of drowning by seeking the mollusc on the sea bottom; without exploiting the deep to multiply the attractions of courtesans'. The sepulchral monuments at Arlon in the heart of the cloth country, depicting men at work stirring a deep vat, have puzzled the archaeologists, but there can be little doubt that in fact they represent dyers. From the monuments, indeed, it would seem as though fullers and dyers were in a position of special importance and were men of substance as compared with the other workers. This is to be expected in view of the capital equipment they required and the fact that they were concerned with the finishing processes of clothmaking. Even more important were the cloth merchants with their expert knowledge of the foreign markets on which the very life of the industry depended. Such were the Secundini, commemorated by the sumptuous monument at Igel near Trier, whereon may be seen their bales of precious cloth in course of transport, first by barge along a river, then on mule-back over a lofty mountain range, doubtless up the Rhine, over the Alps and into Italy itself.

In Britain, last of all the western provinces to be developed, we hear nothing of the production of cloth for export until the fourth century. But by the time of Diocletian's edict there were on the market two varieties of Britannic *tapete* (coverlets or hangings) and a Britannic *birrus* which fetched a fair price, above that of the Canusian if below that of the Nervian *birrus*. There was also one imperial *gynaecium*, at Venta probably Winchester. Beyond this we know nothing for certain of the British woollen industry in Roman times. All else is conjecture. The remains of troughs vaguely reminiscent of those depicted in the *fullonica* at Pompeii have been found in three villas – at Titsey and Darenth in Kent and at Chedworth in Gloucestershire – and since in each case they are in close proximity to beds of fullers' earth it has been argued that there were fulleries there. Recent excavations have, however, shown those at Chedworth to be part of a complex of both buildings, and those at Titsey and Darenth may well be similarly explained. Traces of what were perhaps, but not certainly, dye-works have also been found at Silchester. All that can be said with confidence is that a British export industry in high quality cloths existed, though it was slower to develop than that of Belgica, and never reached comparable proportions in Roman times.

II. *The Northern Industry in Transition*

What then became of this flourishing industry, with its trading connections throughout Europe and perhaps beyond, when the Empire disintegrated? Most probably it never wholly disappeared, but of its fate in the first few centuries after the collapse of Roman rule little can be known for lack of records. Certainly sheep were still reared, even if on a diminished scale; some tradition of manufacturing techniques persisted, and clothmaking continued, not merely as a domestic craft for supplying the needs of the family, but as an industry of expert artisans, working at least for a local if not for an international market. In the glimpses that we have of sixth-century Gaul the independent artisan working on commission appears in the pages of Gregory of Tours, who tells of an *artifex lanariae* called in to manufacture the royal stock of wool and of the manager of a corn mill who also 'pectinibus insedit lanasque conposuit'. In England, when at the end of the seventh century the first clear picture of Anglo-Saxon life emerges in the pages of Bede, sheep-flocks are part of the scene; it was while Cuthbert lay awake on the mountains one night tending a flock entrusted to his care as his companions slept, that he saw the vision which tempted him to enter a monastery. And early in the following century woollen cloaks and tunics such as Anglo-Saxon clerics were accustomed to wear in England ('sicut mos est apud nos habendi') were sent overseas to the English missionaries on the continent, where they proved most acceptable presents to those faced with the unaccustomed rigours of a winter in the heart of Germany. Boniface, though he bought some of his clothing near the scene of his missionary labours in Frisia, looked out none the less eagerly for woollens from England. 'If it would not be too much trouble', he wrote to the abbot of Wearmouth, 'pray send us a cloak, for this would be a great comfort on our journeys.' To the abbess of Thanet he spoke of the comfort of the garments with which she had relieved his distress, while King Ethelbert of Kent included two woollen cloaks in the gift parcel he sent him. In a century when English people were to be found throughout western Europe and the Levant as missionaries, merchants, pilgrims, scholars, bishops, monks or nuns, it is, indeed, not surprising that English woollens should have been found there too.

There seems no reason to suppose that clothing such as was sent to the English missionaries abroad was manufactured by the religious communities themselves rather than by lay artisans. All the evidence points to the contrary. Nuns, indeed, sometimes occupied themselves with weaving, like those nuns of St Andrew at Florence who wove five pieces of solid stuff for the chief of their order from the wool which he sent them. But in general they seem to have been concerned with weaving as an art, for the production of small luxury articles such as altar cloths, rather than as an industry for the production of everyday clothing, and so it continued as a pleasant occupation for ladies of leisure, lay or religious, throughout the Middle Ages. The seventh-century nuns of Coldingham were censured because they spent their leisure in the weaving of fine garments with which to adorn themselves as brides, instead of in the care of their souls. Ordinary clothing was from earliest times purchased at markets often far distant from the monasteries themselves, as is made abundantly clear by monastic charters. A seventh-century charter, for instance, exempted the members of the religious houses of Corbie and St Denis from tolls when they travelled to buy clothing, and the same was doubtless true of similar houses in England and Italy. The real importance of the religious communities, as of the great lay households, in this connection lies in the fact that they provided a steady market for commercially produced cloth.

There can thus be no doubt that a considerable woollen industry existed in western Europe in the seventh and early eighth centuries, and that much cloth was bought and sold on the open market. But of the size, structure and location of the industry little can at present be said, except that in England at least it catered for more than a purely local demand. Clearly it would be a mistake to measure the importance of the industry by the extent of the available evidence, for historical sources of the kind familiar to students of industrial history in the later Middle Ages scarcely exist for this period.

By the end of the eighth century the picture becomes somewhat more distinct, and we can discern what may be described as a North Sea centre of the industry, comprising the English kingdoms and the north-east part of the Carolingian Empire (as it was at Charlemagne's accession). Here, as in Roman days, there was firmly established an export industry in fine quality cloaks highly valued for their wool and for their colour; an industry fostered by wise rulers such as Offa and Charlemagne and second to none in Europe.

Important as it was, the scope of this industry must not be exaggerated, for not everyone depended upon it as in the world of today. Peasants continued to weave, as well as to spin, at home, using the primitive warp-weighted looms that could quickly be set up when they were needed. And some at least of the great households then, as in Roman days, made up their own wool on the spot, setting their domain serfs to card, spin, weave, full and dye. In this way, as Columella had pointed out, the good estate manager could profitably employ much labour in the winter or during bad weather when work in the open was impossible. Thus in the royal capitularies of Charlemagne the *villici* of his rural estates were instructed to see that the women's workshops (*gynaecia*) were well furnished with wool, linen, woad, madder, vermilion, wool-combs, teasels, soap, oil, and other necessaries. To what extent the products of these workshops were marketed, in accordance with the instructions to the *villici* to strive to improve the income of the estates, it is impossible to say. Charlemagne, like Augustus, believed in the virtues of homespun, though only, according to Einhard, as a means of keeping his daughters out of mischief. More important was his encouragement of native woollens by his preference for them over the exotic silks and other stuffs of Byzantium suited to the dignity of an emperor. With his hatred of foreign garments, however beautiful, and his refusal to wear them except when in Rome, and then only at the request of the Pope, he set a vogue for Frankish clothes which must have stimulated sales at home as much as his presents to far-distant monarchs like Haroun al Raschid must have stimulated them abroad.

Much discussion has raged around the precise origin of those Frisian cloaks (*pallia fresonica*) which Charlemagne himself wore and which played so important a part in the international commerce of his day. Were they in fact the produce of Frisia, or were they made elsewhere, in Flanders or in England, and called Frisian because the Frisian traders marketed them? Probably Pirenne was right in seeing in them evidence of an exporting industry either in the Low Countries or in their immediate vicinity. At any rate they assuredly indicate the production somewhere in the region of fine quality cloth, dyed and finished, and much in demand over a wide area. *Pallia fresonica* fetched a high price, according to a capitulary of 808, and though Louis the Pious himself disdained his father's preference for native wear and still on great feasts gave silk to the highest dignitaries at his court, yet *pallia fresonica* were considered sufficiently good for officers of the second rank and were evidently very superior to the common stuffs given to simple domestics. Since such cloth found its way by ancient routes to the Levant and on to Baghdad with Charlemagne's embassy, it may well have excited a demand among the caliph's subjects. Nearer home it gave rise to a vigorous traffic, for the Frisians carried it not only by sea along the coasts of the North Sea, but also inland up the Rhine, where it provided a good exchange for more southerly products. Ernold le Noir, in exile in Strasbourg in the reign of Louis the Pious, remarked that the people of the Vosges were receiving from the Frisians cloaks of diverse colours such as they had not known hitherto, in exchange for the corn and wine which they exported down the Rhine to the sea.

The acceptance of Pirenne's conclusions need not involve the rejection of the idea of an English exporting industry. Nor is such a rejection possible. For, as we have seen, English cloaks were going to the continent in considerable numbers during the first half of the eighth century. And in the second half of the century they were the subject of diplomatic exchanges between the Carolingian Empire and Mercia, paramount power in England. Charlemagne's letter to Offa saying that his subjects were complaining of the 'prolixity' of the cloaks (*saga*) sent from England, and asking that they should be made 'as of old', suggests that the traffic was a regular one of long standing, and that the industry was producing standardised articles susceptible to some measure of state regulation. Whether such cloaks were sold for consumption in Charlemagne's realm or despatched yet further afield by Frankish merchants we have no means of knowing, but Offa, who struck coins in imitation of those of Haroun al Raschid, may at least have dreamed that English, like Frisian, woollens should reach the court of Baghdad.

Thus when at the opening of the ninth century the Vikings began to raid the shore of the North Sea on both sides of the English Channel they descended on a region prosperous industrially as well as agriculturally. Its cloth excited their cupidity as much as its corn and its wine. For they had few sheep in their own country and coveted the comfort of good woollens without as much as that of good wines within. As pirates they captured ships laden with cloth; as peaceful traders they bargained for it, exchanging fish, skins and furs from the North. By the end of the tenth and on into the eleventh century there is abundant evidence of woollens from the North Sea region being sold in Norway. So Egil's saga relates how Thorolf sent his large sea-going ship to England 'to buy woollen cloth and other goods he needed'. So too King Sverrir thanked all those Englishmen who brought to his land 'wheat and honey, flour and cloth'.

If some of the cloth imported by Norway was English and some Frankish, some may also have been Irish. The *saga* brought by Irish merchants to Cambridge in 975 may, or may not, have been of Irish manufacture. But there is evidence of cloth being sent from Ireland to Brittany in pre-Carolingian days, and the Irish were certainly highly skilled in weaving wool as well as linen, as also in dyeing and embroidering it. Fine work was done by the women of the great houses, some of which, like Charlemagne's villas, grew their own dyestuffs; in many a cottage weaving was carried on as a bye-industry, as in the home of the poor widow of Fingal who, when visited by St Brigid, sacrificed the new beam of her loom in order that she might make a fire and cook upon it her only calf; and the important part played by the industry in the economy of the country is shown by the Book of Rights (*circa* 900) which speaks of tribute being paid in thread and wool, in cloaks and in napped cloaks. Such cloaks, often finely embroidered, must have been eagerly sought after by Norse traders as well as by Norse settlers in Ireland.

Thus the Vikings provided themselves with fine woollens from the West as with fine silks and satins from the East, and the splendour of their brightly coloured clothing was the envy of all beholders. And when they ventured forth across the Atlantic it was red cloth that they took to barter with the North Americans for furs. For a good skin, relates the Flatey Book, the natives received a span of cloth, and when the supply began to run out the Norsemen cut the cloth into smaller and smaller pieces, till the fragments measured not more than a finger's breadth.

There can be no doubt of the immense impetus given to the woollen industry in the North Sea region by the expansion of the Viking peoples, whose wealth and prosperity created a new demand, and whose far-flung trade routes facilitated the exchange of fine cloth over a wide area and the development of specialised manufacturing centres importing raw materials and marketing their cloth in distant lands. By the end of the eleventh and the beginning of the twelfth century we can discern not merely small groups of craftsmen gathered around monastery, cathedral or castle as fullers had been gathered at St Riquier in the ninth century, but large congregations of weavers and other cloth workers, contributing not a little to the growth of the cities, to the development of their free institutions, and to the whole urban renaissance of the time.

If the rapid growth of the northern industry in the eleventh century was in part due to the external stimulus of widening markets, it was in part also due to the internal development of the area, to its rising population, and to an intensified exploitation of its natural resources. Such a development was in turn dependent upon a politically stable regime, and it was probably for this reason that the district which at this time leapt most rapidly ahead, outdistancing all its rivals, was that which came under the enlightened rule of the counts of Flanders.

In the county of Flanders, stretching from Arras to the Scheldt, there were unmistakable signs in the eleventh century of a surplus population which could no longer support itself upon the land. Many Flemings joined the Crusades, or enrolled themselves in the armies of the Normans setting out for the conquest of Sicily or of a distracted England. Others flocked to the towns, swelling the number of landless artisans and providing the labour supply for the great urban industry, which lived by the exchange of its manufactures for food. Others again assisted in bringing new lands under cultivation by dyking, draining and clearing the wastes along the coast, and the new pastures thus created sustained many thousands of sheep whose wool fed the looms of the growing industrial towns. More and more Flanders industrialised herself. New towns rose; ancient ones revived and expanded, with suburbs full of cloth workers – weavers, fullers, dyers and others – sprawling over what had once been countryside. Virtually every town in Flanders was a textile town, living by its export trade. Markets grew up, therefore, for the purchase of food and raw materials and for the sale of the finished cloth. Ghent had an active market at the opening of the century, when Adelard of Tournai arrived there with his boat laden with wool and other goods. Wool, dyestuffs and teasels were amongst the goods for which tolls were charged at Arras and St Omer in 1024 and in 1043. At fairs, such as that of Thourout, cloth was bought and sold. Merchant gilds, such as that at Valenciennes with its own cloth hall, concerned themselves both with the import of food and raw materials and with the marketing of the finished products. The reputation of Flemish cloth in the latter part of the eleventh century is shown by the poem in praise of wool by Winric of Trier – *Conflictus Ovis et Lini*. Here Flanders is described as the centre of manufacture for cloth of fine quality, producing a fabric of exquisite finish far superior to that of her neighbours, and exporting it to England, France and Germany.

In the clothing towns of Flanders we begin gradually to discern not only associations of merchants, such as that of Valenciennes, but also associations of artisans, drawn together by common interests, common problems, and common needs in this world and the next. The origins of these associations are still obscure and will probably always remain a matter of conjecture. Yet certain factors in their early development may clearly be discerned. Almost every town possessed its Street of the Fullers and its Street of the Dyers, each on a watercourse. This suggests a specifically industrial factor. Both fullers and dyers required ample supplies of clear water. It was therefore essential that agreements should be reached among themselves to regulate the use of the streams and to prevent their pollution or interruption. Moreover, it was often equally necessary for common action to be taken in securing from the owners the right to use the streams, and in maintaining that right against other claimants; for many disputes arose about these rights, such as that at Douai in 1220 when the canons of St Amé claimed £20 damages on the ground that the working of their corn mill was interrupted by the waste matter thrown into the stream up above it by the dyers. And just as workers living together in close proximity united to protect and regulate their trade, so too they joined together for mutual succour in distress, forming their own philanthropic fraternities; many such fraternities would seem to have been in existence in the twelfth century, though their surviving statutes do not go back beyond the thirteenth. Religion played as important a part as social security in the creation of the craft association, for it prompted the foundation of societies to promote the welfare of their members in the world to come by the erection of a chapel or at least a permanent altar in their parish church, dedicated to a particular saint whom they took as their patron, and provided with a priest to say mass there regularly.

In England, as in Flanders, the expansion of the woollen industry went forward with remarkable rapidity in the twelfth century, though in the previous century it had somewhat lagged behind. The strong rule of the Norman kings, the privileges granted by them to merchants and to towns on royal demesne, and the gradual emergence of a stable system of national government, all favoured its growth. So also did the influx of Flemish artisans in the wake of the conquest. In natural resources England was potentially quite as rich as Flanders. She too had fine pastures on which at the time of the Domesday survey there grazed flocks of many thousands of sheep. Her soil also was rich in fullers' earth and suited to the cultivation of teasels and of dyestuffs such as madder, weld and woad; the instructions in the eleventh-century *Gerefa* for the planting of madder and woad show that their production was common on many estates. Yet in the late twelfth century England's own dyestuffs were insufficient for her needs.

Nowhere is the progress of her industry more clearly shown than by the fact that in the reign of Richard I she was importing large quantities of woad. Clothmaking was clearly England's premier industry, and though primarily she was still an agricultural land her manufactures were by no means negligible. Her cloth was taking its place on the European markets, and by the end of the century was the subject of national legislation. The Assize of Measures (1197) decreed that the production of dyed cloth for the market should be carried on only in cities and capital boroughs; it also fixed a uniform standard of width, proclaiming that cloth, wherever made, should be two ells wide within the lists, and of the same quality in the middle as at the sides.

Inevitably there grew up in England, as in Flanders, gilds of merchants concerned, amongst other matters, with securing the provision of raw materials for the textile industry as well as with the marketing of its finished wares. In cities where such merchant gilds existed all dealing in cloth as well as the dyeing and finishing of cloth for the market, was strictly confined to their members, and it may well have been they who inspired the Assize of Measures. At the same time many of the artisans congregated in the towns were forming gilds of their own, seeking royal sanction for them, as did the merchants, when they were in towns on royal demesne. In the earliest extant account of the royal exchequer (1130–1) there is record of payments made for such gilds by the weavers of London, Winchester, Lincoln, Oxford, Nottingham and Huntingdon, and by the fullers of Winchester. A few years later the York weavers' gild appears, paying £10. From the size of the sums paid for their privileges it is clear that these gilds were greater in number and importance than those of any other artisans.

Thus by the twelfth century the woollen industry of the North Sea region, whose roots stretched far back into the past, had developed afresh with astonishing speed, reaching the stage of large-scale urban manufacture of standardised fabrics for sale to distant markets. On the busy Scandinavian routes along the Baltic and the North Sea, from the Slav lands of the East to Ireland in the West, a lively interchange was carried on. Flemish cloth was wellknown not only in Germany but as far east as Novgorod, where each year the Fraternity of Merchants of Saint John the Baptist gave a whole cloth of Ypres to the bishop when he said mass for them on the feast of their patron saint. English cloth was known on the Rhine and was much in demand in Scandinavian lands; when Sweyn Olaf's son, cruising off Dublin in 1171, captured two ships out from England laden with English cloth, he returned in triumph to the Orkneys, displaying his booty by sewing the cloth to his sails, and ever after his voyage was known as 'the broadcloth cruise' (*skruð víking*).

But already this northern traffic was beginning to be eclipsed by another, surpassing it in volume and importance. Italian merchants, journeying over the Alpine passes, had by the opening of the twelfth century penetrated to Flanders and crossed over to do business in England. By the middle of the century they were regularly visiting the fairs of Champagne at which much cloth was marketed. Flemish merchants too were making their way to Italy, and a steady stream of northern textiles was moving south towards the Mediterranean ports, some of them to be sold in Italy but most destined ultimately for Africa and the Levant. Trade with the East was transformed. Cloth now more and more took the place of the specie that had once gone east to pay for the spices, silk, gold, ivory and precious stones imported thence. Not only was the balance of trade to some extent redressed, but a great expansion of imports followed. Together with the luxuries which from time immemorial had formed the staple of the trade came raw materials for the cloth industry, particularly dyestuffs. The expansion of the Mediterranean trade and the expansion of the northern textile industry, acting and reacting upon each other, had built up in Africa and the Near East an immense new market for Europe's quantity-produced textiles, and immeasurably increased Europe's buying power, creating new demands for oriental luxuries.

No longer content with the native herbs, such as woad and madder, used by their Frankish and Saxon forebears, the northern dyers vastly extended the range and variety of their colours with more exotic products from Asia as well as from the Mediterranean. Kermes, now commonly called grain (*granum*), from Asia Minor, Spain and Portugal was now used in the North as it had been in the South in Roman days; with it was dyed the costly scarlet worn by kings. Other red dyes were of eastern origin. Brasil, for instance, now used in large quantities in England and Flanders, was prepared from the wood of an East Indian tree (*Caesalpina Sappau*); the finest quality came from Ceylon, according to Marco Polo who brought seeds of it to set and sow in Venice, and brasil wood was frequently a return cargo in ships from the Levant, and even more important were the large shipments of alum, one of the principal mordants used in fixing the dyes. The alum of northern Europe was very inferior to that of the South, and the principal sources of supply were now in North Africa, Asia Minor and the Black Sea, particularly in the mines of Phocaea, exploited for over a millennium by the Greeks and now in the possession of the Genoese.

Thus by the end of the twelfth century the northern industry had come to depend in large measure upon far-distant Mediterranean markets both for its raw materials and for the marketing of its finished products. This fact is of cardinal importance for the understanding of its history. For it vitally affected both the progress of the industry and, as we shall see later, its organisation. It is assuredly no coincidence that the period when the Mediterranean trade was at its height, from the late twelfth to the late thirteenth century, was a period of great prosperity for the northern industry, and a period also of stability, when demand was increasing and industry developing, but along lines already well established, with no sharp break in continuity. It is a period which ends with widespread labour troubles and industrial depression in many old centres of the industry, and at the same time with the restriction of the Mediterranean market, as Acre was lost to the Christians and trade with Egypt prohibited, and as the Asiatic markets became more and more uncertain and the direct routes to the Far East, though continuing, more and more curtailed.

III. *The Zenith of Flanders: Thirteenth-Century Capitalism*

While no quantitative estimates are possible of the amounts of cloth marketed in the Levant, yet from the records of Mediterranean ports such as Venice, Genoa, Marseilles and Barcelona it is possible to assess with some confidence the relative importance of the different centres of production concerned in this export trade. All such records emphasise the primary importance of the northern producing region, both for quality and for quantity, and, within that region, the paramount position held by the industry of Flanders and its immediate neighbourhood, with the English industry contributing cloth comparable in quality though less in quantity. Moreover, for the first time the abundance of documents enables us clearly to define the chief production areas.

Densest of all was the concentration of industry in the county of Flanders, one of the wealthiest, if also one of the most troublesome, fiefs of the crown of France. Here, between the Canche and the Zwin, in a region bounded eastwards by the Scheldt, almost every town, great and small, was busy with the manufacture of woollens, and there were at least a dozen centres whose cloth had won so distinctive a reputation as to be marketed under its own name in France, Spain, Italy and beyond. In the South, French Flanders was again renowned for its cloth as in the days of the Atrebates and the Nervii. Here pride of place was taken by five great clothing towns: Arras and St Omer in Artois – rich prize of war severed from the county of Flanders at the end of the twelfth century by Philip Augustus; Douai, Lille, and Tournai. Lesser centres with an active export trade in their own distinctive lines included Hesdin, Aire-sur-Lys and Béthune in Artois, Orchies and Bailleul. Northwards, in Flemish Flanders, whose industrial fame stretched back into no such remote antiquity, there were three pre-eminent centres – Ypres, Ghent and Bruges, and many subsidiary ones such as Poperinghe, Dixmude, Wervicq, Courtrai and Oudenarde. Cloths of Ypres, well known throughout northern Europe in the early twelfth century, surpassed all others on the southern markets towards the end of the century, both in number and variety. And though cloths of Ghent also were then appearing on the Mediterranean market, it was not until the turn of the century that they, with cloths of Bruges, were coming to rival the products of more southerly towns such as Ypres.

While Flanders reigned supreme, there were nevertheless important extensions of the textile region southwards into the adjacent French provinces of Ponthieu and Vermandois and eastwards across the frontiers of the Empire into Brabant, Hainault and the bishopric of Cambrai. In Vermandois, Amiens and St Quentin on the Somme, and Beauvais further south, were of primary importance, while Corbie was a considerable secondary centre. Lower down the Somme in Ponthieu lay Abbeville, with Montreuil-sur-Mer to the north, both primary centres. Even more important were Cambrai and its near neighbour Valenciennes in Hainault, both of which exported large quantities of cloths of many colours, while in Hainault there were also other noted centres such as Maubeuge and Chimay. Brabant, whose industrial development lagged far behind that of Flanders, assumed a steadily growing importance in the course of the thirteenth century, and by its close Brussels cloth, not seen on the markets of Genoa in the late twelfth century, was known in Italy, and was being marketed in France as was that of Louvain. Malines, geographically though not strictly politically a Brabantine town, was probably earlier in the field and certainly more active; in the last years of the century its merchants were travelling in the Baltic, they had their halls in the fairs of Champagne, and their cloth was being sold in Spain.

Yet further, beyond these provinces, lay other outlying textile towns. In particular, cloth was exported from the valley of the Meuse – from Liège, Namur, Huy and Maastricht; while Rheims and Champagne cities such as Châlons-sur-Marne, Provins and Aubenton were all centres of production as well as of exchange. There can be no doubt, however, that first place on the export markets was taken by the cities of Flanders – French and Flemish, with the cities of Brabant a good second by the end of the thirteenth century. It was these which the author of the *Dit de Lendit* singled out not long afterwards, in his detailed enumeration of clothmaking towns exhibiting their wares at the fair of St Denis, as producing the finest merchandise of all:

> En mon dit, vous amenteuvrai
> Gant et Ypres et puis Douay
> Et Maalines et Broiselles;
> Je les dois bien nommer com celes
> Qui plus belles son a veoir.

The whole of this great manufacturing region, stretching across modern Belgium and north-east France, may be regarded as an economic as well as a geographical unity. For its chief clothmaking towns, though divided politically among a number of different feudal principalities, owing fealty some to the emperor and some to the king of France, were yet closely linked one with another for the furtherance of their business. Already by the end of the twelfth century they were associated in a commercial gild or *hanse* known throughout the thirteenth century by the name of 'The Seventeen Towns', though by then its membership had grown to some two dozen and more with the admission of towns later to develop such as Ghent and Bruges. Primarily these towns were concerned with regulating their relations with the fairs of Champagne, premier mart throughout this period for the textiles of the North. Together they determined which fairs should be attended; together they negotiated with the officials of the fairs; together they enforced a common discipline on their merchants. Thus the powerful merchant gilds which in each city governed the trade on which that city's life depended were now themselves linked in an inter-city gild so that they might frame and execute a common export policy.

The stream of northern textiles flowing east and south was augmented, as we have seen, by cloth from England. This was then in high repute on all the markets with which European traders dealt, as it had been in Roman, Merovingian and Carolingian times. But England was much less industrialised than Flanders, and was herself importing considerable quantities from Flanders. There were indeed organised groups of professional weavers, fullers and dyers in almost every part of the country, from the Lake District and Northumberland down to the south-west, all concerned in the making of cloth for sale. Many towns too were doing business in buying up raw cloth woven in the countryside, dyeing and finishing it for sale; Shrewsbury's charter, for instance, restricted to burgesses the right to purchase *pannum crudum*, just as the burgesses of Newcastle acquired from Henry I the sole right to purchase *telas ad tingendam*. But the fine quality cloths famous in the Spanish and Mediterranean trade in the thirteenth century would seem to have come wholly from that part of the lowland eastern plain which drains into the Humber and the Wash, chiefly from the towns of Lincoln, Stamford, York, Beverley, Louth, Northampton and Leicester. It is here that we can detect Europe's second most important cloth-producing region at this time, a region comparable in extent to Flanders with Artois, though much less densely industrialised. Most noted were the cities of Lincoln (*Nichole*) and Stamford. Their high-priced cloths, dyed often in the scarlet kermes ('in grain'), were much in demand for the royal wardrobe and for presents to overseas sovereigns, and they were constantly exported. Lincoln cloths were singled out for special mention in foreign tariffs, as in the Venetian tariff of 1265. Whether Stamford gave its name to the *stamforts* so popular on the continent, or whether this name was derived from *stamen forte* ('strong warp') will probably never be determined, but there is no doubt that much cloth was exported from Stamford even if all the *stamfortes de Anglia*, more numerous than the *stamforts* of Arras, Ypres and elsewhere, were not made there. Further south of this region lay a number of other industrial towns producing some fine cloth, but much cheaper cloth such as russet and burel, mainly for distribution on the home market among the poorer classes of the community and thus comparable to cloth of Canusium in the ancient world. Chief among these were Colchester, London, Oxford and Winchester, but there was also a considerable internal trade in russets from small centres such as Marlborough, Bedwyn and Totnes.

Nothing could more clearly show the advance of the 'great industry' in the twelfth and thirteenth centuries and the growing interdependence of all parts of Europe upon one another than the extent to which the cloth industry in Flanders and, to a lesser degree, in England was based upon raw materials brought from other lands.

The primary raw material, wool, was, as we have seen, produced both in Flanders and England. But by the thirteenth century England was the principal supplier for the industries of both countries. Flanders was importing not only because her own wool was proving insufficient in quantity with the rapid expansion of industrial output, but also because it was less satisfactory in quality than English wool. Already early in the twelfth century many Flemings had come to England purchasing wool for cash. Such were the merchants who travelled over with the canons of Laon; threatened by pirates, they vowed all their money to Our Lady of Laon, but once safe on land, regardless of their vow, they journeyed 'almost all over the country' spending all they had upon wool. And throughout the thirteenth century Flemish cloth manufacturers were contracting for large supplies, purchased either through agents or direct from the growers. It was Lincolnshire wool, especially from the Lindsey region, which was most in demand for fine quality cloth in Flanders as in the Lincolnshire towns themselves; its excellence may indeed have had much to do with the excellence of Lincolnshire cloth. But considerable quantities were bought by the Flemings in other parts of England and also in Scotland, Wales and Ireland.

Spain also was supplying the northern industry with a certain amount of wool from her rapidly developing sheep-farms, at any rate by the mid-thirteenth century. In England, Spanish wool was used in London and Winchester at the end of the century and doubtless in other parts of the south-eastern manufacturing region. Different in character both from the local downland wool and from the finer Lincolnshire wool, it could not be mixed with either, and regulations prohibiting such mixing still survive in some of the oldest weavers' ordinances of London. German wool was also then reaching England and Flanders, though in much smaller quantities.

Dyestuffs were drawn from all parts of Europe and from further afield. As we have already seen, the Mediterranean regions yielded the most brilliant and costly red, kermes, together with most of the alum used in fixing the dyes, while from tropical regions came another red – brasil. North-west Europe yielded madder, woad and weld. Madder and woad, commonest dyes of all, gave those shades of blue and red, light or dark, which predominate in the backgrounds of medieval tapestries, while woad was used also to produce black. In combination they gave various shades of purple such as violet, sanguine, and burnet (a deep almost black shade), while woad with weld gave greens such as 'Lincoln green'. Yellow, from weld alone, was in little demand. Choicest of all blues was perse, a rich deep shade dyed in woad; cloths of this colour sometimes nearly reached the price of scarlet dyed in grain, whereas the lighter blues such as 'clear blue' and 'azure blue' were cheapest of all the coloured cloths. Some of the purples – 'poenac', for instance, and murrey – could be dyed 'in grain', that is with woad and kermes rather than woad and any other red.

Woad and madder continued to be cultivated in the clothmaking districts of Flanders and England throughout the Middle Ages, as they had been in Saxon and Carolingian times and doubtless in Roman times also, and as they continued to be until recently. To some extent, therefore, the industries of both countries drew on local supplies. But there was already a considerable degree of specialisation, more particularly in woad, the dye most in request since it was used not only for blues but as a foundation for so many other colours; indeed England came almost wholly to depend on imported supplies. And as Lincolnshire developed its sheep rather than its woad, acquiring thereby a European reputation for its wool, so Picardy became par excellence not a wool- but a woad-producing region, supplying both England and Flanders. All along the Somme and its tributaries the woad plant was grown and harvested; there its leaves were crushed into pulp in the mills, rolled into balls and sold on the local markets, particularly at Amiens, Corbie and Nesle. The merchants of these towns united to push its sale abroad, shipping it overseas from the estuary of the Somme. Together they secured in 1237, for instance, a convention with the city of London allowing them to warehouse within the city, to sell there to strangers and citizens and, a still more unusual privilege, to take their woad themselves into any part of the country they wished. That their business was very considerable is shown by the fact that they were prepared to pay £50 a year for these privileges and a sum of £100 down towards the cost of a new water supply for the city. Very similar privileges were granted to them elsewhere, as at Norwich and Bristol. The greatness of Amiens was indeed built upon woad. This it was which founded the fortunes of its leading families, who kept for themselves a monopoly of the trade. This too it was which led to the enrichment of Amiens cathedral, where several of the windows were presented by woad merchants who travelled to England with their wares, and where the country folk who brought woad into the city to sell are still commemorated by the life-like statue of two woadmen standing with a bulging sack of woad balls between them.

Though woad was exported mainly from Picardy at this time, it was also reaching the clothing towns from central Germany, as for example from the Altmark, and from south-western France, and both these latter sources of supply became steadily more important. England in particular became increasingly dependent upon the woad farms of Languedoc, where enormous quantities were produced for export in the region of Toulouse, Albi and Montauban. Woad became, next to wine, the principal commodity shipped down the Garonne from Bordeaux, and England, secure as she hoped in her possession of Gascony, tended to abandon the cultivation of woad as she did that of the vine, while south-west France, on the other hand, devoted herself more and more to these crops, looking to northern Europe for much of her food supply. 'Picardy woad' and 'Toulouse woad' were the two varieties most commonly used by English cloth-makers in the fourteenth century. It was scarcely surprising that England clung to Gascony and coveted Ponthieu, since through these two duchies, by the outlets of the Garonne and the Somme, came the principal dyestuff on which her industry depended.

The far north of Europe yielded lichens such as orchil (*roccella tinctoria*), which was imported from Norway and gave a purplish red colour, and from Baltic forests came potash. Potash was even more in demand as a mordant than alum, for it was universally used with woad, as all medieval dyeing regulations, English or Flemish, show; hence it was needed for dyeing not only in blue but in the many colours whose foundation was woad. Thus it was decreed, for instance, that the finest dark blue, perse, must be dyed in woad alone, on white wool, mordanted with ashes, without any attempt to darken it by putting it into madder or alum or by using black or grey wool. Far greater quantities were therefore required than could be secured locally in England or Flanders from wood fires or the burning of whole trees, and ashes were imported in increasing quantities in ships from north Germany and the Baltic. They figure constantly from the mid-thirteenth century in lists of goods on which tolls were paid, both at ports and at inland cloth-making towns such as Northampton (1251) or Winchester, where they are described as ashes 'ke afferte a weide'; they formed part of the stock in trade of almost every dyer, and special ordinances were passed for their sale and measurement, as at Douai (1250).

The remaining raw materials most commonly required for the finishing processes were mainly supplied locally. Beds of fullers' earth (*terra fullonis*) were to be found on both sides of the Channel. The diggings were controlled and turned to the profit of the urban or seigneurial authority in whose domain they lay, and ample supplies appear to have been available. Teasels (*cardones*) for the raising of the nap were also obtained locally and were evidently cultivated as a cash crop on a considerable scale. Tithes on teasels had been paid in England in the twelfth century, and in the same century at Amiens tolls were paid on them, by the thousand. Attempts were made from time to time to substitute iron instruments for the natural teasel, especially when the supply was not equal to the demand as at the opening of the fourteenth century. But such attempts were resisted. Ordinances were passed both in English and Flemish towns forbidding the use of iron implements such as *skrattes* and in England such ordinances were reiterated by Parliament at the close of the Middle Ages. The medieval preference for the teasel was no irrational prejudice. It is shared today by west of England cloth manufacturers, for the teasel, they maintain, has greater elasticity than any metal hook and is less liable to damage the delicate fibres of the wool.

Thus the 'great industry' of England and Flanders in the thirteenth century drew its supplies not only from the fields and pastures of western Europe (thereby stimulating considerably its agrarian development) but also from the forests of the Indies and the Baltic, the mines of the Middle East, and the oak groves of the Mediterranean, just as it marketed its textiles in all these regions. It was therefore an industry peculiarly sensitive to changes in the international situation as well as to changes in the yields of certain primary products, and one subject to many fluctuations, short-term and long-term, often only to be explained by political or economic developments in lands remote from the centres of manufacture.

It will already be apparent that the completion of a piece of fine broadcloth, such as was put on the market by Lincoln, Douai and many other towns, was an operation involving many different craftsmen, each with his own specialised skill. Before turning to a consideration of the organisation of the industry and the position of these craftsmen it may be as well to make clear their various functions by a brief review of the processes involved.

Dyeing might take place at almost any stage in the manufacture of the cloth; the wool might be dyed in the wool, in the yarn or in the piece. In the whole process of clothmaking it was the most intricate operation and the one demanding most skill. The dyer must be thoroughly acquainted with the properties of the various materials he used – wools, dyes and mordants, with the effects to be obtained from different quantities or combinations of them and from different methods of preparation or use. He must be able to judge good alum from bad, fresh madder from old; he must know how to set woad or cut brasil, and he must understand the different treatment required for different qualities of wool. Because of these complexities dyeing was often separated into two distinct crafts – that of the dyers in woad and the dyers in red and in other colours. In either case it was carried out in large circular vats, round which moved the dyer or his assistants turning over the wool or cloth as they went with long poles. This was heavy work, almost invariably done by men.

Least skill was required for the preliminary operations of sorting, beating and washing the wool, each of which was usually in charge of specialised if humble workers. Then came the preparation of the wool for spinning, by carding if it was short staple and combing if it was long staple wool; this was most frequently done by women and it was effected by means of wooden instruments, set either with short metal hooks (for carding) or with long metal teeth (for combing). The wool, duly oiled, was then spun into yarn. This was almost invariably done by women, either with the age-old distaff and spindle, in which case it could be a peripatetic occupation carried on when watching the pot or watching the sheep, or with the newly invented spinning wheel. The introduction of the spinning wheel, probably in the thirteenth century though possibly earlier, was one of the major innovations in the textile industry, but one about which little is at present known.

From the spinners the yarn went on to the weavers, unless it was to be dyed. It was prepared for weaving by workers who were often distinct from the weavers themselves – the warpers, who sized and wound the warp thread, arranging it in the requisite number of threads of the requisite length; and the spoolers, who wound the woof thread on to the bobbin for insertion in the shuttle: warp thread and woof thread were differently spun, since the warp must be the stronger. Warping was no simple task, since the full-size broadcloth which was now the staple of the export trade contained some 2,000 to 3,000 warp threads, each thirty or more yards long before fulling. Weaving, in the case of these broadcloths some two yards wide, was done by two workers, usually men, seated side by side at a broad double loom, infinitely more complex than any known in Carolingian times, for the upright warp-weighted loom in use for two thousand years and more had now been superseded, in the *grande industrie* at least, by the horizontal treadle loom – another major innovation that greatly speeded up output. Narrow cloths were woven on a single loom. In some places the two crafts of broad and narrow loom weaving were kept entirely distinct, as at Winchester; elsewhere a weaver might possess both a broad and a narrow loom.

Fulling was one of the most arduous, if one of the comparatively less skilled, operations. Through most of the thirteenth century it was generally carried out in the principal clothing towns by the wearisome old Roman method of trampling in a trough, though the water-powered fulling-mill had already been invented (pp. 616, 669–70). Hence fullers were usually men and were required to be 'strong', and three were needed on a single cloth, according to an Arras ruling. Even so they were apt to demand a rise of wages on the ground that the weight of the cloth had been increased so that they could not work it 'sans trop grant grief et exil de corps et de membres'. When the cloth had been thus washed and felted in the trough it was hung out to dry on a tenter; this was an upright wooden frame to which the lists of the cloth were fastened by innumerable tenterhooks placed along parallel bars which could be adjusted to the width of the cloth. By this means the cloth could be stretched to precisely the right length and breadth, neither more nor less. Several workers were needed on this job because of the great weight of a full broadcloth, especially when wet. Frequently they were women. Indeed the porportion of women employed in the cloth industry must have been as high then as now, from women entrepreneurs such as the *grandes drapières* of the Béguinage at Bergues St Winoc down to humble spinners and sorters.

After tentering, the fine quality broadcloths were subjected to the finishing processes of raising and shearing, so vividly depicted in the lower lights of the clothworkers' window at Semur. The raising of the nap was done by teasels set in rows on a wooden frame like an ace of spades. This was drawn down the cloth, when damp, as it hung from a wooden bar. Raising was a process often repeated many times, and sometimes carried out first at the fuller's and then at special finishing shops. Finally the cloth was shorn. This was done when the cloth was dry, with shears distinguished from sheep shears both by their size and by their shape; they were at least three to four feet long, and they were flat, not pointed, at the ends. Much skill must have been required of the shear-grinder to give them a cutting edge of some 18 inches, even enough and sharp enough to crop the surface of a fine cloth. Faulty grinding was often the subject of a claim for damages, and good shears were so valuable a possession that they were frequently left by will. The finest cloth was shorn and reshorn a number of times, in each case after redamping, teasling and drying. After shearing the cloth was brushed, pressed and folded. Various subsidiary operations were performed at different stages of manufacture, such as mending to make good any faults in the weaving and burling to remove knots and impurities; these were specialised crafts, often practised by women.

All the circumstances under which the *grande industrie* was working – wide and elastic markets, dependence upon imported raw materials (especially in Flanders), and considerable subdivision of labour – dictated an organisation which cannot but be described as capitalist whether the Marxist or any other criterion be used. Clearly it was most unlikely that the artisans actually carrying out the various processes of manufacture would be in direct relation with the consumer, and in any case not all of them could be. The combination of the many processes alone demanded an entrepreneur; so too did the import of the raw materials and the marketing of the cloth. In each sphere of operations entrepreneurs appeared; sometimes a single individual or a great company combined all three functions, purchasing materials direct from the producers, putting them out to the various craftsmen (some of whom were themselves entrepreneurs on a small scale), and selling the finished cloth. Whatever the precise form of the organisation – and it varied much even in a single centre – everywhere the artisan in the 'great industry' was subject to the entrepreneur, at least in so far as he was working for the export market.

One such captain of industry was Jean Boine Broke, draper (*drapier*) of Douai, who flourished in the second half of the thirteenth century. A man of property and substance, he himself owned all the raw materials and some of the implements of his business. Some wool was produced on his own estates or bought locally, but much more was imported, especially from England, where Boine Broke purchased on his own account from abbeys such as Newbo in Lincolnshire, Holmcultram in Cumberland, and Newminster in Northumberland. A little madder was also grown, but more was bought, with woad and alum and perhaps other dyestuffs too. Boine Broke's house combined the functions of home, office, warehouse and general headquarters of the whole concern. In it were stored raw materials and also the finished cloths – murrey, violet, or white – which he marketed abroad through his agents, some of whom were members of his own family like the Boine Broke who once took merchandise for him to Scotland. Behind his house, down by the river, he possessed a dye-house and not far off a tenter-ground equipped with his own tenter-frames. In these two establishments artisans were much in the position of factory workers of today, directly dependent upon their employer, contracted to him for a definite time, and working for specified wages. Some remained in his service over long periods; one was a washer of wools for a year, another served in the dye-house for three years, and 'Sarah of the Tenters' worked at the tenters for twelve years or more. Cloth was also most probably dressed and shorn in his house, for we know that he owed money to a shear-grinder, and it seems likely that some of the preliminary processes of sorting and beating were done there too. There was thus to a certain extent a concentration of work on the premises of the entrepreneur. For the rest the work was put out to independent craftsmen who fetched the raw material from Boine Broke's house and delivered back the finished product. Sometimes dyeing also was put out in this way. These craftsmen worked in their own homes, owned the implements of their trade, and often themselves had workers under them. Here and there they were more closely bound to the entrepreneur by living in one of his houses, which they occupied on terms which assured them sufficient raw material to enable them at least to earn their rent. Since this work was done outside the entrepreneur's own premises it was inevitably paid for at piece-work rates, while to check any embezzlement of raw material the worker was regarded as having purchased the quantity received, even if only on paper, so that he could be held responsible for its full value should it not all be returned.

A similar pattern of organisation is discernible in England, where the industry was no less highly, if less extensively, developed. Here too there had emerged a class of entrepreneurs owning the raw materials, controlling the whole production of the cloth, and selling it at the fairs, where the English *draparii* rivalled the English *lanarii*. Thus, for instance, Henry Houhil, burgess of Leicester and contemporary of Boine Broke, dyed wool on his own premises, had it made up into cloth, put it out to be fulled, and took it himself to Boston fair, where he had his own stall in a row with the other Leicester drapers, opposite the row of the wool merchants. Similarly the London burellers 'caused cloth to be made', employing the weavers and paying them at piece-work rates, and it was from them that the king bought burel for his alms to the poor. The legend of a medieval world of independent craftsmen, owning both the raw materials and the instruments of their trade and selling direct to the consumer, dies hard. In the principal industry of the time it is far from the truth. All contemporary records, concerning the main cloth-making centres, both in Flanders and England, point to a large class of wage-earning craftsmen – weavers, fullers, and others, subservient to the capitalist draper.

The position of the entrepreneurs was the stronger in that they wielded not only economic but also political power. For they were patricians, leading members of their city governments (Boine Broke was *échevin* nine times) and members too of those merchant gilds which controlled the trade and industry of their cities, and which had become more and more aristocratic; at least by the beginning of the thirteenth century they excluded altogether the wage-earning artisans of the 'great industry'. Neither in Flanders nor in England might weavers, fullers, or dyers who soiled their own hands at the work, so that they were dubbed 'blue-nails', be members of these gilds. Nicholas the Chaloner, admitted to the merchant gild of Leicester on condition that he put weaver's work out of his house, was later expelled from the gild on the ground that he had not done so. The famous laws of the weavers and fullers of Beverley (*circa* 1200) enacted that any weaver or fuller who grew rich and wished to join the ranks of the burgesses must forswear his craft, turning all the instruments of it out of his house; very similar laws are extant for Winchester, Oxford and Marlborough. All dealing in raw materials and in the finished cloth was strictly reserved to members of the merchant gilds. Hence the artisan was wholly dependent upon the entrepreneur for his livelihood, and found every detail of his life regulated by his employers through their all-powerful position in their city's government.

Possessed of full power, the merchant gilds watched over the interests of trade and controlled the 'great industry' often in minute detail, as from time to time seemed to them desirable. An immense mass of industrial legislation has survived from this most regulated economy of the thirteenth century, some of it going back to the very early years of the century. Much of it deals with the technique of the industry. Precise standards of length, breadth and weight were laid down, methods defined, and the use of certain materials prescribed or forbidden. Though more regulations have survived for Flanders and the Flemish industry was doubtless more thoroughly regimented than the English, the character of the legislation is markedly similar in both countries and many of the technical provisions are identical. The use of flocks, for instance, was forbidden in many industrial towns on both sides of the Channel, as was the mixing of different types of wool in the same piece of yarn or cloth. Teasels might only be used on the cloth when it was damp, shears only when it was dry. Perse might only be dyed with woad and ashes. Such statutory provision for good workmanship and specific standards was in part a corollary of the dispersal of production. The entrepreneur's task of supervising work done on the worker's own premises was thereby simplified in that the penalties for breach of such rules were sufficiently severe to act as a considerable deterrent. In addition it assisted in maintaining the reputation of the town's wares on the foreign market by ensuring a certain uniformity of size and quality for the various types of cloth.

To ensure the observance of the regulations, rigid systems of scrutiny were devised. Inspectors were appointed to cover every branch of the trade, investigating workshops, markets and fairs. With rare exceptions they were nominated by the civic authorities, though in part at least there might be a certain representative element, and in almost every case there were merchants among them. The official list of inspectors at Douai in 1250 includes inspectors of dyestuffs, such as the seven inspectors of brasil, three of whom were to act at the fairs and four at Douai, inspectors of crafts such as weaving and shearing, and inspectors 'of England' and 'of Burgundy', i.e. of the principal market outlets. Such inspectors had the right of entry at any time to any premises where production or trade was being carried on, even into the homes of those who spun wool. It was their duty not only to see that rules were enforced and no trickery practised and to present offenders to the city authorities, but also to prevent discord and strife and to intervene in all disputes between the entrepreneurs and the masters or the masters and their servants.

Amongst the most important functions of the inspectors was that of taking part in wage negotiations and enforcing the observance of wage regulations. Almost all wages were fixed, and where this was so no deviation from the standard rates was allowed, nor could the rates be altered unilaterally or jointly by either employers or employed, but only by the civic authorities. The idea that wages should be left to find their own level and that everyone should be free to strike his own bargain, however hard, was abhorrent to the men and women of the thirteenth century. It was generally thought that wages should be 'reasonable' and this, when interpreted, meant that some variation should be allowed in accordance both with changes in supply and demand and, still more, with changes in money values. When money was cheap, and prices consequently high, wages were raised; when money was dear, and prices fell, wages were reduced. Wages in fact were related to the cost of living. The application of this principle can be observed most clearly in the records of St Omer in the first half of the fourteenth century; here the constant fluctuations of official wage rates for weavers, fullers, tenterers and shearmen were directly, and admittedly, related to the monetary changes of Philip the Fair and Charles IV. But there is no doubt that both principles were operative elsewhere and a century earlier. At Douai in 1229, for instance, it was decreed that if demand rose and the shearmen wished to improve their pay then they might appeal to the inspectors who, with two of the shearmen themselves, would put the matter before the *échevins* for their decision. If, on the contrary, work diminished or money became less abundant and the price of the precious metals rose so that the entrepreneurs sought to lower wages and the workers refused to agree, then again appeal was to be made to the *échevins*. Truck payments were strictly forbidden, though from the frequent reiteration of the prohibition it would seem as though it was not always obeyed.

It is evident that wages were often fixed only as the result of disputes between employers and employed, often ending in strikes, when the city authorities stepped in to settle the matter. When, for instance, the sliding scale principle was laid down at Douai in 1229 the shearmen were specifically forbidden to strike in order to force a rise; prohibitions against combining to raise wages were frequent in both Flanders and England; and the detailed schedule of rates for fulling drawn up at Brussels in 1282 was, we are told, the sequel to a conflict. Certainly, employers had the last word through their position of influence on the city's government, but machinery for negotiation at least existed and the craftsmen might at any rate get a hearing for their case. Worst off must have been the humbler craftsmen – beaters, carders, combers, spinners and the like, often working on the entrepreneur's premises, who were neither organised in their own fraternities nor grouped together under separate inspectors. Less in a position to bargain, they must have been compelled to accept whatever wages the city authorities chose to fix. Yet it is unlikely that these wages were wholly unreasonable. At Brussels in 1296, after a dispute about wages among those working on the preparation of wool at the Béguinage, the city authorities agreed that the general town rates should apply also to the béguines, on condition that when the townsmen's wages went down theirs should too; they were accordingly awarded day rates of $2\frac{1}{2}d.$ in winter, $3d.$ in spring and autumn, and $4d.$ in summer.

Piece-work rates were paid for weaving, fulling, tentering, shearing and dyeing (when done on the dyer's premises). They varied much according to the type of material. Weavers were paid by the yard; fullers by the cloth, reckoning according to the number of days fulling required by different types of cloth. Dyeing rates varied according to the dyestuffs used and the dyer was obliged to display in his shop a standard sample showing the standard colours with the statutory prices for each.

In addition to fixing the rates to be given by the entrepreneurs to the master craftsmen the city authorities fixed the rates to be given by the masters to their valets or journeymen. Here payment was sometimes by the day and sometimes by the piece. Thus at Brussels in 1282 it was decreed that of the price paid by the entrepreneur for fulling each cloth, about one-third should go to the master and the rest to the journeymen.

The length of the working day was fixed as rigidly as wages in this regulated economy of the thirteenth century, though more rigidly, it would seem, in the denser industrial region of Flanders than in England. No one might work either more or less than the statutory hours. The principle on which these hours were determined was a simple one – that work should continue as long as there was daylight, except for a midday break of one and a half hours. Though 'night' work, that is work by artificial light, was occasionally allowed, it was universally disliked, not so much for reasons of economy as because of the danger of fire and for the avoidance of bad work. Hence not only hours but also precise times were fixed. Work began at dawn and ended at dusk. And lest there should be any doubt about it a bell was rung four times in the day, often in a belfry specially erected for the purpose, such as the belfry over the cloth hall at Bruges; first came the morning bell as day broke, then the 'dinner bell', then the 'resumption bell' and finally the evening bell. Thus great clothing towns such as Douai, Ypres or Brussels were in effect like one vast factory. In the early morning many thousands of workers might be seen flocking to the workshops of the entrepreneurs or of the weavers, fullers, dyers or shearmen, and the streets would empty as the bell rang out and they 'clocked in' to their labours. The working day therefore varied from some 8 hours in the winter to some 13 hours in the summer, and wages, where they were day wages, varied similarly (see above). There may, however, have been some such merciful provision as at Brussels in the early sixteenth century, when during the long summer hours the workers were allowed a further break both in the morning and in the afternoon. There is certainly no trace of the harsh provisions in force in certain French towns in the late fourteenth century when a king, ignorant of the economic value of rest pauses, compelled the weavers to work without stopping from dawn till dusk, taking with them their bread for the day, and 'if they wished for soup their wives must bring it to the looms where they worked so that they should in no way be interrupted in their work'.

No work was allowed on Sundays or on Saturday afternoons, so that the normal working week varied from 60 hours or more in summer to some 44 hours in winter, though the authorities might stop all work in case of extreme cold or frost. But holidays were frequent, since all Holy Days were usually appointed as obligatory days of rest; even when only the major feast days were observed the total annual holiday would be longer than now, particularly since work commonly stopped at the midday dinner bell on the vigil of each feast, as laid down for instance in the weavers' ordinances of Douai and St Omer. The ordinances of the shearmen of Arras early in the thirteenth century decreed that there should be no work for four days at Christmas, eight at Easter and eight at Pentecost, but the decision of the London weavers at the end of the century to forbid work between Epiphany (6 January) and Candlemas (2 February) was challenged by the employers, and the city authorities decreed that each person might 'boldly' work during that season as well as at any other time of the year. It is impossible now to say whether these longer holiday periods reflected a shortage of work and an attempt to spread it, or an attempt to raise the price of labour by restricting its supply.

While it is permissible and indeed necessary to describe this *grande industrie* of the thirteenth century as a capitalist one, it would be a mistake to conceive of all the workers as being equally in a state of dependence. Their condition varied considerably. Lowest in the scale were the beaters, washers and others engaged in the preliminary processes, who worked usually on the entrepreneur's premises, doing humble and ill-paid tasks, owning none of their own equipment, and apparently quite unorganised among themselves. Equally unorganised were the carders, combers and spinners, but they were slightly more independent in that they worked mostly in their own homes, owned their own equipment, slight as it was, and were free to work for more than one master and, if they wished, to employ workers under them. Higher in the scale came the master weavers, fullers, dyers and shearmen. These also worked in most cases on their own premises and owned capital equipment of some value, such as the weaver's loom, the fuller's troughs and tenters, the dyer's vats, the shearman's special table and shears. They were therefore often men of property and also of necessity employers of labour, with valets or journeymen under them, for, as we have seen, in no case could their work be done alone if they were making heavy broadcloths for the export market. Combination among them to improve their condition, though constantly forbidden, was facilitated by the fact they they were grouped together by the city authorities for the purposes of control, while some of them were also associated in their own religious and social fraternities. Best off among them were probably the master dyers and shearmen, whose work was the most skilled of all. They almost always maintained a position of comparative independence, working on commission for a number of employers, while weavers and fullers at times sank almost into servitude, pledging even their implements to the entrepreneurs.

IV. *The Renaissance of the Italian Industry*

The supremacy of the northern industry remained unchallenged through the twelfth and on toward the close of the thirteenth century. All the circumstances of history and geography had favoured its growth – the long tradition of fine craftsmanship and manufacture for export, the excellence and abundance of the local wool supplies, a measure of political stability ensuring to the city magnate a happy blend of liberty and order peculiarly propitious to his business and, above all, a commanding position both on the ancient north–south route across western Europe and on those highways of the northern seas whereon the Vikings had built up so vigorous a commerce. The whole northern world had been unified as never before. If Russians cut their suits out of Flemish cloth, Russian hats became all the fashion in Norway and Iceland, while for their cloaks Norwegians and Icelanders who could afford it sought the fine scarlets of Lincolnshire. On the Mediterranean markets the northern woollens quite outstripped the local stuffs in quality, quantity and variety. A Venetian tariff of 1265 lists over thirty different kinds of cloth from England and the Flemish region and only some ten Italian varieties; almost without exception the Italian cloths are cheap; even the costliest do not approach in value those of Ypres, Douai and Cambrai, or the English stamforts.

But if in the production of cloth the Italians were at this time far behind the northerners, in its commerce they were second to none. As the flow of northern textiles southwards had increased, so it had tended more and more to concentrate on those central routes down the Rhone valley to the Ligurian coast, or over the Alps to the Lombardy plain, and thence from the ports of Italy to the shores of Africa and the Levant. Italy, in particular its northern towns, held a key position in this lucrative traffic, and it is scarcely surprising that

Italian merchants became its chief intermediaries, purchasing the cloth at the fairs of Champagne and marketing it in Italy, Africa or Asia, whence they returned with those oriental dyestuffs so eagerly sought by the northern manufacturers. Thus they acquired an unrivalled knowledge of eastern and Mediterranean markets and the types of cloth in demand there, a controlling influence over the import of some of the costlier dyestuffs, and very considerable profits. These assets they turned to account by developing an industry of their own in the dyeing and finishing of northern cloths. Capital was invested in dye-works, tenter-yards and finishing shops. Kermes, brasil, orchil and alum were imported less for re-export than for use at home, and once again Italy specialised in producing those shades of scarlet, crimson and purple for which she had been famous in Roman times. Finishing techniques were elaborated and perfected; the soft, closely felted fabrics of the North were raised and shorn again and again after dyeing and were then marketed in Italy or abroad, competing keenly with those wholly manufactured in England or Flanders.

Such a cloth-finishing industry grew up during the late twelfth or early thirteenth century in most of the cities which handled the northern trade. In Genoa, for instance, the dyers were fully organised by 1222, with three *rectores de tinctoria*, and there too shearmen were at work on the northern cloths. Lucca, famous for its vermilion dye, was finishing cloths of Ypres. Best known of all is the finishing industry of Florence. By the middle of the twelfth century Florence was doing a busy traffic in northern cloths. The merchants who dealt in them had their shops in a narrow lane called, since it was a place of ill fame, the *Calimala*, and they were already associated together in the Calimala gild (*Arte di Calimala*), which took as its coat of arms an eagle bearing in his talons a corded bale of cloth. So wealthy and important was this gild that on occasion (as in 1182) its consuls were appointed to deputise for the consuls of the commune, just as they were entrusted with the care of some of the chief city buildings like the old Baptistry. By the end of the thirteenth century, if not before then, the gild was as much concerned with the processing as with the import of northern cloths, and its members had become as expert in matters of dyeing and finishing as the Flemings and Englishmen themselves.

The early fourteenth-century statutes of the Calimala gild and the books of some of its member companies such as that of Francesco Del Bene give us a vivid picture not only of what its members decreed but also of what they did. Cloths, finished and unfinished, were purchased at the fairs of Champagne or at the place of manufacture either by a member of the firm concerned or through the agency of another firm. Thence, packed together in canvas bales that could be laden on a packhorse, they were despatched overland to the ports of Provence and thence through Pisa to Florence on a journey of some four months' duration. The gild itself maintained inns along the route for the safe-keeping of merchants and their merchandise, and organised a postal service for the despatch of letters to and from the fairs and their delivery to the merchant's place of business in the Calimala. It negotiated for the reduction or abolition of tolls along the way, and for the redress of injuries suffered by its members in a foreign land. On arrival in Florence, cloths already finished were sold locally or re-exported, while others were put out to expert dyers, menders and finishers. These craftsmen plied their trade on their own premises but were closely controlled by the gild. On no account might they themselves engage in the buying and selling of cloth, nor might cloth be even displayed to prospective buyers at the dye-works, on the tenters or in the finishing shops, unless in the presence of its owner. They might work only for members of the gild, which took security for their good behaviour, fixed their rates of pay, forbade them to combine, inspected their work, and prescribed precise technical rules very similar to those in force in Flanders, with heavy penalties for their non-observance. Particularly strict was the scrutiny of the precious scarlets. If a scarlet were found to be not wholly dyed in grain (kermes), but with some admixture of brasil, madder or orchil, the perpetrator was condemned to the crushing fine of £105 or, failing payment, to the loss of his right hand.

If the Calimala gild controlled and restricted the activities of its subordinate craftsmen, so too it did those of its own merchant entrepreneurs. The aid of the commune was invoked, not wholly perhaps with success, to ensure that all who handled any transalpine or English cloths joined the gild, so that its control could be effective, and members' shops and warehouses in Florence were subjected to close inspection, while special consuls 'for the realm of France' supervised their doings beyond the Alps. When there was a surplus of cloth on hand the gild forbade all dealings at the fairs. It laid down a schedule of length and breadth for the cloths that might be handled, and it prescribed rigid rules not only for the dyeing and finishing but also for the selling of the cloth. Credit terms were limited (at the beginning of the fourteenth century) to 3½ months, or 2½ months for foreigners, with one week's grace, and rates of discount and of indemnity for late payment were fixed, usually at a level of 10 per cent per annum. That these terms were in fact observed can be seen from the Del Bene books, which show us the whole financing of the business, from the original purchase and the cost of transport, averaging some 16 per cent of the first cost, down to the dyeing, finishing and resale. On balance, after deducting the general expenses of the firm, a Calimala company at this time might expect to make a net profit of some 12 per cent for distribution to its shareholders.

Meanwhile Italy was not entirely without a woollen manufacture of its own. In many cities there was a wool gild (*Arte della Lana*) dealing in the whole process of cloth production from the preparation of the wool onwards. That of Florence, with a fleecy lamb of St John the Baptist as its coat of arms, goes back at least to the early thirteenth century, while in Pisa there is mention of the consuls of the *Arte della Lana* in 1188. In northern Italy as well as in Tuscany the manufacture of woollen cloth on a commercial scale was widespread in the twelfth century, and in the following century it steadily increased. Religious communities as well as laymen engaged in it. Such were the Umiliati, originally a lay brotherhood, who in 1140 joined the Benedictine order. Like the Bogards and Béguines of Flanders they at first worked daily themselves at the actual tasks of clothmaking, differing from the secular craftsmen only in that they lived together, broke their labours for religious observances, and were subject to no control but that of their own community. Later, however, they specialised more and more on entrepreneurial functions, leaving the manual work to hired employees. Capital was obtained not only by the ploughing back of profits but by loans from lay investors and by donations from pious folk who looked for a return less in this world than the next. Their industrial activity was at its height in the mid-thirteenth century but thereafter declined rapidly, ceasing almost entirely by the end of the century. At Florence they had established themselves on an island in the Arno in 1239, but in 1277 they sold their business there and early in the following century they were exempted from all taxation because of the dire distress into which they had fallen.

Now the cloths made by the Umiliati, like almost all Italian cloths at that time, were cheap cloths of inferior quality, as we have seen from the Venetian tariff of 1265. Progress in the production of high grade cloth was impeded by the competition of textiles from the more advanced northern region, by the tendency for capital to be directed into the very profitable channel of the finishing and marketing of these cloths, and above all by the comparative poverty of the raw material which the Italian manufacturers had at their disposal in their own country. Italian woollens could not hope to equal, much less to surpass, northerns in quality as long as they were made from Italian wool. But the immense development of Italy's commercial activity, which had led the Italians to become the principal carriers of northern cloths and to perfect the technique of dyeing and finishing, led them also to deal in wool. Increasingly during the thirteenth century they were competing with English and Flemish manufacturers for the best wools of Europe. Spanish, North African, French, English and Scottish wools were imported into Italy, where the finest of them fetched three to four times the price of the native wools. Most excellent of all were the high-grade wools of England, whose superiority is shown not only by their own price but by the fact that cloth woven from them could command a price sufficiently high to cover the heavy costs of transport across Europe. Before long they had superseded all others for the making of best quality cloths. Italian merchants, profiting from their peculiar position in England as papal collectors, were travelling throughout the land buying up the clip of the great religious houses and of others besides, often for several years in advance, and transferring the proceeds of papal taxation to Italy in the form of wool. By the opening of the fourteenth century they had become the principal dealers in English wool, ousting altogether the Flemings who once had dominated the trade, and themselves supplying the Flemish market. In Italy itself imported wools had so far supplanted home-grown supplies for the manufacture of high-grade cloth that, though it was still worth while to produce the finer wools of the South, in the North wool production was in many places abandoned, and in the plain of the Po lands which had once sustained large numbers of sheep were now devoted rather to the cultivation of woad.

The enterprise of the Italian merchants, which so powerfully contributed to the success of the Italian manufacturers, was assisted by a series of fortunate circumstances, more especially by the difficulties confronting the Flemish producers. From 1269 onwards trade between Flanders and England was constantly interrupted by embargoes and confiscations, so that the supply of wool to the Flemish manufacturers was intermittent and uncertain; at the same time the chief outlet for their cloths, that of the fairs of Champagne, was rendered no less precarious by their uneasy relations with the French king and by his seizures of their goods and credits. To these political difficulties were added labour troubles no less serious, culminating at the close of the century in a general revolt of the workers against the class of merchant capitalists who for so long had dominated the industry and politics of Flanders. Conflicts such as these, as we shall see later, were gravely impairing the position of the Flemish industry, threatening it from within at the very moment that the Italians, now diverting to their own country the finest of Europe's wools, were threatening it from without. And they were contributing even more directly to Italy's success. For as conditions deteriorated in Flanders more and more clothmakers emigrated, either of their own accord or banished by the state. Many went to the rising industrial towns of Italy which, with a growing demand for skilled labour, as well as for skilled direction, gave them a ready welcome. In Padua, for instance, foreigners who came into the city to make cloth were exempted by a statute of 1265 from all tolls and customs duties and later on also from personal taxes; by similar grants of privileges, reiterated in the early fourteenth century, they were allowed to import wool, dyestuffs and implements, and to export finished products, free of duty, while the whole of their profits were exempted from tax.

The inducements offered by the Italian clothing towns were designed to attract workers from neighbouring regions not less than those from across the Alps. They formed indeed in many places part of a fiscal system consciously directed towards fostering a native industry by protecting it not so much against northern manufacturers as against its own immediate rivals. For competition between city and city was more intense, if only because more readily apprehended, than competition between two geographical regions neither of which had a distinct political entity. Thus in the late thirteenth century the merchant oligarchy of Venice, while careful to do nothing that might injure the overseas traffic in northern cloth which was the lifeblood of its city, yet took measures to protect its own nascent industry against Italian competitors. Customs duties were gradually imposed not only on cloth from neighbouring cities such as Padua, Vicenza and Mantua, but also on cloth from Lombardy and Tuscany; a prohibitive export duty on wool imported from Romagna and Apulia checked the drain of raw material to rival cities, while Venetian subjects were forbidden (in 1281) to go to Padua or Treviso to work in the woollen industry there.

Fed by the finest wools of Europe and by dyestuffs from the Orient and the Mediterranean, amply supplied with labour from many lands and with capital from the immense wealth of the Italian merchants, and profiting from the difficulties confronting the Flemish producers, the Italian industry leapt rapidly ahead into the front rank, reaching its zenith in the first half of the fourteenth century. If the *Arte di Calimala* still held first place among Florentine gilds at the opening of the century, only a few decades later it had been outdistanced by its rival the *Arte della Lana*; for though in 1338 Florence might still be importing some 10,000 cloths each year it was then said to be producing some 80,000.

The progress of the Italian industry was as widespread as it was rapid. Throughout the plain of the Po, in innumerable towns of Lombardy and Venetia, the manufacture of woollens had become the principal industry. Towns which had long produced coarse cloth for home consumption were now making fine cloth for the foreign market. Milan, Brescia, Verona, Padua and Parma were as famous for their woollens as they had been in Roman days, and there was an export trade also in many other places such as Como, Monza, Bergamo, Vicenza, Treviso, Mantua and Cremona. In Venice also there had been a marked improvement in the quality of goods produced and the industry flourished exceedingly, though yielding first place to the manufacture of silk. In the Romagna there was an important centre at Bologna, and in Umbria at Perugia. If in Lombardy and Venetia, as in Belgica, such an expansion was but the renaissance of an industry reaching back a thousand years, for Tuscany there was no such ancient precedent. Its industrialisation would appear to be a wholly medieval phenomenon. Now, however, with a number of clothing towns such as Pisa, Pistoia, Prato, Lucca and Florence, it was quite as important a producing region as the plain of the Po, and indeed perhaps more so until the close of the fourteenth century. Lucca had already won a high reputation by 1265, when it was sending to Venice not only cheap white and grey cloths and vermilion-dyed cloths of Ypres but also vermilion broadcloths of its own manufacture – the only high-priced Italian cloths specifically mentioned in the Venetian tariff of 1265. But by the early fourteenth century all other Tuscan towns had been outstripped by Florence, the brilliance of whose achievements in this as in other spheres has so attracted historians as to divert attention from achievements not less substantial, if less spectacular, elsewhere. The Florentine woollen industry, so the contemporary historian Villani proudly relates, then produced each year some 80,000 pieces of cloth and employed some 30,000 persons. Over the Ponte Vecchio in the suburb of Oltrarno, where in 1200 there had been but a few houses, there now lived many thousands of wool workers, and there too many firms of the *Arte della Lana* had their headquarters.

In all these towns the structure of the industry was highly capitalistic and essentially similar to that of Flanders. The Italian *lanaiuolo*, like the English draper and the Flemish *drapier*, was an entrepreneur, supplying capital and skilled direction, employing anything from a few only to many hundreds of craftsmen, and joining together with his fellow *lanaiuoli* in the *Arte della Lana* which controlled the production of the cloth as closely as did the merchant gilds of the North. Often he went into partnership with members of his family or others; in such a case the management was carried out by one or more of the partners or entrusted to a paid manager who sometimes participated in the profits. In Florence in 1338 there were, according to Villani, 200 such woollen manufacturing firms, employing on an average 150 operatives each, if we accept Villani's figures for the total numbers involved. In Milan at the end of the century there were 363 firms; almost all of them had their headquarters in a single parish near the Porta Nuova, for the cloth manufacturers here as everywhere tended to congregate together.

In one respect the organisation of the Italian industry in the fourteenth century differed markedly from that of the North in the thirteenth century. The woollen manufacturers of each city were united together in their own exclusive gild — the *Arte della Lana*, whereas in the North they were members of the more comprehensive merchant gild. Manufacturer and foreign merchant were in fact more clearly separated, though an individual merchant might hold shares in a manufacturing concern, as did Francesco di Marco Datini of Prato, whose accounts and papers give us so much detail about the actual processes and costs of manufacture. The *lanaiuolo*, unlike the northern draper, seldom touched the export side of the business or indeed concerned himself in foreign trade at all, nor did he ever apparently attain such a position of wealth and influence as was occupied by the great international merchants and bankers of his day. Cloth for home consumption might be sold direct to the retailer, but cloth for the foreign market was usually disposed of to export firms; only occasionally did the *lanaiuolo* export it himself, retaining ownership of it until it was sold abroad. In some cases he was definitely excluded from overseas trade. In Milan, for instance, where the manufacturers seem to have been controlled by the foreign merchants, as in Venice, the statutes of the commune of 1396 distinguish carefully between merchants and merchants manufacturing fine wool; these last were effectively prevented from dealing on the foreign market by being forbidden to sell cloth of more than a certain value except on short-term credit. Similarly the *lanaiuolo* seldom imported wool himself but usually purchased from large importing houses or from middlemen.

As the 'great industry' increased in intensity, there was a growing tendency towards the concentration of business in the hands of large units, whether importers, exporters or manufacturers, and towards the elimination of small capitalists, independent craftsmen and middlemen. The number of manufacturing firms in Florence contracted from some 300 to 200 in the great period of expansion between 1308 and 1338, according to Villani, though the value of their total annual production increased from 600 to 1200 thousand florins. In Florence also we can discern at this time the gradual extinction of the *lanivendoli*, small capitalists who bought up raw wool, had it washed and beaten and sold it either to the public or to the *lanaiuoli*. A like fate befell the *stamaiuoli*, dealers in yarn. At first they were small entrepreneurs in their own right; they bought washed, beaten and combed wool from the *lanaiuoli*, had it spun into yarn and delivered it back to them. By the end of the fourteenth century, however, they had become merely employees of the *lanaiuoli*, charged with supervising the whole work of spinning in the countryside, including the transport of wool and yarn to and fro.

The division of labour in the 'great industry' was very similar in Italy and in Flanders, and indeed not dissimilar from that to be found in a west of England broadcloth factory today. Some two dozen specialised wool-working crafts can be discerned in fourteenth-century Florentine records. Almost all of these appear unambiguously in the records of Flanders, where there are also a few trade names which cannot with certainty be identified and one or two more, such as *espouleresse* (spooler), which seem to have no counterpart in Italy. Then as now work was inevitably more highly specialised in the larger concerns, while in the smaller concerns more than one operation was entrusted to the same worker; only a very large finishing shop could, for instance, employ a full-time presser.

Among the workers we find, as in the North, much variety in regard to their command over capital, their economic dependence on the entrepreneur, their standard of living, and their political rights. But in general the growth of a class of industrial capitalists was everywhere accompanied by the growth of a hired proletariat of workers. If at first many of the craftsmen attached themselves spontaneously to the big industrial firms, later they were compelled to do so as they found themselves unable to acquire raw material or to dispose of the finished product and as they were brought compulsorily under the control of the *Arte della Lana*.

The condition of this proletariat may be most clearly illustrated from the history of Florence where its numbers were undoubtedly greater at this time than in any other city of Italy. Least independent, as in Flanders, were the workers engaged in the preliminary processes such as beating, washing, combing and carding. These possessed not even the tools of their trade; they worked mostly in the entrepreneur's central shop, and were under the immediate supervision of his foremen. Propertyless and rightless, they were forbidden to assemble together or to combine in their own fraternities, even for religious purposes, without the permission of the consuls of the gild, to whose jurisdiction they were wholly subjected but in whose election they had no voice. Threatened with mass unemployment and starvation in times of slump, in times of boom or of labour shortage their prospects might materially improve. With the scarcity of workers after the

Black Death, for instance, they were in so favourable a position to bargain for higher wages that for the first time the gild intervened in the matter, abolishing freedom of contract and setting up a committee of eight *lanaiuoli* to fix wages. Paid mostly by the hour or by the day, they had no security of employment. But if it was in the employer's interest not to be burdened with superfluous hands in times of slump, it was equally necessary for him to be able in times of boom to command a body of workers which could not leave him and enter the service of a rival entrepreneur. This he often achieved by granting advances in goods or money, to be repaid later in work. Such a practice favoured the entrepreneur with considerable capital at his disposal and the attitude of the gild towards it varied according to the view that it took of the concentration of business in the hands of big firms. Early in the fourteenth century loans were forbidden, but the trend of opinion was in the opposite direction, the prohibition soon lapsed, and later on the entrepreneur's hold over the workers was tightened by an order forbidding the repayment of advances in money instead of labour.

The spinners also were by the fourteenth century wholly dependent, and tied often to a single entrepreneur whose wool alone they might spin. But their supervision was a more difficult matter, for they carried on their work in their own homes, scattered about in town and countryside, often far from the headquarters of the firm for which they worked. The *lanaiuolo* might cheat them with short weight wool and long delays in payment, despite laws passed for their protection, but they too had opportunities for trickery and bad workmanship. So the employers called to their aid the long arm of the church as well as that of the law, and pressure was brought to bear upon the bishops of Florence and Fiesole that they should instruct their priests to preach thrice yearly from the pulpit, enjoining the spinners to obey the orders of the *stamaiuoli* on pain of excommunication.

Weaving was done mostly in the city, by a cosmopolitan throng, Italian, German and Flemish, assisted often by their wives and by other members of their households. They too became increasingly dependent, working often under the direct supervision of the *lanaiuoli*. Often they ceased even to own the tools of their trade. For in times of trouble they would pledge their looms, often at rates ruinous to themselves but so profitable to the lender that an active business grew up in this form of investment; if some investors were content with 50 per cent, others, like the artist Giotto, took 120 per cent.

Even the fullers and dyers tended to come increasingly under the domination of the *lanaiuoli*. For though these branches of the business required more capital and independent firms were frequently set up to carry them out, serving more than one entrepreneur, the gild itself often invested in them and acquired a controlling influence. In course of time it actually became the owner of many of the fulleries and tenters, letting out small parts of them – one or two stocks and a few frames – to individual fullers and stretchers, who thus became no less dependent than the weavers whose looms had fallen into the hands of their employers. The dyers, who appear to have possessed their own union in the thirteenth century, were in the fourteenth century absorbed by the *Arte della Lana*. They had more rights than other workers in that they were admitted to actual membership as *membra minora*, but since the gild was still dominated by its *membra majora* they had to submit to rates of pay fixed for them by others. Nor could they get redress against the custom of payments in instalments, with postponements even up to five years – a practice which tended to bring them also into dependence upon the entrepreneur. Twice in the fourteenth century they recovered a gild of their own, each time to lose it again, though unlike the other workers they were allowed to retain a religious fraternity, which at least gave them the right of assembly.

Only the finishers were never brought wholly under the control of the *lanaiuoli*, for they kept possession of their own finishing shops and their own tools, though often they worked on the entrepreneur's premises, but they continued to deal with clients as well as with masters.

As the *lanaiuoli* steadily extended their control over almost all branches of the industry, so the *Arte della Lana* in which they were all united, and of which they alone were full members, grew in power and prestige, becoming in effect very like a cartel. Not content with purely regulatory functions, the gild itself engaged in business on a considerable scale. Not only did it invest its funds in dye-works, tenter-yards and fulleries, becoming a dominant partner in, if not the owner of, many of them; it also constructed washing places along the Arno, operated a central woad store and, when supplies of this dyestuff became precarious, undertook its bulk import.

Ever zealous to stimulate sales abroad, the gild gave courteous welcome to foreign buyers, providing them with brokers to conduct them round the shops and also with lavish hospitality. And so that clients might be able to rely on Florentine cloth it attempted to ensure a high level of workmanship by prohibiting the use of inferior tools, methods and materials, and by fixing certain uniform standards of size and of weight. It intervened between members and their employees only when its help was urgently needed. In the case of the economically strong dyers, for instance, it elaborately controlled wages, whereas the wages of the helpless combers were left unregulated until the time of the labour shortage caused by the Black Death. But always it strove to forestall trouble from the workers by keeping them in a position of subservience and refusing to them that right of assembly, of association and of corporate action that was in large measure the secret of their own success.

The gild's powers of enforcement were formidable. A large staff of inspectors was constantly occupied in the detection of any breach of the regulations. The gild had its own police officers for the apprehension of delinquents, its own gaols for their detention, and its own court for their trial. So wide was the competence of this court that a suit brought by a *lanaiuolo* even against an outsider could be heard there. Moreover, the aid of the commune could if necessary be invoked to enforce its judgements. The penalties it was permitted to impose were of the utmost severity. Fines, often exacted in the form of a postponement of wages, were the least to be feared; more serious was deprivation of work, involving ruin or exile. Such sanctions as these were a commonplace of gild regulation throughout the clothing towns of Europe, but in Florence, where industrial capitalism may perhaps be seen in its most intense and ruthless form, they frequently gave place to more savage methods of corporal punishment, from flogging to the loss of a hand and even the loss of life. The wool-carder Cinto Brandini, for instance, accused in 1345 of holding public meetings and exhorting the workers to unite, was arrested during the night with his two sons and, despite a protest strike by all his fellow wool-combers and carders, was hanged on the gallows. And when the prosperity of the first half of the fourteenth century was threatened by increasing problems and difficulties towards its close, the industrial life of Florence became as violent and sanguinary as its political life.

V. *Crisis and Transformation in the North*

(i) *Flanders.* While the Italian industry was reaching its fullest development, the Flemish industry, first to attain maturity, was becoming increasingly conscious of the problems that torment an industrial society. That dependence upon foreign lands for its raw materials and for its markets which had dictated its capitalist organisation had also exposed it to violent fluctuations and, as a result, to widespread labour unrest. Internal and external troubles, acting and reacting upon each other, shook the industry to its foundations, and two centuries of expansion were succeeded by a period of recurrent crises, readjustments and gradual decline.

In the densely peopled clothing cities of the county of Flanders the conflict of capital and labour reached an intensity and a violence never since equalled even in the *Hochkapitalismus* of modern Europe. By the thirteenth century the cleavage between the two had become clearly pronounced. Once there had been a time when all engaged in trade and industry had united to liberate their cities from the common enemy of a feudal overlord. Thus in 1077 the weavers and fullers of Cambrai had joined forces with their fellow citizens to win freedom from the bishop. And in the twelfth century the independent spirit of the weavers, always restless under authority, had shown itself in rebellion against the accepted tenets of the Church, when they championed what were often described both in Flanders and in England as the 'weavers' heresies'. By the thirteenth century, however, their interest in theological disputation had waned, and they were becoming increasingly absorbed in the struggle to improve their own material conditions of life. By this time the craftsman in the 'great industry' had everywhere fallen into dependence upon the entrepreneur. While the craftsman worked for wages the entrepreneur reaped the surplus profits, and as profits mounted a growing disparity of wealth became apparent. Society was sharply divided into *grands* and *petits*, *majores* and *minores*, rich and poor; the one rich in substance but few in numbers, the other poor in substance but to be counted by their tens of thousands.

The discontents of the *minores* were focussed primarily on questions of wages, not only on rates of pay but on abuses such as truck. But they went further than this, taking at times the form of vague socialist and communist aspirations, as when the weavers and fullers of Valenciennes in 1225 deposed the town government, despoiled the plutocrats and declared a commune. Such a spoliation was doubtless partly instigated by mere lust for plunder. As the chronicler Philippe Mousket put it:

Povre gent, telier et foulon
Estoient si privet coulon;
Et li meliour et li plus gros
En orent partot mauvais los.
Et dissoient la povre gent
Qu'il en orent or et argent.

Doubtless too the craftsmen were influenced by the mystical ideals then widely prevalent among the weavers and by the preaching of the friars who, by proclaiming the virtues of poverty and humility, unconsciously inculcated also contempt and hatred for the rich. But many of them were also convinced, and not without reason, that only by putting down the mighty from their seat could they achieve improved conditions of life. For, as we have seen, the craftsmen themselves were wholly excluded from the merchant gilds in which the employers were entrenched, and it was these gilds which dominated the town governments, fixed wages and conditions of work, controlled the import of wool and the export of cloth and, at the same time, forbade the craftsmen to combine or to hold any meetings without their permission. It was this concentration of political and economic power in the hands of the employers which the workers sought to destroy by the establishment of democratic governments, or at least by securing some share in the political life of their cities.

In the county of Flanders the popular movement came to a climax in 1280. After half a century or more of intermittent trade disputes, strikes and lock-outs, there broke out in this year a general revolution which spread in a few days to Bruges, Ypres, Douai and Tournai. The overthrow of the privileges of the communal oligarchies was the primary objective of the craftsmen, and it was this which in the first instance enabled them to ally themselves both with those lesser merchants and drapers who were excluded from the gilds, and with the count, who was no less anxious to reduce the power of his overmighty subjects. Thus in their petition to the count they requested the abrogation of the privileges of the merchant gilds, the abolition of the hereditary *échevinage*, the representation of the craftsmen on the city councils, and freedom for anyone to import wool. Not for long, however, did this threefold coalition endure. Those lesser burgesses who had made common cause with the populace soon realised that if the count wished to destroy the power of the oligarchs it was only in order that he might ultimately destroy the independence of the cities, making himself absolute sovereign in his own land. Valuing civic autonomy more than democracy they abandoned the artisans, rallying to the side of the patricians.

Issue was thus clearly joined between artisans and entrepreneurs, employers and employed. And as the artisans had appealed over the heads of their immediate masters to the count, so the employers appealed over the head of the count to his suzerain. Calling to their aid the king of France they admitted to their cities a 'guardian' appointed by him, renounced their allegiance to the count, and flew from their belfries the fleur-de-lys, thus acquiring their nickname of *Leliaerts*. By so doing they jeopardised the liberty of their country. For as the count supported the artisans in order that he might destroy the authority of the patricians and possess himself of full power over his cities, so the king supported the patricians only in order that he might humble the count, his most mighty vassal, and make himself master of Flanders. Thus the artisans in championing the cause of democracy championed also the freedom of Flanders, and to the cause of freedom, as to that of democracy, they remained steadfast. The invasion and annexation of Flanders by the king of France was the signal for a popular rising in which the textile workers rallied the whole of the populace. At Bruges, fullers, weavers and shearmen and indeed all the proletariat rose in arms, led by a weaver, Pierre de Coninc. The workers of Ghent followed suit. Everywhere the people seized power, massacring or putting to flight both Frenchmen and *Leliaerts*. Their victory was sealed at the battle of Courtrai (1302) when a host of foot-soldiers, recruited from the artisans, armed with pikes, and aided only by some thirty horsemen, utterly routed the cavalry of France. To the astonishment of Europe, Flanders had been liberated by the heroic determination of its working people.

The cause of democracy in the cities had also triumphed at Courtrai. The power of the merchant gilds was destroyed and thenceforward the artisans shared in the government, just as they were permitted to associate together in their own trade gilds. But the victory of the crafts was illusory. The well-being of the workers depended ultimately upon the prosperity of the industry. Absence of class strife may have been one condition of this prosperity, but it was also a result of it. Other conditions were ample and regular supplies of raw materials and adequate markets. Successfully as the artisans might attempt a solution of the problem of the proletariat by limiting the power of the capitalists, these wider problems were more intractable and less susceptible to control. And in the discontents and miseries of the late thirteenth century we may see not so much a cause as a symptom of the onset of a malady to which in due course the industry was to succumb.

A dearth of wool was one of the principal troubles of the time. Despite an increase of production, the supply of English wool, most coveted for high-grade cloth manufacture, was insufficient to meet the demand. Italy, now rapidly developing her own production of high-quality woollens, was competing more and more seriously for English wool, and in the late thirteenth century her merchants were taking a leading part in the English wool trade; though some of the wool they exported was sold to the Flemings, more and more of it went south to feed the looms of Italy. In any event, therefore, the supply of wool to Flanders was precarious. Political developments made it yet more so. As relations between England and France became increasingly strained towards the close of the century both sides tended to use economic weapons. By threatening a cessation of wool exports England could seriously embarrass France and could also enforce the neutrality, if not the active aid, of France's most mighty fief, Flanders.

France might reply by closing her markets to English wool and by seizing English wool merchants and their goods, but only at the expense of ruining Flanders and throwing her into the hands of England. From 1269 onwards trade was interrupted by a succession of embargoes and confiscations which from time to time brought industry completely to a standstill, ruining the employers and bringing misery and destitution to the artisans, who roamed the countryside in starving hordes, begging their bread. In the great wool famine of 1297 the land of Flanders was said to be well-nigh empty (*exinanitam*) 'because the people could not have the wools of England'. It was little wonder that Edward I's tactics on this occasion proved successful and that before long the count, already turning against the French king for his support of the Flemish patricians, signed a treaty of alliance with England; England alone could secure his people's livelihood.

If wool was scarce, it was also expensive, though not only on account of its scarcity. The wool of England, declared Parliament, amounted 'to some half the value of the whole land'. Inevitably, therefore, the needs of Edward's war finance prompted a tax on wool, and in 1275 the first export duty was levied. The original tax of half a mark (6*s.* 8*d.*) per sack was sharply stepped up from time to time by such devices as the 'maltôte' of 5 marks per sack levied in 1294 and that of 3 marks per sack levied in 1297. A part of these duties could be passed on to the English growers in the form of lower payments, but part was necessarily transferred to the continental purchaser. And when in 1303 a yet further duty was imposed on alien exporters only, the whole of the new tax had thus to be passed on, since in dealing with the English producers the aliens were in competition with English merchants.

Prices for the foreign manufacturer thus rose steeply as a result of the English export duties. They rose yet further as a result of the weakening of Flemish money in relation to English, for the devaluation of the currency was among the principal remedies sought by the French king, Philip the Fair, against the financial embarrassments which were afflicting the French, no less than the English, monarchy. Thus the inflationary policy which so raised the cost of living as to justify the growing clamour for higher wages, at the same time so raised the price of raw materials as to make it more difficult for employers to meet these claims if their cloth was still to compete successfully on foreign markets.

If raw materials were a problem for the Flemish manufacturers so too were markets. Italian competition, as we have seen, was steadily growing, menacing sales in Mediterranean markets, while the English market, where Flemings had built up a thriving business, was from time to time completely closed to them when for diplomatic reasons trade between England and Flanders was prohibited. At the same time the principal outlet for Flemish cloths, that to the fairs of Champagne, was frequently interrupted from the moment that Champagne became in effect part of the royal domain of France in 1285. Flanders' export trade in cloth suffered as much from the fiscal and diplomatic needs of the French king as did her import trade in wool from those of the English king. Not only were there many disputes about frontier tolls between the Flemings and the king, to whom his new territories were principally of interest for the replenishing of his exchequer, but the prohibition of all traffic across the frontier was constantly used from then on as a diplomatic weapon against the Flemings. And when in 1297 Flanders became allied to England, all the Flemish merchants throughout France were arrested, their goods and credits confiscated, and their halls seized.

Thus at the close of the thirteenth century political difficulties threatened the two life-lines of the Flemish industry, the wool route across the Channel and the cloth route across the frontier to the great fairs and so to Italy, just at the moment when the competition of clothmakers elsewhere was becoming increasingly serious. The unemployment caused by the cutting of the two life-lines, together with the rise in the cost of living resulting from the devaluation of the currency, exacerbated the discontents of the workers and stimulated their demands for higher wages, while at the same time it was less possible for the employers to meet these demands since production costs were rising, overheads had still to be met even in times of stoppage, and profits were precarious.

Such were the circumstances which made the triumph of the crafts but a Pyrrhic victory, marking indeed the beginning of the decline of the Flemish industry. The battle of Courtrai might put political power into the hands of the textile workers, but it solved none of the problems of an industrial state whose prosperity was dependent upon foreign markets, upon foreign raw materials, and upon the skill and initiative of entrepreneurs in close touch with each. These problems became more rather than less acute with the new century. Industrial conflict continued. For though the craftsmen had sought to secure economic as well as political power by destroying the monopoly of the merchant gilds and throwing open to all the trade in wool and cloth, in practice the great majority of them remained a dependent proletariat, working for others, since the 'great industry' demanded the capitalist entrepreneur. Their situation was fundamentally unchanged, if somewhat ameliorated. Nor was any real improvement possible in their standard of life without the re-establishment of regular imports of wool and exports of cloth. Here no recovery could be looked for along the old lines. The Italian industry, expanding spectacularly in the early decades of the century, made increasing demands on English wool and as the conflict between England and France moved inexorably towards the final rupture of the Hundred Years War traffic in wool and in cloth between England and Flanders was again interrupted. Moreover, the French king still aimed at the absorption of Flanders, while the peoples of Flanders were still as passionately attached to the idea of autonomy; hence periods of peace, when trade was resumed apparently with undiminished vigour, alternated with open warfare and complete embargoes. Unemployment therefore continued. So too did civil war: with the disillusionment of the workers, class hatreds increased rather than diminished. A series of insurrections in the first quarter of the century culminated in that of 1324 when the weavers and fullers of Ypres and Bruges joined the peasants in revolt against the rich, proclaiming the dawn of a new era. The revolt was suppressed only by the intervention of the French, who, outside the walls of Cassel (1328), cut to pieces the armies of peasants and artisans and wreaked upon the cities a terrible vengeance.

The internal and external conflicts that drove the textile workers of Flanders again and again during the early fourteenth century to take up arms, whether against the French or the plutocrats, or among themselves, did not wholly destroy the 'great industry', even if they gravely impaired its strength and stability. But they brought about profound changes in its location, in its organisation, and in the marketing of its products.

The significant Flemish manufacturing region had now shrunk to the maritime lands north of the Lys. Already by the mid-thirteenth century the northern centres were tending to become more important than the southern; in the early fourteenth century this tendency was intensified. For in 1312 Flanders had purchased peace for a few years by the cession to France of her Walloon districts, in which lay the clothing towns of Douai, Lille and Orchies. In these once famous textile centres, now so often the scene of the passage of French armies, industry languished and declined, even as had that of Arras, once the industrial and commercial metropolis of the North, when Artois had been ceded to France at the close of the twelfth century. The paramount manufacturing cities were now Ypres and Bruges and Ghent, whose vigour and vitality, not less than their greater distance from France, had preserved them, though at heavy cost, from annexation.

Within these three cities foreign had replaced native capital in two of the three branches of the trade, dominating the import of the raw material and the export of the finished product, and leaving to the Flemish capitalists only the organisation of the various processes of production. The day of the great individual entrepreneur combining all three functions, as Jean Boine Broke had done, was ended. With the suppression of the merchant gilds and the abolition of the political and economic privileges of the merchant patricians, Flemish enterprise was on a more modest scale. Just as the Flemish ships had now left the seas, so the Flemish merchants had abandoned the foreign trade; no longer did they flock to the great fairs selling their cloth, or travel through England buying up wool; the Hanse of the Seventeen Towns (p. 632) became in the course of the fourteenth century no more than a name. The Flemish draper still put out wool to spinners, weavers, fullers and others, but he bought his wool from foreign importers, most often Italians, and he sold his cloth, usually through the agency of native brokers, to export firms many of whom were also Italian. Sometimes he was himself a master-weaver, for artisans were now allowed to buy wool and sell cloth.

If the decline of the Hanse of the Seventeen Towns was a sign of the decadence of the Flemish merchant patrician class, it was also a sign of the reorientation of the export trade. France was no longer the principal mart for Flemish textiles. The ancient landward route to the fairs of Champagne, now so frequently blocked at the frontier by new toll barriers or by the armies of France, was less and less used. In the fair towns themselves grass grew in the streets, and the halls of the Flemish merchants crumbled into ruins. The cloths of Ypres, Ghent and Bruges now found their chief outlet by sea from the port of Bruges, though some still went over land into Germany and into Central Europe. Bruges, yet more important for its commerce than for its industry, became the principal collecting and exporting centre for northern textiles, as Arras had been in the first phase of expansion. There the Flemish cloths were loaded on the foreign vessels that now crowded the harbour – on the Italian carracks and galleys which since the close of the thirteenth century had opened up a direct sea route from Italy to the North; on English, French, Spanish and Portuguese ships; and, above all, on the sturdy cogs of the German Hanse, now rising to the zenith of its power, which carried Flemish cloth to the newly colonised lands on the Baltic in return for the corn and potash needed by the industrial cities of Flanders.

(ii) *Brabant*. The troubles that afflicted the textile centres of the county of Flanders in the late thirteenth and early fourteenth centuries gave to their neighbours in the duchy of Brabant a golden opportunity. While in Flanders life for both rich and poor became less and less secure, as workshops lay silent for lack of material or for lack of markets and the land was repeatedly ravaged by sanguinary revolts or foreign invasions, Brabant, on the contrary, achieved an astonishing measure of stability and prosperity. Fief of the Empire, she enjoyed a quasi-independence such as Flanders had known two centuries earlier. The skilful policy of a succession of able dukes ensured her autonomy while at the same time it preserved peace with her neighbours and kept open the arteries of trade. John I, his son and his grandson, were deservedly popular with the merchants and people of Brabant. Refusing to become seriously entangled either in the contest between Flanders and France or in that between France and England, now approaching its climax, they nevertheless negotiated from time to time with each of the protagonists, but only so that they might exact greater privileges as the price of their alliance or even of their neutrality. In the Anglo-French war of 1294–7, for instance, when all export of wool from England was forbidden an exception was made in favour of the merchants of Brabant alone, for the duke had been active in urging the count of Flanders to ally himself with the king of England. A few years later, however, he allowed himself to be used by the French king as his agent to bring the Flemings to terms, in return for a commercial treaty giving the merchants of Brabant a privileged status above all others on the markets of France.

Thus, by the astute statesmanship of her dukes, Brabant's wool supply continued almost uninterrupted, and while she maintained and even strengthened her ancient commercial links with the eastern markets of the Rhineland she developed new links with the West, intensifying her trade in the markets of France at the very moment that these markets were being deserted by the Flemings.

Equally successful were the dukes in holding in check those social conflicts which, though less violent and prolonged than in Flanders, nevertheless threatened the peace of Brabant. Never once did they waver in their support of the patricians against the proletariat. The patricians on their part were undeviating in their loyalty to the dukes since in them they saw their only possible protector against the fury of the populace. Industrial unrest had given rise to sporadic, but unsuccessful, outbreaks throughout the thirteenth century. In Brabant, as in Flanders, the right of association was denied to the artisans, and they were wholly under the power of the patrician merchant gilds, from which all manual workers were excluded. The triumph of the Flemish insurgents in 1302 was the signal for a general revolt. Led by the weavers and fullers, the workers of Brussels, Louvain, Antwerp and Léau rose in arms, drove the patricians from their cities, seized the reins of power, and abolished the merchant gilds. But the duke himself took up arms against them, commanding in person the forces of the patricians. On the field of Vilvorde (1306) he utterly defeated a rebel army. The revolt was suppressed with ruthless severity. Many of those weavers and fullers who had been foremost in the fight were banished; some, it seems likely, were even buried alive. The merchant gilds were restored and their powers confirmed; they alone might henceforth make regulations for the weavers, fullers, dyers, carders and spinners. The workers were again forbidden to strike, to assemble together without permission, or to carry arms; at Brussels the death penalty was imposed on any who were found within the walls of the city itself after the curfew had sounded, when they should have been outside it in the workers' suburb in which they were segregated.

If the failure of the popular movement must in part be attributed to the firm alliance between the duke and his patrician subjects, it must in part also be attributed to the vigour of the merchant gilds, whose continuing vitality in Brabant is in striking contrast to their decadence in Flanders at this time. But this vitality is itself no doubt as much the result as the cause of the stability of the Brabantine industry. Free to develop their business undisturbed, the Brabantine merchants were in a position to exploit to the full the opportunity presented by the troubles of Flanders. Hitherto the textile industry of Brabant had lagged behind that of Flanders. In the twelfth century, when cloths of Arras and Ypres were being marketed throughout Europe, it had been of little importance. And though in the middle of the thirteenth century its products were being sold on the Rhine, it was only towards the close of the century that they appear to have reached the fairs of Champagne in any quantity. In the most ancient list of the Hanse of the Seventeen Towns (in the mid-thirteenth century) the cities of Brabant are wholly missing, but in a list of 1285 Louvain and Malines appear, and a few years later Brussels, Nivelles and Diest also. In the next half-century, while retaining their trade to the East and greatly extending their sales throughout Central Europe and Poland, they steadily strengthened their hold in the West.

Cloths of Brussels, Malines and Louvain in particular enjoyed a growing reputation and many, especially of Brussels, were of very high quality. This may be seen, for instance, by the purchases made between 1298 and 1328 for the household of the countess of Artois, whether at the fairs of Champagne or at the place of manufacture: cloths of Brussels are most numerous of all, followed closely by those of Louvain and Malines; together purchases from these three cities outnumber all those from Flanders. In Paris, during the early fourteenth century, cloths of Brabant were steadily gaining on those of Flanders; business was so brisk that Brabantine merchants were seeking fresh space in which to display their wares, and it is significant of the trend of the times that they hired there a part of the halls held by the merchants of Douai since the time of St Louis. It was doubtless by these French routes that some Brabant cloths began to reach the Mediterranean in the early fourteenth century, thence penetrating to the Levant where, when Pegolotti compiled his handbook, cloths of Brussels, Louvain, Malines and Antwerp were to be found on the markets of Constantinople. But some were also going south by a more direct route, now less subject to interruption and hindrance. In the long series of Genoese notarial records beginning in the late twelfth century, to which we owe so much of our knowledge of the trade in northern cloths, the cloths of Brabant appear first in 1310. From this time on it is clear that not only Genoese agents but also Genoese ships were penetrating to Brabant, where at Antwerp they were to be found 'seeking cloths and other goods'. It was with shrewd judgement that John III bestowed upon them special privileges, encouraging them to frequent his rapidly developing port. For thus he secured a third outlet for the cloths of Brabant, and one likely to be less precarious than either the eastern or western land routes.

(iii) *England*. For the English industry, as for that of the Low Countries, the turn of the thirteenth and fourteenth centuries was a time of crisis and transformation, though of transformation which had in it the seeds of progress rather than decline. England's industrial development was as yet much behind that of Flanders. Though her production of cloth was not negligible, she was above all a supplier of raw wool to Flanders and Italy, and was herself a market for considerable quantities of foreign cloth: when Edward I needed new sources of revenue it was wool rather than cloth whose export he taxed. Hence the English clothing towns were on a very small scale compared, for example, with Ypres or Ghent. Yet here too there were signs of industrial conflict, if not of so grave a nature as in Flanders. Wage rates, restrictive practices, the right of association and the right of assembly were all matters hotly disputed between employers and employed. At Leicester the fullers were summoned (in 1275) for holding an illegal meeting not in the presence of members of the gild merchant, and the weavers (in 1264) for 'making by themselves a provision about weaving against the community of the gild merchant'. At Norwich (in 1293) the fullers were accused of having an illegal gild. At Lincoln too (in 1280) the weavers and fullers were at grips with their employers. The London weavers, strongly organised in their own gild with its royal charter going back at least to the early twelfth century, were in a position to defy their employers with some measure of success. Attempts to destroy their gild had proved vain. When the city government offered King John a large sum to abolish the charter, the weavers gave him a still larger sum for its restoration. By the end of the thirteenth century they were meeting the problem of rising prices by raising their own wages, demanding, if their employers the burellers are to be believed, first 2*s.*, then 2*s.* 6*d.* and even 3*s.* 4*d.* for weaving a cloth, where formerly they had been content with 1*s.* 4*d.* or 1*s.* 6*d.*, and enforcing their demands when necessary by strikes. At the same time, complained the burellers, they limited the number of looms from 380 to 80, decreed that no cloth was to be woven in less than four days, and lengthened their holidays, taking a winter break of over a month from Christmas to 2 February.

The restrictive practices in which the London weavers were indulging at this time certainly suggest that there was not enough work to go round. Business in fact was declining, not only in London but also in many other old-established centres of the industry. At Oxford there were said to be only seven weavers left in 1290; by 1323 these seven were dead and none had taken their place. At Lincoln, once renowned for its scarlets, there were said to be no weavers at all; at Leicester in 1322 there was but one fuller 'and he a poor man'; textile workers were already deserting Northampton by 1279, and by 1334 the houses where once 300 clothmakers had lived were said all to have fallen down. The Winchester weavers' gild, finding increasing difficulty in collecting its yearly payments to the crown, excused itself on the ground that large numbers of cloth-workers had left the town; the York, Lincoln and Oxford gilds were also falling into more and more serious arrears. If such complaints are too closely associated with claims for relief from taxation to be taken quite at their face value, yet they are too general and too simultaneous to be ignored.

Such a setback in the once famous clothing cities of England's eastern lowlands may in part be attributed to the intensification of foreign competition. Already early in the thirteenth century Flemish ships coming over to fetch English wool had been bringing in fine Flemish cloth, made from that same English wool, and during the century men and women of fashion bought more and more of the foreign cloth, despite spasmodic prohibitions. Slowly, inexorably, the giant textile cities across the Channel were capturing the luxury market, until they were bringing into England each year, when there was no embargo, enough to make 24,000 complete sets of robes. Meanwhile England grew ever richer by the export trade in raw wool which was draining away the very lifeblood of the English industry, for from the late thirteenth century Brabantine and, even more, Italian manufacturers were taking increasing quantities of this for their own rapidly developing industries. Such was the dearth in England that clothmakers there were resorting to the import of Spanish and

German wool, while at one time early in the fourteenth century the country was said also to be denuded by foreign merchants of other essential raw materials like fullers' earth, teasels and even woad. Thus fine quality English cloth was tending to lose its home luxury market, its foreign market, and even its source of raw materials.

These urban industrial centres were, however, but a very small sector of the whole English woollen industry. Scattered through the length and breadth of the realm, ubiquitous as the sheep, was another less publicised but not less important industry, located not so much in cities as in villages, hamlets and little market towns, and catering primarily each for the needs of its own neighbourhood. It was against this rural industry that the 'cities and capital boroughs' had sought protection away back in the twelfth century by the Assize of 1197 (p. 628) and by their own charters. Never, however, had they succeeded in achieving the monopoly they coveted, and more and more as time went on they felt the force of outside competition, threatening their sales of the cheaper cloths as foreign woollens were threatening their sales of the finer cloths.

If at first this rural industry had been directed towards meeting a purely local demand, increasingly during the thirteenth century it was drawn into the orbit of the *grande industrie*. One potent factor here was the proliferation of markets that was so striking a feature of the English economy in the late twelfth and thirteenth centuries. This brought every countryman within easy reach of a place where he could dispose of surplus produce to dealers in touch with the cities or with merchants at the ports. So too it created new opportunities for acquiring raw materials; the woad merchants of Amiens at the end of the century were doing business not only in cities like Lincoln or London but in widely dispersed and often remote little market towns like Appleby in Westmorland. Even more important was a technical revolution in one of the main branches of the industry as a result of the introduction of the fulling mill – the first innovation to substitute mechanical for human power in the textile industry.

The mechanising of fulling in the Middle Ages was as decisive an event as the mechanising of spinning and weaving in the eighteenth century, but we know neither when nor where, much less by whom, the fulling mill was invented. The evidence available so far points to its having come into general use in western Europe in the course of the twelfth century. The earliest mention of a fulling mill that has yet come to light is in a late eleventh-century charter of St Wandrille's in Normandy; this has been dated 1086–7, and it refers probably to a mill at Annebecq (Orne). No further references have so far been found before 1145. From then, however, until the end of the twelfth century they abound in northern France; at that time no less than twenty-nine fulling mills are recorded in a region stretching from the west of Normandy to Châlons in Champagne. In England the earliest yet known is one recorded at Paxton (Hunts) in 1173; only four others have so far been traced to the twelfth century, including two in the 1185 survey of the Templars' estates – at Newsham in Yorkshire and at Barton in the Cotswolds – but from then on references to such mills become more and more numerous. Two significant changes in terminology confirm the impression that from about the late twelfth century it was being widely substituted for the old-fashioned fullery. The old word 'fullery' (*fullonia*) which was common in earlier documents and clearly implies an installation little different from that in use in Roman times (cf. p. 616) now gradually disappears, giving place to 'fulling mill' (*molendinum fullericum*), and when water mills are mentioned it becomes usual to specify, as was hitherto unnecessary, whether they are for grinding corn or for some other purpose.

In the 'great industry' at least the new device had obvious advantages over the arduous old method of trampling in the trough. For in the mill the feet of men were replaced by two wooden hammers, which were alternately raised and dropped upon the cloth on the tilt hammer system, by means of a revolving drum attached to the spindle of a water wheel. Thus by a simple contrivance water power replaced human energy and a whole series of hammers could be set to work with but one man standing over them to watch the cloth and see that it was kept properly moving in the trough.

The very fact that the new process so greatly reduced the labour force required meant that its adoption was resisted by the old-established fullers in the clothing cities. Seeing in it a threat to their livelihood they strenuously opposed it, urging, like the handloom weavers of the eighteenth century, the inferiority of machine work as well as the unemployment it caused. Such was the double complaint of the Londoners in 1298, when they bewailed that cloth was being sent out to mills at Stratford on the Lea 'to the grave damage of those to whom the cloth belonged and also of the men using this office in the city'.

Despite the opposition of city fullers, however, fulling mills were by this time springing up all over England, wherever water power was available. By the opening of the fourteenth century their use was widespread. London manufacturers were regularly sending cloth to the Stratford mills, and later on also to those at Wandsworth and at Enfield, some ten miles away. Bristol clothmakers were finishing cloths fulled 'up-country'. Everywhere foot-fulling was giving way to mechanical fulling; human labour was being displaced by water power; the fulling industry was being carried on at the mill rather than in the home, and it was dependent, as never before, upon considerable capital equipment. So much business was being drawn to the mills that they had become a form of investment to which much capital was attracted, capital derived from the land as well as from trade. In country districts the venture was a profitable one not only because stuffs woven in the towns were being sent out to the mills, but also because the fulling mill – like the corn mill, the oven, the winepress or the dyepan – had come to be regarded as a manorial monopoly to which the tenants owed suit. The country folk could be compelled to bring their webs to the lord's mill for fulling, instead of fulling them at home with their feet, even if they were woven only for their own use, just as they had to take their corn to the lord's windmill or watermill instead of grinding it at home with handmills. Frequently, therefore, the initiative in building the mills was taken by lords of the manor, lay and ecclesiastical, who spent large sums upon them. The bishop of Winchester, for instance, built a fulling mill on his manor at Brightwell in 1208–9 at a cost of more than £9, spent £16 on another at Taunton and provided one for each of his new boroughs of Downton and Witney. Once erected, the mills were usually leased out, though occasionally they were worked by a fuller on the lord's account. The profits on them varied both according to the amount of commercial business attracted and according to the number of tenants who owed suit to the mill; thus half a share in the fulling mill of Kendal, which had once been worth 10 marks, was by 1274 worth only 8 marks, since another mill had been built higher up the river at Staveley, and to this new mill the tenants in Kentmere did suit, walking only four instead of eight miles down the Kent valley with their cloths.

The monopolistic claims of the lords of the manor, which ensured to them a substantial profit from their investments, were not unnaturally resisted by the populace, in England as on the continent, and here and there the struggle erupted into open revolt. When, for instance, the abbot of St Albans, having spent no less than £100 on his corn and fulling mills, insisted that even the smallest pieces of cloth must be brought there for fulling, the people of St Albans considered this an unwarrantable usurpation and continued to full their cloth at home free of charge. And when in 1274 the abbot sent to search their houses and distrain their cloths they resisted his servants by force, opened a fighting fund and contested the case in the king's court, though in vain.

The rapid extension of the fulling mill affected decisively not only the technique and organisation of the English industry but also its location, creating new opportunities for its development in rural regions. Some of the cities did indeed set up their own fulling mills, despite opposition to an innovation which would throw so many out of work. But the requisite space for constructing mills, with the necessary diversion of the watercourse, cannot always have been readily available. Nor were the slow-moving lower courses of the rivers on which most of the towns lay as well suited to the purpose as their swifter upper courses, where use could more easily be made of the more efficient overshot wheel. Hence fulling came more and more to be carried on outside the cities, often in remote upland valleys and the tendency for one branch of the industry to develop in rural districts gave an immense stimulus to the development of the industry as a whole there.

Yet more important, it was in the hilly regions of England that water power could most readily be obtained. Since, therefore, water was now as decisive a factor as coal was to become in the nineteenth century, the industry tended to decline in the flat eastern plain between Humber and Wash, where once its principal centres had been, and to develop in the North and West and also in the South, especially in those districts where fine wool was to be had as well as water power and clear water for dyeing. In particular it grew with startling rapidity in the West Riding of Yorkshire, the southern marches of Wales, the Cotswolds, the Mendips, and the valleys among the Wiltshire and Berkshire downs. Scarcely less remarkable was its development in the Lake District and in Devon and Cornwall, though in these parts a rougher cloth was made. In all these districts water power was being actively used by the early fourteenth century, though not until later was it exploited to anything like its full extent.

In vain the cities strove against the ever-increasing competition of the countryside. The sending out of cloth to the mills was restricted, as was also the employment of artisans outside the city walls. But such ordinances, though they might do something to prevent city manufacturers from having dealings with workers outside, could not prevent an independent industry from flourishing in the country. Some cities therefore invoked the charters which in times past had granted them the monopoly, within a certain region, of the manufacture of dyed and finished cloth. Thus, for instance, the citizens of York pleaded in 1304 that although by their charter in 1164 the making of such cloth had been restricted to York itself and the other boroughs of the country, yet now 'divers men in divers places in the county, elsewhere than in the city and in other towns, make dyed and rayed cloths'. Their petition to the king did indeed result in an official enquiry and in an order that all found plying the craft in illegal places should be compelled to refrain, but such an order could not effectively succeed in confining the industry within urban walls, much less in preventing its development in far distant parts of England.

Clearly by the turn of the thirteenth and fourteenth centuries the relative advantages of setting up cloth manufacture in cities rather than in the country were no longer as great as they had once been. The rural clothmaker now had ready access to markets other than purely local ones, and ready access also to imported raw materials, and he could make use of fulling mills whose capital costs had been borne by feudal seigneurs. Moreover where lords of the manor had established a market they had frequently also established a borough, where the inhabitants enjoyed a wide measure of personal freedom. It was seigneurial boroughs such as these, tiny at their inception, which often, like Leeds, proved growing points for the industry of the future.

Meanwhile in cities where the industry had long been established controls were many and irksome, labour tended to be restive and better organised than employers might wish and, above all, taxes were onerous, for both craftsmen and entrepreneurs. At Winchester, for instance, in the late thirteenth century, the city authorities levied 5*s*. a year on every broad loom for weaving burels, whereas outside the city's jurisdiction in the bishop's soke no annual tax was exacted, but only a once-for-all fee for a licence to set up a loom. It was not surprising that looms vanished from the city's streets and were set up in certain suburban streets claimed by the bishop where, it was said, 'men became rich and prosperous because they were not burdened by taxes or other things touching the king and his city'. At Leicester, too, and at Northampton, oppressive taxation was said to be the cause of a flight of industry from the city. At Oxford the advantages of moving out into the country, for whatever reason, must have been very apparent to certain entrepreneurs who, in the late thirteenth century, set up looms in Cowley and Bexley and there put weavers to work upon them. This, it was alleged, was the cause of the decline of weaving in the city of Oxford so that the weavers had great difficulty in paying the sum due to the king for their gild.

An exodus such as this, which may well have had parallels elsewhere, cannot but have contributed to the plight of the old-established textile cities. And when in the latter half of the fourteenth century the English industry began to overtake its rivals, its growth points were to be found, with few exceptions, outside these once famous textile cities. Moreover, they were to be found principally not in lowland but in upland regions, for these, since the coming of the fulling mill, possessed in their water power a prime industrial advantage.

VI. *The Triumph of the English Industry*

The advance of the English woollen industry to that position of pre-eminence which it has since enjoyed is one of the cardinal facts of the later Middle Ages. By the close of the fifteenth century its triumph was assured; the once mighty urban industries of Flanders and Italy, having failed to solve the problem of the industrial society, were in the throes of dissolution, rent by increasing dissensions and difficulties, while England was transformed from an exporter primarily of raw material into an exporter primarily of manufactured products.

The new possibilities inherent in the development of the fulling mill gave England, with its abundant water power, one decisive advantage over Flanders. Flanders, like Lincolnshire, is on the whole a land of windmills rather than watermills. Except in the south the mechanising of fulling there on any considerable scale would have been difficult, if not impossible, even had it not been prohibited by the urban gilds, which were not less conservative than those of England, and very much more powerful. Such evidence as is at present available suggests that it was scarcely attempted in the thirteenth and fourteenth centuries. In Artois, in Brabant and in Liège, some fulling mills were built at that time, but there too, as also in northern France, their use was vigorously, and on the whole successfully, opposed by the traditional centres of the industry, if only on the ground that they might prejudice the quality of their products. Only in the sixteenth century did the new techniques triumph in the Low Countries, and then chiefly in the hillier regions, more especially in Brabant, in the valleys of the Meuse and the Vesdre, and in southern Flanders along the Lys, where cheap and medium-priced woollens were the staple products. At Ypres, on the other hand, foot-fulling was still then generally practised. Italy was in this respect more favourably situated than Flanders. In Tuscany, for instance, the Arno and other streams descending from the Apennines provided sufficient power to turn a number of mills in the immediate neighbourhood of Florence, and to these mills the Florentine cloth was sent out, at least as early as the thirteenth century. Unlike the Flemish cities which, each in splendid isolation, attempted to confine the industry within their walls, striving against the competition of rural neighbours and also against one another, Florence exploited the surrounding countryside, over which she herself held sway. Capital for the erection of the mills was contributed both by individual manufacturers and by the corporate *Arte della Lana*, which came gradually to acquire a controlling share in most of them.

In raw materials England had the advantage over both Italy and

Flanders, for those abundant supplies of Europe's finest wools which she herself produced could be bought by her own manufacturers at prices far below those paid by the foreigner. The purchase price abroad had now to take account, as we have seen, not only of transport charges but also of the export duties imposed since 1275, and in the 1330s these duties were increased more than sixfold to a permanent new high level; from the opening of the Hundred Years War to the end of the Middle Ages the rate for English exporters was never less than some 40–50*s.* per sack, while that for alien exporters rose sometimes to over £4 per sack. Cheaper raw materials lowered the relative costs of production and enabled the English manufacturer to put his cloth on the market, at home and abroad, more cheaply than that of the foreigner. Thus the immense margin between the domestic and the foreign prices of English wool provided effective protection for an infant industry, and doubtless did more to foster its growth than did the sporadic export embargoes which could, in any event, be frequently evaded by special licence. The industry was further favoured by the comparative lightness of the export duties on cloth. Cloth, unlike wool, could be shipped from England entirely free of customs at the close of the thirteenth century. The first export duty, that of 1303, affected only alien merchants, and not until 1347 were native merchants taxed. Even then cloth paid a duty of less than 2 per cent, as compared with one of some 33 per cent on wool. Nor was its export restricted by any staple system. There was therefore every incentive to export cloth rather than wool.

The new and lucrative opportunities presented by technical and fiscal developments such as have been described above attracted to the English industry both capital and labour. In the country districts to which it increasingly gravitated much use could be made of part-time workers, and many a cottar, whose time was not fully taken up on his own small holding or by the performance of the comparatively light manorial services demanded of him, took to weaving as a by-industry, as the women had from time immemorial taken to carding, combing and spinning. Doubtless, too, many younger sons who might once have brought new lands under the plough now found careers in industry. Such rural labour tended to be cheaper than urban labour not only because it was wholly unprotected and uncontrolled, and without opportunity for collective bargaining, but also because living costs were lower in the country, where victuals, firewood and other necessaries were much more easily obtained. This was a further factor favourable to English enterprise.

Fresh impetus, too, was given to the immigration of foreign workers, particularly of skilled craftsmen from the Flemish textile centres. Such immigrations were no novelty; in the twelfth century the members of the Flemish colony settled by Henry I in Pembrokeshire were said by Giraldus Cambrensis to be well versed in the making of woollens. But from the late thirteenth century, as tension increased between England and France, their encouragement became an instrument of diplomatic policy. When export of wool and import of cloth were forbidden, to bring pressure upon the count of Flanders or upon his suzerain the French king, such prohibitions were almost invariably accompanied by a general invitation to Flemish artisans to ply their trade in England, often on very favourable terms, and by an injunction to the English public to wear English cloth only. By such means, it was thought, English growers might be provided with an outlet for their wool at home instead of abroad, English consumers with supplies of home-made instead of foreign cloth, and Flemish artisans with the employment of which they had been deprived in Flanders. Thus, for example, during the embargo of 1271 Henry III decreed that 'all workers of woollen cloths, male and female, as well of Flanders as of other lands, may safely come into our realm, there to make cloths', and he granted them freedom from taxation for five years. Though at first the ban on the wearing of foreign apparel did not apply to the upper income levels, as diplomatic relations became strained to breaking point it was extended to all classes of the community. Thus when in 1337 Edward III took the extreme step of claiming the crown of France, all his subjects 'of whatever degree' were bidden to wear English cloth; no import of foreign cloth or export of English wool was allowed, and 'all clothmakers of strange lands of whatever country they be' were taken into the king's protection. Edward's agents, according to the sixteenth-century historian Fuller, were not slow to point out to the Flemings the contrast between the wretched conditions of life in the Low Countries and the rosy prospects in England. Whether or not this is true, it is not surprising that many took advantage of the invitation, abandoning a land so frequently given over to unemployment, civil tumult and foreign invasion for one enjoying an abundance of raw materials, relative freedom from controls, and virtual immunity from conflict. The stream of voluntary emigrants was swollen by that of political refugees. After the defeat of Cassel, for instance, some 500 weavers and 500 fullers of Ypres were banished from Flanders, and in 1344 certain weavers of Poperinghe were specifically condemned to exile in England. It is impossible now to assess the scale and pace of this migration. While individual safe-conducts were often sought by immigrants from territories with which England was, nominally at least, at war, many came over relying solely on the general offer of protection, leaving no trace in the official records of the time. The majority of the settlers would appear to have been well-to-do artisans – weavers chiefly, and also fullers and dyers – who brought with them their own journeymen and apprentices; but there were also entrepreneurs like 'John Bruyn, burgess of Ghent, now making stay in Abingdon, making woollen cloth there and trading in other wares within the realm, and his men and servants'. Some found their way to the West Country, like a certain weaver at Stow-on-the-Wold, and some to the West Riding of Yorkshire, but most of them seem to have settled in eastern and southern England, so that they probably contributed little to the development of the newer industrial districts. Their coming is of importance rather as a symptom than as a cause of the progress of English enterprise.

It is at this point in the history of the English industry that for the first time we begin to get data for some quantitative measure of its advance. With the imposition in 1347 of the duty on native as well as foreign shipments of cloth the customs accounts of the royal exchequer come year by year to record all exports of cloth as well as of wool. A remarkable transformation is thereby revealed. In the mid-fourteenth century England was still predominantly an exporter of raw materials, shipping abroad some 30,000 sacks of wool or more each year, as she had done at the opening of the century, enough to make at least 120,000 broadcloths. Cloth exports recorded for Michaelmas 1347–Michaelmas 1348 were only 4,423 cloths (in terms of full-size broadcloths), though it would be dangerous to dogmatise from this one full year of cloth accounts as to the general level of exports just before the Black Death. But after a marked depression in the years immediately following the Black Death they rose with great rapidity, reaching in 1366–8 an annual average of over 14,000 cloths for the manufacture of which some 3,700 sacks of wool were probably used. A second impressive advance in the last two decades of the century bought them to nearly tenfold the 1347–8 figure, for in 1392–5 they averaged some 43,000 cloths, equivalent to some 11,000 sacks of wool. Wool exports meanwhile had fallen to an average of some 19,000 sacks. It was not surprising that Chaucer, who had lived through so notable a development of England's economy and had himself been a collector of customs, included among his Canterbury pilgrims a vigorous West Country clothier, the much travelled goodwife living near Bath, and wrote of her:

> Of clooth-making she hadde swiche an haunt
> She passed hem of Ypres and of Gaunt.

This spectacular rate of expansion was not maintained. Nevertheless the industry continued to progress, if more slowly, and by the mid-fifteenth century cloth exports had risen to an annual average of some 54,000 cloths, equivalent to some 12,500 sacks of wool. Since wool exports had at the same time declined to some 8,000 sacks a turning point had been reached: England was now predominantly an exporter of manufactured woollens rather than of raw wool. Towards the close of the century, when the civil wars of York and Lancaster were over, the momentum of the advance again increased; by the end of Edward IV's reign woollen exports averaged 63,000 cloths, and in the time of the first two Tudors they doubled, despite temporary setbacks, reaching 84,000 cloths early in Henry VIII's reign and passing the 120,000 mark by the end of it.

The customs accounts record not only the immense increase in the export of English woollens but also the virtual cessation of the import of foreign woollens, except for certain specialities; in the course of the fourteenth century English woollens had captured the English market. Apart from this falling off of imports, however, there is no means of estimating changes in home demand; hence the trend of production, unlike that of export, cannot be satisfactorily measured. A tax was indeed imposed in England from 1353 on all cloths produced for sale, and it would at first sight appear as though we have valuable quantitative evidence of production in the accounts of the royal aulnagers who were responsible for collecting it, as well as for measuring the cloths to ensure that they conformed to the Assize of Measures standardising length and breadth. But the returns are fragmentary and of dubious worth. Those for the late fourteenth century give us perhaps approximate figures of total production, though they can seldom be relied on for figures of individual output. Those for the fifteenth century are still less satisfactory; the majority of them prove at best to be second-hand compilations of doubtful veracity and at worst to be pure invention; they may give a rough measure of the relative importance of different production areas at some point of time, but the figures they yield for the country as a whole towards the end of the century are certainly too low, since they would scarcely account even for the quantity exported, while the names of individual producers and the numbers of cloths so carefully allotted to each can be shown in some cases to be wholly fictitious.

By the late fifteenth century, when the revolution had been accomplished that turned England from an exporter of raw wool into an exporter primarily of manufactured woollens, there had also been completed that revolution in the location of her industry which owed so much to the invention of the fulling mill. No more was now heard of cloths of Lincoln, Louth, Stamford or Leicester; the industries of

York and Beverley were slowly dying. First in importance among England's cloth producing regions was the West of England, which was responsible in the late fifteenth century for possibly half the whole cloth production of the country and for almost all the broadcloths. Thence came those 'Stroudwaters', 'Cotswolds', 'Castlecombes' and 'Westerns' whose reputation on the continent was now as high as that of Lincoln scarlets had once been. The manufacture of fine broadcloths, dyed and finished, was concentrated especially in the southern Cotswolds, in the Stroud valley and along the Bradford Avon and its tributaries, where were abundant supplies of fine quality wools, water power and fuller's earth. Here weaving and spinning were being carried on in almost every village and hamlet; fulling mills crowded the valleys running up into the hills, and new settlements were developing along the streams where none had been before. Thus Stroud and Chalford, for example, grew from nothing into thriving industrial centres, though the wealthy millowners who carried on business down in the valley lie buried in the ancient parish churches on the upland above – at Minchinhampton, Rodborough and Bisley, since there was as yet neither church nor separate parish below. Thus too at Castlecombe there lived down by the river, it is said, some seventy craftsmen – weavers, fullers and dyers – each with his servants and apprentices, and from them the lord of the manor, Sir John Fastolf, bought each year cloth to the value of £100, red and white, for the clothing of his men in the Hundred Years War. All along the southern fringes of the Cotswolds other busy centres of the industry were emerging: Wickwar, Dursley, Wotton-under-Edge, Bath, Trowbridge, Bradford-on-Avon, Cirencester, Malmesbury and many another. South of the Avon, Somerset was famous for its 'Mendips'. Further west, through Bridgwater and Taunton and on into Devon to Barnstaple, Tiverton, Cullompton, Exeter and Totnes, stretched a manufacturing region producing not heavily milled broadcloths but kerseys and other such cheap and light fabrics. An equally notable kersey district lay in south Wiltshire and Berkshire, particularly along the Wylie valley to Salisbury, one of its principal centres, and along the Kennet valley through Marlborough and Newbury to Reading, while there was a less important extension of this kersey region through Hampshire into Surrey and Kent.

If the West of England was second to none as a producer of broadcloths, as a producer of kerseys and suchlike stuffs it had rivals both in Yorkshire and in East Anglia. Clothmaking had long been established in Essex and Suffolk. Colchester, as we have seen, had once been renowned for its cheap russets, and cloths of Maldon, Coggeshall, Sudbury and other parts of the countryside were being shipped abroad when Ipswich compiled its Domesday Book at the end of the thirteenth century. By the fifteenth century a remarkable concentration of industry had developed along the Stour, where there was a manufacturing region comparable for the volume of its production only to that of the southern Cotswolds, and enjoying a prosperity which it has never since recaptured. Almost all the villages on both the Essex and the Suffolk banks of the Stour – from Dedham and East Bergholt through Stratford and Nayland to Sudbury, Long Melford, Glemsford, Cavendish and Clare to Haverhill – were now growing rich by clothing, as the splendour of their perpendicular churches testifies. Not less important were the clothing centres on the tributaries of the Stour, such as Hadleigh, Kersey, Lavenham, Boxford, Great and Little Waldingfield. Beyond these were outlying centres like Bury St Edmunds, Halstead, Braintree and Coggeshall.

In Norfolk there had been established at least since the late thirteenth century the manufacture of a light stuff of high quality made of long wool, combed not carded, and requiring little milling. This was in much demand for the summer clothing of religious orders in this country and abroad – quantities were sent overseas to the Knights of St John and to the Knights Templar – and for the furnishings of churches and houses, particularly for the coverlets and testers which were an indispensable adjunct to the medieval bed. At first called serge or say, it came gradually to be described more often as worsted, most probably because it was produced chiefly at Worstead and in the immediate vicinity at other now insignificant villages like Honing, Tunstead, and Scottow; Norwich too became a centre for its manufacture as well as for its marketing. By the fifteenth century the industry appears to have been in decline, and worsteds were playing but a small part in England's export trade; though John Paston determined with true local patriotism to make his doublet 'all worsted for the honour of Norfolk', and wrote from London to his Norfolk home not five miles from Worstead asking his wife to enquire 'where William Paston bought his tippet of fine worsted which is almost like silk'.

Third in order of importance was the West Riding of Yorkshire, primarily a kersey-producing region. Here, on the rocky becks tumbling down from the Pennine moorlands which nourished a sturdy breed of mountain sheep, fulling mills (or walkmills as they were called in the North) had been springing up far and wide in the thirteenth century. In the succeeding century progress had been impeded as much by the devastations of the Scots as by those of the plague, but by the later fifteenth century there was clearly discernible a thriving industry concentrating on the upper reaches of the Aire and the Calder, where today is the principal seat of England's woollen manufacture. Leeds and Bradford, Wakefield and Halifax, were then as now its leading centres; scarcely less important was Almondbury, and in almost every village, hamlet and homestead people were supplementing the meagre livelihood to be won from agriculture by the profits of industry. The city of York itself had been quite outstripped by the West Riding; its industry, with that of England as a whole, had grown rapidly in the great expansion of the later fourteenth century, but from the mid-fifteenth century its decline became steadily more marked. Elsewhere in Yorkshire a considerable quantity of cloth was being manufactured in and around Ripon and Barnsley.

Beyond these three principal regions a certain amount of cloth was being produced for export in many other parts of the country. One or two centres call for special mention. Westmorland was famous for its cheap but durable 'Kendals', made from the wool of the hardy sheep that roamed the Lakeland fells. Here there was rapid development towards the close of the Middle Ages. The industry spread far beyond Kendal and the valley of the Kent, penetrating the furthest recesses of the Rothay and the Brathay, where there was an abundance of water power and also of cheap land, barren and rocky, worthless for agriculture but suitable for the erection of tenters for stretching and drying the cloth. In the parish of Grasmere alone, in place of the one manorial fulling mill of the early fourteenth century, there were now at least twenty such mills, some in spots as remote as on the becks descending from Stickle and Easedale Tarns. Southwards in Lancashire some cloth, mostly cheap and rough, was made. Wales produced quantities of frieze, and from its southern Marches, whence came wool superior even to that of the Cotswolds and worth twice that of Yorkshire, some finer cloth was made, as at Ludlow. In Warwickshire there was a centre of primary importance at Coventry, famous for its blues, and Northampton had not yet wholly lost its ancient reputation.

While much of this cloth was sold on local markets for home consumption, ever-increasing quantities found their way to the ports by cart, pack-horse, river barge or coasting boat. If Bristol, first of provincial ports, owed much to the industrial activity of its immediate hinterland, it must in turn have greatly stimulated that activity. For with its excellent communications inland and its age-old connections along the Atlantic seaboard – from Ireland to Brittany, Gascony, Spain, Portugal and the Mediterranean – it was admirably suited to be the chief collecting centre for the whole west of England region and also for Coventry and the Marches of Wales. Exeter, too, was doing a thriving trade in Westerns, mainly to France, Spain and Portugal.

Southampton, attracting to itself much of the trade of Wiltshire, was chiefly of importance as a collecting centre for the Italian carracks and galleys, which there took on board each winter rich cargoes of woollens from all parts of England, for despatch south to Italy, Africa and the Levant. Hull, 'Key of the North', was the natural outlet for the Yorkshire vales, whose cloth it shipped not only eastwards to Scandinavia and the Baltic but also westwards with fleets bound for the wines of Gascony. By the later fifteenth century, however, it was already in decline. More and more its business, like that of the East Anglian ports, was being drawn to London, now the cloth mart *par excellence* for the whole of England. The annual fair which opened on the eve of St Bartholomew in the churchyard of the venerable priory church at Smithfield was now the most famous cloth fair in England. Thither every year journeyed cloth manufacturers from all parts of the land, there to display their wares in booths which they held on lease or as their own freehold. In addition, a weekly cloth market had been established at Blackwell Hall, purchased for the purpose by the Mayor and Commonalty in 1396; here, and here alone, between noon on Thursday and Saturday, countrymen might expose and sell their cloths.

Back from the ports to the clothing centres came raw materials for England's industry: madder and teasels from Flanders, ashes from the Baltic, woad from Gascony, Picardy, Brabant, Germany and also Italy, alum from Asia Minor and from the Pope's newly found mines at Tolfa, grain from Spain and Portugal. From Bristol they were distributed throughout the West of England and beyond – up the Severn and so to Ludlow or Coventry, and by sea to Wales and Devon in little boats which brought back frieze and kerseys. From Southampton casks of woad and alum brought in on the Genoese carracks were despatched through the whole south and west of England and much further afield; some went even as far as Kendal in the charge of those vigorous Lakeland carriers who ventured south each winter with cloth for the Italian galleys, taking home with them winter luxuries for the Westmorland housewife – oranges, nuts, wines and dried fruits – in addition to the raw materials of industry.

The structure of the 'great industry' in England at the close of the Middle Ages was inevitably capitalist, as that of the thirteenth century had been. At each stage of the industry the capitalist entrepreneur was in evidence – in the provision of the raw materials, in the combining of the various processes of manufacture and in the marketing of the finished product. Sometimes a single individual combined all three functions, as Boine Broke had done at Douai. More often the trading and manufacturing sides of the business were separated, as in Italy.

But if neither capitalism nor the putting out system were in any sense novel phenomena, even in this country, yet in one respect the fifteenth-century 'clothier' (as the English manufacturer now came to be called) differed radically from his predecessors the Flemish *drapier*, the English *draper*, and the Italian *lanaiuolo*. Not only in name was he a new and specifically English product. For he operated under what can only be described as conditions of free enterprise in contrast to the regimented control once common in England and still then customary abroad.

At the time that England's woollen industry outdistanced its rivals and won first place on the markets of Europe it was concentrated in no such vast urban agglomerations as were those of Flanders or Italy in their heyday. Nourished though it had once been in many an ancient borough behind whose walls weavers, fullers, dyers, and drapers could ply their trade in freedom and security, immune from the restraints and obligations which burdened the members of the feudal society without, the city had never gained a stranglehold upon it. For English cities had never assumed such large proportions or achieved so great a measure of autonomy as their Flemish or Italian counterparts, if only because England had been slower in developing an advanced industrial and commercial economy and quicker in developing an effective central monarchy. And when England's industry reached maturity the relative advantages and disadvantages of doing business in cities or in the countryside were very different from what they had once been. The feudal society was in dissolution; villeinage had all but disappeared; the city with its battlemented walls was becoming as much an anachronism as the baronial castle; its liberties had become privileges for the few, and its economy was more rigidly regimented and more heavily taxed than that of the manor had ever been. Even though controls had been somewhat relaxed – weavers, for instance, were no longer excluded from merchant gilds, the ancient proverb 'city air maketh free' could have had little meaning for an Englishman of the late fifteenth century, least of all for an aspiring captain of industry.

The progressive manufacturer usually, though not invariably, kept away from the city and developed his business unrestricted in the countryside, making his headquarters in some small market town or village, which grew as the industry grew, in haphazard fashion, unregulated, under the aegis of the manor rather than the borough. The pattern of the new industrial centre was strikingly different from that of the old. With no walls to confine and limit it, it was a straggling growth, integrated only by its central market-place and by the stately parish church which dominated it – built originally to serve a small rural parish, but now often wholly rebuilt to meet the needs of an industrial community and as witness to its wealth. Wide open streets with low two-storey houses took the place of the narrow alleys and the tall close-packed houses with their projecting third and fourth storeys almost meeting overhead in which many a city burgess had been content to live. The manor house, if such existed, was now of much less consequence than the comfortable if unpretentious homes of its clothier tenants, like that of the Paycockes at Coggeshall; indeed often its buildings were divided up and let in portions to house clothiers and craftsmen and their stuff. Moreover the new industrial township stood seldom in isolation but merged almost imperceptibly into neighbouring townships; a dozen such lay within a radius of seven miles in the clothing district of the West Riding which included Leeds, Bradford, Halifax and Wakefield; in Suffolk, Cavendish, Long Melford, Glemsford and Sudbury lie along a six-mile stretch of the River Stour, and Dedham, Stratford and Bergholt are within a mile of each other.

Such few manorial incidents as survived did not greatly hamper industry. Here and there, especially on ecclesiastical estates, a manorial fulling mill with monopoly rights remained, but most lords of the manor were very ready to lease out not merely the manorial mill but any portion of the watercourse that could be used for additional mills. Those tenants who were still villeins were not thereby debarred from devoting themselves to business and making their fortunes. William Haynes, one of the villein clothiers of Castlecombe, had to seek permission to marry his daughters outside the manor, but at his death he held three mills and many tenements and was also possessed of wool, dyestuffs, woollen cloth, gold and silver, furniture, debts and miscellaneous chattels which were assessed by a local jury as worth 300 marks and had at first been valued by the lord's officials at 3,000 marks. So considerable was his property that his widow was prepared to pay fines totalling £140 for possession of his movables and for leave to enter into his holdings and to marry again. Death duties might be high, but the country clothier, unlike the city clothier, had not to suffer a constant drain on his purse for local taxation, pageants, liveries, and all the burdens of public office. Nor had he to submit to the industrial controls that bound the city manufacturer. He was free to employ what workers he pleased, whether inside or outside the township; to offer whatever wages would secure them; to engage in manual labour himself if he wished and to use any methods he chose. He had, it is true, to conform to the statutory assize fixing the length and breadth of cloth put on the market, though to this there were many exceptions and many local specialities were permitted. But the quality of his cloth was unregulated, except for spasmodic attempts by the state to ensure certain elementary standards, as by such acts as those forbidding undue stretching of cloth and the use of waste and inferior wools – acts echoing civic ordinances and never wholly effectual since they were enforced only by occasional commissions and not by any regular system of state inspection.

Freedom to experiment had always characterised the rural industry. In an age of expanding business the progressive manufacturer was very ready to welcome new methods of mechanisation which, for a capital outlay, would enable him to reduce costs and increase production without increasing his labour force. By the early fifteenth century, if not before then, a means of mechanising the first finishing process, that of raising, had been invented, and West Country clothiers were using the 'gigmill' for their fine broadcloths. Instead of the tedious process of drawing teasels by hand over the surface of the cloth, the cloth was now passed over a roller set with teasels and kept whirling by being attached to the spindle of a water wheel – a device in all essentials similar to that used today. Such a gigmill was among the possessions of William Haynes of Castlecombe at his death in 1435. That its use was becoming general, and giving rise to considerable opposition as the fulling mill had done, is shown by a petition to Parliament (4 Edward IV) asking for its prohibition – a protest as ineffective as the protests against the fulling mill, for gigmills were still in use in the sixteenth century. Experiments were also being made in the fifteenth century for mechanising shearing – one of the many problems that fascinated Leonardo da Vinci – but the long heavy hand shears remained generally in use.

Such an era of economic individualism favoured diversity of organisation as much as diversity of technique. Indeed there was so great a variety of industrial structure as almost to defy analysis. The ranks of the clothiers were recruited from all sorts and conditions of men – some from within the industry, where they had begun as weavers, fullers, dyers or shearmen; some from without, from among wool farmers, victuallers, butchers, country gentry and many others. Nor was there any sharp dividing line between clothier and artisan, as once there had been in the urban 'great industry', for there was no law compelling a man to forswear his craft if he wished to 'drape' and sell cloth. The small clothier, as for example in Yorkshire, was often himself a weaver, possessing one or two looms in his cottage and employing the members of his family and perhaps one or two others for combing, carding, spinning and weaving; fulling his webs himself, or sending them to the mill, particularly if they were heavy materials; and marketing them locally at frequent intervals. With little capital behind him he led a precarious existence, though less precarious than it might have been in a city since he relied partly on the produce of his small holding. Sometimes he combined clothmaking not only with agriculture but also with some other trade such as that of a miller or a butcher. Such a mixed economy – very like that still practised in recent times by the crofter clothiers of Skye – was characteristic of great as well as small English clothiers in the later Middle Ages. The large-scale manufacturer was often a landowner, possessed of very considerable estates and engaged in stock and arable farming. As the Frenchman pointed out in the *Heralds' Debate*: 'In England your clothiers dwell in great farms abroad in the country, where as well they make cloth and keep husbandry, as also graze and feed sheep and cattle.' On these estates they grew some of the wool they needed, though they usually bought much too, either direct from growers or through middlemen wool-brokers.

The big clothier entrepreneur, at the opposite extreme from the small clothier artisan, was occupied exclusively in management. Usually he owned considerable capital equipment. Like his thirteenth-century predecessors in the clothing cities, he favoured partly the outwork and partly the factory system. His 'head house' comprised both home and office, and here were kept his stores of wool, dyestuffs and finished cloths. The preliminary sorting and beating of the wool was usually carried out on the premises. Close to the head house there was very commonly a dye-house, the property of the clothier, where the intricate processes of dyeing the wool could be performed by his own employees under his supervision with his own carefully prepared materials. Often he also owned a fulling mill, together with tenters for drying and stretching the cloth: Thomas Spring, the noted clothier of Lavenham who died in 1486 possessed of many farms and manors, not only bequeathed his tenters in his will, as did John Hunt of Lavenham, but also remembered his tenterers. Sometimes, however, both dyeing and fulling, together with the final processes of raising and shearing to which the fine broadcloths were subjected, were entrusted to independent firms specialising in these tasks. The dye-works and fulling and finishing establishments of the Stroud valley and Castlecombe, for instance, famous for their 'Bristol reds', were constantly employed by West Country clothiers. It was also quite usual for cloths to be dyed and shorn by expert finishers in or near the ports to which they were sent for export: such a finishing industry flourished in collecting centres like Bristol, Exeter, Ipswich and especially London, and at Southampton cloth was often sent out for dyeing and finishing to Ramsey or Winchester, and sometimes even to London.

For the rest, carding, combing, spinning and weaving were

sometimes done on the clothier's own premises but were much more often put out to a host of local craftsmen working in their own homes but looking to the clothier for employment. The close and friendly relationship that frequently existed between employer and employed is evident from many clothiers' wills. Thomas Spring specially remembered his spinners and fullers as well as his tenterers; Thomas Paycocke of Coggeshall (died 1518), in addition to individual legacies to specific weavers and fullers, left 'to all my wevers, fullers and shermen 12*d.* apece' and willed that 'they that have wrought me verey moch wark have 3*s.* 4*d.* apece'; he also left £4 to be distributed among his combers, carders and spinners. While weaving was to a great extent concentrated in the township, spinning was dispersed all over the countryside – as in Tuscany. John Golding of Glemsford left 12*d.* each to his spinners 'as well out of town as in town'. For this reason alone its supervision presented as difficult a problem in England as in Italy. If unscrupulous clothiers sometimes gave out short weight, unscrupulous spinners sometimes kept back part of the wool to traffic with it, making up the weight by adding more oil and water to the remainder.

Deceits such as these, which were practised by weavers as well as by spinners, may well have encouraged some of the wealthier clothiers to bring as much of the work as possible under their immediate supervision. A concentration of manufacture on the clothier's premises was more easily achieved for weaving than for spinning, for spinning was still to a great extent a part-time occupation combined day by day with housewifery. Moreover weaving demanded a certain capital outlay in the acquisition of a loom, and even those craftsmen who had once owned looms were sometimes compelled by dire necessity to part with them: the hiring out of looms had long been known in England, as abroad. It was not at all unusual for a fifteenth-century clothier to keep a number of looms operating in his own shop, as Thomas Blanket of Bristol had done a century earlier, and the practice became still more common in the early sixteenth century, strenuously opposed though it was by the weavers, who saw in it a threat to their comparative independence. The legends that gathered round Jack Winchcombe, the wealthy clothier of Newbury who died in 1519, may or may not have been true – it was said that he had kept 1,040 persons at work on his premises, in his dyehouse, fulling mill, sorting, carding, spinning, weaving and shearing rooms. But there is no reason to disbelieve the eyewitness account of Leland, who when journeying through Malmesbury shortly after the dissolution of the monasteries found the abbey lodgings converted into a factory by 'one Stumpe an exceding rich clothiar'. 'At this present tyme', he wrote, 'every corner of the vaste houses of office that belongid to thabbay be fulle of lumbes to weve clooth yn.' We know too that Stumpe planned to take over the empty buildings of Osney abbey and to employ there 2,000 skilled operatives, though this scheme never materialised. In general, however, weavers as well as spinners worked in their own homes, even if it was on looms hired from the clothier and in houses built by him and rented from him.

In these young industrial townships, growing up mostly still within the framework of the manor or the little market town, the throng of craftsmen with their servants and apprentices presented a novel social problem. Now and again in the manorial rolls we can glimpse measures taken to keep under control what must at times have been unruly and disturbing elements. Ordinances were passed at Castlecombe, for instance, prohibiting gambling and late hours in taverns and enjoining upon tenants the duty of restraining their servants and apprentices from poaching in the manorial fishponds. At Castlecombe, also, two wardens were appointed to supervise the dyers and fullers (*custodes et conservatores artis tintorum et fullatorum*) and two more to supervise the weavers, though how far these wardens had industrial functions we do not know. The manor courts, too, were called on to deal with cases of debt, contract, wrongful detention of goods, enticement of apprentices, and deceitful work. Here and there the running of a fulling mill on Sunday was forbidden, but beyond this there seems to have been no attempt to control hours, much less wages or industrial processes. *Laissez-faire* reigned supreme.

If the workers prospered when markets were expanding and prices rising, in times of slump their lot was an unenviable one. Wages were depressed, workers dismissed, and the new industrial communities experienced, like those of Flanders, mass unemployment and destitution. The social and religious fraternities in which many of the artisans were enrolled could do little to insure them against such wholesale calamities. The diplomatic crises which from time to time blocked the main arteries of trade in the early sixteenth century brought immediate repercussions. So too did the excessive war taxation which in 1525, for instance, threatened to cripple the woollen industry. 'For soth his name is Povertie, for he and his cosyn Necessitie hath brought us to this day', said the spokesman of the Suffolk rebels in that year, when asked who was the captain of the four thousand men who had risen in arms. 'The clothmakers', he continued, 'have put all these people and a farre greater nomber from worke.'

Just as the workfolk were helpless since, as they put it, 'we live not of ourselves but by the substanciall occupiers of this countrey', so were the clothiers, since they lived by the merchants. Few clothiers exported their own wares. Most of them sold either to the drapers, whose agents travelled up and down the country collecting cloth, or direct to merchants at the port – to the Hanseatics, to the Italians, but above all to the Merchant Adventurers. For as the cloth trade had expanded, so in each of its principal ports the English merchants concerned in it had drawn together into fellowships of Merchant Adventurers – 'adventurers' in that they were engaged not in the regular old-established traffic to and from Calais with wool, but in seeking new outlets for England's manufactures. Their wealth and influence at the close of the Middle Ages is itself eloquent witness to the growth of England's industry. In the great international marts of the Low Countries where now they chiefly congregated, the Merchant Adventurers of England, who went in stately procession to their own richly furnished chapel at the opening of each mart, were then of as much consequence as once the Flemish merchant in London had been, for English cloth and English exporting firms were now second to none.

The steadily growing pressure of English competition on the markets of Europe was accompanied by profound disturbances in Italy and Belgica, leading gradually to a transformation of their economies. Labour unrest in the densely peopled clothing cities increased in intensity, reaching its climax in Italy in the late fourteenth century. In Florence 1378 saw the mass rising of the woolcarders, ruthlessly repressed, while in the following year the weavers of Ypres, Ghent and Bruges rose in rebellion once again, seized the reins of power, and plunged Flanders into a sanguinary civil war in which many thousands of workers were slain. Nor were the cities of Brabant immune from such troubles. A rising in Brussels in 1360 led to the banishment of a hundred weavers and fullers, and in the last quarter of the century there were revolts also in Malines and Louvain, and a mass exodus of textile workers. To dissensions between masters and men were added dissensions between city and city, between town and country, between craft and craft. Such dissensions were both a symptom and a cause of the decline of the industry in these once mighty cities of Belgica and Tuscany, a decline amply corroborated by such figures as still exist for their industrial production at that time. Nor was England alone in profiting by their distresses and contributing to their troubles. In Germany too, and still more so in Holland, there was towards the close of the Middle Ages a woollen industry of formidable proportions. And in Italy and Belgica, as in England, smaller centres, where taxes were lighter, where vested interests and the forces of conservatism were less strong, were adapting themselves to new conditions by experimenting in new methods and new materials to meet a different clientele, challenging successfully the monopoly claimed by the old-established centres. Thus, petty Tuscan towns, of little account hitherto, now grew rich by woollens, while cities and lesser towns of Lombardy and Venetia leapt into the front rank, producing cheap stuffs abhorrent to the Florentines. Thus, too, many small Flemish and Brabantine towns and even villages developed a flourishing business in light stuffs, made frequently from Spanish wool. This transfer of production from the large to the smaller centres and from English wool to Spanish, which is so characteristic a feature of the fifteenth century, cannot be quantitatively measured. Nor can we hope to assess for the whole of Italy or Belgica the trend of production or even, as for England, the trend of the export trade. Yet despite temporary recoveries, especially in the fifteenth century, despite the survival of some few of the larger centres of production, not least Florence, and the blossoming of many smaller ones, the impression remains of a slow contraction in these two regions, while the English industry, halting though the tempo of its advance was at times, moved surely forwards until by the end of the Middle Ages it was in a position of unchallengeable supremacy, producing woollens probably greater in quantity and, if Erasmus is to be believed, finer in quality, than any other region of Europe.

CHAPTER X

Mining and Metallurgy in Medieval Civilisation

Nature endowed Europe with extraordinarily varied and abundant mineral resources. The conquest of this underground wealth by the western peoples has been inseparable from the unprecedented power obtained by men in recent centuries over the physical world.[1]

This power has come from the solution of technical problems which earlier civilisations had never seriously faced. Many of these problems first became acute in connection with mining metallurgy. Three examples will perhaps suffice. It was the search for adequate means of draining coal pits that led to the practical use of the force contained in jets of steam, to the invention of the steam engine. As the quantities of minerals dug out of the earth increased, their bulky character exerted increasing pressure on men's minds to discover cheaper methods of carrying them over land and water. It was the difficulty of hauling ores and coal in wagons along rough, soggy ground that led to the invention and development of the railway. The demand for larger quantities of metal for use in war as well as in peace pressed men on to discover methods of treating ores which would reduce the labour and the waste involved in separating and obtaining metals. It was the persistence of the western Europeans in exploiting a discovery which probably had been made by many earlier peoples[2] – that iron ore actually melted when the fires were hot enough – which has produced metal in overwhelming quantities from cascades of liquid flame.

Upon this abundance the great industrial expansion of modern times partly depended. Had it not been for the blast furnace, the twentieth-century European might be giving his fiancée an iron ring as a token of their engagement, as Pliny tells us was still the custom in the rich Roman world of the first century.[3] Had it not been for the general use of coal fuel, which was no less novel than the production of large quantities of iron, the expansion of heavy industry could hardly have taken place.

[1] On relations between geography and the origins of industrial civilisation, cf. J. U. Nef, *La Naissance de la civilisation industrielle et le monde contemporain* (Paris, 1954), 83–104.

[2] Cf. J. Newton Friend, *Iron and Antiquity* (London, 1926), 92–3, interpreting Pliny, *Natural History*, bk. XXXIV, ch. XLI.

[3] *Natural History*, bk. XXXIII, ch. I.

Fresh technical problems raised by the demand for minerals aroused the curiosity of natural scientists. Modern mining and metallurgy offered them new materials for speculative thought and experiment. Modern mining and metallurgy were among many sources which helped to lead their minds in new directions, hitherto unexplored. Again and again their general scientific discoveries have provided theoretical foundations without which many of the technical industrial achievements of the modern world, that have dazzled and also bewildered mankind, would have been impossible.[4] Indirectly, therefore, as well as directly, the development of the mining and metallurgical industries has contributed to the triumph of industrial civilisation.

Early in the seventeenth century Bacon and Descartes dreamed of a paradise of material plenty. Without the treasures of the subsoil and the attraction they exercised on men's minds, these dreams would hardly have approached fulfilment at the beginning of the twentieth century.

The rich endowment of Asia and North America, as well as western Europe, with mineral resources obviously presented novel challenges to human ingenuity. But such challenges come to nothing unless someone is challenged. Vast mineral resources have been present in many parts of the earth for thousands of years. As is shown in the first chapter of this volume, some use had been made of them in many parts of the world for several millennia before the Christian era. But the pressure on the exceedingly abundant supplies of iron ore and coal had been slight. This continued to be true after the Roman conquests.

It was in Asia that a more intensive attack was first made on the supplies of iron ore and coal. Under the Sung dynasty (A.D. 960–1127) the Chinese initiated new kinds of technological progress in connection with their exploitation. They invented and made a considerable use of the blast furnace. They reduced coal to coke. They used mineral fuel in many manufactures, for example in the production of alum and salt.[5]

All this happened some five hundred years before comparable strides in technology were taken in the use of coal or in iron metallurgy in Europe. But unlike the similar developments which occurred there under the leadership of Great Britain in the late sixteenth and seventeenth centuries,[6] these Chinese innovations had no direct sequel. Nor is there evidence that the comparable technological

[4] Cf. J. U. Nef, *The Conquest of the Material World* (Chicago, 1964), ch. 7.

[5] Robert Hartwell in *Journal of Economic History*, XXVI (1966), 29–58.

[6] J. U. Nef. *The Rise of the British Coal Industry* (London, 1932), pts. I and II; *idem*, *The Conquest of the Material World*, chs. 3 and 4, and see below, p. 704.

innovations in the West, which came so much later and led so much farther, were based on Asian experience. Chinese influence was important in modern Europe rather in the evolution of a baroque economy of commodity and delight,[7] beginning with the introduction of many forms of printing and engraving in the fifteenth and early sixteenth centuries when the communications between Europe and Asia were becoming much more frequent. By this time the stir caused in China by the unprecedented exploitation of iron ore and coal under the Sung had subsided. The production of Chinese coal seems to have dwindled to comparative insignificance even by the time Marco Polo visited Asia towards the end of the thirteenth century, when he mentions the burning of 'this black stone' as a curiosity worth reporting to Italians who had practically no supplies of it in their country. Compared with the West, China has remained, at least until very recently, in a backwater in precisely those areas of technology which the Chinese seem to have been on the point of pre-empting in the eleventh century.

The early inhabitants of Europe and North America, like the highly civilised peoples of the ancient classical world, showed little disposition to ransack the subsoil for its underground riches. Their existence was more a condition of the triumph of industrialism than a cause for it. How did it happen that the western Europeans were first to respond fully to the challenge? Why were they less reluctant than earlier peoples to rob the earth of its treasures? A history of the efforts to exploit mineral resources in Europe during the thousand years which ended with the Reformation is a necessary prelude to any attempt to answer such questions. How far had the technical skill and economic enterprise developed among the medieval Europeans made inevitable the phenomenal progress in modern times of mining and metallurgy, which has been an essential element in the rise of industrial civilisation?

I. *The Industries in Classical Times*

At hundreds of places in Europe seams of ores containing gold and silver, copper, lead and zinc, tin and iron, as well as seams of coal, once broke through the surface, or lay hidden at such short depths below that builders uncovered them in digging foundations, if they had not been already disclosed by the plough of some husbandman.

Some of these ores had been exploited long before the Roman conquests. A growing recognition of the value of the seams, and of

[7] Cf. Ernest Renan, *Oeuvres complètes*, ed. Henriette Psichari (Paris, Calmann-Levy, n.d.), II, 244–5.

the course that they followed below the surface, had led miners to sink shafts and to discover further treasure at greater depths. Already in the fifth and fourth centuries B.C., thousands of work-people, mostly slaves, were employed in mining and working the famous silver-bearing lead ore on the mountain of Laurion near Athens. A few of the pits reached down three hundred feet or more into the earth. The slopes and valleys in the neighbourhood were full of men washing, breaking and preparing the ore, or separating the silver from the lead. During the Hellenistic period of the third and second centuries mining operations were pursued with increased vigour in some of the lands surrounding the Mediterranean, so that the Romans found metallurgical enterprises in nearly all the countries they conquered.

It is not possible to determine whether the Roman conquests and the founding of the Roman Empire slowed down this progress. In any event progress continued in the sense that the production of metals went on increasing at least for several generations. Many mines were opened in Spain, Britain, Gaul and in the Alpine regions south of the river Danube. What was lacking was the zeal, which eventually took possession of the western Europeans, for driving on into the earth regardless of the cost. Like the Greeks, the Romans generally had little scientific knowledge of the nature of minerals. Many well-educated men thought that they grew like plants,[8] a view which persisted even among the intelligentsia in Europe into the eighteenth century. In 1709 the French *intendant* at Lyons actually consoled the *contrôleur-général* for the exhaustion of the surface coal at St Etienne by telling him that these mines had 'the happy property of reproducing themselves'![9]

In classical times mining was generally regarded as a much less desirable occupation than agriculture. A law was passed by the Roman Republic, probably towards the end of the second century B.C., prohibiting the digging of ores in Italy. Modern authorities disagree about the circumstances that led to this particular enactment. But it seems to reflect a distaste felt by classical peoples for labour underground and their preference for agrarian pursuits.

As century followed century across a millennium of highly sophisticated life, lived in the long, hot summers of the Mediterranean, the readily accessible surface ores were eventually largely exhausted in the more populous parts of the Roman Empire. The exhaustion of the more easily worked seams added continually to the arduous and distasteful nature of the miners' work. The difficulties of sinking shafts,

[8] Maurice Besnier, 'L'Interdiction du travail des mines en Italie', *Revue archéologique*, 5th ser., x (1919), 37–8.

[9] A. M. de Boislisle, *Correspondance des contrôleurs généraux...avec les intendants* (Paris, 1897), III, no. 496.

draining off water and hauling ore to the surface were for ever multiplying. While the classical peoples were frequently ingenious in devising machinery, they were backward about harnessing the strength of animals, of flowing streams (which were scarce and subject to drought), and even of the wind to operate their machinery. It is little wonder that labour in the mines seemed more and more intolerable. Convicts and Christians were deported to work them.[10] As a consequence of the difficulties encountered in getting ores worked, the costs of mining in man-power, even with slave labour, drove up the prices of the ores and the metals made from them and discouraged their extensive use.

To a modern European or American who has visited the coalfields of Belgium, South Wales or Pennsylvania, with the mountains of black earth beside the shafts, or who has seen the skies aflame for miles from the fires of blast furnaces in the Ruhr, the English Midlands, or north-western Indiana, the mines and forges of the Roman Empire would not have seemed impressive. Together with the quarries, they formed 'merely small islands in a sea of fields and meadows'.[11]

According to the criteria of a modern European all metals were scarce. Metal was the material of many statues, but it was never the basis for constructing ships, aqueducts, public buildings, theatres, or stadiums. It was used as sparingly as possible in making tools and machinery. Iron was almost always obtained by prolonged and patient heating in a forge fire, followed by reiterated heatings and hammerings on the anvil. Small-scale operations alone were possible and much of the iron present in the ore was lost as slag and scale. The process was very costly in firewood, charcoal and labour. Lead was preferred to iron whenever it could serve, because less fuel was needed to produce it. Bronze and brass were derived from copper, tin, zinc and their ores, all of which required less heat in smelting than iron ore. The greatest development of manufacturing in classical times occurred in regions bordering the Mediterranean, which were exceedingly poor in coal resources compared with the north of Europe or North America. Partly on that account, no attempt was made, except it seems in Roman Britain,[12] to substitute coal for firewood and charcoal either for domestic fuel or in industry. As the price of wood rose under the pressure of growing population and expanding industry, metallurgy and every other kind of manufacture requiring fuel was discouraged. Without the use of coal, oil and hydroelectric power, without also the

[10] Evidence of this is to be found in the early litanies as the late Prof. Ernst Kantorowicz told me.

[11] M. Rostovtzeff, *The Social and Economic History of the Roman Empire* (Oxford, 1926), 296.

[12] R. G. Collingwood and J. N. L. Myers, *Roman Britain and the English Settlements* (Oxford, 1937), 231–2.

wholesale use of wood from the thick forests of northern Europe and America, industrial changes similar to those which transformed the western world before the middle of the twentieth century were impossible.

II. *The Course of Production, c.300–c.1330*

A decline in the output of metal began in Europe in the third century. At first it was probably slight, but it continued for hundreds of years. From the end of the sixth century until the end of the tenth, ores were taken at much shallower depths than those that had been often reached in classical times. More primitive methods of working the mines prevailed. Gone were the long shafts such as had been occasionally sunk, for example in the neighbourhood of Cartagena in Spain, to depths of five or six hundred feet. Gone also – buried in debris – were pits forty feet or more in depth, such as had been fairly common during the second century. All the more ambitious mines of the Roman Empire in the West were eventually abandoned. They disappeared from the sight of local villagers, to be rediscovered only during the last hundred years by modern archaeologists in the course of their excavations. With the decline in the population of Europe which began after the third century, with the accompanying decay of towns, the shrinkage of trade and the reduction of the acreage under cultivation, the descendants of old inhabitants, and the Germanic invaders who settled among them, contented themselves with such ores as could be won near their village huts, mostly in the remnants of old workings accessible without the sinking of shafts. Efforts to find new seams at considerable depths ceased, at least for a time. In many places, forests, cut down in Roman times, grew again.

Iron ore abounded in most of Europe and was easily accessible. From an early period in western history, it seems to have played a somewhat larger part than in classical history. From the third to the eighth century, even in southern Europe, the output of iron diminished less than that of other metals. Iron was still needed by woodsmen and husbandmen for axes, knives and spades, and even for ploughshares in a few places where a knowledge of Roman methods of ploughing was preserved. Iron was wanted, above all, for weapons. As it was the most abundant of the ores dug during the Middle Ages, it could generally be had with less effort than ores containing silver, lead, copper, or tin. At many places in Gaul, the Rhineland, Saxony, Bohemia, and Tuscany, and especially in Spain and possibly on the slopes and along the valleys of the Eastern Alps,[13] iron in small

[13] There is some dispute as to whether iron was worked continuously in the Eastern Alps. The

quantities was produced throughout the Merovingian period (A.D. c.500–c.800).[14] In Lorraine there seems to have been some development of iron metallurgy in that age.

After the eighth century, with the spread of horses and mounted warriors, together with the introduction of the stirrup, more iron was wanted almost everywhere in Europe.[15] Europe also became a source of supplies for the Near East. At the end of the ninth century iron, brought down from the Eastern Alps, was already an item of some prominence in the exports of Venice, then the chief port for European commerce with the Near East.[16] In and beyond the Alps the wood needed to provide charcoal for the iron forges was to be had in abundance. There had long been traffic in surplus timber to Egypt, which had always depended for its wood on imports by sea.

So there is evidence that iron production had increased considerably in Europe by the tenth century.

There is, by contrast, little trace in historical records of mining for copper ore between the beginning of the sixth and the end of the tenth centuries. Brass, an alloy of copper and calamine, the ore of zinc, seems to have gone largely out of use until the discovery of deposits of calamine in the Alps and the north of Europe during the fifteenth century. Bronze, an alloy in which copper is the main element, is historically the oldest of the metals to be extensively used. It was used concurrently with iron, often for the same purposes. The paucity of early medieval references to copper suggests that iron may have been taking the place of bronze to a considerable extent. It would be unreasonable to suppose, however, that the demand for bronze, or even brass, ceased for an extended period, or that the medieval Europeans ever lost touch altogether with the copper ores needed to supply both.

According to Tacitus, one of the considerations that prompted the Claudian invasion of England in the middle of the first century was its mineral wealth. There was perhaps no part of the Empire in which mining occupied as prominent a place in industrial life as in Roman Britain. Other provinces had more impressive mines. But the relative

principal authority on iron mining in Styria argues that when the Slavs settled this area in the sixth and seventh centuries, iron work was abandoned (L. Bittner, 'Das Eisenwesen in Innerberg-Eisenerz,' *Archiv für österreichische Geschichte*, LXXXIX (Vienna, 1901), 458–9). But a later writer, who studied the iron-making industry in Carniola, raises what seem to be weighty objections to this thesis (Alfons Müllner, *Geschichte des Eisens in Krain, Görz und Istrien* (Vienna, 1909), 112–13).

[14] Cf. Ludwig Beck, *Die Geschichte des Eisens*, 2nd edn (Braunschweig, 1890–1903), I, 703ff, 728–39.

[15] As Dr Lynn White suggests to me. See also E. Salin and A. France-Lanord, *Le Fer à l'époque mérovingienne* (Paris, 1943).

[16] H. Pirenne, *Economic and Social History of Medieval Europe* (translated by I. E. Clegg, New York, 1937), 18.

importance of mining in Britain, not one of the most industrialised provinces, was great when compared with the Empire generally. In Britain, lead ore, some of which contained silver, seems to have been worked more extensively than any other mineral. The ancient tin mines of Cornwall were revived by the Romans in the third century; copper was worked in Shropshire and Wales; iron in many places. The rich and abundant mines of coal were dug, it seems, in a number of the fields where they poked their way close to the surface.[17]

Neither the mining of tin nor of lead ore was abandoned altogether in Great Britain after the Saxon conquests of the fifth and sixth centuries, although these conquests were apparently followed by an eclipse of copper ore and coal mining. A more or less steady demand for lead, both in England and in most continental countries, continued after the barbarian invasions, because of the use made of it in roofing the churches which were always being built or at least repaired, during ages when the hold of Christianity tightened on all the European peoples.

In spite of the continued use of metal in small quantities, it is probable that the European production of gold, silver, copper, lead and tin shrank to a fraction of its former amount by the early ninth century, after the Muslim conquests. Lessees of the imperial revenues from mines in Hadrian's reign, if they could have been brought back to life seven centuries afterwards in the Carolingian period, would have been shocked to find how small was the yield of these metals. The mining districts which they had known in prosperous times might have seemed almost deserts. Pliny might have deplored the loss of interest in natural history, which had been associated by the classical peoples partly with mining and metallurgy, though he would perhaps have applauded the reluctance of men to raid underground treasure which in his eyes had bred mainly luxury and vice.

The growth in the output of iron, which began in the Eastern Alps towards the end of the ninth century, if not earlier, was followed in the last half of the tenth by more general progress in mining and metallurgy, especially in Germany. Several new mines were discovered there. The most famous were the rich copper mines and silver-bearing lead ores of the once thickly-wooded Rammelsberg, the fine hill that rises some 1,200 feet above the town of Goslar in the Harz. In German the same word was used for miner as for mountaineer. During the

[17] The late Professor Collingwood accepted the evidence of modern archaeologists as proof that coal was rather extensively worked in Britain during the Roman period (R. G. Collingwood and J. N. L. Myers, *Roman Britain and the English Settlements* (2nd edn, Oxford, 1937), 231–2). No other scholar gives coal in Roman times so much importance (cf. M. Rostovtzeff, *The Social and Economic History of the Hellenistic World* (Oxford, 1941), III, 1615).

eleventh and twelfth centuries mining became primarily an Alpine occupation. In the Harz, the Vosges, the Jura and especially in the Eastern Alps, the working of gold, silver, lead, copper and iron grew in importance. After the middle of the twelfth century progress was intensified and the new interest in mining spread to other regions.

The first great period in the history of mining among the western peoples began around 1170, with the discovery of the rich silver-bearing ores of Freiberg in Saxony. It continued until the fourteenth century. If statistics of output existed, they would probably show that during this stretch of 150 years or so there were few decades in which the production of minerals and metals in Europe failed substantially to increase.

In cultural and intellectual history this period is one of the most brilliant in the annals of Europe. The achievements were summed up in wonderful romanesque and gothic churches. These monuments were the expression of Europe's common form of worship, at a time when the whole of life centred about religious life. The twelfth and thirteenth centuries, like the eighteenth and nineteenth, were times of extraordinary hope and extraordinary economic and social progress in which the whole of Europe shared. The hope was of a different kind and the directions which progress took in the earlier period were less material. The efforts of the twelfth- and thirteenth-century Europeans culminated in the great cathedrals with their spires, some of which, especially in the North, seemed almost to pierce the heavens. But even structures symbolising, as these churches symbolised, a transcendental conception of the destiny of man, required much concrete material to build. The walls were far thicker and firmer than those of the buildings that came afterwards.

All aspects of an era are interrelated. The increase in the production of silver, gold and less valuable metals (combined with a flow of gold from the Muslim countries to Europe) contributed to the growth of wealth, partly by increasing the supply of money but mainly by adding to the material available for industrial purposes. A prodigious expansion of agrarian and industrial production, combined with an even more remarkable growth of trade, transformed the economic face of western Europe between the late eleventh and the fourteenth centuries. The growth of mineral wealth helps to explain how it was possible for the people of the thirteenth century to create such magnificent and costly monuments in stone, and then embellish them with equally wonderful work in glass and metal. The growth of wealth also made possible greater leisure. This facilitated the remarkable philosophical speculations which were the chief glory of the medieval universities.

How strong an influence had the expansion of mining and metallurgy upon evolving European society from the eleventh to the fourteenth centuries? The influence apparently seemed indirect and remote to most medieval writers. Few of them mentioned metal in the works they composed. Albertus Magnus, with his German background, was apparently the only famous thinker who talked much about the metallurgical development of his age. He wrote with enthusiasm of the fine quality of the silver from the great mines discovered at Freiberg shortly before his birth. The most striking progress in mining of all kinds, particularly of silver-bearing ores, took place on the margin of western civilisation, away from the chief centres of cultural and economic life. Paris and the Ile-de-France, the focus from which the culture of the thirteenth century radiated, were greatly favoured by nature. But their riches were of the soil rather than the subsoil. The progress of mining was perhaps less a cause for the economic development of medieval Europe than a result of it. Yet in the mystery of the historical process, cause and effect are so intertwined that the positive conception of them that the modern mind derived from the natural sciences is hardly of service to truth.

Among the driving forces behind the discovery and the development of mining were the increase in population and the growth in tillage, trade and industry. Not until after 1750, not perhaps until after 1785, were the western European peoples again to grow in numbers at as rapid a rate as during most of the twelfth and thirteenth centuries. The area of cultivation and pasturage was extended in every direction, especially into wooded, hilly and mountainous country, hitherto sparsely populated. Frequently the plough of a husbandman struck against one of the outcropping seams of iron or coal with which the northern parts of Europe were so plentifully supplied. The location of more valuable ores was disclosed by the violence of nature in the forests, the Alpine valleys, and even on the slopes of high peaks. When the snows melted, rushing torrents overflowed their banks to strip off surface land and lay bare treasure underneath. Seams of rich ore were also revealed when a great wind uprooted trees, when lightning splintered rocks, or when an avalanche tore its path down some mountain side. As settlers and travelling traders streamed into the uplands and penetrated the woodlands, there were more eyes to watch these accidents, which encouraged prospectors to probe the earth for minerals. The increasing curiosity about the material world and the increasing agricultural, commercial, industrial and artistic needs for gold, silver, iron, lead, copper, tin and alloys of these metals made men eager to explore beneath the soil, to examine and to exploit the substances they found. Not until the eve of the Reformation, when fresh waves of settlers pushed into the same regions, was there another comparable movement of exploration and discovery.

This newly aroused curiosity accounts for the rapid growth of the silver mines at Freiberg in the late twelfth century. Traders carrying salt happened on some argentiferous lead ore where the spring floods had washed away the earth. They took a sample to Goslar to compare with the famous ores from the Rammelsberg. Their sample yielded a larger quantity and a finer grade of silver. As news of their discovery spread, adventurers in considerable numbers, with picks and shovels, hurried to Freiberg. They came in a spirit of adventure not altogether unlike that of the Americans who migrated to California in the gold rush of the mid-nineteenth century.

In the late twelfth and thirteenth centuries traders and colonisers everywhere were on the look-out for ores, and especially for ores containing silver or gold. Rich veins lay waiting for them near the surface, chiefly in Central Europe. Such ores as could be readily reached were especially abundant north of the Danube – in Saxony, Bohemia, Silesia and Hungary. The lands containing them had lain for the most part beyond the borders of the Roman Empire. Partly no doubt on that account there had been relatively little mining here in Roman times. In the Middle Ages these regions – together with greater Austria, the Harz and the Black Forest – assumed a position of dominance, like that of the Spanish peninsula in classical times, in supplying all Europe with silver, copper and small quantities of gold. On the slopes and along the valleys of the Eastern Alps, the Carpathians, the Erzgebirge and the Sudeten Mountains, the thick woods provided abundant lumber for building, firewood and charcoal for fuel needed in preparing ores for the smelters, in separating them from the worthless material with which they were intermingled and in converting them to metals. The rushing brooks and streams in which these regions abounded were hardly less helpful than the woods. As will appear, they came to provide sources of power to drive machinery that crushed and hammered the materials or blew air upon the fires. From the beginning the abundant water courses facilitated the washing away of dirt and impurities; the ore was dressed in artfully constructed containers, made to settle the heavy minerals and to remove the lighter rocky matter.

German emigrants, some of whom were bent on mining, were pushing into regions held by Slavs and Magyars in the great colonising movements towards the east and south-east, which brought Walloons and Flemings into Saxony and Frenchmen into the western Rhineland. It was not only in eastern and southern Germany, it was in almost all Central Europe that the Germans took the leading part in mining. The movements to colonise and to mine went hand in hand. One of the strongest attractions for German settlers was the glitter of precious metals.

Ores near the surface containing silver and gold were fewer and less fruitful west of the Rhine and the Alps. It was partly the accidents of nature that made Germans, rather than other western peoples, the leaders in mining and metallurgy from the twelfth to the sixteenth centuries. Travelling traders and explorers in France, England and the Low Countries were no less eager to discover ores containing precious metal. Kings, princes, bishops and other great landlords in the western part of Europe were not backward in encouraging prospectors. Where silver-bearing ores were discovered, as in Devon and Alsace, they were exploited as vigorously as in central Europe.

While the search for precious metal had a special fascination for the Europeans throughout the later Middle Ages, the demand for minerals of every kind grew rapidly with the rapid growth of population, industry, and trade. The boom in mining extended to ores containing only base metals – copper, lead, tin and iron. It extended even to coal. In the digging of coal and base ores other than copper, the Germans had no such dominance as in the digging of ores rich in silver and gold. Even in copper mining by the beginning of the fourteenth century, the mines of Stora Kopparberg in Sweden, developed under German influence, had come to rival those of the Rammelsberg. The English mines of lead ore – in Somerset, Durham, Cumberland, Shropshire, Flintshire and, above all, in Derbyshire – grew increasingly prosperous during the thirteenth century, and a flourishing export trade in lead developed. Lead production in England rivalled that in Central Europe. The continent was as dependent on Devon and Cornwall for its tin as it was on Saxony and Bohemia for its silver and gold. During the last half of the twelfth century the annual output of tin in south-western England, mostly from Devon, apparently increased nearly five-fold. The early fourteenth century was another time of rapid progress, especially in Cornwall, where the output in 1338 was more than double that in 1301. In the 1330s production in the two counties together apparently reached seven hundred tons in good years. Since the middle of the twelfth century it had increased approximately tenfold. The figures of output for the 1330s were not regularly surpassed until the last half of the seventeenth century.[18]

As the supplies of iron ore were not localised like the supplies of scarcer minerals, there was no such concentration of population about the iron mines as about some mines of argentiferous lead ores, copper

[18] G. R. Lewis, *The Stannaries* (Cambridge (Mass.), 1907), 252–5.

ores and tin. But the medieval people wanted iron in much larger quantities during the great age of gothic building, which lasted from the early twelfth to the early fourteenth century. Iron was more needed than before for ploughshares and other farm implements, for tools, axles, chauldrons and other accessories in the expanding industries, for anchors, keels and nails in shipbuilding, for horseshoes, bits and stirrups with the spread of horsemanship, and for armour, spears, swords and daggers to be used ferociously by our ancestors in their endless fighting in those times of few restraints on ruthless violence. Iron-making prospered all over Europe. An international traffic in iron developed. Styria, Carinthia, the Basque provinces of Biscay and Guipuzcoa in Spain and, to a lesser extent, Hungary, Sweden and Westphalia were the principal exporting countries. Iron was carried thence on pack-horses and in carts, in river barges and in ships, especially to the most populous and civilised parts of Europe – to Italy, northern France and the Low Countries.

All these regions had iron ore; so the imports of iron served only to supplement the local supplies. Italy produced much of its own iron, and additional supplies came from the island of Elba across the water to the rich and populous Tuscany, where at the turn of the thirteenth and fourteenth centuries building and manufacturing were pushed further perhaps than anywhere else in Europe. Both in England and in the provinces which were to form modern France small forges multiplied, especially in the wooded uplands, to supply the needs of the neighbouring towns and villages. These tiny mills required very little capital. It was not difficult for the iron-makers to pick up their equipment when they had thinned out the immediately surrounding woods for charcoal and to move on to new clusters of trees. There were, in addition, some more important centres of production, with rather larger forges – Piedmont, the Forest of Dean, upper Champagne, Lorraine and Dauphiné. Wrought iron was carried thence for longer distances to serve multitudes of smiths and artistic craftsmen.

In spite of the growing prosperity of the iron-making industry, iron was produced even at the beginning of the fourteenth century in quantities which seem to us, in the present great age of iron and steel, almost negligible. The annual output of all the forges in Styria, a leading iron-making centre in Europe, probably seldom exceeded two thousand tons.[19] At the beginning of the twentieth century a single enterprise produced more in a few hours. No wonder that a president of the United States Steel Corporation remarked recently in his report to the shareholders, 'steel is now cheaper than dirt'!

[19] The output could hardly have been greater than it was 150 years later, in the sixties of the fifteenth century (see below, p. 737).

According to modern standards, steel, and iron too, were exceedingly scarce and valuable materials in medieval Europe. The pursuit of new technological methods for iron manufacture in the interest mainly of productivity were first tried, not in Europe, but in eleventh-century China. It has recently been suggested that there, with the spread of the blast furnace, the annual output increased approximately fourfold in the eighty years from A.D. 998 to 1078 when a figure of about 125,000 tons was reached.[20] A comparable output was apparently not obtained in the whole of Europe until about 1530–40.

Although the growth of iron production in Europe still was sluggish during the 150 years that followed, there was a remarkable spurt in output after the Reformation, first in Great Britain and then in Sweden,[21] which after about 1620 exported a considerable quantity of iron to serve the English manufacturers in addition to their native supplies. From about 1540 to 1620 the progress of the blast furnace and the rate of growth in iron production in England and Wales were altogether comparable to the progress which had apparently occurred in eleventh-century China, from 998 to 1078. During the later period of eighty years from 1540 to 1620 the output of England and Wales seems to have increased some fivefold. A total of approximately 35,000 tons per annum was reached in the 1620s,[22] when the entire population of Great Britain (an area then beginning to be served with Swedish and Scottish iron as well) was perhaps not a fifth that of northern China under the Sung. The spread of blast furnaces for making iron in Great Britain, and the growth in per capita consumption, seems to have been more striking during the century following the Reformation than it had ever been before in a period of similar duration anywhere in the world.

That expansion in iron-making in Elizabethan and early Stuart times was a new departure pointing in the direction of a quantitative economy destined to lead to the triumph of industrial civilisation. During the great period of cathedral building, especially during the relatively peaceful thirteenth and early fourteenth centuries, when ever larger multitudes of town craftsmen were learning to make use in new ways of every available material which could serve in fashioning religious images and other works of art, it was natural that so rare a substance as iron, which, in its finer varieties, as prepared in charcoal fires, was not only durable but lustrous, should have been in demand hardly less for aesthetic than for utilitarian purposes. Fine iron was wanted for grilles and other decorative work, especially in

[20] Hartwell, *Journal of Economic History*, XXVI (1966), 32–4.
[21] Nef, *War and Human Progress* (London, 1951), 35, 80–1, 442.
[22] Nef, 'Iron Production in England', *Journal of Political Economy*, XLIV (1936), 398–403.

connection with the cathedrals, churches, abbeys and priories which were going up everywhere in the rising cities and towns, in old villages and in hosts of new settlements. Skilful craftsmen also used iron to fashion for laymen fine window grilles, entrance keys and locks, knockers and decorations for strong boxes. As Roger Bacon explained, iron was made into charms designed to drive away evil spirits.

For the generations brought up in the early twentieth century, and accustomed to an annual output in Europe of several hundred million tons, the use of coal in the thirteenth century will seem even more insignificant than the use of iron. But the generations who lived in the lands surrounding the Mediterranean Sea during the first three centuries of the Christian ere would have found the use of coal, unlike the use of iron, almost entirely novel. While its burning properties were not unknown in classical times, no systematic attempt was made to dig coal out of the earth except, it seems, in Roman Britain. Authentic records of its use in Europe have not been discovered after the Roman period before the last decades of the twelfth century. This contrasts with Chinese experience during the fifteen hundred years after Confucius (*c.*551–479 B.C.), and contrasts most sharply with the increasingly extensive recourse to coal for industrial fuel in parts of China during the eleventh century.

It is hardly until the thirteenth century that documentary references to coal digging in Europe abound. There is no evidence that the new interest taken by the Europeans at this time in what was long regarded as a base mineral, had any important connection with earlier Chinese coal mining. The small but increasing use of coal in Europe during the later Middle Ages seems to reflect rather the growth in European population and the mounting prosperity of the twelfth, thirteenth and early fourteenth centuries. This brought about a continual increase in the need for metals, as well as other industrial products. The fulfilment of that need brought increasing pressure on the European timber supplies both for fuel and for material to be used in construction work. The burning of coal, of which there is abundant evidence after the twelfth century, followed the great expansion in building and in iron working, and was in large measure caused by it. In spite of protests against the dirt and the noxious smells generated by coal fires, when wood and charcoal grew dear the lime-burner (whose product was used for mortar and cement in building and also for fertilizer), like those smiths who made the cruder iron wares, turned to coal when it could be had nearby from outcropping seams. These were found at a great many places. During the thirteenth century local inhabitants began to dig shallow pits in nearly all the coalfields of England, Scotland and the Low Countries, as well as in the neighbourhood of

Aix-la-Chapelle, in Franche-Comté, Lyonnais, Forez, Alais and Anjou.

The chief centres for coal mining were in the Low Countries at Liège and Mons, and in the north of England. The traditional reputation of Newcastle as the inexhaustible source of supplies dates from this age. Coal began to be sometimes loaded into ships leaving the Tyne. It served as ballast in place of the bags of sand usually carried by medieval vessels. It found a small market among smiths and lime-burners in London and, in smaller quantities, at other ports along the eastern and southern coasts of England and the northern coasts of the continent, particularly in the Low Countries. There industry throve at the end of the thirteenth century only less than in Tuscany and northern Italy, where the manufactures of Florence and other Italian towns prospered without any help from coal fuel.

III. *Laws and Customs of Medieval Mining*

As the situation of mines and metallurgical works was determined by the whereabouts of accessible ores and, to a lesser extent, by the whereabouts of woodlands and swiftly moving streams, the organisation of mining and metallurgy from the twelfth to the early fourteenth century presents features which mark these industries off from the other rising medieval crafts. While cloth-making and the making of leather wares were usually the direct concern only of the towns, mining and metallurgy affected every political authority and every kind of country landholder from the emperor to the meanest serf.

The increasing need for revenue felt by almost all overlords, lay and ecclesiastical, provided them with a motive for throwing open the mines in their territories to all comers and for claiming as large a share as possible of the output. By establishing mints to coin silver and later gold, and by ordering the mining communities in the interest of their treasuries, some princes added greatly to their wealth and political power.

In feudal times in western Europe, emperors, kings, popes, bishops and numerous other lesser overlords exercised political authority in varying degrees. The origin of their claims to dispose of mines under private lands subject to their authority (the *Bergregal*) is obscure. It was certainly not Roman but feudal. Regalian rights to mines, like regalian rights to coin silver money, were not recognised before the tenth or even the eleventh century. The new claims probably had much to do with the remarkable growth in mining, particularly in the mining of silver-bearing ores, needed for coinage. As claims to the *regale* were frequently limited, especially until after the thirteenth century, to ores containing gold or silver, there is a temptation to assume that one source of the regalian rights may have been the idea, later set forth in favour of these rights in the English 'case of mines', in 1566, that the overlord had a special title as the most excellent person to the most excellent things within his territorial dominions.[23] As will be seen in a moment, there is solider ground for suggesting that the mining *regale* grew at least partly out of the claims of feudal overlords to dispose of waste land and 'treasure trove' or hidden treasure.[24]

During the twelfth and thirteenth centuries European overlords were claiming with much success the rights to dispose of ores containing gold or silver (then won mainly from seams of argentiferous lead ore), and in some cases of tin and copper ore as well, both in their own lands and in those of their subjects. When the mines were worked, they claimed a share in the produce. This share generally included a settled portion of the ore or metal, frequently a tenth. In addition the overlords usually received coinage duties; they often had the right of pre-emption over the entire output of the best metal – i.e. a right to buy all of it at a lower price than that which it might have commanded if sold on the open market. But as it was in their interest to have the mines worked, and as they seldom cared to bear the risks of operating them, there were practical limits to their demands. They could not afford to be exorbitant. Their claims to revenue were frequently reduced to meet the increased costs which the miners had to undergo in sinking, draining and ventilating the pits.

During the last half of the twelfth century, and possibly even earlier, when the political authority of the German emperor was theoretically very great, the emperors pressed their claims to share throughout the Empire in the revenue of all mines producing silver or gold. At Roncaglia Frederick Barbarossa (1155–89) claimed the *regale* as an attribute of imperial sovereignty.[25] The revival of Roman law was used as a basis for applying attributes of the Roman imperial authority to feudal conditions, for asserting that feudal overlordship everywhere belonged to the emperor. The emperors sought, not without opposition, to make the *Bergregal* a sovereign *regale*, as they tried unsuccessfully to make the *Münzregal*, or right of coinage.[26] They tried to establish the principle that the power to grant concessions for mining ores

[23] Edmund Plowden, *The Commentaries or Reports* (1818 edn), 310ff. Cf. Sir John Pettus, *Fodinae Regales* (1670), 28–9.

[24] Cf. Adam Smith, *Wealth of Nations*, bk. II, ch. I.

[25] P. W. Finsterwalder, 'Die Gesetze des Reichstags von Roncalia von 11 November 1158', *Zeitschrift der Savigny Stiftung für Rechtsgeschichte, Germanistische Abteilung*, XLI (1931), 43–5, 62–9, a reference called to my attention by Professor Kantorowicz. I am indebted to him and to Professor McIlwain for helping me to understand the origin of the mining *regale*. If I have not got matters right, the fault is mine.

[26] F. von Schrötter, *Wörterbüch der Münzkunde* (Berlin, 1930), 430–2.

containing precious metals was exclusively imperial. As it was usually interpreted, that principle put the emperors under an obligation to set up an imperial administration for regulating the labour and the community life of the free men who came to try their luck with their picks and shovels. The emperors treated this participation in the administration of mining, along with the claim to a revenue from the mines, as attributes of sovereign authority, distinguished from those rights which went with the tenure of landed estates. According to this doctrine, no lord of the soil could have valuable minerals dug within his lands without the permission of the emperor. In case the emperor had delegated his authority to an overlord, the overlord's permission was required.

After the death of Barbarossa, the political powers of the emperors diminished throughout the Holy Roman Empire and especially in Germany. Territorial sovereign rights were increasingly split up among their chief vassals. As Charles IV made clear in his famous Golden Bull of 1356, the emperors relinquished their regalian rights to mines whenever they relinquished their sovereign authority. Regalian rights went with lordship of territories. This did not prevent a territorial prince, if he chose, from investing certain of his vassals, or even his rear vassals, with his regalian rights. He could do so while he retained the general authority which went with territorial lordship. In this way, he could rid himself of the obligation to oversee mines in many regions, at a time when mining enterprises were multiplying very rapidly. The emperors, the kings of Bohemia, the dukes of Silesia and other princes of the Empire all took advantage of this opportunity to delegate their mining responsibilities. In consequence the number of overlords exercising regalian (or even sovereign) rights in Central Europe was continually growing. On the eve of the Reformation, the bishops, dukes, margraves, counts and independent towns possessing these rights could be counted by dozens.

The unwary are likely to assume that the regalian authority of the territorial princes in the Empire was more extensive than was actually the case. In the fourteenth century few holders of the *regale* had successfully put forward a claim to base ores in the lands of private owners (*Grundherren*) within their territorial dominions. Someone, however, had to assume responsibility for orderly mining and for settling disputes between groups of miners, at a time when mining was still carried on largely by small bands of work-people who claimed a share in the ownership of the ores by virtue of the technical ingenuity they exercised and the manual labour they performed. Where base ores were dug in considerable quantities in privately owned lands, the lord of the soil frequently took the place of the territorial lord. Like the territorial lord, he set up a mining administration and shared in the produce of the mines or the revenue from them.

Coal invariably and iron ore generally were treated as the property of the landlord. In the margravate of Meissen, which included the rich mines of Freiberg, the lords of the soil also retained the authority to work tin, lead and copper ore without the permission of the margrave. In Bohemia the kings generally limited their claims to ores containing substantial quantities of gold or silver. Consequently much mining was carried on during the twelfth and thirteenth centuries outside the *regale*.

We are here frequently in the presence of a valid distinction which masks a practical reality. The territorial lord was always a private landlord as well. Within the territorial jurisdiction over which he ruled were estates that belonged to him directly. As it happened, a large part of the ores dug in Central Europe during the thirteenth century were in mountainous country, and so in waste land, in no-man's land. Territorial princes claimed such land as part of their demesne. This gave them adequate authority as private landlords to dispose of many base ores in the same way as they disposed, by virtue of their sovereign rights, of ores containing precious metal.

What was the position of a private landlord, who was not a territorial prince, when mines were worked in his soil under the authority of his overlord? His obligations were heavy, but he often had in return certain advantages. Such a landlord was obliged to allow the miners and smelters who obtained concessions from the overlord access to the ore. He was obliged, when necessary, to provide these work-people with land for their cottages, their mills and their forges. In addition the miners and smelters were frequently given parts of his land for farming and for pasture. They were allowed to use the streams for washing their ore and driving their mills. They were generally entitled to take from his manor or lordship at least a part of the lumber that they needed for building, together with fuel for their kilns and furnaces.

The miners and smelters had to pay for these privileges. The landlords received compensation for the use of their lands and for any damage done to them. Sometimes they shared with the regalian lord in the royalty on the produce of the mines containing precious metal. There were cases, for example in Bohemia, where the landlords appointed mining officials of their own to care for their interests. Two mining administrations, those of the territorial lord and of the lord of the soil, operated concurrently.

The problems arising out of mining operations, which called for settlement by administrative, legislative and judicial procedures, were in fact almost endless. Much of the work of mining and making metal was carried on in soil held by tenants of the landlord. These tenants were entitled to compensation when mining and metallurgical operations touched their actual holdings of arable and pasture land. There was no aspect of medieval life – economic, political, cultural, or religious – which was not affected by these expanding industries.

In the other countries of continental Europe, and in Great Britain and Scandinavia, the medieval laws and customs concerning the ownership and the working of mines resembled those in the Empire. But the division of the sovereign authority after the twelfth century, characteristic of Central Europe, was by no means the rule during the Middle Ages.

In France the process was reversed, in the sense that the supreme political authority – the French crown – was continually gaining in actual power throughout the realm. With the revival of Roman law, the legitimisation of illegitimate children was treated as a sovereign, i.e. an imperial, right. In 1205 a decretal of Pope Innocent III declared that this power of legitimisation belonged to the French king, Philip Augustus (1180–1223), within his dominions. Not long afterwards lawyers began to interpret the decretal as evidence that the French king was emperor in his realm–'Rex est imperator in regno suo'.[27]

During and after the reign of Philip Augustus the French kings steadily encroached upon the independent governing authorities, the principal feudal overlords. When it came to contesting the rights of such lords to dispose of minerals within their ancient jurisdictions, the French kings generally proceeded warily. Compared with the emperors, the great German princes and the English kings, they were slow in claiming regalian rights over mines in the lands of their vassals. They were slow about insisting upon a royalty from mining operations outside the territories that formed part of their royal demesne.

Their caution resulted partly from the strength possessed by some of the greater noblemen, foremost among whom were the dukes of Burgundy, who had already begun to exercise regalian rights over mines.[28] To take the *regale* in France from feudal overlords, who had long exercised it, involved many difficulties. It may be questioned whether such a policy could have been embarked upon as soon as it was, had silver-bearing ores been as plentiful in France as they were in Central Europe. It might even have been necessary for the French kings to decentralise the *regale* as the emperors did. In so large a kingdom as France the administrative machinery required in the form

[27] J. Rivière, *Le Problème de l'église et de l'état* (Louvain, 1926), 424–30, another reference for which I thank Professor Kantorowicz.

[28] Henri Beaune, 'Note sur le régime des mines dans le duché de Bourgogne', *Mém. de la Société des Antiquaires de France*, XXXI (1869), 114–15; *Inventaire sommaire des archives départementales de l'Hérault*, c. III (1887), 258.

of clerks, technical experts and judges for regulating mining in many districts would have been beyond the capacity of a medieval ruler to staff. As things were, the French kings seem to have waited until the great expansion in mining and metallurgy of the gothic age was over before acting vigorously. With the early fifteenth century, they set about to deprive French overlords of their mining authority. In 1413 a royal edict was passed making it illegal for any lord but the king to collect the royalty (*dixième*) on the produce of mines.[29] As the strength of the monarchy grew in France, and as administrative, legal and judicial authority was more and more centralised at the end of the Middle Ages and in early modern times, the crown was able bit by bit to centralise the mining *regale*.

In England, government was centralised earlier than in any continental country, during the two centuries following the Norman conquest of 1066. Except in a few areas, like the Palatinate of Durham, the crown became the undisputed sovereign. In the thirteenth century the regalian rights which the English kings exercised in connection with mines seem hardly to have fallen short of those possessed by the emperor, or by leading princes of the Empire to whom the emperor delegated his sovereign authority. While the English kings showed no disposition to codify the customary laws of the mining communities, as some Central European princes were doing, they successfully claimed the authority to dispose of all gold- and silver-bearing ores in the lands of their subjects and to collect a royalty on the produce of gold and silver mines. While their attempts to extend their regalian rights to include base ores were sporadic and ultimately unsuccessful they controlled the prosperous stannaries of Devon and Cornwall. In the thirteenth century the authority of the crown over the stannaries hardly fell short of that exercised over mines of silver-bearing ores by the territorial princes in Central Europe, Tuscany and Sardinia. The privileges of prospectors for and finders of ore were at least as great as those usually allowed them on the continent. Either directly, or through the Prince of Wales as earl and later as duke of Cornwall, the crown had the sole power to grant finders of ore and other miners concessions to tin mines in the unenclosed lands of private landlords in Cornwall and, in Devon, under the enclosed lands as well. Miners were free to search for tin in these lands without permission from the landlords.[30] The crown derived a considerable revenue from the coinage duties and from the purchase and sale of tin, which it could buy at an advantageous price by virtue of its right of pre-emption. As lord of the soil, not apparently as sovereign, the king possessed

[29] *Recueil général des anciennes lois françaises* (Paris, 1825), VII, 386–90.
[30] Cf. Lewis, *The Stannaries*, 158–60; A. K. H. Jenkin, *The Cornish Miner* (London, 1927), 32.

a similar control over some of the richest mines of lead ore in Derbyshire,[31] the leading centre for lead mining in the country.

In the thirteenth century the most productive mines of iron ore were probably those in the Forest of Dean.[32] The crown seems to have claimed successfully a part in the produce of all iron ore and coal mines there, apparently because much of the land belonged to the royal demesne. In other parts of England iron ore and coal were dug independently of the crown in many private lands. Coal and iron ore were then of relatively small importance.

The chief mines in England in the thirteenth century were worked mostly under royal authority. From them the king derived a revenue, either by virtue of his sovereignty or by virtue of his direct possession of soil which formed part of the royal demesne. It was not until the end of the Middle Ages, after the Hundred Years War, that important differences arose between the mineral rights attaching to overlordship on the continent and in England. In the thirteenth century the situation respecting the *regale* was much the same in all European countries. The actual authority of the English king over mineral property in his dominion was hardly inferior to that of any prince in Christendom.

While there was an extraordinary diversity in such matters as weights and measures, European society in the late twelfth and thirteenth centuries had a great unity. Everywhere there was a basic similarity in the manner in which men lived and worked, as well as in the manner in which they worshipped. Conditions in mining and metallurgy were no exception. Whether the minerals were at the disposal of the emperor, a king, a prince or lord, a bishop, or a city council, by virtue of delegated as well as usurped sovereign authority, or at the disposal of the lay or ecclesiastical lord of some manor or vill, by virtue of his property in the land,[33] mining concessions all over Europe resembled one another. When it came to fundamentals, the relations between the miners or smelters and the officials representing the lords were everywhere much the same.

The finder of ore staked out a claim to mine by applying for a

[31] Cf. *Victoria County History, Derbyshire*, II, 325–7.

[32] Rhys Jenkins, 'Iron-making in the Forest of Dean', *Newcomen Society Trans.*, VI (1925–6), 46.

[33] There were districts where the power to grant concessions and to order mining operations was vested neither in a sovereign prince nor in a single lord of the soil. In the lead mines of Mendip, in Somerset, the control was in the hands of four prominent local lords, each of whom controlled an area with its own separate officers, its mining code, and its mineral courts (*Mendip Mining Laws and Forest Bounds*, ed. J. W. Gough, 1931). In the coalfield west of Mons, in Hainault, where, as in the silver-mining districts, property in mines was separated from property in the soil, concessions were granted by the local officials charged with the administration of justice – the *seigneurs haut-justicers* (G. Arnould, *Le Bassin houiller du couchant de Mons* (Mons, 1877), 22; G. Decamps, *Mémoire historique sur l'origine et les développements de l'industrie houillère...de Mons*, 58ff).

concession to the lord's principal officer, generally known in the German mining districts of Central Europe as the *Bergmeister*. This officer, or his representative, invested the miner for an indefinite term with the right to exploit a section of the seam or to extract the minerals under a given plot of land. In many districts, especially in Central Europe, it was the custom to divide up the accessible portion of the seam near the surface into a number of small sections (meers), often square and of a size prescribed by local customs. The lord's officers then granted the finder the section that he had discovered and sometimes an additional section. One or more of the other sections was usually reserved for the lord, to be worked for him directly or leased out (a practice analogous to that of treating sections of agricultural land held by tenants in common as part of their lord's demesne). Each of the remaining sections of the seam was granted to a miner, ordinarily to the first applicant. In return for promises to mine continuously, to pay the customary royalties and to abide by the mining customs of the district as enforced by the lord's officers, the miners had full power to work their concessions.

Wherever the digging and the working of ores were sufficiently important to employ several scores of miners and smelters, little mining communities were formed. These communities were separate from those of the local peasants engaged in tillage and pasture farming. They had their own laws and customs. Such special communities multiplied rapidly in number especially in Central Europe during the late twelfth and thirteenth centuries. They were everywhere the rule in the digging and smelting of silver, gold, copper, tin and lead ores. In the making of iron they were rather less common. In the mining of coal they were found only in the Low Countries and the Forest of Dean. As coal and iron ore mining were less localised than the mining of more valuable ores, there were only a few places, such as Liège and the Erzberg in Styria, where considerable numbers of persons were engaged in either the coal-mining or the iron-making industries. Elsewhere the digging of coal for the most part, and in many cases the digging and smelting of iron ore, were undertaken more informally by a few local peasants, working either for themselves or for some lord of the soil, frequently on days when they were not engaged in husbandry. They were subject to the ordinary local laws and customs concerning labour in the fields and forests.

In Central Europe as far as the Balkans, the principal regions of German colonisation, the overlords generally threw open to all comers the rights to search for minerals, to mine and to convert ores to metals. Elsewhere, in western Europe generally, there were many districts in which such rights were restricted to certain local persons who formed a closed body similar to a town gild. Such exclusive groups were obviously better suited to peoples who remained in their native provinces than to colonisers who came from many different regions and settled far from the countries of their origin. Exclusive communities were fairly common in the iron-making industry, especially in France, where they were also formed in other industries dependent on abundant woods for fuel, like the making of crude glass vessels. In the wooded, hilly country about Alençon, in Perche and upper Normandy, a group of local lords, lay and ecclesiastical, known as *barons fossiers*, were alone entitled to open mines of iron ore or to build iron forges. The actual manual labour of making the charcoal fuel and the iron was in the hands of a corporation of *férons*. Admission was limited to the sons and sons-in-law of members.[34]

There were other cases in which the right to work (and indeed to own) mines was restricted to people living in a certain area. In the eastern Pyrenees no one could search for or exploit iron ore on the mountain of Rancié unless he was an inhabitant of the valley of Vicdessos.[35] Similar restrictions existed in at least one English mining district. Only persons born in the hundred of St Briavels, who had worked with their picks for a year and a day, were eligible to obtain concessions from the king's gaveller to parts in the seams of iron ore or coal within the Forest of Dean.[36]

Whether or not the communities were exclusive, the social status of the miners and metallurgical workers was generally as high as that of the citizens in the rising towns. In the twelfth and thirteenth centuries settlement in the towns offered a means of escape from serfdom. During this age of growing population, peasants became free by taking up the profession of mining as much as by taking up work as craftsmen or traders. In fact, the formation of mining communities and towns may be considered as two parts of a single great movement of industrial and commercial expansion. There were cases in which these two parts converged. At Liège in the thirteenth century the coal miners were organised into a leading municipal gild. An accident of nature at this bend in the river Meuse had placed rich coal seams under one of the most thickly settled spots in the Low Countries, so that coal mining there was actually a municipal industry. There were other cases in connection with the discovery of ores rich in precious metals where the new mining communities were large enough to form actual towns. That happened, for example, at Freiberg, at Iglau, and at Schemnitz

[34] H. de Formeville, *Les Barons fossiers et les férons de Normandie* (Caen, 1852), 1–7, and *passim*.

[35] Henri Rouzaud, *Histoire d'une mine au mineur* (Toulouse, 1908), 11–12, 23–30.

[36] *Laws and Customs of the Miners in the Forest of Dean*, ed. T. Houghton (1687); H. G. Nichols, *Iron Making in...the Forest of Dean* (1866), 71–82; Exchequer Depositions by Commission (Public Record Office, London), 13 Charles I, Mich. 42.

in Hungary. In these places municipal and mining law developed concurrently.[37]

Whether the mining community formed part of a town or not, it was generally a sort of state within a state, with laws and regulations of its own, suited at least to some extent to the special needs and conditions of its members.[38] In it the actual workers possessed, to begin with, special privileges and a considerable amount of self-government. Wherever the miners or makers of metal contributed to the wealth of a sovereign prince, they were exempted from the obligation of paying the ordinary taxes. They generally had a voice in ordering their own labour. The regulations governing the manner of sinking and supporting pits, the manner of raising ore, the hours of work and the division of profits and losses were determined by the lord's officials in company with representatives of the miners and metallurgical workers (*jurés*, *Geschwornen*, jurors). Cases concerning the working of the mines and forges were tried in special courts, in which the work-people were always represented and in which they often formed the majority.

The people in these mining communities were bound to conform to the worship of the Roman Church, whose priests followed the settlers everywhere. They were subject to the general political laws and regulations of the sovereign authority within whose jurisdiction they lived. But to such authority there were invariably limits defined by traditions and customs. The customs that developed in mining, in the formation of which working miners had a share, were actually helping to circumscribe the authority of the political sovereign. When the units of labour were very small, as they were in the beginning in mining and metallurgy, the participation of work-people in political authority had a concrete and immediate reality which is less easy for workers to feel in the large industries of modern times, even when these industries are in the hands of a government which the work-people have a share in choosing. The twelfth- and thirteenth-century miners were powerless to change the overlord, but they were frequently in a strong position to influence the decisions of the local leaders he appointed to supervise and regulate the mining communities.

IV. *The Origin of Medieval Mining Laws and Customs*

In many mining communities, especially in Central Europe, the laws and customs were eventually embodied in codes written in

[37] Cf., for Iglau, Adolf Zycha, *Das böhmische Bergrecht des Mittelalters auf Grundlage des Bergrechts von Iglau* (Berlin, 1900), I, 43–4.

[38] Cf. *Victoria County History of Cornwall*, I (1906), 523.

longhand. Codes were issued by the territorial lords holding regalian rights, or by the lords of the soil when the property in the minerals went with the property in land. The first code of which we have direct evidence is for Trent in the southern Tyrol. It was issued in 1185 by the bishop of Trent. From that time the codification of laws and customs spread. In Central Europe and Scandinavia some codes, originally promulgated for one community, served as a model for many others. The most influential codes were apparently those enacted by the king of Bohemia for the miners of Iglau, the first of which dated from about 1249.[39] The Iglau regulations formed the basis for all the written Bohemain laws relating to the mining of silver-bearing ores during the late thirteenth and fourteenth centuries. These Iglau codes left their trace on those of several mining communities in Germany, Hungary, Transylvania and the Venetian Republic.[40]

It would be a mistake to conclude that all medieval mining laws and customs had a common origin. The most universal customs were the product not of a single lawgiver or even of a single race. They were the product of conditions common to the whole of Europe during the twelfth and thirteenth centuries.

Precedents can be found for them in earlier history. In Attica in the fifth and fourth centuries B.C. the principle that the right to dispose of valuable ores under private lands is an attribute of sovereignty, was apparently established in connection with the silver mines of Laurion. While there is no evidence that this principle ever became a part of imperial Roman law, in the late Roman Empire most mines seem to have belonged to the imperial treasury or to the emperor.[41] The emperor also levied a tax of a tenth on the produce of privately owned mines. References to this tax in the Roman codes studied by jurists in the twelfth and thirteenth centuries may possibly have encouraged medieval princes to claim a similar tax, in somewhat the same way that the emperors and later the French kings apparently used revivals of Roman law as a basis for putting forward exclusive claims to the mining *regale* as a whole.

The work of modern archaeologists has provided us with a knowledge of classical history inaccessible to medieval people. Among other things, it has proved that in the second century A.D. the Roman imperial administration issued written regulations for mining in certain imperial lands at and near Vispasca, in what is now Portugal. These

[39] Zycha, *op. cit.*, I, 49.

[40] Cf. J. A. Tomaschek, *Das alte Bergrecht von Iglau* (Innsbruck, 1897).

[41] We must still regard the thesis of Henri Francotte (*L'Industrie dans la Grèce ancienne* (Brussels, 1900), II, 183–91) that there were privately owned mines in Attica as unproved (G. M. Calhoun, 'Ancient Athenian Mining', *Journal of Economic and Business History*, III (1931), 341–4).

regulations, set forth in the tables of Aljustrel, resemble very strikingly those embodying the customs of the medieval mining communities in the late twelfth and thirteenth centuries. There was the same division of interests between the lord and the occupiers of pits, the same kind of administrative control by the lord's officers over mining operations. There were the same little companies with transferable shares, formed by miners working together at a seam, the same special jurisdictions outside the ordinary courts for settling mining disputes. Regulations of the sort found in second-century Portugal apparently existed even earlier, as far back at least as Hellenistic times, in the countries of the eastern Mediterranean.

A knowledge of such a mining administration could hardly have been brought to medieval Europe by the revival of Roman law in the twelfth century, for there is no trace of such regulations in the code of Justinian, in earlier compilations of imperial legislation, or in classical legal treatises. But it is possible that remnants of the system may have been preserved across many centuries in the customs of a few districts where the working of ores was never entirely abandoned. This would help to explain why in medieval England this system of mining administration is found almost exclusively in connection with lead and tin mining, the only kinds of mining which have left conspicuous traces during the Saxon period. Such laws and customs appear, moreover, at just those places where the Romans are known to have encouraged mining during their occupation of Britain.

At first sight it is more difficult to understand how these mining regulations of imperial Rome could have had any influence in Saxony and Bohemia, which were the chief centres of medieval mining laws and customs. The Romans probably had not worked mines in these countries as they had in Britain. Rome may have had an indirect influence for all that. The remarkable development of mining in Bohemia at the end of the twelfth and during the thirteenth century was brought about by the immigration of German miners who are said to have come from the South German lands, especially from Tyrol and other regions of the Eastern Alps.[42] In the Eastern Alps there is more evidence of continuity between Roman and medieval mining than in any other part of Europe.[43]

We have, then, strong circumstantial evidence of a connection between a mining administration of the kind that is known to have

[42] It was once supposed that the first German miners in Bohemia came from western Germany, from the Harz and the Rhineland. But Zycha gives impressive evidence in favour of their Alpine origin. (Adolf Zycha, *Das bömische Bergrecht des Mittelalters* (1900), I, 17–33.)

[43] Cf. Clamor Neuburg, 'Der Zusammenhang zwischen römischem und deutschem Bergbau', in *Festgaben für Wilhelm Lexis* (Jena, 1907), 278, 298–9.

existed in second-century Portugal and the laws and customs very widely adopted in the medieval mining communities. But why should the western Europeans have adopted this particular form of ancient mining administration rather than another? While Montesquieu and various modern writers were wrong in thinking that classical mining was invariably the labour of slaves, slaves were perhaps the most common labourers in the mines.

For certain limited periods in classical history slave labour may have been almost universal. Somewhat less frequently mining was done by wage-earners who had no more share in ordering their work or governing themselves than the wage-earners in the European mines and factories of the eighteenth and early nineteenth centuries. The wage-earning miners of classical times were in the employ sometimes of private capitalists, sometimes of the state, sometimes of contractors acting for the state, sometimes of farmers of the public revenues. There is no reason for supposing that the different system which existed in ancient Portugal in the second century A.D. gained ground in the later Roman Empire. Professor Rostovtzeff has taught that the emperors interfered more and more with the conduct of economic enterprises of all kinds – commercial, financial and industrial. As part of this policy, the Roman imperial administration took over many mines formerly let out in various ways to private persons. It worked them directly, sometimes employing convicts as miners, a practice for which there were a great many precedents in classical history. Nothing could be further from the spirit of medieval mining than this treatment of the work as a kind of punishment. Mining by independent associations of workmen, whose right to dig for ore rested on a grant by a superior authority representing the imperial fiscal administration, is believed to have decreased in importance after the second century. It is impossible to say whether there was a revival of it on the eve of the barbarian conquests when the imperial enterprises were apparently replaced by small mining ventures under local lords.[44] In any event the tendency of later Roman history was not in the direction of the free mining communities. These appear to have been most exceptional during the thousand years or more when mining operations were of considerable importance in the economy of classical civilisation.

Inventiveness has been characteristic of the people of western Europe at least as far back as the eleventh century. It is a fundamental part of the process of invention to know what and how to borrow. To a greater degree than in any other age in western history, perhaps to a greater degree than in any other age in all history, the eleventh

[44] We have no evidence concerning the form of these ventures (cf. Neuberg, *op. cit.*, 297).

and still more the twelfth and early thirteenth centuries awoke among the humble the talent, the desire, the knowledge and the skill indispensable for co-operating in works of genius. In late romanesque and gothic Europe the same gifts for absorbing, reconciling and unifying divers materials were manifested in the architecture, in which many participated, as in the creative learning on which a very small proportion of the population left a visible trace.

Princes and lords, lay and ecclesiastical, were granting charters to growing towns and freedom to serfs and the sons of serfs in the country. When valuable mines were discovered, the princes and lords who claimed the authority to dispose of them had to attract hands to get them worked. In order to do this they had to offer advantages equivalent to those granted to settlers in the towns.

Work-people in the mining communities derived their privileges and their independence from other circumstances besides their bargaining power. Mining made a positive contribution of its own to the new freedom and also, though this may seem paradoxical, to the new authority exercised during and after the thirteenth century by lesser political rulers, who nominally owed allegiance to the Empire.

The conditions under which mining was generally carried on added to the prestige attaching in a small degree to many kinds of manual labour, and especially to the artistic work in building and decorating churches and monasteries. The early miners and smelters, particularly in Saxony, the Alps, and other regions of Central Europe, were explorers and even climbers attacking forests, venturing into high valleys and scrambling up the sides of mountains. Serfdom was almost unknown among the Germans colonising these regions; so freedom was the virtually inevitable status for the miner.[45] The magic of the surroundings in which he often worked helped to class him in the hearts of men not with the slave but with the pioneer.

At the same time this connection of medieval mining and metallurgy with the highlands and woodlands helped to bring mining under the control of princes, lay and ecclesiastical, instead of under the control of private landlords. New seams were found very often in places where there had been little or no tillage and relatively few settlers before the twelfth and thirteenth centuries. In such areas the claims of strong private persons to the possession of the soil were weaker than in some thickly settled regions, where the land had been systematically exploited with little or no interruption since Roman times. The Alpine character of medieval mining, which marked it off from modern and from classical mining, facilitated the divorce, characteristic of medieval

[45] Cf. Gustav Schmoller, 'Die geschichtliche Entwicklung der Unternehmung,' *Jahrbuch für Gesetzgebung, Verwaltung und Volkswirtschaft im deutschen Reich*, xv (1891), 677.

mining law, between the use of the surface and the possession of mines. As lordship of the soil was inclined to remain rather indefinite in the forests and Alpine regions, the minerals underneath could be more readily claimed by the overlords than would have been possible where the surface landlords were generally men of greater substance with traditional power over their estates.[46] Peasants who drove flocks to pasture in the Alpine regions were always moving about. They generally left during the winter. So the rights of the owners of cattle were rarely identified with any particular plots of land. If, as frequently happened, some of their animals tumbled into the miners' pits, the shepherds were outraged. They demanded compensation. But it did not occur to them to claim a share in the mines. That left the territorial princes, lay and ecclesiastical, an excellent opportunity to stake out claims to take the miners and metallurgical workers under their tutelage, at a time when they granted such working people much independence and welcomed their participation in local government.

An astonishing feature of early western history in the Pyrenees, Normandy, England, Wales, the southern Low Countries, the Rhineland, as well as in the Alps and the Erzgebirge, was the disposition of overlords and lords of the soil to grant similar privileges and adopt similar regulations and similar administrative arrangements in hundreds of communities formed to exploit ores and metals. It was almost as if an invisible lawgiver inspired miners, landlords and territorial rulers from one end of Europe to the other with a single conception of right and wrong, which could be translated into custom and positive law. For a brief spell, which in some regions hardly lasted through the thirteenth century, the western Europeans almost managed to universalise among the miners freedom and partial self-government. The conditions of industrial work in the country as well as in the town were helping to strengthen in western Europe an allegiance that was largely new to the small semi-independent unit of enterprise which came with other units to form part of a local community. This allegiance came to exist concurrently with the allegiances to the authority of a centralised state and a universal church, which the Europeans had inherited from the more distant past.

Like the gothic arch and the great cathedral spires, the community of free miners was a creation of western Europe. Like the philosophical *Summae* of Thomas Aquinas and Duns Scotus, it was indicative of a genius extensively awakened among the Europeans of the twelfth and thirteenth centuries. This genius consisted in the desire and the capacity to exploit for fresh purposes ideas, forms and principles, including

[46] Cf. Schmoller, *op. cit.*, 676, 679.

forms of industrial organisation, suggested by earlier advanced peoples, to generalise these ideas, forms, and principles in ways that made them accessible to all. The power to universalise through small units for the benefit of western Christendom as a whole gave the age its special unity. To a degree apparently unknown in the past, the many and the one complemented and fortified without absorbing each other.

V. *The Collapse of Prosperity in the Fourteenth Century*

The balance was a delicate one. So far as mining and metallurgy are concerned it became increasingly imperfect as the Middle Ages waned. The conditions of enterprise which prevailed during the period of expanding output at the end of the twelfth and in the thirteenth century were partly dependent upon the fortunes of nature which spread rich mineral resources out near the surface along the upland valleys and on the sides of hills and mountains, readily accessible to adventurers with little capital. These surface resources obviously had limits.

During the fourteenth century the rapid progress in the output of minerals and metals, characteristic of most of Europe for several previous generations, came to an end. Except in a few districts, notably in eastern Franconia and perhaps in Bohemia, the miners began to encounter hard times early in the century or at least before the middle of it, when the bubonic plague swept away a substantial part of the European population. Both Franconia and Bohemia suffered relatively little from the Black Death. Their escape may have had something to do with the revival of the prosperity of the mines of silver-bearing ore in Bohemia during the third quarter of the fourteenth century. Progress was made also in the output of gold in Bohemia, Silesia and Hungary.[47] But mining in Central Europe generally was not in a flourishing state during the fourteenth and early fifteenth centuries. The production of gold and silver in Europe as a whole actually declined. To judge from conditions at the famous copper mines on the Rammelsberg and at the equally famous tin mines in Devon and

[47] Cf. Kaspar Sternberg, *Umrisse einer Geschichte der böhmischen Bergwerke* (Prague, 1838), I, ii, 32–4. E. J. Hamilton, *Money, Prices and Wages in Valencia, Aragon, and Navarre, 1351–1500* (Cambridge, Mass., 1936), 195. But the Silesian mines generally were in a depressed state throughout the fourteenth and fifteenth centuries (Konrad Wutke, 'Die Salzerschliessungsversuche in Schlesien in vorpreussischer Zeit', *Zeitschrift des Vereins für Geschichte und Altertum Schlesiens*, XXVIII (1894), 107). Some of the gold used for the development of coinage in late fourteenth-century Europe came from the Sudan, a source of supplies since at least the twelfth century (Fernand Braudel, 'Monnaies et Civilisations', *Annales: Economies, Sociétés, Civilisations*, I (1946), 11).

Cornwall, the production of copper and tin also diminished somewhat. In spite of frequent warfare, which kept up the demand for iron and steel, the forges in the chief iron-making districts were seldom prosperous. In many districts their number dwindled. The traffic in sea coal from from England to the continent was not increasing.

What were the causes for this long slump which lasted for several generations? The prosperity of the mining and metallurgical industries was bound up with general prosperity. The depression in mining was partly a reflection of the economic and political troubles which beset most of Europe. After at least two hundred years of exceptionally rapid increase, the population was growing slowly, if at all. The peasants, who formed the great majority in every country, found it much more difficult to improve either their social status or their material welfare. In most towns there was no marked increase in the number of craftsmen or in industrial production. Except perhaps in the Low Countries under the Burgundian duke, Philip the Good (1419–67), there was nowhere any sustained economic boom until the last decades of the fifteenth century. Consequently there were few places where the demand for metal grew. Wars and political disputes between various European princes and between the rising national states of France and England were more frequent and more destructive than in the thirteenth century. They interfered with the growth of trade in all products, including metals. In some cases the armies attacked mines and forges, filled the pits with earth and rubbish, smashed the furnaces and bellows and massacred some of the miners and smelters. The Hussite wars of the early fifteenth century (1415–36) left the celebrated Bohemian mining towns of Kuttenberg (Kutná Horá), Eyle, and Deutsch-Brod in ruins.

A renewal of prosperity in mining depended upon general improvement in economic and political conditions. In turn, economic progress as a whole depended on a renewal of prosperity in mining. In addition to their other ills, most of the states of Europe suffered from a shortage of gold and silver during the fourteenth and most of the fifteenth centuries, especially after about 1375. Except in those states where princes resorted to the expedient of reducing the gold or silver content of their coins, this was a period of stable or slightly falling prices. Industry and trade were stagnant partly because of the difficulties encountered in trying to sell commodities at a profit. The markets provided by the territorial princes, lay and ecclesiastical, were clogged up. One of the reasons for this sluggish demand was the unsatisfactory yield of the mines and the mints from which these princes often derived a portion of their revenues. To a degree that is difficult for modern men to grasp, orders for industrial products came from the great princes and still more from the Church – from the Pope and from innumerable ecclesiastical foundations (large and small) spread through the whole of Europe.

In Saxony and the Harz, in Bohemia and Hungary, in Sweden, Alsace, and Devon, some of the most productive mines of silver-bearing ores were exhausted in the fourteenth century. Others were worked so deep that many miners were forced to flee before the onrush of water breaking through into the workings, if they had escaped being buried alive when the badly supported walls of underground passages caved in. Progress depended upon the discovery of new seams and better methods of draining the mines and supporting the walls. It also depended upon the invention of new and cheaper processes for extracting precious metals from the ores and for combining ores and metals.

VI. *The Progress of Industrial Technology*

Heavier capital expenditures were necessary if deeper shafts were to be dug and more machinery installed. During the earlier medieval silver rushes, mining had been generally carried on by rather primitive methods. Much has been written recently about the backwardness of the peoples of the Roman Empire in engineering skill. But archaeologists have now shown that the Romans actually used more ingenious machinery in mining than the Europeans adopted extensively during the twelfth and thirteenth centuries. If miners in the gothic age had learned of the shafts that had been sunk in Roman times to depths of some six hundred feet in Spain, if they had learned of the adits that had been driven for more than a mile to drain the workings, or of the costly drainage machinery in the forms of water-wheels and cochlea, moved apparently by human labour, their admiration for the technical skill of the ancients might have approached that felt by the schoolmen for the thought of the greatest classical philosophers. No such deep mines were to be found in medieval Europe before the end of the thirteenth century; nor were the attempts to rid the pits of water yet as enterprising as those sometimes made by ancient peoples.

Most of the coal and base ore was got either by quarrying or by digging a sort of cave, widening out at the bottom like a bell or cone, with its base only a few feet below the surface. It was only in the digging of rich silver-bearing ores in Central Europe that shaft mining had become at all general by the end of the thirteenth century. Even in silver mining the shafts seldom penetrated deeply below the surface. The normal procedure in attacking silver-bearing ores was to puncture a sloping field with dozens of very shallow pits. As soon as water interfered with the hewers' work, a pit was usually abandoned. In this way hundreds of pits were sometimes sunk in a small area in the space of a few years. Some were so close together that a man could leap the whole distance between them.[48]

The first attempts at drainage were of two kinds. Trenches open to the sky were dug for short distances from the bottom of the shafts down into the valley. Again, leather buckets filled with water were wound up from a pit by a hand-turned windlass, or passed along a chain of men stationed in an inclined shaft. In a few districts such methods of drainage went back to the beginning of the thirteenth century and probably much earlier. They seldom proved adequate for any long stretch of years, if the demand for ore grew at all rapidly. Long before medieval mining reached the depths that had been attained in the Roman Empire, such primitive drainage devices were unable to cope with the floods. The soil of the Alps and the countries to the North is much damper than that of most Mediterranean lands. At depths of from sixty to a hundred feet, flooding was likely to become a much more serious danger than it had been commonly in the mines of the Hellenistic age or of the Roman Empire.

The only way to meet the difficulties was to drain off the water continuously in fairly large quantities. This called for heavy expenditures in digging drainage tunnels or installing machines. At the end of the thirteenth century or at the beginning of the fourteenth, the first experiments were apparently made with long adits in Bohemia. Some had to be driven more than a mile underground before they reached an opening in the valley below the level of the shaft bottom or sump, in which the water that had seeped into the workings was collected. But as the adits were seldom kept in repair, they were soon clogged up. Water worked its way back into the pits.

In Bohemia at the end of the thirteenth century, and a little later in Saxony, the Harz and southern Bavaria, water- and horse-driven machines were tried for drawing water from the pits and also for raising brine water from deep salt springs. The mechanical use of water and horse power was not new. For generations water power and occasionally horse power had been employed in metallurgy and some other surface industries. But, if water and horse power were to be effective in draining deep mines, more substantial wheels, axles, and gears than those hitherto in use were indispensable. The early machines for fulling cloth, pounding rags to pulp, even those for driving the bellows and the hammers in metallurgy were not equipped with the

[48] Schmoller, 'Die geschichtliche Entwicklung der Unternehmung', 664.

powerful wheels needed to raise enough water out of mines to staunch a flood underground. Some thirteenth-century Europeans saw what was wanted better apparently than the Romans had seen. But the idea hardly brought important results for another two hundred years.

In the preparation and the smelting of ores and the refining of metals during the thirteenth century the methods for the most part were little more efficient mechanically than in mining. Washing, breaking, and crushing were usually done out-of-doors by hand labour. Smelters showed much resourcefulness and imagination in devising a variety of hearths, trenches, pots, ovens and furnaces, suited to the species and the quality of the ore they had to treat. But however artful these forges and mills might be, they were not large or expensive to build and equip. Sometimes, as in the making of lead, smelting was undertaken in open air hearths on the side of some hill where the fires were fanned by the wind. More often, as in the treatment of iron ore, the metal was produced at tiny forges equipped with hand- or foot-driven bellows. The capital invested in such forges seldom exceeded that required to set up the workshop of a smith. In the woodlands near the seams forges and hammers were almost as numerous as the pits and open works dug down to the ore. They were abandoned almost as lightly.

In metallurgy, as in mining, the first heavy capital expenditures were made in connection with silver. The extraction of this beautiful metal from argentiferous lead ore was a more complicated and expensive task than the preparation of gold or of base metals. After the ore had been raised from the shafts, it was washed, then broken and crushed, then smelted. The resulting argentiferous lead was next subjected to oxidation in a cupelling hearth to remove the lead or litharge, and the residual silver was finally refined in a separate 'test' with bellows. During the twelfth century, the hammers and stamps for breaking and crushing the ore, and the bellows used in heating it, were probably mostly driven by hand or foot labour, as had been the practice at Laurion in the halcyon days of Attic mining in the fifth and fourth centuries B.C. But primitive power-driven machinery could be more effective in many metallurgical operations than in draining mines. Industrial development occurred in many places where nature invited the use of water power. Rushing streams poured down the slopes and ran through the mountain valleys of Central Europe in a profusion unknown in the drier lands of Greece and in most of the Mediterranean basin. By the first decade of the thirteenth century, if not earlier, water-driven wheels were set up at the silver mines of Trent, in the southern Tyrol, both for driving the hammers and the bellows. A hundred years later, in the principal silver-mining districts, water-driven machinery was frequently employed for breaking and crushing the ores as well as for blowing.

Similar water-driven wheels were introduced for operating the bellows and the hammers in the chief iron-making regions – in Styria, Carinthia, Bohemia, Lorraine and Dauphiné. Some bellows were already more skilfully constructed than seems to have been common in classical smelting. The modern type of heart-shaped bellows with a flap-valve, never extensively used in Hellenistic or in Roman times, is said to have appeared even before the twelfth century. In the early fourteenth century there were double and fairly sophisticated bellows producing a constant, instead of a panting, blast.[49] The hotter flame from the new and longer water-driven bellows produced bigger salamanders, or masses of metal, than had been made by the older methods. Consequently larger furnaces had to be devised to hold the ore and the fuel, while power-driven tilt hammers were needed to reduce the salamanders to blooms of wrought iron at nearby mills.

Three types of furnace had begun to replace the older bloomery forges in the fourteenth century: the Catalan forge, which had an ancient origin and was adopted mainly in the Pyrenees and the adjoining parts of Spain and France; the Osmund furnace, introduced in Scandinavia; and what was called in German the *Stückofen*. The *Stückofen*, the highest and most effective of the three, was found mainly in Central Europe, eastern France, and the Alpine districts between. Unlike the tiny woodland bloomery forges, which rose only three or four feet from the ground, the *Stückofen* was a fairly substantial structure of brick or stone, usually built close to the streams to make possible the use of water power. It was some 10 feet high, and consisted of a circular or quadrangular shaft, about 2 feet across at the top and bottom, and widening out to 5 feet or so in the middle. Such a furnace could turn out 40 or 50 tons of iron in a year, about three times the quantity ordinarily produced at the more primitive bloomery forges.

Like the long adits and the water-driven machinery for draining the silver mines, the improved methods for manufacturing iron were not widely adopted in Europe for more than a hundred years after their introduction. While more progress was made during the fourteenth and early fifteenth centuries with water-driven bellows and hammers than with water-driven drainage engines or even with adits, the less powerful methods of making iron at small bloomery forges remained the rule in all except the leading centres.

[49] Karl Sudhoff, *Beiträge zur Geschichte der Chirurgie im Mittelalter* (Leipzig, 1914), plate xxxi, a reference which I owe to Dr Lynn White.

In most of Europe the miners, smelters and refiners of metal went on digging and treating ores in the fashion to which their ancestors had become accustomed. Neither the material condition of the European peoples nor the state of learning during the fourteenth and early fifteenth centuries were as favourable to exploration and discovery as in the gothic age. In the universities, students of natural science worked the views of the schoolmen and of the classical philosophers into dogmatic systems that left little room for the kind of re-examination which some of the great men themselves would have welcomed. Scholars, whose experiences led them to distrust authority, kept their own counsel for fear of trouble with their colleagues or with the Church.

A new period of widespread prospecting for fresh seams of ore, and of remarkable technical progress in mining and metallurgy, began in the second half of the fifteenth century. It was an expression of the same forces that led to the discovery of new lands beyond the seas and to advances in natural science. The larger mines and metallurgical establishments of Central Europe became laboratories. The occasional association with them of learned men, such as Paracelsus (1493–1541) and Agricola (1494–1555), and of Biringuccio (d. 1540), a master craftsman in metal work, all of whom devoted a considerable part of their lives to science and engineering, helped to prepare the way for the destruction of the barrier which had existed during the Middle Ages between the work of the industrial craftsman and that of the speculative thinker. In the medieval hierarchy the separation of the liberal from the servile arts was perhaps as complete as the separation between two departments in some large modern university. It would be a mistake to suppose that the 'servility' of handling matter in the Middle Ages was the same sort of servility that came later to attach to the wage-earning manual labourer in mines and factories. But it was the accepted medieval convention that the manipulation of material substances was a servile art and that the more abstract labour of the intelligence belonged to a separated category. For material progress and the rise of modern science the decay of this convention was of great advantage. It persisted through the sixteenth century, but the progress of mining and metallurgy weakened it by providing a meeting ground for technical experts and some learned men.

The efforts of miners and metallurgical workers bore much fruit during the last half of the fifteenth century and the early decades of the sixteenth. New seams of rich ore were found in many districts, especially in those parts of Central Europe that had been famous for their mines already in the thirteenth century. Prospectors also came upon valuable supplies of cinnabar, the ore of mercury, and of alum stones. True brass, as distinguished from bronze, is an alloy of calamine and copper. Its production became common after centuries of neglect. The discovery of abundant calamine in the Tyrol and Carinthia, and especially at Moresnet, near Aachen, led to an extensive manufacture of brass in Germany and the Low Countries. This increased notably the demand for copper.

An invention of the mid-fifteenth century was of even greater importance than the working of calamine in the development of the copper mines. It was discovered that the separation of silver from the argentiferous copper ores, which abounded in Central Europe, could be effectively accomplished with the help of lead. The new method, which seems to have been discovered in the eleventh century in China (to be forgotten there), was apparently introduced in Saxony about 1451 by a certain Johannsen Funcken. The rich copper ores had been little exploited before this time because of the difficulty of extracting silver from them or of using them to produce brass. No other invention had so stimulating an effect as the new treatment of copper ore upon the development of the mining and metallurgical industries in Central Europe on the eve of the Reformation.

Just as this invention was helping to make profitable the working of deeper seams of copper ore, the invention of more powerful drainage engines combined with the digging of more skilfully constructed adits to make it possible to cope with the water at greater depths. Better methods of ventilating the underground passages made it possible to blow away some of the noxious and explosive gases.

The most ingenious of the new machines were apparently constructed in Hungary and Saxony. The most curious of all was at Schemnitz in the Carpathian mountains. There the water from the bottom of the deepest pit was pumped up in three flights before it reached a sufficient height to be carried off down an adit. Each pump was set in motion by the rotation of a large horse-driven wheel. The animals to turn these wheels were led down to their labour along inclined shafts which sloped and twisted like screws. In construction these shafts apparently resembled the ramps that enable modern automobile owners to park their cars in congested city areas. The work required ninety-six horses. They were employed in relays at each of the three wheels.[50] The peoples of antiquity had apparently never devised so powerful a drainage engine.

Less important than improvements in drainage for the progress of mining and metallurgy at the end of the Middle Ages, but far more important in its *eventual* consequences for the rise of modern industrial

[50] Cf. Georgius Agricola, *De re metallica* (Hoover edn, London, 1912), 194–5.

civilisation, was the rediscovery of the blast furnace. The heavy manual labour and the great waste of metal involved in producing iron had restrained its use both in war and peace among earlier peoples than the western Europeans. Once iron ore could be made into metal cheaply, masses of men could be outfitted with weapons based on gunpowder and other explosives, and with carriages, cars, tanks, armoured ships and aeroplanes on which the weapons could be mounted. Machines and conveyances of all kinds to supply commodities intended for peaceful use and new structural materials of iron and steel for building could be produced in an equally bewildering profusion. The blast furnace was not by any means the only invention needed to bring the modern age of metal, but it was an essential one. As the supplies of iron ore proved to be almost unlimited, the widespread use and mechanical improvement of the blast furnace prepared the way for a revolutionary increase in the output of iron and steel. The blast furnace was an open sesame to the production of *abundant* metal.

Let us consider more closely its history in medieval Europe. The discovery that led to its invention was apparently accidental. Bronze, a compound of copper and tin, melts more readily than iron ore. In the later Middle Ages, in the early twelfth century or perhaps before, a liquified mixture of copper and tin, produced by a strong heat, was run into holes prepared in the earth where the liquid solidified in such shapes as were desired. In this way bronze was cast into the marvellous church bells of medieval Europe, as well as into statues and domestic utensils. During the great age of gothic cathedral building bells of cast bronze were hoisted into the towers of churches, where they tolled their message, summoning the faithful, across a continent. The first guns were made of bronze by a process learned from bell and statue makers. The early bronze founders contributed unintentionally to the discovery of one of man's most awful weapons.[51]

The more powerful water-driven bellows, introduced in iron-making during the thirteenth century, if not sooner, sometimes generated so fierce a flame in smelting that even the intractable ore of iron ran before the eyes of the astonished iron-masters. As the casting of bronze was already known, it was natural that the new discovery should be exploited in the same way for casting iron. It is not certain when the first cast iron objects were made, but clearly by the beginning of the fifteenth century and probably somewhat earlier. Cannon made of cast iron appeared before the middle of the fifteenth century in the dominion of the powerful and enterprising dukes of Burgundy, and somewhat later in Italy. These cannon were clumsy,

[51] Charles Ffoulkes, *The Gun-Founders of England* (Cambridge, 1937), 2.

ineffective pieces. It was not until after the Reformation that cast iron cannon did effective execution or were turned out in any number, and then they were manufactured not on the continent but in south-eastern England. Meanwhile it was mainly cannon of wrought iron that helped to revolutionise the art of war at the turn of the fifteenth and sixteenth centuries.[52]

By this time, and possibly earlier, genuine blast furnaces, with auxiliary forges, were built in north-eastern France and northern Italy.[53] There were few of them at the end of the Middle Ages however.

In a few instances where these furnaces were introduced, cast iron replaced wrought iron as the primary product. In large fires the ore was maintained for long periods in contact with carbon at high temperatures, and the carbon was absorbed by the reduced iron forming an alloy, cast iron, of much lower melting point than the pure metal. The molten metal was allowed to collect in the hearth and was run periodically through a tap hole into an open oblong mould where it solidified into pieces called 'sows'. As larger amounts were cast at one time, bars branching from the sow were added, called 'pigs' – a name suggested by their relationship to the maternal sow. The melting of the product permitted efficient recovery of the iron present in the ore and the cast iron produced was of great use in making a whole range of new products at the foundry – such as guns, shot, fire-backs, andirons and grave slabs – but it was not in a form fit to use for wrought products – such as tools, weapons and armour. The cast iron therefore had to be given subsequent treatment to decarbonise it. This consisted of reheating under oxidising conditions, giving an unlimited, spongy mass, that by continued forging became equivalent, and for *modern* industrial purposes even superior, to the old directly reduced iron. The new roundabout process not only facilitated the production of larger quantities of iron with less labour; it reduced the amount lost in the manufacture. Blast furnaces with their dependent forges were larger than the *Stückofen* of Styria, Carinthia and other regions of Central Europe. They were equipped with more powerful bellows and hammers. Their establishment involved a heavier investment in land, buildings, machinery and other equipment.

The possibilities for stimulating a quantitative economy with the help of cheaper iron and steel were little exploited during the late fifteenth and the early sixteenth centuries by the two or three

[52] Rhys Jenkins, 'The Rise and Fall of the Sussex Iron Industry', *Transactions of the Newcomen Society*, fifth series, I (1920–1), 17; Ernest Straker, *Wealden Iron* (London, 1931), 38–40, 141ff; V. Biringuccio, *Pirotechnia*, Cyril S. Smith (ed.) (New York, 1942), 226.

[53] Straker, *op. cit.*, 40–3; Biringuccio, *op. cit.*, 146–8.

generations of Europeans born before the Reformation. The widespread preoccupation of craftsmen in that age with iron as material for the fashioning of beautiful objects – ornamental locks and keys for example – and for steel instruments (such as the burin) used in engraving, widely introduced with the spread of printing and the flowering of the Renaissance visual arts, influenced the Europeans in the kinds of techniques they chose to develop in connection with iron work and even iron metallurgy. Wrought iron was better suited than cast iron for almost all the needs of the artist and the artistic craftsman. The Europeans made haste slowly with the blast furnace on the eve of the Reformation not mainly because of technological ineptitude but because their inventive skill, when not absorbed with the development of new firearms, was directed towards the goals of beauty and quality more than towards the goals of efficiency and quantity. One wonders whether similar preoccupations with art may have helped deter the Chinese earlier from multiplying and developing their blast furnaces. One is tempted also to search for those factors that turned the Europeans, long before the Chinese, towards more modern economic goals. Whatever these factors were, the *extensive* development in Europe of the roundabout process (better suited to quantitative ends) started only later in the sixteenth and during the early seventeenth century. It seems to have started first in the Low Countries, then in Great Britain, then in Sweden.

Whatever direction they took, the inventions connected with iron metallurgy and the fashioning of iron wares were not the only interesting technical innovations of the miners and metallurgical workers in the fifteenth century and at the beginning of the sixteenth. Few years passed without some important mechanical discovery, such as mills for flattening metal or for drawing wire. Machines driven by the rush of streams came into widespread use in some metallurgical districts. Dams were built to store the water used to turn the larger and more powerful overshot wheels.

All the peoples of Europe made contributions to these technical discoveries. There was a good deal of interchange of mechanical knowledge between countries. In iron-making it was the Italians and the French, not the Germans, who led the way on the eve of the Reformation towards larger and more powerful enterprises. It is common to think of the English as backward in technique at the beginning of the sixteenth century. They were backward, but not unqualifiedly backward. Earlier in the Middle Ages they had had many things to give as well as to receive from foreigners. Even in the fifteenth century they were not without their influence on continental mining. A celebrated English master miner was brought to Saxony in 1444 by the Elector Friedrich II to help search for fresh seams of ore. But the stream of mechanical knowledge flowed in the opposite direction, with Central Europe as its source.

It was generally experts from Hungary, Bohemia, the Low Countries, the Tyrol and Saxony who excelled in the technical development of mining and metallurgy. Miners and mechanics of German origin were the leaders in the discovery and the dissemination of new methods, particularly in the mining and working of ores containing silver, copper, zinc and quicksilver, and in the manufacture of brass. New methods discovered in Central Europe spread to Scandinavia, Spain, France and England. 'In no place of the world shalt thou finde more witty engins and excellent peeces of workemanship than in Germany', wrote Thomas Coryate, the parson's son from Somerset, after he had travelled through much of Europe at the beginning of the seventeenth century. By this time Germany was on the point of losing this pre-eminence. She owed it mainly to the ingenuity of Germans and of some Slavs during the late fifteenth and early sixteenth centuries.

Inventions were essential to the great progress made in mining and metallurgy at the close of the Middle Ages. In the coalfields of the Low Countries and to some extent in those of the north of England shaft mining was becoming common; depths of 150 feet or so were reached. Still deeper shafts, descending some 400 feet or so below the surface, were sunk for mining cinnabar at Idria in Carniola and at Almadén in Spain.[54] The greatest depths of all were reached in working argentiferous copper ores in Saxony, Bohemia and Hungary, where a few pits went down 600 feet or more. At such depths the problem of drainage could be met only by driving long adits and pumping up water with powerful engines.

Remarkable though the inventions of the later Middle Ages were, they hardly revolutionised mining. Without them there would have been considerable, though less remarkable, progress in output, for new seams were still turning up at shallow depths. Only where the surface minerals were exhausted was recourse had to new methods. Horse- and water-driven drainage engines were installed almost exclusively at argentiferous copper ore mines. For the most part, the older ways of the thirteenth century prevailed. Though shaft mining was introduced for getting tin and lead ore, at the time of the Reformation most of these ores were still obtained at shallow depths of less than fifty feet, simply by surface workings. In Central Europe coal and iron ore were dug entirely from the outcropping seams, by means of open

[54] P. Hitzinger, *Das Quecksilber–Bergwerk Idria* (Laibach, 1860), 16; K. Häbler, *Die Geschichter der Fugger'schen Handlung in Spanien* (Weimar, 1897), 98.

works or caves. The use of even a hand windlass for raising ore was exceptional in connection with iron.

Mining deep below the surface was actually rare even in connection with silver-bearing ores in the most advanced districts. At Mansfeld, one of the chief centres for such mining on the eve of the Reformation, the initial progress was in working seams near the surface which, for want of demand, had not hitherto been exploited. These surface veins, overlooked in earlier times, were now rendered profitable without heavy investments. Except perhaps on the Schneeberg in Saxony, where shafts reaching down 200 feet and more seem to have been common,[55] the usual depth in the principal copper mines in Central Europe was about 75 or 80 feet. Many productive argentiferous copper mines were worked without horse- or water-driven engines, or even long adits. In the valley of the Inn, at Schwaz, the leading mining centre in Tyrol and one of the most productive in Europe of silver and copper, men were still engaged in 1537 to pass buckets full of water up an inclined shaft. That had been the universal method at Schwaz until about 1522, when the first attempt was made to introduce an expensive water-driven pumping machine. It is not certain that the attempt succeeded, although some sort of water pump was then installed.[56]

Folklore and superstition concerning their craft were still rife among the miners.[57] Special sight was attributed to a few experts who roamed over the hills, holding the ancient divining rod – a forked twig – straight out in front of them, until it turned and twisted as they passed over a hidden seam of ore. The mining communities still depended upon these mystery men for guidance, except when accidents of nature put them directly on the scent of new veins.

In metallurgy, as in mining, the important changes in methods were largely confined to silver and copper. At the time of the Reformation, water power had hardly begun to replace hand and foot power in the crushing, smelting and hammering of tin or lead ore, except perhaps at a few places in Germany. Even when water power was used for driving the bellows, the forges were generally small. The making of lead and tin did not require as fierce a flame as the making of iron. While blast furnaces had been built in north-eastern France,[58] in Piedmont, along the valleys of the Rhine and the lower Meuse, and in Sussex, most iron was still made directly from the ore even in these regions. In southern Germany and the eastern Alps, while the blast

[55] Oswald Hoppe, *Der Silberbergbau zu Schneeberg bis zum Jahre* 1500 (Freiberg, 1908), 158–9; cf. 92–3.

[56] M. R. von Wolfstrigl-Wolfskron, *Die Tiroler Erzbergbaue, 1301–1665* (Innsbruck, 1903), 39–41.

[57] Cf. Agricola, *De re metallica*, 37–41.

[58] Marcel Bulard, L'Industrie du fer dans la Haute-Marne', *Ann. de géog.*, XIII (1904), 232.

furnace was apparently unknown, water power had become the common force both for driving the bellows and the hammers in the leading iron-making districts, such as Styria and Carinthia, where the *Stückofen* had come into widespread use. But hand- or foot-driven bellows remained the rule at the pervasive bloomery forges in less advanced districts.

It is by no means certain that the European peoples had attained in the early sixteenth century a much higher level of technical proficiency in mining and metallurgy than the classical peoples in the early Roman Empire. But they had made discoveries never exploited by the ancients, of which the blast furnace and the *Saigerhüte*[59] are outstanding examples. They were using water power for turning machinery much more extensively than the Greeks or Romans had ever used it. The respect for the miners as pioneers, the freedom and dignity which their calling had come to possess during the twelfth and thirteenth centuries, had relieved the processes of mining and metallurgy from some of the stigma frequently associated with them in earlier societies. Was it not partly on that account that the western Europeans already in the later Middle Ages seem to have been less reluctant than the classical peoples were to exploit relentlessly the mineral riches of the earth, to devote their intellectual energies wholeheartedly to methods of cheapening the costs of mining and metallurgy?

By the period of the Reformation the study of engineering was beginning to claim greater attention than in classical times. Two books out of thirty-seven in Pliny's *Natural History*, written in the first century, are concerned with metals. Other Graeco-Roman works, mostly known to the moderns only at second hand, also treated the subject. But mining and metallurgy apparently never engaged the undivided attention of any classical writer[60] to the extent that they engaged men early in the sixteenth century, especially two men, a German and an Italian, Georgius Agricola and Vannoccio Biringuccio. The former devoted several treatises to it, the best known being a large book *De re metallica*. The latter was concerned with nothing else in his one long piece of writing, the *Pirotechnia*. Both treatises, and especially the *Pirotechnia*, are largely free from superstition. Neither Agricola nor Biringuccio took the divining rod seriously, and the Italian scorned the pseudo-magic of the alchemists.[61] Several of their contemporaries composed works on the same subjects, but the books

59 For a description, see below p. 746.

60 Cf. M. Rostovtzeff, *The Social and Economic History of the Hellenistic World* (Oxford, 1941), II, 1212.

61 Cyril S. Smith's introduction to *The Pirotechnia* (New York, 1942), xv. His admirable piece of editing has added substantially to knowledge of industrial history.

have been forgotten. This novel disposition to give undivided and accurate attention to mining and metallurgy was indicative of the respect felt by western Europeans for the occupation of the miner, which had been so distasteful to classical men that they had felt little inclination to explore, even with their minds, the world underground, shunned as it was by all who could avoid the labour of mining.

VII. *The Boom in Mining and Metallurgy, 1460–1530*

The wonderful artistic achievements of the late fifteenth and early sixteenth century, when much of continental Europe was built or rebuilt in the new Renaissance style of architecture, were accompanied by a remarkable industrial development, especially striking in northern Italy, parts of Spain, the southern Low Countries and in eastern and southern Germany. The progress of mining and metallurgy played an important part in this industrial development, above all in Central Europe. At some of the leading mines, as at Schneeberg in Saxony, the production of silver reached its zenith by the eighties of the fifteenth century. At others, as at Freiberg, the zenith was not reached until after the middle of the sixteenth century. For most mines the time of greatest prosperity was from about 1515 to 1540, when Agricola and Paracelsus reached maturity, when Dürer (1471–1528) and Holbein (1497–1543) painted many of their incomparable masterpieces, and when the doctrines of Luther (1483–1546), Zwingli (1484–1531) and other reformers fired the German people with a new religious enthusiasm. Between 1460 and 1530 the annual output of silver in Central Europe increased several times over, perhaps more than fivefold. It probably reached a maximum during the decade 1526–35. Nearly three million ounces were then produced each year, a figure not again attained until the fifties of the nineteenth century.[62] The output of copper grew at least as rapidly as the output of silver. By the thirties of the sixteenth century, it amounted to several thousands of tons annually.

The wealth of the Germans in silver, copper and brass had become a marvel for the rest of Europe. The most productive mines were in the Erzgebirge (at Schneeberg, Annaberg and Joachimstal), at Schwaz, at Neusohl in Hungary, and at Mansfeld, where Luther spent part of his childhood in the mountain air after his father had moved there to earn his bread as a miner. Several thousand men were drawn to each

[62] J. U. Nef, 'Silver Production in Central Europe', *Journal of Political Economy*, XLIX (1941), 584–6.

place to work underground, in carrying materials, in preparing charcoal, and in smelting, separating and refining the ores and metals.[63] With their families, they formed some settlements nearly as large as Leipzig and the other great towns of southern and eastern Germany which were growing rich and prosperous partly through the prosperity of the mines.[64] Emperor Charles V was probably not exaggerating in 1525 when he placed at a hundred thousand the number of persons employed in mining and metallurgy in all the countries of the Empire.[65]

The rapid growth in the output from mines was not limited to Central Europe. In Sweden and Alsace the production of silver, while inferior in volume to that of Saxony, Bohemia, Hungary, the Tyrol, or even Silesia, increased at nearly as rapid a rate as in those countries. During the first half of the sixteenth century the cinnabar mines at Almadén in Spain were almost if not quite as productive as those at Idria in Carniola.[66] Italy led in the new alum-making industry. The principal enterprise was at Tolfa, near Civita Vecchia, in the Papal States.[67] Rich deposits of alum stones were discovered there in 1462, by John de Castro, the general 'commissar' of the revenue for the Papal Chamber. A decade later in 1471, the output at Tolfa amounted to over a thousand tons – almost twice the quantity of alum imported from the Near East at Genoa on the eve of Castro's discovery, when Genoa was the chief receiving centre in Europe.[68] Castro predicted that the vast works set up under his direction for the popes would assure the defeat of the infidel by freeing Europe from its long dependence upon the Near East for alum. The alum manufacture at Tolfa was actually one of the largest industrial ventures operating under a single management in sixteenth-century Europe. It employed 711 work-people in 1557.[69] Alum was an essential element in the dyeing of fine cloth, at a time when textiles employed a great many more hands than any other industry. In the early sixteenth century alum-making on a considerable scale spread to other parts of Europe. Newly found deposits of alum stones were exploited in southern Spain, near Cartagena, and also in Central Europe. By 1549 the alum works in Bohemia were considered by the king of Bohemia as sufficient to supply his entire kingdom.[70] The papal manufacture

[63] Cf. Zycha, *Das bömische Bergrecht des Mittelalters*, II, 299; Wolfstrigl-Wolfskron, *Die Tiroler Erzbergbaue*, 45, 66–7.

[64] Cf. Ernst Kroker, 'Leipzig und die sächsischen Bergwerke', *Schriften des Vereins für die Geschichte Leipzigs*, IX (1909), 26–7, 32–3, and *passim*.

[65] Jakob Strieder, *Studien zur Geschichte kapitalistischer Organisationsformen* (2nd edn, Munich, 1925), 3–4, 376–7.

[66] Häbler, *Fugger'schen Handlung in Spanien*, 102; Hitzinger, *Quecksilber-Bergwerk Idria*, *passim*.

[67] Jean Delumeay, *L'Alun de Rome XVe–XIXe siècles* (Paris, 1962).

[68] *Ibid.*, 124.

[69] *Ibid.*, 76–7.

[70] Kasper Sternberg, *Umrisse einer Geschichte der böhmischen Bergwerke* (Prague, 1836), I, pt. II, 83–4.

suffered from the new competition, which some popes sought ineffectually to curb by trying to force the faithful to buy only papal alum. But Castro was proved right in his prediction about the independence from the Near East which his initiative in the alum manufacture could help to achieve. By the mid-sixteenth century Europe had become virtually self-sufficient for its supplies of alum.

All over the continent the manufacture of iron and steel grew rapidly to meet the demands of a large number of expanding industries. Cannon, mainly of wrought iron, were coming into widespread use for the first time, as kings and princes stored up ordnance in anticipation of a coming struggle for authority and dominion and tried out their artillery, especially in Italy where the fields were stained with the blood from frequent battles. At many places on the continent the manufacture of salt was expanding. Pumping machinery with iron parts, and iron pans the length and breadth of a fair-sized room, were installed to raise and to hold the water from the rich brine springs in Franche-Comté and Lorraine, where the new salt works in the enclosures built at Salins and Dieuze, each with many scores of work-people, were among the largest industrial units in Renaissance Europe, second in size perhaps only to the arsenal at Venice and the alum works at Tolfa.[71] Tools, gears and machine parts, and various other iron wares, were wanted in larger quantities than before in mining and metallurgy, in shipbuilding and in construction work of all kinds. In Styria the output of iron seems to have quadrupled between the sixties of the fifteenth century and the thirties of the sixteenth, when it amounted to some eight thousand tons or more a year.[72]

As this expansion in Styria was apparently achieved without the blast furnace, which provided the most productive technique for iron-making, it is reasonable to suppose that such an expansion in iron production was by no means exceptional. Scattered figures concerning the iron mills in the Ardennes forest and the Meuse valley indicate that the growth of the industry there at the beginning of the sixteenth century was at least as rapid as in Styria. In Carinthia, Carniola, Westphalia and the Harz, in Lorraine, Champagne, Dauphiné and Nivernais, in Tuscany and Piedmont, in the eastern Pyrenees and the Basque provinces of Spain, the development characteristic of Styria

[71] Nef, *The Conquest of the Material World*, 43, 51–2, 89–90, 104–6.

[72] L. Bittner, 'Das Eisenwesen in Innerberg-Eisenerz', *Archiv für österreichische Geschichte*, LXXXIX (Vienna, 1901), 628–9. These statistics of output are for Innerberg-Eisenerz only. There production increased from about 1,300 tons in 1466 to about 5,000 tons in 1536. At Vordernberg, the other iron-producing district of Styria, the annual output is said to have averaged more than 3,000 tons between 1535 and 1537 (*ibid.*, 490, n.). I have assumed that in 1466 the output at Vordernberg was more than half that at Innerberg-Eisenerz, as in 1536.

and the Low Countries was repeated. The iron-masters deserted the highlands, with their woods, for the streams and rivers with their water power. They built larger mills and stayed much longer in one spot than they had done when the location of forges had been more dependent upon clusters of trees, which were soon hewed down to serve the charcoal burners. The new labour-saving machinery made it economical sometimes to bring wood and charcoal considerable distances on packhorses and in carts. Thus, even without the introduction of a blast furnace, the area serving a single iron-making enterprise was extended in a number of regions where more costly and more permanent iron-works were established.

Old peasants in the valleys complained that the new furnaces, forges and mills were converting once quiet villages into noisy bedlams. The machinery swished and creaked as the large wooden wheels, for transmitting the power, rotated in the streams or under the force of water poured from the end of an elevated wooden trough running from a newly built reservoir. The blows of great power-driven hammers, sometimes weighing 200 lb and more, echoed through the forests and hills. As larger iron-works were installed, as stronger bellows were introduced, the air was often filled with such a stench and smoke as to trouble travellers as well as old inhabitants. In some places, according to the villagers, the waste products from the forges and furnaces so polluted the streams as to deprive them of fish.[73]

The growth and multiplication of enterprises for mining and making metals put strains upon the forests in many parts of Europe. Lumber of various kinds was used for pit props, in making machinery, in building houses, shops, dams and small factories needed for manufacturing metal. The demand for logs and charcoal grew almost as rapidly as the output of metal, for most of the new furnaces and mills effected little saving in fuel. They caused the destruction every year of the trees and shrubbery on thousands of acres.

Increasing pressure on timber supplies aroused a fresh interest in the coal seams. In several provinces of southern and central France, notably in Lyonnais and Forez, where coal outcropped, and also in Germany – in Westphalia, Saxony and Silesia – the digging of coal early in the sixteenth century began to employ larger numbers of local peasants than in the past. Some of them loaded the black stones and gravel into sacks and carried the stuff to nearby towns on pack horses, or, if river traffic was possible, in flat-bottomed boats. The dirty fuel was beginning to command a price at some distances from the pits among lime-burners and those smiths who specialised in the rougher

[73] A. Meister, 'Die Anfänge des Eisenindustrie in der Grafschaft Mark', *Beiträge zur Geschichte Dortmunds und der Grafschaft Mark*, XVII (1909), 140.

kinds of iron work. But most of the peasants who dug and carried coal had other work, usually in husbandry. They handled the mineral as a by-occupation.

It was only in the principality of Liège that coal mining actually became an industry of some importance, employing considerable numbers of trained miners. The wide gently flowing Meuse, so convenient for the transport of cheap, bulky commodities, veers at almost a right angle from east to north. At Liège the production of coal had been more noteworthy during the fourteenth and fifteenth centuries than at any other place on the continent. Charles the Bold, the fiery duke of Burgundy, had ordered his soldiers to erase the city from the map and had vowed that even its name should not be revived. Yet in the decades that followed his death, in 1477, it became one of the great armouries for the European princes who followed him. The output of coal tripled or quadrupled to help feed with fuel the growing metal and armament manufactures in the town itself and at many places up and down the river. Liège coals were not quite carried to Newcastle! But fuel from the land of 'Luick' actually competed at Calais and other channel ports with 'seacoals' from the Tyne. At Liège the long adits which drained the coal pits were driven and interconnected in such a way as to provide the main city water supply. The mounds of black earth thrown up beside the pits were hardly less prominent a sight than the spires of the churches. They were more portentous of the future that awaited the western peoples than the city halls, the courts of justice and the merchant palaces that were rising in profusion in a host of European towns.

VIII. *The Cleavage between Capital and Labour*

The long adits and the drainage engines, the largest of the new furnaces and mills with their horse- and water-driven machinery, were costly to construct, to maintain and to operate. They added greatly to the capital required in mining and in extracting metals from the ores. Even when it was possible to supply the increased demand for ores and metals without fundamental changes in industrial technology, the increase in the demand often made it profitable to increase the scale of enterprise. Under the spur of technical changes and of expanding markets, a striking cleavage was taking place between capital and labour in many of the mining districts on the continent, especially in southern and eastern Germany, Bohemia, Hungary and the Eastern Alps.

While mining and metallurgy had always required some capital, and had always lent themselves to enterprise on a considerable scale more readily than most other medieval industries except building, it would be a mistake to suppose that from the beginning the organisation of the workmen resembled in miniature that in a modern mine or factory. During the late twelfth and early thirteenth centuries it was common for the finders of the ore and their fellows who held adjoining meers in the same seam to band together in associations. They worked many concessions as a single undertaking much as the peasants ploughed and sowed their holdings in common. Thus, companies of working miners were formed with a number of parts, in some cases as many as thirty-two. These parts could be passed from father to son. They could be sold or exchanged. In some cases they could be leased.

Working partnerships of this kind were not unknown during the thirteenth century in the preparation, the smelting, separating and refining of ores and metals; but they were rare. Sometimes forges and hammers were provided by the miners themselves. Sometimes, especially in the production of silver, the metallurgical establishments belonged to the princes who coined money and granted mining concessions. In fourteenth-century Germany furnaces for separating silver from lead ore, and for making silver, lead and copper, came frequently to be farmed out to a working master, generally under short-term leases with a year or so to run. In the production of iron, as we have seen, the works were frequently owned by the local lords of the soil. The iron forges themselves, or the sites on which to build them, were often leased out by these lords either to some of their chief tenants or to traders in metal from the nearby towns. In many cases the early iron forges, hammers and mills were manorial ventures like corn mills or wine presses. The work was done for wages or under contract by local villagers, many of whom held small plots of land and were occupied in husbandry a part of their time. As it was rare before the late thirteenth century for more than four or five persons to work in one pit at a time, it was probably also rare in metallurgy for more than four or five persons to work at a single forge or stamping mill.

In many parts of Europe little manorial enterprises employing less than a dozen local villagers remained the normal type in mining and metallurgy even at the time of the Reformation. That was the case in the digging of coal except in the Low Countries, along the Tyne in Durham and in southern Nottinghamshire. It was the case with the mining of iron ore and its conversion to metal in the numerous iron-making districts where tiny bloomery forges still prevailed. It was frequently the case in tin mining and lead mining, except in those districts of Central Europe where silver was won in substantial quantities from argentiferous lead ores.

Wherever the demand for minerals and metals grew rapidly, independent partnerships of working miners or smelters were placed on the defensive. As the expenses of mining and smelting increased, the miners and smelters were obliged to borrow money. They often borrowed from the traders with whom they had been accustomed to enter into contracts for the sale of their coal, ore, or metal. It is an almost universal rule in economic history that such loans give the creditor the upper hand. During the late Middle Ages, they put him in a position to take over the enterprise when the workers were unable at a specified time to pay off the loans or the interest due on them. Creditors who foreclosed might then work the mine on their own account. More frequently they either employed an expert to operate it for them or, if they could find someone with funds willing to assume the risks, leased it. In any case the work-people, once independent adventurers in a small way, were turned into wage-earning employees.

In the principality of Liège by 1520 or so the independent working partnership of coal miners had given way almost entirely before small capitalistic enterprises, usually owned and managed by partnerships of town traders. Farther west in the neighbourhood of Mons, where coal had also been dug and sold for centuries, the disintegration of the working partnership under the impact of similar financial forces was already well under way. In England were a few new capitalistically organised collieries on the south bank of the Tyne opposite Newcastle and north of the Trent near Nottingham.

On the continent in the principal iron-making districts a few of the chief ventures were staffed by scores of wage-earners, engaged in digging and carrying the ore, in preparing charcoal, and in tending the furnaces, forges and hammers. The introduction of the roundabout process for producing iron increased the number of operations that had to be co-ordinated, and, at the same time, added to the capital equipment required in each process. The landlords generally seem to have maintained their share in the ownership of the iron-works. But they frequently leased the establishments for short terms to merchants from the nearby towns. Such merchants might form small smelting companies with transferable shares, as in the Schmalkalden district in South Hesse.

In the mining of quicksilver, copper and all other silver-bearing ores, in the making of silver, copper, brass and alum, the partnerships of working miners and the small manorial ventures, characteristic of mining and metallurgy in the thirteenth century, gave way almost entirely (especially in the industrial regions of Central Europe) before new forms of enterprise requiring greater resources in capital. Argentiferous copper ore mining involved especially heavy expenditures. It was almost inevitable, therefore, that the great expansion in the mining of silver-bearing copper ore at the close of the Middle Ages should help to destroy the type of mining enterprise characteristic of the thirteenth century. Under the pressure of expanding production, larger concessions were granted. It was out of the question for a single miner to work one of these alone.[74] In any case several concessions were often combined in the interest of a more efficient administration.

As a consequence of the growing need for capital the old companies of working miners, common in the late twelfth and thirteenth centuries, were replaced by new companies of absentee shareholders. Parts grew more numerous. They were sold to local noblemen and landed gentry, to monasteries, merchants, sometimes to municipal governments and even to universities. By the beginning of the sixteenth century a division of mining companies into 128 parts (*Kuxen*) was usual in silver and copper mining in Saxony and Bohemia. There were companies with as many as 256, with 384, and (in at least one case) 640 parts.[75] Even these numerous parts were sometimes subdivided.

After the original capital had been raised, all the partners could be called on to meet their share in any additional expenditures. Dividends were sometimes paid in ore, the ore being separated near the mines into a number of piles of various sizes, one for each partner. When the company sold the ore, or smelted it and sold the metal, dividends were paid in cash. The actual direction of the enterprise was left increasingly to managers and foremen. They hired the hewers, barrowmen and winders to work in the pits, paid them and supervised their labour. As the number of partners and the partners living at some distance from the mine multiplied, it became difficult, if not impossible, for the shareholders to meet frequently to settle matters of policy. In the late fifteenth and early sixteenth centuries the weekly meeting gave way to the bi-weekly, the monthly, the quarterly and the semi-annual meeting. There were partners who never appeared even at these infrequent meetings. They appointed local agents to manage their interests and to represent them in dealing with the managers.

In spite of such absentee proprietorship and of the wide distribution of mining shares, the actual enterprises were seldom large even in the

[74] Cf. E. Gothein, 'Beiträge zur Geschichte des Bergbaus im Schwarzwald', *Zeitschrift für die Geschichte des Oberrheins*, N.F., II (1887), 435–6.

[75] Cf. Hoppe, *Der Silberbergbau zu Schneeberg*, 149–56.

chief silver-mining districts. In each district there were commonly a number of separate competing units. At Joachimstal the chief companies had normally only from sixteen to thirty-two work-people on their payrolls. There were actually small ventures with only four or five employees. So far as can be ascertained, even the largest units of private enterprise in mining at the time of the Reformation maintained only a small labour force compared with several of the larger collieries in Great Britain a century afterwards, following the great expansion between 1575 and 1640 in the English and Scottish coal-mining industry.

Yet, as a result of the cleavage between capital and labour, the miners of argentiferous copper ores, together with some of the miners of tin and lead ores, had lost by the mid-sixteenth century most of the special privileges granted by the princes and overlords who had claimed regalian rights during the twelfth and thirteenth centuries. It was the owners of parts in the mining companies and the experts in the new mining technique who fell heir to such privileges, in so far as they persisted, and in so far as fresh privileges were granted in connection with newly developed mines. The exclusion of craftsmen from access to the mastership in some towns led to the organisation of journeymen's gilds. In a somewhat similar way the creation of large groups of wage-earning miners led to the formation of pitmen's associations for keeping up wages and maintaining decent working conditions. Such associations appeared at Freiberg early in the fifteenth century and at the principal mining districts in the Erzgebirge early in the sixteenth. At Joachimstal and Schneeberg dissatisfied miners struck work. The new associations and the strikes indicate how little was left of the community which the European peoples had sometimes achieved in connection with industrial labour during the first great wave of economic progress and prosperity in the twelfth and early thirteenth centuries.

To reach Strieder's conclusion that the modern struggle between capital and labour originated at the juncture of the fifteenth and sixteenth centuries would be too simple. The mining communities were split at this time not in two ways but in three. In addition to the working wage-earners and their capitalist employers, there were the holders of regalian rights. As we shall see in a moment, this third group was gaining tremendously in strength and assertiveness on the eve of the Reformation. It held the balance of power in so far as mining enterprise was concerned, though probably not to the same extent in connection with metallurgical enterprise. While the princes can hardly be represented as defenders of the wage-earning miners against their employers, they were unwilling to have the private companies gain the ascendancy in the mining communities. That ascendancy princes reserved for themselves.

The princes and other regalian lords were obliged to call on wealthy merchants or financiers for help. The problems of draining pits and of ridding underground passages from noxious and explosive gases concerned these lords. They found it desirable not to leave such matters to the numerous groups of concessionaires, to be dealt with piecemeal by each group. It was recognised that the drainage of a mining field was actually a single task, which could be met most effectively by a single drainage system. Some of the greatest merchant-financiers of the Renaissance helped the regalian lords in meeting the costs. These wealthy men, who patronised the leading artists and lent money to kings, popes and emperors, furnished much of the capital needed to drive long adits and to set up expensive drainage machinery. The Fuggers and Welsers and other leading mercantile families of Augsburg, Nuremberg, Leipzig and other flourishing German towns participated in many ventures of the kind throughout Central Europe. They extended their investments into Spain and Sweden. In return they received shares in the mining companies whose pits they helped to drain.

What was the condition of the workers in the mines after the cleavage that took place between capital and labour in some of the most prosperous mining districts during the late fifteenth and early sixteenth centuries? In spite of their loss of economic independence, the working miners in Germany retained something of the dignified social status that had attached to their profession earlier in the Middle Ages. In his best-known treatise, which appeared first in 1556, when the labour struggles at the ore mines of Central Europe had been going on for two generations, Agricola wrote that 'not even the common worker in the mines is vile and abject'. He knew at first hand conditions in the most populous and highly developed mining settlements of Saxony and western Bohemia. He had spent a considerable period as a physician at Joachimstal, where the cleavage between the miners and their employers was perhaps as wide as anywhere in Europe.

Carried on even more than during the thirteenth century in the mountains and high valleys, amid some of the most dramatic scenery in the world, mining retained a romance and even a certain magic which accompanies the conquest of nature. The work of the mountain men, as the miners were called in German, also encouraged the kind of courage and resourcefulness that proved invaluable in the army and that so warlike a people held in particular esteem. With the help of their experience in driving subterranean passages, miners brought from the silver-mining districts of the eastern Alps in 1529 to defend Vienna are said to have met and outwitted the Turks, who were trying to tunnel their way under and into the city.[76]

Later, in seventeenth-century England, a customs officer, engaged in pressing men into the navy for war with the Dutch, spurned the keelmen who loaded coal into ships from the mines near Newcastle, saying it 'would do more harm than good...to have such nasty creatures on board' the men-of-war.[77] Such an attitude towards members of the German mining settlements would have been hardly conceivable at the time of the Reformation. In recruiting their units the German army officers preferred miners to townsmen and even to peasants. The search for silver-bearing ores in medieval Europe had not stained the bodies of the workmen or made them social outcasts as coal mining later was to do. Many miners had their Saturday night baths with an efficient regularity that we associate with the Germans. Silver was thought of as an excellent thing in itself. Digging for it was still widely regarded as a more honourable way of earning a living than accumulating it in strong boxes by sharp financial practices. The calling of the miner, Agricola remarked, 'excels in honour and dignity that of the merchant trading for lucre'.[78]

In France, as well as in Germany, princes frequently treated the miners with a consideration that they did not always accord the greatest merchants of the age. After confiscating mines of silver-bearing lead and copper ores in Lyonnais and Beaujolais belonging to Jacques Coeur, perhaps the richest French merchant of the time, Charles VII was faced with the task of reviving these enterprises. In 1454 the royal officials engaged for this purpose a large number of miners, some of the most skilful of them Germans. These work-people were sumptuously housed and lavishly nourished with varied meats, wines and fruits, such as might have aroused the envy of the most ambitious twentieth-century trade-union leader if he had had the taste for excellent dining common among the wealthy in nineteenth-century Europe.[79]

Large-scale private enterprise seems to have made its most striking progress in some branches of metallurgy, rather than in mining. The principal establishments for producing silver and copper represented a heavier concentration of buildings and labour than was apparently

[76] Wolfstrigl-Wolfskron, *Die Tiroler Erzbergbaue*, 393; Leopold Ranke, *History of the Reformation in Germany* (trans. by Sarah Austin, London, 1905), 582–3.

[77] Nef, *The British Coal Industry*, II, 151.

[78] *De re metallica* (Hoover edition), 24. Biringuccio took the same view of the moral superiority of the miner to the merchant.

[79] S. Luce, 'De l'exploitation des mines et de la condition des ouvriers mineurs en France au XVe siècle', *Revue des Questions Historiques*, XXI (1877), 192–5.

to be found in any single mining company. It was the discovery of the new method of separating copper and silver that led to the erection of the most impressive metallurgical works. These *Saigerhütten* were built in Saxony, Thuringia, the Tyrol and Carinthia. Agricola described one of them in *De re metallica*. It consisted of four parallel walls, the longest more than a hundred metres long, broken by transverse walls into a series of rooms of various sizes and with diverse costly equipment. This included a great many hearths and furnaces, bellows, hammers and stamping machinery – mostly driven by water power – and a variety of tools and crucibles, all for treating the metals in different stages of manufacture.[80] At Hohenkirchen near Georgental in Thuringia, where the Fuggers built such a factory, scores of workmen were employed.[81] The same family had another equally impressive factory near Villach, at Arnoldstein.[82] Supplies of argentiferous ore were brought to both these establishments from mines at Neusohl in Hungary, hundreds of miles away.

Nowhere else in Europe, perhaps, was there a greater concentration of capital and labour in a single plant than in these *Saigerhütten*, except at the alum works of the Pope at Tolfa, at a few salt springs like those at Salins in Franche-Comté, where the houses and pans were huddled into an enclosure as large as a fair-sized medieval village,[83] and at a few shipbuilding yards, especially the famous arsenal at Venice. Unlike the chief alum and salt works and the largest shipyards, the chief *Saigerhütten* were owned and operated by private capitalists, and not by the sovereign rulers or under their direction. The assertion of regalian authority in connection with ores was hardly possible so far away from the mines.

IV. *The Growth in the Authority of the Prince*

Nothing limited so much the power of private capitalists in the principal mining districts as the growing authority of the regalian lords. In the later Middle Ages medieval constitutionalism was breaking down. The time of Machiavelli was an age of growing despotism. The kings of France and Spain and the emperors, who were

[80] *De re metallica* (Hoover edition), 491–535.

[81] Ernst Koch, 'Das Hütten- und Hammerwerk der Fugger zu Hohenkirchen bei Georgenthal in Thuringen, 1495–1549', *Zeitschrift des Vereins für Thüringische Geschichte*, N. F., XXVI (1926), 296–306.

[82] F. Dobel, 'Ueber den Bergbau und Handel des Jacob und Anton Fugger in Kärnten und Tirol, 1495–1560', *Zeitschrift des Historischen Vereins für Schwaben und Neuburg*, IX (1882), 194–6.

[83] Nef, *The Conquest of the Material World*, 104–6.

Machiavelli's contemporaries, together with scores of other princes, lay and ecclesiastical, in Italy and Central Europe, set about increasing their power at the expense of all independent authority. Mining communities were governed more and more paternally and even despotically. The capitalists, as well as the workers, were expected to obey the laws and orders of the prince and his officers.

The independence of the mining companies, and of such metallurgical enterprises as were closely dependent on the mines, was curtailed by the enactment of regulations far more comprehensive and rigid than those of the thirteenth and fourteenth centuries. During the first forty years of the sixteenth century the issue of mining laws reached a high point.[84] More mining officials were always being appointed and their authority was always being extended. Saxon mining law, as embodied in a code of 1509 issued by the duke of Saxony for his newly developed mines of Annaberg, became the basis for mining law throughout northern and eastern Germany. In southern Germany and Central Europe generally, the regulations were somewhat less comprehensive. But everywhere the new codes, notable among which were the Austrian regulations of 1517, curbed the initiative of private investors in the mines, forges and mills.

Problems connected with the digging of long adits, which the princes often helped to finance, provided them with an excuse for increasing their supervision over all kinds of mining operations.[85] Any small scheme for draining or ventilating the pits, or for using fire to shatter the rock that was encountered in sinking shafts, had to be approved by the prince's mining officials. An *Oberberghauptmann* was given general authority by the regalian lord over the entire administration. At periodic intervals of thirteen days or so, one of the chief officers, the *Bergmeister*, accompanied by a group of technical experts, visited each mining enterprise to see that the regulations contained in the codes and in the supplementary orders issued by the central mining administration were enforced. The wage rates and the hours of labour for the miners and the metallurgical workers were settled by this administration. Managers and foremen who worked for the mining companies and for the masters of forges could be appointed only with the approval of the prince's officials. They could be discharged without the consent of their employers, but the shareholders in the mining companies could not discharge their own managers and foremen without the approval of the prince's officers.

Officers appointed by the regalian lords had frequently participated in the working partnerships of the thirteenth and fourteenth centuries.

[84] Cf. Schmoller, 'Die Entwicklung der Unternehmung', 979–82.

[85] Cf. *ibid.*, 972, 976.

But the new regulations forbade such officials to hold parts in the mining companies, in order to ensure their loyalty to the prince. The number of these officials was continually increasing, as the work of the prince's administration was amplified. In some cases, as at Kuttenberg in Bohemia, the officials were almost as numerous as the hewers in the mines.[86] Many princes took advantage of the dissatisfaction felt by the mining companies and the buyers of ore with the private masters of the local smelting works to engross those enterprises into their own hands.[87] They provided chapels for the miners and smelters, and looked after the health as well as the religious instruction of all the workmen. Rules were passed forbidding the introduction of prostitutes into the industrial communities. Swearing was prohibited, probably because of the superstitious dread of its consequences.

In every direction the princes and other regalian lords tightened their grip on the expanding mining communities. The real directing unit ceased to be the individual enterprise and became the ruler's administration. By the Reformation many of the rulers were coming to treat as their property, not only the minerals which contained precious metals but also the mines.[88] Some, like those at Mansfeld and Goslar, actually became state enterprises.

This movement towards an administrative control of mining by political rulers was not confined to the German countries. It was general on the continent. The abundance of silver-bearing ores in Central Europe made the movement especially prominent there. But the French kings were proceeding in the same direction. In the late fifteenth and early sixteenth centuries they set out to gain control of mining enterprise throughout the realm. The problem of control was in some ways more difficult than in the small principalities of Central Europe. Size was a considerable handicap to effective government. Furthermore the French kings had the problem of absorbing and making their own the regalian authority exercised by territorial lords, whilst in Germany, as we have seen, it was the territorial lords who absorbed the regalian authority.

A royal mining administration was eventually created for the entire French kingdom. In general character it resembled the smaller territorial mining administrations of Central Europe. While private landlords were allowed to dig for ore in their own lands and those of their tenants, Louis XI issued an edict in 1471 requiring them to report within forty days the discovery of any minerals, and to signify their intention of working them. If they failed to comply, or if they

[86] *Ibid.*, 973. [87] Cf. Schmoller, *op. cit.*, 692–3.

[88] Cf. A. Zycha, *Das Recht des ältesten deutchen Bergbaues bis ins 13. Jahrhundert* (Berlin, 1899), 157; Schmoller, *op. cit.*, 1018.

did not wish to finance an enterprise of their own, the royal mining administration was instructed either to lease the mine or to work it directly. All mining, even that carried on by private landlords in their own lands, was placed under the supervision of the royal mining administration. The crown could send experts to search for ore in privately owned lands without the consent of the owner. All mines which they found were at the disposal of the royal mining administration. If, in accordance with the edict, the crown worked or leased mines in privately owned lands, the landlords were to receive compensation for damage to the soil. They were to receive also a portion of the returns, beyond the 'tenth' due to the sovereign. The holders of royal concessions and their workmen were exempted from the payment of ordinary taxes. All mining disputes, except those touching the property of the landlords, were to be settled, not by the ordinary courts, but by the king's principal mining official, the *maistre général*, or his lieutenants.[89]

While the *parlement de Paris* modified the edict of 1471 in minor respects before registering it, its main provisions were apparently upheld. During the next seventy years, the royal mining administration occasionally organised enterprises under its direct control for working silver-bearing ores. More often concessions were leased to royal favourites or capital was raised for mining by selling to merchants and traders parts in companies organised in much the same way as those in Germany.[90] Results were meagre, mainly no doubt because France was poor compared with Central Europe in silver-bearing ores, partly because of the administrative difficulties of supervising activity in remote parts of what was for the medieval European a vast realm. But practical disappointments interfered little with the assertion of the principle that the king had a title to all valuable mines within his dominion.

By the middle of the sixteenth century the regalian claims of the French crown covered most of the country north and east of the Pyrenees and west of the Spanish Netherlands, Lorraine, Franche-Comté, and the Alps. Concessions were granted by royal patent to mine in almost every part of the kingdom, though not all the French nobles willingly permitted the royal concessionaires access to ores in their lands.[91] In Lorraine and Franche-Comté, which were not yet a part of France, the local rulers regulated and supervised the operations of their

89 *Recueil général des anciennes lois francaises*, x, 626–7.

90 Archives nationales, Paris, Minutier central, fonds XIX, liasse 152 (documents concerning André de Rozembourch of Bohemia and Nicholas Hermans of Brussels, masters of the French king's mines and forges of gold and silver, 1539).

91 Archives nationales, XI A8624, ff. 271–4 (Ordonnance sur les mines et leur exploitation, 1560).

mining concessionaires, as in France. In Lorraine the dukes apparently threw open the mines to all comers, as had been the general practice of medieval rulers in Central Europe.[92]

With the growth of sovereign political power on the continent, efforts were made to extend regalian rights to cover base ores. In Central Europe several territorial rulers successfully brought seams of iron ore, as well as of lead and tin, into the same category with ores containing silver or gold. Iron-making enterprises in Styria, Austria and the upper Harz were subjected by the duke of Styria, the emperor and the duke of Brunswick to taxes, regulations and inspections similar to those which had become the rule in the silver-mining communities. The French king, François I (1515–47), also interested himself in iron production. In 1542 he levied a tax on all forges and furnaces throughout the kingdom. Its collection was confided to the royal mining administration.

The reception of Roman law in France and other continental countries in the late fifteenth and early sixteenth centuries helped rulers to stretch their regalian claims, both because a very large proportion of all mines had belonged to the state in the late Roman Empire, and because the imperial tax of a tenth on the produce of mines in privately owned lands had been levied indiscriminately on all ores or metal,[93] at a time when all metals were scarce. Here we have an illustration of the difference between the classical revival of the twelfth century and that of the later Middle Ages. One side of ancient experience – the administrative practices of a few districts as these practices were handed across the centuries by custom and tradition – helped the Europeans in the gothic age almost to universalise the essentially democratic community of free miners. Another side of classical experience – formal Roman law, as recorded in the codes and digests of the Empire – helped the European rulers in a later age of waxing political authority almost to universalise the claim of the state to a revenue from all mining operations.

With the increasing need for capital in mining and metallurgy in

[92] Archives nationales, K. 876, no. 14 (Des mines de Lorraine, 1520).

[93] As we now know that Roman law did not deprive the private landlord of the ownership of mines under his land (see above, p. 706), it seems inconsistent, at the first sight, to argue that the revival of Roman law helped the European princes to extend their regalian rights at the end of the Middle Ages, to cover base ores. It is true nevertheless. The use to which Roman law was put rested, to some extent, on a misinterpretation. Until the work of Achenbach was published in 1869, European jurists quite generally assumed that property in mines had been divorced from property in land under the Roman Empire. In the Middle Ages such a view was probably widely held by men learned in the law. It was encouraged by a misconstruction by Lombard commentators of passages in the Theodosian code and the code of Justinian (cf. Lewis, *The Stannaries*, 66–8). Roman law, moreover, could be legitimately invoked in favour of putting base in the same category with precious metals, for the tax that had been levied by the Roman emperors on the produce of mines had fallen on both indiscriminately (cf. Alfons Müllner, *Geschichte des Eisens in Krain, Görz und Istrien*, 195–6).

the age of the Renaissance, a point had been reached, especially in the production of silver and copper, where the costs could be met only by the richest merchants, whose power came from their skill in trade and in managing money and credit, or by kings, princes and overlords, whose power rested on their inherited position and their political rights. In mining and metallurgy, earlier than in other great industries, Europe faced a choice between the dominance of private capitalists or the dominance of sovereign authorities. On the continent the sovereign authorities generally prevailed, at least insofar as the principal mining enterprises were concerned.

This fact had been obscured by the conspicuous place occupied by certain enormously rich merchants, among whom the Fuggers of Augsburg have received the most attention from historical writers, at least since the time, a century ago, when Michelet wrote his chapters on 'la banque'. The cost of maintaining an elaborate mining administration strained the resources of sovereign political authorities at the end of the Middle Ages. They had recourse in this connection, as in so many others, to the money bags of merchants of great wealth – among whom these same Fuggers occupied a place of the greatest prominence. Territorial princes, who borrowed money in large amounts, sometimes repaid the loan by granting their creditors, for a term of years, a portion of the revenue which they derived from their regalian rights. In extreme cases they even put the merchants in possession for a time of their entire mining administration, with all its duties and privileges, including the authority to grant mining concessions. This happened at Reichenstein, in Silesia, where the *regale* belonged to the dukes of Münsterberg-Oels.[94] Again, the important quicksilver mines of Almadén, which had once played a considerable role in the economy of the Romans, were leased for four-year periods to the Fuggers.[95]

For all this, the ultimate authority of the political rulers to control the mines was hardly questioned. If the merchant fell out of favour, it was always possible for the prince to confiscate his property. In 1453 the French king, Charles VII, acting in what nineteenth-century Europeans would have almost universally condemned as an arbitrary and despotic manner, confiscated the three mining enterprises in Lyonnais and Beaujolais belonging to Jacques Coeur of Bourges, the most glamorous merchant of the fifteenth century.[96]

Princes, lay and ecclesiastical, welcomed the participation of mer-

[94] E. Fink, 'Die Bergwerksunternehmungen der Fugger in Schlesien', *Zeitschrift des Vereins für Geschichte und Altertum Schlesiens*, XXVIII (1894), 308.

[95] Konrad Häbler, *Die Geschichte der Fugger'schen Handlung in Spanien* (Weimar, 1897), 93–5.

[96] Cf. Pierre Clément, *Jacques Coeur et Charles VII* (Paris, 1866), 147ff, 342–4, 420–6.

chants in mining. They borrowed from them freely to get money to exercise their rights of pre-emption. They even shared control of the mining administration with them. But in continental Europe the course of history was not running in favour of mercantile leadership, as it was destined to run for a time in the late eighteenth and nineteenth centuries. When it came to a show-down, the prince and not the merchant held the brute force that was decisive. In a cruel age, which was not to be the last, he was capable of exercising this force in the most ferocious ways. In the sphere of art alone was the subject left any real independence. In the last analysis, everything material was claimed by the prince, at a time when the material aspects of existence were coming into the foreground of thought, worship and conduct to a greater extent than ever before in western history. The absolute authority that the prince exercised over the bodies as well as the economic existence of his subjects has been described in unforgettable detail by Ranke, in his chapter on Ferrara under Alphonso II. The duke had concentrated every scrap of prosperity in the court itself. The country was poverty-stricken. His control over industry extended to food, including the prime necessities of flour and bread. Even nobles were limited in their right to hunt, and one day the bodies of six men were left hanging in the market-place, with dead pheasants tied to their feet, to show, it was said, that the culprits had been shot while poaching on the duke's preserves.[97] On the continent the growing strength of despots made fleeting the control exercised by mercantile capital in the mining administrations of the political rulers. At the close of the Middle Ages in most European states it was the political ruler who held the reins which guided the chief mining enterprises.

In England and Scotland no such bulwarks against the independent power of private capital in mining were built up during the later Middle Ages. Henry VIII retained the regalian rights that his predecessors had exercised during the twelfth and thirteenth centuries. He collected a revenue from mines royal and he continued to appoint officials to oversee and protect the royal rights over mineral property. But the share of the crown in the direction of mining had not been extended. No national mining administration, like that introduced in France by the Valois kings, had been established. No legislation had been passed like the French edict of 1413, making it lawful for the crown, and the crown alone, to collect a royalty on the produce of all mines worked throughout the realm. No legislation had been passed like the French edict of 1471, permitting the crown to send experts to search for ore in privately owned land. No new codes governing

[97] Leopold Ranke, *The Ecclesiastical and Political History of the Popes of Rome* (trans. Sarah Austin, London, 1841), bk. VI, ch. vii.

mining were issued, at a time when mining legislation in Central Europe reached a peak. No apparent effort was made to regulate more minutely operations of private mining companies holding concessions from the royal authority. While the crown maintained its control over mines containing precious metals and mines under the royal demesne, while it maintained the rights of the royal family in the stannaries, elsewhere all base ores and minerals were left at the disposal of private landlords.

The resources of Great Britain in gold- and silver-bearing ores proved to be negligible. The crown was to sell a great part of the royal demesne in the late sixteenth and seventeenth centuries. The English tin mines were not again to occupy as prominent a place in European mining history as in the Middle Ages. For all three reasons the power of the sovereign in mineral matters was on the point of contracting in England, at the very time when it was expanding strikingly on the continent. Stronger than the French crown in its control over mining in the twelfth and thirteenth centuries, the English crown was potentially much weaker at the time of Henry VIII's break with Rome.

These differences between English and continental mining history in the later Middle Ages had an influence upon industrial development in modern times. They helped to make possible the regime of free economic enterprise which is associated primarily with the English speaking countries. What are the explanations for the failure of the English kings during the late fifteenth and early sixteenth centuries to follow the course taken by so many continental rulers and to add to their authority over mines?[98]

The lack in Great Britain of ores which contained large quantities of precious metals and which were generally acknowledged as royal property was undoubtedly something of a stumbling block. The great abundance of such ores in Central Europe enabled the princes to establish a control over mines in many districts. When an opportunity presented itself to extend regalian rights to mines of base ores, the form of administration was ready to hand. Again England's size proved a disadvantage. While it is common today to think of Great Britain as a small island, in the sixteenth and seventeenth centuries the area covered by England and Wales was much larger than that of the most of the principalities of Central Europe. The division of sovereignty within the Empire during the later Middle Ages made it easier than in England to strengthen the regalian rights which went with sovereignty. In an age when the slowness of travel and communication

[98] For a development of this subject, see J. U. Nef, *Industry and Government in France and England, 1540–1640* (Ithaca, N.Y., 1957), 5–12.

added to the difficulties of governing distant regions, this division often reduced to manageable dimensions the territory within which a single ruler exercised his authority over mines, and made it comparatively easy for him to maintain a staff of obedient officers sufficient to enforce his authority.

But such explanations of the divergence between the history of the mining *regale* in England and on the continent are inadequate. Neither the size of France, considerably larger than England, nor the lack of abundant supplies of ores rich in precious metals, prevented the French kings from strengthening their regalian rights. More adequate explanations of the special position occupied by England in the development of mining law in the later Middle Ages are to be found in two legal conditions. Sovereign authority was centralised earlier than in any continental country, and property claimed by the subjects, over which the crown had failed to establish its control possessed greater immunity through the greater effectiveness of the English parliament as compared with any restraining bodies on the continent.

Sovereign authority was centralised in England during the late eleventh and twelfth centuries, at a time when medieval constitutionalism was strong. This made the medieval estates, in which mercantile interests were represented, a more essential part of the machinery of government in England than in other countries. Early centralisation also made it necessary to create a system of legal principles common to the whole realm, before imperial Roman law had been sufficiently recovered by medieval jurists to permit it to take its place as that system.[99] In imperial Roman law the sovereign political authority was much more pre-eminent than in the European practice of the eleventh and twelfth centuries.

The early authority of the English crown, which was a limited authority, fixed limits to the exercise of regalian rights. They proved less elastic than the regalian rights of most continental rulers. Partly as a result of the development of common law, the English kings were unable to use the revival of Roman law in the late fifteenth and early sixteenth centuries as so many continental rulers were doing, to help them to claim a royalty on the produce of mines of every description. In Europe generally the authority of great vassal landlords had been stronger in feudal times than in the later Middle Ages. The early strength of the English parliament and of the English common law helped landlords to conserve their property rights.

The first Tudor monarchs, Henry VII and Henry VIII, might nevertheless have made an energetic bid to extend their authority over

[99] See C. H. McIlwain, 'Medieval Estates', *Cambridge Medieval History* (Cambridge, 1932), VII, 709–14.

mines, as the French kings were doing, if mining and metallurgy had been growing in importance as rapidly in England as on the continent, and if they had not been confronted by a parliament, composed of lawyers and propertied men, determined to resist encroachments upon the property rights they represented. The early Tudors showed great skill in exercising their political powers, at a time when the will of the king was still regarded by nearly all Englishmen as supreme in matters of government. According to the Spanish ambassador, Henry VII expressed the desire 'to keep his subjects low, because riches would make them haughty'.[100] It is improbable that he would have been more disposed than continental rulers to give merchants a free hand to dominate the mines if their value had been as obvious in England as it was in Central Europe. His son, Henry VIII, was out to raise all the money he could. If he bothered little with the mines it was very likely because his advisers regarded them as of trifling importance. He had a hard time, moreover, in getting his way with parliament in matters of property, as is shown by its not ineffective opposition to the dissolution of the lesser monasteries in 1536, and by its emasculation in 1539 of the king's proposed Statute of Proclamations as finally passed.

Scarce metals were still the principal objective for which mining and metallurgical operations were carried on in Europe before the mid-sixteenth century. Great Britain was poor in the ores providing those metals, rich in the ones of *base* metals and in coal. Partly perhaps on that account the development of mining in England during the late fifteenth and early sixteenth centuries was very slow. The searches for silver-bearing ores, conducted on the eve of the Reformation with the help of miners from Germany, gave disappointing results. The production of tin increased only some 60 or 70 per cent between 1470 and 1540,[101] as compared with an increase of four- or fivefold in the production of metals in Central Europe. The increase little more than offset the slump in output that had occurred in England during the first half of the fifteenth century. The supremacy retained during the Middle Ages by the tin of Devon and Cornwall in continental markets was threatened by the progress of tin mining in Spain, Bohemia, Bavaria and Saxony. In Saxony alone, around 1518, something like a third as much tin was being produced as in England. English lead was also finding more competition abroad than in the past. In 1539 one of Thomas Cromwell's correspondents described the lead mines of England as 'dead'.[102] Until after the dissolution of the monasteries,

[100] *Calendar of State Papers, Spanish, 1485–1509*, 177.
[101] G. R. Lewis, *The Stannaries* (Cambridge (Mass.), 1907), 253.
[102] W. Gough, *The Mines of Mendip* (Oxford, 1930), 65.

mining and metallurgy were carried on mainly by the tiny enterprises, which used the methods prevalent on the continent in the thirteenth and fourteenth centuries. The sluggish growth of English metallurgy in an age of remarkable metallurgical expansion in many European countries, helped to keep the field open to private mining enterprise, unfettered by government control, at a time when the crown was strong. Later, during the late sixteenth and early seventeenth centuries, an even more remarkable industrial expansion connected especially with the use of coal, occurred in England. But, by that time, royal authority had grown so weak that the kinds of state control over economic development which had been effectively set up in many continental countries, proved impracticable.[103]

The English crown held on to the very considerable mineral rights which it inherited from an earlier age. But a variety of conditions blocked it from extending these rights at the very time when such an extension had become the price of effective political authority in mineral matters even more in England than on the continent.[104] Such resources as the English crown held by virtue of medieval law crumbled to dust in its hands when coal and iron ore replaced silver and gold as the main treasure of the subsoil.

X. *The Transition to Modern Times*

At the end of the Middle Ages the rapid development of continental mining and metallurgy showed signs of waning. The discovery of ores extraordinarily rich in silver in South and Central America, and particularly the opening about 1546 of the famous mines of Potosí in Bolivia, dealt a heavy blow to the European silver-mining industry. Treasure from the new world could be delivered in Europe, even by the unwieldy Spanish galleons, more cheaply than the trained miners of Saxony, Bohemia, Tyrol, Hungary and Silesia could dig and smelt their ores and ship their metal, with the help of the most skilful German, Hungarian and Bohemian engineers and technical experts. While a few mining communities in Silesia, and at Freiberg and Goslar in Germany, continued to prosper after the middle of the sixteenth century, a slump had begun by that time in the output of silver and gold in most parts of Central Europe and also in Alsace and Sweden.

Fifty years later this slump in the production of precious metals had gone very far. On the eve of the Thirty Years' War (1618–48), which was to bring mining in Central Europe temporarily almost to a standstill, the annual output of silver was perhaps less than a third as

103 Nef, *Industry and Government in France and England*, 149ff.

104 See also the discussion in Nef, *Rise of the British Coal Industry*, I, 267–85.

great as it had been in the twenties and thirties of the sixteenth century.[105] Even in Sweden, which unlike most of Central Europe prospered industrially during the hundred years following the Reformation, the production of silver in the best years of the mid-seventeenth century was hardly half what it had been in the 1540s.[106]

At the close of the Middle Ages the progress of continental mining was bound up, almost as much as in the twelfth and thirteenth centuries, with the prosperity of mines rich in silver. The collapse of the market for European silver brought a reduction in the value of argentiferous copper and lead ore. Conditions proved almost equally unfavourable to other kinds of mining. Before the end of the sixteenth century, the rapid expansion in iron production[107] and coal mining on the continent came to an end. Thus the signs of industrial revolution at the end of the Middle Ages proved deceptive. The remarkable growth in the output from mining and some other heavy industries lasted only during the interval between the Hundred Years War and the beginning of the religious wars in the mid-sixteenth century. It was two hundred years more before the rate of growth in industrial output again became as rapid on the continent generally as it had been during the late fifteenth and the early sixteenth centuries.

What was lacking to bring about a development of mining and metallurgy that would lead directly to the wealthy industrial civilisation destined to dominate the whole of Western Europe in the nineteenth century? Why was the new machinery for draining and ventilating mines at considerable depths, devised in connection with the mining of argentiferous copper ores, not taken over extensively in the mining of tin, lead and, above all, coal on the continent, as it was in Great Britain in the late sixteenth and seventeenth centuries?

After the Reformation warfare on the continent became more destructive and more damaging to heavy industry.[108] The dissolution of the English monasteries and other ecclesiastical foundations played into the hands of private landlords and merchants eager to exploit mineral wealth.[109] But in continental mining districts, the course taken by the religious struggle was different and the Church retained a greater portion of the landed property. Some churchmen possessed

[105] J. U. Nef, 'Silver production in Central Europe, 1450–1618', *Journal of Political Economy*, XLIX, no. 4 (1941), 589.

[106] Eli F. Heckscher, *Sveriges Ekonomiska Historia* (Stockholm, 1936), II, 439.

[107] In Styria the output of iron reached a high point during the middle decades of the sixteenth century. From 1601 to 1625 the annual production at Innerberg-Eisenerz was considerably less than from 1536 to 1560 (Bittner, 'Das Eisenwesen', 490, 628–9). In Siegerland the number of forges was reduced by half in the late sixteenth century (Richard Utsch, *Die Entwicklung und volkswirtschaftliche Bedeutung des Eisenerzbergbaues und der Eisenindustrie im Siegerland* (Görlitz, 1913), 34).

[108] Cf. Nef, *War and Human Progress*, esp. Pt. I.

[109] Nef, *The Conquest of the Material World*, Ch. 5.

regalian rights by virtue of their political authority. Ecclesiastical foundations were less ready than lay landlords to invest large capitals in mines and metallurgical plant. They were unwilling to lease their mines on as favourable terms as lay landlords. Again, the natural difficulties of carriage through mountainous country and the numerous tolls and taxes, which stood in the way of transporting heavy ores and coal for considerable distances, imposed handicaps upon the progress of mining on the continent. The great authority over the mines and the mining ventures, established at the end of the Middle Ages by so many continental rulers, discouraged private enterprise.

At the time of the Reformation political considerations frequently outweighed economic in the guidance of mining and metallurgy. While this helped European rulers to strengthen their authority over their subjects, it was on the whole unfavourable to the growth of industrial output, at least to the growth in the output of products like iron and coal,[110] upon whose abundance the progress of modern industrial civilisation has been so largely based.[111] It was only in the eighteenth and nineteenth centuries, after changes in the mining laws first of France and later of Germany made conditions more favourable to the initiative of private capitalists,[112] that the output of mines again grew rapidly in either country.

In exploiting their silver resources, the western European peoples were only following in the footsteps of their classical predecessors, who had exploited the surface supplies of *argentiferous* ores in Spain and all along the shores of the Mediterranean. If the western Europeans had turned aside from the supplies of iron and coal, as the classical peoples had done, or had retreated after starting to exploit coal and iron ore as the Chinese had done, they could hardly have created the industrial world of the late nineteenth century, which seemed to offer a foretaste of the millennium for those who measured happiness primarily in material terms.

[110] Cf. Nef, *Industry and Government*, 68–76.

[111] The late Professor Strieder made much of the collaboration between the German princes and the merchants as an element in the great expansion of mining and metallurgy in Germany and Central Europe in the late fifteenth and early sixteenth centuries (*Studien zur Geschichte kapitalistischer Organisationsformen*, 2nd edn, 362–3). To some extent, he seems to have put the cart before the horse. As Inama-Sternegg pointed out, in connection with the progress of the German salt-making industry at an earlier period, it was less that the princes' control caused the expansion, than that the expansion enabled the princes to strengthen their control. 'So ist schliesslich mehr von einer Beförderung des Regalitätsgedanken durch die Entwicklung der Salinen, als von einer Beförederung des Salinenwesens durch die Entwicklung der Regalität zu sprechen.' (K. T. von Inama-Sternegg, 'Zur Verfassungsgeschichte der deutschen Salinen im Mittelalter', *Sitzungsberichte der kaiserlichen Akademie der Wissenschaft*, CXI (1866), 578.) Otto Hue found these remarks applicable to German mining. 'Dieselbe Wechselwirkung vollzog sich auch zwischen der Bergbauentwicklung und der Ausdehnung de Bergregal anspruche' (*Die Bergarbeiter* (Stuttgart, 1910), I, 93).

[112] Marcel Rouff, *Les Mines de charbon en France* (Paris, 1922), esp. part I, chaps. ii, iv, and pp. 63–4; Schmoller, 'Die Entwicklung der Unternehmen', 1027–8.

It is perhaps beyond the scope of history to enquire what would have happened if there had been no America, and no regions in the north of Europe rich in mineral resources and rich also in industrious work-people.[113] But it is certain that the progress of heavy industries in early modern times was not in those European countries which had been in the vanguard of civilised life during the Middle Ages. The progress occurred in Sweden, Holland, and above all in Great Britain. All of these countries were protected for various reasons from the full force of the religious struggles and the actual battles. All established, partly with the help of these favours, traditions of constitutional government which facilitated private initiative in the development of natural resources, as in economic enterprise generally.[114]

Many inventions which abridged labour had been made in Europe during the Middle Ages, from the eighth through to the early sixteenth century.[115] Yet the increase in efficiency, obtained by the progress of medieval technology, should not blind us to the prevailing concern of medieval Europeans with technical innovations whose primary purpose was beauty. The priority given more and more in modern times to the multiplication of industrial products for general use was alien to medieval European technique. The pre-eminence of art and craftsmanship as objectives for invention was reaffirmed in the age of the Reformation. The times of Leonardo da Vinci (1452–1519), Carpaccio, Giorgione and Titian, of Raphael, Michelangelo, Dürer and the younger Holbein, of François Clouet and Pieter Breughel the elder (1520?–69), were full of most ingenious inventions which helped in printing, engraving and the other visual arts and in decorative craftsmanship of every kind. During the period *c.*1460–*c.*1540, the Europeans, as they began to colonise on all the earth's continents, were laying foundations for an economy of commodity and delight, that culminated in the age of the baroque.

As we now know, the north of Europe, and Great Britain in particular, in the mid-sixteenth century were on the threshold of a coal economy. That economy was realised during the later sixteenth and seventeenth centuries.[116] It was accompanied and followed by a revolution in technological invention of the sort the Chinese had begun but had failed to pursue. Unlike those earlier efforts of the Chinese, the early industrial revolution in modern Britain led on to

113 For a consideration of this subject, see Nef, *La Naissance de la civilisation industrielle et le monde contemporain*, chs. 4 and 5.

114 Cf. Nef, *Industry and Government*, esp. ch. 5. For the influence on industrial development of Great Britain's geographical isolation and of peace, cf. Nef, *War and Human Progress*, pt. 1. For the influence of the Reformation and the transfer of ecclesiastical property into private hands, cf. Nef, *Conquest of the Material World*, ch. 5.

115 Cf. Lynn White, *Medieval Technology and Social Change* (Oxford, 1962).

116 Cf. Nef, *Rise of the British Coal Industry* (reprint, 1966).

the astounding conquest of the material world which today confronts all mankind.

How did it happen that so long after a number of inventions for using and increasing the production of iron in China had been made (and apparently forgotten even by the Chinese), the Europeans should have pressed on where their predecessors had abandoned the quest? That is a most complicated story, of which we still have only fragments. But a few suggestions are perhaps not out of order, as the subject is of surpassing interest, and as the suggestions indicate that the history of mining and metallurgy, which has engaged us in this chapter, cannot be kept separate from the history of the mind and of manners.

At least three novel developments in intellectual and cultural history, for which there seem to be no equivalent in Chinese or other earlier societies, help us to understand better the coming of industrialism. All of these developments were identified in their beginnings with the period of the early industrial revolution in Great Britain, with the late sixteenth and early seventeenth centuries. All of them had made remarkable headway by the time of the phenomenal leap in rates of growth in output and in population which started, also in Great Britain, two hundred years later at the end of the eighteenth century[117] and then spread to the entire planet. One was the rise among the Europeans of a quantitative mentality more intense than is to be found among the peoples of any earlier society.[118] The second, to which this quantitative mentality contributed, was the rise of modern science, with novel methods of investigation.[119] These new methods revealed new aspects of the physical universe and of biology, and later the practical applications of this new knowledge revolutionised medicine and surgery, as well as the technology of industry, transportation and communication, in the service of the new quantitative mentality. The third development was the spread of gentle manners and of beautiful furniture, appointments, decorations and other objects of delight, from tableware to musical instruments, into the home life of increasing numbers of Europeans. The coming of conditions, among them limited warfare, which led some writers in the mid-eighteenth century to coin the word 'civilisation', contributed to a new optimism among some of the most intelligent and influential Europeans. They came to believe that, for the first time in history, the good in human nature might prove capable of winning out over the evil. This optimism reassured men of science that they could, with

[117] Cf. Nef, *War and Human Progress*, ch. 15.
[118] Cf. Nef, *Cultural Foundations of Industrial Civilization*, esp. chs. 1 and 2.
[119] Cf. Nef, *Conquest of the Material World*, ch. 7.

good consciences, encourage to the uttermost the exploitation for practical purposes of every revolutionary scientific discovery.[120]

These developments of early modern times were not localised in any particular country. They were pan-European, and the optimism they engendered was to spread among the North American settlers. Yet, while the new rational promises and hopes were shared to an increasing extent during the late seventeenth and eighteenth centuries by all the European peoples, and while they were fostered by the baroque economy of commodity and delight which was primarily continental in origin, the rapid progress of a coal economy in Great Britain after the Reformation made that island the original setting for the technological revolution which earlier societies had missed. If the inventive skill which the Europeans had already demonstrated between the eighth and the early sixteenth centuries was to lead to the conquest of the material world, quantitative goals had to take precedence in the minds of men, and inventions to reduce the costs of production, transport, and communication, and to prolong human life, had to be more undividedly pursued than in the past. At the end of the Middle Ages conditions in continental Europe, where mining and metallurgy had been progressing for centuries, were not as favourable for such precedence or for such intense exploitation as they became in Great Britain in the times of Shakespeare and Milton.

Would the triumph of industrialism have occurred in Europe without a change of scene in connection with mining and metallurgy? The answer is probably 'yes'. But it is certain that the change of scene helped to prepare the way for that triumph.

[120] Cf. Nef, *The United States and Civilization*, new rewritten edition (Chicago, 1967), ch. 2 (iv); *Cultural Foundations*, chaps. 5 and 6; and 'Civilization, Industrial Society, and Love', Centre for the Study of Democratic Institutions, Santa Barbara, California, 1961.

CHAPTER XI

Building in Stone in Medieval Western Europe

In the years which have gone by since Werner Sombart[1] called attention to the desirability of investigating the economic history of building, relatively little has been done in that direction with regard to medieval Europe as a whole though some notable contributions have been made in regard to particular buildings and countries. A major difficulty is the scarcity, especially for the earlier Middle Ages, of the kind of record which is essential. Archaeological and literary evidences, though useful, cannot by themselves do much more than indicate the kind of question which the inquirer must ask; for the answers there are needed accounts of the expenditure on building operations. Unfortunately, those relating to important buildings, such as large royal and ecclesiastical works in France during the early fourteenth century,[2] have in many cases been lost. Large numbers, relating to buildings of various kinds in different countries, have survived sporadically; but probably the fullest series in existence is that relating to works carried out for the crown in England. This is the more valuable because it includes not merely summarised accounts, from which relatively little can be learned, but particulars, in some instances even weekly statements, giving the names of workmen with the amounts paid to them and similarly full detail relating to purchases. The ideal collection, which is rare, is that of which the London Bridge Accounts are a sample; these are particulars, extending from week to week or month to month over several centuries, an invaluable record of changes in wages and prices paid at the same undertaking. Other records, especially valuable in the absence of accounts, are contracts between builders and those who did the work for them, and rules laid down by lay or ecclesiastical authorities for those in their employment.

A study of the accounts for the period during which they are relatively abundant and full, that is from the later part of the thirteenth century, suggests that, however architectural styles might vary, the fundamental economic problems connected with building, and the organisation developed to deal with them, were very much the same in the chief countries of western Europe. It is clear also that

[1] *Der moderne Kapitalismus* (Munich and Leipzig), II (1921 edition), 772–3.
[2] Ch.-V. Langlois, in E. Lavisse, *Histoire de France* (Paris), III, ii, 417n. (1901 edition).

this organisation, as it existed at Caernarvon Castle in the thirteenth century, Beauvais in the fourteenth and Eton in the fifteenth, was something different in kind from that prevailing in most medieval industries, in which production was ordinarily limited by the resources and the markets of the individual country craftsman or town gild master. We shall attempt to make clear the characteristics of the industry by considering in turn (i) the impetus given to building; (ii) some technical changes of importance; (iii) the chief problems of supply; (iv) the system of administration; and (v) the conditions and organisation of master workmen and ordinary operatives in the chief building craft, that of the mason.

I. *The Demand for Building*

Feudal conditions were an important stimulus to building, both directly in themselves and indirectly through the attempt to modify or overcome them. Every man with a fief to maintain needed a place of defence, and the number of these, though it cannot be accurately known, must have run to thousands. Many could, no doubt, be fairly easily destroyed and, under strong monarchs, the number of feudal strongholds might be reduced; but they could be easily rebuilt. Moreover, their existence meant a continuing competition between the weapons of attack and the arts of defence, in the course of which ramparts had to be raised to greater heights, approaches to be complicated, lines of fortification to be multiplied and walls and towers altered in shape and made more solid. The walls of the castle of Langres, for instance, were 21 feet thick.[3] Sovereigns, in order to maintain themselves against neighbours or powerful vassals and to extend their territories, needed similar means. Hence the powerful bastions erected by the Swiss at Schaffhausen, the great Edwardian castles of North Wales and the vast works of Richard Cœur de Lion for the defence of Normandy at Les Andelys, which required more than two miles of towers and walling besides about 4,000 yards of defences across the peninsula.[4] To the fortifications of kings and seigneurs, lay and ecclesiastical, must be added those of the towns. Many of these were first walled by the lords who founded them, and some, like most of the bastides of southern France, were not very large. Neither Aigues Mortes nor Carcassonne, for instance, was more than a mile around. Rich and free cities might need much more; the fourteenth-century defences of Verona stretched for two miles and a

[3] Viollet-le-Duc, *Military Architecture* (English translation, Oxford and London, 1879), 185.
[4] Plans in Viollet-le-Duc, *op. cit.*, 82, 85.

half,[5] and Nuremberg in the same century had grown so wealthy and populous that its two chief churches had to be enlarged and new defences begun, which extended to four miles of double walling. Altogether the military needs of hundreds of towns in England, France, Spain, Italy and Germany must have required an enormous amount of mason's work.

A second great medieval stimulus to building was religion. Each parish needed its church, eventually of stone. Besides there were abbeys, with their churches, living quarters and other buildings, sometimes, as the ninth-century plan of St Gall shows, designed on an extensive scale. With the cessation of the Scandinavian and other invasions conditions were favourable to the rebuilding of destroyed churches and the extension of monastic building, at times held in check by the puritanical principles of St Bernard but eventually, even with the Cistercians, attaining to great size and splendour. Already in the eleventh century, but more frequently in the twelfth, bishops were energetically renewing or enlarging their cathedrals. Church building also provided a channel of expenditure, and opportunities to acquire spiritual merit and to show local pride, for the rising mercantile class in the towns. The contributions of the second and third Thomas Spring, clothiers, towards the building of Lavenham steeple are instances of a generosity that must have been shown to a greater or lesser degree many times before by their like in the cities of the Low Countries, the Hanseatic League and northern Italy. In towns, as outside them, changes in architectural fashion created a good deal of work for building craftsmen. Once the gothic style had been seen in splendour it was easy for bishops and others to persuade themselves, with the help of master masons eager to be engaged on new work, that an old-fashioned church was unsafe. It could then be pulled down so that, like the thirteenth-century cathedral of Auxerre, *in elegantiorem juvenesceret speciem.*[6]

Other factors affecting the demand for building were rising population and, at any rate in towns and among the richer classes, a desire for greater comfort. Relatively little time would be required to put up a house for a peasant family, and a local carpenter and a thatcher only would be needed. Building for town dwellers might be a slower business; that is suggested by the charters of Bazas, Sauveterre (Gironde) and some other towns of bastide type which required each settler to have one-third of his house finished in the first year and two-thirds in the second.[7] In the larger towns, at any rate, a body of

[5] A. M. Allen, *History of Verona* (London, 1910), 229.

[6] V. Mortet and P. Deschamps, *Recueil de textes relatifs à l'histoire de l'architecture etc.* (Paris, 1911, 1929), II, XV, 203.

[7] T. F. Tout, 'Medieval Town Planning' in *Collected Papers* (Manchester, 1932–4), III, 71.

workmen would be necessary to keep pace with the growth of population and to carry out repairs; but in many towns it would be carpenters and plasterers rather than masons who would be needed. The municipal accounts of Douai make frequent mention of *plakeurs*, or daubers, who were employed not only on houses but on public buildings.[8] In Caen, the centre of a quarrying district, timber houses were being built in the fifteenth and early sixteenth centuries.[9] In Hamburg *domus lapideae* were very rare before 1350 and slates were beginning to be substituted for thatch only about 1460.[10]

In the countryside not every house was purely a fortress. The Carolingian nobility had delighted in country houses and, though these were destroyed in the ninth- and tenth-century invasions, the taste survived. England was rich in manor houses, and in several parts of France, though conditions were less favourable, there were erected, from the twelfth century onwards, residences in which comfort and convenience were more considered than defence. By the fifteenth century these had become more numerous, and doors and windows occupied more space in their elevations; by the sixteenth, despite their moats and turrets, still preserved as ornaments and signs of nobility, they were *chateaux* only in name.[11] Urban houses, protected by city walls, could be designed with even less reference to security. In some French towns, it is true, there were fortified noble houses[12] and the cities of northern Italy bristled with private fortresses – Verona is said to have had 700 at one time or another and the little town of San Gimignano no fewer than 300 – in the shape of towers, sometimes 200 feet high, built by nobles who lived in the cities and slew one another in their feuds.[13] Elsewhere nobles and prelates with town houses built for comfort, though they had an eye also for elegance. Besides walls, habitations and churches, the cities needed public buildings, especially the town hall, the bottom storey of which not uncommonly served as a market while those above were used for administrative, judicial and social purposes. A belfry was not infrequently part of the same structure. Surviving examples in the Low Countries, France, Germany and especially Italy (e.g. the town hall of Siena, built between 1289 and 1309) indicate that the municipal headquarters were often buildings of considerable pretension.

8 C. Enlart, *Manuel d'archéologie française*, II (*Architecture Civile et Militaire*) (Paris, 1902–16), 186.

9 H. Prentout, *Caen et Bayeux* (1921), 48–9.

10 W. Möring, 'Die Wohlfahrtspolitik des Hamburger Rates im Mittelalter', *Abhandlungen z. mittl. und neuer. Geschichte*, XLV, 57–8.

11 Enlart, *op. cit.*, II, 189–95.

12 Mortet and Deschamps, *Recueil de textes* I, lii.

13 M. V. Clarke, *The Medieval City State* (London, 1926), 60–1.

II. *Technical Capacity and Changes*

Before these various demands for building could be met a series of problems had to be solved. Those of an economic and administrative nature will be discussed later, attention being called meanwhile to certain technical matters, on some of which historical records throw comparatively little light. So far as is known, there was not available for medieval architects and engineers any written compendium or manual giving extensive and accurate instruction on the strength of materials and certain other matters now considered necessary parts of the professional curriculum. There is, however, no doubt that a body of technical knowledge did exist and that it was possible for intending builders to consult experts. The chapter at Gerona, for example, in 1416, when its master mason produced a plan for completing the cathedral church with a nave of one span, without the support of aisle columns, called in eleven masters from other churches to answer questions on the matter. All of them agreed that the plan was possible with safety and four of them agreed with the chapter's master mason that it was more suitable than the alternative proposed. The bishop and chapter, having discussed the replies, decided to build the one-span nave.[14] Medieval architects were familiar with the practice of driving piles to make foundations; their advice was sought in regard to the suitability of sites and the safety of structures,[15] though mistakes were made in practice, with disastrous effects at times on the central towers of churches. Masons and quarrymen possessed knowledge with regard to the 'cleaving grain' of stone and the way in which stone ought to be bedded in a building, and they understood the necessity of 'perpend' stones, going right through the thickness of a wall. Building workers were familiar with the block and pulley for lifting and with the windlass;[16] and they could, at need, construct in the scaffolding an inclined 'tramway' by means of which heavy stones could be wheeled to the top of a work.[17] The essential capacity to measure and calculate was also a fairly widespread qualification, used in the surveying and allocation of land, the laying out of sites, preparation of plans and in estimating and certifying work done. Thus Master Simon, *doctus geometricalis operis*, in charge of the preliminary works at the castle of Ardres about 1200, went about busily *cum virga sua*

[14] For the documents, see G. E. Street, *Gothic Architecture in Spain* (London and Toronto, 1914), II, 319ff.

[15] Mortet and Deschamps, *Recueil de textes*, II, 204, 237, 269.

[16] A thirteenth-century illustration reproduced in D. Knoop and G. P. Jones, 'Castle Building at Beaumaris and Caernarvon', *Ars Quatuor Coronatorum*, XLV (1932), 17: cf., possibly, the *ingenium ad levandum lapides* included in a Carcassonne inventory of 1298 (Mortet and Deschamps, *op. cit.*, II, 327ff.).

[17] Viollet-le-Duc, *Military Architecture*, 112.

magistrali more, and Peter, abbot of Andres, about 1164, took a personal part in his building work *cum ligno vel virgula geometrica lapides metiens.*[18] The construction of tracery and vaulting required geometry, in the modern sense of the term, both for designing and execution and there can be no doubt about the capacity of medieval architects to make such geometrical drawings as were required.[19] That is proved by records of payment to master masons for drawing and also entries relating to diagrams, on wooden floors, clay or slate, for the exact fitting of pieces of stonework or carpentry. Architectural drawings on parchment also, dating from the thirteenth century onwards, have survived; twenty-two of them were preserved in the cathedral of Strasbourg.

An important change in the industry occurred when building artificers turned their attention increasingly from timber to stone. The art of building in stone was not entirely lost with the collapse of the Western Empire. Workmen could still be found to erect a church of lovely design for a Visigothic king in seventh-century Spain[20] and in remote Wearmouth Benedict Biscop was able, about 675, with masons and other craftsmen from Gaul to raise a church in the Roman manner which was his delight.[21] Nevertheless, in western Europe generally stone was not then the chief, or even a common, building material. Timber abounded in many districts; it must have been easier to fell and work than stone was to quarry and dress; and, among the migrant Germanic peoples at least, it was material familiar from of old and useful for many purposes which stone could not serve. Accordingly it was used for mills, bridges, defensive works, churches and baronial halls, even large ones, such as that built at Ardres about 1060.[22] For several of these purposes timber continued to be used for centuries, giving place to stone at various times in different countries. In France the substitution began on a marked scale during the last quarter of the tenth century.[23] In the eleventh, stone was being increasingly used not only in the construction of churches but also in the building of castles.[24] Developments in England kept pace with those in France, but in remote Scotland the timber castle did not yield place completely to the stone keep until the fifteenth century.[25] It should be noted that despite the transition large quantities of timber were still needed, for scaffolding, centring for arches, doors, screens and partitions and, where vaulting was not used, for beams and other parts of roofs.

18 Mortet and Deschamps, *Recueil de textes*, I, 390; II, 190.
19 On medieval drawing, see C. Enlart, *Manuel d'archéologie française*, I (*Architecture religieuse*), 65.
20 B. Bevan, *History of Spanish Architecture* (London, 1938), 10, 11.
21 *Bedae Venerabilis Opera Historica* (ed. Plummer), (Oxford, 1896), I, 368.
22 Mortet and Deschamps, *Recueil de textes*, I, 183ff.
23 *Ibid.*, xxxiii. 24 *Ibid.*, xliii.
25 W. M. Mackenzie, *The Mediaeval Castle in Scotland* (London, 1927), 4.

Another change, of which the effects were far-reaching, was an improvement in vaulting, the discovery of what the French call *la voûte sur croisée d'ogives*, the main structural characteristic of the gothic style. Like earlier vaulting, it had the advantage of eliminating timber for roofing and thus reducing the risk of fire and, in addition, it made possible changes amounting to a revolution in construction. The space which could be spanned was greatly increased; the centre of the vault could be carried to a very great height; and it was possible to provide with safety far more window space, so as to fill the building with light. Indeed, with skilful use of buttresses the limits of stone building were reached by French architects in the second half of the thirteenth century, as in the choir of St Peter's at Beauvais which rose to a height of 150 feet. Only in modern times and with steel, as M. Langlois[26] pointed out, could that be exceeded. The new vaulting was in use in the cathedral at Durham early in the twelfth century and at Gloucester some time between 1100 and 1120. At the same time it was known in Normandy, Picardy and the Ile de France, where, in all probability, it was perfected and the gothic style really founded.[27] Between 1160 and 1180 the new style appeared in complete form at Vézelay in Burgundy and before 1220 it had reached Toulouse and also Casamari in Italy. To Germany, where it was known as *opus francigenum*, it came later, a notable instance of its use being the church of Wimpfen, near Heidelberg, begun in 1263. French influence, however, spread much further than that; it has been noted in the cathedrals of Burgos and Toledo, of Cologne, Bamberg and Naumberg, and even in Uppsala and Cyprus; and, in some cases at least, the explanation is known to have been the emigration of French architects and workmen.

III. *The Supply of Materials and Labour*

In addition to making the arrangements which building work of any kind must entail, those in charge of some medieval undertakings might have to cope with special difficulties resulting from one or more of three conditions, namely remoteness, urgency and size. Monastic building, for instance, often had to be carried on in out-of-the-way places; and fortresses, such as English strongholds in Wales or Scotland, might have to be erected not only in sparsely peopled but in hostile territory. In that event it was necessary to build with speed – the vast works of Richard Cœur de Lion at Chateau Gaillard,

[26] In Lavisse, *Histoire de France*, III, i, 423.

[27] On the spread of gothic, see Enlart, *Architecture Religieuse*, I, 435ff.; Ch.-V. Langlois, in Lavisse, *Histoire*, 422; and especially G. Dehio and G. von Bezold, *Die kirchliche Baukunst des Abendlandes, Text* (Stuttgart, 1892), II.

for instance, are said to have been erected in a year[28] – and that was possible only by employing very large numbers of men, such as the 400 masons and 1,200 other workers at Beaumaris in the late thirteenth century. In such cases the managements were faced with a problem of food supply and accommodation not unlike that with which railway contractors had to deal in the nineteenth century, and, so far as accommodation is concerned, the answer appears to have been the same, the wooden hut. An early item in the accounts relating to the building of Vale Royal Abbey in 1277 is a payment for the construction of *mansiones* for the masons and other workmen. Another feature of this temporary congregation of large and fluctuating numbers of men in places which might be far from towns is the unsuitability of the ordinary craft gild as a nexus of the organisation of craftsmen, if organisation there was to be.

(I) SUPPLY OF MATERIALS

In the main medieval builders used local stone, sometimes when it was not very suitable, because the cost of transport was high, and for the same reason as much as possible of the scappling and dressing was done at the quarry. Where funds permitted, however, stone might be brought from a distance: for the cathedral of Sens, for instance, stone was brought not only from Auxerre, at a distance of about 30 miles, but from Ivry, well over 100 miles away.[29] Stone was even exported by sea: the limestone of Istria, easily carried across the Adriatic, was much used in Italy, e.g. in fifth-century Ravenna and eleventh-century Venice,[30] and the oolitic limestone of Caen was widely used in England from the eleventh century onwards. The relative cheapness of water transport was an advantage to such churches as St Victor's at Xanten, to which stone was brought by way of the rivers Lippe, Ruhr and Rhine, but part of the benefit was apt to be lost through payment of tolls. In 1405 the fabric of St Victor's acquired Drachenfels and Andernach stone costing 140 gulden at the quarries; to that amount there were added 44 gulden paid in tolls, 88½ gulden for transport to the quay at Beek, 4½ gulden for carrying from the quay to the church, and 31½ gulden in travelling expenses of officials in connection with the stone, so that very nearly 55 per cent of the cost of the stone on the site was accounted for by transport, tolls and travelling. In this respect the cathedrals of Cologne and Mainz were in comparison fortunately placed.[31] Very high costs of transport were,

28 Viollet-le-Duc, *Military Architecture*, 87.

29 On the transport of materials see Enlart, *Architecture religieuse* I, 77ff.

30 J. Watson, *British and Foreign Building Stones* (Cambridge, 1911) 203.

31 S. Beissel, *Die Bauführung des Mittelalters* (Freiburg i. Breisgau, 1889), II, 44.

naturally, incurred as a rule only for decorative stonework, such as the Tournai fonts found at Lincoln and elsewhere; tombs, such as that of Robert Bruce, made in Paris in 1329 for export to Scotland; and the alabaster of Chellaston, in Derbyshire, imported in large quantities and partly in a worked state, into Normandy[32] in the fifteenth century. Timber, like stone, was mainly obtained locally; but, since medieval carpenters preferred to use only the heart of timber and wood was also needed for other uses, the supply might at times run short, and imported wood was used. Irish timber, for instance, was used at the Louvre in the fourteenth century and, in the fourteenth and fifteenth centuries, Danish timber was used in building work done for the kings of France and the dukes of Burgundy.[33] Bricks (*tegulae murales*), which were known in the eleventh century, were, for reasons not well understood, almost entirely given up in the centuries following, except in districts poorly supplied with good building stone, such as parts of Languedoc, Flanders, North Germany and northern Italy. From the fifteenth century their use, either alone or in conjunction with stone, became widespread. They were, for instance, employed in large quantities for Beverley Bar, Eton College and the fortified houses of Tattersall and Kirby Muxloe.

There were in the main two ways by which medieval builders could provide themselves with stone, namely, by acquiring or leasing quarries, or by buying stone from quarry owners. For England it would be possible to draw up a short list of the latter who sold prepared stone on a fairly large scale, but, though purchases of stone by the crown and other builders were frequent, it is probable that the other method of supply was the commoner. Gifts of quarries, such as that made to the bishop of Laon for his cathedral in 1205, were a frequent form of pious donation in France[34] and in England, and so were gifts of timber. For the transport of stone, timber and other materials the supervisors of a building work either hired carts and carters – and, where necessary, boats and sailors – or had their own or, very commonly, did both. It appears, therefore, that some medieval building operations, in which quarrying, brick-making, timber-felling and transport were all under one management, are to be regarded as large and more or less integrated concerns, comparable in size and the variety of operations entailed to some early firms of the Industrial Revolution.

[32] P. le Cacheux, *Rouen au temps de Jeanne d'Arc*, xcvi.
[33] Enlart, *Architecture religieuse*, I, 78–9.
[34] Mortet and Deschamps, *Recueil de textes*, II, 201 n. 4.

(2) SUPPLY OF LABOUR

The labour required on a large building operation included, besides the more or less skilled masons, carpenters, smiths, plumbers and glaziers, numbers of *minutii operarii*,[35] namely navvies, mortar-mixers, barrowmen and other carriers. Such unskilled labour could probably be found fairly easily in most neighbourhoods. There was, probably, no feudal estate in Western Europe on which some building labour was not available, since building, repairing or roofing the lord's hall or the manorial mill or bakehouse were common obligations of the tenants;[36] and, in addition to unskilled or semi-skilled workers, a mason was sometimes and a carpenter often to be found on a feudal estate. Moreover, should there be a shortage of male labour, women, as some medieval examples show, could be used.

At times, at least, religious obligation, an outburst of pious fervour, or a laudable local patriotism, eased the problem for those in charge of building works. Thus it is provided in a French contract of 1463,[37] made with a mason repairing a parish church, that *les habitans de ladite parroisse... lui feront les maneuvres que seront necesseres*. For the repair of Bodmin parish church between 1469 and 1472 the inhabitants of the town not only raised money through gilds and by rating themselves but also turned out to labour without pay. Similarly, at the building of the church of St Trond, near Liège, in the second half of the eleventh century numbers of people hastened to carry stone and other materials *plaustris et curribus gratis propriisque expensis*;[38] and after the disastrous fire of 1194 at Chartres people of all classes took part in the work of reconstruction.[39] For other works, offering no opportunity to acquire merit, such enthusiasm could not be expected, but the public authority might be used. In ninth-century Germany the Roman tradition of *munera publica* is said to have been behind a decree of Louis II compelling his subjects to take their part in the work of restoring buildings,[40] and in medieval England, as will be shown later, local shortages of labour were remedied at need by means of the crown's power of impressment and purveyance.

The supply and training of skilled labour in the quantities necessary for the building activity of the twelfth and following centuries were matters of greater difficulty. Many masons and other craftsmen learned

[35] Knoop and Jones, 'Castle Building at Beaumaris and Caernarvon', 15; cf. the contemporary French *menus ouvriers*.
[36] For German and other examples, see Sombart, *Der moderne Kapitalismus*, I, i, 81–4.
[37] G. Fagniez, *Documents relatifs à l'histoire de l'industrie, etc.* (Paris, 1877), II, 258–60.
[38] Mortet and Deschamps, *Recueil de textes*, I, 158.
[39] Mortet and Deschamps, *op. cit.*, II, xiv.
[40] Sombart, *Der moderne Kapitalismus*, I, i, 84.

their trades in the workshops connected with abbey and cathedral fabrics but, despite the belief of such authors as Heideloff about the importance of monastic institutions such as Kloster Hirschau under its famous Abbot William (1069–91) as training schools for artisans,[41] and the undoubted fact that some monks and secular clergymen are known to have had competence in architecture and even as craftsmen, there is, so far as we know, no evidence to suggest that monks or seculars played any part of importance in teaching men the practical business of using axe and saw, or mallet and chisel. They did, on the other hand, take good care to provide themselves with the services of laymen skilled in the building crafts. The abbey of St Aubin d'Angers, for instance, agreed, at some date between 1082 and 1106, that a serf called Fulk should, in return for serving as painter and glazier, be made free and given land, which, however, was to return to the abbey at his death unless he should have a son capable of serving the house in the same craft.[42] Similarly the abbey of Cupar stipulated, when hiring a mason in 1497, that 'the said Thomas sal ken and inform the prentys that we or our successouris resawis al craft in masonry or any wther he can'.[43] In general, the skilled craftsmen of the Middle Ages were laymen, and so also, except perhaps in the earlier centuries, were the architects. With the transition from timber to stone the number of masons and the average level of skill may be presumed to have risen. This development occurred in military as well as in ecclesiastical architecture, and there is little likelihood that the craftsmen required to erect stone strongholds owed much to monastic training. They learned their trades on the building works themselves from laymen already masters of them. One nursery of craftsmen in stone, which has so far attracted little attention but which may nevertheless have been important, is the quarry. In an early phase the callings of mason and quarrymen were probably not entirely distinct; some English masons are known to have been quarrymen at one stage in their careers; and sellers of dressed and prepared stone, who are known to have existed both in England and on the continent,[44] may well have had in their employment workers who learned the mason's trade well enough to earn a living by it, as wallers if not as setters, outside the quarry.

[41] *Die Bauhütte des Mittelalters in Deutschland:* the basis seems to be largely the uncritical fifteenth-century writer John Trithemius. For the evidence relating to ecclesiastical and monastic architects in Catalonia and for the importance of the abbey of Ripoll, under Abbot Oliva in the eleventh century, as a centre for the studies required for architecture, see J. Puig y Cadafalch, A. de Falguera and J. Goday y Casals, *L'Arquitectura Romànica a Catalunya* (Barcelona, 1919–21), II, 59ff. One should, however, beware of taking too literally words such as *fabricavit*, *erexit*, *struxit*, and the like, occurring in literary sources.

[42] Mortet and Deschamps, *Recueil de textes*, I, 264–5.

[43] C. Rogers, *Rental Book of ... Cupar-Angus*, I, 310.

[44] For purchases of stone from stone-cutters in the region of Tournai, see Mortet and Deschamps, *op. cit.*, II, 298–9.

It now remains to be seen how craftsmen were recruited by those who required their services. Where the work to be done was on a small scale, or consisted of repairs rather than new construction, masons or carpenters could be hired as need arose or a master craftsman could be found to do the work at an agreed price. Where the work was on a larger scale and likely to last for a long time it was convenient to keep a staff, with a master or warden, or both, in charge in the lodge (*Bauhütte*, *chantier*) attached to every building work of importance. Such a staff could be expanded in times of special activity and reduced to a minimum at other times. On the continent unmarried journeymen were willing enough, as work finished in one place, to go elsewhere. The *tour de France* was a familiar institution, in early modern times and probably before, among building craftsmen, and German workers of the same kind were mobile in the fifteenth century; no fewer than 117 of them came to Ulm in one week when the church tower was in danger of falling in 1493.[45] Lombard masons probably travelled to Urgel in Catalonia in 1175[46] and French masons went to distant Uppsala in 1287.[47] How far the movement of craftsmen was voluntary is not clear, but in most countries the civil authority would no doubt attempt to use its powers at need. Thus Raymond V, count of Toulouse, though not specifically claiming a power to send masons away from home in time of peace, lays down the principle of compulsion in regulations of 1187,[87] requiring the master stone masons of Nîmes, if the count should have building in progress there, to labour for one day in the week for their food only and on the other days for pay. When they joined the army they were to bring their gear, he providing transport for it and food for them as well as a stipulated sum for fortifications destroyed. In Aquitaine, earlier in the same century, there had apparently been a risk of conscription, for a charter of Duke William VIII,[49] between 1127 and 1137, expressly provided that his officers should not have power to seize workmen on one operation and send them to another. The most abundant evidence of conscription of building workers occurs in English records, which leave no doubt that the powers of the crown were being extensively used in the thirteenth century through the sheriffs and during the remainder of the Middle Ages mainly through master masons or administrative officials such as Geoffrey Chaucer, clerk of the works at St George's Chapel, Windsor, in 1390. Masons were taken sometimes by the hundred, but the system was evidently not without difficulties. There was a possibility of gathering too many men at some periods and too few at others; men could not altogether be prevented from deserting either while on the

[45] *Die Chroniken der deutschen Städte*, XXIII (Augsburg iv), 420.
[46] Mortet and Deschamps, *op. cit.*, II, 129, 130.
[47] *Ibid.*, II, 305–6. [48] *Ibid.*, II, 156. [49] *Ibid.*, I, 379.

way or after arrival; and the eagerness of officials to take men from one building might hinder progress with others. Impressment was apt to interfere with ecclesiastical, municipal and private works, where officials were most likely to find the men they needed. Hence, in 1441, Archbishop Chicheley sought a royal order to save the workmen at All Souls' College from being pressed for work at Eton and in 1479 it was requested that the men who had finished Magdalen College should not be taken for Windsor but left to work for the University.

IV. *The Management of Large Building Operations*

The simplest arrangement known to us for the administration of a building operation is that indicated in a document of 1175 relating to the church of St Mary in Urgel, Catalonia.[50] All the funds, from rents and other sources, assigned to the fabric were to be handed over to Raymond the Lombard, apparently the master mason, who agreed to roof the church, construct a dome and raise the towers, taking seven years for the work and employing four other Lombards, to whom other masons were to be added at need. During the seven years and afterwards for his life Raymond was to have *cibum canonicale*. This provision may be compared with that in force until 1374 at St Victor's in Xanten, Germany, where the master mason held a prebend of equal status with those of canons.[51] The system in general use, at any rate from the thirteenth century onwards, differed from that at Urgel in separating the two sides of an undertaking, the financial and administrative on the one hand and the technical or architectural on the other, and putting a different man in charge of each. Thus, at St Victor's in Xanten the *magister fabrice* or *Werkmeister* was in charge of the funds and the master mason (*magister lapicida*) in charge of the building operations. Similarly, in fourteenth- and fifteenth-century Spain, collegiate and cathedral churches entrusted the financial and administrative functions to canons or other clergymen called *canonicos fabriqueros*, *obreros* or *operarii*, leaving the management of the building work itself to the architect or master mason, the *lapicida et magister operis*.[52] In France and in England, and on ecclesiastical, royal, municipal and private buildings, a similar separation was the practice.

[50] *Ibid.*, II, 129–31.

[51] Beissel, *Die Bauführung des Mittelalters*, I, 96, 97. On the separation in general see Dehio and von Bezold, *Die Kirchliche Baukunst*, II, 24.

[52] Street, *Gothic Architecture in Spain*, II, 267, 321. On the administrative function of the *operarii* in an earlier period, see Puig y Cadafalch, Falguera and Goday y Casals, *L'Arquitectura Romànica*, II, 47.

Kings used financial officers, churches used the sacrist or another obedientiary, colleges one of the fellows and great lords their stewards, to deal with accounts, inventories and the like, leaving the master mason or architect free to give his whole attention to matters directly concerned with his art. The relative importance of the two chief officials varied from time to time and from one building to another, and the separation was not always complete; but the system may be presumed to have brought with it the advantages of specialisation and to have been necessary when a building operation was on a considerable scale. It was also in accord with the professional pride of the architect and master craftsman. Michelangelo was probably expressing a conviction shared by men in an earlier age when he told Cardinal Marcello: 'your office is to procure money and take care that thieves do not get the same; the designs for the building you are to leave to my care'.[53] Where the same employer had several building operations in progress, or many buildings to maintain at the same time, as was the case with the crown in England and France and, to a lesser degree, with the princes of the blood and other great nobles, some unification of control was achieved by putting a master workman in general command; with wardens or subordinate masters in charge at each work. Thus, to take one instance, Alexander de Berneval in 1421 functioned as *maistre des oeuvres de machonerie du Roy* throughout the bailliage of Rouen.[54] In England from 1256 onwards there was a central office of works[55] which in the course of time had premises, including stores for materials and traceries from drawings, at Westminster and developed a large technical and administrative staff, some members of which were travelling officials.

The finance of building is outside our present scope and, accordingly, leaving on one side officials such as William of Wykeham whose functions were largely concerned with it, we have to consider their technical colleagues, the master masons, about whom some not altogether correct notions have been current. It has been held that, as craftsmen, they were less individualist than their Renaissance successors; that their work was largely anonymous; and that between the artist responsible for the design of a building and the masons and carpenters who carried it out there was no distinction.[56] By now it is known that medieval craftsmen were proud enough of their individual masterpieces; and to such wellknown names as those of Erwin von Steinbach

[53] J. Foster, *Vasari's Lives of the most eminent Painters, etc.* (London, 1892), v, 304.

[54] For many references to Alexander de Berneval see P. le Cacheux, *Le Livre de comptes de Thomas du Marest* (Rouen, 1905).

[55] John H. Harvey, 'The Medieval Office of Works' in *Journal Brit. Archaeol. Assoc.* (1941).

[56] Sombart, *Der moderne Kapitalismus*, II, ii, 773. Similar notions are corrected in Martin S. Briggs, *The Architect in History*.

of Strasbourg and Hugues Libergier of Rheims others can be added by the dozen. It can be shown that at least as early as the thirteenth century there existed a kind of architect quite distinct in pay and status from the craftsmen who worked under his eye. There is, for instance, no doubting the gap between the ordinary mason working at Caernarvon Castle in the early fourteenth century for *2s. 6d.* a week and the master mason, Walter of Hereford, who received *2s.* a day. Such architects were called masons or carpenters, though they were commonly distinguished by the title *magister* or an adjective, *principalis* or *capitalis*. Biographical detail relating to them is difficult to gather but enough evidence remains to suggest that the more eminent of them had distinct professional qualifications. Those included the capacity to measure the quantity and assess the quality of work done and probably to estimate the quantities necessary for any given piece of work; ability in drawing and making plans; and the ability to arrange and supervise the labours of large numbers of men working at one time in one place. That was especially necessary under a system such as that prevailing in royal building in England, where a large operation was managed directly and as a unity, all the workers being hired and paid by the crown. Some operations were indeed divided into contracts or 'bargains' but with those also it was necessary that someone should be able to plan the building as a whole and to supervise the separate masters who carried out the different parts. An example of that system may be found in the erection of a college at Beauvais in 1387[57] under the general supervision of Master Raymon du Temple. He first made a schedule of the form, materials, order and thickness of the edifice and had this copied by his clerk. It was then read and shown to workmen who were capable of undertaking parts of the work and, after some bargaining, contracts were made with two Paris masons for the stone work and subsequently with other artificers for the carpentry, lead work and the like. From time to time Master Raymon came to measure the quantities performed, bringing on one occasion his clerk, 'who wrote down every particular as the said Master Raymon named it'. His care for design in detail is evident from the fact that the crown of the Virgin, whose statue decorated the college, though made by Marcel the Goldsmith, was *devisée par M. Raymon*.

The best known evidence of the training and interests of such architects is probably the thirteenth-century sketch book of Villard de Honnecourt.[58] He was probably a protégé of the Cistercian house of Vaucelles and travelled as far as Hungary, where the Cistercians were busily building between 1235 and 1250. Besides figures, sketches and

[57] Fagniez, *Documents etc.*, II, 128ff.
[58] For an appreciation, see Ch.-V. Langlois, in Lavisse, *Histoire*, 414–16.

architectural drawings his book contains indications of his interest in mechanics and other aspects of thirteenth-century science, and it is clear that he knew some little Latin. Though he cannot, on the strength of buildings with which he is known to have been connected, be counted among the great architects of his day he was evidently not only professionally trained but a man of some culture, at a considerable remove from the ordinary craftsmen of his time.

V. *Masons' Contracts*

Raymon du Temple and his English contemporary, Henry Yevele, are two instances out of many which could be cited to show that the architect, in the sense not only of a designer but of a man taking charge of a whole building operation, and even several at the same time, had developed before the end of the Middle Ages. A further development, by which the architect or master mason himself contracted for the construction of a whole building or a considerable part of one, is believed to have been reached in Italy in the fifteenth century (Beltramo di Martino of Varese, active about 1450, being an example) and France in the sixteenth.[59] It may indeed be true that the contracting system became dominant only after the end of the Middle Ages, but building contracts, involving relatively large sums of money and the supply of materials by the contractor, were known before the fifteenth century. Some of Queen Eleanor's crosses were erected by such contracts in the latter part of the thirteenth century and about 1380 William Sharnhale undertook work to the value of £456 – a sum equivalent to the earnings of 65 masons in a whole year – at Cowling Castle.[60]

The number of surviving building contracts of one kind or another is so large that space will permit only of general observations upon them. The simplest form of contract work was *opus ad tascam*, whereby a man or group of men received an agreed sum for scappling stone or some similar work easy to estimate quantitatively. This, in effect, was piece work accompanied, where several men did the work, by division of the proceeds. A common type of contract was that whereby an artificer undertook to erect a building, himself supplying the labour only; thus, for instance, in 1224 Master Nicholas of Beaumont-le-Roger agreed to build a castle for the count of Dreux, the count providing stone, sand, lime, timber and transport, and retaining the scaffolding made by the contractor when the work had been

[59] Sombart, *Der moderne Kapitalismus*, II, ii, 774.

[60] On English contracts, see D. Knoop and G. P. Jones, 'The Rise of the Mason Contractor', *Journal R.I.B.A.*, XLIII (1936).

finished.[61] Other types of agreement bind the contractor to provide, in addition to workmanship, either materials or transport or both. The contractors were sometimes ordinary working masons occasionally trying an alternative to their usual wage labour, but it was by no means unknown for master masons in charge of a building to take a contract either for work connected with it or for some quite different building. Henry Yevele,[62] for instance, while King's Master Mason and a member of the royal household as well as master mason at Westminster Abbey and Warden of London Bridge, undertook considerable contracts. Contractors who undertook to supply not only workmanship but materials were likely to be either dealers in them or owners of their own supplies. Beltramo di Martino, who has been taken as marking the advent of the new system of building, owned tileries and lime kilns in Rome; Thomas Crompe, a considerable contractor at Cowling Castle seventy years earlier, was probably a quarry master; his famous contemporary, Henry Yevele, is known to have dealt in stone and tiles in large quantities and may at one time have worked a marble quarry at Purbeck.

Building contracts, probably to an increasing extent after 1350, thus offered chances of greater gain to masons and carpenters of various grades, but they were not the only way by which a craftsman might hope to attain a higher status than that of the ordinary worker in his trade. If he preferred the relative safety of a salaried position to the speculative possibilities of contracting, he might seek to become a foreman or a warden on a large works, *magister secundarius* on the fabric of a church and eventually master mason in the service of a great lord, a municipality or a cathedral chapter. In that event he would commonly be bound by a contract of appointment for a term of years or for life, generally prescribing his salary and not infrequently his entertainment,[63] limiting or prohibiting his absence to do other work without the consent of the chapter or convent, and sometimes providing him with a house and guaranteeing part of his salary or maintenance in case of continued infirmity. At least one contract contained a clause designed to offset possible fluctuations in the value of money; the bishop and canons of Lugo in Spain agreed in 1129 that their master mason should have an annual salary of 200 *sueldos*, but, if the value were to change, he should have six marks in silver and various payments in kind.[64]

[61] Mortet and Deschamps, *Recueil de textes*, II, 234–5.

[62] On whom see D. Knoop and G. P. Jones, 'Henry Yevele and his Associates', *Journal R.I.B.A.*, XLII (1935).

[63] This is done in detail in a French contract of 1261 printed in Mortet and Deschamps, *Recueil de textes*, II, 288–90.

[64] Street, *Gothic Architecture in Spain*, I, 171–2.

VI. *Conditions of Labour*

There is no means of discovering exactly what proportion of medieval building craftsmen succeeded, by one or other of the ways described, in reaching and retaining positions which marked them off from their fellows, but it may safely be regarded as very small, and the great majority of artificers in the industry remained throughout their working lives wage earners. As such they have until recently been little noticed by historians. Of the accounts, by means of which their conditions can be studied, many have perished or are difficult of access or, when found, are insufficiently detailed; but enough evidence is now available to throw light not only on rates of remuneration and changes in them but also on such problems as the length of the working period, the number of holidays and, to a limited extent, on continuity of employment.

Before coming directly to those questions it will be well to indicate certain respects in which the medieval mason and, to some extent, other building craftsmen differed from their contemporaries in other industries. One was their very much greater mobility. Since, not only in the countryside but also in many towns, most houses were of timber, lath and plaster, there could have been little continuous employment, in many districts, for a large number of masons in their own villages, unless those were in a quarrying district such as Tournai where large quantities of dressed stone, pillars and part-manufactured statues were produced for export. In any event, the erection of the great castles and cathedrals of medieval Europe was possible only by gathering hundreds of craftsmen from a wide district. That was the easier to arrange because masons and carpenters were not, like the weaver, tied to a loom but could pack their instruments into a small bundle and take to the road, as they continued to do until modern times. At need the tools might even be provided by the management of the building operation which, in any case, generally paid for the sharpening and steeling of them, often employing a smith or smiths for the purpose and a *portehache* to carry them between the smithy and the work. A second difference between the mason and other workers, such as the weaver, tailor and saddler, was that he had fewer opportunities to acquire, even in small quantities, the material in which he worked, and that he was in consequence more generally in the position of a man having his labour and skill only to sell. Thirdly, unlike most medieval craftsmen, who worked in isolation or in small workshops, the mason was often employed in conditions which must have been similar to those obtaining in the industrial establishments which immediately preceded the modern mill or factory. He was thus subject to an order and discipline which, though probably less harsh in their operation, were similar in essence to those imposed upon the reluctant cotton workers of early nineteenth-century Lancashire and Alsace. Men were fined at the building of Eton College not only for fighting but for hindering their fellows by telling tales and for unpunctuality.

The mason's trade comprised two main branches, the arts practised respectively by the hewer (*cementarius*, *lathomus*) and the layer or setter (*positor*, *cubitor*) but the separation was not rigid and most masons were proficient to some extent in both branches. Hewing was considered the higher, since at its best it included sculpture, the carving of tracery and of pillar capitals and the like difficult and intricate work, but it also included the rough dressing or scappling of stone used in the core or inner part of walls, for only the outer surfaces were of smoothly dressed and squared stone. It is probable that the setting of such work as a rose window was done by the carver; on the other hand the shaping of roughly dressed stone was probably done by the men who laid it. Stones for outer surfaces, including mouldings and other carving, were commonly worked in the lodge, the mason responsible scoring his bench mark upon each one as he finished it, but sometimes the carving was done long after the stone had been laid.[65] When the hewer's work had been tried with square and mould, to see that the angles of the surfaces and the profile or pattern were accurate, it was the layer's business to set the stones truly with a plumb line in a correct bonding. The distinction between hewing and laying corresponded, though not completely, to the difference between 'freemason' and 'rough mason' or 'rowmason', the latter term being sometimes used for bricklayer.

The fact that both hewing and laying included operations requiring different degrees of skill may explain, though only in part, the puzzling variety of wage rates on some large building works. The 131 masons working at Vale Royal Abbey in 1278–80 received no fewer than eighteen different rates, and at Caernarvon and Beaumaris Castles in the early fourteenth century there were twenty-two. That this variety was not exceptional is clear from the fact that 29 masons were employed, at five different rates, on the fabric of York Minster in 1371, and ten masons, at eight different rates, at Ely in 1359–60. Whatever the causes of this multiplicity may have been, the evidence suggests that a man's wage was probably the result of an individual bargain and was not determined simply by custom or by such machinery as that of a gild. As the Middle Ages wore on, the diversity tended to diminish, in part perhaps because, during the last century

[65] Enlart, *Architecture religieuse*, I, 14n.

and a half – say between 1350 and 1500 – masons were more nearly of the same grade in skill than they had been earlier. That will not appear strange if it be borne in mind that very large numbers were employed on similar work, especially in castle building, and also that something like standardisation came in with the perpendicular style.

Of variations in wages between town and country there is little information, though enough to show that in London they were one-sixth to one-third higher than in the country as a whole. There is clearer proof of the common medieval variation according to the season of the year. Thus, at Verona in 1228 master masons were to be paid four *soldi* a day in summer and three in winter, because of the shorter working day.[66] The difference was less for carpenters in Dax, near Bayonne, about 1300, their wages being fixed at 12 *deniers* a day from 1 March to 1 November and ten from thence to 1 March.[67] At St Victor's in Xanten[68] the winter rate, starting on 11 November, was about two-thirds of the summer rate, starting on 22 February; the two journeymen (*Gesellen*) who worked with the master mason there in 1356 were paid from 12 to 14 *denarii* a day in summer and 9 or 10 in winter; Herman von Offenburg and Tilman von Koeln in 1436 and 1437 drew $36\frac{1}{2}$ *denarii* a day in summer and $24\frac{1}{3}$ in winter. In London, according to regulations made between 1275 and 1296, masons were to get 5*d*. a day from Easter to Michaelmas, 4*d*. from Michaelmas to 11 November, 3*d*. from 11 November to 2 February and 4*d*. thence to Easter.

A more important phenomenon, but one far more difficult to trace for western Europe in general, is the secular variation. The trend of money wages in England, from 1300 onwards, is fairly clear and may be summarily stated as follows: (i) from 1300 to the Black Death the wages of masons and craftsmen of the same kind ranged about 4*d*. a day; (ii) about 1350 or 1360 they rose to 5*d*. or 6*d*. and remained, with remarkable constancy and uniformity, at about that level until the beginning of the sixteenth century; (iii) thereafter they rose steeply, to 10*d*. by 1560, 12*d*. by the end of Elizabeth's reign and 18*d*. by the Restoration. There is no reason to suppose that building craftsmen in other countries also did not share in the rise in wages which is known to have followed the Black Death. At St Victor's in Xanten,[69] for instance, the wages of a skilled mason rose from 14 *denarii* in 1350–59 to 21 *denarii* in 1360–69, 36 *denarii* in 1370–89 and 42 *denarii* in 1390–99, and the wages of other artificers on the same fabric moved

[66] Allen, *History of Verona*, 38.
[67] Mortet and Deschamps, *Recueil de textes*, II, 336. The carpenters were partly paid in food.
[68] Beissel, *Die Bauführung*, II, 150, 153, 157.
[69] On wages in Xanten, see Beissel, *op. cit.*, II, 149ff.

in much the same way. Here the rise was a slower process than in England; moreover, after reaching a peak in 1400–9, wages in Xanten did not remain at that level but declined, more rapidly in the second half of the fifteenth century than during the first, falling from 50 *denarii* in 1400–9 to 25 *denarii* in 1510–19. The rise in the sixteenth century, like that in the fourteenth, came more slowly in Xanten than in England but it was of a similar order: the wages of a good artificer were about 54 *denarii* in 1560–69, 115 *denarii* in 1590–99 and 168 *denarii* in 1650–59. Though there are many difficulties in relating these movements to changes in the standard of living, there is little doubt that the period following the Black Death brought with it a rise in real wages. For England, where money wages rose approximately 42 per cent between 1350 and 1510 and food prices may have risen by 33 per cent in the same period, the picture is more pleasant than that which the careful researches of Beissel suggest for Xanten. Money wages there, if measured in wheat, barley and rye, tended downwards on the whole in the century and a half following 1350; the quantity purchasable by 16 days' wages in 1350–59 could be bought for an average of 13 days' wages between 1370 and 1419, but the figure rose to 16 again for the next forty years, to 19 for the period 1460–99 and to 25 for the years 1500–39. Thus, even in Xanten, though to a smaller extent than in England, the later Middle Ages were, on the surface at least, a time of relative stability and perhaps of rough plenty for artificers in the building trades; certainly there, as in England and France, they seem prosperous when compared with the catastrophic period which followed.[70]

Neither in France nor in England was the rise in wages after the Black Death allowed to take place without an attempt by the government and local authorities to prevent it. In the former country an ordinance of 1351 sought to undermine the position of journeymen in Paris not only by fixing their wages and tying them to their work but also by abolishing gild regulations limiting the number of apprentices and local restrictions on the employment of 'foreign' workmen; but the attempt was unsuccessful and further legislation was called for in 1354 and 1356. In England, where municipal regulation of masons' wages goes back as far as 1212, statutes and by-laws dealt with the same subject repeatedly in the fourteenth, fifteenth and sixteenth centuries, aiming generally at a defined working day and a fixed maximum wage. Official views on the working day were probably much the same in all countries. The French ordinance of 1351 required journeymen to work 'loyaument du soleil levant jusques

[70] On the fall of real wages in France see H. Sée, *Histoire économique de la France* (Paris, 1939), 93–4.

au soleil couchant', much as the English Statute of Artificers nearly two hundred years later defined the hours of work, between mid-September and mid-March, as 'from the springe of the daye in the mornynge untill the nyght', limits which probably accorded with the custom of lodges, though masons, like other craftsmen, were known to start late and finish early and to stretch the permitted breaks for meals and drinking. The second object of these regulations was only imperfectly attained even in quarters where the attempt to put the orders into practice was most to be expected. In the heart of the capital the Wardens of London Bridge in the early fifteenth century disregarded the legal obligation to keep to the maximum wage for masons, to reduce their wage in winter and to give no pay for holidays; and on the king's works in the fourteenth century hundreds of men were paid at higher rates than his laws allowed.

Even if we take it that governments failed to prevent the rise in wages, we cannot be sure that medieval building craftsmen enjoyed anything like a golden age until more is known about the amount of their annual earnings. The number of days for which they were paid might be diminished by several factors; fabric funds might be exhausted so that building work would have to stop; the medieval church insisted on the observance of a considerable number of saints' days; and bad weather was a common cause of interruption. Building work was certainly slowed down, and might cease altogether, in winter: the Beauvais account of 1387 noted that *les gelees approchoient et se passoit la saison de maconner*. Many cathedral chapters and other employers probably made arrangements similar to those at Xanten in November 1399, when the staff of masons was reduced from twelve to six, who covered the stonework with straw to protect it from cold and frost, made their wooden lodge weatherproof with turf and settled down to their winter work, cutting stone for the pillars of the choir. On some buildings laying ceased for months at a time and though other work might be found for some of the layers there must have been a good deal of seasonal unemployment. Some idea of the length of the working year may perhaps be gained from a Rochester Castle account for 1368: the majority of the masons employed there received pay for 252 days but no setter was paid for more than 180. Even when the weather was good, however, the medieval mason rarely worked a full week of six days. The number of saints' days observed, and the days themselves, varied from one building to another and from year to year but the number might work out at three or more in each month. With the Rochester account for 1368 the Xanten fabric accounts for 1356 and 1495 may be compared: the former covered 49 weeks, containing 250 working days, and the latter

53 weeks with an aggregate of 270½ working days, giving an average of 265 in a calendar year. If, as there is some evidence to suggest, the daily wage of a mason was approximately equal to three times the cost of his meat and drink, we may conclude that he would be lucky, in the climate of northern Europe, to earn annually the equivalent of 810 days' subsistence. That would give a single man a fair margin, but for a mason with a wife and child it might leave less than 27 days' earnings to meet all expenses other than the cost of food, unless, as may often have been the case, the mason's family contributed to its maintenance.

There were occasional opportunities for masons to add to their ordinary earnings by extra diligence where haste was required, and they might even work at night, as the Xanten staff did in 1399 and the London Bridge masons were in special circumstances required to do in the fifteenth century; but systematic overtime, so far as we know, was not usual until the sixteenth century, when it helped to bridge the gap between wages and rising prices. Friendly relations between employers and employed were shown in donations on special festivals or on the completion of particular pieces of work. Thus, at Beauvais in 1387, we are told, *le jour de caresme...il fust accoustume que l'on donnoit a tous les ouvriers courtoisie, c'est assavoir pour le char d'un mouton*; but the commonest form of present was drink, which, for instance, the London Bridge Wardens gave on Shrove Tuesday and the Chapter of Regensburg on 24 June. The more continuous benevolence of the canons of Xanten provided their masons with a weekly *Trinkgeld* amounting to about 2 per cent of their earnings.

VII. *Organisation of Craftsmen*

Like other medieval workmen, those in the building trades were commonly subject to some degree of organisation, which was either imposed upon them by employers of evolved by the craftsmen themselves; but, because the conditions of the industry differed from those prevailing in most others, the forms of organisation among building workers, and especially masons, were to some extent peculiar. There are, speaking generally, records of two different kinds of association among them: first municipal gilds and secondly associations on a different basis which might be wider or narrower than the ordinary gild. Organisation in such gilds does not appear to have been either early or widespread among masons, the main reason probably being that in most towns the number of masons was too small. Of 603 craftsmen in Coventry in 1450 only seven were masons; at that date there may have been 20 in Norwich and sixty years earlier there were perhaps 23 or 24 in Oxford. It is thus not strange that in most places where municipal gilds are known to have existed the masons were joined to other craftsmen. In thirteenth-century Florence the *maestri di pietra e legname* were associated, as masons and wrights were in Edinburgh in 1475; the Quatuor Coronati gild in fifteenth-century Antwerp included, with the masons, tilers and paviours; that in Bruges included, besides, plasterers and brickmakers.[71] In London, indeed, there were sufficient masons to constitute a gild by themselves, formed between 1356 and 1376, and in medieval Paris, where the number of building workers was considerable,[72] the masons and carpenters were separately organised. The latter in 1268 were subject to the general supervision of Foulques du Temple, who claimed to have been appointed by the crown, and who both drew a revenue from the craftsmen and exercised jurisdiction over practically all workers in wood, each of the separate crafts having regulations of its own. The masons, together with the stone-cutters, plasterers and mortar-makers, were subject to the jurisdiction of the king's master mason, who engaged to rule the trade fairly, 'as well for the poor as the rich, for the weak as for the strong'. Though the workers in these four trades had customs and regulations of their own and were associated in a fraternity of St Blaise they do not appear to have had a monopoly, since any skilled person was free to practice the mason's trade in Paris. The objects of gilds where they existed were to regulate apprenticeship, the employment of journeymen and the examination of materials and workmanship, and also to promote piety and good fellowship amongst the members. Tendencies towards monopoly were apt to be checked by the municipal authorities acting in the public interest. Thus, the city authorities in Florence controlled the price of building materials and by an ordinance in the early fourteenth century permitted craftsmen from outside to work in the city without becoming members of the gild or even paying to it.[73] Similarly, in Antwerp provision was made in 1458 for the introduction of 'foreign' workmen at need.

More widespread than such building trade gilds were the masons' lodges, of which one at least must have existed in connection with every considerable building, whether in town or country, in western Europe and which might well contain a greater number of masons than many municipalities required. Primarily, the lodge was a workshop, but it was also used for meals and for the mid-day *siesta*, and the men working within it, who no doubt discussed their pay and

[71] Count Goblet d'Alviella, 'The Quatuor Coronati in Belgium', *Ars Quatuor Coronatorum*, XIII (1900), 78ff.

[72] In 1300 there were 122 masons, 108 carpenters, 22 plasterers and 6 mortar-makers. On the Paris trades see Fagniez, *Etudes sur l'industrie et la classe industrielle* (Paris, 1877), especially 191ff.

[73] A. Doren, *Das Florentiner Zunftwesen* (Stuttgart and Berlin, 1908), 122.

grievances, were conscious of some solidarity and regarded it as disloyal for a man to reveal to those outside 'the councelle of his felows in logge and in chambere'.[74] From the employer's point of view it was desirable to draw up regulations, or to sanction existing customs, for the lodge; those for the lodges at York Minister in 1352, 1370 and 1408–9 survive and similar regulations may be presumed to have existed in other places and countries. It may also be presumed that the migratory character of the mason's calling would make many craftsmen familiar with the rules of lodges in different places and tend to bring about a certain uniformity in the customs of the craft. The lodge at Xanten at one time or another contained masons not only from the immediate neighbourhood but from Douai, Holland (Utrecht, Kranenberg), Antwerp, Brussels, Westphalia (Borken, Münster), the Rhineland (Düsseldorf, Cologne, Mainz, Trier) and even Nuremberg, and no doubt a similar variety existed in other lodges. This may well have made easier the development of an association to link the lodges together and to safeguard the interests of masons in general.

In Germany that stage was reached in 1459, if not before. The earliest regulations of the *Steinmetzen*[75] set forth what are claimed to be the good old customs of the craft as agreed upon by an assembly held in Regensburg in that year, and these, in a document of 1462, are said to have been accepted by masters from Magdeburg, Halberstadt Hildesheim and other places meeting at Torgau. The regulations were confirmed by imperial authority in 1498 and 1563. English masons may have had a similar organisation in the fourteenth century, for two documents relating to the craft describe an assembly or congregation which masons were bound to attend and which had legislative and judicial functions. There is no proof that such powers were in fact regularly and systematically exercised, but the statutory prohibition of masons' congregations does suggest that assemblies of some kind had occurred. The English documents contain no indication of a regional organisation, such as the German regulations portray, with headquarters in each district. In their general tenor and spirit, however, the English and the German regulations are similar; they assume the existence of the three industrial grades of apprentice, fellow and master and lay stress on apprenticeship; they prohibit the supersession of one master by another without cause and they exhort masons to piety, morality and care of the honour of the craft. In short they attempt to reconcile the interests of the 'lord' or employer with those of the master mason, his warden and the mass of journeymen.

[74] D. Knoop, G. P. Jones and D. Hamer, *The Two Earliest Masonic MSS* (Manchester, 1938), 121.

[75] For text and translation see F. Janner, *Die Bauhütten des deutschen Mittelalters* (Leipzig, 1876), 294ff. and Gould, *History of Freemasonry*, I, 134ff.

Whether a similar organisation existed in medieval France is doubtful, though M. Martin Saint-Léon may well be right in holding that the origins of the *compagnonnages* go back to the lodges connected with twelfth- or thirteenth-century cathedrals.[76] As we know them from later records, the *compagnonnages* were associations adapted to the needs of wandering journeymen requiring employment in the towns to which they came, or hospitality and help on their way. In Germany, no doubt, as in England and Scotland, there was a need to 'receive and cherish strange masons and set them to work' or else 'to refresh them with money to the next lodge'; and in France, Germany and Scotland there may have been a ritual and secret grips or other signs by means of which rightful claimants to this service could be distinguished from pretenders; but the French organisation, if it did indeed exist in the Middle Ages, differed from that prevailing elsewhere by excluding masters and concerning itself solely with the interests of journeymen. Associations limited to one industrial grade were common enough in other trades on the continent and not unknown in England, where the 'young men' of the carpenters had a fellowship in London in 1468. The general factors, apart from the migratory character of the craftsmen concerned, which gave rise to such associations were the increasing exclusiveness of the gilds and the decreasing chance of attaining independent status. When they formed their own organisations the journeymen adopted the model they knew, the masters' gild with its industrial, religious and convivial aspects; and they regarded themselves as being, no less than the masters, custodians of the honour and traditions of the craft. Thus, the *compagnons* who were masons held themselves to be inheritors of a craft and customs in use at the building of Solomon's Temple; but, however traditional their legends might be, their organisation was based on a principle which to the constituted authorities could not but seem detestable. The *compagnonnages* nevertheless survived and were active in the nineteenth century. It may be presumed that the rise in prices and the increasing importance of the large-scale building contractor, which came about after the close of the Middle Ages, did not change one of the main features of the medieval industry, its dependence on a great mass of wage-earning craftsmen.

[76] E. M. Saint-Léon, *Le Compagnonnage* (Paris, 1901), 15.

CHAPTER XII

Coinage and Currency

I. *Roman–Barbarian Discontinuity**

The collapse of the Roman Empire in the West was so prolonged a process that to expect to find any cataclysmic change in the coinage would be unreasonable. No such violent change or lengthy cessation of coinage occurred except in Britain. After the departure of the army and the breakdown of administrative contacts with the rest of the Empire, no further coin entered Britain, and, within a generation, by about A.D. 435, coin ceased to be used there as a medium of exchange. Not until the latter part of the seventh century were coins again used in Britain as money, although many survived as jewellery or were used for gifts or for compensation. Everywhere else in the area of the western Empire the use of money was maintained.

The coinage of the late Roman Empire reflected its economic decrepitude. On the one hand there was highly valued gold coins, the pure gold *solidus*, introduced by Constantine in 309, together with its half, the *semissis*, and its third, the *tremissis* or *triens*. The *solidus* weighed 24 carob seeds or carats, about 4.48 grams in modern terms. On the other hand there was the heavy copper *follis*, revived by Anastasius I in 498 as a coin of forty *nummi*, and its poor relations down to the *nummus*. In between came the sparsely issued silver coins, conventionally termed *siliquae* by numismatists. As units of account 24 *siliquae* were worth a *solidus*. The gold coinage was used for imperial gifts and the payment of subsidies to imperial 'allies', like the 50,000 *solidi* paid by Maurice Tiberius to Chilperic in 584. Its primary importance within the Empire was that land taxes had to be paid in gold. The prolific coinage of the lower denominations of copper was only of use for a multiplicity of small local payments. The silver coinage, of which very little had been issued since the late fourth century, finally came to an end in eastern Europe under Justinian (527–65). This was also the time of the disappearance of silver in western Europe. This decline and disappearance of a silver coinage has been used as an argument for the decline and disappearance of trade at this period.

* I would like to thank Professor Philip Grierson, of the Universities of Cambridge and Brussels, for reading a draft of this chapter and for making a number of most useful criticisms and suggestions.

The barbarian 'allies', although they had no tradition of coinage of their own, took over the Roman mints, which continued to strike in the names of the emperors. It is not clear at precisely what date this took place, but it probably occurred under Clovis (484–511) among the Franks, and under Alaric II (484–507) among the Visigoths. Over the next half-century gold *solidi* and *trientes* in the names of Anastasius, Justin and Justinian were issued by various Merovingian kings in northern Gaul and by Visigothic kings from such mints as Toulouse, without giving any indication of their real issuers.[1]

A similar small series of poor copies of the silver coins of emperors ranging from Valentinian to Anastasius was struck in Gaul at the end of the fifth century and the beginning of the sixth. Surviving examples weigh from 0.91 grams down to as little as 0.3 grams. They were possibly intended as 'half-*siliquae*', although their prototypes weighed from 1.04 to 1.25 grams.

These imitations of imperial coins were followed by a limited number of silver coins struck in their own names by the barbarian rulers. In Italy silver *siliquae* were struck at Rome, Ravenna and Pavia by the Germanic kings from Theodoric (493–526) to Teja (552–3), the last Ostrogothic ruler before Justinian's reconquest. These Ostrogoth issues were so tiny that even the small quantities of imperial *siliquae* that Justinian was able to strike at his Italian mints seem relatively abundant in comparison. However, after the Lombard conquest of much of the Italian peninsula in 568–70, the silver coinage of the remaining imperial mints at Ravenna and Rome again become very much sparser. In the other provinces of the Byzantine Empire it had already stopped altogether. In their early years the Lombard invaders went on striking *siliquae* which bore the names of Justinian and Justin II (565–78), whose coins formed the bulk of the limited circulating medium at the time of their arrival. In Gaul the Merovingian kings of the Franks from Thierry I (511–34) to Sigebert I (561–75) continued in their own names the series of silver coins previously struck in the names of the emperors. These were also probably intended as half-*siliquae*, since the later ones imitated in type the much heavier half-*siliquae* of Justinian (527–65). In the middle of the sixth century, copies in the name of Justinian were also being struck in the Rhineland, where his Italian *siliquae*, like their Ostrogothic predecessors, had a certain restricted circulation.[2]

Such extremely limited issues can hardly have been of much use for

[1] P. Le Gentilhomme, 'Le Monnayage et la circulation monétaire dans les royaumes barbares en Occident, ve – viie siècles', *Rev. Numismatique*, 5th ser. vii (1943), 46–112; and viii (1948), 13–59.

[2] J. Werner, 'Fernhandel und Naturalwirtschaft im östlichen Merowingerreich nach archäologischen und numismatischen Zeugrissen', Settimane di studio del Centro Italiano di Studi sull'alto medioevo, viii (Spoleto, 1961), *Moneta e Scambi nell'alto Medioevo*, 557–618.

commercial purposes, although it is perhaps significant that the Rhineland was one of the places in which some of these few pieces were struck. The final end of the trade patterns of the ancient world might well be placed in the third quarter of the sixth century when the issue of silver coins ceased altogether in both the western and eastern halves of the Roman Empire. This perhaps indicates the 'darkest' period of the 'dark ages' from the point of view of commercial activity.

The coinage of copper had come to an end a little earlier than that of silver. It had borne the names of such barbarian issuers as the Burgundian Godemar (524–34), Theodebert of Austrasia (534–48) and Childebert of Paris (511–58). These issues of small bronze coins had come to an end about the middle of the sixth century, and no further coins of bronze or pure copper were struck in western Europe until the end of the fifteenth century, save briefly in thirteenth-century Hungary. The Byzantine administrators on the mainland of Italy managed to keep a feeble copper coinage going until the eighth century when even that ceased. Only Sicily continued to fit in to the pattern of the central provinces of the Byzantine Empire, for there an abundant copper coinage was maintained by the Byzantine administrators and passed down to their successors, even to the Norman conquerors of the island in the twelfth century.[3] The prime function of a copper coinage is to provide for the enormous number of extraordinarily small payments that are a natural part of urban living, and which play so much smaller a part in a thoroughly rural society. The countryman's transactions are far fewer and in general rather larger than the townsman's. The countryman buys and sells grain by the bushel, the townsman bread by the loaf; the countryman deals with whole beasts, the townsman with his meat in small joints. In a properly urban environment a great deal of small change of some sort is required. It is perhaps a measure of the collapse of urban society that only in Sicily did the necessary copper coinage survive. Elsewhere in the West the great cities of antiquity had dwindled away.

What was left after the disappearance of both copper and silver coinage was gold, and this had a prestige out of all proportion to its utility. The first of the barbarians to have the audacity to put his own name on gold coins was Theodebert I of Austrasia (534–48), an action which brought forth bitter comment in Procopius' *De Bello Gothico*. Neither of his two immediate successors issued coins in their own names, although some of the *solidi* and *trientes* in the name of Theodebert may have been issued by them. From the reign of Sigebert (561–75) and his brother Gontran (561–92) onwards, however, the

[3] P. Grierson, 'Monete Bizantine in Italia dal VII all' XI secolo', *Monete e Scambi nell'alto Medioevo*.

minting of coins bearing the name of their true issuer became regular in the Frankish kingdoms of northern Gaul, although issues in the names of the emperors continued in Provence down to Heraclius (610–41). The Visigothic kings did not strike *trientes* in their own names until Leovigild, around 580, and there was a similar time-lag in Italy under its Lombard rulers, who kept the mints open from their conquest in 568 onwards, but did not use their own names on the coinage until Cunincpert (680–700). Thus, for periods of up to a century, the various barbarian rulers appeared to keep alive the fiction that western Europe was still a part of the Roman Empire, before proclaiming on their gold coinages that they had created new independent kingdoms.

It was basically a non-commercial coinage of gold that the barbarians had inherited. Their *solidi*, whether issued in the names of the emperors or in those of their own kings, were, initially at any rate, as good as those struck in the mints under direct imperial control. They were also used for much the same purposes, prestigious gifts and tribute, exemplified by the annual sum of 12,000 gold *solidi* intermittently paid by the Lombards to the Franks in the late sixth century.[4] Their bronze and silver coinages, before they were given up in the middle of the sixth century, were often much poorer than their imperial prototypes and did not serve well for commercial purposes. After the end of the bronze and silver coinages, even the gold coinage began to diminish in quantity. What sort of an economy was it with only a diminishing gold coinage and neither silver nor copper? Apart from the activities of rulers, we have little direct evidence of the use of money, but it is clear that, at least in the seventh and eighth centuries, in the Lombard territories gold coin was used for capital outlay, such as the purchase of agricultural land, although the rents from such land were received in kind or in services.[5]

In the second half of the sixth century it became more usual to strike the *triens* rather than the whole *solidus*. No whole *solidi* at all were struck by the Visigoths from the reign of Leovigild (568–86) at the latest. In seventh- and eighth-century Italy too, it was *trientes* that the Lombard kings struck from their mints in the Po valley and Tuscany, although further south the Lombard dukes of Benevento, more strongly influenced by Byzantium, did strike *solidi* as well, like the surviving Byzantine mints in Italy and Sicily.

A further indication of the declining use of the *solidus* is provided by two hoards. A hoard from Seville, of the mid-sixth century, contained at least 40 *solidi* and only certainly 18 *trientes*, whereas a

[4] P. Grierson, 'Commerce in the Dark Ages: a Critique of the Evidence', *Trans. Roy. Hist. Soc.*, 5th ser., IX (1959), 132.

[5] E. Bernareggi, *Il sistema economica della monetazione dei Longobardi nell'Italia superiore* (Milan, 1960).

hoard at Escharen, near Nijmegen, deposited half a century later, around 600, contained 54 *trientes*, but only 11 whole *solidi*, and of these 5 were of Byzantine rather than barbarian origin.

Although we may be technically correct today in speaking of later barbarian gold pieces of the seventh century as *trientes*, using the Byzantine *solidus* for comparison, there is some reason to suppose that they were themselves known at the time as *solidi*, or shillings, after the true *solidus* had disappeared from circulation in the West.

All the surviving specimens of the *triens* of the Bonn mint were struck from a single pair of dies, which suggests that the issues were very small, and consisted of only a few thousand pieces from some mints. However, the number of separate mints increased. The Franks set up new mints in addition to those which they had inherited from the Romans. Although these operated in all parts of their kingdoms, there was a certain concentration of mints in those areas in which trade was beginning to revive, for example, in the valleys of the Meuse and the Rhine. These valleys not only lay in the heartland of the Frankish people, but were also routes frequented by Frisian merchants, the new leaders in trade. *Trientes* were also struck in Frisia itself. This was the first extension of coinage to an area where it had not been struck in antiquity. Otherwise minting was restricted to areas that had once been within the confines of the Roman Empire, and the circulation of coin, as shown by both coin hoards and finds of stray coins, barely extended beyond the old Roman frontiers.

Alongside the *triens* the Frisians and Merovingians also began to strike a new *denarius* in the seventh century, of the same weight as the *triens*, but in silver instead of gold. The future lay with the silver *denarius* rather than the declining gold *triens*, for this *denarius* was the ancestor of the Carolingian denier and the whole range of medieval penny coinages.

Gold was about to go out of use in the West for over five centuries. Except in Italy the issue of *trientes* came to an end late in the seventh century. The Merovingians stopped striking their own gold coins under Dagobert II (674–9), and hoard evidence suggests that the circulation of gold coins from the eastern Empire had long since ceased in Merovingian Gaul. The Anglo-Saxons, who had resumed the use of coin only a generation before, and even that in south-east England alone, stopped minting gold around the end of the century. In Spain the last Visigothic *trientes* of Achila II (*c.* 710–14) were succeeded only by a very poor issue of gold *dinars* by the conquering Ummayads.[6]

[6] G. C. Miles, *The Coinage of the Visigoths of Spain: Leovigild to Achila II*, American Numismatic Society (New York, 1952); and G. C. Miles, *The Coins of the Spanish Mulūk al-Tawa'if*, American Numismatic Society (New York, 1954).

No further gold coins were then struck in Spain until the tenth century. Minting of gold continued only in Italy, which was still partially in the orbit of the eastern Mediterranean, and even here the general dearth of gold made it impossible any longer to produce coins of fine gold.

In northern Italy, in Lombardy and Tuscany, the issue of *trientes*, by the Lombards and by Charlemagne, went on through much of the eighth century, and their circulation continued until it was forbidden in 781. By then they had greatly deteriorated in fineness, from nearly pure gold to barely a quarter gold and three-quarters alloy. There had still been direct Byzantine issues of gold coin in northern Italy as late as the middle of the eighth century, for Ravenna did not fall to the Lombards until 751.

In central Italy the Byzantine issues of gold at Rome deteriorated at the same time as those of the Lombards further north. By the mid-eighth century they were only about a third gold, and two-thirds alloy. In the 770s just before Pope Adrian I took over the mint, the last Byzantine coins struck in Rome were only of gilded copper.

In the south of Italy, parts of which remained in Byzantine hands until the eleventh century, the use of gold coins continued without any interruption. The Byzantine provinces were supplied with coin from Sicily until it fell into Muslim hands, and thereafter from Byzantium itself, where the minting of gold *solidi* continued uninterruptedly. The original fourth-century standard of fineness and weight was even maintained until the eleventh century. As late as the ninth century they were extensively imitated in at least one south Italian mint, probably Naples, outside Byzantine control.[7] In addition the Lombard rulers of Benevento continued to strike *solidi* and *tremisses* in their own names until the mid-ninth century, although their pieces were of extremely poor gold. Modern analysis has shown that the worst of them were no more than 8 per cent gold and 92 per cent alloy.

In Sicily itself, gold *solidi* circulated commonly as long as the Byzantine mint at Syracuse remained open – up to 878 – and during the Muslim occupation of the island, gold *taris* or quarter-*dinars* were minted, similar to those of North Africa.

Otherwise, from the eighth century onwards, the coinage of western Europe was minted exclusively of silver for the next five hundred years, apart from a few altogether extraordinary pieces, issued by such rulers as the Carolingian emperor Louis the Pious, Offa king of Mercia, and Edward the Confessor of England, which were almost certainly intended only for prestigious royal alms-givings.

[7] Grierson, 'Monete Bizantine'.

However, before the final disappearance of gold in the West, there was a short period in seventh-century Merovingian Gaul which saw a temporary relationship between gold and silver in which one pound (as a weight of silver) equalled 20 old shillings (which we would now call gold *trientes*) equalled 240 new pence (silver *denarii*). It was at this time that there originated the familiar relationship of pounds, shillings and pence, which was almost universally employed in western Europe before the decimalisation of the last two centuries. On the demise of the gold *triens* (shilling) as a coin, and the decline of the weight of the silver *denarius* (penny) so that 240 no longer weighed a pound, the relationship remained in a fossilised form as a convenient means of counting silver pennies. A shilling came to mean a dozen pennies, and a pound to mean a score of dozens.[8]

When gold coinage had finally disappeared, the West was left with a coinage entirely unlike either that which survived in the East, in the Byzantine Empire, or that which had existed in the later Roman Empire. The discontinuity was complete. The system of coinage based on the silver penny was something essentially new and different from the coinage systems of antiquity. There had been a total transformation. It was not that the barbarians brought something new and differently Germanic into the Roman world, but that a transformation took place after the barbarian peoples were inside the Roman world. There was a total break with antiquity, but it was not a revolutionary break at a single instant as when the Germanic peoples crossed the Rhine frontier in 403, but an evolutionary change, which had taken over two centuries to work out. The disappearance of the coinage systems of antiquity, like the disappearance of the Roman senatorial aristocracy, took many generations. It was none the less complete.[9]

II. *The Denier*

The silver penny or denier, the minting of which began during the tentative revival of trade in the seventh century was, for over five centuries, not merely the characteristic coin of western Europe, but virtually the only coin in use.

The most prolific issues of the seventh century were the pennies or *pennings* of England and Frisia, frequently mis-called 'sceattas' or 'sceats' by numismatists. They were minted in enormous quantities between the end of the seventh century and the third quarter of the

[8] P. Grierson, 'Money and coinage under Charlemagne', *Karl der Grosse: Lebenswerk und Nachleben*, ed. H. Beumann, I (Dusseldorf, 1965), 501–36.

[9] For the whole of this period see the remarkable group of papers in *Monete e Scambi nell'alto medioevo*. Settimane di studio del Centro Italiano di Studi sull'alto medioevo, VIII (Spoleto, 1961).

eighth and had the same weight and general appearance as the contemporaneous Merovingian Frankish denier. It is not very easy to distinguish which pieces were struck on the Anglo-Saxon and which on the Frisian coast of the North Sea. However, certain of the commoner types appear to have been primarily struck on the Frisian side like the 'porcupine' type of around 720–40 which may have been minted in millions. As far as can now be judged the stretch of coastline then settled by 'Frisians' reached from the mouth of the Weser in the north, to the mouth of the Zwin in the south, where Bruges was later to be built, or perhaps even to the mouth of the Canche, where Quentovic was to be founded. The Frisians' trade ran not only coastwise, but also across the North Sea, and up the Rhine to Cologne, Bonn and Mainz. As such its focal point was the mouth of the Rhine, where sea, coast and river traffic all concentrated. The course of the principal branch of the Rhine was more northerly than at present, so that the focal point was not Europapoort-Rotterdam, but Dorstad, not far from Utrecht, the 'capital' of the dukes of the Frisians, and the see of the bishops of the Frisians after their conversion. It seems likely that the principal mint of the Frisians was in Dorstad, even before the nominal Frankish conquest in the 730s. In the later eighth century Dorstad appears, from the evidence of surviving coins, to have been the most prolific minting place as well as one of the most important trading centres of the Frankish kingdom as it grew rapidly into an empire.

The Merovingian silver denier was closely related to the Anglo-Frisian penning, but it does not seem to have been issued in very considerable quantities before the conquest of Frisia, although our evidence for this is based on a very restricted number of coin hoards.[10] The issue of these pieces seems to have been mainly concentrated in the mints of northern Gaul, the area closest to Anglo-Frisian trade. Apart from a single known very early royal issue, by Caribert II of Aquitaine (629–31), these pieces were entirely struck by local enterprise and authority in the period of late Merovingian collapse. The majority of the issuers were ecclesiastical, including both bishops, like St Lambert of Lyons (680–90), and abbeys, such as St Denis and St Martin of Tours. A certain number of issuers were, however, laymen, for example Ebroin, mayor of the palace of Neustria (659–81), and Ansedert and two of his fellow patricians of Marseilles, which was another of the focal points of the trade of the seventh and eighth centuries.

The silver *denarius* of the middle and late seventh century was

[10] J. Lafaurie, 'Monnaies d'argent mérovingiennes des VIIe et VIIIe siècles', *Revue Numismatique*, 6th ser., XI (1969), 98–129.

modelled so exactly on the gold *triens* that they can only be distinguished from one another by the metal in which they were struck. In the early eighth century the types were reduced almost entirely to legends and monograms. Surviving examples suggest that Merovingian deniers were struck either at the rate of 240 to the pound of silver (i.e. 1.36 grams each), or, more frequently, on a standard of 264 to the pound (i.e. 1.24 grams each). Certainly they were struck for long enough at 240 to the pound for this relationship to be the one that was fossilised for the next thirteen hundred years.

The end of the gold coinage in the seventh century saw the closure of many mints which had been striking gold only, whilst some of those which had been striking silver as well as gold appear to have remained in uninterrupted operation until the Carolingian period. It is difficult to be certain of this because the majority of these deniers do not distinguish their issuers as individuals, but merely as the 'bishop of Clermont' or the 'abbey of St Maxentius', for example, and hence cannot be dated exactly.

Silver coinage was revived in the seventh century, not only in Merovingian Gaul and on the Anglo-Frisian coasts, but also in Lombard Italy under Perctarit (678–88) and in Ummayad Spain. In contrast to the thick, dumpy, silver deniers of the Frisians, the Anglo-Saxons and the Franks, the silver *dirhems* of Ummayad Spain were struck on a thinner, broader flan, and this was gradually adopted elsewhere. The Emperor Leo III (717–40) used the thinner, broader flan in Byzantium for his silver *miliaresion*, and the Carolingian ruler, Pepin, did the same in 755 for the expanding kingdom of the Franks.

Pepin's reform of the coinage in 755 also restored the weight of the coin, after a temporary lapse, by reaffirming that no more than 22 sous (i.e. 264 deniers) should be made from the pound of silver. Pepin's reform applied primarily to mints under royal control, but the non-royal mints, mainly in ecclesiastical hands, soon turned from the issue of the smaller to the broader denier, and once more placed the royal title on their issues. This system, in which the mints were still locally controlled, while now again acknowledging the king as the ultimate authority over coinage, continued into the early years of Charlemagne's reign. It was then superseded by a much more centralised system, under which identical coins were struck throughout the 'empire'. After Dorstad, one of the most prolific mints was that at Melle in Poitou, which was close to a rich vein of silver. In addition to the mints inherited from the Merovingian period, an increasing number of new mints were opened in the Carolingian period. The issue of the broader, thinner deniers was not confined to Gaul. They were struck in all parts of the 'empire'; in Spain at such mints as

Barcelona and Ampurias, and in Italy at such mints as Lucca which had been very active under the Lombards, Milan and, above all, Pavia. A joint coinage with the Pope was issued in Rome, and with the Lombard prince in Benevento. The Germanic lands conquered east of the Rhineland were, however, not ready for coinage. Nevertheless the principal concentration of mints in the Carolingian Empire lay, not surprisingly, in the heartland of the Austrasian Franks and coincided with the greatest concentration of Carolingian family property around the 'capital' at Aachen. As well as a palatine mint at Aachen itself, there were also major mints at Cologne and Bonn on the Rhine, and at Maastricht, Huy and Namur on the Meuse and a host of less important mints at such neighbouring places as St Trond, Tongres and Liège.[11]

In the larger part of England coin did not circulate as money in the eighth century. Its monetary use seems to have been limited to parts of the south and east coasts. In south-east England the dumpy Anglo-Frisian 'sceatta' pennies began to be replaced by the new broad pennies about 775–80 by Heahbert and Ecgbehrt, sub-reguli in Kent, who opened a mint at Canterbury, which was taken over about 783/4 by Offa of Mercia. In 792 Offa reformed his coinage to bring it into line with Charlemagne's. It was this new, thin, broad denier, rather than the smaller, thicker 'sceatta' penny, which served as a model for the later pennies of all the Anglo-Saxon kingdoms, apart from Northumbria, where old-fashioned pieces of the smaller, thicker module curiously began to be minted about the 820s.

Almost immediately after Offa had brought his coinage into line with the existing coinage of Charlemagne, the latter inaugurated a major reform of his own coinage. As part of his general reform of weights and measures, he radically increased the weight of the silver denier. Universal acceptance of the new deniers was enjoined at the Council of Frankfurt in May 794. They were still of a very thin module, but even broader than their predecessors, about 20 mm in diameter, instead of 15 mm. They were intended to weigh just over 1.7 grams. Nine of the new deniers were to be worth twelve of the old. Charlemagne's successors tried to maintain their coinages at this weight throughout the ninth century. It was a common standard which applied alike in western Germany and northern Italy, as well as Christian Spain and what is now France, whether the pennies were known as *pfennigs* or *denari*, *dineros* or deniers. It is therefore in relation to this standard that we can measure how far rulers in various parts of Europe allowed, or caused, their different coinages to deteriorate.

[11] A. Suhle, *Deutsche Münz- und Geldgeschichte von den Anfängen bis zum 15 Jahrhundert* (2nd edn, Berlin, 1964), 42 (and Map 1 for distribution of mints).

The degree of control over the coinage, after Charlemagne's reform of it, was reflected in the uniformity of the coinage throughout the Empire. This was in marked contrast to the diversity that had existed at the beginning of his reign. The earlier deniers, although acknowledging his authority, were crudely made, and give the impression of having been designed locally according to the taste of the individual moneyers. The reformed heavy deniers are of careful design, and only differ from mint to mint in the mint name, and use of the additional title of 'king of the Lombards' on pieces struck in Italy. At one stage the idea was even entertained of centralising yet further by producing all the necessary coin at a single palatine mint at Aachen.

Louis the Pious, Charlemagne's son, ordered shortly after his accession that all the coin in circulation, which had been minted during his father's reign, should be brought in for reminting. The evidence of coin hoards shows that this order was actually obeyed. The success of such a proceeding was another measure of the degree of control over the coinage that Charlemagne had established. It was also a measure of the small amount of coinage in circulation. Even if the amount of coinage in circulation was still small enough for such an order to be imposed, it was nevertheless much larger than it had been earlier and went on increasing in quantity until the middle of the ninth century, when prodigious sums were available for payment to Viking armies as Danegeld. The problem arises of where this silver came from. Import from the Islamic world has been postulated, but neither literary sources nor coin hoards suggest that much Islamic silver entered western Europe. The general pattern of both earlier and later commerce would lead the historian to expect that precious metal would have been leaving rather than entering Europe. Northern 'trade' would also suggest that Carolingian silver moved outwards from the Empire along the Frisian trade routes into England and towards the Baltic. The only tenable solution to the problem of the origin of the silver is that it was made available from within the Empire by dis-hoarding and by new mining, for example, at Melle in Poitou, and at 'German Melle'.

Hoard evidence suggests that free movement of coin about the Empire was a reality, although how much this can be correlated with internal trade and free movement of goods is another matter. The movement of goods can be both much less, and much greater than the movement of coin. 'Much less' in that coin can move about for administrative reasons inside a centralised state, however primitive its administration, without any corresponding movement of goods. 'Much greater' in that the exchange of goods can take place without coin. There was not only the barter of commodities in particular places, but also 'gift-exchange' over considerable distances. There is some evidence to suggest that the barbarian custom of 'gift-exchange' survived on quite a considerable scale into Carolingian times.[12] However, there was certainly some correlation between money and trade. Excavations at Dorstad have turned up so large a number of stray deniers, making it quite apparent that money was there in common circulation for so many to have been lost. But how typical was Dorstad? When in 833 Louis the Pious granted the right to open a *moneta publica nostrae auctoritatis* at Corvey on the Weser it was 'quia locum mercationis ipsa regio indigebat'.[13] In the mind of the grantor at any rate, mint and market were firmly associated. This seems to have been the case in practice in the Carolingian heartland, even if the right to open a mint was not yet a useful one east of the Rhineland.

Carolingian Europe was a very rural Europe, and in the countryside the circulation of money, even in this fresh dawn of a 'money' economy, could be socially circumscribed. The *polyptique* of the abbey of St Germain-des-Prés compiled during the abbacy of Irminon (806–29) gives details of the revenues from the abbey's estates which were largely situated in the Paris basin, an area in which money might be expected to have circulated as freely as anywhere in the Carolingian Empire. Only 3 per cent of the revenue from the servile *manses* was received in silver. The rest was in kind or, above all, in services. On the other hand no less than 24 per cent of the revenues from the free *manses* was received in money.[14] Some of this was clearly in commutation of services rendered in the past – a free *manse* at Villeneuve-St-Georges, for example, paid 4 *sous* in silver (48 actual deniers) instead of military service. Free countrymen were increasingly using coin on these estates, but it is not clear how typical they were of Carolingian Europe, or even of the Paris basin. Further from the economic and political heart of the Carolingian Empire the use of money was sometimes more restricted. It is quite clear that money was not always easily available and contracts and leases give alternative means of payment as a matter of course. The abbey of St Gallen lay not far off one of the main routes through the Alps into Italy, and in the reign of Louis the Pious (814–40) there was a mint at Chur on this route. Nevertheless, at this very time, in 836, a dependant of the abbey had the option of paying it each year '3 maldros sive 6 denarios vel precium 6 denariorum in ferramentis qualecumque ex his tribus facilius invenire possimus'.[15] Similar options continued to appear in leases for centuries.

[12] Grierson, 'Commerce in the Dark Ages', 136–9.
[13] W. Jesse, *Quellenbuch zur Münz- und Geldgeschichte des Mittelalters* (Halle-Saale, 1924), Document no. 44, pp. 14–15.
[14] *Polyptique de l'Abbé Irminon*, ed. B. Guérard (Paris, 1844), 892–7.
[15] A. Dopsch, *Naturalwirtschaft und Geldwirtschaft in der Weltgeschichte* (Vienna, 1930), 138.

The use of money in the ninth century was thus not uniform throughout the Carolingian Empire. The distribution of mints and of coin hoards suggests that it was concentrated in Frisia, in the Frankish heartland, and in a 'Lotharingian' corridor leading to the Arelate and Lombardy.[16] It was to the east of this corridor that the use of money was particularly limited.

There were Carolingian mints in the Rhineland, as there had been earlier, but east of the Rhine minting did not generally begin until the tenth century. It was only then that the grant of a mint at Corvey began to become of any use. There was no mint at all east of the Rhine until 817 when Louis 'the German' was created 'King of Bavaria' by his father Louis the Pious and took up residence on the Danube in Regensburg. This was to continue as one of the principal palaces of the line of East Frankish rulers who descended from him. The output of his mint at Regensburg was negligible.[17]

The next development was very different. The Frisian trading area, focussed on the Rhine mouth, reached northwards beyond Frisian territory to the mouth of the Elbe and to the isthmus across which traders went from the North Sea to the Baltic, where the Kiel Canal is now situated. To begin with Frisian merchants carried coin to this area, and it was there that coinage next began to be minted. By about 825 a mint or mints was in operation in this isthmus, perhaps at Hedeby (Haithabu) which was later to be so important. In the first instance this mint, or mints, did not even strike direct copies of Carolingian pieces, let alone an autonomous coinage of its own, but imitations of north Frisian imitations of the deniers of Dorstad of Charlemagne and Louis the Pious. It is strange that it took place in such a roundabout way, for genuine deniers from the early part of the reign of Charlemagne have actually been found in this area, for example in a hoard found at Krinkberg in Holstein. About 834 a mint also appears to have been opened at Hamburg,[18] and the issues of Hamburg and on the isthmus continued until about the middle of the century and then ceased. This beginning was not to lead to a continuous issue of coin in northern Germany, for in 845 the Danes under King Horik sacked Hamburg and its mint ceased operations. At about the same time the mint on the isthmus closed down.

Other mints closed at this time for similar reasons. Even the mint at Dorstad itself, so prolific under Frisian, Merovingian and Carolingian aegis, closed down about 863 after the repeated sack of the place by Vikings. The newly started coinage of the Northumbrian kingdom

[16] See map in: K. F. Morrison and H. Grunthal, *Carolingian Coinage*. Numismatic Notes and Monographs, CLVIII. American Numismatic Society (New York, 1967).
[17] Grierson, 'Money and Coinage under Charlemagne', 501–36.
[18] Suhle, *Deutsche Münz- und Geldgeschichte*, 42.

was cut short by the Vikings in the 860s after only forty years of existence. Scandinavia itself had been on the verge of creating its own coinage in the first half of the ninth century, but its raiders not only turned that possibility away, but also quite violently reduced the minting of coinage in some other parts of western Europe as well.[19]

The genesis of 'feudal' society strictly defined, as opposed to the earlier origins of manorial society, is generally seen in the breakdown of imperial authority in the ninth century. The fragmentation of the control of the minting of coined money was naturally involved at this period with the general fragmentation of regalian authority. Charlemagne had quite clearly established that minting was an undoubted exercise of regalian authority. When the political breakdown of the western half of the Carolingian Empire came about in the course of the ninth century many counts had mints to administer. The counts, whose proper function was to protect imperial or royal interests, instead began to strike coins for their own advantage. Naturally they did not do so at first under their own names, nor, initially, did they allow their deniers to diverge much from the known and universal standards of weight and fineness which they were supposed to maintain. Later they did both. Very many of these post- or sub-Carolingian deniers were anonymous, bearing neither the name of the emperor nor of the feudatory. Others bore the name of some long-dead emperor or king, rather than those of the current emperor or king. The counts of Poitou, for example, went on minting at Melle, from the ninth century to the twelfth, in the name of Charles the Bald (840–77). Since coinage remained, in theory at least, an imperial or royal prerogative, it was natural that the lords who controlled the individual mints should for long refrain from using their own names on their deniers and should produce anonymous or posthumous pieces before declaring on the coins themselves their usurpation, or grant, of the royal minting rights. When they did so, some began by linking the name of their king with their own. As early as 876–80 Bruno, duke of the Saxons, issued an obol in his own name together with that of King Louis. Soon others were, more honestly, declaring that their deniers were issued entirely on their own authority. Hugh, count of the Lyonnais, for example, omitted the king's name entirely from deniers struck between 936 and 948, using only his own name on them. As with the earlier evolution of the independent coinages of the barbarian kingdoms in the fifth and six centuries, there was a considerable time-lag between the actual taking over of the running of the mints and the formal acknowledgement of this act on the coins themselves.

[19] For the Viking period see the articles collected in N. L. Rasmusson and L. O. Lagerquist, (eds.), *Commentationes de nummis saeculorum IX–XI in Suecia repertis*. 2 vols. (Stockholm, 1961–8).

In these circumstances there was a strong incentive to continue issuing the same types over a long period of time. This happened both in the barbarian kingdoms in the West in the fifth and sixth centuries, and in the 'feudal' society evolving between the Pyrenees and the Rhine from the ninth century to the twelfth. In order to maintain these static types, new dies were copied slavishly, and seemingly uncomprehendingly, from those previously in use, and in the process gradual, degenerative, change crept in. The monogram of the ruler, a typical Carolingian reverse type, continued to appear in gradually less and less recognisable forms on deniers from all parts of West Frankia until the eleventh or even the twelfth century, whilst the obverse head at times became grotesque with repeated copying. On the eleventh-century deniers of Chartres and neighbouring mints it became the notorious *tête chartrain*, an abstract arrangement of lines and dots.

The fragmentation of political authority over a period of three centuries was not paralleled at all levels by a fragmentation of mint rights. They were fragmented certainly, but not so completely as some other aspects of political authority. All the successor kings naturally minted, and so did the greatest feudatories of West Frankia, the marquesses of Flanders, the counts of Paris, the dukes of Burgundy and Aquitaine, and the counts of Brittany and Anjou. The next level in the feudal hierarchy, the subordinate counts, did not all operate mints, and below them only a very limited number of lesser seigneurs were ever granted, or usurped, the right of minting. Often their doing so did not in any case become apparent until comparatively late. Alongside the lay hierarchy, quite a number of ecclesiastical feudatories also exercised the rights of coinage. Many bishops did so, and so did the greatest land-holding monasteries such as the abbey of St Martin at Tours, or that of St Martial at Limoges.[20]

Despite the fragmentation of the authority by which coin was minted, the later ninth and the early tenth century witnessed the remarkable resilience of the Carolingian monetary system under very adverse circumstances. Although some of the major mints had to close down, like those in the leading ports of Dorstad and Quentovic, it was still possible right through the second half of the ninth century and into the first half of the tenth to collect Danegeld in rural West Frankia in silver deniers. This was levied at so many deniers on every *mansus* and added up to quite considerable sums, beginning in 845 with the payment by Charles the Bald of seven thousand pounds (well over one and a half million deniers) to persuade one Scandinavian army to leave the Seine valley. It is not surprising that this brought about dis-hoarding

[20] F. Poey D'Avant, *Les Monnaies féodales de la France*. 3 vols. (Paris, 1858–62), reprinted (Graz, 1961) and E. Caron, *Monnaies féodales françaises* (Paris, 1882).

of silver, and that dozens of small new local mints had to be opened to strike the deniers used for paying the Danegeld.[21]

The late ninth and early tenth century witnessed the high watermark of Viking expansion, not only into western Europe, where Frisia, Normandy and the English Danelaw were overrun, but also into eastern Europe. It was in this way that commercial contact was made with central Asia. The 'Rus' collected sable and other kinds of fur in what is to-day Russia, partially, at least, as tribute. These commodities, together with honey, wax and amber from the Baltic area itself, went, like the slaves which had been traded in the same area since time immemorial, to Muslim merchants at Bulgar on the middle Volga. The Muslim merchants paid in 'Kufic' *dirhems*, so-called from Kufah in Mesopotamia, although most of them were in reality Samanid *dirhems* from Transoxiana, which was particularly prosperous in the early tenth century. This prosperity depended in part on the exploitation of rich silver mines in the Samanid provinces, particularly those at Shash, now Tashkent, and at Pendjhir in Afghanistan which were discovered in the second half of the ninth century. In this way these *dirhems* found their way to Scandinavian Russia, to Scandinavia itself, and to other lands bordering on the Baltic. Some 200,000 *dirhems* have so far been found and recorded in hoards in northern, central and eastern Europe, including 85,000 in Scandinavia, and 25,000 in what is now Poland, principally along the Baltic in Pomerania. Most of the rest have been found in Russia.[22]

It was in the period after 890 that this trade was at its most considerable, and that Birka, looking eastwards to Russia from Sweden, was at its most prosperous. 'Kufic' *dirhems* spread westwards from Sweden along the trade routes, through Hedeby, and across the North Sea to the Scandinavian parts of the British Isles. It was in this way that a hoard of 37 coins and other silver objects at Goldsborough in Yorkshire, probably dating from about 925–30, came to contain no fewer than 35 *dirhems*, of which at least 28 were of Samanid origin, struck at such mints as that of Samarkand between 895 and 911.[23]

Since many coin hoards, like this one, in the Scandinavian world also contained silver in the form of silver ornaments or fragments of ornaments and deliberately hacked ingots of silver and cut pieces of *dirhems*, it has been deduced that silver was used as a means of exchange by the Vikings by weight, and that coin was only regarded as one form

[21] E. Joranson, *The Danegeld in France* (Rock Island, Illionois, 1924) and A. d'Hoenens, 'Les Invasions Normandes dans l'Empire franc au IXe siècle', *I Normanni e la loro espansione in Europa nell'alto medioevo* (Spoleto, 1969), 233–98.

[22] P. H. Sawyer, *The Age of the Vikings* (London, 1971).

[23] For this and other British coin hoards, see J. D. A. Thomson, *Inventory of British Coin Hoards AD 600–1500*, Royal Numismatic Society (London, 1956).

of silver. This view is supported by saga evidence and by the fact that no regular coinage was yet minted in Scandinavia itself. It is therefore not clear whether or not these *dirhems* were used as money in the strictest sense of the word once they had reached tenth-century Russia, Sweden, Denmark, Poland or northern England. It is certain, however, that they did circulate in some places in the furtherance of trade. A Jew from Tortosa on the Ebro, in Muslim Spain, travelling through Mainz in 965, commented that he found Indian aromatics and spices – spikenard, pepper, cloves and ginger – exposed for sale, as well as local grain and wine. In addition he noted that *dirhems* were in use which had been struck at Samarkand as recently as the reign of the Samanid Nasr b. Ahmad (913–43).[24] In a quite remarkable way, and for the only time in the Middle Ages, non-European coins formed, in some sense at least, a part of the currency of Europe.

This episode drew to an abrupt close about 965. Hoards concealed in Poland during the second half of the tenth century no longer contained enormous quantities of Islamic *dirhems*. Instead they reflected the influx of a great mass of west European coins, particularly German pfennigs. Other west European coins travelled on to northern Russia. Hoards concealed there, from the first half of the eleventh century onwards, increasingly contained large proportions of German pfennigs and Anglo-Saxon pennies. Similarly, Scandinavian coin hoards, from the end of the tenth century to the middle of the eleventh, consisted almost entirely of German pfennigs and English pennies in place of Islamic *dirhems*. This represents both a new orientation in Scandinavian life, as well as a considerable increase in prosperity in Ottonian Germany and Anglo-Saxon England in the tenth and eleventh centuries.

The means by which this increased wealth was transferred from Germany and England to Sweden were, at least in part, political rather than commercial. Intermittently, from 991 to 1051, the English paid immense sums to Scandinavians as tribute and military wages. This was on a scale, if chronicle sources are to be believed, ten times greater than the Danegeld paid by the West Franks in the later ninth century and the early tenth. The change of scale between the tribute payments made by the ninth-century Franks and the eleventh-century English perhaps reflects a great increase in the amount of money in circulation in western Europe and, in particular, in Germany and England.

There also seems to have been a change inside Scandinavia in the way that coin was treated. The hacked ingots of silver and cut pieces of coins were no longer the characteristic element in coin hoards that

[24] A. Miquel, 'L'Europe occidentale dans la relation arabe d'Ibrâhîm b. Ya'qûb (xe s.)', *Annales E.S.C.*, XXI (1966), 1048–64.

they had been. This could imply that coins had ceased merely to be accepted as one form, amongst others, in which a given weight of silver might be handed over. A changed attitude to coined silver is also suggested by the beginning of minting in Scandinavia itself. Initially copies were minted of the coins most commonly available, particularly the pennies of Æthelred II of England. From the imitation of English pennies, either with the name of the king of England, or with blundered and incoherent inscriptions, it was a simple progression to the creation of a true indigenous coinage, albeit with types based on those of others.[25]

The extension of minting into Scandinavia was only one example of a general expansion in the geographical distribution of mints in operation. In the tenth century minting became much more considerable in northern Italy, France, and south-east England. It was revived in the Rhineland and in the southern Netherlands where it had almost ceased. It was permanently extended from the upper Rhineland through Bavaria to Bohemia and Hungary. It was permanently extended from the middle Rhineland through Saxony to the Elbe and temporarily on to Poland. It was permanently extended from the mouth of the Rhine along the North Sea coast to Denmark, and temporarily into Sweden and Norway. It was permanently extended from the south-east of England to York and Chester, and temporarily into Ireland. With this enormous extension of the area in which silver pennies were minted there naturally went an extension of the system of counting them in pounds and shillings.

In one particular instance this increase in the quantity of coin put into circulation has been directly linked with the mining of silver. Spectrographic analysis of the trace elements of various minor impurities in the commonly surviving pfennigs struck in the name of the Empress Adelaide have shown that the majority of them were minted from the silver mined out of the Rammelsberg above the town of Goslar in the Harz mountains. Adelaide married Otto the Great in 951, and her name appears with his on pfennigs struck in her dowerlands. It later appears in turn with those of her son, Otto II, and of her grandson, Otto III, for whom she was acting as regent when she died in 999. Although silver mining began at Goslar in the 960s, its development, at least as measured by the 'Adelaide-Otto' pfennigs produced from it, seems to have been slow until the reign of Otto III (983–1002), when the most prolific issues of 'Adelaide-Otto' pfennigs came from the Goslar mint.[26] As well as the silver mines in

[25] B. Malmer, *Nordiska Mynt före år 1000*. Acta Archaeologica Lundensia, IV (Lund-Bonn, 1966). With English resumé.

[26] E. Kraume and V. Hatz, 'Die Otto-Adelheid Pfennige und Ihre Nachprägungen', *Hamburger Beiträge zur Numismatik*, NS, XV (1961–3), 13–23 and appendices.

the Harz, of which the 'Alte Lager' of the Rammelsberg was only the first, more silver was discovered and further mines were exploited elsewhere in Germany in the late tenth century and the early eleventh. In this way the stock of silver available for minting in western Europe enormously increased from the second half of the tenth century onwards. Otto I had had to melt down central Asian *dirhems* to produce his own pfennigs at Magdeburg. By the early eleventh century this was no longer necessary, for there was enough German silver available.

One of the striking phenomena of the tenth century in both Germany and England was the great number of 'towns' deliberately favoured with imperial or royal privileges, for example with the twin grants of the right to hold a market and to operate a mint. It is frequently not clear how far such authorisation preceded commercial development or merely gave regalian sanction and encouragement to what had already taken place. What is clear is that mint and market very often went together. The market was not primarily for barter, but for buying and selling with money, and to provide this, a mint on the spot seems to have been felt necessary.

By the reign of Conrad of Franconia (911–18) there was still no mint in Germany east of the Rhine except for that at Regensburg, the 'capital' of the East Franks, and none of the numerous Carolingian mints in the Rhineland were operating any longer except that at Mainz, on which Conrad's family lands were centred. Neither Mainz nor Regensburg had very prolific mints. Conrad's successor, Henry of Saxony (918–36), possessed family lands around Magdeburg, and it was probably here that he had his pfennigs minted. It was Henry's son, Otto 'the Great' (936–73), who presided not only over the discovery of silver at Goslar, but also over the beginning of the transformation of minting in Germany. He himself had coins minted, during the latter part of his reign, not only at Magdeburg but at twelve other mints, all on the Rhine or to the east of it. Of these Cologne was the most important. As well as the mints that he operated directly, Otto made a dozen or so grants to others, mostly ecclesiastics, of the right to operate a mint. Otto III (973–83) and Otto III (983–1002) opened some 17 additional mints for themselves, and granted the right to others, still mostly ecclesiastics, to open 40 or so further mints. By the end of Otto III's reign more than 80 mints existed in 'Germany' instead of 2 under Conrad, only three generations earlier. A fairly high proportion of these new mints were east of the Rhine, and were concentrated in the area of Saxony along the main east–west trade route from Cologne to Magdeburg. At Magdeburg this route crossed the Elbe into the Slav lands beyond. At Cologne it crossed the Rhine into the area in which minting had been most concentrated in Carolingian times.[27]

In England, apart from the abortive attempt to start a coinage in Northumbria which the Vikings cut short, even the beginnings of minting outside the extreme south-east of the country did not take place until the early tenth century. It was not until much later in the century, in the 970s and 980s, that any considerable extension of coinage took place. It is remarkable that this is at exactly the same time as in Ottonian Germany, and, as in Germany, new mints were associated with 'boroughs' and markets. In 1000 money was as commonly in circulation throughout lowland England as in the Rhineland and Saxony. The source of silver for this coin presents some problems. It is probable that in the earlier tenth century such coinage as was produced in Wessex, like that at Magdeburg, was minted from melted down central Asian *dirhems*, of the sort that have been found in contemporary hoards from the Scandinavian-dominated parts of England. It was in the last thirty years of the century that the really dramatic increase in the volume of coin in circulation began to take place, but there was no major development in the mining of silver corresponding to that taking place in Germany. It has been strongly argued that it was German silver that provided the material for the prolific coinage of pennies in late Anglo-Saxon England, and that silver flowed from Germany to England because of England's favourable balance of trade. This argument maintains that continental demand, backed by the new German silver, provoked a much larger scale export of wool and cloth from England than ever before. If this was the case, then the later tenth century was the time at which England effectively began to take that primacy in European wool production that she was to hold for so many centuries.[28] The spread of minting and circulation of coin to all parts of England by the first half of the eleventh century shows how much the enormous import of silver had facilitated monetary changes. The ordinary peasant, even outside the more advanced areas, had, possibly for the first time since antiquity, some coin with which to pay his rent and the landholder some coin to pay his geld.

In late Anglo-Saxon England the denier or penny was perhaps more closely controlled than anywhere else in Europe.[29] The coinage of

[27] Suhle, *Deutsche Münz- und Geldgeschichte*, 157–8.

[28] P. H. Sawyer, 'The wealth of England in the eleventh century', *Trans. Roy. Hist. Soc.*, 5th series, xv (1965), 145–64.

[29] For this and other aspects of late Anglo-Saxon coinage see the essays in *Anglo-Saxon Coins; studies presented to F. M. Stenton*, ed. R. H. M. Dolley (London, 1961).

Wessex alone remained, after the coinages of the various other Anglo-Saxon kingdoms had come to an end during the Scandinavian onslaught of the ninth century. It was soon supplemented by a variety of short-lived Danish and Hiberno-Norse penny coinages of not dissimilar type in northern England. With the West Saxon reconquest a uniform coinage was imposed on the whole of England, with only slight regional deviations, as for example in the mints of the north-west. The mint towns had originally been few in number and the bulk of the coinage had been issued at Canterbury and London, but during the tenth century the coinage rapidly increased in quantity and the number of mints increased more than correspondingly. Under Æthelstan it was stipulated that every borough should have a mint, but this was not a case of extreme decentralisation. Very strict royal control over the coinage was maintained, for the dies were cut for the whole country either in a series of regional workshops or, possibly, at a single central workshop at Winchester or in London. Over the next generation the number of mints increased prodigiously, although the aim of one mint to every borough was never quite achieved, despite the use from time to time of moneyers who were prepared to operate mints in two, or occasionally more, small boroughs close to each other. From the 970s royal control over the coinage was tightened still further, for at frequent intervals, perhaps every six years, the complete currency was reminted and the previous issue demonetised. Hoard evidence shows that this remarkable policy was actually put into execution, and during the reign of Edward the Confessor the lifetime of a coinage was reduced to three years. The contrast with the feudalised coinages of West Frankia, where an immobilised type might be issued with greater and greater degeneration for three centuries, is astonishing. Only the Carolingians had attempted complete recoinages before and even then not as a regularly repeated operation. Repeated coinages were later practised in other parts of Europe, for example, in some of the ecclesiastical principalities of Germany after the breakdown of imperial control and in Poland in the twelfth century. However, in the tenth and eleventh centuries the Anglo-Saxon kings were unique in their control of their currency. No other rulers, not even the Ottonian emperors, had had so much ability to manipulate the coinage. The large number of mints in England proved invaluable for these frequent total remintings, and there is some evidence to suggest that an attempt was made to ensure that no one should be more than fifteen miles distant from a mint. A very considerable measure of royal authority is also implied by the way that Anglo-Saxon pennies were of token value rather than intrinsic value. They fluctuated quite considerably in weight and fineness from one issue to the next and yet their value seems to have remained constant, since it derived not from their intrinsic worth but from the word of the king. Elsewhere in western Europe the value of the denier depended entirely on its silver content or its supposed silver content.

The Normans adopted the Anglo-Saxon system in its entirety. It continued to function, with its triennial change and its basis on royal credit, albeit with a declining number of mints, until the reign of Henry I. The anarchy of Stephen's reign saw, for the only time in England, the emergence of a feudal coinage and the shattering of royal credit. The feudal coinage was on a very limited scale and the only permanent survival from it became the national coinage of Scotland.[30] After Stephen's reign it was no longer possible to validate the coinage by the authority and credit of the monarchy. Henry II abandoned the hope of restoring a triennial change in the coinage and commenced the series of coinages of fixed and known type lasting for many years. He saw to it that, if the coinage had to be based on the intrinsic value of the penny, it should be good, known and stable. He was assisted in this by the vastly increased quantities of silver available in England for coinage from the 1170s. The change in attitude resulting from the adoption based on its *valor intrinsecus* was reflected in the practice of the English exchequer, which less and less accepted coin *per numero*. A penny was no longer a penny because the king said so, it was a penny because, and only if, it contained a pennyworth of silver. Hence the exchequer came more frequently to accept coin by weight or preferably blanched.

The contrast between the centralised monarchy and monetary system of the West Saxon and Norman kings of England and that of the Capetian kings of France is astonishing. The Capetian counts of Paris, as dukes of the Franks, had minted deniers like any other of the major late Carolingian feudatories, and the title of king, which they acquired in the tenth century, made little difference to their issues. Unlike their Anglo-Saxon contemporaries, the early Capetian kings had no control of coinage throughout their 'kingdom', but only in their own domain, where they minted deniers that were indistinguishable from those of their feudal neighbours. Until the mid-twelfth century they did not even ensure a uniformity of issue between the few mints that were under their control.

The increased supplies of silver available in the second half of the twelfth century enabled a handful of the more successful of the

[30] For Scottish coinage see I. H. Stewart, *The Scottish Coinage*, 3rd edn (London, 1967).

multitude of local feudal coinages to dominate the currency of wide areas of France by the end of that century.[31] The deniers of Provins did so in eastern France, the deniers of Melgueil in southern France, those of Paris in northern France, and of Tours in western France.

In eastern France the deniers of Provins, one of the four great fair towns of Champagne, circulated not merely in the vicinity of Provins but much further afield, first overwhelming the money of Troyes and then gradually becoming the basis of a money of account which became standard not only for the whole of Champagne and all its fairs, but also for the Chalonnais, the Barrois and Lorraine. The *deniers provinois* increased from regional to international importance, in parallel with the fairs, from the reign of Henry I of Champagne (1152–80). Through the fairs the mint at Provins was abundantly supplied with silver, partially brought by merchants in ingot form from Germany. From the fairs the *deniers provinois* travelled outwards along the trade routes, particularly to Italy. They circulated so widely in Italy in the twelfth and early thirteenth centuries that successive senators of Rome issued imitative pieces, *denari provisini*, which remained the basic coin of Rome long after the original issues in Champagne had ceased.[32]

In the south of France the *deniers melgoriens* issued by the bishops of Maguelonne, as counts of Melgueil or Mauguio, came to dominate the trade of the whole coastal plain of Languedoc. They became not only the official coinage of the fast-growing nearby city of Montpellier, but were so successful that independent coinages ceased to be issued to the west at Béziers and Carcassonne, and to the east at Uzés, Nîmes and St Gilles in the Rhone delta. All these had stopped by the early thirteenth century, when the *deniers melgoriens* were the common currency from Toulouse to Provence and even circulated to a limited extent as far away as Barcelona.[33]

At the beginning of the twelfth century the *deniers parisis* of the Capetians were still only the money of Paris, but Louis VII (1137–80), by closing most of the other mints in the royal domain, ensured that it became the money of the whole Île-de-France. It was under Philip II Augustus (1180–1223) that it began to be minted on a considerable scale and became the common coin of much of northern France. He had *deniers parisis* struck not only in Paris itself, but also at the then

[31] For the feudal coinages of France, see A. Blanchet and A. Dieudonné, *Manuel de numismatique français*, IV, *Monnaies Féodales Françaises*, (Paris, 1936).

[32] P. Toubert, *Les Structures du Latium medieval...du* IXe *à la fin due* XIIe *siècle*. Bibliothéques des Ecoles Françaises d'Athénes et de Rome, CCXXI (Rome, 1973).

[33] M. Castaing-Sicard, *Monnaies féodales et circulation monétaire en Languedoc* Xe–XIIIe *siécles*. Cahiers de l'Association Marc Bloch de Toulouse, Etudes d'Histoire Meridionale, IV (Toulouse, 1961).

important channel port of Montreuil-sur-Mer and, when he inherited Artois and Peronne in 1191, also at Arras, St Omer and Peronne. Imitative *deniers parisis* were soon struck by the counts of St Pol, Ponthieu and of Boulogne, and by the countess of Vermandois. The independent coinages of the bishops of Beauvais, Laon, and Noyon all came to an end by 1220, so that, in the first quarter of the thirteenth century, the *deniers parisis* were commonly used for both payment and accounting from Orleans to Flanders.

It was really only in the thirteenth century that France acquired a national coinage.[34] In 1204 Philip Augustus enormously increased the scope of his kingship by confiscating Normandy and many of the extensive Plantaganet lands in western France from John of Anjou, who was also king of England. Philip did not try to impose the *denier parisis* on the newly conquered lands in western France, but instead put his authority behind the most successful of the coinages already circulating in this region, the deniers minted at Tours by the abbey of St Martin, which had already been struck in very considerable quantities in the previous half-century. Philip brought the independent coinage of Maine and Anjou to an end and the mint at Tours was brought directly under his own administration. Henceforth *deniers tournois* as well as *deniers parisis* were under royal control, and in the years that followed the lighter money *tournois* was preferred to money *parisis*, so that the *tournois* became the national coinage of France, struck not merely at Tours but at the increasing number of mints under royal control throughout France. Even in northern France *tournois* replaced *parisis*. In eastern France the *denier provinois* was deliberately altered in 1210, or possibly 1224, to bring it into conformity with the *denier tournois*. Later in the century when the king of France married the hieress of Champagne, money *tournois* was minted in Champagne itself, in place of *provinois*. In southern France a royal mint was opened at Sommières, a few miles from Montpellier, to strike *deniers tournois* in deliberate competition with the *deniers melgoriens* which gradually lost their dominance in Languedoc.[35] In 1282 a royal ordinance effectively destroyed the *denier melgorien* as a trading currency by specifically limiting the circulation of *deniers melgoriens* to the diocese of Melgueil, in the same way that the circulation of other 'feudal' coin had already been theoretically limited for a generation to the fief of the issuer, whilst royal coin was free to circulate throughout the kingdom. After the royal acquisition of Montpellier itself in 1293 the

[34] A. Blanchet and A. Dieudonné, *Manuel de numismatique française*, II, *Monnaies Royales Françaises depuis Hugues Capet jusqu'à la Révolution* (Paris, 1936).

[35] T. Bisson, 'Coinages and Royal Monetary Policy in Languedoc during the Reign of Saint Louis', *Speculum*, XXXII (1957), 443–69.

mint at Sommières was moved there. Later in the Middle Ages the Montpellier mint was one of the two most prolific mints in France outside Paris. The bishop of Maguelonne retained his theoretical right of coinage, but money *tournois* was the common coinage of Languedoc in the fourteenth century. By the middle of that century money *melgorien* even ceased to be used for accounts in Montpellier. In the third decade of the fourteenth century the kings of France bought back the right of minting from a number of their feudatories, so that in the later Middle Ages the only effective non-royal coinages in France were those issued by a handful of the greatest, near-autonomous, princes whose actions were not amenable to royal control, such as the duke of Brittany, or the duke of Guyenne who was also king of England.

Whilst the Capetians were valiantly struggling to build up a national coinage out of feudal fragmentation, and whilst the English coinage had been refounded on the basis of sound weight and fineness, the coinage of the Empire fell almost entirely into local hands as the imperial authority declined from the close of the Salian dynasty onwards through the twelfth and thirteenth centuries. In Germany the equivalent of the thirteenth-century 'strong' monarchies of France and England was not to be found at the imperial level but at the princely level. Many thirteenth-century German princes exercised a precociously centralised control over their principalities, even though these were often not very large in area or their economies very highly developed. In this period of devolution two distinct types of coin came to be issued. Local rulers in the southern and western parts of the Empire (Italy, the Rhone valley, Bavaria, Lorraine, the Rhineland, Frisia and parts of Franconia and Swabia) continued to issue ordinary silver deniers. On the other hand, from around the 1130s local rulers in the East (along the Baltic, in Saxony, Thuringia, and the remainder of Franconia and Swabia) struck paper-thin pfennigs or deniers commonly called bracteates. They were struck on very thin silver wafers, and had only an obverse design. They were considerably lighter than the normal deniers and of very slight intrinsic value. In Poland, Silesia and Bohemia, the minting of bracteate deniers also replaced that of the heavier denier in the last quarter of the twelfth century and the first years of the thirteenth. Bracteate deniers similarly replaced the heavier deniers in Hungary under Bela IV (1235–70). In many places the issue of bracteate pfennigs was associated with a regular renewal of the complete currency at intervals, not unlike that in late Anglo-Saxon and Norman England.[36] As then, it was a

[36] S. Suchodolski, 'Renovatio Monetae in Poland in the 12th century', *Wiàdomosci Numizmatyczne*, v (1961), 57–75.

symptom of a relatively strong, central, control over a not very highly developed economy. The bracteate pfennig's lack of intrinsic value was therefore of little importance, since its local value was a token one. We must presume that for long-distance transactions silver would be carried about in other forms, ingots or better coin. The fragility of the bracteate pfennigs was also of little importance since they were designed to circulate only over a limited area and for a limited period. In the most extreme cases the coinage was totally renewed after circulating for only six months.

The number of issuers in the thoroughly fragmented Empire of the thirteenth century seems as infinite, and many of them as insignificant, as the wave of 'feudal' denier-strikers in post-Carolingian France. Amongst the confusion of deniers there were a considerable number of imitations of the English penny, particularly in Westphalia in the first and second decades of the thirteenth century, and in the Rhineland in the middle years of the century. The former copied the English short-cross penny and have been associated with John's subsidies to Otto IV, and the latter copied the English long-cross penny and have been associated with Richard of Cornwall's bid for the imperial throne.[37]

The Low Countries, technically within the confines of the Empire but always very largely independent, were equally the scene of a riotous confusion of seigneurial minting, although with time the more considerable principalities of the Low Countries, such as Flanders (only partially within the Empire) or Brabant, engrossed much of the minting. The Low Countries were an area peculiarly prone to imitation of 'foreign' coins, or of the coins of other principalities within the Low Countries, a phenomenon which later became even more apparent in the period of issue of larger silver and of gold. During the last years of the thirteenth century and the first of the fourteenth century the great vogue was for the imitation of the sterling pennies of Edward I of England.

In Italy, also within the confines of the Empire, there was a similar multiplication of mints in the twelfth and thirteenth centuries. There was also an enormous increase in scale in the quantity of *denari* issued, after the relative shortage of newly coined silver in the late eleventh and early twelfth centuries. The new mints in Italy were not, however, in the hands of lay feudatories, or even ecclesiastics, as they were elsewhere in the empire, but of towns, a natural reflection of the differing political, and economic, structure there. In Tuscany, for example, the old imperial mint at Lucca was joined by five new

[37] P. Berghaus, 'Die Perioden des Sterlings in Westfalen, dem Rheinland und in den Niederlanden', *Hamburger Beiträge zur Numismatik*, 1 (1947), 34–53.

communal mints between 1150 and 1250. By 1151, there was a mint at Pisa, the seaport of Tuscany through which the new Sardinian silver was imported; by 1165 at Volterra; by 1193 at Siena, which had silver mines, admittedly, but not very prolific ones, in its own *contado*; and by 1236 at Florence and Arezzo.[38]

Although there was so great a degree of fragmentation in the issue of deniers in tenth- and eleventh-century France, or in Germany, the Low Countries and Italy in the twelfth and thirteenth centuries, it must not be thought that the currency in use changed at every political frontier across Europe. Apart from the fact that the concept of a frontier is anachronistic, it must be emphasised that a different coinage for every minor seigneury did not mean a different currency for each. Only in England was there a relatively successful attempt to ensure that the 'national' currency consisted exclusively of 'national' coinage. The kings of France from Philip Augustus onwards may have attempted this, but they failed, and elsewhere it was hardly attempted, except where a policy of regular renewal of the whole currency was being implemented. The currency of any principality or city normally consisted not only of the indigenous coinage, but also of deniers from neighbouring territories and cities, sometimes in even larger quantities, together with a few pieces from much farther afield.

III. *The Commercial Revolution: The Silver Mark, the Silver Groat and the Gold Florin*

The transformation of the coinage of Europe in the thirteenth century was only made possible by the vastly increased supplies of precious metals that were being mined throughout the century. The first of the new sources of silver to become of importance at this time was discovered at Freiberg in Meissen in 1168.[39] In the last three decades of the twelfth century it achieved a pre-eminence that was maintained for much of the thirteenth century. The mines at Friesach in Carinthia, although discovered as early as the 1120s, only became very productive in the opening years of the thirteenth century. On the other hand, those discovered in the 1220s at Iglau (Jihlava) on the borders of Bohemia and Moravia were exploited very rapidly and came to replace those at Freiberg and Friesach, where production seems to have dwindled in the second half of the thirteenth century.

[38] D. Herlihy, 'Pisan Coinage and the Monetary Development of Tuscany, 1150–1250', *The American Numismatic Society, Museum Notes*, VI (New York, 1954), 143–68.

[39] W. Herrmann, 'Bergbau und Kultur', *Freiberger Forschungshefte*, series D, II (1953), 7–22.

From the 1250s the mines around Iglesias in Sardinia, which had been known for at least a century, began to be exploited on a large scale by the Pisans and soon came to rival those of central Europe.[40] The last, and greatest, of the major sources of silver to be exploited in thirteenth century Europe was discovered at Kutná Hora (Kuttenberg) in Bohemia in 1298.[41] Various estimates suggest that the Kutná Hora mines were producing over 20 tons of silver a year throughout the first forty years of the fourteenth century, before they too, like all mines, began to be exhausted. The Sardinian mines also seem to have gone into a decline in the 1340s. These were only the richest sources of silver, which, from the 1170s, supplied the ever-increasing currency of Europe for over a century and an half. Other lesser mines were exploited with varying degrees of success throughout Europe, from Beer Alston in England to Brskovo in Serbia, from Montieri near Siena to Mechernich in the Eifel, and from Calabria to Silesia.[42] None of these, not even those in Transylvania or the Black Forest, were worth comparison with the leading mines at Freiberg, Friesach, Iglau, Iglesias and Kutná Hora, which, each in turn, dominated the production of silver in Europe. Although none of the lesser mines were individually of major importance, and some of them even involved their exploiters in considerable financial loss, nevertheless in combination they added significantly to the amount of silver available.

These mines were very rarely directly exploited by rulers or great noblemen themselves. As a general rule the prince took a royalty of an eighth or a tenth of the proceeds,[43] but a wide variety of individual bargains were struck with surface owners, whilst the bulk of the metal, after ecclesiastical tithes had been paid,[44] remained in the hands of the miners themselves. In some areas, for example at Iglesias, the organisation of mining rapidly developed from the self-employed

[40] R. S. Lopez, 'Contributo alla storia delle miniere argentifere di Sardegna', *Studi economico-guidice dall'Universita di Cagliari*, XXIV (1936), 7–13.

[41] K. Castelin, 'Grossus Pragensis', *Arbeits- und Forschungsberichte zur sächsischen Bodendenkmalpfege*, XVI–XVII (1967), 665–75, and B. Homan, 'La circolazione delle monete d'oro in Ungheria dal X a XIV secolo e la crisi europea dell'oro nel secolo XIV', *Rivista Italiana di Numismatica*, 2nd series, V (1922), 132.

[42] Beer Alston, *Close Rolls 1261–1264*, 187 and 227, *Calendar of Patent Rolls 1258–1266*, 249, 253, 304, *Calendar of Liberate Rolls 1260–1267*, 246; L. F. Salzman, *English Industries of the Middle Ages* (2nd edn, 1923), 52–63; A. Sapori, *La compagnia dei Frescobaldi in Inghilterra* (Florence, 1947), 19–20, 39ff; Brskovo-D. Kovacevic, 'Dans la Serbie et le Bosnie medievales: les mines d'or et d'argent', *Annales E.S.C.*, XV (1960), 248–58; Montieri-L. Simonin, 'De l'exploitation des mines en Toscane pendent l'antiquité et le moyen âge', *Annales des mines*, 5th *series*, XIV (1858), 557–615; Mechernich-F. H. Beyschlag *et al.*, *The Deposits of Useful Minerals and Rocks: Ore Deposits* (1909; English trans., London, 1914–16), 702; Calabria – F. B. Pegolotti, *La Pratica della Mercatura*, ed. A. Evans. Medieval Academy of America (Cambridge, Mass., 1936), 291.

[43] Homan, 'La circolazione delle monete d'oro in Ungheria', 109–56.

[44] Eberhard Gothein, *Wirtschaftsgeschichte des Schwarzwaldes und der Angnenzendenlandschaften*, I (Strassburg, 1892), 630–31.

free-miner to the mining company, with absentee shareholders. In others primitive arrangements survived by which the original prospectors went on mining each on a small scale on his own staked out plot. Their royalties made a very great deal of difference to certain princes, the margraves of Meissen, the archbishops of Salzburg, the city of Pisa, and the last Premyslid and early Luxembourg kings of Bohemia. Their share in the production of silver enabled them to undertake extensive political expenditure. The larger part of the silver, which remained in the hands of the miners and mine-shareholders, entered into circulation directly through trade. The mining areas rapidly became good markets for merchants from the most advanced areas of Europe, northern Italy and the southern Netherlands. In the thirteenth century there seems to have been little obligation on the miners to have their silver minted into coins locally. When Wenceslas IV of Bohemia made such a requirement at Kutná Hora in 1300 it was regarded as an innovation and its strict enforcement proved quite impossible. As a consequence most of the new silver travelled from the mining areas to the more economically advanced areas of Europe not as coin, but in the form of bars or ingots of silver of a standard fineness. There is some evidence to suggest that they were also frequently made to weigh a mark, although the mark itself varied in weight from place to place. In the spring of 1204 Wolfger, bishop of Passau, set out for Rome.[45] His chamberlain brought a supply of such silver bars to exchange along the route into local currency to pay for the needs of the bishop's party. In eleven transactions out of thirteen between crossing the Tarvis pass into Italy and Rome itself the chamberlain offered for exchange silver bars which weighed complete numbers of marks, which strongly suggests that most of the bars that he was carrying weighed a mark or an exact multiple. In 1265 in Champagne the Sienese banker, Andrea Tolomei, noted the rate at which marks of bar silver from Freiberg were being exchanged for local currency at the 'cold' fair at Troyes.[46] Around 1300, Bruges and other cities of Flanders were maintaining municipal establishments for the refining and assaying of silver which issued silver bars bearing an assay stamp as a guarantee of fineness.[47] In Venice and Genoa it was the mints which performed this function, sealing bars of standard fineness with their coin dies so that they might be acceptable.[48] No

[45] Jesse, *Quellenbuch zur Münz- und Geldgeschichte*, Document no. 370, 249–52.

[46] A. Schaube, in *Zeitschrift für Sozial- und Wirtschaftgeschichte*, v (1897), 248–308.

[47] R. de Roover, *Money, Banking and Credit in Medieval Bruges* (1948), 230, from G. Bigwood, *Le régime juridique et économique du commerce de l'argent dans la Belgique du Moyen Age*, I (1921), 422–5.

[48] Pegolotti, *La Pratica della Mercatura*, 291; and *Problemi Monetari Veneziani*, ed. R. Cessi, *Documenti Finanziari della Repubblica di Venezia*, 4th series, I, Reale Accademia dei Lincei (Padua, 1937).

Venetian or Genoese bars survive, but the few such bars that have been discovered bear symbols that have been interpreted as city assay marks. For large payments, unminted silver, providing its fineness was known, was more convenient than minted silver which had to be counted out, or weighed, in the form of thousands of separate coins. Many of these bars were eventually turned into coin in European mints, but some went right through the European currency system to Africa or Asia. The da Canal notebook compiled in Venice around 1311 records Venetian bar silver in Lesser Armenia and at the mint of Hama in Syria. Pegolotti, in his notebook compiled over the following three decades, noted the rates for bars of Sardinian silver, not only at the mint of Naples, but also at that of Tunis. He reported 'German' silver in Venetian bars, in Alexandria, Famagusta in Cyprus, and Lajazzo in Lesser Armenia, and also explained how European bar silver was melted down in Pera and Constantinople and recast into fresh bars or *sommi* of a different fineness suitable for Asiatic trade. He refers to these *sommi* again in the Crimea, at Tana on the sea of Azov and elsewhere on the route to China at the frontier of which they were exchanged for paper money.[49]

When this new silver first began to be available at the end of the twelfth century it was minted, if it was minted, into the same sorts of silver deniers or pennies that had been minted for centuries, but in larger quantities. The surviving pieces give the impression that considerably more *denari* were struck at the Venice mint during the twenty years of the reigns of Sebastian Ziani and Enrico Malpiero (doges 1172–8 and 1179–92) than over the whole of the preceding century. It was in the reign of Philip II of France (1180–1223) that the *denier parisis* became the denier not merely of Paris, or even the Île-de-France only, but of much of northern France, and that it came to be minted on a considerable scale. In England the great increase in the scale of minting took place at an early point in the currency of the so-called 'short-cross' pennies, which Henry II began to have issued in 1180. By the 1220s, the two principal English mints, at Canterbury and London, were minting over four million pennies a year.[50]

The natural first stage in the expansion was thus to produce more of the same sorts of coins, the traditional pennies of varying types. The second stage was to produce different and larger coins. This change took place at varying dates between the early thirteenth and the mid-fourteenth century depending on the economic needs of the different parts of Europe. The natural place for this second stage to

[49] Pegolotti, *La Pratica della Mercatura*.

[50] C. E. Blunt and J. D. Brand, 'Mint Output of Henry III', *British Numismatic Journal*, XXXIX (1970), 61–6.

start was northern Italy, not only because it was by far the most economically advanced area of Europe, and because it was the area to which so much of the newly available silver tended to gravitate, but also because the traditional pennies here had become much slighter in silver content than in many parts of Europe. Whereas the prototypical Carolingian denier had weighed 1.7 grams, the *denari* of Pavia and Venice contained only 0.2 grams and 0.1 grams of silver respectively in the 1170s. By way of contrast the English penny still contained over 1.3 grams of silver. A fairly obvious solution to the problem of the diminished silver content of the coinage was simply to attempt to replace the old *denari* by better new *denari*. One attempt of this kind was made between 1155 and 1161 by the Emperor Frederick I, who caused new and better *denari imperiali* to be struck in Lombardy. These were to contain no less than 0.5 grams of silver, and were thus worth twice as much as the pre-existing *denari* of Pavia and Milan. Although the new imperial *denari* fairly rapidly replaced the older *denari*, this was not the radical solution that was required. It merely brought the Lombard *denari* up to the same approximate level as the Tuscan ones.[51]

The occasion for the initiation of the radical change that was required was the Fourth Crusade. The crusaders, mostly from north of the Alps, bargained to pay the Venetians 51,000 marks of silver for their transport onwards by sea. Much of it was needed at once for paying shipwrights and other workmen who were constructing additional ships in the Venetian arsenal, and after that for the provisioning of the fleet and for the wages of mariners. Some intermediate denomination was clearly needed between the *denari* and the silver mark bar, which was worth over 2,400 *denari*, for paying such wages, and for internal commercial transactions. Silver bars were admirable for long-distance trade and for large transactions, but were useless for smaller local purposes like rents and wages for which the *denaro* was by now too small. It was for the specific purpose of paying the men working on the fleet that the doge, Enrico Dandalo, ordered the striking, in 1201, of great coins, or *grossi*,[52] each of which was to be worth no less than twenty-four of the older *denari*. This was no mere replacement of old *denari* by new ones, since the older *denari*, which by contrast were soon called *piccoli*, little ones, went on being struck alongside the new *grossi*. What had happened was that a complete new tier had been added to the monetary system. The new pieces not only weighed about 2.2 grams each, which was heavier than any silver coin struck in western Europe since antiquity, but were also

51 C. M. Cipolla, *Le avventure della lira* (Milan, 1958).
52 M. da Canale, 'Cronaca Venta', *Archivio storico italiano*, VIII (1845), 320.

minted from almost pure silver, 965/1,000 fine.[53] This was in marked contrast with the poor quality *piccoli*, which continued only one-quarter silver and three-quarters alloy.

Venice's greatest rival in Mediterranean trade, Genoa, also struck *grossi* within the first decades of the thirteenth century and similar pieces were struck at Marseilles, which was closely associated with Genoa, from 1218. In the 1220s and the 1230s the striking of *grossi* spread rapidly, to Verona, for example, which had only recently been eclipsed by Venice and was still the key mint city for much of north-eastern Italy, and to Parma, Bologna, Ferrara and Reggio north of the Apennines. Milan was certainly striking *grossi* by this period, and may have been doing so for some time, possibly even as early as the 1190s. South of the Apennines, Siena, then the second city of Tuscany, coined a *grosso* by 1231. Pisa, then the largest city of Tuscany, imitated it a few years later. The fast-growing boom town of Florence, which was to surpass both Siena and Pisa well before the end of the century, also struck silver *grossi* or *fiorini d'argento*, by 1237, and so did Lucca and Arezzo about the same time.[54]

These Tuscan *grossi* seem to have been of an agreed weight from the beginning, but further north the *grossi* were not uniform in weight between one city and another, although they were all of one general size and were distinctly different in scale from the *piccoli* which were already circulating in northern Italy. They were all, initially at least, of good silver, and their weights ranged from the 1.4 to 1.5 grams of the *grossi* of Bologna and Ferrara, through the rather heavier *grossi* of Genoa, Verona and the Tuscan cities, to the 2.2 grams of the Milanese and Venetian *grossi*. Their values in terms of pre-existing *piccoli* equally varied from city to city, depending, of course, not only on the weight of the new *grossi*, but also on the weight and fineness of the *piccoli*. In Genoa the earliest *grossi* were only worth 4 of the older Genoese *denari*, but in Verona the *grossi* were worth 20 of the older Veronese *denari*. In Tuscany the *grossi* were circulating in the 1240s as pieces of 12 *denari*. In other words the Sienese, the Pisan and the Florentine *soldi* had become, temporarily at least, real coins rather than merely convenient accounting multiples.[55] It is quite remarkable that the shilling had survived for half a millennium as an accounting multiple, without any such real coin existing. The last time that there had been a *soldo* as a coin in Tuscany had been as long before as the eighth century, and then it had been a gold coin. On its return in the thirteenth century it was a silver one.

[53] P. Grierson, 'La Moneta Veneziana nell'economica mediterranea del trecento e quattrocento', *La Civilita Veneziana del Quattrocento*. Fundazione Giorgio Cini (Florence, 1957), 77–97.

[54] Herlihy, 'Pisan coinage', 143–68.

[55] Cipolla, *Le avventure della lira*, 37–8.

Unlike the older *denari*, most of the new *grossi* were not changed in weight or fineness over long periods of time. In Venice, for example, the *grosso*, or *matapan* as the Venetian *grosso* came to be called, remained unchanged from 1201 to 1379. Meanwhile the *piccoli* continued to be debased from time to time, particularly from the second half of the thirteenth century, and as a consequence the *grossi* increased in value in terms of *piccoli*. When the *matapan* was introduced it was designed to be worth a neat 2 *soldi*, or 24 *piccoli*, and during the first half of the thirteenth century it stood for long at 26 *piccoli*. However, in the second half of the century it rapidly rose in value in terms of *piccoli*. In 1265 it was valued at 27 *piccoli*, in 1269 at 28 *piccoli*, and in 1282 at 32 *piccoli*.[56]

Thus between 1201 and 1237 every important Italian mint north of Rome began to strike *grossi* of about 2 grams in weight.[57] But these 2-gram *grossi* were not destined to be the standard-sized silver coins of the later Middle Ages. Yet larger coins (also called *grossi*) were to appear, of about double the size. The first such piece appeared in Rome in 1253 during the rule of Brancaleone d'Andolo (Senator 1252–5 and 1257–8).[58] It too began as a *soldo*, a piece of 12 Roman *denari* or *provisini*. These *grossi* or *romanini* were continued by the Senate after his death, and then by Charles of Anjou (Senator 1263–6, 1268–78, 1281–4). After his temporary loss of control over Rome in 1278, Charles struck pieces of a similar size, known as *carlini*, at Naples, by then the capital of his kingdom. When Constance of Hohenstaufen and her husband, Pedro of Aragon, recaptured Sicily from him in 1282, they too struck heavy *grossi*, known as *pierreale*, for the island. Both *carlini* and *pierreale* had very long lives, and they continued to be minted until the close of the Middle Ages. Even in northern Italy itself, the home of the smaller *grosso* of the early thirteenth century, these larger *grossi* began to be struck, for example at Milan at about this time, where they were known as *ambrosini* from the seated figure of St Ambrose on the obverse.

The idea of striking silver *grossi* also percolated gradually across the Alps into the Germanic lands beyond. The 2-gram size *grossi* of Verona provided the prototypes for pieces struck along the trade route that ran down the Etsch or Adige valley. The bishops of Trent, from the 1230s, and the counts of the Tyrol, by 1271, struck pieces at Bozen

[56] G. Luzzatto, 'L'oro e l'argento nell politica monetaria veneziana dei secoli XIII–XIV', *Rivista Storica Italiana* (1937), reprinted in *Studia di Storia Economica Veneziana* (Padua, 1954), 261–3.

[57] P. Grierson, 'The Origins of the Grosso and of Gold Coinage in Italy', *Numismaticky Sbornik*, XII (1971–2), 33–48.

[58] P. Grierson, 'I grossi "senatoriali" di Roma, parte I, dal 1253 al 1282', *Rivista Italiana di Numismatica*, LVIII (1956), 36–69.

and Meran (Bolzano and Merano), valued at 20 Veronese *piccoli*, from the silver mined in the Tyrol. They were issued on a linguistic frontier, and so were known by many names, as *zwanziger* or *vigintiarii* from their value, or as *tirolini* from the source, but also, in Italy, as *aquilini* from their reverse type of an eagle and, in Germany, as kreuzer from their obverse type of the double cross. They were much imitated in what are now Austria, Switzerland and southern Germany.[59] Just as in Italy the 2-gram *grosso* was followed after a time by a 4-gram *grosso*, so the same happened in the silver-producing lands to the north. First came the 2-gram groschen or kreuzer, and it was later followed by the 4-gram groschen. The first and most prolific of these larger groschen was the Prague groschen of Bohemia, struck at the silver-mining town of Kutná Hora from 1300 onwards, with a weight of about 3.8 grams. It too was valued initially at 12 of the pre-existing pfennigs.[60] Pieces of a similar size were soon issued at Freiberg for the margrave of Meissen. Although the Bohemian and Meissen groschen circulated to a certain extent in such neighbouring lands as Silesia, Lausitz and Brandenburg, this part of Europe, outside the silver-mining districts themselves, was not yet ready for such large silver coins when they were first issued. Even the dukes of Austria did not attempt to mint such large groschen at this time, despite the large amounts of silver passing through Vienna into Italy. The mid-fourteenth century attempt of Casimir the Great to issue large groschen at Krakow in Poland failed, and his successors had to be content with the issue of silver *kwartniks*, which were the size of the smaller *grossi*. The Polish economy did not yet have any real use for the large pieces. On the other hand the Bohemian groschen do seem to have had an enormous success in Italy. They flowed freely southwards through Vienna into Italy in exchange for goods that Italians could provide, and circulated not only in North Italy but also the eastern trade routes travelled by the Venetians overseas. Pegolotti noted their existence in a variety of places under the name of *buenmini*, bohemians. When they were first issued, therefore, the Prague groschen only had a major circulation in lands where large *grossi* were already acceptable. It was only a great deal later that they made a major impact on the make-up of the currency of Germany and Central Europe.

In Hungary, in 1329, a generation later than in Bohemia, Charles Robert of Anjou, a great grandson of the first Charles of Anjou, swept away the bracteates of the previous half-century, and introduced a new groschen. He imported workmen, probably Italians, from Kutná Hora

59 Suhle, *Deutsche Münz- und Geldgeschichte*, 157–8.

60 K. Castelin, *Grossus Pragensis. Der Prager Groschen und seine Teilstücke 1300–1547*, 2nd edn (Brunswick, 1973).

to mint them out of the silver from his own mines. In type they drew their inspiration direct from Italy. They were based on the *gigliati* minted at Naples since his grandfather's time.

The use of large silver coins in other parts of Europe spread very gradually. Charles of Anjou's elder brother, Saint Louis, began to strike 4-gram coins for France as early as 1266, as Charles himself did for Provence the next year, and James I of Aragon in his city of Montpellier in 1272. St Louis' *gros tournois*, as they were called, do not seem to have had a very considerable circulation at first. Like the early Prague groschen they seem to have been more usable in Italy than in their native land to begin with. Like many other 'great' coins they had an initial value of 12 of the pre-existing deniers. The *gros tournois* was thus, for its first quarter-century, the *sou tournois* in silver, but in 1290 Philip IV brought this equivalence to an end by reducing the weight of the *denier tournois*, whilst keeping the *gros* unchanged. From then onwards, the *gros tournois*, like so many other 'great' coins, had a variable value in the two French moneys of account, *tournois* and *parisis*, as the *deniers tournois* and *parisis* on which the accounting system rested changed frequently, usually for the worse.

In Barcelona, commercially and politically closely linked with Italy, the use of 'great' coins began early. The Infante Pedro, acting for his father, James I of Aragon, proposed to mint a *grosso de plata* as early as 1268, but withdrew the proposal in the face of opposition from the city. In 1284, Pedro, by now king, did begin to strike the first regular series of 'great' coins in Spain, at about the same time as he began the issue of *reales*, of about the same size, in Sicily. These *grossos de plata*, or groats as they were later called, were initially valued at 12 of the existing *dineros ternales*, in other words the *sueldo* of Barcelona, but since they retained their weight and fineness, and the *dineros* did not, groats also gradually increased in value in terms of local *dineros*.

The experience of Castile, without such close ties to Italy, was quite different. *Maravedis de plata*, at 6 grams the largest silver coins of thirteenth-century Europe, were issued from 1258. Such a large silver coin was not of a scale to be of much use in the Castilian economy at so early a date. Its issue was soon discontinued, but not before enough examples had gone into circulation for this silver *maravedi* rather than the older gold *maravedi* to form the basis of the later Castilian system of accounting. The *maravedi* shortly came to mean not a single large silver coin, but a unit of 10 Castilian *dineros*. It was not until a century later, under Pedro I (1350–69), that the standard 'great' coin of late medieval Castile was successfully introduced. This was the *reale*, a coin clearly modelled on the *gros tournois* of his French allies.[61]

[61] O. Gil Farres, *Historia de la Moneda Espanola*, 2nd edn (Madrid, 1976).

It is at first sight surprising that the minting of larger pieces did not spread more rapidly, particularly to the southern Netherlands, then the second most economically advanced area of Europe. The state of the currency there differed greatly from that in Italy on the introduction of the *grossi* at the beginning of the century. A hoard of over 140,000 silver deniers found in Brussels shows what it was like in Brabant about 1264. This hoard, weighing over 2 cwt (100 kg) is one of the largest hoards of medieval coins yet discovered, and also illustrates the huge number of coins that men were prepared to handle in the era before the introduction of the silver groat and of coined gold. The two major constituents of the hoard were the pennies of England, and the deniers of Brabant itself. The former were substantial coins, quite unlike the *piccoli* in Italy. Indeed some of the smaller of the new Italian *grossi* were not as heavy as the English sterling, which still weighed nearly 1.5 grams and was made of good silver. There was therefore not the same pressing need for a new sort of coin that there was in North Italy.

The first larger silver coin in the area was a double sterling, produced from 1269 by Margaret of Constantinople, countess of Flanders and Hainault. It was known as *cavalier* from its obverse type of a knight on horseback. This weighed about 2.5 grams and was much imitated throughout the Low Countries over the next forty years.[62] As in Italy and the silver-mining lands, the progression to the use of large silver coins came in two stages. After a generation of *cavaliers d'argent* the area was, around 1310, at last ready for the 4-gram size of *gros*. Earlier, from 1285 onwards, a large number of *gros tournois* had been minted for the king of France at the Tournai mint, and small numbers of imitative silver *grooten*, modelled on the French *gros tournois*, had been struck by native princes, from John I in Brabant (by 1294), Florence V in Holland (by 1296), Hugh of Chalon in Liège (by 1301) and John of Namur in Flanders (by 1303). Nevertheless, payments in Artois reckoned in the 1280s in *gros tournois* were confined to commercial transactions over long distances and to the count's dealings with his Italian bankers in Siena.[63] Hoards discovered in this area in the 1290s contained few *gros tournois*.[64] A 4-gram *gros* was still too big for internal use in the North. The same was true of England, where in 1279 Edward I unsuccessfully attempted to introduce a great coin or groat, which weighed nearly 6 grams of silver. England was not ready for a groat until 1351.

In the course of the fourteenth century pieces of the scale of the 4-gram *gros tournois*, many of them direct derivatives, began eventually

[62] A. Engel and R. Serrure, *Traité de numismatique de moyen âge*, III (Paris, 1905), 1431–2.
[63] C. Richebé, *Les Monnaies féodales d'Artois du Xe au début du XIVe siècle* (Paris, 1963).
[64] *Revue Suisse de Numismatique* (1963), 67.

to be minted in the Rhineland by such princes as the archbishop of Cologne. Their minting hardly spread further into Germany than this, however, despite the issues by two of the emperors, Lewis IV of Bavaria, and Charles IV of Luxembourg. Even the Hanseatic cities of the North never produced them, apart from a brief and abortive issue by Lübeck in the 1360s. The scale of their internal commercial activity and urban life did not warrant it. Not until the second half of the fourteenth century did they progress far enough even to mint *witten*, 4-pfennig pieces no larger than an English silver penny.[65] Over a century and a half after the introduction of the first *grossi* in Venice, the currency of the Baltic still consisted almost entirely of silver currency bars and extraordinarily light silver bracteate pfennigs.

This makes it abundantly clear how very different the timing of the progression from pennies to groats was in various parts of Europe. It immediately poses the question of what conditions determined the readiness of an area for the use of coins of a larger denomination than the silver penny. Sometimes the attempt was made before the area was ready, as it was by Alfonso X in Castile, by Casimir the Great in Poland, by Edward I in England and by the city of Lübeck, and it failed. What conditions were lacking in England in 1279 when groats failed, that were present in 1351 when they succeeded? The volume of coined money in England was probably greater in 1279 than it was in 1351. The volume of England's external trade was of the same order of magnitude in 1279 as in 1351. Alteration in the volume of international transactions on its own could not have been the efficient cause of the change. This throws doubt on the assumption, which is frequently made, that 'great' coins, silver *grossi*, *gros*, groschen or groats, were primarily struck for long-distance trade, as well as being incidentally used for it. The *gros tournois* did not circulate widely in the Low Countries in the 1280s when it was too large for ordinary everyday internal transactions, and it was not much used for another generation, until after the cloth manufacture and export of Flanders had started to decline.

Long-distance payments in the thirteenth century were increasingly made by exchange instruments. When and where this was not possible, they were still carried out with bar silver, only partially supplemented by silver coin, until the re-appearance of gold coinage outside Italy. The *gros tournois* acted as such a supplementary means of international payments, but this was not enough to justify its existence. The key need for such large coins was an internal one, not an external one.

[65] W. Jesse, *Der Wendische Münzverein* (Lübeck, 1928).

When the first *grossi* were introduced in Venice they were specifically designed for the payment of wages. It was in the payment of wages, and the spending of them, that standard coins were most used. At the point at which either the basic coin became too small because of debasement or wage rates rose, it became inconvenient not to have a large silver coin. In England in 1279 the penny was perfectly adequate for the payment of wages and the groat was inconveniently large, but in 1351 wage rates were in the process of doubling, and the new silver groat and half-groat were suddenly needed much more.

That urban rents and wages, whether day-wages or, in the cloth trades, piece-rates, should have become determinants of the required scale of silver coinage is in itself an indicator of the growth in complexity of cities and industry in the era of the 'commercial revolution'. Alterations in trading practices and commercial techniques did not directly make for any change in coinage at so low a level. One of the side-effects of the transformation of commercial practices was a reduction in the reliance on precious metals as the sole means of payment.

Within certain of the leading commercial cities money-changers extended their activities from manual money-changing to taking deposits, and then to transferring sums from one account to another on oral orders from the depositors. In Genoa, probably the most precocious centre for such local banking activities, the notarial register of Guglielmo Cassinese (1190–2) indicates that local payments could be made not only by transfer between accounts within the same bank but also between accounts in different banks in the city. By the fourteenth century it had become customary amongst merchants within a limited number of cities to make payments as far as possible by assignment on their bank accounts (*per ditta di banco*).[66] By granting credit under such circumstances and by letting their cash reserves fall below the total of their deposits, such local bankers were not only facilitating payments but also increasing the money supply. It can be argued that the money supply was also increased in the fourteenth century, again in a limited number of cities such as Florence, Genoa and Venice, by the creation of negotiable paper, such as shares in the *monte*, the public debts of the cities.

There was a similar reduction in the reliance on precious metals in long-distance trade. No longer did every peripatetic merchant need to carry with him marks of silver or ounces of gold, depending on the trading area, but the static manager could send and receive remittances from his factors and agents by bills of exchange. The bill

66 R. de Roover, *Business, Banking and Economic Thought. Selected Studies of R. de Roover*, ed. Julius Kirshner (Chicago, 1974).

of exchange seems to have evolved into its definitive form by the end of the thirteenth century. Its evolution had begun over a hundred years earlier with the notarised 'instrumentum ex causa cambii'. The surviving Genoese notarial registers include some such instruments from the late twelfth century, mostly involving transactions between Genoa and the Champagne fairs. In the thirteenth century the Champagne fairs seem to have formed the principal money market of Europe and the forcing house for the evolution of the bill of exchange. In the first half of the fourteenth century it became normal to make commercial payments by bill of exchange between a wide range of cities in western Europe. The merchant-banking network was focussed on the great trading cities of North Italy, particularly of Tuscany, and on the papal curia at Avignon. It extended westwards to Montpellier, Barcelona, Valencia, Seville and sometimes Lisbon; northwards to the Champagne fairs, until they faded from importance, and to Paris, Bruges and London; and southwards to Naples and Palermo.[67] Even between these cities, although the majority of transactions could be carried out by bill of exchange, any eventual imbalances had ultimately to be settled up in gold or silver. When an imbalance became too great, the rate of exchange rose (or fell) to such an extent that it passed one of the specie points. In other words it temporarily became cheaper, in one direction, to transport bullion, with all its attendant costs and risks, than to buy a bill of exchange. Certain international political payments, such as wages to keep whole armies in the field for protracted periods, subsidies for expensive allies, or royal ransoms and dowries, could easily prove too large for the normal commercial system to handle and also had to be transmitted largely, or wholly, in gold or silver.

Outside this range of cities, more ordinary international payments had still primarily to be made in bullion. Even here credit, when extended from buyer to seller, or vice versa, stretched the money supply by deferring payment, and so enabled a greater volume of business to be transacted. Where there was a continuous and large imbalance of trade, as there was between the mining centres of Europe and the commercially advanced areas, a bill of exchange system had little chance of developing. In the fourteenth century papal collectors in Poland still had to take bullion to Bruges or Venice before they could make use of the west European banking system by acquiring bills of exchange to remit to the curia. Until the fifteenth century, even the most prominent trading cities of Germany, such as Lübeck, basically remained outside this network of exchanges.

[67] R. de Roover, *L'Évolution de la Lettre de Change XIVe–XVIIIe siècles* (Paris, 1953).

Between Christian Europe, Muslim North Africa and the Levant, the use of bills was little developed, although the scale of trade was very large and the division of labour between manager, carrier and factor developed early; for here there were not only chronic imbalances of trade, but also decided differences in the values given to gold and to silver in the three areas concerned.

The balance between western North Africa and western Europe seems generally to have been in favour of Europe and to have been settled in West African gold that had crossed the Sahara. The balances both between Christian Europe and the Levant, and between Muslim North Africa and the Levant, were in favour of the Levant and were generally settled in European silver and African gold. The Near East itself had a generally unfavourable balance with the Middle and Far East, so that much African gold and European silver continued further into Asia. Since Europe was a silver producer and Africa a gold producer, silver was less valued in Europe than Africa, and gold less valued in Africa than Europe. When this disproportion in value was sufficiently great to overcome the risks and costs of the voyage across the western Mediterranean, it occasionally became worthwhile to take European silver to Africa in order to purchase African gold.[68] Much more frequently it was common sense to carry additional silver southwards and gold northwards along with other more ordinary merchandise. In the Levant, supplied with both European silver and African gold, the relationship between gold and silver was more variable. At some times it was worthwhile for Venetians to take central European silver to Alexandria and return with gold, whilst at others it was more worthwhile for Genoese to carry thither the gold newly received from North Africa rather than the silver newly received from Champagne.

Until the increase in exchanges in the thirteenth century silver was rare outside western Europe and gold was rare within it, except for Sicily, southern Italy and Spain, where the use of gold for currency had never entirely ceased, and the minting of gold had continued, somewhat hesitantly, through most of the earlier Middle Ages. A certain very restricted number of Byzantine gold *solidi* and Islamic gold *dinars* had found their way further afield, but the extent to which these were used has been the subject of much speculation.

Beyond the Alps the bezant, as the *solidus* was now sometimes called, was a very rare piece, and there is some reason to suppose that its use was even more restricted than documents would at first sight suggest. Sums of money expressed in bezants would seem to have been

[68] A. M. Watson, 'Back to Gold – and Silver', *Economic History Review*, 2nd ser., XX (1967), 1–34.

frequently paid in silver. The English Pipe Roll of 1178/9, for example, indicates that an obligation of twenty bezants was discharged by payment of forty shillings, i.e. 480 silver pennies. The use of the *dinar* was even rarer than that of the bezant. Islamic gold coins hardly circulated until after the tenth century, when access to West African gold brought about a renewal of minting of gold in Spain and Sicily. In southern France some thirteenth-century payments were made in *dinars*, but when they travelled further afield they ceased to be treated as money. In thirteenth-century England, coins, mostly Spanish in origin, were used for jewellery and almsgiving and could be found in such non-commercial contexts as attached to the shrines of saints to which they had been given by pious benefactors.

In Mediterranean Europe things were otherwise. During the Muslim occupation, gold *taris*, or quarter-*dinars*, similar to those of North Africa, were struck in Sicily, and these readily found their way into the hands of their Christian neighbours in southern Italy, who had for long been accustomed to using Byzantine gold coinage. Tenth-century charters of Amalfi reveal that payments for lands, houses and slaves were most commonly made in gold *taris*. It is therefore little wonder that from the mid-eleventh to the late twelfth century derivative *taris* were struck at Salerno, and the mint at Amalfi also produced *taris* from the mid-eleventh century to the reign of the Emperor Frederick II. It was therefore into a society used to gold coinage that in 1231 Frederick II launched his famous *augustale* from the Messina and Brindisi mints. It proved to be the precursor rather than the prototype of the gold coinages of western Europe in the later Middle Ages. This splendid piece, based on classical models, was imitated only by Charles of Anjou when he took over Frederick's kingdom of Sicily. The gold coinages of western Europe drew their inspiration from the coins of trading cities rather than from those of this pre-Renaissance 'prince'.

Save in the ninth century, the minting of gold coins had been maintained continuously in Muslim Spain. These were supplemented in Christian Spain in the eleventh century by derivative *mancusi de oro* from Barcelona, and in the twelfth and thirteenth centuries by *dinars* and double *dinars* from Castile, Leon and Portugal.

Minting of gold coins thus continued not only in North Africa but also in Spain, Islamic and Christian, and in southern Italy and Sicily, so that the western basin of the Mediterranean was largely surrounded by *dinar*-issuing countries. It was therefore natural that cities such as Genoa and Pisa, and later Florence, whose trade was largely carried on in the western Mediterranean, should use the gold *dinar* to a considerable extent. In the twelfth and thirteenth centuries a problem was posed, especially to such trading cities, by the irregular standard of the *dinar*, for it was rapidly becoming unusable for commercial purposes. A replacement for the *dinar* was needed. Fine gold by the ounce, either as dust or as leaf, was of some use, but was not very convenient. The flamboyant *augustale* also proved impractical. However, in 1252 Genoa commenced the issue of the gold *genovino* for her maritime trade, and in the same year Florence began to issue the florin. Both *genovino* and florin weighed about 3.5 grams, which was considerably more than the contemporary Almohade *dinar*, and both were nominally of fine gold, whereas the *dinar* had become very much debased.

The gold *genovino* and its quarter, the *quartarolo*, seem to have been largely used in commercial transactions in the western Mediterranean, hitherto the province of the *dinar* and the *tari*, although they were also used in the Levant. In the thirteenth century the gold florin had a much more limited circulation, although in the fourteenth century it was destined to travel along the increasingly important trade routes into northern and western Europe and to become the prototype of most later European gold coinage.

Meanwhile in the eastern Mediterranean the Byzantine gold *solidus* was also becoming less and less useful for commercial purposes. It had kept its original weight and fineness until the eleventh century, but had then declined rapidly. An attempted return to a higher standard at the end of that century, in 1092, had produced a 'pure' *solidus*, the *hyperperon*, which, despite its name, was never more than 85 per cent gold. It was this restored *solidus* that was known to Italians as the *iperpero* and to other Europeans as the *perper*. The Latin emperors in Constantinople after 1204 had minted no *perpers*, although the exiled Byzantines continued minting gold after a fashion at Nicaea. The last 'pure' *perpers* had been struck by John III Vatatzes at Nicaea (1222–54). The later Nicaean *hyperperon* and those struck at Constantinople, after the Palaeologid restoration in 1261 were so poor as to be no longer satisfactory for trade. From Andronicus II (1282–1328) onwards the issues were very small and the last *solidus* was struck about 1341, over a millennium since Constantine had introduced the denomination. *Hyperperon* minted after 1341 were not gold coins at all but silver ones.[69] The westerners most affected by this decline and disappearance of the *hyperperon* were the Venetians. For much of the thirteenth century they continued to rely for their commercial transactions not on gold, but on silver from Central Europe, either in the form of ingots or *grossi*. However, in 1269 the Great Council

[69] T. Bertelé, 'L'iperpero bizantino dal 1261 al 1453', *Rivista Italiana di Numismatica*, LIX (1957), 70–89.

had an official refinery for gold set up near the Rialto and decreed that gold sold in Venice had to be of a fixed fineness ($23\frac{1}{2}$ carats = 0.979 fine). Most gold at this time still came from West Africa, and reached Venice through southern Italy and Sicily, or else direct from Barbary, or even through Byzantium or the Levant, but a small amount also came across the Alps. In 1284 the official manufacture of bars from gold was replaced by that of *zecchini* or gold ducats (as opposed to the *matapans* or silver ducats). They were marginally heavier than the *genovino* and the florins, and were also of fine gold.

Whilst there had been a lack of gold in western Europe, there had been a parallel lack of silver in the Islamic Near East. This equally changed in the thirteenth century, as mint after mint began to mint silver coins again, starting at the end of the previous century when Damascus began to do so in 1174/5. The silver appears to have come from Christian Europe, where, just at this very time, mining was again commencing to increase the availability of silver. It seems likely that most of this silver reached the Near East by way of trade, but in addition the crusaders attempted to take with them the sort of monetary structure to which they were accustomed at home, as well as the silver from which to mint it. Silver-denier-minting Crusader states were thus planted into a gold-using Palestine in the twelfth century. In the same way they were also planted into a gold-using Greece in the thirteenth century. For example the coinage of the French in the Peloponnese in the thirteenth and fourteenth centuries consisted of deniers which were directly derived from the *deniers tournois* of their homeland.

To summarise, the history of money in the Middle Ages can thus be made to fall into two distinct periods. The first which ran from the seventh century to the twelfth, was an era of silver coins variously called pennies, deniers, *denari*, pfennigs or *pennings* depending on the language used. The second period, which began in the thirteenth century, was a much more complex era of larger silver coins, which since they were 'great' in comparison with the pennies, were variously called groats, groschen, *gros* or *grossi*. There was very little gold coin in circulation in the first period in western Europe, but in the second period gold coin was again regularly issued for the first time since its disappearance in the Dark Ages. Alongside the silver pennies of the first period a certain amount of silver also circulated in the form of ingots or bars of fixed fineness, whilst some payments were fixed in terms of commodities other than silver, such as pepper. Alongside the silver groats and gold florins of the second period certain payments between the more advanced commercial centres of western Europe were made by bills of exchange and, within the most advanced of these cities, by credit transfers in the books of certain banks, the *banche di scritta* or *del giro*.

IV. *The Victory of Gold*

The middle years of the fourteenth century saw the transformation of Europe from an area which primarily used silver for currency to one which primarily used gold. Although gold coinage had already been minted in Genoa, Florence and Venice from the second half of the thirteenth century, its use had been largely limited to Mediterranean lands, and the ultimate source of the gold lay outside Europe. This was to change, for the last of the great sources of precious metal to be exploited on a large scale in the era of medieval expansion were the Hungarian gold deposits, principally around Kremnitz, which were opened up about 1320.

The mining of gold in Hungary was not new in 1320, but the scale of operations changed radically at that point in time. Small quantities of gold had been sent to Venice in the thirteenth century and the early years of the fourteenth century, but by 1324 or 1325 there was enough gold being produced for the king of Hungary, Charles Robert of Anjou, to begin the first considerable coinage of gold beyond the Alps.[70] He had pieces struck of almost the same weight and fineness as the Florentine florin and the Venetian ducat. The first issues even imitated the Florentine florin in type as well.

These gold pieces were known as florins, ducats and gulden at various times in different parts of Europe. On later issues the Hungarian rulers replaced the figure of St John the Baptist, the Florentine patron saint, by their own St Ladislas and the lily of Florence by their own arms. However, they retained the standard of weight and fineness of the Florentine florin so long as the mines continued to produce gold, from the fourteenth century right through to the sixteenth.

The price of gold in terms of silver had been rising in Italy ever since the introduction of the florin and the *genovino* in 1252. Suddenly in the 1320s gold was available in large enough quantities to meet the demand for it, and at the same time an agreement made in 1327 between the kings of Bohemia and Hungary stopped the flow of silver to Italy.[71] The price of gold, in terms of silver, began at last to fall, after rising for three-quarters of a century. In Venice itself gold reached its highest value in terms of silver in 1328 and then began to fall, and had fallen quite considerably by 1335. In Genoa the highest

70 Homan, 'La circolazione delle monete d'oro in Ungheria', 128 and 131.
71 Homan, 'La circolazione', 123–5.

point was reached in 1325/7, in Florence between 1326 and 1331, in Siena in 1329, and in Naples in 1326/7.[72] The mint reforms of 1328 mark the point at which Venice moved from a silver standard to a gold standard and from then onwards the minting of gold ducats greatly exceeded the minting of silver *grossi* in importance. So much so that in 1343 a commission advised the setting up of a duplicate mint organisation to cope with the quantities involved.[73] Venice had hitherto been the leading exporter of silver from Europe to the Levant. It now became the leading exporter of gold, and the gold ducat became the principal trading coin throughout the Middle East from the middle of the century, in Mameluke Egypt and Syria, among the Turkish emirs of Asia Minor and the petty Christian states of Greece and the Aegean. It was, not surprisingly, greatly imitated in the eastern Mediterranean by Christians and Muslims alike, and its circulation followed the trade routes as far as South India.

Meanwhile in Italy itself the quantities of gold available increased everywhere, not merely in Venice. By the late 1330s the Florentine mint was striking no fewer than 350,000 gold florins every year, and in some years 400,000.[74] Whereas the ducat spread outwards from Italy to the Levant, the florin now spread out from Italy to western Europe, where it was widely imitated, a sign of considerable circulation, in Aragon, France, the Low Countries, the Rhineland and even Lübeck.

Unsuccessful attempts had been made earlier to start gold coinages outside Italy, but very little came of them. Henry III, for example, issued a gold penny in England in 1257. A certain amount of gold was available in England at this time, but it was treated as a commodity and not as part of the currency. The import from Spain of West African gold for English goldsmiths to work with was no novelty, and gold was used too for such strictly uncommercial purposes as prestigious alms-giving by the king.[75] In such circumstances Henry III's attempt to initiate a gold coinage came to nothing. Around 1270 St Louis issued an *écu* in France, but with equally little success. Northern Europe in general was not yet ready to use, let alone issue, gold coins. It was St Louis' grandson, Philip IV, who managed to establish the first successful national gold coinage after a number of

[72] F. C. Lane, 'Le Vecchie Monete di Conto Veneziane ed il ritorno all'oro', *Atti del Instituto Veneto di Scienze, Lettere ed Arti*, CXVII (1959), 72–5.

[73] F. Thiriet, *Delibérations des assemblées Vénitiennes concernant la Romanie*, I (Paris, 1966), documents 496 and 497, 201.

[74] *Cronica di Giovanni Villani*, book XI, chapter XCIV.

[75] P. Grierson, 'Oboli de Musc', *English Historical Review*, LXVI (1957), 75–81; and P. Grierson, 'Muslim Coins in Thirteenth-Century England', *Near Eastern Numismatics, Iconography, Epigraphy and History, Studies in Honor of George C. Miles*, ed. D. K. Kouymjian (Beirut, 1974), 387–91.

abortive attempts. In 1303 he introduced a *chaise* of nominally fine gold which initially weighed the same as two Florentine florins. He offered a mint price, in silver, for gold which was higher than that in Italy. As a consequence gold flowed in from Italy, and silver flowed out of France to pay for it. By about 1310 the general master of the French mints estimated that 400,000 marks of silver (around 100 tonnes), coined and uncoined, had already been exported from France. From 1305 the popes were living in the Rhone valley, from 1316 at Avignon, and this drew a certain amount of gold across the Alps to the Curia. In the 1320s the Pope, the dauphin of Vienne and the duke of Burgundy all produced florins based on the Florentine model, but none were really successful.

After 1327, when the agreement between the kings of Bohemia and Hungary virtually ensured that no more Bohemian silver should go directly to Italy through Austria, there began to be a shortage of silver in parts of northern Italy. The Venetians were the most directly affected by this diversion of Bohemian silver supplies, and the minting of silver *grossi* in Venice was greatly reduced. Bohemian silver still went westwards across Germany to the Low Countries and to France, and Italians had to draw their silver indirectly through France, sending gold in exchange.

In the 1330s the French were already complaining of a lack of silver, which had presumably been exported to Italy. Gold, however, was sufficiently available at the end of the decade for Philip VI to pay subsidies in his own gold *écus* to his allies in the Low Countries at the opening of the Hundred Years War. Both he and Edward III of England set about purchasing allies in the Low Countries in 1336 and particularly in 1337 in preparation for war. Edward III, lacking his rival's resources, borrowed heavily, perhaps as much as one and a half million gold florins, from Florentine bankers. Much of this was conveyed in gold from Florence to Edwards III's paymaster at Valenciennes.[76] It can hardly be mere coincidence that North-West Europe came to mint gold coins, and abandon the use of silver ingots for payment at just the same time as these vast political subventions were made in gold.

In the Low Countries the mints of Flanders, Brabant, Hainault, Cambrai and Guelders all began to mint gold for the first time in 1336 and 1337. In type these either followed the Florentine florin or the French *écu*, the two coins in which English and French subsidies entered the area. As a corollary, the system whereby the city of Bruges had ingots of silver assayed and marked as a guarantee of fineness ceases

[76] M. McKisack, *The Fourteenth Century* (Oxford, 1959), 119–32.

to be heard of after the middle of the century.[77] The use of gold up the Rhine and the Main followed soon after. Lewis of Bavaria, another of the recipients of Edward III's subsidies, was the first to commence the minting of gold coins at his imperial mint at Frankfurt in 1339. The four great Rhineland electors, the archbishops of Cologne, Mainz and Trier, and the count palatine, all followed suit over the next fifteen years.[78] However, with the exception of the town of Lübeck, the use of gold coinage hardly spread any further and in fourteenth-century Germany remained limited to the valleys of the Rhine and Main. In England itself the striking of gold coins began in 1344.

In those areas of northern Europe to which the use of gold coin did not spread, the traditional use of ingots of silver for large payments survived much later; in Scotland, for example; or in Scandinavia; in large parts of northern Germany and in Poland. In Scotland a successful gold coinage was not established until around 1400; at Hamburg and Lüneburg until around 1440; in Denmark until 1490; and in Poland not until the 1520s. Elsewhere gold coin became, from the 1330s and 1340s, the prime means of international settlements, whether commercial or political, that could not be coped with by bills of exchange and, indeed, for many considerable payments, such as the purchase of land.

During the fourteenth century French gold coinage kept changing in type. The *écu* of Philip VI was a variant of the *chaise* of Philip IV. The type, the king enthroned, was to be used very considerably in France and the Netherlands throughout the fourteenth century and into the fifteenth. The *écu à la chaise* of Philip VI was distinguished from other pieces of the same general type by the appearance of a shield with the arms of France at the left-hand side of the king's throne. Perhaps as many as a million and a half of these *écus*, each valued at a *livre tournois*, were struck in France between 1337 and 1339. This was probably very much more than any previous issue of gold coins in France. The surviving mint accounts are very incomplete and it is difficult to be certain of the scale of issues, but it seems that the previous largest issue, that of *agnels* between 1311 and 1326, may have totalled no more than half a million pieces over as long a period as sixteen years. The *agnel* or *mouton* also derived its name from its type – the paschal lamb – and, like the *chaise* or *clinkaert*, had a considerable vogue later in the fourteenth century and into the

77 R. de Roover, *Money, Banking and Credit in Medieval Bruges* (Cambridge, Mass., 1948), 230–1 and 244, quoting G. Bigwood, *La Régime juridique et économique du commerce de l'argent dans la Belgique du Moyen Age*, Mémoires de l'Académie royale de Belgique, Classe des lettres et des sciences morales et politiques, XIV (2nd ser., Brussels, 1921), 422–5.

78 P. Berghaus, 'Die Ausbreitung der Goldmünze und des Groschens in deutschen Landen zu beginn des 14 Jahrhunderts', *Numismaticky Sbornik*, XII (Prague, 1971–2), 213–16 and 223–5.

fifteenth as a type not only for royal issues but also for imitations, particularly in the Low Countries. The third French royal type to have wide circulation was the *cavalier* or *franc à cheval* minted by the French kings from 1360 onwards. This was initially associated with the ransom paid to England for King John II and weighed the half of an English noble. This was a piece which had great popularity not only in the fourteenth century but also in the fifteenth when revived by Philip the Good of Burgundy for his, by then, united Netherlands. After very numerous changes and types, of which these three were only the most prolific, French royal gold coinage found its standard type at last in 1385 in the *écu à la couronne*, a coin which continued to be issued with some modification until the reign of Louis XIV. The type was the crowned shield of the arms of France. Initially this *écu* or crown weighed 4.08 grams and was of nominally fine gold, but the weight and fineness gradually sank. The Lancastrian kings of France, Henry V and Henry VI, issued from 1421 to 1449 the *salut*, of nominally fine gold and weighing half an English noble. It was issued in far greater quantities than the Valois *écu* and for a short time it looked as if it might supplant it. As the fortunes of war and politics turned in favour of the Valois, the supremacy of the *écu* as the national coin of France was reasserted.

In England a national gold coinage was a little later in its establishment. After a false start with abortive issues of florins and leopards, from 1344 Edward III minted the noble of fine gold. For over a century this was valued at 6*s*. 8*d*. sterling (half of the mark sterling, or one-third of the pound sterling), and remained of the same fineness from 1344 to 1619, although its weight was reduced by over a fifth during that period. The obverse type, the king standing in a ship, had frequently been supposed to relate to the English naval victory at Sluys in 1340. The noble was one of the largest gold pieces of the Middle Ages, slightly larger even than the double-florin-size pieces that the French monarchs kept trying to create. It retained throughout its existence a particular esteem for goodness in north-western Europe and was much imitated, principally in the Low Countries in the early fifteenth century and again in the second half of the sixteenth. The transformation of the English currency in the second half of the fourteenth century, after the introduction of the noble, may be gauged from the recoinage of 1412–14. In this 97 per cent, by value, of the money recoined was of gold, and only 3 per cent of silver. Seventy years earlier the entire currency had been of silver.

In the Empire the Rhineland electors, the archbishops of Cologne, Mainz and Trier, and the count palatine, were among the most prolific issuers of florins. The electors, and from time to time other Rhineland princes, bound themselves by a series of monetary conventions to issue florins of like type, fineness and weight. By the first of these conventions, that of 1354, they agreed to issue florins of $23\frac{1}{2}$-carat gold, 66 of which were to be struck from the Cologne mark of metal. This was in effect the same standard as that of the Florentine florin. The fineness of these Rhineland florins, or Rhine-gulden, rapidly dropped, but was stabilised from 1419 to 1490 at 19 carats. Whilst the fineness was stabilised in the fifteenth century, the weight continued to drop very slowly. When the issue of these gulden finally ceased in 1626 they were struck of $18\frac{1}{2}$-carat gold, at the rate of 72 to the Cologne mark.[79] In the fifteenth century the Rhine-gulden were used very greatly in commerce not only in the valley of the Rhine, but throughout the Low Countries and in much of Germany. They found imitators in the florins issued in the names of such emperors as Sigismund and Frederick III by imperial free cities like Frankfurt and Nördlingen.

The Low Countries, although the second most commercially advanced area of Europe, produced few distinctive gold coins of their own. The gold pieces of France, England, the Rhineland and, to a lesser extent, of northern Italy itself mingled freely in the independent duchies, counties and bishoprics of Artois, Namur, Tournai, Flanders, Brabant, Hainault, Liège, Luxembourg, Holland, Utrecht and Guelders, and the respective dukes, counts and bishops issued a series of imitations of Florentine florins, French *moutons* and *écus à la chaise*, English nobles, and electoral gulden from the Rhineland. There was no indigenous gold coin of Bruges to be a northern rival to the florin of Florence as the great commercial coin of western Europe, perhaps because Bruges was a great market to which men came from all parts of Europe, whilst Florence was a great production and banking centre from which men set out to all parts of Europe. The florin travelled outwards with the Florentines, and many of the mints which produced derivative florin coinages were in fact run by Florentine officials. Bruges sent out no coin of its own, but took in the coin of all who came to trade there and produced local imitations of them. The county of Flanders alone produced Florentine-style florins in the 1330s, French-style *moutons* and *francs à cheval* in the 1350s and 1360s, and English-style nobles in the 1390s. When the Low Countries were politically united in the fifteenth century there was for the first time an opportunity of producing a 'national' coinage for the new Burgundian 'state'. In 1433 a gold *philippus* was introduced by Philip the Good of Burgundy for concurrent issue in Flanders, Brabant,

[79] W. Diepenbach, 'Der Rheinische Münzverein', *Kultur und Wirtschaft im Rheinischen Raum. Festschrift zu Christian Eckert*, ed. A. F. Napp-Zinn and M. Oppenheim (Mainz, 1949), 89–120.

Holland, Hainault and Namur – although the issues from Namur never materialised. Like the French *franc à cheval* of seventy years before, it displayed the ruler riding a galloping horse and so became known as the *cavalier* or rider. Like the contemporary *salut*, which Philip was issuing in the French mints under his control, it was of the same general standard of weight and fineness as the Venetian ducat and Florentine florin.[80]

Meanwhile in Italy itself the three great commercial cities continued to mint *genovini*, florins and ducats of virtually identical and unchanging weight and fineness in very considerable quantities, and some other cities also began to mint gold pieces of a similar standard. In 1380 Bologna began to strike its own gold 'florin', the *bolognino d'oro*. Some years earlier Galeazzo II Visconti and Barnabo Visconti, both separately and jointly, in Milan and Pavia, had begun an issue of 'florins' which lasted well into the fifteenth century of which the obverse was also of the French *franc à cheval* type of John II.

Gold coinage with paper largely replaced bar silver for international transactions and for large payments, government transactions, land purchase and so forth, but some distinction needs to be drawn between national and international coinages. National coinages, such as the English noble or the French *écu*, were designed for use in their country of issue, and, except in the Low Countries, were relatively rarely found outside. National rulers frequently attempted to enforce the reminting of foreign coin that entered their country and to forbid the export of their own coin. The English were more successful than most because their country was an island. The entry of foreign coin into circulation in England was largely, although nor entirely, prevented by the vigilance of the royal exchanges at Canterbury and London, of the mint at Calais and of the local searchers in seaports like Sandwich. From time to time the system broke down, as it had done over the quantities of imitative sterlings which flooded into England in Edward I's reign. Also, of course, a certain amount of Scottish and Irish coin could never be prevented from coming in.[81] On the other hand, international coinages, such as the florin and the ducat, were designed for long-distance commerce and were used as much outside Florence and Venice as within those cities. Although the variety of gold coins in circulation together in any part of later medieval Europe was considerable, it was probably greatest in the two most commercially advanced areas of the continent, northern Italy and the

[80] P. Spufford, *Monetary Problems and Policies in the Burgundian Netherlands 1433–1496* (Leiden, 1970).

[81] P. Spufford, 'Continental Coins in Late Medieval England', *British Numismatic Journal*, XXXII (1963), 127–39.

southern Netherlands. This variety was coped with by contemporaries in a number of ways.

Since much minting was carried out not from gold in the form of dust or ingots but from either foreign coin or earlier coin of the same place, it was absolutely necessary for every mint to compile and keep up to date extremely accurate lists of all possible coin likely to be in circulation and their exact finenesses and the amount to be paid for them as metal for minting. In some sense deriving from the mint's lists, and in some sense dictating the values in those lists, were the much shorter lists put out by rulers as the official values of foreign or old coins which were to be permitted to circulate freely. Since the prime suppliers of the mints were the money-changers, they too had such lists, frequently derived from the mint lists or the official lists. It was the value of a coin in local currency at the money-changers' tables which was the basis of the accepted value for it, and this was frequently slightly different from the official value at which it should have circulated. Even tax collectors had to take coin at this market value rather than at the official value put on it by their own rulers. To us, in retrospect, this immense variety of pieces and their changing values seems most confusing, but to contemporaries it was a perfectly natural state of affairs to which one accommodated oneself with ease. One of the most natural things for a merchant to put in his notebook was a list of gold coins circulating in a particular city with a note of their fineness, sometimes derived directly from the local mint. Less often he added a note of their values in local currency, a less useful piece of information in view of their changes in value. It is often not clear whether these values when given are official values or market values. Such notebooks survive from the late thirteenth century onwards and examples from Venice, Florence, Pisa and Genoa have been published.[82] Their compilers in the course of a business career were posted as far afield as Bruges, Seville or Famagusta and noted down details of the money circulating in those places. Young men going into business and starting their own notebooks often began by copying down sections of the notebooks already in use by older men, so that it is not always possible to tell whether the coins listed were actually in circulation when the notebook was compiled. For example, Pegolotti's notebook, spanning an active career from around 1310 to around 1340, includes lists of coins which seem more likely to have been currently circulating in the late thirteenth century.

Later, when printing came in, it was rapidly used for disseminating information about coin values. The printed placard of official values replaced the handwritten list and oral proclamation, and printed

[82] See Bibliography, pp. 948–9.

booklets also appeared written by merchants for merchants, which were sometimes derived from existing merchant notebooks.

A side effect of the use of gold for international transactions was the reduction of silver to a regional role. Until the victory of gold a certain range of coins had circulated internationally along with silver in bars. For example in the twelfth century and the first half of the thirteenth, silver *deniers provinois* had followed the trade routes from Champagne to Italy and had circulated there to such an extent that they formed the prototypes for the *denari provisini* struck in Rome. In the latter part of the thirteenth century it was the *gros tournois* which accompanied the bar silver on the road to Italy, and a large part of the silver of Tuscany in the 1290s was made up of them. After the mid-fourteenth century it was only in areas in which gold was not dominant that silver coins, and ingots, had a wide circulation. Central Europe, and indeed much of Germany east of the Rhineland, still used mark bars of silver, and in this area Prague groschen also had a wide circulation. Elsewhere the long-distance use of gold reduced silver to circulation within what some historians have called 'coinage provinces'. These 'coinage provinces' have usually been defined in terms of economics and geography. Within each 'province' silver coins issued by all the mints in that area, on whatever authority, circulated together. This was in some sense a survival from the denier period, except that silver coin from outside, if it came in at all, was much more rigorously reminted. Some of these 'coinage provinces' coincided with areas of unified political authority: others did not. In such places there was a tendency for monetary unions to come into existence by which the different rulers or cities agreed to mint coins of identical weight, fineness and value. From the late 1220s the cities of Tuscany united to produce silver *denari*, and later *grossi*, of identical weight and fineness and of related types. From 1354 the Rhineland electors united to produce the *Weisspfennig* or *Albus* of identical weight and fineness and of closely related types, and other rulers of the Rhineland soon joined them. From 1379 six 'Wendish' towns, Hamburg, Lübeck, Lüneburg, Rostock, Stralsund and Wismar, joined together in the same way to produce a uniform silver currency for the heartland of the Hanseatic League.[83]

V. *Money of Account*

In most parts of late medieval Europe, and in many places up to the eighteenth or even the nineteenth century, a dichotomy existed in the functions of money. On the one hand money of account was

[83] Jesse, *Der Wendische Münzverein*.

the *measure of value*, whilst on the other, the actual coin was the *medium of exchange* and the *store of wealth*.

Money of account derived its name from its function. As a measure of value it was used almost exclusively for accounting purposes. Most financial transactions were first determined and expressed in money of account, although payments were naturally made subsequently in coin or, surprisingly often, in other goods. Coin itself was valued as a commodity in terms of money of account, and, like any other commodity, its value frequently varied. This variation of the value of coin in terms of money of account has been the cause of much confusion of thought about the nature of money of account. This confusion of thought has resulted in the expression of a differing concept of money of account by practically every writer on medieval money.

With the decline of the denier at different rates in different places in the eleventh and twelfth centuries a standard of reference was needed for the wide variety of deniers that might be circulating in any region in addition to the indigenous coinage. Such a need was particularly felt in such regions as Champagne on account of the fairs. With the introduction in the thirteenth century of the fine silver *grosso* and the gold florin in addition to the often base *denaro*, a common denominator became necessary to express the varying values of gold, silver and billon coins. Money of account supplied both these needs.[84]

Although the necessity for money of account did not arise until the eleventh and, more seriously, the twelfth and thirteenth centuries the form taken by money of account dated from a much earlier period. As early as the eighth century, and probably in the seventh, the system of pounds and shillings had been in use. With regional modifications, the relationship of 12 deniers or pennies to the *sou* or shilling, and of 20 shillings to the *livre* or pound, had gradually become established throughout western Europe. As has been seen, this was basically a system of counting coins, rather than a system of money. A shilling meant a dozen coins, and a pound meant a score of dozens. Marc Bloch maintained that before the thirteenth century the *sou* and the *livre* were no more than *unités numériques*.[85] The principal variants on the system were in Bavaria and places like Austria which were settled from Bavaria, where the *schilling* meant 30 coins and *pfund* or *talent* meant 8 sets of 30 coins. In England the mark, which was a weight two-thirds of the size of the pound, had been transformed into a unit of account, two-thirds of the pound sterling, and was freely used alongside it. At

[84] H. van Werweke, 'Monnaie de compte et monnaie réelle'. *Revue belge de philologie et d'histoire*, XIII (1934), 123–52. Reprinted in *Miscellanea Mediaevalia* (Ghent, 1968), 133–58.

[85] M. Bloch, *Esquisse d'une histoire monétaire de l'Europe*. Cahiers des Annales, IX (Paris, 1954).

Cologne and Lübeck, marks were also transformed into units of account, representing 12 and 16 *schillings*.

In some cases the development of money of account was facilitated by a transitional stage in which the new coins neatly represented the old multiples of deniers. The earliest *grossi* of Florence and Rome, the earliest *gros tournois* and the earliest Prague groschen were all originally intended to be *soldi*, *sous* or *schillings*, containing twelve times as much silver as their respective deniers, but they soon ceased to fulfil this function. Similarly the Florentine florin and the French *écu à la chaise* were originally intended to represent the Florentine *lira* and the French *livre tournois*, but both were soon elevated in value. The English noble was only kept at a fixed value, half of the mark sterling or one-third of the pound sterling, by reducing the weight of gold that it contained from time to time.

The habit of counting in dozens and scores of dozens was so ingrained that when a new coin did not coincide neatly with a multiple of the pre-existing coins, a new system of pounds, shillings and pence was automatically constructed on the basis of the new coin.[86] In Venice, after the creation of the *matapan*, two concurrent systems of money of account came into use, the one based on the old little (*piccolo*) denier, the other on the new great (*grosso*) denier. There was no firm relationship between the two systems of accounting, for whereas the base *denaro* of the *lira*, *soldo* and *denaro piccolo* system sank further and further in quality, eventually becoming undisguised copper in the late fifteenth century, the *denaro* of the *£s.d. grosso* system very largely conserved its fineness and weight. Two concurrent, and divergent, systems of money of account similarly came into existence in Florence, with the creation of the silver florin or *grosso*, and in France, with the creation of the *gros tournois*. In Venice and France alike the system of account based on the larger coin expired when the relevant *grosso* or *gros* ceased to circulate, several decades after it ceased to be issued. In Castile although the *maravedi* had only an ephemeral life as a large silver coin, it survived for over two centuries as a unit of account, with the meaning of 10 small Castilian *dineros*.

In other places the newer *gros* ousted the older deniers so completely that methods of accounting based on the denier either ceased or continued to be used only on the basis of a notional relationship between the defunct denier and the surviving *gros*. This occurred in Flanders early in the fourteenth century when the new *groot penning* supplanted the Flemish version of the French *denier parisis* and the Flemish version of the English sterling. The new *groot* was held to be

[86] The examples in the following paragraphs are mostly drawn from P. Spufford, *Handbook of Medieval Exchange* (London, 1986).

worth 3 of the old Flemish sterlings and 12 of the old Flemish *deniers parisis*. The Flemish systems of account based on their *groot*, their sterling and their *parisis* were thereafter fossilised in this relationship. All three moneys of account were thus in reality tied to the *groot*. A similar transition to reckoning in the new great coins took place not only in neighbouring Brabant, which also had its *gros*, but in other places as far away as Naples and Bohemia, where accounting came to be carried out in terms of *gigliati* and Prague groschen respectively. Initially the Prague (and Meissen) groschen were struck at 60 to the local mark weight of silver, so that the mark was a convenient multiple of these groats. Even when they ceased to be minted at 60 to the mark they continued to be reckoned for convenience in multiples of 60, each called a *sexagena* or *schock*. Reckoning in *schocks* or sixties occasionally spread to other denominations and was reinforced in the mid-fifteenth century when a *schock* of the Meissen groschen was temporarily worth an imperial gold gulden.

Not only were new systems of money of account constructed using the larger silver pieces as *denari* or *soldi*, but others were built up using the new gold pieces as *lire*. The Florentine gold florin, the French franc and the electoral Rhine-gulden all became pounds of account. Unfortunately for simplicity of comprehension, all three coins became in time detached from their namesakes as pounds of account.

In Florence the gold florin began as the *lira* in the system of money based on the *denaro piccolo*, whilst the *grosso* or silver florin was still the *soldo*. The gold florin thus began as equal to silver florins or 20 *soldi affiorino*. As the *denaro piccolo* and the *fiorino grosso* evolved differently, the gold florin came to have different values in *grossi* and in *piccoli*. This evolution came to an end in 1279 when the silver *fiorino* ceased to be struck. By that time the gold florin had become worth 29 silver florins (29 *soldi affiorino*). Silver florins remained in circulation until they were withdrawn in 1296. Accounting in *lire*, *soldi* and *denari affiorino* did not, like most other systems based on large silver coins, vanish with *fiorino grosso*, but continued into the fourteenth century, because it had effectively become based on the gold florin, rather than the silver florin, at the fossilised rate of 29 *soldi* to the gold florin.[87]

The French case was much simpler. The gold franc was first issued at the value of a *livre tournois*, it then increased in value in money *tournois* as the silver coinage was debased, but the word franc remained as an alternative term for the *livre tournois*, not only when gold francs of a different, higher value were actually in circulation but for long after gold francs had ceased to circulate.

[87] M. Bernocchi, *Le monete della repubblica fiorentina*, III, *Documentazione* (Florence, 1976).

In the Netherlands the electoral florins from the Rhineland were commercially current in the 1440s at 40 Flemish *grooten*, and in the 1450s officially current at that rate and so became equated in men's minds with the pound of 40 *grooten*. The principal silver coin in circulation in the Netherlands, the Burgundian *stuiver* or *patard*, formed a natural shilling for it, being valued at 2 *grooten*. Although by 1467 the gold Rhine-gulden had officially become worth 42 Flemish *grooten*, and by 1488, 90 Flemish *grooten*, gulden still remained, into the sixteenth century, as the name of the pound of 40 groats. This was indeed a strange fossilised system, yet it continued to attach itself to monetary reality by its fixed relationship to the Flemish groat.

Similar fossilised systems existed elsewhere. In France the system of *livre*, *sou* and *denier parisis* based, until its disappearance in 1365, on the *denier parisis*, continued in use for at least another century and a half, keeping contact with reality by the fossilisation of the mid-fourteenth-century relationship of 5:4 with the *denier tournois*. In Flanders their system of *livre*, *sou* and *parisis* was kept in contact with reality, as has already been seen, through the perpetuated equivalence of the Flemish *sou parisis* to the Flemish groat. After 1433 there was no distinct Brabançon coinage, yet the Brabançon money of account continued to be used; it also was kept in contact with reality by the fossilisation of its relationship with the Flemish money of account, as it had been in 1433, when 3 Brabançon *livres* had equalled two Flemish *livres*. Thereafter Brabançon money of account was based on the Flemish groat.

The misnomer 'imaginary money' has often been applied to late medieval money of account, perhaps because the real coin on which the money of account was resting was not always evident on first inspection, as in the cases above. To untangle the maze of moneys of account which were created in the last centuries of the Middle Ages is beyond the scope of this chapter, but it may be taken as axiomatic that on closer inspection a historical explanation may be found for the existence of each money of account, and that such a historical explanation will indicate to which real coin the system continued to be attached.

For transactions inside any one 'country', accounting naturally took place in local money of account, and payment, unless made by assignment on a bank, was made in coins available on the spot, in gold, silver or billon according to the scale of the transaction. For transactions across 'national' boundaries, however, this was not adequate. The different moneys had to be reduced to a common denominator. Since the people most frequently concerned in such 'international' transactions were papal officials and Italian merchants, it was natural that it should be Italian money that was used as the common denominator, and it was most frequently the Florentine florin that was so used, for the Florentine florin was the gold coin *par excellence* of Tuscany. It was also Tuscan merchants above all others who provided the multi-branched commercial and banking network within which so many of these transactions took place. It was only rarely that papal treasurers and even papal collectors used cameral merchants from outside a charmed circle of Florentines, Lucchese and Sienese for the transmission of funds across Europe, whether from collectors in fourteenth-century England to the papal curia at Avignon, or onwards from Avignon to paymasters in Perugia for papal troops in central Italy. The amount due from a new archbishop of York was thus fixed in florins, although, of course, paid over to the transmitting bankers in sterling. In noting the cost of sending English wool to Porto Pisano for cloth manufacture in Tuscany, Pegolotti expressed the various sums actually to be paid out along the way in the relevant local moneys of account, but then summarised the costs by conversion into Florentine florins. For the purpose of making comparisons between sums in the moneys of different countries, for example, the prices of iron in various parts of Europe, we can do no better than systematise one of the principal threads in the actual accounting procedures of the Middle Ages. Table I on pp. 846–9 purports to give the value of florins, usually Florentine, in the principal moneys of account of western Europe at fifty-year intervals.

Such a table must be used with extreme caution, since although in times and places of monetary stability the exchange rates may stay approximately the same for decades on end, in times of monetary change the exchange rates for one year cannot be applied to another. For example, the effects of the debasements associated with Philip IV's wars against England and Flanders, or the debasements effected in connection with the first phase of the Hundred Years War, mean that the figures given for the value of Florentine florins in French money *tournois* in 1300 and 1350 are not to be taken as general indicators of relevance over several decades. When monetary changes were very sudden and violent, exchange rates altered radically within months.

The other caveat to be entered is that not all the exchange rates are of the same sort. Some are the official exchange rates in royal ordinances, others are the exchange rates offered by money-changers in exchanging gold currency for silver currency (which should theoretically have been the same as the official rates, but were not necessarily so in practice), and yet others are the exchange rates in bills of exchange transferring money from one place to another. The latter, of course were not the same in any two places – Venetian ducats could always buy a bill for a greater quantity of English sterling in Venice than could be obtained in the contrary direction in London in buying Venetian ducats with sterling. The difference represented the interest payable for the use of the money in the time which had to elapse between drawing a bill in one place and having it met in another.

The value of exchange rates derived from bills of exchange is further complicated by the various ways in which medieval business men used bills of exchange. Bills of exchange were of course developed and went on being used primarily for the transfer of money from one place to another, but they could also function as a cloak for loans, by the system of exchange and re-exchange. Re-exchange brought the interest element in the difference in exchange rates back as a profit to the initial deliverer. The price of bills could also be affected by those who played the exchanges in the hope of making a profit from alterations in the exchange rates which they had foreseen and speculated on. Even local money-changers' rates for exchange might conceal loan charges. The rate is obviously different if gold coin is physically exchanged for silver coin over the counter than if the silver is paid out on one occasion and the gold paid in three months later.

When reading Table 1 on pp. 846–9 it should be borne in mind that although most of the rates are quoted in *soldi* or shillings, they are based on *denari* or pennies, so that a value for the florin of 66*s.* 3*d.* could equally be expressed as 795 *denari* or as 3 *li.* 6*s.* 3*d.*

A brief glance at the table will bring out a number of points. In the mid-thirteenth century not only did deniers, and hence *sous*, differ very greatly from one place to another but over the next two and a half centuries they continued to evolve differently. The more debased the denier, the greater the number needed to be worth a florin. The Tuscan, Venetian and Roman *denari* which, in the thirteenth century, had already been worse than Milanese or Genoese *denari*, remained so, even though the latter sank to a ninth and an eighth of their relative values by 1500. Debasement of a denier on such a scale meant that it had practically no silver content at all, and indeed in some places such as Florence, the intrinsic value of a single denier would have been so slight that it was no longer practicable to mint. Instead 4-*denari* pieces, *quattrini*, were in practice the lowest denomination, and even they contained only 1 per cent or 2 per cent of silver. Such coins were known as *monnaie noire*, 'black money'. The table equally shows that reckoning in *gros* stopped in the later fourteenth century in a number of places, for example, in France. In others the *gros* evidently became a much less valuable coin, in Flanders, for example. In most of Europe the good silver *grosso* had, by the end of the fourteenth century, ceased to exist. In its place the standard coin was a half-silver piece, a *blanc*

Table I. *Exchange Rates in Medieval Europe*[88]

	1252	1300	1350	1400	1450	1500
Tuscany						
Florence (gold florin in *piccoli* of Florence)	20*s.*	46*s.* 6*d.*	64*s.* (1351)	77*s.* 11*d.*	96*s.*	140*s.*
Lucca (gold florin in money of Lucca)	20*s.* veteri	38*s.* 6*d.* novi (1292)				
Pisa (gold florin in money of Pisa)	20*s.*	42*s.* (1299)	64*s.* (1348)	70*s.* (1396)	(Pisa under Florence)	
Siena (gold florin in money of Siena)	20*s.*	50*s.* (1302)	63*s.*	78*s.*	95*s.* (1451)	128*s.* 8*d.* (1499)
Italy outside Tuscany						
Sicily (gold florin in *pierreale*)		18 (1315)	$11\frac{1}{2}$ (1344)	12 (1403)	14	$25\frac{1}{3}$ (1506)
Naples (gold florin in *gigliati* or *carlini*)	12 (1280)	$13\frac{1}{2}$	12	10 (1404)	10	12 (1497)
Rome (gold florin in *provisini* of the Roman Senate)	20*s.*	34*s.*	47*s.*	73*s.* (1403)	98*s.* 8*d.* (1452)	130*s.*

Bologna						
(gold florin in money of Bologna)	24*s.* (1264)	40*s.* (1298)	32*s.*	36*s.* (1392)		
(gold *bolognino* in money of Bologna)				36*s.*	49*s.*	70*s.*
Venice						
(gold ducat in *piccoli* of Venice)	48*s.* (1284)	64*s.* (1310)	64*s.*	93*s.*	116*s.* (1452)	124*s.*
Verona/Tyrol						
(gold ducat in *grossi* or *kreuzer*)		33 (1303)	36 (1356)	36 (1411)	49	80
Milan						
(gold florin in *imperiali*)	?10*s.*	17*s.* 3*d.*	32*s.*	36*s.*	65*s.*	91*s.*
Genoa						
(gold *genovino* in money of Genoa)	8*s.*	17*s.* 2*d.*	29*s.*	29*s.* 9*d.* (1402)	44*s.*	64*s.* (1498)
Savoy						
(gold florin in *viennois*)	12*s.* 6*d.* (1275)	18*s.* (1298)	24*s.* (1349)	36*s.* 6*d.* (1384)		
Outside Italy						
France						
(florin in *tournois* money) (£4 *parisis* = £5 *tournois*) (£1 *tournois* = £1 *provinois* of Champagne)	8*s.* (1265)	19*s.*	25*s.*	22*s.* (1398)	25*s.*	38*s.* 9*d.*
(florin in *gros tournois*)	9 (1274)	$11\frac{1}{2}$	10	14 (1390)		

88 The values given here are drawn from the interim listing of the exchange rates of medieval Europe recently compiled by the author and Miss W. Y. Wilkinson with the support of the Social Science Research Council of Great Britain. (*Interim Listing of the Exchange Rates of Medieval Europe*, Keele, 1977). When a date is given in brackets it is that of the nearest year for which a value was known in 1977.

Table I. (*cont.*)

	1252	1300	1350	1400	1450	1500
Iberia						
Barcelona						
(florin in money of Barcelona)	11*s.* (1276)	11*s.* (1310)	12*s.*	15*s.* 3*d.*	17*s.* 1*d.* (1447)	20*s.* (1480)
Aragon						
(Florentine florin in money of Iacca)	9*s.* (1280)	11*s.* 6*d.* (1320)	11*s.*			22*s.* (1479)
Castile						
(florin in *maravedis* and *dineros*) (1 *maravedi* = 10 *dineros*)		5*m.* 8*d.* (1291)	20*m.* (1358)	66*m.*	150*m.*	375*m.* (1497)
Low Countries						
Flanders						
(florin in Flemish *grooten* and *mite*) (1 *groot* = 24 *miten*)		13*gr.* 3*m.* (1317)	16*gr.* 20*m.* (1348)	33*gr.* 12*m.*	49*gr.* (1453)	80*gr.*
England						
(florin in sterling) (mark sterling = 13*s.* 4*d.*)	2*s.* 6*d.* (1277)	2*s.* 8*d.* (1301)	3*s.* ½*d.*	3*s.* (1405)	3*s.* 7*d.*	4*s.* 7*d.*
Empire						
Cologne						
(florin in money of Cologne) (Cologne mark = 12*s.*)	2*s.* 6*pf.* (1277)	6*s.* 8*pf.* (1301)	22*s.* 5*pf.* (1349)	42*s.*	42*s.* (1423)	

Lübeck						
(Florentine florin in money of Lübeck)	8*s.* (1288)	12*s.* (1317)	8*s.* (1345)			
(Lübeck florin in money of Lübeck)			8*s.* 6*d.*	15*s.* 6*d.* (1402)	32*s.* (1449)	32*s.* (1483)
Swabia/Nuremburg						
(florin in *heller*)	10*s.* (1265)	12*s.* (1308)	17*s.* 6*h.* (1351)	25*s.*	26*s.*	28*s.*
Bohemia						
(florin in Prague groschen) (1 *schock* = 60 groschen)		12 (1316)	13 (1343)	29¼ (1405)	45½ (1442)	
Austria						
(florin in money of Vienna) (1 *pfund* = 8 *schillings*) (1 *schilling* = 30 *pfennigs*)	60*pf.* (1262)	66⅔*pf.* (1298)	94*pf.* (1354)	150*pf.*	222*pf.*	330*pf.* (1498)

in France, *Weisspfennig* or *Witten* in Germany, *pegione* in Italy, *patard* in the Netherlands. These half-silver coins were known generically as *monnaie blanche*, 'white money', in distinction to the billon 'black money' beneath them. The 'white money', like the good silver *gros* before it, was used primarily for the larger payments of everyday life – wages and rents, for example – or for small quantities of semi-luxuries – butter or candles by the pound – or for more ordinary commodities in larger quantities – whole cheeses or apples by the bushel. 'Black money' served for the most common purchases in an urban environment – the loaf of bread, the joint of meat, the pint of wine or beer.

As the weight of 'silver' coins generally in circulation was gradually worn down, so the price of fine silver in terms of current coin crept upwards. After a time it naturally passed even the highest price that the mint could afford to pay for bullion in new coins, without reducing the weight or fineness of the coin offered. A slight reduction in the weight of newly minted coin was therefore necessary every generation or so to match the wear and tear on the coin already in circulation. If this was not done, money-changers and other suppliers ceased to bring any bullion to the mint. No fresh coin could then be minted, and the mint naturally had to close until the prince was able and willing to reduce the silver content enough. The lack of a continuous supply of new coins led to a variety of inconveniences. The 'foreign' coins that would otherwise have been reminted remained in circulation, particularly the most wretched ones. On the other hand the best surviving coins were culled out of circulation and frequently exported to a mint in whichever neighbouring state was offering the highest mint price for them as bullion. In return further miserable 'foreign' coins were brought back. Coinage thus rapidly deteriorated in quality when the mints were shut. There also seems to have been a surprisingly rapid fall in the quantity of currency circulating at such times. This is not altogether explicable, but hoarding no doubt played a part.

The amount by which currency was debased or decreased in weight went in many cases far beyond the mild reduction in weight necessary to equal the effects of wear. The table on pp. 846–9 shows a number of examples of such rapid falls in value of various currencies. They represent instead sequences of violent debasements undertaken for no other purpose than to provide extremely large and rapid additional sources of revenue to rulers in financial difficulties, usually because of war. The debasements of the French coinage, for example, can be closely connected with the wars of Philip IV against England and

Flanders,[89] with the first stage in the Hundred Years War under Philip VI and John II and finally with a later stage of the war at the end of the reign of Charles VI and the beginning of that of Charles VII. Between the short crisis periods of violent debasement were long periods of relative stability, and, indeed, as soon as possible after the crisis was over and expenditure had returned to a more normal peace-time level, vigorous efforts were made to restore the coinage, if not to its pre-war standard, at least to a better condition than that to which it had sunk in the darkest days of crisis. Philip IV himself restored the coinage after peace had been made with England, Charles V did the same when he took over the reins of government from John II, and so did Charles VII, even before he had completely driven the English out of France. The values for the florin in *monnaie tournois* in the table are of differing sorts. The wartime figures for 1300 and 1350 can only be taken as figures for those particular years and cannot be used as representative of values over longish periods of time. On the other hand those for 1265, 1398 and 1450 fall in periods of stability and can much more safely be used to suggest values over longer periods of time.

VI. *The Silver Famines of the Later Middle Ages*

As well as the enormous variety of particular changes in exchange rates in particular countries which resulted from local circumstances, a number of long-run trends can be seen right across Europe, depending on the changing relationship in the supplies of gold and of silver available for coinage.

As more and more silver became available in the thirteenth century its value in terms of gold dropped accordingly. When more gold became available after the 1320s, the value of gold in terms of silver dropped back (see above pp. 831–4). When for twenty years, from around 1390, and for a further thirty years, from around 1435, the availability of silver was greatly restricted, its price in terms of gold rose correspondingly, and when it began to become more freely available again in the 1460s its price once more sank. The whole period from 1320s to the 1460s was one of the predominance of gold, and the increased use of gold has already been touched on. The decreased use of silver, event to the point of its nearly total disappearance in some

[89] A. Landry, *Essai économique sur les mutations des monnaies dans l'ancienne France de Philippe le Bel à Charles VII*, Bibliothèque de l'Ecole des Hautes Etudes, Sciences Historiques et Philologiques, CLXXXV (Paris, 1910: reprinted 1969), 203–6.

countries in the mid-fifteenth century, is a separate, although closely related, phenomenon.

It was not the first time that the stock of silver had diminished in western Europe. In the sixth century silver had ebbed out of the West completely, and when penny coinages began in the seventh century, they made a completely new beginning. There may have been other diminutions in the stock of silver in the ninth and eleventh centuries, but the evidence is ambiguous, and in each case the stock of silver was soon rapidly increased – in the late tenth century from the Goslar mines and in the late twelfth century from those at Freiberg and elsewhere. In the light of our present knowledge the silver famines of the late fourteenth and the fifteenth centuries appear more severe than anything that had taken place since the seventh century. Moreover the late medieval silver famines took place in an economy which had grown a great deal more complex than in the eleventh or earlier centuries, and in which men were a great deal more reliant on the use of money than their ancestors had been. Some factors were the same as in earlier periods – the dependence of the money supply on the opening of new mines or the closing of old ones, on the wear and tear on coin in circulation, on hoarding and dishoarding, on loss in use and in recoinage, and on the balances of payments with parts of the world outside Europe. However, the late medieval economy was different in some respects. The money supply no longer consisted exclusively of silver, but also included large and growing quantities of gold and far from insignificant quantities of bank money and other forms of negotiable paper. It was also part of a society in which a great deal more was committed to writing, so that we have a great deal more evidence about what was going on.

At the total recoinage of England's currency in 1278–80, Edward I caused some hundred tonnes of silver to be reminted, and there was also an unknowable quantity of uncoined silver available for large payments in ingots and other forms. Hoard evidence shows that practically none of the previous currency escaped the mints' melting pots. Although a certain amount of foreign silver was drawn into the country by the recoinage itself, this hundred tonnes bears some relationship to the silver currency available in England at that time. At the similar recoinage of England's currency in 1412–14 Henry IV was only able to arrange for some two tonnes of silver to be reminted, together with a quantity of gold equivalent in value to another seventy tonnes of silver. Silver in ingot form was no longer in use. The amount of newly-coined money available in England after the first two years of Henry IV's recoinage was thus under three-quarters of that four generations earlier. This is not in itself startling in view of the vast sums paid out and received back over the intervening period as the costs and profits of a long series of major wars, over and above the changes brought about through trade. What is startling is the reduction in the amount of money available in the form of silver coin for the whole range of ordinary transactions, from the very smallest purchases up to the level of the payment of wages and rents.

England was more fortunate than many countries in Europe in possessing even as much silver money as this at the beginning of the fifteenth century. England was still better off in the second and more severe silver famine of the middle of the century, when a high proportion of the mints of Europe were closed for two decades on end for lack of bullion. How had this situation come about? Quite obviously there had been a mammoth exchange of silver for gold. In certain circumstances, such as recoinages in England itself, in the Low Countries or in northern France, it became worthwhile to transfer coin in one metal in one direction and coin in the other in the opposite direction, as the ratios between the mint purchase price for silver and that for gold were made to differ between a group of countries by a recoinage in any one of them.

One of the bizarre effects of a judicious debasement was that so many different people could benefit from it. The prince obviously benefited first and foremost from the seigniorage, but holders of coin who had it reminted also did so in that they increased their normal purchasing power. Those who brought metal from abroad could also benefit if the price offered exceeded the expense and risk of transporting the metal. The money supply patently increased in the country in which the debasement took place, but it also increased in the neighbouring countries which, in exchange, had received the other precious metal, which was relatively more valued in their territories. In the short run exporters and manufacturers gained from a debasement, and in the longer run anybody who paid fixed dues (the majority of the population of peasant tenants in fact) gained at the expense of their landlords. Part of the decline in rents in the late fourteenth and fifteenth centuries is not accountable for by the drop in population and the lack of tenants, but by the erosion of real rents by debasement. It is no wonder that aristocratic regimes favoured the restoration and maintenance of strong money and found an able spokesman in Nicholas Oresme.[90]

Even when a specific debasement had not made it profitable to exchange gold directly for silver, there was generally a slight difference from place to place in the ratios between the market values of gold

[90] Nicholas Oresme, *De Moneta*, ed. C. Johnson. Latin text with English translation (London, 1956).

and silver. This made it worthwhile to make payments in one direction in one metal and in the reverse direction in the other metal. This applied not only to commercial payments, but also to political ones. For example much of Edward III of England's war expenditure on the continent, or rather that part of it funded from his English resources, was in silver, whilst the profits of war, and in particular the ransom of John II of France were brought to England in gold. 'Political' or rather 'administrative' movements of coin might take place even within a 'state'. In the Burgundian 'state' around 1440 there was a difference in the gold–silver ratios between Holland and Flanders – gold was more valued in the north and silver in the south – and the ducal receiver-general's accounts had a section on the profit to the duke made by taking taxes and dues in one part of his territories and spending them in another. The directions of these flows changed from time to time because of either market conditions or government action. For example, in the second quarter of the fifteenth century it was more sensible to make payments from the Low Countries to England in silver and out of England to the Low Countries in gold, instead of the other way round.

The general pattern was that silver from Saxon and, more importantly, Bohemian mines flowed westwards across Germany through Frankfurt to the Rhineland in exchange for goods. From the Rhineland silver flowed into the Low Countries and France, from which gold was received. Between the Low Countries and France the general flow was of silver southwards and of gold northwards, just as between France and Italy the flow was of gold from Italy into France and of silver from France to Italy. The gold itself reached Italy from Hungary and, less importantly by now, from Africa in return for goods. Italy, particularly Venice, exported either gold or silver to the Levant according to the relative ratios in Venice and Alexandria. Additional sources of silver within the Mediterranean world itself were from Sardinia and from Serbia and Bosnia, but with few exceptions this did not affect Europe outside Italy. The Aragonese controlled the Sardinian silver mines in their declining years, and the Venetians sent Serbian silver to England for the purchase of wool and woollens in the fifteenth century.

Whether or not gold and silver flows in opposite directions equalled each other out depended on the balance of trade and the balance of 'political' and 'religious' payments. The general balance of these was in favour of southern Europe and against northern Europe. In general more goods and services were sold by Italians to those beyond the Alps than the other way round. More was spent by outsiders, Germans, Provençals, Aragonese, Bohemians, Hungarians on military expeditions to Italy, than they received in financial advantage. The flow of payments to the papacy, although small in comparison with commercial or military expenditure, ran to Avignon or Rome, and frequently Avignon to the papal states even when the papacy was in Avignon. Curial visitors and pilgrims brought more money to Avignon and Rome, over and above the dues paid to the papacy itself. From Italy the imbalance continued eastwards. The imports of alum, silk, pepper, other spices and slaves, besides those of grain, oil and wine, far exceeded the linens and woollens exported by the Italians, and the difference had to be made up in gold or silver. Pilgrims to the Holy Land or Sinai regularly added to the imbalance. The occasional crusades did the same, to the Aegean in the 1350s, or to Nicopolis in 1396, as did the ransoms following the latter. All this was supportable, and indeed had been built up on the assumption that a continuous flow of silver from Central European mines was constantly being made available to pay for it. The problem of the later fourteenth century and of the fifteenth was that the supplies of precious metal, and in particular silver, were no longer adequate for the demands put on them. Through the thirteenth century great finds of silver at Freiberg, Iglau and Kutná Hora had succeeded each other, so that when one group of mines began to be exhausted another took over. After the Kutná Hora mines, however, there was no major new discovery of silver until the 1460s. The production of silver at Kutná Hora was in gradual decline throughout the second half of the fourteenth century and came to a standstill in the Hussite wars of the early fifteenth century.[91] Since silver continued to be sent onwards along the trade routes without replenishment from the mines, the accumulated stocks of silver that had been built up in western Europe during the long thirteenth century were gradually eroded by the continuation of export without import or internal production of fresh silver.

In some respects the new supplies of gold coming from Hungary did a great deal to make up for the diminution in supplies of silver. For large-scale transactions, bank transfers, bills of exchange and gold coins were much more convenient than silver, but they were quite unsuitable to cope with the everyday needs of the bulk of the population. Even a skilled master craftsman in the building industry in the Burgundian Netherlands or southern England had to work seven to nine whole days in the 1430s to earn a single gold rider or half-noble.[92] The damaging social effects of a dearth of silver coin can be more

[91] Castelin, *Grossus Pragensis*.

[92] E. H. Phelps Brown and S. V. Hopkins, 'Seven Centuries of Building Wages', *Economica* (1955), reprinted in *Essays in Economic History*, ed. E. M. Carus-Wilson, II (London, 1962), 168–78.

readily understood when it is realised how the availability of gold was for many purposes no substitute. The availability of gold itself was not always something that could be taken for granted in the fourteenth and fifteenth centuries. Although the production of gold in Hungary does not seem to have been much diminished until the 1470s there were periods when its arrival in Italy was temporarily interrupted. The supply of gold from West Africa was much more vulnerable to change.[93] There seems to have been a lack of gold from the late 1390s until the second decade of the fifteenth century, and in some places for another twenty years. A further shortage developed in the 1440s, but it is not clear whether these dearths of gold were in some way a by-product of the silver famines, or a result of interruptions in the supply of fresh gold, either in West Africa itself or in the Mediterranean world.

The imbalances of payments and the working out of the mines were in themselves enough to create a critical lack of silver in Europe, but the dearth of silver was exacerbated by two other factors: wear and fear.

Estimates from the reigns of Richard II in late fourteenth-century England and Charles the Rash in the mid-fifteenth century Netherlands suggest that in three decades or so silver coin lost a fifth or a sixth of its weight by wear. These estimates suggest that even if there had been no other factors involved, the weight of coined silver available in the 1460s would have been a little over half of that available a hundred years before. It seems that there was in practice a great deal less than that available, but wear alone made a continual demand on the supplies of silver for the continual renewal of the coinage.

The exacerbating factor was fear. Fear of disorder made men conceal their coin. Fear of not being able to replace coin made men keener to keep their assets liquid. Fear of debasements and the instability of money made men happier to keep their silver in the form of plate, in addition to their desire for ostentation. Silver cups, weighing precisely a mark in weight,[94] were a handy form in which to maintain a store of wealth. All these methods of hoarding, from the thousands of petty coins put aside by poorer men in earthern vessels to the vast arrays of plate accumulated by the greatest in the land, from the constable of France and John of Gaunt downwards, removed more silver from circulation. They were in some sense a consequence of the shortage of silver, but nonetheless they made that shortage worse. Finally, fear of the failure to repay cut back on credit. This was both a consequence of the shortage of money and a cause

[93] John Day, 'The Great Bullion Famine of the Fifteenth Century', *Past and Present*, No. 79 (1978).

[94] P. Wolff, *Commerces et Marchands de Toulouse (vers 1350–vers 1450)* (Paris, 1954).

of yet further shortage. When money is freely available, so is credit; when it is hard to find, so is credit.[95] The fifteenth century frequently saw 'runs' on the local deposit banks, followed by their collapse. There was consequently a diminution of the possibilities of making payments by assignments on bank accounts or, in other terms, a shrinkage in the amount of bank money available.

The first signs of silver becoming rarer were experienced in the 1350s and 1360s. The mines of Argenteria in Sardinia came to an absolute end around 1365, following a rapid decline in production after an abnormally long lifespan.[96] Not only did the Sardinian mint cease production at this time but there was no silver minted in Genoa either. This was around the same time as the supplies from Kutná Hora began to decline appreciably, and around the same time that the first concern about the supply of silver began to be voiced in the English parliament. These were only the beginnings of a chronic shortage of silver which reached famine proportions in the 1390s. In the two most commercially advanced areas of Europe alike, northern Italy and the southern Netherlands, a desperate lack of silver was felt. The minting of silver ceased in Malines in 1392, in Florence the next year and in Louvain the year after, whilst serious concern was expressed about the lack of silver in Milan at the same time. Only the Venetians partially escaped the effects of this silver famine, for they had access to the mines of Serbia and Bosnia which had begun to make some contribution to the Venetian supply of silver from the late 1370s.[97] Venice had been able to start minting silver *grossi* again in 1379. Even Venice was not immune to the silver shortages of the 1390s, and restrictions were imposed on the export of silver in 1396. It is not surprising that the minting of *dirhems* in Egypt ceased the following year because the supply of silver from Europe had dried up. In 1400 fresh regulations to cope with the continuing shortage were framed in Genoa and in the following year in Bruges. A similar dearth of silver was experienced at the same time outside Italy and the Netherlands, for example, in France and England.

However in the next few years the greatly increased quantities of silver from Serbia radically changed the picture in Italy, at least for the time being. In 1402 the minting of silver *grossi* began again in Florence, and some *piccoli* had even been minted the previous year. By 1404 minting of silver had been resumed in Genoa, and by 1407

[95] F. C. Spooner, *The International Economy and Monetary Movements in France, 1493–1725* (Paris, 1956; English edn, Cambridge, Mass., 1972).

[96] John Day, 'The Decline of a Money Economy: Sardinia in the Late Middle Ages', *Studi in memoria di Federigo Melis*, III (Naples, 1978), 155–76.

[97] D. Kovacevic, 'Dans la Serbie et la Bosnie médiévales: Les mines d'or et d'argent', *Annales, E.S.C.*, xv (1960), 248–58.

there was sufficient silver in Venice for restrictions on its export to be waived. Over the next twenty years the imports from the east through Venice were largely paid for in Venetian silver *grossi*, which for a time were common coins in Syria and Egypt. Outside Italy the end of the famine came rather more slowly. It was not until 1410 that minting of silver was resumed in Flanders, and the negligible amount of silver available in England for the recoinage of 1412–14 has already been discussed (p. 852).

The silver available from Serbia and Bosnia went on increasing in quantity until the 1420s, and then it too began to diminish. Some of the mines were worked out as early as 1420. In the speech attributed to the dying Doge Tommaso Mocenigo in 1423 he indicated that three-quarters of the new silver minted in Venice was immediately sent out of Europe. Only a quarter remained in Europe and very little of that in Venice itself.[98] If these proportions are correct, and Mocenigo had access to detailed returns made at the time, any reduction in the supplies of silver coming from Serbia and Bosnia was bound to have an immediate effect. Mocenigo was in fact speaking near the end of the all-too-brief respite in the silver famine. By 1429 it was apparent in Venice that the supply of Balkan silver on a grand scale was coming to an end. It was already less easy to find enough silver to send to the Levant, and a large proportion of the payments to Alexandria, Beirut and the Aegean was again made in gold ducats. Even in Mocenigo's own lifetime many of the payments by other west Europeans had been made in gold. In his deathbed oration he had gloated over the way in which much of the gold of Europe was already being drawn to Venice.

The continued outflow of precious metals brought about erratic shortages of silver, and less often of gold, until, eventually, by the late 1430s and early 1440s both were lacking together. At this point many mints in western Europe were compelled to close down altogether, for lack of bullion, not merely for weeks or months on end, or even for years (as in the famine of the 1390s), but for decades. The Burgundian mint at Brussels was closed for minting silver for no less than 29 years after 1437, that of Ghent was closed for 17 of the 27 years after 1439 and minted insignificant quantities of silver in the other 10. The English mint at Calais produced next to nothing after 1439 and was closed for ever in 1442. The French mint at Tournai struck only minimal quantities in 7 of the 32 years after 1435, and in the other 25 years nothing at all. Between 1440 and 1443 the great Rhineland electors were forced to close down their mints one after

[98] M. Sanuto, *Vite de Duchi di Venezia*, ed. Muratori, col. 960.

another. At Dieppe, already one of the principal ports of northern France, for 30 years after 1446 there was not enough money to keep even a single money-changer in business.[99] Only at the English royal mint in the Tower of London did minting continue in north-western Europe in the 25 years after 1440, and even here the quantities minted were derisory. In other parts of Europe it was much the same. In 1447 the mints of Languedoc had already been closed for several years[100] and showed no signs of re-opening. The same year the city council of Barcelona, whose mint still remained open although it had struck minimal quantities for several years, acknowledged that the dearth of bullion was universal.[101] In 1451 two galleys, one belonging to Jacques Coeur, the *argentier* of Charles VII of France, the other from Florence, came into the port of Valencia. Neither sold any of their cargoes since there was no money available in the city for anyone to make any purchases from them.[102] In 1455 at a South German meeting to discuss what should be done about the continuing dearth of bullion, even the Austrians had to acknowledge that it was impossible for them to mint.

The production of silver and gold in Serbia and Bosnia had been declining since the 1420s. In the 1450s the Turks overran both countries in turn, and their precious metals abruptly ceased to be available in the West. The long life of the Venetian silver *grosso* was brought to a pitiful close in 1462. The last *grossi* of Cristoforo Moro weighed much less than half the original *grossi* of 1202 which had been the first in Europe. There were no more *grossi* after 1462, and in 1465 Venice suffered the fate that other European cities had been suffering for up to thirty years. The agent of the marquis of Mantua reported to him that Venice had sent off all her liquid currency with the Syrian galleys, leaving the city bled white and temporarily paralysed.[103] The following year it was reported that in the Venetian *terra firma*, by then extending almost to the gates of Milan, there was no other kind of currency than 'black money', debased billon *piccoli* and *quattrini*. This was the last, and worst, of thirty years or so of bullion famine.

In the latter years of the bullion famine even 'black money' began to disappear as well as 'white' silver and gold. It was, perhaps, carried out of Europe as well as hoarded, lost and worn out. At first sight this seems improbable, but it may indeed have been the case. Jacques Coeur was certainly accused of such action. One way or another the

[99] M. Mollat, *Le Commerce Maritime Normand à la Fin du Moyen Age* (Paris, 1952).
[100] Wolff, *Commerces et marchands de Toulouse*.
[101] C. Carrère, *Barcelone, Centre Economique 1380–1462*. 2 vols. (Paris, 1967).
[102] Carrère, *Barcelone*.
[103] F. Braudel, *The Mediterranean*, I (English trans. London, 1972), 378.

lack of 'black money' was protested against, in Limburg and Tournai, in Paris and Barcelona, in Holland and, eventually, even Venice.[104]

And, thus, with a lack of even 'black money', as well as 'white' silver and gold, the bullion famine reached its worst point in the mid-1460s, and by then the economy of Europe had been under severe strain for three decades for lack of the means of payment, and silver had not been plentiful for well over a century.

VII. *Money on the Eve of the Price Revolution*

The extreme difficulties created by the dearth of coin and credit disappeared very suddenly in the mid-1460s with the opening up of new sources of silver. A whole series of new discoveries of silver ore were made in the Alps and in the Erzgebirge, particularly at Schwaz in the Tyrol and at Schneeberg in Saxony. At the same time a series of technical innovations made it profitable to re-open old mines. These revived mines included those at Kutná Hora in Bohemia, at Freiberg in Saxony and at Goslar in the Harz, each of which had already possessed in turn the richest silver mines in Europe. The starving mints of Europe eagerly consumed this silver as fast as they could obtain it. The mints of the Burgundian Netherlands were re-opened in 1466 and those in Bohemia in 1469, the year after the Kutná Hora mines began to be exploited once again.[105] Frankfurt and Milan became the two focal points for the precious metal trade. It was through Frankfurt that a large proportion of this new silver passed to the mints of northern and western Europe. In 1472 the city of Cologne, whilst negotiating with the emperor for the right to mint its own coinage, was also negotiating with a bullion broker in Frankfurt for a supply of silver to mint.[106]

During the long century in which the stock of silver in Europe had shrunk away almost to nothing, individual silver coins had also become progressively lighter and baser.[107] With the return of silver, larger and finer pieces began to be struck. Initially only the lost levels

[104] For Tournai, see P. Spufford, *Monetary Problems and Policies in the Burgundian Netherlands, 1433–1496* (Leiden, 1970); for Paris, see F. de Saulcy, *Recueil de documents rélatifs à l'histoire de monnaies frappées par les Rois de France depuis Philippe II jusqu'à Francois Ie*, 4 vols. (Paris, 1879 and 1892); for Barcelona, see Carrère, *Barcelone*; for Holland, see Spufford, *Monetary Problems and Policies*, 201.

[105] Castelin, *Grossus Pragensis*, 701–2.

[106] *Quellen zur Geschichte des Kölner Handels und Verkehrs im Mittelalter*, ed. B. Kuske, II (Bonn, 1917), 291–2.

[107] R. van Uytven, 'Sociaal-economische evoluties in de Nederlanden voor de Revoluties (veertiende-zestiende eeuw)', *Bijdragen en Mededelingen betreffende de geschiedenis der Nederlanden*, LXXXVII (1972), 61–5.

of the past were regained. In 1466 fine silver double *patards* began to be struck in the Burgundian Netherlands, containing about 3 grams of silver. They had a great success and rapidly replaced the single *patards*, which had been only of half-silver, as the standard coin of the area. In Milan, at about the same time, Galeazzo Maria Sforza began to strike new good silver *grossi da 5 soldi* in place of the *pegione* of half-silver which had been the standard pieces for much of the previous hundred years. The new pieces contained approximately as much silver as the *grossi ambrosini* of the late thirteenth century.

It was in Italy too that the next step was taken, the production of silver coins of a greater weight than ever before, exceeding in silver content even the heaviest and best *grossi* of the late thirteenth and early fourteenth centuries. In 1472 the doge of Venice, Nicolo Tron, ordered the striking of a coin worth a whole Venetian *lira*, containing 6 grams of of the plentiful new Tyrolean silver. This was soon after supplies of gold from Hungary had come to an end. Under these circumstances silver *lire* proved very useful as reasonably convenient substitutes for the more valuable gold ducats which were lacking. In 1474 the duke of Milan, Galeazzo Maria Sforza, followed suit and ordered the striking of a Milanese *lira* which weighed more than 9 grams of silver. The obverse type, a magnificent portrait of the duke's head in profile, gave the pieces their nickname, *testoni*, or 'head-pieces'. Other rulers in the Alps and the duchies between the Alps and the Appenines were not slow to follow the example of Venice and Milan.[108] Although the large-scale issue of *testoni* was for long limited to this area, the pieces themselves spread through Europe like gold coins. Since the victory of gold in the fourteenth century, silver coins had normally tended to remain within the 'coinage province' in which they were issued. Very small issues of *hoofdstukken*, *testoons* and *testons* began in the Netherlands, England and France in 1487, 1504 and 1514 respectively, but such large pieces did not find a regular place in the minting arrangements for north-western Europe for another generation because there was no lack of gold in this area, which had not been affected so immediately by the decline in the Magyar gold mines.

A certain proportion of West African gold was by now being brought back directly from the West African coast by merchants and adventurers and reached Europe through Lisbon where, from 1457 onwards, the kings of Portugal minted it into ducat-sized *cruzados*. This gold found its way into wide areas of western Europe; overland into Castile, for instance, or by sea to Genoa, and thence to Milan and

108 P. Grierson, 'The Monetary Pattern of Sixteenth-Century Coinage', *Trans. Roy. Hist. Soc.*, 5th ser., XXI (1971), 53–5.

even the Tyrol; or, from the 1460s, to Bruges and thence to England and Frankfurt.

It is not yet clear whether this Portuguese gold represented any increase at all in the amount of gold reaching Europe from West Africa, or was merely a diversion of the means by which it came, away from the traditional camel caravan routes across the Sahara. There is some indication that the total quantity of gold coming into Portugal each year at the end of the fifteenth century was very little different from the 1,500–1,800 kilograms of gold passing through Sidjilmassa to the ports of Morocco half a century before.[109]

As well as Portugal with its *cruzado*, a number of other countries renewed their gold coinages at about this time. In England in 1464 Edward IV replaced the noble by a heavier version, the ryal or rose-noble, sometimes known in the Low Countries as the sun-noble, which was valued at 10*s.* sterling and weighed 7.78 grams, and was a variation of the noble. A new piece, the angel, was introduced at 6*s.* 8*d.* sterling, the value of earlier nobles. In the sixteenth century the rose-noble became one of the most common, and most commonly imitated, gold coins in the Netherlands. Gold flowed equally into France, where a high value was also set on gold, and in 1475, Louis X modified the *écu à la couronne*, which had for long been the standard gold coin of France, by issuing the slightly heavier *écu au soleil*, weighing 3.5 grams. This was a weight which was shared by many other fifteenth-century coins. It was the old international ducat standard kept by the Florentine florin, the Genoese *genovino* and the Venetian ducat since the thirteenth century, which had been adopted for the Hungarian ducat from the fourteenth century, and had also been used earlier in the fifteenth century for the Plantagenet–French *salut*, the Burgundian rider, and the Mamluk *ashrafi*. The new *cruzado* of Portugal was also of this standard, and so was the *ducado d'oro* adopted in Aragon in 1475/6. Ferdinand and Isabella introduced the *ducado* into Castile in 1497 and their new gold *excelente* was a double *ducado*. For much of the fifteenth century the English noble was also the double of these ducats. All these were of nearly pure gold, over 23¾ carats fine. A secondary standard was provided by the German gulden, which were not very different in weight, but of much poorer gold, only 19 carats fine. As well as the gulden of the Rhineland electors and the imperial cities, the *andriesgulden* of the Burgundian Netherlands, issued from 1466, was also of this standard. This was the standard of gulden in which the Fuggers reckoned.

By the mid-1460s a general dearth of 'black money' had developed,

[109] P. Vilar, *Oro y Moneda en La Historia 1450–1920* (Barcelona, 1969), pp. 45–56.

which had caused great difficulties in the ordinary small everyday transactions of urban life. Princes and cities made desperate attempts to resolve this problem, attempting to ensure that at least some 'black money' was minted, whatever the cost, but the complete lack of silver had defeated these attempts.[110] It had been during this dearth that in 1463 the Venetians had debated the possibility of striking coins of pure copper, containing no silver at all, instead of 1 or 2 per cent of silver.[111] Paradoxically it was not during the dearth of black money that the first pure copper coins were struck but in the following decade, in 1472 when there was again adequate silver to mint the traditional base silver coinage. The first such coins were not struck in Venice, then the major European centre for the growing trade in the copper of the Alps and the Carpathians,[112] but in Naples. Pure copper *bagattini* followed in Venice in 1473. The change from 'black money' to a true copper coinage was not a revolutionary change, at least not at the beginning, for the Venetians insisted that their new copper coins should contain their value in copper, less the actual cost of minting them. This was precisely the same principle that had been applied to the traditional 'black money' which had, after all, been almost entirely of copper. The use of pure copper spread extraordinarily slowly outside Italy and it is not necessary to draw any distinction between 'black money' and copper coinage. It was the sum total of the two which supplied, or failed to supply, the small change necessary for urban daily life. The problem of the inflationary excess of petty coins of copper was a problem of a later epoch. In the fifteenth century the problem was still the same as it had been since the major growth of cities in the thirteenth century, to find enough small change to go round.[113]

Thus, on the eve of the price revolution, the total stock of coined gold in Europe was more or less static although rather differently distributed from what it had been; the stock of good silver coin was growing rapidly, although by the end of the fifteenth century it was still far from reaching the level of the early fourteenth century; and the stock of small change, whether old 'black money' or new copper was beginning to be enough to satisfy the everyday needs of Europe's townsmen.

[110] G. Lesage, 'La Circulation monétaire en France dans la seconde moitié du xve siècle', *Annales E.S.C.*, III (1948), 315–16. He would like to see this influx of gold as evidence of a favourable balance of trade.

[111] W. Jesse (ed.), *Quellenbuch zur Münz- und Geldgeschichte des Mittelalters* (Halle, 1924, Reprinted, 1968), no. 292, 158–9.

[112] H. van der Wee, *The Growth of the Antwerp Market and the European Economy*, I (The Hague, 1963), 523.

[113] C. M. Cipolla, 'The Big Problem of the Petty Coins', *Money, Prices and Civilisation in the Mediterranean World* (Princeton, 1956), 27–37, provides much useful and interesting evidence of seventeenth-century fears of the inflationary excess of copper coin, but also attributes the same fears to men in the fourteenth century without any supporting evidence.

APPENDIX

A TABLE OF MEDIEVAL MONEY

The coins most commonly in use in the Middle Ages, together with details of their country and period of origin, their weight and fineness, their initial values, and the names under which they were current.

Weight in medieval documents was normally expressed in terms of the number of coins that were struck from a standard weight, usually a pound or a mark, but sometimes from a smaller unit, such as an ounce or lot. These weights naturally varied from time to time and from place to place, although there were some, such as the marks of Cologne or Troyes, that had a long and widespread use. Alternatively, weights were expressed in terms of carats or grains. The carat or *siliqua* (the seed of the carob, *ceratonia siliqua*) was the standard basic weight in antiquity in the Mediterranean world and continued in use in the Byzantine Empire in the Middle Ages. In the Germanic West, however, it fell out of use in the sixth and seventh centuries in favour of systems in which cereal grains were the basic units. Both barley grains, later called Troy grains, and wheat grains, later called Paris grains, were used. The former weighed 0.065 grams and the latter 0.053 grams. The last Merovingian gold *trientes* and the first Merovingian silver deniers could therefore either be described as weighing 20 grains of barley or as weighing 24 grains of wheat. In this table all weights are in grams.

Fineness in medieval documents was normally expressed in terms derived from systems of weight used at an earlier time. For silver, the system used right through the Middle Ages was derived from weighing in grains, as it had been used in the first centuries of the circulation of the denier. At that point a *solidus*, or shilling, had meant twelve silver deniers, and at the critical period each denier had weighed 24 grains (a pennyweight – dwt.). This was fossilised, so that pure silver, or, more often *argent-le-roi* (standard, nearly pure, silver) was described as having a fineness of 12 *d*(eniers). Similarly half-silver and half-alloy was described as having a fineness of 6*d*. (out of twelve being understood), and so forth. Thus, silver coins described as having a fineness of 4*d*. 18gr., consisted of $4\frac{3}{4}$-twelfths silver and $7\frac{3}{4}$-twelfths alloy. An alternative system, used around the Baltic, described fineness in terms of lots. A mark weight was divided into 16 lots. Pure silver was therefore described as having a fineness of 16 lots; half-silver and half-alloy as having a fineness of 8 lots, and so forth. When gold was used again in western Europe, the Byzantine system was taken over. Here the *solidus* was still a gold piece, which weighed 24 carats. Pure gold was accordingly described as 24 carats fine and so forth. Gold coins described as $19\frac{1}{2}$ ct. fine, therefore consisted of $19\frac{1}{2}$ twenty-fourths of gold, and $4\frac{1}{2}$ twenty-fourths of alloy. The finenesses of medieval gold coins were much higher than those of modern jewellery. 18 ct fine was poor for a gold coin, but is rather good for jewellery. In this table a modern fineness is given expressed as a decimal. Unity here represents pure metal.

IMPERIAL GOLD

Solidus or *Solidus Aureus* (in Latin) or *Nomisma* (in Greek)	Byzantine Empire – *c.* 309–963. Nominally fine gold. Initially at least 0.98 fine. Wt 4.48 g. Principal mint: Constantinople. Half = *semissis*; third = *tremissis* or *triens* (1.49 g).

Solidus Mancus or *Mancus* or *Mangon*	Light weight *solidus* struck by Byzantine administration in Italy and Sicily. Under Justinian II (685–711), wt 4.2 g.
Tertarteron	Light weight *nomisma*, struck by Constantinople 963–1092.
Histamenon	Standard *nomisma* 963–1092, retained original weight and fineness until abrupt decline in eleventh century.
Hyperperon or *iperpero* or *perper*	Restored *nomisma*, 1092–*c.* 1341. Initially 0.85 fine. Deteriorated in thirteenth century; last issues very small in number.

BARBARIAN GOLD

Visigoths	
Solidus and *Triens*	In names of Emperors Anastasius, Justin and Justinian; issued by Alaric II (484–507) to Leovigild (568–86).
Triens	In names of kings from Leovigild (from about 580) to Achila II (*c.* 710–14).
Merovingians	
Solidus and *Triens*	In names of Emperors Anastasius, Justin, and Justinian; issued by Clovis (481–511) until, in northern Gaul, Theodebert I of Austrasia (534–48), and in Provence, Heraclius (610–41). In names of kings from Theodebert I to Dagobert II (674–9). Weight in sixth century on two standards: *solidus* at 4.48 and 3.92 g, and *triens* at 1.49 and 1.31 g; surviving *trientes* of the seventh century weigh mostly 1.15–1.3 g. Most *solidi* from Provence.
Lombards	
Triens	In names of emperors from *c.* 571 onwards. In names of kings from Cunincpert (680–700) to Charlemagne (until 781). Fineness and weight initially near Byzantine *triens*, but by Charlemagne 0.39 fine, wt 0.97 g.
Anglo-Saxons	
Triens or *Thrymsa*	Mainly issued in last quarter of seventh century. Mints Canterbury and London. Wt surviving examples 1.25–1.35 g. Value thought to be one shilling.

ISLAMIC

Dinar	Standard gold coin issued by Ummayad and Abbasid Caliphs from Damascus mint. Nominally fine; wt 4.25 g. *Dinar* of Offa of Mercia (after 774), wt 4.28 g.
Dinar or *Mancus*	Issued by later Ummayads in Spain, Abd-al-Rahman III to Sulaijman (928–1013).

	Fineness and weight of surviving *dinars* vary greatly; fineness 0.79–0.98; wt 3.43–4.71 g.
Copies	*Mancusi de oro* of Berengar Raymond I and Raymond Berengar I, counts of Barcelona (1018–76)
Dinar or *Morabetino*	Issued by Almoravides in North Africa and Spain (*c.* 1085–*c.* 1170). Wt 3.88 g. *Morabetinos* or *maravedis* issued by kings of Castile, of Leon and of Portugal (1172–*c.* 1221)
Dobla	Double of *dinar* or *mazmudina* issued by Mazmuda or Almohades in North Africa and Spain, Abdelmumin (1129–62) to fall of Granada (1492). Wt 4.60 g.
Copies	*Doblas* of Kings of Castile from Ferdinand III (1217–52) onwards.
Tari	Quarter-*dinar* issued in Ummayad Spain, North Africa and Moslem Sicily.
Copies	*Taris* of Salerno (*c.* 1050–1194) and Amalfi (*c.* 1050–1220+).
Dirhems	Standard silver coin of Ummayad Caliphate and of successor kingdoms from Central Asia to Spain. Slow decline in weight and fineness. Early eighth-century Spain, fineness 0.95–0.99; wt 2.81 g. Late tenth- and early eleventh-century Spain, fineness 0.73–0.78; wt 3.11–3.13 g. Almoravide Spain (*c.* 1085–*c.* 1170), wt 2 g. Almohade Spain wt 1.5 g.

PENNY COINAGE

Penny = *penning* = *pfennig* = *denarius* = *denaro* = *denier* = *dinero* = *dinhero*
Halfpenny = *obolus* = *obole* = *medaglia* = *maille*
Farthing = *ferling* = *pougeoise* = *pogesa*
12 pennies = shilling = *scilling* = *skillingr* = *solidus* = *sou* = *solde* = *sueldo* (except in Bavaria and Austria where 30 pfennigs = *schilling*)
240 pennies = pound = *pfund* = *pond* = *libra* = *livre* = *lira*

Merovingian Gaul	
Denier or *Denarius*	In name of Caribert II of Aquitaine (629–31) and of many ecclesiastics and some laymen during the remainder of the seventh and first half of the eighth century. Majority of surviving examples weigh 1.2–1.3 g. Probable standard, 1.3 g.
Anglo-Saxon and Frisian coasts	
Penny or *Penning*	From the end of the seventh to the third quarter of the eighth century. Miscalled *Sceat* or *Sceatta*.
Carolingian Empire	
Denier	Replaced Merovingian denier from 755, and Frisian penny. 794 wt 1.7 g. After end of Carolingians, issue continued into eleventh century, with immobilised types, in some places.

	Feudal deniers issued throughout West Francia after break up of Carolingian Empire.
France	
Denier Provinois	Minted at Provins in the name of the count of Troyes and then of the count of Champagne (end tenth century–after 1265). Basis of money of accounts for Champagne, Barrois and Lorraine. From 1210 of same standard as *denier tournois*.
Copies	*Denaro provisino* issued by Senate of Rome.
Denier Melgorien	Issued by counts of Melgeuil or Mauguio, then by bishops of Maguelonne (tenth century–after 1282). 1125: fineness 0.42; wt 1.10 g. 1215: fineness 0.33; wt 1.09 g.
Denier Parisis	Issued by kings of France, Louis VII–Charles V. Louis VII (1137–80): wt surviving examples 0.85–1.28 g. Charles V (last issue 1365): fineness 0.16; wt 1.28 g. Other local deniers issued by Capetians from end tenth century.
Denier Tournois	Issued by Abbey of St Martin of Tours, from tenth century to 1204. Wt declining 1.2–0.95 g. Issued by kings of France (1204–1649). Philip Augustus (*d.* 1223): wt surviving examples 0.78–1.01 g. Charles VIII (1483 issue): fineness 0.08; wt 1.02 g.
Empire	
Italy	
Denari	Issued by or in name of Carolingians, of native kings of Italy and of German emperors from Otto I (962). Initially of Charlemagne's standard, 794 wt 1.7 g, but declining. Principal mint for Lombardy: Pavia; for Tuscany: Lucca.
Lombardy	
Denari imperiali	Reformed *denari*, issued from about 1155/61 by emperors and later rulers of Milan and Pavia. Initially, Frederick I, double preceding *denari*, fineness 0.5, wt 1 g.
Venice	
Denari	Issued by city from ninth century. In name of ruling doge instead of long dead emperor from around 1170.
Tuscany	
Denari	Issued by imperial mint at Lucca, taken over by city, and by new civic mints, at Pisa about 1151, Volterra about 1165, and Siena about 1191. *Denari* of Tuscan cities kept at identical fineness and weight by monetary conventions. Second half twelfth century wt 0.6 g; first half thirteenth century wt 0.25 g.
Rome	
Denari	Issued jointly in names of pope and emperor from Leo III and Charlemagne to late tenth century.

Denari Provisini	Issued by Senate from late twelfth century. Of same type as *Denier provinois* of Champagne.
Germany	
Pfennig	Imperial *pfennigs* theoretically on Charlemagne's standard, 240 to pound, wt 1.7 g, or from twelfth century, 160 to mark of Cologne, wt 1.46 g. In practice: *pfennig* at Trier, 1160, wt 0.97 g, pfennig of Luxemburg, early thirteenth century, wt 0.73 g, *bracteate pfennig* at Minden 1265, fineness 0.8; wt 0.67 g.
Hungary	
Denar	From Stefan I (1008–38) onwards *bracteate denars* Bela IV (1235–70) to Otto (1305–7).
England	
Penny or Sterling	Issued from about 775/80 Heaberht and Ecgberht, kings of Kent, and about 783/4 Offa king of Mercia, onwards, by all Anglo-Saxon kingdoms, by Viking kingdom in York, and by Norman kings. Until 1156/7: fineness and weight fluctuated considerably from issue to issue. Wt within limits 1.0–1.8 g. 1156/7–1279: fineness 0.925; wt 1.46 g: 'Tealby' coinage (1156/7–80) Short-cross pennies (1180–1247) Long-cross pennies (1247–78) 1279 onwards: fineness 0.925; declining weight: Edward I 1.44 g; Henry VII 0.78 g.
Copies	Of Anglo-Saxon pennies in large numbers in Scandinavia, particularly of Æthelred II; Of short-cross pennies in Westphalia; Of long-cross pennies in the Rhineland; Of 'sterling' pennies of Edward I in the Low Countries.
Spain	
Barcelona	
Dinero	Issued from early eleventh century by counts of Barcelona. Declining fineness and weight. mid-eleventh-century: fineness 0.33; wt 1.14 g. mid-twelfth-century: fineness 0.2; wt 0.66 g. About 1174–7, reformed *dinero* of Alfonso II; fineness 0.33; wt 1.08 g. 1256: fineness 0.25; wt 1.08 g.
Aragon	
Dinero Iaccensis or *Dinero Jaquesa*	Issued by kings from Sancho Ramirez (1063–94) at Jacca and other mints. Under Alfonso II (of Barcelona) 1175, fineness 0.33; wt 1.08 g.
Castile	
Dinero	Issued by kings from Fernando I (1035–65) onwards.

LARGER SILVER

Grossus denarius = great coin = *grosso* = *gros* = *groschen* = *groot* = *croat* = groat. Thenceforth older penny coinages became petty coins, *piccoli*, *parvi*, *petits*, *minutii*, *menuts* etc.

Venice	
Grosso or *Ducato d'argento* or *Matapan*	First issued by Doge Enrico Dandolo, 1201 fineness 0.965; wt 2.18 g. Initial value probably 24*d.* = 2 *soldi*.
Genoa	
Grosso	Probably issued in first decade of thirteenth century wt 1.4 g. Initial value probably 4*d.*
Grosso	Probably issued in second decade of thirteenth century wt 1.7 g. Initial value probably 6*d.*
Verona	
Grosso or *Aquilino*	First issued in 1220s wt 1.7 g. Value 20*d.*, hence sometimes called *vigintiarius*
Copies	By bishop of Trento from 1230s. By count of Tyrol, from 1271. Known as *Kreuzer*, *Zwanziger* or *tirolino*.
Siena	
Grosso	First issued in 1220s wt 1.7 g. Initial value 12*d.* = Sienese *soldo*.
Pisa	
Grosso	First issued in 1220s wt 1.7 g. Initial value 12*d.* = Pisan *soldo*. Later thirteenth-century Pisan *grossi*, known as *aquilini*, circulated widely in Tuscany; not to be confused with *grossi aquilini* of Verona and the Tyrol which circulated widely in north-eastern Italy.
Florence	
Grosso or *Fiorino d'argento*	First issued in 1230s wt 1.7 g. Initial value 12*d.* = Florentine *soldo*.
Milan	
Grosso or *Ambrosino*	First issued by second quarter thirteenth century, possibly from 1190s. Initial value probably 12*d.* *imperiali* = Milanese *soldo*.
Rome	
Grosso or *Romanino*	First issued 1253 by Brancaleone d'Andolo (Senator 1253–5) wt 3.5 g. Initial value 12*d.* *provisini* = Roman *soldo*.
Naples	
Grosso or *Carlino*	First issued 1278 by Charles I of Anjou. Fineness 0.93; wt 3.34 g.

Grosso or *Gigliato*	Charles II (from 1302) to Louis XII of France (king of Naples 1501–4). Initially fineness 0.93; wt 4 g. Weight fairly constant, surviving examples Louis XII still 3.4–3.6 g.
Copies	Provence from Robert of Naples (1309–43) onwards. These *gros* appear in papal accounts at Avignon as *iulhati*. Cyprus from Henry II (1288–1324) onwards. Hungary from 1329 (Charles Robert of Naples) onwards. Emirates of Mentesche and Aidin in Asia Minor.
Sicily	
Reale or *Pierreale*	From Pedro of Aragon (1282–5) onwards. Original fineness 0.93; wt 3.34 g.
Spain	
Barcelona (Aragon)	
Grosso de plata or *Croat*	First issued 1284 by Pedro III. Fineness 0.96; wt 3.24 g. Initial value 12*d. ternales* = *sueldo* of Barcelona. *Croats* of same weight and fineness to sixteenth century.
Castile	
Maravedi de plata	Alfonso X, isolated issue 1258, wt surviving examples 5.4–6.0 g.
Real	First issued by Pedro I (1350–69). Standard unchanged to late fifteenth century, fineness 0.93; wt 3.48 g. Initial value 3 *maravedis*.
France	
Gros tournois	St Louis to Charles VI. Fineness 0.96. 1266–1322 wt 4.22 g. 1329–64 wt declining to 2.55 g. 1266–90 valued at *sou tournois*.
Copies	Provence 1267. Otherwise almost entirely fourteenth century, principalities within France, in Low Countries, and in Rhineland.
Low Countries	
Hainault and Flanders	
Cavalier	From 1269 issue by Margaret of Constantinople of double sterlings, with type of mounted knight (*cavalier*) at Valenciennes, lion shield at Ghent, eagle at Alost. Wt about 2.6 g.
Copies	Many principalities in Low Countries to about 1320.
Flanders	
Gros	Derivatives from *gros tournois*, from Jean de Namur (1302–3), for twenty years.
Groot	Distinctive indigenous type from Louis de Nevers (1322–46). Initial wt 3.6 g valued at 3 Flemish sterlings.

Bohemia	
Grossus pragensis or *Prager-Groschen* or *Prague Groat*	From 1300 to 1547. Initially fineness 0.93; wt 3.97 g; value 12*d*. Standard declined, at first slowly: 1378 fineness 0.89, wt 3.62 g., thereafter rapidly: 1405 fineness 0.67, wt 2.7 g.
England	
Groat	Edward I, isolated issue 1279, fineness 0.925; wt 5.77 g. Edward III onwards, from 1351, 0.925 fine; declining in weight: 1351 wt 4.67 g; under Henry VII wt 3.11 g. Valued throughout at 4 English sterlings.
Copies	Scotland from 1357.

GOLD

Italy	
Sicily	
Augustale	Frederick II – 1231 – Messina and Brindisi mints. Fineness 0.854; wt 5.3 g.
Florence	
Florin or *Fiorino d'oro*	Issued 1252–1533. Nominally pure gold. Initial value one *litra*, wt 3.54 g. 1252–1422 *Fiorino d'oro stretto*. 1422–1533 *Fiorino d'oro largo*.
Copies	Rhone valley, Low Countries, Rhineland, Austria, Hungary, Aragon.
Genoa	
Genovino or *Genoin*	From 1252. Nominally pure gold. 3.53 g. Initial value 8*s*. Also *quartarolo* or quarter-florin (cf. *tari* or quarter-*dinar*), and eighth-florin or *soldo d'oro*.
Venice	
Ducato d'oro or Ducat or *Zecchino* or *Sequin*	1284–*c*. 1840. Nominally pure (0.997 by assay); wt 3.56 g.
Copies	Rome, Latin Orient, Moslem Levant, India.

Gold florins also issued by Perugia (*c* 1259), Lucca (by 1275), Milan (*Ambrosino d'oro*, before end of thirteenth century), and Bologna (*Bolognino d'oro*, 1379, wt 3.55 g.)

Papacy	
Cameral Florins	Struck at Avignon from 1322, later at Rome.
Spain	
Castile	
Dobla	From Fernando III (1217–52) to 1497. Nominally pure gold. Wt 4.6 g. Also multiple *doblas*, double, ten-fold, twenty-fold and even fifty-fold! Alongside good *doblas*, also poor *doblas de la banda* under John II and Enrique IV (1406–74), fineness only 0.79, wt still 4.6 g. First *excelente* of Catholic Kings was double *dobla* wt 9.2 g.
Copies	Dobra in Portugal from Pedro I (1357–67) onwards.

Aragon/Barcelona	
Florin	From 1369 (Pedro IV) to 1475/6 (John II). Fineness 0.75, wt 3.48 g.
Ducado d'oro	From 1475/6 to 1535. Fineness 0.99; wt 3.54 g.
Copies	*Ducado* adopted as unit in Castile in 1497, nominally pure gold, wt 3.5 g. New *excelente* was double *ducado*, wt 7 g.
Portugal	
Cruzado	From 1457; fineness 0.99; wt 3.78 g.
France	
Écu	St Louis, from 1266, nominally fine; wt 4.2 g., initial value 10*s*. tournois.
Petit Royal or Florin	Philip IV from 1290; nominally fine; wt 3.55 g.
Chaise or *Clinkaert*	Philip IV from 1303; double of royal or florin.
Mouton or *Agnel*	Philip IV from 1311, continued by his successors.
Écu d'or or *Écu à la chaise*	Philip VI and John II, from 1337 to 1351, wt 4.53 g.; fineness declines; 1337 nominally pure gold; 1351 0.75.
Franc à cheval or *Cavalier*	John II, from 1360; nominally fine; wt 3.89 g, i.e. half English noble.
Écu	Charles VI–Louis XIV: 1385: nominally fine, wt 4.08 g. 1388–1475 *Écu à la couronne* or crown: nominally fine; wt in 1388: 3.99 g. declining. From 1475 *Écu au soleil*: fineness 0.96; wt in 1475: 3.5 g.
Salut	Charles VI – Henry VI; nominally fine. 1421–3 wt 3.89 g. 1423–49 wt 3.5 g.
Hungary	
Florins of St Ladislaus or Ducats	From Charles Robert (1308–42) onwards; nominally fine; wt 3.54 g.
Empire	
Emperors	Imperial *gulden* or florins from Louis of Barvaria (1314–47).
Bohemia	Florins, ducats or *gulden* from 1325.
Lübeck	
Gulden or Ducats	1340–1801. Initially nominally fine gold; wt 3.59 g. Not controlled by the Wendish monetary agreements. Hamburg (after 1435) and Lüneburg (after 1440) issued *gulden* of the same fineness and weight as the imperial *gulden* and Rhine *gulden*.
Rhineland	
Rhine *gulden*, florins of the Rhine, electoral florins, electoral *gulden*	Struck by electors and other Rhineland princes under a series of agreements from 1354–1626, declining in weight and fineness. 1354: fineness 0.98; wt 3.54 g. 1419: fineness 0.79; wt 3.51 g. 1626: fineness 0.77; wt 3.24 g.

England	
Gold Penny	Henry III, isolated issue, 1257. Nominally pure gold; wt 2.92 g = that of two silver pennies; valued at 20*d.* sterling.
Noble	Edward III–James I. Nominally pure gold. 1344–1464 valued at 6*s.* 8*d.* sterling. 1344–6 wt 8.97 g; 1346–51 wt 8.33 g; 1351–1412 wt 7.78 g; 1412–64 wt 7.0 g. From 1464 Rose-noble or Ryal, valued at 10*s.* sterling. In 1464 wt 7.78 g.
Angel	From 1464, valued at 6*s.* 8d. sterling; nominally fine; wt 5.18 g.
Burgundy or Burgundian Netherlands	
Philippus or *Cavalier* or *Rider*	Philip the Good, 1433–51; valued in 1433 at 4*s.* *groot* of Flanders; fineness 0.99; wt 3.63 g.
Lion or *Leeuw*	Philip the Good, 1454–60; valued in 1454 at 5*s.* *groot* of Flanders; fineness 0.96; wt 4.25 g.
Florin of St Andrew or St *Andriesgulden*	Philip the Good to Philip the Handsome, 1466–96; valued in 1466 at 3*s.* 5*d.* *groot* of Flanders; fineness 0.79; wt 3.4 g, as Rhine *gulden*.

BLANCS

White money – *blancs, albus, weisspfennig, blancas.*

France	
Blanc au K	1365–80. Fineness 0.32, wt 2.55 g.
Blanc or *Guenar*	1385–1413. Initially fineness 0.48; wt 3.26 g, declined very slowly. 1413: fineness 0.4; wt 3.06 g. Value 10*d.* tournois.
Blanc à la couronne or *Parpaillole*	1436–1515. Initially fineness 0.4; wt 3.06 g, declined slowly 1507–15: fineness 0.36; wt 2.85 g. 1436–88 value 10*d. tournois*; after 1488 value 12*d. tournois.*
Copies	Dukes of Brittany, Burgundy, Savoy.
Burgundian Netherlands	
Patard or *stuiver* or *vierlander*	From 1433 to sixteenth century. Initially fineness 0.48; wt 3.44 g.
Rhineland	
Weisspfennig or *Albus*	Struck by electors and other Rhineland princes under a series of agreements commencing in 1354.
Hanseatic Cities	Coinage (*pfennigs*, *witten* (*4pf.*), *sechslinge* (*6 pf.*), and *schillinge*) minted by six 'Wendish' towns – Lübeck, Hamburg, Lüneburg, Rostock, Stralsund and Wismar – under a series of monetary conventions commencing in 1379.
Schilling	Minted from 1432 to sixteenth century. Initially, fineness 0.625; wt 2.54 g.

BIBLIOGRAPHIES

EDITORS' NOTE

As in the first edition, and in accordance with the established practice of the Cambridge series of histories, the bibliographies printed below are selective and incomplete. Their purpose is not to list all the publications bearing directly or indirectly on the subject, but to enable a reader to study some of the topics in greater detail. As a rule, books and articles superseded by later publications have not been included, and references to general treatises indirectly relevant to the subject matter of individual chapters have been reduced to the minimum. As most of the chapters are not new pieces of research, but summaries and interpretations of knowledge already available in secondary literature, references to original sources have either been left out altogether or have been confined to the principal and most essential classes of evidence. Within the limits set by these general principles, the individual contributors were given the freedom of composing and arranging bibliographies as they thought best. The 'layout' of the bibliographical lists, therefore, varies from chapter to chapter. The prefatory notes will explain other special features of particular lists of authorities.

CHAPTER I

Trade and Industry in Barbarian Europe till Roman Times

by G. N. BAILEY

I. ANTHROPOLOGICAL STUDIES OF TRADE AND ECONOMY

BAILEY, F. G. *Caste and the Economic Frontier*. Manchester, 1957.

BICCHIERI, M. G. (ed.). *Hunters and Gatherers Today*. New York, 1972.

BOHANNAN, P. and DALTON, G. (eds.). *Markets in Africa*. Northwestern University Press, 1962.

DALTON, G. (ed.). *Tribal and Peasant Economies*. New York, 1967.

FIRTH, R. *Economies of the New Zealand Maori*, 2nd edn. Wellington, 1959.

—— (ed.). *Themes in Economic Anthropology*. London, 1967.

GOODY, J. R. 'Inheritance, Property and Marriage in Africa and Eurasia.' *Sociology*, III (1969), 55–76.

HARDING, T. G. *Voyagers of the Vitiaz Strait: a study of the New Guinea trade system*. Monographs of the American Ethnological Society, 44, 1967.

KAPLAN, D. 'The Formal-Substantive Controversy in Economic Anthropology: reflections on its wider implications.' *Southwestern Journal of Anthropology*, XXIV (1968), 228–51.

LEE, R. B. and DEVORE, I. (eds.). *Man the Hunter*. Chicago, 1968.

MALINOWSKI, B. *Argonauts of the Western Pacific*. London, 1922.

POLANYI, K., ARENSBERG, C. M. and PEARSON, H. W. *Trade and Markets in the Early Empires*. New York, 1957.

SERVICE, E. R. *Primitive Social Organization*. New York, 1966.

II. ARCHAEOLOGICAL THEORY WITH REFERENCE TO ECONOMIC ORGANIZATION

BINFORD, L. R. (ed.). *For Theory Building in Archaeology*. New York, 1977.

CLARKE, D. L. *Analytical Archaeology*. London, 1968.

—— (ed.). *Models in Archaeology*. London, 1972.

HIGGS, E. S. (ed.). *Papers in Economic Prehistory*. Cambridge, 1972.

RENFREW, A. C. (ed.). *The Explanation of Cultural Change*. London, 1972.

III. GENERAL WORKS ON PREHISTORIC TRADE AND ECONOMY

CHILDE, V. G. 'Trade and Industry in Barbarian Europe till Roman Times.' Chap. I in *The Cambridge Economic History of Europe*, I, 1st edn. Cambridge, 1952.

CLARK, J. G. D. *Prehistoric Europe*. London, 1952.

EARLE, T. K. and ERICSON, J. E. (eds.). *Exchange Systems in Prehistory*. New York, 1977.

HIGGS, E. S. (ed.). *Palaeoeconomy*. Cambridge, 1975.

JOCHIM, M. A. *Hunter-Gatherer Subsistence and Settlement*. New York, 1976.

LAMBERG-KARLOVSKY, C. C. and SABLOFF, J. A. (eds.). *Ancient Civilization and Trade*. Albuquerque, 1975.

SIEVEKING, G. de G., LONGWORTH, I. M. and WILSON, K. E. (eds.). *Problems in Economic and Social Archaeology*. London, 1976.

UCKO, P. J. and DIMBLEBY, G. W. (eds.). *The Domestication and Exploitation of Plants and Animals*. London, 1969.

UCKO, P. J., TRINGHAM, R. and DIMBLEBY, G. W. (eds.). *Man, Settlement and Urbanism*. London, 1972.

IV. GENERAL WORKS ON EUROPEAN PREHISTORY

CHILDE, V. G. *The Dawn of European Civilization*. 6th edn. London, 1957.

COLES, J. M. and HIGGS, E. S. *The Archaeology of Early Man*. London, 1969.

COLLINS, D. (ed.). *The Origins of Europe*. London, 1975.

PIGGOTT, S. *Ancient Europe*. Edinburgh, 1965.

RENFREW, A. C. *Before Civilization*. London, 1973.

V. THE GATHERING-HUNTING-FISHING AND AGRARIAN ECONOMIES (Sections II and III)

BALIN, P. G. 'Seasonal Migration in South-West France during the late Glacial Period.' *Journal of Archaeological Science*, IV (1977), 245–57.

BORDES, F. *The Old Stone Age*. London, 1968.

BUTZER, K. W. *Environment and Archaeology*. 2nd edn. Chicago, 1971.

CLARK, J. G. D. 'Traffic in Stone Axe and Adze Blades.' *Economic History Review*, 2nd ser. XVIII (1965), 1–28.

CLARKE, D. L. 'Mesolithic Europe: the economic basis.' In SIEVEKING, G. de G. *et al. Problems in Economic and Social Archaeology*. London, 1976, 449–81.

DE SONNEVILLE BORDES, D. *Le Paléolithique Supérieur en Périgord*. Bordeaux, 1960.

FLANNERY, K. V. 'The Ecology of Early Food Production in Mesopotamia.' *Science*, CXLVII (1965), 1247–56.

JAZDZEWSKI, K. *Poland*. London, 1965.

LEROI-GOURHAN, A. 'Les Fouilles d'Arcy-sur-Cure (Yonne).' *Gallia Préhistoire*, IV (1961), 3–16.

MELLAART, J. *Earliest Civilizations of the Near East*. London, 1965.

MOUTON, P. and JOFFROY, R. 'Les Gisements Aurignaciens des Rois à Mouthiers (Charente).' *Gallia*, Supplement IX (1958).

NANDRIS, J. 'Lepenski Vir.' *Science Journal*, Jan. 1968, 64–70.

PHILLIPS, P. *Early Farmers of West Mediterranean Europe*. London, 1975.

PILBEAM, D. *The Ascent of Man*. New York. 1972.

PRADEL, L. 'La Grotte Périgordienne et Aurignacienne du Fontenioux, commune de Saint-Pierre-de-Maillé (Vienne).' *Bulletin de la Société Préhistorique Française*, XLIX (1952), 413–32.

SHACKLETON, N. J. and RENFREW, A. C. 'Neolithic Trade Routes Re-aligned by Oxygen Isotope Analyses.' *Nature*, CCXXVIII (1970), 1062–5.

SIELMANN, B. 'Die Frühneolithische Besiedlung Mitteleuropas.' In SCHWABEDISSEN, J. (ed.). *Die Anfänge des Neolithikum vom Orient bis Nordeuropa, Teil Va (Westliches Mitteleuropas)*. Cologne, 1972, 1–65.

TRINGHAM, R. *Hunters, Fishers and Farmers of Eastern Europe*. London, 1971.

VERTES, L. 'Das Moustérien in Ungarn.' *Eiszeitalter und Gegenwart*, X (1959), 21–40.

VITA-FINZI, C. and HIGGS, E. S. 'Prehistoric Economy in the Mount Carmel Area of Palestine: site catchment analysis.' *Proc. of the Prehistoric Society*, XXXVI (1970), 1–37.

WATERBOLK, H. T. 'Food Production in Prehistoric Europe.' *Science*, CLXII (1968), 1093–1102.

VI. THE AEGEAN AND MYCENAEAN NETWORKS (Sections III and IV)

BASS, G. F. *Archaeology under Water*. London, 1966.

—— 'Cape Gelidonya: a Bronze Age Shipwreck.' *American Philosophical Society*, LVII (1967), part 8.

BOTTERÓ, J., CASSIN, E. and VERCOUTTER, J. (eds.). *The Near East: the Early Civilizations*. Trans. by R. F. TANNENBAUM. London, 1967.

BRANNIGAN, K. 'Wessex and Mycenae: some evidence reviewed.' *Wiltshire Archaeological Magazine*, LXV (1971), 89–107.

CASSON, S. *Ancient Cyprus*. London, 1937.

CHILDE, V. G. *The Danube in Prehistory*. Oxford, 1929.
EBERT, M. *Reallexikon der Vorgeschichte*. Berlin, 1924–32.
GARDIN, J. C. 'Reconstructing an Economic Network in the Ancient East with the Aid of a Computer.' In D. HYMES (ed.). *The Use of Computers in Anthropology*. The Hague, 1965, 378–91.
HOOD, S. *The Minoans*. London, 1971.
HUTCHINSON, R. W. *Prehistoric Crete*. Harmondsworth, 1962.
LLOYD, S. *Early Highland Peoples of Anatolia*. London, 1967.
MELLAART, J. 'The Royal Treasure of Dorak.' *Illustrated London News*, 28 Nov. 1959.
PALMER, L. R. *The Interpretation of Mycenaean Greek Texts*. Oxford, 1963.
Rencontre Assyriologique Internationale XXIII, 1976. *Trade in the Ancient Near East*. In *Iraq*, XXXIX (1977).
RENFREW, A. C. 'Wessex without Mycenae.' *Annual of the British School at Athens*, LXIII (1968), 277–85.
—— *The Emergence of Civilization*. London, 1972.
SHERRATT, A. 'Resources, Technology and Trade in Early European Metallurgy.' In SIEVEKING, G. de G. *et al. Problems in Social and Economic Archaeology*. London, 1976, 557–81.
SNODGRASS, A. 'Mycenae, Northern Europe and Radiocarbon Dates.' *Archaeologica Atlantica*, I (1975), 33–48.
TAYLOUR, Lord William. *The Mycenaeans*. London, 1964.
VENTRIS, M. G. F. and CHADWICK, J. *Documents in Mycenaean Greek*. Cambridge, 1956.

VII. THE COLONIAL NETWORKS AND EMPIRES (Sections V and VI)

ALEXANDER, J. A. *Yugoslavia*. London, 1971.
ARRIBAS, A. *The Iberians*. London, 1967.
BARFIELD, L. H. *Northern Italy*. London, 1971.
BOARDMAN, J. *The Greeks Overseas*. Harmondsworth, 1964.
—— *Preclassical Greece*. Harmondsworth, 1967.
CARPENTER, R. *Discontinuity in Greek Civilization*. Cambridge, 1966.
FILIP, J. *Celtic Civilization and its Heritage*. Trans. R. FINLAYSON-SAMSOUR and I. LEWITOVA. 2nd rev. edn. Prague, 1976.
GIMBUTAS, M. *The Balts*. London, 1963.
—— *Bronze Age Cultures in Central and Eastern Europe*. The Hague, 1965.
HACKMAN, R. *The Germanic Peoples*. London, 1971.
HARDEN, D. *The Phoenicians*. London, 1962.
HATT, J.-J. *Celts and Gallo-Romans*. London, 1970.
JOFFROY, R. *Le Trésor de Vix*. Paris, 1962.
KIMMIG, W. 'Early Celts on the Upper Danube: the excavations at the Heuneburg.' In BRUCE-MITFORD, R. (ed.). *Recent Archaeological Excavations in Europe*. London, 1975, 32–64.
MEGAW, J. V. S. 'The Vix Burial.' *Antiquity*, XL (1966), 38–44.
MOSCATI, S. *The World of the Phoenicians*. London, 1968.
MÜLLER-KARPE, M. *Beiträge zur Chronologie der Urnenfelderzeit*. Berlin, 1959.
NEUSTUPNY, E. and J. *Czechoslovakia*. London, 1961.
PALLOTINO, M. *The Etruscans*. Trans. J. CREMONA, ed. D. RIDGWAY. London, 1974.
PIGGOTT, S., DANIEL, G. E. and MCBURNEY, C. B. M. (eds.). *France Before the Romans*. London, 1974.
PLEINER, R. 'The Iron Age: a notion in history.' In EHRICH, R. W. (ed.). *The Flagstaff Symposium*. 1969, 13.
POWELL, T. G. *The Celts*. London, 1967.
SANDARS, N. K. *Bronze Age Cultures in France*. Cambridge, 1957.
STENBERGER, M. *Sweden*. London, 1962.
SULIMIRSKI, T. *Prehistoric Russia*. London, 1970.
TALBOT-RICE, T. *The Scythians*. London, 1954.
VON MERHART, L. *Hallstatt und Italien*. Vienna, 1968.

CHAPTER II

Trade and Industry under the Later Roman Empire in the West

The following abbreviations have been used in this bibliography:

Act. arch.	*Acta archaeologica* (Copenhagen)
AJP	*American Journal of Philology*
ANRW	*Aufstieg und Neidergang der römischen Welt*, ed. H. Temporini and W. Haase. Berlin–New York, 1972–
BCH	*Bulletin de correspondance hellénique*
BSA	*Annual of the British School at Athens*
CAH	*Cambridge Ancient History*
Class. Journ.	*Classical Journal*
Class. Phil.	*Classical Philology*
CMedH	*Cambridge Medieval History*
Cod. J.	*Codex Justinianus*
Econ. H.R.	*Economic History Review*
JRS	*Journal of Roman Studies*
Mon. ant.	*Monumenti antichi pubblicati per cura della reale Accademia dei Lincei*
Num. Chron.	*Numismatic Chronicle and Journal of the Numismatic Society*
PBSR	*Papers of the British School at Rome*
P. Oxy.	*Oxyrhynchus Papyri*, ed. Grenfell and Hunt *et al.* London, 1898–
REA	*Revue des études anciennes*
Rom. Econ.	A. H. M. Jones, *The Roman Economy: Studies in ancient economic and administrative history*, ed. P. A. Brunt. Oxford, 1974.
TAPA	*Transactions and Proceedings of the American Philological Association*

I. ANCIENT SOURCES

Literary

For the early Empire, Strabo, Pliny's *Natural History* and Petronius' *Cena Trimalchionis* can be supplemented by scattered references in a wide selection of other authors, including Martial and Juvenal. For the second and third centuries various speeches of Aristides and Dio Chrysostom offer valuable evidence; and the *Historia Augusta*, though it probably reflects to a large extent the conditions of the fourth century (cf. N. H. Baynes, *The H.A., its date and purpose*. Oxford, 1926; A. D. Momigliano, *Secondo contributo alla storia degli studi classici*. Rome, 1960, 105–43; R. Syme, *Ammianus and the Historia Augusta*. Oxford, 1968; *Emperors and Biography*. Oxford, 1971), is important if used critically. For the later Empire in the West, the two main works are: the *Expositio totius mundi* (ed. Riese in *Geographici latini minores*, 105–26; Müller, *Geographici graeci minores*, II, 513–28; Sinko, *Archiv f. lateinische Lexicographie u. Grammatik*, XIII, 1904, 531–71), a work probably composed towards the end of the reign of Constantius, and the *Notitia dignitatum* (ed. O. Seeck, 1876), which dates to the early fifth century in its present form, but incorporates earlier material (cf. A. H. M. Jones, *Later Roman Empire*, III, app. 2, 347–80 for bibliography). The Church historians and Christian Fathers also contain much that is of value for the economic historian.

Legal codes

These are of prime importance, especially the Theodosian Code (*Theodosiani libri XVI cum constitutionibus Sirmondianis*, ed. Mommsen-Meyer. Berlin, 1905; translation: C. Pharr, *The Theodosian code and novels, and the Sirmondian constitutions*. Princeton, 1952; reprint, Westport, 1970) which is invaluable for social and economic problems; also important are the various parts of Justinian's codification.

Inscriptions, papyri, etc

These comprise the most important material of all, including such revealing documents as the Mine-Law of Vipasca in Portugal (Dessau, 6891) and Diocletian's price-edict (see below). The papyri, though all come from the eastern part of the Empire, mainly Egypt, give information which is relevant for the West as well. Finally, there is the evidence of coins and the results of excavation in every province of the West.

The following bibliography should be supplemented from those contained in *CAH.* x, xi and xiii (especially those of Oertel in x, 944–5 and xii, 750–54), in *CMedH.* i (especially pp. 688ff) and in Frank's *Economic Survey of Ancient Rome*; for the coinage, see the works listed by Mattingly in *Num. Chron.* 6, vi (1946), 111–20: the three last volumes of *The Roman Imperial Coinage*, ed. C. H. V. Sutherland and R. A. G. Carson: vi, *From Diocletian's reform, 294, to the death of Maximian, 313*, ed. Sutherland (1967), vii, *Constantine and Licinius (313–337)*, ed. P. M. Bruun (1966) and viii, *The Family of Constantine I (337–364)*, ed. J. P. C. Kent (1981); and the bibliography added by M. H. Crawford to A. H. M. Jones's article on 'Numismatics and History' reprinted in *The Roman Economy*, 80–1. In general, Rostovtzeff, *Social and Economic History of the Roman Empire*, *passim*, and Piganiol, *L'Empire chrétien*, pp. vii–xvi. There is also a useful survey in G. Walser and T. Pekáry, *Die Krise des römischen Reiches. Bericht über die Forschungen zur Geschichte des 3. Jahrh. (193–284 n. Chr.) von 1939 bis 1959.* Berlin, 1962.

The standard text of the *Edictum Diocletiani de pretiis* is now: S. Lauffer, *Diokletians Preisedikt.* Berlin, 1971. It is discussed in the following works:

Bingen, J. 'Notes sur l'édit du maximum,' *BCH*, lxxvii (1954), 349.

Bücher, K. *Die Diokletianische Taxordnung vom Jahre 301.* (Tübing. Beiträge z. Wirtschaftsgeschichte (1922), 179ff. Originally appeared in *Zeitsch f. die gesamte Staatswissensch.*, l (1894), 188–219).

Caputo, G and Goodchild, R. 'Diocletian's Price-Edict at Ptolemais (Cyrenaica).' *JRS*, xlv (1955), 106–15.

Crawford, M. H. and Reynolds, J. 'The Publication of the Prices Edict: a new inscription from Aezani.' *JRS*, lxv (1975), 160–3.

Duncan-Jones, R. *The Economy of the Roman Empire.* Cambridge, 1974. App. 17, pp. 366–9, 'Diocletian's Price-Edict and the Cost of Transport.'

Erim, K. T. and Reynolds, Joyce. 'The Copy of Diocletian's Edict on Maximum Prices from Aphrodisias in Caria.' *JRS*, lx (1970), 120 4.

—— 'The Aphrodisias Copy of Diocletian's Edict on Maximum Prices.' *JRS*, lxiii (1973), 99–110.

Graser, E. R. 'The Edict of Diocletian,' ed. and transl. in Vol. v of Frank's *Economic Survey of Ancient Rome*, 305–421.

—— 'The significance of two new fragments of the Edict of Diocletian.' *TAPA*, lxxi (1940), 157 74.

Guarducci, M. 'Il primo frammento scoperto in Italia dell'editto di Diocleziano.' *Atti della Pontificia Accademia Romana di Archaeologia: Rendiconti*, xvi (1940), 11–24.

Jacopi, G. 'Gli scavi della missione archaeologica italiana ad Afrodisiade nel 1937.' *Mon. ant.* xxxviii (1939), 130–52, 159.

MacMullen, R. 'Diocletian's Edict and the *castrensis modius.*' *Aegyptus*, xli (1961), 3–5.

Michell, H. 'The Edict of Diocletian: a study of price fixing in the Roman Empire.' *Canadian Journ. of Econ. and Pol. Sci.*, xiii (1947), 1–12.

Naumann, Rudolf and Friederike. *Der Rundbau in Aezani mit dem Preisedikt des Diokletian und das Gebäude mit dem Edikt in Stratonikeia. Istanbuler Mitteilungen*, Beiheft 10. Tübingen, 1973.

Seeck, O. 'Die Schatzungsordnung Diokletians.' *Zeitschr. f. Sozial- u. Wirtschaftsgesch.*, iv (1895), 275–342.

Segrè, A. See the articles listed under § V below.

West, L. C. 'Notes on Diocletian's *Edict.*' *Class. Phil.*, xxxiv (1939), 242–4.

—— 'The Coinage of Diocletian and the Edict of Prices.' *Studies in Roman Economic and Social History* (ed. P. R. Coleman-Norton). Princeton, 1951, 290–302.

YEO, C. A. 'Land and Sea Transportation in Imperial Italy.' *TAPA*, LXXVII (1946), 221–44.

II. GENERAL

AUBIN, H. *Vom Altertum zum Mittelalter*. Munich, 1949.
BALDACCI, P. 'Negotiatores e mercatores frumentarii nel periodo imperiale.' *R. Instituto Lombardo di Scienze e Lettere, Rendiconti*, CI (1967), 273–91.
BARROW, R. H. *Slavery in the Roman Empire*. London, 1928.
BAYNES, N. H. 'M. Pirenne and the Unity of the Mediterranean World.' *JRS*, XIX (1929), 230–5.
BERNARDI, A. 'Tendenze di fondo nell'economia del tardo impero romano.' *Studi giuridici e sociali in memoria di E. Vanoni*, Pavia, 1961, 257–321.
BESNIER, M. 'L'Empire romain de l'avènement des Sévères au concile de Nicée.' *Histoire romaine*, IV, 1. Paris, 1938.
BOAK, A. E. R. *Manpower Shortage and the Fall of the Roman Empire in the West*. Ann Arbor, 1955.
BRATIANU, G. I. *La Distribution de l'or et les raisons économiques de la division de l'empire romain*. Paris, 1938.
BRÉHIER, L. 'Colonies d'orientaux en occident au commencement du moyen âge.' *Byzantinische Zeitsch.*, XII (1903), 1ff.
BURFORD, ALISON. *Craftsmen in Greek and Roman Society*. London, 1972.
—— 'Heavy Transport in Classical Antiquity.' *Econ. H.R.*, 2nd ser. XIII (1960–1), 1–18.
BURY, J. B. *History of the late Roman Empire from the death of Theodosius I to the death of Justinian* (*A.D. 395–A.D. 565*). 2 vols. London, 1923.
—— 'Rome and Byzantium.' *Quart. Rev.*, CXCII (1900), 129–55.
CHARANIS, P. 'Observations on the Transformation of the Roman World in the Third Century.' *ANRW*, II, 2, 551–9.
CHARLESWORTH, M. P. *Trade Routes and Commerce of the Roman Empire*, 2nd edn. Cambridge, 1926.
CHASTAGNOL, A. 'Le Ravitaillement de Rome en viande au Ve siècle.' *Rev. Historique*, CCX (1953), 13–22.
COLEMAN-NORTON, P. R. (ed.). *Studies in Roman Economic and Social History in Honour of A. C. Johnson*. Princeton, 1951.
D'ARMS, J. H. *Commerce and Social Standing in Ancient Rome*. Cambridge, Mass., 1981.
—— and KOPFF, E. C. (ed.). *The Seaborne Commerce of Ancient Rome*. (Memoirs of the American Academy in Rome, 36.) Rome, 1980.
DE LAET, S. J. *Aspects de la vie sociale et économique sous Auguste et Tibère*. Brussels, 1944.
DILL, S. *Roman Society in the last Century of the Western Empire*, 2nd edn. London, 1899.
DOPSCH, A. *Wirtschaftliche u. soziale Grundlagen der europäischen Kulturentwicklung aus der Zeit von Cäsar bis auf Karl den Grossen*. 2 vols. 2nd edn. Vienna, 1923–4. (A condensed translation of this work appeared as *The Economic and Social Foundations of European Civilisation*. London, 1937.)
—— 'Frühmittelalterliche u. spätantike Wirtschaft.' *Verfassungs- u. Wirtschaftsgeschichte des Mittelalters*, 219–34. Vienna, 1928.
DUNCAN-JONES, R. P. *The Economy of the Roman Empire: quantitative studies*, 2nd edn. Cambridge, 1982.
FINLEY, M. I. *The Ancient Economy*. London, 1973.
—— 'Technical Innovation and Economic Progress in the Ancient World.' *Econ. HR.*, 2nd ser. XVIII (1965), 29–45.
—— (ed.). *Slavery in Classical Antiquity*. Cambridge, 1960.
FOXHALL, L. and FORBES, H. A. 'Sitometreia. The role of grain as a staple food in classical antiquity.' *Chiron*, XII (1982), 41–90.
FRANK, T. *Economic History of Rome*, 2nd edn. Baltimore, 1927.
—— (ed.). *Economic Survey of Ancient Rome*. 5 vols. and index. Baltimore, 1933–40.
—— 'Notes on Roman Commerce.' *JRS*, XXVII (1937), 72–9.
FRIEDLANDER, L. and WISSOWA, G. *Darstellungen aus der Sittengeschichte Roms*. 10th edn,

4 vols. Leipzig, 1919–23. Translated into English from 7th edn as *Roman Life and Manners under the Early Empire*. London, 1910–13.
GARNSEY, P. (ed.). *Non-Slave Labour in the Greco-Roman world*. (Cambridge Philological Society Supplement Volume 6.) Cambridge, 1980.
GARNSEY, P., HOPKINS, K. and WHITTAKER, C. R. (eds.). *Trade in the Ancient Economy*. London, 1983. (See especially GARNSEY, P., 'Grain for Rome', 118–30; PLEKET, H. W., 'Urban Elites and Business in the Greek Part of the Roman Empire' 131–44; CARANDINI, A., 'Pottery and the African Economy', 145–62; WHITTAKER, C. R., 'Late Roman Trade and Traders', 163–80.)
GARNSEY, P. and WHITTAKER, C. R. (eds.). *Trade and Famine in Classical Antiquity*. (Cambridge Philological Society Supplement Volume 8.) Cambridge, 1983. (See especially MOREL, J.-P., 'La Céramique comme indice du commerce antique', 66–74; MIDDLETON, P., 'The Roman Army and Long Distance Trade', 75–83; HOPKINS, K., 'Models, Ships and Staples', 84–109; WHITTAKER, C. R. 'Trade and Frontiers of the Roman Empire,' 110–27.)
GELZER, M. 'Das Römertum als Kulturmacht.' *Hist. Zeitsch.*, CXXVI (1922), 189–206.
—— 'Altertumswissenschaft u. Spätantike.' *Hist. Zeitsch.*, CXXXV (1927), 173–87.
GUMMERUS, H. *Der römische Gutsbetrieb als wirtschaftlicher Organismus nach den Werken des Cato, Varro und Columella. Klio*, Beiheft 5. Leipzig, 1906.
—— *Die Fronden der Kolonen* (Öfversigt af Finska Vetenskaps-Societetens Förhandlingar, L.3). Helsinki, 1907–8.
—— 'Die römische Industrie.' *Klio*, XIV (1914), 149ff; XV (1918), 256ff.
HARMAND, L. *Le Patronat sur les collectivités publiques des origines au Bas-Empire*. Paris, 1957.
HARRIS, W. V. 'Towards a Study of the Roman Slave Trade' in D'Arms and Kopff, *Seaborne Commerce*, 117–40.
HARTMANN, L. M. *Ein Kapitel vom spätantiken und frühmittelalterlichen Staate*. Stuttgart, 1913. Translated into English with notes by H. LIEBESCHÜTZ as *The Early Medieval State: Byzantium, Italy and the West*. London, 1949.
HAYWOOD, R. M. *The Myth of Rome's Fall*. New York, 1958.
—— 'Some Traces of Serfdom in Cicero's Day.' *AJP*, LIV (1933), 145–53.
HEDEAGER, L. 'A Quantitative Analysis of Roman Imports in Europe North of the *Limes* (0–400 A.D),' in KRISTIANSEN, K. and PALAUDAN-MÜLLER, C. (eds.), *New Directions in Scandinavian Archaeology*. Lyngby, 1977. 191–216.
HEICHELHEIM, F. M. *Wirtschaftsgeschichte des Altertums vom Paläolithikum bis zur Völkerwanderung der Germanen, Slaven und Araber*. 2 vols. Leiden, 1938.
—— 'Welthistorische Gesichtspunkte zu den vormittelalterlichen Wirtschaftsepoken.' *Schmollers Jahrb.*, CVI (1933), 994ff.
HOPKINS, K. 'Taxes and Trade in the Roman Empire.' *JRS*, LXX (1980), 101–25.
JONES, A. H. M. *The Later Roman Empire, 284–602*. 3 vols., Oxford, 1964.
—— *The Roman Economy: studies in ancient economic and administrative history*, ed. P. A. BRUNT. Oxford, 1974.
—— 'The Decline and Fall of the Roman Empire.' *History*, XL (1955), 209–26.
—— 'The Economic Life of the Towns of the Roman Empire.' *Recueil de la Société Jean Bodin*, VII (1955), 161–92 (= *Rom. Econ.* 35–60).
—— 'The Cloth Industry under the Roman Empire.' *Econ. H.R.*, 2nd ser, XIII (1960), 183–92 (= *Rom. Econ.* 350–64).
KATZ, S. *The Decline of Rome and the Rise of Mediaeval Europe*. Ithaca, 1955.
KIECHLE, F. *Sklavenarbeit und technischer Fortschritt im römischen Reich*. Wiesbaden, 1969.
KÖSTER, A. *Studien zur Geschichte des antiken Seewesens. Klio*. Beiheft 32. Leipzig, 1934.
KORNEMANN, E. *Weltgeschichte des Mittelmeerraumes von Philipp II von Makedonien bis Muhammed*, II. Munich, 1949.
—— 'Die unsichtbaren Grenzen des römischen Kaiserreichs', on pp. 96ff of *Staaten, Völker, Männer*. Leipzig, 1934.
LANDRY, A. 'Quelques aperçus concernant la dépopulation dans l'antiquité.' *Rev. Hist.*, CLXXVII (1936), 1–33.

LA PIANA, G. 'Foreign Groups in Rome during the First Centuries of the Empire.' *Harvard Theological Review*, xx (1926), 183–403.

LEFEBVRE DES NOËTTES. *L'Attelage: le cheval de selle à travers les âges*. Paris, 1931.

—— *De la marine antique à la marine moderne*. Paris, 1935.

LOPEZ, R. S. 'Mohammed and Charlemagne: a revision.' *Speculum*, XVIII (1943), 14–38.

—— 'Silk industry in the Byzantine Empire.' *Speculum*, xx (1945), 1ff.

LOT, F. *La fin du monde antique et le début du moyen âge*. Paris, 1927.

MACMULLEN, R. 'Market Days in the Roman Empire.' *Phoenix*, XXIV (1970), 333–40.

MAZZA, M. *Lotte sociali e restaurazione autoritaria nel terzo secolo d. C.* Catania, 1970.

MAZZARINO, S. *Aspetti sociali del quarto secolo: ricerche di storia tardo-romana*. Rome, 1951.

MEIGGS, R. *Roman Ostia*. 2nd edn, Oxford, 1973.

MICKWITZ, G. 'Der Verkehr auf dem westlichen Mittelmeer um 600 n. Chr.' *Festschrift Dopsch*, 1938, 74ff.

MILLER, J. I. *The Spice Trade of the Roman Empire, 29 B.C.–A.D. 641*. Oxford, 1969.

MOMMSEN, Th. 'Die Provinzen von Caesar bis Diokletian.' *Römische Geschichte*, 4th edn, v. Berlin, 1894. Translated into English as *The Provinces of the Roman Empire from Caesar to Diocletian*. London, 1909.

OERTEL, F. 'The Economic Unification of the Mediterranean Region: industry, trade and commerce.' *CAH*, x (1934), 382–424 (bibl. 944–5).

—— 'The Economic Life of the Empire.' *CAH*, XII (1939), 232–81 (bibl. 750–4) (cf. 724–5; note on 'Inflation in the second and third centuries').

PARKER, H. M. D. *A History of the Roman World (A.D. 138–337)*. London, 1935.

PARVÂN, V. *Die Nationalität der Kaufleute im römischen Kaiserreich*. Breslau, 1909.

PASSERINI, A. *Linee di storia romana in età imperiale*. Milan, 1949.

PERSSON, A. W. *Staat und Manufaktur im römischen Reiche*. Lund, 1923.

PIGANIOL, A. 'L'Empire chrétien (325–95).' *Histoire romaine*, IV, 2. Paris, 1947.

—— 'La Crise sociale au bas-empire.' *Journ. des savants* (1955), 5–15.

PIRENNE, H. *Mahomet et Charlemagne*, 3rd edn. Paris, 1937.

POLANYI, K., ARENSBERG, C. and PEARSON, H. W. (eds.). *Trade and Market in the Early Empires: economics in theory and practice*. Chicago, 1957.

POMEY, P. and TCHERNIA, A. 'Le Tonnage maximum des navires de commerce romains.' *Archaeonautica* II (1978), 233–51.

RICKMAN, G. R. *The Corn Supply of Ancient Rome*. Oxford, 1980.

ROBLIN, M. 'Citès ou citadelles? Les enceintes romaines au bas empire d'après l'exemple de Paris.' *REA*, LIII (1951), 301–11.

ROSTOVTZEFF, M. *Social and Economic History of the Roman Empire*. 2nd edn revised by P. M. FRASER. 2 vols. Oxford, 1957.

—— *Caravan Cities*. Oxford, 1932.

—— 'The Decay of the Ancient World and its Economic Explanations.' *Econ. H.R.*, II (1929–30), 197–214.

ROUGÉ, J. *Recherches sur l'organisation du commerce maritime en Méditerrannée sous l'Empire romain*. Paris, 1966.

——'La Navigation hivernale sous l'Empire romain.' *REA*, LIV (1952), 316–25.

RUGGINI, L. *Economia e società nell'Italia annonaria. Rapporti fra agricoltura e commercio dal IV al VI sec. d. Cr.* Milan, 1961.

—— 'Ebrei e orientali nell'Italia settentrionale fra il IV e il VI secolo d. Cr.' *Studia et documenta historiae et iuris*, XXV (1959), 186–308.

—— 'Stato e associazioni professionali nell'età imperiale romana.' *Akten der VI. Internat. Kongr. f. griech. u. lat. Epigraphik*. Munich, 1972, 137–47.

STE-CROIX, G. E. M. de. *The Class Struggle in the Ancient Greek World from the Archaic Age to the Arab Conquest*. London, 1981.

SALMON, P. *Population et dépopulation dans l'empire romain*. Collection Latomus. Brussels, 1974.

SCHAAL, H. *Vom Tauschhandel zum Welthandel*. Leipzig, 1931.

—— 'Flusschifffahrt und Flusshandel im Altertum.' *Festschrift f. die 400. Jahr-Feier des Alten Gymnasiums in Bremen*, 370ff. Bremen, 1928.

SCHMIDT, A. *Drogen und Drogenhandel im Altertum*. Leipzig, 1924.

SEECK, O. *Geschichte des Untergangs der antiken Welt*, 4th edn, 2 vols. and 2 vols. of notes. Stuttgart, 1921.

STEIN, E. *Geschichte des spätrömischen Reiches*, I. Vienna, 1928.

—— *Histoire du bas-empire, II: de la disparition de l'empire d'Occident à la mort de Justinien (476–565)*. Bruges, 1950.

SÜNDWALL, J. *Weströmische Studien*. Berlin, 1915.

THÉVENOT, E. 'La Population des villes gallo-romaines.' *Rev. archéologique de l'est et du centre-est*. III (1952), 121–2.

—— 'Le Peuplement rurale de la Gaule.' *Ibid.*, IV (1953), 78–85.

TOUTAIN, J. *The Economic Life of the Ancient World*. New York, 1930.

VAN BERCHEM, D. *Les Distributions de blé et d'argent à la plèbe romaine sous l'empire*. Geneva, 1939.

VAN SICKLE, C. E. 'Diocletian and the Decline of the Roman Municipalities.' *JRS*, XXVIII (1938), 9ff.

VÁRADY, L. *Késörómai hadügyek, etc.* (*Late Roman Military Affairs and their Social Basis: the last century of the Roman Empire, 376–476*). Budapest, 1961.

VINOGRADOFF, P. *The Growth of the Manor*, 2nd edn. London, 1911.

—— 'Social and economic conditions of the Roman Empire in the fourth century.' *CMedH*, I, 2nd edn. 1924, 542–67 (bibl. 688ff).

WALBANK, F. W. *The Awful Revolution*. Liverpool, 1967.

WEBER, M. *Grundriss der Sozialökonomik: III. Abteilung: Wirtschaft und Gesellschaft*, 2nd edn. Tübingen, 1928.

WEST, L. C. 'The Economic Collapse of the Roman Empire.' *Class. Journ.*, XXVIII (1932–3), 96ff.

WESTERMANN, W. L. *The Slave Systems of Greek and Roman Antiquity*. Philadelphia, 1955.

—— 'On Inland Transportation and Communication in Antiquity.' *Pol. Sci. Quart.*, XLIII (1928), 364.

WHITE, K. D. 'Technology and Industry in the Roman Empire. A study of the interrelations between science, technology and industrial activity in the Roman Empire.' *Acta classica* (Cape Town), II (1959), 78–89.

WHITTAKER, C. R. 'Labour supply in the Later Roman Empire.' *Opus*, I (1982), 171–9.

WIPSCYCKA, E. 'Das Textilhandwerk und der Staat.' *Archiv für Papyrusforschung*, XVIII (1966), 1–22.

YEO, C. A. 'Development of Roman Plantations and Marketing of Farm Products.' *Finanzarchiv* (Tübingen), XIII (1952), 321–42.

III. TECHNIQUES; SPECIAL INSTITUTIONS; GILD ORGANISATION

ALFÖLDY, G. 'Collegium-Organisationen in Intercisa.' *Acta Archaeologica Academiae Scientiarum Hungaricae*, VI (1958), 177–98.

BINAGHI, R. *La metallurgia ai tempi dell'impero romano*. Rome, 1946.

BLOCH, M. 'Le Moulin à eau.' *Ann. d'hist. écon.*, VII (1935), 538ff.

CASSON, L. *Ships and Seamanship in the Ancient World*. Princeton, 1971.

—— *Travel in the Ancient World*. London, 1974.

—— 'The Size of Ancient Merchant Ships.' *Studi in onore di A. Calderini e R. Paribeni*, I. Milan, 1956, 231–8.

CLAUSING, R. *The Roman Colonate*. New York, 1925.

CUMMINGS, A. D., CHALMERS, W. R., and MATTINGLY, H. B. 'A Roman Mining Document.' *Mine and Quarry Engineering* (1956), 339–42.

DAVIES, O. *Roman Mines in Europe*. Oxford, 1935.

DE ROBERTIS, F. M. *Il diritto associativo romano*. (Storia delle corporazioni, I, I.) Bari, 1938.

—— *Il fenomeno associativo nel mondo romano dai collegi della reppublica alle corporazioni del basso impero*. Naples, 1955.

DRACHMANN, A. G. *Ancient Oil Mills and Presses*. Copenhagen, 1932.

ELIOT, C. W. J. 'New Evidence for the Speed of the Roman Imperial Post.' *Phoenix*, IX (1955), 76–80.
FELDHAUS, F. *Die Technik der Antike u. des Mittelalters.* Potsdam, 1931.
FORBES, R. J. *Studies in Ancient Technology*, vols. 1–9. Leiden, 1955–1964.
GORCE, D. *Les Voyages, l'hospitalité, et le port des lettres dans le monde chrétien des IVe et Ve siècles.* Paris, 1925.
GROAG, E. 'Collegien u. Zwangsgenossenschaften im III. Jahrhundert.' *Viertel-jahrsch. f. Sozial- u. Wirtschaftsgesch.*, II (1904), 481ff.
HARDEN, D. B. *Roman Glass from Karanis.* Ann Arbor, 1936.
HOLMBERG, E. J. 'Zur Geschichte des Cursus Publicus' (Dissertation). Uppsala, 1933.
JONES, A. H. M. 'The Roman Colonate.' *Past and Present*, XIII (1958), 1–13.
LANDELS, J. G. *Engineering in the Ancient World.* London–Berkeley–Los Angeles, 1978.
MICKWITZ, G. *Die Kartellfunktionen der Zünfte.* (Societas scientiarum Fennica: commentationes humanarum literarum, VIII, 3.). Helsinki, 1936.
MITCHELL, S. 'Requisitioned Transport in the Roman Empire: a new inscription from Pisidia.' *JRS*, LXVI (1976), 106–31.
MORITZ, L. *Grain-mills and Flour in Classical Antiquity.* Oxford, 1958.
PFLAUM, M. 'Essai sur le *cursus publicus* sous le Haut-Empire romain.' *Mém. présentés à l'Académie des Inscriptions et Belles-Lettres*, XIV (1940), 189–390.
STE-CROIX, G. E. M de. 'Greek and Roman Accounting.' *Studies in the History of Accounting.* London, 1956, 14–74.
—— 'Ancient Greek and Roman Maritime Loans' in EDEY, H., YAMEY, B. S. (eds.). *Essays in Honour of W. T. Baxter.* London, 1974.
SCHÖNBAUER, E. *Beiträge zur Geschichte des Bergbaurechts.* Münch. Beitr. z. Pap.-Forsch. u. ant. Rechtsgesch. XII. Munich, 1929.
SINGER, C., HOLMYARD, E. J., HALL, A. R. and WILLIAMS, T. J. *A History of Technology.* Vol. 2: *The Mediterranean Civilization and the Middle Ages, 700 B.C.–A.D. 1500.* Oxford, 1956.
STÖCKLE, A. *Spätrömische und byzantinische Zünfte. Klio*, Beih. 9. Leipzig, 1911.
TACKHOLM, U. *Studien über den Bergbau der römischen Kaiserzeit.* Uppsala, 1937.
WALTZING, J. P. *Étude historique sur les corporations professionelles chez les Romains depuis les origines jusqu'à la chute de l'Empire de l'Occident.* 4 vols. Louvain, 1895–1900.

IV. PARTICULAR AREAS

AUBIN, H. 'Die wirtschaftliche Entwicklung römischen Deutschlands.' *Hist. Zeitsch.*, CXLI (1930), 1ff.
BEDFORD, O. H. 'The Silk Trade of China with the Roman Empire.' *China Journ.*, XXVIII (1938), 207–16.
BELL, H. K. 'The Economic Crisis in Egypt under Nero.' *JRS*, XXVIII (1938), 1–8.
—— 'Roman Egypt from Augustus to Diocletian.' *Chronique d'Egypte*, XIII (1938), 347–63.
BENOIT, F. 'Un Port fluvial de cabotage. Arles et l'ancienne marine à voile du Rhône.' *Ann. d'hist. sociale*, II (1940), 199–206.
BLANCHET, A. *Les rapports entre les dépôts monétaires et les évènements militaires.* Paris, 1936.
BOEHNER, K. 'Die Frage der Kontinuität zwischen Altertum und Mittelalter im Spiegel der fränkischen Funde des Rheinlandes.' *Trierer Zeitschrift.*, XIX (1950), 82–106.
BOLIN, STURE. *Fynden av romerska mynt i det fria Germanien.* Lund, 1926.
BONNARD, L. *La Navigation intérieure de la Gaule à l'époque gallo-romaine.* Paris, 1913.
BROGAN, O. *Roman Gaul.* London, 1953.
—— 'Trade between the Roman Empire and the Free Germans.' *JRS*, XXVI (1936), 195–222.
BROUGHTON, T. R. S. *The Romanization of Africa Proconsularis.* Baltimore, 1929.
CARANDINI, A. 'Produzione agricola e produzione ceramica nell'Africa di età imperiale. Appunti sull'economia della Zeugitana e della Byzacena.' *Studi miscellanei*, XV (1970), 95–124.
CHARLESWORTH, M. P. *The Lost Province or the Worth of Britain.* Cardiff, 1949.

CHENET, G. *Fouilles et documents d'archéol. antique en France. I. La Céramique gallo-romaine d'Argonne du IVe siècle et la terre sigillée décorée à la molette.* Mâcon, 1941.

CHILVER, G. E. F. *Cisalpine Gaul: Social and Economic History from 49 B.C. to the Death of Trajan.* Oxford, 1941.

COLIN, J. *Les Antiquités de la Rhénanie.* Paris, 1927.

COLLINGWOOD, R. G. 'Roman Britain.' In Frank's *Economic Survey of Ancient Rome*, III. Baltimore, 1937.

—— (with J. N. L. MYRES). *Roman Britain and the English Invasions*, 2nd edn, Oxford, 1937.

D'ARMS, J. H. 'Puteoli in the second century of the Roman Empire: a social and economic study.' *JRS*, LXIV (1974), 104–24.

DOBSON, D. P. 'Roman Influence in the North.' *Greece and Rome*, V (1936), 73ff.

DRAGENDORFF, H. *Westdeutschland zur Römerzeit*, 2nd edn. Leipzig, 1919.

DRINKWATER, J. F. 'Die Sekundinier von Igel und die Woll- und Textilindustrie in Gallia Belgica: Fragen und Hypothesen.' *Trierer Zeitschrift*, XL–XLI (1977–8), 107–25.

ECKHOLM, G. 'Zur Geschichte des römisch-germanischen Handels.' *Act. arch.*, VI (1935), 49ff.

EGGER, R. 'Das Leben der kleinen Leute: neue Ergebnisse der Ausgrabungen auf dem Magdalensberg.' *Anzeiger der österreichischen Akademie der Wissenschaften in Wien*, Phil.-Hist. Klasse, XC (1953), 139–41.

EGGERS, H. J. *Der römische Import im freien Germanien.* Hamburg, 1951.

FILLIOZAT, J. 'Les Échanges de l'Inde et de l'empire romain aux premiers siècles de l'ère chrétienne.' *Rev. Hist.*, CCI (1949), 1–29.

FRANK, T. 'On the export tax of Spanish harbours.' *AJP*, LVII (1936), 87–90.

—— 'Rome and Italy of the Empire,' in his *Economic Survey of Ancient Rome*, V. Baltimore, 1940.

FRERE, S. *Britannia, a History of Roman Britain.* London, 1967.

GREN, E. *Kleinasien und der Ostbalkan in der wirtschaftlichen Entwicklung der römischen Kaiserzeit.* Uppsala-Leipzig, 1941.

GRENIER, A. *Manuel d'archéologie* (ed. Déchelette), V and VI; *Archéologie gallo-romaine.* Paris, 1931–4.

—— 'La Gaule romaine.' In T. Frank's *Economic Survey of Ancient Rome*, III. Baltimore, 1937.

GUMMERUS, H. *Die südgallische Terrasigillata-industrie nach den Graffiti aus La Graufesenque* (Comm. hum. lit. III). Helsinki, 1932.

HAVERFIELD, F. and MACDONALD, G. *The Romanization of Roman Britain*, 4th edn. Oxford, 1923.

HAYWOOD, R. M. 'Roman Africa,' in T. Frank's *Economic Survey of Ancient Rome*, IV. Baltimore, 1938.

HERTLEIN, F., PARET, O. and GOESSLER, P. *Die Römer in Württemberg*, 3 vols. Stuttgart, 1928–32.

JOHANSEN, R. 'The Textile Industry in Roman North Africa.' *Class. Journ.*, XLIX (1953–4), 157–60.

JONES, A. H. M. *The Greek City from Alexander to Justinian.* Oxford, 1940.

—— 'Asian trade in antiquity.' *Rom. Econ.*, 140–50.

JULLIAN, C. *Histoire de la Gaule*, VII and VIII. Paris, 1926.

KAHRSTEDT, U. *Das wirtschaftliche Gesicht Griechenlands in der Kaiserzeit.* Berne, 1954.

—— *Die wirtschaftliche Lage Grossgriechenlands in der Kaiserzeit.* Wiesbaden, 1960.

KOEPP, F. *Die Römer in Deutschland*, 3rd edn. Bielefeld-Leipzig, 1926.

LAMBRECHTS, P. 'Le Commerce des Syriens en Gaule.' *L'Antiquité classique*, VI (1937), 34–61.

LEDROIT, J. *Die römische Schifffahrt im Stromgebiet des Rheines.* Kulturgeschichtlicher Wegweiser durch das röm.-germ. Zentralmuseum, no. 12. Mainz, 1930.

LEWIS, P. R. and JONES, G. D. B. 'Roman Gold-Mining in North-West Spain.' *JRS*, LX (1970), 169–85.

LOANE, H. J. *Industry and Commerce of the City of Rome (50 B.C.–A.D. 200).* Baltimore, 1938.

MAGIE, D. *Roman Rule in Asia Minor*, 2 vols. Princeton, 1950.
NIERHAUS, R. 'Kaiserzeitliche Südweinexport nach dem freien Germanien.' *Acta antiqua Academiae Scientiarum Hungaricae*, XXV (1954), 252–60.
NORLING-CHRISTENSEN, H. 'Danish Imports of Roman and Roman Provincial Objects in Bronze and Glass.' *Congress of Roman Frontier Studies, 1949*, Durham, 1952, 74–9.
PANCIERA, S. *Vita economica di Aquileia in età romana*. Aquileia, 1957.
PIGEONNEAU, H. 'L'Annone romaine et les corps de naviculaires particulièrement en Afrique.' *Rev. de l'Afrique française*, IV (1886), 220–37.
RICKARD, T. A. 'The Mining of the Romans in Spain.' *JRS*, XVIII (1928), 129–43.
SCHIPPSCHUH, O. *Die Händler im römischen Kaiserreich in Gallia, Germania and den Donauprovinzen Rätien, Noricum und Pannonien*. Amsterdam, 1974.
SCHULZ, S. 'The Roman Evacuation of Britain.' *JRS*, XXIII (1933), 36ff.
SCHUMACHER, K. *Siedelungs- und Kulturgeschichte der Rheinlande. II: Die römische Periode*. Mainz, 1923.
SCRAMUZZA, V. 'Roman Sicily.' In T. Frank's *Economic Survey of Ancient Rome*, III. Baltimore, 1937.
SELIGMAN, C. G. 'The Roman Orient and the Far East.' *Antiquity*, XI (1937), 5–30.
SHERWIN-WHITE, A. N. 'Geographical Factors in Roman Algeria.' *JRS*, XXXIV (1944), 1–10.
SPERBER, D. 'Costs of Living in Roman Palestine IV.' *Journ. of the Economic and Social History of the Orient*, XIII (1970), 1–15.
STAEHELIN, F. *Die Schweiz in römischer Zeit*, 3rd edn. Basle, 1948.
STANFIELD, J. A. and SIMPSON, G. *Central Gaulish Potters*. Oxford, 1958.
THOUVENOT, R. *Essai sur la province romaine de Bétique*. Paris, 1940.
TOVAR, A. and BLAZQUEZ, J. M. *Historia de la Hispania Romana*. Madrid, 1975. (Especially pp. 192–348 with bibliography.)
VAN NOSTRAND, J. J. 'Roman Spain.' In T. Frank's *Economic Survey of Ancient Rome*, III. Baltimore, 1937.
VAN SICKLE, C. E. 'The Public Works of Africa in the Reign of Diocletian.' *Class. Phil.*, XXV (1930), 173–9.
VERCAUTEREN, F. 'Notes sur la ruine des villes de la Gaule d'après quelques auteurs contemporains des invasions germaniques.' *Mélanges Bidez*, II (1934), 955–63.
WAGNER, F. *Die Römer in Bayern*, 4th edn. Munich, 1928.
WARD PERKINS, J. B. 'Tripolitania and the Marble Trade.' *JRS*, XLI (1951), 89–104.
WARMINGTON, B. H. *The North African Provinces from Diocletian to the Vandal Conquest*. Cambridge, 1954.
WARMINGTON, E. H. *The Commerce between the Roman Empire and India*. Cambridge, 1928.
WEST, L. C. *Roman Britain: the Objects of Trade*. Oxford, 1931.
—— *Roman Gaul: the Objects of Trade*. Oxford, 1935.
—— 'The cost of living in Roman Egypt.' *Class. Phil.*, XI (1916), 293–314.
—— 'Commercial Syria under the Roman Empire.' *TAPA*, LV (1924), 159–89.
WHEELER, R. E. M. 'Roman Contact with India, Pakistan and Afghanistan.' *Essays presented to O. G. S. Crawford*. London, 1951, 345–81.
—— *Rome beyond the Imperial Frontiers*. London, 1954.
WHEELER, R. E. M., GHOSH, A. and DEVA KRISHNA, K. 'Arikamedu, an Indo-Roman Trading Station on the East Coast of India.' *Ancient India*, 1946, 17–124.
WHITTAKER, C. R. 'Land and Labour in North Africa.' *Klio*, LX (1978), 331–62.
WIELOWIEJSKI, J. 'L'Échange commercial entre la Pologne méridionale et l'empire romain.' *Archeologia* (Warsaw), VIII (1956), 76–103.
WILKES, J. J. *Dalmatia*. London, 1969.
WILLERS, H. *Neue Untersuchungen über die römische Bronzeindustrie von Capua und von Nieder-Germanien*. Hanover-Leipzig, 1907.
WILSON, F. H. 'Studies in the Social and Economic History of Ostia.' *BSA*. XIII (1935), 41–68; XIV (1938), 152–62.

V. COINAGE AND FINANCE: TAXATION

ALTHEIM, F. and STIEHL, R. *Finanzgeschichte der Spätantike*. Frankfurt, 1957.
BOAK, A. E. E. 'Early Byzantine Tax Receipts from Egypt' (on *adaeratio*). *Byzantion*, XVII (1944–5), 16–28.
BOLIN, S. *State and Currency in the Roman Empire to A.D. 300*. Stockholm, 1958.
—— 'Der solidus.' *Acta instituti Romani regni Sueciae*, ser. 2, I (1939) (Δρᾶγμα *Nilsson*), 144ff.
BRUNT, P. 'The *Fiscus* and its Development.' *JRS*, LVI (1966), 75–91.
CALLU, J.-P. *La Politique monétaire des empereurs romains*. Paris, 1969.
—— 'La Fonction monétaire dans la société romaine sous l'empire.' *Ve Congrès internat. d'histoire économique*. Leningrad, 1970.
CRAWFORD, M. H. 'Money and Exchange in the Roman world.' *JRS*, LX (1970), 40–8.
DE LAET, S. J. *Portorium, Étude sur l'organisation douanière chez les romains surtout à l'époque du Haut Empire*. Bruges, 1949.
DÉLÉAGE, A. *La Capitation du Bas-Empire*. Mâcon, 1945. (Cf. review by Piganiol, *Journ. des Savants* (1946), 128–39).
DOPSCH, A. *Naturalwirtschaft und Geldwirtschaft in der Weltgeschichte*. Vienna, 1930.
ERIM, K. T., REYNOLDS, JOYCE and CRAWFORD, M. 'Diocletian's Currency Reform: a new inscription.' *JRS*, LXI (1971), 171–7.
GIESECKE, W. *Antikes Geldwesen*. Leipzig, 1938.
GRANT, M. *Roman Imperial Money*. London, 1954.
HEICHELHEIM, F. M. 'Zur Währungskrise des romischen Imperiums im 3. Jahrhundert n. Chr.' *Klio*, XXVI (1933), 96ff.
—— 'New Light on Currency and Inflation in Hellenistic and Roman Times.' *Econ. Hist.* (Suppl. to *Econ. Journ.*), Feb. 1935.
HENDY, M. 'Mint and Financial Administration under Diocletian, his Colleagues and his Successors, A.D. 305–324.' *JRS*, LXII (1972), 75–82.
JONES, A. H. M. 'Inflation under the Roman Empire.' *Econ. H.R.*, 2nd ser. V (1953), 293–318. (Expanded version in *Rom. Econ.*, 187–227.)
—— 'Numismatics and History.' *Essays presented to Harold Mattingly*. Oxford, 1956. (*Rom. Econ.*, 61–81 with bibliography by M. H. Crawford.)
—— '*Capitatio* and *iugatio*.' *JRS*, XLVII (1957), 88–94. (= *Rom. Econ.* 280–92.)
—— 'Over-Taxation and the Decline of the Roman Empire.' *Antiquity*, XXXIII (1959), 39–49 (= *Rom. Econ.* 82–9.)
KARAYANNOPULOS, J. *Das Finanzwesen des frühbyzantinischen Staates*. Munich, 1958.
KUBITSCHEK, W. 'Der Übergang von der vordiokletianischen Währung ins vierte Jahrhundert: Randbemerkungen zu Schriften von G. Mickwitz.' *Byzantinische Zeitsch.*, XXXV (1935), 340ff.
LIEBESCHÜTZ, W. 'Money Economy and Taxation in Kind in Syria in the Fourth Century A.D.' *Rheinisches Museum*, CIV (1961), 242–56.
MATTINGLY, H. *Roman Coins*. London, 1928.
—— 'The Monetary Systems of the Roman Empire from Diocletian to Theodosius I' (with full bibliography). *Num. Chron.* 6, VI (1946), 111–20.
—— and SYDENHAM, E. A. (and others). *The Roman Imperial Coinage*. 8 vols. London, 1923–81.
MICKWITZ, G. *Geld und Wirtschaft im römischen Reich des IV. Jahrhunderts nach Chr.* (Comm. hum. lit. IV, 2). Helsinki, 1932.
—— *Die Systeme des römischen Silbergeldes im IV. Jahrhundert*. (Comm. hum. lit. VI, 2). Helsinki, 1935.
—— 'Le Problème de l'or dans le monde antique.' *Ann. d'hist. économique et sociale*, VI (1934), 239ff.
—— 'Ueber die Kupfergeldinflationen in den Jahren der Thronkämpfe nach Diokletians Abdankung.' *Trans. Internat. Numism. Cong. 1936* (Oxford, 1938), 219ff.
MILLAR, F. 'The Fiscus in the First Two Centuries.' *JRS*, LIII (1963), 29–42.
MOMMSEN, Th. *Geschichte des römischen Münzwesens*. Berlin, 1860 (reprinted Graz, 1956).

Passerini, A. 'Gli aumenti del soldo militare da Commodo a Massimino.' *Athenaeum*, N.S. XIV (1946), 145–59.
—— 'Sulla pretesa rivoluzione dei prezzi durante il regno di Commodo.' *Studi in onore di Gino Luzzatto*. Milan, 1949, 1–17.
Pearce, J. W. E. 'The *vota*-legends on the Roman coinage.' *Num. Chron.*, 5, XVII (1937), 112–23.
—— 'Gold coinage of the reign of Theodosius I.' *Num. Chron.*, 5, XVIII (1938), 205–46.
Pekáry, T. 'Studien zur römischen Währungs- und Finanzgeschichte von 161 bis 235 n. Chr.' *Historia*, VIII (1959), 443–89.
Piganiol, A. 'Le Problème de l'or au IVe siècle.' *Ann. d'hist. sociale* (1945), 47ff.
—— 'La Capitation de Dioclétien.' *Rev. hist.*, CLXXVI (1935), 1–13.
Sedgwick, W. B. 'The gold supply in ancient and mediaeval times, and its influence on history.' *Greece and Rome*, V (1936), 148ff.
Seeck, O. 'Die Münzpolitik Diokletians u. seiner Nachfolger.' *Zeitsch. f. Numismatik*, XVII (1890), 63ff.
Segrè, A. *Metrologia e circolazione monetaria degli antichi*. Bologna, 1928.
—— 'Inflation and its implications in early Byzantine times.' *Byzantion*, XV (1940–1), 249–79.
—— 'The *annona civica* and the *annona militaris*.' *Byzantion*, XVI (1942–3), 393–444.
—— 'Note sulle monete romane dal I sec. d. Cr. all' età byzantina.' *Maia*, XVI (1964), 265f.
Sperber, D. '*Denarii* and *aurei* in the time of Diocletian.' *JRS*, LVI (1966), 190–5.
Strack, P. L. *Untersuchungen zur römischen Reichsprägung des zweiten Jahrhunderts*, 3 vols. Stuttgart, 1931–7.
Szilagyi, J. 'Prices and wages in the western provinces of the Roman Empire.' *Acta antiqua Academiae Scientiarum Hungaricae*, XI (1963), 325–89.
van Berchem, D. 'L'Annone militaire.' *Mém. de la soc. nat. des antiqu. de France*, LXXX (1937), 117–202.
Várady, L. 'Contributions to the late Roman military economy and agrarian taxation.' *Acta archaeologica Academiae Scientiarum Hungaricae*, XIV (1962), 403–38.
Wallace, S. L. *Taxation in Egypt from Augustus to Diocletian*. Princeton, 1938.
West, L. C. *Gold and Silver Coin Standards in the Roman Empire*. (Numismatic notes and monographs, 94.) New York, 1941.
—— 'The Roman Gold Standard and the Ancient Sources.' *AJP*, LXII (1941), 289–301.
West, L. C, and Johnson, A. C. *Currency in Roman and Byzantine Egypt*. Princeton, 1944.
Whittaker, C. R. 'Inflation and the Economy in the Fourth Century A.D.' in King, C. E. (ed.). *Imperial Revenue, Expenditure and Monetary Policy in the Fourth Century A.D.* B.A.R. Suppl. 76, 1–26. Oxford, 1980.

Valuable material will be found in the following articles in the *Real-Encyclopädie der Classischen Altertumswissenschaft* (ed. Pauly-Wissowa-Kroll-Ziegler): *Adaeratio* (Seeck), Berufsvereine (Suppl.-B. IV: Stöckle), *collatio lustralis* (Seeck), *collegium* (Kornemann), *colonatus* (Seeck), Domänen (Suppl.-B, IV: Kornemann), *fabri* (Kornemann), *fabricenses* (Seeck), *follis* (Seeck), *frumentum* (Rostovtzeff), Industrie u. Handel (Gummerus), Inflation (suppl.-B, VI: Mickwitz), Kapitalismus (Sigwart), Monopol (Heichelheim), Münzkunde (Regling), *navicularii* (Sigwart), *siliqua* (Regling), Sklaverei (Suppl.-B. VI: Westermann).

CHAPTER III

Byzantine Trade and Industry

I. ORIGINAL SOURCES

Note: Relevant information can be obtained from all the Byzantine chroniclers and writers. See Bibliographies in the *Cambridge Medieval History*, vols. II and IV, and the *Cambridge Economic History*, vol. I, chap. V. Below are given sources particularly concerned with Byzantine trade and industry.

(1) *Collections of Sources*

Corpus der Griechischen Urkunden des Mittelalters. Ed. F. Dölger. Munich/Berlin, 1924 – (in progress).

Jus Graeco-Romanum. Ed. K. E. Zachariae von Lingenthal. 7 parts. Leipzig, 1856–84.

Jus Graeco-Romanum. Ed. J. and P. Zepos. 8 vols. Athens, 1931.

MIKLOSICH, F. and MULLER, J. *Acta et Diplomata Graeca Medii Aevi.* 6 vols. Vienna, 1860–90.

SATHAS, C. N. Μεσαιωνικὴ Βιβλιοθήκη (Medieval Library). 6 vols. Venice, 1872.

TAFEL, G. L. F. and THOMAS, G. M. *Urkunden zur älteren Handels- und Staatsgeschichte der Republik Venedig mit besonderer Beziehung auf Byzanz und die Levante von 9ten bis zum Ausgang des 15ten Jahr.* 3 parts in *Fontes Rerum Austriacarum*, 2nd sect., vols. XII–XIV. Vienna, 1856–7.

(2) *Individual Sources*

BENJAMIN OF TUDELA. *Itinerary.* Ed. M. N. Adler. London, 1907.

CODINUS. *De Officialibus Palatii Constantinopolitani et de Officiis Magnae Ecclesiae.* Corpus Scriptorum Historiae Byzantinae. Bonn, 1839.

CONSTANTINE VII PORPHYROGENNETUS. *De Ceremoniis Aulae Byzantinae.* 2 vols. *De Thematibus et De Administrando Imperio.* 1 vol. Bonn, 1829–40.

COSMAS INDICOPLEUSTES. *Christian Topography.* Ed. O. Winstedt. London, 1909.

Ἐπαρχικὸν Βίβλιον: *Le Livre du Préfet.* Ed. with Latin transl., by J. Nicole. Geneva, 1893.

—— Ed. in English under title of *Roman Law in the later Roman Empire*, by E. H. Freshfield. Cambridge, 1938.

LEO VI SAPIENS. *Les Nouvelles de Léon VI le Sage.* Ed. P. Noailles and A. Dain. Paris, 1944.

TIMARION. Ed. Hase, in *Notes et Extraits*, vol. IV, 2me partie. Paris, 1813.

II. MODERN WORKS

AHRWEILER, H. 'Fonctionnaires et bureaux maritimes à Byzance.' *Revue des études byzantines*, XIX (1961), 239–52.

—— 'Nouvelle hypothèse sur le tétartèron d'or et la politique monétaire de Nicéphore Phocas.' *Zbornik de l'institut byzantin de l'Academie Serbe*, VIII (1963), 1–9.

ANDREADES, A. Ἱστορία τῆς Ἑλληνικῆς Δημοσίας Οἰκονομίας (History of Greek Political Economy). Athens, 1918.

—— 'Byzance, paradis du monopole et privilège.' *Byzantion*, IX (1934), 171–81.

—— 'Deux livres récents sur les finances byzantines.' *Byzantinische Zeitschrift*, XXVIII (1928), 287–323.

ANKORI, Z. *Karaites in Byzantium*. New York, 1959.

ANTONIADES-BIBICOU, H. *Recherches sur les douanes à Byzance*. Paris, 1963.

—— *Etudes d'histoire maritime de Byzance*. Paris, 1966.

—— 'Problèmes d'histoire économique de Byzance au XIe siècle.' *Byzantinoslavica*, XXVIII (1967), 255–61.

ASHTOR, E. 'Essai sur l'alimentation des diverses classes sociales dans l'orient médiéval.' *Annales: Economies, Sociétés, Civilisations*, XXIII (1968), 1017–53.

BELAIEW, N. 'The Daric and the Zolotnic' (in Russian with English résumé). *Seminarium Kondakovianum*, IV (1931), 179–204.

BOISSONADE, P. *Le Travail dans l'Europe Chrétienne au Moyen Age*. Paris, 1921.

BRAND, C. M. 'Two Byzantine Treatises on Taxation.' *Traditio*, XXV (1969), 30–60.

BRATIANU, G. I. *Recherches sur le commerce Génois dans la Mer Noire au XII siècle*. Paris, 1929.

—— 'Une Expérience d'économie dirigée: le monopole du blé à Byzance au XIe siècle.' *Byzantion*, IX (1934), 643–62.

—— *Études byzantines d'histoire économique et sociale*. Paris, 1938.

—— *Privilèges et franchises municipales dans l'Empire byzantin*. Paris/Bucharest, 1934.

BURY, J. B. *The Imperial Administrative System in the IXth Century*. London, 1911.

CARANDINI, A. 'Produzione agricola e produzione ceramica nell' Africa di età imperiale. Appunti sull'economia della Zeugitana e della Byzacena.' *Studi miscellanei*, XV (1970), 95–124.

CHARANIS, P. *Social, Economic and Political Life in the Byzantine Empire*. London, 1973.

—— 'Observations on the demography of the Byzantine Empire.' Thirteenth International Congress of Byzantine Studies, *Main Papers*, XIV. Oxford, 1966, 445–63.

CICOTTI, E. *Il tramonto della schiavitù nel mondo antico*. Turin, 1899.

CIPOLLA, C. M. *Money, Prices and Civilization in the Mediterranean World, 5th to 7th century*. Princeton, 1956.

CONSTANTELOS, D. J. *Byzantine Philanthropy and Social Welfare*. New Brunswick, 1968.

DIETERICH, K. 'Zur Kulturgeographie und Kulturgeschichte der byzantinischen Balkanshandels.' *Byzantinische Zeitschrift*, XXXI (1931), 37–57, 334–49.

DÖLGER, F. 'Beiträge zur Geschichte der byzantinischen Finanzverwaltung.' Byzantinische Archiv, IX. Leipzig/Berlin, 1927.

—— 'Das Αερικόν'. *Byzantinische Zeitschrift*, XXX (1929–30), 450–7.

—— 'Beitrage zum Geschichte des byzantinischen Finanzverwaltung besonders des 10 und 11 Jahrhunderts.' *Byzantinische Archiv*, IX, 2 auflage (1960).

DUNLOP, D. M. *The History of the Jewish Khazars*. Princeton, 1954.

EBERSOLT, J. *Constantinople byzantine et les voyageurs du Levant*. Paris, 1919.

—— *Les Arts somptuaires de Byzance*. Paris, 1923.

FRANCES, E. 'L'État et les métiers à Byzance.' *Byzantinoslavica*, XXIII (1962), 231–49.

—— 'La Disparition des corporations byzantines.' *Actes du XII Congrès International d'Études Byzantines*, II. Belgrade, 1964, 93–101.

GORYANOV, B. T. 'The Byzantine Town, 11th to 15th centuries' (in Russian). *Vizantiiskii Vremennik*, XIII (1958), 162–83.

GRIERSON, P. 'Nomisma, tetarteron et dinar: un plaidoyer pour Nicéphore Phocas.' *Revue Belge de Numismatique*, C (1954), 75–94.

—— 'The Debasement of the Bezant in the Eleventh Century.' *Byzantinische Zeitschrift*, XLVII, 2 (1954), 379–94.

—— 'Notes on the fineness of the Byzantine solidus.' *Byzantinische Zeitschrift*, LIV, 1 (1961), 91–9.

—— 'Coinage and Money in the Byzantine Empire, 498-c. 1090.' *Settimani di Studio del centro italiano di studi sull' alto medioevo*, VIII (1961), 411–23.

GUILLAND, R. *Recherches sur les institutions byzantines*, 2 vols. Berlin/Amsterdam, 1967.

HENDY, M. F. *Coinage and Money in the Byzantine Empire, 1081–1261*. Dumbarton Oaks, 1969.

—— 'Byzantium, 1081–1204: an economic reappraisal.' *Trans. Roy. Hist. Soc.* ser. 5, xx (1970), 31–52.
HERRIN, J. 'The Collapse of the Byzantine Empire in the Twelfth Century: a study in medieval economy.' *University of Birmingham Historical Journal*, XII (1970), 186–203.
HEYD, W. *Histoire du commerce du Levant*, 2 vols. (rev. edn in French). Leipzig, 1936.
HROCHOVÁ, V. *Byzanska Mésta ve 13–15 stoleti*. Prague, 1967.
JACOBY, D. *Société et démographie à Byzance et en Romanie Latine*. London, 1975.
JEANSELME, E. and OECONOMOS, L. *Les Oeuvres à assistance et les hopitaux byzantins*. Antwerp, 1921.
KARAYANNOPULOS, J. *Das Finanzwesen des frühbyzantinischen Staates*. Munich, 1958.
—— 'Fragmente aus dem Vademecum eines byzantinischen Finanzbeamten.' *Polychronion: Festschrift F. Dölger*. Heidelberg, 1966, 318–34.
KAZHDAN, A. P. 'Corporations and Government workshops of Constantinople in the 9th and 10th centuries' (in Russian). *Vizantiiskii Vremennik*, VI (1953), 132–55.
KAZHDAN, A. P. and CONSTABLE, G. *People and Power in Byzantium*. Washington, Dumbarton Oaks, 1982.
LAIOU-THOMADAKIS, A. E. *Peasant Society in the late Byzantine Empire*. Princeton, 1977.
LOMBARD, M. 'L'Or Musalman du VIIe au XIe siècle.' *Annales: Economies, Societes, Civilisations*, No. 2 (1947).
LOPEZ, R. S. *Byzantine Studies*. New Haven, 1968.
—— *The Commercial Revolution of the Middle Ages*. New Haven, 1971.
—— *Byzantium and the World around it. Economic and industrial relations*. London, 1978.
—— 'Mohammed and Charlemagne, a revision.' *Speculum*, XVIII (1943), 14–39.
—— 'Silk Industry in the Byzantine Empire.' *Speculum*, XX (1945), 1–43.
—— 'La Crise du besant au Xe siècle et la date du Livre du Préfet.' *Annuaire de l'Institut de Philologie et d'Histoire Orientales et Slaves*, X (Brussels, 1950), 403–18.
—— 'Harmenopoulos and the downfall of the Bezant.' *Tomos Constantinou Harmenopoulou* (Thessalonica, 1952), 111–25.
MACRI, C. M. *L'Organisation de l'économie urbaine dans Byzance*. Paris, 1925.
MANGO, C. *Byzantium: the Empire of New Rome*. London, 1980.
MEIGGS, R. *Roman Ostia*, 2nd edn. Oxford, 1973.
MENDL, B. 'Les Corporations byzantines.' *Byzantinoslavica*, XXII (1961), 302–19.
MICKWITZ, G. *Geld und Wirtschaft im römischen Reich des 4ten Jahrh*. Helsinki, 1932.
—— 'Byzance et l'occident médiévale.' *Annales d'Histoire Economique et Sociale*, VIII (1936), 21–8.
MILLET, G. 'Sur les sceaux des commerciaires byzantins.' *Mélanges G. Schlumberger*. Paris, 1924.
MONNIER, H. *Les Nouvelles de Léon le Sage*. Bordeaux, 1923.
OIKONOMIDES, N. 'Quelques boutiques de Constantinople au Xe siècle: prix, loyers, imposition.' *Dumbarton Oaks Papers*, XXVI (1972), 345–56.
OSTROGORSKY, G. 'Lohne und Preise in Byzanz.' *Byzantinische Zeitschrift*, XXXII (1932), 293–333.
—— 'Byzantine Cities in the Early Middle Ages.' *Dumbarton Oaks Papers*, XIII (1959), 47–66.
PATLAGEAN, E. *Pauvreté économique et pauvreté sociale à Byzance, 4e – 7e siècles*. Paris/The Hague, 1977.
PIGULEWSKAJA, N. *Byzanz auf den Wegen nach. Indien*. Berlin/Amsterdam.
SEGRÈ, A. 'Inflation and its implications in Early Byzantine times.' *Byzantion*, XV (1941), 249–80.
—— 'Essays on Byzantine Economic History.' *Byzantion*, XVI (1942–3), 393–445.
SOUTZO, M. 'Les Origines du sesterce et du miliarense et leur continuité jusqu'au temps Byzantins.' Académie Roumaine, *Bulletin de la Section Historique*, XIII (1927), 54–9.
SPULBER, C. A. *L'Éclogue des Isauriens*. Cernauti, 1934.
STARR, J. *The Jews in the Byzantine Empire*. Athens, 1939.
STEIN, J. *Studien zur Geschichte des byzantinischen Reiches*. Stuttgart, 1919.
STÖCKLE, A. *Spätrömische und byzantinische Zünfte. Klio*, IX. Leipzig, 1911.
SVORONOS, N. 'Recherches sur le cadastre byzantin et la fiscalité aux XIe et XIIe siècles:

le cadastre de Thebes.' *Bulletin de Correspondence Hellenique*, LXXXIII (1959), 1–145, 800, 806–25.

—— 'Société et organisation intérieure dans l'empire byzantin au XIe siècle: les principaux problèmes.' Thirteenth International Congress of Byzantine Studies, *Main Papers*, XII, Oxford, 1966, 373–89.

TAFRALI, O. *Thessalonique au quatorzième siècle*. Paris, 1913.

—— *Thessalonique des origines au XIVe siècle*. Paris, 1919.

TEALL, J. L. 'The Grain Supply in the Byzantine Empire.' *Dumbarton Oaks Papers*, XIII (1959), 89–139.

VASILIEV, A. A. 'Economic Relations between Byzantium and Russia.' *Journal of Economic and Business History*, IV, 2 (1932), 314–34.

VASILIEVSKY, V. 'Material for the Internal History of the Byzantine Empire' (in Russian). *Journal of the Russian Ministry of Public Instruction*, CCII (1879), 160–232, 368–438; CCX (1880), 98–170, 355–440.

VERLINDEN, C. *L'Esclavage dans l'Europe médiévale: Italie, Levant latin, Empire byzantin*. Ghent, 1977.

VRYONIS, S. 'The Question of the Byzantine Mines.' *Speculum*, XXXVII (1962), 1–18.

—— 'Byzantine *democratia* and the Guilds in the Thirteenth Century.' *Dumbarton Oaks Papers*, XVII (1963), 287–314.

WALZING, J. P. *Étude historique sur les corporations professionelles chez les romains*, 4 vols. Louvain, 1895–1900.

ZACHARIAE VON LINGENTHAL, K. E. *Geschichte des griechisch-römischen Rechts*. Berlin, 1892.

ZAKYNTHINOS, D. 'Crise monétaire et crise économique à Byzance du XIIIe au XVe siècle.' *L'Hellenisme Contemporain*, I, 2 (1947), 162–92; II, 2 (1948), 150–67.

—— 'La Ville byzantine.' *Diskussions-beitrage zum XI Internationalen Byzantinisten-kongress*. Munich (1958), 43–57.

ZORAS, G. *Le Corporazioni Bizantini*. Rome, 1933.

CHAPTER IV

The Trade of Medieval Europe: the North

Annales	*Annales d'Histoire Économique et Sociale* and *Annales (Économics, Sociétés, Civilisations)*
EconHR	*Economic History Review*
EHR	*English Historical Review*
HG	*Hansische Geschichtsblätter*
BMHG	*Bijdragen en Mederdeelingen van het Historisch Genootschap*
RBPH	*Revue Belge de Philologie et d'Histoire*
TRHS	*Transactions of the Royal Historical Society*
VSW	*Vierteljahrschrift für Sozial- und Wirtschaftsgeschichte*

I. PRINTED SOURCES

FAGNIEZ, G. *Documents relatifs à l'histoire de l'industrie et du commerce en France (au moyen âge)*, 2 vols. Paris, 1898, 1900.

GREGORY OF TOURS. *The History of the Franks*, I and II (transl. by O. M. Dalton). Oxford, 1927.

HÖLBAUM, K., KUNZE, K. and STEIN, W. *Hansisches Urkundenbuch.* Verein für Hansische Geschichte. Halle and Leipzig, 1876–1907.

KOPPMANN, K. *Die Recesse und Andere Akten der Hansetäge, von 1236–1340*, I–VIII. Die Historische Kommission bei der Königl. Akad. der Wissenschaften. Leipzig, 1870–97.

KUNZE, K. *Hanseakten aus England, 1275 bis 1412. Hansische Geschichtsquellen*, VI. Verein für Hansische Geschichte. Halle, 1891.

KUSKE, B. *Quellen zur Geschichte des Kölner Handels und Verkehrs im Mittelalter.* 3 vols. Gesellschaft für Rheinische Geschichtskunde. Bonn, 1918–23.

LANGE, C. C. A., UNGER, C. R. and others. *Diplomatarium Norvegicum*, vols. I ff. Oslo, 1847, etc.

LAPPO-DANILEVSKY, N. *Recueil des documents relatifs à l'histoire de la Neva.* Petrograd, 1916. (Edition of the Imperial Academy of Sciences.)

LECHNER, G. *Die Hansischen Pfundzollisten des Jahres 1368.* Quellen z. Hansisch. Gesch., N.F. vol. x. Lübeck, 1935.

NEALE, E. W. W. *The Great Red Book of Bristol.* Text (pt. I). Bristol Record Society's Publications, vol. IV, 1937.

POELMAN, H. A. *Bronnen tot de Geschiedenis van den Oostzeehandel*, I. Rijks Geschiedenkundige Publicatiën. The Hague, 1917.

POSTHUMUS, N. W. *Bronnen tot de Geschiedenis van de Leidsche Textielnijverheid, 1333–1795.* Rijks Geschiedenkundige Publicatiën. The Hague, 1910–22.

ROPP, G. VON DER. *Hanserecesse 1431–76.* Zweite Abteilung, I–VII. Verein für Hansische Geschichte. Leipzig, 1876–92.

SEVEREN, L. GILLIODTS VAN (ed.). *Cartulaire de l'ancienne Estaple de Bruges.* 4 vols. Société d'Emulation. Bruges, 1904–6.

SMIT, H. J. *Bronnen tot de Geschiedenis van den handel met Engeland, Schotland en Ierland, 1150–1485.* Rijks Geschiedenkundige Publicatiën. The Hague, 1928.

SNELLER, Z. W. and UNGER, W. S. *Bronnen tot de Geschiedenis van den handel met Frankrijk*, I. Rijks Geschiedenkundige Publicatiën. The Hague, 1930.

THOMAS, A. H. *Calendar of Early Mayor's Court Rolls of the City of London, 1298–1307.* Cambridge, 1924.

—— *Calendar of Plea and Memoranda Rolls of the City of London.* 2 vols., *1323–64, 1364–81.* Cambridge, 1926, 1929.

—— *Calendar of Select Pleas and Memoranda of the City of London, 1381–1412.* Cambridge, 1932.

UNGER, W. S. *De Tol van Iersekeroord: documenten en rekeningen, 1321–1572.* The Hague, 1939.

—— *Bronnen tot de Geschiedenis van Meddelburg in het landsheerlijken tijd*. Rijks Geschiedenkundige Publicatiën. The Hague, 1923.
WARNER, G. (ed.). *The Libelle of Englyshe Polycye*. Oxford, 1926.

II. SECONDARY AUTHORITIES

ABEL, W. 'Bevölkerungsgang und Landwirtschaft im Ausgehenden Mittelalter in Lichte der Preis- und Lohnbewegung.' *Schmoller's Jahrbücher*, 58 Jahrg., 1934.
—— *Agrarkrisen und Agrarkonjunktur im Mitteleuropa*. Berlin, 1935.
—— *Die Wüstungen des ausgehenden Mittelalters*, 2nd edn. Stuttgart, 1955.
AGATS, A. *Der Hansische Baienhandel*. Heidelberg, 1904.
ARENS, FRANZ. 'Wilhelm Servat von Cahors zu London.' *VSW*, 1904.
ARUP, E. *Studier i Engelsk og Tysk Handels Histoire, etc. 1350–1850*. Copenhagen, 1907.
AVENEL, G. DE. *Histoire économique de la propriété, des salaires, des denrées et de tous le prix*. 6 vols. Paris, 1886–1920.
BÄCHTOLD, H. *Der Norddeutsche Handel im 12. und beginnenden 13. Jahrhundert*. Abhandlungen zur mittleren und neuen Geschichte, hrsg. von. G. v. Below, H. Finke und F. Meinecke, Heft 21. Berlin and Leipzig, 1910.
BAHR, C. *Handel und Verkehr der deutschen Hanse in Flandern während des vierzehnten Jahrhunderts*. Leipzig, 1911.
BAKER, J. L. N. *Medieval Trade Routes*. Historical Association Pamphlet, no. 111. 1938.
BEARDWOOD, ALICE. *Alien Merchants in England 1350–1377. Their Legal and Economic Position*. Cambridge (Mass.), 1931.
BECK, L. *Die Geschichte des Eisens*. 4 vols. Brunswick, 1891–9.
BELOCH, J. 'Die Bevölkerung Europas im Mittelalter.' *Zeitschrift für Sozial- und Wirtschaftsgesch.*, III, 405. Freiburg i. B., 1894.
BELOW, G. VON. *Aus Sozial- und Wirtschaftsgeschichte*. Stuttgart, 1928.
—— *Probleme der Wirtschaftsgeschichte*. Tübingen, 1920.
BENS, G. *Der deutsche Warenfernhandel im Mittelalter*. Breslau, 1926.
BEVERIDGE, W. 'Wages in the Winchester Manors.' *EconHR* (1936), VII, no. 1.
—— 'Yield and Price of Corn in the Middle Ages.' *Economic History* (Suppl. to *Econ. Journ.*), no. 2 (1927).
BIGWOOD, G. 'Les Financiers d'Arras.' *RBPH* (1924).
—— 'La Politique de la laine en France sous les règnes de Phillipe le Bel et de ses fils.' *RBPH* (1936).
BLOCH, M. 'Le Problème de l'or au Moyen Age.' *Annales* (1933).
BLOCKMANS, Fr. *Het Gentsche Stadspatriciaat tot Omstreeks 1302*. Antwerp, 1938.
BOUQUELOT, G. *Les foires de Champagne*. 2 vols. Mémoires d'Académie des Sciences et Belles Lettres. Paris, 1938.
BOUTRUCHE, R. *La Crise d'une société: seigneurs et paysans du Bordelais pendant la Guerre de Cent Ans*. Paris, 1947.
BOUVIER, R. *Un Financier Colonial au XV Siècle. Jacques Cœur*. Paris, 1928.
BOYER, H. *Histoire de l'industrie et du commerce à Bourges*. Bourges, 1884.
BRUNS, F. (ed.). *Die Lübecker Bergenfahrer und ihre Chronistik*. Hansische Geschichtsquellen, N.F., Bd. II. Verein für Hansische Geschichte. Berlin, 1900.
BUCHER, K. *Die Entstehung der Volkswirtschaft*. 2 vols. Leipzig, 1920.
BUGGE, A. *Den Norske Traelasthandels Historie*, I. Skien, 1925.
—— 'Handelen mellem England og Norge indtil Begyndelsen af det 15de Aarhundrede.' *Historisk Tidskrift*, Raekke III, Bind 4, pp. 1–149. Oslo, 1898.
—— 'Die nordeuropäischen Verkehrswege im früheren Mittelalter.' *VSW*, IV (1906).
—— 'Der Untergang der Norwegischen Seeschiffahrt.' *VSW*, 1904.
CARUS-WILSON, E. M. (ed.). *The Overseas Trade of Bristol in the later Middle Ages*. Bristol Record Society's Publications, VII (1936).
DAENELL, E. R. *Die Blütezeit der deutschen Hanse. Hansische Geschichte von der zweiten Hälfte des XIV. bis zum letzen Viertel des XV. Jahrhunderts*. 2 vols. Berlin, 1905–6.
DEROISY, ARMAND. 'Les Routes terrestres de laines Anglais vers la Lombardie.' *Revue du Nord*, XXV (1939).

DES MAREZ, G. *Études sur la propriété foncière dans les villes du Moyen Age et spécialement au Flandre*. Université de Gand. Recueil des travaux publiés par la Faculté de Philosophie et Lettres, 1898.
DION, R. 'Orléans et l'ancienne navigation de la Loire.' *Annales de Géographie*, XLVII (1938).
DOPSCH, A. *Economic and Social Foundations of European Civilisation*. (Transl.) London, 1937.
—— *Die Wirtschaftsentwicklung der Karolinger Zeit*. 2 vols., 2nd edn. Weimar, 1922.
EBEL, W. 'Das Rostocker Transportgewerbe.' *VSW* (1938).
ECK, A. *Le Moyen Age Russe*. Paris, 1933.
ESPINAS, G. *La Vie urbaine de Douai au Moyen Age*, I–IV. Paris, 1914.
—— *Les Origines du capitalisme*. 2 vols. Lille, 1933, 1936.
FEAVERYEAR, A. E. *The Pound Sterling*. Oxford, 1931.
FLOWER, C. T. *Public Works in Medieval Law*, I and II. Selden Society Publications, 1923.
DE FREVILLE. *Mémoires sur la commerce maritime de Rouen*. 2 vols. Rouen and Paris, 1857.
GILLIARD, CH. 'L'Ouverture du St Gothard.' *Annales* (1929).
GIRY, A. *Histoire de la ville de Saint-Omer*. Paris, 1877.
GOETZ, L. K. *Deutsch-Russiche Handelgeschichte des Mittelalters*. Hansische Geschichtsquellen, N.F., Bd. v. Lübeck, 1922.
GRAS, N. S. B. *The English Customs System*. Cambridge (Mass.), 1918.
—— *The Evolution of the English Corn Market*. Cambridge (Mass.), 1915.
GRAY, H. L. 'The Production and Exportation of English Woollens in the Fourteenth Century.' *EHR*, XXXIX (1924), 13–35.
GRIERSON, P. 'The Relations between England and Flanders before the Norman Conquest.' *TRHS*, 4th ser. XXIII (1941).
GUIRAUD, L. *Recherches et conclusions nouvelles sur le prétendu rôle de Jacques Cœur*. Paris, 1900.
HÄNSELMAN, L. 'Braunschweig in seinen Beziehungen zu den Harz- und Seegebieten.' *HG* (1873).
HAPKE, R. *Brugges Enwicklung zum Mittelalterlichen Weltmarkt*. D. Schaffer's Abhandlungen zur Verkehrs- und Seegeschichte, no. 1. Berlin, 1908.
—— *Der Deutsche Kaufmann in Niederlanden*. Hansische Pfingsblätter, no. 7. Lübeck, 1911.
—— *Der Untergang der Hanse*. Lübeck, 1923.
HARTWICH, C. *Die menschlichen Genussmittel*. Leipzig, 1911.
HAYEM, J. *Mémoires et documents pour servir à l'histoire du commerce et de l'industrie en France*. Paris, 1922.
HENAUX, F. *Fabrique d'armes de Liège*. Liège, 1858.
HEWITT, H. J. *Medieval Cheshire*. Manchester, 1929.
HIRSCH, T. *Danzigs Handels- und Gewerbsgeschichte unter der Herrschaft des deutschen Ordens*. Leipzig, 1858.
HOOPT, C. G. T. *Het ontstaan van Amsterdam*. Amsterdam, 1917.
HUVELIN, P. *Essai historique sur le droit des marchés et des foires*. Paris, 1897.
IMBERTIN, F. 'Les routes médiévales.' *Annales* (1939).
INAMA-STERNEGG, K. T. VON. *Deutsche Wirtschaftsgeschichte*. 3 vols. Leipzig, 1899.
JASTROW, IGNAZ. 'Über Welthandelstrassen in d. Geschichte d. Abendlandes.' *Volkswirtschaftliche Gesellschaft, Volkswirtschaftl. Fragen*, Jahrg. VIII. Berlin, 1887.
JENKINSON, H. 'A Money-lender's Bonds of the Twelfth Century.' *Essays in History presented to R. L. Poole*. Oxford, 1927.
JOHNSEN, O. ALBERT. *Norgesveldets Undergang, et Utsyn og et Opgjør Nedgangstiden*. Oslo, 1924.
JULLIAN, C. *Histoire de Bordeaux depuis les origines jusqu'en 1895*. Bordeaux, 1895.
KENDRICK, T. D. *A History of the Vikings*. London, 1930.
KETNER, F. *Handel en Scheepvaart van Amsterdam in de Vijftiende Eeuw*. The Hague, 1936.
KEYSER, E. 'Der bürgerliche Grundbesitz der Rechtsstadt Danzig im 14. Jahrhundert.' *Zeitschrift d. Westpreussischen Geschichtsverein*, Heft LVIII (1918).
KIESSELBACH, G. A. 'Schleswig als Vermittlerin des Handels zwischen Nordsee und

Ostsee vom 9. bis in das 13. Jahrhundert.' *Zeitschrift für Schleswig-Holsteinischen Lauenburgische Gesch.*, 1907.

KLETTLER, P. *Nordwesteuropas Verkehr, Handel und Gewerbe im frühen Mittelalter.* Deutsches Kultur, Historische Reihe, geleitet von A. Dopsch. Vienna, 1924.

KÖSTER, G. 'Die Entwicklung der nordostdeutschen Verkehrstrassen bis 1800.' *Forschungen zur Brandenburgischen und Preussischen Gesch.* Bd. 48 (1936).

KOSTER, A. *Schiffahrt und Handelsverkehr des Östlichen Mittelmeeres.* Leipzig, 1924.

KOWALEWSKY, M. *Die ökonomische Entwicklung Europas bis zum Beginn der kapitalistischen Wirtschaftsform.* 8 vols. Berlin, 1901–14.

KROCKER, E. *Handelsgeschichte der Stadt Leipzig. Die Entwicklung des Leipziger Handels und der Leipziger Messen.* Vol. VII of von Schulte's and Hoffmann's *Beiträge zur Stadtgeschichte.*

KULISCHER, J. *Allemeine Wirtschaftsgeschichte des Mittelalters und der Neuzeit.* 2 vols., 2nd edn. Munich, 1958.

—— *Russische Wirtschaftsgeschichte*, I. Jena, 1925.

LAMPRECHT, K. *Beiträge zur Geschichte des Französischen Wirtschaftslebens im XI. Jahrhundert.* Leipzig, 1878.

LAPSLEY, G. T. 'The Account Roll of a Fifteenth-Century Iron Master.' *EHR*, XIV (1899).

LAUFFER, V. 'Danzigs Schiffs- und Waarenverkehr.' *Zeitschr. d. Westpreussischen Geschichtsvereins*, Heft XXXIII. Danzig, 1894.

LAURENT, H. *Un Grand commerce d'exportation au moyen âge: La draperie des Pays Bas en France et dans les Pays Mediterranéens, XII–XVe siècle.* Paris, 1935.

—— *Choix de documents inédits pour servir à l'histoire de l'expansion commerciale des Pays Bas en France au Moyen Age (XIIe-XVe siècle).* Brussels, 1934.

—— 'Marchands du palais et marchands d'abbayes.' *Revue Historique*, CLXXXIII (1938).

LESTOCQUOY, J. *Les Dynasties bourgeoises d'Arras du XIe au XVe siècle (Patriciens du moyen-âge).* Arras, 1945.

—— 'Les Etapes du développement urbain d'Arras.' *RBPH* (1944).

LEVASSEUR, E. *Histoire du commerce de la France*, I. Paris, 1910.

—— *Histoire des classes ouvrières et de l'industrie en France avant 1789.* 2nd edn. Paris, 1901.

—— *Histoire de la population française avant 1789....* 3 vols. Paris, 1889–92.

LEWIS, G. R. *The Stannaries, a study of the English tin mines.* Cambridge (Mass.), 1908.

LOT, F. *L'État des paroisses et des feux de 1328.* Paris, 1929.

LOT, F. and FAWTIER, R. *Le premier budget de la monarchie francaise (1202).* Paris, 1932.

LUNT, W. E. *Financial Relations of the Papacy with England to 1327.* Cambridge (Mass.), 1939.

LUZZATTO, G. *Storia del Commerzio.* Florence, 1914.

MAGNUSEN, F. 'Om de Engelskes Handeel og Foerd paa Island i det 15de Aarhundrede.' *Nordisk Tidskrift for Oldkyndighed*, II. Copenhagen, 1833.

MALOWIST, M. 'Le Développement des rapports économiques entre la Flandre, la Pologne et les pays limitrophes du XIIIe au XIVe siècle.' *RBPH*, X (1931).

MARQUANT, R. *La Vie économique à Lille sous Philippe le Bon.* Paris, 1940.

MICKWITZ, G. *Die Kartellfunktionen der Zünfte.* Helsingfors, 1936.

MOERMAN, H. J. 'Bijdragen tot de Economische Geschiedenis van Kampen in de Middeleuwen.' *Economisch Historisch Jaarboek*, 1920.

NAUDE, W. *Getreidehandelspolitik der europäischen Staaten, XIII.–XVIII. Jahr.* Berlin, 1901.

NEF, J. U. 'Silver Production in Central Europe, 1450–1618.' *Journal of Political Econ.*, XLIX (1941).

NETTA, GHERON. *Die Handelsbeziehungen zwischen Leipzig und Ost- und Südosteuropa bis zum Verfall der Warenmessen.* Zurich, 1920.

NEUBURG, C. *Goslars Bergbau bis 1552.* Hanover, 1872.

NEUMANN, G. *Heinrich Castorp.* Lübeck, 1932.

NIERMEYER, J. F. *De Wording van onze Volkshuishouding.* The Hague, 1946.

NÖE, ALBERT. *De Handel van Noord-Nederland op Engeland in de XIIIe Eeuw.* Haarlem, 1918.

OCHENKOWSKI, W. VON. *Englands wirtschaftliche Entwicklung im Ausgange des Mittelalters.* Jena, 1879.

PIGEONNEAU, H. *Histoire du Commerce de la France.* I. Paris, 1885.

PIRENNE, H. *Histoire de Belgique,* vol. I, 5th edn. Brussels, 1929 and vol. II, 3rd edn., Brussels, 1922.

—— *Medieval Cities. Their origins and the revival of trade.* Princeton, 1925.

—— *Mahomet et Charlemagne.* Paris, 1937.

—— 'Un Contraste économique: Mérovingiens et Carolingiens.' *RBPH,* II (1923).

—— 'Les Périodes de l'histoire sociale du capitalisme.' *Bulletins d'Académie Royale de Belgique,* no. 5 (1914).

POSTHUMUS, N. W. *De Geschiedenis van de Leidsche Lakenindustrie,* I. The Hague, 1908.

POWER, E. E. 'The English Wool Trade in the reign of Edward IV.' *Camb. Hist. Journ.* II. Cambridge, 1926.

—— *The Wool Trade in English Medieval History.* Oxford, 1941.

POWER, E. E. and POSTAN, M. M. *Studies in English Trade in the Fifteenth Century.* London, 1933.

PÜSCHEL, A. *Das Anwachsen der deutschen Städte in der Zeit der mittelalterlichen Kolonialbewegung.* Berlin, 1910.

RENOUARD, YVES. *Les Hommes d'affaires Italiens du Moyen Age.* Paris, 1949.

REYER, E. *Zinn: eine geologisch-montanistisch-historische Monographie.* Berlin, 1881.

REYNOLDS, R. L. 'The Market for Northern Textiles in Genoa, 1179–1200,' *RBPH,* VIII (1929).

—— 'Merchants of Arras and the Overland Trade with Genoa, XIIth Century.' *ibid.,* IX (1930).

RHODES, W. E. *The Italian bankers in England and their loans to Edward I and Edward II.* In *Owens College Essays* (eds. T. F. Tout and J. Tait). Manchester, 1902.

ROGERS, J. E. THOROLD. *A History of Agriculture and Prices in England.* Oxford, 1866–1902.

RÖRIG, F. *Hansische Beiträge zur Deutschen Wirtschaftsgeschichte.* Breslau, 1928.

—— *Der Markt von Lübeck. Topographisch-statistische Untersuchung zur deutschen Sozial- und Wirtschaftsgeschichte.* Leipzig, 1922.

—— *Mittelalterliche Weltwirtschaft.* Jena, 1933.

RUDING, R. *Annals of the Coinage of Great Britain.* London, 1840.

RUINEN, J. *De Oudste Handelsbetrekkingen van Holland en Zeeland met Engeland.* (Dissertation.) Amsterdam, 1919.

RUSSELL, J. C. *British Medieval Population.* Albuquerque, 1948.

RUTKOWSKI, J. *Histoire économique de la Pologne avant les partages.* Paris, 1927.

SABBE, E. 'L'Importation des tissus orientaux.' *RBPH* (1935).

SALZMAN, L. F. *English Trade in the Middle Ages.* Oxford, 1931.

SAPORI, A. *Studi di Storia Economica (Secoli XIII–XIV–XV).* 2 vols. Florence, 1955.

—— *La Crisi delle Compagnie Mercantili dei Bardi e dei Peruzzi.* Florence, 1926.

SCHÄFER, D. *Die Hanse.* Monographien zur Weltgeschichte, no. XIX. Bielefeld and Leipzig, 1903.

—— *Das Buch des Lübeckschen Vogts auf Schonen.* Hansische Geschichtsquellen, IV. Halle, 1887.

SCHANZ, G. *Englische Handelspolitik gegen Ende des Mittelalters, mit besonderer Berücksichtigung des Zeitalters der beiden ersten Tudors, Heinrich VII und Heinrich VIII.* 2 vols. Leipzig, 1881.

SCHEFFEL, P. H. *Verkehrsgeschichte der Alpen.* 2 vols. Berlin, 1908–14.

SCHREINER, J. *Pest og Prisfall i Senmiddelalderen.* Oslo, 1949.

SCHULTE, A. *Geschichte der grossen Ravensburger Handelsgesellschaft.* 3 vols. Stuttgart and Berlin, 1923.

SCHULZ, F. *Die Hanse und England von Edwards III bis auf Heinrichs VIII Zeit.* Abhandlungen zur Verkehrs- und Seegeschichte, V. (ed. D. Schäfer.) Berlin, 1911.

SÉE, H. 'Peut-on évaluer la population de l'ancienne France?' *Revue d'économie politique.* Paris, 1924.

SEEGER, H.-J. *Westfalens Handel und Gewerbe.* Studien zur Geschichte der Wirtschaft und Geisteskultur. Bd. I. Berlin, 1926.
SMIT, H. J. 'De betekenis van den Noordnederlandschen in 't bijzonders van den Hollandschen en Zeeuwschen handel in de laatste helft der 14er eeuw.' *BMHG*, Utrecht, 1930.
—— 'Handel en Scheepvaart in het Noordzeegebied gedurende de 13e eeuw.' *Bijdragen voor Vaderlandsche Geschiedenis en Oudheidkunde*, 1928.
SNELLER, Z. W. 'De Hollandsche Korenhandel in het Sommegebied in de 15e eeuw.' *BMHG* (1925).
—— 'De entwikkeling van den handel tusschen Noord-Nederland en Frankrijk tot het midden der vijfteinden eeuw.' *BMHG* (1922).
—— 'Wijnvaart en wijnhandel tusschen Frankrijk en de Noordelijke Nederlanden in de tweede helft der 15e eeuw.' *BMHG* (1924).
SÖDERBERG, T. *Storra Kopparberget ander Medeltiden.* Stockholm, 1932.
—— 'Det Svenska Bergsbrukets uppkomst.' *Historisk Tidskrift* (1936).
SOMBART, W. *Der moderne Kapitalismus*, 3rd edn., I. Munich and Leipzig, 1913.
STEIN, W. 'Die Hanse und England beim Ausgang des hundert-jährigen Krieges.' *HG*, XXVI (1921), 27–126.
STEINHAUSEN, G. *Der Kaufmann in der deutschen Vergangenheit.* Jena, 1912.
STERCK, J. F. M. 'De opkomst van Aemstelredam godsdienstig en economik.' *Tijdschrift voor Geschiendenis* (1926).
STIEDA, W. *Hildebrand Veckinchusen.* Leipzig, 1921.
—— 'Uber die Quellen der Handelsstatistik im Mittelalter.' *Abhandlungen d. Königl. Preussischen Akad. der Wissenschaften* (1903).
STURLER, J. DE. *Les Relations politiques et les échanges commerciaux entre le duché de Brabant et l'Angleterre au moyen âge.* Paris, 1936.
SWANK, J. M. *History of the Manufacture of Iron in All Ages.* Philadelphia, 1892.
TYLER, J. E. *The Alpine Passes.* Oxford, 1930.
UNGER, W. S. 'De Hollandsche graanhandel en graanhandelspolitiek in de middeleeuwen.' *De Economist* (1916).
UNWIN, G. (ed.). *Finance and Trade under Edward III.* Manchester, 1918.
—— *The Gilds and Companies of London.* The Antiquary's Books, ed. J. C. Cox, 1908.
—— *Studies in Economic History* (Collected Papers), 1927.
USHER, A. P. *The History of the Grain Trade in France.* Cambridge (Mass.), 1913.
VERCAUTEREN, F. *Étude sur les Civitates de la Belgique Seconde.* Brussels, 1934.
VOGEL, W. *Geschichte der deutschen Seeschiffahrt*, I. *Von der Urzeit bis zum Ende des XV. Jahrhunderts.* Berlin, 1915.
—— 'Ein seefahrender Kaufmann um 1100.' *HG* (1912).
VOLLBEHR, F. *Die Holländer und die deutsche Hanse.* Jena, 1930.
WALSH, A. *Scandinavian Relations with Ireland during the Viking Period.* Dublin and London, 1922.
WILLARD, J. F. *Parliamentary Taxes on personal property 1290–1334.* Cambridge (Mass.), 1934.
—— 'Inland Transportation in England during the Fourteenth Century.' *Speculum*, I (1926).
ZYCHA, A. *Das Recht des ältesten deutschen Bergbaues bis ins 13. Jahrhundert.* Berlin, 1899.

III. SUPPLEMENTARY BIBLIOGRAPHY

ADELSON, H. L. 'Early Medieval Trade Routes.' *American Hist. Rev.*, LXV (1960).
AMMANN, H. 'Deutschland und die Tuchindustrie Nordwesteuropas im Mittelalter.' *HG*, LXXII (1954).
BAUTIER, R. H. 'Notes sur le commerce de fer en Europe occidentale du XIIIe au XVIe siècle.' *Revue d'Histoire de la Siderurgie*, I, part 4, 1966.
BOLIN, S. 'Mohammed, Charlemagne and Ruric.' *Scandinavian Econ. Hist. Rev.*, I (1953).
BRANDT, A. VON. *Die Hanse und die nordischen Mächte im Mittelalter.* Cologne, 1962.
BRANDT, L. (ed.). *Die deutsche Hanse als Mittler zwischen Ost und West.* Cologne, 1963.

BRULEZ, W. 'Brugge en Antwerpen in de 15e en 16e eeuw: een tegenstelling?' *Tijdschrift voor Geschiedenis*, LXXXIII (1970).

CARUS-WILSON, E. M. 'La Guède francaise en Angleterre: un grand commerce du moyen âge.' *Revue du Nord*, XXXV (1953).

—— *Medieval Merchant Venturers*. 2nd edn. London, 1967.

CARUS-WILSON, E. M. and COLEMAN, O. *England's Export Trade, 1275–1547*. Oxford, 1963.

CHILDS, W. R. *Anglo-Castilian Trade in the Later Middle Ages*. Manchester, 1978.

CHRISTENSEN, E. 'Scandinavia and the Advance of the Hanseatics.' *Scandinavian Econ. Hist. Rev.*, V (1957).

COORNAERT E. *Les Français et le commerce international à Anvers*. 2 vols. Paris, 1961.

CRAEYBECKX, J. *Un Grand commerce d'importation: les vins de France aux anciens Pays Bas, XIIIe–XVIe siècles*. Paris, 1958.

DE LAET, M. 'De Vlaamse actieve handel op Engeland in de erste helft de 14e eeuw, aan de hand van de Customs Accounts.' *Histoire économique de la Belgique*, I, Brussels: Archives Générales du Royaume, 1972.

DE ROOVER, R. *The Bruges Money Market around 1400*. Brussels, 1968.

DOEHAERD, R. *Études anversoises*. 3 vols. Paris, 1962–3.

DOLLINGER, P. *La Hanse (XIIe-XVIIe siècles)*. Paris, 1964 (English translation by AULT, D. S. and STEINBERG, S. H., *The German Hansa*. London, 1970).

ENNEN, E. *Die europaïsche Stadt des Mittelalters*. Göttingen, 1972.

FRYDE, E. B. *Studies in Medieval Trade and Finance*. London, 1983.

GADE, J. A. *Hanseatic Control of Norwegian Commerce during the Late Middle Ages*. Leyden, 1951.

GRIERSON, P. 'Commerce in the Dark Ages: a critique of the evidence.' *TRHS*, 5th ser., IX (1959).

HANHAM, A. (ed.). *The Cely Letters, 1472–88*. London, 1975.

HATCHER, J. *English Tin Production and Trade before 1550*. Oxford, 1973.

HEERS, J. *L'Occident aux XIVe et XVe siècles: aspects économiques et sociaux*. Paris, 1963.

HILDEBRAND, W. 'Der Goslarer Metalhandel im Mittelalter.' *HG*, LXXXVII (1969).

HIMLY, F. J. 'Y a-t-il emprise musulmane sur l'économie des états Européens du VIIIe au Xe siècle?" *Schweizerische Zeitschrift für Geschichte*, V (1955).

HOLMES, G. A. 'Florentine Merchants in England, 1346–1436.' *EconHR*, 2nd ser., XIII (1960).

JAMES, M. K. *Studies in the Medieval Wine Trade*, ed. E. M. VEALE. Oxford, 1971.

JANKUHN, H. 'Der fränkische-friesische Handel zur Ostsee im frühen Mittelalter.' *VSW*, XI (1953)

JAPPE ALBERTS, W. *De Nederlandse Hansesteden*. Bussum, 1969.

JELLEMA, D. 'Frisian Trade in the Dark Ages.' *Speculum*, XXX (1955).

JOHANSEN, P. *Der hansische Russlandhandel, insbesondere nach Novgorod, in kritischer Betrachtung*. Cologne/Opladen, 1962.

KAEUPER, R. W. *Bankers to the Crown: the Riccardi of Lucca and Edward I*. Princeton, 1973.

—— 'The Frescobaldi of Florence and the English Crown.' *Studies in Medieval and Renaissance History*, Lincoln: Nebraska, X (1973).

KELLENBENZ, H. 'Die Aufstieg Kölns zur mittelalterlichen Handelsmetropole.' *Jahrbuch der Kölner Geschichtsvereins*, XLI (1967).

KERLING, N. J. M. *Commercial Relations of Holland and Zeeland with England from the late Thirteenth Century to the Close of the Middle Ages*. Leyden, 1954.

LATOUCHE, R. *Les Origines de l'économie occidentale (IVe–XIe siècle)*. Paris, 1956.

LESNIKOV, M. 'Lübeck als Handelsplatz für osteuropaïsche Waren im 15. Jahrhundert.' *HG*, LXXVIII (1960).

LEWIS, A. R. *The Northern Seas: shipping and commerce in Northern Europe, A.D. 300–1100*. Princeton, 1958.

LLOYD, T. H. *Alien Merchants in England in the High Middle Ages*. Brighton, 1982.

—— *The English Wool Trade in the Middle Ages*. Cambridge, 1977.

LOMBARD, M. *Espaces et réseaux du haut moyen âge*. Paris, 1972.

LOPEZ, R. S. 'Majorcans and Genoese on the North Sea route in the 13th century.' *RBPH*, XXIX (1951).

LOPEZ, R. S. and MISKIMIN, H. A. 'The Economic Depression of the Renaissance.' *EconHR*, 2nd ser., XIV (1962).

LÜTGE, F. *Strukturwandlung im ostdeutschen und osteuropaïschen Fernhandel des 14. bis 16. Jahrhunderts.* Munich, 1964.

MALLETT, M. E. 'Anglo-Florentine Commercial Relations, 1465–1491.' *EconHR*, 2nd ser., XV (1962).

—— *The Florentine Galleys in the Fifteenth Century.* Oxford, 1967.

MALOWIST, M. *Croissance et régression en Europe, XIVe-XVIIe siècles.* Paris, 1972.

—— 'Pologne, Russie et commerce occidental aux XVe et XVIe siècles.' *Past and Present*, no. 13 (1958).

—— 'The Economic and Social Development of the Baltic countries from the Fifteenth to the Seventeenth Centuries.' *EconHR*, 2nd ser., XII (1959).

—— 'The Problem of the Inequality of Economic Development in Europe in the Later Middle Ages.' *EconHR*, 2nd ser., XIX (1966).

MOLLAT, M. *Le Commerce maritime normand à la fin du moyen âge.* Paris, 1951.

—— (ed.). *Le Rôle du sel dans l'histoire.* Paris, 1968.

MUNRO, J. H. *Wool, Cloth and Gold: the struggle for bullion in Anglo-Burgundian trade, 1340–1478.* Toronto, 1973.

NIERMEYER, J. F. (ed.). *Bronnen voor de economische geschiedenis van het Beneden-Maasgebied*, I (1104–1399). The Hague, 1968.

PERROY, E. 'Le Commerce Anglo-Flamand au XIIIe siècle: la Hanse Flamande de Londres.' *Revue Historique*, CCLII (1974).

POSTAN, M. M. 'Economic Relations between Eastern and Western Europe', in BARRACLOUGH, G. (ed.). *Eastern and Western Europe in the Middle Ages.* London, 1970.

—— *Medieval Trade and Finance.* Cambridge, 1973.

RENOUARD, Y. 'Le Grand commerce des vins de Gascogne au moyen âge.' *Revue Historique*, CCXXI (1959).

—— 'Les Cahorsins, hommes d'affaires français du XIIIe siècle.' *TRHS.*, 5th ser., XI (1961).

—— (ed.). *Histoire de Bordeaux*, III: *Bordeaux sous les rois d'Angleterre.* Bordeaux, 1965.

RÖRIG, F. *Wirtschaftskräfte im Mittelalter: Abhandlungen zur Stadt- und Hansegeschichte*, ed. KAEGBEIN, P. Cologne/Graz, 1959.

RUDDOCK, A. A. *Italian Merchants and Shipping in Southampton, 1270–1600.* Southampton, 1951.

SPROEMBERG, H. 'Die Hanse in europaïscher Sicht.' *Annales de la Société Royale d'Archéologie de Bruxelles*, L (1961).

THIELEMANS, M. R. *Bourgogne et Angleterre: relations politiques et économiques entre les Pays-Bas bourguignons et l'Angleterre, 1435–1467.* Brussels, 1966.

TOUCHARD, H. *Le Commerce maritime breton à la fin du moyen âge.* Paris, 1967.

VAN DER WEE, H. *The Growth of the Antwerp Market and the European Economy (fourteenth to sixteenth centuries).* 3 vols. The Hague, 1963.

VAN HOUTTE, J. A. 'Anvers aux XVe et XVIe siècles: expansion et apogée.' *Annales*, XVI (1961).

—— 'Bruges et Anvers, marchés "nationaux" ou "Internationaux" du XIVe au XVIe siècle.' *Revue du Nord.* XXXIV (1952).

—— 'Die Beziehungen zwischen Köln und den Niederlanden vom Hochmittelalter bis zum Beginn des Industriezeitalters.' *Kölner Vorträge zur Sozial- und Wirtschaftsgesch.*, I (1969).

—— 'The Rise and Decline of the Market of Bruges.' *EconHR*, 2nd ser., XIX (1966).

VAN WERVEKE, H. *Miscellanea Mediaevalia: Verspreide Opstellen over Economische en Sociale Geschiedenis van de Middeleeuwen.* Ghent, 1968.

VEALE, E. M. *The English Fur Trade in the Later Middle Ages.* Oxford, 1966.

VERHULST, A. *Der Handel im Merowingerreich.* Ghent, 1970.

WARNKE, C. *Die Anfänge des Fernhandels in Polen.* Würzburg, 1964.

WATSON, W. B. 'The Structure of the Florentine Galley Trade with England and Flanders in the Fifteenth Century.' *RBPH*, XXXIX–XL (1961–2).
WYFFELS, C. 'De Vlaamse handel op Engeland vóór het Engels-Vlaams konflikt van 1270–74.' *Bijdragen voor de Geschiedenis de Nederlanden*, XVII (1962).

CHAPTER V

The Trade of Medieval Europe: the South

Written in 1946, but published in 1952, the original version of the present chapter has served for almost thirty years as the only available essay that tried to cover the medieval trade of southern Europe as a whole. The author, who more recently presented his latest views on the subject in a little book encompassing the entire economic history of medieval Europe – *The Commercial Revolution of the Middle Ages* (2nd edn, Cambridge, 1976) – cannot bring himself to destroy the child of his youth in order to produce what would have to be a duplication of the product of his advanced maturity. The best solution for a revised edition of the present chapter seemed to be the addition of three fresh introductory sections (I(1); II(1); III(1)) and a limited number of indispensable corrections on the balance of the old text. The bibliography needed a different treatment. The explosion of scholarly publication in the latest thirty to forty years would make it impractical to reprint all of the old titles and add new ones on the same full scale. What follows is only an alphabetical sampling of post-1946 books that seemed noteworthy because of their originality, their method, their coverage, or merely their bibliographical refererences. To fill the gaps and keep abreast with current research, the reader is invited to peruse the most important specialised magazines, the proceedings of international conferences and the collections of essays in honour or in memory of distinguished scholars.

BABEL, A. *Histoire économique de Genève*. 2 vols., Geneva, 1963.
BAER, J. *A History of the Jews in Christian Spain*. 2 vols., Philadelphia, 1961–6.
BARATIER, E. and REYNAUD, F. *Histoire du commerce de Marseille*, II. Paris, 1951.
BAUTIER, R. *The Economic Development of Medieval Europe*. London, 1971.
BECHTEL, H. *Wirtschafts- und Sozialgeschichte Deutschlands: Wirtschaftsstile und Lebensformen*. Munich, 1967.
BERGIER, J. F. *Problèmes de l'histoire économique de la Suisse*. Berne, 1968.
BERNARD, J. *Navires et gens de mer à Bordeaux*. 3 vols., Paris, 1968.
BOWSKY, W. M. *The Finance of the Commune of Siena, 1287–1355*. Oxford, 1970.
BRAUDEL, F. *Civilisation matérielle et capitalisme, XVe–XVIIe siècles*. Paris, 1967.
BRUCKER, G. *Florentine Politics and Society, 1343–1378*. Princeton, 1967.
BURKE, P. *Economy and Society in Early Modern Europe*. New York, 1972.
CAMERON, R. (ed.). *Essays in French Economic History*. Homewood, Ill., 1971.
CARRÈRE, C. *Barcelone, centre économique à l'époque des difficultés*. Paris, 1967.
CASTER, G. *Le Commerce du pastel et de l'épicerie à Toulouse*. Toulouse, 1962.
CIPOLLA, C. M. *Literacy and Development in the West*. Harmondsworth, 1969.
—— *Money, Prices and Civilization in the Mediterranean World*. Princeton, 1956.
—— (ed.). *Storia dell'economia italiana*, I. Turin, 1959.
Constructions civiles d'intérêt public dans les villes d'Europe au Moyen Age. Bruxelles, 1971.
COORNAERT, E. *Les Corporations en France avant 1789*. Paris, 1949.
CORTAZER, J. A. G. *Vizcaya en el siglo XV*. Bilbao, 1966.
CRACCO, G. *Società e stato nel medioevo veneziano*. Florence, 1967.
DE ROOVER, R. *The Rise and Decline of the Medici Bank*. Cambridge, Mass., 1963.
DION, R. *Histoire de la vigne et du vin en France*. Paris, 1959.
DOEHAERD, R. *Le Haut moyen âge occidental: économies et sociétés*. Paris, 1971.
Essays in Memory of Robert L. Reynolds. Kent, Ohio, 1969.
FERGUSON, W. (ed.). *The Renaissance: Six Essays*. New York, 1962.
FICHTENAU, H. *Das Karolingische Imperium*. Zurich, 1949.
Fontana Economic History of Europe, I. London, 1972.
FOSSIER, R. *Histoire sociale de l'Occident médiéval*. Paris, 1970.
FOURNIAL, E. *Les Villes et l'économie d'échange en Forez, XIIIe et XIVe siècles*, Paris 1967.
FOURQUIN, G. *Histoire économique de l'Occident médiéval*. Paris, 1969.
GIMPEL, J. *The Industrial Revolution of the Middle Ages*. New York, 1976.
GIOFFRÉ, D. *Il mercato degli schiavi a Genova nel secolo XV*. Genoa, 1971.

Glénisson, J. and Day, J. *Textes et documents d'histoire du moyen âge*, I, Paris, 1970.
Godinho, V. M., *L'Économie de l'empire portugais aux XVe et XVIe siècles*. Paris, 1969.
Guide international d'histoire urbaine, I, Paris, 1976.
Hale, R. J. (ed.). *Renaissance Venice*. London, 1973.
Handlin, O. and Burchard, J., (eds.). *The Historian and the City*. Cambridge, Mass., 1963.
Havighurst, A. (ed.). *The Pirenne Thesis*. Lexington, Mass., 1958.
Heers, J. *L'Occident aux XIVe et XVe siècles, aspects économiques et sociaux*. Paris, 1966.
Herlihy, D. *Pisa in the Early Renaissance*. New Haven, 1958.
—— *Medieval and Renaissance Pistoia*. New Haven, 1967.
Higounet, C. (ed.). *Histoire de Bordeaux*, II–IV. Bordeaux, 1963–6.
Kedar, B. *Merchants in Crisis, 1270–1400*. New Haven, 1976.
Krekic, B. *Dubrovnik in the XIVth and XVth Centuries*. Norman, Okla., 1972.
Lach, D. *Asia in the Making of Europe*, I. Chicago, 1965.
Lane, F. *Navires et constructeurs à Venise pendant la Renaissance*. Paris, 1965.
—— *Venice, a Maritime Republic*. Baltimore, 1973.
Le Goff, J. *Marchands et banquiers du Moyen Age*. Paris, 1956.
Leighton, A. C. *Transport and Communication in Early Medieval Europe*, Newton Abbot, Devon, 1972.
Lestocquoy, J. *Les Villes de Flandre et d'Italie sous les patriciens*. Paris, 1952.
Lopez, R. S. *The Birth of Europe*. London, 1966.
—— *Il ritorno all'oro nell'Occidente duecentesco*, Naples, 1955.
—— *Su e giù per la storia di Genova*. Genoa, 1975.
—— *The Three Ages of the Italian Renaissance*. Charlottesville, Virginia, 1970.
Lopez, R. S. and Raymond, I. *Medieval Trade in the Mediterranean World*. New York, 1955.
Lütge, F. *Deutsche Sozial- und Wirtschaftsgeschichte*. Berlin, 1966.
Luzzatto, M. *Giovanni Villani e la compagnia dei Buonaccorsi*. Rome, 1971.
—— *An Economic History of Italy to the Beginning of the XVIth Century*. London, 1961.
—— *Storia economica di Venezia dall'XI al XVI secolo*. Venice, 1961.
—— *Studi di storia economica veneziana*. Padua, 1954.
Martines, L. *The Social World of the Florentine Humanists*. Princeton, 1963.
Mélanges en l'honneur de Fernand Braudel. 2 vols., Toulouse, 1974.
Melis, F. *Aspetti della via economica medievale*. Siena, 1962.
—— *Documenti per la storia economica dei secoli XIII–XVI*. Florence, 1972.
Milano, A. *Storia degli Ebrei in Italia*. Turin, 1963.
Miskimin, H. *The Economy of Early Renaissance Europe*. Cambridge, 1975.
Miskimin, H. and Udovich, A. L. (eds.). *The Medieval City: in honor of R. S. Lopez*. New Haven, 1977
Molho, A. *Florentine Public Finances in the Early Renaissance*. Cambridge, Mass., 1971.
Mollat, M. *Le Rôle du sel dans l'histoire*. Paris, 1968.
Mols, R. J. *Introduction à la démographie historique des villes d'Europe*. Louvain, 1954.
Moneta e scambi nell'alto medioevo (XII Settimana, Centro italiano di studi sull'alto medioevo). Spoleto, 1961.
Peyer, H. C. *Zur Getreidepolitik oberitalienischer Städte in 13. Jahrhundert*. Vienna, 1950.
Rau, V. *A exploração e o comercio do sal de Setúbal*. Lisbon, 1951.
Rau, V. and Macedo, J. *O açucar da Madeir aos fins do século XV*. Funchal, 1962.
Renouard, Y. *Études d'histoire médiévale*. Paris, 1968.
—— *Les hommes d'affaires italiens du Moyen Age*, rev. edn., Paris, 1968.
Reynolds, R. L. *Europe Emerges*. Madison, Wis., 1961.
Romero, J. L. *La revolucion burguesa en el mundo feudal*. Buenos Aires, 1967.
Ruiz Martin, F. *La banca en España hasta 1782*, s.d.
Sapori, A. *Le Marchand italien au Moyen Age*. Paris, 1952.
—— *Studi di storia economica*. 3 vols., Florence, 1956–65.
Schnyder, W. *Handel und Verkehr über die Pässe in Mittelalter*, I. Zurich, 1973.
Shatzmiller, J. *Recherches sur la communauté juive de Manosque*. Paris, 1973.

Sociétés et compagnies de commerce en Orient et dans l'Océan indien (VIII Colloque International d'histoire maritime). Paris, 1970.
SPRANDEL, R. *Das Eisengewerbe im Mittelalter*. Stuttgart, 1968.
Storia di Milano (Fondazione Treccani). Milan, 1953–66.
Studi dedicati a Franco Borlandi. Bologna, 1977.
Studi in onore di Gino Luzzatto. 4 vols., Padua, 1949–50.
Studi in onore di Armando Sapori. 2 vols., Milan, 1957.
TANGHERONI, M. *Politica, commercio, agricoltura a Pisa nel Trecento*. Pisa, 1973.
VALDEAVELLANO, G. *Sobre los burgos y los burgueses de la etad medieval*. Madrid, 1960.
VALERI, N. (ed.). *Storia d'Italia*, I. Turin, 1965.
VERLINDEN, C. *L'Esclavage dans l'Europe médiévale*, I. Bruges, 1955.
VICENS VIVES, J. *An Economic History of Spain*. Princeton, 1969.
VIOLANTE, C. *La società milanese nell'eta precomunale*. Bari, 1953.
WALEY, D. *The Italian City-Republics*. London, 1969.
WHITE, L. *Medieval Technology and Social Change*. Oxford, 1962.
WOLFF, P. *Commerces et marchands de Toulouse, 1350–1450*. Paris, 1954.
WOLFF, P. and MAURO, F. *Histoire générale du travail*, I. Paris, 1961.
ZIEGLER, P., *The Black Death*, London, 1969.

CHAPTER VI

Asia, Africa and the Trade of Medieval Europe

The following abbreviations have been used in this bibliography:

EcHR	*Economic History Review*
EI²	*Encyclopaedia of Islam*, 2nd edition. Leiden
ITA	*Islam and the Trade of Asia: a colloquium*, D. S. Richards (ed.). Oxford, 1970
JAH	*Journal of African History*
JESHO	*Journal of the Economic and Social History of the Orient*
JRAS	*Journal of the Royal Asiatic Society*
SCCO	*Sociétés et compagnies de commerce en Orient et dans l'Océan indien. Actes du huitième colloque international d'histoire maritime (Beyrouth, 1966)*, M. Mollat (ed.), Paris, 1970
SCI	*Settimane di studi del Centro italiano di studi sull'alto medioeve*
SEH	*Studies in the Economic History of the Middle East from the rise of Islam to the present day*, M. A. Cook (ed.). London, 1970.
VSW	*Vierteljahrschrift für Sozial- und Wirtschaftsgeschichte*

I. GENERAL

ARNE, T. J. *La Suède et l'Orient: études archéologiques sur les relations de la Suède et de l'Orient pendant l'age des Vikings*. Uppsala, 1914. (= Archives d'Etudes orientales, VIII.)

ASHTOR, E. *Les Métaux précieux et la balance des payements du Proche-Orient à la basse époque*. Paris, 1971.

—— *A Social and Economic History of the Near East in the Middle Ages*. London, 1976.

—— 'Quelques problèmes que soulève l'histoire des prix dans l'Orient médiéval'. M. Rosen-Ayalon (ed.). *Studies in Memory of Gaston Wiet*, Institute of Asian and African Studies, Hebrew University of Jerusalem, 1977, 203–34.

—— 'The Jews in the Mediterranean Trade in the Fifteenth Century', *Wirtschaftskräfte und Wirtschaftswege*, I: *Mittelmeer und Kontinent. Festschrift für Hermann Kellenbenz* (= *Beitrage zur Wirtschaftsgeschichte*, IV). Nuremberg, 1978, 441–54.

—— 'Il regime portuario nel Califfato', *SCI*, XXV: *La navigazione mediterranea nell'alto medioevo*. Spoleto, 1978, 652–88.

—— 'Gli Ebrei nel commercio mediterraneo nell'alto medioevo (sec. X–XI)'. *SCI*, XXVI: *Gli Ebrei nell'Alto Medioevo*. Spoleto, 1980, 401–87.

BLOCH, M. 'Le Problème de l'or au moyen âge', *Annales d'histoire économique et sociale*, V (1933), 1–34 and in: *Land and Work in medieval Europe*. London, 1967.

CAHEN, C. 'L'Histoire économique et sociale de l'Orient musulman médiéval'. *Studia islamica*, III (1955), 93–115.

—— 'Quelques problèmes concernant l'expansion économique musulmane au haut moyen âge', *SCI*, XII (1965), 391–432.

—— 'Quelques mots sur le declin commercial du monde musulman à la fin du Moyen Age', *SEH*, 31–6.

COOK, M. A. (ed.). *Studies in the Economic History of the Middle East from the rise of Islam to the present day*. London, 1970.

DE PLANHOL, X. *Les Fondements géographiques de l'histoire de l'Islam*. Paris, 1968.

DESOMOGYI, J. *A Short History of Oriental Trade*. Hildesheim, 1968.

FISCHEL, W. J. 'The Origins of Banking in Medieval Islam', *JRAS* (1933).

GOITEN, S. D. *Studies in Islamic history and institutions*. Leiden, 1966.

—— 'The Main Industries of the Mediterranean Area as Reflected in the Records of the Cairo Geniza', *JESHO*, IV (1961), 168–97.

—— 'Mediterranean Trade in the Eleventh Century: some facts and problems', *SEH*, repr. from *Diogenes*, LIX (1967).

HINZ, W. *Islamische Masse und Gewichte*. Leiden, 1955.

HODGES, R. and WHITEHOUSE, D. *Mohammed, Charlemagne, and the origins of Europe*. London, 1983.

JACOB, GEORG. *Der nordisch-baltische Handel der Araber im Mittelalter*. Leipzig, 1887.

LAMBTON, A. K. S. 'The Merchant in Medieval Islam'. *A Locust's Leg. Studies in honour of S. H. Taqizadeh*. London, 1962, 121–30.

LAPIDUS, I. M. *Muslim Cities in the Later Middle Ages*. Cambridge, Mass., 1967; new edn, Cambridge, England, 1984.

LEVY, R. *The Social Structure of Islam*. Cambridge, 1965.

LIEBER, A. E. 'Eastern Business Practice and Medieval European Commerce', *EcHR*, 2nd ser., XXI (1968), 230–43.

LØKKEGAARD, F. *Islamic Taxation in the Classical Period*. Copenhagen, 1950.

LOMBARD, M. *The Golden Age of Islam*, transl. Joan Spencer. Amsterdam–New York–Oxford, 1975 (transl. from *L'Islam dans sa première grandeur*. Paris, 1971).

RABINOWITZ, L. I. *Jewish Merchant Venturers*. London, 1948.

RICHARDS, D. S. (ed.). *Islam and the Trade of Asia: a colloquium*. Oxford, 1970.

RODINSON, M. *Islam and Capitalism*. (Eng. transl.) London, 1974.

—— 'Le Marchand musulman', *ITA*, 21–35.

—— 'Histoire économique et histoire des classes sociales dans le monde musulman', *SEH*, 139–55.

SABBE, E. 'L'Importation des tissues orientaux en Europe occidentale au Haut Moyen Age (IXe et Xe siècles)'. *Revue belge de philologie et d'histoire*, XIV (1935), 811–48 and 1261–88.

SCHAUBE, A. *Handelsgeschichte der Romanischen Völker des Mittelmeergebiets bis zum Ende der Kreuzzüge*. Munich–Berlin, 1906.

SERJEANT, R. B. 'Material for a History of Islamic Textiles up to the Mongol Conquest'. *Ars islamica*, XIII–XIV (1948), 75–117.

SIMONSEN, D. 'Les Marchands juifs appelés "Radanites"', *Revue des études juives*, LIV (1907), 141–2.

UDOVITCH, A. L. *Partnership and Profit in Medieval Islam*. Princeton, N.J., 1970.

—— 'At the Origins of the Western *Commenda*: Islam, Israel, Byzantium?' *Speculum*, XXXVII (1962), 198–207.

—— 'Credit as Means of Investment in Medieval Islamic Trade'. *Journal of the American Oriental Society*, LXXXVII (1967), 260–4.

—— 'Labor partnerships in medieval Islamic law', *JESHO*, X (1967), 64–80.

—— 'Commercial Techniques in Early Medieval Islamic Trade'. ITA, 37–65.

WATSON, A. *Agricultural Innovation in the Early Islamic World*. Cambridge, 1983.

—— 'Back to Gold – and Silver', *EcHR*. 2nd ser., XX (1967), 1–34.

II. EGYPT AND SYRIA

ALLMENDINGER, K.-H. *Die Beziehungen zwischen der Kommune Pisa und Ägypten im hohen Mittelalter. Eine Rechts- und Wirtschaftshistorische Untersuchung. VSW*, Beiheft no. 54. Wiesbaden, 1967.

AMARI, M. 'Nuovi ricordi arabici su la storia di Genova', *Atti della Società ligure di storia patria*, V (1873).

ASHTOR, E. *Levant Trade in the later Middle Ages*. Princeton, N.J., 1983.

—— 'L'Exportation de textiles occidentaux dans le Proche Orient musulman au bas Moyen Age (1370–1517)'. *Studi in memoria di Federigo Melis*, II, Naples, 1978, 303–77.

—— 'The Karimi Merchants', *JRAS* (1956), 45–56 and in *Studies on the Levantine Trade in the Middle Ages*. London (Variorum), 1978.

—— 'New Data for the History of Levantine Jewries in the Fifteenth Century', *Bulletin of the Institute of Jewish Studies* (London), III (1975), 67–102.

—— 'The Volume of Levantine Trade in the Later Middle Ages (1370–1498)', *Journal of European Economic History*, IV (1975), 573–612, and in *Studies...(Supra)*.

ATIYA, A. S. *Egypt and Aragon. Embassies and diplomatic correspondence between 1300 and 1330 A.D. Abhandlungen für die kunde des Morgenlandes*, XXXIII, 7. Leipzig, 1938.

AUBIN, J. 'La Mine de Siraf et les routes du Golfe Persique', *Cahiers de civilisation médiévale*, X–XII (1959), 287–99.
AYALON, D. 'The System of Payment in Mamluk Military Society', *JESHO*, I (1958), 37–65 and 257–96.
BALOG, P. *The Coinage of the Mamluk Sultans of Egypt and Syria*. New York, 1964.
BARTHOLD, W. *Turkestan down to the Mongol Invasion* (E. J. W. Gill Memorial Series, n.s., v.). London, 1968.
BLAKE, R. P. 'The Circulation of Silver in the Moslem East down to the Mongol Epoch', *Harvard Journal of Asiatic Studies*, II (1937), 291–328.
CAHEN, C. 'Un Text peu connu relatif au commerce oriental d'Amalfi au Xe siècle', *Archivio storico per le provincie napoletane*, N.S. XXXIV (1953/54).
—— 'Douanes et commerce dans les ports mediterranéens de l'Egypt mediévale après le *Minhadj* d'al-Makhzumi', *JESHO*, VII (1964), 217–314. Cf. 'Un Traité financier inédit de l'époque Fatimide-Ayyubide', *ibid.*, V (1962), 139–59. 'Contribution à l'étude des impots dans l'Egypte médiévale', *ibid.*, V (1962), 244–78.
—— 'Le Commerce musulman dans l'océan Indien au Moyen Age', *SCCO*, 179–93.
DARRAG, A. *L'Égypte sous le règne de Barsbay 825–841/1422–1438*. Damascus, 1961.
DE BOÜARD, M. 'Sur l'évolution monétaire de l'Égypte médiéval'. *L'Égypte contemporaine*, XXX. Cairo, 1939.
EHRENKREUTZ, A. 'Studies in the Monetary History of the Near East in the Middle Ages', *JESHO*, II (1959), 128–61; VI (1963), 243–77.
—— 'Monetary Aspects of Medieval Near Eastern Economic History'. *SEH*, 37–50.
FISCHEL, W. J. *Jews in the Economic and Political Life of Medieval Islam*, Royal Asiatic Society monographs, XXII. London, 1937.
—— 'Uber die Gruppe der Karimi-Kaufleute. (Ein Beitrag zur Geschichte des Orienthandels Ägyptens unter den Mameluken).' Fr. ROSENTHAL, G. von GRÜNEBAUM, W. J. FISCHEL, *Studia Arabica*, I (*Analecta Orientalia*, XIV), 67–82. Rome, 1937.
—— 'The Spice-Trade in Mamluk Egypt', *JESHO*, I (1958), 157–74.
GOITEIN, S. D. 'From the Mediterranean to India: documents on the trade to India, South Arabia and East Africa from the eleventh and twelfth centuries', *Speculum*, XXIX (1954), 181–97.
—— 'New Light on the Beginnings of the Karimi Merchants', *JESHO*, I (1958), 175–84.
—— 'Letters and documents on the India trade in medieval times', *Islamic Culture*, XXXVII (1963), 188–205.
—— *A Mediterranean Society: the Jewish communities of the Arab world as portrayed in the documents of the Cairo Geniza*. I: *Economic Foundations*. Berkeley–Los Angeles, 1967.
HEYD, W. *Histoire du commerce du Levant au moyen âge*, édition française de Furcy Raynaud, 2 vols., Leipzig, 1885–6.
LABIB, S. Y. *Handelsgeschichte Ägyptens im Spätmittelalter* (*1171–1517*), *Vierteljahrschrift fur Sozial- und Wirtschaftsgeschichte*, Beiheft nr. 46. Wiesbaden, 1965.
—— 'Egyptian Commercial Policy in the Middle Ages', *SEH*, 63–77.
—— 'Geld und Kredit. Studien zur Wirtschaftsgeschichte Ägyptens im Mittelalter'. *JESHO*, II (1959), 225–46.
—— 'Les Marchands Karimis en Orient et sur l'Océan Indien', *SCCO*, 209–14.
—— 'Karimi, *EI*²', IV, 640–3.
LAPIDUS, I. M. 'The Grain Economy of Mamluk Egypt', *JESHO*, XII (1969), 1–15.
LEWIS, B. 'The Fatimids and the Route to India', *Revue de la Faculté des sciences économiques de l'Université d'Istambul*, XI (1949/50).
NAURA, R. 'Les Karimis aux Archives de Venise' (lettre). *JESHO*, I (1958), 333.
POPPER, W. *Egypt and Syria under the Circassian Sultans, 1382–1468 A.D. Systematic notes to ibn Taghri Birdi's chronicles of Egypt*. 2 vols., Berkeley-Los Angeles, 1955 and 1957.
RABIE, H. *The Financial System of Egypt, A.H. 564–741/A.D. 1169–1341*. London oriental series, XXV. London, 1972.
—— *The size and value of the iqta' in Egypt, 564–741/1169–1341*.' *SEH*.
RILEY-SMITH, J. 'Government in Latin Syria and the Commercial Privileges of Foreign

Merchants', in D. Baker (ed.), *Relations between East and West in the Middle Ages*. Edinburgh, 1973.

SHAKED, S. *A Tentative Bibliography of Geniza Documents*. Paris–The Hague, 1964.

SOBERNHEIM, M. 'Das Zuckermonopol unter Sultan Barsbai', *Zeitschrift für Assyriologie und verwandte Gebiete*, XXVII (1912).

STERN, S. M. 'An original document from the Fatimid Chancery concerning Italian Merchants', *Studi orientalistici in onore di G. Levi della Vida*, II (1956), 529–38.

—— 'Ramisht of Siraf, a merchant millionaire of the twelfth century', *JRAS* (1967), 10–14.

WIET, G. 'Les Marchands d'épices sous les soultans mamlouks', *Cahiers d'histoire égyptienne*, VII (1955), 81–147.

ZIADA, N. *Urban Life in Syria under the Early Mamluks*. Beirut, 1953.

III. NORTH AFRICA AND THE SAHARA

ABDUL-WAHAB, H. H. 'Deux dinars normands de Mahdia', *Revue tunisienne*, N.S., I (1930), 215–18.

ABULAFIA, D. S. H. *The Two Italies: economic relations between the Norman Kingdom of Sicily and the northern communes*. Cambridge, 1977.

—— 'L'attivita genovese nell'Africa normanna: la citta di Tripoli', *Atti del Congresso internazionale di studi sulla Sicilia normanna*. Palermo, 1973.

—— 'Maometto e Carlomagno: le due aree monetarie italiane dell'oro e dell'argento', *Storia d'Italia: Annali*, VI: *Economia naturale, economia monetaria*, ed. R. ROMANO and U. TUCCI. Turin, 1983, 223–70.

ABUN-NASR, J. M. *History of the Maghrib*. Cambridge, 1971.

AMAR, E. *La Pierre de touche des fetwas*, 2 vols. (= *Archives marocaines* XII-XIII, Paris, 1908–9 (al-Mi'yar of al-Wansharishi)).

AMARI, M. *I diplomi arabi del R. Archivio Fiorentino*. Florence, 1863.

BOVILL, E. W. *The Golden Trade of the Moors*, 2nd edn, rev. by Robin Hallett. London, 1968, cf. 1st edn, 1958; cf. *Caravans of the Old Sahara*, 1933.

BRAUDEL, F. 'De l'Or du Soudan à l'argent des Ameriques', *Annales* (1946).

BRETT, M. 'Ifriqiya as a Market for Saharan Trade from the 10th to the 12th Century A.D.', *JAH*, X (1969), 640–51.

—— 'Problems in the Interpretation of the History of the Maghrib in the light of some recent publications', *JAH*, XIII (1972), 489–506.

BRUNSCHVIG, R. *La Berbérie orientale sous les Hafsides*. 2 vols., Paris, 1940, 1947.

COURTOIS, C. 'Remarques sur le commerce maritime en Afrique au XIe siècle', *Mélanges G. Marçais*, Algiers, 1957, II, 51–9.

DE MAS LATRIE, L. *Traités de paix et de commerce et documents divers concernant les relations des Chrétiens avec les Arabes de l'Afrique septentrionale au Moyen Age*, 2 vols. Paris, 1866, 1872.

DUFOURCQ, C. E. *L'Espagne catalane et le Maghrib au XIIIe et XIVe siècles. De la bataille de Las Navas de Tolosa (1212) à l'avènement du sultan merinide Abou-l-Hasan (1331)*. Paris, 1965.

GOITEIN, S. D. 'Sicily and Southern Italy in the Cairo Geniza Documents', *Archivio storico per la Sicilia orientale*, LXVII (1971).

GOLVIN, L. *Le Magrib central a l'époque des Zirides, recherches d'archéologie et d'histoire*. Paris, 1957.

HAZARD, H. W. *The Numismatic History of Late Medieval North Africa*. American Numismatic Society, Numismatic Studies No. 8. New York, 1952.

IDRIS, H. R. *La Berbérie orientale sous les Zirides, Xe-XIIe siècles*, 2 vols. Publications de l'Institut d'Études orientales, Faculté des Lettres et Sciences humaines d'Alger, no. XXII. Paris, 1962.

IMAMUDDIN, S. M. *Some Aspects of the Socio-Economic and Cultural History of Muslim Spain, 711–1492 A.D.* Leiden, 1965.

JOHNSON, M. 'The Cowrie Currencies of West Africa', *JAH*, XI (1970), 331–53.

JULIEN, C. A. *History of North Africa, to 1830*. London, 1970.

KIRKMAN, J. S. 'The Coast of Kenya as a Factor in the Trade and Culture of the Indian Ocean', *SCCO*, 247–53.
KRUEGER, H. C. 'Genoese Trade with Northwest Africa in the Twelfth Century', *Speculum*, VIII (1933), 377–95.
—— 'Wares of exchange in Twelfth-Century Genoese–African Trade', *Speculum*, XII (1937), 57–71.
LEVTZION, N. *Ancient Ghana and Mali*, Studies in African History, VII. London, 1973.
—— 'Ibn Hawqal, the Cheque and Awdaghust', *JAH*, IX (1968), 223–33.
LOPEZ, R. S. 'Back to gold, 1252', *EcHR*, 2nd ser. IX (1956), 219–40.
MAGALHAES GODINHO, V. *O Mediterraneo saariano e as caravans de ouro*. São Paulo, 1956.
MAUNY, R. *Les Siècles obscurs de l'Afrique noire: histoire et archéologie*. Paris, 1970.
OLIVER, R. (ed.). *The Middle Age of African History*. London, 1967.
PACHA (née SOUISSI), N. *Le Commerce du Maghreb du XIe au XIVe siècles*. Faculté de Lettres et Sciences humaines de Tunis, Quatrième serie: Histoire, XVII. Tunis, 1976. (French & Arabic texts.)
SAYOUS, A. E. *Le Commerce des Européens à Tunis depuis le XIIe siècle jusqu'à la fin du XVIe*. Paris, 1929.
STERN, S. M. 'Tari', *Studi medievali*, 3rd ser. XI (1970), 177–207.

IV. EAST AFRICA

CHITTICK, N. 'East African Trade with the Orient', *ITA*, 97–104.
DUYVENDAK, J. J. L. *China's Discovery of Africa*. London, 1949.
FILESI, T. *Le relazioni della Cina con l'Africa nel Medio Evo*. Milan, 1962 (also Eng. transl. London, 1972, *China and Africa in the Middle Ages*).
FREEMAN-GRENVILLE, G. S. P. *The Medieval History of the Coast of Tanganyika*. London, 1962.
KIRKMAN, J. S. *Monuments and Men on the East African Coast*. London. 1964.
—— 'The Coast of Kenya as a Factor in the Trade and Culture of the Indian Ocean', *SCCO*, 247–53.
WHEATLEY, P. 'The Land of Zanj – Chinese knowledge of E. Africa', *Geographers and the Tropics: Liverpool Essays*. London, 1964.

V. THE INDIAN OCEAN

CARSWELL, J. 'Archaeology and the Study of Later Islamic Pottery', *ITA*, 63–5.
DIGBY, S. 'The Maritime Trade of India', *Cambridge Economic History of India*, I (*1200–c. 1790*). Cambridge, 1982, 125–59.
GROSSET-GRANGE, H. 'Les Procédés arabes de navigation en Océan Indien au moment des grandes découvertes', *SCCO*, 227–46.
HOURANI, G. F. *Arab Seafaring in the Indian Ocean in Ancient and early Medieval Times*. Princeton, N.J., 1951.
POUJADE, J. *La Route des Indes et ses navires*. 1949.
MOLLAT, M. (ed.). *SCCO*.
RICHARD, J. 'Les Navigations des Occidentaux sur l'Océan Indien et la Mer Caspienne (XIIe-XVe siècles)', *SCCO*, 353–63.
SERJEANT, R. B. 'Maritime Customary Law off the Arabian Coasts'. *SCCO*, 195–207.
VERIN, P. 'Les Éstablissements islamiques sur les côtes de Madagascar', *SCCO*, 225–9.

VI. INDONESIA AND MALAYA

BASTIN, J. and ROOLVINI, R. (eds.). *Malayan and Indonesian Indies: essays presented to Sir Richard Winstedt*. Oxford, 1964. (Wheatley, Wang Gungwu, etc.)
COEDÈS, G. *Les États hindouisées d'Indochine et d'Indonésie*, 3rd edn. Paris, 1964. *The Indianized States of Southeast Asia*, trans. S. B. Cowing, ed. W. F. Vella. Honolulu, 1968.

ARMANDO CORTESÃO and TOMÉ PIRES (eds.). *The Suma Oriental and the Book of Francisco Rodrigues*. Hakluyt Soc., 2nd ser. LXXXIX & XC. 2 vols., London, 1944.

DI MEGLIO, R. R. 'Arab Trade with Indonesia and the Malay Peninsula from the 8th to the 16th century', *ITA*, 105–35.

FERRAND, G. 'L'Empire sumatranais de Çrivijaya', *Journal Asiatique*, XX, (1922).

JOHNS, A. H. 'Sufism as a Category in Indonesian Literature and History'. Unpublished: typewritten copy in the Sociological-historical seminar for S.E. Asia of the Univ. of Amsterdam, 1955.

KROM, N. J. *Hindoe-Javansche Geschiedenis*. 'sGravenhage, 1926.

MEILINK-ROELOFSZ, M. A. P. *Asian Trade and European Influence in the Indonesian Archipelago between 1500 and about 1630*. The Hague, 1962.

—— 'Trade and Islam in the Malay-Indonesian Archipelago prior to the Arrival of the Europeans', *ITA*, 137–57.

SCHRIEKE, B. J. O. *Indonesian Sociological Studies*, vols. I and II. The Hague–Bandung, 1955, 1957.

TIBBETTS, G. R. 'Early Muslim Traders in S.E. Asia', *Journal of the Malayan Branch of the Royal Asiastic Society*, XXX (1957), 1–45.

TICHELMAN, FRITJOF. *The Social Evolution of Indonesia: the Asiatic mode of production and its legacy*. (International Institute of Social History, Amsterdam). The Hague–Boston–London, 1980.

VAN LEUR, J. C. 'On Early Asian Trade'; 'The World of S.E. Asia'; in: J. C. VAN LEUR, *Indonesian Trade and Society, Essays in Asian Social and Economic History*. The Hague–Bandung, 1955. 2nd edn, 1967.

WANG GUNGWU, 'The Nanhai Trade', *Journal of the Malaysian Branch of the Royal Asiatic Society*, XXXI (1958), 31–61, 118–23.

—— 'Early Ming Relations with S.E. Asia', in: *The Chinese World Order*, ed. J. K. FAIRBANK. Cambridge, Mass., 1968, 34–62.

WHEATLEY, P. *The Golden Khersonese. Studies in the historical geography of the Malay Peninsula before A.D. 1500*. Kuala Lumpur, 1961.

WOLTERS, O. W. *Early Indonesian Commerce. A study of the origins of Srivijaya*. Ithaca, 1967.

—— *The Fall of Śrīvijaya in Malay History*. London, 1970.

VII. CHINA

DI MEGLIO, R. R. 'Il commercio arabo con la Cina dalla Gahiliyya al X secolo'. *Annali dell'Istituto universitario orientale di Napoli* (1964), 539–40; and 'Il commercio arabo con la Cina dal X secolo all'avvento dei Mongoli', *ibid.* (1965), 89–95.

FERRAND, G. *Relations de voyages et textes géographiques arabes, persans et turks relatifs à l'Extrême-Orient du VIIIe au XVIIe siècles* (Documents historiques et géographiques relatifs à l'Indochine). Paris, 1914.

HIRTH, F. and ROCKHILL, W. W. *Chau Ju-Kua*. St Petersburg, 1911.

HUDSON, G. F. 'The Medieval Trade of China', *ITA*, 159–67.

LO JUNG-PANG, 'Chinese Shipping and East-West Trade from the Tenth to the Fourteenth Century', *SCCO*, 167–76.

NEEDHAM, J. 'Abstract of Material Presented to the International Maritime History Commission at Beirut'. *SCCO*, 139–65.

ROCKHILL, W. W. 'Notes on the Relations and Trade of China with the Eastern Archipelago and the Coasts of the Indian Ocean during the XIVth century'. *T'oung Pao*, XVI (1915).

ROGERS, M. 'China and Islam – the Archaeological Evidence in the Mashriq', *ITA*, 67–80.

SATO, K. 'On the Form of Maritime Trade and Commerce in the Near East and the Far East from the 20th to the 13th century CE', *Proceedings of the Second Biennial Conference of the International Association of Historians of Asia*. Taipei, 1962.

SCANLON, G. T. 'Egypt and China: trade an imitation', *ITA*, 81–95.

SPULER, B. 'Trade in the Eastern Islamic Countries in the Early Centuries', *ITA*, 11–20.

WANG GUNGWU, '"Public" and "Private" Overseas Trade in Chinese History', *SCCO*, 215–26.

VIII. TURKEY

CAHEN, C. *Pre-Ottoman Turkey*. London, 1968.
—— 'L'Alun avant Phocée, un chapitre d'histoire économique islamo-chrétienne au temps des Croisades'. *Revue d'histoire économique et sociale*, XLI (1963), 433–47.

CHAPTER VII

Trade and Industry in Eastern Europe before 1200

The following abbreviations have been used in this bibliography:

AESC	*Annales: Economies, Sociétés, Civilisations*
EcHR	*Economic History Review*
KHKM	*Kwartalnik Historii Kultury Materialnej*
SSCI	*Settimane di Studio del Centro italiano di studi sull'alto medioevo*
VI	*Voprosy Istorii*

I. INTRODUCTION

Gieysztor, A. 'Les Structures économiques en pays slaves à l'aube du Moyen Age jusqu'au XIe siècle et l'échange monétaire.' *SSCI*, ix. Spoleto, 1961. 455–518.

—— 'Local Markets and Foreign Exchanges in Central and East Europe before 1200.' *KHKM*, xiv (1966) (= *Ergon*, v), 761–77.

—— 'Villes et campagnes slaves du Xe au XIIIe siècle.' *Deuxième conférence internationale d'histoire économique, Aix-en-Provance 1963*, Paris, 1965, ii, 38–105.

Grierson, Ph. 'Commerce in the Dark Ages.' *Trans. Royal Historical Society*, 5th Ser. ix (1959), 123–43.

Istoriya kultury drevney Rusi, i, Moscow, 1948 (History of the Old Russian Civilisation). (Contributions by P. N. Tretyakov, B. A. Rybakov, N. N. Voronin and B. A. Romanov.)

Manteuffel, T. and Gieysztor, A. (eds.). *L'Europe au IXe – XIe siècles. Aux origines des États nationaux.* Warsaw, 1968. (Contributions by H. Bulin, A. V. Soloviev, H. Łowmiański, R. Kiersnowksi.)

Słownik Starożytności Słowińskich – Lexicon Antiquitatum Slavicarum. Summarium historiae, cultus humanitatis Slavorum. I–III (A–I), Wrocław, 1961–7. (Contributions by G. Labuda, H. Ziółkowska, A. Gieysztor, Wł. kowalenko, T. Lewicki, T. Wasilewski, A. Poppe, H. Chłopocka and R. Kiersnowski.)

Studien zu den Anfangen des europäischen Städtewesens. Reichenau-Vorträge, 1955–6. *Vorträge und Forschungen*, ed. Th. Meyer, iv. Lindau-Konstanz, 1958. (Contributions by W. Schlesinger, B. Schwineköper, H. Jankuhn, P. Johansen and H. Ludat.)

Widera, B. 'Waren-Geld Beziehungen, Silber- und Silberbergbau im frühen Mittelalter in Osteuropa im Lichte neuer Literatur.' *Jahrb. für Wirtschaftsgeschichte*, ii (1961), 321–31.

II. LONG-DISTANCE TRADE IN CENTRAL AND EASTERN EUROPE FROM THE EIGHTH TO THE TWELFTH CENTURY

(1) *General Works*

Agus, I. A. *Urban Civilization in pre-Crusade Europe. A Study of Organized Town-life in Northwestern Europe during the Tenth and Eleventh Centuries based on the Response Literature.* 2 vols., Leiden, 1965.

Blake, R. P. 'The Circulation of Silver in the Moslem East down to the Mongol Epoch.' *Harvard Journal of Asiatic Studies*, ii (1937), 291–328.

Blumenkranz, B. *Juifs et chrétiens dans le monde occidental 430–1096.* Paris–The Hague, 1960.

Bolin, S. 'Mohammed, Charlemagne and Ruric.' *Scandinavian Economic History Review*, i (1953), 5–29.

Cahen, C. 'Quelques problèmes concernant l'expansion économique musulmane au haut Moyen Age.' *SSCI*, xii. Spoleto, 1965, 391–432.

Cipolla, C. 'Sans Mahomet, Charlemagne est inconcevable.' *AESC*, xvii (1962), 130–6.

Davidovitch, E. A. 'Gorod, remeslo i denezhnoe obrashchenie v sredney Azii perioda tak nazyvaemogo "serebrianogo krizisa" XI–XIII v.' (Town, craft and money

circulation in middle Asia during the so-called silver crisis, XI–XIII centuries). *Materialy Vtorogo soveshtchania arkeologov i etnografov sredney Azii*. Moscow, 1959.
GRIERSON, P. 'The Monetary Reforms of Abd al-Malik.' *J. Econ. and Social History of the Orient*, III (1960), 241–64.
HENSEL, W. *Słowianszczyzna wczesnośredniowieczna. Zarys kultury materialnej* (The Slavs in the early Middle Ages. Outline of their material civilization), 3rd edn. Warsaw, 1965.
HIMLY, FR. 'Y a-t-il une emprise musulmane sur l'économie des états européens du VIIIe au Xe siècle?' *Rev. suisse d'histoire*, V (1955),
KIERSNOWSKI, R. *Pieniadz kruszcowy w Polsce wczesnośredniowiecznej* (Metallic money in early medieval Poland). Warsaw, 1960.
KUPFER, FR., and LEWICKI, T. (eds.). *Zródła hebrajskie do dziejów Słowian i niektórych innych ludów środkowej i wschodniej Europy* (Hebrew sources for the history of the Central and East European Slav nations). Wrocław, 1956.
LEWICKI, T. *Zródła arabskie do dziejów Slowiańszczyzny* (Arabic sources for the history of the Slavs), I. Wrocław, 1956.
—— 'Les Sources hebraïques consacrées à l'histoire de l'Europe centrale et orientale, et particulièrement à celle des pays slaves de la fin du IXe siècle au milieu du XIIIe siècle.' *Cahiers du Monde Russe et Soviétique*, II (1961), 228–41.
LIEBER, A. E. 'Eastern Business Practices and Medieval European Commerce.' *EcHR*, 2nd ser., XXI (1968), 230–43.
ŁOWMIAŃSKI, H. *Podstawy gorspodarcze formowania się państw słowiańskich* (Economic basis of Slavonic states). Warsaw, 1953.
—— 'La Génèse des états slaves et ses bases sociales et économiques.' *La Pologne au Xe Congrès international des Sciences historiques à Rome*. Warsaw, 1955, 29–53.
Mezhdunarodnyie svyazi Rossii do XVII v. (Russia's international ties up to the 17th century). Moscow, 1961. (Contributions by B. N. ZAKHODER, M. V. FEKHNER, J. A. LIMONOV, A. V. FLOROVSKY and V. M. POTIN.)
NOVOSELTZEV, A. P. and PASHUTO, V. T. *Vneshnaya torgovlya drevney Rusi (do serediny* XIII *v.)* (Foreign trade of old Russia until the mid-13th century). *Istoriya SSSP*, v. 3 (1967), 81–107.
SZTETYŁŁO, J. 'Handel a wymiana. Z problemów spornych ekonomiki starożytnej i wczesnośredniowiecznej.' (Trade and exchanges. Some controversial problems in ancient and medieval economy). *KHKM*, IX (1961), 809–18.
WATSON, A. M. 'Back to Gold – and Silver.' *EcHR*, 2nd ser., XX (1967), 1–34.

(2) *Eastern Europe between Scandinavia and Central Asia*

ARTAMONOV, M. I. *Istoriya Khazar* (History of the Khazars). Leningrad, 1962.
BIRNBAUM, H. 'An Old Russian and Old Scandinavian Legal Language.' *Scando-Slavica*, VIII (1962), 115–40.
HRBEK, J. 'Vývoj a dnésni stav studiû arabských prámenû o slovanstvu' (Past development and present state of studies on Arabic sources about the Slavs). *Vznik a počatký slovanů* (Prague), V (1964), 26–95.
LEWICKI, T. 'Il commercio arabo con la Russia e con i paesi slavi d'Occidente nei secoli IX–XI.' *Annali dell' Istituto Universitario Orientale di Napoli*, N.S. VIII (1959), 47–61.
—— 'O cenach neiktórych towarów na rynkach wschodniej Europy w IX–XI w' (Prices of certain goods in East European markets in the 9th–11th centuries). *KHKM*, V (1953), 113–32.
ŁOWMIAŃSKI, H. *Zagadnienie roli Normanów w genezie państw słowianskich* (Problem of the Norman role in the origins of the Slav states). Warsaw, 1957.
—— 'Critique de la théorie de l'origine normande des états slaves.' *Studi in onore di Armando Sapori*. Milan, 1957, I, 149.
MARKOV, A. *Topografiya kladov vostoc nykh monet (sasanidskikh i kufitcheskikh)* (Topography of eastern (Sassanid and kufic) coin hoards). St Petersburg, 1910.
MINORSKY, V. F. *Istoriya Sirvana i Derbenta X–XII vv* (History of Shirvan and Derbent). Moscow, 1963.

SAWYER, P. H. *The Age of the Vikings*. London, 1962.

ZAJĄCZKOWSKI, A. 'Khazarian and its inheritors.' *Acta Orientalia Academiae Scientiarum Hungariae*, XII (1961), 299–307.

(3) *Slavonic Slaves in the Mediterranean*

HOFFMAN, J. 'Die östliche Adriaküste als Hauptnachschubbasis für den venezianischen Sklavenhandel bis zum Ausgang des 11.Jh.' *Vierteljahrsschrift für Sozial- und Wirtschaftsgeschichte*, LV (1968), 165–81.

LEWICKI, T. 'Osadnictwo slowianskie i niewolnicy slowianscy w karjach muzulmanskich wedlug średniowiecznych pisarzy arabskich' (Slavonic settlements and Slavonic slaves in the Muslim countries in medieval Arabic writings). *Przegląd Historyczny, Warszawa*, XLIII (1952), 473–91.

VERLINDEN, C. *L'Esclavage dans l'Europe médiévale*. I, *Péninsule Ibérique-France*. Bruges, 1955.

(4) *The Call of Byzantium*

ANTONIADIS-BIBICOU, H. *Recherches sur les douanes à Byzance. L'*octava, *le* kommerkion *et les commerciaires*. Paris, 1963.

DUJCEV, I. 'Rapporti economici fra Bisanzio e gli Slavi.' *Bollettino dell' Istituto Storico Italiano per il Medioevo*, LXXVI (1964), 1–30.

GRIERSON, P. H. 'Byzantine Coinage as Source Material.' *Thirteenth International Congress of Byzantine Studies. Main Papers*, X. Oxford, 1966.

KROPOTKIN, V. V. *Klady vizantiyskikh monet na territorii SSSR* (Hoards of Byzantine coins in USSR territory). Moscow, 1962.

LEVTCHENKO, V. M. *Otcherki po istorii russkovizantiyskikh otnoshenii* (Essays on the history of Byzantino-Russian relations). Moscow, 1956.

LITAVRIN, G. G., KAZHDAN, A. P. and UDALTSOVA, Z. V. 'Otnosheniya drevney Rusi i Vizantii v XI-pervoy polovine XIII v' (Contacts of old Russia with Byzantium, 11th–mid-13th century). *Thirteenth International Congress of Byzantine Studies, Main Papers*, III. Oxford, 1966.

POŜVAR, J. 'Die byzantinische Wahrung und das grossmährische Reich.' *Byzantinoslavica*, XXVI, 2 (1965), 308–17.

STENDER-PETERSON, A. 'Das Problem der ältesten byzantinisch-russisch-nordischen Beziehungen.' *X Congresso internazionale di scienze storiche, Relazioni*, III. Florence, 1955, 165–88.

(5) *The Baltic Trade and the Slavs*

ARBMANN, H. *Schweden und das karolingische Reich. Studien zu den Handelsverbindungen der 9.Jh.* Stockholm, 1957.

CHRISTIANSEN, A. E. 'Scandinavia and the Advance of the Hanseatics.' *Scandinavian Economic History Review* (1958), 89–117. *IX–XI in Suecia repertis*. Stockholm, 1961. *Commentationes de nummis saeculorum.*

HOFFMEISTER, A. *Der Kampf um die Ostsee vom 9. bis 12.Jh.*, 3rd edn. Lübeck, 1960.

JANKUHN, H. *Haithhabu. Ein Handelsplatz der Wikinger*. 4th edn, Neumünster, 1963.

JOHANSEN, P. 'Novogorod und die Hanse.' *Städtewesen und Bürgertum als geschichtliche Kräfte. Gedächtnisschrift für F. Rörig*. Lübeck, 1953.

KMIETOWICZ, F. 'Drogi napływu srebra arabskiego na południowe wybrzeza Bałtyku i przynależnosc etniczna jego nosicieli' (The routes of the flow of Arabic silver to the southern coast of the Baltic and the nationalities of its carriers). *Wiadomości Numizmatyczne*, XII (1968), 65 — 86.

LABUDA, G. *Zródła skandynawskie i anglosaskie do dziejów Słowiańszczyzny*. Excerpta e fontibus gentium septentrionalium atque Anglo-Saxonum. Warsaw, 1961.

LEWICKI, T. 'Écrivains arabes du IXe au XVIe s. traitant de l'ambre jaune de la Baltique et de son importation en pays arabes.' *Folia Orientalia*, IV (1962), 1–40.

LEWIS, A. *The Northern Seas. Shipping and commerce in northern Europe A.D.300–1100.* Princeton, 1958.

MAŁOWIST, M. 'Z problematyki dziejów gospodarczych strefy bałtyckiej' (Some problems of the economic history of the Baltic zone). *Roczniki Dziejow Spolecznych i Gospodar Lizych*, x (1948), 81–120.

SLASKI, K. 'Ekonomitcheskiye otnosheniya zapadnykh Slavyan so Skandinavyey i drugimi pribaltiyaskimi zemlami v VI–XI vekach' (Economic contacts of western Slavs with Scandinavia and other Baltic countries in 6th–11th centuries). *Skandinavskiy Sbornik*, VI (1963), Tallin, 61–93.

STENBERGER, M. *Die Schatzfunde Gotlands der Wikingerzeit*, I–II, Stockholm, 1958.

ŻAK, A. *Studia nad kontaktami handlowymi społeczenstw zachodnio-słowianskich ze skandynawskimi od XI do XIII w. n.e.* (Studies on the commercial relations between West Slavs and Scandinavia from the 11th to 13th centuries). Poznan, 1964.

ZBIERSKI, A. *Port gdański w X–XIII wieku* (The port of Gdańsk in the 10th–13th centuries). Gdańsk, 1964.

ZIÓŁKOWSKA, H. 'Pomorze a handel bałtycki w okresie wczesno-sredniowiecznym' (Pomerania and the Baltic trade in the early Middle Ages). *Przegląd Zachodni*, 1–2 (1951), 45–52.

(6) *Overland Trade between Slavs and Western Europe*

ALBRECHT, G. *Das Münzwesen im niederlothringischen und friesischen Raum vom 10.bis zum beginnenden 12.Jh.* Hamburg, 1959.

ALEKSANDROWICZ, St. 'Stosunki handlowe polsko-ruskie do roku 1240' (Commercial ties between Poland and Russia until 1240). *Zeszyty Naukowe Uniwersytetu A. Mickiewicza, Historia*, 3 (1958), 21–67.

FLOROVSKY, A. V. *Tchekhi i vostotchnyie slavyane* (Czechs and East Slavs), I. Prague, 1935.

La Grande Moravie. Tradition millénaire de l'état et de la civilisation. Prague, 1963 (Contribution by J. POAULIK).

LÁSZLÓ, G. 'A magyar penzyeres kezdebreiröl' (Origins of the Hungarian mint). *Századok*, 97 (1963), 382–97.

LEWICKI, T. *Polska i kraje sąsiednie w świetle Ksiegi Rogera geografa arabskiego* (Poland and its neighbours in Roger's book of the 12th-century Arabic geographer, al-Idrizi), I, Cracow, 1945; II, Cracow, 1954.

—— 'Znaczenie handlowe Drohiczyna nad Bugiem we wczesnym średniowieczu i zagadkowe plomby ołowiane znalezione w tej miejscowości' (Commercial importance of Drohiczyn on the Bug in the early Middle Ages and the problem of the lead seals found in this locality). *KHKM*, IV (1956).

—— 'Certaines routes commerciales de la Hongrie du haut Moyen Age.' *Slavia Antiqua*, XIV (1967), 15–29.

ŁOWMIANSKI, H. 'Economic Problems of the Early Feudal Polish State.' *Acta Poloniae Historica*, III (1960), 7–40.

MORRISON, K. F. 'Numismatics and Carolingian Trade. A Critique of the Evidence.' *Speculum*, XXXVIII (1963), 403–32.

SKALSKY, G. 'Ĉesky obchod 10.a 11.stolêti ve svêtle nalezů minci' (Czech trade in the 10th and 11th centuries and the coin-finds). *Numismatický Sbornik*, Prague, I (1953), 13–42.

SZEKELY, G. 'Wallons et Italiens en Europe centrale aux XIe–XVIe s.' *Annales Universitatis Budapestinae*, VI (1964), 3–71.

SZYMAŃSKI, W. *Kontakty handlowe Wielkopolski w IX–XI wieku* (Commercial contacts of Great Poland in the 9th–11th centuries). Poznan, 1958.

TIMME, F. 'Schessel an der Wümme und das Diedenhoferer Capitulare vom Jahre 805. Zur Frage nach Lage und Aufgaben der karolingischen Grenzkontrollorte von der Elbe bis zum Donau.' *Blätter fur deutsche Landesgeschichte*, C (1964), 122–44.

WALLACE-HADRILL, J. M. (ed.). *The Fourth Book of the Chronicle of Fredegar with its continuations.* London, 1960.

WARNKE, C. *Die Anfänge des Fernhandels in Polen 900–1025.* Würzburg, 1964.

WIDERA, B. 'Wirtschaftliche Beziehungen zwischen Deutschland und der Kiever Rus,' *Zeitschrift fur Geschichtswissenschaft*, I (1954), 5–22.

III. LOCAL MARKETS AND CRAFT PRODUCTION IN CENTRAL AND EASTERN EUROPE FROM THE TENTH TO THE TWELFTH CENTURY

ARISTOV, N. *Promyschlennost' Drevney Rusi* (Crafts in Old Russia). St Petersburg, 1866.

'L'Artisanat et la vie urbaine en Pologne mediévale.' *Ergon*, III (1961), fasc. suppl. *KHKM*, x. (Contributions by A. Gieysztor, W. Hensel, G. Labuda, K. Tymieniecki, H. Ziolkowska, T. Lalik and others.)

BRANKAĈK, J. *Studien zur Wirtschaft und Sozialstruktur der Westslawen zwischen Elbe, Saale und Oder aus der Zeit vom 9.bis zum 12.Jh.* Bautzen, 1964.

DANILOVA, L. V. and PASHUTO, V. T. 'Tovarnoe proizvodstvo na Rusi (do XVII v.)' (Commodity production in Russia until the 17th century). *Voprosy is storii*, I (1954), 121–7.

FRANCASTEL, P. (ed.) *Les Origines des villes polonaises*. Paris–The Hague, 1960.

GIEYSZTOR, A. 'Aux origines de la ville slave: ville de grands, ville d'état aux IXe–XIe siècles.' *Cahiers Bruxellois*, XII (1967), 97–106.

—— 'From Forum to Civitas: Urban Changes in Poland in the 12th and 13th centuries.' *La Pologne au XIIe Congrès international des sciences historiques à Varsovie*, Warsaw, 1965.

Goroda feodalnoy Rossii. Sbornik statey pamyati N. V. Ustiugova (Towns of the feudal Russia. Studies in honour of N. V. USTIUGOV). Moscow, 1966. (Contributions by A. L. KHOROSHKEVITCH, V. K. YATSUNSKIY and V. T. PASHUTO.)

HOŁUBOWICZ, W. *Opole w wiekach X–XII* (Opole in the 10th–12th centuries). Katowice, 1956.

JAKOBSON, A. L. *Srednevekovy Krym* (Medieval Crimea). Moscow–Leningrad, 1964.

KAMINSKA, J. and NAHLIK, A. *Włokiennictwo gdańskie w X–XIII w.* (Textile production in Gdańsk, 10th–13th centuries). Łódź, 1958.

KARGER, M. K. *Drevniy Kiev* (Old Kiev), I–II. Moscow–Leningrad, 1958.

KIERSNOWSKI, R. 'Coin finds and the Problem of Money Hoarding in the Early Medieval Poland.' *Polish Numismatic News* (1961), 67–90.

—— *Wstep do numizmatyki polskiej* (Introduction to Polish Medieval Numismatics). Warsaw, 1964.

KORZUKHINA, G. F. *Russkiye klady IX–XIII v.v.* (Russian hoards in the 9th–13th centuries). Moscow–Leningrad, 1954.

KOSTRZEWSKI, J. *Kultura prapolska* (Proto-Polish civilization), 3rd edn. Warsaw, 1962.

KULISHER, M. *Istoria russkoy torgovli* (History of Russian trade). St Petersburg, 1923.

Kultura drevney Rusi (Civilization of Old Russia. Studies in honour of N. N. Voronin). Moscow, 1966. (Contributions by A. V. ARCIKHOVSKIY, T. N. NIKOLSKAYA and G. V. FEDOROV.)

LECIEJEWICZ, L. *Miasta Słowian północnopołabskich* (Towns of the North Elbe Slavs). Warsaw, 1968.

MIKHALEVSKY, F. I. *Otcherki istorii deneg i denezhnogo obrachtcheniya* (Essays on the history of money and money circulation), I. Moscow, 1947.

MODZELEWSKI, K. 'La Division autarchique du travail à l'échelle d'un état: l'organisation *ministériale* en Pologne médiévale.' *AESC*, XXII (1964), 1125.

POPPE, A. *Materiały do słownika terminów budownictwa staroruskiego* (Materials for a Dictionary of Old Russian Building-terms). Wrocław, 1962.

—— *Materiały do dziejów tkaniny staroruskiej. Terminologia źrodeł pisanych* (Materials for the history of Old Russian textiles. Terminology of written sources). Wrocław, 1965.

POTIN, V. M. 'Nekotorye voprosy torgovli drevnej Rusi po numizmatičeskim dannym' (Some Problems of the Ancient Russian Trade in the light of numismatic evidence). *Vestnik Istorii Mirovoy Kultury*, no. 4 (1961), 67–79.

RABINOVITCH, M. G. 'Iz istorii gorodskikh poselenii vostotchnykh Slavyan' (On the history of urban settlements of eastern Slavs). *Istoriya, kultura, folklor i etnografiya slavyanskikh norodov*, VII. *Mezhdunarodny syezd slavistov*. Moscow, 1968, 130–48.

RAPPORPORT, P. A. 'Die altrussische Burgwälle.' *Zeitschrift für Archaelogie*, I (1967), 61–87.

—— 'O tipologii drevnerusskikh poselenii' (On the typology of old Russian settlements). *Kratkiye soobshchtcheniya Instituta Archaeologii*, AN SSSR, CX (1967), 3–9.

RYBAKOV, B. A. *Remeslo drevney Rusi* (Crafts in Old Russia). Moscow, 1948.

SPITSYN, A. *Torgovyye puti Kievskoy Rusi* (Trade roads of Kievan Russia). St Petersburg, 1911.

STĚPKOVA, J. 'Über das Wesen und die Funktion der Dirhambruchstücke.' *Charisteria Orientalia* (1956), 329–35.

STRUVE, K. V. 'Die baltischen Burgen in Wagrien.' *Offa*, XVII/XVIII (1959/61), 57–108.

SUCHODOLSKI, S. '*Renovatio monetae* in Poland in the 12th century.' *Polish Numismatic News* (1961), 57–71.

SZTETYŁŁO, J. 'Czeski i morawski pieniadz pozakruszcowy wczesnego średniowiecza' (Czech and Moravian non-metallic money in the early Middle Ages). *KHKM*, XI (1963), 505–20.

TABACZYNSKI, S. 'Quelques aspects principaux de la circulation monétaire dans les villes polonaises du haut Moyen Age.' *Archeològia Polona*, VII (1964), 165–79.

—— 'Les Fonctions pécuniaires des trésors.' *AESC*, XVII, II (1962), 223–31.

TIKHOMIROV, M. N. *Drevnerusskiye goroda* (Old Russian Towns), 2nd edn. Moscow, 1956.

VORONIN, N. N. and RAPPOPORT, P. A. 'Arkheologitcheskiye izutcheniya drevnorusskogo goroda' (Archeological studies on the old Russian towns). *Kratkyie soobshchtcheniya Instituta Archeologii*, AN SSSR, XCVI (1963), 3–17.

WIDERA, B. 'Novgorods Beziehungen zu Ural und Westsibirien in der Vorhansezeit.' *Hansische Studien. Festschrift H. Spromberg*. Berlin, 1967, 388–89.

YANIN, V. L. *Denezhno-vesovyie sistemy russkogo srednevekovya. Domongolskiy period* (Coins and weight systems of the Russian Middle Ages. Pre-Mongol period). Moscow, 1956.

—— 'Les Problèmes généraux de l'échange monétaire russe en IXe–XIIe siècle.' *SSCI*, VIII. Spoleto, 1961, 485–509.

CHAPTER VIII

The Trade of Eastern Europe in the Later Middle Ages

The following abbrevation has been used in this bibliography:
HGbl *Hansische Geschichtsblätter*

I. BOHEMIA

Ahlhorn, J. 'Die Nürnberger Fernkaufleute Markus und Matthäus Landauer und deren Handelsbeziehungen zum Osten im 15. Jahrhundert.' *Zeitschrift f. Ostforschung*, xix, 2 (1970), 303–21.

Ammann, H. 'Deutschland und die Tuchindustrie Nordwestdeutschlands im Mittelalter.' *HGbl*, lxxii (1954).

Bachmann, A. *Geschichte Böhmens.* 2 vols., Brünn, 1899–1903.

Bastian, F. *Das Runtingerbuch 1383–1407 und verwandtes Material zum Regensburger-Südostdeutschen Handel und Münzwesen.* 3 vols. Deutsche Handelsakten des Mittelalters und der Neuzeit, vi–viii. Regensburg, 1935–44.

Bretholz, B. *Geschichte der Stadt Brünn.* Brünn, 1911.

Castelin, K. *Česka drobna mince doby předhusitské a husitské 1300–1471* (Bohemian small coins before and during the Hussite period). Prague, 1953.

Dejiny Slovenska (The History of Slovakia). Bratislava, 1961.

Florovski, A. V. *Česke sukno na vychodoevropskym trhu v XIV až XVIII véku* (Bohemian cloth on the east European markets from the 14th to the 18th centuries). Prague, 1947.

—— *Česko-ruske obchodni styky v minulosti X–XVIII stoleti* (Bohemian trade with Russia in the past: from the 10th to the 18th centuries). Prague, 1954.

Graus, F. *Chudina městska v době předhusitske* (Poor people in Bohemian cities in the pre-Hussite period). Prague, 1949.

—— *Česky obchod se suknem ve 14 a počatkem 15 stoleti* (Bohemian cloth trade in the 14th and beginning of the 15th century). Prague, 1950.

—— *Dejiny venkovského lidu v Čechach v době předhusitske* (The history of the peasants in Bohemia before the Hussite period). Prague, 1957.

—— 'Die Handelsbeziehungen Böhmens zu Deutschland und Österreich im 14 und zu Beginn des 15. Jahrhunderts.' *Historica* (Prague), ii (1960).

Janaček, J. *Dejiny obchodu v předbelohorske Praze* (The Trade of Prague in the period before the battle of Bela Hóra). Prague, 1961.

—— *Remeslna vyroba v českych městech v 16 stoleti* (Crafts in Bohemian cities in the 16th century). Prague, 1961.

—— 'Der böhmische Aussenhandel in der zweite Hälfte des 15. Jahrhunderts.' *Historica* (Prague), iv (1962).

Juritsch, G. *Handel und Handelsrecht in Böhmen bis zur hussitischen Revolution.* Leipzig–Vienna, 1907.

Kavka, F. 'Česky a slovensky obchod s textilnimi vyrobky v rumunskych zemich' (Bohemian and Slovakian cloth trade in Romania). *Sbornik Historicky* (Prague), v (1957).

Koran, J. *Dejiny dolováni v rudnim okrsku Kutnohorském* (The history of mining in the Kuttenberg basin). Prague, 1950.

—— *Přehledne dejiny československeho hornictvi* (Outline of the history of Czechoslovakian mining). Prague, 1955.

Leminger, E. *Královská mincovná v Kutné Horé* (The Royal Mint in Kuttenberg). Prague, 1912.

Lippert, J. *Sozialgeschichte Böhmens in vorhussitischer Zeit ausschliesslich aus Quellen*, 2 vols. Prague–Vienna–Leipzig, 1896–8.

Macek, J. *Tabor v husitském revolucnim hnuti* (Tabor during the Hussite revolution), 2 vols. Prague, 1952–3.

MAJER, J. *Težba cinu ve Slovenskom Lese v 16 stoleti* (Tin exploitation in the region of Slovensky Les in the 16th century). Prague, 1970.

MAYER, T. *Der auswärtige Handel des Herzogtums Österreich im Mittelalter*. Innsbruck, 1909.

MENDL, B. *Vývoj remesel a obchodu v městech prazskych* (The development of crafts and trade in the cities of Prague). Prague, 1947.

MIKA, A. 'Feodalni velkostatek v jižnich Čechach (XIV–XVII stoleti)' (The great estate in southern Bohemia in the 14th–17th centuries). *Sbornik Historicky*, I, 1953.

—— 'Česke rybnikařstvi a problem počatku akumulace kapitalu v českych zemich' (Bohemian fishing and the question of primary capital accumulation in Bohemia). *Česky Časopis Historický*, II (1954).

Přehled Českoalovenských Dějin (Outline of Czechoslovakian history). Prague, 1958.

REINCKE, H. 'Machtpolitik und Wirtschaftspläne Kaiser Karls IV.' *HGbl*, XLIX (1924).

SCHENK, H. *Nürnberg und Prag. Ein Beitrag zur Geschichte der Handelsbeziehungen im 14. und 15. Jahrhundert*. Wiesbaden, 1968.

SCHULTE, A. *Geschichte des mittelalterlichen Handels und Verkehrs zwischen Westdeutschland und Italien mit Ausschlus von Venedig*. Leipzig, 1900.

SIMONSFELD, H. *Der Fondacho dei Tedeschi in Venedig und die deutsch-venetianische Handelsbeziehungen*. Stuttgart, 1887.

SKALSKY, G. *Stručny přehled vyvoje českeho mincovnictvi* (Outline of the history of Bohemian minting). Prague, 1937.

VON STROMER, W. *Oberdeutsche Handelsfinanz (1350–1450)*, I. Wiesbaden, 1970.

WERUNSKY, E. *Dějiny řemesel a obchodu v Čechnach v XIV–XV stoleti* (The history of crafts and trade in Bohemia in the 14th–15th centuries). Prague, 1906.

VLACHOVIČ, J. *Slovenska méd v XVI a XVII storoci* (Slovakian copper in the 16th and 17th centuries). Bratislava, 1966.

II. POLAND

AHNSEL, K. O. *Thorns Seehandel und Kaufmannschaft um 1370*. Marburg on Lahn, 1961.

AMMANN, H. 'Wirtschaftsbeziehungen zwischen Oberdeutschland und Polen im Mittelalter.' *Vierteljahrschrift für Sozial- und Wirtschaftsgeschichte*, XLVIII, 4 (1961), 433–43.

ASSMANN, E. *Stettins Seehandel und Seeschiffahrt im Mittelalter*. Kitzingen on Main, 1950.

AUBIN, H. *Geschichte Schlesiens*, I. Breslau, 1938.

BISKUP, M. *Zjednoczenie Pomorza Wschodniego z Polska w połowie XV wieku* (Poland's union with eastern Pomerania in the middle of the 15th century). Warsaw, 1959.

—— 'Handel wiślany w latach 1454–1466' (Trade on the Vistula in 1454–66). *Roczniki Dziejow Społecznych i Gospodarczych* (Annals of Social and Economic History, (Poznan), XIV (1953).

BOGUCKA, M. *Gdańsk jako ośrodek produkcyjny XIV–XVII w.* (Danzig – centre of industry in the 14th–17th centuries). Warsaw, 1962.

BÖHNKE, W. 'Der Binnenhandel des Deutschen Ordens in Preussen und seine Beziehungen zum Aussenhandel um 1400.' *HGbl*, LXXX (1962).

CHAREWICZOWA, L. *Handel średniowiecznego Lwowa* (The trade of Lvov (Lemberg) in the Middle Ages). Lwów/Lvov, 1925.

D'OLIVEIRA, MARQUES. *Hansa e Portugal na idade media*. Lisbon, 1959.

ENGEL, E. and ZIENTARA, B. *Feudalstruktur, Lehn–Bürgertum und Fernhandel im spätmittelalterlichen Brandenburg*. Weimar, 1968.

GIEYSZTORAWA, I. 'Research into the Demographic History of Poland.' *Acta Polaniae Historica*, XVIII (1968), 49–68.

GUMOWSKI, M. *Handbuch der polnischen Numismatik*. Graz, 1960.

HERBST, ST. *Toruńskie cechy rzemieślnicze* (The craft corporations of Toruń). Thorn/Toruń, 1933.

HIRSCH, T. *Handels- und Gewerbsgeschichte Danzigs unter der Herrschaft des Deutschen Ordens*. Leipzig, 1858.

Historia Śląska (The History of Silesia). 2 vols. Wrocław/Breslau, 1961.

HOSZOWSKI, S. 'The Polish Baltic Trade in the 15th–18th Centuries.' *Poland at the XIth International Congress of Historical Sciences in Stockholm 1960*. Warsaw, 1960, 117–55.

KEHN, W. *Der Handel im Oderraum im 13. und 14. Jhrdt.* Cologne–Graz, 1968.

KIERSNOWSKI, R. *Wstep do numizmatyki polskiej wieków średnich* (Introduction to Polish numismatics in the Middle Ages). Warsaw, 1964.

KOCZY, L. *Handel Poznania do Polowy XVI wieku* (The trade of Poznań to the middle of the 16th century). Poznań, 1930.

KUTRZEBA, S. 'Handel Krakowa w wiekach średnich' (The trade of Cracow in the Middle Ages). *Rozprawy Polskiej Akademii Umiejętności* (Transactions of the Polish Academy of Sciences, Cracow), XLIV (1903).

—— 'Handel Polski ze wschodem w wiekach średnich' (Poland's trade with the East in the Middle Ages). *Przeglad Polski* (Polish Review), 148–50, Lwów (1903).

KUTRZEBA, S. and PTAŚNIK, J. 'Dzieje handlu i kupiectwa krakowskiego' (The History of the Cracow merchants). *Rocznik Krakowski* (Cracow's Annals), XIV (1910).

LABUDY, G. (ed.). *Historia Pomorza* (History of Pomerania), I. Poznań, 1969.

ŁADOGORSKI, T. *Studia nad zaludnieniem Polski XIV w.* (Studies in the history of Poland's population in the 14th century). Wrocław/Breslau, 1958.

LOEWE, K. 'Commerce and Agriculture in Lithuania, 1400–1600.' *Economic History Review*, 2 ser. XXVI (1973).

MALECZYŃSKI, K. (ed.). *Dzieje Wrocławia* (History of Wrocław), I. Wrocław/Breslau, 1948.

MAŁOWIST, M. *Kaffa – kolonia genueńska na Krymie i problem wschodni w latach 1453–1475* (Caffa – Genoese colony in the Crimea and the eastern question in 1453–1475). Warsaw, 1947.

—— *Studia z dziejów rzemisła w okresie kryzysu feudalizmu w Zachodniej Europie w XIV i XV wieku* (Essays on the history of western crafts during the crisis of feudalism in the 14th and 15th centuries). Warsaw, 1954.

—— *Wschód a Zachód Europy w XIII–XVI wieku* (Eastern Europe and the West in the 13th–16th centuries). Warsaw, 1973.

—— 'Le Développement des rapports économiques entre la Flandre, la Pologne et les pays limitrophes du XIIIe au XIXe s.' *Revue Belge de Philologie et d'Histoire*, X (1931).

—— 'Podstawy gospodarcze przywrocenia jednosci państwowej Pomorza Gdańskiego z Polskę w XIV wieku' (The economic premises of Poland's union with eastern Pomeranian in the 15th century). *Przeglad Historyczny* (Warsaw), XLV (1954)).

—— 'Über die Frage der Handelspolitik des Adels in den Ostseeländern in 15. und 16. Jahrh.' *HGbl*, LXXV (1957).

—— 'Croissance et régression en Europe XIVe–XVIIe siècles. Recueil d'articlees.' *Cahiers des Annales*, XXXIV (1972).

MĄCZAK, A. *Sukiennictwo wielkopolskie w XIV–XVII wieku* (The woollen industry of Great Poland, 14th–17th centuries). Warsaw, 1955.

MASCHKE, E. *Die Schäffer und Lieger des Deutschen Ordens in Preussen*. Hamburg, 1966.

MENDL, B. 'Breslau zu Beginn des 15. Jahrhunderts.' *Zeitschrift des Vereins fur Geschichte Schlesiens* (Breslau), LXIII (1929).

MOLENDA, D. *Górnictwo kruszcowe na terenie złóz ślasko – krakowskich do połowy XVI w.* (Metal mining in the Silesia–Cracow region). Wrocław, 1963.

NISTOR, J. *Die auswärtigen Handelsbeziehungen der Moldau im XIV, XV und XVI Jahrh.* Gotha, 1911.

PELC, J. *Ceny w Krakowie w latach 1369–1600* (Prices in Cracow 1369–1600). Lwów, 1935.

POSTHUMUS, N. W. *De Oosterse Handel te Amsterdam* (The Baltic trade in Amsterdam). Leiden, 1953.

PTAŚNIK, J. *Italia Mercatoria apud Polonos saeculo XV ineunte*. Rome, 1910.

—— *Miasta i mieszczaństwo w dawnej Polsce* (Towns and townspeople in the old Poland), 2nd edn. Warsaw, 1949.

—— *Kultura włoska wieków średnich w Polsce* (Italian culture in medieval Poland), 2nd edn. Warsaw, 1959.

RENKEN, F. *Der Handel der Königsberger Grosschäfferei des Deutschen Ordens mit Flandern.* Weimar, 1937.

SAMSONOWICZ, H. *Untersuchungen über das Danziger Bürgerkapital in der zweiten Hälfte des 15. Jahrhunderts.* Weimar, 1969.

—— 'Handel zagraniczny Gdańska w drugiej połowie XV wieku' (Danzig's foreign trade in the second half of the 15th century). *Przeglad Historyczny* (Historical Review, Warsaw), LIII (1962/4), 695–715.

—— 'Über Fragen des Landhandels Polens mit Westeuropa im 15/16 Jahrhundert.' *Neue Hansische Studien*, Berlin, 1970.

—— 'Recherches polonaises sur l'histoire de la Baltique au déclin du Moyen Age (XIVe–XVe siècle).' *Acta Poloniae Historica* (Warsaw), XXIII (1971), 150–61.

SATTLER, C. *Handelsrechnungen des Deutschen Ordens.* Leipzig, 1887.

SCHIMSCH, A. *Die Handelsbeziehungen zwischen Nürnberg und Posen im europäischen Wirtschaftsverkehr des 15. und 16. Jahrhundert.* Wiesbaden, 1970.

SCHIPPER, J. *Studia nad stosunkami gospodarczymi Żydów w Polsce podczas wieków średnich* (Investigations into the economic history of the Jews in Poland in the Middle Ages). Lwów, 1911.

SCHOLZ-BABISCH, M. 'Oberdeutscher Handel mit dem deutschen und polnischen Oster nach Geschäftsbriefen von 1444.' *Zeitschrift des Vereins für Geschichte und Alterthum Schlesiens* (Breslau), LXIV (1908).

TOPOLSKI, J. *Rola Gniezna w handlu europejskim od XV do XVII w.* (The city of Gnesen in European trade from the 15th to the 17th centuries). Poznań, 1962.

TOPOLSKI, J. (ed.). *Dzieje Wielkopolski* (History of Great Poland). Poznań, 1969.

WAWRZYŃCZYK, A. *Studia z dziejów handlu Polski z Wielkim Księstwem Litewskim i Rosja w XVI wieku* (Studies in the history of Poland's trade with the Great Duchy of Lithuania and with Russia in the 16th century). Warsaw, 1956.

WENDT, H. *Schlesien und der Orient.* Darstellungen und Quellen zur Schlesischen Geschichte, XXII. Breslau, 1916.

WYROBISZ, A. *Szkło w Polsce od XIV do XVII wieku* (The glass industry in Poland from the 14th to the 17th centuries). Wrocław, 1968.

WYROZUMSKI, J. *Państwowa gospodarka solna w Polsce do schyłku XIV w.* (Polish state economy in the salt mines until the end of the 14th century). Cracow, 1968.

—— *Tkactwo malopolskie w późnym średniowieczu* (The woollen industry in Little Poland in the later Middle Ages). Cracow, 1972.

Zarys dziejów górnictwa na ziemiach polskich (An outline of the history of mining in the Polish territories), I, Katowice, 1960.

ZIENTARA, B. *Dzieje małopolskiego hutnictwa żelaznego XIV–XVII wieku* (The history of iron smelting in Little Poland 14th–17th centuries). Warsaw, 1954.

—— 'Rola Szczecina w odrzańskim i bałtychim handlu zbożem w XIII i XIV wieku' (Stettin in the corn trade on the Oder and in the Baltic zone). *Przeglad Historyczny*, LII (1961).

III. RUSSIA AND LIVONIA

AHVENAINEN, J. *Der Getreidehandel Livlands im Mittelalter.* Helsinki, 1963.

ALEKSEYEV, YA. G. *Agrarnaya i sotsialnaya istorya severo-vostotchnoy Rusi v XV–XVI vv. Pereyaslavski Uyezd* (Agrarian and social history of north-western Russia in the 15th–16th century. The District of Pereyaslavl). Isdatels tvo Nauka, Moscow–Leningrad, 1966.

AMBURGER, E. 'Zur Geschichte des Grosshandels in Russland: die Gosti.' *Zeitschrift f. Sozial- und Wirtschaftsgeschichte*, XLVI (1959).

ARTSIKHOVSKI, A. V. *Arkheologitscheskye izutchenye V. Novgoroda* (Archaeological research in Novgorod the Great). Moscow, 1956.

BAHRUSHIN, S. V. *Nautchnye Trudy* (Historical Researches). I: *Otcherki po istorii remesla, torgovli i gorodov Russkogo Centralizovannogo Gosudarstva XVI – natchala XVII vv.* (Essays in the history of crafts, trade and cities in the Russian Centralized State in the 16th to the beginning of the 17th centuries). Moscow, 1952. II: *Stati po ekonomitcheskoy, sotsialnoy i polititcheskoy istorii Russkogo Centralizovannogo Gosudarstva XV–XVII vv.* (Studies on the economic, social and political history of the Russian Centralized State). Moscow, 1954. III: *Izbrannye raboty po istorii Sibiri v XVI–XVII vv.* (Selected works on the history of Siberia in the 16th–17th centuries). Moscow, 1955.

BERINDEI, M. and VIENSTEIN, G. 'La Tana – Azaq de la présence italienne à l'emprise ottomane (fin du XIIIe – milieu du XVIe siècle).' *Turcica* (Paris-Strasbourg) VIII/2 (1976), 110–201.

BERNADSKI, V. N. *Novgorod i Novgorodskaya Zemla v XV veke* (Novgorod and its territory in the 15th century). Leningrad, 1958.

DANILOVA, L. V. *Otcherki po istorii zemlevladenya i khozyaystva Novgoroda i Novgorodskoy zemli v XIV i XV vv.* (Studies in history of agriculture in Novgorod and its territory). Moscow, 1955.

DOVNAR ZAPOLSKI, U. M. *Torgovla i promyshlennost Moskvi v XVI i XVII veke* (Trade and industry in Moscow in the 16th and 17th centuries). Moscow, 1910.

FEDOROV, G. B. *Dengi Moskovskogo Knyazhestva vremery Dimitrya Donskoyste i Vasylya Dimitryevitcha (1359–1425)* (The mints of the Moscow Principality during the reign of Dimitri Donskoy and Vasili Dimitryevitch (1359–1425)). Moscow–Leningrad, 1949.

FEHNER, M. V. *Torgovla Russkogo Gosudarstva so stranami Vostoka v XVI veke* (Russian trade with the East in the 16th century). Moscow, 1956.

GOEHRKE, C. *Die Wüstungen in der Moskauer Rus. Studium zur Siedlunds- Bevolkerungs- und Sozialgeschichte.* Wiesbaden, 1968.

GOETZ, L. K. *Deutsch–russische Handelsgeschichte des Mittelalters.* Lübeck, 1922.

Goroda feodalnoy Rosii. Sbornik Statey (The cities of feudal Russia. Collection of articles). Moscow, 1966.

GORSKI, A. D. *Otcherki ekonomitcheskago polozhenya krestyan severo – vostotchnoy Rusi v XIV–XV vv* (Essays on the economic life of the peasants in north-eastern Russia in the 14th–15th centuries). Moscow, 1960.

GREKOV, B. D. *Krestyanye na Rusi s drevneyshikh vremen do XVII veka* (Russian peasants since the earliest times up to the 17th century). Moscow–Leningrad, 1945.

GREKOV, B. D. and YAKUBOVSKI, YA. *La Horde d'or. La Domination tatare au XIIIe et au XIVe siècle de la Mer Noire.* Paris, 1939.

Istorya Sibiri (The History of Siberia). 2 vols, Leningrad, 1968.

JOHANSEN, P. 'Novgorod und die Hanse.' *Gedächtnisschrift für F. Rörig.* Lübeck, 1953.

—— *Der hansische Russlandhandel, insbesondere nach Novgorod, in kritischer Betrachtung.* Cologne–Opladen, 1962.

KHOROSHKEVITCH, A. L. *Dogovory Polotska 1405–1406 kak istotchniki po istorii yego vneshney torgovli i torgovoy politiki* (The treaties of Polotsk 1405–1406 as sources for the history of its internal and foreign trade). Arkheologitcheski Ezhegodnik za 1962 god. (Archeological Annals, 1962). Moscow, 1963.

—— *Torgovla Velikogo Novgoroda s Pribaltikoi i Zapadnoy Evropoi v XIV–XV vv.* (Novgorod's Trade with the Baltic Countries and the West in the 14th–15th centuries). Moscow, 1963.

KOPPE, W. 'Schiffsverkehr und Seehandel in den Jahren 1378/1384.' *HGbl*, LXIV (1940).

KOZAKOVA, N. A. *Russko-livonskie i russko-ganzeyskie otnoshenya. Konec XIV–natchalo XVI veka* (The relations of Russia with Livonia and the Hanse from the end of the 14th to the beginning of the 16th centuries). Moscow, 1975.

LESNIKOV, M. P. 'Niderlandy i Vostotchnaya Baltika v natchale XV veka' (The Netherlands and the eastern Baltic countries at the beginning of the 15th century). *Izvestya Akademii Nauk SSSR* (Transactions of the Academy of Sciences of USSR), V, 1951.

—— 'Torgovye snoshenya V. Novgoroda s Tevtonskim Ordenom v konce XIV i natchale XV veka' (Trade relations of Novgorod with the Teutonic Order at the end of the 14th and beginning of the 15th centuries). *Istoritcheskye Zapiski* (Historical Notes), 39 (1952), 259–78.

—— *Ganzeyskaya torgovla pushninoy v natchale XV veka* (Hanseatic fur trade in the beginning of the 15th century). Zapiski Ped. Instituta V.P. Potemkina (Publications of the V.P. Potemkin Institute), XIII, 1954.

—— 'Die livländische Kaufmannschaft und ihre Handelsbeziehungen zu Flandern am Anfang des 15. Jahrhunderts.' *Zeitschrift für Geschichtswissenschaft* (1958), 285–303.

—— 'Lübeck als Handelsplatz für osteuropäische Waren im 15. Jahrhundert.' *HGbl*, LXXVIII (1960), 37–66.

—— *Die Handelsbücher des hansischen Kaufmanns Veckinghusen*. Forschungen zur mittelalterlichen Geschichte, Bd. 19. Berlin, 1973.

LEVTCHENKO, M. V. *Otcherki po istorii russko – vizantiyskich otnoshenyi* (Studies in the history of Russian relations with Byzantium). Moscow, 1956.

LYASHTCHENKO, P. Y. *Istorya narodnogo khozyayastva SSSR* (Economic History of USSR), I. Moscow, 1947.

MANKOV, A. Y. *Tseni i ikh dvizhenye v Russkom Gosudarstve XVI veka* (Prices and their movements in Russia in the 16th century). Moscow–Leningrad, 1951.

Mezhdunarodnye Svyazi Rossii do XVII veka (Russian international relations to the 17th century). Moscow, 1961.

MICKWITZ, G. 'Aus Revaler Handelsbüchern.' *Societas Scientiarum Fennica*, IX, 8 (1938).

MIKHALEVSKI, F. Y. *Otcherki istorii deneg i denezhnogo obrashtchenya* (Studies in the history of money and monetary circulation). Leningrad, 1948.

NASONOV, A. N. *Mongoli i Rus* (The Mongols and Russia). Moscow–Leningrad, 1948.

NIITEMAA, W. 'Die undeutsche Frage in der Politik der livländischen Städte im Mittelalter.' *Annales Academiae Scientiarum Fennicae*, LXIV (1949).

—— 'Der Binnenhandel in der Politik der livländischen Städte im Mittelalter.' *Annales Academiae Scientiarum Fennicae*, LXXVI (1952).

NIKITSKI, A. Y. *Istoria ekonomitcheskogo bita Velikogo Novgoroda* (The economic history of Great Novgorod). Moscow, 1893.

Otcherki istorii SSSR XIV–XV vv. (Studies in the history of USSR, 14th–15th centuries). Moscow, 1953.

POKROVSKI, S. A. *Vneshnaya torgovla i vneshnaya politika Rossii* (Foreign trade and foreign policy of Russia). Moscow, 1947.

RENKEN, F. *Der Handel der Königsberger Grosschäfferei des Deutschen Ordens mit Flandern*. Weimar, 1937.

RIBAKOV, B. A. *Remeslo drevney Rusi* (The crafts in Russia in the past). Moscow, 1948.

SAKHAROV, A. M. *Goroda Severo–vostotchnoy Rusi XIV i XV vv.* (The cities in north-eastern Russia in the 14th and 15th centuries). Moscow, 1959.

SASS, K. H. *Der Hansische Einfuhrhandel in Reval um 1430*. Marburg on Lahn, 1955.

SIROETCHKOVSKI, V. E. 'Puti i uslovya snoshenii Moskvi s Krimom' (The routes and conditions of Moscow's trade with the Crimea). *Izvestya Akademii Nauk SSSR*, III (1932).

—— *Gosti–Surozhanye* (The merchants called Surozhanye). Moscow, 1935.

SKRSHINSKAYA, E. C. 'Storia della Tana.' *Studi Veneziani*, X (1968). Florence, 1969.

SMIRNOV, P. P. *Posadskie lyudi i ikh klassovaya borba do seredini XVII veka* (The 'burghers' and their class struggle to the middle of the 17th century). Moscow–Leningrad, 1947.

SPASSKI, I. G. *Russkaya monetnaya sistema* (The Russian monetary system), 3rd edn. Leningrad, 1962.

STIEDA, W. *Revaler Zollbücher und Quittungen des 16. Jahrhunderts*. Halle, 1887.

—— *Hansisch–Venetianische Handelsbeziehungen im 15 Jahrhundert*. Rostock, 1894.

—— *Hildebrand Veckinghusen*. Leipzig, 1922.

TCHEREPNIN, L. V. *Russkie feodalnye arkhivi XIV i XV vv.* (Russian feudal archives). 2 vols. Moscow, 1948–50.

—— *Obrazovannye Russkogo Centralizovannogo Gosudarstva* (The formation of the Russian centralized state). Moscow, 1960.

TIKHOMIROV, M. N. *Drevnerusskie goroda* (The old Russian cities), 2nd edn. Moscow, 1956.

—— *Srednevekovaya Moskva* (Medieval Moscow), 2nd edn. Moscow, 1957.

—— *Srednevekovaya Rossia na mezhdunarodnikh putyakh* (Medieval Russia in international life). Moscow, 1966.

VERLINDEN, C. *L'Esclavage dans l'Europe médiévale*, I. Bruges, 1955.

—— 'La colonie vénitienne de Tana, centre de la traité des esclaves au XIVe et au début du XVe siècle.' *Studi in onore di Gino Luzzatto*, II. Milan, 1950, 1–25.

—— 'Le Commerce en Mer Noire des débuts de l'époque Byzantine au lendemain de la conquête de l'Egypte par les Ottomans (1517).' *XIIIe Congrès International des Sciences Historiques*. Moscow, 1970, 1–11.

VESOLOVSKI, S. B. *Selo i derevnya v Severo-Vostotchnoy Rusi XIV–XV v.* (Town and village in north-eastern Russia in the 14th–15th centuries). Moscow–Leningrad, 1936.

—— *Feodalnye zemlevladenye v Severo-Vostotchnoy Rusi XIV–XV vv.* (Feudal agriculture in north-eastern Russia in the 14th–15th centuries). Moscow–Leningrad, 1947.

ZABELIN, J. E. *Istoria goroda Moskvi* (The history of the city of Moscow), 2nd edn. Moscow, 1905.

CHAPTER IX

The Woollen Industry

by N. B. HARTE

The following bibliography includes the standard works drawn upon in the original version of the chapter, as well as a selection of the considerable literature which has appeared since. It is based upon various drafts compiled by Professor Carus-Wilson before her death in 1977. It takes no account of the original sources she used, except in the case of a few printed collections concerned primarily with the woollen industry. Nor does it attempt to acknowledge either unpublished theses or discussions with scholars, though to these, as to the source material, published and unpublished, the revised version of the chapter is much indebted. Only works relating to the regions specifically dealt with in the chapter are included, and, with few exceptions, only those primarily concerned with cloth or its raw materials. Works are listed only once, though several could well appear under more than one heading.

The field of study remains unevenly covered by modern works, despite the quantity that have been published since the first version of the chapter appeared in 1952, some of them – for Italy and the Low Countries, as well as for England – directly inspired by it. Professor Carus-Wilson's own work on the English cloth industry was surveyed in a masterly way in her Ford lectures at Oxford in 1965, but regrettably the lectures remain unpublished. A number of further contributions to the field appeared in 1983 in N. B. Harte and K. G. Ponting (eds.), *Cloth and Clothing in Medieval Europe*, an international *Festschrift* in memory of the author.

The following abbreviations have been used in this bibliography:

Annales	*Annales d'Histoire Économique et Sociale* and *Annales* (*Économies, Sociétés, Civilisations*)
ES	*Economia e Storia*
EconHR	*Economic History Review*
JEBH	*Journal of Economic and Business History*
RBPH	*Revue Belge de Philologie et d'Histoire*
RHES	*Revue d'Histoire Économique et Sociale*
RN	*Revue du Nord*
TH	*Textile History*
VSW	*Vierteljahrschrift für Sozial- und Wirtschaftsgeschichte*

I. GENERAL, TECHNOLOGY AND RAW MATERIALS

BAUTIER, A. M. 'Les Plus anciennes mentions de moulins hydrauliques industriels et de moulins à vent.' *Bulletin philologique et historique du comité des travaux historique* (Paris), II (1960).

BORLANDI, F. 'Note per la storia della produzione e del commercio di una materia prima. Il guado nel medio evo.' *Studi in onore di Gino Luzzatto*. Milan, 1950.

CAHEN, C. 'L'Alun avant Phocée: un chapitre d'histoire économique islamo-chrétienne au temps des Croisades.' *RHES*, XLI (1963).

CARUS-WILSON, E. M. 'La Guède francaise en Angleterre: un grand commerce du moyen âge'. *RN* XXXV (1953).

DAVIDSOHN, R. 'Garbowolle und Garbotuch.' *Historische Vierteljahrschrift* (Leipzig), VII (1904).

DELAMEAU, J. *L'Alun de Rome, XVe–XIXe siècle*. Paris, 1962.

DE POERCK, G. *Esquisse d'une histoire de la draperie: introduction historique*. Ghent, 1968.

—— *La Draperie médiévale en Flandre et en Artois: technique et terminologie*. Bruges, 1951.

ENDREI, W. 'Changements dans la productivité de l'industrie lainière au moyen âge.' *AESC*, XXVI (1971).

—— *L'Évolution des techniques du filage et du tissage*. Paris, 1968.

GERVERS, V. (ed.). *Studies in Textile History*. Toronto, 1977.

HEERS, M. L. 'Les Génois et la commerce de l'alun à la fin du moyen âge.' *RHES*, XXXII (1954).

HEYD, W. *Histoire du commerce du Levant au moyen âge*, 2 vols. Leipzig, 1923.

HOFFMAN, M. *The Warp-Weighted Loom*. Oslo, 1964.

HURRY, J. B. *The Woad Plant and its Dye*. London, 1930.

KLEIN, J. *The Mesta; a study in Spanish economic history, 1273–1836*. Harvard Economic Studies, XXI. Cambridge, Mass., 1920.

LEMON, H. 'The Development of Hand Spinning Wheels.' *TH*, I (1968).

LIAGRE, L. 'Le Commerce de l'alun en Flandre au moyen âge.' *Le Moyen Age*, LXI (1955).

LLOYD, T. H. *The English Wool Trade in the Middle Ages*. Cambridge, 1977.

—— *The Movement of Wool Prices in Medieval England*. *EconHR*, Suppl. VI, 1973.

LOMBARD, M. *Les textiles dans le monde musulman, VIIe–XIIe siècles*. Paris, 1978.

MUNRO, J. H. 'Wool-Price Schedules and the Qualities of English Wools in the Later Middle Ages, c. 1270–1499.' *TH*, IX (1978).

—— 'The Medieval Scarlet and the Economics of Sartorial Splendour.' N. B. HARTE and K. G. POINTING (eds.). *Cloth and Clothing in Medieval Europe*. London, 1983.

NAHLIK, A. 'Les Techniques de l'industrie textile en Europe Orientale du Xe au XVe siècle à travers les vestiges de tissus.' *AESC*, XXVI (1971).

—— 'The Wool of the Middle Ages: some results of the searching of the textiles excavated in Central and East Europe.' *La lana come materia prima*. Florence, 1974.

PIPONNIER, F. *Costume et vie sociale: la cour d'Anjou, XIVe–XVe siècle*. Paris–The Hague, 1970.

POWER, E. *The Wool Trade in English Medieval History*. London, 1941.

RAMSAY, G. D. 'The Merchants of the Staple and the Downfall of the English Wool Export Traffic.' *La Lana come Materia Prima*. Florence, 1974.

RYDER, M. L. *Sheep and Man*. London, 1983.

—— 'The Origin of Spinning.' *TH*, I (1968).

SAVARY DES BRUSLONS, J. *Dictionnaire universel de commerce*. 3 vols. Geneva, 1742.

SCHULTE, A. 'Garbo und Florenz. Zur Geschichte der Wollproduktion im Mittelalter.' *Zeitschrift für die gesamte Staatswissenschaft* (Tübingen), LVIII (1901).

SPALLANZANI, M. (ed.). *Produzione Commercio e Consumo dei Palmi di Lana (nei Secoli XII–XVIII)*. Instituto Internationale di Storia Economica 'F. Datini', Prato. Florence, 1976.

—— *La lana come materia prima: i fenomeni della sua produzione e circolazione nei secoli XIII–XVII*. Instituto Internationale di Storia Economica 'F. Datini', Prato. Florence, 1974.

VAN UYTVEN, R. 'Cloth in Medieval Literature of Western Europe.' N. B. HARTE and K. G. PONTING (eds.). *Cloth and Clothing in Medieval Europe*. London, 1983.

WECKERLIN, J. B. *Le Drap 'escarlate' du moyen âge. Essai sur l'étymolgie et la signification du mot écarlate, et notes techniques sur la fabrication de ce drap de laine au moyen âge*. Lyons, 1905.

ZIPPEL, G. 'L'Allume di Tolfa e il suo commercio.' *Archivio della Reale Societa Romana di Storia Patria*, XXX (1907).

II. THE ROMAN EMPIRE

Cambridge Ancient History, 12 vols. Cambridge, 1928–39.

CAPUTO, G. and GOODCHILD, R. 'Diocletian's Price-Edict at Ptolemais, Cyrenaica.' *Journal of Roman Studies*, XLV (1955).

CHARLESWORTH, M. P. *Trade Routes and Commerce of the Roman Empire*, 2nd edn. Cambridge, 1926.

ESPÉRANDIEU, E. *Recueil général des bas-reliefs, statues et bustes de la Gaule romaine*, 10 vols. Paris, 1907–28.

Fox, G. E. 'Notes on some probable traces of Roman fulling in Britain.' *Archaeologia*, LIX (1904).
Frank, T. and others (eds.). *An Economic Survey of Ancient Rome*, 5 vols. Baltimore, 1933–40.
Jones, A. H. M. 'The Cloth Industry under the Roman Empire.' *EconHR*, 2nd ser., XIII (1960).
Mau, A. *Pompeji in Leben und Kunst*, 2nd edn. Leipzig, 1908.
Moeller, W. O. *The Wool Trade of Ancient Pompeii*. The Hague, 1976.
Rostovtzeff, M. I. *The Social and Economic History of the Roman Empire*. Oxford, 1926.
Vercauteren, F. *Étude sur les civitates de la Belgique Seconde*. Mémoires de l'Académie royale de Belgique, Classe des Lettres et des Sciences morales et politiques. Brussels, 1934.
West, L. C. *Roman Britain: the objects of trade*. Oxford, 1931.
—— *Roman Gaul: the objects of trade*. Oxford, 1935.
Wild, J. P. *Textile Manufacture in the Northern Roman Provinces*. Cambridge, 1970.

III. THE LOW COUNTRIES

Ammann, H. 'Deutschland und die Tuchindustrie Nordwest-Europas im Mittelalter.' *Hansische Geschichtsblätter*, LXXII (1954).
—— 'Die Anfänge des Aktivhandels und der Tucheinfuhr aus Nordwest-Europa nach dem Mittelmeergebiet.' *Studi in onore di A. Sapori*. Milan, 1957.
—— 'Maastricht in der Mittelalterlichen Wirtschaft.' *Mélanges Félix Rousseau. Etudes sur l'histoire du pays Mosan au moyen âge*. Brussels, 1958.
Anould, M. A. 'La Ville de Chiévres et sa draperie (XIVe–XVIe s.).' *Bulletin Scientifique de l'Institut Supérieur de Commerce de la Province de Hainaut*, II (1954).
Aymard, M. 'Production, commerce et consommation des draps de laine du XIIe au XVIIe siècle.' *Revue Historique*, CCXLVI (1971).
Bautier, R. H. 'La Place de la draperie brabançonne et plus particulièrement bruxelloise dans l'industrie textile du moyen âge.' *Annales de la Société royale d'archéologie de Bruxelles*, LI (1966).
Bonenfant, P. 'Achats de draps pour des pauvres de Bruxelles aux foires d'Anvers de 1393 à 1487. (Contribution à l'histoire des petites draperies).' *Beiträge zur Wirtschafts- und Stadtgeschichte: Festschrift für Hektor Ammann*. Wiesbaden, 1965.
Brulez, W. 'Engels lakert in Vlaanderen in de 14e–15e eeuw.' *Handelingen van het Genootschap 'Société d'Emulation' te Brugge*, CVIII (1971).
Coornaert, E. 'Draperies rurales, draperies urbaines. L'évolution de l'industrie flamande au moyen âge et au XVIe siècle.' *RBPH*, XXVIII (1950).
—— *L'Industrie de la laine à Bergues-Saint-Winoc*. Paris, 1930.
—— *La Draperie-sayetterie d'Hondschoote (XIVe–XVIIIe siècles)*. Paris, 1930.
Derville, G. A. 'Les Draperies flamandes et artésiennes vers 1250–1350.' *RN*, LIV (1972).
De Sagher, H. E. 'L'Industrie drapière à Bruges.' *Revue de l'Instruction Publique en Belgique*, LIII (1910).
De Sagher, J. H., Van Werveke, H. and Wyffels, C. (eds.). *Recueil de documents relatifs à l'histoire de l'industrie drapière en Flandre. IIe pt: le Sud-Ouest de la Flandre depuis l'époque bourguignonne*, 3 vols. Brussels, 1951, 1961, 1966.
Des Marez, G. *L'Organisation du travail à Bruxelles au XVe siècle*. Mémoires couronnés l'Académie royale des Sciences, des Lettres et des Beaux-Arts de Belgique, LXV. Brussels, 1904.
Doehaerd, R. *Les Relations commerciales entre Gênes, la Belgique et l'Outremont d'après les archives notariales génoises aux XIIIe et XIVe siècles*. Institut historique belge de Rome; Études d'histoire économique et sociale. 4 vols. Brussels, 1941.
Espinas, G. 'Essai sur la technique de l'industrie textile à Douai aux XIIIe et XIVe siècles (1229–1403).' *Mémoires de la Société nationale des antiquaires de France*, LXVII (1909).
—— *La Vie urbaine de Douai au moyen âge*. 4 vols. Paris, 1913.
—— *La Draperie dans la Flandre francais au moyen âge*. 2 vols. Paris, 1923.
—— 'La Draperie rurale d'Estaire (1428–1434).' *RHES* (1923).

—— 'Une Petite correspondance de drapiers de Douai et de Paris en 1313.' *Mélanges d'histoire offerts à Henri Pirenne*. 2 vols. Brussels, 1926.

—— 'La Confrérie des tisserands de draps de Valenciennes (1337).' *Annales*, II (1930).

—— 'L'Organisation corporative des métiers de la draperie à Valenciennes, 1362–1403.' *Annales de la Société scientifique de Bruxelles*, LII (1932).

—— *Les Origines du capitalisme*. I. *Sire Jehan Boinebroke, patricien et drapier Douaisien*. Bibliothéque de la Société d'histoire du droit des pays flamands, picards et wallons (Lille), VII, 1933.

—— G. and PIRENNE, H. *Recueil de documents relatifs à l'histoire de l'industrie drapière en Flandre*. 4 vols. (Additions in *Bulletins de la Commission royale d'histoire*, XCIII (1929). Brussels, 1906–23.

FAVRESSE, F. *Études sur les métiers bruxellois au moyen âge*. Brussels, 1961.

JORIS, A. 'Une création hutoise: la draperie d'Yvois (1304)'. *Mélanges Félix Rousseau. Études sur l'histoire du pays Mosan au moyen âge*. Brussels, 1958.

—— *La Ville de Huy au moyen âge*. Paris, 1959.

LAURENT, H. *Un Grand commerce d'exportation au moyen âge: La draperie des Pays-Bas en France et dans les pays méditerranéens* (*XIIe–XVe siècle*). Paris, 1935.

MALOWIST, M. 'Le Développement des rapports économiques entre la Flandre, la Pologne et les pays limitrophes du XIIIe au XIVe siècle.' *RBPH*, X (1931).

MARQUANT, R. *La Vie économique à Lille sous Philippe le Bon*. Paris, 1940.

MELIS, F. 'La Diffusione nel Mediterraneo occidentale dei panni di Wervicq et della altre città della Lys attorno al 1400'. *Studi in Onore di Amintore Fanfani*, III. Milan, 1962.

MUNRO, J. H. A. *Wool, Cloth and Gold: the struggle for bullion in Anglo-Burgundian Trade, 1340–1478*. Brussels–Toronto, 1972.

MUS, O. 'De verhouding van de waard tot de drapier in de Kortrijkse draperie op het einde van de 15e eeuw.' *Annales de la Société d'Emulation de Bruges*, XCVIII (1961)

PIRENNE, H. 'Draps de Frise ou draps de Flandre? Un petit problème d'histoire économique à l'époque carolingienne.' *VSW*, VII (1909).

—— 'Draps d'Ypres à Novgorod au commencement du XIIe siècle.' *RBPH*, IX (1930).

—— *Histoire de Belgique*. I. *Des origines au XIVe siècle*, 5th edn. Brussels, 1929. II. *Du Commencement du XIVe siècle à la mort de Charles de Téméraire*, 4th edn. Brussels, 1947. III. *Dè la mort de Charles le Téméraire à l'arrivée du duc d'Albe dans les Pays-Bas*, 4th edn. Brussels, 1950.

POSTHUMUS, N. W. *De Geschiedenis van de Leidsche lakenindustrie*. I. *De Middeleeuwen*. The Hague, 1908.

—— *Bronnen tot de Geschiedenis van de Leidsche textielnijverheid*. Rijks Geschiedkundige Publicatiën 8, 6 vols. The Hague, 1910–22.

REYNOLDS, R. L. 'The Market for Northern Textiles in Genoa, 1179–1200.' *RBPH*, VIII (1929).

—— 'Merchants of Arras and the Overland Trade with Genoa.' *Revue Belge de Philologie et d'Histoire*, IX (1930).

—— 'Genoese Trade in the late Twelfth Century.' *JEBH*, III (1931).

VÁCZY, P. *La Transformation de la technique et de l'organisation de l'industrie textile en Flandre aux XIe-XIIIe siècles*. Budapest, 1960.

VAN DER WEE, H. *The Growth of the Antwerp Market and the European Economy*, 3 vols. The Hague, 1963.

—— 'Het sociaal-economisch leven te Lier in de Middeleeuwen.' *'t Land van Ryen*, II (1952, 1953).

—— 'Die Wirtschaft der Stadt Lier zu Beginn des 15. Jahrhunderts.' *Beiträge zur Wirtschafts- und Stadtgeschichte: Festschrift für Hektor Ammann*. Wiesbaden, 1965.

—— 'Structural Changes and Specialisations in the Industry of the Southern Netherlands, 1100–1600.' *EconHR*, 2nd ser., XXVII (1975).

VAN HOUTTE, J. A. 'Stadt und Land in der Geschichte des flandrischen Gewerbes im Spätmittelalter und der Neuzeit.' *Wirtschaft, Geschichte und Wirtschaftsgeschichte. Festschrift für F. Lütge*. Stuttgart, 1966.

VAN UYTVEN, R. 'La Flandre et le Brabant, "terres de promission" sous les ducs de Bourgognes?' *RN*, XLIII (1961).

—— 'Stadsfinanciën en stadsekonomie te Leuven de XIIe tot de XVIe eeuw.' *Verhandelingen van de Koninklijke Vlaamse Academie van België. Klasse der Letteren*, XLIV (1961).

—— 'De omvang van de Mechelse lakenproduktie vanaf de 14e tot de 16e eeuw.' *Noordgouw, Cultureel Tijdschrift van de Provincie Antwerpen*, III (1965).

—— 'The Fulling Mill: Dynamic of the Revolution of Industrial Attitudes.' *Acta Historiae Neerlandica*, V (1971).

—— 'La Draperie brabançonne et malinoise du XIIe au XVIIe siècle: Grandeur éphémère et decadence.' *Produzione Commercio e Consumo dei Panni di Lana*. Florence, 1976.

VAN WERVEKE, H. 'De koopman-ondernemer en de ondernemer in de Vlaamsche lakennijverheid van de middeleeuwen.' *Mededelingen van de Koninklijke Vlaamse Academie voor Wetenschappen, Letteren en Schone Kunsten van België, Klasse der Letteren*, VIII (1946).

—— 'De Omvang van de Ieperse Lakenproductie in de veertiende eeuw.' *Ibid.*, IX (1947).

—— 'Industrial Growth in the Middle Ages: the cloth industry of Flanders.' *EconHR*, 2nd ser., VI (1954).

—— 'Die Stellung des Hansischen Kaufmanns dem flandrischen Tuchproduzenten gegenüber.' *Beiträge zur Wirtschafts- und Stadtgeschichte: Festschrift für Hektor Ammann*. Wiesbaden, 1965.

VERELLEN, J. R. 'Lakennijverheid en lakenhandel van Herentals in de XIVe, XVe en XVIe eeuw.' *Taxandria*, XXVII (1955).

VERHULST, A. 'La Laine indigène dans les anciens Pays-Bas entre le XIIe et le XVIIe siècle.' *Revue Historique*, XCVI (1972).

—— 'La Laine indigène dans les anciens Pays-Bas entre le XIIe et le XVIIIe siècle. Mise en oeuvre industrielle, production et commerce.' *La lana come materia prima*. Florence, 1974.

VERLINDEN, C. 'L'Expansion commerciale de la draperie flamande dans la Péninsule ibérique au XIIIe siècle.' *RN*, XXI (1935).

—— 'Draps des Pays-Bas et du Nord de la France en Espagne au XIVe siècle.' *Le Moyen Age*, ser. 3, VII (1937).

—— 'Brabantsch en Vlaamsch laken te Krakau op het einde der XIVe eeuw.' *Kon. Vlaamse Academie voor Wetenschappen, Letteren en Schone Kunsten van België, Klasse der Letteren*, V, 2 (1943).

—— 'Paños belgas en fuentes literarios españoles medievales.' *Cuadernos de Historia de Espana* (1959).

—— 'Draps des Pays-Bas et du Nord-ouest de l'Europe au Portugal au XVe siècle.' *Annuario de Estudios Medievales*, III (1966).

—— 'Deux pôles de l'expansion de la draperie flamande et brabançonne au XIVe siècle: la Pologne et la péninsula ibérique.' *Kwartalnik Historii Kultury Materialnej* (Warsaw), XVI (1968).

—— 'Marchands ou tisserands? A propos des origines urbaines.' *Annales*, XXVII, 2 (1972).

—— 'Aspects de la production, du commerce et de la consommation de draps flamands au Moyen Age.' *Produzione Commercio e Consumo dei Panni di Lana*. Florence, 1976.

WYFFELS, C. 'De oorsprong der ambachten in Vlaanderen en Brabant.' *Verhandelingen van de Koninklijke Vlaamse Academie van België. Klasse der Letteren*, XIII, 12 (1951).

IV. ITALY

BAUTIER, R. H. 'Marchands siennois et "draps d'outremont" au foires de Champagne, 1294.' *Annuaire Bulletin de la Société de l'histoire de France* (1947).

BENSA, E. *Francesco di Marco da Prato. Notizie e documenti sulla mercatura italiana del sec. XIV*. Milan, 1928.

BINI, T. *I Lucchesi a Venezia. Alcuni studi sopra i secoli XIII e XIV*. Lucca, 1853–6.

BRUN, R. 'A Fourteenth Century Merchant of Italy: Francesco Datini of Prato.' *JEBH*, II (1930).

BYRNE, E. H. 'Commercial Contracts of the Genoese in the Syrian Trade of the Twelfth Century.' *Quarterly Journal of Economics*, XXXI (1916–17).

CESSI, R. 'La corporazioni dei mercanti di panni e della lana in Padova fino a tutto il secolo XIV.' *Memorie del R. Instituto Veneto di Scienze, Lettere ed Arti* (Venice), CXXVIII (1908).

CIPOLLA, C. 'L'economia milanese: i movimenti economici generali 1350–1500.' *Storia di Milano*, VIII (1957).

DAVIDSOHN, R. *Geschichte von Florenz*. Vol. IV, *Die Frühzeit der Florentiner Kultur*, pt. II, *Gewerbe, Zünfte, Welthandel und Bankwesen*. Berlin, 1925.

—— 'Blüte und Niedergang der Florentiner Tuchindustrie.' *Zeitschrift für die gesamte Staatswissenschaft* (Tübingen), LXXXV (1928).

DE ROOVER, R. 'A Florentine firm of cloth manufacturers; management and organisation of a sixteenth century business.' *Speculum*, XVI (1941).

DOREN, A. *Studien aus der Florentiner Wirtschaftsgeschichte*, I. *Die Florentiner Wollentuchindustrie vom XIV. bis zum XVI. Jahrhundert*. Stuttgart, 1901.

—— *Italienische Wirtschaftsgeschichte*, I. Jena, 1934.

EDLER, F. *Glossary of Medieval Terms of Business, Italian Series 1200–1600*. The Medieval Academy of America. Cambridge, Mass., 1934.

FANO, N. 'Richerce sull' arte della lana a Venezia nel XIII e XIV secolo.' *Archivo Veneto*, ser. V, nos. 35–36 (1936).

GRUNZWEIG, A. 'Les Soi-disant statuts de la Confrérie de Sainte-Barbe de Florence.' *Bulletin de la Commission Royal d'Histoire* (Brussels), XCVI (1932).

HERMES, G. 'Der Kapitalismus in der Florentiner Wollenindustrie.' *Zeitschrift für die gesamte Staatswissenschaft* (Tübingen), LXXII (1916).

HOSHINO, H. 'The Rise of the Florentine Woollen Industry in the Fourteenth Century.' N. B. HARTE and K. G. PONTING (eds.). *Cloth and Clothing in Medieval Europe*. London, 1983.

LIAGRE-DE STURLER, L. *Les Relations commerciales entre Gênes, la Belgique et l'Outremont d'après les archives notariales génoises, 1320–1400*, 2 vols. Brussels-Rome, 1969.

LOPEZ, R. *Studi sull' economia genovese nel medio evo*: II. *Le origini dell' arte della lana*. Turin, 1936.

LUZZATTO, G. *Enciclopedia Italiana di Scienze, Lettere ed Arti, Istituto della Enciclopedia Italiana fondata da Giovanni Trecanni*, sub. voc. 'Lana'. Rome, 1933.

MAZZAOUI, M. F. *The Italian Cotton Industry in the Later Middle Ages, 1100–1600*. Cambridge, 1981.

MELIS, F. 'La formazione dei costi nell' industria laniera alla fine del trecento.' *ES*, I (1953).

—— 'Mercanti-imprenditori italiani in Fiandra alla fine del trecento.' *ES*, V (1958).

—— 'Uno sguardo al mercato dei panni di lana a Pisa nella seconda metà del trecento.' *ES* (1959).

—— *Aspetti della Vita Economica Medievale: studi nell' Archivio Datini di Prato*, I. Siena, 1962.

MIRA, G. 'Provvedimenti viscontei e sforzeschi sull' arte della lana in Como 1335–1535.' *Arch. Storico Lombardo*, II (1937).

RENARD, G. *Histoire du Travail à Florence*, 2 vols. Paris, 1913.

RODOLICO, N. 'The Struggle for the Right of Association in Fourteenth Century Florence.' *History*, VII (1922).

—— 'Proletariato operaio in Firenze del secolo XIV.' *Archivio storico italiano*, I (1943).

—— *I Ciompi. Una pagina di storia del proletariato operaio*. Florence, 1945.

SAPORI, A. 'Una compagnia di Calimala ai primi del Trecento.' *Biblioteca storica toscana*, VIII (1932).

SILVA, P. 'Intorno all' industria e al commercio della lana in Pisa.' *Studi Storici* (Pisa), XIX (1911).

TRASSELI, C. 'Il mercato dei panni a Palermo nella prima metà del XV secolo.' *ES* (1957).

ZANAZZO, G. B. 'L'arte della lana in Vicenza.' *Miscellanea di storia Veneta*, ser. 3, VI (1914).
ZANONI, L. *Gli Umiliati nei loro rapporti con l'eresia, l'industria della lana ed i comuni nei secoli XII e XIII, sulla scorta di documenti inediti*. Milan, 1911.
ZERBI, T. *Aspetti economico tecnici del mercato di Milano nel trecento*. Como, 1936.

V. ENGLAND

ARMITT, M. L. 'Fullers and Freeholders of the Parish of Grasmere.' *Transactions of the Cumberland and Westmorland Antiquarian and Archaeological Society*, N. S., VIII (1908).
ASHLEY, W. *The Early History of the English Woollen Industry*. Baltimore, 1887.
—— *An Introduction to English Economic History and Theory*, vol. I, pt. I, *The Middle Ages*, 3rd edn. London, 1894; pt. II, *The End of the Middle Ages*, 4th edn. London, 1906.
BRIDBURY, A. R. *Medieval English Cloth Making: an economic survey*. London, 1982.
CARUS-WILSON, E. M. and COLEMAN, O. *England's Export Trade, 1275–1547*. Oxford, 1963.
CARUS-WILSON, E. M. 'The Aulnage Accounts: a criticism.' *EconHR*, II (1929).
—— 'The Trade of Bristol.' *Studies in English Trade in the Fifteenth Century*. Ed. E. POWER and M. POSTAN. London, 1933.
—— 'An Industrial Revolution of the Thirteenth Century.' *EconHR*, XI (1941).
—— 'The English Cloth Industry in the late Twelfth and Early Thirteenth Centuries.' *EconHR*, XIV (1944).
—— 'The Origins and Early Development of the Merchant Adventurers' Organisation in London.' *EconHR*, IV (1933).
—— 'Trends in the Export of English Woollens in the Fourteenth Century.' *EconHR*, 2nd ser., III (1950).
—— *Medieval Merchant Venturers*. London, 1954; 2nd edn, 1967. (This volume reprints all the above articles by Professor Carus-Wilson.)
—— 'The Significance of the Secular Sculptures in the Lane Chapel, Collompton.' *Medieval Archaeology*, I (1957).
—— 'Evidences of Industrial Growth on Some Fifteenth-Century Manors.' *EconHR*, 2nd ser., XII (1959); reprinted in E. M. Carus-Wilson (ed.). *Essays in Economic History*, II. London, 1962.
—— 'The Woollen Industry before 1550.' *Victoria History of the Counties of England: Wiltshire*, IV. London, 1959.
CONSITT, F. *The London Weavers Company*. I, *From the Twelfth Century to the close of the Sixteenth Century*. Oxford, 1933.
DE SAGHER, H. 'L'Immigration des tisserands flamands et brabançons en Angleterre sous Edward III.' *Mélanges d'histoire offerts à Henri Pirenne*, 2 vols. Brussels, 1926.
FRYDE, E. 'The English Cloth Industry and the Trade with the Mediterranean, *c.* 1370–*c.* 1480.' *Produzione Commercio e Consumo dei Panni di Lana*. Florence, 1976.
GRAY, H. L. 'The Production and Exportation of English Woollens in the Fourteenth Century.' *English Historical Review*, XXXIX (1924).
HARVEY, P. D. A. 'The English Trade in Wool and Cloth, 1150–1250: some problems and suggestions.' *Produzione Commercio e Consumo dei Panni di Lana*. Florence, 1976.
HEATON, H. *The Yorkshire Woollen and Worsted Industries*. Oxford, 1920; 2nd edn, 1965.
JENKINS, J. G. (ed.). *The Wool Textile Industry in Great Britain*. London, 1972.
KERLING, N. J. M. *Commercial Relations of Holland and Zealand with England from the late 13th Century to the Close of the Middle Ages*. Leyden, 1954.
LENNARD, R. 'Early English Fulling-Mills: Additional Examples.' *EconHR*, 2nd ser., III (1951).
LIPSON, E. *The History of the English Woollen and Worsted Industries*. London, 1921.
—— *The Economic History of England*. I. *The Middle Ages*, 7th edn (revising much that is in previous editions and in *The History of the English Woollen and Worsted Industries* above). London, 1937.
MCCLENAGHAN, B. *The Springs of Lavenham and the Suffolk Cloth Trade in the XV and XVI Centuries*. Ipswich, 1924.

MILLER, E. 'The Fortunes of the English Textile Industry in the Thirteenth Century.' *EconHR*, 2nd ser., XVIII (1965).

PONTING, K. G. *The Woollen Industry of South-West England*. Bath, 1971.

POWER, E. *The Paycockes of Coggeshall*. London, 1920.

PREVENIER, W. 'Les Perturbations dans les relations commerciales anglo-flamandes entre 1389 et 1407. Causes de désaccord et raisons d'une réconciliation?' *Mélanges Edouard Perroy: Publications de la Sorbonne, Série Études*, v (1973).

PRITCHARD, F. A. 'Late Saxon Textiles from the City of London'. *Medieval Archaeology*, XXVIII (1984).

RAMSAY, G. D. *The Wiltshire Woollen Industry in the Sixteenth and Seventeenth Centuries*. Oxford, 1943; 2nd edn, London, 1965.

ROGERS, J. E. THOROLD. *History of Agriculture and Prices in England*, 7 vols. Oxford, 1866–1902.

SALZMAN, L. F. *English Industries of the Middle Ages*, new edn. Oxford, 1923.

SELLERS, M. 'The Textile Industries.' *Victoria History of the Counties of England: Yorkshire*, II. London, 1912.

SZÉKELY, G. 'Niederländische und Englische Tucharten im Mitteleuropa des 13–17 Jahrhunderts.' *Annales Universitatis Scientiarum Budapestensis, Sectio historica*, VIII (1966).

THORNTON, G. A. *A History of Clare, Suffolk*. Cambridge, 1930.

UNWIN, G. 'Woollen Cloth – the Old Draperies.' *Victoria History of the Counties of England: Suffolk*, II. London, 1907.

—— *The Gilds and Companies of London*, 3rd edn. London, 1938.

VON ROON-BASSERMAN, E. 'Die Handelsperre Englands gegen Flandern, 1270–74, und die lizenzierte englische Wollausfuhr.' *VSW*, L (1963).

WOLFF, P. 'English Cloth in Toulouse, 1380–1450.' *EconHR*, 2nd ser., II (1949–50).

CHAPTER X

Mining and Metallurgy in Medieval Civilisation

The following abbreviations have been used in this bibliography:

Annales	*Annales d'Histoire Économique et Sociale* and *Annales* (*Économies, Sociétés, Civilisations*).
EconHR	*Economic History Review*
JEBH	*Journal of Economic and Business History*
ZSSR	*Zeitschrift der Savigny-Stiftung für Rechtsgeschichte*
ZVGAS	*Zeitschrift des Vereins für Geschichte und Altertums Schlesiens*

I. SOURCES

AGRICOLA, GEORGIUS. *De Re Metallica*. Transl. from the Latin edition of 1556 by H. C. and L. H. Hoover. London, 1912.

BIRINGUCCIO, VANNOCCIO. *De la Pirotechnia*. Transl. from the Italian edition of 1540 and edited by Cyril S. Smith and M. T. Gnudi. New York, 1942.

ERCKER, LAZARUS. *Beschreibung allerfürnennstett mineralischen Ertzt und Berckwercksarten*. Prague, 1574. Transl. from the German edition of 1580 by A. G. Sisco and Cyril S. Smith. Chicago, 1951.

ERMISCH, HUBERT. *Das sächsische Bergrecht des Mittelalters*. Leipzig, 1887.

Laws and Customs of the Miners in the Forest of Dean. Ed. T. Houghton, 1689.

LOUVREX, M. G. de. *Recueil contenant les édits et règlements faits pour le pais de Liège et comté de Looz*. 4 vols. Liège, 1749–52.

MATHESIUS, JOHANN. *Sarepta Darinnen allerlei Bergwerck und Metallen*. Munich, 1571.

Mendip Mining Law and Forest Bounds (ed. J. W. Gough). Somerset Record Society Publications, XLV (1931).

PARACELSUS (THEOPHRASTUS BOMBASTUS VON HOHENHEIM). *Von der Bergsucht und anderen Bergkrankheiten* (*1533–34?*). Dillingen, 1567. (Engl. transl. in *Four Treatises of Paracelsus*. Ed. Henry E. Sigerist. Baltimore, 1941.)

PLOWDEN, EDMUND. *The Commentaries or Reports*. 1818 edn.

Recueil général des anciennes lois françaises. Par MM. Jourdan, Decrusy, Isambert. 28 vols. Paris, 1822–33.

WUTKE, KONRAD. *Schlesiens Bergbau und Huttenwesen – Urkunden und Akten* (*1529–1740*). *Codex Diplomaticus Silesiae*, XX and XXI. Breslau, 1900–1.

ZIVIER, E. *Akten und Urkunden zur Geschichte des Schlesischen Bergwesens*. Kattowitz, 1900.

ZYCHA, ADOLF. *Das böhmische Bergrecht des Mittelalters auf Grundlage des Bergrechts von Iglau*. 2 vols. Berlin, 1900.

II. MODERN WORKS

(1) *General*

ALLEMAGNE, HENRY RENÉ D'. *Ferronnerie ancienne*. 2 vols. Paris, 1924.

ARNDT, ADOLF. *Bergbau und Bergbaupolitik*. Leipzig, 1894.

BAUERMAN, H. *A Treatise on the Metallurgy of Iron*, 5th edn. London, 1882.

BECK, LUDWIG. *Die Geschichte des Eisens in technischer und kulturgeschichtlicher Beziehung*. 5 vols., 2nd edn. Brunswick, 1890–1903.

BECKMANN, JOHANN. *A History of Inventions, Discoveries and Origins*. (Transl. by Wm. Johnston. 2 vols., 4th edn. London, 1846.)

BENNETT, RICHARD and ELTON, JOHN. *History of Corn Milling*. London, 1898–1904.

BRAUDEL, FERNAND. 'Monnaies et Civilisations: de l'or du Soudan à l'argent d'Amérique.' *Annales*, I (1946), 10–21.

BRAUNSTEIN, P. 'Le Fer et la production du fer en Europe de 500 à 1500.' *Annales*, XXVII (1972).

CLEMENT, PIERRE. *Jacques Cœur et Charles VII*. Paris, 1866.
EHRENBERG, RICHARD. *Das Zeitalter der Fugger, Geldkapital und Creditverkehr im 16. Jahrhundert*. Jena, 1896. (Transl. in part as *Capital and Finance in the Age of the Renaissance* by H. M. Lucas. London, 1928.)
FELDHAUS, FRANZ M. *Die Technik der Antike und des Mittelalters*. Potsdam, 1931.
GILLE, B. 'L'Organisation de la production du fer au moyen âge.' *Revue d'Histoire de la Sidérurgie*, IX (1968).
HECKSCHER, ELI F. *Sveriges Ekonomiska Historia fran Gustav Vasa*. 2 vols. Stockholm, 1935–6.
JARS, G. *Voyages métallurgiques ou recherches et observations sur les mines...en Allemagne, Suède, Norvège, Angleterre et Ecosse*. 3 vols. Lyons, 1774–81.
LEJEUNE, JEAN. *La Formation du capitalisme moderne dans la principauté de Liège au XVIe siècle*. Liège, 1939.
LESTOCQUOY, J. 'The Tenth Century.' *EconHR*, XVII (1947).
LEXIS, W. 'Beiträge zur Statistik der Edelmetalle.' *Jahrbücher für Nationalökonomie und Statistik*, XXXIV (1879), 361–417.
LOMBARD, M. *Les Métaux dans l'ancien monde du Ve au XIe siècle*. Paris, 1974.
—— *Monnaie et histoire d'Alexandre à Mahomet*. Paris, 1971.
MçILWAIN, C. H. 'Medieval Estates.' *Cambridge Medieval History*, VII (1932), 664–715.
NEF, J. U. *The Conquest of the Material World*. Parts 1 and 2 and Part 3 (chap. 7). Chicago, 1964.
—— *Cultural Foundations of Industrial Civilisation*, Chapters 1, 2 and 3. Cambridge, 1958.
—— *Industry and Government in France and England, 1540–1640*. New York, 1957.
—— *La Naissance de la civilisation industrielle et le monde contemporain*. Paris, 1954.
—— *The United States and Civilisation*, 2nd edn. Chapters 2, 3 and 4. Chicago, 1967.
—— *War and Human Progress*, Part I. London, 1951.
PERCY, JOHN. *Metallurgy*, II. London, 1880.
PIRENNE, HENRI. *Economic and Social History of Medieval Europe*. New York, 1937. (Transl. by I. E. Clegg. London, 1936.)
—— *Histoire de Belgique*, I–III, 3rd edn. Brussels, 1909, 1922, 1923.
POSTAN, M. M. in *Congrès des Sciences Historiques*. Paris, 1950, 230–31.
POWER, EILEEN E. 'Peasant Life and Rural Conditions.' *Cambridge Medieval History*, VII (1932).
SMITH, J. RUSSELL. *The Story of Iron and Steel*. New York, 1908.
SOETBEER, ADOLF. *Edelmetall-Producktion und Werthverhältnis zwischen Gold und Silber seit der Entdeckung Amerikas bis zur Gegenwart*. Gotha, 1879.
SOMBART, WERNER. *Der Moderne Kapitalismus*. 4th edn. 4 vols. Munich and Leipzig, 1916.
SPRANDEL, R. *Das Eisengewerbe im Mittelalter*. Stuttgart, 1968.
—— 'La Production du fer au moyen âge.' *Annales*, XXIV (1969).
STRIEDER, JACOB. 'Werden und Waschsen des europäischen Frühkapitalismus.' *Propyläen Weltgeschichte*, IV. Ed. Walter Goetz. Berlin, 1932.
—— *Zur Genesis des modernen Kapitalismus*. Leipzig, 1904.
SWANK, JAMES M. *History of the Manufacture of Iron in All Ages*, 2nd edn. Philadelphia, 1892.
USHUR, ABBOTT PAYSON. *The Early History of Deposit Banking in Mediterranean Europe*. Cambridge, Mass., 1943.
—— *A History of Mechanical Inventions*. New York, 1929.
WEBER, MAX. *General Economic History*. (Transl. by F. H. Knight.) London, 1927.
WHITE, LYNN. *Medieval Technology and Social Change*. Oxford, 1962.

(2) *On Mining and Metallurgy in Antiquity and in Ancient China*

ARDAILLON, EDOUARD. *Les Mines du Laurion dans l'antiquité*. Paris, 1897.
BESNIER, MAURICE. 'L'Interdiction du travail des mines en Italie sous la république.' *Revue Archéologique*, ser. 5, X (1919), 31–50.

—— 'Le Commerce de plomb a l'époque romaine.' *Revue Archéologique*, ser. 5, XII (1920), 211–44; XIII (1921), 36–76; XIV (1921), 98–121.
CALHOUN, G. M. 'Ancient Athenian Mining.' *JEBH*, III (1931), 333–61.
COLLINGWOOD, R. G. and MYERS, J. N. L. *Roman Britain and the English Settlements*, 2nd edn. Oxford, 1937.
DAVIES, OLIVER. *Roman Mines in Europe*. Oxford, 1935.
FRANCOTTE, HENRI. *L'Industrie dans la Grèce ancienne*. 2 vols. Brussels, 1900–1.
FRANK, TENNEY. *An Economic History of Rome*, 2nd edn. Baltimore, 1927.
FRIEND, J. NEWTON. *Iron in Antiquity*. London, 1926.
HARTWELL, ROBERT. 'A Revolution in the Chinese Iron and Coal Industries during the Northern Sung, A.D. 960–1126.' *Journal of Asian Studies*, XXII (1962), 153–62.
—— 'A Cycle of Economic Change in Imperial China: coal and iron in Northeast China, 750–1350.' *Journal of the Economic and Social History of the Orient* (1966).
—— 'Markets, Technology and the Structure of Enterprise in the Development of the Eleventh-Century Chinese Iron and Steel Industry.' *Journal of Economic History*, XXVI (1966), 29–58.
HAUDRICOURT, A. G. 'La Fonte en Chine.' *Techniques et Civilisations*, II (1952), 37–41.
MISPOULET, JEAN-BAPTISTE. *Le Régime des mines à l'époque romaine et au moyen âge d'après les tables d'Aljustrel*. Paris, 1908.
NEEDHAM, JOSEPH. *Science and Civilisation in China*. Cambridge, 1954.
NEUBURG, CLAMOR. 'Untersuchungen zur Geschichte des römischen Bergbaus.' *Zeitschrift für die gesamte Staatswissenschaft*, LVI (1900).
NEUBURGER, ALBERT. *Die Technik des Altertums*. Transl. by Henry L. Brose. *The Technical Arts and Sciences of the Ancients*. London, 1930.
ROSSIGNOL, JEAN PIERRE. *Les Métaux dans l'antiquité*. Paris, 1863.
ROSTOVTZEFF, M. 'Geschichte der Staatspacht in der römischen Kaiserzeit bis Diokletian.' *Philologus*, Suppl., IX (1904).
—— *Studien zur Geschichte des römischen Kolonates*. Leipzig, 1910.
—— *The Social and Economic History of the Hellenistic World*. 3 vols. Oxford, 1941.
—— *The Social and Economic History of the Roman Empire*. Oxford, 1926.

(3) *Central Europe and Italy*

ACHENBACH, H. *Das französische Bergrecht und die Forbildung desselben durch das preussische allgemeine Berggesetz*. Bonn, 1869.
—— *Das gemeine deutsche Bergrecht*. Bonn, 1871.
—— 'Geschichte der Cleve-Märkischen Berggesetzgebung und Bergverwaltung bis zum Jahre 1815.' *Zeitschrift fur Bergrecht*, XXXIII (1887).
AMRHEIN, AUGUST. 'Der Bergbau im Spessart unter der Regierung der Churfursten von Mainz.' *Archiv des historischen Vereins von Unterfranken und Aschaffenburg*, XXXVII (1895).
ARNDT, AD. *Zur Geschichte und Theorie des Bergregals und der Bergbaufreiheit*. Halle, 1878.
—— 'Noch einmal der Sachsenspiegel und das Bergregal.' *ZSSR*, Germanische Abt., XXIII (1902).
—— 'Einige Bemerkungen zur Geschichte des Bergregals.' *ZSSR*, Germanische Abt., XXIV (1903).
BERNHARD, LUDWIG. 'Die Entstehung und Entwicklung der Gedingeordnungen im deutschen Bergrecht.' *Staats- und sozialwissenschaftliche Forschungen*. Ed. G Schmöller, vol. XX, no. 7. Leipzig, 1902.
BITTNER, L. 'Das Eisenwesen in Innerberg-Eisenerz.' *Archiv. für osterreichische Geschichte*, LXXXIX (ii). Vienna, 1901.
BOYCE, HELEN. *The Mines of the Upper Harz from 1514 to 1589*. Menasha, Wisconsin, 1920.
BRUCHMÜLLER, W. *Der Kobaltbergbau und die Blaufarbenwerke in Sachsen bis zum Jahre 1653*. Crossen a. O., 1897.
CSALLNER, ROBERT. 'Alte deutsche Bergwerkskolonien im Norden Siebenbürgens.' In *Studium Lipsiense*, by Karl Lamprecht. Berlin, 1909.
DELUMEA, JEAN. *L'Alun de Rome XVe–XIXe*. Paris, 1962.

DOBEL, FRIEDRICH. 'Ueber den Bergbau und Handel des Jacob und Anton Fugger in Kärnten und Tirol, 1495–1550.' *Zeitschrift des historischen Vereins für Schwaben und Neuburg*, IX (1882), 193–213.

FINK, E. 'Die Bergwerksunternehmungen der Fugger in Schlesien.' *Zeitschrift des Vereins für Geschichte und Altertum Schlesiens*, XXVIII (1894).

FÖHRENBACH, OTTO. *Der badische Bergbau in seiner wirtschaftlichen Bedeutung vom Ausgang des Mittelalters bis zur Gegenwart*. Zell im Wiesenthal, 1910.

GOTHEIN, EBERHARD. 'Beiträge zur Geschichte des Bergbaus im Schwarzwald.' *Zeitschrift für die Geschichte des Oberrheins*, N.F. II (1887), 385–448.

—— *Wirtschaftsgeschichte des Schwarzwaldes und der angrenzenden Landschaften*. Strasbourg, 1892.

GRÉAU, E. *Le Fer en Lorraine*. Nancy, 1908.

HASSLACHER, A. 'Geschichtliche Entwicklung des Steinkohlenbergbaues im Saargebiete.' *Zeitschrift für Bergbau, Hütten und Salinenwesen im preussischen Staate*, XXXII (1884).

HASSLER, FRIED. 'German Miners in Foreign Lands in the Sixteenth Century.' *Research and Progress*, March/April, 1939.

HILLEBRAND, W. 'Der Goslarer Metallhandel im Mittelalter.' *Hansische Geschichtsblätter*, LXXXVII (1969).

—— 'Von den Anfangen des Erzbergbaus am Rammelsberg bei Goslar.' *Niedersächsisches Jahrbuch für Landesgeschichte*, XXXIX (1967).

HITZINGER, PETER. *Das Quecksilber-Bergwerk Idria*. Laibach, 1860.

HOPPE, OSWALD. *Der Silberbergbau zu Schneeberg bis zum Jahre 1500*. Freiberg, 1908.

HUE, OTTO. *Die Bergarbeiter. Historische Darstellung der Bergarbeiterverhältnisse von der ältesten bis in die neueste Zeit*, 2 vols. Stuttgart, 1910, 1913.

HÜLLMAN, KARL D. *Geschichte des Ursprungs der Stände in Deutschland*. Frankfurt-an-der-Oder, 1806.

INAMA-STERNEGG, K. T. von. *Deutsche Wirtschaftsgeschichte des 10. bis 12. Jahrhunderts*. Leipzig, 1891.

JACQUOT, E. 'Notice sur la fabrication de la fonte, du fer et de l'acier dans la Thüringerwald et le Frankenwald.' *Annales des mines*, ser. 4, II (1842).

JÄGER, ALBERT. 'Beiträge zur Tirolisch-Salzburgischen Bergwerksgeschichte.' *Archiv für österreichische Geschichte*, LIII (1875), 337–456.

JANAČEK, J. 'L'Argent tchèque et la Méditerranée, XIVe et XVe siècles'. *Mélanges en l'Honneur de Fernand Braudel*, I. Paris, 1973.

JANSEN, MAX. *Jakob Fugger der Reiche*. Studien zur Fugger-Geschichte, 3. Heft. Leipzig, 1910.

KOCH, ERNST. 'Das Hütten- und Hammerwerk der Fugger zu Hohenkirchen bei Georgenthal in Thüringen, 1495–1549.' *Zeitschrift des Vereins für Thüringische Geschichte*, N.F., XXVI (1926).

KROKER, ERNST. 'Leipzig und die sächsischen Bergwerke.' *Schriften des Vereins für die Geschichte Leipzigs*, IX (1909).

LANGER, JOHANNES. 'Der ostelbische Bergbau im und am Gebiet der Dresdner Heide und der sächs. Schweiz.' *Neues Archiv für sächsische Geschichte und Altertumskunde*, I (1929), 1–66.

MANNEL, GOTTFRIED. *Die Eisenhütten und Hämmer des Fürstentums Waldeck*. Leipzig, 1908.

MEISTER, A. 'Die Anfänge des Eisenindustrie in der Grafschaft Mark.' *Beiträge zur Geschichte Dortmunds und der Grafschaft Mark*, XVII (1909).

MUCK, WALTER. *Der Mansfelder Kupferschieferbergbau in seiner rechtsgeschichtlichen Entwicklung*. 2 vols. Eisleben, 1910.

MÜLLNER, ALFONS. 'Die historische Entwicklung des Bergbaues in den österreichischen Alpenlandern.' *Berg-u. huttermännisches Jahrbuch* (1906).

—— *Geschichte des Eisens*. Erste Abteilung. In *Krain, Görz und Istrien*. Vienna, 1909.

NEF, J. U. 'Silver Production in Central Europe, 1450–1618.' *Journ. of Political Economy*, XLIX (1941), no. 4.

NEUBURG, CLAMOR. *Goslars Bergbau bis 1552*. Hanover, 1892.

—— 'Der Zusammenhang zwischen römischem und deutschem Bergbau.' *Festgaben für Wilhelm Lexis*. Jena, 1907.

Opet, Otto. 'Das Gewerbschaftsrecht nach den deutschen Bergrechtsquellen des Mittelalters.' *Zeitschrift für Bergrecht*, xxxiv (1893).
Peter, Karl. 'Die Goldbergwerke bei Zuckmantel und Freiwaldau.' *ZVGAS*, xix (1885).
Pflug, Karl. 'Zur Geschichte des Bergbaues im Waldenburger Berglande.' *ZVGAS*, xliii (1909).
Schmöller, Gustav. 'Die geschichtliche Entwicklung der Unternehmung.' *Jahrbuch für Gesetzgebung, Verwaltung und Volkswirtschaft im deutschen Reich*, xv (1891).
Schnürlen, Mathilde. *Geschichte des Württembergischen Kupfer- und Silbererzbergbaus.* Berlin, 1921.
Simonin, L. 'De l'exploitation des mines et de la métallurgie en Toscane pendant l'antiquité et le moyen âge.' *Annales des mines*, ser. 5, xix (1858), 557–615.
Steinbeck, Aemil. *Geschichte des schlesischen Bergbaues.* Breslau, 1857.
Sternberg, Kaspar. *Umrisse einer Geschichte der böhmischen Bergwerke.* 2 vols. Prague, 1836, 1838.
Stoddart, Anna M. *The Life of Paracelsus.* Philadelphia, 1911.
Strieder, Jakob. *Studien zur Geschichte kapitalistischer Organisationsformen*, 2nd edn. Munich, 1925.
Tomaschek Edler Von Sradowa, J. A. *Das alte Bergrecht von Iglau.* Innsbruck, 1897.
Utsch, Richard. *Die Entwicklung und volkswirtschaftliche Bedeutung des Eisenerzbaues und der Eisenindustrie im Siegerland.* Görlitz, 1913.
Westermann, E. *Das Eislebener Garkupfer und seine Bedeutung für den europaïschen Kupfermarkt, 1460–1560.* Cologne, 1971.
Weyhmann, Alfred. *Geschichte der älteren Lothringischen Eisenindustrie.* Metz, 1905.
Wick, Wilhelm. *Die landesherrlichen Eisenhütten und Hämmer im ehemaligen Kurhessen bis zum Ende des XVII. Jahrhunderts.* Cassel, 1910.
Wolfstrigl-Wolfskron, M. R. von. *Die Tiroler Erzbergbaue, 1301–1665.* Innsbruck, 1903. (This is the only comprehensive work on mining in the Tyrol during the Middle Ages, but it has not been well received by scholars. It is rather unintelligently and clumsily put together, and it is said by Stephan Worms to contain many errors of fact and of interpretation.)
Worms, Stephan. *Schwazer Bergbau im fünfzehnten Jahrhundert.* Vienna, 1904.
Zycha, Adolf. *Das Recht des ältesten deutschen Bergbaues bis ins 13. Jahrhundert.* Berlin, 1899.
—— 'Zur neuesten Literatur über die Wirtschafts- und Rechts-geschichte des deutschen Bergbaus.' *Vierteljahrschrift für Sozial- und Wirtschaftsgeschichte*, v (1907); vi (1908).

(4) *France, Spain, and the Low Countries*

Arnould, G. *Le Bassin houiller du couchant de Mons.* Mons, 1877.
Bardon, Achille. *L'Exploitation du bassin houiller d'Alais sous l'ancien régime.* Nîmes, 1898.
Beaune, Henri. 'Note sur le régime des mines dans le duché de Bourgogne.' *Mém. de la société des antiquaires de France*, xxxi (1869).
Borlase, W. C. *Tin Mining in Spain, Past and Present.* London, 1898.
Bouchayer, Auguste. *Les Chartreux maîtres de forges.* Grenoble, 1927.
Bouzy, Alf. 'Essai hist. sur l'ancien mandement d'Allevard.' *Bull. de la soc. de statistique de l'Isère*, i (1839).
Bulard, Marcel. 'L'Industrie du fer dans la Haute-Marne.' *Annales de geographie*, xiii (1904), 223–42, 310–21.
Chabrand, Ernest. *Essai historique sur la métallurgie du fer et de l'acier en Dauphiné et en Savoie.* Grenoble, 1898.
Chazaud, A. M. 'Les Mines de houille de Charbonnier (Puy-de-Dome) au XVe siècle.' *Bulletin de la soc. d'émulation du dépt. de l'Allier*, x (1868).
Clément, Pierre. *Jacques Cœur et Charles VII.* Paris, 1866.
Corbier. 'Notice sur les forges impériales de la Chaussade.' *Bull. de la soc. nivernaise des lettres, sciences et arts*, ser. 2, iv (1869).

COUFFON, OLIVER. *Les Mines de charbon en Anjou*. Angers, 1911.

DÉCAMPS, G. 'Mémoire historique sur l'origine et les développements de l'industrie houillère dans le bassin du couchant de Mons.' *Société des arts et des lettres du Hainaut, publications*, ser. 4, v (1880); ser. 5, I (1889).

DESTRAY, P. 'Note sur les anciennes forges du prieuré de la Charité.' *Mém. de la soc. acad. du Nivernais*, XVII (1913).

—— 'Les Houillères de la Machine (Nivernais) au 16e siècle.' *Mémoires et documents pour servir à l'histoire du commerce et de l'industrie en France* (ed. Julien Hayem). Ser. 4. Paris, 1916.

FEBVRE, LUCIEN. *Phillippe II et la Franche-Comté*. Paris, 1912.

FINOT, J. 'La Seigneurerie de Ronchamp et l'origine de l'exploitation des houillères de cette localitè, 1220–1789.' *Rev. d'hist. nobilliaire et d'archéol. héraldique*, 1882.

FORMEVILLE, A. de. *Les barons fossiers et les férons de Normandie*. Caen, 1852.

GÉRIN, RICHARD, H. de. 'Mines et mineurs autrefois et aujourd'hui. Etude économique sur les charbonnages de Provence du 15 au 19 siècle.' *Soc. stat. de Marseille*, XLVII (1906–7).

GIRAUD, J.-B. *Documents pour servir à l'histoire de l'armement au moyen âge*, I. Lyons, 1895.

—— *Documents pour l'histoire de l'armement au moyen âge et à la renaissance*, II. Lyons, 1904.

GORIS, J. A. *Études sur les colonies marchandes méridionales à Anvers de 1488 à 1567*. Louvain, 1925.

GRAS, L. J. *Essai sur l'histoire de la quincaillerie et petite métallurgie à Saint-Etienne et dans la région stephanoise comparée aux régions concurrentes*. Saint-Etienne, 1904.

—— *Histoire économique générale des mines de la Loire*. Saint-Etienne, 1922.

HÄBLER, KONRAD. *Die Geschichte der Fugger'schen Handlung in Spanien*. Weimar, 1897.

HAMILTON, EARL J. *American Treasure and the Price Revolution in Spain, 1501–1650*. Cambridge, Mass., 1934.

—— *Money, Prices and Wages in Valencia, Aragon, and Navarre, 1351–1500*. Cambridge, Mass., 1936.

HAUSER, HENRI. *Ouvriers du temps passé*. Paris, 1899.

HENAUX, F. *Fabrique d'armes de Liège*. Liège, 1858.

LAMÉ-FLEURY. *De la législation minérale sous l'ancienne monarchie*. Paris, 1857.

LECORNNU, L. 'Sur le métallurgie du fer en Basse-Normandie.' *Mém. de l'acad. nat. des sciences, arts, et belles-lettres de Caen*, 1884.

LEJEUNE, JEAN. *La Formation du capitalisme moderne dans la principauté de Liège au XVIe siècle*. Paris, 1939.

LEROUX, MAURICE. *L'Industrie du fer dans le Perche*. Paris, 1916.

LEVAINVILLE, J. *L'Industrie du fer en France*. Paris, 1922.

LOPEZ, ROBERTO. *Contributo alla storia della miniere argentifere di Sardegna*. Milan, 1936.

LUCE, SIMÉON. 'De l'exploitation des mines et de la condition des ouvriers mineurs en France au XVe siècle.' *Revue des questions historiques*, XXI (1877).

MALHERBE, RENIER. 'Historique de l'exploitation de la houille dans le pays de Liège jusqu'à nos jours.' *Mémoire de la société libre d'émulation de Liège*, N.S., II. Liège, 1862.

MASSÉ, ALFRED. *Monographies nivernaises*. Nevers, 1913.

MIGNERON, M. 'The Mining Laws of France.' *Trans. Roy. Geog. Soc. Cornwall*, VI, 239–58.

NIMAL, H. DE. 'La Métallurgie à l'exposition de Charleroi en 1911 avec des notes historiques sur la forgerie.' *Livre d'or de l'exposition de Charleroi*. Charleroi, 1913.

PAGÉ, CAMILLE. *La Coutellerie depuis l'origine jusqu'à nos jours*. 6 vols. Chatellerault, 1896–1904.

PIRENNE, HENRI. *Histoire de Belgique*, I–III. Brussels, 1900–32.

PRINET, MAX. *L'Industrie du sel en Franche-Comté avant la conquête française*. Besançon, 1900.

ROUZAUD, HENRI. *Histoire d'une mine au mineur. La mine de Rancié depuis le moyen âge jusqu'à la Révolution*. Toulouse, 1908.

SAINT SAUD, COMTE DE. 'Privilèges concernant les maîtres de forges.' *Bulletin de la société archaéologique du Périgord*, XXVII (1900).

SALIN, EDOUARD. 'Un Aspect de la civilisation mérovingienne.' *Annales*, II (1955), 161–72.
SALIN, EDOUARD and FRANCE-LANORD, ALBERT. *Le Fer a l'époque mérovingienne*. Paris, 1943.
SCLAFERT, THÉRÈSE. *L'Industrie du fer dans la région d'Allevard au moyen âge*. Grenoble, 1926.
VASQUEZ DE PRADA, V. 'Las antiquas ferrarias de Vizcaya, 1450–1800.' *Mélanges en l'honneur de Fernand Braudel*, I. Paris 1973.
VERNEILH, BARON DE. 'Notes sur les anciennes forges du Périgord et du Limousin.' *Revue des sociétés savantes*, ser. 6, IV (1876).
VILLEFOSSE, HÉRON DE. *De la richesse minérale*. 3 vols. Paris, 1810, 1819.
YERNAUX, Y. *La Métallurgie liègeoise et son expansion au 17e siècle*. 1939.

(5) *Great Britain and Scandinavia*

ABRAHAMS, ISRAEL. 'Joachim Gaunse: a mining incident in the reign of Queen Elizabeth.' *Jewish Hist. Soc. Trans.*, IV. London, 1899–1901.
ASHTON, T. S. *Iron and Steel in the Industrial Revolution*. Manchester, 1924.
ATKINSON, STEPHEN. *The Discoverie and Historie of the Gold Mynes in Scotland, written in 1619*. Edinburgh (Bannatyne Club), 1825.
AWTY, B. G. 'Continental Origins of Wealden Ironworkers.' *EconHR*, 2nd ser., XXXIV (1981).
BLAKE, J. B. 'The Medieval Coal Trade of North East England: some fourteenth-century evidence.' *Northern History*, II (1967).
BLANCHARD, I. S. W. 'The Miner and the Agricultural Community in Late Medieval England.' *Agricultural Hist. Rev.*, XX (1972).
—— 'Seigneurial Entrepreneurship: the bishops of Durham and the Weardale iron industry, 1406–1529.' *Business History*, XV (1973).
—— 'Derbyshire Lead Production, 1195–1505.' *Derbyshire Arch. Jnl.*, XCL (1974).
'Labour Productivity and Work Psychology in the English Mining Industry'. *EconHR*, 2nd ser., XXXI (1978).
CHILDS, W. R. 'England's Iron Trade in the Fifteenth Century'. *Economic History Review*, 2nd ser. XXXIV (1981).
CUNNINGHAM, A. S. *Mining in the Kingdom of Fife*. Edinburgh, 1913.
FFOULKES, CHARLES. *The Gun-Founders of England*. Cambridge, 1937.
GALLOWAY, ROBERT L. *A History of Coal Mining in Great Britain*. London, 1882.
—— *Annals of Coal Mining and the Coal Trade*. London, 1898.
GOUGH, JOHN W. *The Mines of Mendip*. 2nd edn. Oxford, 1967.
HAMILTON, HENRY. *The English Brass and Copper Industries to 1800*. London, 1926.
HATCHER, J. *English Tin Production and Trade before 1550*. Oxford, 1973.
—— 'Myths, Miners and Agricultural Communities.' *Agricultural Hist. Rev.*, XXII (1974).
HECKSCHER, ELI F. *Sveriges Ekonomiska Historia fran Gustav Vasa*. 2 vols. Stockholm, 1935–6.
—— 'Un Grand chapitre de l'histoire du fer: le monopole suédois.' *Annales*, II (1932), 127–39, 225–41.
HOUGHTON, THOMAS. *The Compleat Miner; or a Collection of the Laws, Liberties, ancient Customs...and Privileges of the several Mines and Miners in the Counties of Derby, Gloucester and Somerset*. 3 pts. London, 1687–88.
JENKIN, A. K. HAMILTON. *The Cornish Miner*. London, 1927.
JENKINS, RHYS. 'The Rise and Fall of the Sussex Iron Industry.' *Newcomen Soc. Trans.*, I (1920–1).
—— 'Iron-Making in the Forest of Dean.' *Newcomen Soc. Trans.*, VI (1925–6).
LAPSLEY, G. T. 'The Account Roll of a Fifteenth-Century Iron Master.' *Engl. Hist. Rev.*, XIV (1899).
LARSON, HENRIETTA M. 'Notes and Documents: a medieval Swedish mining company.' *JEBH*, II, 545–59. Cambridge, Mass., 1930.

LEADER, R. E. *History of the Company of Cutlers of Hallamshire*, I. Sheffield, 1905.
LEWIS, E. A. 'The Development of Industry and Commerce in Wales during the Middle Ages.' *Trans. Roy. Hist. Soc.* N.S., XVII (1903), 121–73.
LEWIS, G. R. *The Stannaries*. Cambridge, Mass., 1907.
LLOYD, G. I. H. *The Cutlery Trades*. London, 1913.
LOWER, MARK ANTONY. 'Historical and Archaeological Notices of the Iron Works of the County of Sussex.' *Sussex Arch. Collections*, II (1849), 169–220.
MACADAM, I. 'Notes on the Ancient Iron Industry of Scotland.' *Proc. Soc. Antiq. Scot.*, XXI (1886–7).
NEF, J. U. *The Rise of the British Coal Industry*. 2 vols. Reprinted London, 1966.
—— 'Note on the Progress of Iron Production in England, 1540–1640.' *Journ. Political Economy*, XLIV (1936), 398–403.
NICHOLL, JOHN. *Some Account of the Worshipful Company of Ironmongers*, 2nd edn. London, 1866.
NICHOLLS, HENRY GEORGE. *Iron-Making in the Olden Times as instanced in the Ancient Mines, Forges, and Furnaces of the Forest of Dean*. London, 1866.
PATRICK, ROBERT W. C. *Early Records Relating to Mining in Scotland*. Edinburgh, 1878.
RAISTRICK, A. and JENNINGS, B. *A History of Lead Mining in the Pennines*. London, 1965.
SALTZMAN, LOUIS FRANCIS. *English Industries of the Middle Ages*, 2nd edn. Oxford, 1923.
SOPWITH, THOS. *An Account of the Mining Districts of Alston Moor, Weardale and Teesdale in Cumberland and Durham*. Alnwick, 1833.
STRAKER, ERNEST. *Wealden Iron*. London, 1931.
Victoria County History of: Cornwall, Derby, Durham, Gloucester, Lancaster, Nottingham, Shropshire, Warwick, York.

CHAPTER XI

Building in Stone in Medieval Western Europe

by H. M. COLVIN

This bibliography is directed towards building as an economic rather than as an artistic activity; it concentrates on organisation rather than style, on construction rather than design. At a time when aesthetic aims and technical means were so closely linked the distinction is an artificial one, and what follows is only an economically biased selection from the vast literature of medieval European architecture, to which the bibliographies appended to the relevant volumes of the Pelican History of Art provide a convenient introduction. For further bibliographical guidance on the topics dealt with here see especially the works cited below by Aubert, Binding and Nussbaum, Du Colombier, Knoop and Jones (1967), Maier, Shelby and Sosson.

I. GENERAL

BINDING, G., (ed.). *Beiträge über Bauführung und Baufinanzierung im Mittelalter.* Cologne 1974.

CHENEY, C. R. 'Church-building in the Middle Ages.' *Bulletin of the John Rylands Library*, XXXIV, 1951.

GEM, R. 'A recession in English architecture during the early eleventh century, and its effect on the development of the Romanesque style.' *Journal of the British Archaeological Association*, 3rd ser., XXXVIII (1975).

JOHNSON, H. T. 'Cathedral Building and the Medieval Economy', in *Explorations in Entrepreneurial History*. Spring 1967.

LOPEZ, R. S. 'Economie et architecture médiévale. Cela a-t-il tué ceci?' *Annales*, VII (1952).

MUSSET, L. 'Les Conditions financières d'une réussite architecturale: les grandes églises romanes de Normandie', in *Mélanges offerts à René Crozet*. Poitiers, 1966.

VERPLAETSE, A. 'L'Architecture en Flandre entre 900 et 1200.' *Cahiers de civilisation médiévale*, VIII (1965).

WARNKE, MARTIN. *Bau und Überbau, Soziologie der Mittelalterlichen Architektur nach dem Schriftquellen.* Frankfurt, 1976.

II. SOURCES

BAR, M. *Der Koblenzer Mauerbau Rechnungen 1276–1289* (Publikationen des Gesellschaft für Rheinische Geschichtskunde, Leipsig, 1888).

COLVIN, H. M. *Building Accounts of King Henry III.* Oxford, 1971.

ERSKINE, AUDREY M. *The Accounts of the Fabric of Exeter Cathedral, 1279–1353.* 2 vols. Devon & Cornwall Record Society, N.S., XXIV and XXVI, 1981–3.

GÜMBEL, A. 'Baurechnungen vom Chor von St. Lorenz zu Nürnberg 1462–1467.' *Repertorium für Kunstwissenschaft*, XXXIII (1910).

LEHMANN-BROCKHAUS, OTTO. *Lateinische Schriftquellen zur Kunst in England, Wales und Schottland, vom Jahre 901 bis zum Jahre 1307.* 5 vols. Munich, 1955–60.

MORTET, V. and DESCHAMPS, P. *Recueil de textes relatifs a l'histoire de l'architecture et à la condition des architectes en France au Moyen Age*, 2 vols. Paris, 1911, 1929.

RAINE, JAMES. *The Fabric Rolls of York Minster* (Surtees Society, 1859).

SIMPSON, W. DOUGLAS. *The Building Accounts of Tattershall Castle 1434–1472.* Lincoln Record Society, LV, 1960.

STHAMER, EDUARD. *Die Bauten der Hohenstaufen in Unteritalien: Dokumente zur Geschichte der Kastelbauten Kaiser Freidrichs II und Karls I von Anjou.* 2 vols. Leipzig, 1912, 1926.

III. BUILDING ORGANISATION

(1) *Royal and other State Works*

BROWN, R. A., COLVIN, H. M. and TAYLOR, A. J. *The History of the King's Works*, vols. I–2: *The Middle Ages*. London, 1963.

CANAT DE CHIZY, N. 'Etude sur le service des travaux publics et spécialement sur la charge de maîtres des oeuvres de Bourgogne sous les ducs de la race des Valois (1363–1477).' *Bulletin Monumental*, LXIII (1898).

FAVREAU, R. 'Les Maîtres des oeuvres du roi en Poitou au XVe siècle,' *Mélanges offerts à René Crozet*, II (1966).

(2) *Municipal Works*

BRAUNFELS, W. *Mittelalterliche Stadtbaukunst in der Toscana*. Berlin, 1959.

FOWLER, ANGUS. 'Der Stadhof und die spätere Stadtbaumschule am Grün 1428–1803,' in *Vom 'Staithobe' zum Bauhof der Stadt Marburg*, Marburger Stadtschriften zur Geschichte und Kultur 5. Marburg, 1982.

KNOOP, D. and JONES, G. P. 'London Bridge and its Builders: a study of the municipal employment of masons mainly in the fifteenth century.' *Ars Quatuor Coronatorum*, XLVII (1934).

LLOYD, T. H. *Some Aspects of the Building Industry in Medieval Stratford-upon-Avon*. Dugdale Society Occasional papers No. XIV, 1961.

SALVI, G. *L'Operarius del Porto di Genova: Architetto o Amministratore?* Genoa, 1934.

SOSSON, J. P. *Les Travaux publics de la ville de Bruges XIVe–XVe siècles*. Brussels, 1977.

SWANSON, HEATHER. *Building Craftsmen in late medieval York* (University of York, Borthwick paper No. LXIII, 1983).

(3) *Ecclesiastical Works*

ASSIER, A. *Comtes de l'Oeuvre de l'église de Troyes ou nouvelles recherches sur la construction des églises et sur les usages du Moyen Age*. Troyes, 1855.

BIGET, J. L. 'Recherches sur le financement des cathédrales du Midi au XIIIe siècle,' in *La Naissance et l'essor du gothique méridional au XIIIe siècle* (Cahiers de Fanjeaux, IX. Toulouse, 1974).

BRUTAILS, J. A. 'Deux chantiers bordelais 1486–1521.' *Le Moyen Age*, XII–XIV (1899–1901).

DAVID, M. 'La Fabrique et les manoeuvres sur les chantiers des cathédrales de France jusqu'au XIVe siècle'. *Études de droit, d'histoire du droit canonique dédiées à Gabriel Le Bras*, II. Paris, 1965.

DE MELY. 'Nos Vieilles cathédrales et leurs maîtres d'oeuvre.' *Revue Archéologique*, 5th ser., XI (1920) and XIII (1921).

DU COLOMBIER, P. *Les Chantiers des cathédrales*, 2nd edn. Paris, 1973.

GIMPEL, J. *Les Batisseurs des cathédrales*. Paris, 1959; *The Cathedral Builders*. London, 1983.

JUSSELIN, H. 'La Maîtrise de l'oeuvre à Notre Dame de Chartres.' *Mémoires de la Société archéologique d'Eure-et-Loir*, XV. Chartres, 1921.

KRAUS, HENRY. *Gold was the Mortar. The Economics of Cathedral Building*. London, 1979.

QUICHERAT, J. 'Notice sur plusieurs registres de l'oeuvre de la cathédrale de Troyes.' *Mélanges d'archéologie et d'histoire*, I. Paris, 1886.

ROOTTHOFF, G. *Organisation und Finanzierung des Xantener Dombaues in 15 Jahrhundert*. Xanten, 1973.

SWARTWOUT, R. E. *The Monastic Craftsman*. Cambridge, 1932.

VROOM, W. H. *De financiering van de kathedraalbouw in de middeleeuwen: in het bijzander van de dom van Utrecht*. Maarsen, 1981.

(4) *The Mason's Trade and Conditions of Employment*

AUBERT, MARCEL. 'La Construction au Moyen Age. Loges d'Allemagne, Maçons et Francs-maçons en Angleterre.' *Bulletin Monumental*, CXVI (1958), CXVIII (1960), CXIX (1961).

BAULANT, M. 'Le Salaire des ouvriers du bâtiment à Paris, de 1400 à 1726.' *Annales*, XXVI (1971).

GIMPEL, J. 'Le Liberté du travail et l'organisation des professions du bâtiment a l'époque des grand constructions gothiques.' *Revue d'Histoire Économique et Sociale*, XXXIV (1956).

HARVEY, JOHN. *The Mediaeval Architect*. London, 1972.

KNOOP, D. and JONES, G. P. *The Mediaeval Mason*, 3rd edn. Manchester, 1967.

RIBAULT, Y. 'Chantiers et maîtres d'oeuvre à Bourges durant la première moitié du XVe siècle. *Actes du 93e Congrès national des Sociétés savantes, section d'archéologie*. Tours, 1968 (Paris, 1970).

III. BUILDING TECHNOLOGY

ANDREWS, D. D. 'The Medieval Masonry of Northern Lazio', in *Papers in Italian Archaeology*, ed. H. MCK. BLAKE, J. W. POTTER, D. B. WHITEHOUSE *et al.* Oxford, 1978.

BINDING, G. and NUSSBAUM, N. *Der mittelalterliche Baubetrieb nördlich der Alpen in zeitgenössischen Darstellungen*. Darmstadt, 1978.

BOOZ, R. *Der Baumeister der Gotik*. Münster–Berlin, 1956.

BUCHER, FRANÇOIS. 'Medieval Architectural Design Methods, 800–1560.' *Gesta*, XI (2) (1972).

CLASEN, K. H. *Deutsche Gewölbe der Spätgotik*. Berlin, 1961.

CSEMEGI, J. 'Die Konstruktionsmethoden den mittelalterlichen Baukunst,' in *Acta historiae Artium*, II (Budapest, 1954–5).

DENEUX, H. 'Signes lapidaires et épures du XIIIe siècle à la cathédrale de Reims.' *Bulletin Monumental*, LXXXIV (1925).

FITCHEN, JOHN. *The Construction of Gothic Cathedrals, a study of vault erection*. Oxford, 1961.

FRIEDRICH, K. *Die Steinbearbeitung vom 11 bis zum 18 Jahrhundert*. Augsburg, 1932.

JAMES, JOHN. *Chartres les constructeurs*. Société archéologique d'Eure-et-Loir, 1977; *The Contractors of Chartres*, 2 vols. Mandorla Publications, Wyong, New South Wales, 1979, 1981.

KIMPEL, D. 'Le Développement de la taille en série dans l'architecture médiévale et son rôle dans l'histoire économique.' *Bulletin Monumental*, CXXXV (1977).

LEEDY, W. C., JR. *Fan Vaulting*. London, 1980.

LEISTIKOW, D. 'Aufzugsvorrichtungen für Werksteine im mittelalterlichen Baubetrieb: Wolf und Zange.' *Architectura*, XII (Munich) (1982).

MAIER, KONRAD. 'Mittelalterliche Steinbearbeitung und Mauertechnik als Datierungsmittel, Bibliographische Hinweise.' *Zeitschrift für Archäologie des Mittelalters*, III (1975).

MARK, ROBERT. *Experiments in Gothic Structure*. Massachusetts, 1982.

PLAT, G. *L'Art de bâtir en France des Romains á l'an 1100*. Paris, 1939.

SALZMAN, F. *Building in England down to 1540*. Oxford, 1952.

SHELBY, LON R. *Gothic Design Techniques: the fifteenth-century design booklets of Mathes Roriczer and Hanns Schmuttermayer*. S. Illinois University Press, 1977.

TAYLOR, H. M. *Anglo-Saxon Architecture*, III. Cambridge, 1978.

VIOLLET-LE-DUC, E. M. *Dictionnaire raisonné de l'architecture française du XIe au XVIe siècle*, 10 vols. Paris, 1858–68.

IV. QUARRYING AND BUILDING-STONES

ARKELL, W. J. *Oxford Stone*. London, 1947, and review by E. M. Jope in *Oxoniensia*, XIV (1949), 90–8.

CAMERMAN, C. and ROLLAND, P. *La Pierre de Tournai*. Mémoires de la société belge de géologie, de paléontologie et d'hydrologie, N.S. (4°) I. Brussels, 1944.

COURTOY, F. 'Le Travail et le commerce de la pierre à Namur avant 1500.' *Namurcum*, XXI (1946).

JOPE, E. M. 'The Saxon building-stone industry in southern and midland England.' *Medieval Archaeology*, VIII (1964).

KLAPISCH-ZUBER, C. *Les Maîtres du marbre, Carrare 1300–1600*. Paris, 1969.

KNOOP, D. and JONES, G. P. 'The Medieval English Quarry.' *Economic History Review* (1938).

PIETRESSON DE SAINT-AUBIN, P. 'La Fourniture de la pierre sur les grands chantiers troyens du Moyen Age et de la Renaissance.' *Bulletin Archéologique* (1928–9).

WARD-PERKINS, J. B. 'Quarries and Stoneworking in the Middle Ages: the heritage of the ancient world.' *Settimane di studio del Centro italiano di studi sull' alto medioevo*, XVIII (2). Spoleto, 1971.

CHAPTER XII

Coinage and Currency

The following abbreviations have been used in this bibliography:

Annales	*Annales d'Histoire Économique et Sociale and Annales (Économies, Sociétés et Civilisations)*
BNJ	*British Numismatic Journal*
EconHR	*Economic History Review*
JEH	*Journal of Economic History*
NS	*Numismatický Sbornik*
NZ	*Numismatische Zeitschrift*
RN	*Revue Numismatique*
RIN	*Rivista Italiana di Numismatica*
RBPH	*Revue Belge de Philologie et d'Histoire*
TRHS	*Transactions of the Royal Historical Society*

I. GENERAL

The standard bibliography is Philip Grierson, *Bibliographie numismatique* 2nd. ed., Brussels, 1979. This can be supplemented by:

Martin Price and others. (eds.). *A Survey of Numismatic Research 1978–1984. I. Ancient, Medieval and Modern Numismatics.* International Numismatic Commission, London, 1986. Similar bibliographical surveys are published every six years, which bring the literature up to date.

From the point of view of the economic historian the nearest that is available to a general history of money is provided by the incomplete and posthumously published Marc Bloch, *Esquisse d'une histoire monétaire de l'Europe.* Cahiers des Annales, IX. Paris, 1954, and the suggestive, but brief, series of lectures published as Carlo M. Cipolla, *Money, Prices and Civilization in the Mediterranean World.* Princeton, 1956, and see now P. Spufford, *Money and its Uses in Medieval Europe.* Cambridge, 1986. From the point of view of the numismatist the best introductory work is: John Porteous, *Coins in History.* London, 1969. Economic historians and numismatists joined together at a remarkable conference in 1975, the proceedings of which are published as *La Moneta nell'Economia Europea Secoli XIII–XVIII.* Settima Settimana di Studio, 1975. Istituto Internazionale di Storia Economica 'Francesco Datini'. Prato, ed. V. Barbagli Bagnoli. Florence, 1982.

The standard work of reference for the coinage of medieval Europe is A. Engel and R. Serrure, *Traité de numismatique du moyen âge* (3 vols., Paris, 1891–1905. Reprinted 1964). This is, however, outdated in many particulars and it is in many ways now preferable to refer first to the magnificently illustrated single volume: Philip Grierson, *Monnaies du Moyen Âge* (Fribourg, 1976) and to follow up the references given there. Other useful reference works are the volume of documents: Wilhelm Jesse (ed.), *Quellenbuch zur Münz- und Geldgeschichte des Mittelalters* (Halle, 1924. Reprinted 1968) and the dictionary: F. von Schrötter, *Wörterbuch der Münzkunde* (Leipzig, 1930). An interesting introductory essay on numismatics as an ancillary discipline of history is Philip Grierson, 'Numismatics', in Powell, J. M. (ed.), *Medieval Studies. An introduction* (Syracuse, N.Y., 1976, 103–50).

The standard work on numismatics is now Philip Grierson, *Numismatics* (Oxford, 1975) which does not quite entirely replace A. Luschin von Ebengreuth, *Allgemeine Münzkunde und Geldgeschichte* (2nd edn., Munich, 1926. Reprinted 1969).

A particular range of new numismatic techniques is covered by the proceedings of a specialist conference: E. T. Hall and D. M. Metcalf (eds.), *Methods of Chemical and Metallurgical Investigation of Ancient Coinage* (Royal Numismatic Society, London, 1972). Particularly useful is D. M. Metcalf, 'Analyses of the Metal Contents of Medieval Coins', 383–434.

II. BARBARIAN DISCONTINUITY

BERNAREGGI, ERNESTO. *Il sistema economico della monetazione dei Langobardi nell'Italia superiore*. Milan, 1960.

DOEHAERD, RENÉE. *Le Haut moyen âge occidental: économies et sociétés*. Paris, 1971.

GRIERSON, PHILIP. 'Commerce in the Dark Ages: a Critique of the Evidence.' *TRHS* 5th ser., IX (1959), 123–40.

LAFAURIE, JEAN. 'Essai sur le monnayage d'argent franc des Ve et VIe siècles.' *Annales de Normandie*, XIV (1964), 173–222.

LATOUCHE, ROBERT. *The Birth of Western Economy*. English translation London, 1961.

LE GÉNTILHOMME, PIERRE. 'Le Monnayage et la circulation monétaire dans les royaumes barbares en Occident Ve–VIIIe siècles.' *RN*, 5th ser., VII (1943), 46–112 and VIII (1948), 13–59.

MILES, G. C. *The Coinage of the Visigoths of Spain: Leovigild to Achila II*. American Numismatic Society. New York, 1952.

Moneta e scambi nell'alto medioevo. Settimane di studio del Centro Ìtaliano di Studi sull'alto medioevo, VII. Spoleto, 1961.

TOMASINI, W. H. *The Barbaric Tremissis in Spain and Southern France. Anastasius to Leovigild*. Numismatic Notes and Monographs, CLII. American Numismatic Society. New York, 1964.

WROTH, W. *Catalogue of the Coins of the Vandals, Ostrogoths and Lombards...in the British Museum*. London, 1911.

III. BYZANTINE EMPIRE

BERTELÉ, T. 'L'iperpero bizantino dal 1261 al 1453', *Rivista Italiana di Numismatica*, LIX (1957), 70–89.

—— 'Lineamenti principali della numismatica bizantina', *RIN*, LXVI (1964), 33–118.

GRIERSON, PHILIP. Introductions to BELLINGER, A. R. and GRIERSON P. *Catalogue of Byzantine coins in the Dumbarton Oaks Collection and in the Whittemore Collection 491–1081*. 5 vols. Dumbarton Oaks Center for Byzantine Studies, Washington, 1966ff.

—— *Byzantine Coins*. London, 1982.

HENDY, MICHAEL F. *Coinage and Money in the Byzantine Empire 1081–1261*. Dumbarton Oaks Studies. XII. Washington, 1969.

—— *Studies in the Byzantine Monetary Economy, c. 300–1450*. Cambridge, 1985.

—— 'Byzantium 1081–1024: An Economic Reappraisal', *TRHS*, 5th ser. XX (1970), 31–52.

IV. FROM THE ORIGINS OF THE DENIER TO THE CAROLINGIANS

GRIERSON, PHILIP. 'Money and Coinage under Charlemagne', in *Karl der Grosse: Lebenswerk und Nachleben*, ed. W. Braunfels. I. Dussdeldorf, 1965. 501–36.

LAFAURIE, JEAN. 'Monnaies d'argent mérovingiennes des VIIe et VIIIe siècles', *RN*, 6th ser., XI (1960), 98–219.

MORRISON, KARL F. 'Numismatics and Carolingian trade: a critique of the evidence', *Speculum*, XXXVIII (1963), 403–32.

MORRISON, KARL F. and GRUNTHAL, HENRY. *Carolingian Coinage*. Numismatic Notes and Monographs, CLVIII, American Numismatic Society. New York, 1967.

V. THE 'AGE OF THE VIKINGS'

BLUNT, CHRISTOPHER E. 'The Coinage of Athelstan 924–939. A Survey'. *British Numismatic Journal*, XLII (1974), 35–160.

DOLLEY, R. H. M. (ed.). *Anglo-Saxon Coins: studies presented to F. M. Stenton*. London, 1961.

—— *Anglo-Saxon Pennies*. London, 1964.
—— *Viking Coins of the Danelaw and of Dublin*. London, 1965.
DUMAS-DUBOURG, FRANÇOISE. *Le Trésor de Fécamp et le monnayage en Francie Occidentale pendant la seconde moitié du Xe siècle*. Paris, 1971.
GRIERSON, PHILIP. 'The Volume of Anglo-Saxon Currency', *EconHR*, 2nd ser., XX (1967), 153–60.
HATZ, GERT. *Handel und Verkehr zwischen dem Deutschen Reich und Schweden in der späten Wikingerzeit*. Lund, 1974.
KRAUME, EMIL and HATZ, VERA. 'Die Otto-Adelheid Pfennige und Ihre Nachprägungen', *Hamburger Beiträge zur Numismatik*, New Ser., XV (1961–3), 13–23 and appendixes.
MALMER, BRITA. *Nordiska Mynt före år 1000*. Acta Archaeologica Lundensia in 8°, IV. Lund-Bonn, 1966. (With English resumé.)
METCALF, D. M. 'How Large was the Anglo-Saxon Currency?' *EconHR*, 2nd ser., XVIII (1965).
PETERSSON, H. and BERTIL A. *Anglo-Saxon Currency, King Edgar's Reform to the Norman Conquest*. Lund, 1969.
RASMUSSON, N. L. and LAGERQVIST, L. O. (eds.). *Commentationes de nummis saeculorum IX–XI in Suecia repertis*. 2 vols. Stockholm, 1961–8.
SAWYER, P. H. 'The Wealth of England in the Eleventh Century', *TRHS*, 5th ser., XV (1965). 145–64.
—— *The Age of the Vikings*, 2nd edn. London, 1971.
SUCHODOLSKI, S. 'Études sur la monnaie polonaise de la fin du Xe et du début du XIe siècle', *Archaeologia Polona*, XI (1969), 91–129.
YANIN, V. . 'Les Problèmes généraux de l'échange monétaire russe aux IXe–XIIe siècles', *Moneta e Scambi nell'alto medioevo*. VIII. Settimane di studio del Centro Italiano di Studi sull'alto medioevo. Spoleto, 1961, 485–505.

VI. RURAL USE OF MONEY

BLOCH, MARC. 'Natural economy and money economy: a pseudo-dilemma', in *Land and Work in Medieval Europe*. London, 1967. 230–43.
DOLLINGER, PHILIPPE. *L'Évolution des Classes Rurales en Bavière*. Paris, 1949.
DUBY, GEORGES. *Rural Economy and Country Life in the Medieval West*. Paris, 1961. (English translation, 1968.)
—— *Guerriers et paysans VIIe–XIIe siècles*. Paris, 1973.
FOSSIER, ROBERT. *La Terre et les Hommes en Picardie jusqu'a la fin du XIIIe siècle*. Paris–Louvain, 1968.
HERLIHY, DAVID. 'Treasure Hoards in the Italian Economy, 960–1139', *EconHR*, 2nd ser., X (1957), 1–14.
—— 'The Agrarian Revolution in Southern France and Italy 801–1150', *Speculum*, XXXIII (1958), 23–41.
MEUVRET, J. 'Circulation monétaire et utilisation économique de la monnaie dans la France du XVe et du XVIIe siècle', *Études d'Histoire Moderne et Contemporaine*, I (1947), 15–28. Reprinted in *Études d'Histoire Économique*. Cahiers des Annales, XXXII. Paris, 1971, 127–37.
POSTAN, M. M. 'The Chronology of Labour Services', *TRHS*, 4th ser., XX (1937).
—— 'The Rise of a Money Economy', *EconHR*, XIV (1944), 123–34.

VII. MINING AND TRADE IN PRECIOUS METALS

AGRICOLA, GEORGIUS. *De veteribus et novis metallis*. Basle, 1546. English translation in Georgius Agricola, *De re Metallica*, trans. and ed. HOOVER, H. C. and L. H. London, 1912.
ALBERTUS MAGNUS. *Book of Minerals*. Trans. and ed. WYCKOFF, DOROTHY. Oxford, 1967.
CIPOLLA, CARLO M. 'Argento Tedesco e Monete Genovesi alla fine del quattrocento', *RIN*, LVIII (1956), 100–7.

HERRMANN, WALTHER. 'Bergbau und Kultur', *Freiberger Forschungshefte*, series D, II (1953), 7–22.

HILLEBRAND, WERNER. 'Der Goslarer Metallhandel im Mittelalter', *Hansische Geschichtsblätter*, LXXXVII (1969).

KOVACEVIC, DESANKA. 'Dans la Serbie et la Bosnie médiévales: les mines d'or et d'argent', *Annales*, XV (1960), 248–58.

NEF, J. U. 'Silver Production in Central Europe 1450–1618', *Journal of Political Economy*, XLIX (1941), 575–91.

VIII. MONEY IN THE COMMERCIAL REVOLUTION

BARNARD, F. P. *The Casting-counter and the Counting-Board*. Oxford, 1916.

CASTELIN, K. *Grossus Pragensis. Der Präger Groschen und seine Teilstücke 1300–1547*, 2nd edn. Brunswick, 1973.

CIPOLLA, C. 'Currency Depreciation in Medieval Europe', *EconHR*, 2nd ser., XV (1963), 413–22. Reprinted in THRUPP, SYLVIA (ed.). *Change in Medieval Society*. New York, 1964, 227–36.

COURTENAY, WILLIAM J. 'Token Coinage and the Administration of Poor Relief during the Later Middle Ages', *Journal of Inter-disciplinary History*, III (1972), 275–95.

DE ROOVER, R. *Business, Banking and Economic Thought: Selected Studies*, ed. KIRSHNER, J. Chicago, 1974.

GRUNZWEIG, A. 'Les Incidences internationales des mutations monétaires de Philippe le Bel', *Moyen Âge*, LIX (1953), 117–72.

HERLIHY, DAVID. 'Pisan Coinage and the Monetary Development of Tuscany, 1150–1250', *American Numismatic Society, Museum Notes*, VI (1954), 143–68.

HOMAN, BALINT. 'La circolazione delle monete d'oro in Ungheria dal X a XIV secole e la crisi europea dell'oro nel secolo XIV', *RIN*, 2nd ser., V (1922), 109–56.

HOMER, SIDNEY. *A History of Interest Rates*. Rutgers, 1963.

KOCH, BERNHARD. 'Goldgeld und Groschen-münzen im österreichischen Geldverkehr des Mittelalters', *NZ*, LXXXI (1965), 3–13.

LANE, F. C. 'Le vecchie monete di conte Veneziane ed il ritorno all'oro', *Atti del Istituto Veneto di Scienze, Lettere ed Arti*, CXVII (1959) 51–78.

LOPEZ, R. S. 'Back to Gold, 1252', *EconHR*, 2nd ser., IX (1956), 219–40.

—— 'Prima del Ritorno all'oro nell'occidente duecentesco: i primi denari grossi d'argento', *Rivista Storica Italiana*, LXXIX (1967), 174–81.

NAGL, ALFRED. 'Die Goldwährung und die handelmässige Geldrechnung im Mittelalter', *NZ*, XXVI (1894), 41–258.

NOHEJLOVA-PRATOVA, E. (ed.). 'Les Commencements de la grosse monnaie et de la monnaie d'or en Europe Centrale (1250–1350)', special number of *NS*, XII. Prague, 1971–2.

SPUFFORD, PETER. 'Le Rôle de la monnaie dans la révolution commerciale du XIIIe siècle', in DAY, JOHN (ed.). *Études d'histoire monétaire*. Lille, 1984.

WERVEKE, HANS VAN. 'Monnaie, lingots ou marchandises? Les instruments d'échange aux XIe et XIIe siècles', *Annales*, IV (1932), 452–68. Reprinted in *Miscellanea Mediaevalia*. Ghent, 1968, 191–208.

—— 'Monnaie de compte et monnaie réelle', *RBPH*, XIII (1934), 123–52. Reprinted in *Miscellanea Mediavalia*. Ghent, 1968, 133–58.

ZERBI, TOMMASO. *Moneta effectiva e moneta di conto nelle fonti contabile di storia economica*. Milan, 1955.

A great deal of information about money is to be found in merchants' notebooks. The following are arranged in the order of the date of their compilation:

ORLANDINI, V. (ed.). *Tarifa zoe Noticia dy Pexi e Mexure di Luogi e Tere che s'adovra Mercandantia per el mondo*. Introduction by R. Cessi. Reale Instituto superiore di scienze economiche e commerciali di Venezia. Venice, 1925.

STUSSI, ALFREDO (ed.). *Zibaldone da Canal, Manoscritto Mercantile del sec. XIV*. Fonti per la Storia di Venezia. Venice. 1967.

PEGOLOTTI, FRANCESCO BALDUCCI. *La Pratica della Mercatura*. EVANS ALLEN (ed.). Medieval Academy of America. Cambridge, Mass., 1936, together with: EVANS, ALLAN. 'Some Coinage systems of the Fourteenth Century', *Journal of Economc and Business History*, III (1931), 481–96, and GRIERSON, PHILIP. 'The Coin List of Pegolotti', *Studi in Onore di Armando Sapori*, I. Milan, 1957. 483–92.

CIANE, CESARE (ed.). *La 'Pratica di Mercatura' Datiniana*. Milan, 1964.

BORLANDI, ANTONIA (ed.). *Il Manuale di Mercatura da Sanminiato de' Ricci*. Genoa, 1963.

BORLANDI, FRANCO (ed.). *El Libro di Mercatantie et Usanze de' Paesi*. Turin, 1936.

PAGNINI della VENTURA, G. F. (ed.). 'La Pratica della mercatura scritta de Giovanni di Antonio da Uzzanno', *Della Decima e delle Altre gravezze*, IV. Lisbon–Lucca, 1766.

IX. THE INTERNATIONAL MONEY MARKET

CIPOLLA, CARLO M. *Studi di Storia della moneta*, I. *I Movimenti dei Cambi in Italia dal Secolo XIII al XV*. Pavia, 1948.

DE ROOVER, RAYMOND. *L'Évolution de la lettre de change XIVe–XVIIIe siècles*. Paris, 1953.

—— 'Le Marché monétaire au moyen âge et au début des temps modernes. Problèmes et méthodes', *Revue Historique*, CCXLIV (1970).

EINZIG, PAUL. *The History of Foreign Exchange*. London, 1962.

FAVIER, JEAN. *Les Finances pontificales á l'époque du grande schisme d'Occident 1378–1419*. Bibliothèque des écoles Françaises d'Athènes et de Rome, CCXI (1966).

LUNT, W. E. *Papal Revenues in the Middle Ages*. 2 vols. New York, 1934.

PIQUET, J. *Des banquiers au moyen âge. Les Templiers. Étude de leurs opérations financières*. Paris, 1935.

RENOUARD, Y. *Les Relations des papes d'Avignon et des compagnies commerciales et bancaires*. Paris, 1941.

SCHÄFER, H. *Die Ausgaben der apostolichen Kammer unter Johann XXII*. Vatikanische Quellen zur Geschichte der päpstlichen Hof- und Finanzverwaltung, 1316–1375, II. Paderborn, 1911.

SPRANDEL, ROLF. 'Exkurs über Geld', *Das Eisengewerbe im Mittlelalter*. Stuttgart, 1968.

SPUFFORD, PETER. *Handbook of Medieval Exchange*. London, 1986.

USHER, A. P. *The Early History of Deposit Banking in Mediterranean Europe*. Cambridge, Mass., 1943.

X. THE FLOW OF MONEY AND BULLION IN AND OUT OF WESTERN EUROPE

ASHTOR, ELIYAHU. *Les Métaux precieux et la balance des payements du proche-orient à la basse époque*. Paris, 1971.

BACHARACH, JERE L. 'The Dinar versus the Ducat', *International Journal of Middle Eastern Studies*, IV (1973), 77–96.

BAUTIER, R–H. 'L'Or et l'argent en occident de la fin du XIIIe siècle au début du XIVe siècle', *Académie des Inscriptions et Belles Lettres, Comptes Rendus des Séances* (1951), 169–74.

BLOCH, MARC. 'The problem of gold in the middle ages', *Land and Work in Medieval Europe*. London, 1967, 186–229.

BRAUDEL, F. 'Economies: Precious Metals, Money and Prices', *The Mediterranean and the Mediterranean World in the Age of Philip II*, I. 2nd edn. Paris, 1966. English translation, London, 1972, 462–542.

CAHEN, CLAUDE. 'Quelques problèmes concernant l'expansion économique musulmane au haut moyen âge', *L'Occidente e l'Islam nell'alto medioevo*. Settimane di studio del Centro italiano di Studi sull'alto Medioevo, XII. Spoleto, 1965, 391–432.

DUPLESSY, JEAN. 'La Circulation des monnaies arabes en Europe occidentale du VIIIe au XIIIe siècle'. *RN*, 5th ser., XVIII (1956), 101–63.

GOITEIN, S. D. *A Mediterranean Society. The Jewish communities of the Arab World as portrayed in the Documents of the Cairo Geniza*, I. *Economic Foundations*. Berkeley, 1967.

HEYD, WILHELM VON. *Histoire du Commerce du Levant au Moyen Âge*. 2 vols. Leipzig, 1885–6.

MAŁOWIST, MARIAN. 'Quelques observations sur le commerce de l'or dans le soudan occidental au moyen âge', *Annales*, XXV (1970), 1630–6.

RICHARDS, J. F. (ed.). *Precious Metals in the Late Medieval and Early Modern Worlds*. Durham, North Carolina, 1983.

SCHLUMBERGER, G. *Numismatique de l'Orient Latin*. Paris, 1878. Supplement, 1882. Reprinted, Graz, 1954.

WATSON, ANDREW M. 'Back to Gold – and Silver', *EconHR*, 2nd. ser., XX (1967), 1–34.

WEE, HERMAN VAN DER and PEETERS, THEO. 'Un Modèle dynamique de croissance interséculaire du commerce mondial XIIe–XVIIIe siècles', *Annales*, XXV (1970), 100–26.

XI. MINT ORGANISATION

BAILHACHE, J. 'Chambre et cour des Monnaies XIVe, XVe, XVIe siècles. Aperçu historique', *RN*, 4th ser., XXXVII (1934), 63–99, 175–97; XXXVIII (1935), 67–89; and XXXIX (1936), 157–79 and 327–45.

BEARDWOOD, ALICE. 'The Royal Mints and Exchanges', in *The English Government at Work 1327–1336*. WILLARD J. F. and MORRIS, W. A. (eds.). III. Cambridge, Mass., 1950. 35–66.

CARSON, R. A. G. (ed.). *Mints, Dies and Currency*. London, 1971.

CRAIG, JOHN. *The Mint*. Cambridge, 1953.

LOPEZ, ROBERTO S. 'An Aristocracy of Money in the Early Middle Ages', *Speculum*, XXVIII (1953), 1–43.

MATE, MAVIS. 'A Mint of Trouble 1279–1307', *Speculum*, XLIV (1969), 201–12.

REDDAWAY, T. F. 'The King's Mint and Exchange in London 1343–1543', *English Historical Review*, LXXXII (1967), 1–23.

XII. MONEY AND GOVERNMENT

BISSON, T. *Conservation of Coinage*. Oxford, 1979.

BLOCKMANS, WILLEM P. 'La Participation des sujets flamands à la politique monétaire des ducs de Bourgogne 1384–1500', *Revue Belge de Numismatique*, CXIX (1973), 103–34.

BOLIN, STURE. 'Tax Money and Plough Money', *Scandinavian Economic History Review*, II (1954), 3–21.

CAMPBELL, JAMES. 'Observations on English Government from the Tenth to the Twelfth Century', *TRHS*, 5th ser., XXV (1975). 39–54.

SPUFFORD, PETER. 'Assemblies of Estates, Taxation and Control of Coinage in Medieval Europe', *Studies Presented to the International Commission for the History of Representative and Parliamentary Institutions*, XXXI. Louvain–Paris, 1966, 115–30.

—— 'Coinage, Taxation and the Estates General of the Burgundian Netherlands', *Standen en Landen*, XL (1966), 61–87.

—— 'Mint Organization in the Burgundian Netherlands in the Fifteenth Century', in BROOKE, C. N. L. and others (eds.). *Studies in Numismatic Method presented to Philip Grierson*. Cambridge, 1983.

—— and MAYHEW, N. J. (ed.). *Late Medieval Mints: Organisation, Administration and Techniques*. Oxford, 1986.

XIII. THEORY OF MONEY

BABELON, ERNEST. 'La Théorie féodale de la monnaie', *Mémoires de l'Académie des Inscriptions et Belles-Lettres*, XXXVIII (first part) (Paris, 1908), 279–347.
BIEL, GABRIEL. *Treatise on the Power and Utility of Moneys.* Trans. and ed. R. BURKE. Philadelphia, 1930.
BRIDREY, E. *La Théorie de la monnaie au XIVe siècle, Nicole Oresme.* Caen, 1906.
DE ROOVER, R. 'Les Doctrines économiques des scolastiques: à propos du traité sur l'usure d'Alexandre Lombard', *Revue d'Histoire Ecclesiastique*, LIX (1964), 854–66.
GORDON, BARRY. *Economic Analysis before Adam Smith.* London, 1975.
IBANES, J. *La Doctrine de l'Église et les réalités économiques du XIIIe siècle. L'interêt, le prix et monnaie.* Paris, 1967.
MONROE, A. E. *Monetary Theory before Adam Smith.* Harvard, 1923.
ORESME, NICHOLAS. *De Moneta*, ed. and trans. CHARLES JOHNSON. London, 1956.

XIV. THE SILVER FAMINES OF THE LATER MIDDLE AGES

DAY, JOHN. 'The Decline of a Money Economy: Sardinia in the Late Middle Ages', *Studi in memoria di Federigo Melis*, III. Naples, 1978.
—— 'The Great Bullion Famine of the Fifteenth Century', *Past and Present*, No. 79 (1978), 3–54.
GIRARD, A. 'Un Phénomène économique: La Guerre Monétaire (XIVe–XVe siècles)', *Annales*, II (1940), 207–218.
GRAUS, FRANTISEK. 'La Crise monétaire du 14e siècle', *RBPH*, XXIX (1951), 445–54.
HEERS, JACQUES. 'Il commercio nel Mediterraneo alla fine del sec. XIVe nei primi anni del XV', *Archivio Storico Italiano*, CXIII (1955).
——*L'Occident aux XIVe et XVe siècles. Aspects économiques et sociaux*, 2nd edn. Paris, 1966.
MISKIMIN, HARRY A. *Money, Prices and Foreign Exchange in Fourteenth Century France.* Newhaven, Conn., 1963.
——'Monetary Movements and Market Structure: Forces for Contraction in Fourteenth and Fifteenth Century England', *JEH*, XXIV (1964), 470–95.
MUNRO, JOHN H. *Wool, Cloth and Gold. The Struggle for Bullion in Anglo-Burgundian Trade 1340–1478.* Brussels–Toronto, 1973.
PERROY, E. 'À l'origine d'une économie contractée: les crises du XIVe siècle', *Annales*, IV (1949), 167–82.
——'Wage Labour in France in the Later Middle Ages', *EconHR*, 2nd ser., VIII (1955), 232–9. Reprinted in THRUPP, SYLVIA (ed.). *Change in Medieval Society.* New York, 1964, 237–46.

XV. MONEY ON THE EVE OF THE PRICE REVOLUTION

EHRENBERG, R. *Das Zeitalter der Fugger. Geldkapital und Kreditverkehr im 16 Jahrhundert*, 3rd edn, Jena, 1922. Shorter English version *Capital and Finance in the Age of the Renaissance.* London, 1928.
GRIERSON, PHILIP. 'The Monetary Pattern of Sixteenth-Century Coinage', *TRHS*, 5th ser., XXI (1971), 45–60.
LESAGE, GEORGES. 'La Circulation monétaire en France dans la seconde moitié du XVe siècle', *Annales*, III (1948), 304–16.
SPOONER, F.C. *The International Economy and Monetary Movements in France 1495–1725.* Harvard, 1972.
VILAR, P. *Oro y Moneda en la Historia 1450–1920.* Barcelona, 1969.

XVI. MONEY AND COMMERCE – GENERAL BIBLIOGRAPHY, ARRANGED BY COUNTRIES:

The States of Italy

BERNOCCHI, MARIO. *Le Monete della repubblica fiorentina*, I. *Il Libro della Zecca*. Florence, 1974. II. *Corpus Nummorum Florentinorum*. Florence, 1975. III. *Documentazione*. Florence, 1976. IV. *Valuti del fiorino d'oro*. Florence, 1978.

CESSI, ROBERTO (ed.). *Problemi Monetari Veneziani*. Documenti Finanziari della Repubblica di Venezia, 4th series, I, Reale Accademia dei Lincei. Padua, 1937.

CHIAUDANO, MARIO. 'La Moneta di Genova nel Secolo XII', *Studi in Onore di Armando Sapori*, I. Milan, 1957. 189–214.

CIPOLLA, CARLO M. *Le avventure della lira*. Milan, 1958.

——*Storia dell'economia italiana. Saggi di storia economica*, I. Secoli VII–XVII. Turin, 1959.

Corpus Nummorum Italicorum. 20 out of 21 volumes published. Rome, 1910 onwards.

DAY, JOHN. *Les Douanes de Gênes 1376–1377*. Paris, 1963.

——'La circulation monétaire en Toscane en 1296', *Annales*, XXIII (1968), 1054–66.

DE ROOVER, R. *The Rise and Decline of the Medici Bank 1397–1494*. Cambridge, Mass., 1963.

GNECCHI, F. AND E. *Le Monete di Milano*. Milan, 1884.

GRIERSON, PHILIP. 'La Moneta Veneziana nell' economia mediterranea del trecento e quattrocento', *La Civilta Veneziana del Quattrocento*. Fundazione Giorgio Cini. Florence, 1957, 77–97.

——'I Grossi "senatoriali" di Roma, parte I, dal 1253 al 1282', *RIN*, LVIII (1956), 36–69.

——'The Origins of the Grosso and of Gold Coinage in Italy', *NS*, XII (1971–2), 33–48.

HEERS, JACQUES. *Gênes au XVe siècle: activité économique et problèmes sociaux*. Paris, 1961.

HERLIHY, DAVID, LOPEZ, ROBERT S., and SLESSAREV, VSEVOLOD. *Economy, Society and Government in Medieval Italy. Essays in Memory of Robert L. Reynolds*. Kent, Ohio, 1969.

LANE, FREDERIC C. *Venice and History; Collected Papers*. Baltimore, 1966.

——*Venice. A Maritime Republic*. Baltimore, 1973.

——and MUELLER, REINHOLD C. *Money and Banking in Medieval and Renaissance Venice*, I. Baltimore, 1985.

LA RONCIÈRE, CHARLES DE. *Un changeur florentin du trecento, Lippo di Fede del Sega 1285 env.-1363 env*. Paris, 1973.

——*Florence. Centre économique régional au XIVe siècle*. Aix-en-Provence, 1976.

LUZZATTO, GINO. *Studi di Storia Economica Veneziana*. Padua, 1954.

PAPADOPOLI, N. *Le Monete di Venezia*. 4 vols., Venice, 1893–1919.

PESCE, G. AND FELLONI, G. *Le Monete Genovesi*. Genoa, 1975.

SAMBON, G. *Repertorio generale delle monete coniate in Italia*, I. Paris, 1912.

SAPORI, A. *Studi di storia economica medievale*. 3 vols., Florence, 1956–67.

SCHULTE, ALOYS. *Geschichte des mittelalterlichen Handels und Verkehrs zwischen Westdeutschland und Italien mit Ausschuss von Venedig*. Leipzig, 1900.

TRASELLI, CARMELLO. *Note per la Storia dei Banchi in Sicilia nel XV secolo*. I. *Zecche e Monete*. Palermo, 1959. II. *I Banchieri e i loro affari*. Palermo, 1968.

The Kingdoms of the Iberian Peninsula

CARRÈRE, CLAUDE. *Barcelone, Centre Economique 1380–1462*. 2 vols., Paris, 1967.

GIL FARRES, OCTAVIO. *Historia de la Moneda Espanola*, 2nd edn, Madrid, 1975.

HAMILTON, EARL J. *Money, Prices and Wages in Valencia, Aragon and Navarre 1351–1550*. Cambridge, Mass., 1936.

MACKAY, ANGUS. *Money, Prices and Politics in Fifteenth-Century Castile*. London, 1981.

MAGALHÃES-GODINHO, VITORINO. *L'Economie de l'Empire Portugais aux XVe et XVIe siècles*. Paris, 1969.

MILES, GEORGE C. *The Coinage of the Umayyads of Spain*. American Numismatic Society, New York, 1950.

——*The coins of the Spanish Mulūk al-Tawā'if*. American Numismatic Society, New York, 1954.
TEIXEIRA DE ARAGÃO, A. C. *Descripção general e historica das moedas cunhadas em nome dos reis, regentes e governadores de Portugal*. 3 vols., Lisbon, 1874–80.

France

BARATIER, E. and REYNAUD, F. *Histoire du commerce de Marseille*. II. *1291–1480*. Paris, 1951.
BISSON, T. 'Coinages and Royal Monetary Policy in Langeudoc during the Reign of Saint Louis', *Speculum*, XXXII (1957), 443–69.
BLANCHARD, LOUIS. *Essai sur les Monnaies de Charles I Comte de Provence*. Paris, 1868.
BLANCHET A. and DIEUDONNÉ, A. *Manuel de numismatique française*, 4 vols. Paris, 1912–1936. II. *Monnaies royales françaises depuis Hugues Capet jusqu'à la Révolution*. Paris, 1916. IV. *Monnaies féodales françaises*. Paris, 1936.
CARON, E. *Monnaies féodales françaises*. Paris, 1882.
CASTAING-SICARD, MIREILLE. *Monnaies féodales et circulation monétaire en Languedoc Xe–XIIIe siècles*. Cahiers de l'Association Marc Bloch de Toulouse, Études d'Histoire Méridionale, IV. Toulouse, 1961.
CASTELLANI, C. 'Le Rôle économique de la communauté juive de Carpentras au début du XVe siècle', *Annales* XXVII (1972), 583–611.
CAZELLES, R. 'Quelques réflexions à propos des mutations de la monnaie royale française, 1295–1360', *Le Moyen Âge*, LXXII (1966), 83–105 and 251–78.
——La Stabilisation de la monnaie par la création du franc (décembre 1360)-blocage d'une société', *Traditio*, XXXII (1976), 293–311.
COMBES, JEAN. 'Les Commercants et les capitalistes de Montpellier aux XIIIe et XIVe siècles', *Revue Historique*, CLXXXIX (1940), 341–77.
DE ROOVER, R. 'Le Marché monétaire à Paris du règne de Philippe le Bel au début du XVe siècle', *Comptes rendus de l'Académie des Inscriptions et Belles Lettres* (1968), 548–58.
DUBOIS, HENRI. *Les Foires de Chalon-sur Saône et le commerce dans la vallée de la Saône à la fin du Moyen Age*. Paris, 1975.
EMERY, R. W. *The Jews of Perpignan in the XIII Century*. New York, 1959.
FAVREAU, ROBERT. 'Les Changeurs du royaume sous le règne de Louis XI', *Bibliothèque de l'École des Chartes*, CXXII (1964), 216–51.
FOURNIAL, ETIENNE. *Les Villes et l'économie d'échange en Forez aux XIIIe et XIVe siècles*. Paris, 1967.
GANDILHON, RENÉ. *Politique économique de Louis XI*. Rennes, 1940.
GIARD, JEAN-BAPTISTE. 'Le Florin d'or au Baptiste et ses imitations en France au XIVe siècle', *Bibliothèque de l'École des Chartes*, CXXV (1967), 94–141.
GUERREAU, ALAIN. 'L'Atelier monétaire royal de Mâcon (1239–1421)', *Annales*, XXIX (1974), 369–92.
GUILHERMOZ, P. and DIEUDONNÉ, A. 'Chronologie des documents monétaires de la numismatique royale des origines à 1330 et 1337', RN, XXXII (1929) and XXXIII (1930).
LAFAURIE, JEAN. *Les Monnaies des rois de France*. I. Paris, 1951.
LANDRY, A. *Essai économique sur les mutations des monnaies dans l'ancienne France de Philippe le Bel à Charles VII*. Bibliothèque de l'École des Hautes Études, IV, Sciences Historiques et Philologiques, CLXXXV. Paris, 1910, reprinted 1969.
NAHON, GERARD. 'Le Crédit et les juifs dans la France du XIIIe siècle', *Annales*, XXIV (1969), 1121–48.
POEY D'AVANT, FAUSTIN. *Les Monnaies féodales de la France*, 3 vols., Paris, 1858–62. Reprinted, Graz, 1961.
REY, MAURICE. *Le Domaine du roi et les finances extraordinaires sous Charles VI 1388–1413*. Paris, 1965.
——*Les Finances Royales sous Charles VI. Les Causes du Déficit 1388–1413*. Paris, 1965.

RICHEBÉ, CLAUDE. *Les Monnaies féodales d'Artois du Xe au début du XIVe siècle*. Paris, 1963.

ROLLAND, HENRI. *Monnaies des Comtes de Provence, XIIe–XVe siècles. Histoire monétaire, économique et corporative*. Paris, 1956.

SAULCY, F. DE. *Recueil de documents relatifs a l'histoire des monnaies frappées par les rois de France depuis Philippe II jusqu'à François Ier*. 4 vols., Paris, 1879–92.

WOLFF, PHILIPPE. *Commerces et Marchands de Toulouse (vers 1350–vers 1450)*. Paris, 1954.

Principalities of the Low Countries

BIGWOOD, GEORGES. *Le Régime juridique et économique du commerce de l'argent dans la Belgique du moyen âge*. Brussels, 1920–1.

CHALON, R. *Recherches sur les monnaies des comtes de Hainaut*. Brussels, 1848. Supplements 1852, 1854, 1857 and, by A. DE WITTE, 1891.

CHAUTARD, J. *Les Imitations des monnaies au type Esterlin*. Nancy, 1871.

CHESTRET DE HANEFFE, J. DE. *Numismatique de la principauté de Liège*. Brussels, 1890.

CHIJS, P. O VAN DER. *De Munten der Nederlanden van de vroogste tijden tot aan de Pacificatie van Gend (1576)*. 9 vols., Haarlem, 1851–66.

DE ROOVER, R. *Money, Banking and Credit in Medieval Bruges*. Cambridge, Mass., 1948.

—— *The Bruges Money Market around 1400*. Brussels, 1968.

DESCHAMPS DE PAS, L. 'Essai sur l'historie monétaire des comtes de Flandre de la maison de Bourgogne', *RN*, N.S., VI (1861), VII (1862), XI (1866), XIV (1869), XV (1874), and *Revue Belge de numismatique*, XXXII (1876).

DE WITTE, A. *Historie monétaire des comtes de Louvain, ducs de Brabant*. 3 vols., Antwerp, 1894–9.

ENNO VAN GELDER, H. *De nederlandse Munten*. Utrecht–Antwerp, 1966.

—— and HOC., M. *Les Monnaies des Pays-Bas Bourguignons et Espagnols*. Amsterdam, 1960. Supplement, 1964.

GAILLARD, VICTOR. *Recherches sur les monnaies des comtes de Flandre...jusque'à l'avènement de la maison de Bourgogne*, 2nd edn. Ghent, 1857.

GHYSSENS, J. *Les Petits deniers de Flandre du XIIe et XIIIe siècles*. Brussels, 1971.

GRIERSON, PHILIP. 'Coinage in the Cely Papers', *Miscellanea Mediaevalia in Memoriam Jan Frederik Niermeyer*. Groningen, 1967, 379–404.

HOC, M. *Histoire monétaire de Tournai*. Brussels, 1970.

KETNER, F. 'The Utrecht Monetary System' in POSTHUMUS, N.W. *Inquiry into the History of Prices in Holland*, II. Leiden, 1964, p. 12–30.

LAURENT, H. *La Loi de Gresham au Moyen Age. Essai sur la circulation monétaire entre la Flandre et le Brabant à la fin du XIVe siècle*. Brussels, 1933.

SPUFFORD, PETER. *Monetary Problems and Policies in the Burgundian Netherlands 1433–1496*. Leiden, 1970.

VAN UYTVEN, RAYMOND. 'La Flandre et le Brabant, "Terres de Promission" sous les ducs de Bourgogne', *Revue du Nord*, XLIII (1961), 281–317.

—— 'What is new socially and economically in the sixteenth century Netherlands', *Acta Historicae Neerlandicae*, VII (1975), 18–53.

WERVEKE, HANS VAN. 'De economische en sociale gevolgen van de muntpolitiek der graven van Vlaanderen 1337–1433', *Annales de la Société d'Emulation de Bruges*, LXXIV (1931), 1–15. Reprinted in *Miscellanea Mediaevalia*. Ghent, 1968, 243–54.

—— 'Currency Manipulation in the Middle Ages. The Case of Louis de Male, Count of Flanders', *TRHS*, XXXI (1949), 115–27. Reprinted in *Miscellanea Mediaevalia*. Ghent, 1968, 255–67.

British Isles

BLUNT, C. E. and BRAND, J. D. 'Mint Output of Henry III', *BJN*, XXXIX (1970), 61–6.

CHALLIS, C. E. *The Tudor Coinage*. Manchester, 1978.

CRUMP, C. G. and JOHNSON, C. 'Tables of Bullion coined under Edward I, II and III', *Numismatic Chronicle*, 4th ser., XIII (1913), 200–45.

Dolley, Michael. 'Anglo-Irish Monetary Policies, 1172–1637', *Historical Studies*, vii. London, 1969, 45–64.
Feaveryear, A. E. *The Pound Sterling*. 2nd edn, Oxford, 1963.
Fryde, E. B. 'Financial Resources of Edward I in the Netherlands, 1294–98', *RBPH*, xl (1962), 1168–87.
——'Financial Resources of Edward III in the Netherlands, 1337–1340', *RBPH*, xlv (1967), 1142–1216.
——'Parliament and the French War 1336–40', *Essays in Medieval History presented to Bertie Wilkinson*, ed. T. A. Sandqvist and M. R. Powicke. Toronto, 1969, 250–69. Reprinted in Fryde, E. B. and Miller, Edward (eds.). *Historical Studies of the English Parliament*, i. Cambridge, 1970, 242–61.
Harvey, P. D. A. 'The English Inflation of 1180–1220', *Past and Present*, lxi (1973), 3–30.
Ives, Herbert E. *Foreign Imitations of the English Noble*. Numismatic Notes and Monographs, xciii. American Numismatic Society, New York, 1941.
Mate, Mavis. 'Monetary Policies in England 1272–1307', *BNJ*, xli (1972), 34–79.
——'High Prices in Early Fourteenth-Century England: Causes and Consequences', *EconHR*, 2nd ser., xxviii (1975), 1–16.
Mayhew, N. J. 'Numismatic Evidence and Falling Prices in Fourteenth-Century England', *EconHR*, 2nd ser., xxvii (1974), 1–15.
—— (ed.). *Edwardian Monetary Affairs (1279–1344)*. British Archaeological Reports, 36. Oxford, 1977.
North, J. J. *English Hammered Coinage*. 2nd edn. London, 1975–80.
Oman, Charles. *The Coinage of England*. Oxford, 1931.
Prestwich, Michael. 'Edward I's Monetary Policies and their Consequences', *EconHR*, 2nd ser., xxii (1969), 406–16.
Ruding, R. *Annals of the Coinage*, 3 vols. 3rd edn, London, 1840.
Spufford, Peter. 'Continental Coins in Late Medieval England', *BNJ*, xxxii (1963), 127–39.
——'Burgundian Double Patards in Late Medieval England', *BNJ*, xxxiii (1964), 110–17.
Stewart, I. H. *The Scottish Coinage*, 3rd edn. London, 1967.
Stokes, Ethel. 'Tables of Bullion Coined from 1377 to 1550', *Numismatic Chronicle*, 5th ser., ix (1929), 27–69.
Sylloge of Coins of the British Isles. British Academy. London, 1958 onwards.
Thompson, J. D. A. *Inventory of British Coin Hoards AD 600–1500*. Royal Numismatic Society. London, 1956.

German States

Bastian, F. (ed.). *Das Runtingberbuch 1383–1407 und verwandtes Material zum Regensburger–südostdeutschen Handel und Münzwesen*. 3 vols., Regensburg, 1935–44.
Berghaus, Peter. 'Die Münzpolitik der deutschen Städte im Mittelalter', *Finances et Comptibilité Urbaines du XIIIe au XVIe siècle*. Pro Civitate, Collection Histoire in 8°, vii. Brussels, 1964, 75–85.
—— 'Die Perioden des Sterlings in Westfalen, dem Rheinland und in den Niederlanden', *Hamburger Beiträge zur Numismatik*, i (1947), 34–53.
—— 'Umlauf und Nachprägung des Florentiner Guldens Nördlich der Alpen', *Congresso Internazionale di Numismatica*, ii. Rome, 1965, 595–607.
Berghaus, P. and Hatz, G. (eds). *Dona Numismatica – Walter Hävernick zum 23 Januar 1965 dargebracht*. Hamburg, 1965.
Cahn, Julius. *Der Rappenmünzbund*. Heidelberg, 1901.
Diepenbach, W. 'Der Rheinische Münzverein', *Kultur und Wirtschaft im Rheinischen Raum. Festschrift zu Christian Eckert*, ed. A. F. Napp-Zinn and M. Oppenheim. Mainz, 1949, 89–120.
Hävernick, Walter. *Der Kölner Pfennig im 12 und 13 Jahrhundert*. Stuttgart, 1931.
Metcalf, D. M. *The Coinage of South Germany in the Thirteenth Century*. London, 1961.

SCHULTE, A. *Geschichte der Grossen Ravensberger Handelsgesellschaft 1380–1530*. Stüttgart–Berlin, 1923.

STROMER, W. VON. *Oberdeutsche Hochfinanz 1350–1450*. Vierteljahrschrift für Sozial- und Wirtschaftsgeschichte, Beiheft, LV–LVII. 1970.

SUHLE, A. *Deutsche Münz- und Geldgeschichte von den Anfängen bis zum 15 Jahrhundert*. 2nd edn. Berlin, 1964

Northern Europe

BENDIXEN, KIRSTEN. *Denmark's Money*. Copenhagen, 1967.

GALSTER, G. *Coins and History*. Copenhagen, 1959.

JENSEN, J. S. 'Danish Money in the Fourteenth Century', *Mediaeval Scandinavia*, VI (1973), 161–71.

JESSE, WILHELM. *Der Wendische Münzverein*. Lübeck, 1928.

LAGERQVIST, L. O. *Svenska mynt under Vikingtid och Medeltid ca.995–1521 samt Gotländska mynt ca.1140–1565*. Stockholm, 1969.

MAŁOWIST, MARIAN. *Croissance et régression en Europe XIVe–XVIIe siècles: recueil d'articles*. Cahiers des Annales, XXXIV. Paris, 1972.

SPRANDEL, ROLF. *Das Mittelalterliche Zahlungs-system nach Hansisch-Nordischen Quellen des 13–15 Jahrhunderts*. Stuttgart, 1975.

Central and Eastern Europe

BAUMGARTNER, EGON. 'Die Blütezeit der Friesacher Pfennige', *NZ*, LXXIII (1949), LXXVIII (1959), LXXIX (1961).

CASTELIN, K. *Česka drobná mince doby předhusitské a husitské 1300–1471*. Prague, 1953. With resumé in French.

GRAUS, F. 'Die Handelsbeziehungen Böhmens zu Deutschland und Österreich in 14 und zu Beginn des 15 Jahrhunderts', *Historica*, II (1960).

GUMOWSKI, M. *Handbuch der polnischen Numismatik*. Graz, 1960.

KIERSNOWSKI, R. *Wstep do numizmatyki polskiej wieków średnich*. Warsaw, 1964.

LÖHR, A. *Österreichische Geldgeschichte*. Vienna, 1946.

METCALF, D. M. *Coinage in South-Eastern Europe, 820–1396*. London, 1979.

PROBSZT, GUNTHER. *Quellenkunde der Münz- und Geldgeschichte der ehemaligen Österreichisch-Ungarischen Monarchie*. Graz, 1953. Supplements, 1960 and 1963.

RÉTHY, L. (ed.). *Corpus Nummorum Hungarie*. *1899–1907*. German translations, Graz, 1958.

SPASSKIJ, I. G. *The Russian Monetary System*. Amsterdam, 1967.

SUCHODOLSKI, STANISLAW. 'Renovatio Monetae in Poland in the 12th. century', *Wiadomosci Numizmatyczne*, V (1961), 57–75.

INDEX